For Pete.

One for your...
from
Jenny + Ph...
Christmas...

Let's Go
ALASKA &
THE PACIFIC NORTHWEST

is the best book for anyone traveling on a budget. Here's why:

▓ No other guidebook has as many budget listings.

In Alaska and the Pacific Northwest we list over 4,500 budget travel bargains. We tell you the cheapest way to get around, and where to get an inexpensive and satisfying meal once you've arrived. We give hundreds of money-saving tips that anyone can use, plus invaluable advice on discounts and deals for students, children, families, and senior travelers.

▓ Let's Go researchers have to make it on their own.

Our Harvard-Radcliffe researcher-writers travel on budgets as tight as your own—no expense accounts, no free hotel rooms.

▓ Let's Go is completely revised each year.

We don't just update the prices, we go back to the place. If a charming café has become an overpriced tourist trap, we'll replace the listing with a new and better one.

▓ No other guidebook includes all this:

Honest, engaging coverage of both the cities and the countryside; up-to-the-minute prices, directions, addresses, phone numbers, and opening hours; in-depth essays on local culture, history, and politics; comprehensive listings on transportation between and within regions and cities; straight advice on work and study, budget accommodations, sights, nightlife, and food; detailed city and regional maps; and much more.

▓ Let's Go is for anyone who wants to see Alaska & The Pacific Northwest on a budget.

Books by Let's Go, Inc.

EUROPE

Let's Go: Europe

Let's Go: Austria & Switzerland

Let's Go: Britain & Ireland

Let's Go: Eastern Europe

Let's Go: France

Let's Go: Germany

Let's Go: Greece & Turkey

Let's Go: Ireland

Let's Go: Italy

Let's Go: London

Let's Go: Paris

Let's Go: Rome

Let's Go: Spain & Portugal

NORTH & CENTRAL AMERICA

Let's Go: USA & Canada

Let's Go: Alaska & The Pacific Northwest

Let's Go: California

Let's Go: New York City

Let's Go: Washington, D.C.

Let's Go: Mexico

MIDDLE EAST & ASIA

Let's Go: Israel & Egypt

Let's Go: Thailand

Let's Go

The Budget Guide to

ALASKA &
THE PACIFIC
NORTHWEST
1995

Brian J. Erskine
Editor

Amy E. Cooper
Associate Editor

Written by
Let's Go, Inc.
A subsidiary of
Harvard Student Agencies, Inc.

MACMILLAN

HELPING LET'S GO

If you have suggestions or corrections, or just want to share your discoveries, drop us a line. We read every piece of correspondence, whether a 10-page e-mail letter, a velveteen Elvis postcard, or, as in one case, a collage. All suggestions are passed along to our researcher-writers. Please note that mail received after May 5, 1995 will probably be too late for the 1996 book, but will be retained for the following edition.

Address mail to: Or send e-mail to:
Let's Go: Alaska & The Pacific Northwest   **letsgo@delphi.com**
Let's Go, Inc.
1 Story Street
Cambridge, MA 02138
USA

In addition to the invaluable travel advice our readers share with us, many are kind enough to offer their services as researchers or editors. Unfortunately, the charter of Let's Go, Inc. and Harvard Student Agencies, Inc. enables us to employ only currently enrolled Harvard-Radcliffe students.

Published in Great Britain 1995 by Macmillan, Cavaye Place, London SW10 9PG.

10 9 8 7 6 5 4 3 2 1

Maps by David Lindroth, copyright © 1995, 1994, 1993, 1992, 1991, 1990, 1988 by St. Martin's Press, Inc.

Published in the United States of America by St. Martin's Press, Inc.

Let's Go: Alaska & The Pacific Northwest

ISBN: 0 333 62231 6

Let's Go: Alaska & The Pacific Northwest is

written by the Publishing Division of Let's Go, Inc., 1 Story Street, Cambridge, MA 02138.

Contents

Maps

About Let's Go

Back in 1960, a few students at Harvard University got together to produce a 20-page pamphlet offering a collection of tips on budget travel in Europe. For three years, Harvard Student Agencies, a student-run nonprofit corporation, had been doing a brisk business booking charter flights to Europe; this modest, mimeographed packet was offered to passengers as an extra. The following year, students traveling to Europe researched the first full-fledged edition of *Let's Go: Europe*, a pocket-sized book featuring advice on shoestring travel, irreverent write-ups of sights, and a decidedly youthful slant.

Throughout the 60s, the guides reflected the times: one section of the 1968 *Let's Go: Europe* talked about "Street Singing in Europe on No Dollars a Day." During the 70s, *Let's Go* gradually became a large-scale operation, adding regional European guides and expanding coverage into North Africa and Asia. The 80s saw the arrival of *Let's Go: USA & Canada* and *Let's Go: Mexico*, as well as regional North American guides; in the 90s we introduced five in-depth city guides to Paris, London, Rome, New York City, and Washington, DC. And as the budget travel world expands, so do we; the first edition of *Let's Go: Thailand* hit the shelves last year, and this year's edition adds coverage of Malaysia, Singapore, Tokyo, and Hong Kong.

This year we're proud to announce the birth of *Let's Go: Eastern Europe*—the most comprehensive guide to this renascent region, with more practical information and insider tips than any other. *Let's Go: Eastern Europe* brings our total number of titles, with their spirit of adventure and reputation for honesty, accuracy, and editorial integrity, to 21.

We've seen a lot in 35 years. *Let's Go: Europe* is now the world's #1 best selling international guide, translated into seven languages. And our guides are still researched, written, and produced entirely by students who know first-hand how to see the world on the cheap.

Every spring, we recruit over 100 researchers and 50 editors to write our books anew. Come summertime, after several months of training, researchers hit the road for seven weeks of exploration, from Bangkok to Budapest, Anchorage to Ankara. With pen and notebook in hand, a few changes of underwear stuffed in our backpacks, and a budget as tight as yours, we visit every *pensione*, *palapa*, pizzeria, café, club, campground, or castle we can find to make sure you'll get the most out of *your* trip.

We've put the best of our discoveries into the book you're now holding. A brand-new edition of each guide hits the shelves every year, only months after it is researched, so you know you're getting the most reliable, up-to-date, and comprehensive information available. The budget travel world is constantly changing, and where other guides quickly become obsolete, our annual research keeps you abreast of the very latest travel insights. And even as you read this, work on next year's editions is well underway.

At *Let's Go*, we think of budget travel not only as a means of cutting down on costs, but as a way of breaking down a few walls as well. Living cheap and simple on the road brings you closer to the real people and places you've been saving up to visit. This book will ease your anxieties and answer your questions about the basics—to help *you* get off the beaten track and explore. We encourage you to put *Let's Go* away now and then and strike out on your own. As any seasoned traveler will tell you, the best discoveries are often those you make yourself. If you find something worth sharing, drop us a line. We're at Let's Go, Inc., 1 Story Street, Cambridge, MA, 02138, USA (e-mail: letsgo@delphi.com).

Happy travels!

Acknowledgments

To Mark, who loves the Northwest and fishes there still. To Cara, a source of bound-less inspiration. To Dad and Mom for unconditional love and support. To all five RWs and especially Amy, without whom this book would have been impossible. To Alexis, who is amazing. To Mr. Waterbury from AlaskaPass for his help. To Colin and all 3-seats, heavy or light. To the Domestic Room. To Matt for Alaska. To Brooke for Olympia. To Luiza for W. Canada and concerts and dinners and ice cream. To Ms. Susan for her generosity, to Pat in DC and Russia, and Emily and Phoebe. To views of Portland with friends and good beer, and nights lingering over dinner with R.M., sketching salmon. To John and Ward and Grace and Dr. H and Peter and Orwell's essay for giving me a better understanding of the deeper meaning of words. To old friend Brendan and his family and all my friends in Oregon and the Northwest.—**BJE**

"Once upon a time there was princess, and she lived in a castle on Story St..." Thanks to Mamacita, Papala, and Jay-Jay. To Jeffrey M. Miller, for "convos" that saved me more than once (and for narrating a better Princess story than either mom or Let's Go knew how to tell). To Kiki and Amy for being there. To Brian for sharing the grim hilarity of caffeinated sleep-deprivation and imminent deadline. To Jahan for a Room-13 hug and a slew of semicolons. To Pete for a honed GI. To the Domes-tic Room, especially Mary and Cisneros, and to Sucharita, Emily, Sean, Dan, Jim, Tim, Matt, et al. for infinite support. To Jed for the backrub. To Liz for being a grown-up, and Alexis for being The Shit (especially when the server crashed and my psyche self-destructed). This princess is renouncing her royal format manual.—**AEC**

STAFF

Editor	Brian J. Erskine
Associate Editor	Amy E. Cooper
Managing Editor	Jahan Sagafi-nejad
Publishing Director	Pete Keith
Production Manager	Alexis G. Averbuck
Production Assistant	Elizabeth J. Stein
Financial Manager	Matt Heid
Assistant General Manager	Anne E. Chisholm
Sales Group Manager	Sherice R. Guillory
Sales Department Coordinator	Andrea N. Taylor
Sales Group Representatives	Eli K. Aheto
	Timur Okay Harry Hiçyılmaz
	Arzhang Kamerei
	Hollister Jane Leopold
	David L. Yuan
President	Lucienne D. Lester
General Manager	Richard M. Olken

Researcher-Writers

James Bronzan
On his demanding trek through eastern Oregon (among the bedouin), eastern Washington, the Kootenay, Banff, and Calgary, James somehow managed to stay apprised of both the O.J. Simpson play-by-play and the NBA play-offs. Hostel-owners would rave about him weeks after his departure, but he also harbors a penchant for solitude; if you hadn't heard of it before, chances are it made the guide because James rediscovered it. Sincere thanks for consistently excellent copy and an irrepressible sense of humor, even through Stuart Smalley conversations with Amy. Finally, special kudos to James for never failing to grapple with that most erudite of inquiries, "What *kind* of fish?"

Colin Chant
Colin may have sampled every kind of breakfast and corndog the Alaskan interior has to offer. This is one personality in whom humility is misplaced; few other individuals could so smoothly have weathered such awful driving conditions (his suspension, shattered; his storytelling abilities, intact; his ability to castigate his lighter, fellow starboard oarsman and editor, sharpened, on the road to Eagle.) Thanks to Colin for spending sleepless nights in coffee shops, rewriting introductions, and capturing in astute social commentary a land where even RVers fear to tread. ("Square dancing is good for the soul.") Through the delirium, the stubble, the Neil Diamond, and the endless copybatches, Colin delivered again and again.

Meredith FitzGerald
Very early in her itinerary, Meredith seized upon the secret of successful travel: pal around with older people. The presence of mind that propelled her through the Queen Charlotte Islands also gave her the patience to endure countless (actually, she counted) nights in a sleeping bag beneath the dripping skies of the Alaska Panhandle. We are eternally indebted to you for enduring Whittier. Thanks for confident and thorough research, an eye for detail, and a comfort with candor ("Can you libel an entire town?")

Ken Fleming
Despite an abysmal string of bad luck—including, but not limited to, one car break-in and two car break-downs (in Canada!)—Ken managed to pull it off where it most counted. Eager to add an excellent new nightspot or an undetected vegetarian offering, Ken's urban audacity was particularly well-suited to Seattle and Vancouver. For writing his copy while carless, sleepless, and penniless, we thank Ken; we hope the view from Mt. Rainier made it all worthwhile.

Catherine Galbraith
Kate's copybatches were thicker than than the 4-lb. sirloin at the Circle S in Pendleton, Oregon...lucky for us. When Kate managed to navigate Eugene the very weekend the Deadheads descended, we knew there was nothing she couldn't accomplish. Her scrupulous research and onslaught of pamphlets kept us working, but her box of cranberry candies from the Oregon Coast kept us smiling while we slaved. With wit and irreverence ("In this writeup, 'grunge' means people trying to imitate Metallica's hairstyle,") Kate traipsed through Oregon, the Olympic Peninsula, and the occasional art-museum burglar alarm.

How To Use This Book

Let's Go: Alaska & The Pacific Northwest is written for the budget traveler. The **Essentials** section provides information you will need to know before you leave. **Planning Your Trip** lets you know where to write for information about the region; what to do about customs, visas, and bureaucracy; how to stay safe and healthy; what to do if you'd like to work or study on your sojourn; and how to pack. **Getting There and Getting Around** sorts out the various modes of transportation to and around the region. Once There helps you to find the cheapest and cleanest in **Accommodations**, with detailed information on **Camping** and the **Outdoors**.

The main body of this guide is divided into two parts: **Alaska** and the **Pacific Northwest**. **Alaska** opens with coverage of Anchorage and the southcentral part of the state: the Kenai, Kodiak, Prince William Sound, and Wrangell-St. Elias National Park. The second chapter discusses the ferry voyage north along the Panhandle, from Ketchikan to Skagway. The third section heads toward Fairbanks and the Interior, including Denali National Park. The Alaskan wilderness is discussed at length in The Bush; unfortunately, reaching many points in the Bush can be expensive.

The Pacific Northwest regions include British Columbia, the Yukon Territory, Alberta, Washington, and Oregon. The coverage of each of these areas, excluding the Yukon, begins with a major metropolitan area. These exciting cities lead into detailed descriptions of parks and wilderness areas, usually region by region, in an easy-to-follow format. **British Columbia** begins with Vancouver, crosses to Victoria and Vancouver Island, then heads east to Okanagan and Kootenay country. The **Yukon** follows detailed coverage of Yellowhead Highway 16, the Cassiar Highway (Hwy. 37), and the Alaska Highway to best serve readers driving to Alaska. **Alberta** is next, from Edmonton south through Jasper and Banff National Parks to Calgary, including information about the Stampede. **Washington** begins in Seattle, covers Puget Sound and the San Juan Islands, moves to the rainforests of Olympic National Park and south along the coast, takes the Cascades south to north, including Mount St. Helens, Mt. Rainier, and incredible Rte. 20, and moves east to Spokane and wine country. **Oregon** begins with Portland, Mt. Hood, and the Columbia Gorge, moves south along the coast, back north into the Willamette Valley through Eugene, and crosses the Cascades to the outdoor mecca of Bend and Eastern Oregon.

For each specific area, the guide lists Practical Information and Orientation, Accommodations, Food, Sights, and Entertainment. A discussion of exploring the Outdoors follows Sights when appropriate. It may be useful to flip through a few sections to familiarize yourself with the book; understanding its structure will help you make the most of the wealth of information we offer. Amy Cooper and I hope this book is of the greatest service and meets your high standards for budget travel, urban cultural experience, and true wilderness exploration. —Brian J. Erskine '96

A NOTE TO OUR READERS

The information for this book is gathered by *Let's Go*'s researchers during the late spring and summer months. Each listing is derived from the assigned researcher's opinion based upon his or her visit at a particular time. The opinions are expressed in a candid and forthright manner. Other travelers might disagree. Those traveling at a different time may have different experiences since prices, dates, hours, and conditions are always subject to change. You are urged to check beforehand to avoid inconvenience and surprises. Travel always involves a certain degree of risk, especially in low-cost areas. When traveling, especially on a budget, you should always take particular care to ensure your safety.

ESSENTIALS

■ Planning Your Trip

Ideally, a vacation is supposed to be a reckless, spontaneous affair, but you'll have a better time if you plan ahead. Set aside a few hours well before your trip begins to make calls, write letters to organizations with useful information, and compile lists of things to bring along. Conscientious preparation will save you in moments of unexpected crisis, and will help you to take unforeseen circumstances in stride.

As you plan your itinerary, it's a good idea to consult the *Let's Go* listings for the specific destinations you intend to include. Tourist Bureaus and Chambers of Commerce can send you information in advance that can help you to plan (see addresses listed below, and also check the Practical Information sections within cities and regions). Remember that businesses must pay to appear in Chambers' literature; listings may not include the least expensive alternatives. For organizations catering to travelers with specific interests or needs, see Specific Concerns below.

■■■ WHEN TO GO

Traveling is like comedy —timing is everything. In the Pacific Northwest, your rival concerns will be the tourist season and the weather. In general, summer (June-Aug.) is high season; during those months, you can expect to share the warm weather with crowds of fellow tourists. If you prefer to experience the region as the natives do, go during the off-season when crowds are smaller and rates are lower. Beware the disadvantages of winter travel in certain parts, however—slush, icy roads, and prohibitively cold weather (especially in northern Canada and Alaska) will constrain your movement and limit your desire to be outdoors. May and September may be the best times to travel in the Northwest.

■■■ USEFUL ORGANIZATIONS AND PUBLICATIONS

■ TOURIST BUREAUS

Each state and province has its own travel bureau (listed below), which can refer you to other useful organizations, send you brochures and maps, and answer your questions about the region. One good resource is the **U.S. Government Printing Office,** Superintendent of Documents, Washington, DC 20402 (202-783-3238; fax 202-275-2529), with a wide selection of travel and recreation references. *Let's Go* lists many of the most useful, but you can call or write for complete bibliographies. Bibliography #17 deals with outdoor activities in general, and #302 with travel to particular regions. The pamphlet *Travel and Tourism* covers travel within the U.S.

Alaska Division of Tourism, P.O. Box 110801, Juneau, AK 99811 (907-465-2010).
Alberta Tourism, Commerce Place, 10155 102 St., Edmonton, AB T5J 4L6 (800-222-6501; 800-661-8888 outside Alberta).
Tourism British Columbia, 1117 Wharf St., Victoria, BC V8W 2Z2 (604-387-1642 or 800-663-6000) for travel information and accommodations reservations.
Oregon Tourism Division, 775 Summer St. NE, Salem, OR 97310 (800-543-8838; 800-547-7842 outside Oregon; fax 503-373-7307).

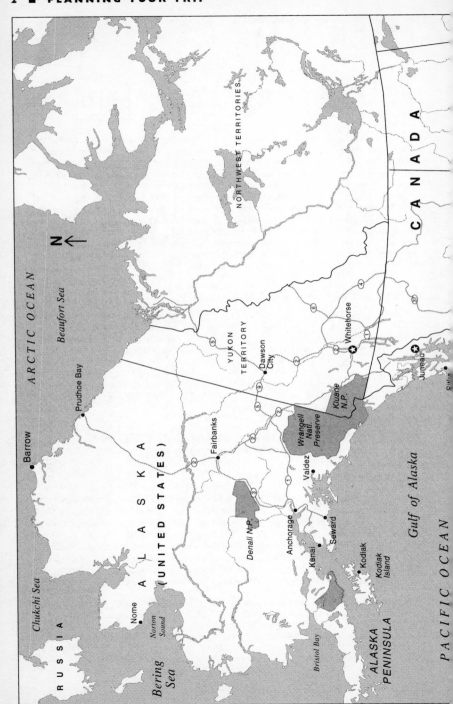

Pacific Northwest, Western Canada, and Alaska

Washington Division of Tourism, Dept. of Trade and Economic Development, P.O. Box 42500, Olympia, WA 98504-2500 (800-544-1800 or 206-586-2088).

Yukon Department of Tourism, P.O. Box 2703, Whitehorse, YT Y1A 2C6 (403-667-5340; fax at 403-667-2634).

U.S. Travel and Tourism Administration (USTTA), Department of Commerce, 14th St. and Constitution Ave. NW, Washington, DC 20230 (202-482-4752). USTTA has branches in Australia, Canada, Japan, Mexico, and the U.K, and in many other countries (contact the Washington office).

■ BUDGET TRAVEL SERVICES

Most of the following budget travel services offer discounted flights, railpasses, ISICs, hostel memberships, and general budget travel expertise.

Campus Travel, 52 Grosvenor Gardens, London SW1W OAG (tel. (0171) 730 8832; fax (0171) 730 5739). 37 branches in the UK. Booklets with general information for British travelers. Telephone bookings from Europe (0171) 730 3402, from North America (0171) 730 2101, worldwide (0171) 730 8111.

Council on International Educational Exchange (CIEE), 205 East 42nd St., New York, NY 10017 (212-661-1414). A private, not-for-profit organization, CIEE administers work, academic and professional programs around the world. A range of publications, among them the magazine *Student Travels* (postage $1).

Council Travel, a subsidiary of CIEE, is a chain of budget travel agencies. 41 U.S. offices, including: 729 Boylston St., #201, **Boston,** MA 02166 (617-266-1926); 1153 N Dearborn St., 2nd floor, **Chicago,** IL 60610 (312-951-0585); 6715 Hillcrest, **Dallas,** TX 75205 (214-363-9941); 1093 Broxton Ave. #220, **Los Angeles,** CA 90024 (310-208-3551); 205 East 42nd St., **New York,** NY 10017 (212-661-1450); 715 SW Morrison #600, **Portland,** OR 97205 (503-228-1900); 530 Bush St., Ground Floor, **San Francisco,** CA 94108 (415-421-3473); 1314 Northeast 43rd St. #210, **Seattle,** WA 98105 (206-632-2448). Offices in Europe, including: 28A Poland St. (Oxford Circus), **London** WIV 3DB ((0171) 437 77 67).

Educational Travel Centre (ETC), 438 North Frances St., Madison, WI 53703 (800-747-5551; fax 608-256-2042). Budget travel agency.

Federation of International Youth Travel Organisations (FIYTO). For the office closest to you, write to FIYTO Secretariat, 25H Bredgade, 1160 Copenhagen K, Denmark. Organization of suppliers of youth and student travel services.

International Student Travel Confederation (ISTC), Store Kongensgade 40H, 1264 Copenhagen K, Denmark (tel. (45) 33 93 93 03). Affiliate of travel agencies around the world; sponsors the Student Air Travel Ass. for European students.

International Student Exchange Flights (ISE), 5010 East Shea Blvd., #A104, Scottsdale, AZ 85254 (602-951-1177). Budget travel agency.

Let's Go Travel, Harvard Student Agencies, Inc., 53A Church St., Cambridge, MA 02138 (800-553-8746). Railpasses, HI/AYH memberships, ISICs, *Let's Gos* at a discount), bargain flights, and mail-order line of travel gear (see catalog insert).

STA Travel, 17 E 45th St., New York, NY 10017 (800-777-0112 or 212-986-9470). A chain of budget travel agencies. 11 offices in the U.S. and more than 100 offices in the world. **Boston,** 297 Newbury St., MA 02116 (617-266-6014), **San Francisco,** 51 Grant Ave., CA 94108 (415-391-8407). **New York,** 48 E 11th St., NY 10003 (212-477-7166). **Washington, DC,** 2401 Pennsylvania Ave., 20037 (202-887-0912). In the **U.K.,** STA's main offices are at 86 Old Brompton Rd., London SW7 3LQ and 117 Euston Rd., London NW1 2SX (tel. (0171) 937 99 71 for N American travel). In **New Zealand,** 10 High St., Auckland (tel. (09) 398 9995). In **Australia,** 222 Faraday St., Melbourne VIC 3053 (tel. (03) 349 2411).

Travel Management International (TMI), 39 JFK St., 3rd Floor, Cambridge, MA 02138 ((617-661-8187 or 800-245-3672). Budget travel agency.

USIT Ltd., Aston Quay, O'Connell Bridge, Dublin 2 (tel. (01) 679 8833; fax (01) 677 8843). Budget travel agency.

■ USEFUL PUBLICATIONS

Animal and Plant Health Inspection Service (APHIS), U.S. Department of Agriculture, 6505 Belcrest Road, Hyattsville, MD 20782-2058 (301-436-7799; fax 301-436-5221). Provides information about restrictions in the wildlife trade.

Forsyth Travel Library, P.O. Box 2975, Shawnee Mission, KS 66201 (800-367-7984). Call or write for their catalog of maps, guides, railpasses and timetables.

Hippocrene Books, Inc., 171 Madison Ave., New York, NY 10016 (212-685-4371; orders 718-454-2360; fax 718-454-1391). Publishes travel references.

Rand McNally publishes one of the most comprehensive road atlases of the U.S. and Canada, available in most bookstores for $8.

Travelling Books, P.O. Box 77114, Seattle, WA 98177. Travel guides.

Wide World Books and Maps, 1911 N 45th St., Seattle, WA 98103 (206-634-3453). A good selection of hard-to-find maps. Open Mon.-Fri. 10am-7pm, Sat. 10am-6pm, Sun. noon-5pm.

■■■ DOCUMENTS & FORMALITIES

Be sure to file all applications several weeks or (better) months in advance of your planned departure date. Applications can take a considerable amount of time to process. Some offices suggest that you apply in the fall and winter off-season (Aug.-Dec.) for speedier service.

When you travel, *always carry on your person two or more forms of identification, including at least one photo ID.* A passport combined with a driver's license or birth certificate usually serves as adequate proof of your identity and citizenship. Many establishments, especially banks, require several IDs before cashing traveler's checks. It is also wise to carry several extra passport-size photos for any additional IDs you may eventually acquire. Students should bring proof of their status to get discounts on sights and transportation. For students at U.S. universities, a current college ID will do. Never carry your passport, tickets, ID, money, traveler's checks, insurance, and credit cards all together; one instance of absentmindedness or thievery could leave you bereft of IDs and funds. If you plan an extended stay, you might want to register your passport with the nearest embassy or consulate.

■ ENTRANCE REQUIREMENTS

U.S. or Canadian citizens who are adults may cross the **U.S.-Canadian border** with only proof of citizenship (passport, birth certificate, or voter registration card). U.S. citizens under 18 need the written consent of a parent or guardian, while Canadian citizens under 16 need notarized permission from both parents. Naturalized citizens should have their naturalization papers with them; occasionally officials will ask to see them. At the U.S.-Canadian border, persons who are not citizens of either country will need a visa to cross in either direction (citizens of Greenland excepted). See the Visas section on page 7 for further exceptions and restrictions.

Mexican citizens may cross into the U.S. with an I-186 form. Mexican border crossing cards (non-immigrant visas) prohibit you from staying more than 72 hours in the U.S., or traveling more than 25 mi. from the border.

Visitors from other countries to either the U.S. or Canada must have a passport, visa, and proof of intent to leave in order to enter either the United States or Canada.

■ PASSPORTS

As a precaution in case your passport is lost or stolen, carry a photocopy of all of its pages, including all visa stamps, apart from your actual passport, and leave a duplicate copy with a relative or friend. These measures will help prove your citizenship and facilitate the issuing of a new passport. Consulates also recommend that you carry an expired passport or a *notarized* copy of your birth certificate (not the one issued at birth, of course) in a part of your baggage separate from other documents.

Losing your passport can be a nightmare. It may take weeks to process a replacement, and your new passport may be valid only for a limited time. In addition, any visas stamped in your old passport will be lost. Immediately notify the local police and the nearest consulate or embassy of your home government.

British citizens are required to obtain a full passport for entrance into the U.S. or Canada. Full passports are valid for 10 years (5 years for under 16); apply in person or by mail to the London Passport Office or to an office in Liverpool, Newport, Peterborough, Glasgow, or Belfast. Applications can also be picked up at post offices. The fee is £18; leave 4-6 weeks for processing. The London office offers same-day walk-in rush service, so arrive early.

Irish citizens can receive passports valid for 10 years in exchange for a £45 fee, though citizens younger than 18 and older than 65 can request a 3 year passport that costs only £10. Apply by mail to the **Department of Foreign Affairs,** Passport Office, Setanta Centre, Molesworth St., Dublin 2 (tel. (01) 671 1633). Applications can also be obtained from local Garda stations.

Australian citizens must apply for a passport in person at a local post office, an embassy or consulate, an Australian diplomatic mission overseas, or one of the Passport Offices in Adelaide, Brisbane, Canberra, Darwin, Hobart, Melbourne, Newcastle, Perth, and Sydney. Application fees are adjusted every three months; call the toll free information service for current details (tel. 13 12 32).

New Zealand citizens can obtain passports valid for up to 10 years. Pick up an application from your local Link Centre, travel agent, or New Zealand Representative, and mail the completed forms to the **New Zealand Passport Office,** Documents of National Identity Division, Dept. of Internal Affairs, Box 10-526, Wellington (tel. (04) 474 81 00). The application fee is NZ$130, NZ$65 for under age 16.

South African citizens can apply for a passport at any Home Affairs Office. For more information, contact the nearest Home Affairs Office.

■ TOURIST VISAS

A visa is an endorsement that a foreign government stamps into a passport; it allows the bearer to stay in that country for a specified purpose and period of time. Most visas cost $10-30 and allow you to spend about a month in a country, within six months to a year from the date of issue.

To acquire a visa for entrance to the **U.S.,** called a B-2, or "pleasure tourist" visa, you will need your passport and proof of intent to leave. Contact the nearest U.S. consulate to obtain your visa. Alternatively, contact the **Center for International Business and Travel (CIBT),** 25 West 43rd St. #1420, New York, NY 10036 (800-925-2428). This organization secures visas for travel to and from all possible countries. The service charge varies; the average cost for a U.S. citizen is $15-20 per visa. The I-94 form is the arrival/ departure certificate attached to your visa upon arrival; if you lose this, replace it at the nearest U.S. Immigration and Naturalization office. Extensions for visas (max. 6 months) require form I-539 and a $70 fee, and are also granted by the INS. For a list of offices, write the **INS Central Office,** 425 I St. NW #5044, Washington, DC 20536 (INS informational voice mail, 202-514-4316).

Visitors from certain nations may enter the U.S. without visas through the **Visa Waiver Pilot Program.** Travelers qualify as long as they are traveling for business or pleasure, are staying for 90 days or less, have proof of intent to leave and a completed form I-94W, and enter aboard particular air or sea carriers. Participating countries are Andorra, Austria, Belgium, Brunei, Denmark, Finland, France, Germany, Iceland, Italy, Japan, Liechtenstein, Luxembourg, Monaco, the Netherlands, New Zealand, Norway, San Marino, Spain, Sweden, Switzerland, and the U.K. Contact the nearest U.S. consulate for more information.

To acquire a visa for entrance to **Canada,** you will need your passport and proof of intent to leave, which could include a detailed itinerary for travel, proof of employment or other ties to a home country, a valid travel document, a letter of invitation from a Canadian family, or a return airline ticket. Visas are issued on a first come, first serve basis at Canadian consulates or by mail; personal interviews are sometimes required. To visit Canada, you must be healthy, have a clean criminal record (a drunk driving offense may be enough to keep you out), and be able to demonstrate the ability to support yourself financially during your stay. Contact the nearest Canadian consulate to obtain your visa.

Visitors from certain nations may enter Canada without visas. Travelers qualify if they are staying for 90 days or less, have proof of intent to leave, and are citizens of Australia, the Bahamas, Barbados, Costa Rica, Dominica, the E.C., Singapore, Swaziland, the U.S., Venezuela, Western Samoa, or Zimbabwe. Contact the nearest Canadian consulate for more information.

If you want to stay longer, apply for a visa at a U.S. or Canadian embassy or consulate in your home country well before your departure. Unless you are a student, extending your stay once you are abroad is more difficult. You must contact the country's immigration officials or local police well before your time is up. See Work and Study on page 21 for information on Non-tourist Visas.

■ CUSTOMS: COMING TO THE U.S. & CANADA

Unless you plan to import something as exotic as a BMW or a barnyard beast, you will probably pass right over the customs barrier with minimal ado. U.S. and Canada prohibit or restrict the importation of firearms, explosives, ammunition, fireworks, controlled drugs, most plants and animals, lottery tickets, obscene literature and films, and articles made from the skins and furs of certain animals. To avoid problems when you transport **prescription drugs,** ensure that the bottles are clearly marked, and carry a copy of the prescription to show the customs officer. Women especially should be aware that certain prescription drugs are illegal in the U.S.

If you fail to declare an article acquired abroad, the article is subject to seizure and forfeiture, and you will be liable for a personal penalty or criminal prosecution. You may bring the following into the U.S. duty free: 200 cigarettes, 50 cigars, or 2kg smoking tobacco; $100 in gifts (this may include 100 cigars); and personal belongings such as clothing and jewelry. Travelers ages 21 and older may also bring up to 1L alcohol, although state laws may further restrict the amount of alcohol you can carry. You can bring any amount of currency into the U.S., but if you carry over US$10,000, you'll need to report it. In general, customs officers ask how much money you're bringing and your planned departure date in order to ensure that you'll be able to support yourself while in the U.S. Articles imported in excess of your exemption will simply be subject to varying duty rates, to be paid upon arrival.

■ CUSTOMS: RETURNING HOME

Upon returning home, you must declare all articles acquired abroad and pay a duty on the value of those articles that exceeds your country's established allowance. Holding onto receipts for purchases made abroad will help establish values when you return. It is wise to *make a list*, including serial numbers, of any valuables that you carry from home; register this list with customs before your departure and have an official stamp it, and you will avoid import duty charges and ensure an easy passage upon return. Be especially careful to document items manufactured abroad.

Keep in mind that goods and gifts purchased at duty-free shops abroad are not exempt from duty or sales tax at your point of return. **"Duty-free"** merely means that you need not pay a tax in the country of purchase.

British citizens are allowed an exemption of up to £36 worth of goods purchased outside the EC, not more than 200 cigarettes, 100 cigarillos, 50 cigars, or 250g tobacco, and no more than 2L of still table wine plus 1L of alcohol (over age 17 only). Citizens are also allowed 60mL perfume and 250mL toilet water. Contact **Her Majesty's Customs and Excise,** Customs House, Heathrow Airport North, Hounslow, Middlesex, TW6 2LA ((0181) 750 15 49).

Irish citizens may return home with the equivalent of IR£34 of goods purchased outside the EC, and 200 cigarettes, 100 cigarillos, 50 cigars, or 250g tobacco, 1L liquor or 2L wine, 2L still wine, 50g perfume, and 250ml toilet water. Contact **The Revenue Commissioners,** Dublin Castle (tel. (01) 679 2777; fax (01) 671 2021).

Australian citizens may import AUS$400 (under 18 AUS$200) of goods duty-free, as well as 250 cigarettes, 250g tobacco, and 1L alcohol if over the age of 18. Contact the **Australian Customs Service,** 5 Constitution Ave., Canberra, ACT 2601.

New Zealand citizens may bring home up to NZ$700 worth of goods duty-free if they are intended for personal use or are unsolicited gifts. They may also bring in 400 cigarettes, 250g tobacco, or 50 cigars, or a combination of all three not to exceed 250g. In addition, they are allowed 4.5L beer or wine, 1.125L liquor, 250mL toilet water, and 50ML perfume. Consult the *New Zealand Customs Guide for Travelers,* available from customs houses, or contact **New Zealand Customs,** 50 Anzac Avenue, Box 29, Auckland (tel. (09) 377 35 20; fax (09) 309 29 78).

South African citizens are allowed 100 cigarettes, 50 cigars, 250g tobacco, 2L wine, 1L spirits, 250mL toilet water, 50mL perfume, and other items up to a value of R500. Citizens should address their inquiries to: **The Commissioner for Customs and Excise,** Private Bag X47, Pretoria, 0001, which distributes the pamphlet *South African Customs Information.* South Africans who reside in the U.S. should contact the **South African mission to the IMF/World Bank,** 3201 New Mexico Ave. #380, NW, Washington, DC, 20016 (tel. 202-364-8320/1; fax 364-6008).

For more information, including the helpful pamphlet *U.S. Customs Hints for Visitors (Nonresidents),* contact the nearest U.S. Embassy or write the **U.S. Customs Service,** P.O. Box 7407, Washington, DC 20004 (202-927-2095).

■ HOSTEL MEMBERSHIP

Hostelling International (HI) is the new and universal trademark name adopted by the International Youth Hostel Federation (IYHF). The more than 6000 official youth hostels worldwide will normally display the new HI logo (a blue triangle) alongside the symbol of the national organization. A one-year Hostelling International (HI) membership permits you to stay at youth hostels all over the U.S. and Canada for $5-22. Most national branches vend ISICs, arrange student and charter flights, arrange reservations, and sell travel equipment and literature on budget travel. See page 49 for more information. Hostel cards are available from Council Travel and STA and from the hostelling organization of your own country:

Hostelling International Headquarters, 9 Guessens Rd., Welwyn Garden City, Herts AL8 6QW England (tel. (44) 0707 33 24 87). An umbrella organization for more than 200 hostels in the U.S. and more than 6000 worldwide. Publishes the annually updated *Hostelling North America Handbook* (free to members, non-members $6) listing hostels across Canada and the U.S.

American Youth Hostels (AYH), 733 15th St. NW #840, Washington, DC 20005 (202-783-6161). 1-yr. membership $25, under 18 $10, over 54 $15, family $35.

Canada: Hostelling International-Canada (HI-C), 400-205 Catherine St., Ont., Canada K2P 1C3 (613-237-7884; fax 613-237-7868). 1-yr. membership CDN$26.75, under 18 CDN$12.84, 2-yr. CDN$37.45. Life membership available.

United Kingdom: Youth Hostels Association of England and Wales (YHA), Trevelyan House, 8 St. Stephens Hill, St. Albans, Hertz AL1 2DY (tel. 727 855 215); fee £9, under 18 £3, children aged 5 to 18 enrolled free when a parent joins.

Ireland: An Óige (Irish Youth Hostel Association), 61 Mountjoy Sq., Dublin 7 (tel. (01) 830 4555; fax 830 5808); fee £7.50, under 18 £4, family £15.

Australia: Australian Youth Hostels Association (AYHA), Level 3, 10 Mallet St., Camperdown, NSW 2050 (tel. 02 565 1699; fax 565 1235); fee AUS$40, under 18 AUS$12.

New Zealand: Youth Hostels Association of New Zealand (YHANZ), P.O. Box 436,173 Gloucester St., Christchurch 1 (tel. (03) 379 9970; fax (03) 365 4476); fee NZ$24.

Independent hostels vary widely in quality and service. Many neither require nor offer membership. Many fine hostels are not HI-affiliated.

■ YOUTH AND STUDENT IDENTIFICATION

In the world of budget travel, youth has its privileges. Two main forms of student and youth identification are accepted worldwide; they are extremely useful, especially for the insurance packages that accompany them.

The **International Student Identity Card (ISIC)** is the most widely accepted form of student ID. Some one million plus students flash it every year. Carrying this card can garner you discounts for sights, theaters, museums, accommodations, train, ferry, and airplane travel, and other services throughout the U.S. and Canada. Present the card wherever you go, and ask about discounts even when none are advertised. The card provides up to $3000 of accident **insurance,** $100 per day of in-hospital care, accidental death or dismemberment benefits, emergency evacuation coverage, and, in a particularly morbid touch, "$3000 to cover reasonable expenses for repatriation of remains." Cardholders have access to a toll-free **Traveler's Assistance Hotline** whose multilingual staff can provide help in medical, legal, and financial emergencies overseas.

Many student travel offices issue ISICs (see page 4). When applying for the card, procure a copy of the *International Student Identity Card Handbook,* which lists by country some of the available discounts. Applicants must be between 12 and 25 years old and students at secondary or post-secondary schools. The fee is $17. Because of the proliferation of improperly issued ISIC cards, many airlines and other services require double proof of student identity; it is wise to carry your school ID.

The new, $17 **International Teacher Identity Card (ITIC)** offers identical discounts, in theory, but because of its recent introduction many establishments are reluctant to honor it. The application process is the same as that for the ISIC, except that teachers need to present an official document from a school official. The **International Youth Discount Travel Card** or the **GO 25 Card,** is issued by the **Federation of International Youth Travel Organizations (FIYTO)** (see page 4) and offers many of the same benefits as the ISIC. A brochure that lists discounts is free when you purchase the card. The fee is $16.

■ INTERNATIONAL DRIVER'S PERMIT

Unless they have valid driver's licenses from the U.S. or Canada, foreigners who drive in either country should have International Driving Permits (IDP) to accompany their home driver's licenses. The IDP helps visitors from non-English speaking-nations, whose licenses might confuse American authorities, particularly police officers. The IDP must be issued by your home country- you can't get one here. Check with your national automobile association.

■■■ MONEY

Money will always cause you trouble—even when you have it. Design a **budget** and expect to exceed it. If you stay in hostels and prepare your own food, anticipate spending anywhere from $25-50 per day, depending on local cost of living and your needs. No matter how low your budget, if you plan to travel for more than a couple of days you will need to keep handy a much larger amount of cash than usual. Carrying it around, even in a money belt, is risky. Personal checks from home may not be acceptable no matter how many forms of iD you carry (even banks may shy away). Travelers checks and ATM accounts are good alternatives.

■ CURRENCY AND EXCHANGE

CDN$1 = US$0.73	US$1 = CDN$1.37
UK£1 = US$1.54	US$1 = UK£0.65
IR£1 = US$1.52	US$1 = IR£0.66
AUS$1 = US$0.77	US$ = AUS$1.35
NZ$1 = US$0.60	US$1 = NZ$1.66

U.S. currency uses a decimal system based on the **dollar ($).** Paper money ("bills") comes in six denominations, all the same size, shape, and dull green color. The bills now issued are $1, $5, $10, $20, $50 and $100. You may occasionally see denominations of $2 and $500, which are no longer printed but are still acceptable as currency. Some restaurants and retail stores may not accept $50 bills and higher. The dollar divides into 100 **cents (¢);** fractions such as 35 cents can be represented as 35¢ or $0.35. The penny (1¢), the nickel (5¢), the dime (10¢), and the quarter (25¢) are the most common coins. The half-dollar (50¢) and the one-dollar coins (which come in two sizes) are rare but valid currency.

It is nearly impossible to use **foreign currency** in the U.S., although in some regions near the Canadian border shops may accept Canadian money at a very unfavorable rate of exchange. In some parts of the country you may even have trouble **exchanging your currency** for U.S. dollars. Convert your currency infrequently and in large amounts to minimize fees. Buy U.S. traveler's checks, which can be used in lieu of cash (when an establishment specifies "no checks accepted" this usually refers to checks drawn on a bank account). **Personal checks** can be very difficult to cash in the U.S.; most banks require that you have an account with them to cash one. You may want to bring a U.S.-affiliated credit card such as Interbank (Master-Card) or American Express. For more information on credit cards see page 13.

In both the U.S. and Canada, public telephones and most laundromats take coins and not tokens, and drivers of local buses generally do not give change for dollar bills. Keep this in mind and make sure to carry coins with you.

The main unit of currency in **Canada** is the Canadian **dollar,** which is identical to the U.S. dollar in name only. You will need to exchange your currency when you cross the border. As in the U.S., Canadian currency uses a decimal system, with the dollar divided into 100 **cents (¢);** fractions are represented in the same way: 35¢ or

$0.35. Paper money comes in denominations of $2, $5, $10, $20, $50, and $100, which are all the same size but color-coded by denomination. Several years ago, the Canadian government phased out the $1 bill and replaced it with a **$1 coin,** known as the loony for the loon which graces its reverse.

Many Canadian shops, as well as vending machines and parking meters, accept U.S. coins at face value (which is a loss for you). Many stores will even convert the price of your purchase for you, but they are under no legal obligation to offer you a fair exchange. Banks provide a reasonable exchange rate, but often charge a handling fee and shave off several percentage points; **ATM Cirrus** and **Plus** networks allow you to draw Canadian currency from American or British bank accounts at the official exchange rate and are spreading rapidly. Exchange houses have the best rates and hours; most are open on weekends when banks close. During the past several years, the Canadian dollar has been worth 15 to 20% less than the U.S. dollar; the **exchange rate** hovers around 18%. *All prices in the Canada section of this book are listed in Canadian dollars unless otherwise noted.*

■ TIPPING

Tipping is expected in restaurants with waitstaff in both the United States and Canada. Fifteen to twenty percent of the bill, depending on the quality of service, is appropriate, and should be left on the table for the waiter or waitress. Cab drivers receive fifteen to twenty percent of the fare in tips; hairdressers should get ten percent of the bill; bellhops expect $1 per bag; and bartenders usually make 50¢ to $1 per drink and $1-2 per pitcher. Tipping is both an expected politeness and a way of ensuring better service in the future.

■ TRAVELER'S CHECKS

Traveler's checks are the safest way to carry large sums of money. Most tourist establishments will accept them, and almost any bank will cash them. Usually banks sell traveler's checks for a 1% commission, although your own bank may waive the surcharge if you have a large enough balance or a certain type of account. In addition, certain travel organizations, such as the American Automobile Association (AAA), offer commission-free traveler's checks to their members. Try to purchase traveler's checks in small denominations ($20 is best, never larger than $50)—otherwise, after having made a small-to-medium purchase, you'll find yourself carrying a large amount of change.

Always keep the receipts from the purchase of your traveler's checks, a list of their serial numbers, and a record of which ones you've cashed. Keep these in a separate pocket or pouch from the checks themselves and leave a copies at home, since these contain the information you will need to replace your checks if they are stolen. Larger firms like American Express can provide immediate refunds at their branch offices. Sign travelers checks at the time of purchase; sign again to cash them in the presence of the shopkeeper accepting them. Be sure to bring your passport with you any time you plan to use your checks! Also keep a quantity of cash on hand, as some smaller establishments are hesitant to accept traveler's checks.

American Express: 800-221-7282 in U.S and Canada. From elsewhere, call collect 800-964-6665, or contact the U.K. office at (01800) 52 13 13 and ask for the *Traveler's Companion,* which gives full addresses for all their travel offices and lists benefits, including a **Global Assist Hotline** with emergency medical, legal, and financial services and advice. Their traveler's cheques are perhaps the most widely recognized in the world, and the easiest to replace if lost or stolen—just contact the nearest AmEx Travel office or call the 800 number.

Citicorp sells Visa traveler's checks. Call 800-645-6556 in the U.S. and Canada; 0171 982 4040 in London; from elsewhere call collect 813-623-1709. Commission is 1-2% on check purchases. Check holders automatically enrolled in **Travel Assist Hotline** (800-523-1199) for 45 days after checks are bought. This service

TRAVELER'S CHECKS

Don't forget to write.

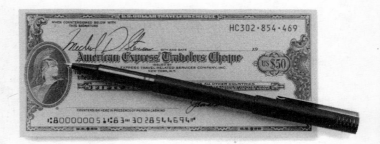

Now that you've said, "Let's go," it's time to say "Let's get American Express® Travelers Cheques." If they are lost or stolen, you can get a fast and full refund virtually anywhere you travel. So before you leave be sure and write.

provides travelers with an English-speaking doctor, lawyer, and interpreter referrals as well as traveler's check refund assistance. Citicorp also has a World Courier
Service which guarantees hand-delivery of traveler's checks anywhere.

Mastercard International: 800-223-9920 in the U.S. and Canada; from abroad, call
collect 609-987-7300. Issued only in US$. Free from Mastercard, though bank
commissions may run 1-2%.

Thomas Cook: call 800-223-7373 from the U.S. to report loss or theft, 800-223-
4030 for orders. Elsewhere call collect 212-974-5696. Thomas Cook and Mastercard International have formed a "global alliance;" Thomas Cook now distributes
traveler's checks which bear both the Mastercard and Thomas Cook names.

Visa: 800-227-6811 in U.S. and Canada; from abroad, call (0171) 937 80 91 (London) or call New York collect 212-858-8500.

▪ CREDIT CARDS

With a major credit card you can rent cars, make reservations, obtain cash advances
at most banks, and make large purchases without depleting ready cash. But many
places mentioned in *Let's Go* will not honor major credit cards. This is just as well—
if you rely on them too much, your trip will no longer qualify as "budget travel."

Mastercard (800-999-0454) and **Visa** (800-336-8472) credit cards are sold by individual banks, and each bank offers different services in conjunction with the card.
Visa and MasterCard are accepted in more establishments than other credit cards,
and they are also the most useful for getting an instant cash advance. Visa holders
can generally obtain an advance up to the amount of the credit line remaining on
the card, while Mastercard imposes a daily limit. Be sure to consult the bank that
issues your card, however, since it may impose its own rules and restrictions. Note
that the British **"Access"** is equivalent to Mastercard. You can often reduce conversion fees by charging a purchase instead of changing traveler's checks. At a bank,
you should be able to obtain cash from a teller, who will essentially "charge" you as
if you had made a purchase. Remember, not all ATMs will honor your credit card;
those that do require you to enter your personal access code. Expect a service
charge for electronic cash advances.

American Express (800-843-2273 for a green card; 800-843-4653 for a gold card)
charges a hefty annual fee, but also offers a number of services to cardholders. Local
AmEx offices will cash personal checks up to $5000 every seven days. Note that the
money is drawn from your personal checking account, not your AmEx account.
Green Card holders can also get money from ATMs, if enrolled in Express Cash Service. Cash advances are available in certain places to Gold Card holders. At some
major airports, American Express also operates machines from which you can purchase traveler's checks with your card. Cardholders can take advantage of the American Express Travel Service. Benefits include assistance in changing airline, hotel,
and car rental reservations, sending mailgrams and international cables, and holding
your mail (if you contact them well in advance; see Keeping in Touch below), as
well as **Global Assist** (800-333-2639), a 24-hour helpline that provides legal and
medical assistance. You can pick up a copy of the *Traveler's Companion,* a list of
full-service offices throughout the world at any American Express Travel Service
office. For more information, contact the American Express Travel Service office or
affiliate nearest you.

If you're a **student** or your income level is low, you may have difficulty acquiring
a recognized credit card. American Express, as well as some of the larger, national
banks have credit card offers geared especially toward students, even those who
bank elsewhere. Otherwise, you may have to find someone older and more established (such as a parent) to co-sign your application. If someone in your family
already has a card, they can usually ask for another card in your name (this encourages travel economy, as they will see the bill before you do).

■ ELECTRONIC BANKING

Automatic Teller Machines (frequently abbreviated as ATMs; operated by bank cards) offer 24-hour service in banks, groceries, gas stations, and telephone booths across the U.S. You will find that most banks in the larger cities are connected to an international money network, usually **PLUS** (800-THE-PLUS/ 843-7587) or **CIRRUS** (800-4-CIRRUS/ 424-7787). Depending on the system that your bank at home uses, you will probably be able to access your own personal bank account whenever you're in need of funds. However: some small and inaccessible towns (in Alaska, the Yukon, and northern B.C., in particular) do not have ATM machines: *be sure to bring enough cash!* You will be charged $5 to withdraw money in Canada, but this will be offset by the wholesale exchange rate garnered by using the ATM network. American Express is planning to begin disbursing travelers checks from ATM machines; inquire about this service before departing (see Credit Cards on page 13).

■ SENDING MONEY

If you run out of money on the road, you can have more mailed to you in the form of **traveler's checks** bought in your name, a **certified check,** or through **postal money orders,** available at post offices (75¢ fee; $700 limit per order; cash only). Certified checks are redeemable at any bank, while postal money orders can be cashed at post offices upon display of two IDs (one of which must be photo). Keep receipts since money orders are refundable if lost.

Money can be **wired** directly from bank to bank for about $30 for amounts less than $1000, plus the commission charged by your home bank. Once you've found a bank that will accept a wire, write or telegram your home bank with your account number, the name and address of the bank to receive the wire, and a routing number. Also notify the bank of the form of ID that the second bank should accept before paying the money. **Bank drafts** or **international money orders** are cheaper but slower. You pay a commission of $15-20 on the draft, plus the cost of sending it registered air mail. As a *last, last* resort, **consulates** will wire home for you and deduct the cost from the money you receive, but they won't be very happy about it.

Another alternative is **cabling money.** Through **Bank of America** (800-346-7693), money can be sent to any affiliated bank. Have someone bring cash, a credit card, or a cashier's check to the sending bank—you need not have an account. You can pick up the money one to three working days later with ID, and it will be paid out to you in U.S. currency. If you do not have a Bank of America account, there is a $37 flat fee for receiving incoming funds, and an $8.50 flat fee if you are a Bank of America member; if you are not a member, you will pay any charges requested by the sending bank (at least $15 and up). **American Express' Moneygram** service (800-543-4080) will cable up to $10,000 to you within 30 minutes. It costs $36 for the first $1000 sent domestically and $70 for the first $1000 sent abroad (subsequent thousands cost less). Non-cardholders may use this service for no extra charge, but money can only be sent from England, Germany, and some locations in France—other European and Australian AmEx offices can only receive Moneygrams. Some offices may require the first $200 to be received in cash and the rest as a money transfer check which may be cashed at a bank; others will allow the entire sum to be received as a money transfer check.

To take advantage of a time-honored, almost-instantaneous, and expensive service, use **Western Union** (800-325-6000). You or someone else can phone in a credit card number, or else someone can bring cash to a Western Union office. As always, you need ID to pick up your money. Their charge is, by credit card, $50 for $500, $60 for $1000; the service is $10 less (and faster) if by cash.

■ SALES TAX

Sales tax is the **U.S.** equivalent of the Value Added Tax. Expect to pay 5 to 10% depending on the item and place. See the state introductions for information on local taxes. Some areas charge a hotel tax; ask in advance.

Prices in general tend to be higher in **Canada** than in the U.S., as are taxes; you'll quickly notice the much-maligned 7% **goods and services tax (GST)** and an additional **sales tax** in some provinces. See the provincial introductions for information on local taxes. Oddly enough, you will often find yourself being taxed on taxes; in Quebec, for example, provincial sales tax is 8%, so that the total tax will be 15.56%. Visitors to Canada can claim a rebate of the GST they pay on accommodations of less than one month and on most goods they buy and take home, so be sure to save your receipts and pick up a GST rebate form while in Canada. The total claim must be at least CDN$7 of GST and must be made within one year of the date on which you purchased the goods and/or accommodations for which you are claiming your rebate. A brochure detailing numerous other restrictions is available from local tourist info booths or by contacting **Revenue Canada,** Customs and Excise Visitor's Rebate Program, Ottawa, Ont. K1A 1J5 (800-668-4748 in Canada, 613-991-3346 outside Canada). Some provinces offer refunds of provincial sales tax as well; contact the Provincial Tourist Information Centres for details (see Practical Information listing of each province).

■■■ HEALTH

For **medical emergencies** in the U.S. and Canada, dial 911. This number works in most places. If it does not, dial 0 for the operator and request to be connected with an ambulance service or hospital.

■ BEFORE YOU GO

For minor health problems on the road, a compact **first-aid kit** should suffice. Some hardware stores carry ready-made kits, but it's easy to assemble your own. Items you might want to include are bandages of several sizes, aspirin, antiseptic soap or antibiotic cream, a thermometer in a sturdy case, a Swiss Army knife with tweezers, moleskin, a decongestant (to clear your ears if you fly with a cold), motion sickness remedy, medicine for diarrhea and stomach problems, sunscreen, wet-ones, insect repellent, burn ointment, baby powder to keep your feet moisture-free, and an elastic bandage.

Always go prepared with any medication you regularly take and may need while traveling, as well as a prescription from your doctor and a statement of any preexisting medical conditions you may have, especially if you will be bringing insulin, syringes, or any narcotics into a foreign country. It is always a good idea to see a doctor before traveling, especially if you will be abroad for more than a month or two or if you will be hiking or camping. If you wear glasses or contact lenses, carry an extra prescription and a backup pair. If you wear contacts, be sure to carry a pair of glasses as the stress of travel can dry out lenses.

Any traveler with a medical condition that cannot easily be recognized (i.e. diabetes, epilepsy, heart conditions, allergies to antibiotics) may want to obtain a **Medic Alert Identification Tag.** In an emergency, the internationally recognized tag indicates the nature of the bearer's problem and provides the number of Medic Alert's 24-hour hotline. Lifetime membership (tag, annually updated wallet card, and 24-hr. hotline access) begins at US$35. Contact Medic Alert Foundation, P.O. Box 1009, Turlock, CA 95381-1009 (800-432-5378). The **American Diabetes Association,** 1660 Duke St., Alexandria, VA 22314 (800-232-3472), provides copies of an article "Travel and Diabetes" and diabetic ID cards—messages in 18 languages on the carrier's diabetic status. Contact your local ADA office for information. In your passport, write the names of any people you wish to be contacted in case of medical emergency, and also list any allergies or medical conditions.

WOMEN'S HEALTH

Women traveling in unsanitary conditions are vulnerable to **urinary tract and bladder infections,** common and severely uncomfortable bacterial conditions which cause a burning sensation and painful and sometimes frequent urination. Drink tons of juice rich in vitamin C (like cranberry) and plenty of clean water, and urinate frequently, especially right after intercourse. Untreated, these infections can become very serious and lead to kidney infections, which in themselves can lead to sterility and death. If symptoms persist, see a doctor. If you tend to develop **vaginal yeast infections**, be sure to take an over-the-counter medicine along with you, as treatments may not be readily available elsewhere. Other diseases that women may be more susceptible to while traveling are vaginal thrush and cystitis, two treatable but uncomfortable diseases. Women also needs to be aware that **tampons** and pads are sometimes hard to find in the Alaskan wilderness; certainly your preferred brands may not be available, so it may be advisable to take supplies along. O.b. tampons have very little packaging and take up less space in a backpack or suitcase. Refer to the *Handbook for Women Travellers* by Maggie and Gemma Moss for more extensive information specific to women's health on the road.

EVERYTHING YOU WERE AFRAID TO ASK

All travelers should be concerned about **Acquired Immune Deficiency Syndrome (AIDS),** transmitted through the exchange of body fluids with an infected individual (HIV-positive). The World Health Organization (WHO) reports that worldwide, 10-13 million people are infected with HIV, the virus that weakens a person's immune system and leads to AIDS. Remember that there is no assurance that someone is not infected: HIV tests only show antibodies after a six-month lapse. People can be healthy with HIV for 5-10 years after infection before they develop symptoms of AIDS, so HIV infection is invisible. Never have sex with people whom you do not know or with people you know to engage in high risk behaviors (i.e., IV drug use or promiscuous or unprotected sexual activity).

While you my be able to recognize some of the symptoms of full-blown AIDS, you can never tell by looking at or even examining someone whether he or she carries the HIV virus. Medical authorities recommend using a condom during vaginal, anal, and oral sex, and to use either a latex condom lubricated with spermicide (nonoxynol-9) or to apply spermicide to the tip of the condom separately. Performing oral sex carries much less risk than vaginal or anal sex does, and receiving carries even less, but if you have reason to suspect that your partner is HIV-positive, do not have unprotected oral sex with him or her. An unlubricated condom is best for use during oral sex. Women can create dental dams from saran wrap or by cutting a square of latex from a condom. Do not use lambskin condoms- they have bigger pores than latex and the HIV virus can penetrate, even if semen does not. Do not use oil-based lubricants, which can destroy latex. Do not share intravenous needles with anyone. Be aware, too, that drugs and alcohol are associated with higher rates of unprotected rates of unprotected sex; keep condoms with nonoxynol-9 or dental dams with you at all times, and implant the need for protection deep enough in your subconscious that it will still occur to you if you are drunk or high. Remember, too, that it is risky to share piercing or tattoo equipment. Of course, none of these protective methods is 100% effective, but they do significantly reduce the danger.

Neither the U.S. nor Canada require a medical exam for those visiting their countries, meaning that HIV-infected individuals may enter. The Center for Disease Control's **AIDS Hotline** provides information on AIDS in the U.S. and can refer you to other organizations with information on Canada (800-342-2437 24 hrs.; Spanish 800-344-7432 8am-2am; TTD 800-243-7889 8am-2am). The **World Health Organization** (202-861-3200) provides written material on AIDS internationally.

Reliable **contraception** may sometimes be difficult to come by while traveling. Women on the pill should bring enough to allow for possible loss or extended stay, as should women who use diaphragms and need contraceptive jelly. **Condoms** are increasingly available from drugstores and pharmacies throughout the U.S. and Canada. They are the most commonly used form of protection against AIDS and unwanted pregnancies in these countries.

■ MEDICAL ATTENTION ON THE ROAD

While you travel, eat well, drink lots of fluids, get enough sleep, and don't overexert yourself– in other words, listen to your body. Pay attention to signals of pain and discomfort; these may be due to a new climate, diet, water quality, or pace when you first arrive or even after a couple of weeks. Your increased exertion may wear you out and make you more susceptible to illness, and some of the milder symptoms that you may safely ignore at home may be signs of something more serious on the road. The following paragraphs list some health problems you may encounter, but should not be your only information source on these common ailments. Check with the publications and organizations listed above for more complete information, or send for the **American Red Cross** *First-Aid and Safety Handbook* ($15), available by writing to your local office. If you are interested in taking one of the many first-aid and CPR courses that the American Red Cross offers before leaving on your trip, contact your local office—courses are well-taught and relatively inexpensive.

When traveling in the summer, or at any time in tropical or desert regions, protect yourself against the **dangers of the sun and heat,** especially to the possibility of heatstroke. The term **heatstroke** is often misapplied to all forms of heat exhaustion, but it actually refers to a specific reaction caused by continuous heat stress, lack of fitness, or overactivity following heat exhaustion. In the early stages of heatstroke, sweating stops, body temperature rises, and an intense headache develops, which if untreated is followed by mental confusion and, ultimately, death. Experts recommend cooling a heatstroke victim off immediately with fruit juice or salted water, wet towels, and shade, then rushing him to the hospital. Less debilitating, but still dangerous, is sunburn (and its predecessor, suntan). If you're prone to sunburn, carry sunscreen with you and apply it liberally and often. Be wary of sunscreens of SPF (skin protection factor) higher than 20, however; SPFs of 15 or 20 are strong enough for the fairest skin, and higher ratings won't make a measurable difference, but will cost more. Wear a hat and sunglasses and a lightweight long sleeve shirt to avoid heatstroke. If you get sunburned, drink even more water and other fluids than you otherwise might; they'll cool you down and help your skin recover faster.

Extreme **cold** is no less dangerous than heat–overexposure to cold brings risks of hypothermia and frostbite. **Hypothermia** is a result of exposure to cold, and can occur even in the middle of the summer, especially in rainy or windy conditions or at night. The signs are easy to detect: body temperature drops rapidly, resulting in the failure to produce body heat. Other possible symptoms are uncontrollable shivering, poor coordination, and exhaustion, followed by slurred speech, sleepiness, hallucinations, and amnesia. Doctors recommend to *not* let victims fall asleep if they are in advanced stages—if they lose consciousness, they might die. Seek medical help as soon as possible. To avoid hypothermia, always keep dry. Wear wool or polypropylene, *especially* in soggy weather—they retain their insulating properties even when wet. Dress in layers, avoid cotton, and stay out of the wind, which carries heat away from the body. Remember that most loss of body heat is through your head, so always carry a wool hat with you. In freezing temperatures, **frostbite** may occur. The affected skin will turn white, then waxy and cold. To counteract the problem, the victim should drink warm beverages, stay or get dry, and gently and slowly warm the frostbitten area in dry fabric or with steady body contact. NEVER *rub* frostbite—the skin is easily damaged when frozen. Take serious cases to a doctor or medic as soon as possible.

Travelers in **high altitudes** should allow their bodies a couple of days to adjust to the lower atmospheric oxygen levels before engaging in any strenuous activity. This particularly applies to those intent on setting out on long alpine hikes. Those new to high-altitude areas may feel drowsy and get headaches, and one alcoholic beverage may have the same effect as three at a lower altitude.

If you plan to **romp in the forest,** scope out your terrain and pack food, water and equipment accordingly. Try to learn of any regional hazards. Know that any three-leaved plant might be poison ivy, poison oak, or poison sumac—pernicious plants whose oily surface causes insufferable itchiness if touched. (As Marge Simpson tells Bart and Lisa before they leave for camp, "Leaves of three, let it be; leaves of four, eat some more.") If you touch poison oak or other varieties, wash your skin as soon as possible in cold water and soap (heat will dilate your pores and drive the poison deeper into your skin). Taking an antihistamine may help the itching. Some people have allergic reactions to poison oak, ivy, or sumac, causing asthma-like reactions in which their breathing passages close up. If you begin to have a severe reaction, try to remain calm and seek immediate medical attention.

Many areas have their own local snakes, spiders, insects and other **creepy-crawlies.** Be sure to wear repellent, long sleeves, long pants, and socks. Calamine lotion or tropical cortisones (like Cortaid) may stop insect bites from itching. More soothing, but harder to get on the road, is a bath with baking soda or oatmeal (**Aveeno** packages several oatmeal mixtures, or you could just dump a half-cup or so of baking soda into a lukewarm bath.) See the Wilderness Concerns section on page 58, below, for more thorough information on safety concerns while in the wilds.

Food poisoning can spoil any trip. Some of the cheapest and most convenient eating options are also the most susceptible, including street vendors' wares, tap water, and perishable foods (like mayonnaise) carried for hours in a hot backpack. Fried or greasy foods, especially prevalent in the U.S., may weigh you down or cause indigestion (especially for those not used to eating them).

One of the most common symptoms associated with eating and drinking in another country is **diarrhea.** Known variously as *turista, Montezuma's revenge,* and "what a way to spend my vacation," diarrhea *symptoms* can be cured with over-the-counter remedies (such as Pepto-Bismol). However, since dehydration is the most common side effect of diarrhea and does not necessarily cease with medication, those suffering should drink plenty of fruit juice and pure water. The simplest anti-dehydration formula is still highly effective: 8oz. of water with a ½ tsp. of sugar or honey and a pinch of salt. Down several of these a day.

Trudging around the world is a romantic undertaking, but be sure to take care of your **feet** along the way; bring moleskin for blisters (the U.S.A. brand **2nd Skin** is highly effective), wear durable, comfortable shoes with arches, and change your socks often. If you are ever bitten by an animal, be concerned about **rabies**; be sure to clean the wound carefully and seek medical help to determine whether you need special treatment.

■■■ INSURANCE

Beware of unnecessary coverage—your current policies might well extend to many travel-related accidents. **Medical insurance** (especially university policies) often cover costs incurred abroad. **Medicare's** foreign travel coverage is limited, but is valid in Canada. Canadians are protected by their home province's health insurance plan: check with the provincial Ministry of Health or Health Plan Headquarters. Your Homeowners' Insurance (or your family's coverage) often covers theft during travel. Homeowners are generally covered against loss of travel documents (passport, plane ticket, railpass, etc.) up to $500.

Buying an **ISIC** in the U.S. provides $3000 worth of accident and illness insurance and $100 per day up to 60 days of hospitalization while the card is valid (see Youth and Student Identification on page 9, above). **CIEE** offers the inexpensive Trip-Safe plan with options covering medical treatment and hospitalization, accidents, baggage loss, and even charter flights missed due to illness; **STA** offers a more expensive, more comprehensive plan (see page 4). **American Express** cardholders receive automatic car-rental and flight insurance on purchases made with the card.

Insurance companies usually require a copy of the police report for thefts, or evidence of having paid medical expenses (doctor's statements, receipts) for illness, before they will honor a claim, and many have time limits on filing. Have documents written in English to avoid translating fees. Always carry policy numbers and proof of insurance. Note that some of the plans listed below offer cash advances or guaranteed bills; be sure to check with each insurance carrier for specific restrictions.

Access America, Inc., 6600 West Broad St., P.O. Box 11188, Richmond, VA 23230 (800-294-8300; fax 804-673-1491). Covers trip cancellation/interruption, on-the-spot hospital admittance costs, emergency medical evacuation. 24-hr. hotline.

ARM Coverage, Inc./Carefree Travel Insurance, 100 Garden City Plaza, P.O. Box 9366, Garden City, N.Y. 11530-9366 (800-323-3149 or 516-294-0220; fax 516-294-1821). Offers 2comprehensive packages. Trip cancellation/interruption may be purchased separately at a rate of $5.50 per $100 of coverage. 24-hr. hotline.

Travel Assistance International, by Worldwide Assistance Services, Inc., 1133 15th St. #400, NW, Washington DC 20005 (800-821-2828; fax 202-331-1530). Short-term and long-term plans available. 24-hr. hotline.

Travel Guard International, 1145 Clark St., Stevens Point, WI 54481 (800-826-1300 or 715-345-0505; fax 715-345-0525). "Travel Guard Gold" packages; Basic ($19), Deluxe ($39), and Comprehensive (9% of total trip cost) for medical expenses, delays, and trip cancellation/interruption. 24-hr. hotline.

Travel Insured International, Inc., 52-S Oakland Avenue, P.O. Box 280568, East Hartford, CT 06128-0568 (800-243-3174; fax 203-528-8005). Insurance against accidents, travel delay, and default.

Wallach & Company, Inc., 107 W Federal St., P.O. Box 480, Middleburg, VA 22117-0480 (800-237-6615; fax 703-687-3172). Comprehensive medical insurance. Other optional coverage available. 24-hr. hotline.

■■■ SAFETY AND SECURITY

> For emergencies in the U.S. and Canada, dial 911. This number works in most places. If it does not, dial 0 for the operator and request to be connected with the appropriate emergency service (i.e., police, fire, ambulance, etc.).

■ STAYING SAFE

Tourists are particularly vulnerable to crime for two reasons: they often carry large amounts of cash and they are not as savvy as locals. To avoid such unwanted attention, the best tactic is to blend in as much as possible: the gawking camera-toter is much easier prey than the casual local look-alike. Muggings are more often impromptu than planned; walking with nervous, over-the-shoulder glances can be a tip that you have something valuable to protect. Carry all your valuables (including your passport, railpass, traveler's checks and airline ticket) either in a **money belt** or **neckpouch** stashed securely inside your clothing. These will help protect you from skilled thieves who use razors to slash open backpacks and fanny packs (particular favorites of skilled bag-snatchers). Making **photocopies** of important documents will allow you to recover them in case they are lost or filched. Carry one copy separate from the documents and leave another copy at home. Keep some money separate from the rest, to use in an emergency or in case of theft. Label every piece of luggage both inside and out.

When exploring a new **city,** extra vigilance may be wise, but no city should force you to turn precautions into panic. When you get to a place where you'll be spending some time, find out about unsafe areas from tourist information, from the manager of your hotel or hostel, or from a local whom you trust. Both men and women may want to carry a small **whistle** to scare off attackers or attract attention, and it's not a bad idea to jot down the number of the police if you'll be in town for a couple days. When walking at night, you should turn day-time precautions into mandates. In particular, stay near crowded and well-lit areas and do not attempt to cross through parks, parking lots or any other large, deserted areas.

Among the more colorful aspects of large cities are the **con artists.** Although less prevalent in the U.S. and Canada than in Europe, these hucksters use tricks which are many and adaptable. Be aware of certain classics: sob stories that require money, rolls of bills "found" on the street, mustard spilled (or saliva spit) onto your shoulder distracting you for enough time to snatch your bag. Always put on a bag so that the strap passes over your head and runs diagonally across your torso.

If you choose to sleep in a **car,** be aware that this is one of the most dangerous ways to get your rest—when you lock other people out, you also lock yourself in. It is foolish. Sleeping outside can be even more dangerous—camping is recommended only in official, supervised campsites or in wilderness backcountry.

There is no sure-fire set of precautions that will protect you from all situations you might encounter when you travel. A good self-defense course will give you more concrete ways to react to different types of aggression, but it might cost you more money than your trip. **Model Mugging** (East Coast 617-232-7900; Midwest 312-338-4545; West Coast 415-592-7300), a national organization with offices in several major cities, teaches a very effective, comprehensive course on self-defense. (Course prices vary from $400-500. Women's and men's courses offered.) Community colleges frequently offer self-defense courses at more affordable prices.

For official **Department of State** travel advisories on the U.S. and/or Canada, including crime and security, call their 24-hour hotline at 202-647-5225. Also available are pamphlets on traveling to specific areas. More complete information on safety while traveling may be found in *Travel Safety: Security and Safeguards at Home and Abroad,* from **Hippocrene Books, Inc.,** 171 Madison Ave., New York, NY 10016 (212-685-4371; orders 718-454-2366; fax 718-454-1391).

■ DRUGS AND ALCOHOL

In Oregon, Washington, and Alaska, the drinking age is 21 years of age and is strictly enforced. British Columbia and the Yukon Territory prohibit drinking below the age of 19, while in Alberta you can drink at 18. In both the U.S. and Canada, the law is strictly enforced. Particularly in the U.S., be prepared to show a photo ID (preferably some government document—driver's license or passport) if you look under 30. Some areas of the country are still "dry," meaning they do not permit the sale of alcohol at all, while other places do not allow it to be sold on Sundays.

Drugs and traveling are not a good combination. If you carry **prescription drugs** while your travel, it is vital to have a copy of the prescriptions themselves readily accessible at country borders. As far as **illegal drugs** are concerned, possession of marijuana no longer constitutes a misdemeanor in a *state's* reckoning, but is a U.S. *federal* offense subject to imprisonment. At the Canadian border, if you are found in possession of drugs, you will be subject to an automatic seven-year jail term, regardless of how small an amount you are found with, and if you are a foreigner, you will be permanently barred from entering the country—and that's just the beginning. Police attitudes towards drugs vary widely across the region. In some cities, police tend to ignore pot smokers who mind their own business. But don't be fooled by their seeming lack of interest; arrests are not uncommon. And while private use of marijuana used to be legal in **Alaska,** the law was recently *repealed,* and possession of the drug, even on private property, is now a punishable offense.

Officials at both the United States and Canadian borders also take **drunk driving** very seriously. No matter what kind of transportation you use for entry, if the customs guards discover a drunk driving conviction, you will be denied access.

■■■ WORK AND STUDY

■ WORK

Don't come looking for work unless you're steeled for a lot of adventure and a little hardship; bring extra money and a return ticket in case things go awry. Your best leads in the job hunt often come from local residents, hostels, employment offices and Chambers of Commerce. Temporary agencies often hire for non-secretarial placement as well as for standard typing assignments. Marketable skills (e.g. touch-typing, dictation, computer knowledge, and experience with children) will prove very helpful, if not necessary, in your search for a temporary job. Consult local newspapers and bulletin boards on local college campuses.

VISA REQUIREMENTS FOR NON-RESIDENTS

Working in the **U.S.** while carrying only a B-2 tourist visa is grounds for deportation. Before an appropriate visa can be issued to you, you must—depending on the visa category you are seeking—join a USIA-authorized Exchange Visitor Program (J-1 visa), enroll in a U.S. academic or language program (F-1 visa), or locate an employer who will sponsor you (usually an H-2B visa) and file the necessary paperwork with the Immigration and Naturalization Service (INS) in the United States on your behalf. In order to apply to the U.S. Embassy or Consulate for an J-1 or F-1 visa you must obtain an IAP-66 eligibility form, issued by a U.S. academic institution or a private organization involved in U.S. exchanges. The H-2 visa is difficult to obtain, as your employer must prove that there are no other American or foreign permanent residents already residing in the U.S. with your job skills. For more specific information on visa categories and requirements, contact your nearest U.S. Embassy or Consulate and Educational Advisory Service of the Fulbright Commission (a U.S. embassy-affiliated organization).

If you intend to work in **Canada,** you will need an **Employment Authorization,** which must be obtained before you enter the country; visitors ordinarily are not allowed to change status once they have arrived. The processing fee is CDN$100. Employment authorizations are only issued after it has been determined that qualified Canadian citizens and residents will not be adversely affected by the admission of a foreign worker. Your potential employer must contact the nearest **Canadian Employment Centre (CEC)** for approval of the employment offer. For more information, contact the consulate or embassy in your home country. Residents of the U.S., Greenland, St. Pierre, or Miquelon only may apply for employment authorization at the point of entry.

PAID EMPLOYMENT

Finding work in Alaska or the Pacific Northwest depends largely on pure persistence. The once-rapid expansion in industries such as construction, fishing, lumber, and oil has slowed somewhat, and as more people head to the region each year in search of employment, jobs become harder to find. Summer is the best season for job hunting, as warm weather and long daylight hours are put to good use before winter closes many industries down.

Paid employment can occasionally be found through the **USDA Forest Service;** in **Alaska,** write USDA Forest Service, Chugach National Forest, 3301 "C" St., #300, Anchorage, AK 99503 (907-271-4126).

Agriculture in the Northwest generates a huge variety of temporary unskilled jobs, but expect low wages and poor conditions. **Fruit pickers** are often needed in Oregon, Washington, and B.C.'s Okanagan Valley, since shortages of workers cause tons of fruit to spoil each year.

Cannery and **fish processing** jobs are currently the most popular forms of summer employment in Alaska. Many processing plants in the southeast, on Kodiak Island, and in the Aleutians have long waiting lists, and nearly two-thirds of their employees are hired through company offices in Washington, Oregon, or California.

WORK

However, canneries that need help often have jobs available on short notice. You can obtain a list of processing plants from the **Alaska Department of Fish and Game,** Commercial Fisheries Management and Development Division, P.O. Box 25526, Juneau, AK 99802-5526 (907-465-4210; open Mon.-Fri. 8am-4:30pm). Inquiries about the current employment outlook should be addressed to job service agencies in the towns where you wish to work. The major fish seasons are in July, August, and September.

To some, the continued popularity of **cannery** work is baffling. The work (gutting fish by hand) is difficult, boring, and unpleasant. Strenuous 16- to 18-hour days are often demanded (sometimes non-stop for up to 45 days). Cannery workers sleep in primitive tents and are exposed to sweeping rain. Hourly pay is only about $6 per hour, but this can bring you tons of money, especially since all overtime pays time-and-a-half, and you're almost guaranteed to save what you earn (you'll probably be too tired to spend it).

Don't count on earning thousands on an Alaskan **fishing boat;** skippers on profitable boats rarely hire inexperienced deck hands, and a job on an unprofitable boat nets you little sleep and poor pay. The work is dangerous, and you will be paid with a percentage of the profits; if it is a bad season for halibut, it will be a bad season for you. For an excellent brochure about fish processing jobs write to **Seafood FTU,** Alaska State Employment Service, P.O. Box 25509 Juneau, AK 99802-5509.

VOLUNTEERING

Volunteer jobs are readily available throughout the Pacific Northwest and Alaska. Some jobs provide room and board in exchange for labor. Write to **CIEE** (see Budget Travel Services on page 4) for *Volunteer! The Comprehensive Guide to Voluntary Service in the U.S. and Abroad* ($9, postage $1.50). CIEE also administers the **International Voluntary Service Program,** an international work-camp program which places young people interested in short-term voluntary service with organizations conducting projects worldwide, including the United States. Two- to four-week projects include restoring historical sights, working with children or the elderly, constructing low-income housing, and taking part in nature conservation. Room and board are provided. There is a $165 program fee and an 18 year age minimum. Request the initial application materials as early as January, and apply no later than April to ensure placement. For a brochure, write to CIEE, International Voluntary Service Department, 205 East 42nd St., NY 10017-5706, or call 212-661-1414 x1139. The **USDA Forest Service** invites everyone to volunteer as hosts to visitors to the woods. Contact the **USDA Forest Service,** Human Resource Program Office, P.O. Box 96090, Washington, DC 20090-6090 (703-235-8834; fax 703-235-1597).

WORK EXCHANGE PROGRAMS

Many student travel organizations arrange work-exchange programs. Both CIEE and YMCA place students as summer camp counselors in the U.S. In some areas you may be able to work a desk job at an HI Hostel in exchange for a bed. Check at hostels in the area you in which you are interested for opportunities. Foreign university-level students can get on-the-job technical training in fields such as engineering, computer science, agriculture, and natural and physical sciences from the **Association for International Practical Training,** which is the U.S. member of the **International Association for the Exchange of Students for Technical Experience (IAESTE).** You must apply through the IAESTE office in your home country; application deadlines vary. For more information, contact the local IAESTE committee—try universities or colleges in your area —or write to IAESTE, c/o AIPT, 10 Corporate Center, #250, 10400 Little Patuxent Pkwy., Columbia, MD (410-997-2200). If you are interested in staying with an American family and learning firsthand, check out World Learning **Homestay/USA.** Programs are available to international visitors aged 15 and up for stays from several days to several months in urban, suburban, and rural areas, in volunteer hosts' homes. Contact Homestay/USA at P.O. Box 676 Brattleboro, VT 05302 (800-257-7751). Other organizations to contact are:

CIEE (Council on International Educational Exchange) (see Budget Travel Services on page 4) runs a summer travel/ work program designed to provide students with the opportunity to spend their summers working in the U.S. University students studying in Australia, Canada, Costa Rica, the Dominican Republic, France, Germany, Ireland, Jamaica, New Zealand, Spain, and the U.K. are eligible and should contact CIEE for the appropriate addresses in their home countries.

SCI—International Voluntary Service, Route 2, Box 506B, Crozet, VA 22932 (804-823-1826). Established after WWI as a means to promote international understanding, SCI arranges placement in workcamps in Europe and the US for people over 18 and 16, respectively. Fees $40 (US) to $200 (former USSR).

■ STUDY

VISA REQUIREMENTS FOR NON-RESIDENTS

International students who wish to study in the **U.S.** must apply for either a J-1 visa (for exchange students) or a F-1 visas (for full-time students enrolled in an academic or language program). To obtain a J-1, you must fill out an IAP 66 eligibility form, issued by the program in which you will enroll. Neither the F-1 nor the J-1 visa specifies any expiration date; instead they are both valid for the duration of stay, which includes the length of your particular program and a brief grace period thereafter. In order to extend a student visa, fill out an I-538 form. Requests to extend a visa must be submitted 15 to 60 days before the original departure date.

To study in **Canada** you will need a Student Authorization in addition to any entry visa you may need (see Documents and Formalities above). To obtain one, contact the nearest Canadian Consulate or Embassy. Be sure to apply well ahead of time; it can take up to six months, and there is a fee of $75. You will also need to prove to the Canadian government that you are able to support yourself financially. A student authorization is good for one year. If you plan to stay longer, it is extremely important that you do not let it expire before you apply for renewal.

LANGUAGE EDUCATION PROGRAMS

If you are interested in studying in the **U.S.,** there are a number of different paths you can take. One possibility is to enroll in a language education program, particularly if you are interested in a short-term stay. Contact **World Learning, Inc.,** which runs the **International Students of English** program, offering intensive language courses at select U.S. campuses. The price of a four-week program averages US$1800. For more information, write to World Learning, PO Box 676, Brattleboro, VT 05302-0676 (802-257-7751).

TOEFL/TSE

Almost all institutions accept applications from foreign students directly. If English is not your native tongue, you will likely be required to take the Test of English as a Foreign Language and Test of Spoken English (TOEFL/TSE), which is administered in many countries. Requirements are set by each school. Contact the **TOEFL/TSE Application Office,** PO Box 6151, Princeton, NJ 08541-6151 (609-951-1100).

ENROLLING IN A U.S. OR CANADIAN COLLEGE OR UNIVERSITY

If you would rather live the life of an American or Canadian college student, you might consider a visiting student program lasting either a semester or a full year. Contact colleges and universities in your country to see what kind of exchanges they administer. Many colleges in the Pacific Northwest welcome visiting students. The colleges and universities listed below all offer summer terms (3-11 weeks). Direct all correspondence to the **Director of Admissions** unless otherwise noted. **University of Alaska Fairbanks,** P.O. Box 757480, Fairbanks, AK 99775-7480 (907-474-7521). **University of Alaska, Anchorage,** 3211 Providence Dr., Anchorage, AK 99508 (907-786-1480). **Lewis & Clark College,** 0615 SW Palatine Hill Rd., Portland,

OR 97219 (503-768-7040 or 800-444-4111). **University of Oregon,** 240 Oregon Hall, Eugene, OR 97403 (503-346-3201; fax at 503-346-5815). **Oregon State University,** Administrative Services B-104, Corvallis, OR 97331-2106 (503-737-4411). **University of Washington,** Smith Hall, 1400 NE Campus Pkwy., Seattle, WA 98195 (206-543-9686). **Washington State University,** 342 French Administration Bldg., Pullman, WA 99164-1036 (509-335-5586; fax at 509-335-4902). **University of Alberta,** 120 Administration Bldg., Edmonton, AB T6G 2M7 (403-492-3113). **University of Calgary,** 2500 University Dr. NW, Calgary, AB T2N 1N4 (403-220-6640). **Simon Fraser University,** Burnaby, BC V5A 1S6 (604-291-3111). **University of British Columbia,** Office of the Registrar, Brock Hall, 2016-1874 East Mall, Vancouver, BC V6T 1Z1 (604-822-3159; fax at 604-822-5945). **University of Victoria,** P.O. Box 3025, Victoria, BC V8W 3P2 (604-721-8111).

Most U.S. and Canadian colleges have offices that give advice and information on studying in the U.S. To help you choose the college which suits you, seek out one or all of the following annually revised reference books which provide summaries and evaluations of various colleges, describing their general atmosphere, fields of study, tuition, and enrollment data. Among the most useful are *The Insider's Guide to the Colleges* (St. Martin's Press, $20), the *Fiske Guide to Colleges* by Edward Fiske (N.Y. Times Books, $16), and *Barron's Profiles of American Colleges* ($19).

One excellent source of information on studying in the U.S. and Canada is the **Institute of International Education (IIE),** which administers many exchange programs in the US and abroad. IIE publishes *Academic Year Abroad,* which describes over 2,100 semester and academic-year programs offered in the US and Canada ($43 plus $4 shipping); *Vacation Study Abroad,* with information on 1,500 short term programs in the US and Canada ($37, shipping $4); and *English Language and Orientation Programs,* detailing language and cultural programs, (1993/4 edition $43, plus $4 shipping). Many **Central Bureau** books (see Work-Exchange programs above) are also available from IIE. Contact IIE Books, Institute for International Education, 809 United Nations Plaza, New York, NY 10017-3580 (212-984-5412; fax 212-984-5358).

■■■ PACKING

■ WHAT TO PACK

Pack light. Set out everything you think you need, then pack only half of it. Include lots of T-shirts, underwear, and socks, even if it means skimping on everything else. And leave room for gifts. Irrepressible luggage freaks should read Judith Gilford's *The Packing Book* (US$8), which provides various checklists and suggested wardrobes, addresses safety concerns, includes advice for traveling with children, imparts packing techniques, and more. Order from **Ten Speed Press,** P.O. Box 7123, Berkeley, CA 94707 ((800) 841-2665)

First decide what kind of luggage will be necessary for your trip. If you'll be biking or hiking a great deal, a **backpack** is in order (see Tent Camping and Hiking on page 56). If you plan to stay in one city or town for a while, you might prefer a light suitcase. Large shoulder bags or duffels are good for stuffing into lockers, crowded baggage compartments, and all-purpose lugging. Be sure to have a **daypack** for carrying a day's worth of food, camera, first-aid essentials, and valuables. Guard your money, passport, and other important articles in a moneybelt and keep it with you at *all times.* Refrain from using frontal "fannypacks;" these are visible invitations to theft. The best combination of convenience and invulnerability is the nylon, zippered pouch with belt that should sit inside the waist of your pants or skirt.

In the Northwest, be prepared for a wide range of weather conditions no matter what time of year you travel. To cover the most bases, stick with the "**layer** concept:" start with several T-shirts, over which you can wear a sweatshirt or sweater in cold or wet weather. It is a good idea to have at least one layer that will **insulate** while wet, such as polypropylene, polarfleece, or wool. For winter, and depending on which regions you visit, you may want a few heavier layers, as well as a winter coat with a breathable, waterproof shell. Dark colors are less likely to show the dirt they're bound to accumulate. A rain **poncho,** which will cover both you and your pack, can double as a groundcover for a night outdoors. And, of course, never go anywhere without your **towel.**

Shoes are very important, whether you'll be doing serious hiking or not. Buy comfortable shoes; Birkenstocks or Tevas can be worn with or without socks, and medium-weight hiking boots are an obvious necessity. Break your shoes in before you leave. Don't be caught without some type of rainproof footwear.

Other **odds and ends** to consider bringing: sleeping bag, sleep sack (required at many hostels—see Accommodations below), flashlight, pens and paper, travel alarm, plastic canteen or water bottle, padlock, plastic garbage bags (for isolating damp or dirty clothing), sewing kit, string, rubber bands, safety pins, pocketknife, earplugs for noisy hostels, waterproof matches, clothespins and a length of cord, sunglasses, insect repellent, and assorted toiletries, including toilet paper, sunscreen, and mild, *biosafe* liquid soap (Dr. Bronner's and Mountain Suds are two popular brands) for campers. A rubber squash ball can be a sink stopper; soap or shampoo should do for handwashing clothes.

■■■ MEASUREMENTS

Although the metric system has made considerable inroads into American business and science, the British system of weights and measures continues to prevail in the U.S. The following is a list of U.S. units and their metric equivalents:

1 inch = 25 millimeters (mm)	1mm = 0.04 inch
1 foot (ft.) = 0.30 meter (m)	1m = 3.33 ft.
1 yard (yd.) = 0.91m	1m = 1.1 yd.
1 mile = 1.61kilometers (km)	1km = 0.62 mile
1 ounce = 25 gram (g)	1g = 0.04 ounce
1 pound (lb.) = 0.45 kilogram (kg)	1kg = 2.22 pound
1 quart = 0.94 liter	1 liter = 1.06 quarts

Here are the comparative values of some U.S. units of measurement:

1 foot	= 12 inches
1 yard	= 3 feet
1 mile	= 5280 feet
1 pound	= 16 ounces (weight)
1 cup	= 8 ounces (volume)
1 pint	= 2 cups
1 quart	= 2 pints
1 gallon	= 4 quarts

It should be noted that gallons in the U.S. are not identical to those across the Atlantic; one U.S. gallon equals 0.83 Imperial gallons.

The U.S. uses the Fahrenheit **temperature scale.** To convert Fahrenheit to Centigrade temperatures, subtract 32, then multiply by 5/9. To convert from Centigrade to Fahrenheit, multiply by 9/5 and then add 32. Or, just remember that 32° is the freezing point of water, 212° its boiling point, normal human body temperature is 98.6°, and room temperature hovers around 70°.

■ ELECTRICITY

Electricity is 110V AC in the U.S. and Canada, only half as much as that of most European countries. Visit a hardware store for an **adapter** (which changes the shape of the plug) and a **converter** (which changes the voltage). Do not make the mistake of using only an adapter, or you'll fry your appliances. Travelers who heat-disinfect their **contact lenses** should consider switching to a chemical disinfection system.

■ PHOTOGRAPHY

At every turn in the Northwest, you'll want to photograph your breathtaking surroundings. You will have to carefully consider before you leave, though, how much equipment you absolutely *need:* camera gear is heavy, fragile, and costly to replace. Buy film before you leave, or in the big cities as you go. Often large discount department stores have the best deals. The sensitivity of film to light is measured by the **ASA/ISO number:** 100 is good for normal outdoor or indoor flash photography, 3200 is necessary for night photography. A variety of 12-exposure film rolls in different speeds will afford you the greatest flexibility.

Although most tourists visit Alaska during the period of its endless summer light, residents maintain that their land is most beautiful in the winter. One reward for the intrepid winter traveler is the *aurora borealis,* or **"northern lights."** Shimmering spectrums of color dance like smoke, visible whenever the sky is dark. The brightest displays occur in fall and spring when the earth's tilt toward the sun accentuates their light most. To photograph the Northern Lights, you'll need 10- to 30-second exposures on a tripod-based 35mm camera with a locking cable release. For 400 ASA film, use the following scale as a guide: f 1.2 for 2 seconds; f 1.4 for 3 seconds; f 2 for 10 seconds; f 2.8 for 20 seconds; and f 3.5 for 30 seconds. September and March are the best months in which to view the Aurora.

Even the greatest photographs cannot do the scenery perfect justice, so don't let the need to snap the perfect photo fill your every waking hour. To preserve some of the grandeur, shoot slides instead of prints—they're also cheaper to process.

Process your film after you return home; you will save money, and it's much simpler to carry rolls of film as you travel, rather than easily damaged boxes of slides or packages of prints and negatives. A less cumbersome and worrisome option is a disposable camera available at most supermarkets and drug stores. These gadgets enable you to take 36 pictures and then trash the camera, which is no more than a paper box. More expensive models even include a flash or wide-angle lens. In any event, protect exposed film from extreme heat and the sun. Despite disclaimers, **airport X-ray equipment** can fog film; the more sensitive the film, the more susceptible to damage: anything over ASA 1600 should not be X-rayed. Ask security personnel to inspect your camera and film by hand. Serious photographers should purchase a lead-lined pouch for storing film.

■■■ SPECIFIC CONCERNS

■ WOMEN AND TRAVEL

Women exploring any area on their own inevitably face additional **safety concerns**. In all situations it is best to trust your instincts: if you'd feel better somewhere else, don't hesitate to move on. Always carry extra money for a phone call, bus, or taxi. You may want to consider staying in hostels which offer single rooms which lock from the inside. Stick to centrally-located accommodations and avoid late-night treks or metro rides. Remember that **hitching** is *never* safe for women. Choose train compartments occupied by other women or couples. In general, dress conservatively, especially in more rural areas. If you spend time in cities, you may be harassed no matter how you're dressed. Look as if you know where you're going (even when you don't) and ask women or couples for directions if you're lost or if you feel uncomfortable. In crowds, you may be pinched or squeezed by oversexed slime-balls; wearing a conspicuous **wedding band** may help prevent such incidents. Don't hesitate to seek out a police officer or a passerby if you are being harassed.

A **Model Mugging** course (see Safety and Security: Staying Safe on page 19) will not only prepare you for a potential mugging, but will also increase your feeling of confidence in unfamiliar areas. Offices exist in 14 U.S. states, as well as in Quebec.

For additional tips and suggestions, consult *The Handbook for Women Travelers* (£9) by Maggie and Gemma Moss, published by Piatkus Books, 5 Windmill St., London W1P 1HF England (tel. 44 071 631 0710). Also consult *Women Going Places* ($14), a new women's travel and resource guide emphasizing women-owned enterprises. The guide is geared towards lesbians, but offers advice appropriate for all women and is available from Inland Book Company, P.O. Box 120261, East Haven, CT 06512 (203-467-4257). The latest option is *A Journey of One's Own,* by Thalia Zepatos (Eighth Mountain Press, $15), which includes a specific and manageable bibliography of books and resources. **Wander Women,** 136 N Grand Ave. #237, West Covina, CA 91791 (818-966-8857) is a travel and adventure networking organization for women over 40, and publishes the quarterly newsletter Journal 'n Footnotes (Membership $29 per year.) Finally, the **National Organization for Women** has branches across the country, and can refer women travelers to rape crisis centers, counseling services, and lists of feminist events in the area. Main offices include 22 W 21st, 7th floor, New York, NY 10010 (212-807-0721; 425 13th St. NW, Washington DC 20004 (202-234-4558); and 3543 18th St., San Francisco, CA 94110 (415-861-8880).

■ BISEXUAL, GAY, AND LESBIAN TRAVELERS

Generally, in the larger cities of the Pacific Northwest, you need not compromise your freedom to enjoy your trip. Be warned, however, that smaller communities may not be so receptive to openly gay and lesbian travelers. The most open atmospheres can be found in large cities and tourist and college towns. Wherever possible, *Let's Go* lists local gay and lesbian information lines and community centers.

Damron, P.O. Box 422458, San Francisco, CA 94142 (800-462-6654 or 415-255-0404). Publishers of the Damron Address Book ($14), which lists over 800 bars, restaurants, guest houses, and services catering to the gay male. Covers the U.S., Canada, and Mexico. Also publishes the *Damron Road Atlas* ($13), which contains color maps of 56 major U.S. and Canadian cities and listings of gay and lesbian resorts, bars and accommodations, and *The Women's Traveler* ($10), which includes maps of 50 major U.S. cities and listings of bars, restaurants, accommodations, bookstores, and services catering to lesbians. Mail order add $4 shipping.

Ferrari Publications, P.O. Box 37887, Phoenix, AZ 85069 (602-863-2408). Publishes *Ferrari's Places of Interest* ($16), *Ferrari's Places for Men* ($15), *Ferrari's Places for Women* ($13), and *Inn Places: US A and Worldwide Gay Accommodations* ($15). Available in bookstores, or by mail order (postage $3.50).

Gay's the Word, 66 Marchmont St., London WC1N 1AB, England (tel. 071 278 7654). Tube: Russell Sq. A gay and lesbian bookshop which also sells videos, jewelry, and postcards. Mail order service also available. Open Mon.-Fri. 11am-7pm, Sat. 10-6, Sun. and holidays 2-6pm.

Gayellow Pages (U.S./Canada edition $12) an annually updated listing of accommodations, resorts, hotlines, and other items of interest to the gay traveler. Available through Renaissance House. For further details, send a self-addressed, stamped envelope to Box 292, Village Station, New York NY 10014-0292 (212-674-0120).

Giovanni's Room, 345 S 12th St., Philadelphia, PA 19107 (215-923-2960; fax 215-923-0813). International feminist, lesbian and gay bookstore with mail-order Call or write for a free mail-order catalogue.

Renaissance House, P.O. Box 533, Village Station, New York, NY 10014 (212-674-0121; fax 212-420-1126). Send self-addressed stamped envelope for a free mail-order catalogue.

Spartacus International Gay Guide, ($30). Published by Bruno Gmunder, P.O. Box 301345, D-1000 Berlin 30, Germany (49 30 25 49 82 00). Extensive list of gay bars, restaurants, hotels, bookstores and hotlines throughout the world for men.

Women Going Places, a new women's travel and resource guide emphasizing women-owned enterprises. Geared towards lesbians, but offers advice appropriate for all women. $14. Available from Inland Book Company, P.O. Box 120261, East Haven, CT 06512 (203-467-4257).

■ OLDER TRAVELERS

Seniors are eligible for a wide range of discounts on transportation, museums, movies, theater, concerts, restaurants, and accommodations. Proof of age is usually required (e.g., a driver's license, Medicare card, or membership card from a recognized society of retired persons).

Hostelling International (HI) sells membership cards at a discount to those over 54 ($15). Write the **American Youth Hostel (HI/AYH)** National Headquarters, P.O. Box 37613, Washington DC 20013-7613 (202-783-6161). See Youth Hostels on page 49 for more information. To explore the outdoors, seniors 62 and over can buy a lifetime **Golden Age Passport** ($10), allowing entry into all national parks and a 50% discount on recreational activities. See Parks & Forests on page 54 for more information. Check out Joan Rattner Heilman's *Unbelievable Good Deals and Great Adventures That You Absolutely Can't Get Unless You're Over 50* (Contemporary Books, $8). Also consult the following organizations for information:

AARP (American Association of Retired Persons), 601 E St. NW, Washington, DC 20049 (202-434-2277). U.S. residents over 50 and spouses receive benefits which include travel programs and discounts, as well as discounts on lodging, car and RV rental, air arrangements, and sight-seeing. $8 annual fee per couple.

Elderhostel, 75 Federal St., 3rd floor, Boston, MA 02110. You must be 60 or over, and may bring a spouse who is over 50. Programs at colleges and universities in over 40 countries focus on varied subjects and generally last one week.

Gateway Books, 2023 Clemens Rd., Oakland, CA 94602 (510-530-0299 or 800-669-0773 for credit card orders; fax 510-530-0497). Publishes Gene and Adele Malott's *Get Up and Go: A Guide for the Mature Traveler* ($11, postage $2), and Adventures Abroad ($13), which offer tips for the budget-conscious senior.

National Council of Senior Citizens, 1331 F St. NW, Washington, DC 20004 (202-347-8800). For $12 a year, $30 for three years, or $150 for a lifetime, an individual or couple of any age can receive a range of discounts.

Pilot Books, 103 Cooper St., Babylon, NY 11702 (516-422-2225). Publishes *The International Health Guide for Senior Citizens* ($6) and *The Senior Citizens' Guide to Budget Travel in the United States and Canada* ($6).

■ TRAVELERS WITH DISABILITIES

Travelers with disabilities should arrange transportation well in advance. **Hertz, Avis,** and **National** have hand-controlled vehicles at some locations (see By Car in the Getting There and Getting Around section below). **Amtrak** and all **airlines** can better serve passengers with disabilities if notified in advance; tell the ticket agent when making reservations which services you'll need. Both **Greyhound** and Canada's **VIA Rail** allow a person with disabilities and a companion to ride for the price of a single fare with a doctor's statement confirming that a companion is necessary. Wheelchairs, seeing-eye dogs, and oxygen tanks are not counted against your luggage allowance. If you are without a fellow-traveler, call Greyhound's special hotline (800-752-4841) at least 48 hours before you plan to travel so that they can make arrangements to assist you. Many **ferries** that run up and down the Pacific coast can also accommodate travelers who are disabled; consult the companies listed under By Ferry on page 42.

American Foundation for the Blind, 15 W 16th St., New York, NY 10011 (212-620-2147). ID cards ($10); write for an application, or call the Product Center (800-829-0500). Also call this number to order AFB catalogs in Braille, print, or on cassette or disk. Open Mon.-Fri. 9am-2pm.

Directions Unlimited, 720 North Bedford Rd., Bedford Hills, NY 10507 (800-533-5343 or 914-241-1700; fax 914-241-0243). Specializes in arranging individual and group vacations, tours and cruises for those with disabilities.

Facts on File, 460 Park Ave. S, New York, NY 10016 (800-829-0500, 212-683-2244 in AK or HI). Publishers of *Access to the World* ($17), a guide to accessible accommodations and sights. Available in bookstores or by mail-order.

Mobility International, USA (MIUSA), P.O. Box 10767, Eugene, OR 97440 (503-343-1284 voice and TDD; fax 503-343-6812). International headquarters in Britain, 228 Borough High St., London SE1 1JX (071 403 5688). Contacts in 30 countries. Travel programs, international work camps, accommodations, access guides, and organized tours. Membership $20 per year, newsletter $10. Sells *A World of Options: A Guide to International Educational Exchange, Community Service, and Travel for Persons with Disabilities* ($14, nonmembers $16).

Society for the Advancement of Travel for the Handicapped, 347 Fifth Ave. #610, New York, NY 10016 (212-447-7284; fax 212-725-8253). Publishes quarterly travel newsletter *SATH News* and information booklets (free, nonmembers $3). Advice on trip planning. Annual membership $45, students and seniors $25.

Twin Peaks Press, P.O. Box 129, Vancouver, WA 98666-0129 (206-694-2462, orders only 800-637-2256). *Travel for the Disabled* lists tips and resources ($20). Also available: *Directory for Travel Agencies of the Disabled* ($20),*Wheelchair Vagabond* ($15), and *Directory of Accessible Van Rentals* ($10). Postage $2.

■ TRAVELERS WITH CHILDREN

If you're planning a family vacation with the kids, you'll need to adapt your travel pace to their needs. Consult local newspapers or travel bureaus to find out about events that might be of special interest for young children, such as the Cannon Beach Sandcastle Festival in Oregon or the annual Magicazam magic show that visits Portland in the summer. Most national parks offer **Junior Ranger** programs, which introduce kids ages 8-12 to nature in half- or full-day trips (see Parks & Forests in the Camping & the Outdoors section on page 54).

Many fares, admission prices, and fees are lower for children and/or families. Some lodgings, such as the **Days Inn,** offer special rates for rooms with kitchenettes (see Accommodations below). By **airplane,** children under 2 sit on your lap for free, ages 2 to 4 can ride for 10% of the fare, and ages 4 to 12 are half-off. By **Amtrak,** children under 2 are free, and ages 2-15 are usually half-off. However, it may be best to travel by car, as it allows you the freedom to make frequent stops and your children the freedom to spread out.

Children require additional health and safety considerations while on the road. If you're renting a car, be sure that the company supplies a child safety seat for children under five years old. Have children carry some sort of ID in case of emergency or in case they get lost. Before forging into the wilderness, consider picking up one of the following publications:

Lonely Planet Publications, Embarcadero West, 155 Philbert St., #251, Oakland, CA 94607 (510-893-8555 or 800-275-8555); also P.O. Box 617, Hawthorn, Victoria 3122, Australia. Publishes Maureen Wheeler's *Travel with Children* ($11, postage $1.50 in the U.S.).

John Muir Publications, P.O. Box 613, Santa Fe, NM 87504 (800-285-4078). The *Kidding Around* series ($10 each; $4.25 shipping) are illustrated books intended for children, depicting mostly U.S. destinations.

Wilderness Press, 2440 Bancroft Way, Berkeley, CA 94704 (800-443-7227 or 510-843-8080). Publishes *Backpacking with Babies and Small Children* ($11) and *Sharing Nature with Children* ($9).

■ TRAVELING ALONE

Single accommodations are usually much more costly per person than are doubles. In addition, if you do travel alone, you should be extremely careful about where you sleep: outdoor locations make the lone traveler an easy target.

Even if you're alone, chances are you won't be hurting for company along the way. If you carry your copy of *Let's Go,* you might be noticed by others doing the same. Another trick for finding people with whom you may have some connection is to wear a baseball cap or T-shirt from your home state or college. Hostels are great places to schmooze with fascinating wanderers like yourself.

■ KOSHER AND VEGETARIAN TRAVELERS

The Northwest heaps blessings on vegetarian and kosher travelers alike. Fresh fish, fruits, and vegetables abound in both the larger cities and smaller towns of the region. Delicious apples and Chinook salmon are just a couple of the area's indigenous treats. Alaska, however, offers largely fatty fare. Vegetarian travelers can obtain *The Vegetarian Travel Guide* and *Vegetarian Times Guide to Natural Foods Restaurants in the U.S. and Canada* (each costs $16 plus $2 postage) from the **North American Vegetarian Society,** P.O. Box 72, Dolgeville, NY 13329 (518-568-7970).

Kosher travelers should contact synagogues in Seattle, Portland, Vancouver, Edmonton, and Calgary for information about kosher restaurants in those cities; your own synagogue or college Hillel should have access to lists of Jewish institutions across the continent. *The Jewish Travel Guide* ($12 plus $1.75 postage) from **Sepher-Hermon Press,** 1265 46th St., Brooklyn, NY 11219 (718-972-9010), lists Jewish institutions, synagogues, and kosher restaurants in over 80 countries.

■ MINORITY TRAVELERS

As elsewhere in the U.S. and Canada, many smaller towns in the Pacific Northwest and Alaska can be uncomfortable for individuals who are obviously nonwhite. Some establishments do discriminate against individuals of color; Let's Go instructs its researchers not to list such establishments should they experience or witness such discrimination. If you encounter such a situation, remain calm and, if you feel confident, make it clear that another establishment will receive your business.

Recent years have seen a rise in the frequency of hate crimes against East and Southeast Asians, even in the larger cities of Portland, Seattle, and Vancouver. While these incidents have been widely publicized, be assured that the vast majority of travelers to the Pacific Northwest and Alaska have safe and enjoyable trips. Be aware of your surroundings, and do not hesitate to contact local police should you fear for your safety.

Getting There and Getting Around

■■■ ON A JET PLANE

■ COMMERCIAL AIRLINES

Be sure to check with your travel agent for system-wide air passes and excursion fares, especially since these generally have fewer advance-purchase requirements than standard tickets. Consider **discount travel agencies** such as **Travel Avenue,** 10 S Riverside Plaza, Chicago, IL, 60606 (800-333-3335), which rebates 4-7% on the price of all airline tickets (domestic and international) minus a $15 ticketing fee. Student-oriented agencies such as **CIEE, Travel CUTS,** and **STA Travel** (see Useful Organizations: Budget Travel Services above) sometimes have special deals that regular travel agents can't offer. The weekend travel sections of major newspapers (especially *The New York Times*) are good places to seek out bargain fares from a variety of carriers. If you're looking to bypass travel agents altogether, consult a library copy of the *Official Airline Guide (OAG),* 2000 Clearwater Dr., Oakbrook IL 60521 (800-323-3537), which publishes North American (twice a month) and worldwide (once a month) editions.

When dealing with any commercial airline, buying in advance is always the best bet. The commercial carriers' lowest regular offer is the **APEX** (Advanced Purchase Excursion Fare); specials advertised in newspapers may be cheaper, but have correspondingly more restrictions and fewer available seats. APEX fares provide you with confirmed reservations and often allow "open-jaw" tickets (landing and returning from different cities). APEX tickets must usually be purchased two to three weeks ahead of the departure date.

Last-minute travelers should also ask about **"red-eye"** (all-night) flights which are common on popular business routes. Be wary; It is unwise to buy **"frequent-flyer" coupons** from others—it is standard policy on most commercial airlines to check a photo ID, and you could find yourself paying for a new, full-fare ticket. Chances of receiving discount fares increase on competitive routes; flying smaller airlines instead of the national giants can also save money. When buying a ticket, be sure to inquire about additional student discounts, travel restrictions, and flexibility.

A total **smoking** ban is in effect on all scheduled service flights within and between the 48 contiguous U.S. states, within Hawaii and Alaska, and to and from Hawaii and Alaska if the flight is under six hours. This ban applies to both U.S. and international carriers operating within these areas. Flights touching a point outside the U.S. are not affected. The Canadian policy is still more stringent: a total smoking ban is in effect on all aircraft registered in Canada. This includes service within and between points in Canada as well as all international service (except Japan).

WITHIN NORTH AMERICA

The major carriers serving Alaska and the Pacific Northwest are listed below; call for sample fares:

Air Canada, P.O. Box 14000, St. Laurent, Que. H4Y 1H4 Canada (800-776-3000). Ask about special discounts for youths ages 12-24 on stand-by tickets for flights within Canada. Discounts can be substantial, although youth tickets can sometimes be more expensive than advance purchase fares.

Alaska Airlines, P.O. Box 68900, Seattle, WA 98168 USA (800-426-0333 for reservations and information).

Northwestern Air Lease Ltd., P.O. Box 249, Fort Smith, NWT X0E 0P0, Canada (800-661-2214). Travel within Alaska.

Other airlines to consider when flying into Alaska and the Pacific Northwest include **United,** P.O. Box 66100, Chicago, IL 60666 (800-241-6522); **USAir,** Crystal Park Four Dr., Arlington, VA 22227 (800-428-4322); and **Continental,** 2929 Allen Parkway, Houston, TX 77210 (800-525-0280).

Many major U.S. airlines offer special **"Visit USA"** air passes and fares to international travelers. You must purchase these passes outside the U.S., paying one price for a certain number of "flight coupons." Each coupon is good for one flight segment on an airline's domestic system within a certain time period; typically, all travel must be completed within 30-60 days. Some cross-country trips may require two segments. The point of departure and the destination must be specified for each coupon at the time of purchase, but dates of travel may be changed once travel has begun at no charge. **United** offers three vouchers for $305, and additional vouchers (up to 5 more) sell for $97 apiece. **USAir** (800-428-4322) offers three vouchers for $389 from July through mid-September, and for $349 off-season. Additional vouchers (up to 5 more) run $80 apiece year-round. **Continental, Delta** (800-221-1212), and **TWA** (800-892-4141) all offer programs as well.

Mexican residents who live more than 100 mi. from the border may be eligible for "Visit USA" discount flight passes on some carriers. Otherwise, because flying in the U.S. is expensive, it may be cheaper to fly on a Mexican airline to one of the border towns, and then to travel by train or bus from there. Contact **AeroMexico** (800-237-6639; fax 713-460-3334) or **Mexicana** (800-531-7921) for more information.

In recent years **American Express** has run promotions whereby students are offered a pre-approved green card along with vouchers for inexpensive domestic flights. Of course, you have to pay the $55 annual fee for the card, but the savings on longer flights can be substantial. Be sure to read the fine print about black-out dates and other restrictions. See Money: Credit Cards on page 13 for more information.

If all you need is a short flight, scout **local airfields** for prospective rides on private, non-commercial planes. Some airfields have ride boards. If not, a good place to begin is the operations counter, where pilots file their flight plans. Remember that propeller planes have a much higher accident rate than their larger commercial counterparts.

FROM EUROPE

Travelers from Europe will experience the least competition for inexpensive seats during the off-season. Peak season rates generally take effect on either May 15 or June 1 and run until about September 15. You can take advantage of cheap off-season flights within Europe to reach an advantageous point of departure for North America. (London is a major connecting point for budget flights to the U.S.; New York City is often the destination.) Once in the States, you can catch a coast-to-coast flight to make your way out West; see Within North America on page 31 for details.

If you decide to fly with a commercial airline rather than through a charter agency or ticket consolidator (see below), you'll be purchasing greater reliability, security, and flexibility. The worst crunch leaving Europe takes place from mid-June to early July, while August is uniformly tight for returning flights; at no time can you count on getting a seat right away. Reduced-rate fares are often available; check with a travel agent or inquire at the airline.

TWA (800-892-4141) offers a variety of international flights. **American,** P.O. Box 619616, Dallas/Ft. Worth Airport, Dallas, TX 75261-9616 (800-433-7300), often has good fares from London. **British Airways,** P.O. Box 10, Heathrow Airport (London), Hounslow TW6 2JA, England (800-247-9297) has extensive service from London to North America. Smaller, budget airlines often undercut major carriers by offering bargain fares on regularly scheduled flights. Competition for seats on these smaller carriers during peak season is fierce—book early. Discount trans-Atlantic airlines include **Virgin Atlantic Airways** (800-862-8621 daily 7am-11pm) and **Iceland-Air** (800-223-5500).

FROM AUSTRALIA, NEW ZEALAND, ASIA, AND SOUTH AFRICA

Whereas European travelers may choose from a variety of regular reduced fares, their counterparts in Asia, Australia, and South Africa must rely on APEX. A good place to start searching for tickets is a branch of one of the budget travel agencies listed above in Budget Travel Services. **STA Travel** is probably the largest international agency you will find: they have offices in Sydney, Melbourne, and Auckland.

Qantas (800-227-4500), **Air New Zealand** (800-663-5494), **United,** and **Northwest** fly between Australia or New Zealand and the United States, and both **Canadian Pacific Airlines** and **Northwest** fly to Canada. Many travelers from Australia and New Zealand reportedly take Singapore Air or other Far-East based carriers during the initial leg of their trip. Check with STA or another budget agency for more comprehensive information.

From Japan, U.S. airlines such as **Northwest** (800-225-2525) and **United Airlines** (800-241-6522) offer rates slightly higher than those of **Japan Airlines** (800-525-3663). **British Airways** (800-247-9297), **American** (800-443-7300), and **South African Airways** (800-722-9675) all connect South Africa with North America.

■ CHARTER FLIGHTS

Those wishing to bypass the larger commercial airlines should consider booking through a charter company or through a ticket consolidator. **Charter flights** can save you a lot of money. They are roughly equivalent to flying a commercial airline: your reservation guarantees you a seat on the plane, and you can be certain that if you don't get on the flight someone (other than you) is to blame. Many charters book passengers up to the last minute—some will not even sell tickets more than 30 days in advance. For more information, contact the charter companies listed below:

CIEE Travel Services, 205 E 42nd St., New York, NY 10017 (212-661-1450; fax 212-972-0194). A variety of flights from Europe to the U.S., although none originating from London. Phones open Mon.-Fri. 8am-8pm, Sat. 9am-5pm. (For more information on CIEE, see Useful Organizations above).

Travel CUTS, 187 College St., Toronto, Ont. M5T 1P7 (416-979-2406; fax 416-979-8167). The Canadian equivalent to CIEE. One program, open to all Canadians, flies directly into major Canadian destinations from the larger European cities; peak season (and rates) run May-Oct. A second program for students and youths (under 26) is similar to the first, except that all European flights connect through London and the fares are somewhat less. (For more information on Travel CUTS, see Useful Organizations on page 1.)

Unitravel, 1177 N Warson Rd., St. Louis, MO 63132 (800-325-2222; fax 314-569-2503). Specializes in trans-continental and long distance flights within the U.S. Phones open Mon.-Fri. 8am-8pm, Sat. 8am-4pm.

Also try **DER Tours,** 9501 West Devon Ave. #400, Rosemont, IL 60018 (800-782-2424; fax 800-282-7474), **Travel Charter International,** 1301 W Long Lake #270, Troy, MI 48098 (800-521-5267 or 313-528-3500; fax 800-FAX-3888), both of which offer charter flights to a more limited range of cities.

■ TICKET CONSOLIDATORS

Ticket Consolidators are companies which sell unbooked commercial and charter airline seats; tickets gained through them are both less expensive and more risky than those on charter flights. **Airhitch,** 2790 Broadway #100, New York, NY 10025 (212-864-2000; fax 212-864-5489), works through more cities and to a greater number of destinations, although their prices are slightly higher and flights are less desti-

nation-specific (meaning that often you must list, in order of priority, two or three cities within a given region which you are willing to fly to; Airhitch guarantees only that you will get to one of these cities). For most flights you must give a range of three to five days within which you are willing to travel. Be sure to read *all* of the fine print (especially since payment occurs well in advance of the actual flight), and to check all flight times and departure sites directly with the carrier. All fares are one-way in either direction. (East Coast phone lines open Mon.-Fri. 10am-6pm, Sat. 11am-4pm; off-season open Mon.-Fri. 10am-4pm, Sat. 11am-1pm.)

■■■ BY CAR

■ GETTING REVVED UP

If you'll be relying heavily on car travel, you would do well to join an automobile club. For $54 per year the **American Automobile Association (AAA)** (check your local yellow pages), offers free trip-planning services, roadmaps and guidebooks, discounts on car rentals, emergency road service anywhere in the U.S., free towing, the International Driver's Permit (see Documents & Formalities on page 5), and commission-free AmEx traveler's cheques. Your membership card doubles as a $5000 bail bond (if you find yourself in jail) or a $1000 arrest bond certificate (which you can use in lieu of being arrested for any motor vehicle offense except drunk driving, driving without a valid license, or failure to appear in court on a prior motor-vehicle arrest). Many clubs also have an "AAA Plus" membership program, costing about $76 per year, which provides more extensive emergency road service, insurance protection, and 100 mi. of free towing. AAA has reciprocal agreements with the auto associations of many other countries which often provide you with full benefits while in the U.S.

Other automobile travel service organizations are affiliated with oil companies or other large corporations. These include:

AMOCO Motor Club, P.O Box 9041, Des Moines, IA 50368 (800-334-3300). $50 annual membership.24-hr. towing (5 mi. free or free back to the tower's garage), emergency road service, trip planning, and travel information. Membership doubles as bail bond. Discounts for car rental at Avis, Alamo and Hertz and for selected hotels and motels. Premier membership ($75) brings 50 mi. free towing.

Mobil Auto Club, 200 N Martingale Rd., Schaumburg, IL 60174 (800-621-5581). For $52 per year, membership includes locksmith, free towing (up to 10 mi.) and other roadside services, as well as car-rental discounts with Hertz, Avis, and National. Free travelers checks, bail bond, and car repair discounts as well.

Montgomery Ward Auto Club, 200 N Martingale Rd., Schaumberg, IL 60173-2096 (800-621-5151). For $52 per year, get legal aid, and roadside assistance.

If you'll be driving during your trip, make sure that your **insurance** is up-to-date and that you are completely covered. Car rental companies often offer additional insurance coverage, as does American Express if you use them to rent the car. *In Canada, automobile insurance with coverage of CDN$200,000 is mandatory.* If you are involved in a car accident and you don't have insurance, the stiff fine will not improve the experience, and your car may be impounded to boot. U.S. motorists are advised to carry some form proving that they have insurance, the most effective of which is the **Canadian Non-Resident Inter-Provincial Motor Vehicle Liability Card.** The cards are available through U.S. insurers. For more information on insurance issues within Canada, contact **The Insurance Bureau of Canada,** 181 University Ave., Toronto, Ont. M5H 3M7. For information on the **International Driver's Permit,** see Documents & Formalities on page 5.

Let's Go lists U.S. highways in the following format: "I" (as in "I-90") refers to Interstate highways, "U.S." (as in "U.S. 1") to United States Highways, and "Rte." (as in "Rte. 7") to state and local highways.

■ ON THE ROAD

Learn a bit about minor automobile maintenance and repair before you leave, and pack an easy-to-read manual—it may at the very least help you keep your car alive long enough to reach a reputable garage. Your trunk should at least contain the following **bare necessities:** a spare tire and jack, jumper cables, extra oil, flares, a blanket (several, if you're traveling in winter), extra water (if you're traveling in summer or through the desert), and a flashlight. If there's a chance you may be stranded in a remote area, bring an emergency food and water supply. Always have plenty of gas and check road conditions ahead of time when possible, particularly during the winter. (*Let's Go* provides road condition hotline numbers where available.) Carry a good map with you at all times. **Rand McNally** publishes the most comprehensive road atlas of the U.S. and Canada, available in bookstores for around $8.

Gas is generally cheaper in towns than at interstate service stops. Don't be surprised to find that gas stations are, by law, solely full-service in Oregon. And when planning your budget, remember that the enormous travel distances of the Pacific Northwest and Alaska will require you to spend more on gas than you might expect. Burn less money by burning less fuel. Tune up the car, make sure the tires are in good repair and properly aligned and inflated, check the oil frequently, and avoid running the air conditioner unnecessarily. Don't use roof luggage racks—they cause air drag, and if you need one, you've probably over-packed. Check college campus ride boards, bulletin boards, and the classified ads (particularly those in newspapers geared to students) to find traveling companions who will split gasoline costs. Those in Alaska should **gas up whenever possible.** Filling stations can be few and far between. And it's also a good idea to carry and emergency supply of cash, since many filling stations in the more remote areas don't accept credit cards.

If you take a car into a major city, try not to leave valuable **possessions**—such as radios or luggage—in it while you're away from the car. Park your vehicle in a garage or well-traveled area. Sleeping in a car or van parked in the city is extremely dangerous—even the most hardcore budget traveler should not consider it.

Be sure to **buckle up**—it's the law in Washington, British Columbia, and Alberta. Before you hit the road, check rental cars to make sure that the seatbelts work properly. In general, the speed limit in the U.S. is 55mph, but rural sections of major interstates may well be 65mph (when posted).

Shockingly, the **interstate** system in the U.S. actually makes sense. Even-numbered interstates run east-west and odd ones run north-south, decreasing in number the further north or west they are. If the interstate has a three-digit number, it is a branch of another interstate (i.e., I-285 is a branch of I-85), often a bypass skirting around a large city. An *even* digit in the *hundred's* place means the branch will eventually return to the main interstate; an *odd* digit means it won't. North-south routes begin on the West Coast with I-5 and end with I-95 on the East Coast. The southernmost east-west route is I-4 in Florida. The northernmost east-west route is I-94, stretching from Montana to Wisconsin.

The greatest difficulty posed by interstates is not the state troopers, the other drivers, or even bad road conditions (although these can be imposing)—it's the sheer **boredom.** For a normally active brain, license plate games only stave off the soporific monotony for so long. To prevent "frozen vision," don't keep your eyes glued to the road. If you feel drowsy, pull off the road to take a break, even if there are no official rest areas in the vicinity. To avoid over-exhaustion, start driving in the wee hours of the morning and stop early in the afternoon (this way, you'll also have more time to find accommodations). When you're driving with companions, insist that one of them is awake at all times, and keep talking. If you can't pull over, try listening to an aggravating radio talk show (music can be as lulling as silence). A thermos of coffee is also helpful. And remember that turning up the heat too high in the car can also make you sleepy.

Never drive if you've had anything alcoholic to drink or if you've used drugs or any potentially impairing substance. Don't believe the myth that a cup of hot coffee or a cold shower can sober you up; the only remedy for a buzz is time, preferably spent doing some sort of activity (it burns off the alcohol faster), but several hours' sleep should do. Also, avoid the open road on weekend nights and holidays, when more drivers are likely to be drunk.

■ DRIVING IN ALASKA

Juneau, the only state capital in the nation that cannot be reached by automobile, is emblematic of Alaska's inaccessibility. In fact, roads reach only a quarter of the state's area. In 1942—under pressure to create wartime supply routes for Alaska's far-flung military bases—the U.S. Army Corps of Engineers built a 1500-mi. road from British Columbia to Fairbanks in an astonishingly quick eight months. The **Alaska Highway,** as it is now called, runs from Dawson Creek, B.C., to Fairbanks. The Canadian stretch of the road is poorly maintained, causing the entire drive to take three to five days. Only hardsiders should attempt this trip; lodgings en route are hard to come by. Winter and summer travelers alike are advised to let a friend or relative know of their position along the highway several times during the trip.

The **Haines Highway** connects Haines with the Alaska Hwy. at Haines Junction. Similarly, **Rte. 2** connects Skagway with the Alaska Hwy. in Whitehorse. In Fairbanks, the Alaska Hwy. merges into the **Dalton Highway,** which runs all the way north to Prudhoe Bay. Running south from the Alaska Hwy., the **George Parks Highway** goes to Denali and Anchorage from Fairbanks; the **Richardson Highway** goes to Glennallen from Delta Junction and continues on to Valdez; and the **Tok Cut Off** goes to Glennallen from Tok and merges into the **Glenn Highway,** which continues to Anchorage. From Anchorage, the **Seward Highway.** goes to Seward, and the **Sterling Highway** splits off to go to Homer. The highways that traverse the southern part of the state are narrow, often gravelly ribbons extending from town to town with few services in between.

Many major roads in Alaska are still in **desperately bad shape.** Dust and flying rocks are major hazards in the summer, as are the road construction crews, which interrupt long-distance trips with miserable 10- to 30-mi. patches of gravel as they repave the road. Many of the worst roads in Alaska (such as the Dalton Hwy. from Fairbanks to Prudhoe Bay) have been treated with calcium chloride to minimize the dust flying up from the road. Calcium chloride can be very hard on your car's paint, though, and you should take every opportunity to wash your car. And *drive slowly—* it will not only make the trip much easier on your own car, it will also keep dust from flying into the windshields of those behind you. Melting and contracting permafrost in the north causes "frost heaves," creating dips and Dali-esque twists on the road. Radiators and headlights should be protected from flying rocks and swarming bugs with a **wire screen;** plastic **headlight covers** can protect your lights; good **shocks** and a functional **spare tire** are absolutely essential. Wintertime snow cover can actually smooth your ride a bit: the packed surface and the thinned traffic it brings permit easy driving without the summer's mechanical troubles (although the dangers of avalanches and driving on ice offer a different set of concerns). Check road conditions before traveling; in Anchorage call 243-7675 (winter only) or tune in to local radio stations.

As a final precaution, keep in your car at all times the following in case of emergency or break-down: flares, a good set of tools and wrenches, a good jack, electrician's tape, a fan belt, a blanket and canned food.

Two valuable guides which include maps, detailed, mile-by-mile car routes and general travel information are available from **Vernon Publications, Inc.,** 3000 Northup Way, #200, Bellevue, WA, 98004 (800-726-4707; fax 206-822-9372). *The MILEPOST* is an exceptional guide to Alaska and northwestern Canada ($19), and, for off-the-road travel in Alaska, *The Alaska Wilderness Guide* covers bush communities and remote national parks, monuments, wilderness areas, and refuges ($17).

■ DRIVING IN THE NORTHWEST

Unlike the more densely populated regions of the continent, the Northwest does not have an extensive system of quality secondary roads. Older highways predominate; they merge with the main street of each town in their path, and are slower to drive—but far more rewarding—than most interstate freeways. Venture down unpaved roads for some unforgettable vistas, but be sure to have plenty of gas and a healthy driving machine. And before you hit the road, particularly during the winter, check out the **road conditions.**

Several major interstate highways provide connections between cities in the Northwest. Running north-south through Oregon and Washington are **I-5** and **US 101.** I-5 connects Portland and Seattle and is the fastest route through the region, while 101 hugs the coast and is known for its scenery. **I-84,** running east-west, connects with I-5 near Portland and runs along the Oregon/Washington border before dipping southeast toward Boise, Idaho and Salt Lake City, Utah. **I-90** runs east from its junction with I-5 near Seattle through Spokane and then into northern Idaho and Montana.

The **Trans Canada Highway** (Hwy. 1) is Canada's major east-west artery and connects Calgary and Vancouver. The **Mackenzie Highway** (Hwy. 2) runs north-south through Alberta and connects Calgary and Edmonton. Hwy. 97, the **Cariboo Highway,** joins southern and northern BC, including the towns of Prince George and Dawson Creek. For those continuing north from Dawson Creek, it's the 2647-km-long **Alaskan Highway,** which goes through the Yukon Territory and into northeastern Alaska, ending in Fairbanks (see Driving in Alaska). To more easily picture the roads listed above, see the map to the Yukon Territory and Alaska.

■ RENTING

Although the cost of renting a car for long distances is often prohibitive, renting for local trips may be reasonable. **Auto rental agencies** fall into two categories: national companies with thousands of branches, and local agencies that serve only one city or region. The former usually allow cars to be picked up in one city and dropped off in another (for a hefty charge). By calling a toll-free number you can reserve a reliable car anywhere in the country. Drawbacks include steep prices and high minimum ages for rentals (usually 25). If you're 21 or older and have a major credit card in your name, you may be able to rent where the minimum age would otherwise rule you out. Student discounts are occasionally available. Try **Alamo** (800-327-9633), **Avis** (800-331-1212), **Budget** (800-527-0700), **Dollar** (800-800-4000), **Hertz** (800-654-3131), **National** (800-328-4567), or **Thrifty** (800-367-2277). Dollar, Thrifty, and Alamo rent to those 21 to 25; expect to pay an additional charge of $10-20 per day, even when renting for a week or more.

Local companies are often more flexible and cheaper than major companies, but you'll generally have to return the car to its point of origin. Some local companies will accept a cash deposit ($50-100) or simply proof of employment (e.g., check stubs) in lieu of a credit card. Companies such as **Rent-A-Wreck** (800-421-7253) supply cars that are long past their prime. Sporting dents and purely decorative radios, the cars sometimes get very poor mileage, but they run and they're cheap. *Let's Go* lists addresses and phone numbers of local rental agencies in most towns.

When dealing with any car rental company, make certain the price includes **insurance** against theft and collision. This may be an additional charge (commonly $12 per day), though **American Express** automatically insures any car rented with the card. If using AmEx to rent over a long period, you must enter a new contract with the rental company every 15 days for the card to continue its coverage; call AmEx's car rental, loss, and damage division (800-338-1670) for more information. **Rates** change on a day-to-day basis without notice, so be sure to call for information. Basic rental charges for a compact car run $17-45 per day and $85-250 per week (bills are commonly the same for 5 days as for 7), but most companies offer specials. Standard shift cars are usually a few dollars cheaper than automatics. Most packages allow you a certain number of mi. free before the usual charge of 30 to 40 cents per mi. takes effect; if you'll be driving a long distance (a few hundred mi. or more), ask for an unlimited-mileage package. For rentals longer than a week, look into **automobile leasing,** which costs less than renting. Make sure, however, that your car is covered by a service plan to avoid the risk of outrageous repair bills.

■ AUTO TRANSPORT COMPANIES

Automobile transport companies match drivers with car owners who need cars moved from one city to another. Would-be travelers give the company their desired destination; the company finds the car. The only expenses are gas, food, tolls, and lodging. The company's insurance covers any breakdowns or damage. You must be at least 21, have a valid license, and agree to drive about 400 mi. per day on a fairly direct route. Companies regularly inspect current and past job references, take your fingerprints, and require a cash bond. Cars are available between most points, although it's easiest to find cars for traveling from coast to coast; New York and Los Angeles are popular transfer points.

If offered a car, look it over first. Think twice about accepting a gas guzzler, as you'll be paying for the gas. With the company's approval, however, you may be able to share the cost with several companions. For more information, contact **Auto Driveaway,** 310 S Michigan Ave., Chicago, IL 60604 (800-346-2277). Also try **A Anthony's Driveaway,** P.O. Box 502, 62 Railroad Ave., East Rutherford, NJ 07073 (201-935-8030; fax 201-935-2567).

■■■ BY TRAIN

Locomotion is still one of the cheapest and most comfortable ways to tour the Northwest. You can walk from car to car to stretch your legs, buy overpriced edibles in the snack bar, and shut out the sun to sleep in a reclining chair (the budget traveler should avoid paying unnecessarily for a roomette or bedroom). It is essential to travel light; not all stations will check your baggage and not all trains carry large amounts (though most long-distance ones do).

Amtrak, 60 Massachusetts Ave. NE, Washington, DC 20002 (800-872-7245), offers a discount **All-Aboard America** fare which divides the Continental U.S. into three regions—Eastern, Central, and Western. Amtrak charges the same rate for both one-way and round-trip travel, with three stopovers permitted and a maximum trip duration of 45 days. During the summer, rates are $198 if you travel within one region, $278 to travel within and between two regions, and $338 among three (from late Aug.-mid Dec. and early Jan.-mid June, rates are $178, $238, and $278). Drawing a line from Chicago south roughly divides the first region from the second; drawing a north-south line through Denver roughly divides regions two and three. Your itinerary, including both cities and dates, must be set at the time the passes are purchased; the route may not be changed once travel has begun, although times and dates may be changed at no cost. All-aboard fares are subject to availability, and Amtrak recommends reserving two to three months in advance for summer travel.

Another discount option, available only to those who aren't citizens of North America, is the **USA Rail Pass** which allows unlimited travel and unlimited stops over a period of either 15 or 30 days. As with the All-Aboard America program, the cost of this pass depends on the number of regions within which you wish to travel. The pass allowing 30 days of travel nationwide sells for $399 peak season and $319 off-season; the 15-day nationwide pass sells for $318 peak season and $218 off-season. The 30-day pass which limits travel to the western region only (as far east as Denver) sells for $239 peak season and $219 off-season; the 15-day pass for the western region sells for $188 peak season, and $168 off-season.

Full fares vary according to time, day, and destination: Amtrak seldom places advance purchase requirements on its fares, although the number of seats sold at discount prices is often limited. These discount tickets are naturally the first to sell, so it's best to plan in advance and reserve early. One-way fares don't vary with the season, but round-trip tickets can be significantly cheaper if traveling between late August and late May, excepting Christmas time. Several routes, such as the *Coast Starlight* between Seattle and L.A., cross stunning countryside; round-trip tickets sell for $128 peak-season and $108 off-season.

Amtrak offers several **discounts** from its full fares: children under 15 accompanied by a parent (half-fare); children under age two (free on the lap of an adult); seniors (15% off for travel Mon.-Thurs.) and travelers with disabilities (25% off); current members of the U.S. armed forces and active-duty veterans (25% discount) and their dependents (12.5% discount). Circle trips and special holiday packages can save you money as well. Keep in mind that discounted air travel, particularly for longer distances, may be cheaper than train travel. For up-to-date information and reservations, contact your local Amtrak office or call. Travelers with hearing impairments may use a teletypewriter (800-872-7245).

A final discount option on Amtrak is the **Air-Rail Travel Plan,** offered in conjunction with United Airlines, which allows you to travel in one direction by train and then fly home, or to fly to a distant point and then return home by train. The train portion of the journey allows up to three stopovers, and you have 180 days to complete your travel. A multitude of variations on these plans are available; call for details.

VIA Rail, Place Ville Marie, Lobby Level, Montreal, Quebec H3C 3N3 (800-561-3949 or 800-561-7860; from Hawaii and Alaska, call collect 506-857-9830), is Amtrak's Canadian analogue, and makes British Columbia, Alberta, and the Yukon accessible to the Northwestern traveler. Routes are as scenic as Amtrak's, and the fares are often more affordable.

A number of **discounts** apply on full-fare tickets. During the off season (late Sept.-early June) rates are 40% lower than at other times of the year (min. 7-day advance purchase required). Rates are also significantly lower for travel to remote areas. Seniors (60 and over) and youths (12 to 24) receive 10% discounts at all times; children under 12 pay half-fare. Special rates are available for groups of twenty or more. Travelers with certain disabilities may travel with a companion who will be offered free transportation. Remember when scheduling that the price of a round-trip ticket is just twice the amount of a one-way fare.

Reservations are required for first-class seats and sleeping car accommodations. VIA RAil allows passengers to check up to 100 lbs. of baggage and to carry on two bags of reasonable size and weight. Bicycles must be packaged in boxes and are subject to a fee of CDN$15 plus tax.

If you're planning a long trip you may save money with the **Canrail Pass,** which allows travel on 12 days within a 30-day period; distance traveled is unlimited. Between early June and late September, passes cost CDN$545.70, CDN$493 for seniors and youths under 24. Off-season passes cost CDN$373, CDN$341 for youths and seniors.

For Alaskans in the most isolated regions, the **Alaskan Railroad** may be the only link to civilization. North America's northernmost railroad covers 470 mi. of land—connecting Seward and Whittier in the south with Anchorage, Fairbanks, and Denali National Park farther north—much of which is inaccessible by road or boat. In 1984, the railroad, one of the last nationally-owned railroads in the country, was sold into private hands, changing its name to the **Alaska Railroad Company (ARRC),** P.O. Box 107500, Anchorage, AK 99510-7500 (800-544-0552;fax at 907-265-2623). ARRC runs daily between Anchorage and Fairbanks (with a stop in Denali National Park) for $135 one-way and $270 round-trip; and between Anchorage and Seward (summer only) for $50 one-way and $80 round-trip. Given advance notice in the winter, the engineer will drop cargo or passengers along the way. The train is the only overland route to Whittier (round-trip $16 from Portage; add bus fare from Anchorage to Portage), and the 30-minute ride runs from Portage several times per day to coincide with the schedule of the ferry *M.V. Bartlett.* Advance reservations are required for all except Portage-Whittier trips.

On the Panhandle, the 90-year-old **White Pass and Yukon Route** offers round-trip train rides in vintage parlor cars along routes forged during the Klondike Gold rush of the late 1890's. The Summit Excursion is a 3-hour/40-mi. round-trip for $72 per adult. The Lake Bennett Adventure is a 5.5-hour round trip that includes box lunch and a 40-minute layover to see the exhibits in the 1903 station, all for $119. Lake Bennett also offers Thru-Service by train and bus between Skagway and White-horse, YT (4.5 hours each way, $92), and a regularly-scheduled hiker's pick-up from the end of the Chilkoot Trail at Lake Bennet ($59 to Skagway; $20 to Fraser). Daily Service for all routes between mid-May and mid-September. For more information, contact the White Pass and Yukon Route, P.O. Box 435, Skagway, AK 99840 (800-343-7373 or 907-983-2217; fax at 907-983-2734).

■■■ BY BUS

Buses generally offer the most frequent and complete service between the cities and towns of the Pacific Northwest. Often they are the only way to reach smaller locales without a car. The exceptions are some rural areas and more open spaces, particularly in Alaska and the Yukon, where bus lines are sparse. Your biggest challenge when you travel by bus is scheduling. *Russell's Official National Motor Coach Guide* ($12.80 including postage) is an indispensable tool for constructing an itinerary. Updated each month, *Russell's Guide* contains schedules of literally every bus route (except Greyhound) between any two towns in the United States and Canada. Russell's also publishes a semiannual *Supplement,* which includes a Directory of Bus Lines, Bus Stations, and Route Maps. The schedules change frequently and the guide is updated monthly, so look at a copy in a library reference room.

Greyhound, P.O. Box 660362, Dallas TX 75266-0362 (800-231-2222 in the U.S.), operates the largest number of routes in both the U.S. and Canada. Within specific regions, other bus companies may provide more exhaustive services. Greyhound is a useful organization for the budget traveler; its fares are cheap, and its tendrils poke into virtually every corner of America. Be sure, however, to allow plenty of time for connections, and be prepared for possibly unsavory traveling companions. By all means avoid spending the night in a bus station. Though generally guarded, bus stations can be hangouts for dangerous, or at least frightening, characters. Try to arrange your arrivals for reasonable day or evening times. This will also make it easier for you to find accommodations for the night.

A number of **discounts** are available on Greyhound's standard-fare tickets (restrictions apply): seniors (15% off); children ages two to 11 (50% off); children under age two travel free (if they'll sit on your lap); travelers with disabilities and their companions together ride for the price of one.

Greyhound allows passengers to carry two pieces of luggage (up to 45 lbs. total) and to check two pieces of luggage (up to 100 lbs.). Whatever you stow in compartments underneath the bus should be clearly marked; get a claim check for it, and watch to make sure your luggage is on the same bus as you. Take a jacket, too; surprisingly efficient air-conditioning brings the temperature down to arctic levels.

If you plan to tour a great deal by bus within the U.S., you may save money with the **Ameripass,** which entitles you to unlimited travel for seven days ($250), 15 days ($350), or 30 days ($450); extensions for the seven- and 15-day passes cost $15 per day. The pass takes effect the first day used, so make sure you have a pretty good idea of your itinerary before you start. Before you purchase an Ameripass, total up the separate bus fares between towns to make sure that the pass is indeed more economical, or at least worth the unlimited flexibility it provides. **TNM&O Coaches** and **Vermont Transit** are actually Greyhound subsidiaries, and as such will honor Ameripasses. The Canadian equivalent is the **CanadaPass**; a seven-day pass is CDN$179, a 15-day pass is CDN$239, and a 30-day pass is CDN $329. Check with the companies for specifics. Greyhound also offers an **International Ameripass** for those from outside North America. A seven-day pass sells for $175, a 15-day pass for $250, and a 30-day pass for $325.

BY BUS

Greyhound schedule information can be obtained from any Greyhound terminal, or from the reservation center at the new toll-free number (800-231-2222). Greyhound is implementing a reservation system much like the airlines, which will allow you to call and reserve a seat or purchase a ticket by mail. If you call seven or more days in advance and want to purchase your ticket with a credit card, reservations can be made and the ticket mailed to you. Otherwise, you may make a reservation up to 24 hours in advance. You can also buy your ticket at the terminal, but arrive early. If you are boarding at a remote "flag stop," be sure you know exactly where the bus stops. It's a good idea to call the nearest agency and let them know you'll be waiting at the flag-stop for the bus and at what time.

For a more unusual and social trip, consider **Green Tortoise,** 494 Broadway, San Francisco, CA 94133 (800-227-4766, in CA 415-956-7500, in Canada 800–867-8647; fax 956-4900). These funky "hostels on wheels" are remodeled diesel buses done up with foam mattresses, sofa seats, stereos, and dinettes; meals are prepared communally. Bus drivers operate in teams so that one can drive and the other can point out sites and chat with passengers. Prices include transportation, sleeping space on the bus, and tours of the regions through which you pass. Deposits ($100 most trips) are generally required since space is tight and economy is important for the group.

Green Tortoise can take you coast-to-coast, one-way, for a night on the town in Chicago, a midnight dip in Lake Michigan, or a mass "mud yoga" session. A "commuter" line runs between Seattle and Los Angeles; hop on at any point.

For the vacation-oriented, Green Tortoise also operates a series of round-trip "loops" which start and finish in San Francisco and travel to Yosemite National Park, Northern California, Baja California, the Grand Canyon, and Alaska. The Alaska trip includes a ferry ride through the Inside Passage and forays into the Canadian Rockies (35 days, $1700, plus $250 for food). Much of Green Tortoise's charm lies in its low price and the departure it offers from the impersonality of standard bus service. To be assured of a reservation, book one to two months in advance; however, many trips have space available at departure.

Alaskon Express, 745 W 4th Ave., Anchorage 99501 (907-277-5581), a subsidiary of **Gray Line of Alaska** (800-544-2206; fax 206-281-0621; open Mon.-Fri. 8am-5pm, Sat. 9am-1pm), based in Anchorage, runs four buses per week to a variety of cities in Alaska and the Yukon, including Whitehorse, Tok and Skagway. Several enterprising van owners run small operations from Haines to Anchorage, synchronized with the ferry. Fares can be as low as $115, but service is sometimes unreliable. **Homer and Seward Bus Lines** (278-0800) is a small, affordable bus company that runs to Seward ($30) and Homer ($38) on the Kenai Peninsula.

Try to use the **local bus systems** to travel within a town. The largest cities also have subways and commuter train lines. In most areas, however, mass public transport remains limited; local buses, while often cheap (fares 50¢-$1.50), are sparse. Call city transit information numbers and track down a public transport map with schedules (often found at a visitors information center). *Let's Go* helps you find this information wherever possible.

■■■ BY FERRY

Along the Pacific coast, ferries are an exhilarating and occasionally unavoidable way to travel. Some Alaskan towns can only be reached by water or air—Juneau, the state capital, for example. In addition to basic transportation, the ferry system gives travelers the chance to enjoy the beauty of the water and the coast, one of the Northwest's finest outdoor experiences. Ferry travel, however, can become quite expensive when you bring a car along with you. In Alaska, schedule an overnight ferry ride; sleep free in the Solarium, on the top deck, or spread out in the lounge. Free showers are also a bonus on all but the smallest boats.

Ferries traveling along the coast also serve the area between Seattle, Vancouver Island, and the northern coast of British Columbia. Contact these companies for more information.

BC Ferries, 1112 Fort St., Victoria, BC V8V 4V2 (604-386-3431 for information or reservations; 604-656-0757 for 24-hour schedule information). Passenger and vehicle ferry service on 24 routes throughout coastal British Columbia. Service areas include Vancouver-Vancouver Island, Sunshine Coast, Gulf Islands to Vancouver and Vancouver Island, the Inside Passage, and the Queen Charlotte Islands. Special facilities for passengers with disabilities. Send away for their excellent, complete scheduling and fare **pamphlets,** *Northern Gulf Islands, Southern Gulf Islands,* and *Sunshine Coast.*

Black Ball Transport, Inc., 430 Belleville St., Victoria, BC. V8V 1W9 (604-386-2202); Foot of Laurel, Port Angeles 98362 (206-457-4491). Ferries daily between Port Angeles and Victoria, with a crossing time of 95 min. Fare for an adult around $6 each way; for car and driver, around $25 each way; for a motorcycle and driver, $15.50 each way. Bicycles $3 extra. All prices in U.S. funds.

Washington State Ferries, 801 Alaskan Way, Seattle, WA 98104 (206-464-6400 or 206-464-2000). Ferries to Sidney, BC, and throughout Puget Sound. See below for information.

WASHINGTON STATE AND PUGET SOUND FERRIES

The ferry system in the Seattle and Puget Sound area are complex, There are, in fact, more than 10 different routes. Using a **touch-tone phone,** however, it is possible to get **current schedule and fare information** from Washington State Ferries. The system offers two numbers to call from outside Washington: 206-464-6400 and 206-464-2000. These numbers offer partially overlapping information. The following table will make clear how quickly to get schedule and rate information on any Puget Sound ferry. You may have to listen to the entire schedule before hearing any fare information. Ferries are not overly expensive. Reservations are usually unnecessary, except for travel to the San Juan Islands or British Columbia (**K** and **L**).

Ferry service is frequent, especially in summer. In winter, service is reduced. Schedules change seasonally. Fares fluctuate, but are reasonable. The ferry accepts only cash or checks from Washington banks. It is usually possible to buy a ferry ticket just before boarding; if the first ferry is full, wait a few minutes for the next one. Ferries run approximately between 5am and 1:30am.

Throughout the book, ferries will be identified by letter, and there will be a cross-reference directing you to this page. These letters are for *Let's Go* cross-referencing only, making it easy for you to identify your ferry; they will mean nothing to the ferry authority.

206-464-6400

Push 1. Push 1. Push 1. Push 1. Pause and wait for the new voice to step in after each keystroke. After pushing 1 for the fourth time, push the following numbers to obtain **schedule and fare information** about the following ferries:
Push 1 (again): Downtown Seattle Colman Dock (Pier 52) to Bainbridge Island (**A**)
Push 2: Downtown Seattle-Bremerton (Kitsap Peninsula) (**B**)
Push 3: Edmonds (north of Seattle)-Kingston (Kitsap Peninsula) (**C**)
Push 4: All four ferries touching Vashon Island. Push another key:
  Push 1 for the Fauntleroy (West Seattle)-Vashon ferry (**D**)
  Push 2 for the Point Defiance (Tacoma)-Vashon ferry (**E**)
  Push 3 for the Southworth (Kitsap Peninsula)-Vashon ferry (**F**)
  Push 4 for the passenger-only Downtown Seattle-Vashon ferry (**G**)
Push 5: Fauntleroy (West Seattle)-Southworth (Kitsap Peninsula) (**H**)
Push 6: Mukilteo (north of Seattle)-Clinton (southern tip of Whidbey Island) (**I**)
Push 7: Port Townsend (Olympic Peninsula)-Keystone (central Whidbey Island) (**J**)
Push 8: Anacortes-San Juan Islands (Friday Harbor, Orcas, Lopez, and Shaw) (**K**)

206-464-2000

Push 5500. After pushing 5500, push the following numbers to obtain **schedule and fare information** for the following ferries:
Push 7: Anacortes-Sidney, British Columbia (**L**)

Push 8: Other ferry service to Victoria (**M**)
Push 9: passenger-only Seattle-Bremerton (Kitsap Peninsula) (**N**)

PLANNING YOUR FERRY TRIPS

The **Alaska Northwest Travel Service, Inc.,** 130 2nd Ave. S, Edmonds, WA 98020 (206-775-4504), is an agent for Alaska and British Columbia ferries, as well as a full service travel agency specializing in Alaska; they can book ferries, cruise ships, and airline reservations. They will also plan individualized itineraries. Ferry scheduling information can also be found in *The Milepost,* published by Vernon Publications; see By Car above for information on how to obtain a copy.

Information about fares, reservations, vehicles, and schedules varies greatly throughout the year (see sections on Seattle, southwestern BC, and Alaska). Be sure to consult each ferry company when constructing your itinerary in order to clear up any additional questions before finalizing your plans.

■ ALASKA MARINE HIGHWAY

The Alaska Marine Highway consists of two completely unconnected ferry systems administered by one bureaucracy. The **southeast** system runs from Bellingham, WA up the coast to Skagway, stopping in Juneau, Ketchikan, Haines, and other towns. The **southcentral/southwest** network serves Kodiak Island, Seward, Homer, Prince William Sound, and, occasionally, the Aleutian Islands. For both systems, the ferry schedule is a function of tides and other navigational exigencies. **Stopovers** are encouraged. There is no additional charge for stopovers if they are reserved at the same time as the rest of your itinerary. Once your itinerary is reserved, you may still add stopovers at the port-to-port rate, which may result in a slightly higher fare. Write ahead; for all schedules, rates, and information, contact Alaska Marine Highway, (907-465-3941) P.O. Box 25535, Juneau SOUTHEAST. Practically none of southeast Alaska (the Panhandle) is accessible by road; most of this area can be reached only by plane or on the Marine Highway ferry from Bellingham, WA. Connections can also be made from most towns via **Alaska Airlines,** or overland from Haines and Skagway. (See **Alaskon Express** under By Bus on page 41.)

The full trip from Bellingham to Skagway takes three days—an adventure in itself, peppered with whales, bald eagles, and the majesty of the Inside Passage. (The Love Boat's notorious Alaskan voyages took this same route.) All southeast ferries have free showers, cafes, lectures on history and ecology, and a heated top-deck "solarium" where cabinless passengers can sleep (bring a sleeping bag). Ferries depart Friday evenings; departure times are dictated by the tides. Spaces for vehicles are very limited; reservations are crucial and often necessary six months in advance for summer trips. For more information, see Bellingham: Practical Information and Orientation in the Washington section.

A different Marine Highway ferry travels from **Prince Rupert, BC to Skagway** for $118 (half the price of the Bellingham-Skagway route). The ferry from Bellingham to Skagway does not stop in Prince Rupert; to get there, you must travel overland through British Columbia or fly. (See Prince Rupert: Practical Information in the British Columbia section).

SOUTHCENTRAL

The ferries in southcentral Alaska are more expensive and less swank than those in the southeast. The boats are older, the food is worse, and the solariums are smaller. They also ride the open seas, where your vessel is bound to be rocked to and fro. For information on schedules and rates in the southcentral, see individual entries in the Practical Information sections of Whittier, Valdez, Cordova, Homer, Seward, Kodiak, and the Aleutian Islands.

■■■ BY MOTORCYCLE

It's cheaper than driving a car, but the physical and emotional wear and tear of motorcycling may negate any financial gain. Fatigue and the small gas tank conspire to force the motorcyclist to stop more often on long trips; experienced riders are seldom on the road more than six hours per day. Lack of luggage space can also be a serious limitation. If you must carry a load, keep it low and forward where it won't distort the cycle's center of gravity. Fasten it either to the seat or over the rear axle in saddle or tank bags. Invest in really good rain gear and outerwear, or you'll be a wretched, miserable cur.

Annoyances, though, are secondary to risks. Despite their superior maneuverability, motorcycles are incredibly vulnerable to crosswinds, drunk drivers, and the blind spots of cars and trucks. *Always ride defensively.* The dangers skyrocket at night; travel only in the daytime. Half of all cyclists have an accident within their first month of riding. Always wear the best **helmet** you can get your hands on. For information on motorcycle emergencies, ask your State Department of Motor Vehicles for a motorcycle operator's manual.

■■■ BY BICYCLE

Travel by bicycle is about the cheapest way to go. You move much more slowly for much more effort, but that doesn't mean you'll be ill-rewarded. The leisurely pace gives you a chance to take in the view. In addition, cycling is pollution-free and a good way to exercise.

Get in touch with a local biking club if you don't know a great deal about bicycle equipment and repair. When you shop around, compare knowledgeable local retailers to mail-order firms. If the disparity in price is modest, buy locally. Otherwise, order by phone or mail and make sure you have a local reference with which to consult. Make your first investment in an issue of *Bicycling* magazine (published by Rodale Press; see below), which advertises low sale prices. **Bike Nashbar,** 4111 Simon Rd., Youngstown, OH 44512 (800-627-4227 for a catalog, 216-788-6464 for questions about repair and maintenance; fax 216-782-2856), is the leading mail-order catalog for cycling equipment and accessories. They will beat any nationally advertised price by 5¢. They regularly ship anywhere in the U.S. and Canada and to overseas military addresses. Their own line of products, including complete bicycles, is the best value. Another exceptional mail-order firm which specializes in mountain bikes and full suspension cycles, starting at $700, is **Superego Bikes,** 1660 9th St., Santa Monica, CA 90404 (800-326-2453 or 310-450-2224).

Safe and secure cycling requires a quality helmet and lock. A **Bell** or **Tourlite** helmet costs about $40—much cheaper than critical head surgery or a well-appointed funeral. **U-shaped Kryptonite** or **Citadel locks** start at around $30, with insurance against theft for one or two years if your bike is registered with the police.

Long-distance cyclists should contact **Adventure Cycling Association,** P.O. Box 8308-P, Missoula, MT 59807 (406-721-7776, fax at 721-8754), a national, non-profit organization that researches and maps long-distance routes and organizes bike tours for members. Their 4450-mi. TransAmerican Trail has become the core of a 19,000-mi. route network of cycling-specific North American maps. Adventure Cycling also offers members discounted maps, guidebooks (including the *Cyclists' Yellow Pages*), nine issues of *Bike Report,* the organization's bicycle touring magazine, and a catalog describing their extensive organized tour program, including trips from Anchorage to Denali National Park and from Seattle to Eugene, OR through the Olympic Peninsula. Annual fees are $25 per person in the U.S, $35 in Canada and Mexico, and $45 overseas. (Phones open Mon.-Fri. 8am-5pm.) American Youth Hostels and the Sierra Club also help plan bike tours. **The Canadian Cycling Association,** 1600 James Naismith Dr., #810, Gloucester, Ont. K1B 5N4 (613-748-5629; fax 748-5692) is the place to go for information about cycling in Canada. This group publishes *The Canadian Cycling Association's Complete Guide to Bicycle Touring* *in Canada* (CDN$20), plus oodles of touring guides to specific regions of Canada, Alaska and the Pacific Coast The association also sells maps and general titles on bicycling technique, maintenance, safety, and off-road cycling. **Rocky Mountain Cycle Tours,** Box 1978, Canmore, AB T0L 0M0 (403-678-6770 or 800-661-2453; fax 403-678-4451), organizes summer bicycle tours in Alberta and B.C. for groups of fewer than 20 ($710-1375 for 6 days, 5 nights of chi-chi digs and gourmet meals).

There are also a number of good books about bicycle touring and repair in general. **Rodale Press,** 33 E Minor St., Emmaus, PA 18908 (610-967-8447; fax 967-8962), publishes *Mountain Biking Skills, Basic Maintenance and Repair,* and *Bicycle Touring in the 90's* ($7 apiece) and other general publications on prepping yourself and your bike for an excursion. *Bike Touring* ($11, Sierra Club) discusses how to equip and plan a bicycle trip. *Bicycle Gearing: A Practical Guide* (US$9) is available from **The Mountaineers Books,** 1011 SW Klickitat Way, #107, Seattle, WA 98134 (800-553-4453; fax 206-223-6306), and discusses in lay-terms how bicycle gears work, covering everything you need to know in order to shift properly and get the maximum propulsion from the minimum exertion. *The Bike Bag Book* ($5), available from **10-Speed Press,** Box 7123, Berkeley, CA 94707 (800-841-2665 or 510-524-1052; fax 510-524-1052), is a bite-sized manual with broad utility.

Information about cycling in the Northwest is available from tourist bureaus, which often distribute free maps. You can obtain the *Oregon Bicycling Guide* and *Oregon Coast Bike Route Map* from the Bicycle/Pedestrian Program, Room 210 Transportation Building, Salem, OR 97310 (503-378-3432). Mountaineers Books publishes a series about bicycling through Washington and Oregon. Some good guides are *Bicycling the Pacific Coast,* by Tom Kirkendall and Vicky Spring ($15, Mountaineers Books), *and Bicycling the Backroads of Northwest Oregon,* by Jonas and J. Henderson. Contact **Umbrella Books,** a subsidiary of Epicenter Press, at 18821 64th Street NE, Seattle, WA 98155 (206-485-6822), for a number of regional guides, including *Bicycling the Oregon Coast,* by Robin Cody ($11), and *Alaska's Wilderness Highway, Traveling the Dalton Road,* by Mike Jensen.

Bikers should keep in mind that the Northwest possesses fewer well-paved back-roads than other regions of the U.S. When traveling the coast and the mountains, bikers should be wary of strong winds from the northwest. You can transport your bike with you by bus, train, or air—check with each carrier for regulations.

■■■ BY THUMB

> *Let's Go* urges you to consider the risks and disadvantages of hitchhiking before thumbing it. We do not recommend hitchhiking, particularly for women.

If you feel you have no other alternative, *insist* on ignoring our warnings, and decide to hitchhike anyway, there are many precautions that must be taken. First, assess the risks and your chances of getting a ride. **Women** traveling alone should never, ever, *ever* hitch in the United States. It's too big of a risk. It is slightly less dangerous for single men, but also much more difficult to get a ride. A woman and a man is perhaps the best compromise between safety and utility. Two men will have a hard time getting rides and if they do, it will probably be in extremely uncomfortable circumstances (e.g. the back of a pickup). Three men won't be picked up.

Next, don't take any chances with drivers. Choosy beggars might not get where they're going the fastest, but at least they'll get there alive. Experienced hitchers won't get in the car if they don't know where the driver is going. Hitchers never get into the back seat of a two-door car, or into a car whose passenger door doesn't open from the inside. Beware of cars that have electric door locks which lock you in against your will. Automatically turn down a ride when the driver opens the door quickly and offers to drive anywhere. Never put yourself in a position from which you can't exit quickly, never let your belongings out of your reach, and *never* hesitate to refuse a ride if you will feel at all uncomfortable alone with the driver.

Experienced hitchers talk with the driver, they but never divulge any information that they would not want a stranger to know. They also won't stay in the car if the driver starts making sexual innuendoes. If at all threatened or intimidated, experienced hitchers ask to be let out no matter how uncompromising the road looks, and they know *in advance* where to go if stranded and what to do in emergencies.

People who travel by thumb often consider hitchhiking in the Pacific Northwest—and Alaska in particular—as generally safer than in other areas of the U.S. and Canada (see Hitching in Alaska below). However, they still take care to observe the many precautions that lower the dangers inherent in hitchhiking. Don't toy with your life, and don't compromise your safety.

All states prohibit hitchhiking while standing on the roadway itself or behind a posted freeway entrance sign; hitchers more commonly find rides on stretches near major intersections where many cars converge.

■ HITCHING IN ALASKA

To reiterate, *Let's Go* does not recommend hitchhiking as a means of transportation. The information provided below is not intended to do so.

Many people hitchhike instead of depending on buses in Alaska. In fact, Alaska state law prohibits moving vehicles from *not* picking up stranded motorists, as the extreme weather conditions can be life-endangering. However, hitchhiking backpackers may only legally thumb for rides on the on-and-off ramps of major highways—not on the highways themselves. (Sticking to the ramps makes sense anyway; motorists need space to slow down and stop.) Hitchhikers keep their placement in mind even on smaller thoroughfares and are careful of being stranded on lightly traveled stretches of road. A wait of a day or two between rides is not unusual on certain stretches of the Alaska Hwy., especially in Canada. Luckily, Alaskans are generally a friendly and cooperative group, and most rides last at least a day.

HITCHING IN ALASKA

Campgrounds and service stations make the best bases for hitching, providing an opportunity for mutual inspection of both driver and hitchhiker before a journey.

Women should never hitchhike alone. It is safer for them to travel in pairs or with men. Drivers will often pick up females and then proceed to warn them sternly against hitching alone.

Carrying a large cardboard sign clearly marked with your destination can improve your chances of getting a ride. Drivers may not want to stop if they don't know where you're going. When it gets particularly tough, hitchers add "SHARE GAS."

Catching a ride from Canada into Alaska on the Alaska Hwy. involves passing the **Alaska-Yukon "border" check,** which is a series of routine questions about citizenship, residency, insurance, contraband, and finances, followed by an auto inspection. In the event that a hitchhiker is turned back, it is the driver's responsibility to return the hitchhiker to the "border." Hitchers should walk across the border to avoid hassles, and *never attempt to carry illegal drugs across the border.*

A popular alternative to hitching the entire length of the Alaska Hwy. is to take the **Marine Highway** (see By Ferry on page 42) to Haines and hitch a ride with cars coming off the ferry. Often the competition for rides in summer is heavy; it may be easier to remain on the ferry to Skagway, take a bus or train to Whitehorse in the Yukon, and hitch the Alaska Hwy. from there. Always carry extra money, food, and warm sleeping gear. The next town or ride could be days away.

■ Once There

■■■ ACCOMMODATIONS

After a long day rediscovering the Northwest, a good night's sleep is an abbreviated measure of bliss. Try to locate places to stay along your route and make reservations, especially if you plan to travel during peak tourist seasons. Even if you find yourself in dire straits, don't spend the night under the stars in an unsupervised campground; it's often uncomfortable, unsafe, and sometimes illegal, even in national parks and forest areas. The local crisis center hotline may have a list of persons or groups who will house you in an emergency.

■ YOUTH HOSTELS

Youth hostels offer unbeatable deals on indoor lodging, and they are great places to meet traveling companions from all over the world; many hostels even have **ride boards** to help you hook up with other hostelers going your way. As a rule, hostels are dorm-style accommodations where the sexes sleep apart, often in large rooms with bunk beds. (Some hostels allow families and couples to have private rooms, often for an additional charge.) You must bring or rent your own sleep sack (two sheets sewn together will suffice); sleeping bags are often not allowed. Hostels frequently have kitchens and utensils available, and some have storage areas and laundry facilities. Many also require you to perform a communal chore daily, usually lasting no more than 15 minutes.

Hostelling International/American Youth Hostels (HI/AYH) maintains over 300 hostels in the U.S. Hostelling International is the newly-adopted trademark name of the International Youth Hostel Federation; rates and services remain the same. HI memberships are valid at all HI/AYH hostels. Basic HI/AYH rules (with some local variation): check-in between 5 and 8pm, check-out by 9:30am, maximum stay three days, no pets or alcohol allowed on the premises. All ages are welcome ($5-22 per night). Hostels are graded according to the number of facilities they offer and their overall level of quality—consult *Let's Go* listings in each town.

HI/AYH membership is annual: $24, $15 for ages over 54, $10 for ages under 18, $35 for a family. Non-members who wish to stay at an HI/AYH hostel usually pay $3 extra, which can be applied toward membership. Regional AYH Councils schedule recreational activities and trips, ranging from afternoon bike rides to extended trips. Councils within Alaska and the Pacific Northwest include: **Anchorage International Hostel,** 700 H St., Anchorage, AK 99501 (907-562-7772); **Washington State Council,** 419 Queen Anne Ave. North #102, Seattle, WA 98109 (206-281-7306); **Oregon Council,** 1520 SE 37th Ave., Portland, OR 97214 (503-223-1873).

Hostelling International-Canada (HI-C), 400-205 Catherine St., Ontario, Canada K2P 1C3 (613-237-7884; fax 613-237-7884), was founded in 1933, and maintains over 80 hostels throughout the country. HI-C also publishes *Canada on a Budget,* a summer newsletter available free at hostels across Canada, with tips on travel and information about hostel programs like bungee jumping and white water rafting. Graded "basic," "simple," "standard," or "superior," hostels (CDN$9-18 per night) usually have kitchens, laundries, and often meal service. Open to members and non-members, most hostels allow a maximum stay of three nights. For hostels in busy locations, reservations are recommended. As with U.S. hostels, most Canadian hostels require that you have a "sleepsack"—two sheets sewn together will do; rentals are usually available for CDN$1. Sleeping bags are sometimes acceptable, but often they are not. Most Canadian hostels have full-day access, and quiet hours are generally between 11pm and 7am. Otherwise, regulations are generally the same as in U.S. hostels.

HI encourages visitors to make **reservations** ahead of time. Do so by mail by sending a letter or postcard with the date and estimated time of your arrival, the number of nights you plan to stay, and the number of male and female beds or private rooms you will need. Also send a check for the first night and a SASE in order to receive confirmation of the reservation. You can also make reservations by phone or fax, but have your credit card number and expiration date on hand to guarantee the first night's fee. HI has recently instituted an **International Booking Network.** To reserve space in high season, obtain an International Booking Voucher from any national youth hostel association (in your home country or the one you will visit) and send it to a participating hostel four to eight weeks in advance of your stay, along with US$2.75 in local currency. Locations are listed in the Accommodation sections of the particular cities or regions. If your plans are firm enough to allow it, pre-booking is wise. Note that effective use of this pre-application is how populous school groups always manage to get dibs on rooms.

■ HOTELS AND MOTELS

Those interested in bypassing hostels and moving up to mid-range hotels should consider joining **Discount Travel International,** 114 Forrest Ave. #203, Narberth, PA 19072 (215-668-9182). For an annual membership fee of $45, you and your household gain access to a clearing-house of discounts on organized trips, car rentals (with National, Alamo, and Hertz), and unsold hotel rooms.

Many budget motels preserve single digits in their names (e.g. Motel 6), but the cellar-level price of a single has matured to just under $30. Nevertheless, budget chain motels still cost significantly less than the chains catering to the next-pricier market, such as Holiday Inn. Chains usually adhere more consistently to a level of cleanliness and comfort than locally operated budget competitors; some budget motels even feature heated pools and cable TV. In bigger cities, budget motels are normally just off the highway, often inconveniently far from the downtown area; so, if you don't have a car, you may well spend the difference between a budget motel and one downtown on transportation. Contact these chains for free directories:

Motel 6, 3391 S Blvd., Rio Rancho, NM 87124 (505-891-6161).
Super 8 Motels, Inc., 1910 8th Ave. NE, P.O. Box 4090, Aberdeen, SD 57402-4090 (800-800-8000 or 605-229-8708; fax 605-229-8900).
Choice Hotels International, 10750 Columbia Pike, Silver Springs, MD 20901-4494 (800-453-4511).
Best Western, 6201 N 24th Parkway, Phoenix, AZ 85016-2023 (602-957-5751; fax 602-957-5505).

It is fortunate that the **Canadian hostel system** is somewhat more extensive than that of the U.S., because that country's dearth of budget motel chains puts most Canadian hotels and motels beyond the means of most budget travelers.

■ BED AND BREAKFASTS

As alternatives to impersonal hotel rooms, bed and breakfasts (private homes with spare rooms available to travelers, abbreviated B&Bs) range from the acceptable to the sublime. B&Bs may provide an excellent way to explore an area with the help of a host who knows it well, and some go out of their way to be accommodating—accepting travelers with pets or giving personalized tours. Often the best part of your stay will be a home-cooked breakfast (and occasionally dinner). Many B&Bs do not provide phones or TVs, and showers must sometimes be shared.

Prices vary widely. B&Bs in major cities are usually more expensive than those in out-of-the-way places. Doubles can cost anywhere from $20-300 per night; most are in the $30 to $50 range. Some homes give special discounts to families or seniors. Reservations are almost always necessary, although in the off-season (if the B&B is open), you can frequently find a room on short notice.

For information on B&Bs, contact **Pacific Bed and Breakfast,** 701 NW 60th St., Seattle, WA 98107 (206-782-4036 9am-5pm Mon.-Fri.), or consult CIEE's *Where to Stay USA* ($14) which includes listings for hostels, YMCAs and dorms, along with B&Bs with singles under $30 and doubles under $35. Two useful guidebooks on the subject are *Bed & Breakfast, USA* ($14), by Betty R. Rundback and Nancy Kramer, available in bookstores or through Tourist House Associates, Inc., RD 1, Box 310-A, Greentown, PA 18426 (717-676-3222); and *The Complete Guide to Bed and Breakfasts, Inns and Guesthouses in the U.S. and Canada,* by Pamela Lanier ($17) from Lanier Publications, Box 20467, Oakland, CA 94620 (510-644-8018; fax 510-644-2541). If you're interested in "delightful" or "charming" accommodations at slightly less than charming prices, you might want to look at *America's Wonderful Little Hotels and Inns* ($20), by Sandra W. Soule, St. Martin's Press. In addition, check local phone books, visitors' bureaus, and information at bus and train stations.

Most every city in **Canada** offers at least one B&B to give rest to those who aren't so needy that they have to stay in hostels (rooms generally run $25-70 per night for a double room).

■ YMCAS AND YWCAS

Not all **Young Men's Christian Associations** (YMCAs), 224 East 47th St., New York, NY 10017 (212-308-2899; fax 212-308-3161), offer lodging; those that do are often located in urban downtowns, which can be convenient though a little gritty. Rates in YMCAs are usually lower than a hotel but higher than the local hostel, normally about $40 per night depending on the size of the city and whether you want a single or a double room. Renting a room often allows you use of the showers (usually communal), library, pool, and other facilities. Economy packages (3-8 days; $38-343), which include lodging, some meals, and excursions are available in a few of the larger cities. The maximum stay is most often 25 nights. Reservations (strongly recommended) cost an additional $3 in the US and Canada, except Hawaii and overseas ($5), and key deposits are $10. Payment for reservations must be made in advance,

with a traveler's check (signed top and bottom), US money order, certified check, Visa, or Mastercard; personal checks are not accepted. To obtain information and make reservations, write the Y's Way to Travel at the above address. Send a self-addressed envelope with a 65¢ stamp for a free catalogue.

Most **Young Women's Christian Associations (YWCAs),** 726 Broadway, New York, NY 10003 (212-614-2700), accommodate only women. Non-members can also rent rooms. For more information, write YWCA of the USA.

The network of YMCAs and YWCAs extends to many larger **Canadian** cities. You will generally find the same types clean and affordable rooms as those offered in the States, mostly in downtown areas. For further information, and to make reservations at YMCAs around Canada, contact the YMCA in Montreal at 1450 Stanley St., Montreal, PQ H3A 2W6 (514-849-8393; fax 514-849-8017), or the YW/YMCA in Ottawa at 180 Argyle St., Ottawa, Ont. K2P 1B7 (613-237-1320; fax 613-233-3096).

■ ALTERNATIVE ACCOMMODATIONS

Many **colleges** and **universities** in the U.S. and Canada open their residence halls to travelers when school is not in session—some do so even during term-time. No general policy covers all of these institutions, but rates tend to be low, and some schools require that you express at least a vague interest in attending their institution. Since college dorms are popular with many travelers, you should call or write ahead for reservations. In general, college campuses are some of the best sources for information on things to do, places to stay, and possible rides out of town. To contact colleges and universities in Alaska and the Pacific Northwest, make use of the addresses and phone numbers given in the Work and Study section on page 21.

If you wish to stay in a U.S. home during your vacation, try **Servas,** run by the U.S. Servas Committee, 11 John St. #407, New York, NY 10038 (212-267-0252). Servas is an international cooperative system which matches hosts and travelers in about 100 countries. Stays are limited to two to three nights, unless your host invites you to stay longer; guests must complete arrangements with hosts in advance of their stay. Travelers pay a $55 fee per year to Servas, plus a $25 refundable deposit for up to five host lists which provide a short description of each host member. No money is exchanged between travelers and hosts—rather, they share conversation and ideas. Travelers must submit an application, provide two letters of reference, and arrange for an interview at least one month before the trip.

The World Learning's **Homestay/USA** coordinates homestay programs for international visitors over 14 wishing to join a U.S. family for three to four weeks. Homestays are arranged for all times of the year. Contact Homestay/USA, 25 Bay State Rd., Boston, MA 02215 (800-327-4678 or 617-247-0350). The **Institute of International Education (IIE)** publishes a "Homestay Information Sheet" listing homestay programs for foreign visitors. For a more thorough description and a contact address, see Work and Study above. **CIEE** can also help arrange homestays.

■■■ CAMPING & THE OUTDOORS

■ USEFUL PUBLICATIONS

For information about camping, hiking, and biking, write or call the publishers listed below to receive a free catalog.

PUBLICATIONS

A variety of publishing companies offer hiking guidebooks to meet the educational needs of novice or expert.

The Mountaineers Books, 1011 Kilickitat Way, #107, Seattle, WA 98134 (800-553-4453 or 206- 223-6303; fax 206-223-6306). Publishes the 100 Hikes series, abounding in information on backpacking, climbing, biking, natural history, and environmental conservation.

Sierra Club Bookstore, 730 Polk St., San Francisco, CA, 94109 (415- 923-5500). Books on many national parks, as well as *The Best About Backpacking* ($11) and *Cooking for Camp and Trail* ($12). For information on Alaska in particular, consult *Adventuring in Alaska* ($12), by Peggy Wayburn.

Wilderness Press, 2440 Bancroft Way, Berkeley, CA, 894704-1676 (800-443-7227 or 510-843-8080; fax 510-548-1355). Offers Backpacking Basics ($11) and Backpacking with Babies and Small Children ($11). Hiking Guides and maps for the Western U.S. are also available.

Woodall Publishing Company, P.O. Box 5000, 28167 N Keith Dr., Lake Forest, IL 60045-5000 (800-323-9076; fax 708-362-8776). Woodall publishes the ever-popular and annually updated *Woodall's Campground Directory* ($12) and *Woodall's Plan-it, Pack-it, Go!: Great Places to Tent, Fun Things to Do* ($13), both of which are generally available in American bookstores.

The Mountaineers Books, 1011 Klickitat Way #107, Seattle, WA 98134 (800-553-4453 or 206-223-6303). Numerous titles on hiking (the *100 Hikes* series), biking, mountaineering, natural history, and environmental conservation.

For excellent **topographical maps** starting at $2.50, write the **U.S. Geological Survey,** Map Distribution, Box 25286, Denver, CO, 80225 (303-236-7477) or the **Canada Map Office,** 130 Bentley Ave., Ottawa, Ont., K1A 0E9 (613-952-7000), which distributes geographical and topographical maps as well as aeronautical charts. All maps are less than $10.

■ PARKS & FORESTS

At the turn of the century it may have seemed unnecessary to set aside parts of the vast American and Canadian wilderness for conservation, but today that act is recognized as a stroke of genius. **National parks** protect some of America and Canada's most spectacular scenery. Alaska's crowning Denali (Mt. McKinley), Oregon's

stone-still Crater Lake, and Alberta's Banff and Jasper are treasures that will remain intact for generations. Though their primary purpose is preservation, the parks also make room for recreational activities such as ranger talks, guided hikes, skiing, and snowshoe expeditions. Most national parks have backcountry camping and developed tent camping; others welcome RVs, and a few offer opulent living in grand lodges. A mixed blessing, internal road systems allow you to reach the interior and major sights even if you are not a long-distance hiker.

Write to one or all of the following addresses for information on camping, accommodations, and regulations: for **Washington** and **Oregon** contact Forest Service/ National Park Service, Outdoor Recreation Information Center, 915 2nd Ave. #442, Seattle, WA 98174 (206-220-7450); for **Alberta** and **British Columbia** contact Canadian Parks Service #520, 220 4th Ave., Calgary, AB T2P 3H8 (403-292-4401); for Manitoba, Saskatchewan, and the **Northwest Territories** contact Canadian Parks Service, Prairie and Northern Region Information Office, 4th floor, 457 Main St., Winnipeg, Manitoba R3B 3E8 (204-983-2290; 204-983-0551 for the hearing impaired; fax 204-984-2240); and for **Alaska** contact **Alaska Public Lands Information Center**, 605 W 4th Ave. #105, Anchorage, AK 99501 (907-271-2737). Forsyth Travel Library publishes a *Campers' Guide to U.S. National Parks West of the Rockies* ($19); see Useful Publications on page 1 for more information.

Entry fees vary from park to park. The larger and more popular national parks charge a $5-10 entry fee for vehicles and sometimes a nominal one for pedestrians and cyclists. Most national parks offer **discounts** such as the annual **Golden Eagle Passport** ($25), which allows the bearer and family free entry into all parks. Visitors ages 62 and over qualify for the **Golden Age Passport**, $10, entitling them to free entry and a 50% discount on recreational fees; travelers with disabilities enjoy the same privileges with the **Golden Access Passport**. Both the Golden Age and Golden Access Passports are free, and both are also valid at national monuments. For more information, visitors centers at parks offer excellent free literature and information, and the U.S. Government Printing Office publishes two useful pamphlets: *National Parks: Camping Guide* ($3.50) and *National Parks: Lesser-Known Areas* ($1.50). The Canadian equivalent to the Golden Eagle Pass in the U.S. is the **Annual National.** The pass costs CDN$30, can be purchased at the entrance to any Canadian National Park, and covers vehicle entrance fees (generally about $5 per day) for a year. The Winnipeg office of the Canadian Parks Service (see address above) distributes free of charge *Parks West*, a thorough and beautiful book about all the national parks and historic sites of western and northern Canada.

Many states and provinces have parks of their own, which are often smaller than the national parks but offer some of the best camping around—handsome surroundings, elaborate facilities, and plenty of space. In contrast to national parks, the primary function of **state and provincial parks** is recreation. Prices for camping at public sites are almost always better than those at private campgrounds. Don't let swarming visitors dissuade you from seeing the large parks—these places are huge, and even at their most crowded they offer many opportunities for quiet and solitude. Reservations are absolutely essential at the more popular parks in the Pacific Northwest; make them through **MISTIX** (800-365-2267). U.S. states will also have a State Division of Parks which you can contact for information and brochures; find their addresses and phone numbers listed in the Practical Information sections following the introductions to the respective states. Lodges and indoor accommodations are generally in the shortest supply and should be reserved months in advance. However, most campgrounds are strictly first-come, first-camped. Arrive early: many campgrounds, public and private, fill up by late morning. Some limit your stay and/ or the number of people in a group (usually no more than 25).

If the national parks are too developed for your tastes, **national forests** provide a purist's alternative. While some have recreation facilities, most are equipped only for primitive camping—pit toilets and no running water are the rule. Fees range from US$10-20. Forests are well marked and accessible, but can often get crowded, especially in the summertime. Backpackers can take advantage of specially designated **wilderness areas,** which are even less accessible due to regulations barring all vehicles. **Wilderness permits,** required for backcountry hiking, can usually be obtained (usually free, sometimes US$3-4) at parks; check ahead. Adventurers who plan to explore some real wilderness should always check in at a USDA Forest Service (see phone number below) field office before heading out. Write ahead to **USDA Forest Service,** 14th and Independence, SW, P.O. Box 96090, Washington, D.C. 20090-6090, to order detailed, accurate maps (US$3-6). Always try the regional office for the region you are visiting first, as they are more helpful and less busy than the central office.

The USDA Forest Service oversees more than 200 scenic and well-maintained wilderness **log cabins** for public use, scattered throughout the southern and central regions of Alaska. User permits are required along with a fee of $25 per party (of any size) per night. Reservations are usually necessary several months in advance. Most cabins have seven-day use limits (hike-in cabins have a 3-day limit May-Aug.), and are usually accessible only by air, boat, or hiking trail. Cabin sizes vary, and facilities at these sites rarely include more than a wood stove and pit toilets, but some cabins provide skiffs. For maps or further information write to the USDA Forest Service (see Visitors Information). For general information, contact the Forest Service's regional office in the **Pacific Northwest** (503-326-3816) or **Alaska** (907-271-2500)

The **U.S. Fish and Wildlife Service,** 1011 E Tudor Rd., Anchorage 99503 (786-3486), maintains numerous campgrounds within the National Wildlife Refuges of the Alaska, including the Kenai National Refuge (907-262-7021; 15 campgrounds with sites from $5 (max. stay of either 3 or 14 days depending on the campground).

Believe it or not, the U.S. Department of the Interior does more than grant public lands to oil companies for exploitative development. Its **Bureau of Land Management (BLM),** Public Affairs, Rm. 5600, 1849 C St., NW, Washington D.C., 20240 (202-208-5717), offers a wide variety of outdoor recreation opportunities—including camping, hiking, mountain biking, rock climbing, river rafting and wildlife viewing—on the 270 million acres it oversees in ten Western states and Alaska. These lands also contain hundreds of archaeological artifacts and historic sites like ghost towns. The BLM's many **campgrounds** include 20 sprinkled throughout Alaska, all free (except for the Delta BLM campground on the Alaska Hwy.).

The **Pacific Crest Trail,** which stretches 2620 mi. from the Mexico-California border into Canada, is particularly attractive for one- or two-week hiking trips along its shorter segments. Heated cabins and some running tap water along the trails add convenience. Consult BLM or an area tourism bureau for maps of the trail; another valuable source is *The Pacific Crest Trail, Vol. 2* (Wilderness Press, $25), which covers Oregon and Washington.

■ TENT CAMPING AND HIKING

EQUIPMENT

Whether buying or renting, finding sturdy, light, and inexpensive equipment is a must. Spend some time examining catalogs and talking to knowledgeable salespeople. Mail-order firms are for the most part reputable and cheap—order from them if you can't do as well locally. Look for prices on the previous year's line of equipment to decline precipitously (sometimes by as much as 50%) when the new year's line starts to sell, usually sometime in the fall.

At the core of your equipment is the **sleeping bag.** What kind you should buy depends on the climate of the area you'll be camping in and climbing through. Most of the better sleeping bags are rated according to the lowest outdoor temperature at which they will still keep you warm. Bags are sometimes rated by season rather than temperature: keep in mind that "summer" translates to a rating of 30-40°F, "three-season" means 20°F, and "four-season" or "winter" means below 0°F. Sleeping bags are made either of down (warmer and lighter) or of synthetic material (cheaper, heavier, more durable, and warmer when wet). When choosing your bag, get the most specific temperature rating you can. The following prices are reasonable for good bags: $65-80 for a summer synthetic, $136-$180 for a three-season synthetic, $170-225 for a three-season down bag, and upwards of $270-550 for a down sleeping bag you can use in the winter. If you're using a sleeping bag for serious camping, you should also have either a foam pad ($13 and up for closed-cell foam, $25 and up for open-cell foam) or an air mattress ($25 to $50) to cushion your back and neck. Another good alternative is the **Therm-A-Rest,** which is part foam and part air-mattress and inflates to full padding when you unroll it (from $50-90). Watch out for big, bulky air mattresses, which can be a pain if you're planning on doing much hiking.

When you select a **tent,** your major considerations should be shape and size. The best tents are free-standing, with their own frames and suspension systems; they set up quickly and require no staking (though staking will keep your tent from blowing away). Low profile dome tents are the best all-around. When pitched their internal space is almost entirely usable, which means little unnecessary bulk. One drawback to keep in mind: if you're caught in the rain and have to spend a day or two holed up inside your tent, A-frames can be cramped and claustrophobic. Dome and umbrella shapes offer more spacious living, but tend to be bulkier to carry. As for size, two people *can* fit in a two-person tent but will find life more pleasant in a four-person tent. If you're traveling by car, go for the bigger tent; if you're hiking, stick with a smaller tent that weighs no more than 3.5 lbs./1.5kg. For especially small and lightweight models, contact **Sierra Design,** 2039 4th St., Berkeley, CA 94710, which sells the "Clip Flashlight," a two-person tent that weighs less than 1.4kg (3 lbs.) Good two-person tents start at about $135; $200 for a four-person. You can, however, often find last year's version for half the price. Be sure to seal the seams of your tent with waterproofer, and make sure it has a rain fly.

If you intend to do a lot of hiking or biking, you should have a **frame backpack.** Buy a backpack with an internal frame if you'll be hiking on difficult trails that require a lot of bending and maneuvering—internal-frame packs mold better to your back, keep a lower center of gravity, and can flex adequately to follow you through a variety of movements. In addition, internal frame packs are more manageable on crowded trains, and are less likely to be mangled by rough handling. An excellent choice is a conversion pack, an internal frame pack which converts easily into a suitcase. External-frame packs are more comfortable for long hikes over even terrain since they keep the weight higher and distribute it more evenly. Regular packs don't travel as well; bring a duffle to protect your pack when in baggage compartments. Make sure your pack has a strong, padded hip belt, which transfers much of the weight from delicate shoulders to sturdier legs. The size of a backpack is measured in cubic inches (cu. in.). Any serious backpacking requires at least 3300 of them, while longer trips require around 4000. Tack on an additional 500 cu. in. for internal-frame packs, since you'll have to pack your sleeping bag inside, rather than strap it on the outside as you do with an external-frame pack. Backpacks with many compartments generally turn a large space into many unusable small spaces; use separate stuff-sacks instead. Packs that load from the front rather than the top allow you access to your gear more easily (see Packing above for more hints). Sturdy backpacks start anywhere from $200-300. This is one area where it doesn't pay to economize—cheaper packs may be less comfortable, and the straps are more likely to fray or rip quickly. Test-drive a backpack for comfort before you buy it.

Other necessities include: **battery-operated lantern** (gas is inconvenient and dangerous), **plastic groundcloth** for the floor of your tent, **nylon tarp** for general purposes, a **waterproof backpack cover,** and a **"stuff sack"** or plastic bag to keep your sleeping bag dry. **Rain gear,** including polypropylene tops, socks, and long underwear, will keep you warm when wet. When camping in autumn, winter, or spring, bring along a "space blanket," a technological wonder that helps you to retain your body heat (US $3.50-13; doubles as a groundcloth). Don't go anywhere without a **canteen** or water bottle. Plastic models keep water cooler in the hot sun than metal ones do, although metal canteens are a bit sturdier and leak less. Large, collapsible **water sacks** will significantly improve your lot in primitive campgrounds and weigh practically nothing when empty, though they can get bulky. If you'll be car-camping at sites with no showers, bring **water sacks**. Although most campgrounds provide campfire sites, you may want to bring a small **metal grate** of your own, and even a grill. For those places that forbid fires or the gathering of firewood, you'll need a **camp stove** (Coleman, the classic, starts at $30). Consider GAZ-powered stoves, which come with bottled propane gas that is easy to use and widely available in Europe. Make sure you have **waterproof matches,** or your stove may do you no good. A **swiss army knife** and **insect repellent** are also essential camping items.

Shop around locally before turning to mail-order firms; this allows you to get an idea of what the different items actually look like (and weigh), so that if you later decide to order by mail you'll have a more exact idea of what it is you're getting. The mail-order firms listed below offer lower prices than those you're likely to find in stores, and they can also help you determine which item you need. Call or write for a free catalog:

Cabela's, 812 13th Ave., Sidney, NE 69160 (800-237-4444). Offers great prices on quality outdoor equipment and holds seasonal sales. Particularly well-stocked in hunting and fishing gear.

Campmor, P.O. Box 700, Saddle River, NJ 07458-0700 (800-526-4784). Has a monstrous selection of name brand equipment at low prices. One year guarantee for unused or defective merchandise.

Eastern Mountain Sports, One Vose Farm Rd., Peterborough, NH, 03458 ((603) 924-7231). EMS has stores from Colorado to Virginia to Maine. Though slightly higher priced, they provide excellent service and guaranteed satisfaction (ie. a full refund if you're unhappy) on all items sold.

Recreational Equipment, Inc., P.O. Box 1700, Sumner, WA 98352-0001 (800-426-4840). Long-time outdoor equipment cooperative. Stocks a wide range of the latest in camping gear and holds great seasonal sales. Huge selection, and many items are guaranteed for life. Lifetime membership (not required) US$10.

L.L. Bean, Casco St., Freeport, ME 04033-0001 (800-878-2104; outside U.S. and Canada, 207-865-3111; fax 207-878-2104). Equipment and preppy outdoor clothing favored by northeastern Americans; high quality and chock-full of information. Call or write for their free catalog. The customer is guaranteed 100% satisfaction on all purchases; if it doesn't meet your expectations, they'll replace or refund it. Open 24 hrs. per day, 365 days per year.

Sierra Design, 3029 4th St., Berkeley, CA 94710 (510-843-0923). Has a wide array of especially small and lightweight tent models including the two person "Clip Flashlight ($160) which weighs less than 1.76 kg (4 lbs.) you can often find last year's version for half the price.

Cheaper equipment can also be obtained on the used market, but, as with anything used, know what you're buying. Consult publications like the want-ads and student bulletin boards. Retail outlets like **L.L. Bean** may save you money, but remember that with camping gear you usually get what you pay for. Spending a little more money up front may save money down the line.

WILDERNESS CONCERNS

The first thing to preserve in the wilderness is you—health, safety, and food should be your primary concerns when you camp. See Health above for information about basic medical concerns and first-aid. A comprehensive guide to outdoor survival is *How to Stay Alive in the Woods* ($8), by Bradford Angier; to order, write or call **Macmillan Publishing Co.,** Front and Brown St., Riverside, NJ 08075 (800-257-5755). Many rivers, streams, and lakes are contaminated with bacteria such as **giardia,** which causes gas, cramps, loss of appetite, and violent diarrhea. To protect yourself from the effects of this invisible trip-wrecker, always boil your water vigorously for at least five minutes before drinking, or use a purification tablet or solution made from iodine (Polarpure is one good solution). Filters do not remove all bacteria, but they can be useful when drawing water from small streams withered by drought. *Never go camping or hiking by yourself for any significant time or distance.* If you're going into an area that is not well-traveled or well-marked, let someone (perhaps a ranger) know where you're hiking and how long you intend to be out. If you fail to return on schedule or if someone needs to reach you, searchers will at least know where to look.

The second thing to protect while outdoors is the wilderness. The thousands of would-be woodspeople who pour into the parks every year threaten to slowly trample the land to death. Because firewood is scarce in popular parks, campers are asked to make small fires using only dead branches or brush. Using a campstove is the more cautious way to cook; check ahead to see if the park prohibits **campfires** altogether. Travelers in Alaska and the Yukon are asked not to build campfires on the Arctic Tundra.

To avoid allowing rain to swamp your tent, pitch it on high, dry ground. Don't cut vegetation, and don't clear campsites. If there are no toilet facilities, bury human waste at least 4 in. deep and 100 ft. or more from any water supplies and campsites. Avoid using toilet paper—use a rock or the rounded surface of a stick if possible, use leaves only if certain they're free of noxious oils. **Biosafe soap** or detergents may be used in streams or lakes. Otherwise, don't use soaps in or near bodies of water. Always pack up your trash in a plastic bag and carry it with you until you reach the next trash can; burning and burying pollute the environment. In more civilized camping circumstances, it's important to respect fellow campers. Keep light and noise to a minimum, particularly if you arrive after dark.

BEAR NECESSITIES

No matter how tame a bear appears, don't be fooled—they're dangerous and unpredictable animals who are simply not impressed or intimidated by humans. As a basic rule, if you're close enough for a bear to be observing you, you're too close. To avoid a grizzly experience, *never feed a bear* or tempt it with such delicacies as open trash cans; contact with food can make them hungry for more, and you may end up as dessert. What's more, your action could force the rangers to put to death a previously harmless animal. Keep your camp clean, and don't cook near where you sleep. Do not leave trash or food lying around camp.

The best way to keep your toothpaste from becoming a condiment is to **bearbag**. This amounts to hanging your edibles from a tree, out of reach of hungry paws. Ask a salesperson at a wilderness store or a park ranger to show you how. In order to do it properly, you'll need heavy nylon strapping, thin nylon rope, and caribiners, as well as a bit of instruction. Food and waste should be sealed in airtight plastic bags, all of which should be placed in duffel bags and hung in a tree 10 ft. from the ground and 5 ft. from the trunk.

Also avoid indulging in greasy foods, especially bacon and ham. Grease gets on everything, including your clothes and sleeping bag, and bears find it an alluring dressing for whatever or whomever is wearing it. Bears are attracted to perfume smells; do without cologne, scented soap, and hairspray while camping. Park rangers can tell you how to identify bear trails (don't camp on them!). *Leave your packs empty and open on the ground so that a bear can nose through them without ripping them to shreds.*

Wear bells or sing loudly when wandering through areas populated by bears, and shine a flashlight when walking at night; bears will avoid you if given sufficient warning. If you stumble upon a sweet-looking bear cub, leave immediately, lest its over-protective mother stumble upon you. And stay away from dead animals and berry bushes—these are *Le menu* for bears.

If you see a bear at a distance, calmly walk (don't run) in the other direction. If it seems interested, some old hands recommend waving your arms or a long stick above your head and talking loudly; the bear's dull vision gives it the impression that you're much taller than a person, and it may (if you're lucky) decide that *you* are threatening to *it*. A bear standing on its hind legs is not necessarily going to attack;

growling is a more reliable danger sign. If you're charged, try to stand your ground. If the bear attacks, assume the fetal position with your hands clasped behind your neck. The aggressiveness of bears varies from region to region; ask local rangers for details before entering any park or wilderness area.

ORGANIZED ADVENTURE

Begin by consulting tourism bureaus, which can suggest parks, trails, and outfitters as well as answer more general questions. *Outside Magazine*, Outside Plaza, Santa Fe, New Mexico 87501 (505-989-7100), publishes an Expedition Services Directory in each issue. The **Sierra Club,** 730 Polk St., San Francisco, CA 94109 (415-923-5630), plans a variety of outings. So does **Trekamerica,** P.O. Box 470, Blairstown, NJ 07825 (800-221-0596); call or write for more information.

■ OUTDOOR SPORTS

WATER SPORTS

The latticework of fast-flowing rivers in the Pacific Northwest is ideal for canoeing, kayaking, and whitewater rafting. Boating opportunities are suggested in the Activities sections throughout the book. Travel agents and tourism bureaus can recommend others.

The **River Travel Center,** P.O. Box 6, Pt. Arena, CA 95468 (800-882-RAFT or 7238), can place you in a whitewater raft, kayak, or sea kayak through one of over 100 outfitters. Trips range in length from three to 18 days and range in price from $350 to $1200. British Columbia rafting trips (half day $42, full day $89) and a multiplicity of other outdoor adventures are planned by **Clearwater Expeditions Ltd.,** R.R. 2, Box 2545, Clearwater, BC V0E 1ND (604-674-3354). **Hells Canyon Adventures, Inc.,** Box 159, Oxbow, OR 97840 (800-422-3568; in OR, 503-785-3352; fax 503-785-3353), is the place to call for Snake River whitewater rafting, whitewater jet boat tours, float trips, and fishing charters. Rafting trips on class 4 rapids cost $90 per person for a 7-hour trip; 2- hour jet boat tours start at $25, 3- hour tours at $30.

Sierra Club Books publishes a kayaking and whitewater rafting guide entitled *Wildwater* ($12). The club offers kayaking trips to the Pacific Northwest and Alaska every year. *Washington Whitewater* ($19) and *Canoe Routes: Northwest Oregon* ($11), published by The Mountaineers Books, might also interest you.

Swimmers in the North country should consult locals before diving into any unsupervised lake or gravelly pit. Some of these may contain the feisty larvae which can lead to **"swimmer's itch."** Symptoms include red and irritated skin beginning almost immediately and usually lasting seven to ten days.

SNOW SPORTS

Tourism bureaus can help you locate the best sports outfitters and ski areas. *Let's Go* suggests options in the Activities sections throughout the book. For Oregon and Washington skiing guides and information (both downhill and cross country), write the **Pacific Northwest Ski Areas Association,** P.O. Box 2325 Seattle, WA 98111-2325 (206-623-3777). The Sierra Club publishes *The Best Ski Touring in America* ($11), which includes Canada as well. The Mountaineers Books publishes good skiing guides for Oregon and Washington.

Pay attention to cold weather safety concerns. Know the symptoms of hypothermia and frostbite (see Health above), and bring along warm clothes and quick energy snacks like candy bars and trail mix. Drinking alcohol in the cold can be particularly dangerous: even though you *feel* warm, alcohol can slow your body's ability to adjust to the temperature, and thus make you more vulnerable to hypothermia.

FISHING AND HUNTING

Should you wish to take advantage of the regions' well-stocked lakes and streams, contact the appropriate department of fisheries for brochures that summarize regulations and make sport fishing predictions. Some fishing seasons are extremely short, so be sure to ask when the expected prime angling dates occur. Licenses are available from many tackle shops, or you can purchase them directly from the state or provincial department of fisheries. You need not reside in a state or province in order to hunt there, but steep license and tag fees will probably discourage you. Consult the appropriate departments of game to purchase licenses and receive regulations pamphlets.

Alaska: Fish and Game Licensing Section, P.O. Box 25525, Juneau, AK 99802-5525 (907-465-2376; fax 465-2604; open Mon.-Fri. 8:30am-4:30pm). Nonresident fishing license $10 for 1 day, $15 for 3 days, $30 for 14 days, $50 for a year. Nonresident hunting licenses $85 ($20 for small game only), plus tags from $150 (deer) to $1100 (musk ox). $135 combined annual nonresident license for hunting and fishing for a full year.

Alberta: Fish and Wildlife Service, 9945 108th St., Edmonton, Alb. T5K 2G6 (403-427-3590). Nonresident fishing license CDN$15 for Canadians, CDN$30 for non-Canadians. Nonresident hunting license CDN$22 (wildlife certificate and resource development stamp), plus tags from CDN$24 (wolf) to CDN$306 (sheep). CDN$20 limited 5-day fishing license for non-Canadians.

British Columbia: Fish and Wildlife Information, Ministry of Environment, 780 Blanshard St., Victoria, BC V8V 1X4 (604-387-9737). Non-Canadian angling license CDN$25 for 8 days, CDN$40 for a year; CDN$20 for steelhead tags. Non-Canadian hunting license CDN$155, for wolf CDN$27, for grizzly bear CDN$535; prices for other animals range somewhere in between.

Oregon: Department of Fish and Wildlife, 2501 SW 1st Ave., P.O. Box 59, Portland 97207 (503-229-5400). Nonresident fishing license $40.50, plus $10.50 each for salmon/steelhead, sturgeon, and halibut tags. Nonresident hunting license $53 Combination license $29.50 (residents only).

Washington: Department of Fish and Wildlife, 600 Capitol Way, Olympia 98501-1091 (206-753-5700). Nonresident game fishing license $48. Nonresident Personal Use Food Fish License $20. Nonresident Shellfish/ Seaweed License $20. Nonresident hunting license $150. Combination license $29 (residents only).

Yukon Government, Department of Renewable Resources, Fish and Wildlife Branch, 10 Burns Rd., P.O. Box 2703, Whitehorse Y1A 2C6 (403-667-5221). Non-Canadian fishing license CDN$5 for 1 day, CDN$20 for 6 days, CDN$35 for a year. Non-Canadian small-game hunting license CDN$20 for 1 year; large-game hunting license CDN$150 for a year, plus tags from CDN$5 (moose) to CDN$25 (grizzly bear). All Non-Canadians must work with a registered guide when hunting large game.

Many outfitters plan fly-in fishing trips or boating trips designed for anglers. These expeditions are expensive. If interested, consult a travel agent or tourism bureau for possibilities.

■■■ KEEPING IN TOUCH

■ MAIL

Individual offices of the **U.S. Postal Service** are usually open Monday to Friday from 9am to 5pm and sometimes on Saturday until about noon; branches in many larger cities open earlier and close later. All are closed on national holidays. **Postcards** mailed within the U.S. cost 19¢; **letters** cost 29¢ for the first ounce and 23¢ for each additional ounce. Domestic mail takes from two days to a week to reach its destination, depending on distance. To Canada, it costs 30¢ to mail a postcard, 40¢ to mail a letter for the first ounce, 23¢ for each additional ounce. It costs 30¢ to mail a postcard to Mexico; a letter is 35¢ for a half- ounce, 45¢ for an ounce, and 10¢ for each additional half-ounce up to two pounds. Each additional ounce after two ounces and up to 12 ounces costs 25¢. Postcards mailed overseas cost 40¢, and letters are 50¢ for a half-ounce, 95¢ for an ounce, and 39¢ for each additional half-ounce up to 64 ounces. Within the U.S., up to 2 pounds of material can be sent Priority Mail (two to three days to domestic locations) at a cost of $2.90.

Aerogrammes, printed sheets that fold into envelopes and travel via air mail, are available at post offices for 45¢. Mail to northern Europe, Canada, and Mexico takes a week to 10 days to arrive; to southern Europe, North Africa, and the Middle East, two weeks; and to South America or Asia, a week to 10 days. Of course, all of the above estimated times of arrival are rough estimates, and may vary where other national postal services are involved. Be sure to write "Air Mail" on the front of the envelope for the speediest delivery. Large cities' post offices offer an **International Express Mail** service, which is the fastest way to send an item overseas: delivery is guaranteed to a major city overseas in 40 to 72 hours for between $11.50 and $14.00; often takes only a day). In **Canada** mailing a letter (or a postcard, which carries the same rate as a letter) to the U.S. costs CDN$0.50 for the first 30 grams and CDN$.74 for 31-50 grams. To every other foreign country, a 20-gram letter costs CDN$0.88, a 50-gram letter CDN$1.33, and a 51- to 100-gram letter CDN$2.25. The domestic rate is CDN$0.43 for a 30-gram letter, and CDN$0.69 for a letter between 31 and 50 grams. Aerogrammes can be mailed only to other locations in Canada (CDN$0.88). Letters take from three to eight working days to reach the U.S. and a week or two to get to an overseas address.

Canada Post's most reliable and pricey service is **Priority Courier,** which offers speedy delivery (usually next-day) to major American cities (CDN$23.50 for a document). Delivery to overseas locations usually takes two days and costs CDN$63 for a document. Guaranteed next-day delivery exists between any two Canadian cities and costs CDN$8.10 within a single province and CDN$11.50 between provinces; for the purposes of Priority Courier, Quebec and Ontario represent one region, so that mail traveling between those provinces costs CDN$8.10.

Depending on how neurotic your family is, consider making arrangements for them to get in touch with you. Mail can be sent **General Delivery** to a city's main branch of the post office. Once a letter arrives it will be held for about 30 days; it can be held for longer if such a request is clearly indicated on the front of the envelope. Family and friends can send letters to you labeled like this:

Mr. Jeffrey M. Miller (underline last name for accurate filing)
c/o General Delivery
Main Post Office
Portland, OR 97208

Customers should bring a passport or other ID to pick up General Delivery mail.

The U.S. is divided into postal zones, each with a five-digit **ZIP code** particular to a region, city, or part of a city. Some addresses have nine-digit ZIP codes, used primarily to speed up delivery for business mailings. Writing this code on letters is essential for delivery. The normal form of address is as follows:

Jay A. Cooper
Creative Director (title or name of organization, optional)
4000 Northup Way, #290 (address, apartment number)
Bellevue, WA 98009 (city, state abbreviation, Zip)
USA (country, if mailing internationally)

In Canada, **postal codes** are the equivalent of U.S. Zip codes and contain letters as well as numbers (for example, H4P 1B8). The normal form of address is nearly identical to that in the U.S.; the only difference is that the apartment or suite number can *precede* the street address along with a dash. For example, 23-40 Sherbrooke St. refers to Room #23 at 40 Sherbrooke St.

If in the U.S. and ordering books and materials from abroad, always include with your request an **International Reply Coupon**—a method of "pre-paying" in the

U.S. for postage on letters to be mailed from foreign countries that belong to the Universal Postal Union (95¢). IRCs should be available from your home post office. Be sure that your coupon has adequate postage to cover the cost of delivery. Canada Post also offers an IRC service (CDN$1.25).

American Express offices throughout the U.S. and Canada will act as a mail service for cardholders if you contact them in advance. Under this free **"Client Letter Service,"** they will hold mail for 30 days, forward upon request, and accept telegrams. The last name of the person to whom the mail is addressed should be capitalized and underlined. For "Traveler's Companion," a complete list of offices and instructions on how to use the service, call 800-528-4800.

Most major cities features the **Postal Answer Line (PAL),** which provides information on first-class surface mail at ext. 319, International Express Mail at ext. 318, Parcel Post at ext. 317, customs at ext. 308, special services at ext. 142, and IRCs at ext. 307.

Other alternatives include a variety of private mail services. **DHL** (800-225-5345 in USA and Canada) will send mail to almost all of Western Europe in two to three days for approximately $30. **Federal Express** (800-238-5355 in USA and Canada) will send mail express to Western Europe in two business days for about US$30; other destinations are more variable.

■ TELEPHONES

Most of the information you will need about telephone usage—including area codes for the U.S., foreign country codes, and rates—is in the front of the local **white pages** telephone directory. The **yellow pages,** published at the end of the white pages or in a separate book, is used to look up numbers of businesses and other services. Federal, state, and local government listings are provided in the **blue pages** at the back of the directory. To obtain local phone numbers or area codes of other cities, call **directory assistance** at 411. Dialing "0" will get you the **operator,** who can assist you in reaching a phone number and provide you with general information. For long-distance directory assistance, dial 1-(area code)-555-1212. The operator will help you with rates and other information, and will give assistance in an emergency. You can reach directory assistance and the operator free from any pay phone.

Telephone numbers in the U.S. consist of a three-digit area code, a three-digit exchange, and a four-digit number, written as 123-456-7890. In a **local call,** it is not necessary to use the area code. **Non-local calls** *within* the area code from which you are dialing require a "1" before the last seven digits, while **long-distance calls** outside the area code from which you are dialing require a "1" and the area code. Canada and much of Mexico share the same system. Generally, **discount rates** apply after 5pm on weekdays and Sunday and **economy rates** every day between 11pm and 8am; on Saturday and on Sunday until 5pm, economy rates are also in effect.

Many large companies operate **toll-free numbers** to provide information to their customers at no charge. These consist of "1" plus "800" plus a seven-digit number. To obtain specific toll-free numbers, call 800-555-1212. Be careful—the age of technology has recently given birth to the **"900" number.** Its area code is deceptively similar to the toll-free code, but "900" calls are staggeringly expensive.

Pay phones are plentiful, most often stationed on street corners and in public areas. Be wary of private, more expensive pay phones—the rate they charge per call will be printed on the phone. Put your coins (10-25¢ for a local call depending on the region) into the slot and listen for a dial tone before dialing. If there is no answer or if you get a busy signal, you will get your money back after hanging up; connecting with answering machines will prevent this. To make a long-distance direct call, dial the number. An operator will tell you the cost for the first three minutes; deposit that amount in the coin slot. The operator or a recording will cut in when you must deposit more money. A rare type of pay phone can be found in some train stations and charges 25¢ for a one-minute call to anywhere in the continental U.S.

If you are at an ordinary telephone and don't have barrels of change, you may want to make a **collect call** (i.e., charge the call to the recipient). First dial "0" and then the area code and number you wish to reach. An operator will cut in and ask to help you. Identify yourself and tell him or her that you wish to place a collect call; anyone who answers may accept or refuse the call. The cheapest method of reversing the charges is MCI's new 1-800-COLLECT (205-5328) service: just dial 1-800-COLLECT, tell the operator what number you want to engage (it can be anywhere in the world), and receive a 20-44% discount off normal rates. Finally, if you'd like to call someone who is as poor as you, simply bill to a third party, also by dialing "0," the area code, and then the number; the operator will call the third party for approval. Note that in some areas, particularly rural ones, you may have to dial "0" alone for any operator-assisted call.

You can place **international calls** from any telephone. To call direct, dial the universal international access code (011) followed the country code, the city code, and the local number. **Country codes** are as follows: the **United Kingdom** (44); **Ireland** (353); **Australia** (61); **New Zealand** (64); **South Africa** (27).Country codes and city codes may sometimes be listed with a zero in front (e.g. 033), but when using 011, drop successive zeros (e.g., 011-33). In some areas you will have to give the operator the number and he or she will place the call. AT&T offers international calling through AT&T USADirect and AT&T World Connect. Each country is assigned an access number, and by combining the access code with one's calling card number, callers can bill charges to their AT&T Calling Card; call (800-331-1140) for information and access code lists. MCI has a similar program called WorldPhone which also provides access to MCI's Traveler's Assist, a service which gives legal and medical advice, exchange rate information, and translation services. Call (800-444-3333 for information or to obtain a calling card. Rates are cheapest on calls to the United Kingdom and Ireland between 6pm and 7am (Eastern Time); to Australia between 3am and 2pm; to New Zealand between 11pm and 10am; and to South Africa between 5pm and 6am.

■■■ CLIMATE

In **Alaska,** the weather varies from the coast inland. In general, summer and early fall (i.e. June-Sept.) are the warmest and sunniest times of year. However, wet, windy, and cold days even during the summer should be no real surprise. In Anchorage, the average temperature is around 20°F in January and 60°F in July. In Alaska's interior, the temperatures range from the 70s in the summers to the -30s in the wintertime. As you progress farther north, summer days and winter nights become longer. In Alaska and the Yukon, summer days may last from 6am to 2am.

In **Alberta,** the north and south of the province differ in temperature, although the entire area tends to be dry and cool. In January, the average temperature is around 15°F in the south, closer to -20°F in the north; in the summer, both regions warm to around 70°F.

In British Columbia, Washington, and Oregon, the key weather-making factor is the **mountains.** West of the mountains it rains quite a bit; to the east it is relatively dry. On the BC coast, the average temperature is about 35°F in January and a cool 65°F in the summer. Inland, winter temperatures hover around 0°F, while summer temperatures rise near 70°F. Temperatures in Washington range from an average of 35°F in January to 70°F in July—the west slightly colder, the east slightly warmer in the summer, and the other way around in the winter. Oregon is, on average, a little warmer than Washington.

ALASKA

Alaska's beauty is born of extremes. Here lie the highest mountain, the deepest gorge, and the broadest expanse of flatlands in all of North America. Alaska's oceans and rainforests teem with wildlife, even while its icy wastelands receive less rainfall than most deserts. Harsh weather and an unforgiving landscape resisted successful human habitation in Alaska's interior until the 19th century, and the human presence in this vast land is still so minute as to be virtually negligible. Yet human quests for fur, gold, and oil have indelibly altered the once-pristine landscape.

The native Aleuts, who thrived for millennia in the harsh climate of the Aleutian island chain, called the spectacular and enormous expanses to the northeast "Alashka," meaning "The Great Land." To the Europeans and followers of "manifest destiny" who journeyed into the northwestern hinterlands, Alaska was the "Last Frontier." For the tourists and the sunlight-starved who trek to Alaska each summer, this region is the "Land of the Midnight Sun." Alaska has as many names as it has distinguishing characteristics, but the least appropriate is its popular identity as a "frozen wasteland;" indeed, for half of the year, all but the northernmost reaches of the state turn green with vegetation.

Physically, Alaska truly is "The Great Land." The state contains 586,000 sq. mi., more than one-fifth of the land mass of all of America. The 33,000-mi. coastline stretches 11 times the distance from New York to San Francisco. Alaska is also home to Wrangell-St. Elias, the largest national park in America, which covers an area of 13 million acres and is twice the size of Massachusetts. Nineteen Alaskan peaks reach over 14,000 ft., more than 3 million lakes are larger than 20 acres, and several glacial ice fields occupy areas larger than the state of Rhode Island. Four major mountain ranges, the Wrangell Mountains, the Chugach Mountains, the Brooks Range, and the Denali-topped Alaska Range, cross the state.

But despite its monumental natural endowments, Alaska necessarily maintains a combative relationship with Nature. The Aleutian Islands are located on the "Ring of Fire" at the edge of the Pacific Plate and are positioned almost due north of the Hawaiian volcanic chain; predictably, they are perpetually wracked by earthquakes and active volcanoes. The rest of the state, too, has reason to scoff at California's hyperbolized fear of tremors. In 1964, the Good Friday quake, centered in Miner's Lake (located between Whittier and Valdez), registered 9.2 on the modern Richter Scale and lasted eight terrible minutes. Its aftershocks continued for several days. Many coastal towns, including Kodiak and Whittier, were demolished by the *tsunami* which followed the earthquake; Valdez was completely destroyed and was forced rebuild on a new site.

Although the wounds inflicted by the disaster visibly linger, a trip to Alaska will still thrill nature lovers. Photographers will find the wilderness full of unsuspecting subjects, including caribou, bear, moose, Dall sheep, and mountain goats. Anglers will be satisfied by millions of spawning salmon, huge off-shore halibut, and trophy-sized grayling and trout churning in countless untouched interior lakes. For hikers and campers, Alaska provides unparalleled opportunities for a truly solitary wilderness experience (only one-quarter of Alaska is accessible by highway). But you do not need to be a hard-core outdoorsperson to see much of the state's beauty—many of Alaska's most stunning glaciers can also be reached by road.

Geography

Alaska is home to several distinct geographic zones. On the archipelago of the **Southeastern Panhandle,** the isolated state capital of Juneau resides among numerous fjord-scarred islands, verdant rainforests, and primordial swamps known as *muskeg*. **Southcentral Alaska**, home of Kodiak Island, the Kenai Peninsula, and Prince William Sound, is filled with an abundance of wildlife, including the Kodiak

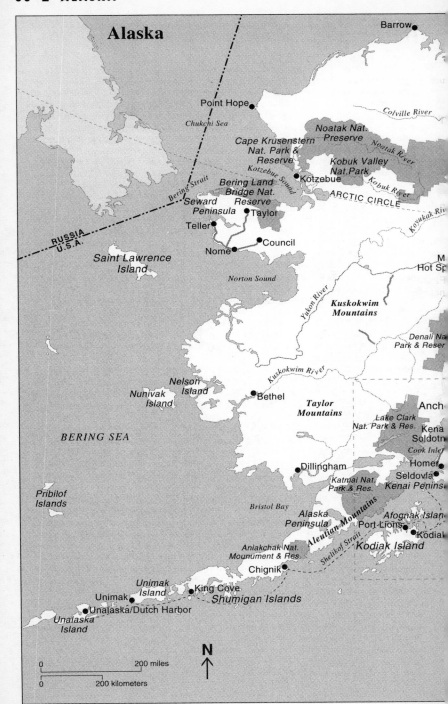

Alaska

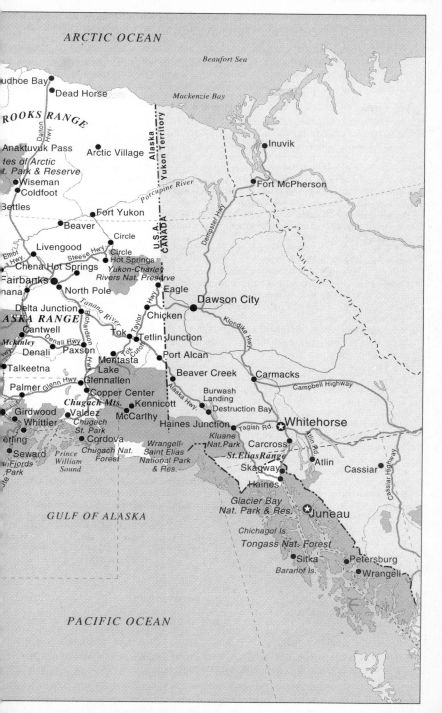

ARCTIC OCEAN

Beaufort Sea

Mackenzie Bay

...dhoe Bay

Dead Horse

BROOKS RANGE

Dalton Hwy.

Anaktuvuk Pass

...tes of Arctic
...t. Park & Reserve

Arctic Village

Inuvik

Alaska
Yukon Territory

Porcupine River

Fort McPherson

Wiseman

Coldfoot

Bettles

Fort Yukon

Beaver

U.S.A.
CANADA

Circle

Livengood

Steese Hwy.

Elliot Hwy.

Circle
Hot Springs

Chena Hot Springs

Yukon-Charley
Rivers Nat. Preserve

Dempster Hwy.

Fairbanks

...nana

North Pole

Eagle

Dawson City

Tanana River

Delta Junction

Richardson Hwy.

Chicken

Klondike Hwy.

ALASKA RANGE

Cantwell

Denali Hwy.

Tok

Tok Taylor Hwy.

Mckinley
Hwy.

Denali

Paxson

Tetlin Junction

Tok Cutoff

Port Alcan

Talkeetna

Mentasta
Lake

Beaver Creek

Carmacks

Palmer

Glenn Hwy.

Glennallen

Burwash
Landing

Campbell Highway

Chugach Mts.

Copper Center

Kennicott

Alaska Hwy.

Girdwood

Valdez

McCarthy

Destruction Bay

Whitehorse

Whittier

Chugach
St. Park

Haines Junction

Tagish Rd.

Atlin Rd.

...erling

Cordova

Wrangell-
Saint Elias
National Park
& Res.

Kluane
Nat. Park

Carcross

Seward

Prince
William
Sound

Chugach Nat.
Forest

St. Elias Range

Atlin

...ai Fjords
...Park

Skagway

Cassiar

Haines

Cassiar Highway

GULF OF ALASKA

Glacier Bay
Nat. Park & Res.

Juneau

Chichagof Is.

Tongass Nat. Forest

Sitka

Petersburg

Baranof Is.

Wrangell

PACIFIC OCEAN

INTRODUCTION

brown bear. To the north and east from Anchorage, the interminable flatlands of the **Interior** are dominated by the highest mountain in North America: 20,320-ft.-tall Denali. The **Bush** encompasses the vast and empty areas north and west of the Interior, including the Brooks Range and the Arctic Circle, the Seward Peninsula, and all of western Alaska along the Bering Sea. The Alaska Peninsula and the storm-swept **Aleutian Islands** poke into the extreme southwestern reaches of the Bush, offering small purchase to a handful of hardy human inhabitants.

History

The first humans arrived in the region some 20,000 years ago, migrating over the Bering Land Bridge from Siberia to Alaska. Today, four distinct native ethnic groups inhabit Alaska. The Southeast is home to the Tlingit and Haida peoples, who are renowned for their exquisitely carved totem poles and the nearly impenetrable wooden forts from which they almost staved off Russian invaders in the 19th century. The Interior and Southcentral regions harbor the once-nomadic Athabasca nation. The Aleutian Island Chain is populated largely by the Aleuts, a peaceful people who were enslaved by the Russians as fur trappers. The Inuits (commonly given the misnomer of "Eskimos," or "raw meat-eaters,") reside almost exclusively within the Arctic Circle, and share a common language and heritage with the Native Siberians across the Bering Strait.

Under orders from Peter the Great to find a route from the Arctic to the Pacific, Russian seafarers landed on Kayak Island of Prince William Sound In 1733. Bering's expedition brought the fur of sea otters back to Russia, and inaugurated intense competition for control of the lucrative trade in "soft gold." In initiating a massive colonization of the Alaskan wilderness, the Russians located their base of operation primarily in the southern coastal region, which even today retains an unmistakably Slavic imprint. By the mid-1800s, the once-bountiful supply of fur-bearing animals was nearly exhausted, the populations of Aleuts had diminished through forced labor, and the Russians welcomed an American bid for the "dead land." Such frenzied and profit-seeking exploitation of natural resources, ending only with total depletion, would provide the pattern for much of Alaska's future.

The United States purchased Alaska for $7,200,000, or approximately 2¢ per acre, on October 18, 1867. Critics mocked the transaction, popularly called "Seward's Folly" after the Secretary of State who negotiated the deal under President Johnson. At this time, Native Alaskans restated their claims to their ancestral lands, but received only limited recognition from Washington. The issue went unresolved, and titles were to be held in abeyance for more than a century.

James Seward was vindicated a scant 15 years post-purchase, when large deposits of gold were unearthed in the Gastineau Channel and the Eldorado-esque Juneau was born. As deposits on the Gastineau were exhausted, other rivers such as the Yukon, the Charley, the Fortymile, and the Klondike were each, in turn, swarmed by gold-panning prospectors. Hundreds of millions of dollars in gold eventually made their way, pipeline-style, to the continental U.S. Alaska became the 49th state in 1959, decades after the last major deposits of gold had been pulled from the ground. Throughout the 1960s, Alaskan Natives watched with growing consternation as the federal and state governments divvied up vast tracts of land without regard for the Natives' 20,000-year-long occupancy. The discovery in 1968 of huge oil deposits beneath the shore of the Beaufort Sea in the Arctic Ocean brought matters to a head. Natives increased the pressure for settlement of the claims which had for so long been ignored and sought a share in the anticipated economic boom.

In December of 1971, the federal government finally made its peace with the native peoples, state and federal courts, and environmental groups by passing the Alaska Native Claims Settlement Act (ANCSA). The natives, who then numbered around 60,000, received $1 billion and 40 million acres of land. The natives became, collectively, rich; but their victory came at the cost of an attitudinal readjustment. In a land where natives once could follow caribou over lands without borders and fish for subsistence without permits, "no trespassing" signs have shot up, and the native corporations have been compelled to sell off natural resources in exchange for the almighty dollar.

Meanwhile, economic development continued unimpeded. In 1973, the Alyeska Pipeline Service Company received the official go-ahead to build a pipeline from Prudhoe Bay to Valdez—800 mi. through the heart of the Alaskan wilderness. The pipeline has brought jobs, money, and people to Alaska, and with them, many of the undesirable features of the lower 48 states: pollution, overcrowding, and profligate spending. It is hard to imagine overcrowding in a land so huge; then again, it is hard to believe that a single pipeline, in relative size only as thick as a thread across Staten Island, could have such a drastic effect on the state's political, social, and economic landscape. By 1981, four years after the Trans-Alaska pipeline was installed, $7,200,000 worth of crude oil flowed from the Arctic oil field every 4½ hours, forever curtailing dismissal of "The Folly." State revenues from oil taxation have created a trust fund in the name of the people of Alaska, providing the government with enough money to operate without the need for any additional private taxation.

But even the most lucrative of industries has its price tags. Twenty-five years to the day after the Good Friday earthquake of '64 leveled the port city of Valdez, the Exxon oil tanker *Valdez* ran aground on Bligh Reef, spilling over 250,000 barrels (11 million gallons) of syrupy crude into the blue waters of Prince William Sound and onto shores as far away as Kodiak Island, several hundred mi. to the south. Thousands of marine mammals and birds, saturated with the sticky black sludge, suffered horrible deaths. Clean-up crews were completely unprepared and grossly underfunded and understaffed. A full 10% of the Sound was poisoned by oil, and 2% of Alaska's total coastline was polluted. Though by the summer of 1990 no oil was visible to the casual observer, the long-term effects of the spill are uncertain at best; in addition to poisoning thousands of marine mammals and birds, the oil has disrupted feeding cycles in the sound.

Exxon has spent $2.5 billion to clean up the spilled oil, and in October, 1991, the company agreed to pay an additional $900 million over the next 11 years for future clean-up operations, plus $100 million in restitution to the state and federal governments and $25 million in criminal fines. Hundreds of lawsuits filed against Exxon by private individuals, including Native Alaskans, are still pending. But the payments have put little more than a dent in the oil company's earnings and have done little to ameliorate the basic problem; recent federal and state environmental reports have revealed that marine biologists (and the courts) may even have underestimated the extent of the damage caused by the spill.

The tremendous uproar surrounding the spill helps to underscore the present shift taking place within the Alaskan economy. As the pipeline's profits have been securely divided among the oil companies, the native corporations, and the state and federal governments, the rush which sprang up around its discovery and exploitation has begun to subside. In its place has developed an environmentally-spurred interest in the state's wilderness. The vast expanses of unspoiled land, not to be found anywhere else in the U.S., are at present Alaska's hottest commodity. The astounding extent of Exxon's payment (and the serious threat that it may be required to pay still more) attests to the growing political clout of those controlling and promoting the state's unpopulated lands.

In 1990, political eccentric Walter Hickel, an early advocate for the of the oil industry, swept into the governor's mansion once again on an independent ticket, supported by a small but dedicated party of Alaskan secessionists. Hickel made a slew of attempts at further commercializing the state. The governor bears the dubious distinction of being the introducer of the shopping mall into Alaska, has proposed construction of a gigantic "garden hose" through which Alaskan fresh water would be pumped to drought-stricken California, and once suggested building an "ice highway" over the top of the world to Norway in order to spur trade with Europe.

In the fall of 1992, with Hickel still at the state's helm, the Alaska Board of Game voted to allow the tracking and shooting of wolves from the air, hoping that a smaller population of wolves would lead to larger herds of moose and caribou, and, in turn, to larger crowds of tourists to the state's public park lands. A *New York Times* article quoted David Kelleyhouse, director of the Alaska Division of Wildlife Conservation: "We feel we are going to create a wildlife spectacle on par with the major migrations in East Africa. Mom and pop from Syracuse can come up here and see something that they can't see anywhere else on earth." Kelleyhouse's grand vision was clearly in keeping with that of Governor Hickel, who had appointed both Kelleyhouse and the members of the state Board of Game following his election in 1990.

The vote by the Board of Game quickly drew vociferous protest, both from within Alaska and from the Lower 48. The Fund for Animals, Inc., took out a prominent ad on the *Times's* Op-Ed page displaying a large picture of a wolf, tongue lolling from its mouth. The ad exhorted readers to "make a call for the wild" by contacting the Governor and voicing their dissent. On December 5, the *Times* published a selection of the reader mail it had received on the matter, the gist of which was captured in the section's accompanying illustration: a wolf blindfolded and roped to a stake, the muzzles of five rifles pushing into its chest.

Such negative publicity was certainly not what Hickel had hoped for, and, following several governmental gatherings in early 1993, the state Board of Game rescinded its decision to allow shooting and tracking from the air, opting instead to permit shooting from the ground only, and solely by officers of the state's Department of Fish and Game. The hunting is to take place in a more limited area than was first proposed, and the newly-revised goal of the hunting is more specific and more acceptable—to reverse the decline of a certain herd of caribou near Fairbanks whose numbers had been falling for several years. Mom and pop from Syracuse will have to wait.

Literature

A good way to catch up on the ABCs to Alaska is to peruse John McPhee's *Coming Into the Country*, which sketches a fascinating overview of Alaskan issues and wilderness life-styles. *Village Journey*, by Thomas Burger, gives a first-hand perspective on emerging Native corporations. A depiction of Eskimo culture and heritage can be found in Lael Morgan's *Art and Eskimo Power*. Walter Hickel's *Who Owns America* outlines the Governor's plans for future development of the state. The venerable Native newspaper *Tundra Times,* founded in part by the legendary Eskimo journalist Howard Rock, publishes out of Anchorage and provides the most up-to-date discussions of current Native American issues without glossing over internal diversity and factionalism. Finally, *Going to Extremes* by Joe McGinniss and *Alaska: The Sophisticated Wilderness* by Jon Gardey both acquaint the reader with Alaskan settlers seeking refuge from the lower 48. (Eccentrics or mavericks? You decide.)

PRACTICAL INFORMATION

Capital: Juneau.

Visitors Information: Alaska Division of Tourism, 33 Willoughby St. (465-2010). Mailing address: P.O. Box 110801, Juneau 99811-0801. Open Mon.-Fri. 8am-5pm.

Alaska Public Lands Information Center, 605 W 4th Ave. #105, Anchorage, 99501 (271-2737 or 258-PARK for a recording), in the Old Federal Bldg. Help in crossing any and all wilderness areas. Branch office in Fairbanks; others under construction in Ketchikan and Tok. Open daily 9am-5:30pm.

Alaska State Division of Parks, 3601 C St., Anchorage 99510 (762-2617). Open Mon.-Fri. 8am-4:30pm.

United States Forest Service, 1675 C. St., Anchorage, AK 99501-5198 (271-4126). General information regarding national parks and reserves. Open Mon.-Fri. 8am-5pm.

National Park Service, Parks and Forests Information Center, W 4th Ave., Anchorage 99503 (271-2737). Open Mon.-Fri. 9am-7pm.

Alaska Department of Fish and Game, P.O. Box 25526, Juneau, AK 99802-5526 (465-4190). Hunting and fishing regulations available here.
Alaska State Employment Service, 10002 Glacier Highway, #200, Juneau 99801 (465-4562).
Legislative Information Office, 716 W 4th Ave. #200, Anchorage 99501-2133 (258-8111). For those who would like to delve into Alaska's juicy political debates. Or call the **Alaska State Government General Information** service at 561-4226.
United States Customs Service: 202-927-6724. This Washington, DC office will connect you with the Canadian Customs and Excise office for information regarding the rules and regulations of traveling through Canada on your way to Alaska.
Payphones: In many towns, phones will not return coins, even if the party you're calling doesn't answer. Dial, wait until party picks up, and *then* deposit coins. They will understand the lag.
Population: 550,000. **Nicknames:** The Last Frontier; Land of the Midnight Sun. **Motto:** North to the Future. **Flower:** Forget-Me-Not. **Bird:** Willow Ptarmigan. **Tree:** Sitka Spruce. **Date of Incorporation:** Jan. 3, 1959 (49th state). **Land Area:** 570,373 sq. mi.
Emergency: 911.
Mountaineering Info.: 243-7675.
State Troopers: 269-5511 in Anchorage, 452-2114 in Fairbanks.
Time Zones: Alaska (most of the state; 4 hr. behind Eastern); Aleutian-Hawaii (Aleutian Islands; 5 hr. behind Eastern).
Postal Abbreviation: AK
Drinking Age: 21.
Area Code: 907.

GETTING AROUND

The cost of travel both to and through Alaska is exorbitant no matter how you go. Bringing a car is not necessarily the wisest plan—if at all feeble, the car may not survive the rocky drive up the largely unpaved **Alaska Highway.** Even if you and your car do arrive safely, there often aren't enough usable roads to justify the time and expense of driving (gas is expensive, breakdowns are common, and traveling with a car on the ferry is costly). Many people do, of course, venture onto Alaska's roads despite the difficulties, and anyone so inclined should consult the By Car: Driving in Alaska section of the Essentials chapter.

The shortcomings of Alaska's sketchy road and rail networks are quick to explain why one in 36 Alaskans has a pilot's license. Given Alaska's size, air travel is often a necessity, albeit an exorbitantly expensive one (the hourly rate exceeds $100). Several intrastate airlines, almost exclusively based at the Anchorage airport, transport passengers and cargo virtually to every village in Alaska: **Alaska Airlines** (to larger Bush towns and Cordova; 800-426-5292); **Mark Air** (to larger Bush towns, Kodiak, and the Aleutians; 800-426-6784); **ERA Aviation** (southcentral; 243-6633); **Southcentral Air** (southcentral; 243-2761); **Reeves Aleutian Airways** (Aleutians; 243-4700); and **Ryan Air Service** (practically anywhere in the Bush; 561-2090). Many other charters and flight-seeing services are available. Write **Ketchum Air Service Inc.,** P.O. Box 190588, Anchorage 99519 (243-5525), on the North Shore of Lake Hood, to ask about their charters. One-day flights and overnight or weekend trips to isolated lakes, mountains, and tundra usually range from $165 up.

Those who intend to hit the ground running, and keep running, would be smart to check out the **AlaskaPass.** The pass offers unlimited access to Alaska's railroad, ferry, and bus systems; a 15-day pass sells for $569, a 30-day pass for $799. The fare may seem expensive, but with a network that extends from Bellingham, WA to Dutch Harbor on the Aleutian Islands, the pass is a good deal for those who want to see a lot of Alaska in a short amount of time. If interested, call 800-248-7598, 7am-7pm (Alaska time).

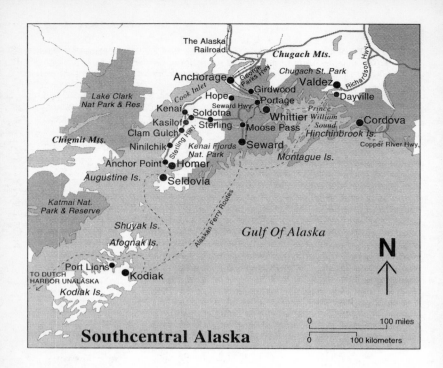

Southcentral Alaska

Southcentral Alaska

Southcentral Alaska stands on the threshold of Alaska's future. Anchorage, Prince William Sound, the Kenai Peninsula, and Kodiak Island are becoming less isolated as opportunity and an expanding network of well-maintained roads draw more and more people up from the Lower 48. The cost of living is slowly declining and Alaska's isolation, while in no danger of ending shortly, is gradually eroding.

Massive and challenging peaks, rivers churning with fish, and a diverse cast of animal life can be reached in less than a day from Anchorage. But as the state makes itself more presentable to guests and export industries, the kinds of nature that to many people define Alaska, the pristine and untouched expanses devoid of human presence, are receding into a distance open only to the most diligent.

Valdez is the southern terminus of the Alaska Pipeline, attracting heavy tankers to pump themselves full. It was in this area that the tanker Exxon *Valdez* made its toxic, intoxicated blunder, defacing miles of coastline and poisoning wildlife. The big oil and fishing interests have been at loggerheads since the environmental disaster. In August 1993, fishermen blockaded Valdez harbor in protest of the oil conglomerate's insufficient efforts at compensation and cleanup.

■■■ ANCHORAGE

Only 80 years ago, cartographers wasted no ink on what is now Alaska's major metropolis. Approximately half the state's population, about 250,000 people, live in "Los Anchorage," the term that some rural residents use to mock the city's urban pretensions. Not surprisingly, the city has an air of prefabrication; writer John

McPhee called it "condensed, instant Albuquerque." Extremely spread out, the low buildings of Anchorage extend in many directions. But more than merely a decentralized jumble of fast-food joints and discount liquor stores, Anchorage supports a full range of popular culture: semi-professional baseball and basketball teams, frequent performances by internationally known orchestras and music stars, dramatic theater, and opera. The *Anchorage Daily News* won a Pulitzer Prize in 1989 for its reporting on suicide and alcoholism among Native Alaskans. Moose and bear not only occasionally wander downtown but are actually hunted legally within the municipality. Still, this is as close to "big city" as Alaska gets.

PRACTICAL INFORMATION AND ORIENTATION

Visitors Information: Log Cabin Visitor Information Center, W 4th Ave. (274-3531) at F St. Open daily 7:30am-7pm; May and Sept. 9am-6pm; Oct.-April 9am-4pm. The Log Cabin is usually crammed with visitors and a staff of volunteers. Plenty of **maps** and brochures; 25¢ will buy the *Bike Trails* guide. Smaller visitors information outlets are at the **airport** (266-2437), in the domestic terminal near the baggage claim, and in the overseas terminal in the central atrium, as well as in the **Valley River Mall,** first level.

Visitor Language Assistance: 276-4118. Pre-programmed assistance in dozens of languages. Anchorage is home to **consulates** from Japan and many European countries.

Alaska Public Lands Information Center, Old Federal Bldg., 605 W 4th Ave., (271-2737), between F and G St. An astounding conglomeration of 8 state and federal offices (including the **Park Service, Forest Service, Division of State Parks,** and the **Fish and Wildlife Service**), all under one roof, provides the most current information on the entire state. Here you will find popular **topographic maps,** a computerized **sportfishing map,** and an interactive trip-planning video unit. Films daily at 10am, noon, 2 and 4pm. Open daily 9am-5:30pm.

Alaska Department of Fish and Game, 344-0541; 344-4687 for recorded info.

Alaska Employment Center, P.O. Box 107224, 3301 Eagle St. (269-4800). Take bus #3 or 60. Open Mon.-Fri. 8am-noon and 1-4:30pm.

Airport: Alaska International Airport, P.O. Box 190649-VG, Anchorage 99519-0649 (266-2525). Serviced by 8 international carriers and 15 domestic carriers, including **Delta** (249-2110 or 800-221-1212), **Northwest Airlines** (266-5636, 800-225-2525), **United** (800-241-6522), and **Mark Air** (266-6802 or 800-627-5247); and 3 Alaskan carriers, including **Reeve Aleutian, Pen Air,** and **Era.** Nearly every airport in Alaska can be reached from Anchorage, either directly or through a connecting flight in Fairbanks.

Alaska Railroad, 411 W 1st Ave., Anchorage 99510-7500 (265-2494, 800-544-0552 out of state), at the head of town. To: Denali ($88); Fairbanks ($125); and Seward ($50). In winter, 1 per week to Fairbanks; no service to Seward. A summertime "flag-stop" also runs between Anchorage and Hurricane (a stop between Talkeetna and Denali) on Sat. and Sun. ($88). The train will normally make unscheduled stops anywhere along this route. Just wave it down with a white cloth and wait to be acknowledged with a whistle. For more information write to Passenger Service, P.O. Box 107500, Anchorage. Office open daily 6am-10pm; ticket sales Mon.-Fri. 5:30am-5:30pm, Sat. 5:30am-4pm, Sun. 5:30am-2:30pm.

Buses: Alaska Backpacker Shuttle (344-8775). Van service to towns and trailheads in the vicinity. To: Denali ($35, $60 round trip, $5 bike). Leaves daily from the youth hostel at 8am. Also to: Talkeetna ($30), Girdwood ($15), Portage Train Station ($17.50), and trailheads north and south of Anchorage ($5-10 depending on distance). Call to arrange pick-up. **Moon Bay Express** (274-6454). To: Denali (1 per day, $35, $60 round-trip, $10 bike). Pickup at Anchorage Youth Hostel (see Accommodations) at 8am. **Fireweed Express** (452-0521). To: Denali ($25, $45 round-trip, $5 bike). Several pickups, including the visitors center. Call for reservations. **Homer and Seward Bus Lines** (800-478-8280). To: Seward (1 per day, $30), Homer (1 per day, $38). Leaves from the Alaskan Samovar Inn, 720 Gambell St. **Alaskon Express** (800-544-2206). To: Valdez ($59, leaves daily at 8am), Haines ($194, leaves Sun., Tues., and Fri. at 7am), and Fairbanks ($109, leaves

PRACTICAL INFORMATION

Sun., Tues., and Fri. at 7am). **Alaska Direct** (277-6652). To Whitehorse, YT (Mon., Wed., and Sat. at 6am, $145).

People Mover Bus: (343-6543), in the Transit Center, on 6th Ave. between G and H St., just up the street from the Anchorage Youth Hostel. Buses leave from here to all points in the Anchorage area, including a few per day to the airport, 6am-10pm; restricted schedule on weekends. Cash fare $1, tokens 90¢, day pass $2.50. Exact change. The downtown region, border by 5th Ave., Denali St., 6th Ave. and K St., is a **free fare zone** Mon.-Fri. 9am-3pm and 6-8pm, Sat. 9am-8pm, Sun. 11am-6pm. The Transit Center office is open Mon.-Fri. 8am-5pm and sells a helpful transit **map** (50¢).

Alaska Marine Highway, 333 W 4th St. (272-4482), in the Post Office Mall. No terminal, but ferry tickets and reservations. Open Mon.-Fri. 8am-4:30pm.

Taxi: Yellow Cab, 272-2422. **Checker Cab,** 276-1234. **Alaska Cab,** 563-5353. **Anchorage Cab,** 278-8000. About $13 from airport to downtown hostel.

Car Rentals: Affordable Car Rental, 4707 Spenard Rd. (243-3370), across from the Regal Alaskan Hotel. $24 per day, 40 free mi., 30¢ each additional mi. **Budget,** 243-0150. $39 per day, unlimited mileage. For both, must be at least 21 with major credit card. Both are at the **airport.** Ask about a free drop-off and pick-up downtown.

Road Conditions: 243-7675.

Bicycle Rental: At the **Anchorage Youth Hostel** (see Accommodations). $7 per day. Also at **Downtown Bicycle Rental** (279-5293), at the corner of 6th and B St., 7 blocks from the Coastal Trail. $10 per 4 hrs., $14 per 24 hrs. Single speeds $10 per 24 hrs. Lock, helmet, **map,** and gloves included. Also rents tennis equipment. Must have MC or VISA. Open daily 9am-10pm.

Alaska Mountain Biking Club: 694-0900 for recorded info.

Camping Equipment: Recreational Equipment, Inc. (REI), 1200 Northern Lights Blvd. (272-4565), near Spenard, at Minnesota. High-quality packs, clothing, tents, stores, and dried foods. Open Mon.-Fri. 10am-9pm, Sat.-Sun. 10am-6pm. 10% off non-sale items for AYH members. The **Army-Navy Store** (279-2401), on 4th Ave., across from the Post Office Mall, offers even lower prices. Open Mon.-Fri. 9am-8pm, Sat. 9am-6pm, Sun. 11am-5pm. For buying or selling **used equipment,** try **Play It Again Sports** (278-7529), at 27th and Spenard near REI. A frequently-rotating inventory of quality fishing and camping equipment at discount. Open Mon.-Fri. 10:30am-8pm, Sat. 10:30am-6pm, Sun. 11:30am-5:30pm.

Bookstore: Cyrano's Bookstore and Cafe, 413 D St. (274-2599), between 4th and 5th Ave. Anchorage has come a long way since writer John McPhee reported 20 years ago that books were selling for 47¢ per lb. Mosey over for a cappucino or an artsy film. Tasty morsels cooked up inside at the cafe; try the killer cheesecake ($3). Late-night comedy improv. on Fridays at 10pm, acoustic music on weekend evenings downstairs in the living room. Open daily 8am until late-ish. For a dog-eared copy of *White Fang,* try **C&M Used Books,** 215 E 4th Ave. (278-9394). Open Mon.-Tues. and Thurs.-Fri. 10am-7pm, Wed. and Sat. 10am-6pm. **Cook Inlet Book Company** (258-4544), 415 W 5th Ave., stocks an extensive collection of paperbacks, magazines, and Alaskan books. Open Mon.-Sat. 8:30am-10pm, Sun. 8:30am-8pm.

Library: ZJ Loussac Library (261-2975), at 36th Ave. and Denali St. The most architecturally intriguing building in Anchorage. Take bus #2 or #60. Devotes an entire wing to Alaskan material. Open Mon.-Thurs. 11am-9pm, Fri.-Sat. 10am-6pm; winter also Sun. 1-5pm.

Secondhand Tickets: An entire section of the classified ads in the *Daily News* lists tickets for travel within the state and to the Lower 48. **The Ticket Exchange,** 505 W Northern Lights (274-8153), also buys and sells tickets at rates between the newspaper and over-the-counter prices. Open Mon.-Fri. 9am-6pm and Sat. 10am-4pm. **Warning:** If you travel under someone else's name, the airline is under no obligation to honor the ticket. Before paying for a secondhand ticket, call the airline and ask if they require identification at check-in with the particular ticket you want to buy. Be especially careful about frequent-flyer tickets.

Anchorage

A **B** **C** **D**

Knik Arm

Ship Creek

Viking Dr.

W. 1st Ave. E. 1st Ave.

Post Rd.

Imaginarium
Visual Arts Center

W. 2nd Ave.

Elderberry
Park

W. 3rd Ave.
Alaska Public Lands
Information Center
E. 3rd Ave.

Log Cabin Visitor
Information Center

W. 4th Ave. E. 4th Ave.

Hyder St.

TO
GLENN HWY. →

W. 5th Ave. E. 5th Ave.

Old City Hall

Medfra St.

E. 6th Ave.

Youth
Hostel

Performing
Arts Center

Kimball
Building

Anchorage
Museum
of
History and Art

E. 7th Ave.

Juneau

Karluk St.

L St.
K St.

Bus
Station

F St.
E St.
D St.
C St.

E. 8th Ave.

E. 9th Ave.

Latouche St.

W. 9th Ave.

W. 10th Ave.
I St.
H St.
G St.
Cordova St.
Denali
Eagle
E. 10th Ave.

W. 11th Ave. E. 11th Ave.

P St.

W. 12th Ave. E. 12th Ave.

N St.
L St.
W. 13th Ave.
B St.
E. 13th Ave.

W. 14th Ave. E. 14th Ave.

Campbell

W. 15th Ave. E. 15th Ave.

E. 16th Ave.

TO HUMANA →
HOSPITAL

**CHESTER
CREEK
PARK**

Chester Creek

Arctic Blvd.

A St.

Eagle St.

Spenard Rd.

W. Fireweed La.

EARTHQUAKE PARK,
← WORZENOF POINT

W. 27th Ave.

Northern

Heritage Library
and Museum

Lights Blvd. E.

TO UNIVERISITY
OF ALASKA →

Northern
Lights Center

Benson Blvd.

Benson Blvd.

Minnesota Dr.

Eureka St.

Bering St.

32nd Ave.

Denali St.

E. 33rd Ave.

Redwood St.

TO
CHUGACH
STATE
PARK →

W. 36th Ave. E. 36th Ave.

N
↑

0   1/2 mile
0   1/2 kilometer

Loussac Public
Library

University
Center

Cedar Union Drive

W. 40th Ave.

Old Seward Hwy.

1

Seward Hwy.

TO ANCHORAGE
INTERNATIONAL AIRPORT,
LAKE HOOD,
← LAKE SPENARD

Tudor Rd.

TO
ALASKA
ZOO
↓

Laundromat: K-Speed Wash, 600 E 6th St. (279-0731). Wash $1.50, 7½-min. dry 25¢. Open Mon.-Sat. 7am-10pm. **Anchorage Youth Hostel** (see Accommodations) also has laundry facilities. Wash $1, dry 50¢. Open for laundry 5pm-10pm.

Weather: 936-2525. **Motorists and Recreation Forecast:** 936-2626. **Marine Weather Forecast:** 936-2727.

24-hr. Crisis Line: 272-0010. **24-hr. Rape Crisis Line:** 563-7273.

Disabilities Access Line: Challenge Alaska (563-2658). The Log Cabin Visitors Center (see listing above) is equipped with a **TTY** for people with communications disabilities.

Hospital: Alaska Regional Hospital, 2801 DeBarr Ave. (264-1224).

Emergency: 911. **Police:** 786-8400.

Post Office (279-3062), W 4th Ave. and C St. on the lower level in the mall. Open Mon.-Fri. 10am-5:30pm, Sat. 10am-4pm. **General Delivery ZIP Code:** 99510. The **state's central post office** (266-3259) is next to the international airport. It does *not* handle general delivery mail, but is open 24 hrs.

Area Code: 907.

From its seat 114 mi. north of Seward on the Seward Hwy., 304 mi. west of Valdez on the Glenn and Richardson Hwy., and 358 mi. south of Fairbanks on the George Parks Hwy., Anchorage is the hub of Southcentral Alaska.

The city can be reached by road, rail, or air. **Anchorage International Airport** (see above), a few mi. southwest of downtown off International Airport Rd., is served by all Alaskan airlines, as well as by major American and international airlines. The **People Mover Bus** (see above) runs from the airport to downtown (3 per day, weekdays only); the visitors center near the baggage claim can direct you a short distance from the terminal to more frequently-serviced routes. Many **courtesy vans** run from the airport to the larger hotels downtown.

Military bases to the north, the Chugach Mountains to the east, and the Knik and Turnagain Arms of the Pacific to the west and south frame the **Anchorage Bowl,** within which the city sprawls some 50,000 acres. The **downtown area** of Anchorage is laid out in a grid. Numbered avenues run east-west, and addresses are designated East or West from **C Street.** North-south streets are lettered alphabetically west of **A Street,** and named alphabetically east of A Street. The rest of Anchorage spreads out—*way* out—along the major highways. The **University of Alaska, Anchorage** campus lies on 36th Ave., off Northern Lights Blvd.

ACCOMMODATIONS

Although Anchorage is blessed many times over with affordable lodgings, few are downtown. The best option is the hostel (see listing below). Several **Bed and Breakfast** referral agencies have set up shop in Anchorage. Try **Alaska Private Lodgings,** 1010 W 10th Ave., P.O. Box 200017, Anchorage 99520-0047 (258-1717), or **Stay With a Friend,** 3605 Arctic Blvd., #173, Anchorage 99503 (278-8800). Both can refer you to B&Bs with singles from $50 and doubles from $55.

Anchorage International Youth Hostel (HI/AYH), 700 H St. (276-3635), at 7th, 1 block south of the Transit Center downtown. A great gateway hostel in a convenient location. Three kitchens, 2 balconies, and scads of info. on traveling throughout the state. Family and couple rooms available. Frequently filled to the rafters in summer; write ahead for reservations. Bring a sleeping bag. The **Alaska Black Book,** in the 2nd floor reference room, is an invaluable compendium of previous travelers' (mis)adventures all over Alaska. Wheelchair accessible. Lockout noon-5pm. Curfew midnight, watchman can check you in until 3am. 4-day max. stay in summer. $12, non-members $15; photo ID required. Weekly and monthly rates during the off-season's "winter community" program. Towel 25¢, bag storage $1 per bag per day. Overflow and long-term guests are directed to a smaller, less convenient hostel near the airport.

International Backpackers Inn, 3601 Peterkin (274-3870 or 272-0297), at Mumford. Take bus #45 to Bragaw and Peterkin. As you watch the bus depart, turn left and walk 3 blocks. The office is upstairs. Anchorage's "other hostel," this quiet, family-run complex houses 45 dorm-style beds, common kitchens, bathrooms, and TVs. Free local phone and linen. Chore required. Key deposit $10. Beds $12-15 (go for the $15 building). Tentsites $10. Weekly and monthly rates available.

Eagle Crest (276-5913), 9th Ave. and Eagle St. Clean and well-managed by the Salvation Army. For many, the next stop after they've stayed their limit at the hostel. Many long-term residents. Common kitchen and laundry. Free coffee. No curfew. Bed in 4-person room $15, chore required. Singles $27.50, doubles $40, both with private baths. Low weekly and monthly rates.

Midtown Lodge, 604 W 26th (258-7778), off Arctic Blvd. Take bus #9. Simple, spotless rooms with shared bath. Free continental breakfast; free soup and sandwiches in the lobby for teatime snack. These people get an "A" for effort. Singles $43. Doubles $49. Reservations essential up to 2 weeks ahead in summer.

CAMPING

Both camping areas within the city welcome tents and RVs. Many of the state's best sites lie in the free **State Division of Parks and Outdoor Recreation campgrounds,** just outside the city limits. These state campgrounds have water and toilets. Most sites hide along dirt roads off the highway. Bring your own food and supplies. Among the best of the state campgrounds are **Eagle River** (688-0998) and **Eklutna** (EE-kloot-nah; 694-2108), respectively, 12.6 mi. and 26.5 mi. northeast of Anchorage along Glenn Hwy. For more information on these and other campsites, contact the State Parks Service (762-2261) or the Alaska Parks and Recreation Dept. (762-2617).

Centennial Park, 5300 Glenn Hwy. (333-9711), north of town off Muldoon Rd.; look for the park sign. Take bus #3 or #75 from downtown. 90 sites for tents and RVs. Showers, dumpsters, fireplaces, pay phones, and water. 7-day max. stay. Check-in daily 7am-midnight. Flexible noon check-out. Sites $13, Alaskans $11. Open May 1-Sept. 30.

Lions' Camper Park, 800 Boniface Pkwy. (333-9711), south of the Glenn Hwy. In Russian Jack Springs Park across from the Municipal Greenhouse, 4 blocks from the Boniface Mall. Take bus #12 or 45 to the mall and walk. Connected to the city's bike trail system. Overflow for Centennial Park. 50 campsites with showers, dumpsters, fireplaces, pay phones, and water. 7-day max. stay. Office at Centennial Park. Sites $13, Alaskans $11. Open June 15-Sept. 30.

John's Motel and RV Park, 3543 Mt. View Dr. (277-4332). Only 2 mi. from downtown. Take bus #45. 50 RV sites. Full hookups $20. Singles $45. Doubles $50.

FOOD

Anchorage presents budget travelers with the most affordable and varied culinary fare in the state.

Cheap Eats

In addition to the places listed below, check out the following: **Nordstrom's Cafe** (279-7622), on the second floor of the department store on 603 D St., pours a bottomless 25¢ cup of coffee (open Mon.-Fri. 9:30am-9pm, Sat. 9:30am-6pm, Sun. 11am-6pm); yesterday's sandwiches are half-price at the **4th Avenue Theater** (see Entertainment below) and today's sandwiches achieve "yesterday-status" at about 8pm; the affable **hot dog man** who sets up shop at 4th Ave. and G St. not only serves a large Polish dog with chips and a drink for $3, but he's also a friend to half the city; the **Wonder and Hostess Bakery Thrift Shop** (277-6151), on Spenard and 23rd Ave., purveys discount bread (open Mon.-Sat. 9am-7pm, Sun. 10am-5pm). In town, you can pick up minimal provisions at the **4th & E St. Grocery and Deli.** The place offers mongo $1 cookies (open Mon.-Sat. 7am-10pm, Sun. 8am-10pm).

For a wider selection of brand name groceries, the 24-hour **Carr's** (272-4574), at 13th and Gamble, is a 1½-mi. walk from the hostel. After dark, take bus #11; this neighborhood is dubious.

F
O
O
D

Downtown

Phyllis' Cafe and Salmon Bake, 436 D St. (274-6576). The black and white polka-dot tables and hunter-green carpets could decorate a Dalmatian's den. The all-day breakfast (2 eggs, sausage, hash browns, and toast, $6) will fill the hungriest of hounds. Dinners, served with salad, vegetable, potato, beans, and a roll, also satisfy (try the stir-fry shrimp, $8). Salmon dinners are more expensive at $16. Indoor/outdoor seating. Open daily 7am-11pm.

Scottie's Sub Shop (276-2784), 331 W 5th Ave. Like a fast food restaurant in someone's living room. 4-in. ham, roast beef and turkey sandwich $3. Daily 8-in. sub with fries, $4.75. Hamburger with fries $3.50. Open Mon.-Sat. 9am-9pm.

Legal Pizza, 1034 W 4th Ave. (274-0686). Home to a noteworthy buffet: all-you-can-eat pizza, salad bar, soup, and beverages ($6) served Mon.-Fri. 11:30am-3pm. Arrive by 12:30 for the best selection of pizzas. You can catch leftovers afterward for $1 per slice. Open Mon.-Fri. 10am-11pm, Sat.-Sun. 5-11pm.

Blondie's Cafe (279-0698), at the corner of 4th and D St. Bizarre combination of neon-pink zebra carpeting and Iditarod memorabilia (or just sit outside and away from it all). All-day breakfast includes 3 hotcakes for $5. Ham and cheese sandwich $5. Open daily 5am-10pm.

White Spot Cafe, 109 W 4th Ave. (279-3954). An unrivaled cheeseburger with homecut fries ($3.50) has made this tiny establishment an Anchorage favorite since 1959. Two eggs, potato, toast, and coffee ($2.75). Open daily 6:30am-7pm.

Federal Building Cafeteria, 222 W 7th St. (277-6736), in the Federal Building on C. St. Hot entrees like teriyaki chicken with rice ($4.75) and Mexican lasagna with cornbread ($4.50). Daily soups ($2 per cup, $2.65 per bowl). After 1:30pm, muffins, donuts, and pizza are ½-price; after 1:30pm on Fri., everything is half price. Open Mon.-Fri. 7am-3:30pm, hot lunch stops at 1:30pm.

Maharaja's, 328 G St. (272-2233), between 3rd and 4th Ave. The gilded decor and spicy lunch buffet provide a feast for all the senses at this authentic Indian restaurant. All-you-can-eat buffet ($7) served Mon.-Fri. 11:30am-2pm. Vegetarian dinner specialties ($6.50-8.50) served Sun.-Thurs. 5:30-9:30pm, Fri.-Sat. 5:30-10pm.

Wing and Things, 529 I St. (277-9464), between 5th and 6th St. Unbelievably good chicken wings barbecued amid wing memorabilia and inspirational poetry. The "nuke" sauce is a wonderfully masochistic experience. 10 wings for $6. Open Mon.-Sat. 10:30am-11pm.

Thai Cuisine, 444 H St. (277-8424). Therrific Thai fare on white linen amid patio furniture. Big bowl of soup ($7-8). 18 vegetarian dishes ($7-9). Lunch specials include entree, rice, soup, and salad ($6.50-8). Open Mon.-Sat. 11am-10pm, Sun. 4-10pm.

Kumagoro Restaurant, 533 4th St. (272-9905). The combination of Alaskan fish and Japanese expertise make this an excellent sushi restaurant. Daily lunch specials (served 11:30am-2pm), such as halibut teriyaki with soup, rice, and vegetables ($6). Chicken teriyaki ($6.50). At night, karaoke crooners ham it up at the mike. Bar and restaurant open daily 11am-10pm.

Midtown Restaurants

Alaska Flapjacks, 1230 W 27th Ave. (274-2241). The best breakfast spot in town advertises itself as a family restaurant, possibly because you could almost feed a family with a single one of their breakfast specials. Three eggs, bacon, biscuit and gravy, and hash browns ($6). Open daily 6am-8pm.

Pickle Barrel Deli, 1241 W 27th St. (258-6108). Wide variety of bread, trimmings, cheese and dressings, and cheap. House specials include the 8-in. veggie sub, avocado, sprouts, pickles, and cheese ($4), and the 8-in. Pepper Tom with genoa salami, turkey, and cheese ($4.25). Foosball table and magazine racks transform the place into a good rainy-day hangout.

The Hogg Brothers Cafe and Watering Trough, 2421 Spenard Ave. (276-9649). Come here to escape the sprout-loving set. Pig paraphernalia. Try the Hogg Muffin (one egg, ham, and cheese on a toasted muffin, $3.50) or the Bacon Blue Cheeseburger ($5.25). Open daily 6am-10pm.

SIGHTS AND ACTIVITIES

Watching over Anchorage from Cook Inlet is **Mt. Susitna,** known to locals as the "Sleeping Lady." For a fabulous view of Susitna, and Denali on a clear day, head to the top of the parking garage over the People Mover Transit Office (see Practical Information). The same view is available from a more attractive setting about 4 mi. from downtown at **Point Warzenof,** on the western end of Northern Lights Blvd. **Earthquake Park** recalls the 1964 Good Friday earthquake, a day Alaskans refer to as "Black Friday." The quake was the strongest ever recorded in North America, registering 9.2 on the Richter scale. Either drive, walk, skate, or bike along the **Tony Knowles Coastal Trail,** an 11-mi. paved track that skirts Cook Inlet on one side and the backyards of Anchorage's upper-crust on the other. Built for a million dollars per mi., critics originally complained that the trail would only be an expensive invitation for burglars to prey on wealthy homeowners. Fears have proved unfounded, though, and the heavily-traveled trail has become a major asset. In the winter it is groomed for **cross-country skiing.**

A four-hour **walking tour** of downtown Anchorage begins at the visitors center. You can absorb the tour in smaller segments while wandering about downtown. The **Captain Cook Monument,** at 5th and K, presents an interesting synopsis of this restless explorer's travels from Antarctica to the Aleutian Islands. **Alaska Guest Tours** (268-4295), at 5th and F St., offers an inexpensive city tour (1½ hrs., $15).

The public **Anchorage Museum of History and Art,** 121 W 7th Ave. (343-4326), at A St., is without a doubt the best of the public and private museums that fill downtown Anchorage. The museum features permanent exhibits of Native Alaskan artifacts and art, and a traditional dance series three times per day in summer ($4). The gallery gives free tours daily at 10am, 11am, 1pm and 2pm. (Open daily 9am-6pm; Sept. 16-May 14 Tues.-Sat. 10am-6pm, Sun. 1-5pm. $4, seniors $3.50, under 18 free.) The **Alaska Aviation Heritage Museum,** 4721 Aircraft Dr. (248-5325), provides a fun look at Alaska's incredible pioneer aviators. The collection includes 22 rare planes, dated 1928-1952, some salvaged from remote Bush areas. The museum also houses a theater where rare footage is shown continuously. Take bus #6 to the airport; the museum is within easy walking distance (open daily 9am-6pm, $5, seniors $3.75, youths $2).

The **Imaginarium,** 725 5th Ave. (276-3179), a hands-on "science-discovery center," recreates Arctic marine environments, glacier formation, and other scientific oddities of the North (open Mon.-Sat. 10am-6pm, Sun. noon-5pm; $4, seniors $3, under 12 $3). The **Heritage Library** (265-2834), in the National Bank of Alaska Office Building at Northern Lights Blvd. and C St., contains a display of rare books and Native Alaskan artifacts (open Mon.-Fri. noon-5pm; free).

To see real Alaskan wildlife without the danger of being trampled or otherwise mauled, visit the **Alaska Zoo,** Mile 2 on O'Malley Rd. (346-2133). Take bus #91. In salmon season, walk down C St. to the water and watch fin-to-fin traffic jams heading upstream. Best viewing is from the plant lookout.

SHOPPING

For an unconventional shopping experience, head to the close confines of the non-profit gift shop at the **Alaska Native Medical Center,** 255 Campbell (257-1150), at 3rd St. Many Native Alaskans pay for medical services with their own arts and handicrafts, and the Alaska State Museum in Juneau has sent buyers here to improve its exhibitions. Walrus bone *ulus* (knives used by Native Alaskans, $27-85), fur moccasins, parkas, and dolls highlight the selection (open Mon.-Fri. 10am-2pm, and occasionally Sat. 11am-2pm). Downtown holds several more traditional shops.

Works from Alaska's Bush country, similar to those on display at the Museum of History and Art (see above), are sold at the **Alaska Native Arts and Crafts Showroom,** 333 W 4th Ave. (274-2932). Birch baskets (from $25), beadwork and other jewelry ($2.75-50), and ivory carvings ($30) tempt you here (open Mon.-Fri. 10am-5pm). More made-in-Alaska products, as well as fresh produce, fish, and arts and crafts, can be picked up at the **Saturday Market** (276-7207), at the Lower Bowl

Parking Lot at the corner of 3rd and E. The outdoor market is held Saturdays May 28-Sept. 3, 10am-6pm.

The gigantic **Fifth Avenue Mall** houses typical American chain stores, including Eddie Bauer, Foot Locker, Waldenbooks, and Burger King, along with the not-so-standard **Northwind Kites,** 320 W 5th Ave. #156 (279-4386). Find a delightful array of puzzles, hackey sacks, juggling paraphernalia, and, of course, kites (open Mon.-Fri. 9:30am-9pm, Sat. 9:30am-6pm, Sun. 11am-6pm).

ENTERTAINMENT

Trek to the **Alaska Experience Theater,** 705 W 6th Ave. (276-3730), to see brown bears and traditional dancers come alive on the inner surface of a hemispherical dome. The 70mm film (40 min.) will make your head spin (every hr. 9am-9pm; $7, children $4). An earthquake exhibit at the theater will cost you another $5, $3 for kids. The earth quakes for 35 min. each time between, 9am and 8:30pm. The **Capri Cinema,** 3425 E Tudor Rd. (275-3799), runs a mix of art flicks and intelligent mainstream works (oxymoron though it may seem) that have finished their first run. Take bus #75 (shows $4). On a rainy day, park yourself at the **Denali Theater,** 1230 W 27th St. (275-3106), at Spenard, where double-features of popular movies in limbo between the big screen and video release show for $1.01. The **Fireweed Theaters** and **University Cinemas** show first-run flicks at first-run prices. For both, take the #60 bus route; for Fireweed Theaters, get off on Fireweed at Denali and walk three blocks east on Fireweed, while University Cinemas is at University Center.

Yearning for a touch of Arctic Broadway? The **4th Avenue Theatre,** 630 4th Ave. (257-5678), 1 block west of the Log Cabin visitors center (see Practical Information) and 5000 mi. west of Broadway, has been faithfully restored to its original 1940s decor. The neon-clad building now contains a cafeteria, and gift shop, and is home to the "Alaska, Where We Live Show," a song/story combo that runs from June 1 to August 28 from Wednesday to Sunday at 8pm ($10, $5 under 13). Charitable gambling also takes place right after the show, 9:30pm-midnight. The theater contains a free museum that presents the "History of Anchorage: From the Beginning in 1915 to the 1964 Earthquake" (open daily 10am-11pm).

NIGHTLIFE

Downtown bars get nastier around C St., but several places on the west side of town fill each night with merry tipplers. The **F Street Station,** 325 F St. (272-5196), attracts half the yuppies in Alaska on a weekend night. The bar offers free cheddar cheese and crackers and serves sandwiches from the kitchen (open 11:30am-2:30am, food served until 1am). **Darwin's Theory,** 426 G St. (277-5322), between 4th and 5th Ave., is often packed with a friendly, local crowd. Darwin dishes out free popcorn to increase your thirst (open Sun.-Thurs. 10am-2am, Fri.-Sat. 10am-3am). The **Pioneer Bar,** 439 W 4th Ave. (276-7996), claims to be the oldest bar in Anchorage (meaning that it's still younger than your grandparents; open Sun.-Thurs. 10am-2:30am, Fri.-Sat. 10am-3am).

Around midtown, Alaskans from all tax brackets party at **Chilkoot Charlie's,** 2435 Spenard Rd. (272-1010), at Fireweed. Take bus #7 or #60. Six bars fill this huge and heavily commercial space, in addition to a rockin' dance floor and a quiet lounge. Ask about the nightly drink specials, or you'll pay an outrageous price. Two different bands at each end of this behemoth "log cabin" play nightly from 9:30pm (open Mon.-Thurs. 10am-2:30am, Fri.-Sat. 10am-3am, Sun. noon-2:30am).

Less crowded and more interesting is **Mr. Whitekey's Fly-by-Night Club,** 3300 Spenard Rd. (279-SPAM/7726). Take bus #7. Mr. Whitekey's is a "sleazy bar serving everything from the world's finest champagnes to a damn fine plate of Spam." The Monty Python-esque house special gives you anything with Spam at half-price when you order champagne (free with Dom Perignon). Try Spam nachos or Spam and cream cheese on a bagel ($3-7). Nightly music ranges from rock to jazz to blues. They also feature *Whale Fat Follies,* a new anti-tourist tourist attraction or "musical off-color follies;" *Follies* plays 8pm nightly (bar open Tues.-Sat. 4pm-2:30am). The

Great Alaskan Bush Co., 631 E International Airport Rd. (561-2609), is a world-famous strip-joint where there is no cover for guests...or employees (open Mon.-Thurs. 4pm-2am, Fri.-Sat. 4pm-2:30am, Sun. 7pm-2am).

EVENTS

For more spontaneous entertainment, watch for annual events celebrated Alaska-style. Call the **event hotline** (276-3200) to see what's coming up. The **Anchorage Music Festival** has been held from mid-June through early July since 1956. For information and tickets for this mostly classical festival, call 263-2787. The summer solstice (June 21) brings dancing to the streets and runners from all over the world to the inspirational **Mayor's Marathon.** The **Iditarod,** a grueling 1049-mi. sled-dog race traversing two mountain ranges, 150 mi. of the frozen Yukon River, and the ice pack of the Norton Sound, begins in Anchorage on the first weekend in March. Twelve to 18 days later, the winner, and, hopefully, the other competitors, arrive in Nome. The tortuous route commemorates and duplicates a part of the heroic journey of early-day Anchorage mushers who carried serum to halt a diphtheria epidemic in Nome. The **Fur Rendezvous,** held the second week of February, revives the era when fur trappers gathered to whoop it up. Today, affectionately referred to as "Fur Rondy," it includes the world sled-dog championship races, a grand prix, and snowshoe softball games.

The Anchorage Bucs (272-2827) and Pirates (274-3627), the city's two **semi-professional baseball** teams, play a more traditional version of the game in the summer. Games take place at Mulcahy Park on 16th Ave. and A St.; call ahead for times and ticket prices. Reggie Jackson and Dave Winfield once impressed the Anchorage crowds here.

OUTDOORS

To counteract urban claustrophobia, hike to the summit of **Flattop Mountain** in the "Glenn Alps" of the Chugach Range near Anchorage. The excellent view of the city and, if it's clear, sun-soaked Denali, is well worth the hour-long hike. The most frequently climbed trail in Alaska is deceptively difficult due to its steepness and slippery shale, but even novices will find it manageable. Wear long pants, as you may find yourself sliding down. To reach the trailhead, jump on bus #92 to the intersection of Hillside Rd. and Upper Huffman Rd. From there walk ¾ mi. along upper Huffman Rd. and take a right on Toilsome Hill Dr. Proceed for 2 mi. Trail signs at the park entrance point the way up the 4,500-ft. mountain.

People Mover bus #92 will also bring you to the foot of 4455-ft. **Wolverine Peak,** overlooking eastern Anchorage. At the intersection of O'Malley Rd. and Hillside Dr., head east ½ mi. along O'Malley to Upper O'Malley Rd. Turn left at the intersection with Prospect Dr. and head 1.1 mi. to the park entrance. The return hike from bus stop to the peak is a long 13.8 mi., but the views of the Alaska Range and Cook Inlet will keep you hopping.

Rabbit Lake is a beautiful alpine bowl that collects water in the shadow of 5,000-ft. **Suicide Peak.** People Mover bus #92 is again your montane chariot; hop off at the corner of Hillside Dr. and De Armour Rd. Follow Upper De Armour Rd. from here 1 mi. east, and then turn right onto Lower Canyon Rd. for 1.2 mi. The round-trip from where you debark the bus to the lake is a gentle 15.4 mi. Camping at the lake or along the way makes for a pleasant two-day hike.

Although neither the Forest Service nor the City of Anchorage publishes a guide to nearby trails, the widely available *55 Ways to the Wilderness in Southcentral Alaska* by Helen Nienhueser and Nancy Simmerman (The Mountaineers Books, 306 2nd Ave. West, Seattle, WA 98119; $11) offers an excellent description of many trails around Anchorage and the Kenai Peninsula. **Midnight Sun,** P.O. Box 221561 (338-7238), offers a three-and-a-half-hour float-trip excursion down Eagle River, about 15 min. from Anchorage ($55, Ages 4-12 $40). Trips leave daily at 9am and 4pm.

■ NEAR ANCHORAGE: SOUTH

The Seward Hwy. runs south along the **Turnagain Arm** of the Cook Inlet. English explorer Captain Cook named it in 1778 while looking for the Northwest Passage. Cook left disappointed, having had only to turn, again. The Turnagain Arm is known for dramatic tidal fluctuations. Miles of the arm are temporarily uncovered at low tide, only to be inundated by 10-ft. high "bores," or walls of water created as the 15mph riptide races in. *Do not walk on the exposed sand at low tide; the sand is quicksand and you risk getting stuck and being killed by hypothermia or drowning when the tide comes in.*

Just beyond the Anchorage city limits on the Seward Highway is **Potter's Marsh,** created when the Alaska Railroad bed dammed the surface run-off from the nearby mountains and further enhanced when the 1964 earthquake caused the land to drop a few feet. Potter's Marsh was declared a wetlands bird and wildlife sanctuary in the mid-70s. The marsh's boardwalk, one of the state's best centers for wildlife photography, is an ideal place for viewing a variety of birds and mammals. When not inundated with bus tour groups, the boardwalk offers a peaceful haven for travelers fed-up with traffic-clogged Seward Highway. The area is across the highway from a rifle range; a quick comparison of the number of cars in each parking lot will speak volumes about a societal value system gone awry.

15 mi. down the arm sits the **Potter Section House Historical Site** (345-5014), the last of the Alaska Railroad's original roadhouses. The site is now the headquarters for **Chugach State Park** (for info. on Chugach State Park see below; open Mon.-Fri. 8am-4:30pm). To catch a glimpse of an incoming bore tide or a pod of Beluga whales chasing salmon up the inlet, pull over at **Beluga Point,** about 4 mi. south of the section house. The bore tides generally reach Turnagain Arm two hours after the low tide in Anchorage; consult the *Daily News* for a tidal report.

Dall sheep often appear in the rocky crevices of **Bird Ridge,** another 9 mi. down the highway at Mile 102. Sheep even wander down to the roadside in summer. A convoy of RVs pulled over beside the ridge is usually the first giveaway that something is astir. Sadly, the RV tourists often display no respect for wildlife; the animals pathetically approach the roadside for free handouts. Do not compromise the dignity of the wild animals, or your own dignity, by feeding them.

The **Birdhouse Bar** sits off the highway in a sunken cabin a few mi. past the ridge. A large blue and orange bird protrudes from the cabin wall, the only exterior indication of the hilarious antics within. Every square inch of the small bar room is padded with the personal effects of past patrons, from business cards and lingerie to a prosthetic leg. Many believe it's all that holds the place together. (Try to find the two *Let's Go* researcher-writer ID cards.) The lewd lyrics of the blaring bluegrass detract somewhat from the bar's hushed and intimate atmosphere; patrons will have to strain to hear the bartenders' endless supply of jokes. The bar itself slants at the 20° angle it achieved in the 1964 earthquake; a few key knotholes provide a purchase for your beer. Before leaving, ask to call the ptarmigans, or better yet, ask for a friend; a special horn brings them right to the window.

Off of Seward Hwy. lies the **Alyeska Ski Resort** (783-2222), a site perennially proposed to host the Winter Olympics. The resort is open Nov.-April for skiing (a full-day lift ticket runs about $30). While in Alyeska, stay at the **Girdwood-Alyeska Home Hostel (HI/AYH),** run by the same folks who manage the Anchorage Hostel (783-2099; see Accommodations above). To get there, turn left onto Alyeska Blvd. off Seward Hwy., right on Timberline Dr., then right on Alpina. The hostel has six beds and a sauna, but no hot showers ($10, non-members $13). Winter or summer, it's worth the detour into Alyeska just to visit the **Bake Shop,** an outstanding restaurant below the Alyeska Resort. People from across the state sing the praises of their towering sweet rolls ($2), bottomless bowls of soup ($3.75), and...mmmm...sourdough ($1.25). (Open Mon.-Fri. and Sun. 7am-7pm, Sat. 7am-8pm.)

Four mi. up Crow Creek Rd. is **Crow Creek Mine,** a National Historic Site with eight original buildings and an active gold mine. The $5 admission for miners includes a pan, a sluice box, and instructions. Most people turn up a few flakes, but don't expect to make back your entrance fee. This strike predates even those in Fairbanks and the Klondike. The site is non-restored and genuine, not a Disney-esque theme park. Crow Creek is still a fully operational gold mine during the fall. (Campsites with water and toilets $5; hikers and sightseers $3. Open June-Aug. daily 9am-6pm.) As you leave Crow Creek Rd., stop in at the **Double Musky** (783-2822), set back from the road in the trees. The Musky deserves its reputation as one of the best restaurants in Alaska. If you can't swing a spicy Cajun-style dinner ($16-30), at least treat yourself to a drink or dessert (about $4). The jambalaya, a spicy creole concoction served over rice, and the double musky pie (a blend of chocolate and pecans with a pecan, meringue, and cracker crust) both deserve special attention (open Tues.-Thurs. 5-10pm, Fri.-Sun. 4-10pm).

PORTAGE

Portage is 45 min. from downtown Anchorage along the Seward Hwy. It's just a train and bus stop, a point of transshipment from Whittier. The **Alaska Backpacker Shuttle** runs buses between the train station and Anchorage for $17.50 ($20 with kayak). For hitchers, rides are reportedly easy to find. (*Let's Go* does not recommend hitchhiking.)

Four roadside glaciers sit staunchly along the **Portage Valley.** Imperceptibly grinding and gouging, the glaciers gradually recede as spectacular blue ice chunks fall into Portage Lake and float near shore. On the lakeside, the **Begich-Boggs Visitors Center** (783-2326) houses what are perhaps the most modern displays of any Alaskan information outlet. The center's glacial exhibitions attract throngs of visitors. The collection of animal skulls is worth a quick look. The first-person descriptions attached to the skulls read like confessions from an animal therapy group. "I have a big nose," reads the moose placard. "Why is my skull so thick?" says the musk ox. Brochures will cost you some spare change. (Open daily 9am-7pm; in winter Sat.-Sun. 11am-4pm.) To reach the center, take the 5-mi. detour off Seward Hwy., south of Alyeska, along the well-paved **Portage Hwy.** The cheapest may be the one given by **Gray Line** (277-5581), which conducts the six-hour, mother-of-all-tours of Portage Glacier, including stops at the **Begich-Boggs Visitor Center** and **Alyeska Ski Resort** (daily tours at 9am and noon; $54, under 12 $25). Grayline also runs a one-hour tour five times daily ($20). Both tours run from May 16 to September 21.

Two state-run **campgrounds** on Portage Hwy. have excellent sites ($6) with panoramic glacial views. **Black Bear** and **Williwaw** provide water and toilets; Williwaw also has a short hiking trail and a viewing ledge overlooking salmon-spawning areas (salmon run from early July to late Aug.). Naturalists introduce travelers to the easy hiking trails that begin from the visitors center. For more information on the hikes and trails, call the **Anchorage Ranger District Office** (271-2500), or write to Chugach National Forest, Anchorage Ranger District, 201 E 9th Ave., #206, Anchorage 99501. The **Alaska Public Lands Information**, 605 W 4th, Anchorage 99501 (271-2737) has information on the Chugach as well.

■ NEAR ANCHORAGE: NORTH

If Flattop doesn't satisfy your craving for wilderness (see Outdoors above), head for **Chugach State Park,** covering over 770 sq. mi. north, east, and south of the city. The **Eagle River Visitors Center** (694-2108) is at Mile 12.7 on Eagle River Rd., off Glenn Hwy. In addition to the wildlife displays, hiking trails, and a new outdoor telescope, they can explain the many **hiking** opportunities in this area (open Thurs.-Mon. 11am-7pm). If you're long on time and short on dollars, take **People Mover** bus #74, 76, or 78 on a 48-mi. round-trip excursion to the satellite communities of **Eagle River, Chugiak,** and **Peters Creek,** north of Anchorage. Even without getting off the bus, you're likely to catch a glimpse of a moose between Fort Richardson and Eagle River.

Due north is **Matanuska Valley,** settled by Scandinavian-American farmers in 1935 as part of a New Deal program. President Roosevelt wanted to transplant families from the depressed Midwest to Alaska to experiment with agriculture. Several thousand people moved to the valley and watched as the long summer daylight turned garden-variety vegetables into mastodon-sized meals. 75-pound (34kg) cabbages and watermelons that require several people to lift are common; **fist-sized strawberries** are popular snacks. In summer, fresh produce is available (in bulk, of course) from roadside stands along Glenn Hwy. between its junction with George Parks Hwy. and the town of **Wasilla.** The drive through the Matanuska is powerfully beautiful, running parallel to glacier fingers, winding through steep, lush passes, and crossing and re-crossing turbid rivers of glacier silt.

The valley's biggest annual event is the **Alaska State Fair,** on the fairgrounds at Mile 40.2 on Glenn Hwy. The 11-day event, ending on Labor Day, includes parades, rodeos, livestock, and agricultural sideshows starring the aforementioned cabbages. (Open daily 10am-10pm. Admission $6, seniors $3, ages 6-12 $2.) For more information, call 745-4827.

Relive the days when dogsleds carried medical supplies across endless windswept, frozen tundra at the **Knik Museum and Mushers Hall of Fame** (376-7755), at Mile 14 on Knik Rd. While not Cooperstown, the museum features mushing memorabilia and famous dog sleds in its Canine Hall of Fame. (Open June-Aug. 31 Wed.-Sun. noon-6pm. $2, seniors $1.50, under 18 free.) The **Iditarod Race Headquarters** is just down the road at Mile 2.2 on Knik Rd. (376-5155; open daily 8am-5pm, free). Fifteen minutes south of Palmer on the Glenn Highway, **Eklutna Village Historical Park** (276-5701) is an Athabascan village dating back to 1650. Today, the restored village is a place for observing traditional native artisans, fishermen, and culture firsthand. The park documents the interaction between Russian settlers and the Athabascans, and is home to the St. Nicholas Russian Church. Constructed in 1830, the church is the oldest standing structure in greater Anchorage. The park is open daily from mid-May to mid-Sept. 8am-8pm ($3.50). **Independence Mine State Historic Park** (745-5897), 22 mi. from downtown Wasilla in Hatcher Pass, features hiking, fishing, restored mine buildings, and a lodge. Take either Glenn Hwy. to Mile 50 and the Fishhook-Willow Rd. to the park, or Parks Hwy. to Mile 71, the other end of Fishhook-Willow Rd. (Open Fri.-Mon. 11am-6pm. 1-hr. tours at 1:30 and 3:30pm, Sat.-Sun. also at 4:30pm. $3, seniors and under 12 $2, parking $2.)

Head to **Big Lake** (Mile 52 on Parks Hwy.) and **Nancy Lake** (Mile 67.5 on Parks Hwy.) for excellent camping, lodging, canoeing, fishing, and more. Or splash in whitewater on the lower **Matanuska River** for a fair price with **NOVA Riverrunners** (745-5733). NOVA also runs thrilling whitewater trips, including the 14-mi. class IV Lionshead, featuring a 16-ft. drop when the water is high, and the boiling class V Sixmile Creek requiring previous whitewater experience ($60 and $100, respectively). Call collect for reservations, or write NOVA, P.O. Box 1129, Chickaloon, AK 99674. For more information, go to **Matanuska Visitors Center** at Mile 35.5 on the George Parks Hwy. (746-5003 or 800-770-5003).

PALMER

An agricultural hamlet cradled by the stunning scenery of the Matanuska Valley, Palmer evokes the feel of a small mid-western town. Learn more about its history at the **visitors center** (745-2880), a log cabin downtown, across the railroad tracks on South Valley Way at E Fireweed Ave. (open May-Sept. daily 8am-6pm). Next to the visitors center are a garden and greenhouse with samples of the regions's **mammoth fruits** and large legumes.

A few mi. off Parks Hwy., on Hatcher Pass Rd. at Mile 50.1 of the Glenn Hwy., lies the world's only **domesticated musk-ox farm** (745-4151). Neither bovines nor producers of perfume, these beasts are actually hairy cousins of goats and antelopes. Hunted to extinction in the 1850s by Inuit hired and armed by Arctic whalers, musk oxen were reintroduced to Alaska from Greenland in 1934. Descendents of this herd, Palmer's domesticated oxen are prized for their fleece, called *qiviut. Qiviut* is finer than cashmere, does not shrink, and is eight times warmer than regular wool. This wonder fleece, gathered when the oxen shed, supports a healthy cottage industry for traditional Inuit weavers under the auspices of a state-wide organization. Visitors to the farm will be overwhelmed by the friendliness and enthusiasm of its volunteers (open daily 9am-7pm; $6, seniors and students $5, under 6 free).

Fall asleep to the distant bellows of these furry behemoths at the **Matanuska River Park,** at Mile 18 of the Glenn Hwy (sites with water and pit toilets $8).

WASILLA

Wasilla shares Palmer's overgrown agricultural heritage. Despite its location only 42 mi. north of Anchorage on the Parks Hwy., the town lives in the wild outback of rough frontier days, a fact reflected by the nearby **Dog Musher's Hall of Fame.** If you want to try dog mushing, call **Mush Alaska,** P.O. Box 871752, Wasilla 99687 (376-4743). Half-hour excursions start at $20 per person.

The **Wasilla Museum** (376-2005) and the town's **visitors center** are on Main St., off the Parks Hwy. Behind the museum is **Frontier Village,** containing Wasilla's first school, sauna, and ferris wheel (open daily 10am-6pm; $3, seniors $2.50, under 18 free). The **Alaska Historical and Transportation Museum** (745-4493), ¾ mi. off the Parks highway (turn at Mile 46.7 onto Rocky Ridge Rd.), displays implements from the loggers, miners, fisherfolk, and farmers of Alaska past (open Mon.-Sat. 10am-6pm; $3, ages 6-12 $1.50, family $7).

Anchorage's **Stay-With-A-Friend B&B** (344-4006) projects its sphere of influence north to Wasilla (singles start at $50, doubles at $55). Campers should continue south toward Anchorage for another 13 mi. to **Eklutna Campground,** a state-run spot with water and toilets. For more information on the area, contact the **Wasilla Chamber of Commerce,** #C18 Cottonwood Creek Mall, Wasilla 99687 (376-1299).

KENAI PENINSULA

■■■ HOPE

Most people know Hope, the only town on the southern side of Turnagain Arm, as a twinkle of lights seen across the water from the Seward Hwy. Without a major salmon run or ferry terminal, this former gold rush town of 200 remains untrampled, unlike other communities within a daytrip of Anchorage.

Prospectors made an early gold strike at Hope in 1889. The town grew to 3000 people years before Anchorage existed. The boom was short-lived, but many of its relics remain, and much of the federal land around Hope is still open to recreational mining. Hope lies at the end of the scenic 17-mi. Hope Hwy. This road joins the Seward Hwy. 71 mi. outside of Anchorage, just where it turns sharply south down the Peninsula toward Seward.

Practical Information and Sights The Hope **visitors center** (782-3268) can be reached by heading ¼ mi. out on Palmer Creek Rd., just before the townsite (open daily 10am-7pm; in winter Sat.-Sun. noon-6pm). The center provides information on mining and hiking near Hope; more thorough literature on mining is found at the Ranger Station in Seward. The Forest Service permits amateur mining along Sixmile Creek from Mile 1.5 to 5.5 on the Hope Rd. They will even allow you to bring a dredge in here from May 15 to July 15 with a permit. Closer to town, another 20-acre claim (beginning at the Resurrection trailhead foot bridge of Resurrection Trail Rd.) is also open to weekend sourdoughs.

Resurrection Creek at the edge of town supports a healthy run of **salmon** in July and August. The **Hope Salmon Derby** of July 1994 might become an annual event.

During the third week in July, Hope puts on a series of community events, including a bazaar, a raffle, a square dance, and a 5km fun run. Nostalgic Republicans can relive the halcyon days of President Bush's administration at Hope's municipal horseshoe pit across from the Seaview. Read my lips: it's free. Stay the course. The **post office** sits next to the museum (open Mon.-Fri. 8:30am-4:30pm, Sat. 10am-2pm; **General Delivery ZIP Code:** 99605).

Accommodations, Camping, and Food Hope is happily endowed with a number of affordable accommodations. At about Mile 17 of the Hope Hwy., **Henry's 1-Stop Grocery and Motel** (782-3671) has motel rooms for $50, showers for $2, basic groceries, and laundry facilities (open daily 9am-6pm; wash $1, dryer 75¢). Next door, **Bear Creek Lodge** has cabins for $75. In town, the **Seaview Motel** (782-3364) occupies a choice location near the mouth of Resurrection Creek. Rooms with separate baths go for $25 for singles, $45 for doubles. They also rent private cabins sleeping 2 to 5 people ($25 for 2, up to $50 for 5), and have tent sites ($7). Campers will find sweet respite at the Chugach National Forest **Porcupine Campground,** at the end of the Hope Hwy. (sites $8, water and pit toilets).

In the late afternoon, the sun slants into the peaceful **Seaview Cafe** (782-3364), and a light breeze blows through the screen door. Avail yourself of their all-you-can-eat ribs, chicken, and pork chop barbecue with baked beans, potato salad, and a sourdough roll ($9). The pie, however, is average ($3).

Outdoors Hiking is excellent here. In addition to enjoyable day hikes, this is the northern end of a 70-mi. series of trails crossing the Kenai from Seward to Hope.

The **Gull Rock Trail,** an easy 5-mi. trek along Turnagain Arm, affords fine views of the water, the shore, and, on an exceptionally clear day, Denali. The trek initially follows an old wagon road out of the Porcupine Campground at the end of the Hope Hwy. It passes the site of an old sawmill and a homestead along the way to the rock. The terrain does not favor camping, so plan on making the 4-6 hr. round-trip.

Also beginning from the Porcupine Campground, the **Hope Point Trail** is a more challenging hike up to a peak above treeline. This 5-mi. round trip initially follows Porcupine Creek, then climbs steeply up to treeline and on to Hope Point. The trail becomes less distinct after passing a microwave tower but is still easy to follow.

The **Resurrection Pass Trail,** originally a 19th-century gold miner's byway, leads 39 mi. through the Chugach National Forest from Hope to the Sterling Hwy. This popular hike traverses a beautiful area of abundant wildlife. To reach the trailhead in Hope, turn south onto Resurrection Creek Road at Mile 15 of the Hope Hwy. The trail begins 4 mi. in at a parking area. No less than seven **Forest Service cabins** punctuate this hike. They can be reserved in Anchorage (and often are, far in advance) and at the **Seward Ranger Station** in Seward. Fine fishing in Juneau and Trout Lakes comes as a reward near the end of the trail. The southern trailhead lies on the Sterling Hwy. near Cooper Landing, 106 mi. south of Anchorage and 53 mi. east of Soldotna. An alternative endgame is to take the **Devil's Creek Trail** just south of Resurrection Pass, 19 mi. along the trail from Hope, and end up on the Seward Hwy. instead. For more information on the Resurrection Pass Trail and the extension to Seward, contact the USDA Forest Service for the Seward Ranger District, P.O. Box 390, 334 4th Ave., Seward 99664 (224-3374).

■■■ SEWARD

Seward holds paramount importance as the gateway to the stupendous **Kenai fjords.** It also commands respect for surviving the 1964 earthquake that rang in at 8.3 on the old Richter scale (9.2 on the new scale) and sent six successive *tsunamis* sweeping across the peninsula.

The streets in Seward are named after the U.S. Presidents from Washington to Van Buren, in chronological order, so read up on your history before you visit.

PRACTICAL INFORMATION AND ORIENTATION

Visitors Information: Chamber of Commerce (224-8051), Mile 2 on Seward Hwy. Encyclopedic knowledge of Seward. Assortment of pamphlets. Open daily 9am-5pm, Labor Day-Memorial Day Mon.-Fri. 9am-5pm. Also operates a **railroad car** (224-3094), 3rd and Jefferson St., where you can pick up a self-guided walking tour and mark your home town on the world map. Open daily in summer 11am-5pm. Another **information center** in the small boat harbor (open in summer daily 11am-5pm).

National Park Service Visitors Center, 1212 4th Ave. (224-3175), at the small-boat harbor. Information and maps for the spectacular **Kenai Fjords National Park.** Dockside talks on marine life daily at 3pm, slide show inside (open in summer daily 8am-7pm; winter Mon.-Fri. 8am-noon and 1-5pm). **Seward Ranger Station, Chugach National Forest,** 334 4th Ave. (224-3374), at Jefferson. Extensive trail information, maps, advice on trails close to town, and the complete Iditarod route. Chugach cabin reservations ($25 per night, 3-day max. stay; see Hope: Outdoors). Open Mon.-Fri. 8am-5pm.

Employment Office, Seward Employment Center, P.O. Box 1009, Seward (224-5276), 5th and Adams, on the 2nd floor of the City Building. Open Mon.-Fri. 8am-4:30pm.

Airport: 2 mi. north of town on Seward Hwy. No regularly scheduled flights to Anchorage. **Harbor Air** offers charters and hr.-long flightseeing trips over the fjords ($85 per person; 3-person min.).

Winter Road Closure Information: 800-478-7675.

Alaska Railroad, 224-3133, 278-0800 for reservations, depot at the northern edge of town. To: Anchorage (May 23-Sept. 6, 1 per day, 6pm; $40).

Buses: Homer and Seward Bus Lines, 550 Railway Ave. (224-3608, next door to the Chamber of Commerce. To: Anchorage (2 per day, 9am, $30). Call about service to Homer.

Alaska Marine Highway (224-5485; 800-478-7675 for road closure info.), ferry dock, 4th and Railway Ave. Served by the *Tustumena*. About 1 per week in summer to: Kodiak ($54), Valdez ($58), and Homer ($98). No service during one week of every month. Call for schedule.

Trolley: Just wave it down and it will take you anywhere on its route through town, or call for pickup (50 ¢, round-trip $3). Operates daily 10am-6pm.

Taxi: Independent Cab, 224-5000. **PJ's Taxi,** 224-5555. Both 24 hrs.

Car Rental: Seward Tesoro (224-8611), at Mile 1.9 of the Seward Hwy. $59 per day with unlimited free mi. Must be at least 25 with credit card.

Kayak Rental: Sea Kayak (224-3960), next to the National Park Visitors Center. Single-seats $35 for the first day, $25 per day thereafter; $15 per day after a week. Doubles $55 first day, $45 thereafter; $25 after a week. $200 deposit per boat. Guided day trips start at $45 per day. Open daily 9am-6pm.

Bike Rental: Murphy's Motel (224-8090). Mountain bikes available for $15, $20, or $25 per day. 1-speed wonders available for $10 per day.

Laundromat and Showers: Seward Laundry, 224-5727, at 4th and C St. Wash, dry, and fold $1.30 per lb. Showers $3 (unlimited time). Open daily 8am-10pm. **Public Showers,** also at the Harbormaster Bldg. 5-min. shower $1.

Public Restrooms: On the waterfront near Adams St. and at the Harbormaster Building.

Pharmacy: Seward Drug, 224 4th Ave. (224-8989). Open Mon.-Sat. 9am-9pm, Sun. 10am-6pm; winter Mon.-Sat. 9:30am-6:30pm.

Fishing: Rod rentals from **Seward Drug** (see above) $10 per day with a $50 deposit. No tackle included. Buy tackle from **The Fish House,** across from the Harbormaster. Wide selection of all necessary equipment. Open daily 6am-10pm.

Crisis Line: 224-3027. 24 hrs.

Hospital: Seward General (224-5205), 1st Ave. and Jefferson St.

Emergency: 911.

Police: 244-3338.

Post Office: 224-3001, 5th Ave. and Madison St. Open Mon.-Fri. 9:30am-4:30pm, Sat. 10am-2pm. **General Delivery ZIP Code:** 99664.

Area Code: 907.

Seward is on the south coast of the Kenai Peninsula, on beautiful **Resurrection Bay.**
Anchorage, 127 mi. north, is connected to Seward by the **Seward Hwy.**

ACCOMMODATIONS AND CAMPING

The only hostel on the Kenai Peninsula lies 16 mi. outside Seward and lacks a telephone, but the hotel rates in town may give you the adrenaline surge you'll need to
hike there. A rooming scarcity in Seward has driven accommodation prices up.
Seward's municipal campground is clean and inexpensive, though there are private
alternatives offering more solitude. At Mile 29 on Seward Hwy., the nearby town of
Moose Pass has four **campgrounds** with excellent fishing: **Primrose** at Mile 18,
Ptarmigan Creek at Mile 23, **Trail River** at Mile 24, and **Wye** at Mile 36. All are run
by the **Chugach National Forest;** for information, write Alaska Public Lands Information, 605 W 4th, Anchorage 99501 (271-2737).

Snow River International Home Hostel (HI/AYH), at Mile 16 of Seward Hwy.
No phone; call the central hosteling number in Anchorage (276-3635). Beautiful
new house in a scenic, inconvenient location with 30 beds, showers, and sauna.
$12, nonmembers $15. Private rooms also available ($30, $36 for nonmembers).

Van Gilder Hotel, 308 Adams St. (224-3079), just off 3rd Ave. Constructed in
1916, the Van Gilder is probably the only National Historic site with garish pink
window trim. Beautiful rooms with TV, sink, and toilet area $60, with private
bath area $80. Reservations necessary, especially on weekends.

Municipal Waterfront Campground, stretching along Ballaine Rd. from Railway
Ave. in the south to D St. in the north. Tent lawns and RV lots occupy some of
Seward's choicest (and windiest) real estate, with a stunning view of the mountains across Resurrection Bay. Most tenting between Adams and Jefferson St. Toilets are scattered throughout the campground, and restrooms with showers are at
the Harbormaster Bldg. 2-week max. stay. Check-out 4pm. Open May 15-Sept. 30.
Sites $8, parking spots $8; collected by strict honor code.

Bear Creek RV Park (224-5725). Turn off Seward Hwy. at Mile 6.5 and take Bear
Leg Rd. ½ mi. Free showers. Laundry $1.50 wash, $1 dry. Small area for tents
$7.50 per person. Full hookup $20.

FOOD

Seward offers the usual spread of greasy diners and tourist traps. Stock up on groceries at the **Eagle Quality Center** at Mile 2 of Seward Hwy. (open 24 hrs.). It's a bit of
a walk from downtown, but you can reward yourself with a massive $1 ice cream
cone from the in-store soda fountain.

Don's Kitchen, 4th Ave. and Washington St. (224-8036). Big breakfast specials
$5.75-9. Their biscuits-and-gravy plate ($4) is available in ½–portion. 2 eggs, 2 hotcakes or hashbrowns, and 2 sausage links ($5). Specializes in home-style cooking.
Open 5am-10pm.

Breeze Inn (224-5298), in the small-boat harbor. Not your average hotel-restau-
rant. Breeze in for the huge all-you-can-eat lunch buffet ($8). Slighter appetites
should try the 2-trips-to-the-soup-and-salad-bar ($4.25). Breakfast all day. Open
daily 6am-9pm.

Peking, 338 4th Ave. (224-5444), at Jefferson St. Tasty lunch specials with rice and
soup ($5.45-6.45) served 11:30am-3pm. Open Mon.-Fri. 11:30am-10:30pm, Sat.-
Sun. noon-10:30pm.

Christo's Palace, 4th Ave. and Railway Ave. Cavernous pizza joint and bar. Large
15-in. pizza ($12). Wide variety of Italian and Mexican fare, too. Dinner served
until 11pm, pizza until 1am. Open daily noon-1am.

SIGHTS AND EVENTS

The self-guided **walking tour** of Seward, detailed on the **map** available at the visitors
center, passes many turn-of-the-century homes and businesses. A complete tour
takes 2-3 hrs. The **Resurrection Bay Historical Society Museum,** in the Senior Center, 3rd and Jefferson St., exhibits traditional Alaskan artifacts, including a fine col-

lection of woven baskets. (Museum open Memorial Day-Labor Day Mon.-Fri. 11am-5pm, Sat.-Sun. noon-6pm. Extended hours when tour ships are in town. $1, children 50¢.) From June 15 to Labor Day, you can see the "Earthquake Movie" at the **Seward Community Library** (224-3646), 5th Ave. and Adams St. The movie shows actual footage of the 1964 Good Friday earthquake, with a supporting cast of fires and tidal waves, which destroyed much of Seward and Southcentral Alaska. (Library open Mon.-Fri. noon-8pm, Sat. noon-6pm. Screenings Mon.-Sat. at 2pm and Mon., Wed., and Fri. at 7pm. $1.50 donation requested.) **Liberty Theater,** 304 Adams St. (224-5418), projects current films. In the spring of 1994, the Liberty began to release films on their national release date (a source of community pride).

The **Silver Salmon Derby** opens each year on the second Saturday in August and closes eight days later. Prizes are awarded for the largest fish and the tagged fish (up to $10,000). No one has ever caught the tagged fish during the derby.

The other annual event that gets Seward hopping is the **Mountain Marathon** on the 4th of July. Alaska's oldest footrace, the marathon began when one sourdough challenged a neighbor to make it up and down the 3022-ft. peak in less than an hour. That was in 1915, and the poor guy just couldn't do it. The current records for men (43 min.) and women (50 min.) demonstrate that humankind is on the move. The race has been joined by a parade, the governor, and hundreds of enthusiasts running, sliding, falling, and bleeding down the steep mountainsides to the shores of Resurrection Bay. Thousands of sadistic spectators set up lawn chairs anywhere in town and watch the painful spectacle with binoculars. The annual **Seward Silver Salmon 10K Run** takes off during the Labor Day weekend, and the **Exit Glacier 5K and 10K Run** kicks off in mid-May. Though these races may sound tough, Seward's truest test of physical endurance comes in the third weekend of January during the 3-day **Seward Polar Bear Jump,** sending participants plunging right into the freezing water.

OUTDOORS

The southern terminus of the Alaska railroad, Seward is also the point of entry into the **Kenai Fjords National Park.** The **Park Service Visitors Center** is near the small-boat harbor (see Practical Information). Protecting a coastal mountain system packed with wildlife and glaciers, the best way to see the park is from boats in the bay. Pick up the list of charters and prices at the Chamber of Commerce (see Practical Information) or from shops along the boardwalk next to the harbormaster's office. **Alaska Renown Charters** (224-3806) offers the cheapest tour; their 2½-hr. tour of the Sound costs $40, under 12 $20 (4 per day). **Kenai Fjords Tours** (224-8030) has 4-hr. cruises for $58 (depart twice daily May-Sept. at 8:30am and 1pm). Call for information about day-long trips. **Mariah Charters** (243-1238) gives tours that are worth the cost, gratifying visitors with incredible sights: glaciers, pods of **orcas** diving and gliding under the boat, and playful sea lions in the wild.

For a less-expensive glimpse of wildlife, loiter near the small-boat harbor when the charter fishing trips return in the evening. A sea lion often prowls below the docks waiting for remains of fish tossed into the water as the catch is cleaned.

Seward is a great base for day hikes. Nearby **Mt. Marathon** offers a **view** of the city and ocean. From 1st and Jefferson St., take Lowell St. to reach the trail. The trail begins with a steep ascent up a rocky stream bed. Once above vegetation, a network of trails continue up the rocky ledge to the left. Another route climbs through scree to the right. The rocky route provides better footing for the ascent, and the scree can be fun to run through on the way down. Unless you're training for the race, plan on a 2-hr. climb to the top and a 45-min. hop-and-slide to come down. There is no final peak at the end of the trail, but the **views** out over Resurrection Bay are phenomenal. Travelers wishing to stay closer to shore can hike along the **McGilvrey Trail.** 1½ mi. into the 7-mi. trail, there is a 3-mi. stretch negotiable only at low tide. Consult the newspaper, the Chamber of Commerce, the Coast Guard, or any commercial fisherman for tide information. The last two ½ mi. lead along sand, ending at South Beach, where camping is free.

Exit Glacier, billed as Alaska's most accessible glacier, is 9 mi. west on the road that starts at Mile 3.7 of Seward Hwy. Kenai Fjords Tours runs 2½-hr. tours of Exit Glacier for $19 (under 12, $9.50). Tours depart daily at 2pm, May through Sept., from the small boat harbor. If you're feeling energetic and have 7 hrs. of free time, take the steep, slippery, 4-mi. trail from the ranger station to the magnificent **Harding Ice Field** above the glacier. The rangers will prevent you from getting within 50 ft. of the glacier face, as chunks of ice weighing several tons are continually breaking off, or "calving." Check the **ranger station** (see Practical Information) for information on a campground and other trails in the Seward area. Every Sat. a ranger leads a hike to the Harding Ice Field. A campsite is about 1 mi. from the glacier's face (9 sites, pit toilets, water. No RVs; free).

Fishing is heavenly in the Seward area. Salmon and halibut can be caught in the bay, grayling and dolly varden right outside of town. Charters are available for both halibut and salmon throughout the summer; prices run from $95-145, with all gear provided. Call **The Fish House** (800-257-7760; see Practical Information), the largest charter-booking service in Seward. You can also fish for free from the docks.

■■■ SOLDOTNA

As the peninsula's premier fishing spot, Soldotna draws vacationers from far away. Prize-winning salmon are caught regularly in the Kenai River, a few minutes from downtown. Kenai Riverbend Campground, halfway between Soldotna and Kenai, offers a $10,000 reward to the person who catches a salmon weighing more than 97 lbs., the current record (that's $103.09 per lb.). That would go a long way toward paying for a budget vacation, even in Alaska.

Both Soldotna and neighboring Kenai resemble a slice of greater Anchorage more than typical Alaskan towns, but Soldotna provides budget travelers with a comfortable campground. If you have to stay overnight in one of these ugly service strips, even if you're not a single-minded angler, Soldotna is the clear choice.

PRACTICAL INFORMATION AND ORIENTATION

At the north end of town, the **Sterling Highway** forks in one direction to continue to Anchorage, and forks in the other as the **Kenai Spur Road** to Kenai. This fork is known as the **Y,** and many businesses describe their locations in relation to it. The 22-mi. **Kalifornsky Beach Road** (no, that's not Russian for "California") also intersects Sterling Hwy. at the southern end of town and begins its mi. marking from the Kenai end. Hence, an address at Mile 3 is actually 19 mi. from Soldotna.

Visitors Information: Visitors Center, 44790 Sterling Highway (262-1337), between Miles 95 and 96, just across the river from downtown. Modern facility with photo displays, friendly staff, and stairs down to the river. The world-record 97-lb. king salmon caught in the Kenai River is here on permanent display, as well as a multitude of mounted mammals. Open daily mid-May-Labor Day 9am-7pm. **Chamber of Commerce,** P.O. Box 236, Soldotna 99669 (262-9814), next to the visitors center. Especially good for Bed and Breakfast lists, trail information, fishing guides, and sundry Soldotna souvenirs. Open Mon.-Fri. 9am-5pm.

Division of Parks and Outdoor Recreation, P.O. Box 1247 (262-5581), on Morgans Rd. at Mile 85 on Sterling Hwy. Information on campgrounds and fishing.

Fishing Licenses: Available at any sporting goods store or **Payless.** 1-day $10, 3-day $15, 14-day $30, annual $50. Alaska residents $15 for the year.

Car Rental: Ford Rent-A-Car, 43465 Sterling Hwy. (262-5491). $43 per day, unlimited mi. Must be at least 21 with credit card. **Hertz** (262-5857), based at Kenai Airport but will deliver. $45 per day, unlimited mi. Must be at least 25 with credit card.

Buses: Homer and Seward Bus Lines, 800-478-8280. To: Homer (1 per day; $10), Seward (1 per day; $27), and Anchorage (1 per day; $30).

Taxi: AAA Taxi, 262-1555.

Laundromat: Alpine Laundromat (262-9129), on Sterling Hwy. next to the Dairy
Queen. Wash $1.75, 7-min. dry 25¢. Shower $3. Open daily in the summer 7am-
noon; in winter 8am-9pm.
Pharmacy: Payless Drug, next to the Safeway on Sterling Hwy. Open Mon.-Fri.
9am-9pm, Sat. 9am-6pm, Sun. 10am-6pm.
Crisis Line: 283-7257. 24 hrs.
Ambulance: 262-4792.
Hospital: Central Peninsula General, 250 Hospital Pl. (262-4404).
Emergency: 911.
Post Office: (262-4760), Corral and Binkley St., downtown. Open Mon.-Fri.
8:30am-5pm, Sat. 10am-2pm. **General Delivery ZIP Code:** 99669.
Area Code: 907.

Soldotna is 140 mi. southwest of Anchorage on Sterling Hwy., at its junction with
Kenai Spur Rd. Take the Seward Hwy. south from Anchorage and turn right onto
Sterling at the second fork in the road (the Hope Hwy. is the first).

ACCOMMODATIONS AND CAMPING

Soldotna is mobbed by thousands of crazed anglers willing to pay any price for a
room or campground close to the Kenai River, especially during **"the run,"** a three-
week period in July when the river is choked with millions of spawning salmon.
Competition for scarce rooms and tentsites drives prices up; your best rooming
option may be a bed and breakfast. The Chamber of Commerce (see Practical Information above) has a complete list of local establishments starting at $45 per night.
Fortunately for itinerant pedestrian campers, the Soldotna city elders have decreed
a price of only $2 per night at the attractive municipal campgrounds.

The Duck Inn (262-1849), Mile 3 on Kalifornsky Beach Rd., by the Red Diamond
Mall. Tiny, clean rooms with private bath and TV. Room with 1 queen-sized bed
$59.50, $69.50 during peak fishing frenzy.
The Goodnight Inn (262-4584), across the river from the visitors center. Recently
remodeled rooms with cable TV and full bath. 10% discount for seniors. Singles
$85. Doubles $95. Off-peak, the same rooms cost $59 and $69.
Swiftwater Park Municipal Campground, south on Sterling Hwy. at Mile 94, and
Centennial Park Municipal Campground, off Kalifornsky Beach Rd. near the
visitors center. Both are in the woods, both have boat launches on the river, and
both offer excellent fishing spots and tables set aside for cleaning fish. 1-week
max. stay. Pit toilets and water. Quiet, well-groomed sites $2, with a vehicle $7.

FOOD

The Kenai-Soldotna area has boomed in the past 20 years, attracting swarms of fast-
food joints. There are, however, many good local restaurants for true budget travelers. The 24-hr. **Safeway** downtown, on Sterling Hwy., is the place for groceries, and
in the summer they sell cheap and delicious **fruit** from a tent in the parking lot. A
weekly **Farmer's Market** meets next to the fire department on Sterling Hwy. (Sat.
10am-2pm).

Sal's Klondike Diner, 44619 Sterling Hwy. (262-2220), ½ mi. from the river and
several hundred mi. from the Klondike. A model train circles overhead. Menu
"loded" with gold rush trivia. Newspaper columns of breakfast items ($3.50 each
or 2 for $6) served all day. The massive $3 cinnamon roll is a meal. Open 24 hrs.
Black Forest Restaurant, 44278 Sterling Hwy. (262-5111). Nostalgic foreign travelers and polyglots should stop in, as the owners, fluent in English, French, German, and Filipino, love swapping stories in any language. They also speak the
international language of the budget diner. Whopping ½-lb. cheeseburger
($5.25), 12-in. subs ($4.50-5.25). Drink a cold shake ($2.50). Open Mon.-Fri.
11am-7pm, Sun. 10am-6pm.

Bull Feathers (262-3844), in the back of the Peninsula Center Mall, on Sterling Hwy. Substantial ½-lb. burger with 3 Jo-Jos (deep-fried potato slices) and a packed "burger fixin's bar" ($5). Open Mon.-Sat. 10am-9pm, Sun. noon-6pm.

Diamond K Cafe, in the small mall at Sterling Hwy. and the Kenai Spur Rd. A family-run restaurant with no-nonsense American food. The Hungry Man's breakfast could satisfy a grizzly: 3 eggs, bacon, pancakes, biscuits and gravy, and coffee ($7.50). Wide range of sandwiches ($4.85-6.65). Open 24 hrs.

EVENTS AND ENTERTAINMENT

Soldotna Progress Days, celebrated at the end of July, commemorates the completion of the natural gas pipeline in 1961. Festivities include a parade, rodeo, and airshow. Mid-June brings the ecology-oriented **Kenai River Festival,** held across from the Soldotna Safeway.

If you feel like stomping your heels, check out the rough-and-tumble, local **Maverick Saloon** (262-7979), on Sterling Hwy., across from the Goodnight Inn, for live country music (Mon. 9:30pm-4:30am; club open daily 8am-5am). A little bowling to pass the time? At **Gold Strike Lanes,** behind Sal's Klondike Diner (262-9065), games are a piddling $2.50 ($1 more if you left your shoes at home). Games are only $1 on Monday nights (open daily 9am-5pm in winter, 4pm-10pm in summer).

OUTDOORS

The **Kenai River** wriggles with fish. Pink, king, red, and silver salmon glide through at various times during the summer, and steelhead and dolly varden do the underwater tango all summer long. Many **fishing charters** run the river, usually charging $100-125 for a ½-day of either halibut or salmon fishing (or $150 for both kinds of fishing). Contact the visitors center for more information. Such expense isn't necessary, however. The downtown area is loaded with equipment rental shops that will fully outfit you with everything from bait to licenses for under $15 per day, and you can angle from the shore. **Kenai Motorboat Rental** (262-3736), on Knight Dr., ¾ mi. off the Spur (turn at Mile 1½ of the Spur), provides 16-ft. power boats ($125 per day plus a $5 launching fee; gas not included). The best places to throw out a line are those where the current runs slowly (e.g. near a bridge), since salmon often rest in eddies on their journeys upstream. Unfortunately, fishermen pack elbow to elbow in the same pockets.

If you're tired of maniacal, rubber-suited anglers, wander over to the **Kenai National Wildlife Refuge Visitors Center** (262-7021), off Funny River Rd. at the top of Ski Hill Rd., directly across from the Soldotna Visitors Center, with a great source of information on this 197-million acre refuge for moose, Dall sheep, and other wild animals. Don't count on seeing any beasts from here; most of them are wandering the several million acres. The center also houses dioramas and various victims of taxidermy. Scratch-and-sniff wooly patches of caribou, moose, and sheep hair. If you're feeling saucy, pick up a phone and talk dirty to a loon or a wolf. Several nature trails are nearby (open Mon.-Fri. 8am-5pm, Sat.-Sun. 10am-6pm).

Fast-paced rivers weave into the **Kenai National Wildlife Refuge,** and dozens of 1 to 4-day **canoe routes** wind their way through the forest. **The Sports Den** (262-7491) has canoes for $35 per day, $25 per day for 3 days or more (open daily 8am-8pm). Boats are also available alongside the highway; residents put their vessels in their front yards and hang "for rent" signs. Boat rentals are expensive, but it's hard to put a price on gliding through some of the nation's most remote waterways. For free **canoe route maps** drop by the visitors center (above), or write or call the Refuge Manager, Kenai National Wildlife Refuge, P.O. Box 2139, Soldotna (262-7021).

■■■ KENAI

Kenai (KEEN-eye) is the largest and fastest-growing town on the peninsula. The Kenaitze Native people lived here first; Russia and later the United States built forts here. Kenai is now evidence of oil's importance to Alaska. Over seven major international oil firms pump from near the shore. Rigs with pet names like "Spark" and "King Salmon" pump out about 70,000 barrels of crude per day. In the shadows of the rigs, remnants of each historical era lie scattered among the strip malls and RV parks that constitute Kenai. During the summer months, Alaska's largest pod of Beluga whales dodge the hunks of metal as they chase spawning salmon through the mouth of the Kenai River. The rest of the town isn't a lot prettier than the rigs; Kenai boasts the world's largest K-mart.

PRACTICAL INFORMATION AND ORIENTATION

Visitor and Cultural Center, 11471 Kenai Spur Hwy. (283-1991), just past the corner of Spur and Main St. A veritable palace of visitation, erected for the town's 1991 bicentennial. Usual array of pamphlets is supplemented by a room full of stuffed native wildlife, an area dedicated to traditional Alaskan artifacts, and a small theater with films on the area's development ($1 suggested donation for exhibits). Open Mon.-Fri. 9am-6pm, Sat. 10am-5pm, Sun. 11am-4pm; winter Mon.-Fri. 9am-5pm.

National Park Service, 502 Overland Dr., P.O. Box 2643, Kenai 99611 (283-5855). Best source of information on **Lake Clark National Park and Preserve,** across Cook Inlet from Kenai. Hours vary.

Airport, 1 mi. north of downtown. Take Kenai Spur Rd. to Willow St.; follow signs for Airport Loop. Serviced by **ERA** (800-426-0333), and **Mark Air** (800-627-5247, from out of state 800-426-6784). To Anchorage (rates start at $37).

Taxi: Alaska Cab, 283-6000. **Inlet Cab,** 283-4711. Both open 24 hr.

Car Rental: National (283-9566). Must be 21 with credit card. June-Aug. $45 per day with unlimited mileage; Sept.-May $38. **Avis** (283-7900), $40 per day, unlimited mi. Must be 21 with credit card. **Hertz** (283-7979), $47 per day, unlimited mi. Must be 25 with credit card. All three at the airport.

Buses: Homer and Seward Bus Lines (278-0800). 1 per day to Anchorage ($30) and Homer ($19).

Library, 163 Main St. Loop (283-4378). Open Mon.-Thurs. 8:30am-8pm, Fri.-Sat. 8:30am-5pm.

Laundromat and Showers: Wash-n-Dry (283-9973), Lake St. and Kenai Spur Rd. Wash $1.50, 7-min. dry 25¢. 20-min. shower $3.50. Open daily 8am-10pm.

Pharmacy: Kenai Drug Inlet Pharmacy (283-3714), in the Sea Plaza, at Spur and McKinley. Open Mon.-Sat. 10am-6pm.

Crisis Line: 283-7257. 24 hrs.

Women's Resource Center, 325 S Spruce St. (283-9479). 24 hrs.

Hospital: Central Peninsula General Hospital, 250 Hospital Pl., Soldotna (262-4404).

Emergency: 911.

Police: 283-7879.

Post Office, 140 Bidarka (283-7771). Open Mon.-Fri. 8:45am-5:15pm, Sat. 9:30am-1pm. **General Delivery ZIP Code:** 99611.

Area Code: 907.

Kenai, on the western Kenai Peninsula, is about 148 mi. from Anchorage and 81 mi. north of Homer. It can be reached via **Kalifornsky Beach Rd.,** joining the Sterling Hwy. from Anchorage just south of Soldotna, or via **Kenai Spur Rd.,** running north through the Nikishka area and east to Soldotna. Kalifornsky **mile markers** measure distance from Kenai, while the Kenai Spur mile markers measure distance from Soldotna. Both roads lay open the peninsula's lakes and peaks: on a clear day, you can see the 10,000-ft. **Mt. Redoubt Volcano** across Cook Inlet.

ACCOMMODATIONS AND CAMPING

The annual invasion of tourists and anglers has put Kenai's hotel rates into orbit. Check the visitors center (see Practical Information) for listings of local bed and breakfasts, starting at $45. Backpackers used to stay in a free municipal campground that has since banned overnight camping. This leaves not a single affordable accom-

K
E
N
A
I

modation in Kenai, although one lodge 9 mi. out of town offers inexpensive bunks (*men only;* see North Star Lodge below).

Katmai Hotel, 10800 Kenai Spur Hwy. (283-6101), 1 block from downtown. Small rooms with nice decor and cable TV. Singles $75. Doubles $87.

Kenai Merit Inn Hotel, 260 S Willow St. (283-6131), just off the Kenai Spur Hwy. Complimentary Airport pick-up, cable TV. Singles and doubles $85 during peak summer season; $75 non-peak.

North Star Lodge, Mile 21 Kenai Spur Hwy. (776-5259). A hotel and restaurant 9 mi. north of town with space for 12 men in a bunkhouse. $10. Showers $4. Rooms from $55.

FOOD

Carr's Quality Center (283-7829), in the Kenai Mall next to the K-Mart on Kenai Spur Rd., is the city's largest grocery store. They have a bakery, fruit and juice bar, natural foods section, pharmacy, and fast food for reasonable prices (open 24 hrs.).

Little Ski-Mo's Burger-n-Brew (283-4463), on Kenai Spur Rd. across from the visitors center. Stunning array of burgers. Try the Polynesian ($6.50) or the Shaka burger ($5.25). Burger-n-brew or soda ($5) all day, every day. Open Mon.-Sat. 11am-11pm, Sun. 11am-10pm.

Katmai Hotel Restaurant, 10800 Kenai Spur Rd. (238-6101), near Kalifornsky Beach Rd. Full platters of lip-smacking (artery-stopping) fried foods. 2 eggs, ½-order of biscuits and gravy, and coffee ($5). Deluxe burger with fries ($5). Tall iced tea ($1). Open 24 hrs.

Arirang Chinese Restaurant, 145 S Willow St. (283-4662), off Kenai Spur Rd. Refuel at the all-you-can-eat lunch buffet ($7) served Mon.-Fri. 11:30-2pm. Open daily 11am-10pm.

SIGHTS AND ACTIVITIES

The most breathtaking sight in Kenai is **Cook Inlet,** framing white sand, two mountain ranges, and volcanic **Mt. Augustine** and **Mt. Redoubt.** Imbibe the magic of the inlet and its beluga whales, salmon, and gulls from the overlook at the end of Main St. A small **caribou** herd, often spotted trotting along Kenai Spur Hwy. or Kalifornsky Beach Rd., roams the flatlands between Kenai and Soldotna. The town is a diffuse jumble of asphalt and malls that has more in common with suburban sprawl than with Alaska's frontier towns.

The only worthwhile indoor attraction in Old Kenai is the town's oldest building, the **Holy Assumption Russian Orthodox Church,** on Mission St. off Overland. Originally built in 1846 and rebuilt in 1896, this National Historic Landmark contains a 200-year-old Bible (tours in summer daily 11am, 1pm, and 3pm). Cultural Kenai is closeted inside the cement-block **Kenai Fine Arts Center** (283-7040). The **Kenai Peninsula Artists Exhibit** rests in the Gallery (open Mon.-Sat. 10am-4pm).

Recreational opportunities in the Kenai area abound. Check at the Chamber of Commerce for fishing charter information (prices are comparable to those in Soldotna), or with the Forest Service (see Practical Information) for canoeing and hiking activities. The **Captain Cook State Recreation Area,** 30 mi. north of Kenai at the end of Kenai Spur Rd., offers swimming, fishing, free **camping,** and landing points for canoes on the Swanson River. Contact the State Division of Parks for rules and regulations. **Nikiski,** a few mi. north of Kenai, is home to a **geodesic-domed pool** behind the school. The dome is a stunning contrast to its forest setting, and in winter you can swim next to the snowdrifts that pile high outside the arched windows. (Open Tues.-Fri. 7am-5pm and 6-9pm, Sat. noon-5pm, Sun. 6-9pm. $2.50, seniors free, ages 17 and under $1.) If swimming under a dome has you tuckered out, take the gravel paths at the end of Spruce St. in Kenai. Slide down the sandy slope to lounge on the local **beaches.** Despite the oil rigs in the distance, the beaches are clean. Use the rope to haul yourself back up.

■ BETWEEN KENAI AND HOMER: NINILCHIK

Ninilchik, between Kenai and Homer on the Sterling Hwy., is another small town with spectacular fishing and fantastic scenery. Its strong Russian heritage, however, distinguishes it from other hamlets on the peninsula. The only sightseeing attractions are the old **Russian fishing village** on Village Rd. north of town, and the **Holy Transfiguration of Our Lord Orthodox Church,** built in 1901. Both overlook Cook Inlet, and the church, high up on a bluff, offers an unparalleled view of the Redoubt and Iliamna volcanoes. The church and cemetery are still in use, but the Russian village sits abandoned and dilapidated.

The nearby **Deep Creek Recreation Area** is one of the most popular on the peninsula. Locals stake the claim that it has the world's best salt-water king salmon fishing; dolly varden and steelhead trout also swim here.

If you decide to stay in town for the night, head for the **Beachcomber Motel and RV Park** (567-3417) on Village Rd. Each of the motel's four cabins has a shower, full kitchenette, TV, and unimpeded view of Mt. Redoubt across the Cook Inlet. (Singles $45. Doubles $55. Full hookups for RVs $12.) For campers the choice is obvious: stay at one of the **state campgrounds** near town, each with water and toilets (sites $6). Superb sites in **Ninilchik State Recreation Area** are less than 1 mi. north of the library. RV hookups rattle and hum closer to town at **Hylea's Camper Park,** Mile 135.4 of Sterling Hwy. (567-3393).

Buy groceries early at the **General Store** (567-1091) on Sterling Hwy. (open daily 6am-noon). On the east side of Sterling Hwy., a long low restaurant and bar sits back on a gravel plot. The **Inlet View Cafe,** Mile 135.4 on Sterling Hwy. (567-3337), offers a sterling view of the Cook Inlet and hearty sandwiches named for the mountains you can see across the water: the Redoubt, Iliamna, and others ($5.50-9). A halibut basket, cole slaw, and fries is $8. (Open daily 5:30am-midnight.) The bar is a laid-back local hangout (open 10am-5am).

The library's visitor information section is also the local **visitors center** (567-3333; open Mon.-Sat. 11am-4pm). The library is across from the General Store.

■■■ HOMER

Homer seems little different than other small coastal towns in Alaska. Dented pickup trucks and RVs barrel over dusty roads, a large fleet of commercial halibut boats strain at their moorings in the harbor, and an indifferent backdrop of immense natural beauty; the town rises up on bluffs above Kachemak Bay at one end with wide views of the blue mountains and pale glaciers across the water. And yet, Homer supports its own theater group, scores of galleries stocked with the work of local artists, and one of the best small newspapers in Alaska.

The town extends into the bay along the improbable 3½-mi. tendril of sand and gravel known as the **Spit.** The ruggedly beautiful island and wilds of **Kachemak State Park** lie across the Kachemak Bay, where the southern end of the **Kenai Mountains** reaches the sea. Also on the south side of the bay are the artist/fishing colony of **Halibut Cove,** the Russian/hippy **Yukon Island,** the **Gull Island** bird rookery, and the Russian-founded town of **Seldovia.**

PRACTICAL INFORMATION AND ORIENTATION

Homer Chamber of Commerce and Visitor Information Center, on Homer Bypass near the Eagle Quality Center (235-5300). All the necessary information and pamphlets. Open Memorial Day-Labor Day daily 9am-9pm. If you can't make it here, go to the **Pratt Museum,** 3779 Bartlett St. (235-8635), for brochures. Open daily 10am-6pm; Oct.-April Tues.-Fri. 10am-6pm, Sat. 10am-5pm.

Park Information: Alaska Maritime National Wildlife Refuge Visitor Center, 509 Sterling Highway, next to the Best Western Bidarka Inn (235-6961). Wildlife exhibits, marine photography, and helpful advice on backcountry adventures in Kachemak Bay. Open daily 9am-6pm. **Southern District Ranger Station,**

Kachemak Bay State Park, P.O. Box 321, Homer 99603 (235-7024), 4 mi. outside town on the Sterling Hwy. **Fishing Licenses:** $15 for 3 days, available at local sporting goods stores and charter offices, or contact the **Alaska Dept. of Fish and Game,** 3298 Douglas St., Homer 99603 (235-8191).

Employment Service, 601 E Pioneer Ave. #123 (235-7791). Open daily 8am-noon and 1-4:30pm.

Airport: Turn left at the beginning of the Spit. **Era Aviation,** (243-6633 or 800-426-0333). To: Anchorage ($90) and Kodiak ($250). Substantial discounts available through Kodiak Charter and hotel companies. **Homer Air** (235-8591) to: Seldovia ($26).

Buses: Homer and Seward Bus Lines, 235-8280 from Homer, 278-0800 from Anchorage. Daily to: Soldotna ($19), Kenai ($19), Anchorage ($38) and Seward ($35). Leaves Homer from 455 Sterling Hwy. and leaves Anchorage from Alaskan Samovar Inn (720 Gambell St.).

Alaska Marine Highway, P.O. Box 166, Homer 99603 (235-8449 or 800-382-9229). Ferry terminal just across the road beyond the small boat harbor. Ferry office toward the end of the Spit, on the right. Open Mon.-Fri. 10am-noon and when ferry is in. The *M/V Tustumena* sails from Homer to Cordova ($138), Seward ($96), Seldovia ($18), Kodiak ($48), and once a month to Dutch Harbor ($242).

Taxi: Chux Taxi, 235-2489. **Maggie's Taxi,** 235-2345. To downtown from the airport ($4) or ferry ($8). **Day Breeze Shuttle** (399-1168) will run you from Land's End to the Fishing Hole for $1.

Ride Line: KBBI Public Radio, AM 890. Call 235-7721 for more info.

Car Rental: Polar Car Rental, 4555 Sterling Hwy. Suite B (235-5998). $45 per day, 30¢ per mi. after 100 free mi. **National Car Rental,** at South Central Air at the airport (235-5515). $50 per day, plus 33¢ per mi. after 100 mi. Must be 21 with a credit card for both.

Bike Rental: Quiet Sports, 144 W Pioneer Ave. (235-8620). Mountain bikes $12 per 4 hrs., $20 per 24 hrs. They also have the best selection of **camping equipment** in town. Open Mon.-Fri. 10am-6pm, Sat. 10am-5pm. **Homer Rental Center** on the Spit (see below). Mountain bikes 4 hr. $10, 24 hr. $18. $50 deposit required for bike rentals.

Bookstore: The Bookstore, 436 Sterling Hwy. (235-7496) next to the Eagle Quality Center. Open Mon.-Sat. 10am-7pm, Sun. noon-5pm.

Homer Public Library, 141 Pioneer Ave. (235-3180), near Main St. Open Tues. and Thurs. 10am-8pm, Mon.,Wed., and Fri.-Sat. 10am-6pm.

Laundromat and Showers: Homer Cleaning Center, Main St. (235-5152), downtown. Wash $1.65, 5-min. dry 25¢. Last load 1 hr. before closing. 30-min. shower $2.50, towel and shampoo included. Open Mon.-Sat. 8am-9pm, Sun. 9am-8pm. **Washboard,** 1204 Ocean Dr. (235-6781), not far off the Spit, 2 doors up from Sourdough Express. Wash $1.50-2, 8-min. dry 25¢. 30-min. shower $3. Lockers and dirt-purging products. Open daily 6am-midnight; winter daily 6am-11pm. Last wash at 10:30pm, last shower at 11:30pm. **Homer Rental Center,** on the Spit (see above). Wash $2, dry $1. Shower $3.75, towel and soap included.

Women's Crisis Line: 235-8101. 24 hrs.

Hospital: South Peninsula Hospital, 4300 Bartlett (235-8101), off Pioneer.

Emergency: 911. **Police:** 235-3150.

Post Office: 3261 Wadell Rd. (235-6125), off Homer Bypass. Open Mon.-Fri. 8:30am-5pm. **General Delivery ZIP Code:** 99603.

Area Code: 907.

Surrounded by 400 million tons of coal, Homer rests on **Kachemak ("Smoky") Bay,** named after the mysteriously burning coal deposits that greeted the first settlers. Mild 20°F (-7°C) weather in January and 60°F (20°C) days in June have since earned Homer the dubious title "Banana Belt of Alaska." Homer is on the southwestern Kenai Peninsula, on the north shore of Kachemak Bay. The Sterling Hwy. links it with Anchorage (226 mi. away) and the rest of the Kenai Peninsula.

ACCOMMODATIONS AND CAMPING

The visitors center has a list of bed and breakfasts, starting at $50 per night. Contact them at P.O. Box 541, Homer (235-7740), for further information. Homer's closest approximation to a hostel, the **Seaside Farm,** lies in the meadows outside of town, on East End Rd. Of Homer's two **municipal campgrounds,** one is in town and one is on the Spit. Most budget travelers choose the oceanfront locale and become "Spit rats." Town camping and Spit camping are governed by different sets of rules.

Seaside Farm, 58335 East End Rd. (235-7850), by the shore, 4½ mi. out. Equestrian Bed and Breakfast with bunks for backpackers ($12 with shower). Tentsites $6, showers an additional $3. Kitchens also available.

Ocean Shores Motel, 3500 Crittendon (235-7775), off Sterling Hwy. One block from downtown. Fair to excellent mountain and ocean views, depending on the room. Singles from $50, in winter from $35. Tentsites $3, including a shower. Badminton, bonfires, croquet and horseshoes. Yippee!

Driftwood Inn, 135 W Bunnell (235-8019), a short walk from downtown. Take the Homer Bypass, turn right on Main St., then right again on Bunnell. Rustic and family-run with barbecues on the porch. Courtesy van. Singles $58. Doubles $68.

Homer Cabins, 3601 Main St. (235-6768). Seven tidy owner-built cabins, each with a flower box in the window, kitchenette, shower, and double bed. For 1-2 people $65, for 3 people $80. Weekly rates available.

Municipal Campgrounds on the Spit: Harbormaster's Office, 3735 Homer Spit Rd., across from the Fishing Hole, about 4 mi. out the spit, Homer 99603 (235-3160). *Do* camp on the beach or on the 30-acre fill north of Harbor. *Don't* camp between road and harbor, within 50 ft. of road, on private property east of road before the Harbor, between freight deck and Land's End (used for barge landings), or on beach near Spit Lagoon. Check with the office for specifics. Portable toilets at the top of each harbor ramp and in camp areas. 2 permanent city restrooms with fresh water. Pitch tents high to avoid the extremely high tides, or you may wake up in the water. Windy, but shockingly scenic. Campers can usually share a bonfire built by cannery workers in their tent enclaves. Sites $3. RVs $7. Pay next to the visitors center.

Municipal City Campground, office at Parks and Recreation Dept., City Hall, 491 E Pioneer (235-6090). Take Pioneer to Bartlett St., go uphill, and take a left at the hospital entrance on Fairview St. Water and pit toilets. Tentsites $3. RVs $7.

Kachemak Bay State Park, 7 water mi. across from the Spit (it may cost you $40-50 just to get there, by boat). Free. No facilities. For further information, contact: State of Alaska Division of Parks, Kenai area, Box 1247, Soldotna 99603. March-Oct., call 235-7024. Also, a **public use cabin** available with two separate bedrooms (each with bunks), living room, and outside water ($35 for first 4, $10 each additional person up to a total of 8). Call Soldotna State Park Headquarters (262-5581) for cabin information.

FOOD

Homer's grocery stores range from the earthy **Smoky Bay Cooperative,** 248 W Pioneer Ave. (235-7252), carrying only health food and housing an excellent lunch counter (open Mon.-Fri. 8am-8pm, Sat. 9am-6:30pm, Sun. 10am-5pm; lunch counter open daily 11am-3pm); to the 24-hr. **Eagle Quality Center,** 436 Sterling Hwy. (235-2408), a spin-off from the Carr's Chain.

On the Spit, you can usually hook or snag a salmon from the **Fishing Hole.** Buy fresh seafood for campfire cookouts directly from fishermen or at one of the large retail outlets: **The Coal Point Trading Co.,** 4306 Homer Spit Rd. (235-3877), will sell it to you raw, or vacuum-pack and deep-freeze your catch for 65¢ per lb.; or **Dragnet Fisheries,** 800 Fish Dock Rd. (235-6023). Those seeking a restaurant meal in Homer will find themselves buffeted with buffets. Five restaurants advertise reasonable all-you-can-eat specials within five blocks.

Downtown

Cafe Cups, 162 Pioneer Ave. (235-8330). A gathering place for artists and young travelers. Tasty, unusual sandwiches ($6.50-8 with salad). Espresso milkshake ($4.50). Good music; wood decor. Outdoor seating. Open daily 7am-10pm.

Fresh Sourdough Express Bakery and Coffee Shop, 1316 Ocean Dr. (235-7571), on the main drag to the Spit. Dine indoors or out on the deck, or just pick up some fresh baked goods. Try the all-you-can-eat breakfast buffet ($7.25); it includes almost everything on the breakfast menu: great sourdough rolls, organic coffee, fresh fruit, sausage gravy and biscuits, bread pudding with blueberries, and more. Filling ½-sandwiches ($3.75). Open daily 7am-10pm.

Smith's Restaurant, 412 Pioneer Avenue (235-8600). Food keeps 'em coming! Roast beef with gravy and mashed potatoes $6.75, pancake special of 2 cakes, 1 egg, 2 sausages and a fruit cup for a mere $4.25. Open daily 5am-2pm.

Pioneer Pizzeria, 265 E Pioneer Ave. (235-3663). Order the all-you-can-eat pizza dinner ($7, served 5pm-9pm), including soda and a small salad bar. Decent pizza encourages you to lose count of the slices. 8-in. personal pizza with 1 topping ($3.50). Pizza buffet 5-9pm. Open Mon. 4-11pm, Tues.-Sat. 11:30am-11pm.

Kachemak Bowl and Beachcomber's Restaurant, Lake St. and Pioneer Ave.(235-5639). A favorite with anglers, especially for breakfast. The all-you-can-eat sourdough hotcakes ($3.50) will keep you anchored all day. Features 9 flavors of milkshakes. Open daily 6am-9pm.

The Thai and Chinese Restaurant, 601 E Kachemak Center (235-7250). Food is of varying quality, but the all-you-can-eat Thai and Chinese buffet ($6) is the best of the bunch (served 11am-3pm). Much of the same fare appears again for the dinner buffet ($7, served 5-9pm). Open daily 11am-10pm. Similar lunch buffets are served for the same price at **Young's Oriental Restaurant,** 365 E Pioneer St. (235-4002) next door, and at the **Blue Dragon Chinese Restaurant,** 3798 Lake St. (235-8523) between the Homer Bypass and Pioneer Ave.

On the Spit

Glacier Drive-In, 3789 Homer Spit Rd., next to the Spit Campground. You can't drive in, but you can take it out. Cajun dog ($2.30), hamburger ($3.90) and milkshakes ($2.10). Grab a 50¢ cup of coffee. Open daily 11am-8pm.

Betty's, near the end of the Spit. A mobile provender of substantial, inexpensive Mexican meals. Bulging bean burritos ($1), black beans with rice and french bread ($2). Picnic table seating. The whole operation may pack up and roll away for the Talkeetna Bluegrass Festival during Aug.

Barb's Seafood, Steak, and Casa di Pizza, 4241 Homer Spit Rd. (235-6153). Filling entrees served with warm and buttery garlic bread. Try the spaghetti ($8) with a colossal ice cream sandwich ($2) for dessert. Ten-inch pizza ($9-10), also beer and wine. A bit chilly; bring your sweater. Open daily 11:30am-midnight.

Boardwalk Fish 'n Chips (235-7749), at the end of Cannery Row Boardwalk, across from the Harbormaster's Office. A local favorite. Halibut with chips ($7). Open daily 11:30am-10pm.

Addie's Porpoise Room, 4262 Homer Spit Rd., (235-8132). Items on the menu range from a $2.75 hot dog to a $36 steak and lobster dinner, all served up by dudes in tuxes. Open daily 5am-midnight.

SIGHTS AND EVENTS

The **Pratt Museum,** 3779 Bartlett St. (235-8635), is the best museum on the peninsula. Recently remodeled, the Pratt houses a gallery of local art and historical exhibits of Kenai artifacts. "Eclectic" doesn't quite capture it; displays range from homesteader cabins to artifacts of the Inuit and Denali peoples, and include some of the best displays of dead and living marine mammals. View the skeleton of the Bering Sea beaked whale or take part in the feeding frenzy in the salt water aquarium (fish frenzied Tues. and Fri. 4-5pm). If you're at the Pratt on a Friday afternoon, be sure to help feed the resident octopus. The museum houses a permanent exhibit on the March, 1989 Exxon *Valdez* oil spill that dumped 11 million gallons of oil into

Prince William Sound. (Open daily 10am-6pm; Oct.-April Tues.-Sun. noon-5pm. $3, seniors and students $2.)

Homer has any number of **art galleries,** such as **Homer Artists,** 202 W Pioneer (235-8944; open Tues.-Fri. 10am-6pm, Sat. 10am-5pm), and **Ptarmigan Arts,** 471 Pioneer Ave. (235-5345; open Mon.-Sat. 10am-7pm, Sun. 10am-6pm), with the work of over 40 Alaskan artists and craftspeople. The town's active theater group performs at **Pier One Theater,** P.O. Box 894 (235-7333), near the start of the buildings on the Spit. You can catch plays there on the Main Stage throughout the summer (Thurs. and Sun. at 7:15pm, Fri.-Sat. at 8:15pm; tickets $9, seniors $6, children $6, Thurs. $1 off night shows). 1994 productions included *Prelude to a Kiss, The Foreigner,* and *Steel Magnolias.* A series of other performances take place Sunday through Thursday, many featuring Homer's most famous son, Tom Bodett, of National Public Radio and Motel 6 ("We'll leave the light on for ya") fame. Check the *Homer News* for up-to-date schedules. **Homer Family Theater** (235-6728), at Main St. and Pioneer Ave., features current blockbusters and feel-good movies. Tickets are $5; get advance tickets at The Bookstore or at the door ½ hr. before showtime.

Homer never sleeps in the summer; nightlife ranges from beachcombing at low tide in the midnight summer sun to hanging out at the sourdough-filled **Salty Dawg Saloon** under the log lighthouse at the end of the Spit (open 11am-whenever, as the sign says). **Alice's Champagne Palace,** 196 Pioneer Ave. (235-7650), is a wooden barn with honky-tonk music (Tues.-Sat. from 10pm into the morning). The **Waterfront Bar,** 120 Bunnell Ave. (235-9949), has all the gritty character of its name, smoke-filled pool room and all (live music Wed.-Sat. 10pm-3am; bar open daily 1pm-5am). *Beware of the moose* crossing outside the bar with their calves in June. (No, you haven't been drinking too much.)

Since Homer is often billed as the halibut capital of the world, it should perhaps come as no surprise that a massive halibut derby is the town's most popular annual event. The **Homer Jackpot Halibut Derby,** from May 1 to Labor Day, offers prizes from $250 to $20,000 for catching the biggest fish and the tagged fish. Every year several would-be winners are left crying at the scales after they land prize-winning fish with no ticket. Tickets are available in local charter offices on the Spit; $5. The annual **Winter Carnival,** held during the first week in February, features sled dog races and snow machine competitions.

OUTDOORS

Nearly everyone who comes to Homer spends some time on the **Homer Spit.** This 5-mi. strip of sand juts into Kachemak Bay, and is home to many fishing charter services and typical boardwalk candy and ice-cream stores. The Spit is a hot-spot for in-state tourism and a magnet for scores of RVs that scream down Homer Spit Rd. Unfortunately for pedestrians and bicyclists, there is no sidewalk. The Spit is virtually devoid of any small-town charm; the complete lack of greenery and concentration of vehicles makes the area seem more like a parking lot. However, if you can get off the road to enjoy the view, it is magnificent. High winds make for great kite flying, but bring your own; no kite shop is to be found. Before you stray too far, BEWARE of strolling into the sand, especially where the city has posted warning signs. *People have been killed by being sucked into quicksand.* Near the start of the boardwalks on the bay side of the Spit, the **Fishing Hole** offers almost anyone who can hold a rod the chance to catch a salmon. A vigorous stocking program plants salmon fry in this tidal lagoon, which return years later to spawn. It's all a cruel ruse, though. The lagoon is unsuitable for spawning, and anglers manage to hook or snag most of the fish that return.The forecast in 1994 was for 5,000 king and 6,000 silver salmon.

Fleets of **halibut charters** depart from the Homer Spit daily in summer; many are run by **Central Charters** (235-7847), near the middle of the Spit's buildings. Full-day trips start at $140, varying depending on boat size and meals provided. All tackle and bait are included, and there is a refund policy for foul weather. A fishing license (3 days $15) earns you a daily one-fish limit. Scads of smaller charters, some just for touring, have offices on the boardwalks up and down the Spit. Choosing a charter, like the fishing itself, is something of a crap shoot. Although most charter companies run reputable business, there are some that strip their customers more cleanly than a filleted halibut. Check with the tourist office for a list of companies in the Homer Charter Association; not every reliable business will necessarily be a member, but those that are should be reputable. Have your 300-lb. halibut vacuum-packed and deep-frozen at **The Coal Point Trading Co.,** across the street from Central Charters (65¢ per lb.).

The easiest way to see the sloping bluffs that rise behind Homer is to cruise **Skyline Drive,** along the rim of the bluffs. Wildflowers (mostly fireweed, accompanied by scattered bunches of geranium, paintbrush, rose, etc.) bloom here from June to September. On a clear day, the view of the Kenai Mountains is unrivaled.

■ NEAR HOMER

KACHEMAK BAY

For a closer look at the Kachemak Bay and its wildlife, hike or boat into **Kachemak Bay State Park,** State of Alaska Department of Natural Resources, Pouch 7-0001, Anchorage 99510 (262-5581 in Soldotna). Contact them for park regulations and precautions. The park's trails offer the only **hiking** near Homer, and visitors' facilities are limited. A **water taxi** run by St. Augustine's Charters in Homer will bring you to the park any morning and arrange for a flexible pick-up date and time. ($40 per person round-trip with a 2-person min. For reservations call Inlet Charter at 235-6126 and ask for Seabird.) Pick up *The Kachemak Bay Park Pamphlet* at the Spit's visitors center (see Homer: Practical Information) for details on eight varied **trails.** Central Charters (235-7847) also offers **kayaking** daytrips to the Park, with equipment, guide, and lunch ($140).

One of the best natural history tours of Kachemak Bay is conducted by the nonprofit **Center for Alaskan Coastal Studies.** Their daily expedition passes by the 15,000 nesting seabirds on **Gull Island,** surveys beaches and intertidal areas, and includes discussion of Native history. For reservations, call **Rainbow Tours** (235-7272; outing from 9am-6pm; $49, seniors $39, children $20). **St. Augustine Charters,** P. O. Box 2083, (235-6126) runs a 2-3 hr. wildlife cruise including Gull Island and the south slope of Kachemak Bay ($35, under 12 $20). For $50, they will also do a drop-off and pick-up for people interested in hiking to a glacier. The drop-off/pick-up option is the same thing as the "water taxi" above. It leaves Homer at 9:30am and Kachemak at 5pm, but you do not have to return on the same day. **Kachemak Bay Adventures** (book through Central Charters at 235-7847) offers a quick $10 tour of Gull Island (departs daily at 10am, returns at 11:30am).

HALIBUT COVE

Make your visit to Halibut Cove a daytrip; camping is prohibited. **Danny J. Cruise Tours** (235-7847) leaves from the small-boat harbor in Homer for Halibut Cove daily at noon and returns at 5pm ($35 round-trip, seniors $28, children $17.50). The tour passes **Gull Island** for a close view of puffins, ptarmigans, red-legged cormorants, and other birds up from the Aleutian chain to roost for the summer. The charter stops for three hours at the artist/fishing colony of **Halibut Cove,** with its few dozen residents. Walk the raised boardwalk village to the **Experience Art Gallery** and view a collection of works by residents. Then head to the **Saltry** (296-2223), the cove's only restaurant, for lunch (open 1-9pm). Their menu offers a variety of raw and cooked fish. Try the halibut salad ($8), the chocolate cheese cake, or the nori maki ($9). The *Danny J.* also makes a daily dinner trip to the Saltry at 5pm, returning at 9pm ($17.50 round-trip). On Thursday nights the trip is half-price ($8.75); reservations are critical. Explore the octopus-ink paintings at **Diana Tillion's Cove Gallery.** Diana extracts ink from stranded octopi with a hypodermic needle, eats the octopi, and then paints with their body fluids. She and her husband were the first artists to raise a family here and begin the integration of fish and art that now characterizes Halibut Cove. **Alex Combs'** private oil gallery lies at the end of the beach in the two small red buildings.

■ ■ ■ SELDOVIA

Directly across Kachemak Bay from Homer, this small town has been virtually untouched by the tourist mania prevailing on the rest of the peninsula. The Russians named Seldovia for its herring; the fishing industry has kept the town afloat for centuries. Seldovia overlooks four active volcanoes: **Mts. Augustine, Iliamna, Redoubt,** and **Spur.**

Practical Information Synergy Artworks, 220 Main St. (234-7479), across from the boat harbor, houses the Chamber of Commerce and has visitor information, including the free and detailed **map** (open daily 10am-5pm). The **airport** is about a mi. out of town on Airport Ave. Seldovia is served by **Homer Air** (235-8591; to: Homer $25.50, $46.50 round-trip) and **Great Northern Airlines** (800-243-1968; to: Anchorage, $88). The **ferry** *M/V Tustumena* runs between Homer and Seldovia several times per week ($32 round-trip). You have the choice of spending either a few hours (while the *Tustumena* refuels) or two days (until the next ferry arrives) in Seldovia. Once in town, the **Seldovia Taxi** (234-7841; open 8:30am-1am) will shuttle you about, or you can rent a bike at **The Buzz,** on the harbor side of Stamper's Market on Main St. (234-7479). Cost is $10 for half-day (6am-noon or noon-6pm), $15 for full day (6am-6pm) or $20 for 24 hrs. They also rent fishing tackle for $15 per day (open daily 6am-6pm). **Lost Horizon Books,** 235 Main St. (234-7679), has a surprisingly good selection of rare and out-of-print texts (open Mon.-Sat. 10am-5pm, Sun. noon-5pm). The **Magistrate Library,** on Seldovia St. near Main St., is less amply endowed (open Tues. 2:30-4:30pm and 7:30-9:30pm, Thurs. 3:30-6pm and 7:30-9:30pm, Sat. 11:30am-4:30pm). The phone at the **Seldovia Clinic** is 234-7825; in an **emergency** call 911. The **police** can be reached at 234-7640. Call the **firehall** at 234-7812. The **post office** is at the corner of Main St. and Seldovia St. (234-7831) and is open Mon.-Fri. 9am-5pm. The general delivery **ZIP Code** is 99663; the **area code** is 907.

Accommodations, Camping, and Food Simple rooms are available at the **Seldovia Lodge,** at the corner of Young and Anderson St. (234-7654). The lodge resembles a barn, but the rooms are cheap, relatively tidy, with TV and private baths. (Singles $36. Doubles $43.) In town, you can dish out the dough to stay at **Annie's McKenzie's Boardwalk Hotel** (234-7816 or 800-238-7862; singles $68, doubles $88). The Chamber of Commerce keeps a list of Seldovia's B&Bs, most of which cost $60-85 (234-7479). The camp manager may or may not come to collect the $5 tent fee; good citizens can pay in person at the city office (234-7643). RV camping is available for $8 at **Wilderness Park,** as are additional and more secluded tent spots for $5. The Park is approximately ½ mi. past the marked turnout for Outside Beach on Anderson Way. **Stamper's Market,** on Main St. (234-7633), stocks a modest supply of groceries, hardware, tackle, pharmaceuticals and liquor (open Mon.-Sat. 9am-8pm, Sun. noon-6pm). Hot, clean showers are available at the **Harbor Laundromat,** also on Main St. (234-7420; cost $4, towel and soap included; laundry is $3 to wash, $1.50 to dry). The laundromat doubles as an ice cream stand that dishes up $1.75 cones and $3.50 milkshakes (open daily 10am-8pm).

The cheapest eats in town are at the **Seaport Sandwich Shop,** next to the Harbormaster overlooking the harbor (234-7483). A $3.50 turkey sandwich, $2 slice of lukewarm pizza, and a $1.50 taco can be chomped on their outside deck (open daily noon-8pm). If the elements require inside dining, the towns two restaurants are relatively satisfying, but put a large dent in the wallet. **The Kachemak Cafe** (234-7494) serves up burgers form $5-6.75, and cold sandwiches $3.75-7). A short stack is $3.50 (open daily 7am-5pm, Fri. night is "pizza night" 5pm-8pm). **The Buzz** (234-7479) serves coffee and espresso and provides a good place to loiter on a rainy afternoon.

The cappucino ($2) and raspberry rhubarb tart ($2.75) is a delectable combination (open daily 6am-6pm).

Sights and Entertainment Stop by the small **museum,** 206 Main St. (234-7625), sponsored by the Seldovia Native Association (open Mon.-Fri. 8am-5pm). On a hill overlooking the water, the beautiful **St. Nicholas Orthodox Church** was built in 1891 (open daily 1-2pm).

The **Otterbahn Hiking Trail,** starting at the Susan B. English School and winding 1.15 miles to Outside Beach, takes you up to a small lighthouse perched above cliffs that plunge into the bay. On a clear day, the **view** of the volcanoes is magnificent. There is also a 6-mi. hike up the bay on Dirt Rd.; consult the **Seldovia Map** on how to get there. If the weather chases you inside, you can stop at the **Berry Kitchen Museum/Gift Shop,** 328 Main St. Seldovia Native Association Building (234-7898). Ask for a sample of their superb blueberry jam (open daily 11am-5pm). Across the street, you can scale a hill to the beautiful **St. Nicholas Orthodox Church,** built in 1891. Although the doors are usually locked, the view of the harbor is fabulous. If getting back to nature grows stale (shame on you!), you can head to the **Knightspot** (234-7882) or **Linwood Bar** (234-7857) in town, or to the bar at the **Seldovia Lodge** for a cold one.

Seldovia triples in size on **Independence Day.** The old-fashioned celebration draws hundreds of visitors from all over the peninsula and includes parades, log-rolling, the 5K "Salmon Shuffle" race, horseshoe tournament, greased pole climbing, and a pancake feed at the Fire Hall.

KODIAK ISLAND

Kodiak Island is both astonishingly beautiful and the victim of amazingly hard luck. In this century, Kodiak has been rocked by earthquakes, washed over by tsunamis, hit by the oil of the Exxon *Valdez,* and blanketed in nearly 2 ft. of volcanic ash. Rain falls 180 days per year. It doesn't bother the wildlife, however; the island shelters the **Kodiak National Wildlife Refuge,** home to about 2600 Kodiak brown bears. The refuge's 800 mi. of coastline ring the island's sharp peaks. As for Kodiak's human population, the rich waters around the island have made its fishing and crabbing fleet the state's most productive, drawing flocks of young people each summer to work its canneries. Islanders here take their seafood seriously. The fishing is excellent, and the island is (thankfully) not yet a tourist hot spot.

■■■ KODIAK

Kodiak was the first capital of Russian Alaska before Alexander Baranov moved the Russian-American Company headquarters to Sitka. While the glittering ladies of St. Petersburg achieved a new level of fur-fashion opulence, the Russians enslaved the Aleut people to hunt Kodiak Island's sea otters to near extinction.

Mt. Katmai, on the other hand, is anything but extinct. It erupted in 1912, covering Kodiak Island with 18 in. of ash and obliterating much of the area's wildlife; ash remains in the forests. In 1964, the biggest earthquake (9.2 on the Richter Scale) ever recorded in North America shook the area, creating a tsunami that destroyed much of downtown Kodiak and causing $24 million in damage. The swamped fishing port was rehabilitated by the Army Corps of Engineers and local resourcefulness; one 200-ft. vessel, *The Star of Kodiak,* was cemented into the ferry dock and converted into a cannery.

PRACTICAL INFORMATION AND ORIENTATION

Visitors Information: Kodiak Island Convention and Visitors Bureau, 100 Marine Way, (486-4782; fax 486-6545), in front of the ferry dock. Hunting and fishing information, charter arrangements, and a **map.** Open Mon.-Fri. 8am-5pm, Sat. 10am-3pm, and for most ferry arrivals; winter Mon.-Fri. 8am-noon. **Fish and Wildlife Service and Visitor Center,** 1390 Bustkin River Rd. (487-2600), just outside Buskin State Recreation Site, 4 mi. southwest of town. Wildlife displays, 150 films, and information on the Kodiak National Wildlife Refuge and its cabins. Open Mon.-Fri. 8am-4:30pm, Sat.-Sun. noon-4:30pm.

State Department of Parks: SR Box 3800, Kodiak, AK 99615; 1200 Abercrombie Dr. at Fort Abercrombie (486-6339). Has information on local state parks and campgrounds. Open Mon.-Fri. 8am-noon and 1-4:30pm.

Sport Fishing Division: Alaska Department of Fish and Game, Box 686, Kodiak, at 211 Mission Rd. (486-1880). Information on regulations and seasons.

Employment: Alaska State Employment Service, 309 Center St. (486-3105), in Kodiak Plaza. Open Mon.-Fri. 8am-4:30pm.

Airport: 4 mi. southwest of town on Rezanof Dr. Served by **Mark Air** (487-9798 at the airport, 800-627-5247). To: Anchorage ($97); to Homer ($149).

Alaska Marine Highway: Terminal next to the visitors center (800-642-0066; fax 486-6166 or 486-3800). The *Tustumena* docks in Kodiak May-Sept., 1 to 3 times per week; in winter less frequently. To: Homer ($48); Seward ($54); Valdez ($98); Cordova ($98). Five-day run to Dutch Harbor once every month ($202). Terminal open Mon.-Fri. 8am-5pm and when boats are in.

Car Rental: Rent-A-Heap (486-5200), at the Mark Air terminal. $27 per day and 27¢ per mi. Open daily 7am-7pm. **National Car Rental,** 122 Rezanof Dr. (487-4435). $39 per day; unlimited mileage. Must be 25 with a credit card.

Taxis: A&B Taxi, 486-4343. $3 plus $2 per mi. $13.40 to the airport. 24 hrs.

Bike Rental: Elkay Bicycle Shop, 118 Rezanof (486-4219), across from Kraft's. 4 hrs., $10; 8 hrs. $15; 24 hrs. $25; weekend $45. Open Mon.-Sat. 10am-6pm.

Camping and Fishing Equipment: Mack's Sports Shop, 117 Lower Mill Bay (486-4276), at the end of Center Ave. Open Mon.-Sat. 7am-7pm, Sun. 9am-5pm. **Cy's Sporting Goods,** 202 Shelikof St.(486-3900) near the harbor. Open Mon.-Sat. 8am-7pm, Sun. 10am-5pm.

Bookstore: Shire Bookstore, 104 Center Ave. (486-8680) the alley beside Kraft's Grocery (see below). Open Mon.-Sat. 9:30am-7pm, Sun. 1-5pm.

Library: 319 Lower Mill Bay Rd. Has a **courtesy phone** for free local calls. Open Mon.-Fri. 10am-9pm, Sat. 10am-5pm, Sun. 1-5pm.

Laundromat and showers: Ernie's, 218 Shelikof (486-4119), across from the harbor. Wash $2, 4-min. dry 25¢. 20-min. shower $4. Drop-off available. Open daily 8am-8pm. Last shower 7:30pm, last wash 6:30pm.

Weather: Local forecasts, 487-4313. **Marine forecasts,** 487-4949. When in doubt, expect rain; it falls one day out of two.

Pharmacy: Wodlinger Drug and Photo (486-4035), 312 Marine Way, across from the harbormaster. Pharmacy open Mon.-Fri. 10am-6pm. Store open Mon.-Sat. 9:30am-6:30pm, Sun. noon-4pm

Hospital: Kodiak Island Hospital, 1915 E Rezanof Dr. (486-3281).

Women's Crisis Line: 486-3625, 422 Hillside Dr.

Emergency: 911. **Police:** 217 Lower Mill Bay Rd., 486-8000.

Fire: 219 Lower Mill Bay Rd., 486-8040

Post Office: 419 Lower Mill Bay Rd. (486-4721). Open Mon.-Fri. 9am-5:30pm, Sat. 10am-1pm. **General Delivery ZIP Code:** 99615. Substations in **Kraft's Grocery,** 111 Rezanof, and **Safeway,** 2685 Mill Bay Rd. Open Mon.-Sat. 10am-6pm. **Area Code:** 907.

The city of Kodiak is on the eastern tip of Kodiak Island, 100 mi. off the Kenai Peninsula and roughly 200 mi. south of Homer. Kodiak Island is about the size of Connecticut. One hundred mi. of rutted gravel roads follow the scenic coastlines north and south of the city.

ACCOMMODATIONS AND CAMPING

Kodiak is a good place to check out the local B&Bs. Call the visitors center (see Practical Information) for a list and remember to reserve in advance; finding a room

K
O
D
I
A
K

becomes almost impossible when, as often happens, the airport shuts down due to bad weather.

Backpackers can head for **Gibson Cove,** 2 mi. west off Kodiak on Rezanof. Built by the city for transient cannery workers, Gibson Cove looks and feels like a gravel parking lot and stinks of fish, but at $2 per night with free hot showers, who can quibble? If you can't deal, 2 mi. farther off Rezanof is the prettier and less fishy **Buskin River Recreation Area.**

Shelikof Lodge, 211 Thorsheim Ave. (486-4141; fax 486-4116), a small street to the right of McDonald's. Comfortable rooms with cable TV. Courtesy van to the airport. Singles $60. Doubles $65.

Star Motel, 119 Yukon St. (486-5657), a small street to the left of McDonald's. Twenty-five dimly-lit rooms brightened by color TV's, some have refrigerators. Singles $55. Doubles $60 with a $5 key deposit.

Gibson Cove Campground (Tent City), 2 mi. from ferry terminal. From terminal take Center St. to Rezanof and turn left. 45 tentsites. Transient-worker community can get rowdy; bypass the main lot and head for the trails that lead to wooded sites to avoid most of the riff-raff. Friendly on-site manager. Raised gravel platforms for tents, hot showers, toilets, drinking water. No max. stay. Sites $2, vehicles an additional $3. Open May 16-Sept. 14.

Buskin River State Recreation Site, 4½ mi. southwest of the city (486-6339). Water and pit toilets, RV dumpstation, 18 sites. Over 50% of Kodiak's sport fish is caught on the Bushkin River. 14-night max. stay. Sites $6.

Fort Abercrombie State Park Campground, 4 mi. northeast of town on Rezanof-Monashka Rd. (486-6339). Water, shelters, and toilets. No RV hookups; designed for backpackers. WWII ruins, a trout-fishing lake, and spectacular sunsets. **Pasagshak State Recreation Site,** 40 mi. from the city at the mouth of the Pasagshak River (486-6339), which reverses direction 4 times daily with the tides. Water and toilets. Noted for king salmon fishing. 14-day max. stay. 7 sites. Free.

FOOD

No, the Russians didn't build the enormous **Safeway,** 2 mi. from town at 2685 Mill Bay Rd. (486-6811). Besides cheap groceries and a wide selection of produce, the store houses a popular **Chinese deli** (store open daily 6am-midnight). Other markets in town include **Kraft's Grocery,** 111 Rezanof (486-5761, open daily 7am-midnight) and **Cactus Flats Natural Foods,** 338 Mission St. (open Mon.-Sat. 10am-6pm). Hobgoblins of mass culture can always trudge to **McDonald's,** at Rezanof and Lower Mill Bay Rd. (486-3030, open daily 6am-11pm), **Subway,** at 326 Center Ave.(486-7676, open Mon.-Sat. 11am-midnight, Sun. 11am-11pm), or **Pizza Hut,** 2625 Mill Bay Rd. in front of Safeway.

El Chicano, 103 Center Ave. (486-6116), in the building across from the Orpheum Theater. Some of the best and biggest Mexican specialties north of the border. Try a bowl of black-bean soup with homemade Mexican bread ($4.75) or a filling burrito ($4.75-7.25). Complimentary corn chips and hot salsa, ¡ole! Open Mon.-Sat. 11am-10pm, Sun. 4-9pm.

Fox Inn, 211 Thorsheim (486-4300), a windowless room in the Shelikof Lodge. Locals rave about the Fox's straightforward American fare. Half sandwich with soup or salad ($4.50). Bowl of chili ($3.50), chicken pasta ($6.50). Open Mon.-Sat. 7am-9:30pm, Sun. 8am-9pm.

Beryl's, 202 Center Ave. (486-3323), to the right of the First National Bank of Anchorage. $5.45 sandwiches, a variety of ice cream and sweets. Try a pineapple milkshake ($2.50). Open Mon.-Fri. 7:30am-6pm, Sat. 10am-6pm, Sun. noon-5pm.

Henry's Sports Cafe (486-8844), in the mall on Marine Way. Surprisingly swank for Kodiak, with a circular bar and shaded lamps, but the sandwich prices remain within the realm of reason. Chili dog and fries $4.25, burgers $6-8. Open Mon.-Thurs. 11am-11pm, Fri.-Sat. 11am-midnight, Sun. noon-10pm.

Sizzler Burger and Peking Chinese Restaurant, 116 W Rezanof (486-3300). Eat a weekday lunch for the sweet and sour pork, soup, wonton, and rice ($5.50; served 11:30am-2:30pm). Open Mon.-Sat. 11:30am-10pm, Sun. noon-10pm.

SIGHTS AND EVENTS

Built in 1808 as a storehouse for sea-otter pelts, the **Baranov Museum,** 101 Marine Way (486-5920), is the oldest Russian structure standing in Alaska. The museum displays Russian and traditional Alaskan artifacts, and a library displays period photos and literature ranging from the Russian period to the present. (Open Mon.-Fri. 10am-4pm, Sat.-Sun. noon-4pm; Labor Day- Jan. and March-Memorial Day Mon.-Wed., Fri. 11am-3pm, Sat. noon-3pm. $2, under 12 free.) The **Resurrection Russian Orthodox Church** (486-3854), not far from the museum, houses the oldest parish in Alaska. Built in 1794, its elaborate ikons date back to the early 19th century, and its church bells are still rung by hand (open Mon.-Fri. 1-3pm).

Several interesting sights in Kodiak make little effort at self-promotion. The **Alutiiq Culture Center,** 214 W Rezanof Dr. (486-1992), displays archaeological treasures from recent digs around the island and a model of a communal Alutiiq dwelling (open Mon.-Fri. 10am-5pm; free). The **Kodiak Alutiiq Dancers** perform (May 1-Sept. 30 Mon.-Sat. at 3:30pm) at the **Kodiak Tribal Council Barabara,** 713 Rezanof Dr. Tickets cost $15 (486-3524). **St. Herman's Seminary** (486-3524), up the hill from the double-domed church on Mission St., contains a small collection of ikons, clothing, and Aleut prayer books for viewing (open Mon.-Fri. 1-3pm). Across the bridge on Near Island, engineers at the **Fisheries Industry Technology Center,** 900 Trident Way, rack their brains trying to invent new mass-marketable fish foods. Stop by to tour their laboratories and sample tomorrow's fish products (open Mon.-Fri. 8am-5pm; call to arrange a tour).

For information on the **Frank Brink Amphitheater,** on Minashka Bay, write the Kodiak Arts Council, P.O. Box 1792, Kodiak, or call them at 486-5291. Meanwhile, you can count on first-run films at the **Orpheum Theater** (486-5449), on Center St. (tickets $5, balcony seats $6).

Beautiful **Fort Abercrombie State Park** (486-6339), 3½ mi. north of town, was the site of the first secret radar installation in Alaska (shhh!). The fort is also the site of a WWII defense installation; after Attu and Kiska in the Aleutian chain were attacked and occupied by the Japanese in 1942, American military minds assumed that Kodiak would be the next target. Bunkers and other reminders of the Alaskan campaign remain, including an old naval station 6½ mi. southwest of Kodiak.

The six-day **Kodiak Crab Festival,** held just before Memorial Day, celebrates a bygone industry with parades, fishing derbies, kayak and crab races, and a blessing of the fleet. The event culminates with the **Chad Obden Ultramarathon,** a super-human race along 42 mi. of hilly roads from Chiniak to Kodiak. **St. Herman's Days** (486-3524), held August 7-9, celebrates the first saint of the Russian Orthodox Church in North America (canonized 1970). On one of these days, depending on the weather, visitors are welcome to join the faithful in an annual pilgrimage to St. Herman's former home on Spruce Island. The Thursday evening service at the Resurrection Church also relates a narrative of the life of St. Herman. The **State Fair and Rodeo,** beginning in early September, includes crafts and livestock.

OUTDOORS

The sheer number of fish in the island's rivers and surrounding waters can send you reeling. The 100-mi. road system permits access to good **salmon streams.** Right in Kodiak, surfcasting into Mill Bay around high tide often yields a pink or silver salmon. **Red salmon,** running from early June to early August, appear in the Buskin and Pasagshak Rivers along the road system. **Pink salmon** run up the Buskin, Russian, American, and Olds Rivers in astounding numbers from July 20 to August 20. Better-tasting but scarcer **silver salmon** run up the same rivers from about August 20 into September. **Dolly varden,** the most frequently hooked fish on Kodiak, may be taken year-round from the Pasagshak and Buskin Rivers.

On a clear day, **hikers** can obtain a commanding view stretching from the Kenai Peninsula to the Aleutian Peninsula atop **Barometer Mountain.** To reach the trailhead, take the first right past the end of the airport runway on the way out of town. After passing through thick alders, the trail climbs steadily and steeply along a grassy ridge, marked by several false peaks, before arriving at the summit. Most hikers require about two hours to reach the top, and they usually descend in half that time. The trail up **Pyramid Mountain,** beginning from the parking lot at the pass on Anton Larsen Bay Rd., is another popular hike near town.

Guided **sea kayaking trips** are a great way to experience the natural wonders that Kodiak has to offer. You can come eye-to-eye with sea otters, puffins, and bald eagles, even view the giant Kodiak bear from a comfortable distance. **Wavetamer,** P.O. Box 228 (486-2604), offers two-hour tours of Near Island and Mill Bay ($35) and a four-hour coastal kayak trek for $65. All gear is provided, and there is a 2-person minimum for the two- and four-hour trips. Two-hour tours are available daily; all others Friday through Sunday only.

A large **bison herd** roams a private ranch at the end of Rezanof Hwy. at the southeast tip of Kodiak near Ugak Island. The animals were transplanted to Kodiak and have managed to defend themselves against marauding brown bears; imported cattle herds have not fared so well.

If you have a vehicle, the 42-mi. coastal drive to Chiniak offers the chance to see beautiful seascapes with small coastal islands muted in fog (and dozens of mufflers lying along the j-j-jarringly rough road). If the potholes haven't rearranged your dental work, stop in for a deluxe high-rise hamburger with fries ($5) at the **Road's End Restaurant and Bar,** 42 Roads End in Chiniak. They also serve a generous grilled-cheese sandwich with fries ($3.50) and premier pies ($3.50 per slice) of many varieties (open Tues.-Wed. 2-10pm, Thurs.-Sun. noon-10pm).

Shuyak Island State Park, an undeveloped area with ample hunting, fishing, and kayaking, lies 54 mi. north of Kodiak. The park rents four **cabins,** each with room for two to six people ($50 per night; winter $30 per night). Reserve in advance at the Division of Parks and Outdoor Recreation, SR Box 3800, Kodiak (486-6339), or call for more information.

KODIAK NATIONAL WILDLIFE REFUGE

The Wildlife Refuge, on the western half of Kodiak Island, includes two-thirds of Kodiak Island. Kodiak bears share the island with a variety of other mammals and several hundred bald eagles. The bears are most commonly seen in July and August during their fishing frenzy. They hibernate from December to April, bearing cubs in February and March. Though the bears are omnivorous and usually avoid contact with humans, be careful: Kodiaks are the largest and most powerful bears in North America, and they can and do kill humans. Because of the bears' relatively small numbers, hunters are permitted to kill only one Kodiak bear apiece every four years.

Other mammals native to the area are red foxes, land otters, weasels, tundra moles, and little brown bats. Deer, snowshoe hares, beavers, muskrats, Dall sheep, mountain goats, and red squirrels have been transplanted from other parts of the state to Kodiak. The refuge's 800-mi. coastline is home to thousands of waterfowl and about 20 seabird species. Off the coast, whales, porpoises, seals, sea otters, and sea lions frolic.

About the only affordable way to reach the refuge is to join a scheduled **Mark Air** (487-9798) mail run to any of the several small villages scattered throughout the wilderness. Although stopovers cost extra and are brief, the aerial view is stunning. The flights to Karluk and Larsen Bay ($60) and to Old Harbor ($50) are two of the best. Both routes are flown frequently; call for schedules and information. For information about the park, contact the **Kodiak National Wildlife Refuge Managers,** 1390 Buskin River Rd., Kodiak 99615 (487-2600). If you're in Kodiak, drop by the **Fish and Wildlife Headquarters and Visitor Center** (see Practical Information).

PRINCE WILLIAM SOUND

■■■ WHITTIER

Flanked by massive glaciers and waterfalls, Whittier is surrounded by natural beauty. This gorgeous setting cannot compensate for the town, a prime example of human-kind's ability to scar its environment. Over half of the population lives in the hulking 14-story Begich Towers; the other eyesore is the deserted Buckner Building, once an Army outpost. The harbor area is the most pleasant place in town, home to the res-taurants and boats and the exit to **Portage** via the Alaska Railroad. Whittier is a stra-tegically-located port of transfer; frequent rail and ferry connections won't strand you in Whittier for long.

Practical Information The **Visitors Center,** P.O. Box 604 (472-2329), is in the center of town, slyly camouflaged in a refurbished railroad car next to the tracks. Get information on hiking, boating, camping, or fishing (open daily 11am-6:30pm). Get information on how to leave Whittier from the **Alaska Railroad,** P.O. Box 107500, Anchorage, AK 99501 (800-544-0552 or 265-2494; 265-2607 record-ing), running four to six trips between Whittier and Portage daily ($13). From Por-tage, catch an **Alaska Backpacker Shuttle** (344-8775) bus that runs between Portage and Anchorage ($17.50). Call ahead for pickup and drop-off. To leave by water, call the **Alaska Marine Highway** (472-2378; fax 472-2381), ½ mi. east of town, by the small boat harbor. Ferries run to Valdez ($58) and Cordova ($36).

If you must stay in Whittier, rent a kayak at **Prince William Sound Kayak Center** (562-2866 or 472-2452), at Billings and Glacier St. Single boats are $40 per day; dou-bles $60 per day, including shuttles and all necessary equipment. Call and leave a message to arrange a rental. Until the train to Portage arrives, kill time at the **library,** on the 2nd floor of the Begich Towers (472-2406; open Tues. 10am-noon and 2-5pm, Wed.-Thurs. 2-5pm and 7-9pm, Sat. 11am-4pm). Wash clothes at the Begich Towers. A wash costs $1.50; a dry, 25¢ (open daily 10am-midnight). Take a **shower** at the Harbormaster Office (472-2320), in the small boat harbor. Spend $3 for a 17½-min. pressure-wash (open Sun.-Tues. and Fri.-Sat. 8am-9pm, Wed.-Thurs. 8am-5pm).

There are trained EMTs in Whittier, but **no doctor** or full-time clinic. A **part-time medical clinic** is in Begich Towers Apt. 302 (472-2303; open Thurs.-Mon. 10am-6pm). Over-the-counter **pharmaceuticals** are available at the Anchor Inn Grocery (472-2354). The **emergency** number is 911. Reach the **police** at 472-2340; in case of **fire,** call 472-2560. The **post office** (472-2552) is on the 1st floor of Begich Towers (open Mon., Wed., and Fri. 11:30am-5:30pm). The **General Delivery ZIP Code** is 99693. The **area code** is 907.

Whittier, Portage, Billings, and Maynard Glaciers surround Whittier, 63 mi. south-east of Anchorage and 105 mi. west of Valdez. At the head of nearby College Fjord, **Harvard and Yale Glaciers** loom. Harvard Glacier is, of course, larger than its sec-ond-rate neighbor, proof that even in Alaska they know what's what. Indeed, Yale Glacier is widely regarded as generally a poor excuse for a glacier and an embarrass-ment to Harvard Glacier. Like other towns in the Sound, Whittier is no stranger to rain. More than 21 ft. drips on this soggy hamlet each year.

Accommodations, Camping, Food, and Sights Avoid spending any more time than necessary in Whittier. Make train reservations to Portage before you arrive. Hotels are expensive. If you must spend the night, there is one public camp-ground in Whittier, the **Whittier Campgrounds,** behind Begich Towers next to the Whittier Glacier Falls. It has limited facilities, including water and toilets. Don't keep food in your tent; the summer bear trail passes right through camp. Take showers at the Harbormaster Office (see Practical Information). Sites are $5 on the honor sys-tem; no maximum stay.

Whittier's few restaurants offer standard Alaskan fare at standard Alaskan prices. The **Anchor Inn** (472-2354) is the best place to buy groceries, and your best chance to get your hands on a recent magazine. Don't hold out for a bargain: a box of cereal can run a nightmarish $6.35! Babs, the piemaker at the **Hobo Bay Trading Company** (472-2374; open Wed.-Mon. 11am-7pm), in the Harbor Area, presides over a political salon that doubles as a first-rate short-order restaurant. A ray of sunshine in this otherwise dreary town, she creates the most welcoming atmosphere in Whittier. Try a hearty taco ($2.50) or a piece of fresh baked pie with ice cream ($4). For a tasty sandwich ($6.50) or Arctic Lox bagel ($3.50) to take with you on the train or boat, go to **Cafe Orca & Bakery** (472-2496; open Mon.-Fri. 6am-7pm, Sat.-Sun. 8am-7pm) in the Triangle by the ferry. For dessert, have espresso cake ($2.25).

Your best chance for amusement is to quickly pack off to the beautiful areas that surround the town. **Hiking** opportunities abound; the best day hike climbs the 4½-mi. **Portage Pass Trail** to the stunning Portage Glacier overlook. To reach the trailhead, take W Camp Rd. out of town along the railroad tracks and cross the tracks toward the airstrip; the trail forks off to the left.

■■■ VALDEZ

During the Klondike gold rush in 1897-98, Valdez (val-DEEZ) was the trailhead of the tortuous "all-American route" to the Klondike (other overland routes passed mainly through Canada). Ironically, Valdez today is a terminus of wealth, rather than the start of the trail for goldpanners. The Trans-Alaska Pipeline deposits its "black gold" into waiting oil tankers at the port.

Whether approached by land or sea, the scenery on the journey into Valdez is as beautiful as any in the state. Plummeting into Valdez, the Richardson Hwy. passes by the face of a glacier, through a canyon, and beside two high waterfalls. Coming into Valdez by boat, the trip across Prince William Sound leads past the immense **Columbia Glacier.** Nearly every spot in this busy port affords a gorgeous alpine view. Valdez is the only town on Prince William Sound linked by road to the rest of Alaska, and opponents of road-building projects in Cordova and Whittier often build their case around the example of the town's excess of RVs; in the harbor, camera-toting tourists mingle with iron-tough fishermen while cannery workers huddle under the blue tarp atop the harbor bluff.

The infamous Exxon *Valdez* oil spill of March 1989 despoiled the shores, fouled the water, and killed wildlife only a few mi. away from Valdez, although you won't see much evidence of the disaster in the town itself. The mayor of Valdez appeared in a series of television commercials in 1991 to promote the overestimated success of Exxon's cleanup. To obtain the most thorough, impartial, and up-to-date information on the spill and the ongoing clean-up measures, contact **APLIC** (Alaska Public Lands Information Center) in Anchorage (see page 73).

PRACTICAL INFORMATION AND ORIENTATION

Visitors Information: Valdez Convention and Visitors Bureau, P.O. Box 1603 (800-874-2749 or 835-2984), at Fairbanks and Chenega St. Information on sights, accommodations, hiking, and camping. Shows "Though the Earth Be Moved," a classic film about the devastating 1964 earthquake, daily every ½ hr. 9am-7pm. $2.50. Open daily in summer 8am-8pm; winter Mon.-Fri. 8:30am-5pm. Free local phone. **Parks and Recreation Hotline:** 835-2555.

Job Service (835-4910 or 800-495-5627), on Meals Ave., in the State Office Bldg. Information on working canneries in Valdez. Open Mon.-Fri. 8am-noon and 1-4:30pm.

Fishing Information: Alaska Dept. of Fish and Game, 310 Egan Dr., (835-4307). Booming canneries in Valdez attest to the abundance of fish in the Valdez Arm.

Telegrams: Western Union (800-325-6000), at Eagle Quality Center. Open 7am-midnight.

Airport: Valdez Airport, 4 mi. out of town off Richardson Hwy. Serviced by **Mark Air** (800-478-0800) and **Alaska Airlines,** 800-426-0333. Both airlines fly to Anchorage 4 times daily. Fares identical. To: Anchorage ($79).

Buses: Alaskon Express (800-544-2206) runs from the Westmark Hotel in Valdez to Anchorage daily ($59).

Alaska Marine Highway, P.O. Box 647 (835-4436), in the City Dock at the end of Hazelet Ave. To: Whittier ($58); Cordova ($30); and Seward ($58). Whittier run makes a stop at Columbia Glacier.

Taxis: Valdez Yellow Cab, 835-2500. The 4-mi. trip to airport will cost you $7, each additional person $1.

Car Rental: Valdez-U-Drive, P.O. Box 852 (835-4402), at the airport. $35 per day; 25¢ per mi. after 100 mi. Rates fluctuate. **Avis** (800-835-4774), also at the airport. $42 per day for a compact; unlimited mileage. Open daily 6:30am-10:15pm.

Camping Supplies: The Prospector (835-3858), beside the post office on Galena Dr. One of the best places in the state. Immense supply of clothing, shoes, tarps, freeze-dried food, and fishing tackle. Open Mon.-Sat. 8am-10pm, Sun. 9am-6pm.

Kayak Rental: Keystone Raft and Kayak Adventure, P.O. Box 1486 (835-2606), at Pioneer and Hazelet. Valdez is within easy reach of superb whitewater, with class II, III, and IV rapids. 1-hr. trip $30, daytrip $65. Make reservations at least 1 day in advance. **Anady Adventures** (835-2814), on South Harbor Dr. Guided daytrips begin at $140. Single kayak $45 per day. 3-hr. tours $52. Damage deposit ($200-300) and a 90-min. orientation class ($10) required.

Bike Rental: (835-3773) Directly behind Anady Adventures, the camera and gift shop has bikes for rent ($5 per hr., $30 per day). Must have credit card. Open daily in summer 9am-9pm; winter 10am-7pm).

Library: 200 Fairbanks Dr. Open Mon. 10am-6pm, Tues.-Thurs. 10am-8pm, Fri. 10am-6pm, Sat. noon-6pm.

Laundromat: Like Home Laundromat, 110 Egan (835-2913). Wash $1.50, 7-min. dry 25¢. Open daily 8am-9pm.

Public Showers: $3 for 10 min. at the Harbormaster, or you can cough up another $1 and go to **Bear Paw RV Park** (see below). You'll get a spotlessly clean private bathroom with sink, etc., plus all the time you want.

Weather: 766-2491. Live from the National Weather Service, Valdez.

Crisis Line: 835-2999. 24 hrs.

Pharmacy: Valdez Drug and Photo, 321 Fairbanks Dr. (835-4956). Open Mon.-Fri. 9am-9pm, Sat. 9am-6pm, Sun. noon-5pm.

Hospital: Valdez Community Hospital, 911 Meals Ave. (835-2249).

Emergency/Ambulance: 911. **Police:** 835-4560.

Post Office: 835-4449, at Galena St. and Tatitlek St. Open Mon.-Fri. 9am-5pm, Sat. 10am-noon. **General Delivery ZIP Code:** 99686.

Area Code: 907.

Valdez lies 304 mi. east of Anchorage at the head of the Valdez Arm, in the northeast corner of Prince William Sound. From Valdez, the spectacular **Richardson Hwy.** runs north to Glenallen, where it intercepts the Glenn Hwy. to Anchorage and Tok.

ACCOMMODATIONS AND CAMPING

The **South Harbor Dr. Campground,** home to many of Valdez's transient cannery workers, is also the cheapest place for transient budget travelers. The Visitors Bureau (see Practical Information) also lists over 70 bed and breakfasts, generally charging about $65 for singles and $75 for doubles (about $30 less than a hotel room). The **free reservation center** (835-4988) for Valdez will set you up with bed and breakfasts, glacier tours, rafting trips, helicopter tours, etc. "One call does it all."

South Harbor Drive Campground (835-2531), on S Harbor Dr., overlooking the small boat harbor. This campground occupies a prime location on a bluff overlooking town, but the hard gravel surface and late-night expletives exchanged between the cannery workers may sour your sleep. 50 sites with wooden tent platforms, water, and pit toilets. Sites $6, collected in an honor box.

Valdez Glacier Campground (835-2531), 5½ mi. east of town on the Richardson Hwy., 1½ mi. past the airport. Look for small sign on left. 110 campsites, first-come, first-served. Amazing view of the Valdez glacier. On the site of Old Valdez, destroyed in the 1964 earthquake, this campground is difficult to reach without a car or bicycle, although rides are reportedly easy to find given the steady stream of traffic to and from the airport. (*Let's Go* does not recommend hitchhiking.) Be careful storing food here; as bounteous signs warn, it's a favorite bear hangout. Water and pit toilets. 14-day max. stay. Sites $8.

Bear Paw Camper Park, P.O. Box 93 (835-2530), in the small boat harbor downtown. RV sites $14, with hookups $20. A separate colony of tentsites covers a small hill, $15 for 2 people, $2.50 per additional person. Free showers for guests.

Sea Otter RV Park, P.O. Box 947 (835-2787), on S Harbor Dr. 200 sites. Free showers for guests. Full hookups $18. Tentsites $12.

Gussie's Bed and Breakfast, 354 Lowe St. (835-4448), ½ mi. from downtown. In a quiet residential neighborhood. Clean, comfortable rooms. Singles with shared bath $55. Doubles $60.

FOOD

The busiest town on Prince William Sound, Valdez supports a variety of restaurants. For those who must stick to tight budgets, there's always the **Eagle Quality Center** (835-2100) at Meals and Pioneer (open 24 hrs.), or the **Red Apple Market** (835-4496) on Egan, a deli where a 3-piece chicken dinner with Jo-Jos is $4 (open daily 6am-midnight). If you're staying at the Valdez Glacier Campground, **Top Dog** (835-2001), at the airport, serves up inexpensive chili and assorted fast-food items.

Oscar's (835-4700), on N Harbor Dr., next to Bear Paw RV. The best bet for breakfast in town, and the locals know it. Stack of pancakes ($4). Sausage, hashbrowns, 2 eggs, biscuits and gravy ($7). Homemade chowder in a sourdough bread bowl ($3.75). Open daily 6am-11pm.

Mike's Palace (also called the Pizza Palace), 201 N Harbor Dr. (835-2365). Locals and tourists alike line up along the sidewalk here for the great Italian-Mexican-American fare. You know you're in Alaska when the "low-calorie plate" consists of cottage cheese, fruit, and a beef patty for $6. Baklava ($2.75).

Alaska Halibut House (835-2788), at Meals Ave. and Pioneer Dr. A small halibut basket with fries with emphasis on the fries ($5.75). Ketchup pumps, plastic trays, and his-and-hers halibut on the restroom doors. Open daily 10am-11pm.

A Rogue's Garden & Wildflower Cafe (835-5580), at the intersection of Galena and Tattlek, across from the post office. A small selection of natural foods. Healthy sandwiches on homemade bread with chips ($6.25). Open Mon.-Fri. 9:30am-5:30pm, Sat. 9:30am-4:30pm. Sandwiches served 11am-2pm.

No Name Pizza (835-4419), on Egan Dr., next to the Like Home Laundromat. Pizza that would make Goldilocks smile: 12-in. Mama ($12) and 16-in. Papa ($17), each with up to 3 toppings. The pizza bomb ($8.50) is "just right." Open daily 3pm-midnight; in summer 1am.

SIGHTS AND EVENTS

After an 800-mi. journey from the fields of Prudhoe Bay, the **Alaska Pipeline** dumps its oil at Valdez. Across the bay from town, the monolithic terminal spews millions of gallons of crude oil every day into the maws of awaiting tankers. **Alyeska** (835-2686) offers free 2-hr. tours that leave seven times per day from their visitors center at the airport. In response to anti-pipeline sentiment following the Exxon *Valdez* disaster, the tours strive to make Alyeska appear "environment-friendly." Even the most ardent proponents of solar energy will appreciate the care that goes into transforming the thick crude into marketable petroleum products. (Reservations required; see Practical Information about taxis from the airport.)

The **Salmon Gulch Hatchery** (835-4874), on Dayville Rd., 14 mi. out of town, off the Richardson Hwy., offers guided tours (6 per day, $1). Half a mile outside of town on the Richardson Hwy., tour buses pull over at Cripple Creek, where a strong run of silver salmon battle upstream in July.

In town, head to the **Valdez Museum** (835-2764) on Egan Dr. Inside, you'll see Valdez's original 1907 Ahrens steam fire engine, and exhibits on Alaskan earthquakes and the Columbia Glacier (open daily 8am-7pm; $2, under 18 free). Valdez is also home to **Prince William Sound Community College,** featuring a 30-ft. carved wooden head by renowned traditional sculptor Peter Toth, on the lawn near the corner of Meals Ave. and Pioneer Dr.

In an attempt to spice up small-town life and milk tourists for all they're worth, Valdez created the **Gold Rush Days** celebration (slated to take place during the first week in August). The month-long town fund-raiser includes a fashion show, banquet, dance, and an ugly-vehicle contest. Look out for...hell, chase (if you're 21 and have deadened taste buds) the traveling jail, picking up aimless tourists and making them drink gallons of warm beer. If you'd rather pay for cold beer, head to the **Pipeline Club and Lounge,** 112 Egan Dr. (835-4332). Dance to live bands Saturday nights from 9:30pm to 1am. (Bar open daily 10:30am-2pm.) Get loaded and make a fool of yourself singing Karaoke on Friday and Monday nights starting at 10pm. The **Glacier Bar,** 113 Fairbanks (835-4794), "rocks" to live rock 'n' roll Wednesday through Sunday 10pm to 3am.

OUTDOORS

For all its mountainous grandeur, Valdez has few developed hiking trails. A good place to begin is the 1.2-mi. **Mineral Creek,** just north of downtown, following a magnificent gorge through uninhabited backcountry (but look out for bears). The trail begins 8 mi. down a gravel road at the end of Mineral Creek Dr. and winds up at a turn-of-the-century gold mine. The 1.3-mi. **Solomon Gulch** trail starts 150 yd. northeast of the hatchery on Dayville Rd. near Valdez's hydro-electric plant (which, surprisingly, supplies 80% of the power for this oil-exporting region) and ends at breathtaking **Solomon Lake.** The **Goat Trail** follows an old Native Alaskan footpath that was the only route from Valdez to the Interior prior to the opening of the Richardson Hwy. It begins near Mile 13½ of the highway, just past Horsetail Falls, and accompanies the Lowe River for 5 mi.

By boat, helicopter, or plane, and with a thick wad of cash, you can investigate two of the Sound's most prized possessions: **Columbia** and **Shoup Glaciers. Stan Stephens Charters** (800-478-1297 or 835-4731) offers a 5½-hour red-eye (7am) economy cruise to Columbia ($63.50 per person), while **Glacier Charters** (835-5141) offers a 4½-5 hour cruise ($60). For an economy cruise, simply take the **Alaska Marine Hwy.** (see Practical Information above) from Whittier to Valdez (or vice-versa). The *Bartlett* makes a brief 10- to 15-minute stop at Columbia and gets about as close as the other tours. The price ($60) is the same and you'll be getting somewhere as you sightsee.

■■■ CORDOVA

Cordova is easily one of the most beautiful and welcoming places in the state. Accessible only by sea or air, its isolation has preserved its intense natural beauty in a relatively tourist-free setting. Cordova marks the convergence of three rich ecological systems: the Chugach National Forest, the Copper River delta, and the Pacific Ocean. The ocean keeps this fishing town afloat; blocky, worn seiners and gill-netters crowd Cordova's harbor. Copper originally placed Cordova on the map. With horses, manual labor, and financial backing from J. P. Morgan and the Guggenheim brothers, engineer Michael J. Heney, who had already made railroad history in constructing the White Pass and Yukon route, built the 200-mi. Copper River Railroad from Cordova to the Kennicott mines deep in the Wrangell Mountains. $300 million worth of copper ore passed through Cordova between 1911 and 1938, when the mine was exhausted. The railroad had fallen into disrepair even before the 1964 earthquake snapped its longest bridge. Tentative plans exist for connecting Cordova's highway with the rest of Alaska's road net, but no action has yet been taken.

C
O
R
D
O
V
A

Cordova is within easy reach of **Childs Glacier,** one of the least visited and most spectacular sights in all of Alaska. Fortified by rugged mountains of volcanic rock and salmon-filled waters, Cordova has been known to lure visiting nature-lovers and anglers, and never let them go. **Hiking** and **fishing** are both among the best in Alaska.

PRACTICAL INFORMATION AND ORIENTATION

Visitors Information: Cordova Historical Museum, P.O. Box 391, 622 1st St. (424-6665). Friendly women, including an original Hippy Cove resident (see Accommodations), have all the details. Open summer Mon.-Tues. and Thurs.-Sat. 9am-5pm, Wed. noon-5pm; off-season Tues.-Sat. 1-5pm.

Chugach National Forest, Cordova Ranger District, Box 280 (424-7661), on the 2nd floor, at the building on 2nd between Browning and Adams. Excellent information on hiking trails and fishing. Also a good place to head for pamphlets when the Chamber is closed. Reserve any of the 17 **Forest Service cabins** here. Most cabins provide no water. Open Mon.-Fri. 8am-5pm.

Fishing Information: Alaska Dept. of Fish and Game, Box 669 (424-3212). Recorded information., 424-7535. **Licenses** available at Davis' Super Foods on 1st St. (open Mon.-Sat. 8am-8pm, Sun. 10am-1pm) or A.C. Company (424-7141) in the Small Boat Harbor (open daily 7am-midnight).

Airport: 13 mi. east of town on the Copper River Hwy. Serviced by **Alaska Airlines** (800-426-0333 or 424-3278) and **Mark Air** (800-627-5247 or 424-5982). Either airline to: Juneau ($176), Anchorage ($86).

Alaska Marine Highway, P.O. Box 1689, Cordova 99574 (800-642-0066 or 424-7333), 1 mi. north of town on Ocean Dock Rd. One way to: Valdez ($30), Whittier ($36), Seward ($58), Kodiak ($98), and Homer ($138).

Taxis: J-B Transportation (424-3272) runs a shuttle to and from the airport for $9 per person. Shuttle meets every flight arrival, and departs town from the Reluctant Fisherman Inn at 7:30, 11:15am, 3:15 and 6pm. Regular taxi service: **A-Cab,** 424-7131. **Harbor Cab Co.,** 424-7575. **Wild Hare Taxi,** 424-3939. All 24 hrs. Rates start at $3 and go up.

Car Rental: Reluctant Fisherman Inn (424-3272). $45 per day, 25¢ per mi. after 50 mi. Free shuttle on J-B from airport. Must be 25 with major credit card.

Camping Equipment: Flinn's Clothing & Sporting Goods Store (424-3282), on 1st St. Open Mon.-Sat. 9am-6pm, Sun. 10am-1pm.

Bookstore: Orca Book Store (424-5305) on 1st St. Not a huge selection, but the cappucino bar in the back is a nice touch. Open Mon.-Sat. 8am-5pm.

Library: On 1st St., next to the museum (424-6667). Open Tues.-Sat. 1-9pm.

Laundromat: Whirlwind Laundromat, 100 Adams St. (424-5110), where Adams meets 1st St. Open Mon.-Sat. 8am-8pm, Sun. 8am-5pm.

Showers: Harbormaster's, 602 Nicholoff Way (424-6400) $3 for 5 min. Tokens available Mon.-Fri. 8am-5pm. Showers open 24 hrs.

Public Pool: Bob Korn Memorial Swimming Pool (424-7200), on Railroad Ave. Open daily, complicated schedule. Call ahead. Swim and shower, $4 for first ½hr., $1 per additional hr.

Pharmacy: Cordova Drug Co., P.O. Box 220, (424-3246), on 1st St. Open Mon.-Sat. 9:30am-6pm, Sun. 10am-1pm.

Hospital: Cordova Community Hospital, 602 Chase Ave. (424-8000), off Copper River Hwy.

Ambulance: 424-6100.

Police: 424-6100, next to post office on Railroad Ave.

Emergency: 911.

Post Office: at Council St. and Railroad Ave. (424-3564). Open Mon.-Fri. 10am-5:30pm, Sat. 10am-1pm. **General Delivery ZIP Code:** 99574.

Area Code: 907.

Cordova is on the east side of Prince William Sound on **Orca Inlet,** connected to the rest of the world only by boat or plane. Airline rates listed above for flying into Cordova from Juneau or Anchorage can, with advance purchase, be reasonable and much cheaper than taking a bus from Haines or Skagway to Valdez; you'll have a faster, more pleasant trip. West of town, the braided channels of the Copper River weave a wide delta where 20 million migrating shore birds pause to feed on their way to the Arctic.

ACCOMMODATIONS AND CAMPING

Cordova's accommodations reflect in many ways the lack of concern that residents have for the tourist trade; most of the hotels look like hell. If camping is your game, there's always **"Hippy Cove,"** a private, extremely bizarre place where you can crash for free. A municipal campground offers a more tranquil alternative, with showers for $3. Unsanctioned tents often spring up near the reservoir at the top of a rocky trail off of Whiteshed Rd., and near the ski area behind town.

Hippy Cove, ¾ mi. north of the ferry terminal on Orca Inlet Dr.; cross a few small streams to get there. With its own unique social life, Hippy Cove is guaranteed to keep you entertained. Most inhabitants are short-term cannery workers, although there are some lifers left from the Psychedelic Era. There is also a wood stove **sauna,** where townspeople and Cove dwellers gleefully roast at up to 200°F (93°C), then soak themselves in an icy stream-fed bath. Sauna dress code suggests a birthday suit. Hippy Cove is free and has drinking water. More crowded when fishing is good.

Odiak Camper Park (424-6200 Mon.-Fri. 8am-5pm; at other times call 424-6100), 2 mi. outside of town on Whiteshed Rd. Tentsites with water by the water for $3, with a vehicle $10, $15 with electricity. Free showers for guests; pick up a token in town at City Hall. Register 24 hrs. with city hall or police station. Open May-Sept. No reservations.

Alaskan Hotel and Bar, P.O. Box 484 (424-3288), on 1st St. The only building on the street with a fresh coat of paint. Clean, simple rooms occupy the upper floors. Rooms above the bar a bit noisy at night. Singles $35, with bath $55.

Harborview Bed and Breakfast (424-5356), on Observation Ave. off 1st St. Nice room, private bath, great view of the inlet. $45, with breakfast $50. Also has referral for 2 other B&Bs.

FOOD

The best selection of groceries at the most reasonable prices can be found at the colossal **A.C. Company** (424-7141), on Nicholoff St. in the small boat harbor (open daily 7am-midnight).

The Cookhouse Cafe (424-5926), ¼ mi. south of the ferry terminal on 1st St. Good eats and bright, clean decor make this one of Cordova's bright spots. A fine place to meet younger, talkative, and cheerful workers who are well-acquainted with Hippy Cove. Bins of condiments form the centerpieces on the long, white picnic tables. Try the *rigatoni al forno* ($7)...mmm...superb. Open Mon.-Thurs. 6am-3pm, Fri.-Sat. 6am-3pm and 5:30-9:30pm, brunch Sun. 9am-2pm.

The Reluctant Fisherman's Restaurant (424-3272), 407 Railroad Ave., near the harbor. Good food; cheery dining area with service to match. Stack of pancakes "as light as the first blush of dawn" ($3). 2 eggs, 2 biscuits, and gravy ($5.25). "One of Cordova's favorites:" 2 salmon tacos ($4). Open daily 6:30am-10pm.

Club Cafe (424-3405), on 1st St., behind the Club Bar. The angler's breakfast spot of choice. They gather around a single table in an ever-widening circle. "Hot and Hearty Breakfast Specials" include the sausage 'n muffin for $2.25. Deli sandwiches $3.50 at the take-out window. Open Mon.-Sat. 6am-9pm, Sun. 7am-5pm.

Baja Taco (424-5599), in a red bus by the Small Boat Harbor. A rolling taco stand whose owner goes south of the border in winter for research and development. Breakfast burrito ($5.75), chicken burrito ($6.25). Espresso (50 ¢). Open Mon.-Fri. 8am-4pm, Sat. 9am-4pm, Sun. 10am-4pm.

Killer Whale Cafe (424-7733), on 1st St. in the back of the groovy Orca Bookstore. It seems that every Alaskan town, no matter how tiny, has an earthy espresso-laden cafe; Cordova is no exception. Killer sandwiches ($5.50-8), espresso (50¢), and cappucino ($2). Open Mon.-Sat. 8am-4pm.

C
O
R
D
O
V
A

SIGHTS AND EVENTS

If it's raining (since this area averages 200 in. a year, it probably is), dry off in the **Cordova Historical Museum,** P.O. Box 391, 622 1st St. (424-6665), in the same building as the library on 1st St. Inside the museum you'll find real iceworms *(Mes-enchytraeus solifugus)* that live inside the glaciers. Bigger and more exciting is Prince Willie, an erratic leatherback turtle who strayed several thousand miles and wound up in a local fisherman's net (open summer Mon.-Tues. and Thurs.-Sat. 9am-5pm, Wed. noon-5pm; off-season Tues.-Sat. 1-5pm).

For the past 32 years, Cordova residents have held an **Iceworm Festival** in winter to honor the semi-legendary creature and to relieve cabin fever. The celebrations break loose the first weekend in February (Feb. 5-7 in 1995) and include the parade of a 100-ft. iceworm propelled by Cordova's children down frozen 1st St. Like most coastal towns in Alaska, Cordova also hosts an annual **Salmon Derby** (P.O. Box 99, 424-7260), the last weekend in August and the first weekend of September. At other times of the year, locals seek solace from the rainy nights at the **Alaskan Hotel and Bar** (424-3288), housing the original oak bar front from 1906 (open Sun.-Thurs. 8am-2am, Fri.-Sat. 8am-4am). Most nights feature live blues and rock bands from 10pm until closing.

OUTDOORS

Childs Glacier is both as breathtaking as Glacier Bay to the southeast and as accessible as Mendenhall near Juneau. Under the heat of the summer sun, the glacier calves ten-story chunks of ice, falling hundreds of ft. before crashing into the Copper River's deep, silty water. The largest icefalls are capable of sending 20-ft. waves washing over the observation area on the opposite bank of the river, ¼ mi. from the glacier. Splintered trees and boulders strewn throughout the woods are evidence of the awesome power of this water. Although falls of this size might happen rarely, perhaps once a season, they are unpredictable events and, as several alarming signs suggest, viewers should be prepared to run. Another set of signs prohibits harvesting the salmon flung into the woods by the waves. They have been left high and dry in the parking lot. The Childs Glacier provides an incredible chance to see geological change happen. If you spend much time in Cordova and don't see this glacier, you are missing the point of going to Alaska.

Childs Glacier is 50 mi. north of Cordova along a rough gravel road optimistically called the **Copper River Hwy.** Groups should rent a car, pack a picnic lunch and make a day of it. Travelers have been known to hitchhike and get stranded, since Childs is not a major tourist attraction. If you're traveling alone or can't get a rental car, **Footloose Tours** (424-5356) offers a free ride to town and complimentary refreshments. The tour lasts five to six hours and includes a delicious lunch spread during the three-hour stopover at Childs. The tours are given on demand for $35 per person.

While you're at the glacier you might also explore the **Million Dollar Bridge,** only a few hundred yds. from the glacier viewing area. Built in 1910, the bridge was considered an engineering marvel because of its placement between two active glaciers. One has retreated, but Childs is now less than ½ mi. away. The structure was heavily damaged in the 1964 earthquake and a primitive patch job keeps it standing today; many people drive safely across the span, but officially at their own risk.

Closer to town along the Copper River Hwy. is the vast **Copper River Delta,** a preserve covering over 1100 sq. mi. **Fishing** here is superb, as all five species of Pacific salmon, namely king, silver, red, chum, and pink, spawn seasonally in the Copper River. Catch salmon and halibut right off the city dock, but along Orca Inlet Road, on the Eyak River, or at Hartney Bay the fishing is usually better. It's possible to fish during a major run almost all year. King salmon run in the winter; sockeye and pink run in the mid- and late summer; dolly varden in the summer and early fall; and coho salmon in late summer and fall. The Delta also swarms with bears, moose, foxes, wolves, coyotes, eagles, and sea otters.

Hiking in the Delta is often wet and tough, but the neighboring **Chugach Mountains** provide dry trails and excellent climbing opportunities. An easy hike from town is the 2.4-mi. **Crater Lake Trail,** reachable by Power Creek Rd., 1½ mi. north of Cordova. From Crater Lake cradled high in an alpine bowl, there are excellent views across the sound, delta, and mountains. For a more strenuous and equally scenic hike, continue among mountain goats along a 5½-mi. ridge to connect with the **Power Creek Trail.** The ridge-route meets the Power Creek Trail midway on its 4.2-mi. ascent to a Forest Service **cabin,** one of the three in the Cordova area easily accessible by foot. The Power Creek Trail terminates on Power Creek Rd., 5 mi. from town. The Crater Lake Trail with the Power Creek connection is a 13-mi. hike. Other, shorter trails branch off the Copper River Hwy.; check with the **Forest Service** (see Practical Info.) for an excellent **pamphlet** on hiking around Cordova.

■■■ WRANGELL-ST. ELIAS NATIONAL PARK

Wrangell-St. Elias National Park and Preserve is Alaska's best-kept secret. The largest national park in the U.S., it could contain more than 14 Yosemites within its boundaries. Four major mountain ranges converge within the park: the Wrangells, St. Elias Mountains, Chugach Mountains, and the Alaska Range. Nine peaks tower at more than 14,000 ft. within the park, including the second highest mountain in the U.S. (18,008-ft. **Mt. St. Elias**). The heights are covered in eternal snow and ice; the Bagley Icefield is the largest non-polar icefield in North America, and the Malaspina Glacier, a piedmont glacier near the coast, is larger than the state of Rhode Island. Mountain sheep populate the jagged slopes within the park, and moose and bear are commonly sighted in the lower elevations.

The park is in the southeast corner of Alaska's mainland and is bounded by the Copper River to the west and Kluane National Park in the Yukon to the east. Park access is through two roads: the **McCarthy Road**, entering the heart of the park, and the **Nabesna Road,** entering from the northern park boundaries. Home to Alaska's most rugged, most beautiful, and wildest wilderness, the majority of tourists don't know it exists: fewer than 45,000 people visited the park in 1992 (compared to the 600,000 in Denali). There is a direct correlation between "unknown" and "wilderness;" if you have any time at *all* to spend in Alaska, come *here*, although the condition of the McCarthy Rd. is a deciding factor in your ability to get here, so be sure to check ahead.

The **visitors center** (822-5234) can be found 1 mi. off the Richardson Highway on the side road toward **Copper Center.** (Open in summer daily 8am-6pm, in winter Mon.-Fri. 8am-5pm.) Informed rangers will give you the low-down on all the to-dos and to-sees in the park. There are also **ranger stations** in **Chitina** (CHIT-na; 823-2205, open Fri.-Mon. 9:30am-4:30pm) and in **Slana** on the northern park boundary (822-5238, open daily 8am-5pm).

FROM THE PARK PERIMETER TO MCCARTHY

Find the turnoff for the town of Slana amid the deep ruts and dirt piles of the under-construction Richardson Highway. The Nabesna Road, running southeast for 42 mi. from Slana, offers vehicle access to the park's interior. Although the Nabesna is in better condition, offers better scenery, and is a full six feet wider than the other access road, the McCarthy Road (slack you may need in the face of unyielding RVs) the Nabesna Road's terminus is the uninspiring, abandoned mining town of Nabesna. Stay away; a privately owned abandoned gold mine here leaks toxic chemicals. Those traveling on the Nabesna should also be aware of the three streams crossing the road's path. All of these streams are subject to sizable, sudden fluctuations, especially during the spring and early summer; drivers should always get out of their cars to check stream depth.

Most travelers eschew Nabesna altogether and head to **McCarthy,** a town of fewer than 50 permanent residents and recent *National Geographic* notoriety. To reach McCarthy, turn onto the Edgarton Hwy. at its junction with the Richardson Hwy. 33 mi. south of Glenallen and follow the Edgarton east for 34 mi. to the town of Chitina. On a clear day along the Edgarton Hwy., look north to see 12,010-ft. Mt. Drum, 16,237-ft. Mt. Sanford, and 14,113-ft. Mt. Wrangell, Alaska's tallest active volcano. Steam can be seen rising from the flat summit of Mt. Wrangell on exceptionally clear days. Once the largest town in Alaska and heralded as a potential future capital, Chitina bucked the yoke of greatness and today remains a sleepy town of 300 with a single cafe (open daily 6am-10pm), a general store (823-2111, open daily June-Aug. 8am-11pm; Spring and Fall 9am-8pm; Winter 10am-7pm), and a ranger station (see below).

Since there isn't a grocery store in McCarthy, stock up in **Chitina,** a town perhaps best known as a center for fishwheeling and dipnetting in the nearby Copper River. Because its turbid, silt-ridden waters make fishing with conventional tackle infeasible (fish can't eat what they can't see) the Cooper River is one of only four rivers in Alaska where the use of dipnets and fishwheels is legal.

From Chitina, the **McCarthy Road** follows the old roadbed of the **Copper River and Northwestern Railway** for 58 mi. to the Kennicott River. This road is arguably the roughest state road in Alaska (Dalton Hwy. included). Severe washboard, potholes, and the occasional railroad spike in the road make this a two- to three-hour one-way trip (bring a spare tire). Because of trees and brush, the drive is not particularly scenic, although the 525-ft. long **Kuskulana Bridge** (a former railroad trestle) at Mile 17 passes 238 ft. above the Kuskulana River and was the greatest thrill of the McCarthy Road before it was upgraded and guard rails were added in 1988. The road terminates on the western edge of the Kennicott River, a silt-laden river originating within the Kennicott Glacier. There are two parking lots here, and it is recommended that visitors park in the upper lot as sudden glacial releases of water can raise the river several feet in a matter of minutes, submerging the lower lot. Be especially wary in late July and early August. The only way across the river is by a hand-operated **tram** (a metal "cart" with two seats, running on a cable). It is far easier to have somebody pull you across than to do it yourself, so return the favor if somebody helps you out. Just riding the tram over the roaring river is almost worth the drive out here. McCarthy is an easy ½-mi. walk from the opposite side of the river.

In the early 1900s, the richest copper ore ever discovered was found in the nearby mountain ridge on the east side of the Kennicott Glacier. The ore averaged a 12.79% copper content but ranged as high as 70% pure copper (today's mined ore averages only around 2% copper). The find attracted Stephen Birch, a young mining engineer, who gained backing from men such as the Guggenheim brothers and J.P. Morgan. In 1906, the Kennecott Copper Corporation was formed. (Misspelled, the company and mine's name remained Kennecott while the town and glacier are named Kennicott.) To transport the ore, the Copper River and Northwest Railway was constructed between 1908-1911. The CR&NW (jokingly called "Can't Run and Never Will") did run for 196 mi. from the Kennecott mines to the warm-water port of Cordova. A company town with a reputation for being proper and maintaining strict conduct rules, **Kennicott** was home base for the mining operations until 1938, when falling copper prices forced the mine to shut down. The last train left in November, 1938, after having transported more than $200 million worth of copper ore during its 27-year life-span.

Today, Kennicott remains remarkably intact, and has earned the name "American's largest ghost town." Kennicott awaits asbestos removal before it makes the formal transition from its current status as a privately owned facility to that of a restored national historical site.

MCCARTHY

McCarthy, 5 mi. south of Kennicott, was developed as a free-wheeling alternative to its abstemious neighbor. Both women and alcohol, prohibited in Kennicott by the male powers-that-were, were abundant in McCarthy, making the town more attractive to miners. Today, clustered along a few mainly nameless streets, McCarthy retains a distinctive, if considerably less bawdy, charm.

Practical Information Walking from the river, the first building encountered houses the rather unimpressive **McCarthy-Kennecott Historical Museum,** with artifacts and documents from the mining days (open daily 8am-6pm). This is a good place to get general info about the area and pick up a walking tour of Kennicott and McCarthy ($1 donation).

Getting to McCarthy isn't too difficult. Drive on your own if you want to test your car's suspension. **Backcountry Connections** (822-5292, in AK 800-478-5292) will take you aboard their roomy, comfortable vans complete with friendly and knowledgeable drivers. One-way from Glenallen is $69, from Chitina $35. Vans depart Mon.-Sat. from Glenallen (7:15am) and Chitina (8:30am) and return from McCarthy (4:30pm). They also offer day-long adventure trips from Glenallen and Chitina ($89 and $69, respectively) including lunch, shuttle service to Kennicott, and a walking tour of the abandoned mining town. **Wrangell Mountain Air** (see below in the Outdoors section) flies here daily from Chitina for those who would rather not tackle the highway ($60 each way). Regular traffic makes hitchhiking a possibility (although *Let's Go* does not recommend it).

There are no **phones** in McCarthy. Telecommunication is via the "bush phone" (a CB system) and most businesses have "phone bases" elsewhere. To reach a **business** in town, phone 333-5402, and they will be dispatched by CB. The McCarthy Lodge has **showers** for $5. There is no **post office;** local mail is flown in weekly.

Accommodations, Camping, and Food Beds in the bunk house at the **McCarthy Lodge** (333-5402), in downtown McCarthy, cost only $20. **Camping** is free on the west side of the Kennicott River (no water, pit toilets). Because almost all of the land around McCarthy and Kennicott is privately owned and local drinking water comes from nearby creeks, camping is prohibited in all areas on the eastern side of the Kennicott River, except on land north of Kennicott. Keep it clean.

The town has no general store, though the **Nugget Gift Shop** has some snacks and fruit (open daily 9am-12:30pm and 3-8pm). The **McCarthy Lodge** (see above) serves an affordable breakfast ($5-8) and enormous "McCarthy burgers" for lunch ($9). Alternating every night, the four dinner entrees comprising the dinner menu range in price from $10 to $22.50 (open daily from whenever the owners get up until they feel like closing). **Tailor-Made Pizza** serves breakfast for $5-9, sub sandwiches for $7 and pizzas for $12 to $21 (open Mon.-Sat. 8am-10pm, Sun. 8am-9pm). Dinner is more expensive ($14-17). Rumor has it that a pizzeria is soon to open in town, which will hopefully make its own dough rather than taking most of yours.

OUTDOORS

If you go **flightseeing** anywhere in Alaska, do it here. Because of the close proximity of 16,390-ft. Mt. Blackburn and the spectacular glaciers, a short 35-min. flight offers amazing views of even more incredible scenery. On **Wrangell Mountain Air** (800-478-1160 for reservations), based in downtown McCarthy, a 35-min. flight takes you over Kennicott and the amazing icefalls of the Kennicott and Root Glaciers ($40). A 50-minute trip will take you up the narrow Chitistone Canyon to view the thundering Chitistone Falls and over 15 glaciers and five mountain peaks ($60). You'll fly completely around majestic Mt. Blackburn in a 70-min. flight ($77) or fly out to see 18,000-ft. Mt. St. Elias and 19,800-ft. Mt. Logan in a longer 90-min. flight ($100). There is a 3-person minimum on all flights. **McCarthy Air** (800-245-6909), also in McCarthy, offers similar flights and rates.

St. Elias Alpine Guides (277-6867) organizes day trips (a ½-day glacier walk costs $55). You can rent bikes here to explore some of the old, obscure roads that are everywhere around town ($25 per day, ½-day $15). **The Bike Shop** also rents bikes ($8 per hour, $20 per day). **Copper Oar** (522-1670), at the end of the McCarthy Rd., offers a 2-hr. whitewater trip down the Kennicott River for $40. Get wet! For those on a serious shoe-string, just walking around McCarthy and Kennicott is plenty interesting, as many original buildings remain in both towns, and Kennicott is nearly intact. A **shuttle bus** runs out to Kennicott from McCarthy on a regular schedule ($8 round-trip). It's a 5-mi. hike between the two towns.

Most **hikers and trekkers** use the McCarthy Road or McCarthy as a base. The park maintains no trails, but miners and other travelers from decades past have established various routes and obscure roads that follow the more exciting pathways. The most common route, a hike out past Kennicott to the Root Glacier, takes from 1-3 days for the 16-mi. round-trip and follows road-bed and glacial moraine with three moderate stream crossings. A hike to **Dixie Pass** has the advantage of easy accessibility (it starts from Mile 13 of the McCarthy Road) and hikers should allow 3-4 days for the 24-mi. round-trip. Those with a little more money and a thirst for real adventure should try the **Goat Trail.** The trail is a 25-mi. one-way trek from Lower Skolai Lake to Glacier Creek and traverses the ridge high above **Chitistone Canyon and Falls,** one of the park's more spectacular features. Access is only by air taxi. Allow between $150-200 per person for the drop-off and pick-up. Though only 25 mi., the extremely rugged terrain and many stream crossings make this a 4 to 8-day trek for experienced hikers only. For any overnight trip, the park service requests a written itinerary; though it's not required, it's in your own best interest. This is bear country, so be aware of the precautions necessary to reduce risk. Make sure to have extra food, warm clothing, and know what you're doing, especially in stream crossings. And travel with someone, so you can make it back and share the memories.

Southeastern Alaska

Southeastern Alaska (the Panhandle) encloses the waters of the Inside Passage, spanning 500 mi. north from the breathtaking Misty Fjords National Monument, past Juneau, to Skagway at the foot of the Chilkoot Trail. This network of islands, inlets, and saltwater fjords hemmed in by mountains is distinguished by a cold-temperate rainforest climate, over 60 major glaciers, and 15,000 bald eagles. The beautiful land-and-waterscape make this region ideal for incredible hiking, fishing, kayaking, and other outdoor adventures.

Some communities of the Interior and Southcentral Alaska have experienced what Alaskans consider urban sprawl, but the towns in the southeast cling to the coast. Gold Rush days haunt Skagway, while Sitka preserves artifacts of Russian occupation. Petersburg, Wrangell, and smaller communities prosper with the logging and fishing industries. Throughout the region the Tlingit (TLING-kit), Haida (HI-duh), and Tsimshian (sim-SHEE-an) Native nations preserve and persevere.

The Alaskan Marine Highway system provides the cheapest, most exciting way to explore the Inside Passage. In order to avoid the high price of accommodations in towns without hostels, plan your ferry trip at night so you can sleep on deck.

■■■ KETCHIKAN

Near Alaska's southeasternmost point, at the base of Deer Mountain, Ketchikan is the first stopping point in Alaska for northbound cruise ships and ferries, disgorging loads of tourists and dumping hordes of students looking for the big summer bucks offered by the canneries. Many backpackers risk the wrath of the Ketchikan police by illegally camping in the state forest north of town, where they are largely undisturbed. However, being ousted from your campsite is a possibility. Plan carefully: most campgrounds set weekly limits, and the youth hostel only guarantees four nights out of the rain. "People don't tan in Ketchikan," according to a local proverb, "they rust." If the locals didn't learn to ignore the rain in this fishing-and-lumber town, they would scarcely step outside. Fourteen feet of rain per year explain the ubiquitous awnings projecting over the streets.

Many of the boats and float planes continually buzzing through Ketchikan's busy harbor travel to nearby Misty Fjords National Monument. Only 20 mi. from Ketchikan at its nearest point, this region of long, narrow waterways and old-growth forests, home to both killer whales and mountain goats, invites hikers and kayakers to play in a wilderness the size of Connecticut.

Ketchikan rests on Revillagigedo Island, 235 mi. southeast of Juneau, 90 mi. northwest of Prince Rupert, BC, and 600 mi. northwest of Seattle, WA.

PRACTICAL INFORMATION AND ORIENTATION

Visitors Information: Ketchikan Visitors Bureau, 131 Front St. (225-6166 or 800-770-3300), on the cruise ship docks downtown. Offers **map** of a good walking tour, along with friendly advice and a cup of coffee. Open Mon.-Fri. 7:30am-4:30pm, and Sat.-Sun. depending on cruise ship arrival times.

Forest Service: Ranger District Office, Federal Building at 648 Mission St. (225-3101). Informational packets on hiking and paddling in Misty Fjords and the Ketchikan area (free). They also sell a kayaker's **map** of Misty Fjords ($3) and reserve cabins around Ketchikan and Prince of Wales. Ask for the little green guide to recreation facilities for complete cabin listings. Open in summer Mon.-Fri. 7:30am-4:30pm, Sat.-Sun. 8am-4:30pm; closed weekends in off-season.

Alaska Employment Service, 2030 Sea Level Dr. #220 (225-3181), at the west end of town. Open Mon.-Fri. 8am-noon, 1-4:30pm. This facility is helpful for researching fishing seasons in advance, and offers advice on how to find work in fisheries and canneries.

Public Phones: Alascom Teleservices Center, 315 Mill St. (225-9700). Sixteen phones for long-distance calls, with metered charges that allow you to pay at a cash register rather than plugging in fistfuls of dollars. Fax service available (fax 225-9707). Hours vary with cruise ship schedules, posted on door.

Airport: Across from Ketchikan on Gravina Island. A small ferry runs from the airport to just above the state ferry dock ($2.50). The Alaska Marine Highway terminal is only a short walk from the airport ferry dock. **Alaska Airlines** (225-2141 or 800-426-0333), in the Ingersoll Hotel at the corner of Front and Dock St., provides flight information from Ketchikan. Daily flights to Juneau ($124). Open Mon.-Fri. 9:30am-5pm. **Weather:** Ketchikan airport weather report (874-3232).

Alaska Marine Highway (225-6181), at the far end of town on N Tongass Hwy. Turn right leaving the terminal to reach the city center. Buses run into town until 6:45pm; after that you have to pay the $8 cab fare.

Buses: Local transit fare $1, seniors and under 11 75¢. Buses run every 20 min. Mon.-Sat. 6:40am-7pm. The main bus route runs a loop with turnaround points at the airport parking lot near the ferry terminal at one end, and Dock and Main St. downtown at the other. Stops about every 3 blocks.

Taxi: Sourdough Cab, 225-5544. **Alaska Cab,** 225-2133. **Yellow Taxi,** 225-5555. All can be chartered for $40-45 per hour.

Air Taxis and Tours: Taquan, 225-8800. **Ketchikan Air Service,** 225-9888. **Misty Fjords Air and Outfitters,** 225-5155. Tours $120 per person.

Car Rental: Alaska Rent-A-Car, airport office (225-2232) or 2828 Tongass Ave. (225-5000 or 800-662-0007). Free local pick-up and delivery. $6 per hour, $43 per day, with unlimited free mileage. Open Mon.-Sat. 8am-5pm, Sun. 8am-3pm.

Kayaking: Southeast Exposure, 507 Stedman St. (225-8829). Required 1½-hr. orientation class $20. Single fiberglass kayak rental, $35 per day; 4 or more days, $30 per day. Double kayak, $45 per day; 4 or more days $40 per day. $200 damage deposit. Open daily 8am-5pm.

Bookstore: Parnassus (Ms. Lillian's), 5 Creek St. (225-7690). An upstairs special-subject bookshop with an eclectic selection of used and new books. Discernible emphasis on women's studies. Open daily noon-7pm; in winter closed on Mon.

Seamen's Center (225-6003), on Mission St. next to St. John's. A warm, dry lounge where workers and others can clean up, watch television, and sometimes find free food. Meals served on weekends in summer 6-8pm. Showers $1, laundry 75¢. Open daily June 6-10pm, July-Aug. 3-10pm; winter Wed., Sat.-Sun. 6-9pm. Volunteers can help cook or clean for 2 hrs. any evening.

Public Radio Station: KRBD 105.9. Drop by their station at 123 Stedman St. (225-9655) to learn about who's playing and where.

Laundromat: Highliner Laundromat, 2703 Tongass (225-5308). Wash $1.75, 7-min. dry 25¢. Showers ($2 for 10 min.). Open 6:30am-9:30pm.

Pharmacy: Downtown Drugstore, 300 Front St. (225-3144). Open Mon.-Fri. 8am-6:30pm, Sat. 8am-6pm, Sun. 10am-4pm.

Hospital: Ketchikan General Hospital, 3100 Tongass Ave. (275-5171).

Fire Dept.: Main St., near Dock St. (225-9616). **Police Station:** Main St. and Grant St. (225-6631), across from the hostel.

Post Office: (225-9601) Main office next to the ferry terminal. Open Mon.-Fri. 8:30am-5pm. Substation at corner of Race and Tongass (225-4153) open Mon-Fri 9am-6pm, Sat. 9am-5pm. Another substation (225-2349) in the back of The Trading Post, at Main and Mission St. Open Mon.-Sat. 9am-5:30pm. **General Delivery ZIP Code:** 99901.

Area Code: 907.

ACCOMMODATIONS

Besides hostels, rooms here are relatively expensive. The **Ketchikan Bed and Breakfast Network,** Box 3213, Ketchikan 99901 (225-8550), provides rooms from $65-75.

Ketchikan Youth Hostel (HI/AYH), P.O. Box 8515 (225-3319), at Main and Grant St. in the basement of the First Methodist Church. Although there are no beds, 4-in.-thick foam mats on the floor are comfortable if you have a sleeping

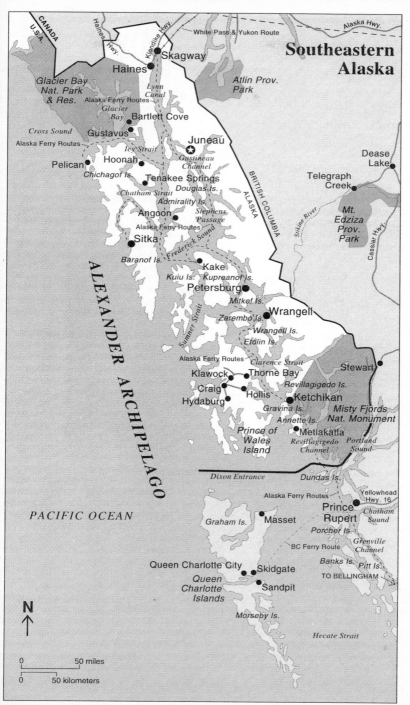

CANADA
U.S.A.

Haines Hwy.

White Pass & Yukon Route

Alaska Hwy.

Klondike Hwy.

Skagway

Haines

Southeastern Alaska

Atlin Prov. Park

Glacier Bay Nat. Park & Res.

Lynn Canal

Alaska Ferry Routes

Glacier Bay

Bartlett Cove

Gustavus

Juneau

Dease Lake

Telegraph Creek

Cross Sound

Alaska Ferry Routes

Pelican

Hoonah

Icy Strait

Gastineau Channel

Chichagof Is.

Tenakee Springs

Douglas Is.

Mt. Edziza Prov. Park

Chatham Strait

Admirality Is.

Angoon

Stephens Passage

BRITISH COLUMBIA

ALASKA

Sitkine River

Alaska Ferry Routes

Sitka

Cassiar Hwy.

Baranof Is.

Frederick Sound

Kake

Kuiu Is.

Kupreanof Is.

Petersburg

Mitkof Is.

Wrangell

Zarembo Is.

Wrangell Is.

Etolin Is.

Summer Strait

Alaska Ferry Routes

Clarence Strait

Stewart

Klawock

Thorne Bay

Revillagigedo Is.

Craig

Hollis

Ketchikan

Hydaburg

Gravina Is.

Misty Fjords Nat. Monument

ALEXANDER ARCHIPELAGO

Annette Is.

Prince of Wales Island

Metlakatla

Revillagigedo Channel

Portland Sound

Dixon Entrance

Dundas Is.

Yellowhead Hwy. 16

Alaska Ferry Routes

PACIFIC OCEAN

Prince Rupert

Chatham Sound

Graham Is.

Masset

Porcher Is.

Grenville Channel

BC Ferry Route

Banks Is.

Pitt Is.

TO BELLINGHAM

Queen Charlotte City

Skidgate

Queen Charlotte Islands

Sandpit

Morseby Is.

Hecate Strait

N

0   50 miles

0   50 kilometers

bag. Clean kitchen, common area, 2 showers, tea and coffee. Houseparents change, and their management styles vary widely. Lockout 9am-6pm. Lights out at 10:30pm, on at 7am. Curfew 11pm. Call ahead if arriving on a late ferry. $7, non-members $10. 3-day max. stay subject to availability. Overflow sleeps in the sanctuary. Baggage storage. Open June 1-Sept. 1. No reservations.

New York Hotel and Cafe, 207 Stedman St. (225-0246). A painstakingly restored 8-room hotel beside the Creek St. boardwalk. Cable TV, queen-size beds, and luxurious bathtubs. $69; Oct.-April $49. Reservations recommended.

Shelter, 628 Park Ave. (225-4194). 28 beds in the 3 rooms with separate quarters for men and women. Check-in 7-10pm, check-out 7:30 am. Kitchen facilities and luggage storage for residents. 5-night max. stay. Free, but $3 donation requested of those who can afford it.

Rain Forest Inn, 231 Hemlock St. (225-9500). Rooms are passably clean, but bring thongs to the showers. Dorm bed $21. Double with two beds $47.

CAMPING

If you plan in advance, camping provides an escape from Ketchikan's high accommodation prices. The sporting goods stores in town cater more to the fatigues-and-fishhooks crowd than to backpackers, but you might want to check out **The Outfitter,** 3232 Tongass (225-6888; open Mon.-Fri. 8am-7pm, Sat. 8am-6pm, Sun. 8am-4pm), or **Plaza Sports,** in the Plaza Mall (225-1587). Campgrounds have time limits of a week or two, but the occasional cannery worker has been spotted carrying supplies to tent illegally up in the public forests for longer periods. There is no public transportation to the campgrounds, so plan on hiking, biking, or paying the exorbitant cab fare out there. **Ketchikan Ranger District** (225-2148) runs the **Signal Creek, Last Chance,** and **Three C's Campgrounds,** and also supplies information about cabins with stoves ($25) in remote locations in the **Tongass National Forest.**

Signal Creek Campground, 6 mi. north on Tongass Hwy. from the ferry terminal. 25 units on the shores of Ward Lake. Water, pit toilets. Sites $5. Open summer. 2-week max. stay.

Last Chance Campground, 2 mi. north of Ward Lake's parking lot entrance. 25 sites, mainly RV. Water, pit toilets. Sites $5. Open summer. 2-week max. stay.

Three C's Campground, ½ mi. north of Signal Creek. Four units for backpackers. Water, pit toilets, firewood. Sites $5. 2-week max. stay.

Clover Pass Resort, P.O. Box 7322-V (247-2234), 14 mi. north of Ketchikan. 30 complete RV hookups with electricity, sewer, water, laundry, and a dump station. $20 per night. Open in summer.

FOOD

The supermarket most convenient to downtown is **Tatsuda's,** 633 Stedman at Deermount St. just beyond the Thomas Basin, (225-4125). Open daily 7am-11pm. You can pick up single items at **Junior's Convenience Store,** at Dock and Main St., including a yummy microwave roast beef "Philly" sandwich for $1.39 (open Mon.-Sat. 7am-11pm, Sun. 8am-11pm). **McDonald's** supplies the cheapest meal at the Plaza Mall, 1 mi. north of the tunnel (a prayer meeting is held here every Wed. morning at 7:30am…"What you want is what you get."). For a $3.19 "cold cut combo" head to **Subway,** at 417 Dock St. (open daily 10am-midnight). The freshest seafood swims in Ketchikan Creek; anglers frequently hook king salmon from the docks by Stedman St. in the summer, and, if you should be so lucky, **Silver Lining Seafoods,** 1705 Tongass Ave. (225-9865), will custom-smoke your catch for $2 per pound. Look for boats along the waterfront selling shrimp. **KetchiCandies** (225-0900), on Mission St. next to the Trading Post, is an aromatic experience not to be missed; you won't be able to keep yourself from the Frangelica Truffles ($15 per lb.; open daily 9am-6pm).

5 Star Cafe, 5 Creek St. (247-7827). Savory salads and scrumptious sandwiches smothered in sprouts. Try the smoked turkey on dark rye ($6) or the daily soup

($2.50). The atmosphere is homey, and an art gallery in back gives you an excuse to linger. Open Mon.-Wed. 8am-5pm, Thurs.-Sat. 8am-8pm, Sun. 8am-8pm.

Chico's (225-2833), at Dock and Edmond St. Tortellini meets the tortilla. Zesty Mexican/Italian decor and music. Lunch specials 10am-3pm. Spicy dinners $8.50-14.50. Large pizza $13. Open daily 10am-11pm.

Pioneer Pantry Cafe (225-3337), on Mill St., across from cruise ship docks. Chicken strip sandwich with cup of chowder $7. Open Sun.-Tues. 6am-midnight, Wed.-Sat. 24 hrs.

Jimbo's Cafe, 307 Mill St. (225-8499), across from the cruise ship docks. Try a 1-lb. Alaskan burger for $9. Stack of 3 pancakes $3.75. Where the inebriated head after the bars have closed. Open daily 6am-3 or 4am.

Latitude 56 Restaurant (225-9011), in the bowling alley across from the mall. Eat a steak sandwich ($9) before you bowl a turkey. Open daily 6am-10pm.

SIGHTS AND ENTERTAINMENT

Fortune-seeking prospectors turned Ketchikan into a mining boom-town, and some of this history is preserved on **Creek Street,** once a thriving red-light district where sailors and salmon went upstream to spawn. Creek St. itself is a wooden boardwalk on pilings lined with shops along Ketchikan Creek; there is no actual street. Older women in black fishnets and red-tasseled silk still beckon passersby into **Dolly's House,** 24 Creek St. (225-6329), a former-brothel-turned-museum. Countless antiques from the 1920s and 30s are set amidst bawdy colors and secret caches. Hours vary with cruise ship arrivals; call ahead ($2.50).

Also on the walking tour is the **Totem Heritage Center,** 601 Deermount St. (225-5900), the largest collection of authentic totem poles in the world. The center houses 33 well-preserved totem poles from Tlingit, Haida, and Tsimshian villages, composing the largest collection of authentic totem poles in the U.S. (Open daily 8am-5pm. $2, under 18 free, Sun. afternoon free.) Across the creek, at the **Deer Mountain Fish Hatchery** (225-6760), a self-guided tour explains artificial salmon sex. (Open daily 8am-4:30pm. Free.) The **Tongass Historical Museum** (225-5600), on Dock St., explains the town's historical pastiche of Native Americans, rain, salmon, and prostitutes. (Open mid-May-Sept. daily 8am-5pm. $2, under 13 free; Sun. afternoon free.) Under the same roof as the museum, the **Ketchikan Library,** overlooking a waterfall and rapids, is the best place to pass a rainy day (open Mon. and Wed. 10am-8pm; Tues., Thurs., Fri.-Sat. 10am-6pm, Sun. 1-5pm). A free **funicular** ascends the street slope behind Creek St. near the library. Enjoy the amazing **view** of the harbor from the top of the Westmark Hotel.

Some of the finest ancient and contemporary totems stand near Ketchikan. Pick up the guided walking totem tour at the visitors bureau. World-renowned totem carver Nathan Jackson lives here; his work stands in front of the Federal Building. If you can see only one thing in Ketchikan, visit the best and largest totem park in the world: the **Saxman Native Village** (225-5163), 2½ mi. southwest of Ketchikan on Tongass Hwy ($8 by cab). The village has a traditional house, dancers, and an open studio where artisans carve new totems. (Open daily 9am-5pm and on weekends when a cruise ship is in.) Also, 10 mi. north of Ketchikan on Tongass Hwy. is **Totem Bight,** featuring 14 totems. Entry to both parks is free, and visitors are welcome during daylight hours. The **Shotridge Cultural Center and Museum,** 407 Stedman St. (225-0407), is both a commission gallery with the best prices in town and the workshop of master carver Israel Shotridge (open Mon.-Sat. 10am-4pm. $1.)

Bars jostle for position along Water St. leading towards the ferry. The **Arctic Bar** (225-4709) on the other side of the tunnel is a fishermen's land-lubbing haunt (open Sun.-Wed. 8am-midnight, Thurs.-Sat. 8am-2am). Throughout the year, **Ketchikan's First City Players** present an intriguing variety of plays to sell-out crowds Thurs.-Sat. at 8pm. In July and Aug., check out the bawdy *Fish Pirate's Daughter,* a melodrama about Prohibition Ketchikan. Shows are $8, and performed at the **Main Street Theatre,** 338 Main St. (225-4792).

Like most towns in the Alaskan Southeast, Ketchikan celebrates the 4th of July with a vengeance. Ketchikan's festivities coincide with the annual **Timber Carni-**

val, a spirited display of speed-chopping, axe-throwing, choker-setting virtuosity. The second Sat. in Aug. brings crafts, food, and live music to the streets along with a fiercely contested **slug race** at the **Blueberry Festival.** If all the excitement wears you down, you can pick up a free cup of coffee at the visitor's center on Dock St. and stroll out onto the wooden deck. The surrounding wooded hills, outdoor vendors, and flags waving from the masts of gift shops offer an excellent atmosphere to watch the cars and ships cruise by. Check out the "Liquid Sunshine Gauge: Busted in 1949, 202.55 inches."

OUTDOORS

Although Ketchikan offers boundless hiking and kayaking opportunities within the nearby **Misty Fjords National Monument,** you scarcely have to go beyond the city limits to find a trailhead leading into the hills. A good dayhike from Ketchikan is 3,001-ft. **Deer Mountain.** Walk past the city park on Fair St. up the hill towards the town dump. The marked trailhead branches off to the left just behind the dump. A steep but manageable ascent leads 2 mi. up the mountain, and though most hikers return the same way they came up, an extended route leads over the summit and past an A-frame shelter that can be reserved at the ranger station in town. The trail continues above treeline along a steep-sided ridge, where snow and ice may remain into the summer. **Blue Lake,** an alpine pond stocked with trout, lies at the middle of the ridge walk. At the summit of the 3,237-ft. John Mountain, the **John Mountain Trail** descends from the ridge, passing the **Stivis Lakes** on its way down to the **Beaver Falls Fish Hatchery** and the **South Tongass Highway,** 13 mi. from Ketchikan. This section of the hike is poorly marked and may test hikers' ability to read **topographic maps.** The entire hike, manageable by experienced hikers in a full day, is 10 mi. long. A less strenuous and equally accessible outing is the trek along a boardwalk built over muskeg up to Perseverance Lake. The **Perseverance Trail,** beginning 6 mi. north of the city just before the Three C's campground, climbs 600 ft. over 2.3 mi. to a mountain lake, an excellent opportunity for a **trout**-fishing respite.

The incredible **Misty Fjords National Monument** lies 20 mi. east of Ketchikan and is accessible by kayak, power boat, or float plane. This 3420-sq.-mi. park offers great camping, kayaking, hiking, and wildlife viewing. Walls of sheer granite, scoured and scraped by retreating glaciers, rise up to 3,000 ft. from saltwater bays. More than 12 ft. of annual rainfall and runoff from large ice fields near the Canadian border feed the hundreds of streams and waterfalls emptying into two long fjords, **Behm Canal** (117 mi.) and **Portland Canal** (72 mi.), on either side of the monument. Four first-come, first-serve shelters (free) and fourteen Forest Service cabins dot the preserve, most requiring a chartered floatplane to reach. Even the two cabins accessible by boat may be available in mid-week during the summer; it's always worth asking at the ranger station (225-2148).

Although seasoned kayakers prepared to navigate the difficult currents between Ketchikan and Behm Canal can paddle straight into the park, another option is to have **Alaska Cruises** (215 Main, Box 7814; 225-6044) bring you and your boat on one of their four sightseeing tours per week. They will drop off paddlers and pick them up again anywhere along their route for $150. Walker Cove, Punchbowl Cove and Rudyard Bay, off Behm Canal, are several of the destinations of choice for paddlers. In planning a trip, keep in mind that these waters are frigid, and extended stretches of coast have no good shelter. A reliable cooking stove is also essential since wood in Misty Fjords tends to be soggy.

A slew of charter operations visit the monument; plan on spending at least $125 for a day trip. Alaska Cruises offers a 10-hour **boat tour** with meals. An **air tour** of the park costs more than $1 for every minute in the air, with the length of the flight depending on what your wallet can sustain. Call the Ketchikan Visitors Bureau (see above) for more information.

■■■ METLAKATLA

Metlakatla ("salt water channel passage" in Tsimshian) lies 15 mi. southwest of Ketchikan on Annette Island in the Tsimshian Reservation (sim-SHEE-an). While the 1800 residents are friendly to the few visitors, the village is uninterested in bolstering tourism. Although island officials do not rigorously enforce the regulation, visitors are legally required to obtain permits in Metlakatla.

Apart from the totem pole outside the **library** (open Mon. noon-3pm and 6pm-8pm, Tues.-Fri. noon-4pm) at the west end of town, there are few outward clues to reveal the town's heritage, but residents still observe the matrilineal custom; children inherit their mothers' totems and property. Only Native Americans and their spouses may work in Metlakatla without a permit. While not a hotbed of excitement, Metlakatla is a good place to escape the crowds. While in the summer the harbor is clogged with fishing vessels and the cannery is busy, Metlakatlans prefer a slower pace, and the town and island are worth a relaxing daytrip for scenery and a unique experience.

Practical Information Getting to Metlakatla is easy. **Ketchikan Air** (886-1007) has five flights per day from Ketchikan for $35 round-trip; **Taquan Air** (886-6868) offers comparable service. The ferry *Aurora* makes several round trips, usually Mon. and Sat., between Metlakatla and Ketchikan on the main line of the **Alaska Marine Highway** (1-800-642-0066). Be aware that Metlakatla observes Pacific Time and does not observe Daylight Savings Time.

Obtain a visitor's permit at the **Municipal Office Building** (on Upper Milton St.; street names mean little in Metlakatla). The **National Bank of Alaska** (886-6363), next to the Municipal Building, provides Visa traveler's checks. The **Island Laundro-Mat** offers showers for $2, wash from $1.25 and an 8-minute dry for 25¢ (one block west of the GTE building in the center of town). There is also a **health clinic** on Upper Milton (open Mon.-Tue., Thurs.,-Fri. 8am-noon and 1-5pm; Wed. 8am-noon). Reach the **police** by calling 886-6721, or visit the station on 8th Ave. The **post office** (886-6712) is also on 8th Ave. past the police station (open Mon.-Fri. 8am-12:30pm and 1-5pm, Sat.10am-noon).

Accommodations and Food Staying overnight in Metlakatla involves considerable expense, as there is little competition for the budget traveler's dollar. For $75 you can sink into the lap of luxury with a queen bed, private bath, and cable TV at the **Metlakatla Hotel and Cafe** at Lower Main and 3rd St. (886-3456). Or, for $70, you might take one of the two rooms at **Scudero's Bottega**, a bed and breakfast in a blue home across from Leasks Market.

Food is surprisingly reasonably priced. The hungry snacker should head to the **Mini Mart** at the south end of Upper Milton St. (886-3000) for free coffee and hot dogs ($1) or mammoth cinnamon rolls ($1; open Mon.-Thurs.7:30am-10pm, Fri. 7:30am-11pm, Sat. 9am-11pm, Sun. 9am-10pm). For a bigger selection but higher prices, buy groceries at **Leasks Market** at the east end of Western Ave. (886-4881; open Mon.-Fri. 10am-6pm, Sat. 10am-5:30pm, Sun. noon-5pm). **The Metlakatla Hotel and Cafe** (see above) offers the best venue for a sit-down meal, with a hamburger, fries, and soft drink for a mere $4 and a full shrimp dinner for $8. If you crave caffeine, head to **Cindy's Seafood and Coffee** at the western end of Western Ave. (886-7187). Cindy brews espresso and amaretto mocha in this sunny extension of her kitchen, but seafood is sold raw by the pound. (Open Mon.-Sat. 7:30am-6pm.)

Sights and Outdoors Camping is discouraged in Metlakatla, but two short, colorful hikes offer a chance to explore the island and appreciate beautiful scenery. Reach both the easier Yellow Hill hike and the steeper, tougher Purple Lake Trail hike by trekking south along Airport Rd. Once you arrive, Lucille Ryan will gladly take you on a free **walking tour** if she isn't hard at work at the Annette Island Packing Co. (907-886-6543; Box 73, 99926). As a detour, call Jack Hudson (886-4923) for a showing of his impressive collection of traditional carvings, lithographs, and jewelry. Evelyn Littlefield, another Tsimshian artist, crafts beaded moccasins. If conversing with the locals doesn't satisfy your appetite for Metlakatlan anecdotes, the **Duncan Museum** (886-6926, open Mon.-Fri. 1pm-4pm) is a free alternative. The museum, once the home of founding father William Duncan, is in a bright yellow cottage at the south end of town. Duncan, and Anglican church layman, led about 800 Tsimshians from British Columbia to Alaska on Aug. 7, 1887, after difficulties with the Canadian religious authorities. The date is annually commemorated with festivities at the island's cannery.

■■■ PRINCE OF WALES ISLAND

Prince of Wales Island sits quietly less than 30 mi. west of Ketchikan. Most beautiful at its edges, where countless bays and protected inlets cradle calm waters, the island lies beneath a dense rain forest broken only by mountain peaks, patches of muskeg, and large clear-cuts. A branch line of the Alaska ferry makes reaching Prince of Wales a cinch, but getting around on the island proves more challenging. The towns on the island are separated by long, potholed roads, and bike and car rentals are not readily available. A 1000-mi. road system (30 mi. paved, 970 mi. gravel), allows mountain bikers and drivers thorough access to the island, but unless you bring your own wheels, be prepared to thumb it. (*Let's Go* does not recommend hitchhiking.) The **Prince of Wales Transporter** (755-2348) meets almost every ferry and rolls on to Craig ($20), and hitchhikers are rarely seen waiting long for rides.

The extensive logging on Prince of Wales recently uncovered a vast network of limestone **caves** in the north of the island. Most of these have yet to be mapped, and only two are now easily accessible. But speleologists are all abuzz over the discovery of another Alaskan superlative, the deepest cave in the U.S., and paleontologists take interest in a prehistoric bear that fell to its death and was preserved at the bottom of another cave. To ensure that visitors don't meet a similar fate, the Forest Service only provides the public with information on two easily accessible caves, both equipped with visitor facilities. If you want to dig deeper, contact **Glacier Grotto,** Alaskan Chapter of the National Speleological Society, P.O. Box 376, Haines 99827.

The Alaska state ferry *Aurora* makes the 2¾-hr. crossing from Ketchikan to Hollis on Prince of Wales roughly eight times per week ($20). Even so, few people other than relatives of the 6000 residents make this detour beyond the foaming wakes of the main ferry route. The small communities on the island meet visitors with a combined expression of warmth and bemusement. These fish and timber towns, where two trucks never pass without a wave, offer few standard services to visitors, but an excellent chance to see Alaskans plying the tourist trade only as an afterthought. Both **Ketchikan Air** (826-3333) and **Taquan Air** (826-8800) buzz over to Craig and Klawock ($65) and Thorne Bay ($50) about eight times per day in the summer.

CRAIG

Craig, on the west coast of Prince of Wales and the local service center, is the most "visitable" town on the island. A short causeway flanked by two small harbors leads out to a small hump of an island, where there are views from the town's center of peaceful waters and islands in nearly every direction. With Craig's commercial enterprises spilling out of town and breaking ground along the road to Klawock, the town seems to be riding a different economic wave than other island communities.

Practical Information and Sights Send glowing postcards from the **Craig Post Office (General Delivery ZIP Code: 99921)** on Craig-Klawock St. next to Thompson House (826-3298; open Mon.-Fri. 8am-5pm, Sat. noon-2pm), or buy reading material at **Voyageur Book Store** across the street (open Mon.-Fri. 10am-6pm, Sat. 11am-5pm, Sun. noon-5pm). The **public library** up the hill on 3rd St. (826-3281) shelves a strong Alaskan section (open Mon. 7-9pm; Tues., Thurs.-Fri. 10:30am-12:30pm and 2:30-5:30pm; Wed. 10-11:30am and 2:30-5:30pm; Sat.-Sun.

2:30-5:30pm). For information on the 19 wilderness cabins on Prince of Wales Island, caves, and camping, drop by the **Forest Service Office** at 9th Ave. and Main St. (826-3271; open Mon.-Fri. 7am-5pm). **Ketchikan Air Island Travel**, on Front St., sells fishing and hunting licenses (open Mon.-Sat. 5:30am-7:30pm); **JT Brown** handles tackle (open Mon.-Sat. 9am-6pm). The **Craig Health Clinic** (826-3257) is on 3rd St., next to the library (open Mon.-Tues., Thurs.-Fri. 9am-1pm, 2-6pm; Sat. 10am-12:30pm, 1:30-4pm.) The **police** (826-3330) are across from the library on 3rd St.

Accommodations, Camping, and Food   After absorbing the sunset from the docks and inspecting a faded fish-packing plant, visitors can mingle with fishermen and loggers in the triangle marked out by three local bars. Both the **Hill Bar** and the **Craig Inn** resound with live music at least five nights a week, more when the fleet is in town. The Inn, which has no accommodations, displays the most hostile decor and atmosphere in town with its chiseled and slashed bar top. **Ruth Ann's** (826-3376), a quieter, more intimate spot, lines its walls with photos from the fishing days of yore. Lunch, tasty and more reasonably priced than dinner, is available from 11am until closing time (open Sun.-Thurs. 6:30am-9:30pm, Fri.-Sat. 6:30am-10pm, off-season 7am-9pm).

Though most of Prince of Wales Island falls within the **Tongass National Forest,** allowing free unimpaired camping, Craig is surrounded by private tribal lands where camping is prohibited. Follow Hamilton Dr. along the water to reach the campsites within city limits beside the baseball field on Graveyard Island. The city has posted signs discouraging camping there, but locals still take advantage of the waterside views and nearby cooking pits. The **TLC Laundromat and Rooms** (826-2966), on Cold Storage Rd. behind the supermarket, offers the only affordable slumber space in Craig. Their singles ($36) and doubles ($47) with hall baths fill fast in summer. The laundromat ($1.75 wash, 25¢ dry) also has showers ($1.50 for 5 min.; open daily 7am-9pm). There are new **public showers** at the corner of Hamilton and Craig-Klawock St., but be prepared to soap up fast; pay 25¢ for less than 1 min.

Several island communities do their food shopping in Craig. Thompson House groceries on Craig-Klawock St. is adequate (open Mon.-Sat. 7am-9pm, Sun. 8am-6pm). There's always a place for the ravenous traveler at the **Captain's Table** (826-3880) on Front. St. The captain serves huge portions of soup, immense sandwiches ($6), and a big breakfast special ($7) of two eggs, three hotcakes, and bacon (open daily 5:30am-9pm). **Lacie's Pizza** (826-3925), across the street from the market, serves up satisfying slices at lunch time for $1.75 plus 30¢ per topping; also 8 flavors of hard ice cream (open Tues.-Thurs. 11:30am-8pm, Sat. 11:30am-9pm, Sun. 4-8pm). **Sub Marina,** open summers on Water St., offers substantial sandwiches at reasonable prices, including their vegetarian special, "The Empty Net" ($4). Their soft-serve ice cream cone packs the most calories to be had for a buck in Craig. Wash it all down with an Italian soda (large for $2.25) or a cappucino ($1.75) at **Cherilyn's Espresso** on Front St. (open Mon.-Fri. 7am-7pm, Sat.-Sun. 9am-6pm).

KLAWOCK, THORNE BAY, AND HYDABURG

The village of **Klawock**, 7 mi. north of Craig, sits by a river of the same name. Home to Alaska's first cannery (1878), Klawock still revolves around fishing. The local totem park, the largest on Prince of Wales Island, contains 21 original and replicated totems from the abandoned village of Tuxekan. The largest structure in Klawock today is the newly constructed **Bell Tower Center** on East Klawock Hwy. housing the colossal **Klawock Super Valu**, the cheapest option for groceries on the island (open Mon.-Sat. 7am-9pm, Sun. 7am-6pm). Next door sits **Papa's Pizza** (755-2244), where marinated artichoke hearts, sun-dried tomatoes, and Canadian bacon are heaped on warm, crunchy homemade dough. A one-person cheese pizza costs $5; dine-in or take-out (open Sun.-Thurs. 11am-10pm, Fri.-Sat. 11am-11pm).

A narrow, dusty logging road cuts northeast across the island from Klawock to **Thorne Bay (Hospital:** 828-3906; **Police:** 828-3905; **Fire:** 828-3313) an unpretentious town recently created through the incorporation of a logging camp. For many of the helicopter pilots, loggers, and mechanics working in the logging industry, Thorne Bay is one in a long series of temporary homes that move with the timber harvest. For others living in float-houses and cabins along the beautiful bay, the town is primarily a postal address and grocery supply point. Thorne Bay provides attractive waters to kayakers, and its tributary rivers win the praise of anglers. Unlike Craig, Thorne Bay lies fully within **Tongass National Forest,** and campers may pitch tents for up to two weeks on any suitable site. **Sandy Beach Picnic Area,** 6 mi. north of Thorne Bay on Forest Rd. 30, offers campers a view and a toilet, as does **Gravelly Creek Picnic Area** 4 mi. northwest of town on Thorne Bay Rd. (free). Locals recommend the **Eagles Nest Campground,** 12 mi. north of Thorne Bay; a camp unit ($5) includes access to bathroom, water, cooking grates, a canoe launch, picnic tables, and RV parking. The flocking hordes of tourists support a single place of lodging in Thorne Bay, **Brenda's Beehive B&B** (828-3945) on Bayview Ct., which has just two beds in the summer; fortunately, they're comfortable ($55, $70 with dinner). Brenda and her husband can also field questions about the Tongass National Forest. You may see them again at the **Forest Service Station** (828-3304) in town. The **Thorne Bay Market,** where a gallon of milk goes for $4, sits back in a cove beyond the docks (open Mon.-Sat. 8am-8pm, Sun. 9am-6pm). **Some Place to Go** (828-8888), the outdoor hamburger stand beside the high school, serves a tasty cheeseburger for $3 (open 10am-7pm), while **D-International Restaurant** (828-3440) on Rainy Lane across from Island News offers friendly sit-down service (open Mon. and Wed.-Fri. 6:30am-1pm and 4-7pm, Sat.-Sun. 6:30am-1pm and 3:30-7pm). Pack your dirty laundry up the hill past St. John's Church to **Dan's Laundromat** for a $2 wash and $1 dry (open daily 8am-9pm).

Hydaburg, the Alaskan stronghold of the Haida people, lies 20 mi. off the Hollis-Craig highway. The predominantly Haida community receives few visitors, but welcomes those that come. The only standard attraction in this little village centered on fishing and subsistence activities is the excellent collection of restored totems in front of the school. Fran Sanderson (285-3139) offers a room and three meals in her blue home across from the totem park for $75 (ask about student discounts). Caroline Natkong (283-3301) does the same for $70 in her home by the Hydaburg River. For grub, head to **TJ's Cafe** on the water, or to **Do Drop-In Groceries**, where a loaf of bread costs $3.05 (open Mon.-Sat. 9am-5:30pm, Sun. 1pm-4pm). The **Hydaburg Clinic** (285-3462) is open Mon.-Fri. 8am to 5pm.

■■■ WRANGELL

The only place in Alaska to have been ruled by four different nations, the tidy town of Wrangell (RANG-gul) harvests the riches of the forest and the sea amidst a wealth of sights and history. This spot, near the mouth of the torrential Stikine River, had long supported a Tlingit Native village when the Russian-American Company built a fort here in 1834. After some wrangling with the British over the Stikine River fur trade, the Russians leased their holding to the British-owned Hudson Bay Company in 1840. Soon after the United States purchased Alaska from Russia in 1867, Britain turned over control of the fort to the Americans. As the only gateway to Canada's interior between Prince Rupert and Skagway, the Stikine River became a key transportation corridor during three gold rushes over the next four decades. Meanwhile, Wrangell exploded into a tramping ground for miners traveling to and from the goldfields. The renowned explorer and ecologist John Muir passed through the town in this era and was unimpressed: "It was a lawless draggle of wooden huts and houses, built in crooked lines, wrangling around the boggy shores of the island."

Wrangell now presents a more appealing front to visitors. An orderly, prosperous, lumber-and-fishing town with a picturesque harbor, Wrangell's attractions are convenient enough to allow a brief visit during a ferry layover and plentiful enough to merit a night's stay. A youth hostel and a free campground make these options easy.

PRACTICAL INFORMATION AND ORIENTATION

Chamber of Commerce Visitors Center (874-3901), in the A-frame on Outer Dr. beside City Hall. Open Mon.-Sat. noon-5pm, Sun. and mornings when the ferries are in.

Forest Service, 525 Bennett St., ¾ mi. east of town (874-2323). Open Mon.-Fri. 8am-5pm. Reserve cabins here.

Alaska Dept. of Fish and Game (874-3822) in green Kadin Building on Front St.

Alaska Marine Highway (874-2021), at Stikine Ave. and 2nd St., 5 min. from the visitors center. Frequent service to Sitka ($38), Juneau ($56), and Ketchikan ($24). 24-hr. recording of arrivals and departures (874-3711). Open 2 hrs. before arrivals and Mon.-Fri. 10am-4pm. Luggage lockers 25¢.

Airport: Alaska Air (874-3309) makes daily stops in Wrangell, once on a flight to Petersburg and Juneau, and again on a flight to Ketchikan and Seattle.

Taxi: Porky's Cab Co., 874-3603, 24 hrs. **Star Cab,** 874-3622, 5:30am-3am.

Car Rental: Practical Rent-A-Car, Airport Road near the airport (874-3495). Compact car $42 per day, van $46, unlimited mileage.

Air Charter Services: Sunrise Aviation, P.O. Box 432 (874-2319). **Ketchikan Air Service,** P.O. Box 874 (874-2369). **Temsco Helicopters,** P.O. Box 5057 (874-2010).

Library on 2nd St. near the museum (874-3535). Good Alaska section. Open Tues.-Thurs. 1-5pm and 7-9pm, Mon. and Fri. 10am-noon and 1-5pm, Sat. 9am-5pm.

Laundromat: Thunderbird Laundromat, at Front St. and Outer Dr. Wash $2, dry 25¢. Open daily 7am-8pm.

Public Swimming Pool: Indoors at Wrangell High School on Church St. (874-2444). Also weight room, racquetball, and showers. Hours vary; closed Sun. Pool, weight room, gym $1.50, under 18 $1. Racquetball: first two players $6, additional players 50¢.

Pharmacy: Wrangell Drug, 202 Front St. (874-3422). Standard array of personal hygiene products (open Mon.-Sat. 9am-6pm, Sun. 11am-6pm). They support Linsey for 4th of July Queen.

Hospital: 874-3356, next to the elementary school on Airport Rd.

Emergency: 911. **Police** (874-3304) and **Fire** (874-3223), both in the Public Safety Building on Zimovia Hwy.

Post Office, on the corner across from the library (874-3714). The town rejected proposed delivery boxes in 1983 in favor of maintaining the ritual of coming in to check P.O. boxes. Open Mon.-Fri. 8:30am-5pm, Sat. 11am-1pm. **ZIP Code:** 99929.

Area Code: 907.

Wrangell (pop. 2500) lies on the northern tip of Wrangell Island, about 85 mi. northwest of Ketchikan and 150 mi. southeast of Juneau. The Stikine River flows west from British Columbia and, after passing through Alaska for the last 30 mi. of its run, empties into the straits and narrows of the Panhandle 5 mi. north of Wrangell. At its mouth, the river branches out into a wide, sandy delta, where the world's second-largest congregation of bald eagles gathers in the spring.

ACCOMMODATIONS AND CAMPING

First Presbyterian Church Hostel (HI/AYH), 202 Church St., five blocks from the ferry terminal (874-3534). An independent hostel run with high and admirable standards. Sleep on foam mats; four rooms, five to a room. Bring your own sleeping bag. Showers, kitchen, and piano. $10. Curfew 10pm unless late ferry. Open mid-June-Labor Day daily 5pm-9am.

Clarke's Bed and Breakfast, P.O. Box 1020, 732 Case Ave., above the inner harbor (874-3863 or 874-2125). Double bed, queen-sized sofa, private bath and cooking facilities, ferry pickup, flexible noon checkout. Clean and comfortable. Breakfast included. Singles $40, doubles $50. Marlene Clarke, the proprietor, prefers reservations with a $25 deposit, but don't call past 11pm. Winter long-term rates negotiable.

City Park, 1 mi. south of town on Zimovia Hwy. (2nd St. changes names several times before becoming Zimovia Hwy. south of town.), immediately beyond the cemetery and the baseball field. Picnic tables and shelters, drinking water, toilet, bumpy tent spots, and a beautiful view of the water. A bit close to the sewage treatment plant. 24-hr. max. stay. Free. Open Memorial Day-Labor Day.

Shoemaker Bay RV Park, 5 mi. south of town on the Zimovia Hwy. 29 RV sites, wooded tent camping area, picnic tables, water tap, and flush toilet. Trail to Rainbow Falls (¾ mi.) across the highway. Sites $8.

Pats Lake, 11 mi. south of town, near where the Zimovia Hwy. becomes a narrow Forest Service road. Drinking water from Pats Creek (boil it first!). Trout swim in the lake and the creek, and salmon run up the creek in the fall. Sites $8.

Rooney's Roost B&B (874-2026), on the corner of 2nd St. and McKinnon. Two tastefully decorated rooms with private baths are the reward for trekking through the weeds sprouting from Mrs. Rooney's front stairs. Kitchen privileges upon request. Comfortable sitting room with TV. Transport to and from ferry. Breakfast included. Singles $55, doubles $60. For other Wrangell B&B information, call or write the **Alaska Bed & Breakfast Association,** 390 South Franklin #200 (586-2959).

FOOD

Not a wellspring of haute cuisine, Wrangell's eateries fry most of their fare. Buy deli sandwiches at **Benjamin's Groceries** (874-2341) on Outer Drive. (Open Mon.-Sat. 8am-8pm.) Good places to lunch outside are the picnic tables near the Chamber of Commerce and the huge stump at the corner of Grief and Church St.

Diamond C Cafe, 215 Front St., beside the laundromat on Front St. (874-3677). A favorite of Wrangellites (and about the only place open before noon on a Sun.). Sausage and cheese omelette with hashbrowns and toast $7.25; fish and chips $8. Breakfast until 11:15am. Open Tues.-Sat. 6am-8pm, Sun.-Mon. 6am-4pm.

Dock Side Restaurant, 109 Stikine Ave. in the Stikine Inn at the city docks (874-3737), across from the post office. Dinners range in price from $11-16, but daily lunch specials are $5.50-6.50, and breakfast (french toast, $3.50) won't break the bank. The back room sits right on the water, a good perch for watching the cruise ships. Breakfast until 11:30am Mon.-Sat., until 1pm Sun. Dinner starts at 5pm. Open 6am-9pm daily.

Duke's Diner, on Front St. (874-2589). The place to eat a late night breakfast before going to bed. Biscuits and gravy $4.75; 3 eggs, ham, hashbrowns and toast $6.50; chicken burger with fries $5. Breakfast all day. Open Sun.-Thurs. 6am-3pm and 6pm-midnight, Fri.-Sat. open 24 hrs.

SIGHTS AND OUTDOORS

If the ferry schedule permits you to spend only 45 minutes of your life in Wrangell, a walk out to **Shakes Island** might be the best use of your time. Follow Front St. to Shakes St., where a short bridge leads out to the island in the middle of Wrangell's snug harbor. Outdoor totems stand before the **Shakes Tribal House,** a meticulous replica of the communal home of high-caste Tlingit people. A Civilian Conservation Corps work team built it during the Depression without the aid of a sawmill or a single nail. Inside, finely carved totems and a sunken floor stand below large timbers showing the countless adze marks that hewed them into shape. The house is open during the summer whenever a ship or ferry docks for more than 1 hr., and Mon.-Tues. 2 to 4pm, Wed. 10am to 1:30pm, Fri. 1 to 3pm. (Also by appointment (874-2023) for a donation of $10 or more. Regular donation $1.)

The **Wrangell Museum** (874-3770) temporarily occupies the basement of the Community Center on Church St. Besides the interesting but predictable collections of Native American artifacts, the museum houses a communications and aviation room and an exhibit about the region's natural history (open May to mid-Sept. Mon.-Sat. 1-4pm and when ferry ships are in; mid-Sept. to April, Wed. 1-4pm, or by appointment. $2, under 16 free). The museum is also the place to buy permits to try your hand at mining garnets from the **Wrangell Garnet Ledge.** Previously owned by the first all-female corporation in America, the mine was deeded to the Boy Scouts and children of Wrangell in 1962. The children now chip garnets out of the rock by hand and line up to hawk their wares whenever a ship arrives. The mine, by the mouth of the Stikine River, can only be reached by boat. Permits are $10 per day; 10% of the garnets must be left with the Scouts.

Garnets aren't the only interesting rocks in Wrangell. Strewn across **Petroglyph Beach**, ¾ mi. north of the ferry terminal on Evergreen Ave., are the stone carvings of Wrangell's first inhabitants. Archaeologists remain uncertain about the age of these petroglyphs; estimates range from centuries to millennia. Unlike the garnets, you can't take these rocks home with you. Many people make rubbings with nearby ferns on a special rice paper sold by several stores in town. Concerned about excessive wear and tear, the city is now encouraging people to take photos instead of rubbings. The petroglyphs photograph well in the rain.

Hikers can follow in John Muir's footsteps and scramble up nearby Mt. Dewey to an observation point with a commanding view of town and the Stikine River flats. Walking down 2nd St. toward the center of town, McKinnon St. is on the left. Follow McKinnon St. 2 blocks away from the water where it intersects with 3rd St. Turn left on 3rd St. and look for a white sign marking the trailhead. The trail is primitive and not regularly maintained, so bring your boots if it's wet.

Three mi. beyond City Park on Zimovia Hwy., **Rainbow Falls Trail** runs 1km up to the waterfall and then continues on as the Institute Creek Trail. This trail climbs steeply through spruce and hemlock forest, then follows a boardwalk past several muskeg openings to a ridgetop with views and space to pitch a tent. A three-sided Forest Service shelter sits on the ridge, available on a first-come basis. The trail's condition ranges from fair to excellent (bring your boots), and the terrain ranges from easy to difficult. Finish in about 1½ hours round trip. For more information on the trails, campsites, and cabins in the Wrangell area, contact the **Wrangell Ranger District** (874-2323), Box 51 (open Mon.-Fri. 8am-4:30pm). The rangers stress that all groundwater be boiled for at least five minutes before drinking, and that you make noise (to scare off the bears!) while hiking the trails.

The Stikine River is the fastest navigable river in the Northwest. Charter boat operations regularly run up the Stikine and over to Garnet Lodge. There are six Forest Service cabins throughout the Stikine delta and two bathing huts at **Chief Shakes Hot Springs**, a few mi. upriver. The only developed black bear observatory in Southeast Alaska, the **Anan Bear Observatory** is also accessible by boat. Here you can watch rapacious bears feast on the pink salmon that climb the falls to spawn. Call **TH Charters**, Box 934, 107 Front St. (874-2085 or 1-800-874-2085; fax 874-2285) for information; they will schedule departures around your ferry schedule (open Mon.-Fri. 9am-5pm). For a complete listing of charter boat services (Wrangell has 16 of them), contact the **Wrangell Chamber of Commerce** (874-3901). The Chamber of Commerce also provides information on scuba-diving tours, whale-watching, fishing and hunting trips, and sightseeing outings. Several charter organizations transport rafts and kayaks up the river.

The **Eagle's Wings Fine Arts Gallery** (874-3888) on Front St. (open daily 10am-5pm; sometimes later for the ferries) and the **Eagle's Nest Craft Gallery** at 407 Church St. (874-3243; open Mon.-Fri. 8am-5pm, Sat. 10am-5pm) display the creative works of local artists. For a real dose of Wrangell culture, visit on the 4th of July for the parade, logging show, and fireworks, or during Memorial Day weekend (May 28-30) for the "special derby days" of the Salmon Derby (May 14-30). The derby's biggest fish nets a $5000 prize.

■■■ PETERSBURG

In 1897, Norwegian immigrant Peter Buschmann saw opportunity in the natural harbor, abundant fish, and convenient glacier ice, and built a cannery here. Petersburg now claims the world's largest halibut fleet and a strong Scandinavian legacy. The greeting signs at the ferry dock proclaim *Velkommen*, and it's more than a tourism gimmick: nearly everyone in town claims to be descended from Buschmann. Petersburg clings fast to a hard-working, hard-playing Norwegian character. Fishing is the mainstay of the local economy, and Petersburg draws a horde of summer workers. By virtue of its position at the top of the Wrangell Narrows, a section of the Inside Passage that challenges ferry captains to navigate within a shallow, narrow channel subject to ferocious tidal currents, Petersburg (pop. 3500) lies outside the range of the large cruise ships. This isolation has lent this island community an uncommon cohesiveness: when one of the canneries a few years ago found itself understaffed with a heap of salmon to process, the management went through the phone book calling for extra hands. Retirees, housewives, and people just home from work all rallied to help.

Unfortunately, Petersburg's strong sense of community has made it somewhat suspicious of strangers. Students or backpackers planning to stay in the city should be forewarned that there are no youth hostels and no storage facilities for packs. Rumor has it that townspeople consider such visitors "transients."

PRACTICAL INFORMATION AND ORIENTATION

Visitors Information: Chamber of Commerce and Visitor Information Center, P.O. Box 649, Petersburg 99833 (772-3646), at 1st and Fram St. Home of a replica of the world-record *126½-lb.* king salmon. Reserve Forest Service cabins here. Helpful, informed staff. Open Mon.-Fri. 8am-4:30pm, Sat. 10am-2pm, Sun. noon-4pm; winter Mon.-Fri. 10am-noon, 1-3pm.

Forest Service (722-3871), P.O. Box 1328, above the post office. Information on hiking trails and fishing. Reserve cabins here, too. Open Mon.-Fri. 8am-5pm.

Airport: Alaska Airlines (772-4255), 1 mi. from the Federal Bldg. on 1506 Haugen Drive. To: Juneau ($105), Seattle ($346). For sightseeing, contact **Temsco Air** (772-4220).

Alaska Marine Highway (772-3855), terminal at Mile 0.9 on the Mitkof Hwy., 1 mi. from the center of town. To: Ketchikan ($38), Sitka ($26), Wrangell ($18), and Juneau ($44).

Taxi: City Cab, 772-3003. Rates start at $4. Open 24 hrs. **Chris West Cab,** 772-9378.

Car Rental: Allstar Car Rentals (772-4281), at the Scandia House Hotel. $45 per day with unlimited mileage. Also rents 18-ft. **boats** ($150 per day, $125 for guests of the hotel).

Bike Rental: Northern Bikes, 114 Harbor Way (772-3777). $4 for 1 hr., $3.50 each additional hr.

Bookstore: Sing Lee Alley Books, 11 Sing Lee Alley (772-4440). Open Mon.-Sat. 10am-5pm, Sun. noon-4pm.

Employment: Petersburg Job Service (772-3791), at Haugen Dr. and 1st St. Provides information on all three canneries. Openings posted in the window. Write ahead for the straight-talking pamphlets *Alaska Job Facts* and *Seafood Processing Jobs in Alaska.* Open Mon.-Fri. 8am-noon and 1-4:30pm.

Laundromat: Glacier Laundry (772-4144), downtown at Nordic and Dolphin. Sleeping bags dry-cleaned for $14. Wash $1.75, 7-min. dry 25¢. Open daily 6am-10pm. Also at **LeConte RV Park** (772-4680), at 4th and Haugen.

Showers: LeConte RV Park (772-4680), at 4th and Haugen, **Tent City** (see below), and **Glacier Laundry:** $1.75 for 7 min.

Pharmacy: Rexall Drug, 215 Nordic Dr., downtown. Open Mon.-Fri. 8am-9pm, Sat. 8am-6pm, Sun. noon-6pm.

Library: at Haugen and Nordic above the Fire Hall. Open Mon.-Thurs. noon-9pm, Fri.-Sat. 1-5pm.

Hospital: Petersburg General Hospital (772-4291), at Fram and N. 1st St.

Emergency: Police, 772-3838. **State Troopers,** 772-3100.

Police, (772-3838), 16 South Nordic Dr.

Post Office: (772-3121), at Haugen and Nordic Dr. Open Mon.-Fri. 9am-5:30pm, Sat. 11am-2pm. **General Delivery ZIP Code:** 99833.

Area Code: 907.

If you're looking for Nordic Drive, Main St., or Mitkof Hwy., you're probably on it. The only main drag goes by several names. The ferry drops you off 1 mi. south of downtown; be prepared to walk, as there is no bus. Cabs to the center run about $4, $6 out to Tent City.

ACCOMMODATIONS AND CAMPING

The only two places in town for backpackers are often packed sardine-like with summer cannery workers; beyond them, there is no camping within city limits. A stagnant swamp surrounds Petersburg; the next nearest campground is 17 mi. away. Contact the Visitor's Center (see above) for more comprehensive bed and breakfast listings.

Tent City (772-9864), on Haugen Dr. past the airport, 2.1 mi. from the ferry. This ramshackle collection of tarps and wooden platforms rests atop Alaska's most fascinating terrain, muskeg swamp, and is home to most of Petersburg's "transient" workers. Administered by Parks and Recreation, camp manager Charlie Freeman has added several amenities (pay phone, griddle, hot-plate, cooking appliances, refrigerator, and a barn-like shelter with no walls) and a dose of order to what used to be largely self-governed; the "No Alcohol" policy is new. A true Alaskan experience. Water, toilet, 4 showers (50¢) and pit fires with wood. Quiet hours 10pm-noon. Open May-Sept. $4 per night, $25 per week, and $85 per month.

LeConte RV Park, P.O. Box 1548 (772-4680), at 4th and Haugen. 1 mi. from ferry, 3 blocks from downtown. Limited space for tent sites ($5); rates vary for RV hookups. Grounds are worn but still close to town. A **coin-op laundry** (wash and dry both 75¢) and **showers** ($1.25 per 9 min.) are open to the public (bring shower shoes!).

Jewells By the Sea, 806 Nordic Dr. (772-3620), ¼ mi. north of the ferry terminal. Small B&B with a great view of the mountains and the Wrangell Narrows. 3 beautifully furnished rooms with a shared bath. Airport or ferry pickup and delivery. Singles $55, doubles $70. Breakfast included; kitchen privileges on request. Laundry $1.50 per load.

Narrows Inn, Box 1048 (772-4284). Mile 1 of Mitkof Hwy., across from the ferry. Surprisingly pleasant, clean rooms, with private baths and cable TV. Complimentary coffee in lobby. 25 units. Singles $55. Doubles $65. Call for summer reservations before June.

Scandia House, 110 Nordic Dr. (772-4281), between Fram and Gjoa (JOE-uh) St. Exceptionally clean rooms, with TV and free HBO. Courtesy van available. Boat and car rental offices based here. Singles $55, with bath $70, with kitchenette $83; $5 each additional person. Doubles with kitchenette $88. 24 units. Continental breakfast included. Hotel open 24 hr. for registration and check-out.

Ohmer Creek Campground, Mile 22 of Mitkof Hwy. Maintained by Forest Service. 15 sites. 14-day max. stay. Gravel trail takes you to the perfect spot for first-hand fish habitat voyeurism. Water, pit toilets. Free.

FOOD

Although it should be as easy as finding fish in the sea, reasonably priced seafood is rare in Petersburg. **Hammer and Wikan** (772-4246), on Nordic Dr., has a huge selection of groceries and sells camping gear and insect repellent (open Mon.-Sat. 8am-7pm, Sun. 9am-6pm). **The Trading Union** (772-3881), on Nordic and Dolphin, has a similar selection (open Mon.-Fri. 8am-7pm, Sat. 8am-5:30pm, Sun. 9am-5pm). Crowds assemble for free soup and sandwiches Wednesdays June 2-August 11 5 to 6:30pm at the St. Andrews church at 3rd and Excel.

Helse-Health Foods and Deli (772-3444), on Sing Lee Alley off Nordic Dr. With flowers, ferns, little wooden stools, and plenty of reggae, this earthy and progressive place is a favorite port of call for the Rastafarian halibut fleet. Soup and bread $5, "Cheese Breeze": avocado, shrimp, mushrooms, and havarti ($6.75). Chocolate brownie $1.35. Lots of yummy juices. Open Mon.-Fri. 7:30am-5pm, Sat. 10am-3pm; winter Mon.-Fri. 7:30am-3pm, Sat. 10am-3pm.

Cafe Agapé (772-9300), three doors north of the post office on Nordic Dr. New Age Jazz and green marble-esque tables soften the impact of the fluorescent lights. Try the fresh squeezed orange juice ($2) with the quiche ($3.25). Breakfast until noon (the menu greets you in Norwegian: *God Morgen!*). Lunch begins at 11am. Open Mon.-Sat. 6am-9pm, Sun. 7am-8pm.

Pellerito's Pizza (772-3727), across from the ferry. Where the locals get stuffed. Try the chicken primavera on noodles with garlic bread ($6.65) or, if you're really hungry, order a football-sized calzone ($9). Offers pizza by the slice ($2.50). Open Sun.-Thurs. 7am-11pm, Fri.-Sat. 7am-midnight.

Homestead Cafe (772-3900), Nordic Dr. at Excel, across from the general store. Run by fishermen's wives who understand large appetites, frequented by fishermen who know how to eat. Not a "friendly" place, but lots of local character. Go ahead and try to finish their stack of pancakes ($3.50). We dare you. Prodigious plate of biscuits and gravy $5.50. Hearty Viking burger and fries $8. The good ol' boys of Petersburg play dice on the tables and convene at the counter. Open Mon.-Sat. 24 hrs. Lunch starts at 11am.

SIGHTS AND ENTERTAINMENT

This is the best place on the Panhandle to see a fishing town at work, as long as the fish are biting. Only one of the town's three canneries is open to the public: Patty Norheim leads groups of four or more on 3-hr. tours through the shrimp cannery next to the harbormaster's office, through the rest of the city, through a hatchery, and finally back to her home for cocktails. Find out about the **"Patty Wagon"** ($25) at 772-4837 or stop in at the Tides Inn.

To learn about the development of this pristine Norwegian village, head to the **Clausen Memorial Museum** (772-3598), P.O. Box 708, at 2nd Ave. and Fram St., which displays native artifacts and an inspiring history of fishing techniques. Outside the museum is the bizarre **Fisk Fountain**, dedicated to Petersburg's sustenance: fish (open Mon.-Sat. 10am-4pm, Sun. 1-4pm; $2, under 12 free). Sat. at 7pm sharp, head to the Sons of Norway Hall for **bingo.**

On the weekend closest to May 17, Petersburg joins its international brethren in joyous celebration of Norwegian independence (1905) from Sweden. During the **Little Norway Festival,** mock Vikings dance, sing (Spam spam spam spam...lovely SPAM, wonderful SPAM!), parade, hunt their own furs, wear horns, and sail in Viking boats. Memorial Day weekend brings the **Salmon Derby,** with its ubiquitous salmon bakes. Tall tales are made reality at the derby's contest for biggest fish; last year's 10-yr.-old winner netted $5000 in prizes with her catch! A search for the tagged fish, and the accompanying $10,000 prize, has been sadly unsuccessful in recent years. Last year a local inhabitant caught the tagged fish, thought he had won, and celebrated publicly...only to be reminded that one must catch the fish *during the festival* to win! The **4th of July** in Petersburg is a merry flight, especially during the **competitive herring toss.**

OUTDOORS

You needn't wander far in Petersburg to find bountiful fishing sites yielding salmon, halibut, crab, shrimp, dolly varden, and cutthroat trout. The island is teeming with brown and black bears, deer, moose and waterfowl. For more information, or to obtain Alaska state sportfishing and hunting licenses, contact the **Alaska Dept. of Fish & Game** (See Fishing and Hunting in the Essentials section). If you're content with the easily obtained smaller catch, or if you're just amused, **jigging** for herring from the docks can be good for kicks. Morning and evening are the best times to glimpse the island's wildlife. Petersburg is now home to five wild deer, often seen aimlessly wandering the town roads.

Petersburg is almost surrounded by scenic hiking trails; most are in the Tongass National Forest. The trails vary both in length (from ½ to more than 10 mi.) and difficulty. Contact the **Forest Service** for advice on necessary equipment, safety considerations, Forest Service Recreation Cabin reservations, and the pamphlet *Hiking Trails: Petersburg Ranger District, Tongass National Forest.* Also contact them for information on necessary equipment and questions about safety.

Of the several Forest Service cabins around Petersburg ($25 per night), only one is easily accessible by foot. The trail to the **Raven's Roost** cabin begins near the large orange and white tanks behind the airport. After traversing a section of muskeg on a boardwalk, the trail climbs steeply to an alpine region with excellent views of Petersburg and the Wrangell Narrows. The cabin with a second-story sleeping loft sits at the end of the 4-mi. trail.

Another popular walk entails traversing what locals call the **Loop;** from Nordic Drive, past Eagle's Roost Picnic Area and Sandy Beach Park, onto the Frederick Pt. Boardwalk (where your chances of seeing bears and indigenous petroglyphs are excellent at low tide), and back on Haugen Drive. The Loop takes about 1½ hours to complete, unless you linger to watch the boats and floatplanes on Frederick Sound. Pick up the *Petersburg Map* at the Chamber of Commerce (see Practical Information) for a complete illustration of the trails and logging roads on Mitkof Island.

Several area outfitters offer reasonably priced outdoor adventures. Scott Roberge at **Tongass Kayak Adventures,** P.O. Box 707 (772-4600), offers guided sea kayak tours up the Petersburg Creek. Tours daily June-Aug., $45 per person, children under 12 $30; includes gear. Or do it yourself: kayak rentals are $40 per day for a single, $50 per day for a double with a three day minimum. Skipper Stephen Berry offers four-hour boat tours of Le Conte Bay and Glacier for $75 at **Sights Southeast,** P.O. Box 934 (772-4503). **Alaskan Scenic Waterways,** 114 Harbor Way (772-3777) also offers river trips, including a $15 1-hr. tour of Petersburg and Petersburg Creek, and air glacier tours ($75 per person for a 3½- to 4-hr. tour).

If you find the mind-boggling number of options daunting, contact David Berg at **Viking Travel,** P.O. Box 787 (772-3813; fax 327-2571), and ask him to book your outing for you; be sure to give advance notice to allow him to find you the best deal (open Mon.-Fri. 8:30am-5:30pm, Sat. 10am-5pm). The planked **Petersburg Creek Trail,** ½-mi. across the Wrangell Narrows on neighboring Kupreanof Island, runs 11½ mi. up to Petersburg Lake through a wilderness area to another Forest Service cabin. If the tide is high enough, you can also go up the creek a few mi. by boat to make a 6½-mi. hike to the lake. Although many charter operators in town ferry people across the narrows and rent skiffs, this can cost more than $100. Try asking at the harbormaster's office about boats making the crossing with space for an extra passenger. A small number of people also live across the narrows and make the afternoon commute home. (*Let's Go* does not recommend hitchhiking).

Twenty-two mi. south of town on Mitkof Hwy., Three Lakes Loop Rd. runs up to **Three Lakes Loop Trail.** This easy 3-mi. loop passes three small lakes, all known for trout. Another 1½-mi. trail leads from the middle lake out to **Ideal Cove** on Frederick Sound. Adjacent to Tent City, **Frederick Boardwalk** leads to the sea through the local flora; a 1-mi. walk each way passes muskeg quagmire. A foolhardy dusk activity for Tent City campers is to follow Nordic Dr. 1 mi. north to the city dump, a gourmet restaurant for local black bears. This can be extremely dangerous; the hungry bears here no longer fear humans.

To access the **Stikine Wilderness and Icefield,** rent a skiff in town, take it 35 mi. south to the end of Mitkof Hwy., and jump in. **Green Rocks Lodge,** P.O. Box 110 (772-3245), offers affordable 4-day package tours to fish salmon at **Blind Slough.** The package is cheaper than four nights at a local bed and breakfast, and includes hot breakfasts, kitchen facilities, 16-ft. skiff with radio, fishing gear, protective wear, and transportation.

■ ■ ■ SITKA

The only major Panhandle town with direct access to the Pacific Ocean, Russians settled Sitka in 1799. The native Tlingits grew to resent the Russians' presence; in 1802 they burned and razed the settlement, massacring nearly all the Russian inhabitants. In 1804, the manager of the Russian-American Company, Alexander Baranov, arrived with a fleet and began a naval bombardment of the fort the Tlingits had constructed in anticipation of Russian counterattack. After a bloody 10-day battle, the

Tlingits withdrew under cover of darkness. Baranov made "New Archangel" the capital of Russian Alaska. The fur trade made it a wealthy cultural center preeminent in the Northwest; for several decades in the 19th century, Seattle and San Francisco were quaint fishing villages compared to Sitka. When Russia sold Alaska to the United States in 1867 for $7.2 million, the transaction was officiated here.

The broken cone of Mt. Edgecumbe dominates the view across Sitka Sound. Dormant for 11,000 years, the volcano was the site of an infamous prank by an eccentric millionaire: about 20 years ago, a huge pile of burning tires in the caldera spewed clouds of dense black smoke and nearly caused the town's evacuation. Although home to a University of Alaska campus and Sheldon Jackson College, in summer, hordes of elderly tourists emerging from cruise ships transform Sitka from a college town into a retirement village.

PRACTICAL INFORMATION AND ORIENTATION

Visitors Information: Sitka Convention & Visitor's Bureau, P.O. Box 1226 (747-5940). In the Centennial Bldg. at 330 Harbor Dr. The visitors bureau is well-organized. Open Mon.-Fri. 8am-5pm, weekends only when cruise ships are in and when the Centennial Bldg. hosts events.

Forest Service, Sitka Ranger District, Tongass National Forest, 201 Katlian, #109 (747-6671). Open Mon.-Fri. 8am-5pm. For a modest charge, pick up a copy of *Sitka Trails.* Also distributes pamphlets about cabins ($25 per night).

Luggage Storage: Fire station holds packs for free, as will the hostel for its visitors. The Centennial Bldg. will hold them for $1 per bag per day, and the ferry terminal has 25¢ lockers with 24-hr. max.

Bookstore: Old Harbor Books, 201 Lincoln (747-8808). Superb Alaska section and lots of information about local arts events. Marine charts and **topographical maps.** Check out the skull collection on loan from the Alaska Dept. of Fish and Game. The owner, a member of Greenpeace, is infamous for chaining himself to the mill to protest their former lack of pollution control. Open Mon.-Fri. 9am-6pm, Sat.-Sun. 9am-5pm.

Library: Kettleson Memorial Library, 320 Harbor Dr. (747-8708). Open Mon.-Thurs. 10am-9pm, Fri. 1-6pm, Sat.-Sun. 1-5pm.

Laundromats and Shower Facilities: Homestead Laundromat, 713 Katlian Ave. (747-6995). Wash $1.75, 30-min. dry $1.25. Showers $2. Open Mon.-Sat. 7am-8pm, Sun. 8am-5pm. **Duds 'n Suds Laundromat,** 906 Halibut Point Rd. (747-5050), near the hostel. Wash $1.75, 10-min. dry 50¢. Shower $2 for 10 min. Open Mon.-Fri. 7am-8pm, Sat. 8am-8pm, Sun. 9am-10pm.

Airport: Alaska Airlines, 800-426-0333 or 966-2266. Service to Juneau ($87) and Ketchikan ($124). Also to Seattle, Anchorage, Wrangell, and Petersburg.

Alaska Marine Highway, 7 Halibut Rd. (747-8737 or 800-642-0066), 7 mi. from town. To: Ketchikan ($54), Petersburg ($26), and Juneau ($26).

Buses: Baranof Tours (747-1016), runs a shuttle and tour guide service from the ferry terminal, whenever ferries are in port ($2). Tours $10. In summer, the shuttle will also pick you up or drop you off at the hostel on the way to or from the ferry, at a bargain price of $1. **Sitka Tours** (747-8443) offers the same shuttle service for $2.50, and a 1-hr. tour for $10.

Taxis: Arrowhead Taxi, 747-8888. **Sitka Taxi,** 747-5001.

Car Rental: Advantage Car Rental, 713 Katlian St. (747-7557). From $31.45 per day with unlimited mileage. Must be 21 with credit card.

Bike Rental: J&B Bike Rental (747-8279), on Lincoln St. near Southeast Diving & Sports. Mountain bikes $4 per hr., $12 per day, $20 overnight. Open Mon.-Sat. 10am-5:30pm.

Kayak Rental: Baidarka Boats (747-8996), on Lincoln St. above Old Harbor Books. Single $25 per ½-day, $35 per day. Double $35 per ½-day, $45 per day. Rates less with longer rentals. Required 1-hr. instructional class for novices ($25). Open Mon.-Sat. 10am-6pm, earlier and Sun. by appointment.

Public Pool: Hames P.E. Center, 801 Lincoln St. (747-5231), at Sheldon Jackson College. $3 (seniors and children under 12 $2) buys a day's access to the gym, weights, and pool. Racquetball an extra $10 per hour. Pool open Mon.-Fri. 6-8am,

SOUTHEASTERN ALASKA ■ 137

noon-1:30pm, and 6-8pm; Sat.-Sun. 3-5pm and 6-8pm. Other facilities open Mon.-Fri. 6am-8pm, Sat.-Sun. 2-9pm.

Pharmacy: Harry Race Pharmacy, 106 Lincoln St. (747-8666), near Castle Hill. Also has 1-hr. photo. Open Mon.-Sat. 9am-6pm; Sun. 9am-1pm.

Hospital: Sitka Community Hospital, 209 Moller Dr. (747-3241), near the intersection of Katlian and Halibut.

Post Office: 1207 Sawmill Creek Rd. (747-3381), a long hike from downtown. Open 8:30am-5:30pm. In town (and for all General Delivery mail), go to the **Pioneer Station** at 201 Katlian (747-5525), inside the Westmark Hotel Annex across from Pioneer Home, open Mon.-Sat. 8:30am-5pm. **ZIP Code:** 99835.

Area Code: 907.

Sitka is on the western side of **Baranov Island,** 95 mi. southwest of Juneau and 185 mi. northwest of Ketchikan. The O'Connell Bridge connects downtown to Japonski Island and the airport. The snow-capped volcano of **Mt. Edgecumbe** dominates the western horizon. Although drier than other parts of the Panhandle, Sitka still receives a full 6 ft. of rain per year.

ACCOMMODATIONS AND CAMPING

The youth hostel is your choicest option in Sitka. Camping facilities are decent, but are at least 5 mi. from town. Cannery workers practice renegade camping closer to town along the Indian River and Gavon Hill trails. Sitka also has 20 **B&Bs** from $40 per night. The Chamber of Commerce lists rates and numbers.

Sitka Youth Hostel (HI/AYH), 303 Kimshan St., Box 2645 (747-8356). In the United Methodist Church at Edgecumbe and Kimshan St. Find the McDonald's 1 mi. out of town on Halibut Point Rd., and walk 25 yds. up Peterson St. to Kimsham. 20 cots, kitchen facilities, free local phone calls, TV and VCR with several movies. Sleeping bags required. Free showers. Lockout 8:30am-6pm. Curfew 11pm. $7, nonmembers $10. Will store packs during the day. Open June-Aug.

Sheldon Jackson College Campus Housing (747-2518), at the east end of Lincoln St., next to the Sheldon Jackson Museum. A reasonably priced dormitory alternative to the hostel. No curfew. 85 units at "S.J." may be full, so call ahead. Provides bedding, towel, and shared bath. Meals available in the cafeteria. Rooms available summer only; register in Sweetland Hall. Singles $30, doubles $50.

Sitka Hotel, 118 Lincoln St. (747-3288; fax 747-8499). Owner Larry Snyder has beautifully remodeled the hotel, dating to 1939. 60 units, each a little different; rooms $50-60. Free local calls, cable TV, laundry facilities. Key deposit $5.

Starrigaven Creek Campground, at the end of Halibut Point Rd., 1 mi. from the ferry terminal, 8 mi. from town. A Forest Service campground. 28 sites for tents and RVs. Water, pit toilets, picnic shelter. Secluded sites, good fishing from shore. Near a scenic estuary trail. 14-day max. stay. Sites $5. Reserve a site for an additional $7.50 by calling the Forest Service at 900-280-2267.

Sawmill Creek Campground, 13 mi. southeast of the ferry terminal, 6 mi. out of town. Take Halibut Point Rd. to Sawmill Creek Rd. junction in Sitka. Follow Sawmill Creek Rd. to Pulp Mill, then take the left spur for 1.4 mi. Unmaintained 9-unit campground with spots for tents and RVs. Boil water from Sawmill Creek. No showers. Picnic tables, fireplaces, 2 outhouses. Great scenery and decent fishing in nearby Blue Lake. Quiet hours 10pm-6am. 14-day max. stay. Free.

FOOD

Do your grocery shopping close to the hostel at **Lakeside Grocery,** 705 Halibut Point Rd. (747-3317); open daily 6am-midnight. You can also pick up fresh seafood along the docks or at **Alaskan Harvest,** 320 Seward St. (747-6867), a store run by Sitka Sound Seafood (open Mon.-Sat. 8am-6pm). Though Sitka Sound is going upscale, food is still affordable at **Seafood Producers Coop,** at 507 Katlian Ave.

Sheldon Jackson College Cafeteria, at the east end of Lincoln St. The best deal in Sitka, if not the state. Make a sacrifice to your god or goddess of budget travel and come ready to feast. All-you-can-eat breakfast ($4.50), lunch ($5.50), dinner ($8). No breakfast on Sun. Open daily 6:45-8am, noon-1pm, and 5-6pm.

Ginny's Kitchen, 236 Lincoln St. (747-8028). Deli sandwiches on freshly baked bread for $5.25; milkshake $1.75. Ginny is also the source of all the baked goods at Coffee Express. Open Mon.-Fri. 9am-7pm, Sat. 10am-7pm.

Coffee Express, 104 Lake St. (747-3343), downtown. Good coffee (80¢), and filling soup and sandwich ($7.50). Cinnamon rolls rolled big and buttery ($1.85); muffins ($1.25). Open Mon.-Fri. 7am-4pm, Sat. 8am-4pm.

The Backdoor, 104 Barracks St. (747-8856), behind Old Harbour Books. An amicable coffee shop, and a popular college hangout, with attractive watercolors on display and unpredictable poetry readings. Thurs. nights feature live accordion music. Double-shot 12oz. Buzzsaw (coffee with espresso) for $2.25, salad plate-sized chocolate chip cookies for $1. Open Mon., Wed., and Fri.-Sat. 7am-5pm; Thurs. 7am-9pm; Sun. 1-4pm. The door swings open frequently after hours.

The Bayview Restaurant, 407 Lincoln St. (747-5440), upstairs in the Bayview Trading Company. Everything from *pirogies,* Russian dumplings (complete with salad and borscht, $7.50) to tandem towed in the hole (2 eggs and toast) with potatoes, gravy, and sausage ($6). More than 25 variations on the hamburger theme. Open Mon.-Sat. 6am-8pm, Sun. 6:30am-4pm.

El Dorado, 714 Katlian St. (747-5070). Mexican-American cuisine and pizzas. Lunch specials: enchilada, burrito or taco with beans and rice, $4.75. Pasta dinners $7. Open daily 10:30am-11pm.

Lane 7 Snack Bar, 331 Lincoln St. (747-6310), next to the Cathedral. Chomp on hotter 'n hell chili dogs ($3), mini-salads ($4), and ice cream cones ($1-1.75) while you bowl some turkeys (games $2.25, seniors $1.25). Tackier than wallpaper paste. Open Mon.-Sat. 7am-11pm, Sun. 7am-10pm.; Sept. 15-May 15 Mon.-Sat. 10am-11pm, Sun 10am-10pm.

Channel Club, 2906 Halibut Point Rd. (747-9916), 3 mi. from downtown. The restaurant every Sitkan recommends. Fantastic salad bar with over 35 individual salads ($12). Open Sun.-Thurs. 5-10pm, Fri.-Sat. 5-11pm.

Chocolate Moose, 120 Lincoln St. (747-5159) next to the Sitka Hotel. Sitka's only candy store with a colorful display of treats. Espresso ($1.50) and cappuccino ($2.25). Open daily 10am-6pm, winter Mon.-Sat.

SIGHTS, EVENTS, AND ENTERTAINMENT

Modern Sitka treasures its rich Russian heritage. Its lasting symbol of Slavic influence is the onion-domed **St. Michael's Cathedral,** built in 1848 by Bishop Innocent. In 1966, fire claimed the original structure, though Sitka's citizens saved the majority of priceless artifacts and paintings. The Cathedral was promptly rebuilt in strict accordance with plans for the first building, and today haunting ikons gleam on its walls. Among the Cathedral's most valued works are the *Sitka Madonna* and the *Pantocrator,* both by Vladimir Borbikovsky, and several neo-Baroque paintings from a movement supported by Catherine the Great. Services are open to the public, and are conducted in English, Tlingit, and Old Slavonic. (Hours vary with cruise ship schedules; generally open Mon.-Sat. 11am-3pm., Sun. noon-3pm; $1 "donation.")

Two blocks down Lincoln St. is the meticulously refurbished **Russian Bishop's House,** one of four remaining Russian colonial buildings in America. Upstairs is a magnificent chapel, dedicated to the Annunciation of the Virgin Mary and adorned with beautiful gold and silver ikons (unlike those in St. Michael's, these may be photographed). For history and architecture buffs, this sight is a must (open 8:30am-4:30pm, tours every ½-hr., except 12:30pm. Call 747-6281 for tour reservations).

The **Sheldon-Jackson Museum** (747-8981), at the east end of Lincoln St., is one of Alaska's best museums for Native artifacts and history. Housed in a single octagonal room, the organized collections date back to the 1880s and represent Athabascan, Aleut, Inuit, and Northwest Coast artistic styles. Don't miss the pull-out drawers holding the Inuit children's toys and the raven helmet worn by Chief Katlean, the Tlingit hero in the 1804 battle (open daily 8am-5pm; $2, free with student ID). For a glimpse of old Sitka, drop by the **Isabel Miller Museum** (747-6455), next to the Centennial Bldg. (Open summer daily 9am-5pm and with cruise ships and ferries, winter Mon.-Fri. 10am-noon and 1-4pm. Free.)

The **Alaska Raptor Rehabilitation Center** (747-8662), in Island Community College on Sawmill Creek Rd., has a fantastic collection of recovering bald eagles and owls. Most summer days, when ships are in town, there are guided tours for $10. Schedule varies; call ahead to confirm. Open daily 8am-5pm and with cruise ships.

The second-best place to view eagles, and a good place to watch seaplanes land, is from the **McDonald's** by the water on Halibut Point Rd. Stroll down the manicured trails of the **Sitka National Historic Park** (Totem Park, as locals call it), at the end of Lincoln St. (747-6281), 1 mi. east of St. Michael's. The trails pass by 15 masterfully replicated totems placed along the shoreline among old-growth trees. At one end of the 1-mi. loop stands the site of the **Tlingit Fort,** where the hammer-wielding chief Katlean almost held off the Russians in the battle for Sitka in 1804. The park **visitors center** offers an audio-visual presentation on the battle and the opportunity to watch traditional artists at work in the Southeast Alaskan Native American Cultural Center (747-8061). Demonstrations are given in woodcarving, silver carving, costume making and weaving. There is also a small **museum** here, dedicated entirely to the local Kiksadi Tlingits (open daily 8am-5pm).

Across town from the college, **Castle Hill,** at one time site of Baranov's Castle, the seat of Russian administration in Alaska, and Tlingit forts, provides an incredible view of Mt. Edgecumbe (open daily 6am-10pm).

The June **Sitka Summer Music Festival** ranks as one of the state's most popular events and draws world-renowned musicians to play chamber music. The concerts, held in the Centennial Building on Tuesday, Friday, and some Saturday evenings, can be crowded. Reservations are a good idea. Rehearsals, however, are free and rarely crowded. (All shows $12, seniors $10; $72 seasonal passes available. Order tickets by phone (277-4852 or 747-6774) or mail (Sitka Summer Music Festival, P.O. Box 3333), or stop by McDonald's Bayview Trading Co., 407 Lincoln St. (Mon.-Fri. noon-1pm and 4:30-6pm, Sat. 1-3pm. Contact the visitors bureau at 747-8601 for information and advance ticketing. The **New Archangel Dancers,** a local all-women troupe, perform energetic Russian folk dances in the Centennial Building throughout the summer ($4, check the variable schedule at the visitors bureau).

The **All-Alaska Logging Championships** take place the weekend before Independence Day. Other summer events include the **King Salmon Derby** (Sitka Sportsmen's Association; 747-8886) at the end of May. A permit costs $10 for a day, but the person who catches the largest salmon wins $6000. Softball fans will enjoy the **Mudball Classic Slowpitch,** on Labor Day. If you're in town in Oct., check out the **Alaska Day** celebrations marking the sale of Alaska to the U.S. on Oct. 18, 1867 (it's a statewide holiday). Castle Hill is the site of a reenactment of the transfer ceremony, taking place at 3pm. Men are encouraged to grow beards, and women to dress in the style of 1867. A road race, the Baranof Ball, concerts, teas, a parade, and beard-judging contests are among the highlights.

The **Pioneer Bar** (747-3456) on Katlian St. is clearly the nightspot of choice for both permanent and transient Sitkans (open daily 8am-2am). **Ernie's Old Time Saloon,** 130 Lincoln St. (747-3334), a down-home pool-hall, is also popular (open Mon.-Sat. 8am-2am, Sun. noon-2am).

OUTDOORS

The Sitka area offers excellent **hiking** opportunities. Don't forget to bring rain gear, and make sure to pick up the thick booklet *Sitka Trails* at the Forest Service information booth or office. One of the gentlest and most intimately beautiful walks is the **Indian River Trail,** a 5½-mi. riverside trek up to the base of Indian River Falls. The walk begins close to town where Indian River Rd. meets Sawmill Creek Rd. beside the Public Safety Academy. Salmonberries abound along this stretch, as do squatters from the canneries. At the pump house at the end of the road the trail branches off into the old growth forest and meanders through muskeg and tall trees alongside the clear pools of the Indian River. The rocky Sisters Mountains occasionally come into view, and it is sometimes possible to see spawning salmon in early fall. The trail gains no more than 250 ft. in elevation; plan on a 4- to 5- hr. round trip.

A shorter, steeper hike leads from downtown up to the summit of **Gavan Hill.** With excellent views of Sitka and the Sound, this 2500-ft. ascent breaks out above the tree-line at about 2100 ft. Hike 3 or 4 hours on a clearly marked trailhead, continuing just past the house at 508 Baranof St. walking towards the Old City Cemetery. If you plan to camp in the alpine areas around Gavan Hill, bring a canteen, since no water is available in the higher regions. The trail was built in 1937 to provide access for hunters; it connects to the Harbor Mountain Trail. Plan on a 6- to 8-hr. round trip, and watch out for bears.

The **Mount Verstovia Trail** offers another direct route to the views. Beginning beside the Kiksadi Restaurant 2 mi. from town on Sawmill Creek Hwy., this strenuous hike begins as an easy stroll through alder groves to the site of the Old Russian Charcoal Pits. The trail soon begins to climb with a series of switchbacks and, at approximately 2 mi., breaks out onto a sparsely vegetated ridge. Many hikers choose to turn back after the ridge meets a steep hillside topped by a rocky outcrop. Stalwarts can continue on through beautiful displays of alpine flowers to reach the summit in another hour. The round-trip to the outcrop takes about four hours.

A fine 3-mi. walk from downtown crosses the runway at the Japonski Island airport, heading across the old WWII causeway leading past abandoned fortifications, finally arriving all the way out at **Makhanati Island.** Access by small boat is best, since waltzing across the runway without special permission is illegal.

■■■ TENAKEE SPRINGS

The only thing people seriously pursue in Tenakee is relaxation, and of this they have an abundance. Many of the homes are summer dwellings of Juneau residents. Tenakee's street is a dirt path beside a row of houses and outhouses along the shore of Tenakee Inlet. Flowers and berries spill into this path,where residents push their belongings in hand carts. An oil delivery truck and a fire truck make rare appearances as the only automobiles in town. The city provides no water, sewer, or sanitation services.

Practical Information The **city office** of Tenakee (736-2207), in the library building, fields questions (Mon.-Wed., 9am-12:30pm and 1:30-4:30pm). To get to the **library** (736-2248), take a left from the ferry, continue about ¼ mi., and enter the big wooden building on your right (open Tues., Thurs., and Sat. 11am-3pm). Check out the decent selection of "trade-'em" paperbacks. The **Post Office** (736-2236; open from Mon.-Fri., 8am-noon and 12:30-4:30pm, Sat. 8am-noon) has a **general delivery ZIP Code** of 99841.

Tenakee is on Chichagof Island, but residents are adamantly opposed to Forest Service proposals to construct a road link with neighboring **Hoonah.** The **state ferry** *LeConte* makes a one-hour stopover in Tenakee on its Friday-evening and Sunday-morning trips between Juneau and Sitka. The Friday ferry leaves you in Tenakee for about 21 hours before the next returning boat to Juneau, the Sunday ferry about 30 hours. The one-way fare to Tenakee from either Sitka or Juneau is $22. **Wings of Alaska** (736-2247 or 2209) soars from Juneau to Tenakee (8am and 5:30pm, $61).

The Hot Spring Tenakee's namesake, a natural hot spring that feeds the public bath house, is the town's epicenter and a short walk from the ferry dock. Miners and fishermen have been soaking out their aches and worries in these therapeutic 106°F (41°C) waters for more than a century. Many of Tenakee's retirees and urban refugees from Juneau poach themselves daily in this sublimely soothing bath.

The weathered yellow bathhouse sits on the end of the ferry dock, so the one-hour layover in Tenakee on trips between Juneau and Sitka provides ample time for a good soaking. Bathing in Tenakee follows a simple but strict protocol: no clothes in the bath, wash beside the pool before entering, and observe the different hours for men (2-6pm and 10pm-9am) and for women (9am-2pm and 6-10pm). Bring your own soap; many people take their actual baths here, as few homes have showers. The bathhouse includes a changing room, heated in winter, from which a door opens onto steps leading down to the pool set in a concrete floor. The acoustics are great if you like to sing in the bath. One naked bulb and the sun or stars shining through an overhead skylight provide the only illumination. The bath is free, but donations are welcome at Snyder Mercantile across the street.

To reach an even higher echelon of relaxation, follow the bath with a visit to **Moon Feather Therapeutic Massage**, P.O. Box 44. Diane Ziel runs this business out of her home just around the corner from the bath beside the Blue Moon Cafe. Pink decor. Sign up for appointments on her door (½ hr. $25, 1 hr. $35, 1½ hr. $55).

Accommodations, Camping, and Food About the only affordable indoor option is to rent one of five available cabins from **Snyder Mercantile** (736-2205). The smaller, more basic cabins sleep 2-3 people comfortably (from $30). Larger cabins sleep 4-5 people (from $35). Both have outhouses and cooking facilities; bring your own towels and bedding. A more plush option is to pay $60 for the cabin that sleeps seven, with carpet, fireplaces, and a rare find in Tenakee: a flush toilet. Reservations are a good idea. The more adventurous can brave the bears (Chichagof Island has about one bear per sq. mi.; only Admiralty Island has a denser population of grizzlies) and head for the woods. Walking from the ferry dock to town, a right turn on the dirt path points you east. After about ¾ mi. walking east, the path leads into a wooded area with several free, primitive **campsites.** Another ¾ mi. along the trail, the free **Indian River Campground** provides tentsites, a shelter, and a picnic table beside the Indian River, a spot favored by bears in summer.

Other than the berries along the main path, food in Tenakee can be difficult to obtain. **Snyder Mercantile** stocks a small supply of groceries but little that doesn't require a can opener as a fourth utensil (open Mon.-Sat. 9am-noon and 1-5pm, Sun. 9am-2pm). At first glance, Tenakee seems well-endowed with restaurants. This is partly because the ghosts of restaurants past haunt Tenakee's street, places that haven't seen a customer in years but still leave out a sign. The **Blue Moon Cafe,** unassuming as it may appear, is a Tenakee institution. A sign over the door reads, "Credit is extended to those past 80, and when accompanied by their grandparents. Rosie." If Rosie is there, and if she feels like cooking, try the french fries. Ham and eggs are $7.25; a chicken dinner, $8.50. The **Quick Stop Cafe** (open daily 7am-10pm) has a wide selection of microwave fare and fried hamburgers ($3.75).

Outdoors Tenakee's street extends several mi. in either direction from town. To the west it leads along the water past a communal saw mill and small homesteads lying farther and farther apart. Tread carefully around private land here; some residents greet tourists with antipathy. Some mi. from town the path turns out onto the shore of the inlet, where silver salmon leap from the water in midsummer and smooth rocks make good footing for an extended walk along the beach. Avoid the beach in town; outhouses and garbage make the beach unappealing.

To the east, the wide beach may make for better walking than the faint path through the woods that parallels the shore. About 4 mi. from town, an abandoned cannery decays by the water. An excellent **paddling** adventure begins in Hoonah and follows the long inlet of Port Frederick back to its end. From there, a 100-yd. portage leads to the upper region of Tenakee Inlet. Paddlers can explore the unbroken shores and hidden coves of the inlet on their way out to Tenakee Springs. The 40-mi. trip could also be made in the reverse direction, but the hot springs are probably best savored at the end. Rent a kayak in Juneau for this trip, since they are not available in Hoonah or Tenakee, and bring it over on the ferry for $9.

For **chartered expeditions** to fish, view wildlife, and learn the intricacies of the inlet from someone who has been on the water around Tenakee all his life, contact Jason Carter (736-2311). His day-long trips, including lunch, cost $90 per person for two, $80 each for three, etc. Jason also conducts ½-day trips and transports kayaks.

JUNEAU

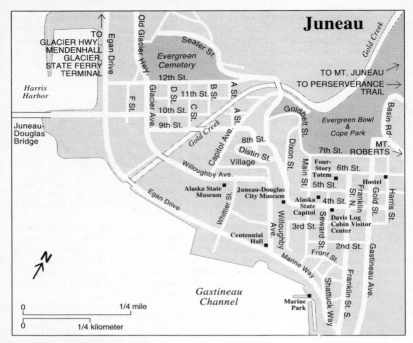

■■■ JUNEAU

Confined to a tiny strip of land at the base of imposing Mt. Juneau, Alaska's capital refuses to accept its small size. Instead, Victorian mansions crowd against log cabins, and hulking state office buildings compete for space with simple frame houses. Accessible only by water and air, Juneau's settlers didn't have civil engineering in mind when founding the city. In October 1880, in a move he probably regretted later, Tlingit Chief Kowee led Joe Juneau and Richard Harris to the gleaming "mother lode" in the hills up Gold Creek. Next summer found boatloads of prospectors digging in the staked, claimed mines. Harris' greedy, irritating habit of staking multiple claims extended to his choice for the town name: angry miners vetoed "Harrisburg." In 1906, the capital moved from Sitka. Mining ended in 1941; fishing, lumber, government, and North Slope petrodollars now fuel the economy. Alaskans voted to move the capital to Willow, north of Anchorage, but rejected funding for the move in 1982; a move now seems highly unlikely. Mines might reopen soon; the character of the city remains divided between a natural-resource-based Southeast town and a capital striving for more cosmopolitan status.

Though full of tourists in the summer, Juneau offers some of the most spectacular **hiking** in the Southeast. Leave the mobs downtown and enjoy the glaciers and trails.

PRACTICAL INFORMATION AND ORIENTATION

Visitors Information: Davis Log Cabin, 134 3rd St., Juneau 99801 (586-2284 or 586-2201; fax 586-6304), at Seward St. Excellent source for pamphlets on walking tours, sights, and the natural wonders in the vicinity. Open Mon.-Fri. 8:30am-5pm, Sat.-Sun. 9am-5pm; Oct.-May Mon.-Fri. 8:30am-5pm. **Marine Park Kiosk** (no phone), Marine Way at Ferry Way, right by the cruise-ship unloading dock (*not* the ferry dock). Manned by enthusiastic volunteers armed with pamphlets and information. Open May-Sept. according to cruise-ship schedules.

Forest and National Park Services, 101 Egan Dr., corner of Egan and Willoughby (586-8751), in Centennial Hall. Helpful staff and extensive pamphlets provide information on hiking and fishing in the Juneau area, and particulars pertaining to Forest Service **cabins** in **Tongass National Forest.** Write here for cabin reservations. Also pick up a copy of the valuable *Juneau Trails* booklet ($3) listing many 5 to 12-mi. hikes. Free, informative 20-min. films on 16 topics, from wildlife to Glacier Bay, shown upon request. Open daily in summer 8am-5pm; winter Mon.-Fri. 8am-5pm.

Alaska Dept. of Fish and Game, 465-4008. **Fishing Hotline,** 465-4116.

Public Phones: Alascom Teleservices Center, 245 Marine Way (463-3582). 17 phones for long-distance calls, payable with cash, travelers checks, and credit cards. Hours vary with cruise ships.

Airport: Juneau International Airport, 9 mi. north of Juneau on Glacier Hwy. Serviced by Alaska Air, Delta Airlines, and local charters. **Alaska Airlines** (789-0600 or 800-426-0333), on S Franklin St. at 2nd St., in the Baranov Hotel. To: Anchorage ($99-222, with 21-day advance purchase $140); Sitka ($87); Ketchikan ($124); and Gustavus ($65; round-trip $95). Flights every morning and afternoon. Open Mon.-Fri. 8:30am-5pm. Closed holidays. Check **Log Cabin Visitors Center** for schedules and routes of all airlines.

Buses: Capital Transit, 789-6901. From downtown to Douglas, the airport, and Mendenhall Glacier Mon.-Sat. 7am-10:30pm, Sun. 9am-5:30pm. To get to Mendenhall Campground, tell the bus driver to let you off at the nearest point on the loop and walk the 2 mi. from there. Hourly express service downtown Mon.-Fri., 8:30am-6pm. The closest stop to the ferry is at Auke Bay, 1½ mi. from the terminal. Fare $1.25; drivers cannot make change. **Schedules** available at municipal building, library, Davis log cabin, and on buses.

MGT Ferry Express, 789-5460. Call between 6-8pm to reserve a ride from any major hotel to the airport or ferry (whether you're staying at a hotel or not). Rides $5. From the hostel, the Baranov is the closest hotel. Also offers a 2½-hr. guided tour of Mendenhall Glacier ($12.50). Tour times vary; call ahead.

Alaska Marine Highway, 1591 Glacier Ave., P.O. Box 25535, Juneau 99802-5535 (800-642-0066 or 465-3941; fax 277-4829). Ferries dock at the Auke Bay terminal 14 mi. from the city on the Glacier Hwy. To: Bellingham, WA ($226, $534); Ketchikan ($74, $168); Sitka ($26, $52); and Haines ($20, $39). The second prices are for vehicles up to 15 ft.; prices higher for larger vehicles and for those making a stopover before their final destination. Lockers 25¢ for 48 hrs.

Taxis: Capital Cab, (586-2772) and **Taku Taxi** (586-2121). Both run a 1-hr. charter to Mendenhall Glacier for about $45, to the ferry about $20. Exact services differ slightly; both let you split charter cost. Call and inquire.

Car Rental: Rent-A-Wreck, 9099 Glacier Hwy. (789-4111), next to the airport. $30 per day with 100 free mi. plus 15¢ per extra mi. Must be at least 21 with a credit card or piles of cash.

Bike Rental: Mountain Gears, 210 N Franklin St. (586-4327). Mountain bikes $6.50 per hr., 2 hr. minimum. $25 per day during business hours, $30 for 24 hrs. Prices include helmet and lock. Open Mon.-Fri. 10am-6pm, Sat. 10am-5pm, Sun. noon-5pm. Informal group rides often meet here at 6pm.

Kayak Rental: Alaska Discovery, 5449-4 Shaune Dr. (780-6226). Single kayak $40 per day. Offers guided kayak tours to Glacier Bay (up to 10 days) and elsewhere. Open daily 9am-5:30pm.

Camping Equipment: Foggy Mountain Shop, 134 N Franklin St. (586-6780), at 2nd. High-quality, expensive gear. Open Mon.-Sat. 10am-6pm, Sat. 10am-6pm, Sun. noon-5pm.

Luggage Storage: In an unlocked closet at the **hostel,** or inside if you are staying the night. Free for the day if you're staying the night, otherwise $1 per bag. Lockers are also available for 25¢ at the **ferry terminal;** 48-hr. max. Also try the counter at the **Alaskan Hotel** (see below). If they're in the mood they'll store bags for free.

Bookstore: Big City Books, 100 N Franklin St. (586-1772). Open Mon.-Fri. 9am-8pm, Sun. 9am-6pm. **The Observatory,** 235 2nd St. (586-9676). A used and rare

bookstore with a knowledgeable proprietress and many **maps** and prints. Open
Mon.-Fri. 10am-5:30pm, Sat. noon-5:30pm; in winter Mon.-Sat. noon-5:30pm.
Library, (586-5249), Over parking garage at Admiral Way and S Franklin (586-
5249). It's worth coming up just for the views and a great stained-glass window.
Open Mon.-Thurs. 11am-9pm, Fri.-Sun. noon-5pm. The **State Library** and the
Alaska Historical Library hold large collections of early Alaskan photographs.
Both are on the 8th floor of the State Office Bldg. Both open Mon.-Fri. 9am-5pm.
Laundromat: The Dungeon Laundrette (586-2805), at 4th and Franklin St. Wash
$1.25, dry $1.25. Open daily 8am-8pm. Also at the **hostel** (see below). Wash
$1.25, dry 75¢.
Public Showers: The Alaskan Hotel (see below) $3.12.
Events Hotline: 586-5866.
Weather: 586-3997.
Pharmacy: Juneau Drug Co., 202 Front St. (586-1233). Open Mon.-Fri. 9am-9pm,
Sat. 9am-6pm, Sun. 10am-7pm.
Hospital: Bartlett Memorial (586-2611), 3½ mi. north off Glacier Hwy.
Emergency and Ambulance: 911. **Police,** 210 Admiral Way (586-2780), near
Marine Park. Visitors can pick up a permit here to allow 48-hr. **parking** in a 1-hr.
zone. Open for permits Mon.-Fri. 8am-4:30pm.
Post Office: Main Office 709 W 9th St. (586-7138). Open Mon. 8:30am-5pm,
Tues.-Fri. 8:30am-5pm, Sat. 1-3pm. **ZIP Code:** 99801. **Substation** (outgoing mail
only) 221 S Seward St. (586-2214). Open Mon.-Fri. 9:30am-5pm, Sat. 9:30am-2pm.
Area Code: 907.

Juneau sits on the Gastineau Channel opposite Douglas Island, 650 mi. southeast of
Anchorage and 900 mi. northwest of Seattle. **Glacier Hwy.** connects downtown,
the airport, the residential area of the Mendenhall Valley, and the ferry terminal.

ACCOMMODATIONS AND CAMPING

If you can't get into Juneau's hostel, the **Alaska Bed and Breakfast Association,**
P.O. Box 3/6500 #169, Juneau 99802 (586-2959), provides information on rooms in
local homes year-round. Most Juneau B&Bs are uphill, beyond 6th St., and offer singles from $45 and doubles from $55. Reservations are recommended. Both campsites are carefully groomed by the Forest Service (see Practical Information).

Juneau International Hostel (HI/AYH), 614 Harris St. (586-9559), at 6th atop a
steep hill. A spotless, highly efficient hostel. Operates by a structured set of rules.
Kitchen available 7-8:30am, 5-10:30pm; common area, smoking area. Chores
assigned. 48 beds. Will store packs during the day. Free showers, laundry (wash
$1.25, dry 75¢), small charges for sheets, towels, soap, detergent. 3-day max. stay
if beds are full. Lockout 9am-5pm. The 11pm curfew is not negotiable. Beds $10.
Popular; make reservations by May for expected stays in July and Aug.
Alaskan Hotel, 167 Franklin St. (586-1000 or 800-327-9347 from the lower 48
states). A handsome hotel built of dark wood, right in the center of downtown.
Has been meticulously restored to original 1913 decor. Bar on 1st floor features
live tunes and dancing. Hot tubs noon-4pm $10.40 for 1 hr., after 4pm $21. Free
luggage storage for guests. Singles $50, with bath $66.60. Doubles $61, with bath
$77.70. Kitchenettes and TVs available. Rates lower in winter.
Inn at the Waterfront, 455 S Franklin (586-2050), over the Summit Restaurant.
Clean, comfortable, carpeted cubicles with attractive wooden dressers, double
bed, and hall bath. Singles $42. Doubles $54. Private bath extra. 1 room has futon.
Mendenhall Lake Campground, Montana Creek Rd. Take Glacier Hwy. north 9
mi. to Mendenhall Loop Rd.; continue 3½ mi. and take the right fork. If asked, bus
driver will let you off within walking distance (2 mi.) of camp (7am-10:30pm
only). About 6 mi. from ferry terminal. View of the glacier, with trails that can
take you even closer. 60 sites. Fireplaces, water, pit toilet, picnic tables, free firewood. 14-day max. stay. Sites $5, Golden Age $2.50. Call the Forest Service in
Juneau (907-586-8800), or reserve for an extra $7.50 by calling 1-800-280-2267.
Auke Village Campground, on Glacier Hwy., 15 mi. from Juneau. Near a scenic
beach. 1.5 mi. west of ferry terminal. 12 sites. Fireplaces, water, flush toilets, pic-

nic tables. Call the Forest Service, Juneau Ranger District (907-586-8800) for information. No reservations. 14-day max. stay. Sites $5.

FOOD

Juneau tries to accommodate those seeking everything from fresh salmon to filet-o'-fish sandwiches. The local grocery store is the **Foodland Supermarket,** 631 Willoughby Ave., near the Federal Building, will ship anywhere (586-3101; fax 586-6775; open daily 7am-9pm). More expensive health-food items can be bought at **Rainbow Foods** (586-6476), at 2nd and Seward St. (Open Mon.-Fri. 10am-7pm, Sat. 10am-6pm, Sun. noon-6pm.) Seafood lovers haunt **Merchants Wharf,** next to Marine Park. The corner of Front St. and Seward is home to Juneau's fast food huts: **McDonald's** (open Mon.-Thurs. 6:30am-11pm, Fri. 6:30am-midnight, Sun. 7am-11pm), **Subway** (open Mon.-Thurs. 10am-10pm, Fri. 10am-midnight, Sat.-Sun. 10am-9pm), and **Taco Bell** (open Mon.-Thurs. 10am-9pm). Taco Bell has the dubious distinction of pricing no item over $2.80.

Armadillo Tex-Mex Cafe, 431 S Franklin St. (586-1880). Fantastic food and always packed with locals and tourists alike. Hunker down to a heaping plateful of T. Terry's nachos ($8). The *chalupa,* a corn tostada heaped with chicken, beans, guacamole, and cheese, goes for $7.50. 2 enchiladas $6. Free taco chips. Open Mon.-Thurs. 11am-9pm, Fri.-Sat. 11am-10pm.

Fiddlehead Restaurant and Bakery, 429 W Willoughby Ave. (586-3150), ½ block from the State Museum. Fern-ishings for the sprouts-loving set. Lures mobs with its beef, salads, seafood, exquisite desserts, and fresh Alaskan sourdough. Great sandwiches and burgers on fiddlehead buns with soup or salad $9-10. Big, buttery ginger-crinkle cookies $1. Dinner $9-15. Open daily 6-10pm; Sun.-Thurs. 11:30am-2pm. The **Fireweed Room** upstairs serves more expensive fare with weekend jazz throughout the summer. Come just to listen. Open daily 6:30-10pm.

Channel Bowl Cafe, across from Foodland on Willoughby Ave. A small breakfast spot with blaring blues and an aspiring musician manning the grill. Try the pancakes with berries, pecans, and real maple syrup ($5.50). Open daily 7am-2pm.

Heritage Coffee Co., 625 W 7th St. (586-1752), across from the Senate Bldg. A popular place to escape for an hour or two from Juneau's often wet and tourist-ridden streets. Jocular staff assembles large sandwiches ($5.20) and pours excellent 16-oz. cups of coffee ($1.25). Open Mon.-Fri. 6:30am-8pm, Sat.-Sun. 7am-8pm. Sandwiches can be had only before 7pm.

Thane Ore House Salmon Bake, 4400 Thane Rd. (586-3442). A few mi. outside of town, but "Mr. Ore" will pick you up at your hotel. All-you-can-eat salmon, halibut, ribs, and fixings ($17.50). Open April 26-Oct. 1 daily 11:30am-9pm.

SIGHTS

The **Alaska State Museum,** 395 Whittier St. (465-2901), leads you through the history, ecology, and cultures of Alaska's four major indigenous groups (Tlingit, Athabascan, Aleut, and Inuit). It also houses the famous "First White Man" totem pole, a carved likeness of Abraham Lincoln. (Open Mon.-Fri. 9am-6pm, Sat.-Sun. 10am-6pm; Sept. 18-May 17 Tues.-Sat. 10am-4pm. $2, seniors and students free.) The **Juneau-Douglas City Museum,** 114 W 4th St. (586-3572), has displays on mining, hand-woven quilts, traditional crafts, and a flattering antique scale that knocks a few pounds off your actual weight. (Open Mon.-Fri. 9am-5pm, Sat.-Sun. 11am-5pm; winter Thurs.-Sat. noon-4:30pm; closed Jan.-Feb.; $1, students and children free.)

The unimpressive, domeless **State Capitol Building** is at 4th and Main (tours summer Sun.-Fri. 9am-4:30pm), but your time is better spent wandering uphill to check out the gold-onion-domed 1894 **St. Nicholas Russian Orthodox Church** on 5th St. between N Franklin and Gold St. Services, held Sat. at 6am and Sun. at 10am, are conducted in English, Old Slavonic, and Tlingit. Tours are open to the public ($1 donation requested, open daily 9am-5pm). The **State Office Building** (the S.O.B.) has an 8th-floor **observation platform** overlooking Douglas Island and the channel.

A large atrium on the same floor contains a totem pole and a pipe organ fired up for a free **concert** every Friday afternoon.

Farther downhill along N Franklin, the **Historic Senate Building** lures tourists with specialty shops, including an authentic Russian gift store. In nearby **Marine Park,** rambunctious children play as tourists picnic and watch the slow passage of ships through the **Gastineau Channel** (free concerts held Fri. mid-June-mid-Aug. 7-8:30pm). Check a newspaper or call 586-2787 to find out who's playing. The **House of Wickersham,** 213 7th St. (586-9001), was home to one of the Alaska's founding fathers, Judge James Wickersham. As a U.S. District Court judge, Wickersham steamed and sledded around Alaska to oversee a region extending from Fort Yukon to the Aleutian Islands. His contributions to the state include founding the Alaska Railroad, establishing the University of Alaska, and pushing for statehood as early as 1917 (open May-Sept. Sun.-Fri. noon-5pm; free).

The **Alaska Brewing Co.,** 5429 Shaune Dr. (780-5866), offers free tours complete with a free sample of its award-winning brew ($5.50 per pint at the Alaskan Hotel). Thurs. and Fri. are bottling days with the most to see. To reach the brewery, take the hourly city bus to Lemon Creek, turn onto Anka Rd. from the Glacier Hwy., and Shaune Dr. is the first on the right. (Tours available on the ½-hr. Tues.-Sat. 11am-4:30pm; Oct.-April Thurs.-Sat. 11am-4:30pm.)

ENTERTAINMENT

The doors swing and the cash registers ring at the **Red Dog Saloon,** 278 S Franklin (463-3777), Juneau's most popular tourist trap, with live music on weekends (open Sun.-Thurs. 10am-midnight, Fri.-Sat. 10am-1am, off-season Sun.-Thurs. noon-midnight, Fri.-Sat. noon-1am). The **Alaskan Hotel,** 167 Franklin St., hosts frequent live Cajun and blues. The **Triangle Club,** 251 Front St. (586-3140), attracts the hard-drinking set, as does the **Penthouse** (463-4141), on the 4th floor of the Senate Building (open Sun.-Thurs. 8pm-1am, Fri.-Sat. 8pm-2am. Must be 21 with a $2 cover on the weekends). The **Lady Lou Revue** (586-3686), a revival of Gold Rush days based on Robert Service's poems, presents weekly toe-tappin' musicals. A major family and tourist attraction, the revue is performed in the **Perseverance Theatre** in Merchants' Wharf, 2 Marine Way. Tickets can be purchased at the door or at Sunburst Tanning in the Wharf Mall Outlet or Marine Way ($15, children $7.50). The show runs May 15-Sept. 27; call ahead for show times.

OUTDOORS

If you're looking for the best view of Juneau and are willing to sweat for it, go to the end of 6th St. and head up the trail to the summit of **Mt. Roberts** (3576 ft.). It's a steep 4-mi. climb, but worth it. Though mining in these hills is, for now, no longer an active industry, the mines remain in business as (of course) tourist attractions and occasionally host salmon bakes.

Juneau is a top hiking center in southeast Alaska. After a ½-hr. hike from downtown, one can easily forget the city left behind. In addition to the ascent of Mt. Roberts, the **Perseverance Trail,** which leads past the ruins of the **Silverbowl Basin Mine** behind Mt. Roberts and to some booming waterfalls, makes for a pleasant day's trek. The trail is suitable for mountain biking. Pick up a free **map** from the Forest Service office. Yell or sing to scare off the bears. To reach this trailhead, follow Gold St. uphill until it turns into Basin Rd. The trail begins on the left, just past a bridge. For more details on this and other area hikes, drop by the state museum bookstore, the Park Service Center, or any local bookstore to pick up *Juneau Trails,* published by the Alaska Natural History Association ($3). Rangers provide free copies of **maps** from this book at the Park Service Center. (See Practical Information.)

In winter, the slopes of the **Eaglecrest Ski Area,** 155 S Seward St., Juneau 99801, on Douglas Island, offer decent alpine skiing (586-5284 or 586-5330; $24 per day, children grades 7-12 $17, up to 6th grade $12; rental of skis, poles, and boots $20, children $14). The Eaglecrest ski bus departs from the Baranof Hotel at 8:30am and returns at 5pm on winter weekends and holidays (round-trip to the slopes $6). In the summer, the Eaglecrest "Alpine Summer" trail is a good way to soak in the mountain scenery of virtually untouched Douglas Island.

There are some **road races** in this fleet-footed city; for information call Juneau Parks and Recreation (586-5226) Mon.-Fri. 8am-4:30pm.

Mendenhall Glacier

The 38 glaciers of the **Juneau Icefield** cover an area larger than Rhode Island. The most visited glacier is the **Mendenhall Glacier,** about 10 mi. north of downtown Juneau. The ice flows forward but recedes slightly faster due to melting and "calving," or ice breaking off from the low end. This process produces the icebergs floating in Mendenhall Lake, which is tinted a milky color by rock crushed into a powder when the glaciers grind against one another. Calving also reveals brilliant blue ice faces. At the **Glacier Visitors Center** (789-0097), rangers will explain everything you could possibly want to know about the glacier (open daily late May-mid Sept., 8:30am-5:30pm). The rangers also give an interesting walking tour Sun.-Fri. at 9:30am, beginning from the flagpole. The best view of the glacier without a helicopter is from the 3½ mi. **West Glacier Trail.** If pressed for time, the 3½ mi. **East Glacier Loop Trail** affords a good way to catch a side view of the glacier in about an hour, though you will spend most of your time surrounded by greenery and tourists. Take the local public bus down Glacier Hwy. and up Mendenhall Loop Rd. until it connects with Glacier Spur Rd. ($1.25). From there it's less than a ½-hr. walk to the visitors center.

■■■ GLACIER BAY NATIONAL PARK

In 1879, when naturalist John Muir became the first white man to see what nature had uncovered in Glacier Bay, he wrote, "These were the highest and whitest mountains, and the greatest of all the glaciers I had yet seen." He wasn't kidding. Crystal boulders float in the 65-mi.-long fjords of Glacier Bay, while humpback whales glide smoothly through the icy blue depths. **Glacier Bay National Park** encloses 16 tidewater glaciers and Mt. Fairweather of the St. Elias Range. Charter flights, tours, and cruise ships all make the spectacular voyage into **Muir Inlet,** offering close-up views of glaciers, rookeries, whales, and seals.

To avoid disturbing the wildlife, the number of people allowed into the park is limited. Visitors should contact the **park superintendent** at P.O. Box 140, Gustavus 99826 (697-2230, Mon.-Fri. 8am-4:30pm). Wilderness camping and hiking are permitted throughout the park, and tour-boat skippers drop passengers off at points designated by the Park Service; you'll have to arrange to be picked up later.

Any visit to this park is expensive. **Glacier Bay Air** (789-9009) flies one-way to Gustavus from Juneau for $55, round-trip $90. Call for schedule and flight availability. **Alaska Airlines** (800-426-0333) offers the same service for slightly more (one way $65, round-trip $95). An **information center** is maintained in **Bartlett Cove** (697-2230) by the park service (open June-Sept. daily 9am-5:30pm; winter 789-0097 Mon.-Fri. 8am-4:30pm, Sat.-Sun. 9am-4pm). Once at Bartlett Cove, backpackers can stay in the free state campground, which has 25 sites and is rarely full.

To see the most impressive part of the park, the **West Arm,** one must take a boat tour. The *Spirit of Adventure* conducts an 8-hr. tour of the glaciers for $289 (flight from Juneau included). For $177.50 (not including airfare), the boat will drop off campers or kayakers, and pick them up again at pre-arranged times. The *Spirit* is owned by the **Glacier Bay Lodge** (800-622-2042), which is next to Bartlett Cove and offers six different **sightseeing packages** for the glacier. Your best bet is to find a buddy with a thick billfold: packages (including all flights, a night at the bed & breakfast, and an 8-hr. tour) start at $369 per person for doubles, $422 per person for singles. **Puffin Travel, Inc.** (697-2260) runs a bed and breakfast and provides free bicycles and transfers to and from the airport (singles $40-75, doubles $60, each additional person $15). Puffin also operates a travel-booking service for other accommodations, and sightseeing, fishing, and photography tours. For more information, write to Puffin Travel, Inc., Box 3-LG, Gustavus, AK 99826. They also sell a package trip including round-trip airfare between Juneau and Gustavus, one night at the Puffin B&B, and a one-day tour of the park on the *Spirit of Adventure* for $315 per person (slightly lower for groups of 3 or 4).

Cruises into the park are also available, though costly. **Alaska Sightseeing Tours** (800-426-7702) operates a three-day, two-night trip from Juneau that includes both the east and west arms of the bay ($500-700 per person). The cruise sails May 28-Sept. 11 Mon., Wed., and Fri. at 4pm. **Alaska Discovery** organizes guided kayaking trips into Glacier Bay from Juneau (see Juneau: Practical Information).

■■■ HAINES

Haines occupies one of the most strikingly beautiful settings of any city on the Southeast Coast, with its clear blue water, granite, snow-covered coastal range, glaciers, sunny days, and breathtaking trails winding in and out of beaches, forests, and mountains. The area's star attraction arrives in late fall or early winter, when warm upwellings in the Chilkat River encourage an out-of-season salmon run that draws over 3000 bald eagles, more than double the town's human population, to the Chilkat Peninsula's "Council Grounds" for a midwinter feast.

Originally named *Dershu*, Tlingit for "End of the Trail," Haines now marks one end of the **Haines Hwy.,** the more heavily traveled overland route between the Yukon and Southeastern Alaska. In the early 1890s adventurer Jack Dalton improved an already well-developed trail, formerly used by Native Alaskans, from Pyramid Harbor to the Yukon. Dalton's investment paid off during the Gold Rush of 1897-1900, when stampeding gold-seekers paid outlandish tolls to cross the quickest road to the Klondike.

PRACTICAL INFORMATION AND ORIENTATION

Visitors Information Center: (766-2234 or 800-458-3579, from British Columbia and the Yukon 800-478-2268), 2nd Ave. near Willard St. Information on accommodations, hiking around town, and surrounding parks. Make sure to pick up the free pamphlet *Haines is for Hikers*. Free tea and coffee inside. Open Mon.-Sat. 8am-8pm, Sun. 10am-6pm; Oct.-April Mon.-Fri. 8am-5pm. Remains open until 10pm if a ferry is arriving.

State Park Information Office, 259 Main St. between 2nd and 3rd Ave., P.O. Box 430 (766-2292), above Helen's Shop. Legendary Ranger Bill Zack can tell you all you need to know about hiking in the area, the dangers of bears, and the Chilkat Bald Eagle Preserve. Officially open Tues.-Sat. 8am-4:30pm, but call ahead to be sure that someone is in the office.

Air Service: L.A.B. Flying Service (766-2222), and **Wings of Alaska** (766-2030) both fly several times per day to Juneau ($50, round-trip $90). Wings has the cheapest flight to Glacier Bay ($88, $168 round-trip).

Buses: Alaskon Express, Box 574 (766-2030 or 800-544-2206), on 2nd Ave., across from the Visitors Center in the Wings of Alaska office. Buses leave Haines traveling north on Tues., Thurs., and Sun., with an overnight stop in Beaver Creek, YT, near the Alaska border. To: Anchorage ($194), Fairbanks ($169), and Whitehorse ($79). Open Mon.-Sat. 7:30am-6:30pm, and Sun. 10am-6pm.

Alaska Marine Highway: 766-2111. Terminal on 5 Mile Lutak Rd., 4 mi. from downtown. Hitchers can usually get into town. (*Let's Go* does not recommend hitchhiking.) A taxi runs $5. Daily ferry to Juneau ($20), to Skagway ($14).

Water Taxi: 766-3395. To Skagway, on a 40-ft. passenger boat (2 per day, $18, round-trip $29).

Taxi: Haines Taxi, 766-3138. 45-min. city tour for $5. **Other Guy's Taxi,** 766-3257. $5 from ferry to downtown. Ask about long-term ferry parking. 24 hrs.

Car Rental: Hertz (766-2131), in the Thunderbird Hotel. $45 per day, 30¢ per mi. after 100 mi. **Eagle's Nest Car Rental** (766-2891), at Eagle's Nest Motel. $45 per day, 30¢ per mi. after 100 mi. **Avis** at Hotel Halsingland (766-2733) offers an 8-hr. time limit deal; 35¢ per mi. after 100 mi. for $30. Must be 25 with a credit card. Don't be late, or you'll pay the standard $69 per day.

Bike and Kayak Rental: Sockeye Cycle (766-2869), Portage St. in Fort Seward. $6 per hr., $20 per ½-day, $30 per day. Open Mon.-Fri. 10am-6pm, Sat. 11am-5pm. Helmets and locks included. Kayaks $35 per day. 2- to 3-day rentals.

Bookstore: Glass Onion Music and Books (766-3100), across from visitor's center on 2nd Ave. Small selection of current magazines and recent books, along with a larger selection of CDs. Even sells old editions of *Let's Go* (the classics!) (Open Mon.-Sat. 10:30am-6pm, Sun. 1-5pm.)

Library: (766-2545), 1 block from Main St. on 3rd Ave. Open Tues.and Thurs.-Fri. 10am-4:30pm, 7-9pm; Wed. 10am-9pm; Sat. 1-4pm; Sun. 2-4pm.

Laundromat and Showers: Port Chilkoot Camper Park (766-2000), across from Halsingland Hotel. Wash $2, 7 min. dry 25¢. Showers $1.50. Open daily 7:30am-9pm. **Susie Q's** (766-2953), on Main St. near Front St. Wash $2, dry 50¢. Showers $2. Open daily 8am-8pm; winter 8am-6pm.

Health Center: 766-2521.

Ambulance and Emergency: 911. **Police:** 766-2121.

Post Office: On Haines Hwy., between 2nd Ave. and Front St. Open Mon.-Fri. 9am-5:30pm, Sat. 1-3pm. **General Delivery ZIP Code:** 99827.

Area Code: 907.

Haines lies on a thin peninsula between the Chilkat and Chilkoot Inlets. Below this narrow neck of land, the two inlets merge into **Lynn Canal.** Don't confuse your Chilkats and Chilkoots! The former refers to the storehouses for salmon taken from that inlet, and the latter to the storehouses for bigger salmon taken from the other. Both the U.S. and Canada have **customs offices** (767-5511 and 767-5540) at Mile 42 of the Haines Hwy. (open daily 7am-11pm). Travelers must have at least $150, a credit card, and valid proof of citizenship to cross into Canada, although the border officials generally enforce this requirement at their whim.

ACCOMMODATIONS AND CAMPING

In addition to the campgrounds listed below, there are several **state campgrounds** in and around Haines which compete for budget travelers. **Portage Cove**, ¾ mi. from town on Beach Rd., accepts only backpackers and bicyclists (sites $6). **Chilkat State Park,** 7 mi. south on Mud Bay Rd. by the sea, has good king salmon and halibut fishing, and guided nature walks near the hiking trail to Seduction Point. (35 sites; $6). **Chilkoot Lake,** 10 mi. north of town on Lutak Rd., provides views and sockeye salmon fishing (32 sites; $8). **Mosquito Lake,** 27 mi. north on Haines Hwy., is a small spot which earns its name in late summer (5 sites; $6). All state campgrounds have water and toilets.

Bear Creek Camp and International Hostel, Box 1158 (766-2259), on Small Tract Rd. 2 mi. outside of town. From downtown, follow 3rd Ave. out Mud Bay Rd. to Small Tract Rd. A ring of basic cabins around a circular drive, 2 of which are hostel dorms. Rarely full. Musical instruments on loan for use around the campfire, clean 24-hr. kitchen facilities, free showers for guests, and laundry (wash $1.50, dry 25¢). Day care available for $4 per hr. per child. Showers $2 for non-guests. No curfew or lockout. Ferry terminal pick-up (call, or look for the orange truck by the dock) and drop-off. Though Bear Creek is not affiliated with AYH, it gives member discounts: $12, nonmembers $15, family cabins $37. Tentsites for $5 may be the best way to go ($2.50 per additional person).

Hotel Halsingland, Box 1589MD, Haines 99827 (766-2000). Good hotel; in old Ft. Seward officers' quarters. Intriguing decor. Rooms $30, with bath $35. Doubles $40. Next door is **The Officers' Inn Bed and Breakfast** (800-542-6363). Singles $50, doubles $55 (shared bath, more for private baths). Breakfast included. Courtesy shuttle will pick up/drop off all over Haines.

Fort Seward Lodge, Box 307, Haines 99827 (766-2009 or 1-800-478-7772). Fine view of Lynn Canal from another historic Fort Seward building. 10 rooms at rea-

HAINES

sonable rates. Singles with shared bath $45. Doubles from $55. Private bath $10 extra. Oct-April rooms are $10 less.

Summer Inn Bed and Breakfast, 247 2nd Ave., P.O. Box 1198 (766-2970). Nice rooms, full breakfast, and great view of the Lynn Canal and surrounding mountains. Shared bath. Singles $55, doubles $65, triples $85. Winter rates $10 less.

Port Chilkoot Camper Park, Box 41589 (766-2000 or 800-542-6363), across from Hotel Halsingland. 60 sites for tents ($6.75) and RVs (full hookup $15). Laundromat (see Practical Information), showers ($1.50), and telephone available. Noon checkout. Summer only.

FOOD

Howser's Supermarket (766-2040) on Main St. has a great deli counter and tasty muffins. Try the Jo-Jos (deep-fried potato wedges) and golden 3-piece fried chicken ($4). (Open daily 8am-8pm. Deli open daily 7am-7pm.) You can pick up bulk health foods at **The Mountain Market** (766-3340) at Haines Hwy. and 3rd Ave., P.O. Box 1189 (open Mon.-Fri. 7:30am-7pm, Sat. 8:30am-6pm, Sun. 9am-3pm). For fresh seafood head to **Bell's Seafood** (766-2950) on 2nd Ave. under the "Old City Jail and Firehouse" sign. Try the salmon for $7 per lb. or the prawns for $13 per lb. (open Sun.-Tues. and Thurs.-Sat. 9am-6pm, Wed. 9am-10pm).

Porcupine Pete's (766-9999), Main and 2nd Ave. Rustic, cheap food. The carved duo depicted on a totem by local artist David Stead is meant to represent "Pete" and his porcupine mascot from mining days in the Porcupine mines of the northern Yukon and Alaska. The hamburger pita, a tasty sourdough-calzone concoction, fills your plate like a small bowling ball ($6.25). Open daily 11am-10pm.

Bamboo Room (776-2800), 2nd Ave. near Main St., next to the Pioneer Bar. What bamboo? Great breakfast spot, until 3pm crowded with fisherfolk downing the buckwheat hotcakes and coffee ($4.25), and omelets with hash browns and toast (from $6.25). Lunch specials $6, dinner specials $9-10. Open daily 6am-10pm.

Chilkat Restaurant and Bakery (766-2920), on 5th Ave., near Main. Family-style restaurant with healthy portions. Haines' best baked goods: bread loaves ($2.10), cinnamon rolls ($1.50). All-you-can-eat soup-and-salad bar ($9). Sandwiches $4-11. Open Mon.-Sat. 7am-9pm, Sun. 9am-9pm.

The Lighthouse (766-2442), where 2nd Ave. meets the water. True to its name, the Lighthouse offers a commanding view of the harbor. Dinner expensive, but lunch sandwiches around $5. Try the roast beef ($3.75) or ham-n-egg with potato salad ($6.25). Breakfast too (open daily 6am-10pm).

Port Chilkoot Potlatch (766-2040), at the Tribal House of Ft. Seward. All-you-can-eat salmon bake and BBQ with all the trimmings ($20). The Potlatch is a tourist trap, but the salmon is unbeatable. Reservations recommended later in the week; tickets are pre-sold to cruise ships. Salmon served 5-8pm Fri.-Wed.

SIGHTS AND ENTERTAINMENT

Fort William Seward, on the west side of town, was established in 1901 to assert an American presence during a border dispute with Canada. With little else to do other than shovel snow and watch for fires, the colonial-style post quickly became known as a gentle assignment. Boredom was the soldiers' only enemy: "Even among men with the most modern arms, time is the hardest thing to kill," lamented one observer in a 1907 newspaper. After being declared surplus after WWII, five veterans bought the entire 400-acre compound with plans of making a commune out of the old fort. Their utopian venture never succeeded, but most of these settlers became free-enterprising members of the community; today Fort Seward lies at the center of Haines's tourist activity. In the middle of the grounds sits a replica of a **Totem Village** (766-2160), complete with a tribal house, where the salmon bake is held. The **Chilkat Dancers** perform traditional Tlingit dances with interpretive narration at the **Chilkat Center for the Arts.** Performances are usually at 8pm, but revolve around cruise ship and ferry schedules. Call the Hotel Halsingland (766-2000) for information and tickets ($8, students $4, under 5 free). The village is also home to the **Sea Wolf Studio-gallery** (766-2540), where you can watch artist Tresham Gregg carve Tlingit masks (open Mon.-Fri. 10am-5pm). Crossing to the far side of the parade grounds takes you to the **Alaska Indian Arts Center** (766-2160). Inside, visitors are welcome to watch artisans in their workshops and marvel at the craft of totem pole carving (open Mon.-Fri. 9am-noon and 1-5pm).

In town, the worthwhile **Sheldon Museum** (766-2366), 25 Main St., houses traditional art and artifacts upstairs and exhibits on the history of Haines downstairs. Movies about Haines are shown starting at 1:15pm (open daily in summer 1-5pm and Wed. 6:30-9pm; $2.50, under 18 free). Haines is also an artists' colony. Check out the works of local artists near the visitors center; the **Northern Arts Gallery** (766-2318, open daily 10am-5pm), and the **Chilkat Valley Arts** (766-2990; open daily 10am-6pm), in Fort Seward, are noteworthy. Galleries here offer high quality craft work in fur, wood, and on film rather than the usual tourist cache.

OUTDOORS

The **Haines Hwy.** winds 40 mi. from Haines through the **Chilkat Range** north through the Yukon. The views are guaranteed to blow you though the back of your Winnebago. **Chilkat State Park,** a 19-mi. drive up the highway, protects the largest population of bald eagles (3500) in North America. From Nov. through Jan., travelers can see great numbers of eagles perched on birchwoods in the rivers or flying overhead. To get the best view of these rare birds, go see the most excellent Ranger Bill Zack for trail tips. Pick up *Haines is for Hikers* there or at the Visitors Information Center (see above).

Three main **trails** head into the hills around Haines. The closest trailhead to the hostel is that of the moderate hike up to the 1760-ft. summit of **Mt. Riley,** where heads spin with the amazing 360° view. The trail begins at a marker about 1½ mi. down Mud Bay Rd. past the hostel. The 2.1-mi. route clears the treeline just before reaching the summit. Two longer trails lead up Mt. Riley from closer to town. To reach the **Port Chilkoot trail,** walk out the FAA road behind Officers' Row in Fort Seward. After 1 mi., the road leads to a city water route, and after 2 mi. along this byway a 5-minute spur trail branches to connect with the Mud Bay route. From Fort Seward to the summit is a 3.8-mi. trek.

The **Portage Cove route,** follows the road along the cove to the level Batter Point trail beside the shore. Just before the Batter Point trail reaches the beach, a right fork leads up to Mt. Riley. This approach is a 5½-mi. hike.

The long but not laborious **Seduction Point trail** offers 6¾ mi. of birds, beaches, ocean bluffs, berry picking, wildflowers, and a view of Davidson Glacier. Take Mud Bay Rd. out of Haines 7 mi. and look for the trailhead. Try to time the last part of the hike along David's Cove to coincide with low tide.

Mt. Ripinsky, the 3920-ft. mountain looming over town to the north, provides a challenging hike over two summits connected by an alpine ridge. On a clear day, the view from the ridge extends all the way to Juneau. To reach the trailhead, follow 2nd Ave. north to Lutak Rd. Branch off Lutak onto Young St. at the hill, and then turn right along a buried pipeline for 1 mi. The trail cuts off to the left a few yards after the pipeline right of way begins to descend steeply towards the tank farm. After cresting at the 3610-ft. **North Summit,** the trail dips down along the ridge where it may be difficult to follow in poor weather. At the end of the ridge, it climbs again to the 3920-ft. peak, and then descends steeply to its terminus at Mile 7 of Haines Hwy. This 10-mi. hike makes for a long day's walking or a more relaxed overnight trip.

Alaska Nature Tours, P.O. Box 491 (766-2876; fax 766-2876), leads you to the eagles for a 3-hr. tour ($45, fall is the best time to spot eagles) and offers a variety of other tours, from 2½ hrs. to a full day. Reservations expected; call 10am-5pm, Mon.-Fri. The people with Nature Tours are experts at observation and photography of bears, moose, and sea lions. **Chilkat Guides,** P.O. Box 170 (766-2491), leads four-hour raft trips down the Chilkat River, leaving several times daily in the summer. Rubber boots, ponchos, and transportation to and from the river are provided ($70, children $30). The office is open Mon.-Fri. 7am-9pm. The **Southeast Alaska State Fair** lights up the fairground here from August 11 to 15 in 1995, while concurrently blues and bluegrass artists strut their stuff at the **Alaska Bald Eagle Music Festival.**

The **Master Anglers Tournament** runs in late August, and **Alcan 200 Snowmobile Races** January 20-22 in 1995 makes the winter livelier for those in the area.

■■■ SKAGWAY

In late 1896 George Carmack, Skookum Jim, and Tagish Charley made a discovery in a tributary of the Klondike River: gold lying thick between slabs of rock "like cheese in a sandwich." Skagway sprang up almost overnight in July 1897 as hordes of prospectors arrived to follow the Chilkoot and White Pass trails to the Yukon. Indescribable madness followed: by October, Skagway was a town of 20,000. (A town of 20,000 in Alaska would be large *today*.) From Skagway, the stampeders drove their pack horses mercilessly along the rocky but relatively gradual White Pass Trail. Thousands of horses expired along this route in the winter of 1897-98, earning it the name **Dead Horse Trail.** The shorter Chilkoot Trail, starting in the nearby ghost town of **Dyea,** climbs too steeply for pack animals, but was just as popular. On the other side of the mountains, miners built boats on Lake Bennett and floated north on the Yukon River to the diggings. To prevent food riots, the Canadian Mounties would not let prospectors into the Yukon without one ton of food and supplies; to carry this much, a person might make 30 or 40 trips over the pass. As Klondike yielded to a Nome gold rush in about 1900, Skagway dwindled but survived as a port and terminus of a railway over White Pass.

Skagway was a lawless gold-boom town, dominated for a few months by the organized-crime boss Jefferson "Soapy" Smith. An enigmatic figure and a master of bizarre, creative criminal schemes, he was notorious for use of bribes, coercion, intimidation, and violence to control Skagway's booming underworld. In July 1898, in a classic shoot-out, Soapy died violently with his heroic opponent, town surveyor Frank Reid, whose tombstone reads, "He gave his life for the honor of Skagway."

Today, Dyea (pop. 11,000 in 1898) is a ghost town. But Skagway, kept alive by the railroad built along the White Pass Trail, has been restored by the National Park Service to its original 1898 condition, down to the wooden sidewalks. Visitors come to enjoy Skagway's history and to enjoy an amazing array of **hiking** opportunities second only to those found around Juneau, including the heavily hiked **Chilkoot Trail.** A scant 29 in. of annual rainfall means that hikers are almost always rewarded with clear views. Because of the sheer bluffs which line the way, the 1-hr. ferry ride from Haines to Skagway is one of the most impressive stretches in the Inside Passage.

PRACTICAL INFORMATION AND ORIENTATION

Visitors Information: Klondike Gold Rush National Historical Park Visitor Center (983-2921), 2nd and Broadway. Walking tours daily at 9:30 and 11am, 2 and 4pm. An excellent introduction to Skagway's history is the film *Days of Adventure, Dreams of Gold,* narrated by Hal Holbrook and shown on the hr. Open May-Sept. daily 8am-8pm. **Skagway Convention and Visitors Bureau** (983-2855), in the Arctic Brotherhood building on Broadway, between 2nd and 3rd. Pick up the free *Skagway Trail Map* here. The *Skagway Story* is performed at 10am, 12:15, 2:45, and 4:45pm; $2.50. Open daily 8am-5pm.

Forest Service: Skagway Office (983-3088) on 2nd St. near Spring Ave., in a yellow building. Open Sun.-Mon. and Thurs. 10am-1pm and 2-5pm; Tues.-Wed. and Fri.-Sat. 8-11:30am and 12:30-5pm. To reserve a cabin call the Juneau office (586-8751).

Long Distance Phone: Alascom Phone Service (983-9150), on Broadway, between 5th and 6th. Open when cruise ships are in.

Flights: Skagway Air Service, 983-2218. 7 flights per day to Juneau ($70).

Trains: White Pass and Yukon Route, P.O. Box 435 (800-343-7373 or 983-2217), 1 block off Broadway on 2nd. All trains wheelchair accessible. 3-hr. round-trip excursion to White Pass Summit, on one of the steepest railroad grades in

North America. Trains leave daily at 8:50am and 1:20pm ($72, under 13 $36). Combined train and bus service to and from Whitehorse, YT leaves daily at 12:40pm ($92 one way, under 13 $46).

Buses: Alaskon Express (800-544-2206 or 983-2241), in the Westmark Inn, 3rd Ave. between Broadway and Spring. Buses Sun., Tues., and Thurs. To: Anchorage and Fairbanks ($200). All trips include overnight stop in Beaver Creek in the Yukon near the border. Also 1 per day in summer to Whitehorse, YT ($52) at 7:30am. **Alaska Direct** (800-770-6652) runs vans from the hostel and hotels. To: Whitehorse ($35) daily, with connections on Tues., Fri., and Sun. to Fairbanks ($155) and Anchorage ($180).

Alaska Marine Highway: 983-2941. Ferries daily to Haines ($14), Juneau ($26).

Water Taxi: 776-3395. 40 passengers; twice daily to Haines ($18, round-trip $29).

Taxi: Pioneer Taxi, 983-2623. To Dyea and Chilkoot Trail ($15). Combination tour of town, waterfront, and White Pass ($24). **Klondike Tours** (983-2075) also runs to the Chilkoot Trail head 5-6 times per day ($10); call for schedule.

Car Rental: Sourdough Van & Car Rentals (983-2523; 800-478-2529), at 6th Ave. and Broadway, is cheapest at $30-50 per day. 30¢ per mi. after the first 100. **Avis** (983-2247; 800-478-2847), 2nd and Spring. $58 per day, unlimited free mi., must be 21.

Bike and Kayak Rental: Sockeye Cycle (983-2851), on 5th Ave. off Broadway. Rates begin at $6 per hr., $30 per day, including helmet and lock. Rents sea kayaks for $35 per 8 hrs. Open Mon.-Sun. 9am-6pm. **Corner Cafe,** 4th and State St. Bikes rent out quickly at $5 per hr., $25 per day. Hours same as cafe.

Bookstore: Skagway News Depot (983-2543), Broadway between 2nd and 3rd. Small collection of Alaskan travel books. Variety of newspapers. Open daily 8:30am-7:30pm.

Library: 8th Ave. and Broadway (983-2665). Open Mon.-Fri. 1-9pm, Sat. 1-5pm.

Laundromat: Service Unlimited Laundromat, 2nd Ave. and State St. Wash $2, 5-min. dry 25¢. Open daily 8am-9pm.

Hospital: Skagway Medical Service, 983-2255 or 983-2418.

Post Office: Broadway and 6th, next to the bank (983-2320). Open Mon.-Fri. 8:30am-5pm. **General Delivery ZIP Code:** 99840. Lobby open 24 hrs. for postage machine.

Area Code: 907.

At the northernmost tip of the Inside Passage, Skagway is the terminus of the Alaska Marine Hwy. From here, travelers on wheels can connect to the Alaska Hwy. by taking the **Klondike Hwy.** (Rte. 98 in AK; Hwy. 2 in YT) to Whitehorse via Carcross. Haines is 12 mi. away by water. Hitchers say they do better by spending $14 on the ferry to Haines and try the more heavily traveled Haines Hwy. to Kluane and interior Alaska. (*Let's Go* does not recommend hitchhiking.)

Only about 700 people spend the winter in Skagway. Another 1500 arrive for summer jobs in the tourist industry, and on a busy day 3000 visitors may spill off the cruise ships and ferries.

ACCOMMODATIONS AND CAMPING

With a recently refurbished bunkhouse and a friendly hostel, Skagway is good to budget travelers. Campers can either shell out $8 for sites at **Hanousek Park,** on 14th at Broadway, or head out for the **Chilkoot Trail** in Dyea, 9 mi. from Skagway, to stay at the free ranger-staffed campground there. It is wise to make reservations at least one month in advance at all Skagway hotels. Also see the **Forest Service cabins** in the Outdoors section below.

Skagway Home Hostel (983-2131), 3rd and Main, P.O. Box 231, ½ mi. from the ferry. In a turn-of-the-century house, 5-10 min. walk from ferry. Pick-up at every ferry. Sign up for dinner before 4:30pm, $5 to join dinner; free if you'd like to cook. No lockout, no curfew, free showers, kitchen. $3 for wash, dry, and detergent. 19 beds and 2 rooms for couples, overflow in nearby church. Chore required. Will store packs. Check-in 5:30-9pm. $10, nonmembers $12; sheets and towels $1.

Hanousek Park (983-2768), on Broadway at 14th, 1½ mi. north of the ferry. Privately run. Drinking water, modern bathrooms with showers (25¢ for 2 min.), fire rings. Sites $8, with RV hookup $15.

Portland House and Inn (983-2493), 5th Ave. and Main. A no-frills cheap-sleep above the Greek place. 1 bed in a 3-bed room, $30. Doubles $45. Shared bath.

Golden North Hotel, P.O. Box 431 (983-2294), at 3rd Ave. and Broadway. A splendid hotel, the oldest (1898) operating in the state. Each room is restored to period style in unique fashion, some with canopy beds, claw-footed bathtubs, and the like. Singles $45, with bath $60. Doubles $55, with bath $75.

Skagway Inn, P.O. Box 500 (983-2289), on Broadway at 7th. Built in 1897 as a brothel, the inn is now respectably refurbished, except for the unaltered practice of naming the 12 rooms after women. Courtesy van to the head of the Chilkoot Trail. Pickup/delivery to ferry, airport. Separate baths. Hearty breakfast included. Expensive restaurant below. Singles $59. Doubles $74.

Pullen Creek Park Campground (983-2768) on the waterfront, by the small boat harbor. Showers and 42 RV sites with full hookup. Call ahead to reserve showers; $1 for 7 min. Sites $18.

Dyea Camping Area, 9 mi. northwest of Skagway on the Dyea Rd. Free; near base of the **Chilkoot Trail.** 22 sites. Pit toilets, fire rings, no drinking water or showers. 2-week max. stay.

FOOD

Campers can pick up last-minute groceries for the Chilkoot trail at the small **Fairway Supermarket** at 4th and State (open daily 8am-10pm). Most restaurants in Skagway are in the Historic District, on Broadway between 2nd and 7th St.

Corner Cafe, 4th and State (983-2155). Where the locals head for grub. Open-air seating lets you avoid the smoke. Hear that fryer sizzle! Kitchenesque atmosphere. Stack of sourdough pancakes ($3.25); biscuits and gravy ($3.75). Burgers and sandwiches ($4.50-7). Open daily 6am-9pm.

Sweet Tooth Cafe (983-2405), on Broadway between 3rd and 4th St. Sandwiches and soup or salad ($3.60-5.75). The cheapest halibut burger in town ($5.60). This cafe scoops a mean ice cream cone ($1.65). Take-out orders 25¢ extra. Frilly decor. Open daily 6am-6pm.

Broadway Bistro (983-6231), across from the Sweet Tooth Cafe on Broadway. One of the few spots in town rooted in the 1990s. Try the State Street Roll-up: sprouts, tomato, onion, guacamole with whipped cream cheese in a flour tortilla ($6), or the granola with sundried cranberries for breakfast ($4). Pizza, beer, wine, and Starbucks coffee. Open daily 8am-8pm, coffee from 6:30am.

Prospector's Sourdough Restaurant (983-2865), on Broadway between 3rd and 4th Ave. All-you-can-eat salad bar and soup in a cafeteria setting ($7.50 11am-4pm, $8 after 4 pm). Open daily 6am-10pm.

The Popcorn Wagon, Broadway and 5th. Down on your luck, or just plain tired of sit-down meals? Stop here for chili ($3) and a large lemonade ($1.50).

SIGHTS AND EVENTS

Most of Broadway (which is most of town) is preserved in pristine 1898 form as the **Klondike Gold Rush National Historic Park.** The Park Service has assembled a small museum beside the visitors center and restored a vintage saloon on Broadway. Many other period pieces have been leased to local businesses. Check out the worthwhile hourly film at the Park's visitors center (see Practical Information). Then wander down Broadway to peep at the **Red Onion Saloon,** Skagway's first bordello, on 2nd Ave. A century ago, each lady marked her availability by placing one of the dolls on the rack downstairs in the appropriate position: upright or prostrate. Now the Red Onion is a locally favored bar with an enviable collection of bed pans adorning one wall. Come for live afternoon jazz on ship days or for the open jam Thursday nights, and check out the fading photos (open daily 10am-?; free).

Farther down Broadway is the 1899 **Arctic Brotherhood Hall,** Alaska's first gold-mining fraternity. Founded in 1899 as the Fraternal Order of Klondike Gold Stampeders, it had as its motto "No Boundary Line Here." Driftwood covers the facade of the Hall, making for a bizarre example of Victorian rustic architecture.

True gold rush buffs can mine for pleasure at the **Trail of '98 Museum** (983-2420), on the second floor of City Hall, at 7th Ave. and Spring St. (open daily 9am-5pm; $2, students $1). Check out the world's only duck-neck robe patterned out of throttled mallard throats, and view the Frank Reid-Soapy Smith paraphernalia for some real frontier flavor. Soapy's blood-stained tie hangs here. If you care to delve deeper into this Manichean clash, wander along State St. until it meets 23rd Ave. and look for the sign pointing to Soapy's grave across the railroad tracks in the **Gold Rush Cemetery.** Frank Reid pushes up grass here, too, along with many other stampeders who never made it to the gold fields. Beyond the cemetery and farther out of town, booming **Reid Falls** cascades 300 ft. down the mountainside.

If you happen to be near these Elysian fields at 10:30pm on July 8, you can witness the celebration of **Soapy's Wake,** an ironic event that was never meant to be an event at all. Several years ago on the anniversary of Soapy's death, a few locals gathered in the cemetery to down some champagne, recite amateur poetry, and relieve themselves on Frank Reid's grave. Tour guides publicized the impromptu gathering as an "event" and people began arriving to see the spectacle. A small group now obliges the crowd with a perfunctory wake, but the police object to the defacing of public monuments. For a more genuine display of Skagway's town spirit, try the lively **Solstice Party** the weekend after June 21.

Back in town, the museum in the back of the **Corrington Alaskan Ivory Co.** (983-2580), 5th and Broadway, contains an intriguing display of expensive carved bone and ivory pieces (open daily 8am-9pm). **Inside Passage Arts** (983-2585), Broadway and 4th St., sells some of the finest works of local Native artists. Come in to view even if you can't buy (open daily 9am-4pm; later when cruise ships are in).

At night, go to the **Skagway Days of '98** show in the Eagles Dance Hall (983-2234), 6th and Broadway. For decades the show has featured song and dance, play-money gambling by the audience, and audience-actor interaction. Definitely worth the money ($14, kids $7). You'll learn all you ever wanted to know about Soapy Smith here (daily in summer; 7:30pm gambling, 8:30pm show). Check the marquee for morning performances that vary with cruise ships ($12, kids $6).

Built as the gold craze calmed in 1900, the **railroad cars** of the White Pass & Yukon Route have been resurrected from the West's locomotive graveyards and now run from Skagway to the summit of White Pass and back. The scenery of this narrow passage is overwhelmingly beautiful. (Trains run May 16-Sept. 22 daily at 8:30am and 1:20pm. Irregular service before May 16. Fare $72, under 13 $36.)

Dyea, near the head of the Chilkoot Trail, lies 9 mi. out of Skagway on the unpaved Dyea Rd. The town crashed following the gold rush, and scavengers quickly moved in to dismantle houses, banks, hotels, and other buildings for scrap wood. Today the only evidence of Dyea's former glory are scattered foundations, the remnants of wooden pilings that once supported a large wharf, and **Slide Cemetery,** where more than 200 victims of an 1898 avalanche on the crowded Chilkoot Pass are buried. The Park Service runs walking tours of Dyea during the summer at Wed.-Fri. at 1:30pm and Sat.-Sun. at 10:30am. They will explain, among other things, why the wharves are now hundreds of feet from the water. Taxi fare to Dyea is roughly $10, but the beautiful scenery of the inlet on the way to Dyea is better seen from a rented bike. The friendly, knowledgable folk at **Klondike Tours** (P.O. Box 320, 983-2075) give a 3-hr. tour of Skagway and Dyea (with an Alaskan Sled Dog Show at the end!) for $34. They also offer flightseeing at **Glacier Bay** ($110).

OUTDOORS

Although the Chilkoot Trail is the marquee name in Skagway hiking, excellent shorter hikes in the area have inspiring views and fewer people around you to block them. You need a permit for overnight camping; get one free at the **Dyea Ranger**

CHILKOOT TRAIL

Station, less than ½ mi. south of Chilkoot trailhead. All train tickets for transportation to these areas should be purchased at least one day in advance. Reserve cabins in advance by calling 586-8751.

The **Dewey Lake Trail System** provides some of the best hikes near town, ranging from a 20-min. stroll to a strenuous climb up to a 3700-ft. elevation and two alpine lakes. To reach the trail system, walk east toward the mountains along 2nd. Ave. Cross the railroad tracks and follow a dirt road to the left, where you'll shortly find signs pointing out the trail. **Lower Dewey Lake,** a long, narrow pond surrounded by woods, lies less than a mile up the trail. Here one trail branches out around the lake (about 2 mi.), and another towards **Icy Lake** and Upper Reid Falls (about 1½ mi.). Both of these walks are gentle, with little change in elevation. A third trail to **Upper Dewey Lake** branches off the Icy Lake trail near the northern end of Lower Dewey Lake. A steep climb leads 2¼ mi. up to the upper lake, which occupies a stunning amphitheater of serrated peaks. A small **cabin** with space for four and a permanent smoky odor sits by the lake. It is available on a first-come, first-served basis. The best **camping sites** are along the opposite shore. An extension of the Upper Dewey trail leads south from the lake 1 mi. across a rocky alpine bench to the limpid waters of the **Devil's Punchbowl.** Excellent views of the inlet below make this sidetrip worthwhile. Watch for bears; yell to alert them to your presence. Chunks of ice float in this transparent pool into June and July, and the water is so clear that you'll have no trouble spotting the freckles on the trout. Plan on a 3-hr. trip one-way from town to the Punchbowl.

A.B. Mountain, named for the pattern created by the melting snow on its side each spring, dominates the skyline on the west side of town. The **Skyline Trail** leads up this mountain. A 1½-mi. walk from town leads out to the Skyline Trailhead. Cross the Skagway River footbridge at the north-west end of First Ave., and turn left on Dyea Rd. The trailhead lies to the right at the crest of a hill. It is a poorly marked and steep 5-mi. hike to the 3500-ft. summit.

Two other hikes near Skagway combine cabins, glaciers, and the White Pass and Yukon Route railroad. The trail to the **Denver Glacier** begins just short of Milepost 6 on the White Pass and Yukon Railroad. This trail passes below the towering walls of the Sawtooth Range and winds down in the brush of the Denver Glacier moraine. The 4½-mi. hike ends near a Forest Service **cabin** close to the glacier. Bear-sightings are frequent. Inquire at the Park Visitor Center (see above) about the availability of the cabin. Don't chance a walk out to the trailhead along the tracks. The WP&YR train will deposit hikers at the trail on its two daily trips to White Pass (leaves daily at 8am and 12:40pm) and make a flag stop to bring them back to town (pickup daily at 11:35am, 4:10pm, round-trip $10).

The clearly marked **Laughton Glacier Trail,** beginning at milepost 14 along the train tracks to White Pass, makes an easy 1½-mi. ascent to an immense wall of hanging glaciers. The **cabin,** for up to six people, sits about 1 mi. from the ice at the junction of two rivers. The round-trip train fare to and from the trailhead (leaves daily at 8am, 12:40pm, pickup daily at 11am, 3:30pm; round trip $30).

The Chilkoot Trail

The winter of 1898 saw nine out of every 10 Klondike-bound stampeders slog through Skagway and Dyea. Formerly a major trade route controlled by the powerful Chilkat Tlingit nation, the Chilkoot Trail extends 33 mi. from the ghost town of **Dyea** to the shores of **Lake Bennett** over the precipitous **Chilkoot Pass.** The 4- to 5-day hike (3 days for seasoned hikers) is littered with wagon wheels, horse skeletons, other ballast the prospectors jettisoned, and informative plaques placed by the U.S. and Canadian National Park Services.

The Chilkoot Trail was a vital link in the extensive Native Alaskan trading network before the Klondike gold rush. As the shortest, best-known route to the Klondike, during the rush it was thick with prospectors on their way to the Yukon. No longer a path to quick riches, the trail offers dramatic changes of climate, terrain, and vegetation through spectacular and rugged scenery, climbing above the treeline before descending into the forests of extreme northern British Columbia. Pick up the complete *Hiker's Guide to the Chilkoot Trail,* a joint publication of the U.S. and Canadian National Park Services, before attempting the grueling, highly rewarding hike.

Although the Chilkoot is considered one of the best trails in Alaska, it is also one of the busiest. It's not mobbed as it was between 1897 and 1900 when gold-seekers stepped on each other's heels as they trudged ant-like over the pass, but the trail sees 3000 hikers setting out each summer. This adventure offers grand scenery and an exciting chance to retrace history, if not a solitary communion with the mountains. Despite its popularity, the Chilkoot is demanding. Weather conditions change rapidly, especially in the summit area; avalanches are common even in June. Check with the ranger at the visitors center at 2nd and Broadway in Skagway (see above) for current trail conditions before you leave. Rangers patrol the U.S. side of the trail and are also usually at the trailhead in Dyea (daily 5-7pm). If you're planning to continue into the Yukon, be sure to call **Canadian customs** (403-821-4111) before leaving Skagway (Dyea has no phones), and have proof of solvency ($150 and a credit card, plus a valid photo ID and birth certificate) before crossing the border.

To return to Skagway, leave the trail between Lake Bennett and Bare Loon Lake and follow the White Pass railroad tracks (be careful, this is private property) back to the Klondike Hwy. Rides are reportedly easy to find. (*Let's Go* does not recommend hitchhiking.)

Interior Alaska

Alaska's vast Interior sprawls between the Alaska Range to the south and the Brooks Range to the north, covering 166,000 sq. mi. of the nation's wildest and most stunning terrain. Most of the Interior alternates between flat forest and marshy, treeless tundra, punctuated by immense mountain ranges. The Yukon River, the Tanana River, and hundreds of other major and minor rivers have created the sloughs, inlets, lakes, and bogs that sustain a huge waterfowl population. The unofficial state bird, the mosquito, outnumbers all other animals by over a thousand to one in summer. Larger mammals, including moose, grizzlies, wolves, caribou, Dall sheep, lynx, beavers, and hares, roam the parks and wild country of the Interior. Few people live here; outside Fairbanks, Alaska's second-largest city, the region is sparsely inhabited.

Interior Alaska is the home of the Athabascan Native people, many of whom still trap, hunt, and fish within the Interior's network of waterways. These nomadic hunters' traditional domain followed the migration of caribou and the spawning cycles of salmon. Unlike the Native Americans in the Lower 48, Athabascans have not been confined to reservations; instead, they own title to their own land, a result of the Alaska Native Land Claims Settlement Act of 1971. Although many have left their remote villages and traditional lifestyle for modern living in Fairbanks and Anchorage, their pride in their unique cultural heritage and in their physical endurance is preserved in traditional stories and games. Today Athabascans still compete in dogsled races and in the annual World Eskimo-Indian Olympics (*sic*), where thousands of spectators watch spectacles of pain and stamina, including competitions that involve tying 10-lb. weights to participants' earlobes.

■■■ DENALI NATIONAL PARK

Denali National Park is the home of Denali ("The Great One" in Athabascan), the highest mountain in North America. Despite the blundering audacity of the Princeton-educated prospector who in 1896 renamed the peak after Republican Presidential nominee William McKinley, locals and visitors alike call it Denali or simply "the mountain." From base to summit, Denali is the greatest vertical relief in the world; even Mt. Everest rises only 11,000 ft. from its base on the Plateau of Tibet. Denali is 18,000 ft. of rock scrape toward the sky with hardly a hill intervening. It's so big that it manufactures its own weather: when moist air from the Pacific collides with the cold mountaintop, sudden storms encircle the peak. Denali's top is visible only for about 20% of the summer, but even if you can't see the peak, you can still experience the glories of the park's stunning terrain, wildlife, and lesser mountains.

Be prepared. Most visitors come to Denali between late May and mid-Sept.; arriving at either end of the summer will mean thinner crowds. Unfortunately, both ends of summer can also mean unpredictable weather. Mid-Sept. should see the fewest mosquitoes. Summer is cool, wet, and windy; snow is possible. Prepare for temperatures of between 35-75°F (1-24°C). Bring tough, warm gloves, rain gear, and strong, sturdy footgear. Insect repellent, binoculars, and a camera will improve your trip.

PRACTICAL INFORMATION AND ORIENTATION

Denali National Park commands respect. If you land in the park unprepared, you'll probably lose a day or more just getting your bearings. Only the first 14 mi. of the park are accessible by private vehicle; the remaining 71 mi. of dirt road can be reached only by shuttle or camper bus. Without preparation, moving through the park can be a complex, time-consuming, and highly confusing process. *Conduct all administrative business at the Visitor's Center as early in the day as possible.*

The park is larger than Massachusetts. If you go no farther than Savage River, the last campground accessible by private vehicle, you'll be missing out on 98% of the park's landscape and wildlife. You need no permit for driving or dayhiking in the first 14 mi. **Dayhiking** in the backcountry is unlimited. There are no wildlife restrictions or permit requirements, but you will need to reserve a spot on a **shuttle bus** ($12-30). You need to get a **campground permit** ($6-40) if you plan to stay at one in the park. If you are planning an **overnight backcountry expedition** into the wilderness of Denali, you need to obtain a **backcountry permit** (free). If you have a campground permit or a backcountry permit, or plan to get one, you are eligible to reserve a spot on a **camper bus** ($16), which may or may not be to your advantage. Permits cannot be reserved by phone; you have to apply in person. Bus spaces can be reserved by phone. Backcountry permits are issued 1 day in advance at the Visitor's Center; campground permits are issued on a space-available basis (usually a 1-day wait). A **bear-resistant food container** is free with your permit. Before you depart, watch the five short backcountry simulator programs, check the quota board at the backcountry desk for unit availability. There are 43 units, each with two to 12 overnight backcountry explorers at a time, and some might be closed for a variety of reasons. Read the description guides. The longest backcountry trips last about 7 days, limited by the amount of food one can carry.

Summer Visitors Information: Denali Visitor Center (V.C.) (683-1266 or 683-2294; 24-hr. emergency number 683-9100), 0.7 mi. from Rte. 3. All travelers stop here for orientation. The headquarters of the shuttle-bus service (to Tolkat, Mile 48 $12; to Eielson Visitor Center, Mile 65 $20; to Wonder Lake, Mile 85 $30. Under 13 free; 3-day pass is twice the price of a single day ticket). Registration or park entrance fee $3, families $5. **Maps**, shuttle-bus schedules, and free permits for campground ($6-40) and backcountry camping (free permit; $16 camper bus for permits beyond Mile 15). Information on campsites, wildlife tours, sled-dog demonstrations, and campfire talks. Denali Park's indispensable publication *Alpenglow* is also available (free). The center is new and has installed a backcountry simulator which provides useful information for wilderness hikers. Open in summer daily 7am-6pm. First shuttle bus departs 5:30am. Lockers outside 50¢.
Eielson Visitors Center, 66 mi. into the park, is staffed by helpful rangers who post day-to-day sightings of the mountain and is accessible by shuttle bus. Open daily in summer 9am-early evening. Write to **Denali National Park and Preserve,** P.O. Box 9, Denali Park, AK 99755 (683-1266), for information on the park; or consult one of the **Public Lands Information Centers** (see page 73 or page 166).
Winter Visitors Information: Skiing and sled-dog racing are popular winter-time activities in Denali. Visit the Park Headquarters (683-2294) at Mile 3.5, on the left side of the park road. For information write to Denali National Park and Preserve, P.O. Box 9, Denali Park 99755.
Bike Rental: Denali Mountain Bike, P.O. Box 1023, Denali 99755(683-1295), next to the Denali Hostel. Mountain bikes $7 per hr. and $25 per day. Repairs and 1- and 2-day guided tours. Unlike private vehicles, bikes *are* permitted on all 85 mi. of the park road.
Kayak Rental: Denali Park Paddling Center, P.O. Box 1171 (683-1925), for $35 per day. Tours $85.
Laundromat and Showers: McKinley Campground, P.O. Box 340, Healy 99743 (683-1418), 12 mi. north of park entrance. Showers ($2.50 for 7½ minutes) and the only public laundromat in the area (wash $2, dry $1). **Mercantile Gas and Groceries,** 1½ mi. into the park. Unlimited showers $2, plus a $5 key deposit. Showers open daily 7:30am-9pm.
Medical Clinic: 683-2211, in Healy. Open Mon.-Fri. 9am-5pm. Registered nurse on call 24 hrs.
Emergency: 911.
Post Office: (683-2291) next to Denali National Park Hotel, 1 mi. from the V.C. (see above). Open Mon.-Fri. 8:30am-5pm, Sat. 10am-1pm; Oct.-May Mon.-Sat. 10am-1pm. **General Delivery ZIP Code:** 99755.
Area Code: 907.

Transportation to the Park

Denali National Park can be easily reached by air, road, or rail. The best place to catch a flightseeing tour is **Talkeetna.** The **George Parks Hwy.** (Rte. 3), the road connecting Anchorage (240 mi. south of Denali) and Fairbanks (120 mi. north), offers direct access to the Denali park road. Leading east away from Denali is Rte. 8, the gravel **Denali Hwy.,** connecting the towns of Cantwell and Paxson. Closed in winter, the Denali Hwy. is one of Alaska's most breathtaking, skirting the foothills of the Alaska Range amid countless lakes and streams teeming with grayling, trout, and Arctic char. Several bus companies have service connecting Denali with Anchorage and Fairbanks. **Moon Bay Express** (274-6454) has 1 bus daily to Anchorage ($35 one way, $60 round-trip). **Fireweed Express** (452-0251) provides daily van service to Fairbanks ($25 one way). Call for times and reservations. **Alaska Direct** (277-6652) has competitive bus service; Fairbanks to Anchorage via Denali ($23; Tues., Fri., and Sun. 7am) and back ($42; Mon., Tues., and Sat. 7am). The **Alaska Backpacker Shuttle** runs a bus one-way from Anchorage to Denali ($35). The **Alaska Railroad,** P.O. Box 107500, Anchorage 99510 (683-2233, out of state 800-544-0552), makes regular stops at Denali station 1½ mi. from the park entrance, going to Fairbanks (1 per day, 4pm; $47); and Anchorage (1 per day, 12:30pm; $88). Check bags at least ½ hr. prior to departure. Call for tickets and reservations.

The helpful, free **Riley Creek Loop Bus** runs the 30-min. loop to the V.C., the Denali Park Hotel, the Alaska Railroad station, and the Riley Creek campground.

Buses within the Park

If you're going beyond Savage River at Mile 14, you must take a bus. The park's concessioner recently took over the **bus system** within the park, expanding both the number of available seats and the fee you'll have to pay for one. Cost depends on how far into the park you plan to go (**shuttle** to Tolkat, Mile 48, $12; to Eielson Visitor Center, Mile 65, $20; to Wonder Lake, Mile 85, $30; **camper** buses $16). A **3-day pass** is available, costing double the price of a single-day ticket for your destination. Tickets can be purchased in advance by phone (800-622-7275), or in person at the V.C. Calling ahead is strongly recommended. If you wait until you get to the park to purchase tickets, arrive at the V.C. as close to opening as possible (7am). Space on buses leaving in 2 days begins to get tight in late afternoon.

Shuttle buses leave the V.C. daily (5:30am-2:30pm). Go for the less frequent Wonder Lake bus if you can, as the best views of Denali are beyond Eielson. The 11-hr. round trip to Wonder Lake sounds grueling, but if the sun and the wildlife are out, you'll be glad you went. If it's raining, you can always hop off at Eielson and catch another bus back to the V.C. (round-trip to Eielson is 8 hrs.). **Camper buses** move faster, transporting *only* people with **campground permits** and **backcountry permits.** However, camper buses will stop to pick up dayhikers along the road. Camper buses leave the V.C. five times daily. The final bus stays overnight at Wonder Lake and returns at 7:10am. You can get on and off these buses **anywhere along the road;** flag the next one down when you want to move on or back. This is a good strategy for dayhiking and extremely convenient for Park explorers.

Blue and White School Bus is a courtesy bus owned by the chalets and makes runs from the Denali Park Hotel to the chalet near Lynx Creek Pizza. Hop on one and head to dinner.

ACCOMMODATIONS AND CAMPING

With one exception, accommodations within the park are open in the summer only. Any hotel room in or near the park will be expensive. **ARA,** 825 W 8th Ave., #240, Anchorage 99501 (800-276-7234), runs the park's tourist services, including the **Denali National Park Hotel** (683-2215), centrally located and near the railroad station, airstrip, trails, park headquarters, a grocery store, and a gas station, but our most expensive listing (singles $121). Since you don't have $121, backpackers who lack vehicles and who are waiting for a backcountry or campground permit are assured a space for $3 per night in **Morino Campground,** next to the hotel, centrally located, and with water and toilets. Permits are distributed on a first-come, first-served basis, so park your tent where you can and arrive at the visitors center as early as possible in the morning. Many people find it helpful to set up camp in Morino the first day while they take the shuttle bus in and preview potential campsites within the park. A wait of several days to get a permit is not uncommon, so be patient and make sure you've brought along plenty of food. You can camp a total of 14 days in park campgrounds. As with the shuttle buses, campgrounds work on the coupon system. Reserve ahead by phone (800-622-7275) or get to the V.C. early in the morning 2 days in advance to assure yourself a site.

Hardsiders are going to have a hard time in Denali. There are few hookups or dump stations, and driving is allowed on only 14 mi. of Denali Park Rd. RV drivers can pay $12 per night to park at **Riley Creek, Savage River,** and **Teklanika River Campgrounds** near the hotel, the visitors center, and the train depot, or they can head to the numerous RV parks huddled near the park entrance.

Riley Creek, Mile ¼ Denali Park Rd. The only year-round campground in Denali (no water in winter). 100 sites, all assigned at V.C. Often has the only sites still open at mid-morning. Piped water, flush toilets, and sewage dump. 100 sites, $12.

Morino Creek, Mile 1.9 Denali Park Rd., next to the train tracks. 60 sites for backpackers without vehicles. Water, chemical toilets. Self-registered sites $3 per person. Nearest showers at the Mercantile, ¼ mi. back up the road.

Savage River, Mile 13 Denali Park Rd. Flush toilets and water. Accessible only by shuttle bus or by a vehicle with a permit. 33 sites, $12.

Sanctuary River, Mile 23 on Denali Park Rd. Chemical toilets but no water. Accessible only by shuttle bus. No fires; stoves only. 7 sites, $12.

Teklanika River, Mile 29 Denali Park Rd. Piped water and chemical toilets. Accessible only by shuttle bus or by a vehicle with a permit. 53 sites, $12.

Igloo Creek, Mile 34 Denali Park Rd. Pit toilets but no water. No open fires. Accessible only by shuttle. No vehicles. 7 tentsites, $6.

Wonder Lake, Mile 85 Denali Park Rd. You are a happy camper indeed if, when you reach the park, Wonder Lake is not full. Spectacular, incredible views of Denali. Piped water, flush toilets. No vehicles allowed. About a bizillion mosquitoes (give or take a few trillion). Tents only. 28 sites, $12.

Several accommodations cluster near the park entrance; most are expensive.

Denali Hostel, P.O. Box 801 (683-1295), Denali Park. Drive 9.6 mi. north of park entrance, turn left onto Otto Lake Rd., drive 1.3 mi. 2nd house on the right (log house with blue trim) is the hostel. Friendly owners preside over bunks, showers, and kitchen facilities. Morning shuttles to the park, daily pick-ups from the V.C. (see Practical Information) at 5pm and 9pm, and from the Alaska Railroad. Open May-Sept., check in 5:30-10pm. Beds $22.

McKinley Campground (683-1418), P.O. Box 340, Healy 99743, 11 mi. north of park entrance. Showers and the only public laundromat in the area (see Practical Information). Tentsites for 1-2 people $15.75, $4.50 per additional person; full hookup $26.

FOOD

Food in Denali is expensive. Try to bring groceries into the park with you. Meager provisions in the park are available at **Mercantile Gas and Groceries,** 1½ mi. along Denali Park Rd. (683-2215). A monster cinnamon roll can be had for $2.40 (open daily 7am-10pm). The **Lynx Creek Grocery** (683-2548) has similarly priced items 1 mi. north of the park entrance and is open 24 hrs.

Lynx Creek Pizza (683-2547), 1 mi. north of park entrance. Monster portions of Italian and Mexican favorites ($7-8.25) and good pizza (16 in. from $15.75). Go for the slice-salad-soda-scoop lunch special ($6.50). Open daily 11am-11:30pm.

Whistle Stop Snack Shop (683-2215), in the Denali Park Hotel. Decent fast food with a variety of sandwich platters ($3.55-6). Open daily 5am-11pm. The neigh-

DENALI NATIONAL PARK

boring hotel **Dining Room** has mouth-watering, pricier entrees. Luckily some of the more reasonably priced meals are available at dinner. Try the vegetarian lasagna ($10) or the crab cakes ($13). The linen tablecloths and the excellent service are fine touches. Open daily 7-10:30am, 11-2:30pm, and 5-10pm.

McKinley/Denali Steak and Salmon Bake Restaurant (683-2733), 1 mi. north of park entrance. Tacky signs out front guide you to a reasonably priced tourist trap. Pounds of food doled out in a picnic setting. Try the Sourdough Breakfast (scrambled eggs, ham, reindeer sausage, potatoes, juice, coffee, and all-you-can-eat blueberry pancakes) for $8. All-you-can-eat soup, salad, rolls, and pudding available all day for $9. Open daily 5am-11pm.

Cruiser's Cafe (683-2282), in the Denali Princess Lodge next to the Lynx Creek complex. Snazzier fare for snazzier prices. Sandwiches ($4.50-6), burgers and chicken dishes ($5.75-7.25). Open daily 5-8am and 11am-midnight.

EXPLORING THE BACKCOUNTRY

Although dayhiking is unlimited wherever there are no wildlife restrictions, only two to 12 hikers can camp at one time in each of the park's 43 units. Overnight stays in the backcountry require a free permit, available 1 day in advance at the backcountry desk at the V.C. Come to the desk, look at the **quota board,** and research your options. The rangers will usually leave two or three zones open to unlimited backcountry camping, but these areas tend to be undesirable, thick with mosquitoes, and set back from the road behind other quadrants. Some quadrants are temporarily closed after a fresh wildlife kill or a "bear encounter." Sable Pass, a romping ground for bears, is closed to hikers.

Each quadrant of the park has a different kind of terrain. The first few units of the park consist of spongy tundra and dense taiga forest with a small bear population. Walking on soggy natural mattresses quickly loses its novelty. **Taiga** is low-lying, forested country. **River bars** refer to level, rocky areas by rivers; these offer very good footing for hikers, but be prepared to get wet fording the river. **Low tundra** means brushy, wet areas above the treeline; the soggy terrain is not easily navigable and makes for difficult, exasperating hiking under buggy conditions. **Alpine tundra** or **dry tundra** is high, dry ground above the treeline. The higher elevation means fewer mosquitoes. Some of the choicest hiking and wildlife-viewing is in the middle of the park, near the **Toklat River, Marmot Rock,** and **Polychrome Pass.** Researching the terrain will make your backcountry hiking, backpacking, or camping experience more enjoyable.

Rangers at the backcountry desk will not give recommendations for specific areas because they want to disperse hikers as widely as possible. Generally, the areas on the southern side of the park road have vast glacial river bars and dramatic valleys, while the northern side has higher ground with some of the best views of Denali. River bars and alpine tundra mean excellent footing and fewer mosquitoes. Areas 9, 10, 11, 12, and 13, all south of the road, are especially good and popular. Except near the Park entrance, there are no officially maintained trails in the Park.

No matter where you camp, keep within the zone for which you signed up. Pitch your tent completely out of sight of the road. To keep from getting lost, you can obtain **topographic maps** ($2.50) at the V.C. Before you leave the V.C., rangers will give you a brief introduction to bear management, and you must watch five brief backcountry simulator programs on **bear safety, minimum-impact camping, river crossing techniques, wildlife ethics,** and **backcountry safety and emergencies.** Most zones require that you carry a black, cylindrical **bear-resistant food container,** available free at the backcountry desk. To alert bears of your presence, it is recommended that you sing, shout, or make other loud noises. Using your voice is best, since bears recognize it as human and will be disinclined to investigate. The Rangers recommend that visitor's read Stephen Herrero's book, *Bear Attacks: Their Cause and Avoidance.* Read Bear Necessities (see page 59) before you camp in the backcountry. Though no one has ever been killed by a bear in Denali, you don't want to be the first to claim the honor.

WILDLIFE, SIGHTS, AND MARKED TRAILS

You can dayhike within the heart of the park by riding the shuttle bus to a suitable embarkation point for your hike and asking the driver to let you off. Upon completion, flag down a shuttle bus heading towards your camp. Remember that in the park, hiking is on unmarked terrain. Before heading out, ask rangers about units which may be closed off for wildlife protection. In addition, check the visitors center for interpretive pamphlets on the flowers and wildlife you may encounter on your way.

Catching a glimpse of both Denali's peak and its many wild inhabitants takes good timing and even better luck. **Dall sheep** generally dawdle near the Igloo and Cathedral Mountains and along Primrose Ridge near Savage River in the summer; look for them near Polychrome Pass in the fall. **Caribou** congregate in alpine meadows in the summer and move to the hills between the Eielson Visitors Center and Wonder Lake in the fall. **Moose** meander everywhere, but are especially visible during early mornings and late evenings near the Riley Creek Campground, near Savage River, and between the Teklanika and Igloo campgrounds. The presence of **wolves** is an indication of the quality of the Denali wilderness. If you see a wolf, you have had a rare, privileged experience. **Grizzly bears** are everywhere; 200 to 300 reside in Denali Park. 37 species of **mammals** and over 150 of **birds,** including **eagles,** live in Denali; some of the birds migrate from Africa. Few **fish** live in Denali; the powdered rock in the glacial streams and rivers makes an impossible fish habitat.

The most impressive views of the mountain can be seen early in the morning and late in the evening. Denali emerges completely only about once every 3 days, but odds are better in the late fall. In summer, fog usually shrouds the mountain. In any season, the best **viewpoints** are the highway from Anchorage and the Wonder Lake Campground. Otherwise, take a shuttle to the Stony Hill Overlook, the Eielson Visitors Center, or the overlook near the Savage River Campground at the rise in Sable Pass. If the sky is clear at 2:30am on summer nights, Wonder Lake campers can watch the tip of Denali catching the sun before it is even visible over the horizon. Climbing Denali takes 30 days and costs thousands of dollars (what do you think you're doing, looking for advice on scaling Denali in a budget travel guide?).

Park rangers organize one-hour **tundra walks** daily at 1:30pm from Eielson (take a bus from the V.C. before 9:30am). Check boards at the V.C. entrance for other guided hikes, which are conducted twice daily. The **Naturalist Choice Walks** leave daily at 1:30pm from the Park Hotel Auditorium Porch. The walks last about 2 hrs. and include segments on identifying birds and plants, scaling the Mt. Helay trail, and an exercise in drawing Denali, with all art supplies provided. The daily **Taiga Treks** are more strenuous 3 to 5-hr. hikes, which leave in the mid-afternoons from the V.C. The treks are limited to 16, and and require advance sign-up at the V.C. A ranger will lead you through perhaps a 4-hr. "cross-country scramble" or a moose trail excursion. Many other talks and naturalist programs are also posted at the V.C. The **sled-dog demonstrations** are another worthwhile free offering. The dogs play a critical role in the winter, when the park is accessible only to sled-dog teams and skiers. Buses leave the V.C. at 9:30am, 1:30pm, and 3:30pm.

Most of Denali Park is a trail-less wilderness, but a good way to kill time while waiting for your date with the shuttle bus is to explore the well-maintained **trails** which snake around the VAC and the Denali Hotel. **Horseshoe Lake Trail** is a gentle ¾-mi. trail connecting the hotel to an overlook of the lake; there is also a steep ¾-mi. trail leading down to the lake. The 2.3-mi. **Rock Creek Trail,** near the Park Headquarters at Mile 3.5 of the park road, terminates at the hotel. The hike to **Mt. Healy Overlook** is a steep 2½ mi. from the hotel. If you feel unchallenged, you can keep going up the ridge to the top of 5700-ft. Mt. Healy. Other popular trails include the 9-mi. **Triple Lakes Trail,** which runs along the railway tracks, and the 1.5-mi. **Morino Loop Trail,** which begins and ends at the Denali Park Hotel parking lot.

Several rafting companies run the rapids of Denali's **Nenana River.** Look for a company that offers equipment to stay dry and warm; the water temperature hovers around 37°F (3°C). The best deal in town is at **McKinley Raft Tours,** P.O. Box 138,

Denali National Park (683-2392), which offers a 4-hr. combination float trip and whitewater run (daily at noon; $48) and a shorter, more intense 2-hr. whitewater run (daily 9am, 2:30pm, and 6:30pm; $35). Similar packages at slightly higher prices are offered by **Alaska Raft Adventures** (683-2215) and **Denali Rafting Adventures** (683-2234).

■■■ TALKEETNA

Talkeetna, at the confluence of the Talkeetna, Susitna, and Chulitna Rivers, is the most popular flight departure point for some 1100 annual climbers of **Denali,** only 60 air mi. to the north. Every year between April and June, hundreds of climbers from across the globe converge on Talkeetna, creating an international village in an unlikely place. From the town, climbers are flown to a base camp on the Kahiltna Glacier at 7200 ft.; from there it's all uphill. The Denali climb is one of the world's most demanding tests for a mountaineer: in the spring and summer of 1992, a record 11 climbers lost their lives on the unforgiving slopes.

With a small population of 500, mostly climbers, Bush pilots, and miners, Talkeetna is widely known for its character. The town is just far enough off the beaten path to remain relatively quiet and escape the deluge of tourists.

Practical Information Visitors Information (733-1686) for Talkeetna, including pamphlets about local air charters and walking tours, is located in the **Three German Bachelors Cabin** at Main St. and Talkeetna Spur (open mid-May-Labor Day 10am-5:30pm). If it's closed, **Talkeetna Gifts and Collectibles** (733-2710) next door has most of the same information (open daily 8am-7pm). The **Talkeetna Ranger Station** (733-2231) is on D St. Before heading to Denali, all climbers must check in here first. Safety and weather information are provided, as is an **equipment check.** Even if you're not a heavy climber, stop in for general Denali information and a copy of the Denali Alpenglow (open Apr.-Sept. daily 8am-5pm).

Talkeetna is 113 mi. north of Anchorage, 280 mi. south of Fairbanks, and 14 mi. off the Parks Hwy. on Talkeetna Spur Rd. (Mile 98.5). The **Alaska Railroad Station,** P.O. Box 107500, Anchorage, AK 99510 (733-2268 or 265-2615), is near the Bachelors Cabin. There is one train daily each to: Denali ($48), Anchorage ($40), and Fairbanks ($85). Call 800-544-0552 for ticket information. **Alaska Backpacker Shuttle** (344-8775) stops in Talkeetna between Anchorage and Denali, as does the **Moon Bay Express** (274-8775). Both have the same fares: to Anchorage and to Denali ($35).

The library is 1 mi. from town (open Tues. noon-8pm, Wed.-Sat. 9am-5pm). The **Sunshine Community Health Clinic** (733-2273) is located 14.5 mi. from town on the Talkeetna Spur. The **emergency number** is 911. In a **fire,** call 733-2443. The **Post Office** (733-2275) is in town on the Spur (open Mon.-Fri. 9am-5pm, Sat. 10am-2pm; **General Delivery ZIP Code:** 99676).

Accommodations and Camping Budget travelers will cheer for the town's clean, pleasant, and affordable accommodations. The **Kahiltna Bunkhouse**, P.O. Box 128 (733-1515), around the corner from the McKinley Deli off Main St., is the town's most affordable indoor option. Two cabins house one set of bunkbeds, one with additional space for two sleeping bags. There is water (no showers), cooking facilities, and an outhouse out back. The Bunkhouse ($20 per person) is a magnet for Denali-bound climbers, so call ahead for availability. The **Fairview Inn**, P.O. Box 645, Main St. (733-2423), has good, cheap rooms (singles $31.50, doubles $42, accepts reservations). Also reasonably priced is the **Talkeetna Roadhouse** (733-1351 or 733-2341), at Main and C St. The rooms are simple and there may be a line for the bath, but the warm, folksy atmosphere in the cafe can't be beat. Park yourself in the easy chair in the corner and enjoy a 50¢ bottomless cup of coffee (singles $45, doubles $60, cabin $75; an additional $15 per person after 2 people). Make reservations well in advance for stays during the climbing season (mid-May-July).

Backpackers should head for the free **River Park Campground,** which is quiet despite its location near the center of town. The park has unimproved sites for tents. The neighboring **Three Rivers Tesoro Gas Station** (733-2620), on Main St., has a **laundromat** (wash $1.50, 10-min. dry 25¢) and **showers** ($2). (Open Mon.-Sat. 8am-9pm, Sun. 9am-7pm.)

Food Minimal groceries at low prices can be picked up at the **B&K Trading Post** (733-2411) on Main St. Chomp on an 85¢ muffin and a 50¢ pint of chocolate milk. Open daily 9am-9pm, in winter 11am-7pm. Cheap snacks are also available at the **Homestead** (733-3000) on the Talkeetna Spur; buy 60¢ juices and 45¢ mini-packs of Oreos (open Mon.-Sat. 9am-9pm and Sun. noon-7pm). The best budget food is at **Sparky's** (733-1414), at the corner of Main St. and Talkeetna Spur, where the menu is full of adult-sized portions of "kiddie delights." The heaping $1 ice cream cone and $2.50 grilled cheese please the tummy (open Sun.-Thurs. noon-7pm, Fri.-Sat. noon-10pm). Talkeetna's spot for pizza, sandwiches, and espresso is the **McKinley Deli** (733-1234), at Main and C St. The $6.50 spaghetti dinner with bread and salad is a tasty deal (open daily 6am-11pm). The **Roadhouse Cafe** (733-1351), in the Talkeetna Roadhouse, serves wonderful food, which, as the menu warns, takes a long time to prepare. Luckily, the sofa, lounge chair, and stocked bookcase provide a warm location for relaxation. Try their famous Porky Joe ($5.75) or a stack of sourdough pancakes ($4) made from a 1902 recipe (open daily 7am-9pm).

Sights, Events, and Entertainment If it's raining, check out the **Museum of Northern Adventure,** on the Talkeetna Spur (733-3999), which offers a gruesome re-creation of "the cremation of Sam McGee" (open daily 11am-7pm; admission $3.50, under 12 $2.50, seniors $3). The **Talkeetna Historical Society Museum** (733-2487), off C St., has high-quality displays on Alaskan transportation and mountaineering, including a 12 ft. x 12 ft. x 2 ft. model of Denali (open daily in summer 10am-5pm; $1).

The second Saturday in July brings the **Moose Dropping Festival** (no, we're not talking about chucking hapless moose from a helicopter), capped by the infamous "gilded moose-dropping toss." The coolest, mellowest concert in Alaska is the **Bluegrass Festival** in early August, a 3-day binge of live bluegrass, rock 'n' roll, and tie-dye in Susitna Bluffs, 30 mi. south of Talkeetna at Mile 86 of the Parks Hwy. A $25 pass entitles you to camp for the weekend.

Outdoors You may not be able to climb the mountain, but at least you can look at it. The Denali **overlook,** 1 mi. down the Talkeetna Spur, boasts the state's best road-accessible view of Denali. If the clouds cooperate, you will be treated to a view of 4 mi. of rock climbing straight up to the sky.

Fishing opportunities and river tours abound in the waterways around town. **McKinley View Tours** (733-2223), **Talkeetna Riverboat Service** (733-2281), **Denali River Guides** (733-2697), and **Mahay's Riverboat Service** (733-2223) all offer access to the wet 'n' wild wilderness. If you'd rather head out on your own, rent a bike in Anchorage and bring it on the train ($20). After the climbing season (mid-May-July), **Talkeetna Airport** (733-2277), across the train tracks in east Talkeetna, is full of charter planes with no place to go, so the four local companies offer Denali flightseeing tours at some of the lowest rates in Alaska. **Hudson Air Service** (733-2321) has the cheapest available flight, a half-hour tour of the Kahilta Glacier region ($40 per person with a 4-person min. **K2 Aviation** (733-2291) offers a one-hour tour for $70 with a 4-person min. Also check with **Talkeetna Air Taxi** (733-2218), and **Doug Geeting Aviation,** P.O. Box 42 (733-2366; fax 733-1000). In the flight-seeing market, it really pays to shop around.

■■■ DENALI HIGHWAY

Running 133 mi. through the foothills of the Alaska Range, the Denali Hwy. gives you a preview of what lies ahead in Denali National Park. You pass the same mountains and the same kinds of wildlife, but with fewer people, fewer hassles, and no lines for campsites. All that's missing is Denali itself. The road stretches east-west from Cantwell, 17 mi. south of the Denali Park entrance, to Paxson on the Richardson Hwy. Overlooked by tour buses and RVs, the road offers an escape from Alaska's heavily-touristed routes.

Except for the 21 mi. west of Paxson, the Denali Hwy. is entirely gravel. It is nevertheless well-maintained with few major bumps, a boon to travelers whose suspensions are nearly comatose. At Mile 21 (heading west), the **Tangle Lakes Campground** (water, toilets) and, ¼ mi. further on, the **Tangle River Campground** (water, toilets) are both scenic and free. Both campgrounds provide easy access to the **Delta River Canoe Route** (a 35-mi. canoe route with one difficult stretch of class III rapids) and the **Upper Tangle Lakes Canoe Route** (an easier paddle beginning at Tangle River and ending at Dickey Lake, 9 mi. to the south). Topographic **maps** are necessary for both routes.

On a clear day, spectacular scenery awaits along the rest of the highway, interrupted by an occasional roadhouse or cafe. Glacial features are also common; lakes and a pingo lie at Mile 41, eskers at Mile 59. At Mile 111 rests the free **Brushkana River Campground** (water, toilets).

Backpackers can camp anywhere along the highway, although topographic **maps** are necessary since there are no marked trails. Before hitting the road, pick up the Bureau of Land Management's *Denali Highway Points of Interest* pamphlet, available at most local roadhouses, visitor centers, and pit stops.

■■■ FAIRBANKS

If E. T. Barnette hadn't run aground with his load of goods at the junction of the Tanana and Chena Rivers, and if Felix Pedro, the Italian immigrant-turned-prospector, hadn't unearthed a golden fortune nearby, and if Alaska Territorial Judge James Wickersham hadn't been trying to woo political favors from Senator Fairbanks of Indiana, then this town might never even have existed.

Far more wealth now flows through the Trans-Alaska Pipeline than was ever extracted from the golden pebbles of Alaskan streams. Fairbanks is chiefly a college town and a service and supply center for the surrounding Bush, maintaining the rough-and-ready flavor of an old frontier town. Men noticeably outnumber women, and the streets are filled with 4-WD steeds, complete with a wolf dog in the back (part of the package from the dealer). To the south, the needles of black spruce and their underlying sheets of permafrost roll out a green and gold carpet below Denali and the Alaska Range. To the north, the Yukon completes its long sweep through the Interior and above the Arctic Circle, bridged only by the lonely Dalton Highway as it escorts the pipeline north through the jagged Brooks Range.

PRACTICAL INFORMATION AND ORIENTATION

Visitors Information: Convention and Visitors Bureau Log Cabin, 550 1st Ave., Fairbanks 99701 (456-5774 or 800-327-5774). Pick up the free *Visitor's Guide,* which maps out a self-guided walking tour of Fairbanks and lists tourist offices, transportation services, **maps**, annual events, activities, and shops. Free local calls. Open daily 8am-8pm; Oct.-April Mon.-Fri. 8am-5pm. The **Fairbanks Chamber of Commerce** is at 709 2nd Ave. (452-1105).

Fairbanks Information Hotline: 456-4636. 24-hr. recording for coming events.

Alaska Public Lands Information Center (APLIC) (451-7352), at 3rd and Cushman St. Exhibits and recreation information on different parks and protected areas of Alaska. Free daily films. Staff welcomes requests for information about hiking; write to 250 Cushman St., #1A, Fairbanks. Open daily 9am-6pm; in winter

FAIRBANKS

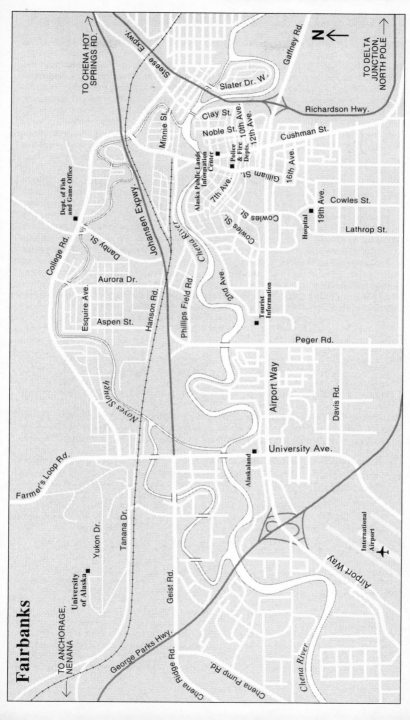

Fairbanks

N ←

TO CHENA HOT SPRINGS RD. →

TO DELTA JUNCTION, NORTH POLE →

Gaffney Rd.

Slater Dr. W.

Richardson Hwy.

Steese Expwy.

Clay St.

Noble St.

Minnie St.

Cushman St.

10th Ave.
12th Ave.

16th Ave.

Police & Fire Depts.

Alaska Public Lands Information Center

Gilliam St.

7th Ave.

Cowles St.

19th Ave.

Cowles St.

Cowles St.

Hospital

Lathrop St.

Dept. of Fish and Game Office

Chena River

College Rd.

Danby St.

Aurora Dr.

Hanson Rd.

Phillips Field Rd.

2nd Ave.

Esquire Ave.

Aspen St.

Tourist Information

Peger Rd.

Johansen Expwy.

Airport Way

Davis Rd.

Noyes's Slough

University Ave.

Alaskaland

Farmer's Loop Rd.

International Airport

Airport Way

Yukon Dr.

Tanana Dr.

University of Alaska

TO ANCHORAGE, NENANA

Geist Rd.

Chena Ridge Rd.

Chena Pump Rd.

George Parks Hwy.

Chena River

Tues.-Sat. 10am-6pm. Fairbanks is also home to the headquarters for the nearby **Gates of the Arctic National Park,** 201 1st Ave. (456-0281; open Mon.-Fri. 8am-5pm) and the **Arctic National Wildlife Refuge,** 101 12th St., Room 266 (456-0250; open Mon.-Fri. 8am-4:30pm).

Airport: Located 5 mi. from downtown on Airport Way, which doubles as the George Parks Hwy. Served by: **Delta** (474-0238), to the lower 48; **Alaska Air** (452-1661), to Anchorage ($184) and Juneau ($283); **Mark Air** (455-5104), to larger Bush towns, including Barrow ($235); **Frontier Flyer Services** (474-0014), to smaller Bush towns: Bettles ($99). These are all immediate departure prices; cheaper fares are possible with advance reservations, but rates vary.

Alaska Railroad, 280 N Cushman (456-4155), next to the *Daily News-Miner* building. An excellent way to see the wilderness. From May-Sept., 1 train daily to: Nenana ($18), Anchorage ($125), and Denali National Park ($47). Ages 2-11 ½-price. Depot open Mon.-Fri. 7am-4:30pm, Sat.-Sun. 6pm-10pm; get there 1 hr. before the train leaves. In winter, a train leaves for Anchorage every Sun. ($70).

Buses: Denali Express, 800-327-7651. Daily to Denali ($25). **Alaskan Express,** 800-544-2206. Daily to Anchorage ($109); 4 times per week to Haines ($169). **Alaska Direct** (1-800-770-6652) has buses to Denali 3 times weekly ($23). **Fireweed Express** (452-0521) provides private van service each day to Denali ($25, round-trip $45). They pick up at the hostel; call for times and reservations.

City Bus: MACS (459-1011), at 6th and Cushman St. Two routes (the red and blue lines) through downtown Fairbanks and the surrounding area. Fare $1.50; seniors, high school students, and disabled people 75¢; under 5 free. Day pass $3. Transfers good within 1 hr. of stamped time. Pick up a schedule at the Convention and Visitors Bureau (see above).

Taxi: King/ Alaska Cab, 451-8294. **Fairbanks Taxi,** 452-3535. Both 24 hrs.

Car Rental: Rent-a-Wreck, 2105 Cushman St. (452-1606). $35 per day, 25 ¢ per mi. after 25 mi. **U-Save Auto Rental,** 3245 College Rd. (479-7060). $37 per day, 26¢ per mi. after 100 mi. At the airport is **Avis** (474-0900 or 800-331-1212). $47 per day, unlimited free mi.

Road Conditions: 456-7623.

Bike and Canoe Rental: Beaver Sports (479-2494), across from College Corner Mall on College Rd. Mountain bikes $11 per day, $18 overnight, $56 weekly. $250 deposit required (cash or credit). Canoes $24 per day; paddles and life jackets included. $500 deposit required per boat. Open Mon.-Fri. 10am-7pm, Sat. 9am-6pm, Sun. 1pm-5pm.

Camping Equipment: Rocket Surplus, 1401 Cushman (456-7078). Fine camouflage fashions. Open Mon.-Sat. 9am-6pm. **Apocalypse Design, Inc.,** 101 College Rd. (451-7555), at Illinois. Fast repairs on zippers and straps. Open Mon.-Fri. 9am-6pm, Sat. 10am-4pm. **Beaver Sports** (see above).

Laundromat and Showers: B & C (479-2696), at University and College, in Campus Mall. $1.75 wash, 8-min. dry 25¢. Showers $2.50. Open Mon.-Sat. 7am-10:30pm, Sun. 9am-10:30pm. **B & L** (452-1355), at 3rd and New St. on Eagle Rd. Wash $1.50, dry $1.50. Showers $2.50 for 20 min. Open daily 8am-11pm.

Bookstore: Gulliver's New and Used Books, 3525 College Rd. (474-9574), in College Corner Mall. Open Mon.-Fri. 10am-8pm, Sat. 10am-6pm, Sun. noon-6pm. Also in the Shopper's Forum, 1255 Airport Way (456-3657). Open Mon.-Fri. 10am-9pm, Sat. 10am-6pm, Sun. noon-6pm.

Library: Noel Wien Library, 1215 Cowles St. (459-1021).

Weather: 452-3553.

24-hr. Help Lines: Rape Emergency, 452-7273. **Poison Control Center,** 456-7182. **Crisis Line,** 452-4357; also provides contacts with gay and lesbian groups.

Pharmacy: Payless Drugstore, 38 College Rd. in the Bentley Mall (452-2072). Open Mon.-Sat. 9am-9pm, Sun. 10am-6pm.

Hospital: Fairbanks Memorial, 1650 Cowles St. (452-8181), off Airport Hwy.

Emergency: 911.

Police: 452-2114.

Post Office: 315 Barnette St. (452-3203). Open Mon.-Fri. 9am-6pm, Sat. 10am-2pm. **General Delivery ZIP Code:** 99707.

Area Code: 907.

Anchorage is 358 mi. south via the **George Parks Hwy.,** and Prudhoe Bay can be reached by 480 mi. of the gravelly **Dalton Hwy.** Delta Junction is 97 mi. southeast of Fairbanks on the Richardson (Alaska) Hwy. The city is centered downtown and along Airport Way, College Rd., and University Ave.

ACCOMMODATIONS AND CAMPING

For information on bed and breakfasts, go to the visitors bureau or write **Fairbanks B&B,** 902 Kellum St., Anchorage (452-4967). The visitors bureau also distributes a flyer listing all the local hostel services. Unless you drive an RV, stay indoors or camp in the scenic, wild country within a short drive of Fairbanks.

> **Fairbanks Youth Hostel (HI/AYH),** 400 Acadia St. (456-4159) on Birch Hill. The hostel has moved around a lot but has settled for the time being at the home of Walter Weesem, who hopes to buy a new hostel building in the upcoming year. There are 6 beds ($12) and plenty of tent space ($6). No curfew, no lockout, free showers, bike rental ($5 per day). Write P.O. Box 72196, Fairbanks 99707 for information.
>
> **Billie's Backpackers Hostel,** 479-2034. Take Westridge Rd. 1 block off College to Mack Rd. Look for the "Billie's B&B" sign. 4 beds in a simple, clean cabin and 8 beds in the main house. Showers and kitchen. Train and airport pickup available. $13.50, plus $5 for a full breakfast.
>
> **Noah's Rainbow Inn,** 474-3666 or 800-770-2177. Take Geist Rd. off University to Fairbanks; make a left and it's right there. During the winter, Noah's rents mainly to U. of Fairbanks students. During the summer, it's a cheap, clean, rarely-crowded, dorm-style hotel. TV, kitchen and laundry facilities available. Shared bathrooms. Singles $35. Doubles $40. $5 less if you can live without a TV.
>
> **Aurora Motel and Cabins,** 2016 College Rd., (451-1935). Cabins lack TV and phones, but they're a bargain. Singles $40. Doubles $45.
>
> **Tanana Valley Campground,** 1800 College (456-7956), next to the Aurora Motel and Cabins. Noisy, but the closest campground to the downtown. Caters to RVs. 4 spots with power hookup available. Free showers, laundromat ($2 wash and dry). Sites $12. Tentsites for travelers with no vehicle $6, with vehicle $10.

FOOD

Fairbanks ferments with fast-food frying; just about every fast-food chain in existence can be found along Airport Way and College Road, and they seem to have squeezed out most locally-owned competition. Groceries are available round the clock at **Carr's,** 526 Gaffney (452-1121), and at **Safeway,** 3627 Airport Way at University Center (479-4231). If you're really stocking up, **Sam's Club,** 48 College Rd. (451-4800), will let non-members buy in bulk for an additional 5% of the total price. Cash only (open Mon.-Fri. 10am-8pm, Sat. 10am-7pm, Sun. 11am-6pm). Catch the best homemade ice cream in Alaska at **Hot Licks** (479-7813), located in the Campus Corner Mall at the intersection of College and University (open Mon.-Fri. 7am-11pm, Sat. 11am-11pm and Sun. noon-10pm). At the fairgrounds at Aurora and College, buy fresh produce at the **Farmers Market** (Wed. noon-5pm; Sat. 9am-4pm).

> **The Whole Earth,** 1157 Deborah St. (479-2052), behind College Corner Mall. A health food store, deli, and restaurant all in one. You can sit here all day over a cup of organic coffee and a Natchester Sandwich (beans, cheese, Greek peppers, and spices in a spread, $4). Locals praise the giant No Bull Burger ($4.25). All sandwiches served on fresh homemade whole-wheat rolls. Store and seating open Mon.-Sat. 8am-8pm, Sun. noon-6pm. Hot food served 11am-3pm, 5pm-7pm).
>
> **Souvlaki,** 112 N Turner (452-5393), across the bridge from the visitors center. You can almost get your fill on the heavenly aroma. Succulent stuffed grape leaves (3 for $1.15). Salad in a pita ($3). Open in summer Mon.-Fri. 10am-9pm, Sat. 10am-6pm; in winter Mon.-Sat. 10am-6pm.
>
> **Dash Deli** (457-3274), at 1st and Cushman. Mama Heidi is a sweetheart, and her deli is a house o' deals. Big, fresh sandwiches $4, with salad $4.75. Top it off with a healthy $1 scoop of ice cream. Open Mon.-Fri. 10am-6pm.

Speedy Submarine Sandwich Shop, 1701 Cushman St. (456-7995). Speedy's is straight out of Chicago and makes the best foot-long subs in Fairbanks ($3.75-6.25). Open daily 10am-6pm.

Food Factory, 36 College Rd. (452-3313), and at 18th and Cushman St. (452-6348). Caters to the Alaskan appetite ("Food just like Mom used to send out for!"). Foot-long hoagies $5-8, but their forte is beer (106 international varieties). Open Mon.-Thurs. 10:30am-11pm, Fri.-Sat. 10:30am-midnight, Sun. noon-10pm.

Royal Fork Buffet, 414 3rd St. (452-5655), at Steese Hwy. Part of a national all-you-can-eat chain dedicated to stuffing gluttonous patrons with cafeteria food. Different menu every day. Lunch ($6.25), dinner ($8.65), and Sunday brunch ($6). Open Mon.-Thurs. 11am-8:30pm, Fri.-Sat. 11am-9pm, Sun. 9am-8pm.

Godfather's Pizza, 3401 Airport Way (479-7652), near Market St. Their all-you-can-eat lunch buffet (pizza, garlic bread, potato wedges) is a miracle of modern mass consumption ($4.29). Salad Bar $1 extra 11am-2pm daily. Open Mon.-Thurs. 11am-10pm, Fri.-Sat. 11am-midnight, Sun. 11am-11pm.

Alaska Salmon Bake (452-7274), at Airport Way and Peger Rd. inside Alaskaland. Genuinely tacky but still the best salmon bake in town. $17 buys enough salmon, halibut, and ribs to satisfy even the most ravenous traveler. Lunch is served mid-June to mid-Aug. noon-2pm ($9). Open mid-June to mid-Sept daily 5-9pm.

The Pumphouse Restaurant and Saloon, Mile 1.3 Chena Pump Rd. (479-8452). Rave local spot. This place is so cool that one of the city's bus lines goes out of its way to drop you here. Out-of-this-world lunch buffet ($9.79). Dinner entrees $10-15. Open daily 11:30am-2pm and 5-10pm. Bar open weekends until 2am.

Two Rivers Lodge, Mile 16 Chena Hot Springs Rd. (488-6815). You'll need a car. *Twin Peaks*-esque place to stop on the way back from Chena Hot Springs. Hefty, reasonably priced appetizers $6-10 make a light dinner, especially if you'd like to try alligator ($10). Check out the mounted, fuzzy one on wall. Entrees $8-72, but the food is so good locals drive out to eat here. Of the series of grapefruit specialties, the grapefruit pie with complimentary grapefruit schnapps is heavenly. Open Mon.-Sun. 5-10pm; lounge opens at 3pm.

SIGHTS

Fairbanks features an extensive **bike trail** system. None of the urban trails is particularly scenic, but it's a lot quicker than walking. Pick up a guide to Fairbank's bike trails at the Visitor's Center. **Beaver Sports** (see Practical Information) offers the best deal on bike rentals.

One of Fairbanks's proudest institutions is the **University of Alaska-Fairbanks,** at the top of a hill overlooking the flat cityscape. Both bus lines stop at the **Wood Campus Center** (474-7033), which has pool tables, lots of video games, and the Student Activities Office, which posts listings of movies ($4-5.50), outdoor activities and occasional music fests (Mon.-Fri. 7am-7:30pm, Sat. 8am-7:30pm, Sun. noon-7:30pm). The **University of Alaska Museum** (474-7505), a 10-minute walk from there up Yukon Dr., houses a fascinating array of exhibits ranging from Russian Orthodox vestments to indigenous crafts to a mummified prehistoric bison, all in one huge room! The most popular exhibit is a 7-min. video of the *aurora borealis*. (Open daily 9am-8pm; May and Sept. 9am-5pm; Oct.-April noon-5pm. Admission $4, seniors and students $3, families $12.50. Oct.-April, free on Fri.) Weekdays at 10am, the university offers free 2-hr. tours of the campus beginning in front of the museum. Travelers can tiptoe through the tulips in the flower garden or ogle the station's resident porcine population at the university's **Agriculture Experimental Station.** The **Large Animal Research Station** offers tours on Tues. and Sat. at 1:30pm and 3pm, and on Thurs. at 1:30pm only ($5, students $2, families $10), although far-sighted tourists can view the station's musk ox and caribou from the viewing stand on Yankovitch Rd.

Alaskaland, P.O. Box 1267, Fairbanks 99707, on Airport Way, is a would-be Arctic Disneyland. The quintessential tourist trap, overrun by kids. But hey, at least there's no general admission (though the park's rides and museums charge nominal fees; Air Museum $1, Boat Tour $3).

The **Dog Mushers Museum** (456-6874), on 2nd Ave. in the Coop Plaza, is little more than a room full of sleds and other mushing paraphernalia, but some cool videos are screened in the theater (open Mon.-Sat. 9:30am-5:30pm. Free, although donations are accepted).

View a technological wonder of the world, the **Alaska Pipeline,** at Mile 8 of the Hwy. heading out of Fairbanks. The Pipeline is elevated on super-cooled posts to protect the tundra's frozen ecological system from the hot oil.

ENTERTAINMENT

With nothing but black spruce to keep them company in the surrounding tundra, Fairbanksians turn to the bars at night. Come carouse with stiff drinks and boisterous, rugged types fresh from the North Slope oil fields. UAF students head for the **Howling Dog Saloon** (457-8780), 11½ mi. down Steese Hwy. for live rock-and-roll. Look for a colorful old wooden structure in the middle of nowhere encircled by pickup trucks. The local eye doctor and his wife dance next to bikers, who dance next to field guides from Denali...Volleyball and horseshoe games go on until 4am or so, as does the band (open Tues.-Fri. 5pm-5am, Sat.-Sun. noon-5am).

Blues Breakers, 1705 S Cushman (452-9890). A biker bar for blues. Get your gear at Harley Davidson's Farthest North (Airport Way and Cushman), then step into a mellow Easy Rider crowd. Don't be fooled by the sign outside that says, "C'mon in, if you're not scared." Open daily 8am-whenever.

Sunset Inn, 345 Old Richardson Hwy. (456-4754). Looks like a warehouse, but since Fairbanksians need only the bare necessities (drinks, dance floor, pool tables), it's usually jam-packed. Live top-40 dance music. Open Wed.-Thurs. and Sun. 10pm-3:30am, Fri.-Sat. 9:30pm-whenever.

Senator's Saloon, Mile 1.3 on Chena Pump Rd. (479-8452), in the Pump House Restaurant. The only oyster bar in Fairbanks. Take drinks out to the deck and watch float planes land and river boats whiz by. Open Sun.-Thurs. 11:30am-1am, Fri.-Sat. 11:30am-2am.

Fox Roadhouse and Motherlode, Mile 11.5 Steese Hwy. (457-7461), across from the Howling Dog. Like Howling Dog, diverse clientele, but older. Don't be surprised if you see horses hitched up to the post out front, and try not to be caught off guard when they collect shotguns at the front door. 24 hrs.

EVENTS

The best time to visit the city is in mid-July; citizens don Gold Rush rags and throw parades, sales, and many other gala events for **Golden Days,** a celebration of Felix Pedro's discovery. Watch out for the traveling jail; if you haven't purchased the silly-looking button commemorating the event, you may be taken prisoner and forced to pay a steep price to spring yourself. (Most stores and businesses in town sell the buttons.) The budget traveler might want to stay on board the paddywagon; it's a free ride and goes all over Fairbanks. For details, contact the Fairbanks Chamber of Commerce (see Practical Information). Make hotel reservations several months in advance if you're coming to town during Golden Days.

The **Tanana Valley Fair** (452-3750), in the second week of August, features shows, competitions, and a rodeo. Follow the line of cars down College Rd. to the fairgrounds. ($6, seniors $3, ages 6-17 $3; $50 family pass covers all family members throughout the fair.)

For a sports spectacular with native flavor, see the **World Eskimo-Indian Olympics,** P.O. Box 72433, Fairbanks (452-6646). At the end of July, Inuit and other Native people from all over Alaska compete in shows of strength and endurance, and celebrate folklore and traditional dance.

Some of the wildest events occur in the days around the summer solstice. The **Yukon 800 Marathon Riverboat Race** sends some high-horsepower people in low-slung powerboats on an 800-mi. quest up the Tanana and Yukon Rivers to the town of Galena and back. A few days before the solstice, the 10km **Midnight Sun Run** happens on a well-lit night, beginning at 10pm. The annual **Midnight Sun Baseball**

Game occurs on the summer solstice. Featuring the Fairbanks Goldpanners pitted against another minor-league team, the game begins at 10:30pm, as the sun dips, features a short pause near midnight for the celebration of the midnight sun, and ends as the sun rises. The Goldpanners play more than 30 home games throughout the summer and have won five minor league national championships since 1970. Barry Bonds and Dave Winfield have played here. Games are played at **Growden Memorial Park** near Alaskaland (451-0095; $4).

Twice weekly Fairbanks' agricultural community assembles at the fairgrounds at Aurora and College for the **Farmer's Market** (Wed. noon-5pm, Sat. 9am-4pm). Enjoy **bluegrass** at the **Fairbanks Folk Festival** runs roughly from July 12 to July 14. In winter, February's **Yukon Quest** Dog Sled Race runs between Fairbanks and Whitehorse, starting in Fairbanks in even years, and in Whitehorse in odd. The Quest is far more rigorous than the more famous Iditarod: fewer dogs, fewer stops, and less compassion for the human condition. Ask about it at the Visitor's Information Office (see Practical Information).

■ NEAR FAIRBANKS

Pick any direction, drive a scant 20 minutes, and find yourself fully enmeshed in complete and utter wilderness. Go soak your feet (or your head) in the plentiful lakes and nearby hot springs. Like Rome, all roads run to Fairbanks. The **George Parks Hwy.** heads to Anchorage by way of **Denali National Park,** and the **Richardson Hwy.** and Alaskarun to Valdez and the Yukon. Two minor roads head north, into the Bush. The **Steese Hwy.** heads north to **Circle,** an outpost on the Yukon River. The **Elliot Hwy.** takes you past to the start of the **Dalton Hwy.** and continues to **Manley Hot Springs.**

STEESE HIGHWAY

The Steese Hwy. heads northeast of Fairbanks for 162 mi. to the town of Circle on the Yukon River. It passes the short side roads that leads to **Arctic Circle Hot Springs** and several potential hikes and floats. The pavement ends at Mile 44, with the exception of a few miles in and near Central. The road is generally good gravel, but the last 20 mi. coming into Circle can get b-b-bumpy.

The Steese Hwy. heads out of Fairbanks as the **Steese Expressway** but becomes the more modest two-lane highway 8 mi. out. Three mi. later comes the junction of the Elliot Hwy. Keep going straight if you're driving to the Dalton Hwy. or just headed for a soak in the Manley Hot Springs, but take a right if you want to follow the Steese. On the highway's north side, at Mile 16, sits a plaque honoring Felix Pedros's 1902 gold discovery which spawned the city of Fairbanks.

Campgrounds at Mile 39 and 60 provide access to the **Chatenika River Canoe Trail,** which parallels the Steese for nearly 30 mi. The stream is clear and Class II, and its biggest dangers to paddlers are low water and overhanging trees.

At **Central** (Mile 127), a small town of about 400 summer residents, the Circle Hot Springs Rd. takes the waiting head-soaker 8 mi. to the **Circle Hot Springs Resort** (520-5113), which has hostel accommodations for $20 ($10 for each additional person; sleeping bags required). Pool use is free for those staying overnight at the resort. Otherwise, a dip in the warm, mineral-rich water will cost $7.

Circle is the pothole at the end of the highway, 35 mi. beyond Central. Few diversions present themselves other than a peek at the Yukon River and the opportunity to have your picture taken in front of the "Welcome to Circle City" sign. For those left starving by the trip, the **Yukon Trading Post** (773-1217) has groceries at Bush prices and a cafe that isn't much cheaper (open daily 9am-8pm). You can find free camping near the river (water, pit toilets).

Useful phone numbers include **medical emergency, 773-7425; village protection safety officer** (the police of Circle): 773-8776. There is a **post office** (773-1220) in the trading post (open Mon., Wed., Fri. 10am-3pm; Tues.-Thurs. 10am-2:30pm). **ZIP Code:** 99733.

CHENA RIVER AND LAKES

The **Chena River Recreation Area** (451-2695), at Miles 26-51 on Chena Hot Springs Rd. covers almost 400 sq. mi., offering fishing, hiking, canoeing, and camping around the Upper Chena River. Tentsites convenient to Chena Hot Springs Rd. are available at quiet, secluded **Rosehip Campground** (Mile 27) and **Granite Bluff** (Mile 39) for $6 (pit toilets and pump water). Hiking trails include **Granite Tors** (trailhead at Mile 39 campground), a 12-16-mi. round-trip hike to granite rocks and great for overnight campouts; **Angel Rocks** (starting at Mile 48.9 campground), an easy 3½-mi. trek through exquisite wilderness; and **Chena Dome Trail** (beginning at Mile 15.5), a more remote 29-mi. adventure overlooking the river valleys. A shooting range is located at Mile 36.5! Wear bright clothing and pay attention to where you are; in Alaska, people shoot first and investigate later.

Harding Lake (Mile 321.4 on Richardson Hwy.), **Birch Lake** (Mile 305.5 on Richardson Hwy.), and **Quartz Lake** (Mile 277.8 on Richardson Hwy.) are Sunday anglers' dreams. The state stocks the lakes with salmon and trout for that extra-tough fishing challenge. Boat ramps ($3) and campsites ($6) are provided at Harding and Quartz Lake. Birch Lake has primitive camping facilities.

CHENA HOT SPRINGS

Fifty-seven mi. northeast of Fairbanks on Chena Hot Springs Rd., the **Chena Hot Springs Resort** (in Fairbanks 452-7867, at the resort 369-4111) allows you the chance to soak out of the rain. Expect fine fishing near this inn once the water temperature has dropped from the spring snow melt. The chalet accommodations are expensive ($80, Alaskans $70, rooms with with sink and toilet $70.), although pool admission is included. Non-patrons may use the hot pool for $8, ages 6-12 $6. Handsome hiking trails and tent and RV campsites ($8, with electricity $10) are nearby. **Two Rivers Lodge and Restaurant** (488-6815) sits at Mile 16 Chena Hot Springs Rd., grilling up ribs and Alaskan specialties (see Fairbanks: Food above).

The **Arctic Circle Hot Springs** (520-5113), discovered in 1893, are 3 hrs. north of Fairbanks on Steese Hwy. The hostel on the fourth floor charges $20 for attic accommodations, $60 for a room. Several campgrounds line Steese Hwy. nearby, amid stunning scenery; you can also camp directly on the banks of the Yukon. Gaze up at Eagle Summit while diving into the Olympic-sized hot springs or indulging yourself at the ice cream parlor. At the peak of summer (June 21-22), you can watch the midnight sun glide across the horizon without setting.

STEESE NATIONAL CONSERVATION AREA AND WHITE MOUNTAIN NATIONAL RECREATION AREA

The 1560-sq.-mi. White Mountain National Recreation Area and the 1870-sq.-mi. Steese National Conservation Area lie side-by-side along the Steese and Elliot Hwy., and boast the **best hiking** and **wilderness fishing** in the Fairbanks area. The region's most popular trail, the 27-mi. **Pinnel Mountain National Recreation Trail** in Steese, begins at Mile 86 of the Steese Hwy. and ends at Mile 107, and is equipped with two shelters for emergencies en route. Allow at least 3 days for the trek. With proper timing you can bask in the midnight sun (June 18-24) or watch caribou (July-Sept.) from many points along the trail. Would-be prospectors should head for **Nome Creek,** where the Bureau of Land Management has established a 4-mi. stretch open to the general public for recreational gold panning. Access is via the Steese Highway to Mile 57, and from there a 6-mi. drive north on U.S. Creek Rd. It is a primitive road that requires at least one crossing of Nome Creek. Flooding and water damage frequently make the road impassable, and while some repair work is slated, additional flooding can destroy improvements overnight. Only travelers with 4wd vehicles should attempt to drive this road; not even that will guarantee passage. White Mountain's **Birch Creek** offers 60 mi. of intermittent class III and IV white water. For more information on the region call the Fairbanks office of the **Bureau of Land Management** (474-2350). Detailed **topographic maps** of the area are available at the

Geologic Survey (456-0244), in the Federal Building at the end of 12th Ave. in Fairbanks. (Also see section on the Steese Hwy.)

NENANA

Nenana (nee-NAH-na) lies 53 mi. south of Fairbanks on George Parks Hwy. Once the terminus of the Alaska Railroad, Nenana is situated at the confluence of the Tanana and Nenana Rivers, and is now famous for the Nenana Ice Pool. Alaskans and Canadian residents of the Yukon, bored out of their skulls during the winter, bet on the exact minute when the ice will thaw in the spring, dislodging two large tripods ceremoniously stuck there. Last year the pot amassed $260,000. Today this tradition is just one of the events at the **Nenana Ice Classic.** For more information write P.O. Box 272, Nenana 99760 (832-5446). The town's nightlife revolves around the two ornery-looking corner **bars** next to the train station. There are no hotels of note, and the nearest campgrounds are another 20 mi. south on George Parks Hwy. The **visitors information center** is open May to September daily from 8am until 6pm (832-9953). The **Alaska Railroad** stops here on the way to Anchorage.

■■■ ALASKA HIGHWAY

From the Yukon border, the Alaska Highway continues northwest through Tok and Delta Junction to Fairbanks, paralleling the Tanana River. The Alaska Hwy. intersects the gravel **Taylor Hwy.** to Eagle and Dawson City, YT, 80 mi. from the Yukon border at **Tetlin Junction** (see page 176). Tok, 92 mi. from the border, is the first noteworthy Alaskan town along the highway. For the Alaska Highway in northwestern Canada, from Dawson Creek, BC to the Yukon/Alaska border, see page 268.

TOK

Tok lies 208 mi. southeast of Fairbanks, 138 mi. northeast of Glenallen, and 387 mi. (619km) northwest of Whitehorse, YT. The **Tok Cutoff,** the road from Tok to Glenallen, offers access to **Wrangell-St. Elias National Park** (see page 115). It has, perhaps, the highest per capita concentration of gift shops and RV parks in the state. Tok proves that, even in God's country, hell maintains a claim to a half acre or so. Those agonizing whether to continue on the Alaska Highway toward Fairbanks or head south along the cut-off toward Anchorage can do some deep thinking at the recently constructed, cavernous **Visitors Center** (883-5775). At the intersection of the two highways, this glorified brochure distribution center is the largest single-story building in Alaska (**WILD CHEERING!** After half a paragraph, the score stands: Tok 1, Rest of Alaska 0!). (Open mid-May-mid-Sept. Mon.-Fri. 7am-9pm and Sun. 9am-7pm.) Adjacent to the visitor center is the **Public Lands Information Center** (883-5667), which has information regarding all national and state parks, monuments, and preserves, a wildlife exhibit, and hourly videos on various national parks. Stop by to plan your field trips (open daily 8am-8pm; winter Mon.-Fri. 8am-4:30pm). The **post office** (883-5880) is near the intersection. (Open Mon.-Fri 8:30am-5pm, Sat. 11:30am-3pm. **ZIP Code:** 99780.) There is a **laundromat** at the Northstar RV Park (see below; wash $1.25, 7-min. dry 25¢). Emergency numbers include: **health clinic/ambulance**, 883-5855; **police**, 883-5111; and **fire**, 883-2333.

Hitchhikers report having a hard time catching a ride out of town. If you're stuck, **Alaska Direct** (800-770-6652) runs buses leaving from the front of Northstar RV Park. Buses to Fairbanks (Tues., Fri., and Sun., $40); to Anchorage (Tues., Fri., and Sun., $65) and Whitehorse (Mon., Wed., and Sat., $80).

The **Tok Youth Hostel (HI/AYH)** (883-3745), an incredibly inconvenient 9 mi. west of town on Pringle Dr., is a huge canvas tent reminiscent of *M*A*S*H**. (Members $7.50; open May 15-Sept. 15; kitchen facilities, no showers or phones.) If you're looking to pitch a tent, the better-situated **Northstar RV Park** (883-4502), ½ mi. east of the visitor center on the Alaska Highway, has tentsites for $5 (free with a gas fill-up), though a shower will cost you another $3 (full hookup with 2 free showers $17; open daily 6am-11pm). **Sourdough Campground** (883-5543), 1¾ mi. south of the junction, has campsites for $11 (shower included) and full hookups for $17. They also operate a breakfast cafe specializing in sourdough pancakes (2 huge cakes $3.50; open 7am-11am). The cheapest place to stay indoors is the **Snowshoe Motel** (883-4511), at Mile 1314 across from the infocenter (singles $57, doubles $62).

Tok offers plenty of expensive roadside food. The town's one exception could be the **Gateway Salmon Bake** (883-5555), on the western edge of town where you can have all the grilled king salmon you want for $16, or all the beef ribs for $13. A free shuttle is available from numerous spots in town to take you there (open Mon.-Sat. 11am-9pm, Sun. 4-9pm). For red-eyed travelers, a dose of caffeine can be had from the **Alcan Espresso Coffee Shop,** tucked just off the highway halfway into town, (mocha $2.25, espresso $2; open Mon.-Sat. 6am-5pm, Sun. 8am-4pm). Tok's answer to wholesale shopping, **Frontier Foods,** is also across from the visitor center; non-restaurant-eaters will rejoice in reasonably priced bulk items (open daily 7am-11pm). Those desperately short of cash can still get food from the Texaco; edibles are ½-price late in the day. Can you say "corn dog?"

Check out **Burnt Paw Northland Specialties** (883-4121), ¼ mi. west of the intersection on the Alaska Highway, which offers nightly sled-dog demonstrations Mon.-Sat. at 7:30pm (open daily 7am-9pm).

DELTA JUNCTION

Like Tok, Delta Junction exists because it lies at the intersection of two main highways, the Alaska and Richardson. Delta Junction lies 111 mi. northwest of Tok, 97 mi. southeast of Fairbanks, and 153 mi. north of Glenallen along the road to Anchorage and Valdez. The huge post in front of the visitor center declares Delta Junction to be the terminus of the Alaska Hwy., though Fairbanks argues otherwise. For $1 you can buy a macho certificate stating that you've successfully reached its end.

The **visitor center** (895-5069) is found (you guessed it) at the intersection of the two highways (open mid-May to mid-Sept. 8:30am-7:30pm). The **post office** (895-4601) is across the street from the bank. (Open Mon.-Fri. 9:30am-5pm, Sat. 10:30-noon. **General Delivery ZIP Code:** 99737.) Important phone numbers: **police,** 895-4344; in an **emergency,** 895-4800; **health clinic,** 895-4879.

Tenters should head to **Delta State Recreation Site,** ½ mi. from the visitor center toward Fairbanks (sites $8, drinking water, pit toilets). The **Delta Youth Hostel (HI/AYH)** (895-5074) is as inconveniently located as the one in Tok, 3 mi. off the road from Mile 272, and has simple but adequate accommodations. (Open June 1-Sept. 1. $7, non-members $8; sleeping bag required.) **Kelly's Country Inn Motel** (895-4667) is ¼ mi. from the intersection toward Fairbanks and has cheery rooms with big country quilts (singles $50, doubles $60).

Delta Junction doesn't offer much in the way of food. **Pizza Bella Restaurant** (895-4841), near the visitors center, has pizzas from $9 as well as plenty o' pasta. Gung-ho grocery grabbers should hit the **Delta Shop-Rite** (895-4653), just north toward Fairbanks (open Mon.-Sat. 7am-11pm, Sun. 8am-9pm).

Attractions in the area include a roaming herd of 450 **buffalo.** Travelers hoping to catch a glimpse of the herd are advised to head either to the herd's summertime calving grounds, 25 mi. south toward Glenallen, or to their winter grounds, 20 mi. to the northwest along the Alaska Hwy. If you stumble into town on the first weekend in August, then welcome to the **Deltana Agricultural Fair!** The most exciting event of the fair is undoubtedly the **Great Alaskan Outhouse Race** which gives new meaning to "the runs." The race features numerous outhouses on wheels, pulled or pushed by four competitors, while one lucky individual sits on the "throne" for the length of the race. The winners receive the coveted "Golden Throne Award" (2nd place, "The Silver Plunger," 3rd place, "The Copper Snake"). Ten mi. north of town is **Big Delta Historic Park,** home of **Rika's Roadhouse** (895-4201), a restored roadhouse full of lewd pioneer spirit. Travelers thirsty for an engineering marvel can go on a tour of **Alyeska Pump Station #9,** the only pump station open to the public. 45 to 60-minute tours run every hour on the hour from 9am-5pm daily (869-3270; reservations are strongly encouraged). Less motivated types can simply observe the Trans-Alaska Pipeline suspended over the Tanana River.

■■■ TAYLOR HIGHWAY

The Taylor Hwy. extends 160 mi. north from **Tetlin Junction,** its junction with the Alaska Hwy., to the interesting town of **Eagle** on the Yukon River. Frost heaves, potholes, and sections of washboard abound along the length of the highway, making this a long and bumpy ride. From Eagle, the highway connects with the **Top-of-the-World Hwy.,** which heads east toward Dawson City, YT. Unfortunately, no scheduled bus service follows this route, and those without a car often hitchhike, difficult as traffic is dominated by the RV crowd. (*Let's Go* does not recommend hitchhiking.) Most hitchers have a good book handy and start early in the morning. Travelers headed to Dawson should keep in mind that the border is open only from 8am to 8pm Alaska time, and entertainment is scarce for those bedding down at the border.

From **Mile 0,** the Taylor Hwy. begins to climb to over 3500 ft. as it winds toward 5541-ft. Mt. Fairplay. An interpretive sign at Mile 35 explains the history of the Taylor Hwy. and offers a good opportunity to stretch your legs and your mind. At Mile 49, the BLM manages the **West Fork Campground,** with 25 sites but no water.

The megalopolis of **Chicken** lies 17 mi. farther north. Free walking tours of historic Chicken leave daily at 1pm from the parking lot in front of the saloon and are the only way to see some of the original pre-Klondike cabins and the roadhouse where Tisha, subject of a nonfictional book about a woman teaching in the Alaskan Bush, taught. Downtown, the **Chicken Cafe** has burgers ($7, or a reindeer burger for $9), and a wide selection of delicious fresh baked goods, which sell out early every day (open daily 7am-7pm). Tent campers and RVs can park or put down on the lawn next to the cafe in Chicken for free (water and pit toilets available). The folks in Chicken aren't scared of expansion: in fact, they're set on creating a bigger and brighter future. New outhouses top 1995's town-improvement to-do list, and there is even talk of installing a phone, although none existed in the summer of 1994. The **post office** is a ¼ mi. down the highway from the downtown Chicken turn-off. The **ZIP Code** in Chicken is 99732.

The **Jack Wade Dredge** lies rusting away right next to the highway at Mile 86. The dredge has deteriorated considerably and isn't all that safe, but that doesn't stop most people from wandering around its hollow insides. At **Jack Wade Junction** the road forks: north for 64 mi. to Eagle and east for 79 mi. via the Top-of-the-World Hwy. to Dawson. Don't forget that the border closes at 8pm and that customs agents often seem to have vendettas against hitchhikers. Make sure you have proof of funds or you might fall victim to an arbitrary decision and get stuck in Alaska 120 mi. from the nearest settlement. The last 64 mi. from the junction to Eagle remain bumpy, dusty, and treacherous.

■■■ EAGLE

Eagle sits on the banks of the Yukon River and the brink of vast stretches of wilderness. Like most towns along the Yukon River, Eagle exists because of the Klondike Gold Rush. Established in 1898 as a permanent mining community, Eagle's central location in the Interior led the War Secretary to establish an adjacent military base in 1899; in 1901, Eagle became the first incorporated city in the Interior. Gold strikes in Nome and Fairbanks, however, soon eclipsed Eagle. The court was moved to Fairbanks and Fort Egbert was almost completely abandoned in 1911. North of town, several original buildings from Fort Egbert sit restored. Extensive restoration work by the BLM and Eagle Historical Society has returned many of the town's buildings to their original conditions.

Practical Information and Sights Eagle has arguably more square feet of museum space for its size than any other town, city, or village in Alaska. The only way to access all of the town's historic buildings and displays is through the town's daily 3-hr. walking tour ($3, under 12 free), which leaves at 10am from the **Courthouse Museum** on Berry St. The courthouse is also open to the general public throughout much of the day. Walking around unguided is interesting but not nearly as informative. **Amundsen Park,** on 1st St. at Amundsen, honors the Norwegian explorer who hiked into Eagle in the *winter* of 1905 from Canada's Arctic Coast. He used Eagle's telegraph to inform the world that he had successfully navigated the Northwest Passage. Several weeks later, Amundsen mushed back to his ship, frozen in the ice floes of the Arctic Ocean. Nine months later, he completed the first successful journey from the Atlantic to the Pacific via the Arctic Ocean.

Bikes can be rented from the Village Store for $10 per day (open Mon.-Sat. 9am-6pm). In case of a **medical emergency** call 547-2300. The **post office** (547-2211) is on 2nd St. at Jefferson (open Mon.-Fri. 8:30am-4:30pm). The **ZIP Code** is 99738.

Camping, Accommodations, and Food Campers will find Eagle a heavenly haven. **Eagle Campground** is a 1-mi. hike from town past Fort Egbert (no fee, no water, pit toilets). Eagle's "mall" is on Front St. The **Eagle Trading Co.** (547-2220) in the mall has it all: groceries (at Bush prices), showers ($4), laundromat ($4 per load), RV hookups ($15), and rooms for rent (singles $50, doubles $60). (Open daily 9am-8pm.) The adjacent **Riverside Cafe** (547-2250) has delicious burgers ($5) and Idaho-sized baskets of fries ($2). (Open daily 7am-8pm.) Groceries and hardware can also be had from the **Village Store** (547-2270), ¼ mi. east of town (open summer daily 9am-6pm, in winter 9am-5pm).

The Float from Eagle to Circle The National Park Service runs a field station for the **Yukon-Charley Rivers National Preserve.** The **visitors center** (547-2233) is on the western end of 1st St. and can provide detailed information on the geography and wildlife of the area (open daily 8am-5pm). The 158-mi. float down the Yukon River through the preserve from Eagle to Circle is popular. The full trip usually takes four to six days and passes through some of Alaska's wildest country. Bear, moose, and beaver abound, as do mosquitoes, though campers can generally avoid them by camping on the numerous gravel bars in the river. Canoes and inflatable rafts are the most common forms of transportation. Investigate outfitters in Eagle or check with the Park Service by writing Superintendent, P.O. Box 167, Eagle, AK 99738.

■ The Bush

Known variously as the Country, the Wilderness Rim, and the Bush, this vast expanse of frozen tundra and jagged coastline is sparsely dotted with small settlements, narrow landing strips, and other insignificant traces of human presence. This harsh country occupies most of Alaska's vast area in the northeast, northwest, and southwest sections of the state.

Nome, Prudhoe Bay, Kotzebue, and Barrow are places even few Alaskans have ever seen. The Bush is the Alaska where polar bears ride ice floes, and where hundreds of thousands of caribou freely roam the tundra. It's the place where Native Alaskan settlements are few and far between, accessible only by plane, boat, or dogsled; where cannery workers and oil drillers swarm to make the big money, knowing it's theirs to save because they'll have nowhere to spend it.

Each area of the Bush has distinctive features. The **Southwest** includes the flat, soggy, buggy terrain of the Yukon-Kushkowin delta and the mountainous **Alaska Peninsula,** a volcanic arc with some of the worst weather on earth. **Western Alaska** includes the Seward Peninsula, a treeless, hilly land of tundra. **Nome,** on the coast of the Bering Sea, is frequently swept by harsh storms. The **Brooks Range,** Alaska's Arctic crown, stretches from the northwest to the Canadian border, while the flat, endless expanses of tundra on the **North Slope** spread northward from the Brooks to the Arctic Ocean, where oil companies employ thousands. The Bush is for the traveler seeking the *National Geographic* experience. Adventure and self-reliance are key concepts when traveling in the Bush; most towns won't expend energy entertaining guests. Revel in the isolation, be prepared to rough it, and remember, caribou and bears always have the right of way.

Transportation in the Bush is not cheap. Tour outfitters abound, ready and willing, for a steep price, to lead you out into the wilds to fish, hunt, hike, kayak, canoe, or photograph. Larger commercial operators like **Alaska Airlines** (800-426-0333) and **Mark Air** (800-MARK-AIR, or 627-5247) service the bigger Bush communities such as Nome, Kotzebue, and Barrow, while smaller companies like **Larry's Flying Service** (474-9169 in Fairbanks) and **Frontier Flying Services** (474-0014 in Fairbanks) fly to the more remote spots like Anaktuvuk Pass and Fort Yukon. Chartering a plane costs over $250 per hour, and it's the only way to get into the middle of the wilderness, away from even the most remote communities.

NORTHEAST ALASKA

■■■ DALTON HIGHWAY

The visitors center in Fairbanks tries to discourage ignorant yokels from attempting the 500 mi. of extremely tough, dangerous road to **Prudhoe Bay.** Services are over 200 mi. apart, and the road's primary function is that of a haul road. Truckers driving 36-wheel rigs spitting rocks and dust dominate the highway. The entire highway is dirt, interspersed with tennis-ball-sized rocks, frost heaves, and large potholes. Bring at least one spare tire, spare gas, and supplies. You do not want to pay to be towed back to Fairbanks.

This breathtaking drive parallels the pipeline from Fairbanks to Prudhoe Bay. Maps often label the road "closed to the public," but the only warning is a weather-beaten sign at Disaster Creek. Hitchers can proceed on the logic that no one will leave someone stranded in the middle of nowhere, but don't expect to catch a ride with a trucker. (Let's Go does not recommend hitchhiking.)

FAIRBANKS TO ARCTIC CIRCLE

The journey begins with an 80-mi. jaunt from Fairbanks along the **Elliot Hwy.** to Mile 0 of the Dalton Highway. Enjoy the 40 mi. of pavement as you head out from Fairbanks; it's the last you'll see for almost 900 mi. Once it becomes gravel, the Elliot Highway remains a good road and not difficult to drive. So also is the first stretch of the Dalton Highway, although you can bet your left leg that there'll be more than a few rough spots. The first landmark heading north is the **Yukon River** crossing. This wood-planked bridge is the only one crossing the mighty Yukon, and unlike most other bridges, it has a pitch: you could virtually put your car in neutral and coast the downhill grade. On the north side of the river exists one of the two **service stations** that can be found on the highway. You can get unleaded gas at **Yukon Ventures** (655-9001) for $1.65 per gallon or rent a room for $50 a person. The gas station and adjacent restaurant are open daily 7am to 2am. The adjacent **restaurant** is open daily 9am to 9pm.

The road next winds through its first tundra region as it gains in elevation and passes **Finger Rock** (to the east) and **Caribou Mountain** (a distance away to the west). You'll pass over several steep hills with names like "Happy Man" and "Beaver Slide." The **pipeline** runs along the highway, as it does for the whole length. The "fins" sticking out of the pipeline's support posts are "thermal siphons" designed to dissipate the heat of the 108°F oil, which would otherwise be conducted through the supports and melt the underlying permafrost, undermining the pipeline's foundation and causing it to sink into a soggy swamp.

Next comes the **Arctic Circle.** A recently constructed place to pull off the road here has several picnic tables and presents the visitor with four placards discussing the Arctic seasons (summer, winter, winter, and winter). The enormous "Arctic Circle" sign is a great photo opportunity, and the spot is good for free camping.

ARCTIC CIRCLE TO PRUDHOE BAY

Continuing north, over 1500-ft. **Gobblers Knob,** past Prospect Camp and Pump Station No. 5, over the Jim River and the South Fork of the Koyukuk River, you'll rattle along to the town of **Coldfoot,** the last services available before Prudhoe Bay (240 mi. away). Coldfoot, "the northernmost truck stop in North America," was originally a mining town which, at its peak, boasted "one gambling hall, two road houses, seven saloons, and 10 prostitutes." Its name originated in 1898, when a group of timid prospectors got "cold feet" about wintering above the Arctic Circle and headed south again. "Downtown" is a huge and muddy parking lot. Around the perimeter of the field is the **Coldfoot Cafe** (678-5201; open 24 hrs.) with good, hot, and (surprise!) expensive food; burgers and fries start at around $7. The **general store** is open daily noon-9pm and has limited supplies. Gas will cost you about $1.50 per gallon for unleaded. The **Arctic Acres Inn** (678-5224) has renovated an old construction-worker bunkhouse into a hotel. (Singles with shared bath $90. Doubles $105.) Several RV sites (full hookups $20) and tentsites ($7.50) are adjacent, but if you just hike 1 mi. out of town in any direction so that you're out of sight, nobody will care where you pitch your tent as long as you leave no trace. You can take a **shower** at the hotel for $3 or wash and dry a load of **laundry** for $4. Just north and around the corner is the **Coldfoot Visitor Center** (678-5209), which is managed jointly by the National Park Service, Bureau of Land Management, and Fish and Wildlife. This is an excellent source of information if you're planning on doing some intense trekking or paddling in the Brooks Range. (Open daily 1-10pm, nightly slide presentations 8:30pm.) For a bit of history, walk across the highway and down the road. You'll pass by the **Coldfoot Cemetery** on your way to historic **Coldfoot,** on the banks of the Koyukuk River, which consists of two weather-worn, broken down cabins dating from the turn of the century. The **post office** is located next to the general store. (Open Mon., Wed., and Fri. 1:30-6pm. **ZIP Code:** 99701.)

Twelve mi. north of Coldfoot is the junction for the historic village of **Wiseman.** 3 mi. off the beaten path, this town was immortalized by Robert Marshall in his 1933 book, *Arctic Village*, which details the winter he spent there. Perhaps the wildest frontier town accessible by road in Alaska, Wiseman is home to many of the dogs appearing in the Walt Disney movie, *White Fang* (including White Fang himself). Do the dogs outnumber the citizens? The **Wiseman Trading Post** (est. 1910), at the end of the road to Wiseman over a narrow footbridge, will confirm all you've imagined about the frontier general store. You can pitch a tent behind the store for $2.50. Wiseman is the Last Frontier, so make the short side trip. It's worth it.

From Wiseman, the highway pierces the heart of the Brooks Range. Wildlife abounds; keep your eyes open for moose, Dall sheep, bear, caribou, hawks, ground squirrels, and other animals. At Mile 235, **the last tree** found along the highway, a surprisingly tall and majestic spruce, is marked by a sign. Then begins the steep and awe-inspiring ascent toward **Atigun Pass** (4752 ft.). The highway cuts steeply into the mountainside as it approaches the pass and offers spectacular **views** of the Dietrich River Valley. Check out the glacial **cirque** (an amphitheater-shaped depression) on the mountainside east of the highway. Once the mountains are breached, the long descent toward the **Arctic Ocean** begins.

In the final stretch of the highway, the mountains gradually transform into low bluffs and hills (with names like "Oil Spill Hill"), and ultimately into broad, flat, monotonous tundra. The road along the northernmost 100 mi. is the worst of the highway. Sharp gravel and small boulders litter the highway. Driving faster than 25mph could cause tooth damage. Your car's suspension and tires might spontaneously disintegrate. The land is generally unattractive. The tundra is perpetually brown except for a short month-long summer in July-August. Although it looks easy, walking on the tundra is a nightmare. It is filled with bumps and lumps of moss, and is underlain by tremendous amounts of water unable to escape through the frozen ground. Try a tundra walk and you're guaranteed a wet, soggy, difficult hike. Despite the rough terrain, you'll see **caribou** roam freely and without difficulty throughout the North Slope. Even with the perpetual sun, the temperature is noticeably cooler on the North Slope, typically about 43 °F (5°C) much of the summer.

Approximately 10 mi. from the end, the land becomes enshrouded in a layer of coastal fog, blocking the sun and causing the temperature to plummet. **Deadhorse** and **Prudhoe Bay** suddenly appear on the horizon in the last few mi. of highway. And then you're there, at the **Arctic Ocean.** The northernmost point accessible by road in North America. Fun, wasn't it? Now you just have to get back.

PRUDHOE BAY

Named in 1826 by English Arctic explorer Sir John Franklin after the fourth Duke of Northumberland, Baron Prudhoe, Prudhoe Bay may not seem an ample reward for those who've endured the grueling 500-mi. trek up the Dalton Highway. Oil was discovered here in 1968. It took less than 10 years for full-fledged oil extraction to begin, and for the 800-mi. Trans-Alaska Pipeline to be strung from Prudhoe Bay south to the warm-water port of Valdez. Oil extraction continues today, and more than 2 million barrels of oil are contained within the length of the pipeline at any given time, slowly moving south at a rate of 6 to 7 mph.

The weather is wretched. Covered by fog and swept by Arctic winds, the temperature can drop below freezing any day of the year, and with windchill, the temperature is usually below freezing. In winter, the official record low-chill factor was recorded at -135 °F (-92°C). Prudhoe Bay receives nine weeks of perpetual daylight and eight of eternal night each year. In winter, the land is blanketed with snow and ice, and the Beaufort Sea freezes solid. It is common for polar bears to wander into town off the Arctic ice floes in search of seals, or perhaps a hapless oil employee.

This is not a regular community. Everything exists for and because of oil. Every building and structure contributes in some manner toward oil production. No permanent residents, no tourist facilities, no "town proper" exist in Prudhoe Bay. The camp of **Deadhorse** is on the southern perimeter of **Lake Colleen,** at the terminus of the Dalton highway. The town owes its home to the gravel company who brought the first road-building materials north, and whose motto was: "We'll haul anything, even a dead horse."

Sights and Practical Information   Prudhoe Bay lacks a visitors center, but any of the hotel desks or travel agencies can supply you with information. If you're interested in getting a look at the oil fields, you'll need to head for Deadhorse. It's the only publicly accessible part of the oil fields, although more than 255 mi. of roads run through them. They are privately owned by the oil companies; access is controlled by two guarded checkpoints. The only way to check them out is aboard a tour. **Arctic Caribou Inn,** Pouch 3401111, Deadhorse 99734 (659-2368), offers excellent tours for $60. You'll stand next to Mile 0 of the pipeline, check out the interior of the worker's bunkhouses (surprisingly nice), and dip your fingers into the icy waters of the Arctic Ocean, among other things. You're here, so you might as well take the tour. What else are you going to do? Fill up your car for $2 per gallon at the **Goodyear** at the end of the Dalton Highway.

The **Deadhorse airport** is served by **Mark Air** (from Fairbanks $248). In case of an **emergency,** call the ARCO operator at 659-5900, as there are no "public" rescue services. Don't expect ARCO to be too happy about it, though. Prudhoe Bay is a dry "community." No alcohol or firearms allowed. The **post office** (659-2669) is located in the general store. (Open daily 1-3:30pm and 6:30-9pm. **ZIP Code:** 99734.) The **area code** is 907.

Accommodations and Food   All hotels in Prudhoe Bay are run by the Northwest Alaska Native Corporation (NANA). The **Prudhoe Bay Hotel** (659-2520) has singles for $110 and shared doubles for $65 (shared bath, meals included). A converted bunkhouse with a spacious rec room and a large TV, darts, pool, and ping-pong, the Prudhoe Bay even has its own **cafeteria** (the only place to eat in town). If you're thinking of camping, **NO!** There is nowhere to pitch a tent. With no budget options, people have slept in their car or the hotel rec rooms, where travelers can sometimes stretch out on their big couches without getting booted.

As far as food and other necessities are concerned, the **Prudhoe Bay General Store** (659-2425), next to the Arctic Caribou Inn, is like a miniature mall and the prices aren't all that steep, considering where you are (open daily 8am-9pm).

■■■ BROOKS RANGE

Defining Alaska's north coast, the magnificent **Brooks Range** describes a tremendous semicircle from the Chuchki Sea in the west, through the Noatak National Preserve and **Gates of the Arctic National Park,** to the **Arctic National Wildlife Refuge (ANWR)** and the Beaufort Sea in the east. Too far from Fairbanks to draw tourists, too isolated (with the exception of Anaktuvuk Pass) to support human habitation, too huge to be patrolled by park rangers, the Brooks Range is the last great stretch of virgin wilderness in U.S. possession. A few remote settlements and the thin trail of the Dalton Highway are the only signs of man's encroachment.

Accessing the Brooks Range and the parks that encompass it is neither difficult nor expensive. Beautiful stretches of the Gates of the Arctic National Park lie just off the Dalton Hwy., near Wiseman (just past Coldfoot) and Atigun Pass. Talk to park officials before planning a trip into the Brooks (the headquarters for both Gates and ANWR are located in Fairbanks; see Fairbanks: Practical Information).

ANAKTUVUK PASS

Literally translated, "Anaktuvuk" means "caribou crap." Twice a year, the swarms of caribou descend upon Anaktuvuk in their migratory grazings. It comes as no surprise, then, that here the Nunamiat (NOON-ah-myoot) are making their last stand. North America's last true nomads, this inland Inuit people began to make permanent settlements only in the last 45 years. Surrounded by **Gates of the Arctic National Park** and nestled in a tundra mountain pass high on the Arctic Divide, the Nunamiat struggle to maintain their subsistence lifestyle amid the pressures and developments of the 20th century. The mountain backdrop encircling the pass is one of the world's most beautiful; this is the side-trip to make if you head out any-where into the Bush.

Larry's Flying Service (474-9169) offers daily flights to Anaktuvuk Pass. If you can stop your stomach from staging a coup, the flight over the tops of the awe–inspiring Brooks Range is worth the money. Wilderness so pristine and beautiful is found few places else on earth. Once in Anaktuvuk, visitors should head to the **Simon Panaek Museum** (661-3413), which has extensive displays on traditional Nunaimut culture. The **Hans van der Laan Brooks Range Library** is also inside and has a huge collection of material on the people and land of Alaska's Far North (open Mon.-Fri. 8am-1pm and 2-5pm; both free). Gorgeous **day-hiking** opportunities abound around the village. Any of the river valleys radiating away from the town will more than suffice. Be prepared for some tough tundra hiking, however, and be sure to cover exposed skin. Even with bug spray, the mosquitoes will eat you alive.

The town has no rooms for rent, but visitors can camp anywhere just outside of town. The hills on the other side of the John River (which runs through town) are often good camping spots. The **Nunamiut Corporation Store** (661-3327) has gro-ceries at steep Brooks Range prices (open Mon.-Thurs. 10am-6pm, Fri. 10am-7pm, Sat. noon-6pm). A small hole-in-the-wall restaurant, the **Nunamiut Corp. Camp Kitchen** (661-3123) on the south end of town has burgers ($5.50) and lobster ($16). (Open Mon.-Sat. 7:30am-7pm, Sun. noon-7pm.) The **washeteria** (661-9713), next to the enormous blue-roofed school, has **showers** (free!) and **laundry** facilities (wash $1, 10-min. dry 25¢. Open Mon.-Tues. and Sat. 1-5pm and 6-8:30pm, Wed. and Fri. 8:30am-8:30pm, Sun. 10am-noon and 1pm-5:30pm). **Emergency numbers include: medical/fire,** 611; **public safety officer,** 661-3911. The **post office** (661-3615) is next to the airstrip (open Mon.-Fri. 8:30am-11:30am, 12:30pm-5:30pm). **ZIP Code:** 99721.

GATES OF THE ARCTIC NATIONAL PARK

With over 11,200 sq. mi. of protected wilderness, Gates of the Arctic National Park is designed to preserve forever the majestic central Brooks Range. Six national wild rivers run through the park and provide excellent floating opportunities. The heavy glaciation has carved huge U-shaped valleys throughout the park that are excellent for hiking and route-finding.

The park is most accessible to those either decidedly wealthy or powerfully deter-mined. Budget backpackers often hitch up the Dalton Hwy. and hike in from several access points along the road. (*Let's Go* does not recommend hitchhiking.) Those with a bit more money can fly commercially into Anaktuvuk Pass and head out from there. Those with still more cash to spare can charter a plane and immerse them-selves in true isolation. The town of **Bettles** lies south of the mountains on the Mid-dle Fork of the Koyukuk River and is the jumping-off point for those chartering a plane. Several companies offer charter service. Ask around for the best deal, and expect to pay several hundred dollars an hour for a plane. **Larry's Flying Service** (474-9169 in Fairbanks) will get you there.

Facility with a compass, bear awareness, and other backcountry skills are neces-sity for any backpacker heading into the park. A sudden drop in temperature can quickly lead to hypothermia. For more information, contact **Park Headquarters, 201 1st Ave.** (456-0281) in Fairbanks, or write Superintendent, Gates of the Arctic National Park, P.O. Box 74680, Fairbanks, AK 99707-4680. The Park Service oper-ates a **Gates of the Arctic Field Station** (692-5494) in Bettles for those seeking information (open daily 8am-5pm). In Bettles, **Sourdough Outfitters** (692-5252) offers guided and unguided adventures in the Brooks Range. Canoes and other kinds of equipment are available for rent, and guides are extremely knowledgeable about the park. Stop by for tips before adventuring out.

Ask around about good places to pitch a tent, or stay in the **Bettles Lodge** (800-770-5111 or 692-5111). The lodge has a bunkhouse ($15, sleeping bag required), which is a better deal than regular rooms ($65). The lodge's **restaurant** has good cheeseburgers ($6.50). (Open daily 8am-10pm.) The **Bettles Trading Post** (692-5252) sells expensive groceries (open Mon.-Sat. 9am-5:30pm, Sun. noon-5pm).

At the lodge, you can also take a **shower** ($3.50) or do some laundry ($7.50 per load). The **post office** (692-5236) is at the northern end of town (open Mon.-Fri. 8am-noon, 1-4pm, Sat. 1-3pm). The **ZIP Code** is 99726.

ARCTIC NATIONAL WILDLIFE REFUGE

Covering a huge swath of northeast Alaska, the Arctic National Wildlife Refuge (ANWR) encompasses more than 31,100 incredibly remote sq. mi., an area larger than Maine. The porcupine caribou herd has its calving grounds here. The Brooks Range's highest mountains are here. The oil companies want to move in for exploration. Three national wild rivers flow in the refuge. The only and very expensive way in is by charter plane. There are wolves, bears, and 53 quintillion mosquitoes. Hike it, float it, soak it up. And know what you're doing. This is wilderness.

■■■ FORT YUKON

Fort Yukon sits at the convergence of the Porcupine and Yukon Rivers, 8 mi. north of the Arctic Circle. It is the largest Native Alaskan community and long an outpost of the Hudson's Bay Company. The town, in a flat between the miles-wide arms of the Yukon, is rich in relics of Native Alaskan history. The town's walking-tour pamphlet (available at **Frontier Flying Services** and the local **Sourdough Hotel**) guides you through a collection of sights: a ghost town, St. Stephen's Church with its beaded-moose-skin altar cloths, the Fort Yukon replica, a museum, and a small town center. Check out the Fort Yukon branch of the **University of Alaska,** which educates mostly Native Alaskans from the surrounding towns of Arctic Village, Beaver, Birch Creek, Central Chalkyitsik, Circle, Circle Hot Springs, Rampart, Stevens Village, and Venetie. Visitors are welcome, and classes offering degree programs are in session throughout the year. The log building housing the university also contains unusual traditional crafts, including a huge wood-block print of the five local Gwich'in chiefs. **Frontier Flying Services** (474-0014) flies twice daily Mon.-Sat., once on Sunday, from Fairbanks to Fort Yukon (round-trip $150). Home-cooked meals are available for $5 to $7 at the time-warped **Sourdough Hotel** (662-2402). It's a bit musty, but spacious and clean with friendly service (singles or doubles $65 with shared bathroom; couples $95).

NORTHWEST ALASKA

■■■ NOME

Alaska's equivalent to the Yukon's Klondike, Nome owes its existence to the "three Lucky Swedes" who discovered gold on nearby Anvil Creek in 1898. Nome today is a transportation hub for western Alaska, where mining remains the economic lifeblood. Built almost entirely upon permafrost, buildings are elevated on pilings to prevent melting, and almost all have extremely ramshackle exteriors. One of the few "wet" towns in the Bush, Nome has an infamous penchant for partying.

PRACTICAL INFORMATION

Visitors Center: P.O. Box 240, Nome 99762 (443-5535), located on Front St. (like everything else) next to the Nugget Inn. Amazing number of flyers. Free nightly slide shows at 7:30pm. Open in summer daily 9am-9pm.

Airport: Located about 1 mi. west of town. Taxi to downtown $5. The airport is served by **Mark Air,** 443-5578; round-trip from Anchorage with 14-day advance purchase $426; **Alaska Airlines** (800-468-2248) offers circuit tours from Anchorage to Nome to Kotzebue (for the touristy route).

Taxis: Checker Cab, 443-5211. **Gold Rush Taxi,** 443-5922. **Nome Cab,** 443-3030. All 24 hrs. Standard fare is $3 for places in town.

Car Rental: Bonanza, compact $65 per day, van $75 per day, unlimited mileage. **Stampede** (443-3838), compact $55 per day, 4x4 pick up $75 per day, unlimited mileage. All renters must be 21 with a major credit card. **Gas** sells for around $2.10 per gallon.

Bookstore: The **Arctic Trading Post** (443-2686), across from the Nugget Inn, has the most extensive selection of local literature. Open daily 7am-11pm.

Library: Kegoayah Kozga Library (443-5133), above the museum on Front St. Open Tues.-Fri. noon-8pm, Sat. noon-6pm.

Laundromat: Blizzard Laundromat (443-5335), at Seppala St. and C St. The only laundromat in town. Wash $3, dry $3. Open in summer Mon.-Sat. 10am-8pm; in winter Mon.-Fri. 10am-6pm, Sat. 10am-7pm.

Shower at the **rec center** (443-5431) on the northern edge of town on East Sixth Ave. Free with the $3 admission price.

Weather: The box outside the visitors center will give you the day's forecast.

Hospital/Pharmacy: Norton Sound Hospital (443-3331), at the end of Bering St.

Emergency: 911. **Police:** 443-2835.

Post Office: 240 Front St. (443-2401). Open Mon.-Fri. 9am-5pm. **ZIP Code:** 99762.

Area Code: 907.

ACCOMMODATIONS

Beds in Nome aren't too costly, but camping is free. Camping is permitted on Nome's flat, good beaches and along the 280-mi. road system through the countryside. No facilities, though. The beach is about a 1-mi. walk east along Front St. past the sea wall. Gold miners dot the slightly golden beaches, so enjoy the company!

Betty's Igloo (443-2419), a luxurious bed and breakfast on the eastern edge of town on E 3rd Ave. Clean and comfortable with kitchen facilities, a spacious common room, and friendly hosts. Singles $55, doubles $70. Shared bath. Reservations strongly recommended.

Ocean View Manor B&B (443-2133), halfway between the visitor center and the beach on Front St. Offers a deck-side view out across Norton Sound and the Bering Sea. TV, phones, shared bath. Singles $40-60. Doubles $50-65.

Ponderosa Inn (443-5737), at Spokane and 3rd Ave. near the visitor center. Generic, clean. TV, phone in some rooms, private bath. Singles $65-85. Doubles $75-95.

FOOD

Don't be scared by the oftentimes dilapidated exteriors of Nome's restaurants; almost all of the buildings look like that. Stock up on groceries and supplies at the **Alaska Commercial Company** (443-2243) on Front St. (open daily 8am-midnight), or **Hanson's Trading Company** (443-5454) on Bering St. (open Mon.-Sat. 8am-10pm, Sun. 10am-6pm). The rowdy bars in town are grouped together on Front St.

Fat Freddie's (443-5899), next to the visitors center. *The* popular place in Nome. Soak in the blue expanses of the Bering Sea while you chow down on a "Poco Loco" (fried chicken patty) for $5.50. Breakfast omelettes for around $7. Open daily 6am-11pm.

Milano's Pizzeria (443-2924), in the old Federal building on Front St. Pizzas start at $9.75. Italian dinners $10-11. Open daily 11am-11pm.

Nacho's (443-5503), also in the old Federal building. Tasty Mexican food. Lunch $8-10, dinner $10-13. Open Mon.-Fri. 7am-9pm, Sat. 9am-9pm, Sun. 9am-4pm.

SIGHTS AND ACTIVITIES

Pick up a free *Historical Walking Tour* pamphlet at the visitors center to see what little history has survived through Nome's numerous natural disasters. One of the more interesting buildings is the office of the **Nome Nugget,** the oldest existing newspaper in Alaska (est. 1901). Walk along Nome's famous beaches 1 mi. east of the visitors center. The beaches are public, and anybody can try a hand at **gold-panning** for that elusive nugget. It's free with your own gold pan, available at the Alaska Commercial Company (see above) for $3.40. The Nugget Inn offers interesting **tours** ($25) which take you out to chat with a local dog musher and long-time resident (after the dog sled demo) and then out towards Anvil Mountain (near the original discovery claims on Anvil Creek) where you get to pan. Tours run twice a day. Stop by the Nugget Inn for specifics.

EVENTS

Being isolated from the rest of the world seems to cause residents to do some strange things. The hilarious **Bering Sea Ice Golf Classic** is held in March on the frozen Bering Sea. Standard golf rules apply (with some interesting exceptions) in this six-hole course. Contestants' bright orange balls skirt the course's unique hazards: crevices, ice chunks, bottomless snow holes, and frost-leafed greens. Extremity-warmers (whisky and Bacardi rum) are provided with contestants' entry fee. Course rules dictate: "If you hit a polar bear with your golf ball (Endangered Species List), you will have three strokes added to your score. If you recover said ball, you will subtract five strokes." The biggest event of the winter, however, is naturally the **Iditarod dogsled race.** The race finishes in mid-March beneath the log "banner" visible year-round next to City Hall. Thousands of spectators journey in, and it isn't uncommon for all local accommodations to be booked nearly a year in advance.

Summer festivities include the **Midnight Sun Festival** on the weekend closest to the solstice (June 21st). After a parade and chicken BBQ, the **Nome River Raft Race,** the city's largest summer event, commences. Home-made contraptions paddle their way down the 1- to 2-mi. course hoping to clinch the prestigious fur-lined Honey-Bucket. On Labor Day, the **Bathtub Race** sends tubs mounted on wheels down Front St. The bathtub must be full of water at the start and have at least 10 gallons remaining by the finish. Teammates outside the tub wear large brim hats and suspenders while the one in the tub totes a bar of soap, towel, and bath mat.

OUTDOORS

Three highways radiate outward from Nome and allow exploration of the Seward Peninsula. The **Council Hwy.** travels 76 mi. from Nome to **Council,** a ghost town and summer home for Nome residents (it's appealingly below the treeline). En route, the highway goes around Cape Nome, passes the fascinating **"Last Train to Nowhere,"** a failed railroad project whose only remnants are the engine and cars that sit slowly rusting on the tundra.

The **Taylor Hwy.** (also known as the Kougarok Road) heads north from Nome for 86 mi., though it pretty much peters out without ever reaching a final destination of note. Along the way is **Salmon Lake,** near Mile 40. Popular with locals, the lake offers excellent fishing and has primitive campsites. North of Salmon Lake and off an 8-mi. gravel road from the highway, **Pilgrim Hot Springs** is an historic landmark. During the gold rush, it was a recreation center for miners with spa baths, saloon, dance hall, and roadhouse. (The saloon and roadhouse burned down in 1908.) From 1917 until 1941, a mission and orphanage existed here, housing up to 120 children. The weary can still soak in the springs. The **Kigluaik Mountains** are accessible via this highway and offer some good hiking opportunities. Evidence of the **Wild Goose Pipeline,** a failed project intended to bring fresh water to Nome, can still be found on the south side of the Grand Central Valley, in the mountains.

The **Nome-Teller Hwy.** winds west from Nome for 76 mi. to the small Native village of **Teller.** Nothing too exciting is out there. A side road heads to **Wooley Lagoon,** where Native families set up summer fish camps. Tourists are few.

All three highways are entirely gravel and can make for rough going. The only solution is to rent a car from any of the companies in Nome (see Practical Information). There are some excellent **fishing** rivers along the highways, including the **Nome River** and **Pilgrim River,** both accessible via the Taylor Highway.

There are many **gold dredges** around Nome. Three of them still operate 24 hrs. a day in the summer. These monstrous machines are littered throughout the Nome vicinity. Ask at the visitors center for locations.

■■■ NORTHWEST COAST

It costs hundreds of dollars to get here. Unless you have a good, specific reason to go to this part of Alaska, there is almost nothing to do here. This is no place for a budget jaunt.

KOTZEBUE

Kotzebue is on the tip of the Baldwin Peninsula, 160 mi. northeast of Nome and 25 mi. north of the Arctic Circle. Kotzebue is principally a hub for Native settlements and other small communities in Alaska's Arctic Northwest. The **Northwest Alaska Native Corporation (NANA)** has its headquarters here. The **visitors center** (442-3760) is a half-block from the airport on Second Ave. Managed jointly by the National Park Service, the BLM, and Fish and Wildlife, the center is geared toward providing information about the national parks, preserves, and wildlife refuges found near Kotzebue. They also offer a free **map** (open daily 8am-5:30pm). The **airport** is on the western edge of town, a 10-minute walk from "downtown." **Mark Air** (442-2737) flies to Anchorage (2 per day, $426 round-trip) and Nome (1 per day; round trip $180). **Alaska Airlines** (442-3474) has almost identical rates. Planes leave 4 times daily for Anchorage.

It is extremely difficult to find a place to stay in Kotzebue. Hotels exist; camping is impossible. For the accommodations or food you find, you'll pay through the nose.

NOATAK RIVER REGION

There are more than 14,000 sq. mi. of protected wilderness in Northwest Alaska. **Kobuk Valley National Park, Noatak National Preserve,** and **Cape Krusenstern National Monument** comprise 11% of all the land administered by the National Park Service. Local Natives legally use the parks for subsistence hunting.

The Northwest Alaska Areas are wilderness at its wildest, and their remoteness all but guarantees that they will remain that way, accessible to only the most dedicated (and rich) outdoorsperson. The **visitors center** for all of the Northwest Alaska Areas is in Kotzebue. For information call 442-3760, or write Superintendent, Northwest Alaska Areas, National Park Service, P.O. Box 1029, Kotzebue 99752.

Cape Krusenstern National Monument was established primarily for archaeological reasons. Within its gravels, in chronological order, lie artifacts from every known Inuit occupation of North America. The monument borders the coastlines of the Chukchi Sea on the west and Kotzebue Sound to the south, and it's mainly marshy tundra. Some hiking is possible in the rolling **Igichuk** or **Mulgrave Hills,** and kayaking along the coast and in the monument's numerous lagoons is another potential activity. Generally, though, the area is best left to the archaeologists. The only way in is by charter plane from Kotzebue (about $275 per hr. for a plane).

The 2650-sq.-mi. **Kobuk Valley National Park** occupies a broad valley along the central Kobuk River, 25 mi. north of the Arctic Circle. One of the more surprising features in the park are the 25-sq.-mi. **Great Kobuk Sand Dunes,** a small piece of the Sahara in Alaska's Arctic, although visitors should watch more for grizzlies here than for camels. The most popular activity is floating the Kobuk. Popular put-in spots are the village of **Ambler** on the park's eastern edge and at the river's headwaters in **Walker Lake,** deep in the Brooks Range. The sand dunes are accessible via a short overland hike from the Kobuk River, once you've floated to within hiking range. The region is accessible via regularly scheduled flights from Kotzebue. **Ryan Air** (442-3342) flies to Ambler from Kotzebue for $215.

The 10,200-sq.-mi. **Noatak National Preserve** contains the broad, gently sloping Noatak River valley. This westward-flowing river has the largest undisturbed watershed in North America. Most visitors see the area by floating. Noatak floaters drift from the arboreal forest's northern edge into a treeless expanse of tundra as they proceed down the river. Wildlife abounds, especially members of the region's 400,000-strong caribou herd. The float is not a difficult one, although its remoteness presents some difficulties. Fewer than 100 visitors floated the Noatak in the 1992 season. The only way in is by (you guessed it) charter airplane, although there are scheduled flights from Noatak, a popular take-out spot on the preserve's western boundary, to Kotzebue for $60.

BARROW

The world's largest Inuit village, Barrow is the northernmost point in the United States. In April and May, villagers carry on the tradition of the whale hunt, both to sustain their culture and themselves. The entire community participates, some hunting, some hauling, others carving up the whale (a bowhead whale can feed entire villages). This event culminates in the **walrus-hide blanket toss,** which bounces Inuit high into the air. **Mark Air** (800-627-5247) flies from Fairbanks daily (14-day advance purchase round-trip $350).

ALEUTIAN ISLANDS

If you're headed to the Aleutians, either you have your own good reason or a lot of idle time and money, because the Aleutian chain is out of the budget-travel price range. At the fiery boundary between two tectonic plates, the snow-capped active and dormant volcanoes that make up the Alaska Peninsula and the Aleutian Islands stretches like an rocky tendril more than 1000 mi. into the stormy North Pacific. The Aleutians are one of the most remote locations on earth, with the westernmost islands coming within a few hundred mi. of Kamchatka. The lava-scarred cones on these green but treeless isles are whipped by some of the world's worst weather. Vicious storms packing winds of over 100 mph can blow in anytime.

Russia used the islands as steppingstones into Alaska. In June 1942, the Japanese Navy bombarded the Aleutian town of Unalaska and occupied the outer islands of Attu and Kiska, land totally without strategic value. A year later, the U.S. military stormed Attu, touching off a bloody, obscure battle which left thousands of American and Japanese soldiers dead on the wind-swept tundra.

The Peninsula and the islands are home to Aleut villages, small military installations, and larger towns dedicated to big-time deep-sea fishing. In the summer, a few hundred tourists come here, despite the cost and time involved, to explore the natural beauty of this volcanic wilderness and to view the millions of migratory seabirds that stop here. Several species of aves nest nowhere else in the world.

GETTING THERE

There are only two ways to see the Aleutians: **plane** or **boat.** Both methods are prohibitively expensive. A round-trip flight from Kodiak to **Dutch Harbor,** the largest town on the Aleutians, costs around $1000 and lasts about 4 hours. The same trip on the **Alaska Marine Hwy.** costs $400 and takes about 5 days. The ferry is the better choice; the whole point of traveling to the Peninsula and the Aleutians is not merely to get somewhere (there is really no place to go) but instead to spend time enjoying the unique panoramas and wildlife. Think of it as a cheap 5-day cruise. If you are seriously considering a ferry voyage to the Aleutians, consider purchasing the **Alaska Pass,** which might make the trip more affordable (see page 71).

By Ferry

The Alaska Marine Highway makes this trip only seven times per year between May and Sept. It is best to go in July, when the weather is mildest. Make reservations at least two weeks in advance; boats often fill in summer.

The *Tustumena* serves the Aleutian chain from Kodiak. It features a dining room with decent food (you can also bring your own from Kodiak), showers 25¢ for 10 min., and a TV room where the on-board naturalist regularly gives slide shows and films on the plants and wildlife often seen from the ship. Cabinless passengers can sleep above decks. The solarium is (cough) right next to the (ack) exhaust tower.

Your companions for the trip will probably be seniors who are taking advantage of the $390 they save on discount tickets, with a scattering of families, students, fisherfolk, and maniacal birdwatcher types who run around with binoculars the size of small children screaming, "It's a Whiskered Auklet!"

The ferry stops briefly at several small towns, ranging from quaint fishing villages to prefabricated cannery quarters, before reaching Dutch Harbor, the most interesting town in the Aleutians. Stock up on Dramamine or another seasickness remedy before you leave. You'll be weathering 5- to 15-ft. seas; they don't call the *Tustumena* the "Vomit Comet" for nothing.

■■■ UNALASKA AND DUTCH HARBOR

Unalaska (YOO-na-las-ka) and Dutch Harbor are at the head of stunning Unalaska Bay, on the eastern coast of Unalaska Island. For years Dutch Harbor referred only to Unalaska's port, but recently a town of Dutch Harbor, complete with its own zip code, has arisen about ½-mile from "the old town" of Unalaska.

Unalaska is a budget traveler's nightmare. Remoteness and unusually high incomes (over $130 million in seafood passes this port every year) keep prices high. But the view, treeless, snow-capped mountains soaring thousands of feet from Unalaska Bay's chilly blue waters, is free.

PRACTICAL INFORMATION AND ORIENTATION

Unalaska Convention and Visitors Bureau, P.O.Box 545 (581-2612), in the Grand Aleutian Hotel. They'll fill you in on the basics. Open Mon.-Fri. 8am-5pm and sometimes on weekends. You can also get local information 24 hrs. from the desk attendant at the Unisea Hotel in downtown Dutch Harbor.

Department of Fish and Game: P.O. Box 308, in the FTS Building, downtown Dutch Harbor (581-1239 or 581-1219). Will fill you in on local fishing and bird-watching opportunities. Open Mon.-Fri. 8am-noon and 1-4:30pm.

Alaska Marine Hwy.: Docks at City Dock about 1½ mi. from Dutch Harbor and 2½ mi. from Unalaska. Arrives about once every 3-4 weeks in the summer. No terminal; call 800-642-0066 for schedule information. One-way to Kodiak; $202.

Airport: Located about ¼ mi. from City Dock on the main road into town. Served by several carriers, including **Reeves Aleutian** (800-544-2248 or 581-3380), **Mark Air** (800-627-5247 or 581-1727), and **Pen Air** (581-1383; to Anchorage one-way $245, to Kodiak via Anchorage $333).

Taxis: 13 different cab companies! Every company charges the same outrageous prices. Tours of the towns are $1 per min.

Bike Rental (581-1297). In the Community Center at 5th and Broadway, in Unalaska. Mountain bikes a cheap $10 per day.

Pharmacy: Alaska Commercial Company ("The A.C."), next to the Grand Aleutian Hotel in downtown Dutch Harbor (581-1245). Open Mon.-Sat. 9am-midnight, Sun. 10am-midnight.

Emergency: Police and Fire, 911.

Hospital: Iliuliuk Family and Health Services, 34 Lovelle Court (581-1202, 581-1233 for after-hours emergencies), near 5th and Broadway. Open Mon.-Fri. 10am-6pm and Sat. 1-5pm.

Post Office: In **Unalaska** (581-1232), on Agnes Rd.. Open Mon.-Fri. 9am-5pm, Sat. 1pm-5pm. **General Delivery ZIP Code:** 99685. In **Dutch Harbor,** in the Intersea Mall (581-1657). Open Mon.-Fri. 9am-5pm, Sat. 1pm-5pm. **General Delivery ZIP Code:** 99692.
Area Code: 907.

Unalaska lies about 300 mi. from the tip of the Alaska Peninsula. It is on the same time as the rest of Alaska. The twin towns have a refreshing lack of concern for the tourist trade; the big money here is in seafood and you will find few tacky t-shirt shops here. The liveliest months in Unalaska are in the fall and winter when the local fish and crab seasons begin. In summer, the two towns are sleepy.

ACCOMMODATIONS AND CAMPING

Most of the potentially cheap hotels have been bought out by canneries or converted into monthly apartments, which leaves the stray tourist a choice among one hotel, one B&B, and one primitive campground.

Jackie's B&B, P.O. Box 534 (581-2964), near the school. 4 rooms, and breakfast, too! Singles $75, doubles $100.
Summer Bay, from the City Dock or the airport, hike 2½ mi. through Dutch Harbor and Unalaska. Pick up Summer Bay Rd., headed out of town, for another 2 mi. to Summer Bay. A bridge, some sand dunes, and a few picnic tables and barbecues mark the spot; there are no other facilities. Set your tent in a sheltered location, or the 100-mph wind gusts will introduce your possessions to Unalaska Bay.

FOOD

The cheapest grocery in town is the **Alaska Commercial Company** or **"AC"** (581-1245), next to the Grand Aleutian Hotel in Dutch Harbor. (Open Mon.-Sat. 9am-midnight, Sun. 10am-midnight.) Remember that "cheap" is a relative term.

Ziggy's, about ½ mi. from the airport on the main road to town. A favorite local hang-out. Full stack of sourdough pancakes $4.50. Sandwiches and burgers $6-8. Mexican dinners $9-16. Open daily 7am-10pm.
Margaret's Bay Cafe (581-7122), in the Grand Aleutian Hotel. Open for breakfast and lunch. Omelettes $7-10 (open daily 7am-3pm).

SIGHTS

If you are traveling by ferry, you have three options: stay 3-4 hrs. while the boat refuels, wait 3-4 weeks until the *Tustumena* returns, or fly back to the mainland, which will cost a minimum of $340. Although Dutch Harbor/Unalaska is an intriguing town, the former option is probably the wisest.

Get a cab (see Practical Information) to drive you the 3 mi. to the **Unalaska Cemetery and Memorial Park** on the eastern edge of Unalaska. These two sights include a description of the Japanese air attacks of June 1942. You can still see the bow of the *SS Northwestern*, sunk during the attack, slowly rusting in the bay.

Heading back toward Unalaska on Beach Front Rd., you will eventually reach the **Holy Ascension Orthodox Church** (built 1824-27, expanded 1894) and the **Bishop's House** (built 1882). The dilapidated church is being restored. This area was once the center of Orthodox missionary activity in Alaska.

Right after you cross the "bridge-to-the-other-side" on the way back to the ferry, you will come up alongside **Bunker Hill.** A quick 420-ft. climb straight up is a large concrete bunker and a spectacular view of the surrounding bays and mountains.

Those planning to stay longer than 3 to 4 hours should ask the locals about the numerous trails and military artifacts strewn across the local countryside. Interesting day hikes are possible.

If you happen to be in Unalaska on any night except Sunday, check out the **Elbow Room Bar** (581-1470) between 2nd and 3rd on Broadway. The Elbow Room was recently voted the second-rowdiest bar in the world.

THE PACIFIC NORTHWEST

The term "Pacific Northwest" generally denotes Oregon and Washington, particularly the western half of each state, including the coast and Cascades. But as a cultural area exceeding national boundaries, the term also refers to British Columbia, Alberta, and the Yukon. The three Canadian jurisdictions probably have more in common with America's libertarian West than with the rest of Canada. Western Canadian opposition parties led by anti-government politicos such as Preston Manning are growing in popularity. Regionalism in the U.S. Northwest has undergone a revival in recent years, but it is unlike that found in other parts of North America: while Californians draw attention to their irrigated paradise on the West Coast, New Englanders take haughty pride in their historic sensibilities, and Southerners lay claim to a better pace of life, inhabitants of the Pacific Northwest are often eager to keep their blessings to themselves. Emmett Watson's "Lesser Seattle" movement has even gone so far as to publish negative (and often misleading) statistics concerning the city in an attempt to dissuade people from moving there. And with good reason: invaders from California threaten to bring their plastic cities and pollution to the Northwest. To some degree they have succeeded.

Those traveling to the Northwest from other parts of the U.S. or Canada will find it by turns charming and awe-inspiring, relaxing and challenging. Visitors may, however, want to keep a handful of miscellaneous points in mind. Drivers do not like to honk, and pedestrians do not jaywalk in the major cities. In general, lines form themselves and tend to proceed just a little more strictly, and slowly, than in some other regions. Finally, folks aren't especially friendly in or-i-GAHN, but residents of the Beaver State *will* be quick to welcome you to OR-i-gun.

History

When the first immigrants crossed the Bering Strait into North America some 20,000 years ago, many of the luckiest settled in a huge swath of land from the Kenai south to the Northern California coast, where natural wealth and good seafood were plentiful. They took advantage of the environment's natural resources, converting the abundant timber into harpoons for whaling and river weirs for snaring salmon. The abundance of food allowed coastal dwellers to abandon their nomadic lifestyle and establish the first permanent settlements in North America.

Life on the coast was so good that altruism became a status symbol in the ceremony of the potlatch ("gift"), in which the chief distributed names, privileges, and material goods such as blankets, copper sheets, and (as times have changed) washing machines and dryers. Receiving these benevolences was proof of a wealth so great that the owner could afford to part with some. Coastal natives were rich in culture and artwork as well; they crafted elaborately symbolic totem poles, inscribed with family crests and animal signs denoting the hereditary lineages through which clans organized social interaction.

Inland on the Plateau region that stretched between the Cascades to the west and the Rockies to the east, life was more difficult and food harder to come by. Plateau natives were on the move nine months of every year, hunting the migratory herds. Their semi-nomadic life-style kept tribal ties in flux, necessitating an egalitarian social system with consensual government. Even wider nomadism was encouraged by the arrival of wild horses around 1730.

An expedition of Russian seafarers, captained by Vitus Bering in 1741, first brought the fur of sea otters back from Alaska, inaugurating the lucrative trade in animal pelts. In 1776, English explorer James Cook traded some rusty nails for a few ragged pelts in Nootka Sound, part of the unclaimed land between Russian and Spanish holdings (now British Columbia). The furs fetched a fortune in China during Cook's return trip, and the fur frenzy was on. The English Hudson's Bay Company engaged in cutthroat fur-trading competition with the French, Montreal-based North West Company, the "Nor'westers;" tales of their wilderness struggle would make frightening reading. The only thing that tied these warring fortune-hunters together was the trading language of the Chinook, who served as the mercenary go-betweens in the Northwest.

U.S. President Thomas Jefferson, eager to attain "geographical knowledge of our own continent," but of course also eager to strengthen American claims to the area newly purchased from Napoleon, commissioned Meriwether Lewis and William Clark to explore the Northwest in 1803. Accompanied by the inept Charbonneau and the indomitable Sacajawea, who was *not* the guide but translated for the explorers into the Shoshone language (Lewis' attempt to impress the Shoshone with *his* limited command of their language involved rushing an armed warrior, waving madly, and yelling "I am your enemy!"). She ensured success not only as a translator, but also her mere presence with her child convinced Native Americans that theirs was not a war party. Lewis and Clark's expedition traveled 4000 mi. from St. Louis to the mouth of the Columbia and back, strengthening American claims to the region. London, for its part, sent Captains James Cook and George Vancouver to map the coast and waterways. In 1818 the two nations hammered out an agreement that divided their claims as far west as the Rockies at the 49th parallel, but left the Oregon question unresolved.

The native population in the Northwest was decimated, partly as a result of whites' deliberate machinations and partly due to the unfamiliar diseases they inadvertently carried along, including measles, small pox, and influenza, which wiped out as much as 90 percent of the natives by the late 1800s. Missionary fervor became an additional means of control and, indirectly, dispossession of indigenous peoples. Whites responded in horror to the Chinook custom of flattening babies' foreheads, and crusaders such as Marcus and Narcissa Whitman rushed west to Walla Walla to "save" their profiles as well as their souls. The Whitmans would have done better to save themselves; Cayuse warriors, convinced that the missionaries were poisoning their tribe to clear the area for white settlers, killed them. The indignation aroused by the incident was a crucial motivating factor in making Oregon an American territory. Those natives who survived the ensuing white invasion were herded, nation by nation, onto reserves on some of the worst land in the region.

Better armed opposition to U.S. control of the Northwest was offered by Britain, prompting President James K. Polk to win the White House with a manifest destiny platform and the jingoistic "54° 40' or fight"—a claim to land west of the Rockies north to present-day Prince George, British Columbia. But Polk pursued neither option, and in 1846 extended westward the 49th parallel as the dividing line between British and American territories, leaving the Russian stake above the 54th parallel intact. Secured, the Oregon Territory split in half. The southern half became the state of Oregon in 1859, and the remaining territory to the north joined it 30 years later, reluctantly giving up the name "Columbia" (reserved for the congressional district back east) for "Washington." Farther north near Vancouver, miners struck gold in 1856, and prospectors swarmed up the coast from Sacramento. Where revenue went, government followed; the governor of Vancouver Island enlarged his jurisdiction to establish a real provincial administration over the mainland in Canada. In 1866, the arrangement was official, and the coastal colony above Washington became British Columbia, Canada. Similarly, the Yukon, which shared Alaska's mineral wealth, and Alberta, whose fertile agricultural plains would later yield valuable oil, became a Canadian territory in 1898 and a Canadian province in 1905, respectively.

Alongside malcontents from the Midwest and New England eager to establish farms and to log huge evergreens were Irish, Scandinavians, and Eastern Europeans lured by promotional literature of a new Eden. Boosterism did not account for the influx of Chinese, who came to the area as railroad workers; Sinophobes drove them from Washington in the 1880s. Many Chinese stuck it out, however, establishing in Vancouver North America's proportionally largest Asian community. The region's population boomed when the railroad roared to the coast, in the American Northwest in the 1870s and in Canada in 1883.

By the beginning of the twentieth century, Northwest history had lost its distinct outlines, becoming national history. Yet the region retains its unique character. The attachment to populist politics in both Western Canada and the Northwest—from the Wobblies labor movement of the early 1900s to BC's Social Credit Party of the 1940s—remains fierce. The Pacific Northwest has spawned history-making liberals such as Washington's Supreme Court Justice William O. Douglas, Senator Henry "Scoop" Jackson, and current Speaker of the House Tom Foley. The floundering lumber industry has largely been replaced by high technology, but Northwestern cities have looked westward to the Pacific Rim in recent years, developing economic and cultural links with Japan and other East Asian nations.

In the '70s and '80s, the high-tech, smokestack-less industries of the region's big cities at first seemed to spread a huge urban umbrella against the recession beating down on the rest of the continent. Few cities in America increased employment as quickly as did Seattle, which solidified its base in the computer software, biotechnology, and airplane industries. But now, as defense industries are downsized and concern grows over the environmental damage involved in logging and salmon fishing (two of the region's longtime economic standbys), Northwesterners are casting about for alternatives. Many proclaim the need for a more diversified economy and reforms of existing industries, including selective tree harvesting, multi-species reforestation, and salmon preservation.

Arts

In the centuries before European settlement, the Kwakiutl tribe on the present-day Canadian coast enacted world-renewal ceremonies with theatrical effects such as tunnels, trapdoors, ventriloquism, and bloody sleight-of-hand beheadings, all while costumed in fantastical, supernatural cedar masks. Performing arts have dazzled audiences in the Northwest ever since.

Native American artists were publicly dormant during most of the twentieth century, awakening only with the renaissance of tribal identity in the 1960s. In its many forms, Native art is a striking and powerful merger of the human, the animal, and the spiritual. Today, some of the best collections of Native American art and artifacts are showcased in the Provincial Museum in Victoria, BC and the Thomas Burke Museum at the University of Washington in Seattle; the Portland Art Museum also houses an impressive collection.

The contemporary art scene in the Northwest maintains a generally convivial and public tone; on the first Thursday evening of each month, Portland and Seattle art galleries fling open their doors (and often their wine cellars) to browsers. The cities' 1% tax on capital improvements is funneled into the acquisition and creation of public art. Contemporary Northwest artists have found an aesthetic silver lining in the clouds that often blanket the region. BC painter Emily Carr blended Native elements with her work to create original Northwest images; in the 1950s, the Northwest School, comprised of the mystic triad Morris Graves, Mark Tobey, and Kenneth Callahan, fashioned magical scenes out of the rainy climes.

The Northwest offers imported artistic treasures as well, such as the Oregon Shakespeare Festival in Ashland, where an estimated annual audience of 450,000 spends a day or a week every summer enjoying the excellent in- and outdoor performances. A number of actors of note have performed here, including William Hurt in *Long Day's Journey into Night* and Kyle MacLachlan (of *Twin Peaks* fame) as Romeo in *Romeo and Juliet*. Seattle, which has a repertory theater community second only to New York's in size, offers a stunning assortment of new dramas in its many fine theaters.

There is entertainment for the discriminating listener here as well. The Seattle Opera puts on a show with classical and modern productions, and has earned an international reputation for its Wagner. Orchestral music aficionados can trek down to the Bach Festival in Eugene, OR, where Helmut Rilling waves his exquisite

INTRODUCTION

Baroque baton. Make your way south for the Mt. Hood Jazz Festival in Gresham, OR; the event has played host to such greats as Wynton Marsalis and Ella Fitzgerald. Or wander north to check out what's playing in Alberta's two Jubilee Auditoriums. Also, Seattle hosts Bumbershoot, a blow-out festival of folk, street, classical, and rock music. Seattle, of course, is home to storefuls of indy-turned-megastar rock.

Literature, Film, and Media

The Northwest has produced no major literary school of its own, but many writers who have lived or wandered there testify to the spiritual power of the frontier and the mountains. Travelers such as John Muir and John McPhee have celebrated the natural wonders of the region and written detailed descriptions of travelers' struggles to survive. Raymond Carver's stories and Alice Munro's novels provide insight into the people and culture of the region. Other authors, like such as Ursula K. Le Guin and Jean M. Auel, have simply drawn upon their surroundings for inspiration in less Northwest-specific works. Poet Theodore Roethke taught at the University of Washington in Seattle, bequeathing his lyric sensibility to a generation of Northwestern poets. Bernard Malamud taught for many years at Oregon State University as he wrote several of his best-known works.

Recent filmmakers and writers, many of them displaying an oddly outrageous comic sense, have lifted the Northwest's veil of fog and introduced the region into the pop culture pantheon. NBC's popular *Northern Exposure,* set in Alaska but filmed in Washington's Cascade range, explores an isolated, tiny timber town, showcasing the inhabitants' bizarre yet average eccentricities. Gary Larson, the Seattle-bred creator of the outlandish cartoon strip "The Far Side," has deified the cow. Matt Groening, creator of the "Life is Hell" strip and FOX's immensely popular *The Simpsons,* hails from Portland. So does John Callahan, unconventional comic-writer. Northwestern pop culture tends not to pay homage to traditional hero figures.

Not incidentally, the Northwest is a popular setting for movies and films—most notably *Sleepless in Seattle, Reality Bites,* Cameron Crowe's *Singles, Say Anything,* and *Fast Times at Ridgemont High,* and David Lynch's *Twin Peaks: Fire Walk With Me.* To get a visual sampling of the area before you go, take a look at some of the following; most are widely available at the corner video rental store: *Drugstore Cowboy; An Officer and a Gentleman; Immediate Family; Ice Station Zebra; Orca; Never Cry Wolf; Shoot to Kill;* and *Vision Quest.* And, of course, flip on the TV for *Northern Exposure* (see Cascade Range: Roslyn, in Washington) and reruns of *Twin Peaks* (see Near Seattle: Snoqualmie, in Washington).

What follows is a brief and idiosyncratic list of books by regional authors and about the region, from travel diaries to children's works. Check your local bookstore or library for other suggestions: *Where I'm Calling From* and *Fires* by Raymond Carver; the *Ramona* series by Beverly Cleary; *I Heard the Owl Call My Name* by Margaret Craven; *Go East, Young Man* by William O. Douglas; *Instructions to the Double* by Tess Gallager; *Julie of the Wolves* by Jean Craighead George; *Notes from the Century Before: A Journal of British Columbia* by Edward Hoagland; *The Country Ahead of Us, The Country Behind* by David Guterson; *Sometimes a Great Notion* by Ken Kesey; *The Lathe of Heaven* by Ursula K. Le Guin; *Journals of Lewis and Clark* by Meriwether Lewis and William Clark; *The Assistant* by Bernard Malamud; *Coming Into the Country* and *The Control of Nature* by John McPhee; *Stories of Flo and Rose* by Alice Munro; *Zen and the Art of Motorcycle Maintenance* by Robert Pirsig; *Another Roadside Attraction* and *Still Life With Woodpecker* by Tom Robbins; *The Lost Sun* by Theodore Roethke; *Sacajawea: American Pathfinder* by Flora Warren Seymour; *Traveling Through the Dark* by William Stafford; *Paul Bunyan* by James Stevens; and *Poet in the Desert* by Charles Erskine Scott Woods (the Erskine clan continues to competently chronicle this legendary region).

British Columbia

British Columbia attracts so many visitors that tourism has become the province's second-largest industry, after logging. Despite excellent skiing year-round, most tourists arrive in the summer and flock to the beautiful cities of Vancouver and Victoria and to the pristine lakes and beaches of the warm Okanagan Valley. Heading north, thick forests, low mountains, and occasional patches of high desert are interrupted only by supply and transit centers, such as Prince George and Prince Rupert. Still farther north, even these outposts of civilization defer to thick spruce and fir forests stretching to the horizon, intermittently logged or blackened by lightning fires. *This chapter covers only the southern part of the province;* for northern British Columbia, including the Cariboo Highway, Yellowhead Highway 16, the Queen Charlotte Islands, the Cassiar and Alaska Highways, and for coverage of Yukon Territory, *see the following chapter.*

Recently the logging industry has prospered, as restrictions on logging in the United States have driven business north. Still, British Columbia is trying to develop beyond its primary-resource economy, vulnerable to economic shocks. Beyond its notorious stock exchange, Vancouver is Canada's window on the Pacific and has long been economically connected with Hong Kong and East Asia. With the largest proportional East Asian minority of any city in North America, the Chinese communist takeover of Hong Kong in 1997 may prove a major boost to Vancouver.

Temperate British Columbia defies the snowy picture many non-natives have of Canada. Vancouver receives even more rain than the American Northwest, but very little snow. The Okanagan country, in the south-central part of the province, grows peaches and other warm-weather fruit. Vacationers bask on sunny beaches along Okanagan and Shuswap Lakes. Kelowna is often the destination of choice, and its high prices and rates reflect this. Nearby towns, offering better recreational opportunities for less money, are covered here.

British Columbia's parks are popular with hikers, mountaineers, cyclists, rafters, and skiers. On Vancouver Island, the coastal rainforests of Strathcona and Pacific Rim Parks are beautiful and largely untrammeled. In the southeastern part of the province, Glacier, Yoho, and Kootenay Parks parks allow visitors to escape into some of Canada's most amazing outdoor country. Here, you can enjoy country just as beautiful as Jasper and Banff without the development or tourist mobs.

This chapter moves from Vancouver to Victoria and Vancouver Island, then crosses back to the mainland from the Fraser River Canyon east of Vancouver, to the Okanogan country, to Kootenay country in the southeast.

PRACTICAL INFORMATION

Capital: Victoria.

Visitors Information: Call 800-663-6000 or write the **Ministry of Tourism and Provincial Secretary,** Parliament Bldgs., Victoria V8V 1X4 (604-387-1642). Ask especially for the *Accommodations* guide, listing prices.

Park Information: Parks Canada, 220 4th Ave. SE, P.O. Box 2989, Station M, Calgary, AB T2P 3H8. **BC Parks,** 800 Johnson St., 2nd Floor, Victoria, BC V8V 1X4 (604-387-5002).

Motto: *Splendor sine Occasu* (Splendor without Diminishment). **Year of Royal Naming:** 1858, by Queen Victoria. **Year to Join Confederation:** 1871. **Provincial Flower:** Pacific Dogwood. **Provincial Tree:** Douglas Fir. **Provincial Bird:** Heron. **Provincial Stone:** Jade.

Emergency: 911.

Time Zone: Mostly Pacific (1 hr. behind Mountain, 2 behind Central, 3 behind Eastern). Small eastern part is Mountain (1 hr. behind Central, 2 behind Eastern).

Postal Abbreviation: BC.

Drinking Age: 19.

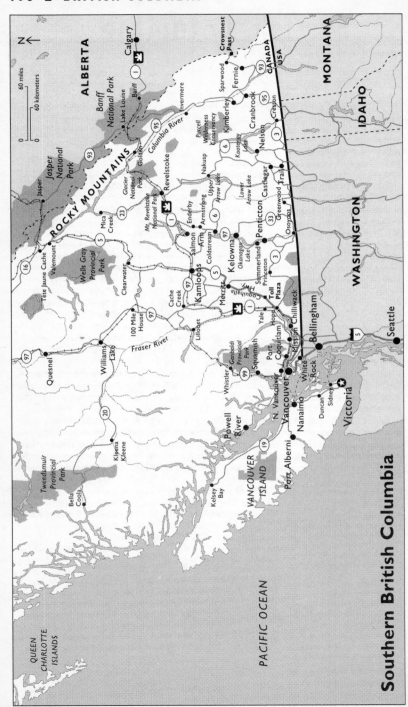

Southern British Columbia

Traffic Laws: Mandatory seatbelt law.
Area Code: 604.

TRAVEL

British Columbia is Canada's westernmost province, covering over 890,000 sq. km, bordering four U.S. states (Washington, Idaho, Montana, and Alaska) and three Canadian jurisdictions (Alberta, the Yukon Territory, and the Northwest Territories). Vancouver, on the mainland, can be reached by interstate highway from Seattle; Victoria, on Vancouver Island to the southwest of Vancouver, requires a ferry trip (see page 42) from Anacortes, Port Angeles, Seattle, or the **Tsawwassen Terminal** near Vancouver. However you travel, get used to thinking of distances in terms of kilometers in three or four digits.

Road travel throughout the province varies with the diverse terrain. If you decide to take your own vehicle, avoid potential hassles by obtaining a **Canadian non-resident interprovincial motor vehicle liability card** from your insurance company before leaving. Border police may turn you away if you are not properly insured. In the south, roads are plentiful and well-paved. Much of B.C. is served by **Greyhound** (662-3222 in Vancouver; 800-231-2222 from the U.S.).

The **Coquihalla Hwy.** (Hwy. 5, more popularly known as "The Coca-Cola") was completed in 1986 to carry tourists comfortably from Hope to Kamloops, a city roughly halfway between Vancouver and Alberta's Banff and Jasper National Parks. The Coquihalla Hwy. costs $10 to ride, but is a much more direct route and constitutes a substantial time savings. Unfortunately, the terrain is very hilly and has assassinated more than one transmission. If you don't think your car is capable, you can always enjoy the Fraser River Canyon's scenery via the Trans-Canada Hwy. instead. **Hwy. 5** brings you from Kamloops straight to Jasper.

■■■ VANCOUVER

Canada's third-largest city will thrill even the most jaded metropolis-hopping traveler. Vancouver has a seamless public transit system, spotless sidewalks, and good safety record; although there are a few dingy alleys scattered through the city, particularly southeast of downtown, Vancouver's citizens display a gentility rare in a city this size.

Vancouver is fast joining the post-industrial age; the unemployment rate has fallen by half in recent years, and electronics and international finance are supplanting timber and mining as the city's economic base. Additionally, a growing wave of Chinese immigrants is orienting Vancouver's culture and economy toward the Far East. Immigration is increasing from Hong Kong in particular; cynics say their city is becoming "Hongcouver" and predict racial tensions will rise. Others regard Vancouver as the prototype of a modern multi-ethnic metropolis. The debate over defining Vancouver's identity remains unsettled, but Mayor Gordon Campbell promises that his city will "not become like a city in the United States." One can only wonder if he reacted so smugly to the extended riots following the Vancouver Canucks' hockey-playoff loss to the New York Rangers.

The range of things to do in Vancouver and its environs is astounding. You can go for nature walks among 1000-year-old virgin timber stands, windsurf, take in a modern art exposition, or get wrapped up in a flick at the most technologically advanced movie theatre in the world, and never leave downtown. Filled with beaches and parks, the cultural vortex that is Vancouver has swallowed hordes of unsuspecting vacationers. If you insist on purchasing a return ticket in advance, be sure to allot yourself ample time to appreciate this marvelous city.

PRACTICAL INFORMATION

Visitors Information: Travel Infocentre, 1055 Dunsmuir St. (683-2000), near Burrard St., in the West End. Help with reservations and tours. If the racks of brochures don't answer all your questions, the staff will. Open daily 8am-6pm.

BC Transit Information Centre, 261-5100. Fare $1.50, exact change. Day passes ($4.50, seniors 75¢, students and children $2.25) available at all 7-11 stores, the Post Office, the Waterfront stop, or the Vancouver International Hostel.

Parks and Recreation Board, 2099 Beach Ave. (681-1141). Open Mon.-Fri. 8:30am-4:30pm.

The Grey Line, 750 Pacific Blvd. (257-8400), in the Plaza of Nations. City tours with several package options. Basic tours leave daily at 9:15am and 1:45pm and last 3½ hrs. $32, seniors $28, ages 5-12 $20. Reservations required.

Taxis: Yellow Cab, 681-3311. **Vancouver Taxi,** 255-5111. Both 24 hrs.

Car Rental: Rent-A-Wreck, 180 W Georgia St. (688-0001), in the West End. (Also 340 W 4th at Manitoba.) From $29.95 per day; 300km free, 10¢ per additional km. Must be 19 with credit card. Open Mon.-Fri. 7am-7pm, Sat. 8am-5pm, Sun. 8am-5pm. Also **ABC Rental,** 255 W Broadway. Starts at $200 per week.

Bike Rental: Bayshore, 745 Denman St. (689-5071). Convenient to Stanley Park. Practically new bikes $5.60 per hr., $20 per 12 hrs., $25 per day. Open May-Sept. daily 9am-9pm. Winter hours vary with the amount of sunlight.

Bicycling Association of BC, 1367 W Broadway, #332, Vancouver V6H 4H9 (290-6455 events line, 737-3034 office). One-page cycling **map** of city ($2.30); more detailed maps available through the mail. Open Mon.-Fri. 9am-5pm.

Road Conditions: 525-4997. 24 hrs. **In Whistler:** 938-4997. 24 hrs.

Camping Equipment Rentals: Recreation Rentals, 2560 Arbutus St. (733-7368), at Broadway. Take bus #10 or #14 from Granville Mall. Backpacks ($9 per day, $25 per week), 2-person tents ($15 per day, $42 per week), and every other kind of camping or sports equipment. Open Mon.-Sat. 8am-7pm, Sun. 10am-7pm.

Scuba Rentals: The Diving Locker, 2745 W 4th Ave. (736-2681). Complete outfit Sun.-Thurs. $45 first day, $25 each additional day. Fri.-Sat. $80 first day, $40 each additional day. Open Mon.-Thurs. 9:30am-7pm, Fri. 9:30am-8pm, Sat. 9:30am-7pm, Sun. 10am-4pm.

Public Library: 750 Burrard St. (665-2280, 665-2276 for a recording), at Robson St., downtown. Open Mon.-Thurs. 10am-4pm, Fri.-Sat. 10am-6pm; Oct.-March also Sun. 1-5pm.

Bookstores: Spartacus, 311 W Hastings (688-6138). Extensive and unique collection spans topics in politics, race relations, and art. Open Mon.-Fri. 10am-8:30pm, Sat. 10am-6pm, Sun. 11:30am-5:30pm. **Little Sisters Book and Art Emporium Inc.,** 1221 Thurlow (669-1753). Selection of literature concerning gays and lesbians. Open daily 10am-11pm.

Arts Hotline: 684-2787. 24 hrs.

Weather: 644-9010.

Crisis Line: Vancouver Crisis Center, 733-4111. 24 hrs.

Women's Services: Rape Crisis Center, 255-6344. 24 hrs. **Rape Relief Center,** 872-8212. 24 hrs. **Emergency,** 872-7774. 24 hrs.

Women's Resource Center, 1144 Robson St. (681-2910), in the West End between Thurlow and Bute St. Open July-Aug. Mon.-Thurs. 10am-2pm; winter Mon.-Fri. 10am-4pm, Sat. 12pm-4pm.

Senior Citizen's Information and Support Network, 524-0516 or 525-2000. Open Mon.-Fri. 10am-4pm.

BC Coalition of People with Disabilities, 204-456 W Broadway (875-0188). Open Mon.-Fri. 9am-5pm. **Postal Code:** V54 1R3.

Gay and Lesbian Switchboard, #2, 1170 Bute St., 684-6869. Counseling and information. Very helpful staff. Open daily 7-10pm.

AIDS Vancouver: 687-2437. Open Mon. 10am-5pm, Tues.-Wed. 10am-9pm, Thurs.-Fri. 10am-5pm.

Poison Control: 682-5050.

Pharmacy: Shoppers Drug Mart, 2979 W Broadway at Carnarvon (733-9128). Open Mon.-Sat. 9am-9pm, Sun. 11am-6pm.

UBC Hospital: 822-7121.

Emergency: 911. **Police:** (665-3321), at Main and Powell.

Post Office: Main branch, 349 W Georgia St. (662-5725). Open Mon.-Fri. 8am-5:30pm. **Postal Code:** V6B 3P7.

Area Code: 604.

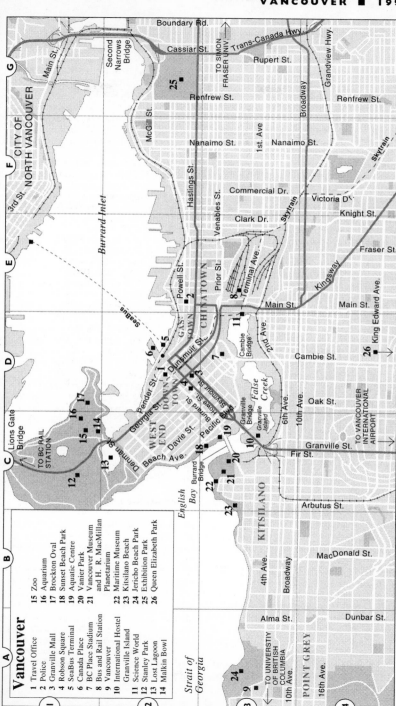

Vancouver

1 Travel Office
2 Police
3 Granville Mall
4 Robson Square
5 SeaBus Terminal
6 Canada Place
7 BC Place Stadium
8 Bus and Rail Station
9 Vancouver
10 International Hostel
11 Science World
12 Stanley Park
13 Lost Lagoon
14 Malkin Bowl
15 Zoo
16 Aquarium
17 Brockton Oval
18 Sunset Beach Park
19 Aquatic Centre
20 Vanier Park
21 Vancouver Museum and H. R. MacMillan Planetarium
22 Maritime Museum
23 Kitsilano Beach
24 Jericho Beach Park
25 Exhibition Park
26 Queen Elizabeth Park

GETTING THERE

Vancouver is in the southwestern corner of the Canadian British Columbia mainland, across the Georgia Strait from Vancouver Island and the city of Victoria. **Vancouver International Airport,** on Sea Island 11km south of the city center, makes connections to major cities on the West Coast and around the world. To reach downtown from the airport, take BC bus #100 to the intersection of Granville and 70th Ave. Transfer there to bus #20, arriving downtown heading north on the Granville Mall. The private **Airport Express** (273-9023) bus leaves from airport level #2 and heads for downtown hotels and the Greyhound station (6am-midnight, 4 per hr., $8.25 per person).

Greyhound makes several runs daily between Seattle and Vancouver. The downtown bus depot provides easy access to the city's transit system. **VIA Rail** runs one train per day east. The **BC Rail** station in North Vancouver launches trains toward northern British Columbia. **BC Ferries** regularly connects the city of Vancouver to Vancouver Island and the Gulf Islands. Ferries leave from the **Tsawwassen Terminal,** 25km south of the city center. To reach downtown from the ferry terminal, take bus #640 to the Ladner Exchange and transfer to bus #601, arriving downtown on Seymour St.

Greyhound, 1150 Station St. (662-3222), in the VIA Rail, see below. Service to the south and across Canada. To: Calgary (7 per day; $90), Banff (6 per day; $85), Jasper (4 per day, $83), and Seattle (4 per day, $25). Open daily 4am-10pm.

Pacific Coach Lines, 150 Dunsmuir St. (662-5074). Serves southern BC, including Vancouver Island, in conjunction with Greyhound. To Victoria $20, including ferry and service into downtown Victoria.

VIA Rail, 1150 Station St. (800-561-8630 or 669-3050), at Main St. Sky Train stop. To: Jasper (3 per week; $131.10), Edmonton (3 per week; $193.67). Open Mon. and Thurs. 8am-8pm, Tues.-Wed., Fri., and Sun. 8am-3:30pm, Sat. 12:30pm-8pm.

BC Rail, 1311 W 1st St. (984-5246), just over the Lions Gate Bridge in North Vancouver. Take the BC Rail Special Bus on Georgia or the SeaBus to North Vancouver, then bus #239 west. Daily to: Garibaldi ($19), Whistler ($19), Williams Lake ($75), Prince George ($107), and points north. Open daily 6am-8:30pm.

BC Ferries (669-1211 general information, 685-1021 recorded information, Tsawwassen ferry terminal 943-9331). Ferry goes to Victoria, the Gulf Islands, Sunshine Coast, Mainland and Vancouver Island ($6.25, car and driver $30.75, motorcycle and driver $15.50, bicycle and rider $8.50; ages 5-11 $3). The terminal serving Victoria is actually in Swartz Bay, north of Victoria.

Bicyclists will find many excellent routes in and near Vancouver, including routes in the Fraser River Canyon, along the shore of the Strait of Georgia, on the Gulf Islands, and on Vancouver Island. The **Bicycling Association of British Columbia** (see Practical Information) can recommend specific trips, and **Tourism BC** publishes a thorough pamphlet on bicycling. Note that the George Massey Tunnel on Hwy. 99, under the Fraser River (which you must use to get to and from the Tsawwassen terminal), is closed to bicycles. A shuttle service transports cyclists through the tunnel. Call the **Bicycling Association of British Columbia** (731-7433) for information on times and fares. (Shuttle service operates daily in summer, less frequently in winter.)

ORIENTATION AND GETTING AROUND

Vancouver looks like a hand with the fingers together pointing west, and the thumb to the north. South of the mitten flows the Fraser River. Beyond the fingertips lies the Georgia Strait. Downtown is on the thumb. At the thumb's tip lie the residential **West End** and Stanley Park. Burrard Inlet separates the downtown from North Vancouver; the bridges over False Creek (the space between the thumb and the rest of the hand) link downtown with **Kitsilano** ("Kits"), **Fairview, Mount Pleasant,** and the rest of the city. East of downtown, where the thumb is attached, lie **Gastown** and **Chinatown.** The **airport** lies south, at the pinkie-tip; the University of British Columbia lies at the tip of the index finger (**Point Grey**). Kitsilano and Point Grey are separated by the north-south Alma Ave. The major highway approaches, Hwy. 99 and the Trans-Canada Hwy., enter the city from the south and east. Most of the city's attractions are concentrated on the city center peninsula and in the fingers of the hand.

Don't try to make any distinction between streets and avenues in Vancouver. There is no apparent standard, and most maps omit the surname. The one exception to this madness are the numbered arterials, always *avenues* in Vancouver proper (running east-west), and always *streets* in North Vancouver (running randomly), across Burrard Inlet. Downtown, private vehicles are not allowed on Granville between Nelson and W Pender St., an area called the **Granville Mall.** Both Chinatown, stretching from east to west between Hastings and East Pender and from Carrall Ave. to Gore Ave., and Gastown, on Alexander as it runs into Water St., are easily reached on foot from the Granville Mall.

Vancouver's **BC Transit** covers most of the city and suburbs, with direct transport or easy connecting transit to the city's points of departure: **Tsawwassen, Horseshoe Bay,** and the airport (see Getting There, above, for specific bus lines). Often one bus will run along a route in one direction, while a bus of a different number will run in the other direction; ask a local or bus driver for assistance. Be forewarned: despite the good transit system, it takes longer to get around in Vancouver than you might expect.

BC Transit subdivides the city into three concentric zones for **fare** purposes. You can ride in BC Transit's central zone for two hours for $1.50 (seniors and ages 5-11 80¢) at all times. During peak hours (6:30-9:30am and 3-6:30pm), it costs $2 (seniors and ages 5-11 $1) to travel between two zones and $2.75 to travel through three zones. During off-peak hours, passengers pay only the one-zone price. **Day-passes** are $4.50, and transfers are free. Single fares, passes, and transfers are also good for the **SeaBus** and **SkyTrain** (running southeast from downtown to New Westminster). Timetables are available at 7-11 stores, public libraries, city halls, community centers, and the Vancouver Travel Infocentre (see Practical Information, above). To retrieve **lost property,** call 682-7887 (Mon.-Fri. 9:30am-5pm); otherwise stop by the lost property office in the Sky Train Stadium station.

BC Transit's **SeaBus** operates from the Granville Waterfront Station, at the foot of Granville St. in downtown Vancouver, to the Lonsdale Quay at the foot of Lonsdale Ave. in North Vancouver. The fares are the same as one-zone bus fares, and all transfers and passes are accepted. While waiting, study *The Buzzer,* BC Transit's weekly pamphlet on transit updates and community events, available on buses and wherever transit timetables are distributed.

Driving in Vancouver is a serious hassle. Rush hour begins at dawn and doesn't end until dusk. Beware of the 7-9:30am and 3-6pm restrictions on left turns and street parking; fines are steep. If you can't find parking at street level, look for underground lots (try the lot below Pacific Centre at Howe and W Georgia St., sometimes called "Garageland"). One-way streets are a curse throughout the city, but many maps have arrows indicating directions. The free **Tourism BC maps** don't cover the area outside the city center in detail; purchase the larger-scale street map, available from the Infocentre (see Practical Information, above) for $2.

If you have a car, consider using **Park 'n Ride** from New Westminster to circumvent the city's perpetual rush hour. Exit Hwy. 1 at New Westminster and follow signs for the Pattullo Bridge. Just over the bridge, you'll see signs for the Park 'n' Ride lot to your right, between Scott Rd. and 110th Ave. A bus will be waiting, where you can purchase tickets for the bus, the SkyTrain, and the SeaBus, or one-day passes for $4. Parking is free, and taking the SkyTrain downtown is faster than driving.

ACCOMMODATIONS

Greater Vancouver is a warren of bed and breakfast accommodations. Cheaper than in the United States, these private homes are usually comfortable and have personable proprietors. Rates average about $45 to $60 for singles and $55 to $75 for doubles. The visitors bureau has a four-page list of B&Bs. Several private agencies also match travelers with B&Bs, usually for a fee; get in touch with **Town and Country Bed and Breakfast** (731-5942) or **Best Canadian** (738-7207). Always call for reservations at least two days in advance.

Near the University of British Columbia

Vancouver International Hostel (HI-C), 1515 Discovery St. (224-3208), in Jericho Beach Park. Turn north off 4th Ave., following the signs for Marine Dr., or take bus #4 from Granville St. downtown. Granville is 1 block north of Seymour. Comely location in park, with a superlative view of the city from Jericho Beach. 285 beds in dorm rooms and 8 family rooms. Good cooking facilities, TV room, laundry facilities, and a convenient, expensive cafeteria. Ask about opportunities to spend a few hours cleaning in exchange for a room. 5-day limit enforced in summer, but flexible in other seasons. Registration 7:30am-midnight. Bedding $1.50. $14.50, non-members $18.50. Reserve at least 2 weeks in advance during summer. Rents top-quality mountain bikes for $20 per day.

University of British Columbia Conference Centre, 5959 Student Union Mall, Walter Gage Residence (822-1010), at the end of Vancouver's largest peninsula. Take bus #4 or 10 from the Granville Mall. Dorm-style rooms available May-Aug. Draws swarms of conventioneers in summer. Check-in after 2pm. Dorm-style singles with shared bath $19, doubles $38; B&B-style singles with shared bath $22, doubles $44; private singles $29, doubles $68.

Downtown and West End

Sylvia Hotel, 1154 Gilford St. (681-9321), at Beach St., 2 blocks from Stanley Park in the quiet, residential West End. Take bus #19 on Pender. Beautiful, ivy-shrouded building overlooking English Bay, with magnificent rooms to match. Singles and doubles $60-80. Additional cots $10. Reservations recommended.

YWCA, 580 Burrard St. (800-633-1424 or 662-8188), at Dunsmuir, 7 blocks from the bus depot. For women, male-female couples, families, and men (when the YMCA is full). Recently remodeled and clean, but expensive. High-quality sports facilities for female guests over age 15 (free). Kitchens on every other floor and cafeteria in basement. Staff on duty 24 hrs., but building locked at midnight; buzz for entry. No male visitors allowed upstairs. Some singles smaller than others, so ask to see a few before choosing. Singles $54. Doubles $66, with private bath $72. 10% discount for YWCA members, seniors, students, and groups. Weekly and monthly rates available when there are sufficient vacancies.

YMCA, 955 Burrard St. (681-0221), between Smithe and Nelson, 4 blocks south of the YWCA. Newly renovated. Concerned staff on duty 24 hrs. Pool, gymnasiums, ball courts, and weight rooms (free). All rooms have shared washrooms and showers. Cafeteria open Mon.-Fri. 7am-5pm, Sat. 8am-2pm. Singles $31. Doubles $47. Rooms with TV $3 extra. Weekly and monthly rates available when there are sufficient vacancies.

Dufferin Hotel, 900 Seymour St. (683-4251), at Smithe. Clean rooms, color TV. Safer than many other hotels in the area. No visitors after 11:30pm. Check-out noon. Singles $55. Doubles $60.

Nelson Place, 1006 Granville (681-6341), at Nelson St., 1 block from the Dufferin. Borders on Vancouver's small and tame red-light district. Great access to downtown. Small rooms with TV and bath. Singles $45. Doubles $50. $5 less in winter. Low-priced **restaurant** on premises. Buttermilk pancakes $3. Sandwiches $4-5.

South of Downtown

Paul's Guest House, 345 W 14th Ave. (872-4753), at Alberta, in Mt. Pleasant, not far from Vancouver General Hospital. Take bus #15. In a beautiful residential area. Shared baths. Complimentary full breakfast. Paul's is part of a network of B&Bs mainly in the Kitsilano and City Hall areas; if Paul's is booked, they can arrange your stay at one of these other B&Bs. Check-in before 11pm. Call ahead for reservations. Tidy and cozy singles $40. Doubles $50-60. Rates $5 lower in winter.

Vincent's Backpackers Hostel, 927 Main St. (682-2441), next to the VIA Rail station, above a big green store called "The Source." Take bus #3 (Main St.) or #8

(Fraser). Super-cheap. 1 washer, 1 dryer. Rents mountain bikes for $5 per day. Office open 8am-midnight. Check in before noon for your best shot at a bed. Shared rooms $10. Singles with shared bath $20. Doubles with shared bath $25. Weekly rates: shared rooms $60, singles $100, doubles $130. Pay before 10am of first morning for 20% discount on all rates.

Burnaby

Simon Fraser University, (291-4503) in Burnaby, 20km east of the city center. Take buses #10 or 14 north on Granville Mall and transfer to bus #135. 190 singles and 9 doubles available May-Aug. Shared bath. Call Mon.-Fri. 8:30am-midnight. Check-in 2-4:30pm. Check-out 11am. Singles $20. Doubles $40. Linen and towels: $6. No reservations necessary.

West Vancouver

Horseshoe Bay Motel, 6588 Royal Ave. (921-7454), in West Vancouver/Horseshoe Bay. Perfect location for passengers on the BC Ferry. Northwest of downtown. Singles $65. Doubles $70. Rooms $45 in winter. No extra charge for kitchens.

CAMPING

Greater Vancouver has few public campgrounds; campers must resort to expensive, private ones. The visitors bureau has a complete list of campgrounds outside Vancouver, but many are for RVs only. **Recreation Rentals** offers tents (see Practical Information), but the high cost makes it more sensible to spend the money on a bed at a hostel. The town of **White Rock,** 30 minutes southeast of Vancouver, has campgrounds with room for tents. Take bus #351 from Howe St. downtown.

Richmond RV Park, 6200 River Rd. (270-7878), near Holly Bridge in Richmond. Take Hwy. 99 to Westminster Hwy., then follow the signs. Unquestionably the best deal within 15km of downtown. Sites offer little privacy, but the showers and a soothing staff are sure to wash those cares right out of your hair. Sites $15, with hookups $19-21. Open April-Oct.

Hazelmere RV Park and Campground, 18843 8th Ave. (538-1167), in Surrey. Off Hwy. 99A, head east on 8th Ave. Quiet sites on the Campbell River with beach access. Showers 50¢. Sites for 1-2 people $14, with hookups $17; add $2 for each additional person, $1 for additional children ages 7-12. 6 and under free.

ParkCanada, 4799 Hwy. 17 (943-5811), in Delta, about 30km south of downtown. Take Hwy. 99 south to Tsawwassen Ferry Terminal Rd., then go east for 2.5km. The campground, located next to a waterslide park, has flush toilets and free showers, though the lines tend to be long. Sites $14, with hookups $19-21.

Dogwood Campground, 15151 112th Ave. (583-5585), 31km east on Hwy. 1 in Surrey. Flush toilets and free showers. Sites $17, with hookups $25.

FOOD

Steer clear of restaurants hawking "Canadian cuisine," an oxymoronic phrase conjuring up nightmarish visions of charred caribou meat soaked in maple syrup. The city's best eateries are the ethnic and natural-foods restaurants. Vancouver's **Chinatown** is second in size only to San Francisco's in North America, and the Indian neighborhoods along Main, Fraser, and 49th St. serve up spicy dishes. Groceries, shops, and restaurants also cluster around E Pender and Gore St., east of downtown.

Restaurants in the **West End** and **Gastown** compete for the highest prices in the city; the former caters to executives with expense accounts, while the latter bleeds money from tourists fresh off the cruise ships. Many of the greasy spoons along Davie and Denman St. stay open late or around the clock. **Buy-Low Foods** at 4th and Alma (597-9122), near the HI-C hostel in Point Grey, will help keep costs down. (Open Mon.-Sat. 9am-9pm, Sun. 9am-6pm.)

The **Granville Island Market,** southwest of downtown under the Granville Bridge, off W 4th Ave. across False Creek, intersperses trendy shops, art galleries, and restaurants with countless produce stands selling local and imported fruits and vegetables. Take bus #50 from Granville St. downtown. The range of delicacies offered by the stalls at the north end of the island will stun your palate. Slurp cherry-papaya yogurt soup (from an edible sugar waffle bowl), down cheese blintzes and potato knishes, or pick up some duck or shrimp stock to take back to the hostel's stew pot. The bakeries also sell day-old bread and bagels at half-price. Picnics tend to break out spontaneously in the parks, patios, and walkways that surround the market. (Market complex open daily 9am-6pm; Labor Day-Victoria Day Tues.-Sun. 9am-6pm.)

Downtown

Frannie's Deli, 325 Cambie (685-2928), at W Cordova St. near Gastown. Doesn't look like much from outside, or inside, but let your stomach be the judge. A variety of sandwiches, including a vegetarian ($3.25). Common ground for the casually- dressed. Open Mon.-Sat. 6:30am-6:30pm.

Chinatown

The Green Door, 111 E Pender St. (685-4194). Follow the alley off Columbia St. to find the hidden entrance. This wildly green establishment takes a prominent place in the annals of Vancouver hippie lore. Huge portions of slightly greasy Chinese seafood ($8-10). No liquor license. Open daily noon-10pm.

The Japanese Deli House Restaurant, 381 Powell (681-6484). Take-out deli with restaurant across the street. All-you-can-eat sushi ($10; take-out only). Open Mon. 11:30am-3pm, Tues.-Sat. 11:30am-8pm, Sun. 11:30am-6pm.

The Only Seafood Cafe, 20 E Hastings St. (681-6546), at Carrall St., within walking distance of downtown. Large portions of great seafood at decent prices and a reputation throughout the Northwest. They've been around since 1912, but they *still* haven't gotten around to building a rest room. Fried halibut steak ($10.70). Open Mon.-Sat. 11am-9pm, Sun. noon-7pm.

Phnom Penh, 244 E Georgia (682-1090), near Main St. Take bus #3 or #8 from downtown. Unquestionably the best Cambodian and Vietnamese food in Vancouver. The truly adventurous can sample the Phnomenal jellyfish salad ($9). The diverse menu can accommodate less daring tastebuds as well. Entrees $5-10. Open Wed.-Mon. 10am-9:30pm.

West End

Cafe La Brocca, 1098 Robson St. (687-0088), at Thurlow. Energetic staff must carbo-load on the pasta ($8.50-10.50). Breakfast served. Open daily 8am-10pm.

Cactus Club Cafe, 1136 Robson St. (687-3278). Trendy cafe and night spot for Vancouver's hippest residents. Many college students. Full vegetarian menu. Entress $5-10. Drink enough of the house brew, "Udder Ale," and maybe you'll be "persuaded" to buy one of the rubber cows that hangs from the ceiling. Open daily 11:30am-1am, some Fri. and Sat. till 2am.

Hamburger Mary's, 1202 Davie St. (687-1293), at Bute. That Northwest institution. Heralded for the best burgers in town, in many varieties ($4-7). Open Sun.-Thurs. 6am-3am, Fri.-Sat. 6am-4am.

Stephos, 1124 Davie St. (683-2555), at Thurlow. Much more elegant than The Souvlaki Place, and the prices are only slightly higher. Full *souvlaki* meal ($7-10), hummus and pita ($3.75), baklava ($2.75). Open daily 11:30am-11:30pm.

Near Stanley Park

Slice of Gourmet, 1152 Denman (689-1112). The pick for tantalizing pizza with original toppings. Try a huge, filling slice of the peppery potato or Devil's Delight pizza ($3.25). Open Sun.-Thurs. 11:30am-midnight, Fri.-Sat. 11:30am-1am.

The Souvlaki Place, 1181 Denman (689-3064). This Greek place pulsates with wailing Mediterranean music. *Spanikopita* ($3.25); *souvlaki* ($5). Open daily 11:30am-11pm.

Jumpstart Cafe, 825 Denman (688-6833). Vegetarian restaurant. Large assortment of vegan foods. Veggie Burger $3, Veggie Lasgna $4. Carrot juice $2.50. Open Mon.-Sat. 9am-6pm, Sun. 11am-4pm.

Commercial Drive

Nuff-Nice-Ness, 1861 Commercial Dr. (255-4211), at 3rd. Vegetable and meat patties ($1.87 each). Jerk chicken with salad and rice $6.25. Daily specials offered in the late afternoon for $5. Open Mon.-Fri. 11am-8pm, Sun. 1-6pm.

Nick's Spaghetti House, 631 Commercial Dr. (254-5633), between Georgia and Frances, in the Italian District. Take bus #20. An old restaurant under new management. Standard Italian food in a traditional atmosphere. The spaghetti is *magnifico* ($10+). Open Mon.-Thurs. 11:30am-11pm, Fri. 11:30am-midnight, Sat. 4pm-midnight, Sun. 4-10pm.

Cafe Du Soleil, 1393 Commercial Dr. (254-1145), near Kitchener. Romper Room meets Boulangerie: a veggie cafe serving breakfast all day, with lots of toys for the kids. 2 eggs, toast, and hashbrowns ($3.50). Mix-and-match sandwiches with soup ($5). Open Mon.-Sat. 8am-6pm, Sun. 8am-5pm.

Granville Island

Isadora's Cooperative Restaurant, 1540 Old Bridge Rd. (681-8816), 1 block on your right near the "Kids Only" complex. This socially conscious natural food restaurant sends its profits to community service organizations. For entertainment, watch the kids douse each other with garden hoses in the wading pool next door. Sandwiches $7, dinner entrees $10-13. *Khatsah lano* burger made with filet of salmon ($8). Open Mon.-Thurs. 7:30am-9pm, Fri.-Sun. 9am-9pm. Closed Mon. evenings in winter.

Kitsilano

The Naam, 2724 W 4th Ave. (738-7151), at Stephens. Take bus #4 or 7 from Granville. Vancouver's oldest natural-food restaurant. With a fireplace and patio, the Naam is a delight. Tofu-nut-beet burgers ($5.50), spinach enchiladas ($8.95), and salad bar ($1.25 per 100g). Live music nightly from 7-10pm. Open 24 hrs.

Nyala, 2930 W 4th Ave. (731-7899). Tasteful, festive environs can't upstage the authentic Ethiopian fare. Marinated chicken with ginger root and cardamon ($9.75). Vegetarian options ($8). All-you-can-eat vegetarian buffet ($8.50). Open Mon.-Tues. noon-3pm and 5pm-10:30pm, Wed. 5pm-10pm, Thurs.-Sat. noon-3pm and 5pm-10:30pm, Sun. 5pm-10pm.

Near Broadway and Cambie St.

Nirvana, 2313 Main St. (876-2911), at 7th. Take bus #8, #3, or #9. Come as you are. Smells like authentic, savory, and possibly spiritual Indian cuisine. Find or lose yourself in the chicken curry ($7.25) or vegetable *biryani* ($8.75). Open Mon.-Fri. 11:30am-11pm, Sat.-Sun. noon-11pm.

Tomato Fresh Food Cafe, 3305 Cambie (874-6020), at 17th. Several blocks south of downtown. Hope you like tomatoes. Try Tomato's tomato sandwich ($5.25) or the more exotic Santa Fe corn pie ($7). Great selection of fruit and vegetable…well, fruit…er…vegetable…drinks ($2.50-3.75). Open Tues.-Sat. 9am-10pm, Sun. 9am-3pm.

The Sitar, 564 W Broadway (879-4333), between Cambie and Ash. Take bus #10 or 14 from Granville. Standard Indian food in a standard Indian setting. You'll have a one-night love affair with the *tandoori* chicken ($9), *mulligatawny* ($3), or full dinners ($12). Lunch specials ($5). The curry cuts like a knife. Open Mon.-Sat. 11am-10:30pm, Sun. 4-10:30pm.

Singapore Restaurant, 546 W Broadway (874-6161), near Cambie. Take bus #10 or 14 from Granville. The mix of Malaysian, Chinese, and Indian cuisine corresponds to the tangled demographics of Singapore. Fried noodles ($6.26), prawns and ginger ($10.90), beef or chicken *satay* ($1.20 each). Lunch specials ($4.50). Open Mon.-Fri. 11am-2:30pm and 5-10pm, Sat. 11am-10pm, Sun. noon-10pm.

SIGHTS AND ACTIVITIES

Vancouver's attractions range from urbane architectural spectacles to serene parks and beaches.

World's Fair Grounds and Downtown

Expo '86 was the first world's fair to be held in two different locations. The **main grounds,** between Granville and Main St., are now gradually devolving into office space, housing for seniors, and a cultural center. The Canada Pavilion, now called **Canada Place,** is about ½km away and can be reached by SkyTrain from the main Expo site. The cavernous pavilion is a conventioneer's dream and an agoraphobe's nightmare; its roof, constructed to resemble gigantic sails, dominates the harbor. The shops and restaurants inside are outrageously expensive, but the promenades around the complex are terrific vantage points for gawking at one of the more than 200 luxury liners that dock here annually.

Also under the sails is the five-story **CN IMAX Theatre** (682-4629). The flat screen doesn't draw you in as much as the domed Omnimax screen, but it has unsurpassed image clarity with no peripheral distortion. So there. (Tickets $6.50-9.75, seniors and children $5.50-8.50. Open daily 11am-9pm.)

The real big-screen star of Expo '86 is the **Omnimax Theatre,** part of the **Science World** complex at 1455 Quebec St. (687-7832) on the Main St. stop of the Sky Train. Gazing on everything from asteroids to zephyrs, you will find yourself delightfully sucked into this celluloid wonderland. The 27m sphere is the largest, most technologically advanced theatre in the world. **Science World** also features more tangible hands-on exhibits for children. (Both attractions $12, seniors and children $8. Only Science World $8 and $5. Tickets for the Omnimax alone can be purchased after 4pm for $9. Shows Sun.-Fri. 10am-5pm, Sat. 10am-9pm. Call 875-6664 for details.)

One block south of Chinatown on Main St. at 777 S Pacific Blvd. is the domed **BC Place Stadium.** Vancouver's so-called "mushroom in bondage" is home to the Canadian Football League's BC Lions. Don't miss the **Terry Fox Memorial** at the entrance to the stadium, erected in honor of the Canadian hero who, after losing a leg to cancer, ran over 5300km across Canada to raise money for medical research. Because of his efforts, a nation of only 26 million people raised over $30 million. A few blocks to the north, at 8 W Penter St., is squeezed the **world's skinniest building.** In 1912, the city expropriated all but six feet of Chang Toy's land in order to expand the street. In a fit of stubbornness, he decided to build on the land anyhow. Currently, the 100 ft. by 6 ft. building is home to Jack Chow's Insurance Company, which might operate on a very slim profit margin.

Newly renovated, the **Lookout!** at 555 W Hastings St. (689-0421), offers fantastic 360° views of the city. Tickets are expensive!, but they're good for the whole day ($6!, seniors $5!, students $4!); after passing a pleasant and panoramic afternoon there, you can leave and come back for the night skyline (open daily 8:30am-10:30pm, in winter 8:30am-9pm; 50% discount with HI membership or receipt from the Vancouver International Hostel).

The **Vancouver Art Gallery,** 750 Hornby St. (682-5621), in Robson Sq., has a small but well-presented collection of classical and contemporary art and photography. An entire floor devoted to the works of Canadian artists features British Columbian **Emily Carr's** surreal paintings of trees and totem poles. The Gallery compensates for its limited holdings with innovative exhibitions. Free tours are frequently given for large groups; just tag along. (Open Mon.-Wed. and Fri.-Sat. 10am-5pm, Thurs. 10am-9pm, Sun. noon-5pm. $5, seniors and students $2.50. Thurs. 5-9pm free, but donations requested.)

Gastown and Chinatown

Gastown is a revitalized turn-of-the-century district rightly disdained by most locals as an expensive tourist trap. The area is named for "Gassy Jack" Deighton, the glib con man who opened Vancouver's first saloon here in 1867. In 1886, a fire leveled

1000 buildings, including the infamous saloon, in 45 minutes. In the 1960s, community groups led the fight for restoration. Today the area overflows with tourist-oriented craft shops, nightclubs, restaurants, and boutiques. It's a nice place to look at, but you wouldn't want to buy anything there. Take the time to stroll along **Water Street,** and stop to listen to the rare steam-powered clock on the corner of Cambie St. The first one in the world, it eerily whistles the notes of the Westminster Chimes on the quarter-hour.

Gastown is a fairly long walk from downtown or a short ride on bus #22 along Burrard St. to Carrall St. It is bordered by Richards St. to the west, Columbia St. to the east, Hastings St. to the south, and the waterfront to the north.

Chinatown, just east of Gastown, is within walking distance of downtown. You can also take bus #22 on Burrard St. northbound to Pender and Carrall St., and return by bus #22 westbound on Pender St. The neighborhood is relatively safe and has some great food, but the area between downtown and Chinatown is definitely sketchy. You will feel safest visiting the area in a small group. At night, women should not enter the area aimlessly or alone.

Parks

Stanley Park

Founded in 1889, the 1000-acre **Stanley Park,** at the tip of the downtown peninsula, is a testament to the foresight of Vancouver's urban planners. Surrounded by a seawall promenade, the thickly wooded park is laced with **cycling** and **hiking** trails. It contains a few restaurants, tennis courts, the **Malkin Bowl** (an outdoor theater), and fully equipped swimming beaches. The **Brockton Oval,** on the park's small eastern peninsula of Brockton Point, is a cinder running track, with hot showers and changing rooms. Nature walks are given May and Sept. Tues. at 10am, and July-Aug. at 7pm. They start from the Lost Lagoon bus loop (in the morning in May, June, and Sept.) or from Lumberman's Arch Water Park (all other times). Note the **orca fountain** by noted Haida sculptor Bill Reid.

Lost Lagoon, an artificial lake next to the Georgia St. entrance, is lively with fish and birds, including the rare trumpeter swan. Exotic aquatic species swim the lengths of their glass habitats at the **Vancouver Aquarium** (682-1118), on the eastern side of the park not far from the entrance. The British Columbian, Tropical, and Amazonian Halls are named for the geographical climes they skillfully replicate. The marine mammal complex features orca and Beluga whales in a sideshow revue. Weather permitting, the aquarium stages several performances per day; on rainy days, you'll have to settle for fish flicks. (Open daily 9:30am-8pm. $10, seniors and students $8.50, under 12 $6.50.)

Stanley Park is small and crowded, but free. The **zoo** next door is worth visiting just to see the maniacal monkeys taunt their poor neighboring polar bears. The brass at the zoo plan to phase out exotic species and replace them with animals indigenous to the region (open daily 9:30am-dusk). Without a doubt, the best way to see the park is on a **bike** (see Practical Information: Bike Rental). If you don't feel like biking or hoofing your way around, horse-drawn carriages will take you on a 50-minute tour (every ½ hr., daily 10:30am-4pm; $10, students and seniors $8, ages 3-12 $6, families of 3 or more $30). Call 681-5115 for more information.

Vanier Park

During the summer, a tiny **ferry** (684-7781) carries passengers from the Aquatic Centre across False Creek to Vanier (van-YAY) Park and its museum complex. (Ferries daily, every 15 min. 10am-8pm. Fare $1.25, youth 50¢.) Another **ferry** runs from the Maritime Museum in Vanier Park to Granville Island ($2.50). Vanier Park can also be reached by bus #22, heading south on Burrard St. from downtown. Once you reach the park, visit the circular **Vancouver Museum,** 1100 Chestnut St. (736-4431), fronted by an abstract crab fountain. The museum displays artifacts from Native Canadian and American cultures in the Pacific Northwest and several rotating exhibits. (Open daily 10am-9pm, Oct.-April Tues.-Sun. 10am-5pm. $5, students, seniors, and kids under 18 $2.50, families $10.) The museum also sponsors dance performances and workshops during the summer.

Housed in the same building, the **H. R. MacMillan Planetarium** (736-4431) runs up to four different star shows per day. **Laser shows** set to rock music illuminate the roof (Tues.-Sun. Star shows $5, laser shows $7, seniors free on Tues.; call for showtimes and programs.) The adjacent **Gordon Southam Observatory** is also open to the public, weather permitting. (Open Fri. 7-11pm, Sat.-Sun. noon-5pm and 7-11pm. Call ahead at 738-2855 to check times. Free.)

The **Maritime Museum** (257-8300) exhibits photographs and models that trace the growth of Vancouver's harbor and port. An exception to the otherwise pacific atmosphere is the well-restored *St. Roch*. This 1928 Royal Canadian Mounted Police Arctic patrol service vessel gained its fame during WWII, when it became the first ship to negotiate the Northwest Passage through the Arctic. The boat is displayed in its hulking entirety, and guided tours of its Leviathan hull are given daily. (Open daily 10am-5pm. $5, seniors, students, and under 13 $2.50, families $10. Tues. free for seniors. Combination tickets to the Maritime Museum, Vancouver Museum, and Planetarium available.) The Maritime Museum displays more wooden boats in the **Heritage Harbour.**

More Parks

The **Van Dusen Botanical Garden,** 37th Ave. and Oak St. (266-7194), has Floral collections ranging from a Sino-Himalayan garden to a growth of heather to an indoor exhibit of Japanese bonsai trees. The garden is also the site of summer concerts and craft shows, as well as special days for seniors and people with disabilities. Take bus #17 from Granville Mall. (Open daily 10am-9pm; winter 10am-4pm. $5.50, seniors and children $3, families $10.)

Only a few blocks away, **Queen Elizabeth Park,** at 33rd Ave. and Cambie St. (872-5513), has metamorphosed from a quarry into an ornamental sunken garden. Take bus #15 from Burrard St. Atop the hill, the **Bloedel Conservatory** gathers a spray of tropical plants and birds together into a geodesic dome overlooking the city center. (Open daily 10am-8pm; winter 10am-5pm. $4, seniors and ages 6-18 $2.)

The **Dr. Sun Yat-Sen Classical Chinese Garden,** 578 Carrall St. (689-7133), is yet another escape from urban bustle. Designed and built by artisans brought to Vancouver from China, the garden boasts many imported plantings and carvings. (Open daily 10am-6pm, winter 10:30am-4pm. $4.50, seniors, students, and children $3, families $10.) Six tours of the grounds depart almost hourly from 10:30am until 4:30pm.

Beaches

Most of Vancouver's beaches are patrolled by lifeguards from Victoria Day (late May) to Labor Day daily from 11:30am to 9pm. Even if you don't dip a foot in the cold waters, you can frolic in true West Coast spirit in Sport BC's weekly **Volleyball Tournament,** featuring all levels of competition. Scare up a team at the hostel, then call 737-3096 to find out where to go to make your opponents eat leather.

For a large city, Vancouver has remarkably clean beaches. Follow the western side of the Stanley Park seawall south to **Sunset Beach Park** (738-8535), a strip of grass and beach that extends all the way to the Burrard Bridge. At the southern end of Sunset Beach is the **Aquatic Centre,** 1050 Beach Ave. (665-3424), a public facility with a 50m indoor saltwater pool, sauna, gymnasium, and diving tank. (Open Mon.-Thurs. 7am-10pm, Sat. 8am-9pm, Sun. 11am-9pm; pool opens Mon.-Thurs. at 7am. Gym use $3.50, pool use $3.)

Kitsilano Beach (731-0011), known to residents of Vancouver as "Kits," on the other side of Arbutus St. from Vanier, is a local favorite. Its heated outdoor saltwater pool has lockers and a snack bar. (Pool open June-Sept. Mon.-Fri. 7am-9pm, Sat.-Sun. 10am-8:30pm. $3.25, seniors $1.60, children $2.10.)

Students hang at **Jericho Beach,** to the west, less heavily used than Kits Beach, despite the massive hostel (see Accommodations). Jericho has free showers. North

Marine Dr. runs along the beach, and a great cycling path at the edge of the road leads to the westernmost edge of the UBC campus. Bike and hiking trails cut through the campus and crop its edges. From the UBC entrance, several marked trails lead down to the unsupervised, inauspicious **Wreck Beach**.

Universities

The high point of a visit to the **University of British Columbia (UBC)** is the university's **Museum of Anthropology**, 6393 NW Marine Dr. (822-3825 for a recording, 822-5087 for an operator). To reach the campus, take bus #4 or #10 from Granville. A high-ceilinged glass and concrete building provides a dramatic setting for the museum's totems and other massive sculptures crafted by the indigenous peoples of the Northwest coast. The *Guide to the UBC Museum of Anthropology* ($1), available at the entrance desk, sorts out the cultural threads of the various nations that produced these works; much of this information does not appear on exhibit labels. Be sure to find the renowned work "The Raven and the First Man," by Bill Reid, an artistic allusion to the Haida creation myth. Hour-long guided walks will help you find your way through the maze of times and places. (Open Tues. 11am-9pm, Mon. and Wed.-Sun. 11am-5pm. Sept.-June closed Mondays. $5, seniors and students $2.50, families $12, under 6 free. Tues. after 5pm free.)

Behind the museum, in a weedy courtyard designed to simulate the Pacific coastal islands, the free **Outdoor Exhibit** displays memorial totems and a mortuary house built by the Haida nation. Each carved figure represents one aspect of the ancestral heritage of the honored dead. Even if you don't make it inside the museum itself, don't miss this silent soliloquy of the Haida culture.

Caretakers of the **Nitobe Memorial Garden** (822-4208 and 822-6038), to the south of the museum across Marine Dr., have fashioned a small immaculate garden in traditional **Japanese** style. (Open daily 10am-6pm; Sept.-June 10am-3pm. $2, seniors and students $1.25. Wed. free.) The **Asian Centre**, 1871 West Mall (822-2746), near the gardens, often showcases free exhibits of Asian-Canadian art. The **Asian Centre Library** contains the largest collection of Asian materials in Canada. (Open Mon.-Fri. 9am-5pm. Call for a schedule of events.)

The **Main Garden,** in the southwest corner of the UBC campus at 16th Ave. and SW Marine Dr., may not be worth the bother, especially to the non-horticulturist. Although pebbles outnumber pistils, the **Physick Gardens** are fascinating; signs alert you to the poisonous nature of some of the plants. In the 30-acre **Asian Garden,** through the tunnel and across the street, quiet paths lead past blue Himalayan poppies and rhododendrons. For more specific information, as well as general and tour information on all the gardens, you can call the Botanical Garden office weekdays 8:30am to 4:30pm. (Open daily 10am-6pm. $3.75, students and seniors $1.50. Wed. free.) Call the **Botanical Garden** for information (822-4208).

Large maps at entrances to UBC's campus indicate other points of interest and bus stops. In addition to its gardens, UBC has a swimming pool open to the public (except in summer in summer) in the **Aquatic Centre** (822-4521), a free **Fine Arts Gallery** (822-2759), free daytime and evening concerts (822-3113), and a museum of geology (822-5586). (Museums and pool open Mon.-Fri. 8:30am-4:30pm.) To arrange a walking **tour** of the campus between May and August, call 822-2211.

Vancouver's other university is the relatively new and somewhat isolated **Simon Fraser University (SFU),** in Burnaby, east of Vancouver. Built in 1965, the campus blends architecture and landscaping with soothing results; the **Main Mall** and **Academic Quadrangle** alone are worth the 35-minute bus ride to the top of "the hill." Take bus #10 or 14 to Kootenay Loop, then the #135 to SFU. The **Athletic Services Department** (291-3611) can fill you in on the details of using the university's gyms and pools, and the **Outdoor Recreation Office** (291-4434; open Mon.-Fri. 10am-4pm) will give you **maps** for the numerous hiking trails around the campus. Free **walking tours** leave the Administration Bldg. every hour on the half-hour daily 10:30am to 3:30pm. Call 291-3439 or 291-3210 for more information.

The Pub in the Main Mall at SFU has the cheapest beer on the lower mainland and a great atmosphere. (Open Mon.-Fri. 9pm-midnight, Sat.-Sun. 9pm-4am.) To find out what else is happening around campus, grab the free weekly *The Peak,* including an extensive arts section on city happenings, from drop-boxes scattered around campus.

Shopping

With pseudo-European delicatessens and shops, the **Robsonstrasse** shopping district, on Robson St. between Howe and Broughton St., tempts tourists to throw around their money under kaleidoscopic awnings. The recently renovated **Pacific Centre,** 700 W Georgia St., is near the Granville SkyTrain station. For more reasonable prices and "idiosyncratic" offerings, stroll down Commercial Dr. for funky stuff, or browse through the numerous boutiques and second-hand clothing stores lining 4th Ave. and Broadway between Burrard and Alma.

Granville Mall, on Granville Ave. between Smithe and Hastings St., is Vancouver's pedestrian and bus mall. From Hastings St. to the Orpheum Theatre, most shops and restaurants on the mall cater to young professionals and business executives on their power-lunch hours. Beyond W Georgia St., the mall takes a much-needed youthful twist as expensive department stores defer to theaters, leather shops, and raucous record stores.

A few blocks to the west, the **Harbour Centre,** 555 W Hastings St., flaunts a mall with distinctly non-budget restaurants, and a fantastic **skylift** providing uplifting views of the cityscape. If you are dying to fill your matching luggage set with chic purchases, head to the ritziest mall west of Long Island: the **Park Royal Shopping Centre** on Marine Dr. in West Vancouver. Take bus #250, 251, or 252 on Georgia St. downtown.

ENTERTAINMENT

To keep abreast of the entertainment scene, pick up a copy of the weekly *Georgia Straight* or the new monthly *AF Magazine,* both free at newsstands and record stores. The 25¢ *West Ender* lists entertainment in that lively neighborhood, and also reports on community issues, while the free *Angles* serves the city's growing gay readership. The free *Common Ground,* a New Age quarterly, lists and advertises restaurants, services, events, bookstores, and workshops. Music of all genres is enjoyed in Vancouver's pubs and clubs; both *Georgia Straight* and the less-thorough *West Ender* have the rundown. Most clubs and bars shut down at 2am.

The Fringe Cafe, 3124 W Broadway (738-6977), in Kitsilano. Working-class crowd mixes with UBC students to create one of the hottest bars in town. Open daily noon-1am.

The Arts Club Lounge, Granville Island (687-1354). Sophiste divas frequent this bar between rehearsals and performances at the theatre. Have a mixed drink ($4.50-6.50) on the terrace overlooking False Creek. Live music (with a $5 cover) Wed., Fri., and Sat. nights. Open Mon.-Sat. 9pm-2am.

Graceland, 1250 Richards St. (688-2648), downtown. Warehouse space pulses to house music on Fri. and Sat. nights, reggae on Wed. Open Mon.-Sat. noon-2am, Sun. noon-midnight.

Celebrities, 1022 Davie St. (689-3180), downtown. Very big, very hot, and very popular with Vancouver's gay community. Sun. features techno music, Mon. spins classic disco. Open Mon.-Sat. 9pm-2am, Sun. 9pm-midnight.

Luv-A-fair, 1275 Seymour St. (685-3288), downtown. Trendy dance space pipes alternative music into the ears of black-clad clubsters. Experiment with the live underground bands Wed. night. Open Mon.-Sat. 9pm-2am, Sun. 9am-midnight.

Hungry Eye, 23 W Cordova St., downtown. This new club prides itself on a wide-ranging selection of live music nightly. Heavy rock, Celtic, world beat. Big dance floor. Beer and drinks from $3.50.

The Odyssey, 1251 Howe St. (689-5956), downtown. Quiet, conversational bar and hangout, also popular with the local gay community. Open Sun.-Thurs. 11am-midnight. Fri.-Sat. 11am-2am.

The **Vancouver Symphony Orchestra** (VSO, 684-9100) plays in the refurbished **Orpheum Theater,** 884 Granville St. (280-4444). The VSO ticketline is 280-3311. The 52-year-old **Vancouver Bach Choir** (921-8012) sometimes performs with the VSO in the Orpheum. Smaller groups, such as the Warblin' Rosen Trio, appeal to a variety of musical tastes. Check the *West Ender* for listings.

Robson Square Conference Centre, 800 Robson St. (661-7373), sponsors events almost daily during the summer and weekly the rest of the year, either on the plaza at the square or in the Centre itself. Their concerts, theater productions, exhibits, lectures, symposia, and films are all free or nearly free. The Centre's monthly brochure, *What's Happening at Robson Square,* is available from the visitors bureau or establishments in the square.

Vancouver theatre is renowned throughout Canada. The **Arts Club Theatre** (687-1644) hosts big-name theatre and musicals, and the **Theatre in the Park** program (687-0174 for ticket information), in Stanley Park's Malkin Bowl, plays a summer season of musical comedy. The annual **Vancouver Shakespeare Festival** (734-0194; June-Aug. in Vanier Park) often needs volunteer ticket-takers and program-sellers, who work for free admission to the critically acclaimed shows. **UBC Summer Stock** (822-2678) puts on four plays in summer at the **Frederick Wood Theatre.**

The **Ridge Theatre,** 16th Ave. and Arbutus (738-6311), often shows European films and works that more commercial theaters may bypass ($6). The **Hollywood Theatre,** 3123 W Broadway (738-3211), also shows art films. (Tickets Mon. $2.25, Tues.-Sun. $3.25, children $2.50. Doors open at 7:30pm.) **Cinema Simon Fraser,** Images Theatre, SFU (291-4869), charges $2.50 for a variety of films (open Sept.-May). The **Paradise,** 919 Granville (681-1732), shows first-run movies (triple-features on weekends) for $2.75.

Cultural activities at Vancouver's universities never cease. The **SFU Centre for the Arts** (291-3514) offers both student and guest-professional theater, primarily from September to May. For **UBC's** activities, call Public Events Information at 822-3131 or pick up a free copy of *Ubyssey.* UBC's film series (228-3698) screens high-quality flicks on Thursday and Friday nights for $2.50.

EVENTS

The famed **Vancouver Folk Music Festival** jams in mid-July in Jericho Park. For three days the best acoustic performers in North America give concerts and workshops. Tickets can be purchased for each day or for the whole weekend. (Tickets $26 per evening, $26 per weekday, $39 per weekend day, $70 per weekend if purchased in advance. Prices increase at the gate.) Buy a whole-weekend ticket before Christmas and pay that year's price; early birds who purchase their tickets before mid-June receive a substantial discount. For more details, contact the festival at 3271 Main St., Vancouver V6V 3M6 (879-2931).

The annual **Du Maurier International Jazz Festival Vancouver** (682-0706) in the third week of June features over five hundred performers and bands such as Randy Wanless's Fab Forty and Charles Eliot's Largely Cookie. Enjoy 10 days of hot jazz. Call 682-0706 or write to 435 W Hastings, Vancouver V6V 1L4 for details. Ask about the free concerts at the Plaza, in Gastown, and on Granville Island.

Vancouver's Chinese community celebrates its heritage on **Chinese New Year** (usually early to mid-Feb.). Fireworks, music, parades, and dragons highlight the event. The **Folkfest** (736-1512) in early June features two weeks of merriness in Gastown and Robson Sq. All the festivities are free. Italian- and Greek-Canadians whoop it up in July and the last week of June, respectively. Food stands, musical performers, carnivals, and more food stands cluster around each community's center.

The Vancouver Maritime Museum in Vanier Park (see Sights and Activities, above) hosts the annual **Captain Vancouver Day** (257-8300) in mid-June to commemorate the 1792 exploration of Canada's west coast by Captain George Vancouver. Thrills include free tours of the Heritage Harbour, tall ships, boat model building, sled dog rides, and appearances by the **Shanty Singers.** In mid-July, the **Vancouver Sea Festival** (684-3378) schedules four days of parades, concerts, sporting events, fireworks, and salmon barbecues. All events take place in English Bay at the BC Enterprise complex and are free, but you have to pay for the salmon. The headline attraction is the notorious **Nanaimo to Vancouver Bathtub Race,** a porcelain journey across the rough waters of the Strait of Georgia.

■ NEAR VANCOUVER

NORTH

For an easy hike with fantastic views of the city, take the SeaBus to **Lynn Canyon Park** in North Vancouver. The **suspension bridge** here is free and uncrowded, unlike its more publicized twin in Capilano Canyon. A walk across the "world's longest suspension footbridge" in Capilano will cost the gullible tourist $10. Try Lynn instead. Take bus #228 from the North Vancouver SeaBus terminal and walk the ½km to the bridge. While there, take in the exhibits of the **Lynn Canyon Ecology Centre** (987-5922; open daily 10am-5pm, Dec.-Jan. Mon.-Fri. 10am-5pm; free).

Grouse Mountain is the ski resort closest to downtown Vancouver and has the crowds to prove it. Take bus #246 from the North Vancouver SeaBus terminal; at Edgemont and Ridgewood transfer to bus #232, which will drop you off at the **Supersky Ride,** an aerial tramway. (Tram runs from 9am to 10pm. $14.50, students $12.50, ages 13-18 $9.25, ages 6-12 $6, entire family $35.) The slopes are lit until 10:30pm from November to May, and the tram ride is popular with sightseers in summer. On sunny days, helicopter tours leave from the top of the mountain, starting at $30 per person. For more information contact Grouse Mountain Resorts, 6400 Nancy Greene Way, North Vancouver V7R 4K9 (984-0661, ski report 986-6262). Ski rental is $21 per day, no deposit required. Lift tickets are $28.

For a secluded and obscure park, head out across the Lions Gate Bridge from Stanley Park along North Marine Dr. to **Lighthouse Park.** Getting there makes for a fantastic and challenging bicycle daytrip; it's a 50km round-trip from downtown, and the inclines can be daunting. This is not for puny pedalers. Bus #250 from downtown will take you right to the park's entrance. From there, numerous trails with peaceful water views will take you all over the 185-acre preserve. The point is punctuated by one of the few remaining human-operated lighthouses, and free guided tours (the only way to the top) ascend on the hour. (Open Wed.-Sun. 11am-5pm.)

Puff along on the **Royal Hudson Steam Locomotive** (688-7246), operated by BC Rail. After a two-hour journey along the coast from Vancouver to Squamish (the gateway to Garibaldi Provincial Park), passengers are loosed for 90 minutes to browse in town before they head back. (Excursions June-Sept. 20 Wed.-Sun. $31.31, seniors and ages 12-18 $27.57, ages 5-11 $8.88.) The train departs once per day at 10am from the BC Rail terminal, 1311 W 1st St., across the Lions Gate Bridge in North Vancouver. Return is around 4pm. Reservations are required.

Fifty-two km north of Vancouver (on the way to Whistler) is the **BC Museum of Mining** in Britannia Beach (688-8735 or 896-2233). An electric mine train pumps passengers through an old copper artery into the mountain that poured out the most metal in the British Empire: over 590,000 metric tons. (Open May-Oct. daily 10am-4:30pm, Sept.-Oct. Wed.-Sun. 10am-4:30pm. $8, seniors and students $6.50, children under 5 free, families $30; pre-booked $1 off.)

Whistler lies about 110km north of Vancouver on Hwy. 99. Expensive development projects have shaken the peaceful foundation of this ski resort town. It seems that only the beautiful hostel allows Whistler to remain on the budget-skiers' itinerary. **Whistler Hostel (HI-C),** 5678 Alta Lake Rd. (932-5492), is a timber cabin with a kitchen, wood stove, sauna, ski tuning room, and ski lockers. They offer free use of their canoes in Alta Lake (i.e. the backyard). (Check-in 8-10am and 5-10pm; $14.50, Canadian non-members $20, international non-members $18. Reservations

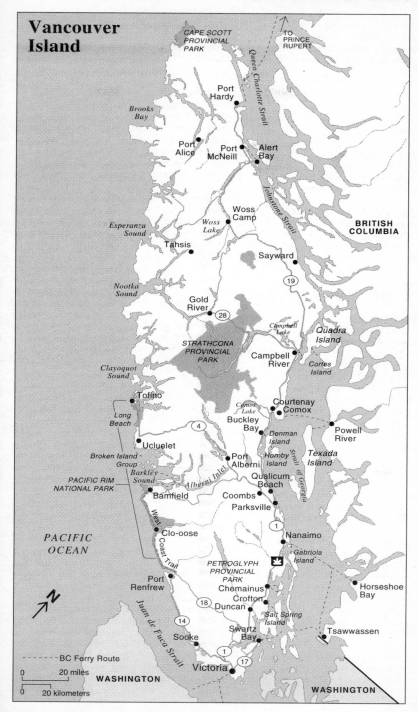

Vancouver Island

CAPE SCOTT
PROVINCIAL
PARK

Queen Charlotte Strait

TO PRINCE
RUPERT

Port
Hardy

Brooks
Bay

Port
Alice

Port
McNeill

Alert
Bay

Johnstone Strait

BRITISH
COLUMBIA

Woss
Camp

Woss
Lake

Esperanza
Sound

Tahsis

Sayward

19

Nootka
Sound

Gold
River

28

Campbell
Lake

Quadra
Island

STRATHCONA
PROVINCIAL
PARK

Campbell
River

Cortes
Island

Clayoquot
Sound

Tofino

Comox
Lake

Courtenay
Comox

Long
Beach

Buckley
Bay

Denman
Island

Powell
River

4

Ucluelet

Broken Island
Group

Port
Alberni

Homby
Island

Texada
Island

PACIFIC RIM
NATIONAL PARK

Barkley
Sound

Qualicum
Beach

Strait of Georgia

Bamfield

Alberni Inlet

Coombs

Parksville

PACIFIC
OCEAN

West Coast Trail

Clo-oose

1

Nanaimo

Gabriola
Island

PETROGLYPH
PROVINCIAL
PARK

Horseshoe
Bay

Port
Renfrew

Chemainus

Crofton

Duncan

18

Salt Spring
Island

14

Sooke

Swartz
Bay

Tsawwassen

1

17

Victoria

Juan de Fuca Strait

------- BC Ferry Route

0   20 miles

0   20 kilometers

WASHINGTON

WASHINGTON

advised Nov.-March.) Outfitters in town have mountain bikes, canoes, kayaks, and ski equipment for rent. For those seeking some solitude, **hiking** in nearby **Garibaldi Provincial Park** is an option to explore. **BC Rail** stops at Whistler on its route from Vancouver and will stop at the hostel if asked.

EAST AND SOUTH

To the east, the town of **Deep Cove** maintains the salty atmosphere of a fishing village. Sea otters and seals cavort on the pleasant Indian Arm beaches. Take bus #210 from Pender St. to the Phibbs Exchange on the north side of Second Narrows Bridge. From there, take bus #211 or 212 to Deep Cove. **Cates Park,** at the end of Dollarton Hwy. on the way to Deep Cove, has popular swimming and scuba waters and is a good destination for a day bike trip out of Vancouver. Bus #211 also leads to **Mount Seymour Provincial Park.** Trails leave from Mt. Seymour Rd., and a paved road winds the 8km to the top. One hundred campsites ($8 per site) are available, and the skiing is superb.

The **Reifel Bird Sanctuary** on Westham Island, 16km south of Vancouver, is just northwest of the Tsawwassen ferry terminal. Bus #601 from Vancouver will take you to the town of **Ladner,** 1½km east of the sanctuary. Two-hundred forty species of birds live in the 850 acres of marshlands, and spotting towers are set up for long-term birdwatching. (Open daily 9am-4pm; nominal fee $3.25, seniors and children $1.) For information contact the **BC Waterfowl Society** at 946-6980.

VANCOUVER ISLAND

Vancouver Island stretches almost 500km along continental Canada's southwest coast, and is one of only two points in Canada extending south of the 49th parallel. The cultural and administrative capital of the island is Victoria, on its extreme southern tip. Victorians seem forthright about their British roots, and the city basks in Englishness.

The Trans-Canada Hwy., approaching the end of its 8000-km trek, leads north from Victoria to Nanaimo, the social hub of the central region. Nanaimo's heritage combines aspects of Native Canadian culture and Welsh coal-miner society, with a dash of Anglo-Canadian pastry chefs' cooking thrown in. Pacific Rim National Park offers some of the most rugged hiking in British Columbia. Beyond Nanaimo, the towns shrink in size. Port Alberni, at the tip of the Alberni Inlet, and Campbell River, along Hwy. 19, are homebases for sublime hiking and fishing; some of the world's largest salmon have met their smoker here. Campbell River guards the entrance to triangle-shaped Strathcona Provincial Park. Hornby Island, off the island's eastern side, is a remarkable post-hippie settlement. Continuing along Rte. 19 into the northern third of Vancouver Island, known to the residents as "North Island," pickups abound and crumpets become clamburgers.

■■■ VICTORIA

The sun set on the British Empire years ago, but Victoria still dresses up and marches to the beat of a bygone era. Set among the rough-hewn logging and fishing towns of Vancouver Island, the capital of British Columbia demonstrates a reserve and propriety worthy of its name. Tourist-filled double-decker buses decorated with the Union Jack meander through the streets. Decked in kilt and sporran, bagpiper ply their trade at the corner of the stately stone Parliament Buildings. The ivy-shawled Empress Hotel, also named for the dour Queen, gazes regally at its own image in the water. On warm summer days, Anglophilic residents take tea on the lawns of Tudor-style homes in the suburbs.

Despite Victoria's refined image, citizens are not at all ashamed of the ornery prospectors who swilled beer in front of rowdy brothels on their way to the Cariboo

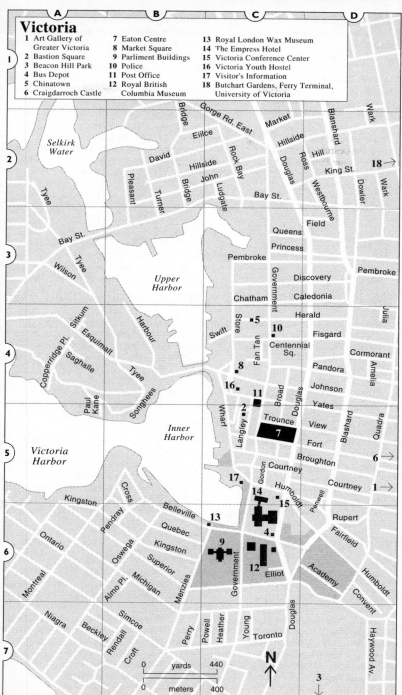

Victoria

1 Art Gallery of
 Greater Victoria
2 Bastion Square
3 Beacon Hill Park
4 Bus Depot
5 Chinatown
6 Craigdarroch Castle
7 Eaton Centre
8 Market Square
9 Parliment Buildings
10 Police
11 Post Office
12 Royal British
 Columbia Museum
13 Royal London Wax Museum
14 The Empress Hotel
15 Victoria Conference Center
16 Victoria Youth Hostel
17 Visitor's Information
18 Butchart Gardens, Ferry Terminal,
 University of Victoria

mines during the 1858 gold rush. The Hudson's Bay Company moved its western headquarters here because the site of its former headquarters in Astoria, Oregon, became U.S. property. When the Canadian Pacific Railway reached the Pacific Coast, Victoria managed to land an additional stretch across the Georgia Strait from Vancouver, and the city stole Vancouver's distinction as Canada's western railroad terminus. The railroad pipe-dream was never fully realized, however, and Victoria did not undergo industrialization as expected, much to its own benefit. Instead of pollution and ugly factory chimneys, Victoria has 250,000 well-heeled citizens who delight in the blessedly un-British annual rainfall of only 27 in. per year.

PRACTICAL INFORMATION AND ORIENTATION

Visitors Information: Tourism Victoria, 336 Government St., Victoria V8W 1T3 (382-2127), on the corner of Wharf St. An unbelievable number of pamphlets on the area. Open daily 9am-9pm; winter daily 9am-5pm.

VIA Rail, 450 Pandora St. (383-4324 for departure/arrival information; 800-561-8630 for general information and tickets). Near the Inner Harbour.

Bus Service: Pacific Coast Lines (PCL) and its affiliate, **Island Coach Lines,** 700 Douglas St. at Belleville (385-4411). Connects all major points and most minor ones, though fares can be steep. To: Nanaimo (7 per day, $15.75); Vancouver (11 per day, $22); Seattle (daily 10am, $28.60). Lockers $2 per hour.

BC Ferry, 656-0757 for a recording, 386-3431 for an operator between 7am-10pm. Between Swartz Bay (Victoria) and Tsawwassen (Vancouver), 20 per day 5:30am-10pm $6.25, bikes $2.50, cars $24.50. Between Tsawwassen and Nanaimo (north Vancouver Island), 10 per day 7am-9pm, same rates. Take bus #70 ($2) to reach the ferry terminal.

Washington State Ferries, 381-1551. From Sidney, BC to Anacortes, WA, via the San Juan Islands: 2 per day in summer, 1 per day in winter. Buy your ticket straight through to Anacortes and stop over in the San Juans for as long as you like; you can rejoin the ferry at any point for no charge as long as you continue traveling eastward (see page 43). Take bus #70 ($1.75) to the ferry terminal.

Victoria Clipper, 254 Belleville St. (382-8100). The only direct ferry service from Victoria to Seattle. April 15-June 5, 2 per day; June 6-Sept. 27, 4 per day; Sept. 28-Dec., 1 per day. Fares vary by season: one way $69, round-trip $92.

Black Ball Transport, 430 Belleville St. (386-2202). Connects Victoria with Port Angeles, WA. Mid-May to late Sept., 4 per day; early Oct. to late Nov. and mid-March-mid-May, 2 per day; Dec.-mid-March, 1 per day. $8.50, car and driver $34, ages 5-11 $4.25. Off-season $6, car and driver $24.

Victoria Regional Transit: 382-6161.

Car Rental: Sigmar Rent-A-Car, 752 Caledonia Ave. (388-6686). $39.07 per day; unlimited km. Must be 21 with a major credit card. Open Mon.-Sat. 8am-5pm. **Budget Discount Car Rentals,** 727 Courtney St. (388-7874). Must be 19 with a major credit card. Used cars in excellent condition for $23-27 per day, plus 15¢ per km, or $37-40 per day, whichever is cheaper. Open Mon.-Fri. 7:30am-6:30pm, Sat.-Sun. 7:30am-6pm.

Canadian Automobile Association, 1075 Pandora (389-6700). Offers full range of services for AAA members. Open Mon.-Sat. 9am-5pm.

Taxi: Victoria Taxi, 383-7111. **Westwind,** 474-4747.

Bike Rental: Harbour Scooter, 843 Douglas St. (384-2133). Mountain bikes $5 per hr., $15 per day. Lock and helmet included. Open daily 9am-6pm; summer 8am-8pm.

Scooter Rentals: Harbour Scooters (see above). $5 per hr., $25 per day.

Camping Supplies and Rentals: Jeune Brothers, 570 Johnson St. (386-8778). 2-person tent $25 for 3 days, $41 per week. Open Mon.-Thurs. 9:30am-6pm, Fri. 9:30am-9pm, Sat. 9:30am-5:30pm, Sun. 11am-5pm.

Library: 735 Broughton (382-7241), at Courtney. Open Mon., Wed., and Fri.,-Sat., 9am-6pm; Tues. and Thurs. 9am-9pm.

Laundromat and Showers, 385-5711, corner of Wharf and Government St., 1 floor below the information center (open 8am, last wash at 7:30pm).

Crisis Line: 386-6323. 24 hrs. **Rape Crisis:** 383-3232. 24 hrs.

Gay and Lesbian Information: 598-4900. Volunteer staff; hours vary.

Disabilities Services for Local Transit: 727-7811. Open 8am-5pm.
Tourist Alert Board: 380-6136. If you need to reach someone in an emergency, this number will put a message at every tourist office in the city and at major tourist attractions.
Poison Control: 595-9211. 24 hrs.
Pharmacy: London Drugs, 900 Yates St. (381-1113), at Vancouver, in the Wilson Centre. Open Mon.-Sat. 9am-10pm, Sun. 10am-8pm.
Emergency: 911. **Police:** 625 Fisgard at Government St. (384-4111 for non-emergency). Staff sergeant on duty 24 hrs.
Post Office: 714 Yates (363-3887). Open Mon.-Fri. 8:30am-5pm. **Postal Code:** V8W 1L0.
Area Code: 604.

While the Seattle and Port Angeles **ferries** dock downtown, the ferry from the San Juan Islands docks at **Sidney,** 28km north on **Hwy. 17;** and the Vancouver/Gulf Islands ferry docks at **Swartz Bay,** 32km north. **Hwy. 1, the Trans-Canada Hwy.,** leads north and reaches the rest of Vancouver Island; **Hwy. 14** leads west to **Port Renfrew** and **Pacific Rim National Park.**

Victoria enfolds the Inner Harbour; **Government Street** and **Douglas Street** are the main north-south thoroughfares. Traditional tourist attractions crowd this area, and locals are few. Residential neighborhoods, wealthier in the east, form a semicircle around the Inner Harbour. **Victoria Regional Transit** (382-6161) provides city bus service, with major bus connections downtown at the corner of Douglas and Yates St. Travel in the single-zone area costs $1.35, multi-zone (north to Sidney and the Butchart Gardens) $2. Daily passes for unlimited single-zone travel are available at the visitors center and 7-11 stores for $4 (over 65 and under 12 $3). Transit **maps** and a riders' guide cost 25¢ and are available wherever day passes are sold; pick up the free pamphlet *Explore Victoria by Bus* at the visitors center.

ACCOMMODATIONS

Victoria Youth Hostel (HI-C), 516 Yates St., Victoria V8W 1K8 (385-4511), at Wharf St. downtown. 104 beds in the newly remodeled Victoria Heritage Building. Big, modern, spotless. Extensive kitchen and laundry facilities. Ping pong, video games, laundry ($2 wash and dry). Family rooms available. Desk open until 11pm; curfew 2:30am. $14, non-members $18.50.
Cherry Bank Hotel, 825 Burdett Ave. (385-5380), at Blanchard. 90-year-old bed and breakfast. Spotless rooms; winding corridors. *Trivial Pursuit* played incessantly in the lounge; they even advertise it. Singles from $43. Doubles from $51.
University of Victoria (721-8395), 20 min. northeast of the Inner Harbour by bus; take bus #7 or #14. Private rooms with shared baths. Coin-operated laundry machines. Register in the Housing Office, near the Coffee Gardens entrance that faces University Dr. Registration after 3pm. Singles $34.60. Doubles $45.80. Breakfast included. Reservations advisable. Open May-Aug.
Renouf House Bunk & Breakfast, 2010 Stanley Ave. (595-4774). 1912 Heritage home with close proximity to downtown. All-you-can-eat buffet breakfast included. Sleep in bunks, 2-4 to a room; $17.75. Singles $35. Doubles $45.
Salvation Army Men's Hostel, 525 Johnson St. (384-3396), at Wharf St. *Men only.* Modern, immaculate, and well run on a first-come, first-sleep basis. Dorms open daily at 4pm. You need a late pass if you plan on returning after 11pm. Dorm beds $15, private rooms $19. Breakfast $1.75, lunch $2.50, dinner $3.50. Weekly room and board $133.
YWCA, 880 Courtney St. (386-7511), at Quadra, within easy walking distance of downtown. *Women only.* Heated pool and new gym. Private rooms with shared baths. Reception 8:30am-6pm. Check out 6-11am. Singles $36.27. Doubles $53.82.
Victoria Backpackers Hostel, 1418 Fernwood Rd. (386-4471). Take buses #1, #10, #11, #14, #27, or #28 to Fernwood and Douglas. No curfew. Shared rooms $10, private $25-30.

Battery Street Guest House, 670 Battery St. (385-4632), 1 block from the ocean between Douglas and Government St. Dutch is spoken in this spacious bed and breakfast. Non-smokers only. Singles from $43. Doubles from $63.

CAMPING

The few grounds on the perimeter cater largely to wealthy RV drivers. Many campgrounds fill up in July and August; reservations are a good idea.

McDonald Park (655-9020), less than 3km south of the Swartz Bay Ferry Terminal, 30km north of downtown on Hwy. 17. Primitive sites. No showers, and no beach access. 30 tent and RV sites, $9.50.

Thetis Lake Campground, 1938 Trans-Canada Hwy. (478-3845), 10km north of the city center. Serves traffic entering Victoria from northern Vancouver Island. Sites are peaceful and removed. Long walk to bathroom. Metered showers and a laundromat. Sites $15 for 2 people, 50¢ per additional person. Full hookups $17.

Fort Victoria Camping, 340 Island Hwy. (479-8112), 7km NW of downtown, off the Trans-Canada Hwy. Free hot showers. Laundromat. Sites $17 for 2 people. Full RV hookups $22.

Goldstream Park, 2930 Trans-Canada Hwy. (387-4363). Set in a deeply forested area along a river, 20km northwest of Victoria. Great short hiking trails, swimming, and fishing. In Nov., the river is crowded with spawning salmon. Flush toilets and firewood available. 150 gorgeous gravelly sites ($15.50). The Goldstream Visitors Center is open from 9am to 6pm. The nearby **Freeman King Visitor Centre** relates the history of the area from the Ice Age to the welfare state. Naturalists will take you for a walk, or roam down the self-guided nature trail. Open in summer daily 8:30am-4:30pm; winter by appointment only.

French Beach, farther west on Hwy. 14, nearly 50km out. Right on the water, park has 70 sites with pit toilets, swimming, and hiking trails. No showers. Sites $8.

FOOD

Victoria's predilection for anachronisms shows in its culinary customs. Victorians actually do take tea; some only on occasion, others daily. No visit to the city would be complete without participating in the ceremony at least once.

As in every big city, the ethnic diversity of Victoria is a recipe for flavorful restaurants. **Chinatown,** west of Fisgard and Government St., fills the air with exotic aromas; European and North American offerings take over by the time you get to Wharf St. If you feel like cooking, head down to **Fisherman's Wharf,** four blocks west at the corner of Harbour and Government St., between Superior and St. Lawrence St. On summer mornings, you can buy the day's catch as it flops off the boats. For bulk food, try **Thrifty Foods** at Simcoe and Menzies, six blocks south of the Parliament buildings. (Open daily 8am-10pm.)

Eugene's, 1280 Broad St. (381-5456). Vegetarian souvlaki $3, dinners $5-7.50. *Rizogalo* or *bougatsa* is a nice change for breakfast ($2). Eugene tells take-out customers, "Call when you leave and it will be ready on your arrival." Ring from a nearby pay phone and freak him out. Open Mon.-Fri. 8am-8pm, Sat. 10am-8pm.

Ferris' Oyster and Burger Bar, 536 Yates St. (360-1824), next to the hostel. BC smoked oysters $2 each. Traditional pub fare, along with a number of vegetarian options. Almond nut burger ($4.50) is a delicious find; try it with the sweet potato fries ($2.25). Open Mon.-Wed. 8:30am-8pm, Thurs.-Fri. 8:30am-10pm, Sat. 8:30am-11pm. HI members discount.

Fan Tan Cafe, 549 Fisgard St. (383-1611), in Chinatown. Fan-tastic food at reasonable prices. Combo plate (chicken chow mein, chicken chop suey, and sweet and sour pork) $6. Fan-cy dinners $7-9. Open Mon.-Thurs. 11am-1am, Fri. 11am-2:30am, Sat. 2pm-2:30am, Sun. 2-10pm.

Bennie's Bagelry, 132-560 Johnson St. (384-3441), between Wharf and Pandora. Whole-grain, environmentally safe bagels 65¢, with cream cheese $2.10. Sandwiches $4.25-6.75. Open Mon.-Sat. 7am-7pm, Sun. 10am-7pm.

Rising Star Bakery, 1320 Broad St. (386-2534). Veggie Pizza Slice ($2.75), Sausage Roll (85¢), Giant cheese croissant, fresh out of the oven and still rising ($1.25). Day-old bread $1 per loaf. Open Mon.-Sat. 7:30am-5:30pm, Sun. 8:30am-2:30pm.

Scott's Restaurant, 650 Yates St. (382-1289), at Douglas St. Real diner feel; you just *know* they serve a mean chicken à la king. "Breakfast 222" (2 hotcakes, 2 eggs, 2 sausages) will cost you $4.50. Daily dinner specials a good bet ($5.25-7). Coffee and Donut special $1.50. 24 hrs.

The Blethering Place, 2250 Oak Bay Ave. (598-1413), at Monterey St. in upright Oak Bay. "Blether" is Scottish for "talk volubly and senselessly," a fact of little relevance to this superb tearoom frequented by elementary school teachers. Afternoon tea served with scones, Devonshire cream tarts, English trifle, muffins, and sandwiches all baked on the premises ($10). Ploughman's Lunch ($7) is a cheesier alternative. Dinners $11. Open daily 7:30am-9pm.

James Bay Tearoom, 332 Menzies St. at Superior (382-8282). Portraits of Queen Victoria, King George V, Sir Winston Churchill and a royal family tree from 900 AD set the scene for regal afternoon tea ($6), daily 1-4:30pm. The place is crowded until 2:30pm. Open Mon.-Sat. 7am-9pm, Sun. 8am-9pm.

Zombies Pizza, 1219 Wharf St. (389-2226). Cheerfully morbid interior decorating and $1.50 slices combine to make this a good, quick stop. Open Mon. 11am-3pm, Tues.-Sat. 11am-4pm, Sun. 11am-2pm.

SIGHTS AND ACTIVITIES

Victoria is a small city; you can wander the **Inner Harbour,** watch the boats come in, and take in many of the city's main attractions, all on foot. The elegant residential neighborhoods and the city's parks and beaches farther out are accessible by car and public transportation.

The first stop for every visitor should be the **Royal British Columbian Museum,** 675 Belleville St. (387-3014 for a recording, 387-3701 for an operator, 800-661-5411). One of the best museums in Canada, it chronicles the geological, biological, and cultural history of the province, and showcases detailed exhibits on logging, mining, and fishing. The extensive exhibits of Native art, culture, and history include full-scale replicas of shelters used centuries ago. The gallery of **Totem Art** is particularly moving. **Open Ocean** is a tongue-in-cheek re-creation of the first descent in a bathysphere. (Open daily 9:30am-7pm; Oct.-April 10am-5:30pm. $5; seniors, handicapped, and students with ID or HI card $3; ages 6-18 $2. Free after 5:45pm and Oct.-April on Mon. Hang on to your ticket; it's good for 2 days.) Behind the museum, **Thunderbird Park** is a striking thicket of totems and longhouses, backed by the green copper towers of the **Empress Hotel.**

Across the street from the front of the museum are the imposing **Parliament Buildings,** 501 Belleville St. (387-3046), home of the Provincial government since 1898. The 10-story dome and Brunelleschi-esque vestibule are gilded with almost 50 oz. of gold. At night, over 300 lights line the facade. Free tours leave from the main steps daily 9am to 5pm, departing every 30 minutes in summer, every hour in winter (open Mon.-Fri. 8:30am-5pm, on weekends for tours only).

Just north of Fort St. on Wharf is **Bastion Square,** which earned Victorians the Vincent Massey Award for Excellence in Urban Environment in 1971. The **Maritime Museum,** 28 Bastion Sq. (385-4222), exhibits ship models, nautical instruments, and a modified 13m Native Canadian canoe that shoved off from Victoria in 1901 on a daring, failed trip around the world. (Open June and Sept. daily 9am-6pm, July and Aug. daily 9am-8:30pm. $5, seniors $4, students $3, ages 6-12 $2, under 6 free.)

Around the corner on Wharf St. is the **Emily Carr Gallery,** 1107 Wharf St. (387-3080). Carr was a turn-of-the-century painter whose originality lay in her synthesis of British landscape conventions and Northwest Native style. The gallery's collection includes many of her paintings of totems and traditional life-styles, forged in a conscious attempt to preserve what she saw as "art treasures of a passing race." Also on display are photographs and manuscripts of other period artists, politicians, and prominent citizens. Free films on Carr's life and work show at 2:30pm. (Open Tues.-Sun. 10am-5:30pm. $2, seniors $1.)

North on Fisgard St., the Government St. entrance to the now-tiny **Chinatown** is marked by the large "Gate of Harmonious Interest." The great restaurants and inexpensive trinket shops make Chinatown a rewarding place for a meal and a jaunt.

South of the Inner Harbour, **Beacon Hill Park** surveys the Strait of Juan de Fuca (take bus #5). Here you can picnic in flower gardens, 350-year-old Garry oaks, and a network of paths. East of the Inner Harbour, **Craigdarroch Castle,** 1050 Joan Crescent (592-5323; take bus #11 or 14), was built in 1890 by Robert Dunsmuir, a coal and railroad tycoon, to lure his wife from their native Scotland to Victoria. The interior detail is impressive; the tower has a mosaic floor and the dining room a built-in oak sideboard. (Open daily 9am-7pm; winter 10am-4:30pm. $6, students $5, ages 6-12 $2, under 6 $1.)

One block back toward the Inner Harbor, on Fort St. at 1040 Moss, is the **Art Gallery of Greater Victoria** (384-4101), never the same museum twice. The museum has no permanent collection save a wooden Shinto shrine, and instead hosts temporary exhibits culled from local and international sources. (Open Mon.-Wed. and Fri.-Sat. 10am-5pm, Thurs. 10am-9pm, Sun. 1-5pm. $4, students and seniors $2, under 12 and Thurs. after 5pm free)

Point Ellice House (387-4697 or 384-0944), a Heritage Conservation House dating from 1861, is decorated exactly as if the residents had just stepped out for a few polo or cricket matches. The dining table is set, the chess set stands ready in the drawing room, and cast-iron pots and period utensils are strewn about the kitchen. Guided tours are given. (Open Thurs.-Mon. 11am-5pm. $3.75, students $2.75.) To get to Point Ellice, head in the opposite direction from Inner Harbor and hop on bus #14, or take Bay St. west off Government and stop just before crossing the Port Ellice Bridge.

Across the bridge, you'll find **Craigflower Farmhouse** (387-4697), at the corner of Craigflower and Admirals Rd. (take bus #14), a complex of historical buildings on a farm built by Hudson's Bay Company in the 1850s. Craigflower is more rustic than Point Ellice, though the kitchen is better-equipped. (Open Sun. 11am-5pm. $3.75, students $2.75, ages 6-11 $1.75.) At **Fort Rodd Hill National Historic Park,** on Ocean Blvd. off Hwy. 1A (388-1601), old defense batteries and **Fisgard Lighthouse,** the first of Canada's Pacific beacons, compete for attention with excellent views of the strait. Take bus #50 or 61 to Western Exchange, and follow Ocean Blvd. to the park. (About a 20-min. walk. No bus service evenings, Sun., or holidays. Park open daily 8am-sunset, exhibit buildings open 10am-5pm.)

The stunning **Butchart Gardens,** 800 Benvenuto, 22km north of Victoria (652-5256 for a recording or 652-4422 for an operator Mon.-Fri. 9am-5pm), are a maze of pools and fountains. Established in 1904 by Jennie Butchart to restore the wasteland that was her husband's quarry and cement plant, the rose, Japanese, and Italian gardens now cover 50 acres in a blaze of color. From mid-May through September, the whole area is lit at dusk, and the gardens, still administered by the Butchart family, host variety shows and cartoons. On Saturday nights in July and August, the skies shimmer with fireworks displays, while seventy thousand Christmas lights compensate for the lack of vegetation in December. Take bus #75 from Douglas and View northbound right into the Gardens, or #70 and walk 1km. The last #75 from the Gardens to the Inner Harbour is at 9:59pm. Motorists should consider approaching Butchart Gardens via the **Scenic Marine Drive,** following the coastline along Dallas and other roads. The 45-minute route passes through sedate suburban neighborhoods and offers a memorable view of the Olympic Mountains across the Strait of Juan de Fuca. (Gardens open 9am; call for closing times. Summer $11, ages 13-17 $8, ages 5-12 $3.50; winter $7.50, $5.50, and $2.50. Hang on to your ticket: readmission within 24 hrs. only $1.)

EVENTS AND ENTERTAINMENT

Nightlife in Victoria doesn't really get off the ground until Thursday night, but once the weekend is under way, the entire city grooves to the rhythms of jazz, blues, country, rock, folk, and more jazz. You can get an exhaustive listing of what's where in the free weekly *Monday Magazine* (inexplicably released every Wednesday), available at the hostel and at most hotel lobbies and tourist attractions. On Tuesdays, first-run movies at Cineplex Odeon theatres are half-price ($4). For more off-beat and foreign films, head to the University of Victoria's **Cinecenta** (721-8365 and 721-8346 for show information) in the student union (bus #7 and #14). non-members pay $6, students $5.

The **Victoria Symphony Society,** 846 Broughton St. (385-6515), performs regularly under conductor Peter McCoppin, and the **University of Victoria Auditorium,** Finnerty Rd. (721-8299), is home stage to a variety of student productions. The **Pacific Opera** performs at the McPherson Playhouse, 3 Centennial Sq. (386-6121), at the corner of Pandora and Government St.

Harpo's Cabaret, 15 Bastion Sq. (385-5333), at Wharf St. An eclectic mix of jazz, blues, folk, and whatever else is in town. Open Mon.-Sat. 9pm-2am, Sun. 8pm-midnight; cover around $5.

The Forge, 919 Douglas St. (383-7137), at Courtney, in the Strathcona Hotel. Specializes in mid-'70s rock with a wattage that could shatter tungsten. Open Tues.-Sat. 8pm-2am.

Spinnakers, 308 Catherine (386-2739). Across the Johnson St. bridge. Locals escape the tourists here and sample the 38 beers brewed on the premises. Live music nightly ranging from jazz to rockabilly. No cover. Open daily 11am-11pm.

Rumors, 1325 Government St. (385-0566). Gay and lesbian clientele; drinking and dancing. Open Mon.-Sat. 9pm-3am.

The **JazzFest** is sponsored by the Victoria Jazz Society (388-4423 or 386-2441). The **Classic Boat Festival** is held Labour Day weekend and displays pre-1955 wooden boats in the Inner Harbour. Free entertainment accompanies the show. Contact the visitor and convention bureau for more information on all Inner Harbour events, or pick up a free copy of *Victoria Today* from the Infocentre.

■ NEAR VICTORIA

SOOKE

West of Victoria on Hwy. 14 lies the town of Sooke, named for the T'sou-ke people and host to the logging events and festivities of **All Sooke Day** on the third Saturday in July. **The Sooke Region Museum** (642-6351), just off Hwy. 14 at 2070 Phillips Rd., delivers an excellent history of the area (open daily 9am-6pm; free). The museum also houses a **travel infocentre.** Next to the park where All Sooke Day takes place, on Phillips Rd. past the museum, is the **Sooke River Flats Campsite** (642-6076), with a phone, showers, toilets, and running water (gates locked 11pm-7am; sites $10). To get to Phillips Rd. from the city, take the #50 bus to the Western Exchange and transfer to #61. Sooke is mostly a haven for wealthier Victorians, making cheap indoor accommodations scarce. Try the **Blackfish B&B** (642-6864), 7 mi. west of Sooke's sole stoplight (singles $35, doubles $40). Large groups should ask about the great **bungalow** down on the pebble beach with free laundry and a full kitchen (sleeps 9; $100 per night).

North of Sooke are some of the best beaches for beachcombing on the southern island. Hwy. 14 continues along the coast, stringing together three provincial parks: **China Beach** and **Loss Creek** (both day use), and **French Beach,** with tentsites (May-Oct.; $9.50).

GULF ISLANDS

Just off the southeastern coast of Vancouver Island lies British Columbia's absolutely beautiful Gulf Island Archipelago. Five islands are serviced by **BC Ferries** (call 656-0757 for details). The three principal members of the chain are **Salt Spring, Pender,** and **Mayne.** Pick up a free copy of *The Gulf Islander* on the ferry to Victoria for a complete listing of area activities. For information on the five main islands, call the **tourist information centres** in Salt Spring (537-5252), Pender (382-3551), Mayne (539-5311), Galiano (539-2233), or Saturna (382-3551). Find a **HI-C hostel** at 640 Cusheon Lake Rd. (537-4149), on Salt Spring Island ($13, non-members $16).

CHEMAINUS

About 70km north of Victoria on Hwy. 1 lies the town of Chemainus. When the closure of the town's sawmill threatened economic disaster in 1980, an ambitious revitalization program, centered on a series of more than 30 enormous murals of the town's history, helped turn things around. In mid-July, **Chemainus Daze** offers arts and crafts and a chance to meet with the mural artists. The **Horseshoe Bay Inn**, 9576 Chemainus Rd. (246-3425) at Henry, has singles for $30, doubles for $38. The **Senior Drop-In Centre**, on the corner of Willow and Alder (246-2111), is open daily from 10am to 4pm with coffee, tea and muffins for anyone who drops in. Call the **Chamber of Commerce** in Chemainus at 246-3944 for more information.

■■■ NANAIMO

Demand for the coal industry floundered after WWII, and British Columbia's first settlement shifted to logging and fishing. When the logging economy turned to pulp throughout the province, Nanaimo turned to tourism to boost its economy. The combination of affable, outgoing people, easy accessibility by car or ferry, and a slow-paced, relaxed atmosphere has drawn many vacationers, especially anglers.

PRACTICAL INFORMATION AND ORIENTATION

Visitors Information: Travel Infocentre, 266 Bryden St. (754-8474), on the Trans-Canada Hwy., just northwest of downtown. Mine of information on all of Vancouver Island. Call before you visit the area for accommodations referrals. Open daily 8am-8pm.

BC Ferries, 680 Trans-Canada Hwy., Nanaimo V9S 5R1 (753-6626 for recorded information, 753-1261 for an operator). To Vancouver (12 per day between 5:30am and 11pm; passenger $6.25, car and driver $30.75). Also to **Gabriola Island** and **Horseshoe Bay** on the mainland, with connections to **Bowen Island** and **Langdale.** Ferries leave from a terminal at the northern end of Stewart Ave. Take the ferry shuttle from Gordon St. Exchange downtown. Check in 15 min. before departure.

Via Rail, 321 Selby St. (800-561-8630). To: Victoria (1 per day;$18, 7 days in advance $10).

Island Coach Lines, 753-4371. At Comox and Terminal, behind Tally Ho Island Inns. To: Victoria (7 per day; $15.75); Port Hardy (1 per day; $60.15); Port Alberni (4 per day; $11.25, with connecting service to Tofino and Ucluelet).

Car Rental: Rent-A-Wreck, 111 Terminal Ave. S (753-6461). Used cars start at $25 per day plus 14¢ per km. Must be at least 21 with a major credit card. Open Mon.-Sat. 8am-6pm, Sun. 10am-4pm. **Budget,** 17 Terminal Ave. S, 754-7368. $200 per week ; unlimited km. Must be at least 19. Free pickup to most areas in town.

Bus Information: 390-4531. Terminal at Front and Wharf. 10 bus routes serve the area. Fares $1.25, seniors 75¢. Day passes $3, students $2.75, seniors $2.25.

Laundromat: at Nicol and Robins at the **Payless Gas Station.** Open 24 hrs.

Crisis: 754-4447. 24 hrs.

Pharmacy: London Drugs (753-5566), in Harbour Park Mall at Island Hwy. and Terminal Ave. Open Mon.-Sat. 9am-10pm, Sun. 10am-8pm.

Hospital: 1200 Dufferin Crescent (754-2141). Open 24 hrs.

Emergency: 911.

Police: 303 Pridaux St. at Fitzwilliam (754-2345). **Fire:** 754-3314. At Fitzwilliam and Milton.

Post Office: 60 Front St., at Church St. Open Mon.-Fri. 8:30am-5pm. **Postal Code:** V9R 5J9.

Area Code: 604.

Nanaimo lies on the eastern coast of Vancouver Island, 111km north of Victoria on **Hwy. 1**, the **Trans-Canada Hwy.**, and 391km south of **Port Hardy** via **Hwy. 19**. The two highways merge downtown at the waterfront and become the major road in town. The **ferry** terminal is 2km north of the junction on Stewart Ave.

ACCOMMODATIONS AND CAMPING

Nicol St. Mini-Hostel (HI-C), 65 Nicol St. (753-1188), 7 blocks southeast of the Island Bus Lines Depot. If you're coming into Nanaimo from the south, ask the driver to let you off by the Nicol St. Hostel, and save yourself a walk. Great management. $13, non-members $15. Tentsites $8. Laundry (wash and dry) $2.50. Registration from 4-11pm.

Malaspina College (754-6338), Morden Hall, 750 4th St., approximately 2km west of downtown. Private rooms with shared baths. Coin-operated laundry, TV rooms, refrigerators, pay phones. Singles $24. Open May-Aug. Must call in advance; desk open from Mon.-Fri. 8am-4pm.

Colonial Motel, 950 N Terminal Ave. (754-4415), on the Trans-Canada Hwy. Immaculate rooms. Kitchenettes available. Singles $41. Doubles $43-52.

Big 7 Motel, 736 Nicol St. (754-2328). Loud, blue-and-pink motel decor, but the rooms are O.K. Waterbed units available for those who don't want to give up that seasick feeling after a long day of open-ocean fishing. Singles $37. Doubles $43.

Westwood Lake (753-3922), west of town off Jingle Pot Road. Full facilities. 66 sites. $13, $18 with hookups. Take bus #5.

Jingle Pot (758-1614), west on Island Hwy. off Jingle Pot Road. 22 sites. $12, with hookup $16. Full facilities.

Brannen Lake Campsite, 4228 Biggs Rd. (756-0404), 6km north of ferry terminal. Follow the signs from Hwy. 19. On a ranch and definitely worth the trip. Clean bathrooms with hot showers (25¢). Free hayrides every night, and you can help with the animals. Hike to a nearby waterfall. Sites $12, with hookup $15.

FOOD

Residents adore the **Nanaimo Bar,** a local concoction comprised of three layers of delicious graham crackers, butter, and chocolate. Locals take great pride in their hometown confection; a 1986 contest uncovered nearly 100 different recipes. Most of the neighborhood restaurants and bakeries offer their own renditions, and the conscientious traveler will sample several (just to get a real feel for the place, of course). Leaving the city without trying a Nanaimo Bar is like hitting a home run and forgetting to touch third.

The Scotch Bakery, 87 Commercial St. (753-3521). The acknowledged home plate of Nanaimo Bar aficionados (75¢). Don't ignore the macaroons ($1) or sausage rolls either. Open Mon.-Sat. 8am-4:30pm.

Doobee's (753-5044), at Front and Church St. Delicious sandwiches $4-5. Sidewalk tables and sunshine. Espresso and cappuccino for $2 will keep you singing. Open Mon.-Fri. 7am-5pm, Sat. 8:30am-5pm.

Nanaimo Harbour Lights Restaurant (NHL), 1518 Stewart Ave. (753-6614). The owner, ex-NHL referee Lloyd Gilmour, is more than willing to "talk puck." Surf-and-turf entrees also let you face off with the salad bar ($9-12). Lunches $6. Open Mon.-Thurs. 11:30am-3pm and 5-9pm, Fri.-Sat. 11:30am-3pm and 5-10pm.

SIGHTS

The **Nanaimo Centennial Museum,** 100 Cameron St. (753-1821), has a full-scale walk-through model of a coal mine. The small museum makes a particular effort to pay tribute to the Chinese laborers who worked the mine (open Mon.-Fri. 9am-6pm, Sat.-Sun. 10am-6pm). Only 300m from the museum, on the water's edge, is the **Bastion** (754-1631), constructed by the Hudson's Bay Company as a storehouse and fort against Native attacks. A 6-pound cannon booms daily at noon. (Open Mon.-Fri. 9am-5pm, Sat.-Sun. 10am-5pm; winter Tues.-Sat. 9am-5pm. Free.)

About 2.5km west of town is the **Nanaimo Art Gallery,** 900 5th St. (755-8790). The gallery features various rotating exhibitions of local and international art and culture. Bus #6 will save you the 30-minute walk uphill (open Mon.-Sat. 10am-5pm and Sun. noon-5pm). About 1km farther west up Nanaimo Lakes Ave. by the city reservoir is the **Morrell Nature Sanctuary.** The tranquil trails are a perfect place to digest those Nanaimo bars.

Three km south of town on Hwy. 1 (also Hwy. 19) is the **Petroglyph Provincial Park.** Hundreds of generations of Salish shamans have carved figures of various animals and mythical creatures into the soft sandstone. Rubbings can be made from concrete replicas at the base of the trail leading to the petroglyphs.

Eight km further south stretches the ever-expanding **Bungy Zone,** P.O. Box 399, Station A, Nanaimo, BC V9R 5L3 (753-5867; from MT, ID, OR, WA, or BC, call 800-668-7771), a dimension of sight, sound, and giant rubber bands. Thrill seekers from all over the continent make a pilgrimage here to drop 140 feet into a narrow gorge, secured against certain death only by a thick elastic bungee cord. The short but exhilarating trip down costs $95 (2 for 1 if you rent a car from Budget). You can also get a video filming your plungy from 'da bungee. To get there, take Hwy. 1 south to Nanaimo River Rd. and then follow the signs (open daily).

Departure Bay washes onto a pleasant beach in the north end of town off Stewart Ave. **North Island Water Sports,** 2755 Departure Bay Rd. (758-2488), rents bikes ($8 per hr., $25 per day), kayaks ($35 per day), and scuppers (they're like kayaks, but you sit on top of them; $8 per hr., $30 per day). **Newcastle Island Provincial Park** has campsites for $9.50 (no hookups), pit toilets, and a fantastic swimming beach. There's no auto access to the park so you'll have to shell out the $4 (round-trip) for the foot ferry (every hr. on the hr. daily 10am-9pm).

The annual **Nanaimo Theatre Group Festival** presents plays in late June and early July. All plays take place at Malaspina College (tickets $11-17). For reservations, contact the festival at P.O. Box 626, Nanaimo V9R 5L9 (754-7587; after June 20 call 758-4484), or stop by the office above the Travel Infocentre.

The week-long **Marine Festival** is held during the second week of July. Highlights include the **Silly Boat Race** and the renowned **Bathtub Race.** Bathers from all over the continent race porcelain tubs with monster outboards from Nanaimo to Vancouver across the 55km Georgia Strait. The organizer of this bizarre but beloved event is the **Royal Nanaimo Bathtub Society,** P.O. Box 656, Nanaimo V9R 5L5 (753-7233). They hand out prizes to everyone who makes it across, and ceremoniously present the "Silver Plunger" trophy to the first tub that sinks.

■ NEAR NANAIMO

HORNBY ISLAND

In the 1960s, large numbers of draft-dodgers fled the U.S. to settle peacefully on quiet Hornby Island, halfway between Nanaimo and Campbell River. Today, Hornby Island and **Denman** comprise an interesting mix of inhabitants: the descendants of pioneering families circa 1850 and hippie-holdovers who offer spiritual awareness readings. Living in a curious symbiosis, the two groups share a thinly veiled disdain for tourists.

With its light traffic and paved roads, Hornby Island is best explored on two wheels. You can rent bikes ($5 per hr., $20 per day) from **Zucchini Ocean Kayak Centre,** at the Co-op (335-2033; open daily 10am-6pm). Zucchini also rents kayaks and sailboards ($20 per 4 hr., $30 per day), and wetsuits ($10 per 4 hr., $20 per day). Low tide at Tribune Bay and Whaling Station Bay uncovers over 300m of the finest sand on Vancouver Island. **Tribune,** at the base of Central Rd., is the more accessible of the two beaches. **Whaling Station Bay** is about 5km farther north.

On the way to Whaling Station Bay from Tribune Bay is Helliwell Rd., the cut-off for stunning **Helliwell Provincial Park.** A well-groomed trail takes you on a one-hour **hike** through old-growth forest to bluffs overlooking the ocean. **Cormorants** are everywhere, diving straight into the ocean to surface moments later with trophy-quality fish. **Bald eagles** cruise on the sea breezes.

The **Hornby Festival** draws musicians, comedians, and artists from all over Canada for ten days in early August. Call the Hornby Festival Society (335-2734) for details. For more information, contact **Denman/Hornby Tourist Services,** Denman Island, BC V0R 1T0 (335-2293), or the post office on Hornby (see below).

If you plan on spending more than a day here, bring a tent and food. The **Hornby Island Resort** (335-0136), right at the ferry docks, is a versatile establishment: a pub/restaurant/laundromat/hotel/campground. The pub fare is standard but reasonably priced; the restaurant has breakfast plates from $4 (restaurant open daily 9am-9pm; sites $13-15 per night, hookup $3). **Bradsdadsland Country Camp,** 1980 Shingle Spit Rd. (335-0757), offers standard plots for your tent (sites for 1-2 people $16 per night; $1 per additional person, $1 per pet; $4 per additional vehicle; full hookup $3). **Tribune Bay,** at the Co-op at the eastern end of Central Rd. (335-2359), has 120 sites on wonderful (you guessed it) Tribune Bay. (Sites $18; 8 sites with electricity $20. Coin-op showers. Open Easter-Labor Day.) **The Joy of Cooking** (335-1487), by the Co-op, serves up BC-style sushi in the form of *nori* rolls, smoked salmon and rice wrapped in seaweed ($3; open daily 8:30am-8pm). **The Co-op,** at the end of Central Rd. by Tribune Bay (335-1121), is a well-stocked grocery store with a deli and post office (open daily 9am-7pm).

Island Coach Lines has a flag stop at **Buckley Bay,** on Hwy. 19, where the ferry docks. **BC Ferries** sails nine times daily (round-trip $4.50, car and driver $12.50). It's a 10-minute ride from Buckley Bay to Denman; disembark and make the 11km trek across the island to the Gravely Bay docks for another 10-minute ride to Hornby. Once on Hornby, there are only two roads to worry about: **Shingle Spit Road** (try saying that 10 times fast) and **Central Road,** separated by the docks. Central Rd. extends to the eastern shore, where all the "action" is. However, it's 15km away, and there's no public transit.

This area is difficult to cover without a bike or car, so some foot-travelers ask friendly faces for lifts at Denman or on the ferry. (*Let's Go* does not recommend hitchhiking.) Those who decide to risk hitching should appear neat; islanders can be somewhat reticent. If you need a **taxi,** call 285-3598. (**Emergency Numbers: ambulance,** 338-9112; **fire,** 338-6522; **police,** 338-6551.) The **post office** is at the Co-op at the terminus of Central Rd. (335-1121), on the eastern shore of the island. **Postal Code:** V0R 1Z0. The **area code** is 604.

PORT ALBERNI

Port Alberni is on Hwy. 4, about 25km west of Hwy. 1 and halfway between Nanaimo and Pacific Rim National Park. This historically lumber-based city is, like many others in the area, shifting toward the tourism industry. And, again like its neighbors, Port Alberni bills itself as the "Salmon Capital of the World" and hosts an annual **Salmon Festival** each Labor Day weekend. The town itself is geared more toward those passing through than to those stopping over. A few attractions do exist, though. Brochures and advice on the general area can be found at the Port Alberni **Infocentre,** on Hwy. 4 (724-6535; open daily 8am-7pm; closes at 5pm in winter). **Nosegaard's,** a bountiful farmer's market off Hwy. 4 just west of town, lets you pick your own strawberries for 90¢ per lb. (open mid-June-mid-July 8am-9pm). **Sproat Lake Provincial Park** (248-3931), 13km west of Port Alberni off Hwy. 4, offers space to explore mysterious petroglyphs, boat, swim, fish, and camp (sites $12). Moored on Sproat Lake in the summer are the **Martin Mars Bombers,** the last two working flying boats of this type in the world. Originally WWII troop carriers, they are now used to fight fires.

■■■ PACIFIC RIM NATIONAL PARK

So different in landscape and seascape are the three regions of Pacific Rim National Park that only a government could have combined them under the same jurisdiction. The park, a thin strip of land on Vancouver Island's remote Pacific coast, can be reached in three distinct ways. To reach the south end of the park, the **West Coast Trail** at **Port Renfrew,** take Hwy. 14 to its end. Hwy. 14 runs west from Hwy. 1 not far from Victoria. In the middle, rough logging roads lead to the **Broken Group Islands** and **Bamfield** from Hwy. 18 and Cowichan Lake. Hwy. 18 connects to Hwy. 1 at Duncan, about 60km north of Victoria. For access to **Long Beach,** the Park's northern reaches, take Hwy. 4 across the center of Vancouver Island to **Ucluelet** (yoo-CLOO-let). Hwy. 4 branches west of Hwy. 1 about 35km north of Nanaimo and leads through **Port Alberni** on the way to the Pacific coast.

Constructed in 1907 to give shipwrecked sailors a path to civilization, the 77km **West Coast Trail** between Port Renfrew and Bamfield is the most demanding and potentially dangerous section of the park. It can be traversed only on foot, and takes anywhere from six to ten days. About halfway along the trail near **Clo-oose** (KLOH-ooze) is the **Carmanah Valley,** where the tallest Sitka spruce in the world tower 90m above the forest floor. This route is for serious hikers only.

Barkley Sound intrudes between Bamfield and Ucluelet, and here you'll find the **Broken Group Islands** unit of the park. Accessible only by boat, these islands are untouched.

Gentle trails and broad vistas of Douglas fir and Western cedar characterize the 23-km **Long Beach,** between Ucluelet in the south and Tofino in the north. Long Beach has two camping facilities (see Accommodations and Camping, below). Begin your explorations at the Wickaninnish Centre, watch a film at the free museum, and then head off to the beach.

Each spring, you can witness the commute of some of the 22,000 **gray whales** streaming past the park. The area also crawls with orcas, sea lions, black-tailed deer, and black bears. Bring rain gear.

WEST COAST TRAIL: PORT RENFREW & BAMFIELD

Port Renfrew, in transition from a logging economy to one based on tourism, is the point of departure for those embarking on the West Coast Trail. It offers only a minimum of resources for hikers and tourists.

The West Coast Trail, linking Port Renfrew and Bamfield, is 77km of rugged coastal hiking weaving through forests and waterfalls and scaling steep wooden ladders and slopes. The treacherous shoreline has been the graveyard of many ships. Only **experienced hikers** should attempt this slick trail, and never alone; gray whales, sea otters, and black bears along the route may provide company, but they can't help you in an accident. A maximum of 52 people per day are permitted to tackle the legendary trail; write the Park Superintendent, Box 280, Ucluelet, BC V0R 3A0, or call ahead for reservations (726-7721). You can order maps, tide tables, information on ferry crossings within the trail, and brochures on trail safety from the Park Superintendent as well.

The **Botanical Beach Provincial Park** is nearly as much a source of local pride as Pacific Rim. Nature enthusiasts have access to varieties of intertidal life, as well as sandstone, shale, quartz, and basalt formations. The park is only accessible to 4WD vehicles; those without must park and make the 45-minute trek to the beach.

Anyone heading into Bamfield will have to pass over a few socket-jarring gravel logging roads, the only routes into town. Luckily, the breathtaking **Lake Cowichan** offers ample reward for the ride. The few patches of clear-cut dotting the lakeshores prove that these logging roads are still active, so be careful. The tactful Forest Service explains that "landscape principles were not fully applied at the time of harvest;" they note, however, that everything will "green-up" as logging continues to decline. **Pacheenaht Bus Service** (647-5521) operates in the area. Take it. Your car will thank you. The town of Bamfield is on two sides of an inlet, and lacks a bridge to connect the halves. A **water taxi** from Kingfisher Marina is the only way to reach the rest of the town.

Practical Information Seek out **maps** and information on the area and registration information for the West Coast Trail at the **Trail Information Center** in Port Renfrew (647-5434; open May-Sept. daily 9am-5pm). The information center in Bamfield is deserted and lacks even a phone.

The **Pacheenaht Bus Service,** 155 Tataxawo, Port Renfrew (647-5521), offers one-way service to Bamfield ($40), Lake Cowichan ($14), and Duncan ($30). In Bamfield, try **Western Bus Lines,** 723-3341. For a **taxi** by road, try **Hawkeye's Marina** (728-3300) in Bamfield. By water, try **Bamfield Kingfisher Marina** (728-3228).

Do your **laundry** and take a **shower** at the Port Renfrew Hotel. The local hospital is the **Bamfield Red Cross Hospital.** The **post office** is in Bamfield, across the inlet near the Bamfield Inn.

Accommodations, Camping, and Food Choices in town are limited, and camping in the park is the best of the lot. The **Seabeam Fishing Resort and Hostel (HI-C)** (728-3286; turn right in Bamfield past the Kamshee Store and it's up the hill on the right) is the only non-camping budget option, and includes a kitchen, laundry, showers, and separate rooms (hostel $10; camping $15, with hookup $18). Campers should head to **Camp Ross** at the West Coast Trailhead in an amazing shore-side spot (outhouses, pay phone; 3-day max.; free).

The **General Store** (647-5587) in Port Renfrew and the **Kamshee Store** (728-3411) in Bamfield are both good markets. Finding a good, cheap restaurant in the area might be impossible.

LONG BEACH: UCLUELET AND TOFINO

Ucluelet and Tofino, at the southern and northern ends of Long Beach, respectively, are both small-town communities complementing the park's outdoor recreational opportunities. From spring through fall, Ucluelet is transformed as binocular-toting tourists arrive to watch the whales migrate. Tofino, an intriguing congregation of artists and environmentalists, is also willing to fulfill tourist demands, although perhaps without trading privacy for dollars.

Practical Information Find **visitor information** in Long Beach, 3km into the Long Beach unit of Hwy. 4, close to the **Port Alberni** junction (726-4212; open mid-April-mid-Oct.); in **Tofino** at 351 Campbell St. (725-3414; open July-Aug. daily 9am-8pm; March-June and Sept.-Oct. Sat.-Sun. 9am-5pm); and in **Ucluelet** at 227 Main St. (726-4641; open daily 10am-6pm; Sept.-June Mon.-Fri. 10am-3pm). It costs $5 per day, $15 per week to remain in the park; annual passes are also available. The **Park Superintendent** can be contacted for advance information at Box 280, Ucluelet, BC V0R 3A0 (726-7721).

Island Coach Lines, 700 Douglas St., Victoria (385-4411; in Port Alberni at 724-1266; in Nanaimo at 753-4371) services the eastern half of Vancouver Island connects Victoria to: Nanaimo (6 buses per day; $15.75); Port Alberni (3 per day; $27); Campbell River (4 per day; $36); and Port Hardy (2 per day; $83.25). **Orient Stage Lines** (in Port Alberni at 723-6924) connects with Island Coach Lines at Port Alberni. During the week they send two buses and on the weekend only one to Ucluelet ($12), and Tofino ($14). **Alberni Marine Transportation, Inc.,** P.O. Box 188, Port Alberni, V9Y 7M7 (723-8313), operates the ferry *Lady Rose* year-round to Bamfield (4 per week; $15, round-trip $30), Ucluelet (3 per week; $18, round-trip $35), and Gibraltar Island in the **Broken Group Islands** (3 per week; $16, round-trip $32); canoe and kayak rental available. **Great Escapes** (725-2384), on Meares Landing in Tofino, rents mountain bikes for $20 per day.

The **laundromat** is Koin Laundrette in Davison's Shopping Plaza on Peninsula in Ucluelet. The **hospital** is at 261 Neill St., Tofino (725-3212). The **police** are at 725-3242, in Tofino. The **post office** is at 1st and Campbell in Tofino (open Mon.-Thurs. 10am-3pm, Fri. 10am-5pm). The **area code** is 604.

Accommodations, Camping, and Food This is campground country. There are no hostels around, and cheap beds are rare. **Ucluelet Hotel** (726-4324), on Main St., offers shared bath, and is located above a rockin' bar (singles and doubles $28.75-34.50). The **Dolphin Motel** (725-3377), 5km south of Tofino near the beach, has singles from $39 and doubles from $45.

Green Point Campground (726-4245), 10km north of the park information centre, has 94 sites equipped with hot water, flush toilets, and fireplaces, and swarms with campers and mosquitoes in July and August. Enjoy an interpreter-led program (June-Sept. daily waiting list; April-June first come, first served. Sites mid-June-Aug. $15; Sept.-March $5; April-mid-June $8.50. No reservations). **Ucluelet Campground,** at Ucluelet Harbor (726-4355), offers showers and toilets for $16 per site, with electricity ($2), water ($1), and sewer ($1) (open March-Oct.).

The small, funky, and colorful **Alleyway Cafe,** 305 Campbell (725-3105), in Tofino, offers the Veggie Burger ($4.80) or the unique taco-in-a-bowl ($4.80; open daily 8am-9pm; closed in winter). At the **Common Loaf Bake Shop,** 131 1st St. (725-3915), in Tofino, everything is dense, delicious and satisfying. The chocolate chunk cookie (75¢) and peasant bread ($1.85) are uncommonly good; so is the conversation (open daily 8am-9pm; winter 8am-6pm). **Porky's Too Pizza and Burgers,** 1950 Peninsula (726-7577), in Ucluelet, has locals squealing over their burgers ($3.20). Quick service, too (open daily 11am-9pm, Fri. 11am-11pm; also located across from the Alleyway Cafe).

Sights and Activities **Whale watching** is the premier outdoor activity on Long Beach from March to November. Local boatsmen will gladly take you on a three-hour ride to observe the grays closely ($40-60). Smooth rides in large boats are available, but the daring venture out in **Zodiacs,** hard-bottomed inflatable rafts with huge outboards that ride the swells at 30 knots. **Remote Passages** (725-3330) offers Zodiac adventures supplemented by an interpretive discussion of the coastal environment (tickets start at $42, under 12 $20). **Subtidal Adventures** (728-7336) offers cruises to the Broken Group Islands ($45, ages 6-12 $21, under 6 $10).

Radar Hill, a few km north of Green Point and connected to the highway by a short paved road, allows you to see far and wide. Learn about the indigenous wildlife and culture at the **Wickaninnish Centre** (726-4212), 3km off Hwy. 4 just past the park entrance (open daily mid-May to Labor Day; free).

Most visitors take advantage of the park's magnificent **hiking trails.** Pick up a *Hiker's Guide* for the Long Beach stretch at the visitors center for a list of nine hikes ranging from 100m to 5km in length. Away from the established trails, the park offers infinite opportunities for wandering. When the rain finally overwhelms you, seek refuge in the Native Canadian art galleries in Ucluelet and Tofino. Ucluelet's **Du Quah Gallery,** 1971 Peninsula Rd. (726-7223), is more modest than Tofino's **Eagle Aerie Gallery,** 350 Campbell St. (725-3235), protecting unusual and striking paintings behind the $17,000 carved wooden doors.

■■■ COMOX VALLEY

Billing itself as the "recreation capital of Canada," the Comox Valley area includes the towns of **Courtenay, Comox,** and **Cumberland.** The area is an intellectual oasis in Vancouver Island's rural north. It boasts the highest concentration of artists in Canada, with many museums and galleries. Along more scientific lines, the discovery of the 80-million-year-old "Courtenay Elasmosaur" in 1989 has transformed the valley into a minor mecca of paleontology as well.

If talk of arts and sciences brings nasty visions of college and coursework, then find relief in nearby **Strathcona Provincial Park.** The park's southern regions are just a llama's trot away from the "Three C's."

Practical Information The **Tourist Office** in Courtenay is at 2040 Cliffe Ave. (334-3234), and in Cumberland on Dunsmuir (336-8313). **Island Coach** (334-2475), in Courtenay at Fitzgerald and Cumberland, connects the area to points north and south along Hwy. 19. **BC Ferries** (339-3310) connects Comox with Powell River on the mainland.

Some useful numbers: **Weather,** 339-5044; **Police,** 338-6551, non-emergency 338-1321; **Fire,** 338-6522; **Ambulance,** 338-7471; **Hospital,** 339-2242. Find the **Women's Resource Center** on Cliffe 2km before the Info. Center. The **Post Office** is on Fourth St. at Cliffe, across from the museum in Courtenay (open Mon.-Thurs. 9am-4pm, Fri. 9am-5:30pm). **Area Code:** 604.

Accommodations, Camping, and Food Pricey motels line the highway south of Courtenay. B&Bs abound and are a better bet. Get a listing at the Infocentre, or try the **Mountain View Bed and Breakfast,** 605 Ellcee Place, Courtenay, BC V9N 7G3 (338-0157), offering spotless bathrooms, a TV lounge area, and a good view from the balcony (singles from $25, doubles from $40; reservations recommended). Campers should try **Kin Beach** (339-4079), Astra Road, Comox. Their 7 tentsites and 8 RV sites are $6.50. **Miracle Beach** (337-5720), Miracle Beach Drive, Black Creek, has trails, picnic tables, BBQ pits, and a playground. It's better than Kin Beach, but harder to reach (showers, flush toilets; $14.50).

The many **Farmers Markets** in the area are cheaper than restaurants. A convenient one is **Farquharson Farms,** 1300 Comox in Courtenay (338-8194). **The Bar None Cafe,** 244 4th St. (334-3112), off Cliffe in Courtenay, purveys exceptional, but expensive, all-vegetarian fare. Choose your own rice and pasta dishes, salads, and fresh salsas, and pay $1.50 per 100 grams. There is also an espresso bar and homemade juices (apple, lime, and mint, $2.50; open Mon.-Sat. 8am-8pm; Fri. night coffee-house until 11pm.) The price is right at **Babe's Cafe,** 2702 Dunsmuir (336-2763), in Cumberland (entrees $4-7). **Safeway** (open daily 8am-10pm) and **Shopper's Drug Mart** (open Mon.-Fri. 9am-9pm, Sat. 9am-6pm, Sun. 9am-5pm) are both on 8th St. in Courtenay.

Sights and Activities The **Arts Alliance,** 367 4th St. (338-6211), in Courtenay, is a focal point for the local arts community, housing craft galleries. (Open Tues.-Sat. 10am-5pm; free.)

The Courtenay and District Museum, 360 Cliffe Ave. (334-3611; open daily in summer 10am-4:30pm), houses permanent exhibits on pioneer life, Native culture and art, industry, and geology. A paleontology annex, next to the museum, holds in storage the bevy of dinosaur bones uncovered in the area (tours free, call the museum). **The Comox Air Force Museum** (339-8635) at the Canadian Forces Base, Ryan and Little River Rd. in Comox, will tell you everything you ever wanted to know (but were afraid to ask) about the Royal Canadian Air Force. Future exhibits will chronicle Native artists who have flown for Canada.

Horne Lake Caves Provincial Park, south of Courtenay on Horne Lakes Rd., opens its caves to the public; equipment is available.

■■■ STRATHCONA PROVINCIAL PARK

Elk, deer, marmots, and wolves all inhabit the more than 2000 sq. km. of Strathcona, one of the best preserved and most beautiful wilderness areas on Vancouver Island. **Buttle Lake,** on Hwy. 28 between Gold River and Campbell River, and **Mt. Washington/Forbidden Plateau** are the park's two visitors centres. The two official **campgrounds,** sharing 161 campsites between them, are Buttle Lake and Ralph River, both on the shores of Buttle Lake and accessible by Hwy. 28 and secondary roads (follow the highway signs). **Buttle Lake,** closer to Campbell River, has comfortable sites, a playground, and the sandy beaches of the lake itself ($12). **Ralph River,** less crowded, provides convenient access to the park's best hiking trails ($9.50). From Ralph River, the difficult 12km **Phillips Ridge** hike takes about five

CAMPBELL RIVER

hours round-trip, passing two waterfalls in a 790m climb and ending at the top of a mountain in a meadow full of wildflowers by an alpine lake.

Visitors wishing to explore Strathcona's **backcountry areas** must camp 800m from main roads. To minimize environmental impact, camp at least 30m away from water sources as well. Backcountry campers are rewarded by lakes, waterfalls, ancient cedar and fir forests, and wildflower meadows. Campfires are discouraged in the park. Those entering the undeveloped areas of the park should notify the park service of their intended departure and return times, and should be well-equipped (**maps** and **rain gear** are essential). The Forbidden Plateau and Mt. Washington, lying outside the park boundaries, hit their high-seasons in the winter with a heavy influx of skiers. For information on the park, contact BC Parks, District Manager, Rathtrevor Beach Provincial Park, Box 1479, Parksville, BC V9P 2H4 (604-248-3931 or 755-2483).

■■■ CAMPBELL RIVER

Campbell's tourist economy is geared toward fishing, diving, and hiking. News of the enormous **salmon** regularly wrestled from the river by Cape Mudge Natives sparked a tremendous influx of sport fishermen in the early 1800s. They could never have expected that today every pamphlet, billboard, and menu would shout "Salmon Capital of the World" in obtrusively large print.

Practical Information The **Travel Infocentre,** 923 Island Hwy. (286-0764), has a helpful staff and brochures (open daily 8am-6pm; winter Mon.-Fri. 9am-5pm, Sat. 10am-5pm). **Island Coach Lines** (287-7151) is at 13th and Cedar. **BC Ferries** runs from Campbell River to Quadra Island (15 daily; $2.75, cars $8, children 5-11 $1.50, bikes and children under 5 free). Find **Rent-a-Wreck** (287-8353) at 1353 Island Hwy. in Lakeland (open daily 8am-5pm). A local laundromat is **Sunrise Laundry Ltd.** (923-2614) in Sunrise Square (open Sun.-Fri. 8am-9pm, Sat. 8am-6pm). Some useful numbers: **Crisis Hotline,** 287-7743; **Emergency,** 911; **Hospital,** 375 2nd Ave., 287-7111 for information; **Poison Control,** 287-7111; **Ambulance,** 286-1155; **Police,** 286-6221.

Accommodations, Camping, and Food Finding inexpensive lodging here is like swimming upstream. The best bet is camping in **Strathcona Provincial Park** (see below). The **Ocean Front Motel,** 834 South Island Hwy. (923-6409), 20 minutes from the city centre, at least gets points for location (singles from $28, doubles $29). The **Parkside Campground** (287-3113), 5km west of Campbell River on Hwy. 28, has appealing wooded sites and hot showers in private, quiet surroundings (sites $14, with hookup $18).

As far as food goes, good budget fare is hard to find. The **Overwaitea Market,** at 13th and Elm St., offers decent sandwiches and other casual cuisine, and it's the best you'll do if you're not cooking your dinner yourself (open daily 9am-9pm). Local supermakets, however, have lots of cheap no-brand canned food.

Sights and Activities Sockeye, coho, pink, chum, and chinook **salmon** are lured each year from the waters of the Campbell River. The savvy can reap deep-sea prizes from **Discovery Pier** in Campbell Harbour (fishing charge $1; rod rentals $2.50 per hr., $6 per ½-day). The pier has 200m of boardwalk plants and an artificial underwater reef built to attract astigmatic fish.

National Geographic once praised Campbell River's **scuba diving** as "second only to the Red Sea." Unfortunately, unless you spy some real treasure in Discovery Pier's artificial reef, it'll be hard to come up with the cash to rent equipment. **Beaver Aquatics,** 760 Island Hwy. (287-7652), advertises a $25 snorkel package that includes suit, mask, snorkel, and fins (open Mon.-Sat. 9am-5pm, Sun. 10am-2pm).

No visit to the self-proclaimed "Salmon Capital of the World" would be complete without a tour of the **Quinsam River Salmon Hatchery** (287-9564). They monitor more smolts before 9am than most people do all day (open daily 8am-4pm). An audio-visual extravaganza introduces you to shiny, happy little fish who are blissfully unaware of the rods and reels lying ahead.

North of Seyward and South of Woss you can frolick around **"The World's Largest Burl."** Weighing over 22 tons and stretching over 15 ft. high, this abnormal tree growth is on the right side of the road northbound, and is marked by a plaque (you can't possibly miss this behemoth).

■■■ ALERT BAY

Alert Bay is on a beautiful, tiny island a short ferry trip from **Port McNeill,** 65km south of Port Hardy on Hwy. 19. It is a major cultural center for the Kwakiutl nation and a great place to watch **orcas** swimming. Travelers are welcome; those coming to observe respectfully and appreciate the culture are in no way interfering.

Practical Information Find **travel information** in **Port McNeil** by the ferry dock. In **Alert Bay,** travel information is at 116 Fir St. (974-5213; open daily 9am-5pm). **BC Ferries** (956-4533) operates a three-point ferry running among Port McNeill, Sointula, and Alert Bay (ferries run daily 8:40am-9:50pm; $3.75, car $10.25). **Island Coach Lines** runs from Port McNeill to Victoria (1 per day, $69, departs from the Dalewood Inn). Those with car trouble should call **Port McNeill Auto Body** (956-3434, 24-hr. towing). You can grab a shower at the pool on Campbell Way past the skating arena (956-3638; $2, children $1).

Some useful numbers: **Ambulance,** 949-7224; **hospital,** 2750 Kingcome Place (956-4461), in Port McNeill; **police,** 956-4441. The **Area Code** is 604.

Accommodations A fabulous **hostel,** 256 Fir St. (604-974-2026), plays host in Alert Bay, complete with piano and a bay view ($13, non-members $15). Reservations are recommended, as group programs can sometimes fill the beds; if the hostel is full, though, lodging can often be arranged elsewhere.

Sights Alert Bay is one of the richest sources of Native culture on Vancouver Island. Half the community is a Nimpkish Native reserve. The tallest totem pole in the world, at 173 ft., is behind the **U'Mista Cultural Centre** (974-5403; open Mon.-Fri. 9am-5pm, Sat.-Sun. noon-5pm; winter Mon.-Fri. 9am-5pm). The totem tells the story of the Kwakiutl Native nation, and the cultural centre houses breathtaking bronzes and masks used in the *Potlatch* (gift-giving ceremony).

The island straits near Alert Bay and Port McNeill boast the continent's highest concentration of **orcas.** Expensive sighting charters are everywhere (and expensive); instead, you can catch a glimpse of the pods surfacing in synchronicity to the water by the ferry or just outside the harbor at Alert Bay.

■■■ PORT HARDY

Port Hardy was completely content to be a quiet logging and fishing community until the BC Ferry made it the drop-off point for southbound visitors from Prince Rupert and Alaska. Virtually overnight, the formerly unassuming town etched a name for itself as a major transportation port, complete with a chainsaw-carved welcome sign. Port Hardy remains a mild coastal town and an excellent place for ferry passengers to spend the night.

Practical Information Pick up a restaurant guide and tour **maps** at the **Travel Infocentre,** 7250 Market St. (949-7622). Take Hardy Bay Rd. off Hwy. 19 to Market St. (open daily 9am-8pm). **Buses** leave from **Island Coach Lines** (949-7532), on Market St. across from the Travel Infocentre (to Victoria: 1 per day; $75.90). **BC Ferry** (949-6722) is 3km south at Bear Creek. (Service between Prince Rupert and

Port Hardy every other day; one way $93, with car $289.) **North Island Taxi** can be reached at 949-8800. **North Star Cycle and Sports,** at Market and Granville, rents bikes for $8 per hour. Other outdoor equipment needs may be taken care of at **MacLean's True Value** on Market. Clean those stinkin' socks at **Payless Gas Co.** (949-2366), on Granville St. (open 24 hrs.).

Some helpful phone numbers: **crisis line,** 949-6033; **police,** 7355 Columbia Ave. (949-6335); **hospital,** 949-6161; and **ambulance,** 949-7224. Port Hardy's **postal code** is V09 2P0. The **area code** is 604.

On the northern tip of Vancouver Island, Port Hardy is the southern terminus for ferries carrying passengers down from Prince Rupert and Alaska. Hwy. 19 runs south from the center of downtown.

Accommodations and Camping   Despite the presence of RVs, the demand for hotel rooms is just as high as you would expect in any port town. Stream to the **Pioneer Inn** (949-7271), off Hwy. 19 on Old Island Hwy., 2km south of town, for rooms next to a salmon hatchery. The Pioneer has laundry facilities and a dining room (singles $56, doubles $60). For current **B&B** listings call 949-7622 (singles from $30). For a quiet, wooded, private setting, tent it at the **Quatse River Campground,** 5050 Hardy Bay Rd. (949-2395), across from the Pioneer Inn. Toilets come in a choice of flush and pit. The campground has showers and a laundromat. (Sites $12, full hookups $15, $1 discount for seniors). The campground shares its grounds with a **fish hatchery;** a visitor viewing area is accessible, and tours are available (call 949-9022 between 8am and 4:30pm). **Wildwoods Campsite** (949-6753), on the road from the ferry within walking distance of the terminal, has comfortable sites strewn with pine needles. Plenty of spaces are crammed into a relatively small forest area, but they are well-designed to afford maximum privacy. There are hot showers, but expect a line in the morning. (Sites $10, with hookup $12.85.)

Food   Groceries can be had at **Giant Foods** on Market St. (open 6am-10pm). A brigade of superb budget restaurants serve dinners for under $10. **Better Burgers** is at 7201 Market St. (949-7633), in the back of the parking lot. The diner offers breakfast all day ($4.50) and burgers and sandwiches ($4.50-5). For more traditional maritime fare, there's **Brigg Seafood House** (949-6532), at Market and Granville St., serving seafood in a large old house. Their "you catch it, we'll cook it" service can get you dinner with all the trimmings for $5; bistro dinners from $7. Children's menu available. (Open daily 4-10pm.) **Sportsman's Steak & Seafood House** (949-7811), on Market St. across from the Infocentre, offers lunch sandwiches stuffed with meat from $4. The salad bar is well-stocked, and a few surf-and-turf entrees are under $9 (open Tues.-Fri. 11:30am-2pm and 5pm-"whenever," Sat.-Mon. 5pm-"whenever"). The **Roadhouse,** a family restaurant at the Pioneer Inn on Old Island Hwy., has sandwiches ($4-7) and pasta entrees ($7-10). Several **markets** line (aptly enough) Market St.

CAPE SCOTT PROVINCIAL PARK

Cape Scott is wild and wet; the elements have spelled doom for two attempts at human settlement. 60km of logging roads (watch for trucks) lead to parking lots near trailheads, the only access to the park. Most trailheads begin from the parking lot on **San Josef Rd.,** near the entrance to the park.

Wilderness camping in the park is not restricted to wilderness sites, although **San Josef Bay** and **Nels Bight** are popular because fresh water is available. Make sure you're not so near the shore that your camp will be swamped at high tide. Good **topographic maps** will be helpful to enterprising trekkers (available from **Maps BC,** Ministry of Environment, Parliament Bldgs., Victoria BC V8V 1XS). For more detailed information on the park, pick up the Cape Scott Provincial Park pamphlet at one of the travel infocentres elsewhere in the region, since none exist anywhere near the park. And finally, while the wildlife you see may vary, bring **rain gear,** because it will rain.

SOUTHERN BRITISH COLUMBIA

■■■ FRASER RIVER CANYON

Simon Fraser braved 1300km of turbulent water to reach the site of Vancouver from Mt. Robson in 1808. Today, a slightly easier path (the **Trans-Canada Hwy.**) snakes down the Fraser River between the towns of Hope and Cache Creek. Fraser's 200km of coiling rapids are not quite as exciting as the Infocentre's pamphlets would have you believe, but the sheer size of the towering, pine-covered canyon walls makes it a striking scene.

HOPE

Hope is a town with little happening, popular chiefly with odd-numbered highways. **Hwy. 1**, the **Trans-Canada Hwy**, leads west into Vancouver and bends north at Hope, running to Yale and Cache Creek where it joins **Hwy. 97, the Cariboo Hwy.**, to northern British Columbia. **Hwy. 7,** from the tinier town of **Haig** near Hope, runs west to Vancouver's suburbs along the north bank of the Fraser River. **Hwy. 3,** the **Crowsnest Trail,** winds east through breathtaking country, close to the U.S. border, to **Osoyoos** near **Penticton,** through **Kootenay country** to **Nelson, Crowsnest Pass,** and into Alberta. Finally, **Hwy. 5,** the **Coquihalla** ("Coca-Cola") **Hwy.,** is a new toll road ($10) running north to **Kamloops** with good access to the **Okanagan country.** If there's anywhere you can't reach from Hope, chances are the province has planned to build "Hwy. 9" directly to it.

The **Travel Infocentre** in Hope, 919 Water Ave. (869-2021), is likelier to know more about the filming here of the original "Rambo" blockbuster, *First Blood,* than anything else. Besides providing the intellectually stimulating "Rambo Walking Tour," (perhaps the guide just grunts?) the Infocentre also has information about the Fraser River Canyon (open daily 8am-8pm; Oct.-May 9am-5pm).

The **Greyhound station,** 833 3rd Ave. (869-5522), is centrally located and provides an easy reference point for visitors. Buses arrive almost hourly from Vancouver and continue onwards toward Dawson Creek or Calgary. 24-hr. **lockers** are available here for $1. Those without the patience (or the cash) to wait for the next departing bus north can hitch a ride along Hwy. 1 without too much difficulty. (*Let's Go* does not recommend hitchhiking.) Those averse to hitching can rent a car at **Gardner Chev-Olds,** 945 Water St. (869-9511), next to the Infocentre ($30 per day; 13 ¢ per km after 100km; optional damage/collision waiver $9 per day; rent for a week for the price of 6 days; open Mon.-Sat. 8:30am-6pm). The **police** in Hope (869-5644) are at 670 Hope-Princeton Hwy. (off Hwy. 3). The **post office** is at 777 Fraser St., across from the Cariboo Restaurant (open Mon.-Fri. 8:30am-5pm).

If you decide to stay overnight, trek a block north from the bus station to Wallace St. and hang a left. The **Hope Motor Hotel,** 272 Wallace St. (869-5641), rents rooms. Singles are from $35; two beds are $45. Be sure to request one of the recently renovated rooms. Breakfast is included in the price of the room, except in July or August. Campers can try **Coquihalla River Park,** 800 Kawkawa Rd. (869-7119), off Hwy. 3 via 7th Ave., just before the Coquihalla River Bridge, providing free showers (116 sites, $14, with electricity and water $18). **Telie Yet Campsite** offers a pretty river view and tentsites for $6, hookup for $15.

Hope has its share of fast-food joints, but if you prefer to order your meal from a resting position, try either the **Cariboo Restaurant** (867-5413), for a good generic meal (hamburger and fries for $6), or **The Suzie Q Family Restaurant** (869-5515) serving both cheap Western *and* Japanese cuisine (hmm…). Both are a block north of the bus station at the intersection of Wallace and 6th. For groceries try the **Overwaiter Foods** across from the Greyhound Station.

FRASER RIVER CANYON

YALE

Abandon Hope and go to…**Yale,** 30km north on the Trans-Canada Hwy. Yale boasted a gold-boom population of 20,000 in 1858, when it was the largest North American city west of Chicago and north of San Francisco. But the city's unfortunate name has permanently condemned it to second-rate status. Yale floundered, and the population has dwindled to 250. Though its decline was entirely predictable, the town could probably still muster an ice-hockey team capable of beating Yale's.

The Information Center lies along Hwy. 1 at the south end of town (open Mon.-Sat. 9am-5pm). If you're not frightened by psychedelic woolly red and orange carpet, the **Gold Nugget Motel** (863-2446), on the highway, offers singles for $28 (cable TV, no phones). Across the street is **Barry's Trading Post** (863-2214), a small general store with lots of cheap, fried food. Hamburgers are $2, cheeseburgers $2.25; groceries are available (open Mon.-Sat. 8am-8pm, Sun. 10am-6pm). The **Emery Creek Provincial Park,** 5km south on Hwy. 1, maintains 34 sites April through October ($10, no reservations; firewood and running water available).

Farther north along Hwy. 1, hard-core campers will enjoy roughing it at **Gold Pan River Campground,** 16km west of **Spences Bridge.** The 12 sites ($6) offer no privacy, but are a mere hop from the rushing **Thompson River.** Less intrepid campers can opt for **Skihist Provincial Park Campground,** 12km east of **Lytton.** The 50 sites ($9.50) are protected by locked gates from 11pm to 6am; water and flush toilets are provided.

OUTDOORS

For a better look at the Fraser River, it is worthwhile to set out on one of the moderately difficult **hikes** that start from trailheads near Hope. The short, lush **Rotary Trail** starts at Wardle St. and meets the confluence of the Fraser and Coquihalla Rivers. If you seek something more challenging, try the two-hour climb to the summit of **Thacker Mountain.** To reach the foot of this trail, cross Coquihalla River Bridge, take a left on Union Bar Rd., and then go left again on Thacker Mtn. Rd. The car park at the road's end marks the beginning of a 5km gravel path to the peak, featuring clear views of Hope and the Fraser River. While hiking to the trailhead, pause for a pleasant diversion at Kawkawa Creek off Union Bar Rd., recently "enhanced" to aid the mid- and late-summer salmon spawnings. The boardwalk along the creek leads to a swimming hole and popular picnicking spot.

For those with a car, the **Coquihalla Canyon Recreation Area** is a five- to10-min. drive out of Hope along Kawkawa Lake Rd. The **Othello Quintet Tunnels** provide mute evidence of the impressive engineering that led to the opening of the Kettle Valley Railway in 1916. Blasted through solid granite, these rough tunnels overlook the Coquihalla River, which has done a more impressive job on the granite by carving out the 300-ft.-deep channe. Take a right on Othello Rd. off Kawkawa Lake Rd., and then take another right on Tunnel Rd. Allow half an hour to walk through the tunnels.

If you're based in Yale and want to escape and enjoy the river, head north and take the first right after the stoplight, then follow the gravel road about 1km; you'll find a close-up view of the majestic **Lady Franklin Rock,** splitting the Fraser into two sets of heavy rapids. If you're interested in getting *on* the river, **Fraser River Raft Expeditions** (863-2336), just south of town, is undoubtedly the way to go. Although the $90 fee for a full-day trip might seem as steep as the canyon walls, those who can pull together the funds shouldn't miss the opportunity to get their hearts pounding and their bodies drenched. One-day and multi-day **rafting trips** down the Fraser, Thompson, Nahatlatch, and Coquihalla Rivers are available, and the friendly guides serve up great meals. Trips leave almost daily; call ahead to make a reservation.

When Simon Fraser made his pioneering trek down the river that now bears his name, he likened one particularly tumultuous stretch of rapids to the "Gates of Hell." Anyone who has spent time in New Haven will not be surprised that Yale lies just beyond **Hell's Gate** on the Fraser. The white foaming waters, 25km north of

Yale on Hwy. 1, make the success of Fraser's journey seem miraculous. When melting snow floods the river in spring, the 60m-deep water rushes through the narrow gorge with incredible force. A cluster of overpriced gift shops and eateries are now embedded in the precipitous cliffs where Fraser once advised "no human beings should venture." The gondolas of **Hell's Gate Airtram** will "fly" you 502 ft. across the canyon ($8.50, seniors $7.50, ages 6-14 $5, families $22) (4 min.); those wishing to stay grounded should opt for the free **hike** down to the river.

■■■ PENTICTON

Indigenous peoples named the region between Okanagan and Skaha Lakes *Pen-tak-tin*, "a place to stay forever." Today, the original inhabitants would spin in their graves if they knew how their eternal paradise has been transformed by heated pools, waterslides, and luxury hotels. Hot weather, sandy beaches, and proximity to Vancouver, Seattle, and Spokane have ushered in the Tourist Age, and it may strain your budget to spend a weekend here, let alone eternity. The human scale of the area still remains small in relation to the surrounding scenery, though, and the warm water and sprawling beaches of the Okanagan and Skaha Lakes make for ideal swimming, sailing and fishing. Camp or stay at the hostel and head away from the city.

PRACTICAL INFORMATION AND ORIENTATION

Visitors Information: Penticton Visitors Information Centre, 185 Lakeshore Dr. (493-4055 or 800-663-5052). Take Riverside Dr. north off Hwy. 97, then right on Lakeshore. Located next to a giant peach; fans of Roald Dahl will be delighted to know that James researched this area for *Let's Go*. A fount of travel brochures and an attentive staff. Open daily 8am-8pm; Sept.-June Mon.-Fri. 9am-5pm, Sat.-Sun. 10am-4pm. In summer, the city also sets up an **Information Centre** on Hwy. 97 S, 7km from downtown. While smaller than the main office, it carries an ample supply of brochures. Open June-Sept. daily 9am-5pm.

Greyhound, 307 Ellis (493-4101). To: Vancouver (5 per day, $43), Vernon (3 per day, $13), Kelowna (7 per day, $12). Open daily 6am-7pm.

Buses: Penticton Transit System, 301 E Warren Ave. (492-5602). Bus service $1, seniors and students 75¢, under 5 free. Day pass $2.50. All drivers carry complete schedules. Many of the routes converge at Wade and Martin St. Transit office open Mon.-Fri. 8am-5pm. Buses run Mon.-Fri. 6:30am-6:30pm, Sat. 8:30am-6:30pm.

Taxi: Klassic Kabs, 492-6666. 24 hrs. **Penticton Taxi,** 492-5555.

Car Rental: Budget Rent-A-Car (493-0212), in the main terminal at the Penticton Airport. $44 per day during the week, $24 on weekends. 100km free, 15¢ per additional km. Must be at least 21 with major credit card.

Bike Rental: The Penticton Hostel (492-3992) has two bikes they will rent to anyone for $15 per day; call ahead to reserve them. **Sun Country Cycle,** 533 Main St. (493-0686). $25 per day, $15 per ½-day, helmet included. Open Mon.-Sat. 9am-5:30pm.

Laundry: Plaza Laundromat, 417-1301 Main St. (493-8710), in the Plaza Shopping Mall. Wash $1.50, 8-min. dry 25¢. TV on premises. Open daily 8am-9pm.

Weather: 492-6991.

Crisis Line, 493-6622. **Women's Shelter,** 493-7233.

Hospital: Penticton Regional, 550 Carmi Ave. (492-4000).

Emergency: 911. **Police:** 1103 Main St. (492-4300).

Post Office: Westminster Postal Outlet (492-8394), in the florist's at 187 W Westminster Ave. Open Mon.-Fri. 8am-5:30pm, Sat. 9am-5pm. **Postal Code:** V2A 5M0. **Area Code:** 604.

The warmest, driest town in the region, Penticton lies 400km east of Vancouver on Hwy. 3, at the southern extreme of the Okanagan Valley. Lake Okanagan borders the north end of town, while smaller Skaha Lake lies to the south. Main Street bisects the city from north to south.

ACCOMMODATIONS AND CAMPING

Because Penticton is a year-round resort city, hotels here charge more than those in the surrounding towns. The hostel is a good deal. Since you'll be paying through the nose for camping, you might as well try to find a campground on the shores of one of the lakes. Make reservations; vacant sites can become scarce in July and Aug.

Penticton Hostel (HI-C), 464 Ellis St. (492-3992). Best bet in Penticton. Conveniently located ½ block from the Greyhound stop and 10 min. from the beach. Comfortable lounge and patio, kitchen, laundry facilities, gas grill. Frequented by a diverse, international crowd. Fills in July and Aug. Accommodates 45. $13.50, non-members $18.50, under 17 $6.25, under 6 free with parent. Linen $2.

Riordan House, 689 Winnipeg (493-5997). More elegant than the neon-glowing concrete-box motels on Lakeshore Dr., and not a penny more expensive. The gorgeous Victorian-style mansion was built in 1921 with stressed oak and fir brought from Nova Scotia. 3 impeccably decorated, enormous rooms include plush carpeting, TV, and VCR. The house even has a library. Mr. and Mrs. Ortiz, the friendly and easygoing proprietors, will make you feel right at home in these palatial surroundings. Mr. Ortiz cooks up a knockout breakfast, included in the room fee, featuring apricots, strawberries, and cherries when in season, and fresh-baked scones. 6 blocks from beach and 2 from center of town. Rooms $50-70.

Club Paradise Motel, 1000 Lakeshore Dr. (493-8400). Great location on Okanagan Lake Beach. Clean, crisp, recently renovated rooms. Each room features a revolutionary revolving television stand invented by the previous owner; you can even watch it from the bathroom. Cool. Showers, A/C, cable TV, refrigerators in every room. Rooms $50.

Wright's Beach Camp (492-7120). Directly off Hwy. 97 on the shores of Skaha Lake at the south end of town. Nearby traffic often noisy. Small, reasonably priced pizza joint on the grounds. Washrooms, showers. Sites $19, with hookups $23-25. Reserve at least 2 weeks in advance.

South Beach Gardens, 3815 Skaha Lake Rd. (492-0628), across the street from the beach, east of the Channel Parkway. 280 sites sprawled over 18 acres. Closely-cropped willows provide shade. Serviced sites $17-20. Unserviced sites $15.

Okanagan Lake Provincial Park (494-7399), 50km north of Penticton on Hwy. 97. 168 sites packed between the highway and the lake in 2 separate units. Sites $11.50. Stay in the north park, where sites are roomier. Good beach swimming. No reservations; always full in summer. Cruise for sites early (8-10am).

FOOD

Intransigent budget travelers may have to swallow their pride and heed the call of the Golden Arches or Burger King. However, a few local sandwich shops do provide workable alternatives. Vegetarians and health-conscious eaters can satisfy all their urges for unsweetened carob and delicious sprouted-out bread (we're serious) at the **Whole Food Emporium.** Stock up on eggs, bacon, sausage, and Spam at **Super Valu Foods,** 450 Martin St., one block west of Main (492-4315; open Mon.-Sat. 9am-9pm, Sun. 9am-6pm).

Penticton Whole Food Emporium, 1515 Main St. (493-2855). A true supermarket of health food, with lots of organic produce, bulk grains and pastas, and herbs. Best of all, the deli counter in the back slaps together fantastic sandwiches for $3-5. Open Mon.-Fri. 9am-8pm, Sat. 9am-6pm, Sun. 10am-5pm; Sept.-June Mon.-Wed. 9am-6pm, Thurs.-Fri. 9am-9pm, Sat. 9am-6pm, Sun. 10am-5pm.

Turtle Island Cafe, 718 Main St. (492-0085). This pleasant indoor/outdoor cafe is a great place to relax with the morning paper. Or relax in the afternoon; breakfast is served all day. Tasty, artery-clogging breakfast $3-6; hot and cold sandwiches $5-6. Open Mon. 7am-4pm, Tues.-Sat. 7am-8pm, Sun. 9am-3pm.

Judy's Deli, 129 W Nanaimo (492-7029). Take-out only; you'll find a large, splinter-free bench in front of the radio station next door. Healthy beach-goers stop here for hearty homemade soups ($1.65-2) and butter-laden sandwiches ($2.80-3.30). Browse the herbs and homeopathic medicines. Open Mon.-Sat. 9am-5:30pm.

Spotted Dog Coffee Bar, 320 Milton. Soda-fountain atmosphere meets espresso bar menu. Go figure. Light food choices. Yummy cookies (42¢). Open Mon.-Fri. 7am-10pm, Sat. 8am-10pm, Sun. 10am-4pm.

SIGHTS AND EVENTS

Known throughout Canada for its bountiful fruit harvests, the **Okanagan Valley** lures visitors with summer blossoms, sleepy towns, and tranquil lakes. Tourists with cars should explore Hwy. 97 and Hwy. 3A south of Penticton; camp in an orchard bursting with newly-ripened cherries, eat the fruit at a family stand, sample the wines at a local vineyard, or fish in one of the pristine lakes.

The Penticton tourist trade revolves around **Okanagan Lake.** A long, hot summer and the sport facilities on the lake make Okanagan a popular hangout for the young. **Sail Inland** (492-2628) arranges cruises, charters, and lessons. **The Marina,** 293 Front St. (492-2628), offers rentals of ski boats. **California Connection** (490-7844), on the beach next to the Coast Lakeside Hotel, rents jet skis (from $35 per ½ hr.), paddleboats ($10 per hr.), and windsurfers. Although renting equipment can blast a hole through your shorts pocket, basking in the plentiful sun and swimming in the warm waters are both free.

For a sample of local culture, take a trip to the **Art Gallery of the South Okanagan,** 11 Ellis St. (493-2928), at Front St. This lovely beachfront gallery exhibits on local and international levels. Good art, absolutely free. Don't miss it. (Open Tues.-Fri. 10am-5pm, Sat.-Sun. 1-5pm.) The **Penticton Museum** (also the **R.N. Atkinson Museum**), 785 Main St. (490-2452), presents one artist's interpretation of the region's history with Native artifacts and wildlife displays. (Open Mon., Wed., and Fri.-Sat. 10am-5pm, Tues. and Thurs. 10am-8:30pm; winter Mon.-Sat. 10am-5pm. Admission by donation.) In the park on Main St. across the road from the lake, the town sponsors free **summer evening concerts** at the Gyro Bandshell, usually beginning around 7:30pm.

Masquerading as an East African wildlife preserve, the **Okanagan Game Farm,** (497-5405) on Hwy. 97 just south of Penticton, covers 560 acres and protects 130 animal species from crazy summer life on the lake. Zebras, rhinos, gnus, aoudads, and ankoli roam free of fences and bars. Cars can drive throughout the park, and animal checklists should keep little kids entertained (open 8am-dusk; $8, ages 5-15 $6). The **Skaha Bluffs,** southeast of town on Valley View Road, have developed into a popular **rock climbing** venue, offering pitches of varying difficulties. For all kinds of information about the area, stop in at **Ray's Sports Den,** 215 Main St. (493-1216). The shop also organizes reasonably-priced classes—if you've been thinking about learning to climb, this might be the place to do it (open Mon.-Fri. 9am-6pm, Sat. 9am-5pm).

Travelers in extremely dire straits may consider signing on to **pick fruit** at one of the many orchards stretching south from Penticton to the U.S. border along Hwy. 97. Pickers are usually allowed to camp free in the orchards, and are paid a per-quart wage; the faster your hands move, the faster the cash flows. Daily earnings of $40 are common. Different fruits reach ripeness from mid-June (cherries) through mid-September (pears). Hitchhiking is a common mode of transportation along this stretch of highway; if you choose to join the fray, you'll face lots of competition. (Let's Go does not recommend hitchhiking.) Contact the Penticton Chamber of Commerce for more info., or cruise Hwy. 97 until you see a "Pickers Wanted" sign.

The colorful **Blossom Festival** in April welcomes the fresh flowers blooming in hundreds of apple, peach, and cherry orchards. The city shifts into full gear with the **Peach Festival** and the hellacious **Ironman Canada Triathlon** in mid-August. The Peach Festival offers recreational and aquatic activities for all ages, including a volleyball tournament and sand castle contest, while the triathalon commits true athletes to 4km of swimming, 180km of bicycling, and 45km of running.

The mists and mellow fruitfulness of fall mark the ripening of the wine season. There are several wineries within easy driving distance of Penticton; the closest one, **Hillside Cellars** (493-44242), at the junction of Vancouver Rd. and Naramata Rd.

northeast of Penticton, has a winery shop offering tastings and tours by appointment (shop open April 1 -Oct. 31 daily 10am-6pm; Nov. 1-Mar. 31 Tues.-Sun. 1pm-5pm). North of Summerland, **Sumac Ridge Estate Winery** (494-0451) offers tours daily at 10am, 2pm, and 4pm in summer, and a winery shop (open daily 9am-6pm). The **Okanagan Wine Festival** (490-8866), held in early October, is fun for those fond of feeling thick pulp squish between their toes. Nearby, **Apex Alpine,** P.O. Box 1060 (492-2880), provides winter diversion with 6 ski lifts, 44 runs, and a 670m vertical drop. (Open Nov. to late April.)

■■■ SALMON ARM

Salmon Arm is a backwoods honky-tonk town just like thousands of others that aren't immortalized in the pages of *Let's Go,* but its setting is extraordinary. Lake Shuswap is sublime, and the mountains cradling the town are breathtaking, especially when the leaves change in autumn.

Practical Information The **Travel Infocentre,** Box 999 (832-6247), is at 751 Marine Park Drive. Follow the "?" signs from the Trans-Canada Hwy. (Hwy. 1). Open daily 9am-7pm; winter Mon.-Fri. 9am-5pm.

The **Salmon Arm Transit System** (832-0191) runs two bus routes Mon.-Fri. 9am-4pm ($1.25) and door-to-door service ($1.50). Call to arrange a ride. You can wash out your grubby clothes at the **B-Line Laundromat,** 456 Trans-Canada Hwy. (835-2300), in Smitty's shopping center (wash $1.25, 12-min. dry 25¢; open daily 7am-11pm). In a medical emergency, call the **ambulance** (833-0188); the **hospital** is at 601 10th St. NE (832-2182). The **police** are at 501 2nd Ave. NE (832-6044). The **post office** is at 370 Hudson St. NE (832-3093; open Mon.-Fri. 8:30am-5pm). Address General Delivery letters to **Postal Code** V1E 4M6. The **area code** is 604.

Accommodations, Camping, and Food When in Salmon Arm, your best option is to overnight at the **Cindosa Bed and Breakfast,** 930 30th St. SE (832-3342), where the Moores will pamper you with nice beds and fantastic, home-cooked breakfasts. They'll even pick you up at the bus station, or bus line #2 will take you right by (singles $35, doubles $45). Only a few blocks away, **Auntie Claire's Bed and Breakfast,** 2930 5th Ave. SE (832-2421) offers pleasant rooms decorated with paintings by family members (singles $35, doubles $45). If you're mobile, it's worth the trek out to the **Squilax General Store Hostel** (675-2977), 50km west of Salmon Arm on the Trans-Canada Highway, for a unique hostelling experience—the sleeping quarters are on board three Canadian National Railway **cabooses,** specially procured and outfitted for the purpose. The mellow and friendly proprietor, Blair, is a wellspring of information about the area, and the sign on the front of the store is home to a remnant of an enormous bat colony displaced when its former haunt, a nearby church, burned down. There is no public transportation, but Greyhound drivers will drop you off at the store if you ask politely. **Glen Echo Resort,** 6592 Trans-Canada Hwy. NW V1E 4M2 (832-6268), 7 mi. west on Hwy. 1, is smack on Lake Shuswap, with a sandy beach, excellent swimming all summer long, and a gregarious owner (open Victoria Day-Sept.; 65 sites, $14).

Despite its name, Salmon Arm's culinary establishments showcase neither fish nor limbs. Stop in at **Golden Pantry Foods,** 452 Trans-Canada Hwy. (832-7910), for healthy foods in bulk (open Mon.-Sat. 9am-5:30pm). Or, check out the classy track lighting over the produce at **Safeway,** 360 Trans-Canada Hwy. (832-8086; open daily 8am-10pm). Restaurants offer standard fare. Try **Mr. Mike's** (832-8428) on Hwy. 1 across from the waterslide. The $6.50 all-you-can-eat salad bar includes soup and dessert. Beat the system and construct primitive, outlaw sandwiches from shredded ham and oddly shaped pieces of French bread. From 10am to 2pm on Sunday, there's an **all-you-can-eat breakfast buffet** for $6.50. (Open Mon.-Thurs. 11am-8:30pm, Fri.-Sat. 11am-9pm, Sun. 10am-8pm). The **Eatery,** 361 Alexander St. (832-7490), serves "Big Magilla" sandwiches (turkey, roast beef, and lamb $4.50) along with other gargantuan servings (open Mon.-Thurs. and Sat. 6am-5pm, Fri. 6am-6pm). **The Chocolate Bean,** 250 Alexander St. NE (832-6681), is a cafe with gourmet coffees ($1-3) and light foods (open Mon.-Fri. 8:30am-5:30pm, Sat. 9am-5pm).

Sights Visit **Heritage Park,** just south of the junction of Hwy. 1 and 97B (832-5243), to experience turn-of-the-century life. Period buildings include a church, a schoolhouse, and the meticulously restored **Haney Heritage House.** The **Salmon Arm Museum,** next to the church, displays an extensive collection of photographs from the early part of the century (open June-Oct. daily 10am-6pm; $2, children $1, preschoolers free).

Learn what curds and whey really are at **Gort's Gouda Cheese Factory,** 1470 50th St. SW (832-4274). The free tours only last a few minutes, getting you to the tasty cheese samples faster (tours Mon. and Fri. at 2pm; call to arrange tours at other times). Even if there's no tour, you can watch the cheesemaking process through viewing windows and stock up on bargain cheeses.

The Salmon Arm area teems with wildlife. Relax at **McGuire Park,** on Hwy. 1 next to the hospital, to view Canada geese, muskrats, turtles, and ducks. Catch kokanee or rainbow trout in **Lake Shuswap,** swim, whitewater raft on nearby **Adams River,** or hike out to **Margaret Falls,** just west of town. Follow the signs for **Heral Park** off Hwy. 1. A 10 km detour and a short hike on the manicured slopes will bring you to the striking falls.

The **Caravan Farm Theatre** (546-8533) presents top-notch performances during the summer on Saturdays through Thursdays at 8pm. The Farm, 5 mi. northwest of Armstrong, is bursting with leftover hippie charm, including musical instruments dangling from the trees and great organic produce ($14, students and seniors $11, children $8).

Every four years in October, the Salmon Arm area experiences two runs: the famous **salmon run** on the Adams River 46km west of Salmon Arm, where more than a million sockeye salmon thrash their desperate way up from the Pacific Ocean to spawn, and the less famous **tourist run,** in which thousands of bystanders cram into tiny Roderick Haig-Brown Provincial Park and strain to catch a glimpse of the colorful fish. The sight of salmon at the end of a 600-km journey from the sea, packed tightly into the river, is truly stunning.

Salmon Arm is also home to world-famous talking horse **Shag-ra** and his faithful companion **Shamus the Wonderdog.** Shag-ra has appeared on network television and performs regularly at local fairs and festivals. In the face of skepticism and plagued with an unappetizing tooth discoloration, Shag-ra perseveres, undaunted. For more information about Shag-ra, contact the Chamber of Commerce or the Travel Infocentre.

■ ■ ■ REVELSTOKE

In the 19th century Revelstoke was straight out of a Sam Peckinpah Western, with dust-encrusted megalomaniacs maiming each other amid the gold-laden Selkirk Mountains. Revelstoke now attracts an older, Winnebago-driving crowd, but has designs on the younger set of skiers and hikers, proposing a major expansion of the ski resort at Mt. MacKenzie, 5km south of town. The projected influx of money and tourism would quickly turn Revelstoke, wedged between the impressive snow-capped peaks of the Selkirk and the Monashee Mountains, into a Banff-like tourist draw, an unwelcome prospect to many Revelstokians.

PRACTICAL INFORMATION AND ORIENTATION

Visitors Information: Travel Information Centre, junction of Hwy. 1 and Hwy. 23 N (837-3522). Open early May-Sept. daily 9am-8pm. **Chamber of Commerce,** 202 Campbell Ave. (837-5345), downtown. Useful and convenient (open Mon.-Fri. 8:30am-4:30pm). For more information write to the Chamber of Commerce, P.O. Box 490, Revelstoke, BC V0E 2S0. **Canadian Parks Service,** at Boyle Ave. and 3rd St. (837-7500). Open Mon.-Fri. 8:30am-noon and 1-4:30pm.

Greyhound, 1899 Fraser Dr. (837-5874), just off Hwy. 1. To: Calgary ($45.50); Vancouver ($54.50); Salmon Arm ($10.65). Open Mon.-Fri. 6:30am-noon, 2-6pm, and 10-11:30pm.

Taxi: Johnnie's, 314 Townley St. (837-3000). 24 hrs.

Car Rental: Tilden Car Rental, 301 W 1st St. (837-2158). New cars at decent rates. $40 per day with 100km free, 15¢ per additional km. Must be 21 with a credit card.

Bicycle Rental: Spoketacular Sports, 111 MacKenzie (837-2220).

Ambulance, 374-5937. **Police,** 320 Wilson St. (837-5255).

Post Office: 307 W 3rd St. (837-3228). Open Mon.-Fri. 8:30am-5pm. **Postal Code:** V0E 2S0.

Area Code: 604.

Revelstoke is situated on the Trans-Canada Hwy., 410km west of Calgary and 575km east of Vancouver. The town can be easily covered on foot or by bicycle. **Mount Revelstoke National Park** is much larger, covering 263 sq. km. Mild temperatures, and much rain support a thick tree cover on the nearby Columbia Mountains.

ACCOMMODATIONS AND CAMPING

Many hotels line Revelstoke's rim along the Trans-Canada Hwy. In town, you'll find a bed for the same moderate price, removed from the sounds and smells of traffic. Local campgrounds tend to favor RV drivers over tenters.

Smokey Bear Campground (837-9575), on Hwy. 1, 5km west of Revelstoke. Close to the noisy highway. Clean bathrooms, metered showers, laundromat, and stocked store. 35-ft. Smokey Bear statue out front. RVs and tents welcome. 30 sites, $10-15. Each additional person 75¢. Electricity $2, sewer $2, water $2. Open all year. Also runs a **hostel** in two mobile trailers with 22 beds and a charcoal grill. $15, discount for cyclists.

King Edward Hotel, 112 2nd St. E (837-2000), at Orton. Down-and-out locals, the nearby train depot, and the lounge beneath make for less-than-tranquil snoozing. Friendly management, lowest prices in town. Rooms vary in quality and upkeep; ask to see one before you accept it. Singles $25.30, $31.05 with bath. Doubles $28.75, $35.65 with bath.

Frontier Motel (837-5119), at Trans-Canada Hwy. and Hwy. 23 N, next to the infocentre. 28 small but pleasant rooms. Color TV. Popular restaurant next door is run by the same management (breakfast before 8am included). Store open 24 hrs. Singles $43. Doubles $50. Prices drop $4 in winter.

Hidden Motel, 1855 Big Eddy Rd. (837-4240). Take Hwy. 23 south from Trans-Canada Hwy., turn left on Big Eddy Rd. to reach this cozy, comfortable, family-operated hotel. Each room has its own stove, refrigerator, kitchen sink, and cable TV. Dutch spoken. No GST. Singles and doubles $48, doubles with twin beds $54. Each additional person $6. Open mid-April-mid-Oct.

FOOD

The downtown dining scene is dominated by Chinese and Western restaurants. You'll have to head far to the west along Hwy. 1 for a Whopper or that much-coveted box of McDonaldland Cookies. Pick up a 5-lb. can of beans at **Cooper's Supermarket** (837-4372), in the Alpine Village Centre on Victoria St. (open Mon.-Thurs. and Sat. 8am-7pm, Fri. 8am-9pm, Sun. 9am-6pm).

Manning's Restaurant, 302 MacKenzie Ave. (837-3258). The best Chinese food in town, plus a wide array of reasonably priced Continental dishes. Beef and broccoli ($6.75), sweet and sour spareribs ($7), 8-oz. steaks ($10). Open Mon.-Sat. noon-10pm, Sun. 4-9pm.

A.B.C. Family Restaurant (837-5491), in the Alpine Village Centre on Victoria St. Link in a chain of "family" restaurants, but nonetheless maintains an original atmosphere. Huge dinner menu ranges from $7-10. Hearty soups ($4) are perfect for a rainy day. Sandwiches, $5.50-7; don't pass up a slice of fresh pie ($3-4). Open daily 6am-10pm.

Frontier Restaurant (837-5119), at the junction of Hwy. 1 and Hwy. 23 N. Wagon wheels and weathered wood. The "Ranchhand" is a ½-lb. cheeseburger with the works ($7.25). Tenderfoots may prefer the "bareback" ($4.50), a plain hamburger with nothing on it. Open daily 6am-9pm.

Alphaus, 604 W. 2nd St., at Garden Ave. (837-6380). The quaint white stucco and brown shingles seem jarring in Revelstoke. Sandwiches on homemade rye $4-6; authentic German dinner specialities run $7.50-12.50. Bottle of Okanagan Stout $3. Open daily 8:30am-8pm.

SIGHTS

The guiding light of tourism in town is the **Revelstoke Dam,** 5km north of Hwy. 1 on Hwy. 23 (837-6515 or 837-6211). The **visitors centre** illustrates the dam's mechanical marvels with a free tour via "talking wand." Extensive videos and exhibits outline the construction, operation, and environmental impact of the dam from a surprisingly even-handed perspective. Ride the elevator to the top of the dam for an impressive view. (Open daily mid-March-mid-June 9am-5pm; mid-June-mid-Sept. 8am-8pm; mid-Sept. to late Oct. 9am-5pm. Wheelchair accessible.)

The **Revelstoke Railway Museum,** off Victoria Road, is a recently-completed shrine to the Iron Horse. Many old photographs and story-board exhibits outline the construction of the first Canadian transcontinental lines, and the museum preserves a steam locomotive and Canadian Pacific Railway office-on-wheels, both indoors in an enormous hangar. Upstairs, an observation deck provides a bird's-eye view of the heavy traffic on the main C.P.R. line right outside (open daily 9am-5pm, winter 10am-4pm. $3, seniors $2, ages 7-17 $1.50, under 7 free.)

Mt. Revelstoke National Park has many of the scenic attractions one comes to expect from Canadian national parks. This small park teems with all sorts of animals that eat, drink, walk, and copulate right in front of you. 35km of established trails lead to spectacular high-alpine lakes. Unfortunately, the small size and cold temperatures of these lakes make fish scarce. At the summit of Mt. Revelstoke are some of the few vehicle-accessible alpine meadows in western Canada; **Summit Road** branches off from the Trans-Canada Hwy. 1.5km east of Revelstoke and takes about one hour to drive.

Two special **boardwalks** just off Hwy. 1 on the eastern border of the park allow exploration of the local brush. The "skunk cabbage" trail leads through "acres of stinking perfection:" brambles of skunk cabbage plants that grow to heights of over 1.5m. Some of the cedars on the "giant cedars trail" are over 1000 years old.

Revelstoke has tried some curious variations on **downhill skiing** to spice up its winter season. **Mount Mackenzie,** P.O. Box 1000, 5km outside of town (call collect at 837-5268), gives you a chance to climb deep bowls of powdered snow in motorized snow cats. For the less adventurous (or wealthy), the mountain also maintains 21 trails with a 2,000 ft. vertical drop. **Cross-country** skiers will find more than enough snow and trails in the nearby national parks to keep them busy all winter. Summer vacationers will want to contact **Monashee Outfitting,** P.O. Box 2958 (837-3538), sponsoring just about every outdoor activity imaginable, including horse rides, fishing and hunting trips, and gold panning.

■■■ GLACIER NATIONAL PARK

For a $5000 salary bonus and immortality on the map, Major A.B. Rogers discovered a route through the Columbia Mountains, finally allowing Canada to build its first transcontinental railway. Completed in 1885, the railway was a dangerous enterprise; more than 200 lives were lost to avalanches during its first 30 years of operation. Today, **Rogers Pass** lies in the center of Glacier National Park, and 1350 sq. km commemorate the efforts of Rogers and other hardy explorers who bound British Columbia to the rest of Canada.

Practical Information   The Trans-Canada Hwy.'s many **scenic turn-offs** offer picnic facilities, bathrooms, and historical plaques. For a detailed description of the park's 19 hiking trails, contact the **Park Administration Office** (837-7500), at 3rd and Boyle, west of the park in Revelstoke (open Mon.-Fri. 8:30am-noon, 1pm-4:30pm), or pick up a copy of *Footloose in the Columbias* at the **Rogers Pass Information Centre,** along the highway in Glacier. The Centre has enough computerized information, scale models, and exhibits to warrant a visit. Don't miss the free 25-minute movie *Snow War,* including a chilling scene from an actual avalanche rescue (open daily 8am-6pm; in winter hours vary). **Park passes** are required if you don't drive straight through ($5 per day, $10 for 4 days, $30 per year, and good in all National Parks). For more information about Glacier National Park, write the Superintendent, P.O. Box 350, Revelstoke, BC V0E 2S0.

Glacier lies right on the Trans-Canada Hwy., 262km west of Calgary and 723km east of Vancouver. **Greyhound** (837-5874) makes four trips daily from Revelstoke to Glacier ($7). In an emergency, call the **Park Warden Office** (837-6274; open daily 7am-11pm; winter daily 24 hrs.). The **area code** is 604.

Accommodations, Camping, and Food   There are two campgrounds in Glacier: **Illecillewaet** (ill-uh-SILL-uh-watt) and **Loop Brook.** Both offer flush toilets, kitchen shelters with cook stoves, drinking water, and firewood (open mid-June-Sept.; sites for both $10.50). Illecillewaet stays open in winter without plumbing; winter guests must register at the Park Administration Office at Rogers Pass. **Back-country campers** must pitch their tents at least 5km from the pavement and register with the Administration Office beforehand. You'd do well to drop by a supermarket in Golden or Revelstoke before you enter the park.

Outdoors   A century after Rogers' discovery, Glacier National Park remains an unspoiled and remote wilderness. The jagged peaks and steep, narrow valleys of the Columbia Range prevent development. One would literally have to move mountains to build here. The Trans-Canada Highway cuts a thin ribbon through the center of the park, affording spectacular views of over 400 glaciers. More than 140km of challenging trails lead away from the highway, inviting rugged mountain men and women to penetrate the near-impenetrable. Try to visit the park in late July or early August, when brilliant explosions of mountain wildflowers offset the deep green of the forests. Glacier receives measurable precipitation every other day in summer, but the clouds of mist that encircle the peaks and blanket the valleys only add to the park's astonishing beauty. Unless you're Sir Edmund Hilary or Tenzing Sherpa, avoid exploring the park in winter, as near-daily snowfalls and the constant threat of avalanches often restrict travel to the Trans-Canada Hwy.

Eight popular **hiking trails** begin at the Illecillewaet campground, 3.4km west of Rogers Pass. The relaxing, 1km **Meeting of the Waters** trail leads to the confluence of the Illecillewaet and Asulkan Rivers. The 4.2-km **Avalanche Crest** trail offers spectacular views of Rogers Pass, the Hermit Range, and the Illecillewaet River Valley; the treeless slopes below the crest testify to the destructive power of winter snowslides. From early July to late August, the Information Centre runs daily **interpretive hikes** through the park beginning at 9am. Come prepared for one of these four- to six-hour tours with a picnic lunch, a rain jacket, and a sturdy pair of walking shoes. Regulations prohibit biking on the trails in Glacier. The park's glacial meltwaters, a startling milky-aqua color due to the fine bits of sediment suspended in the current, don't support many fish; determined anglers can try their luck with the cutthroat in the Illecillewaet River (get a permit, $6 for 7 days, at the Information Centre).

■■■ KOOTENAY NATIONAL PARK

Kootenay National Park hangs off the continental divide to the southwest. Stately conifers, lush alpine meadows, towering peaks, and rushing rivers afford a tremendous range of recreational activites. Kootenay's best feature is what it doesn't have: people. Virtually all the visitors to the park are traveling to or from Banff, and while the majestic Banff-Windermere highway, running the length of the park, is a magnificent drive, it barely scratches the surface of Kootenay National Park. Travelers who step even a short distance off the beaten path will leave the crowds behind and discover the solitude and beauty of the Canadian Rockies as they were meant to be experienced. Paradoxically, the most beautiful natural scenes in Kootenay National Park are also the least visited.

PRACTICAL INFORMATION AND ORIENTATION

Visitor Information: West Gate Information Center (347-9505), on Hwy. 93 just inside the park boundary at Radium Hot Springs, hands out **maps** and pamphlets, and issues wilderness passes for $5-35 (required for overnight backcountry camping). Park entrance fee is $5, $10 for 4 days. Entrance permits are good in Kootenay, Banff, Yoho, and Jasper National Parks. Open June 11-Sept.11 daily 8am-8pm; Sept. 17-Oct. 9 Sat. and Sun. 9am-5pm. On Hwy. 93 near the northeastern entrance to the park, the **Marble Information Centre** fulfills the same purpose. Open June 24-Sept. 25 Mon.-Thurs. 9am-4pm, Fri.-Sun. 8am-8pm. **Park Administration Office** (347-9615) is on the access road to Redstreak Campground, or write Kootenay National Park, P.O. Box 220, Radium Hot Springs, BC V0A 1M0. Open Mon.-Fri. 8am-noon and 1-4pm. The **post office** on Radium St. in Radium Hot Springs is open Mon.-Fri. 8:30am-5pm.

Buses: Greyhound buses stop at the **Esso** station, 7507 W Main St. (347-9369; open daily 7am-11pm), at the junction of Hwy. 93 and Hwy. 95 in the town of Radium Hot Springs just outside the park. Daily service to Banff ($16) and Calgary ($30.50) runs the length of the Banff-Windermere highway through the park.

Emergency: ambulance (342-2055). The nearest hospital is **Windermere District Hospital** in Windermere (342-1201).

Police: Windermere (342-0290) **and Radium Hot Springs** (347-9393).

Area code: 604.

Kootenay National Park lies southwest of Banff and Yoho. Hwy. 93 runs through the park from the Trans-Canada Highway in Banff, to Radium Hot Springs, at the southwest edge of the park, where it joins Hwy. 95 to run 143km south to Cranbrook. From Radium Hot Springs, Hwy. 95 runs north 105km to Golden.

ACCOMMODATIONS AND CAMPING

The flagship campground of the park is **Redstreak,** with 242 sites, flush toilets, showers, firewood, playgrounds, and swarms of RVs. If you're looking for seclusion, look elsewhere: your only chance is in the walk-in sites off **Loop "D."** To get there, don't enter the park on Hwy. 93. Take the access road that departs Hwy. 95 near the south end of Radium Hot Springs. (Open mid-May-mid-Sept.; sites $15, full hookup $18.50.) More appealing from the solitude-seeker's point of view is **McLeod Meadows,** 27km north of the West Gate entrance on Highway 93. The 98 sites are wooded and better spaced than those at Redstreak, and RVs are rare. (Open mid-May- mid-Sept.; sites $11.) **Marble Canyon,** 86km north of the West Gate entrance, or 7km inside the park boundary with Banff, is similar to McLeod Meadows, though the sites are more closely spaced and it's a bit more populated (61 sites; open mid-June to early Sept.; sites $11). In winter, free camping is available at the **Dolly Varden** picnic area, 36km north of the West Gate entrance. Firewood, water, toilets, and a kitchen shelter are provided.

Camping outside the park is plentiful. Try the **Spur Valley Resort** (347-9822), 18km north of Radium Hot Springs on Hwy. 95. This wonderfully undeveloped and sparsely attended commercial campground is worth the trip. Try to nab a site right

K O O T E N A Y   N A T I O N A L   P A R K

on the creek (50 tent sites, $10.60). **Dry Gulch Provincial Park,** 4km south of Radium Hot Springs on Hwy. 95, is just a campground. The 25 pleasant sites on dry, pine-shaded hills cost $9.50 a night and fill up early. If you must have a bed, the **Columbia Motel,** on St. Joseph Street (347-9557), offers clean, well-kept rooms, with friendly, down-to-earth Irish owners and about the lowest rates in town. Lots of seniors keep the place nice and quiet. (Rooms $45-55; $5 extra for a kitchen.)

FOOD

There is no affordable food in the park; the town of Radium supports a few uninspiring eateries. Pop into **JJ's,** 7518 Main St. E (347-9335) for tasty subs (8-inch $3, 12-inch $4), ice cream, and good shakes ($2). Take 'em with you to one of 16 pleasant picnic areas in the park, or sit on the patio out front (open daily, 10am-midnight). If you're looking for a sit-down meal, **Smitty's** at 7513 Main St. W (347-9369) dishes out standard Canadian fare at moderate prices in a family restaurant atmosphere. A 10% senior discount means you'll find lots of silver hair here (open daily 7am-10pm). If you love truck-stop food, the restaurant at the **Husky** station at 4918 Highway 93 (347-9811) offers the most cost-efficient food in town (measured in calories per dollar) short of a five-pound bag of sugar. (Open daily 7am-10:30pm.) If you decide to go with the sugar, get it at **Radium Foods,** 7546 Main St. E (347-9600), which has a decent selection. (Open Mon.-Sat. 9am-6pm, Sun. 10am-7pm.)

OUTDOORS

Kootenay National Park's main attraction is **Radium Hot Springs** (347-9485), the complex of pools just inside the West Gate entrance to the park responsible for the congested traffic and towel-toting tourists. Be thankful this is the closest thing Kootenay has to a "townsite." The complex contains two pools, a hot pool for soaking (40°C; 104°F) and a cooler pool for swimming (27°C; 81°F). The deck overlooking the pools lets you check out the scene for free before you make any investment. (Open daily 9am-10:30pm; $3.50, seniors $3.25, children $3. Lockers 25¢, towel rental $1, suit rental $1.25.)

The 95-km **Banff-Windermere Highway** (Hwy. 93) forms the backbone of scoliosis-afflicted Kootenay. Stretching from Radium Hot Springs to Banff, the highway follows the **Kootenay** and **Vermilion Rivers,** with views of lofty glacier-enclosed peaks, dense stands of virgin forest, and rushing glacial-green rivers. When the route drops into the Kootenay River valley, feast your eyes on the vast, wild landscape. Except for the narrow ribbon of highway, this valley remains in a wild state.

For most visitors, the experience of the park ends with the drive up Hwy. 93. With the exception of two short, photogenic trails, most travelers stalwartly refuse to leave their vehicle and experience nature intimately. One of the places they may stop is **Marble Canyon,** about 15km from the border with Banff, where a 1.6km trail leads along (and over, on numerous bridge crossings) a remarkably deep, narrow gorge cut by Tokumm Creek. Despite the preponderence of video cameras, you won't want to miss this unique geologic feature, and the voluminous falls at the end of the trail. Interpretive signs explain how Nature shaped this landscape.

The other tourist trail is the **Paint Pots Trail,** wheelchair-accessible and leaving Hwy. 93 3.2km south of Marble Canyon. This trail leads to several **springs** rich in iron oxide. Local Native Canadians quarried ochre from this oxide for use in coloring the paints they used to decorate their tipis and bodies. The trail winds through the **ochre flats,** where several early 20th century mining operations produced pigment for the market. Bounce on the suspension bridge over the Vermilion River. The 1.6-km trail is a leisurely 30-minute stroll.

After the two nature trails, the myriad **hiking** trails in Kootenay are blissfully uncrowded. An easy dayhike, the **Stanley Glacier Trail** starts 2.5km north of Marble Canyon and leads 4.8 km into a glacier-carved valley, ending 1.6km from the foot of Stanley Glacier, responsible for gouging out the valley. For the more intrepid dayhiker, the awe-inspiring hike over **Kindersley Pass** is an experience. The 16.5-km hike climbs over 3km, and is rough going, but the reward is incredible **views** of the

Columbia River Valley to the west and the crest of the Rockies to the east. The two trailheads at either end of the route, **Sinclair Creek** and **Kindersley Pass,** are 0.8km apart on Hwy. 93, about 15km inside the West Gate entrance, meaning you won't have to retrace your steps.

Many longer backpacking routes cross the **backcountry.** One popular route is the four-day jaunt along the **Rockwell Trail** from **Floe Lake** to **Wolverine Pass,** though there are many shorter and longer routes. Several trails, and the entire length of Hwy. 93, are open for **mountain biking.** In particular, the 32-km **East Kootenay Trail,** a system of abandoned logging roads, parallels the Hwy. 93 through the Kootenay Valley, making a pleasant loop ride returning along the wide-shouldered highway. Silt-laden rivers make for generally poor, but not impossible, **fishing.**

Backcountry visitors should stop in at an information centre and pick up the free *Kootenay National Park Backcountry Guide,* with its useful **maps,** trail descriptions and profiles. No permit is needed for dayhiking, but overnight backcountry camping requires a **Wilderness Pass,** $5 per person per night, or $35 for an entire season. Wilderness Passes are available from information centres. Both black and grizzly bears roam the woods in prolific numbers, so hikers should use care on the trail, including making noise (using your voice is best) to avoid surprising bears. Poles for suspending food out of bear-reach are provided at all backcountry campsites, and should be used religiously. Surface water is often inhabited by *giardia.* Treat or boil water before drinking it.

■■■ NELSON

In the forested hills at the foot of Kootenay Lake, Nelson is a center of the West Kootenay country. Its long history has bequeathed to the city a large number of landmark buildings. Filmmakers have used Nelson extensively for on-location shooting, including 1986's romantic comedy hit *Roxanne* starring Steve Martin.

Nelson has smoothly assimilated non-traditional lifestyles. In winter, ski bums and affluent outsiders enter the mix peaceably, while in summer a vast influx of hippies and New Agers does not upset the equilibrium of the down-to-earth locals. Whatever you look like, whether you drink mineral water, beer, whiskey, or herbal tea, you'll fit right in here.

PRACTICAL INFORMATION

Nelson and District Infocentre, 225 Hall St. (352-3433), will shower you with information and literature about how to keep busy, whether you plan to spend one day or the rest of your life in and around Nelson. Open daily 8:30am-7pm; Sept.-June Mon.-Fri. 8:30am-4:30pm.

Buses: Greyhound station at 1112 Lakeside, in the Chahko-mika Mall (352-3939). To: Vancouver (2 per day; $74.60), Calgary (2 per day; $72.40), and Banff (2 per day; $58.35).

Nelson Transit Systems: Three lines cover the city, a fourth travels on the North Shore of Kootenay Lake to Balfour. Exact fare required. Within the city, adults $1, seniors and students 80¢. The North Shore route is more expensive, depending on how far you go. Buses run Mon.-Fri. 6:30am-11:30pm, Sat. 8:30am-7:30pm. Call 352-2911 for information.

Taxi: Kootenay Kabs (352-0101). Not kute.

Car Rental: Shellvue Car Rental, at the Shell station, 301 Nelson St. (352-2014). $10 per day plus 12¢ per km, or $169 per week with 1000 free km.

Bike Rental: Gerick Cycle, 702 Baker St. (354-4622). $20 per day, $35 for a weekend. Open Mon.-Thurs. and Sat. 9am-5:30pm, Fri. 9am-9pm.

Pharmacy: Pharmasave, 639 Baker St. (352-2313). Open Mon.-Thurs. 9am-6pm, Fri. 9am-9pm, Sat. 9am-5pm, Sun. 10am-4pm.

Hospital: Kootenay Lake District, 3 View St. (352-3111). If you break your leg, don't try to walk; it's way up the hill in the southeast part of town.

Emergency: Ambulance (352-2112), **fire** (352-3123), **police** (RCMP 352-3511; city 352-2266).

N
E
L
S
O
N

Post Office: 514 Vernon St. (352-3538). Open Mon.-Fri. 8:30am-5pm. **Postal Code:** V1L 5X4.
Area Code: 604.

Nelson lies in the heart of Kootenay County, at the junction of Highways 6 and 3A. From Nelson, Highway 3A heads west to **Castlegar,** 41km distant. Highway 6 leads straight south 65km to the U.S. border, where it becomes Washington Rte. 31, continuing 110 mi. south to Spokane.

ACCOMMODATIONS AND CAMPING

Allen Hotel/Hostel (HI-C), 171 Baker St. (352-7573). This tiny converted hotel has a distinctly European flavor, from the heavy German accent of the manager to the narrow, creaky stairs. The small rooms have one bed or bunk each. Clean. No curfew. Check-in 5-10pm, but call first, or the manager may not be there. Ten beds (reservations recommended). $13.50, non-members $17.50.

Chinook Park Campground, cross the orange bridge over Kootenay Lake and follow Highway 3A 15km (825-0039). This marvelous, rustic campground has spacious, treed sites on the lake. Rough road and rickety bridge keep out most RVs. A burbling brook minimizes highway noise. Hot showers. 25 sites, $10.

Kokanee Creek Provincial Park, 5km beyond Chinook Park on Hwy. 3A (825-4723). 112 closely spaced sites on the shores of Kootenay Lake. Wheelchair-access sites available. No reservations; fills early; $12.

Nelson City Tourist Park, on High St. Take Vernon to its eastern terminus and follow the signs. Packed like sardines. Still, it's the best place to crash if you're unable to get out of town. 40 sites, $11. Showers for non-campers $3.

FOOD

The diverse population of Nelson supports a variety of restaurants. Vegetarians will want to check out the **Alleyway Café,** a "whole foods restaurant" at 620 Herridge Lane (352-5200; open Mon.-Sat. 11:30am-10pm, Sun. 4-10pm). Whatever your lifestyle, you can get the supplies you need at **Super Valu,** 708 Vernon St. (352-2815; open Mon.-Wed., Sat. 9am-6pm, Thurs.-Fri. 9am-9pm, Sun. 10am-5pm). Nelson is the place to stock up on fresh bread. There are many bakeries downtown, including the **Kootenay Baker,** 295 Baker St. (352-2274).

DJ's Restaurant, 561 Baker St. (562-5011). The menu includes Middle Eastern, Greek, and Italian food, but the best deals are on Mexican. Enjoy the tasty and filling $4.50 vegetarian burrito. Partake of laid-back camaraderie with your meal on the patio. Open Mon.-Sat. 11am-10pm.

Mediterranean 57, great pizza at unbeatable prices. Small $5-6, large $9-11. Open Mon.-Thurs. 11:30am-11:30pm, Fri-Sat. 11:30am-2am.

Mimi's, 702 Vernon St. (352-7113). It's always time for breakfast, and this is the place to get it . Try their delicious waffles ($4.50), available in 12 varieties. Sit in the airy, pleasant front room and ponder why people choose to sit in the eerie backroom, which looks like it's straight out of *Twin Peaks.* Huge deli sandwiches to go for $6. Open daily 5:30am-2pm.

SIGHTS AND OUTDOORS

Examine the buildings that made Nelson into a movie backdrop on a walking tour of the historical downtown area. Pick up the free brochure *Architectural Heritage Walking Tour* at the Chamber of Commerce. Extend your tour behind the wheel through the historic homes of the **Uphill District.** The Chamber of Commerce also hands out a free guide to a walking tour of sites filmed in *Roxanne,* but the narrative refers extensively to events in the movie, so if you don't remember it, you'll be lost.

The meticulously restored **Streetcar 23** runs from the end of Hall St. to Kokanee St. along Kootenay Lake, recalling the days when streetcars cruised Nelson's hill, from 1929 to 1949. The streetcar was rescued in the early 1980s from its unfortunate retirement as a dog kennel, and vintage equipment was salvaged from as far

away as Brussels and Melbourne to render the car functional. (Open daily June 15-
Aug. 15 noon-9pm; Aug. 15-Sept. 5 noon-6pm. Fare $2, seniors and ages 6-12 $1.)

The West Arm of Kootenay Lake, bordering Nelson on the north, may look huge,
but its just a tiny part of the enormous lake. Many varieties of **fish** haunt the lake,
notably **dolly varden** and **rainbow trout** up to 30 pounds. **Kokanee** are also abundant in the lake, and **sturgeon** prowl the Kootenay River.

Twenty-five km east of Nelson on Highway 3A, the **West Kootenay Visitor Centre** (825-4723), in Kokanee Creek Provincial Park, displays a range of exhibits on
local human and natural history, and hands-on displays will keep the kiddies
amused. Behind the Visitor Centre, a spawning channel fills up with bright red
kokanee in late August and early September, as they struggle upstream to spawn
and then drift back downstream, dead. The Visitor Centre is also a great place to get
information about outdoor recreation in the area. (Open July-Aug. daily 9am-9pm.)

Forty km northeast of Nelson, Highway 3A crosses Kootenay lake on a **ferry.** The
6-km crossing takes 45 minutes, making it the longest free ferry ride in the world.
(Ferry runs 6am-midnight.)

The Kokanee Creek Road, heading north from Highway 3A, 21km northeast of
Nelson, is a major access to **Kokanee Glacier Provincial Park,** 320 sq. km of rugged
peaks and alpine lakes. The park contains several glaciers and offers numerous dayhiking opportunities. From Gibson Lake at the end of Kokanee Creek Road, it is a
spectacular four-hour hike one-way past Kokanee and Kaslo lakes to the Slocan
Chief Cabin. Try to visit the park during the week, as it gets busy on weekends. Pick
up the **park pamphlet** at the Nelson Chamber of Commerce, or call the Ministry of
Parks District Manager at 825-9509.

The gentle but isolated and densely forested hills of the Kootenay Country are
ideal for mountain biking. Thousands of km of abandoned roads are accessible to
the intrepid explorer. Pick up *Mountain Bike Adventures in the Kootenay* at the
Chamber of Commerce. One popular route begins at the top of Silver King Road in
the southwest part of town, and proceeds through a lush forest to an old, abandoned mine about two hours' ride from town.

During the winter, the phenomenal powder of **Whitewater Ski Area,** 35km
southeast of town, attracts skiers from far away, and Nelson slips comfortably into
the role of ski-resort town. The resort maintains 32 trails and slopes with a 1300 ft.
vertical drop. (Information: 354-4944, 24 hrs. Snow report: 352-7669. Lift tickets
$29, seniors and ages 13-18 $23, ages 7-12 $17.)

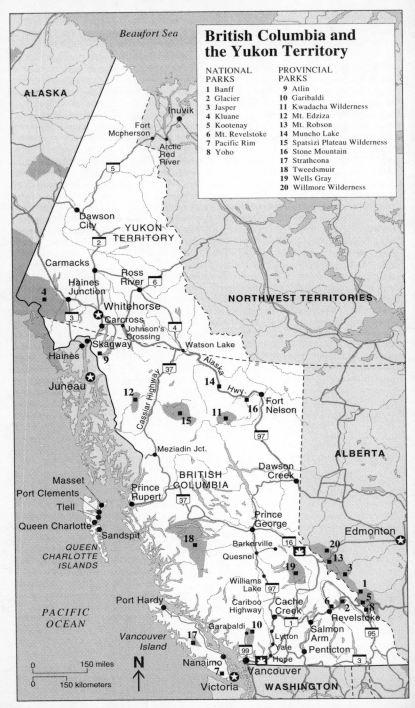

British Columbia and the Yukon Territory

NATIONAL PARKS
1 Banff
2 Glacier
3 Jasper
4 Kluane
5 Kootenay
6 Mt. Revelstoke
7 Pacific Rim
8 Yoho

PROVINCIAL PARKS
9 Atlin
10 Garibaldi
11 Kwadacha Wilderness
12 Mt. Edziza
13 Mt. Robson
14 Muncho Lake
15 Spatsizi Plateau Wilderness
16 Stone Mountain
17 Strathcona
18 Tweedsmuir
19 Wells Gray
20 Willmore Wilderness

Northwestern Canada

Northern British Columbia , the incredible Queen Charlotte Islands, and Yukon Territory remain some of the most untouched, sparsely inhabited regions of North America. Averaging one person per 15 sq. km, the loneliness and sheer physical beauty of the land is overwhelming. In this barely developed area, access is greatly improving. Four major roads cross this region: the **Cariboo Highway (Hwy. 97),** **Yellowhead Highway 16,** the **Cassiar Highway (Hwy. 37),** and the **Alaska Highway.** The **Klondike Loop** and **Dempster Highway** intersect in Dawson City, connecting Whitehorse with Dawson City in Yukon Territory and Dawson City with Inuvik in the Northwest Territories, respectively. The first two are entirely paved, well-maintained, and as good as any highway in Canada or the western U.S. The next two are partly paved and partly seal-coated, have little gravel, and are well-maintained. The Klondike Loop is paved between Whitehorse and Dawson City. The Dempster Hwy. is also seal-coat and gravel, but still a good driving surface. While the Cassiar and Alaska Hwy. trips are several days' driving, they are entirely possible in summer and should present no trouble for the prepared driver. Plan ahead. Make sure your car is in reliable running condition, has good shocks, and can take some wear. Adequate services exist, but are scarce and potentially expensive. It's a good idea to travel with at least one spare tire and some spare gas. Flying rocks abound; buy headlight covers and prepare for a chipped windshield. The Alaska Hwy. is open and maintained year-round, but bring a full set of Arctic clothing, prepare yourself and your heavy-duty 4WD vehicle for temperatures *well* below 0°F (-18°C); bring food, water, etc. Before considering a winter trip, get full information from a local, qualified authority. However, it can be done; some bus services even maintain winter service along these highways. In the warm months, weather is often excellent. Whether you're driving to Alaska or looking for solitude in a true Northwestern wilderness of pristine, seldom-explored areas, you'll enjoy the immense forests, stark mountains, icy glaciers, clear lakes, roaring rivers, yawning canyons, and abundant wildlife of this vast region.

NORTHERN BRITISH COLUMBIA

■■■ CARIBOO HIGHWAY (97)

The portion of Hwy. 97 known as the **Cariboo Hwy.** runs south to north for approximately 450km between Cache Creek and Prince George (see page 251). From Prince George, the highway leads north 406km to the Alaska Hwy (see page 268). The Cariboo region is known for cattle ranching. The road stretches through relatively flat terrain characterized by its mostly unimpressive scenery dominated by rock hills and forests. Dry winds and sagebrush abound along much of the highway as it winds through a series of small towns, many with such prosaic names as "100 Mile House" and "108 Mile Ranch," whose claim to fame is possession of the world's largest pair of cross-country skis. The highway's best pit stops are the towns of Williams Lake, at Mile 155, and Quesnel (kwuh-NEL), halfway between Williams Lake and Prince George. For coverage of the entire Cariboo region, pick up a free copy of *Cariboo Chilcotin Coast,* available at hotels, tourist attractions, and infocentres along the highway.

The **Travel Infocentre** in **Williams Lake** is on the highway and can give you the scoop on activities and events in the area (392-5025; open daily 8am-6pm, Labor Day-Victoria Day Mon.-Fri. 9am-5pm). The **Greyhound** station in Williams Lake is located halfway through town, directly off the highway. Buses going north leave three times daily. You can secure a roof over your head at the **Valley View Motel** (392-4655), to the left northbound on Hwy. 97 heading into Williams Lake. (A/C; singles and doubles $40). Just next door is the **Lakeside Motel** (392-4181), with singles for $44. Williams Lake is home to the province's most active cattle marketing and shipping industry; the town celebrates its cowboy heritage each July with the four-day **Williams Lake Stampede,** held Canada Day Weekend. The festivities include a rodeo, parade, and "pony chuckwagon races."

From Williams Lake, **Hwy. 20** runs 370km to immense, wild **Tweedsmuir Provincial Park** and **Bella Coola** on the remote central coast. Hwy. 20 is mostly paved; the central section is seal-coated gravel and includes an 18% grade. For information on Tweedsmuir, call **BC Parks** in Williams Lake (398-4414; open Mon.-Fri. 9am-5pm).

In **Quesnel** (kwa-NELL), the **Infocentre,** just off Hwy. 97 at 703 Carson Ave. in Le Bourdais Park (992-8716), offers information. (Open May-June daily 8am-6pm, July-Aug. daily 8am-6pm, Labor Day-Victoria Day Mon.-Fri. 8:30am-4:30pm.) The **Cariboo Hotel,** 254 Front St. (992-2333), has rooms starting from $52 (includes continental breakfast), with cable TV, phones, and jacuzzis. Ask about their travel packages. **Roberts Roost Campground,** 3121 Gook Rd. (747-2015), is in **Dragon Lake,** 8km south of Quesnel. Open April to October, the campground has showers, flush toilets, laundry facilities, and a swimming beach (sites $14, full hookup $18).

For those beyond hard-core and right off the deep end, the **Alexander Mackenzie Heritage Trail** might be the ultimate challenge. The over-250km trail begins from Hwy. 97 just north of Quesnel and stretches across western British Columbia as it retraces the final leg of Mackenzie's exploratory journey of 1793, finally terminating in Bella Coola. Allow 14 to 21 days to cover the entire trail.

■■■ YELLOWHEAD HIGHWAY 16

MT. ROBSON TO PRINCE GEORGE (319KM)

In British Columbia, Hwy. 16's quality and surroundings vary more than in Alberta. Hwy. 16 becomes two lanes rather than four and the speed limit is lower, but you'll want to slow down and enjoy the dramatic scenery continuing west of Jasper National Park. 80km west of Jasper stands **Mt. Robson,** at 3954m the highest peak in the Canadian Rockies. Climbers conquered Mt. Robson only in 1913 after five unsuccessful attempts. Those disinclined to tackle the peak can appreciate Robson's beauty from the parking lot beside the **information centre** (565-6340; open May-Sept. Mon.-Fri. 8:30am-4:30pm). Visitors can choose from five nearby hiking trails ranging from 8.5km day-hikes to 70km 6-day treks. Vacillators can stew at the **Emperor Ridge** campground (566-4714; sites $12, $14 with hookup; showers) or ponder their next course of action at **Mt. Robson Provincial Park** ($14.50 with flush toilets and hot showers).

Just west of Mt. Robson is **Tête Jaune Cache.** Here Hwy. 16 intersects **Hwy. 5** leading south to Kamloops (339km) and the Okanagan country. Hwy. 5 is the fastest route from Jasper to Vancouver. Between the Rockies and Cariboo Mountains, 63km west of Tête Jaune Cache, lies the hamlet of **McBride.** Travelers not driving wood-burning vehicles are advised to fill up in McBride, since 205km of timber separate it from Prince George, the next significant town to the west. Exhausted travelers unwilling to negotiate the steep, winding grades to Prince George can find refuge (including flush toilets, showers, and laundry) at the **Beaver View Campsite** in McBride, 1km east of McBride on Hwy. 16 (569-2413). Sites are $11; partial hookup $12. Or stop at scenic **Purden Lake Provincial Park** (565-6340; site $9.50, flush toilets).

The bark chips littering Hwy. 16 from McBride to Prince George indicate heavy **logging** activity. Environmentally-motivated visitors tempted to chain themselves to trees or to extemporize on the practices of the timber industry are invited to read the brochure *Don't Believe Everything That Greenpeace Tells You*, available at tourist information counters, for a brief summary of the locally popular arguments.

This region produces over 6 million cubic meters of lumber annually. Remember that here, as in much of the rural Northwest, terms like "deforestation" and "clear-cutting" are ways of describing how the people make a living.

■ ■ ■ PRINCE GEORGE

At the confluence of the Nechako and Fraser Rivers, Prince George's magnificent riverbanks contrast sharply with the pulp and lumber mills occupying the valley floors. With more than 100 parks, some pleasant museums, and 71,000 friendly residents, Prince George is hoping to move beyond its one-dimensional reputation and become something more to visitors than a simple timber town. If you really want to look like a tourist, jaywalk.

Prince George is also at the junction of Hwy. 16 and Hwy. 97, the **Cariboo Highway** (see page 249), leading south to Cache Creek (441 km) and north to Dawson Creek and the Alaska Highway (406 km).

Practical Information Prince George is roughly equidistant from four major Canadian cities: 780km northeast of Vancouver, 720km east of Prince Rupert, 735km west of Edmonton, and 790km northwest of Calgary. You can pick up a free, detailed map of Prince George at either of the two **Travel Infocentres,** one at 1198 Victoria St. (562-7300) at 15th Ave., and the other at the junction of Hwy. 16 and 97 (563-5493). (Both open daily May-July 9am-6pm; July-Sept. 9am-8pm; the first is also open Oct.-April Mon.-Fri. 9am-6pm.) Call for information at 800-668-7646. Decipher the schedules at **BC Rail** (561-4033), at the end of Terminal Blvd., 2km south on Hwy. 97 (to Vancouver $87 plus tax), or **VIA Rail,** 1300 1st Ave. (564-5233 or 800-561-8630). Station hours change daily. Train service to Vancouver and Edmonton is infrequent; you could be hanging out in Prince George for several days before your train arrives. Rather not wait? Try **Greyhound,** 1566 12th Ave. (564-5454; open Mon.-Sat. 5:30am-midnight, Sun. 5:30-9:30am and 3:30pm-midnight), across from the Infocentre. Buses to Edmonton, AB (2 per day, $85), Vancouver (3 per day, $84), Prince Rupert (2 per day, $80), and other points. Lockers are available for $1.

The **public library** is at 887 Dominion (563-5528 for a recording, 563-9251 for an operator. Open Mon.-Thurs. 10am-9pm, Fri.-Sat. 10am-5:30pm). **Prince George Regional Hospital** is at 2000 15th Ave. (565-2000; emergency 565-2444). The **police** are at 1325 5th Ave. (561-3155). The **post office** is at 1323 5th Ave. (561-5184; open Mon.-Fri. 8:30am-5pm; **Postal Code: V2L 4R8**). The **area code** is 604.

Accommodations, Camping, and Food If you're only stopping in Prince George to get a good night's sleep and stock up on provisions, the closest thing to budget accommodations (not very close) can be found at the **Queensway Motel,** 1616 Queensway (562-5058), at 17th Ave. (singles $43, doubles $49), or at the **Camelot Court Motel,** 1600 Central St. (563-0661), at 15th Ave. and 97 Bypass (singles $52, doubles $57.50; indoor swimming pool). The **Red Cedar Inn** (964-4427), on Bear Rd., 8km west off Hwy. 16, has campsites ($10, full hookups $14) and rooms (singles $32, with kitchen $38; doubles $34) and is close to the highway. Farther from the highway but plagued by RVs, the **South Park Trailer Park** (963-7577), 5km south of Prince George on Hwy. 97, has grassy sites ($12, hookups $16) with clean bathrooms and one metered shower per gender ($1 per 8 min.). The closest campground to downtown is the **City Campground** (563-2313), an approximately 20-minute walk from the Infocentre along 15th Ave. From 15th, take a left on Ospikn Blvd., then a right on 18th Ave. City has showers and a secure fence (gates closed 11am-6pm; sites $11, with full hookup $13).

Those seeking to sate their hunger should find **Safeway,** 1600 15th Ave., across the intersection from the downtown Infocentre. Restaurant fare can be had at **Nick's Place,** 363 George St. (562-2523), where a large plate of good spaghetti costs $7 (open Mon.-Sat. 11am-3:30am, Sun. 4-10pm), or at the **Camelot Court,** right next to the Camelot Court motel, which serves up major portions of burgers, sand-

YELLOWHEAD HIGHWAY 16

wiches, and fries for minor prices. **Graham Lee's,** 910 Victoria St., at 9th Ave. (attached to Slumber Lodge Mall) serves good, cheap eats, including all-day breakfast, in a spartan but brightly-lit setting (open Sun.-Thurs. 7am-8pm, Fri.-Sat. 7am-9pm). For Chinese food, try **Casey's Wonton House,** 193 Quebec St. (near the train station). The Chinese Lunch Smorgasbord allows you to stuff your face for $7 (11am-2pm). However, dinner entrees start at $10 (open Mon.-Fri. 11am-9pm, Sat. 5-11pm, Sun. 5-9pm).

Sights Cottonwood Island Nature Park, a 3-km walk from downtown along Patricia Blvd., has plenty of comfortable walking trails. For a bird's eye view of the rich landscape, climb atop **Connaught Hill Park,** off Queensway on Connaught Dr. **Fort George Park,** on the banks of the Fraser River off 20th Ave., offers huge expanses of green grassy lawns, picnic tables, and barbecue pits. If all the excitement drives you indoors, seek refuge in the **Fort George Regional Museum** (562-1612), which houses frontier artifacts, including several primitive chain saws. (Open daily 10am-5pm; mid-Sept.-mid-May Tues.-Sun. noon-5pm. "Requested donation" $3, students $2.) For a thorough introduction to Canadian rail history, choo-choo on over to the **Prince George Regional Railway and Forest Industry Museum** (563-7351) on River Rd. Visitors can climb aboard and explore the growing collection of rolling stock; the highlight is an original 1914 Grand Trunk Station, one of only three that remain (open Victoria Day-Labor Day daily 10am-5pm; $2.50, students $2).

Mardi Gras, lasting for 10 days in late February, features events such as snow-golf, softball in the snow, and jousting with padded poles. For information call 564-3737 or write P.O. Box 383, Station A, Prince George. Summertime events include the **Canadian Northern Children's Festival,** a four-day event held in mid-May, including live theatre, vaudeville, and plenty of music; and **Sandblast,** the daring third Sunday in August that sends a group of skiers down the steep, sandy Nechako Cutbanks. Prince George's **Oktoberfest** is held on an early October weekend. Enjoy traditional Bavarian oom-pah-pah music while taking in plenty of beer, bands, and bratwurst. Near Prince George, **fishing** is excellent, with more than 1500 stocked lakes within a 150km radius.

■■■ YELLOWHEAD HIGHWAY 16

PRINCE GEORGE TO PRINCE RUPERT (724KM)

West of Prince George, the steep grades and towering timbers of the forest region gradually give way to the gently rolling pastures and tiny towns of British Columbia's interior Lakes District. Aviation enthusiasts are drawn annually to **Vanderhoof,** an unassuming town of 4000 at the geographic centre of the province, for the **International Air Show** taking off annually on the fourth weekend in July. 54km north of Vanderhoof on Hwy. 27 is **Stuart Lake** and great **rainbow trout** fishing.

The world's best hash browns await the hungry at the 24-hr. PetroCan station in **Fort Fraser** (690-7542). Inhale secondhand smoke and vicariously experience the ebb and flow of life in a small town in northern British Columbia. Thanks to a drunken surveyor, Hwy. 16 takes a turn at the town of **Burns Lake.** Virtually every building in Burns Lake is adorned with the likeness of a trout. However, before wetting a line, puffing a hackle, or seating a reel, visitors should consult British Columbia's *Provincial Angling* regulation synopsis, a guide replete with vivid prose and page-turning witticisms. Those wishing to savor the guide at length should consider hunkering down at the **Traveler's Motel** on Hwy. 16 (692-7471; singles start at $35, doubles at $45; continental breakfast included).

Eighty km west of Burns Lake is **Houston** and its Texas-scale contribution to the rampant superlativism of the late 20th century: the world's largest flyrod (60 ft. long and over 800 lbs.). 64km northwest of Houston, **Smithers** offers skiing on the slopes of Hudson Bay Mountain and, in late Aug. and early Sept., the 12-day long

Bulkley Valley Days festival. The **information centre** (847-5072) is in a converted railway car.

Near Moricetown, directly below the highway, the Bulkley River squeezes through the **Moricetown Canyon.** Native Canadians still spear salmon from atop the rocks of the canyon's cragged walls. The Native-totem-pole capital of the world is **New Hazelton,** found just before the **travel infocentre** (842-6071; open May to Sept.; follow the signs for 'Ksan Historic Village). Cross the single-lane **Hagwilget suspension bridge** and gape at the Bulkley River and canyon floor far below. 3.3km north of Hwy. 16 a sign announces Jesus' imminent return. (*Let's Go:* the Bible of the budget traveler….) While waiting for the Second Coming, take in the beauty of **'Ksan,** a restored Gitskan Native village with seven painted tribal houses and totem poles. Visitors can roam the grounds for free (May 3-Oct. 15, daily 9am-6pm; daily Mon.-Fri. 9am-5pm the rest of the year). 'Ksan Historic Village operates a campsite with flush toilets and showers (site $11, hookup $14). Nearby, the Kispiox River has great steelhead **fishing.**

Forty-four km west of New Hazelton is the **junction** with the **Cassiar Hwy. (Hwy. 37)** leading north 733km to the Yukon and the Alaska Hwy. (see page 263). For the remaining 97km to **Terrace,** Hwy. 16 winds along the base of the Hazelton Mountains and follows the thundering Skeena River. With 77km to go to Terrace, join the truckers at **Cedarvale Lodge** for a bite to eat (entrees from $5; open daily 7am-10pm). There is no gas available along the 144km stretch of Hwy. 16 between Terrace and Prince Rupert.

■■■ TERRACE

In 1944, an MIT-esque male-to-female ratio and an extended spell of bad weather caused 3000 Canadian Army troops stationed in Terrace to mutiny and take over the town. For three weeks, the disgruntled soldiers ruled Terrace; officers were forced to find refuge in Prince Rupert, 147km to the west. In the 50 years since the mutiny, Terrace has become considerably less lively. Here on the banks of the Skeena River, fishing has replaced armed rebellion as the most popular means of easing boredom.

Practical Information The **Visitors Center** is at 4511 Keith St. off Hwy. 16 (635-2063; open daily 8:30am-8pm). Bus connections are offered by **Greyhound,** 4620 Keith St. (635-3580; open Mon.-Fri. 7:30am-6pm; Sat. 7:30am-1pm; Sun. 7:30-8:30am, 12:30-1:30pm, 4:30-5:30pm, 9:30-10:30pm). Buses leave daily: **westbound** at 8am and 5:40pm; **eastbound** at 1:20pm and 10:25pm. To catch a train, contact **VIA Rail** (800-501-8630. Trains to Prince Rupert Mon., Thurs., and Sat. 1:09pm; to Prince George Sun., Tues., Fri. 1:45pm). Suds your duds at **Coin Laundry,** 3223 Emerson (635-5119; open Mon.-Sat. 7am-9pm, Sun. 10am-9pm). Suds yourself at the **public showers** at the community pool, 3220 Kalum Ave. Use the pool, hot tub, and gym facilities for $3. Mills Memorial **Hospital** is at 4720 Hangland Ave. (635-2111). For the **police,** go to 3205 Eby St. or call 635-4911. Phone 638-1102 for an **ambulance.** The **public library** is at 4610 Park Ave. (open Tues.-Fri. 10am-9pm, Sat. 10am-5pm, Sun. 1pm-5pm (July-Aug. closed Sun.). Mail your letters at the **post office** at 3232 Emerson (open Mon.-Fri. 9am-5:45pm). The **postal code** is V86 4A1.

Accommodations, Camping, and Food Terrace's simplicity makes for cheap accommodations. **The Alpine House,** 4326 Lakelse (635-7216), is safe, clean, and cheap (singles $42, doubles $46). Campers should head to **Kleanza Creek Provincial Park** (847-7320), the site of an abandoned gold mine19km east of the city on Hwy. 16 (sites $9.50). Another option is **Ferry Island Municipal Campground** (638-4750) just east of Terrace on Hwy. 16 (sites $8.50, hookup $10.50). The community pool is ½-price ($1.50) if you stay here.

Terrace's restaurants are primarily of the fast-food genre. **Safeway,** 4655 Lakelse Ave., is the cheapest place to buy food (open Mon.-Fri. 9am-9pm, Sat.-Sun. 9am-6pm). For a restaurant meal, try the **Grand Trunk Restaurant,** 4702 Lakelse Ave., a good, family-style establishment (open Mon.-Sat. 7am-8pm, Sun. 8am-3pm). Grab breakfast at **The Bear,** 3086 Hwy. 16 East. Try the poached egg breakfast special, including toast, hash browns, and coffee ($3.70; open daily 6am-11pm).

Sights Terrace's most impressive tourist offering is not in Terrace. The **Tseax Lava Beds,** Canada's youngest lava flow and British Columbia's newest provincial park, is 80km north of Terrace. To reach this 54 sq. km swath of lunarscape, follow Kalum Lake Drive through the scenic valleys of the Tseax and Nass Rivers.

Before the **Grand Pacific Trunk Railway** joined Terrace with the rest of humanity in 1914, paddle-wheel boats on the Skeena supplied the city's primary contact with the outside world. **Riverboat Days** celebrates Terrace's pioneer and paddleboat heritage every year in late July.

Amble, sashay, skip, run or walk along Terrace's 11 well-maintained **trails.** More ambitious hikers should consult the **travel infocentre** to find out about the more challenging trails in the area.

■■■ PRINCE RUPERT

Hwy. 16 terminates its mainland course at Prince Rupert, although a ferry trip to the Queen Charlotte Islands from here will take you to the westernmost branch. Named after the Cavalier general and nephew of England's King Charles I, Prince Rupert is the terminus of the second trans-Canada railway and owes its livelihood to forestry, fishing, and the hundreds of thousands of travelers who pass through this "Northwest Gateway to Canada." Anglers seeking salmon and other saltwater fish linger, but Prince Rupert's visitors are usually headed for more interesting places. As a point of embarkation for those wanting to explore the Alaska Panhandle to the north, the Queen Charlotte Islands to the west, and Vancouver Island to the south, Prince Rupert is perhaps best viewed from the stern of an outbound ferry.

Practical Information Most visitors come to Prince Rupert either for fishing or ferries. An afternoon in a guided fishing boat costs upwards of $100; pass the hours before your ship comes in browsing the 15 downtown blocks. The **Travel Infocentre,** 1st Ave. and McBride St. (624-5637; open May 15-Labor Day daily 9am-9pm; winter Mon.-Sat. 10am-5pm), has maps for a self-guided tour, including the Infocentre's free museum, a cornucopia of totem poles, the manicured Sunken Gardens, and a Native Canadian **carving shed.**

The only major road into town is **Hwy. 16,** or McBride at the city limits, curving left to become 2nd Ave. downtown. **Prince Rupert Bus Service** (624-3343) provides local service downtown Mon.-Sat. (fare $1, seniors 60¢, students 75¢; day pass $2.50, seniors and students $2). The #52 bus runs from 2nd Ave. and 3rd St. to within a five-minute walk of the ferry terminal. Or try **Skeena Taxi,** 624-2185 (open 24 hrs.).

From Prince Rupert, **Air BC,** 112 6th St. (624-4554), flies to Vancouver ($283). **Canadian Airlines** (624-9181), on the ground floor of the mall on 2nd Ave. W, offers the same service at the same price. Ask about standby flights; they can be cheaper than the bus or train. **VIA Rail** (627-7589), on the water at the end of 11th St. by car or down the ramp from the corner of 1st Ave. and 2nd St. on foot, runs trains to Vancouver (3 per week, $194) and Prince George ($44 with 7-day advance purchase). (Open Mon., Thurs., and Sat. 1-4:30pm; Tues., Fri., and Sun. 9am-12:30pm.) **Greyhound,** 822 3rd Ave. near 8th St. (624-5090), runs buses twice daily to Prince George ($80), Vancouver ($163), and Seattle ($188). (Open Mon.-Fri. 8:30am-8:30pm, Sat. 9-11am and 6-8:30pm, Sun. 9-11am and 6-8pm, and holidays 9-11:15am and 6-8:30pm.) The **Alaska Marine Highway** (627-1744) runs ferries north from Prince Rupert to Ketchikan (US$38, car US$75), Wrangell (US$56, car US$117), Petersburg (US$68, car US$145), Juneau (US$104, car US$240), and Haines (US$118, car US$273). **BC Ferries** (624-9627), at the end of Hwy. 16, serves the Queen Charlotte Islands (6 per week; $20.75, car $79) and Port Hardy (4 per week;

$93.50, car $192). Vehicle reservations required 3 wks. in advance. Ferrygoers may not leave cars parked on the streets of Prince Rupert. Some establishments charge a daily rate for storage; pick up a list at the Infocentre (see above).

King Koin Laundromat (624-2667) spins at 7th St. and 2nd Ave. (Wash $1.50, 5-min. dry 25¢. Open Mon.-Sun. 7am-10pm; winter 8am-9pm.) The **library** is on McBride at 6th St. (627-1345; open Mon. and Wed. 1-9pm, Tues. and Thurs. 10am-9pm, and Fri.-Sat. 1-5pm; winter also open Sun. 1-5pm). **Star of the West Books,** 518 3rd. Ave., stocks a fine collection of regional titles. (Open Mon.-Fri. 9am-9pm, Sat. 9am-6pm; Jan.-April Mon.-Sat. 9am-6pm).

Prince Rupert's **hospital** is at 1305 Summit Ave. (624-2171); in an **emergency,** call 911. The **police** are at 100 7th Ave. (624-2136). You can receive general delivery mail at the main **post office** at 2nd Ave. and 3rd St. (624-2383; open Mon.-Fri. 8:30am-4:30pm), but only the two **substations** sell stamps and postal supplies. One is in the Shoppers Drug Mart at 3rd Ave. and 2nd St. (open Mon.-Fri. 9am-9pm, Sat. 9am-6pm, Sun. 11am-5pm); another lurks upstairs in the 2nd Ave. Mall (open Mon.-Sat. 9am-6pm). The **Postal Code** is V8J 3P3. The **area code** is 604.

Accommodations, Camping, and Food Nearly all of Prince Rupert's hotels are within the 6-block area defined by 1st Ave., 3rd Ave., 6th St., and 9th St. Everything fills when the ferries dock, so call a day or two ahead. **Pioneer Rooms,** 167 3rd Ave. E (624-2334), has floors clean enough to eat from, a microwave and TV downstairs, and great management. Pick your own berries in the backyard. (Singles with shared bath $15-20. Doubles $25-30. Showers $3. Laundry facilities.) The **Ocean View Hotel,** 950 1st Ave. W (624-6259), just a short stagger upstairs from the 1st-floor tavern, has singles for $30 and doubles for $34. The only campground in Prince Rupert, the **Park Ave. Campground,** 1750 Park Ave. (624-5861 or 800-667-1994), is less than 2km east of the ferry terminal via Hwy. 16 and cheap (sites $9, RVs $16).

The best budget-food options in Prince Rupert begin in the bulk food department at the colossal **Safeway** at 1st. St. and 1st. Ave. (open daily 9am-10pm). When local fisher-families go out for seafood, they head to **Smiles Seafood Cafe** on the waterfront at 113 George Hills Way (624-3072). Entrees hover around $13, but the heaping fish and chips platter for $7.50 is a fine feed (open daily 10am-10pm).

The Stardust Restaurant, 637 3rd Ave. W (627-1221), fries up Chinese food, chicken and seafood for about $9 (open daily 10:30am-10pm). Those craving food in a flash can head to **KFC** at 7th St. and 3rd Ave. (open Mon.-Thurs. 11am-8pm), **Dairy Queen** at 3rd Ave. and McBride (open daily 10am-10pm), or the **Chicken Factory** at 2nd Ave. and 2nd St. (open Mon.-Thurs. and Sat. 11am-8pm, Fri. 11am-9pm, and Sun. noon-7pm). Top it all off with a gigantic cream cheese cinnamon bun ($2) and a cappucino ($2.15) at **Lambada's Cappucino & Espresso,** at 101 3rd Ave. (624-6464, open Mon.-Thurs. and Sat. 9am-5pm, Fri. 9am-9pm).

Sights Few visitors realize that Prince Rupert harbor has the highest concentration of archaeological sites in North America. Large piles of discarded clam shells on nearly every island in the harbor attest to the 10,000-year inhabitance of indigenous peoples and their mollusk-intensive diets. Three-hour **archaeological boat tours** leave from the Infocentre daily. A local expert will take you to **Digby Island;** unfortunately, some of the most interesting petroglyphs are inaccessible to the tour boat, and the tour leaves you staring at your feet too much of the time. (Tours depart June 14-30 daily 12:30pm, July-mid-Sept. daily 1pm. $20, children $12, under 5 free.)

The grassy hills of **Service Park,** off Fulton St., offer a panoramic view of downtown Prince Rupert and the harbor beyond. **Diana Lake Park,** 16km east of town along Hwy. 16, provides a picnic area set against an enticing lake.

QUEEN CHARLOTTE ISLANDS

The Queen Charlotte Islands lie in the Pacific Ocean 130km west of Prince Rupert. Sometimes called the "Canadian Galapagos," these remarkable islands evolved biologically in semi-isolation and contain several plant species found nowhere else amid a profusion of more common Northwestern wildlife. The islands describe a tapering archipelago made up of two principal islands, Graham and Moresby, and 148 surrounding islets. Graham, the northern island, is home to all but one of the islands' communities, the world's only known Golden Spruce tree, a particularly potent (illegal) strain of hallucinogenic mushroom, and the world's largest black bears. Hot springs whisper in the mists of Moresby Island and its smaller neighbors to the south, and the massive wooden monuments of the islands' first denizens decay by the shore in Canada's newest national park.

The Queen Charlottes were the first place in British Columbia to be given a European name. "Discovered" by a Spaniard in 1774, English Captain George Dixon inscribed the islands on the map in 1778, lending them the name of his ship. Despite the European presence, the islands' natives, the Haida (HI-duh), have outlasted most other Native nations in maintaining cultural integrity; they make up a large proportion of the population and an even larger proportion of the islands' many artists. Students in the public schools have a choice between learning Haida or French as a second language, and a recent initiative sought to restore the use of the original Haida name for the islands.

The timber industry is the main employer. Many locals staunchly defend the industry that provides one of the islands' economic mainstays, while others would prefer to put an end to local logging. In the 1980s the debate attracted national attention when environmentalists and Haidas demonstrated in an effort to stop logging on parts of Moresby Island. In 1988, the Canadian government established **Gwaii Haanas South Moresby National Park,** protecting the southern third of the Queen Charlottes. Perhaps not coincidentally, the area's steep terrain makes it unsuitable for logging.

The frequently riotous waters of the Hecate Strait insulate the Queen Charlotte Islands from British Columbia's usual summer tourist moil. The southern beaches are rocky and the water cold, but kayakers and anglers heap praise on the archipelago. Joining a charter group costs money, but it is possible to rent cars, bikes, and kayaks. Cities on Graham and Moresby Islands are not within walking distance of each other, and there is no public transportation. Visitors without cars often have a frustrating time trying to get around the islands. Some travelers try to find others to share the steep car rental fees; many others hitch the 110km between Queen Charlotte City on the south shore of Graham Island and Masset on the north. (*Let's Go* does not recommend hitchhiking.)

■■■ QUEEN CHARLOTTE CITY

The BC Ferry from Prince Rupert docks at **Skidegate Landing,** between **Queen Charlotte City,** 4km west of the landing, and the hamlet of **Skidegate,** 2km to the northeast. Visitors stay and eat in Queen Charlotte City, the largest city in the islands, and usually pass through Skidegate on their way north. Red and golden salmonberries, found in summer along almost every roadside in the Charlottes, make a walk from Skidegate Landing to the town more palatable. Queen Charlotte City extends inland from the water at the southern end of **Graham Island.** The city stretches for 2km along 3rd Ave., becoming **Hwy. 16** to the east, leading to **Skidegate, Tlell, Port Clements, and Masset.** From Skidegate Landing, a frequent ferry connects Graham Island with the town of **Sandspit,** on Moresby Island.

Queen Charlotte City's central location and size make it an ideal base for exploring the two major islands with a car. More than any other settlement on the islands, the town has unrolled a welcome mat to tourists, and visitors enjoy spending time along the attractive waterfront. Queen Charlotte City grew around a sawmill and still relies on logging as its major industry, as the bald hills surrounding the town soberly attest. This small town has yet to undergo large-scale development.

PRACTICAL INFORMATION AND ORIENTATION

Visitors Information: Travel Infocentre, 3922 Hwy. 33 Box 337, Queen Charlotte, BC V0T 1SO (559-4742). Follow 3rd Ave. east out of town for 2km; in a jewelry store. Offers the *Guide to the Queen Charlotte Islands* ($4.25). The zealously helpful staff amplifies the already comprehensive book. Open Mon.-Tues. 9am-5pm, Wed.-Sun. 9am-7pm; Oct.-May Mon.-Sat. 9am-5pm.

Parks Canada: Gwaii Haanas Park Information (559-8818), on 2nd Ave. downtown. Knowledgeable staff will acquaint you with Canada's newest (and least accessible) national park. Register here before setting out into the Park (or at the office in Sandspit). Open Mon.-Fri. 8am-4:30pm.

Ministry of Forests (559-8447), on 3rd Ave. in a new blue bldg. at the far west end of town. Information on free, primitive campsites maintained by the Forest Service on Graham and Moresby Islands. Open Mon.-Fri. 8:30am-noon and 1-4:30pm.

Fishing License: Obtain a saltwater license at **Meegan's Store,** 3126 Wharf St. Box 790 (559-4428). Freshwater licenses are available from the **Government Agent** only (559-4452 or 800-663-7674). Prices vary depending on the length of the license's validity.

BC Ferry: terminal in Skidegate Landing (559-4485), 4.5km east of Queen Charlotte City. To Prince Rupert (July-Aug. 6 per week, Sept. 5 per week, Oct.-June 4 per wee;, $20.75, car $79). Reserve for cars at least 3 weeks in advance.

Inter-island Ferry, 559-4485. Runs between Skidegate Landing on Graham Island and Alliford Bay on Moresby Island (12 trips per day, $2.75 round-trip, car $7).

Taxi: Twin Services, 559-4461.

Car Rental: Rustic Rentals, west of downtown at the Chevron Station (559-4641), and another office at Jo's Bed and Breakfast by the ferry (559-8865). Will rent to 18-yr.-olds with a credit card. Anachronistic autos at contemporary prices. $39 per day plus 15¢ per additional km. Office open Mon.-Fri. 8:30am-6pm, Sat. 9am-5:30pm, but "on call" 24 hrs. Will pick up at the ferry terminal in Skidegate.

Laundromat: 121 3rd Ave. (559-4444). Wash $1.50, dry 25¢. Open daily 6:30am-9pm.

Pharmacy: (559-8315), downstairs in the hospital building. Open Mon.-Fri. 10:30am-12:30pm and 1:30-5:15pm (Wed. open 1:30-5:15pm only).

Hospital: (559-8466), on 3rd Ave. at the east end of town.

Emergency: Police (RMCP), 3211 Wharf St. (559-4421). **Ambulance,** 1-800-461-9911. **Fire,** 559-4488.

Post Office: in the City Centre Bldg. on 3rd Ave. (559-8349). Open Mon.-Fri. 8:30am-5:30pm, Sat. noon-4pm. **Postal Code:** V0T 1S0.

Area Code: 604.

ACCOMMODATIONS AND CAMPING

The small hotels of Queen Charlotte City are clean, cozy, friendly, and expensive. During the summer, make reservations or arrive early in the day to secure a room.

Spruce Point Lodging (559-8234), on the little peninsula across from the Chevron station at the west end of town. 6 hostel beds in a co-ed dorm for $17.50. Dorm reservations accepted for groups; singles can (and should) reserve rooms. Singles $50. Doubles $60.

The Premier Hotel, 3101 3rd Ave. (559-840; fax 559-8198). This friendly hotel dates to 1910 and has been beautifully renovated with veranda and balcony. Singles with shared bath from $25, with balcony from $56, with kitchenette $60. Doubles from $56.

Jo's Bed and Breakfast, 4813 Ferry Loop Rd. (559-8865). Follow the road from the ferry terminal up the hill to the white house with blue trim. Wonderfully clean and convenient. The wood stove will warm your bones after a long day of hiking. Continental breakfast. Singles $25, doubles $35. Reservations a good idea.

Hecate Inn (559-4543 or 800-665-3350), at 3rd Ave. and 4th St. Clean, comfortable rooms with private bath and cable TV. Shared kitchen and refrigerator make Hecate an inn for anglers and work crews. Singles $65. Doubles $70, twins $75. Reservations accepted.

Joy's Island Jewellers, 3rd Ave. at the east end of town (559-4742). A few sites available in the yard next door, with some of the islands' best drinking water from a private spring (free). No toilet facilities. Tents $5, RVs $8, full hookups $10.

Haydn Turner Park Campsite, at the west end of 4th Ave.; a 25-min. walk from the town centre. Forested sites and free firewood. A few spots at the end overlook the water. Toilets and water (boil before drinking). Tents $3, RVs $5.

FOOD

Culinary offerings in Queen Charlotte City are limited in selection and high in price. Buy your own grub at **City Center Stores Ltd.** (559-4444), in the City Center Building (open Tues.-Fri. 9:30am-9pm, Mon. and Sat. 9:30am-6pm).

John's Cafe, on 3rd Ave. just west of the City Centre Building. Tasty Chinese dishes around $10, burgers from $3.20. Open Tues.-Sat. 11:30am-3pm and 4:30-9pm, Sun. noon-3pm and 4:30-9pm.

Margaret's Cafe, 3223 Wharf St. (559-4204), at the east end of town. Locals smoke and linger over filling breakfast and lunch specials. Sandwich, soup, gravy, and fries $6, burgers from $3.50. Try the crab or shrimp omelette with toast and hash browns for $7. Open Mon.-Fri. 6:30am-3pm, Sat. 6:30am-1:30pm.

Charlotte's Own Pizza Factory and Restaurant, 3119 3rd Ave. (559-8940). Don't let the fluorescent lights distract you from the pizza, subs, burgers, chicken, pasta and ice cream. Small pepperoni pizza $8.90, sundae $3.00. Eat-in or take-out. Hours are amorphous: officially open Mon.-Fri. 11am-9pm, Sat.-Sun. 11am-midnight.

Claudette's Place, 233 3rd Ave. (559-8861), just west of city centre. Pleasant patio/garden out front. Best breakfasts in town. Denver omelette ($6.50), or 2 eggs, hashbrowns, and toast ($4). Open daily 9am-9pm.

Isabel Creek Store, Wharf St. (559-8623), next to Margaret's Cafe. Pay a premium for organic fruits and vegetables, health foods, juices and lotions. A refreshing break from fried fare. Open Mon.-Sat. 10am-5:30pm.

Hanging by a Fibre, Wharf St. next to the Pub (559-4463; fax 559-8430). New store and gallery specializing in paper-art also drips out cappuccino ($2), espresso ($1.50), and cafe latte ($3). Regular coffee $1; muffins and cookies 75¢. Open daily 9am-7pm.

SIGHTS

Displays of contemporary Haida artwork sparkle at **Rainbows Art Gallery and Gift Shop,** on 3rd Ave. at Alder (559-8430), a gallery brimming with silver, gold, and argillite (black shale) carvings (open daily 9am-7pm).

In Queen Charlotte City, just south of town, is the **city dump,** open Thurs.-Sun. 9am-3pm. Not known merely for garbage, the dump is a scavenging site for the 40-plus bald eagles and half-dozen black bears that meet there nightly. Go in a car, as garbage bears are capable of trashing any tourist, and the broken glass underfoot can make the bears edgy.

Skidegate Mission, known as "the Village," is a cluster of small, worn houses on Rooney Bay, 2km east of the ferry landing, along Hwy. 16 leading north. Skidegate has been a Haida village for centuries; today's community of 530 is a nexus of Haida art and culture. Visit the **Skidegate Band Council Office** (559-4496), in a Haida longhouse built in 1979 according to ancient design specifications. The frontal totem pole is a favorite perch of bald eagles. Ask the receptionist for permission to view the artwork and old photographs inside (office open Mon.-Fri. 8am-4:30pm). Halfway between Skidegate Landing and Skidegate Mission is the **Queen Charlotte Islands Museum** (559-4643), housing totem poles from remote village sites, an extensive collection of stuffed birds, and beautiful contemporary Haida prints and carvings. The shed next door protects the 50-ft. cedar canoe carved by renowned

Haida artist Bill Reid for Vancouver's Expo '86. (Open June-Aug. Mon.-Fri. 10am-5pm, Sat.-Sun. 1-5pm. $2.50, children free.) On the beach 1km north of Skidegate rests **Balance Rock,** a memento left by a glacial movement thousands of years ago. Search for fossils in the surrounding bedrock, but don't rock the Rock.

■ ■ ■ SANDSPIT

On a thin strip of land that projects into Hecate Strait, and connected by regular ferry to Skidegate Landing near Queen Charlotte City, Sandspit is the only permanent community on **Moresby Island.** The town grew up in the 1940s around a Royal Canadian Air Force airfield; today, the logging operations of TimberWest are the mainstay of the Sandspit economy. The sandy beaches of the spit are a pleasant change from the tidal flats around Queen Charlotte City; birds and shells proliferate on these shores. The best time to visit may be late May or early June when the sawdust flies as axe-wielding men and women climb, chop, and saw in the annual **Loggers Day** competitions.

Practical Information Parks Canada (637-5362) is off Beach Rd. at the north end of town (open mid-June-mid-Sept. Sat.-Wed. 9:30am-6pm, Thurs. and Fri. 9:30am-8:30pm). Register here or at their office in Queen Charlotte City before venturing into the park.

Sandspit is 13km east of the Alliford Bay ferry landing on Moresby Island. There's not much traffic on the connecting road; those hitching from Sandspit to catch a late ferry are known to have a hard time finding a ride. **Inter-island Ferry** (559-4485) runs between Skidegate Landing on Graham Island and Alliford Bay on Moresby Island (12 trips per day; $2.75 round-trip, car $8). **Budget Rent-A-Car** (637-5688), at Beach and Blaine Shaw Rd., rents cars from $59 per day, plus 25¢ per km (must be 21 with a credit card). Another office is at the airport.

The **library** (637-2247) sits off Beach Rd. at the north end of town (open Tues. 3-6:30pm, Thurs. 3-5pm and 7-8:30pm). The **health clinic** (637-5403) is on Copper Bay Rd. in the school building. (Open Mon.-Fri. 10am-noon; after hours, call the **Queen Charlotte City Hospital** at 559-8466.) **Emergency** numbers: **ambulance,** 1-800-461-9911; **fire,** 637-2222; **police,** 559-4421 in Queen Charlotte City. The **Post Office** is at Beach and Blaine Shaw Rd. (637-2244; open Mon.-Fri. 8:30am-5:30pm, Sat. 12:30-3:30pm. **Postal Code:** V0T 1T0). The **area code** is 604.

Accommodations, Camping, and Food The sandy beaches of the spit are the cheapest overnight option (including 20 primitive campsites on the shores of Gray Bay; see Outdoors below), but if you're unwilling to sleep with the fish be prepared to shell out a few clams. The **Moresby Island Guest House** (637-5305), on Beach Rd. next to the post office, provides eight cozy rooms with shared washrooms, kitchen, and billiard table. In the morning, they provide the ingredients and you make the breakfast. (Singles $25. Doubles from $50 can accommodate up to four. Overflow cots for $15. Feign desperation.) Just up the road toward Spit Point, the **Seaport Bed and Breakfast** (637-5678) offers island hospitality with plush couches, cable TV, and breakfast with fresh eggs from the henhouse out back. Reservations nearly essential in summer. (Singles $25, doubles $35, floor space with sleeping bag $15.)

Ramble to **Dick's Wok Inn,** 388 Copper Bay Rd. (637-2275), where a heaping plate of fried rice costs $8 and up (open daily 5-10pm). Or rest your cheeks at the **Bun Wagon,** at 396 Copper Bay Rd. (635-4131). $2.50 dogs and $5.25-7 burgers will satisfy even the most discriminating pioneer (open Mon.-Wed. 11am-2pm and Fri.-Sun. 11am-7pm.). The **Supervalu Supermarket** resides in the mini-mall near the spit (open Mon.-Tues. and Thurs.-Sat. 9:30am-6pm, Wed. 9:30am-7:30pm).

Sights and Outdoors Stroll to the end of the spit for spectacular sunrises and sunsets. Anglers can cast for silver salmon in the surf. Bumpy logging roads lead

20km south of Sandspit to **Gray Bay;** check with the **TimberWest Information Centre** on Beach Rd. (637-5436; open Mon.-Fri. 9am-5pm) to find out when the roads are open to the public (logging trucks are HUGE). Twenty primitive **campsites** line the unspoiled beach (free). A 4.5km trail follows the shore south to **Cumshewa Head. Moresby Camp,** at the end of Cumshewa Inlet (also accessible by logging road) is a perfect launching point for kayakers who wish to explore South Moresby National Park.

In the summer, **TimberWest** will take you out to see the trees (and the stumps) on their free 4½-hour **logging tour.** The tour provides a view of an active logging site and the chance for a frank discussion of logging practices. Some may wince at the sight of glorious spruce trees being reduced to 2x4s, but this is one of the best ways to get away from the highway into the backcountry. Tours leave from the office on Beach Rd. at noon on Wednesday and Friday; call their Information Centre for further information (see above).

Unfortunately, since there's no public relations incentive for any company to take you to South Moresby, the road to Haida Gwaii inevitably begins in your wallet. **Moresby Explorers,** based in Sandspit, offers wilderness trips on a demand basis to points of interest along South Moresby, including Hot Springs Island and the abandoned Haida villages of Skedans and Minstints. Day trips are $110 per person. Overnight trips, during which guests sleep on a 40 by 70 ft. spruce raft, are $140 per person. Contact Doug Gould (637-2215) for information.

■■■ YELLOWHEAD HIGHWAY 16

40KM NORTH OF QUEEN CHARLOTTE CITY: TLELL

Tlell isn't really a town; it consists of a few houses and farms spread thinly along a 7km stretch of Hwy. 16. Its central location and friendly residents make it a perfect stopover for those traveling the 100km between Queen Charlotte City and Masset. Here the rocky beaches of the south give way to sand, and the Tlell River offers excellent trout fishing and water warm enough for swimming.

In December 1928, the wooden log barge **Pezuta** ran aground north of Tlell. A two-hour hike to the wreck from the **Naikoon Park** picnic lot traces the Tlell River, crossing sand dunes and agate-strewn beaches. Look for land otters on the way.

Residents occasionally complain that the exceptionally pure air in their town puts them to sleep. Perk up at **Body Currents Cappuccino Bar** (557-4793), 1km south of Richardson Ranch on Richardson Rd. (off Wiggins Rd.), which serves great chocolate chip cookies and cappuccino. The adjacent **gallery** exhibits and sells handmade local jewelry and crafts (open Mon.-Sat. 10am-5pm, Sun. noon-5pm). **Riverworks Farm & Store** (557-4363), 2km south of Wiggins Rd. next to the post office, boasts island-grown produce and eggs (open daily 10am-5:30pm).

Pitch a tent at **Misty Meadows Campground,** just south of the Tlell River Bridge. Pit toilets, picnic tables, and water grace 30 sites (call Naikoon Provincial Park Headquarters at 557-4390). Or sink into the lap of luxury at **Hltunwa Kaitza Bed and Breakfast** (557-4664), just north of Richardson Ranch on the sea-side of the road; singles start at $25. The friendly folk of Hltunwa Kaitza rent **mountain bikes** and **kayaks.** Out front in the **Glass Shack,** Gayle displays her gorgeous stained glass windows; bring her the bottles you find washed up on the beach and she'll sandblast you a custom design. Ask nicely to sniff the whale skull. Just north of the Tlell River Bridge, the **Haida Gwaii Bed and Breakfast** (557-4434) offers accommodations ($40), laundry facilities, **canoeing,** and **kayak rentals.**

Tlell lies on Hwy. 16 on the east coast of Graham Island, 30km north of Skidegate and 24km southeast of Port Clements. The **post office** is on Hwy. 16 2km south of Wiggins Rd. (557-4551; open Mon.-Fri. 2-5pm; **Postal Code:** V0T 1Y0).

LET'S GO TRAVEL ®

CATALOG

1995

E GIVE YOU THE WORLD... AT A DISCOUNT

scounted Flights, Eurail Passes,
avel Gear, Let's Go™ Series Guides,
stel Memberships... and more

t's Go Travel
vision of
rvard Student
encies, Inc.

**Bargains
to every
corner of
the world!**

Travel Gear

A Let's Go T-Shirt...$10
100% combed cotton. Let's Go logo on front left chest. Four color printing on back. L and XL. Way cool.

B Let's Go Supreme..........$175
Innovative hideaway suspension with parallel stay internal frame turns backpack into carry-on suitcase. Includes lumbar support pad, torso, and waist adjustment, leather trim, and detachable daypack. Waterproof Cordura nylon, lifetime gurantee, 4400 cu. in. Navy, Green, or Black.

C Let's Go Backpack/Suitcase....................$130
Hideaway suspension turns backpack into carry-on suitcase.   Internal frame. Detachable daypack makes 3 bags in 1. Waterproof Cordura nylon, lifetime guarantee, 3750 cu. in. Navy, Green, or Black.

D Let's Go Backcountry I..$210
Full size, slim profile expedition pack designed for the serious trekker. New Airflex suspension. X-frame pack with advanced composite tube suspension. Velcro height adjustment, side compression straps. Detachable hood converts into a fanny pack. Waterproof Cordura nylon, lifetime guarantee, main compartment 3375 cu. in., extends to 4875 cu. in.

E Let's Go Backcountry II............................$240
Backcountry I's Big Brother. Magnum Helix Airflex Suspension. Deluxe bi-lam contoured shoulder harness. Adjustable sterm strap. Adjustable bi-lam Cordura waist belt. 5350 cubic inches. 7130 cubic inches extended. Not pictured.

Order Form

Please print or type — Incomplete applications will not be processed

Last Name	First Name	Date of Birth

Street	*(We cannot ship to P.O. boxes)*	

City	State	Zip

Country	Citizenship	Date of Travel

( ) -		
Phone	School (if applicable)	

Item Code	Description, Size & Color	Quantity	Unit Price	Total Price
			SUBTOTAL:	

Domestic Shipping & Handling		Shipping and Handling (see box at left):	
Order Total:	Add:	Add $10 for RUSH, $20 for overnite:	
Up to $30.00	$4.00	MA Residents add 5% tax on books and gear:	
$30.01 to $100.00	$6.00		
Over $100.00	$7.00	GRAND TOTAL:	
Call for int'l or off-shore delivery			

MasterCard / VISA Order	*Enclose check or money order payable to:*
CARDHOLDER NAME _____	**Harvard Student Agencies, Inc.**
	53A Church Street
CARD NUMBER _____	**Cambridge, MA 02138**
EXPIRATION DATE _____	Allow 2-3 weeks for delivery. Rush orders guaranteed within one week of our receipt. Overnight orders sent via FedEx the same afternoon.

Missing a Let's Go Book from your collection?
Add one to any $50 order at 50% off the cover price!

Let's Go Travel
1-800-5-LETSGO

(617) 495-9649   Fax: (617) 496-8015
53A Church Street
Cambridge MA 02138

20KM NORTH OF TLELL: PORT CLEMENTS

Port Clements is primarily a blue-collar town. A tangled network of logging roads stretches inland from the port; these bumpy byways are open to public use and provide access to the heavily forested interior. Port Clements faces west onto Masset Inlet; the town has the best sunsets in the Charlottes.

The world's only known **Golden Spruce** grows beside the Yakoun River south of Port Clements. A rare mutation causes the tree's needles to be bleached by sunlight. To reach the albino tree, drive 5.5km south of town to a roadside pullover; from there it's a 10-minute walk. Eight km south of the pullover, a trail leads to an unfinished **Haida canoe.** The would-be boat was uncovered by loggers and remains in its original site. Nearby stumps are riddled with test holes where the early builders sampled other trees for their canoe potential. On your way to the spruce, stop by **Golden Spruce Farms,** 1km south of town on Bayview Dr. (557-4583). Dave sells rabbit meat ($2.50 per lb.) and an astonishing variety of fresh vegetables, considering it's nearly impossible to grow potatoes here.

The handful of "reasonably priced" accommodations in Port Clements include the **Golden Spruce Motel,** 2 Grouse St. (557-4325; singles $40, doubles $44; laundry facilities) and the **Millhouse Bed & Breakfast,** 6 Dyson St. (557-4358; singles $35, doubles $50).

Port Clemens has a limited number of food options. Good burgers start around $6.50 at the **Yakoun River Inn** on Bayview Dr. (557-4440). At night, toss back a few pints around the pool table before a stroll on the dock (open Mon.-Sat. noon-2am, Sun. noon-midnight). Or stop by the **III Cheers Family Restaurant,** 9 Cedar Ave., just off Highway 16 (557-9333), for sandwiches and ice cream. (Open 7am-9pm in summer; off-season 7am-8pm.) For the basics, head to **Bayview Market,** on Bayview Dr. (557-4331; open Tues.-Sat. 10am-6pm).

Port Clements is 24km northwest of Tlell on Hwy. 16. Bayview Dr. is the main artery; it follows the shore of Masset Inlet, then breaks south toward the Golden Spruce. The **Port Clements Village Office** (557-4295), on Cedar Ave. between Tingley and Pard St., offers information and free **maps** of the logging roads (open Mon.-Fri. 1-5pm). You can browse for more information at the **Port Clements Islands Regional Library,** at Tingley St. and Cedar Ave. (557-4402; open Wed. 3-5pm and 7-9pm, Fri. 2-6pm). The **Queen Charlotte Islands Health Care Society** operates a medical clinic on Park St. (557-4478) next to the elementary school. (Open Mon. 11am-5pm, Tues. and Thurs.-Fri. 11:30am-1pm and 3:30-5pm, Wed. 2-7pm.) Call **Island Taxi** for a ride at 557-4230. In an **emergency,** call 557-4777. The nearest **police** station is in Masset (626-3991). The **post office** is on Tingley St. between Hemlock and Spruce Ave. (open Mon.-Fri. 8:30am-12:30pm and 1:30-5:30pm, Sat. 1-5pm; **Postal Code:** V0T 1R0). The **area code** is 604.

■■■ MASSET

Resting about 40km north of Port Clements, Masset and the neighboring Haida village of Old Massett (pop. 1600) make up the largest community on the Queen Charlottes. The dispersal of residents between these two settlements and a self-contained Canadian Forces station belie this fact, however, and visitors may search in vain for a focal point to this scattered community. The beautiful beaches of **Naikoon Provincial Park** stretch to the east, inviting beachcombers to search for greatly-prized Japanese fishing floats (glass balls that Japanese fishermen use to float their nets) and elusive razor clams. Masset is at the north end of Graham Island and is the *final* (not merely the mainland) terminus of **Hwy. 16.** Collison Ave. is the main drag. Old Massett Village lies 2km farther up the road.

PRACTICAL INFORMATION AND ORIENTATION

Visitors Information: Travel Infocentre, Old Beach Rd. (626-3982), at Hwy. 16. Plenty of local history and trail maps for choice birdwatching. Open July-Aug.

daily 9am-8pm. The **Masset Village Office** (626-3995) on Main St. has further information. Open Mon.-Fri. 9:30am-4pm.

Car Rental: Tilden Rentals, 1504 Old Beach Rd. (626-3318), at the Singing Surf Inn. New cars from $40 per day, plus 25¢ per km. Must be 21 with a credit card.

Taxi: Jerry's Taxi, 626-5017, or **Island Taxi,** 557-4230. 24 hrs.

Laundromat: Raven & Eagle Gifts & Cleaners, Collison Ave. and Orr St. (626-3511). Wash $1.50, 35-min. dry for $1.50.

Library, at Collison Ave. and McLeod St. (626-3663). Open Tues. and Sat. 2-6pm, Thurs. 2-5pm and 6-8pm.

Emergency: Ambulance, 800-461-9911; **Fire,** 626-5511; **Police** (626-3991), on Collison Ave. at Orr St.

Post Office, on Main St. north of Collison (626-5155). Open Mon.-Fri. 8:30am-5:30pm, Sat. 8:30am-12:30pm. **Postal Code:** V0T 1M0.

Area Code: 604.

ACCOMMODATIONS AND CAMPING

Rooms in a bed and breakfast cost at least $35 per night, and they fill quickly during the summer. There is free **beach camping** 1km past Tow Hill (about 30km east).

Naikoon Park Motel (626-5187), on Tow Hill Rd. about 8km east of town. Close to the beach. 13 rooms at $35, doubles $40, with kitchen $50.

Harbourview Lodging (626-5109), on Delkatla Rd. just north of Collison. B&B right on the harbor. The "blue," "brown," and "pink" rooms downstairs have color TV, shared bath, and sauna. Singles $40. Call for reservations in summer.

Copper Beech House (626-3225), on Delkatla Rd. at Collison. B&B that looks more like an eclectic private museum. Singles $50. Doubles $75.

Masset-Haida Lions RV Site and Campground, on Tow Hill Rd. next to the wildlife sanctuary. 22 gravelly sites, toilets, pay showers. Sites $8, with electricity $10.

Agate Beach Campground, 26km east of town in Naikoon Provincial Park. 32 beachfront sites with an area reserved for tenters. Picnic shelter, firewood, water, flush toilets. Free clamming. Sites: May-Sept. $10, winter free. For more information call Park Headquarters (557-4390).

FOOD

Free razor clams on Agate and North Beach! Best roasted on a stick or chowderized, these clams are rarely affected by the ultra-toxic red-tide (check the hotline anyway). Other types of shellfish, however, should be approached with caution. Ask locally or call the British Columbia red-tide hotline (604-666-3169). You can pick up some lemons at **Masset Grocery** on Old Beach Rd. (626-3666), directly across from the bridge (open daily 11am-11pm).

Sam's Chicken House, at Collison Ave. and Main St. (626-5666). Take-out fish and chips ($7.20) and chicken (1 piece with fries $3.65). Open Thurs.-Sat. 11am-11pm, Wed. and Sun. 11am-7pm.

Cafe Gallery, corner of Collision and Orr (626-9373). Chicken burger with ham and cheese $8.95, pancakes $7.50. Open Mon.-Sat. 9:30am-9pm.

Singing Surf Inn (626-3318), on Old Beach Rd. Breakfast all day; giant milkshakes for $2.70.

SIGHTS AND ACTIVITIES

Search for agates, seashells, and razor clams along the shores of **Agate Beach,** 26km east of Masset in **Naikoon Provincial Park. Tow Hill,** just to the east, rises 100m above Dixon Entrance. The hill is a half-hour walk from the parking area at the Hiellen River; on a clear day you can see Alaska from the top. Another short trail leads to the **Blow Hole,** a small cave that erupts with foaming water when the tide comes in. Across the Hiellen River, **North Beach** is the site of the Haida creation myth, where Raven discovered a giant clam full of tiny men.

Red-breasted sapsuckers, orange-crowned warblers, glaucous-winged gulls, great blue herons, and binocular-toting tourists converge on the **Delkatla Wildlife Sanctuary,** off Tow Hill Rd. in Masset. The best paths for observing the 113 airborne species originate from the junction of Trumpeter Dr. and Cemetery Rd.

With 600 residents, **Old Massett Village,** 2km west of town at the terminus of Hwy. 16, is the largest Haida village on the Charlottes. Many of the houses/stores that line the streets sell Haida prints and carvings. The **Ed Jones Haida Museum** (626-9337), in the old schoolhouse at the north end of town, houses a jumbled collection of old photographs and artifacts from abandoned village sites. The Eagle and Raven totems out front are reproductions of poles from the old village of Yan, across Masset Sound (museum open summer daily 8am-noon and 1-4pm; free). You can apply for permits to visit abandoned Haida villages on Graham Island at the Masset Band Council Office, in the large cedar-and-glass building at the east end of town (626-3337; open Mon.-Fri. 8:30am-noon and 1-4:30pm).

ALASKA APPROACHES

■■■ CASSIAR HIGHWAY (37)

A growing number of travelers prefer **Hwy. 37,** the **Cassiar Highway,** to the Alaska Highway, which has become almost an institution for the RV-driving set. The Cassiar slices 733km through spectacular extremes of charred forest, logged wasteland, and virgin wilderness from Hwy. 16 north to the Alaska Hwy. in the Yukon (Hwy. 16/Hwy. 37 jct. 240km east of Prince Rupert and 484km west of Prince George; Alaska Hwy./Hwy. 37 jct. 434km east of Whitehorse). Completed in 1972, in light of recent improvements, the Cassiar is undeserving of its reputation for gravelly surfaces, flying debris, a dearth of services, and being generally nasty and unforgiving to vehicles and passengers. Today, about 10% of the highway is gravel. Gas stations are still few and far between, so bring along a spare tire extra gas, but if you fill up when you have an opportunity, you need never worry about running out. Observe the general north-country driving guidelines given at the beginning of this chapter. *A Complete Guide for Highway 37,* available at most BC Infocentres, offers a partial list of facilities and campgrounds on the route. Hitchhiking is less popular on the Cassiar than on the Alaska Highway, but the scenery is better, the road less crowded, and the route shorter. (*Let's Go* does not recommend hitchhiking.)

JCT. HWY. 16 TO MEZIADIN JCT. (157KM)

Just north of the junction of Hwy. 37 and Hwy. 16 are the impressive totem poles of **Gitwengak,** relating the history of the Native fort that until 1800 stood on nearby Battle Hill. For Native history mavens looking for additional stimulation, the totem poles of **Kitwancool,** or "place of reduced number," lie another 17km to the north. The village was originally called **Gitenyow,** "the place of many people"; after extended warfare, however, the Natives, sticklers for accurate nomenclature, changed its name. Before heading north, travelers immersed in Native culture should check to see that their fuel tanks are receiving equal attention. The next service station is 113km away at **Elsworth Logging Camp** (open daily 7am-10pm). Elsworth is a great place to buy overpriced groceries and overpriced gas (69¢ per liter, $2.61 per gallon), play a game of baseball (they have their own diamond), or engage in a lively debate on the relative merits of Stihl and Husqvarna chainsaws.

About 63km from the 37/16 junction, **Cranberry River** offers good summer salmon fishing. Services no longer exist at **Meziadin Junction** (meh-zee-AD-in), 18km north of Elsworth. The options, though, are well-defined: 953km to the north lies **Whitehorse,** YT, and 62km west, along Hwy. 37A, are **Stewart,** BC and **Hyder,** AK. The road to Stewart and Hyder offers stunning views of immense glaciers.

■■■ STEWART AND HYDER

Weekly, the Alaska ferry *Aurora* heads south from Ketchikan to the natural Portland Canal, then threads its way back north through the turquoise waters of this scenic fjord to the twin towns of Stewart, BC, and Hyder, AK. The towns lie within 2 mi. of each other at the terminus of the fjord and the end of Rte. 37A, leading to the Cassiar Hwy. In the surrounding mountains, framed perfectly in the view down the main street of either town, glaciers slide down from the clouds, feeding streams and waterfalls that pour into the Canal. Most events in this little international community (including the ferry arrival) happen in Stewart because, with about 900 people, Stewart is ten times the size of Hyder. Hyder's more independently-minded citizens remain on Alaska time while the rest set their clocks to Pacific time (times listed here are in Pacific time unless otherwise noted). Hyderites deal in Canadian currency (except at the post office), use the British Columbia area code, and send their children to school in Stewart. No sign marks the international boundary. From July 1-4, the two communities celebrate an extended birthday party for both nations.

Practical Information and Sights A left turn from the ferry terminal takes you to Hyder; a right turn, to Stewart. Hyder's **information centre** displays the *Hyder Weekly Miner* from 1919-1934 on microfiche for free perusal (open Thurs.-Tues. 10am-2pm). The major tourist activity in Hyder is to sidle up to the bar in the historic **Glacier Inn** and ask to be "Hyderized." About $50,000 in signed bills line the walls of this bar, where early miners would tack up cash as insurance against ever returning to town too broke to buy a drink. In Stewart, a little **museum** housing the **information centre** delves into mining and fashion (miners' fashions? Open Mon.-Fri. 8:30am-4:30pm, Sat.-Sun. 9:30am-4:30pm.) Bears and bald eagles can often be seen plucking salmon from **Fish Creek** 4 mi. from Hyder. **Bear Glacier,** 30 mi. east of Stewart in British Columbia, sits in plain view of the road.

Many visitors never stay overnight in Hyder because if they travel by **ferry,** spending one night means spending a week. The *Aurora's* weekly round-trip from Ketchikan to Stewart/Hyder ($36) includes a three-hour layover that almost gives pedestrians enough time to see both towns. Inquire at the Cornell Travel Agency in Stewart about **bus service** south to Terrace, BC. Buses leave at 10am Mon.-Fri. ($26.75). **Mail flights** zip over to Ketchikan Monday and Thursday ($100); for more information, contact Taquan Air (800-770-8800).

The **Hyder post office** (636-2662), in the HCA building, accepts only US currency (open *Alaska time* Mon.-Fri. 8am-noon and 1-4pm, Sat. 9:30-11:30am) **Stewart's post office** is at Brightwell St. and 5th Ave. (open *Alaska time* Mon.-Fri. 8:30am-5:30pm, Sat. 8:30am-12:30pm). Hyder's **library** (236-2498) also resides in the HCA building (open Tues.-Sat. 1-4pm); as does the **Forest Service** (636-2367; open *Alaska time* Fri.-Sun. 9-10am and 1-2pm, Mon. 9am-noon and 1-2pm). Ask the rangers about hiking trails in the area. The **Police** (636-2233) are posted at 8th Ave. and Conway St. in Stewart. The **area code** is 604.

Camping, Accommodations, and Food Both towns boast campgrounds; the difference between them may be a reflection of national character. Stewart's **Lion's Campground** (636-2537) is orderly and quiet, with tentsites ($10 for 2 people, $2 per additional person), sites with electricity ($12), and incredibly clean showers ($1). It's difficult to tell where the nearby horse pasture ends and Hyder's **Camp Runamuck** begins (tentsites with picnic tables $5). The **Sealaska Inn** (636-2486) offers cheap rates (singles $39, doubles $42). If you can handle the eye strain, the **King Edward Hotel** (636-2244) on 5th Ave. in Stewart provides reasonably priced hotel accommodations. Rooms are decorated with at least four different fabric patterns, each chosen carefully to clash with the others. Rooms in the old motel start at $51, with kitchenette $53. In the new motel, rooms start at $59.

Cut-Rate Foods on 5th Ave. in Stewart fulfills its calling with scores of no-name products for cheap (open daily 9am-9pm). **The King Edward Hotel Coffee Shop,**

on 5th Ave., serves a deluxe burger with fries for quite less than a prince's ransom ($4.50), and a sandwich, soup, and fries special ($6; open daily 7am-9pm). In Hyder, the **Border Cafe** advertises an "internationally famous" burger with potato salad and fries ($6.25). They also do breakfast all day. (Open Tues. and Thurs.-Fri. 8:30am-7pm, Wed. 8:30am-6:30pm, Sat. 8:30am-4pm.)

■■■ CASSIAR HIGHWAY (37)

MEZIADIN JCT. TO JCT. ALASKA HWY. (576KM)

Ninety-five km north of Meziadin Junction is **Bell II Crossing,** an island of civilization in the Cassiar wilderness. Bell II (638-9020) houses a **restaurant** (open 6am-10pm) and a **gas station** (open 6am until 11pm). Minor car and tire repair is available. At Bell II, prices range from the reasonable to the ridiculous. A burger can cost anywhere from $5.75 to $10.25.

Forty km north of Bell II, **Echo Lake** offers a good view of the Coast Mountains to the west, some oddly submerged telegraph cabins, and spectacular cliffs. After 25km more, the immense Iskut burn area is marked by what is rumored by locals to be the largest huckleberry patch in British Columbia. Fifty-three km beyond the patch is **Kinaskan Lake Provincial Park** (847-7320). Campsites are $9.50. Lake, rainbow, and cutthroat trout thrive in the lake. Here also is the head of a 24km hiking trail to Mowdade Lake in **Mount Edziza Provincial Park** (see below). Twenty-six km north on the Cassiar is the **Ealue Lake** turnoff; nearby is another trailhead leading deep into the virgin backcountry of the **Spatsizi Wilderness Plateau** (see below).

For those unwilling to commune with the caribou, there is always a room at the **Red Goat Lodge** (234-3261), just south of **Iskut** (354km north of Meziadin Junction). At the lodge, visitors can choose from bed & breakfast, hostel, or camping style accommodations. At the **bed & breakfast,** singles are $55, doubles $80. The **hostel (HI-C)** has beds for $12 (nonmembers $15); tent sites are $5. Shower and laundry facilities are available (open May 20- Sept. 5). **Canoe** rental starts at $15 per evening on **Eddontenajon Lake** (ed-un-TEN-a-jon). For those wishing to venture further afield, rentals to other lakes start at $27.50 per day.

At the small Native village of **Iskut,** fill the tank and grab some groceries at the **Co-op** (234-3241), which doubles as the village **post office** (general delivery V0J 1K0; in summer, open Mon.-Sat 8am-9pm, Sun. 9am-5pm; winter Mon.-Fri. 9am-noon, 1-5pm, and Sat. 1-5pm). If you and First Tiger Hobbes have enough tuna fish sandwiches and decide to push on (Yukon Ho!), only 84km separate you from tiny Dease Lake.

DEASE LAKE

In 1874, during the peak of the Cassiar gold rush, William Moore cut a trail connecting Telegraph Creek on the Stikine River with Dease Lake, a remote interior trading post. Dease Lake has grown into a simple roadside community and a popular base for exploring the nearby Mount Edziza or Spatsizi wildernesses. Some outdoorspeople pack in by horse.

Practical Information The **Dease Lake Tourist Information Office** is helpful (open Mon.-Fri. 10am-noon and 1-6pm). The **medical clinic** accepts cash or check for medicine (walk-in Mon.-Fri. 8:30am-noon and 1-4:30pm). The **doctor** lives on the premises, and can be reached at 771-3171. For information on local trails or campsites, **British Columbia Parks** (771-4591) and the **Forest Service** (771-4211) share the building next door to the tourist office. **Bonnie and Clyde's Last Hideout** (7710424) has washers ($2) and dryers (25¢ for 10 min.; open Mon.-Fri. 6:30am-11pm, Sat.-Sun. 11am-11pm). The **post office** is in the Shell gas station (771-5600; open Mon.-Fri. 8:30am-5:30pm). The **postal code** is V0C 1L0. Reach the **police** at 771-4111.

Camping, Accommodations, and Food The forest service maintains free **campsites** in remote areas. Get a Forest Service map at the tourist information centre or from the Forest Service (see above). Dease Lake's only motel, the **Northway Motor Inn** (771-5341), offers clean and simple rooms (singles $64, doubles $69). There are two restaurants in Dease Lake. The **Northway Country Kitchen** (771-4114) offers decent food in a clean, spacious setting (open Mon.-Fri. 6am-10pm, Sat.-Sun. 7am-10pm). Agoraphobes should instead head to **Bonnie and Clyde's Last Hideout** (771-4242) to munch standard diner fare (open Mon.-Fri. 6:30am-11pm, Sat.-Sun. 11am-11pm). Groceries and gas are available at both the **Shell station** (771-5600; open daily 7am-11pm) and the **Foodmaster Store** (open Mon.-Sat. 7am-9pm, Sun. 10am-9pm).

Sights Visitors to Dease Lake are presented with four options: drive the remaining 237km to the Alaska Hwy. junction, submit their vehicles to the modern analogue of William Moore's trail, the **Telegraph Creek Road,** explore the **Spatsizi Wilderness Plateau,** or hike through the volcanic wasteland called **Mount Edziza Provincial Park**. The Telegraph Creek Road is an excellent scenic sidetrip for the intrepid traveler who has grown weary of highway driving. The road offers a 113km serpentine ribbon of gravel to **Telegraph Creek.** For the first half of the drive, the road follows the **Tanzilla River** and is remarkable only in its inability to remain level for more than 20 ft. at a stretch. The second half of the trip is considerably more exciting. Drivers must negotiate 20% grades and hairpin turns while sharing the road with the occasional logging truck, as the road clings perilously close to the steep obsidian outbanks of the Taya, Tahltan, and Stikine River canyons. Travelers should allow for a mere two-and-a-half to three-hour drive each way. Those planning to stay overnight in Telegraph Creek without a tent should phone Telegraph Creek's only hotel, the **Stikine Riversong** (235-3196; singles $42, doubles $46), to ensure that it isn't already full.

SPATSIZI WILDERNESS PLATEAU

Long a major hunting ground for the Tahltan people, **Spatsizi Wilderness Plateau** became a provincial park and wildlife reserve in 1975. Supporting one of the largest populations of **Woodland Caribou** in British Columbia, Spatsizi is home to an extensive range of wildlife species. There is no direct vehicle access to the park; **Ealure Lake Road,** near the **Tatogga Lake Junction** 25km north of Kinaskan Lake Provincial Park, offers the only vehicle access to trucks leading into Spatsizi Wilderness Plateau. To reach the trailheads, follow Ealure Lake Road for 22km until it joins with the BC Rail grade, a tertiary road of variable quality described by BC Parks as "rough, but driveable for most vehicles." Because of its isolation, British Columbia Parks strongly recommends that only experienced hikers explore Spatsizi. All hikers, regardless of previous wilderness experience, should make their itineraries and whereabouts known before venturing into the park. For more information, contact **British Columbia Parks Area Supervisor,** General Delivery, Dease Lake, BC V0C 1L0 (604-771-4591).

MOUNT EDZIZA PROVINCIAL PARK

Mount Edziza Provincial Park is a rugged volcanic landscape comprised of over 230,000 hectares of land. The stunning volcanic corners and brilliantly colored volcanic rock are sights to behold, but only for the most experienced hikers. Weather in the park is highly variable. In the summer, daytime temperatures may climb as high as 30°C and then plummet to below freezing at night; snow flurries are not uncommon in mid-summer. In the words of the Park Service, "this is no place for the ill-equipped or the inexperienced." As in the Spatsizi Wilderness, there is no vehicle access. There are three access routes to Edziza, all overgrown and poorly marked. The **Mowdade Trail** leaves from Kinaskan Lake Provincial Park; a boat is required to reach the trailhead. The **Klastine River trail** begins at Iskut (see above). The **Buckley Lake trail** starts on the south shore of the Stikine at Telegraph Creek;

like the Mowdade, this trailhead can only be reached by boat. Travelers should allow a minimum of 5 days to complete the trip, and should be equipped with a - 10°C or better sleeping bag. Travelers may also consider purchasing bear mace, although the Park Service warns that this is an unproven bear deterrent. For a donation, a comprehensive **trail guide** is available at the Stikine Riversong. For more information about the park and possible access routes, contact **British Columbia Parks Area Supervisor,** General Delivery, Dease Lake, BC V0C 1L0 (771-4591).

TELEGRAPH CREEK

Lying 160 miles upstream from Wrangell, Telegraph Creek is the only remaining settlement along the Stikine River. At the highest navigable point on the Stikine, Telegraph Creek was important as a rendezvous point for the coastal Tlingit and interior Tahltan Natives. Obsidian arrowheads fashioned in the Stikine Valley were valued by the Native peoples of the Northwest. While the Tlingits were trading with the Russians in the late 18th century, the Tahltans eluded direct contact with Europeans until 1838, when Robert Campbell of the British Hudson's Bay Company arrived.

Today, Telegraph Creek has 300 residents, most of them Tahltans. The "modern" village revolves around the historic **Stikine Riversong.** Originally the Hudson Bay Company Building in the neighboring, defunct town of **Glenora,** the Riversong was disassembled in 1902 and moved to Telegraph Creek. In 1903, it was reassembled and reopened minus the back quarter of the building so it could fit into the hillside and allow for a road in front of the building's present location. Today, the Riversong acts as Telegraph Hill's sole general store, cafe, and hotel. Take a shower for $4; 50¢ extra to use one of their towels (235-3196; open daily in summer 11am-7pm; closed Sun. in winter. Singles $42. Doubles $46). The staff is extremely helpful and can answer almost any question about the history of the town, the building, or the area.

For a listing of recreation and **camping** facilites in this area, consult the *Stikine Guide to Facilities and Features* or a forest service map. All are available at the Stikine Riversong Cafe or the Dease Lake Tourist Office. There are free Forest Service campsites at **Dodjentin Creek,** 6 mi. west toward Glenora, and **Winter Creek,** 8 mi. west. Take a dip at nearby **Sawmill Lake.** The Dease Lake Tourist Office requires all travelers planning to go into the wilderness to fill out a trip itinerary at the tourist office. The back copy of the itinerary goes to the police, who will be dispatched to retrieve lost or injured travelers. For a listing of recreation and camping facilities in this area, consult the Stikine River Recreation Area pamphlet, the *Valley of the Stikine Guide to Facilities and Features,* or a Forest Service map.

There are no doctors in Telegraph Creek. There is, however, a **health clinic** with two nurses on duty (235-3211; follow signs for Glenora). The police can be reached at 235-3111. For light **mechanical and tire repair,** contact Henry Vance. Flights between Telegraph Creek and Dease Lake run about $260. For more information contact **Tel Air** at 235-3296.

DEASE LAKE TO JCT. ALASKA HWY.

Eighty-five km north of Dease Lake is **Mighty Moe's Place** (no phone), home of the Cassiar's greatest character and collection of paraphernalia. Listen to Moe's Hollywood exploits or sort through his extensive baseball hat collection. Lucky travelers may see Moe perform in his clown suit. Campsites are $7 per night. Canoes are $3 per hr., $15 per day. Cabins for up to three people are $30; for more than three, $45. Moe conducts canoe trips of 6 to 180 mi. For information write Mighty Moe, Box 212, Cassiar, BC, V0C IE0. For those who crave a less cluttered camping environment, **Boya Lake Provincial Park** (847-7320) is 152km north of Dease Lake, 2.5km east of the Cassiar Hwy. Campsites ($9.50) are on a scenic, crystal-blue lake with uncommonly warm waters. Take the plunge in summer.

At the end of the 733km odyssey, dirty, hungry, and weary travelers can grab showers, souvenirs, grub, groceries, and gas at the **PetroCan Station** (536-2744) at the junction of the Cassiar Hwy. and the Alaska Hwy. The PetroCan doubles daily as the office for the RV park next door ($10, $15 with full hook-up). **Showers** are $1 with accommodations, $3 otherwise. They also operate a 24-hr. **laundromat** (washer $1.25, Dryer 25¢ for 14 min.). The **Chevron** nearby is open daily from 8am-8pm. Travelers can splurge on home cooking at the **Junction 37 Cafe** (536-2795) next door to the **PetroCan** (open daily May-Oct. 6am-10pm). For travelers content to carry on, **Whitehorse** lies another 435km west; **Watson Lake** is 33km east.

■■■ ALASKA HIGHWAY

Built during World War II, the Alaska Highway maps out an astonishing 2647km route between Dawson Creek, BC, and Fairbanks, AK. After the Japanese attack on Pearl Harbor in December 1941, worried War Department officials planned an over-land route, out of range of carrier-based aircraft, to supply U.S. Army bases in Alaska. The U.S. Army Corps of Engineers completed the daunting task in just 34 weeks; the one-lane dirt trail curved around swamps and hills (landfill would come only later). Do not use the arbitrarily placed mileposts as official calibration standards, but rather as a general guide. The new kilometer posts are less frequent, though more accurate. Observe the general north-country driving guidelines given at the beginning of this chapter. Take the time to learn some of the history of the highway and the area it runs through. You can make the scenery interesting where it might otherwise get monotonous. Before setting out on your epic Northwestern journey, pick up the exhaustive listing of *Emergency Medical Services* and Canada Highway's *Driving the Alaska Highway* at a visitors bureau, or write the Department of Health and Social Services, P.O. Box H-06C, Juneau, AK 99811 (907-465-3027). The free pamphlet *Help Along the Way* lists emergency numbers along the road from Whitehorse, YT to Fairbanks, AK. (For the Alaska Hwy. in Alaska, see page 174).

■■■ DAWSON CREEK

Dawson Creek, BC (not to be confused with Dawson City, YT) is 590km northwest of Edmonton and the Alaska Hwy.'s official starting point **(Mile 0)** and has calmed down considerably since the heyday of construction. Sixty cases of dynamite exploded close to downtown on February 13, 1943, leveling the business district.

There are two ways to reach Dawson Creek from the south. Drive 590km north-west from Edmonton along Hwy. 43, through Whitecourt to Valleyview. Turn left on Hwy. 34 to **Grande Prairie,** Alberta. From there, continue northwest on **Hwy. 2** to Dawson Creek. Or start in Prince George and drive 406km north on the **Cariboo Hwy.** (Hwy. 97). Either drive takes most of a day.

Practical Information Before you head out on the highway (lookin' for adventure), stop at the **Tourist Information Centre,** 900 Alaska Ave. (782-9595) is in the old train station just off Hwy. 97. If you're stuck in Dawson Creek, **Greyhound,** 1201 Alaska Ave. (782-3131 or 800-661-8747), can bus you to Whitehorse, YT (summer Mon.-Sat; winter 3 per week, $161), Prince George (2 per day, $47), and Edmonton, AB (2 per day, $64). The **King Koin Laundromat,** 1220 103rd Ave. (open daily 8am-9pm), has showers for $2.75 and a $2 wash; 4- min. dry 25¢. **In an emergency,** call for an **ambulance** (782-2211) or contact the **police** (782-5211) at Alaska Ave. and 102nd Ave. The **post office** (782-2322) sits at 104th Ave. and 10th St. **Postal Code:** V1G 4J8.

Accommodations, Camping, and Food Indoor accommodations can be had at the **Cedar Lodge Motel,** 801 110th Ave. (782-8531; singles $32, doubles $40) or the **Sizzler Inn,** 10600 8th St. (782-8136; singles $40, doubles $45). RVers should head for **Tubby's RV Park,** at 20th St. and Hwy. 97 (782-2584; open May-Oct.; sites $10, full-hookups $16, with laundry and showers), while tenters should head for greener pastures at **Mile 0 City Campground,** 1km west of Mile 0 on the Alaska Hwy. (782-2590; sites $10 with laundry and showers). If foraging on your bug-splattered windshield has failed to satisfy you, a great place for nourishment in Dawson Creek is the **Alaska Cafe & Pub** (782-7040), "55 paces south of the Mile 0 Post" on 10th St., with excellent burgers and fries for $6. The Golden Arches of **McDonald's** beckon enticingly at 11628 8th St., just down Hwy. 2.

Sights The town's most inspiring sights have less to do with the town than with the highway running through it: the **Mile 0 Cairn,** on the edge of the rotary next to the Infocentre, marks the beginning of the highway, and the **Mile 0 Post,** a block toward downtown at 10th and 102nd, commemorates the construction of the highway and is much more of a photo-op. Chronically stressed travelers might take a dip in Dawson Creek's **Centennial Swimming Pool,** at 10th and 105th (782-7946; $2.50 per session, students $2.25); the pool also houses a spiraling slide plunking you down in the pool's centre.

■■■ ALASKA HIGHWAY

Tired after only 76 km? Then make a quick pit-stop in **Fort St. John.** The **Travel Infocentre,** 9323 100th St. (785-6037), in the museum complex (open daily 8am-8pm), will quickly make it clear to you that there's really nothing to do or see. The city provides live entertainment on the adjacent oil derrick at **Doin's at the Derrick** every evening from mid-June to mid-August. For those who must spend the night, the **Four Seasons Motor Inn,** 9810 100th St., has singles for $34 and doubles for $38. **Centennial RV Park** is right behind the Infocentre (Phone the infocentre for reservations; sites $11, electricity and water $16; showers and laundry). The only cheap food in town is produced by the flock of fast-food joints lining 100th.

    Fort Nelson, 480 (of the highway's most unexciting) km north of Dawson Creek, is the highway's next pit-stop town on the way to Whitehorse. The **Infocentre** (774-6400) hides itself in the Rec Center on the western edge of town (open daily in summer 8am-8pm) and provides a small brochure, though the fact that the supermarkets are highlighted indicates how much excitement you can expect. The **Fort Nelson Heritage Museum** (774-3536), however, is an exception. Across the highway from the Infocentre, the museum features several beautiful **vintage cars** (museum open daily in the summer 8:30am-7:30pm; $2.50). Rest up at the **Mini-Price Inn** (774-2136), hidden a block off the highway at 5036 51st Ave. W (singles $32; doubles $36; kitchenettes $5 extra). Campers should continue another 1km west to **Westend Campground** (774-2340), an oasis with hot showers (25¢ per 3 min.), a laundromat, a free car wash, and free firewood (sites $12, full hookups $17). Fort Nelson cuisine consists of standard hotel fare and fast food.

    Small hotels, plain but expensive, pockmark the remainder of the highway every 80 to 160km on the way to **Carcross, Whitehorse,** and the Alaska border. Campers' needs are satisfied by the provincial parks that spring up along the road. **Stone Mountain Campground,** about 160km past Fort Nelson, is a park campsite set beside Summit Lake. Tenters should continue on for 19km to the grassy areas, toward the beaver dam, at **One Fifteen Creek.** Each park has sites with toilets and fresh water for $12. Forty km farther down the road lies **Toad River,** a booming town of 60. The **Toad River Cafe** (232-5401) makes an interesting stop to peek up at the 3400 hats hanging from the ceiling. Food is also available at reasonable prices (burgers from $4; open daily in summer 7am-9pm, winter until 7pm).

    After winding its way along beautiful **Muncho Lake,** the highway reaches the **Liard River Hot Springs** near the 800km mark. Soothe your weary bones and ease your frazzled, dazed mind in these naturally warm and hot pools (free). The park service manages **campsites** here ($12) and a free day-use area. Get here early, though, if you want to spend the night. The campground is often full by early afternoon.

    Near the BC-Yukon border, the road winds through vast areas of land scorched by forest fires; gray arboreal skeletons stretch in all directions as far as the eye can see. At night, this area offers prime winter viewing of the *aurora borealis,* as there are no city lights to pollute the view.

The Alaska Highway's winding route crosses the BC-Yukon border several times before it passes through Whitehorse. Just after it crosses into the Yukon for the second time (traveling west), the highway passes through the small town of **Watson Lake** and the famed **"Sign Post Forest,"** at Mile 635. The "forest" was born in 1942 when a homesick Army Engineer erected a sign indicating the mileage to his hometown of Danville, Illinois. More than 17,000 travelers have since followed suit; if you look hard enough, you'll probably find a sign from a town near you. The **Infocentre** is hidden in the forest (open daily 8am-8pm). While in the Yukon, tune in to **road information** at 96.1 FM.

Mile 626 marks the junction with the **Cassiar Hwy. (Hwy. 37)** (see page 267) leading south to **Yellowhead Hwy. 16** (see page 253). At mi. 804, the small community of **Teslin Lake** is best known as the home of the **George Johnston Museum** (390-2550). Born in Alaska in 1889, George Johnston was a Tlingit who made a living running a trap line and a general store. More important, however, was Johnston's interest in photography. The backbone of the museum's collection, Johnston's stunning photographs, capture Tlingit life in Teslin Lake from 1910 to 1940, providing valuable insight into Native culture (open May-Labor Day 9am-7pm. $2, children $1).

YUKON TERRITORY

■■■ WHITEHORSE

Named for the once-perilous Whitehorse Rapids, whose crashing whitecaps were said to resemble an entourage of galloping pale mares before they were tamed by a dam, Whitehorse marks the highest navigable point on the Yukon River. The bone-weary Sourdoughs of the 1898 Gold Rush often stopped here to wring themselves out after successfully navigating the rapids, and then continued on with the floating armada of expectant gold-seekers headed for the Klondike.

Capital of the Yukon since 1953, Whitehorse is developing a cosmopolitan outlook while maintaining much of its century-old Klondike architecture. Whitehorse is a good base for exploring the surrounding country.

PRACTICAL INFORMATION AND ORIENTATION

Visitors Information: Whitehorse Visitor Reception Centre (667-2915), on the Alaska Hwy. next to the airport. The state-of-the-art purple bathrooms lining the circumference of the Centre's rotunda are perhaps the greatest unsung pleasures of the Northwest. Running a close second behind the centre's bathroom facilities are the free brochures and maps, the excellent video overview of the city, and a great stereo-sound slide-show highlighting the Yukon's history and wilderness. Open daily mid-May to mid-Sept. 8am-8pm. You can also get information by writing to **Tourism Yukon,** P.O. Box 2703, Whitehorse, YT Y1A C26. The **City of Whitehorse Information Centre,** at 3rd Ave. and Wood St. (667-7545), offers the same brochures and maps, without the film or the polished fixtures. Open daily mid-May to Sept. 8am-8pm; Oct.-April Mon.-Fri. 9am-5pm.

Canadian Airlines, 668-4466, for reservations 668-3535. To: Calgary (in summer, 3 per day Mon.-Fri., 2 per day Sat.-Sun.; in winter, 2 per day; $519), Edmonton (3 per day, $519), and Vancouver (3 per day, $448). Ask about youth standby fare discounts (ages 12-24).

Buses: Greyhound, 2191 2nd Ave. (667-2223). To: Vancouver ($291), Edmonton ($225), and Dawson Creek ($162). Buses Mon.-Sat.; *no* Greyhound service to Alaska. Open Mon.-Fri. 8:30am-5:30pm, Sat. 8am-noon, Sun. 5-9pm. **Alaskan Express,** (667-2223) at 2nd Ave. and Wood St. (tickets at the Westmark Hotel, 668-3225). Buses late May to mid-Sept. To: Anchorage (3 per week, US$184), Haines (3 per week, US$79), Fairbanks (3 per week, US$155) and Skagway (daily, US$52). **Norline,** in the Greyhound depot (633-3864). To Dawson City (3 per week in summer, 2 per week in winter; $73).

Local Transportation: Whitehorse Transit, 668-2831. Limited service downtown. Buses leave/arrive downtown next to Canadian Tires on the northern edge of town, Mon.-Thurs. 6:15am-6:15pm, Fri. 6:15am-9:15pm, Sat. 8am-7pm. Fare $1.25, seniors 50¢, children and students 85¢.

Taxi: Yellow Cab, 668-4811. 24 hrs.

Car Rental: Norcan Leasing, Ltd., Alaska Hwy. (668-2137 or 800-661-0445), at Mile 917.4. Cars from $30 per day. 100km free; 15¢ per additional km. Must be 21 with credit card.

Bike Rental: The Bike Shop, 2157 2nd Ave. (667-6501). Mountain bikes $20 per day, $12 per ½-day. Credit card imprint as deposit. Open Mon.-Sat. 9am-6pm.

Bookstore: Mac's Fireweed Books, 213 Main St. (668-2434). An extensive collection of Northern literature. Open daily 8am-10pm.

Library: 2071 2nd Ave. (667-5239). Open Mon.-Fri. 10am-9pm, Sat. 1-6pm, Sun. 1-9pm.

Market: Food Fair, 2180 2nd Ave. (667-4278). Open Mon.-Wed. 8:30am-7pm, Thurs.-Fri. 8:30am-9pm, Sat. 8:30am-6pm, Sun. 10am-6pm.

Laundromat: Norgetown (667-6113). Wash $1.90; Dryer 50¢ per 7.5 min. Open daily 8am-9pm.

Public Showers: 4th Ave. Residence, 4051 4th Ave. (667-4471). $3.20, with towel $3.75.

Crisis Line: 668-9111.

Pharmacy: Shoppers Drug Mart, 311 Main St. (667-7304). Open Mon.-Fri. 8am-9pm, Sat. 9am-6pm, Sun. 11am-6pm.

Hospital: (667-8700), on the east side of the Yukon River on Hospital Rd., just off Wickstrom Rd.

Police: 4th and Elliot (667-5555). **Ambulance:** 668-9333.

Post Office: No main office. For general services: 211 Main St. (668-5847). Open Mon.-Fri. 8am-6pm, Sat. 9am-5pm. For general delivery: 3rd and Wood, in the Yukon News Bldg. (668-3824). Open Mon.-Sat. 7am-7pm. **General Delivery Postal Code** for last names beginning with the letters A-L is Y1A 3S7; for M-Z it's Y1A 3S8.

Area Code: 403.

To reach Whitehorse by car, take the downtown exit off the Alaska Hwy. Once there, park the car; the downtown is compact. The airport is a short ride to the west, and the bus station is on the northeastern edge of town, a short walk from downtown.

ACCOMMODATIONS AND CAMPING

Call the **Northern Network of Bed and Breakfasts** (993-5649), in Dawson City, to reserve a room in a Klondike household. Singles start at $50 and doubles at $60. Camping in Whitehorse is a problem: there is only one RV campground and one tenting park near the downtown area. Tenters praying for a hot shower should seek the group of campgrounds clustered 10-20km south of town on the Alaska Hwy.

High Country Inn (HI-C), 4051 4th Ave. (667-4471). Offering long- and short-term housing, this well-run residence boasts cooking and laundry facilities, good security, and free use of the city pool next door. Hostel beds (in a shared twin) $18, nonmembers $20. Private singles $50. Doubles $75. Call to reserve a bed.

Roadside Inn, 2163 2nd Ave. (667-2594), near shopping malls and Greyhound. Bare-bones accommodations. Singles from $40. Doubles from $45.

Robert Service Campground, 1km from town on South Access Rd. on the Yukon River. A convenient stop for tenting folk. Firewood, fire pits, playground, picnic area, drinking water, toilets, metered showers. Island Nature Walk nearby. Open late May-early Sept. Gate closed midnight-6am. 40 sites, $14.

FOOD

Prices are reasonable by Yukon standards.

No Pop Sandwich Shop, 312 Steele (668-3227). This artsy alcove is popular with Whitehorse's small suit-and-tie crowd. You can order a Beltch (BLT and cheese, $4.50), but don't commit the egregious *faux pas* of ordering a Coca-Cola here. Horrors! It's strictly fruit juice and milk. Open Mon.-Thurs. 8am-9pm, Fri. 8am-10pm, Sat. 10am-8pm, Sun. 10am-3pm.

Talisman Cafe, 2112 2nd Ave. (667-2736). Good food in a nondescript environment. Try to get your 4 food groups in a few Russian *pirogies* ($9.50). Burgers from $5 and breakfasts around $5.50. Open daily 6am-10pm.

Mom's Kitchen, 2157 2nd Ave. (668-6620), at Alexander. Breakfast is a specialty. Mom whips up some great omelettes ($6-9). Lunch on the 3-course Chinese special for $7.50. Open Mon.-Fri. 6:30am-8pm, Sat. 6:30am-5pm, Sun. 7am-3pm.

SIGHTS AND ACTIVITIES

Considering the size of its city, the Whitehorse welcoming committee has assembled an astonishing array of scheduled tours and visitor activities. In July and August, the **Yukon Historical and Museum Association,** 3126 3rd Ave. (667-4704), sponsors free daily tours of downtown called **Heritage Walks.** The tours leave from Donnenworth House, in Lepage Park next to the Infocentre (Mon.-Sat. 9:30am-3:30pm, every hr. on the ½-hr.) The **Yukon Conservation Society,** 302 Hawkins St. (668-5678), arranges free hikes Monday through Friday during July and August to explore the Yukon's natural beauty.

The restored *Klondike,* on South Access Rd. (667-4511), is a dry-docked stern-wheeler that recalls the days when the Yukon River was the city's sole artery of survival. Pick up a ticket for a free and fascinating guided tour at the information booth at the parking lot entrance (open June 20-Aug. 13 9am-7:30pm). The **Whitehorse Rapids Fishway** (633-5965), at the end of Nisutlin Drive 2km southeast of town, allows salmon to bypass the dam and continue upstream in the world's longest salmon migration (open daily mid-June to mid-Sept. 8am-10pm; free). Two km south of town on Miles Canyon Rd. off of South Access Rd. whispers **Miles Canyon.** Once the location of the feared Whitehorse rapids, this dammed stretch of the Yukon now swirls silently under the first bridge to span the river's banks.

Visitors desiring a taste of local culture can feed their brains at the **MacBride Museum,** 1st Ave. and Wood St. (667-2709). The exhibits feature memorabilia from the early days of the Yukon, including photographs of Whitehorse as a tent city. The log cabin in the museum courtyard, built by Sam McGee in 1899, has managed to avoid the flames that consumed its occupant ("The Northern Lights have seen queer sights, but the queerest they ever did see, was that night on the marge of Lake Laberge I cremated Sam McGee," —Robert Service) though the proprietors have to mow the grass roof. (Open daily May and Sept. noon-4pm; June and Aug. 10am-6pm; July 9am-6pm. $3.25, seniors and students $2.25, families $7.50.) The **Old Log Church Museum,** 303 Elliot St. (668-2555), at 3rd, has converted its aisles into a museum that fully explicates the history of missionary work in the territories. Built by its pastor, the church required only three months of labor; sub-zero weather has a way of motivating people. (Open June-Aug. Mon.-Sat. 9am-6pm, Sun. noon-4pm. Museum $2.50, children $1.) The incredible three-story **Log Skyscrapers** at 3rd Ave. and Lambert St. were built single-handedly in the 1970s by a local septuagenarian. Vacationing scholars are welcome to browse at the **Yukon Archives,** 80 Range Rd. (667-5321), housing the incredible photographs of Corporal Paxton capturing the construction of the Alaska Hwy. in 1942 (open Tues.-Wed. 9am-5pm, Thurs.-Fri. 1-9pm; Sat. 10am-6pm).

Two-hour river tours are available on two different lines. From June to September, the **Youcon Kat** (668-2927; 668-1252 for ticket reservations) will take you on a jaunt downstream from the hydroelectric dam. Boats leave daily at 1, 4, and 7pm from the ramshackle pier at 1st and Steele ($15, children $7.50). The **Yukon Gardens** (668-7972), 3km southwest of town at the junction of the Alaska Hwy. and South Access Rd., blossom with 22 acres of wildflowers and plants from around the world. (Open early June to mid-Sept. daily 9am-9pm. $5, seniors $4.50, students $3.75, children $1.50.)

Before moving on, needed supplies and fun-time browsing can be had downtown at the **Hougan Center,** on Main St. between 3rd and 4th, a group of specialty shops (open Mon.-Fri. 8am-9pm, Sat. 9am-9pm, Sun. 10am-7pm).

■ ■ ■ CARCROSS

The narrows between Bennett and Nares Lakes has been the site of a seasonal hunting camp of the Tagish Native people since time immemorial. Short for "Caribou Crossing," the herds were obliterated in the early 1900s, but Carcross survived the gold rush nourished by mining and tourism in the Yukon's southern lakes district. Carcross is on the Klondike Hwy. (Hwy. 2), 74km south of Whitehorse and 106km north of Skagway, AK.

Practical Information Old photographs and displays trace the history of the White Pass and Yukon Railroad in the **Carcross Visitor Reception Centre,** inside the depot (821-4431; open mid-May to mid-Sept. daily 8am-8pm). The **Atlin Express** (604-651-7617) connects Carcross with Atlin, BC ($21, seniors $18, children 5-11 $10.50, under 5 free) and with Whitehorse ($15, seniors $7.50, under 5 free). The Express, also the mail van, stops at the Carcross post office Monday, Wednesday, and Friday year-round. The two-story red building in Carcross houses the **health station,** 821-4444. Emergency numbers: **ambulance,** 821-3333; **fire,** 821-2222; **police,** 821-5555 (if no answer call 1-667-5555). Suds your duds at **Montana Services** (see below; wash $2.25, 4 min. dry 25¢). The **post office** is the white building with red trim on Bennett Ave. (Open Mon, Wed., and Fri. 8:30am-noon and1-2pm, Tues. and Thurs. 10-11:45am; **Postal Code:** Y0B 1B0.) Tune in to **visitors information** on 96.1 FM. The **area code** is 403.

Accommodations, Camping, and Food Travelers seeking accommodations in the Crossing may choose to check out the **Caribou Hotel** (821-4501), the oldest operating hotel in the Yukon. The original structure was destroyed in a 1909 fire; the present building was erected shortly thereafter. "She may be old, but she's clean and friendly." (Shared bath. Singles and doubles $35.) **Spirit Lake Lodge** (821-4337), 7km north of town on Hwy. 2, maintains forested tentsites overlooking the lake ($6, showers $3). The Yukon Government maintains 14 rocky sites ($8) with drinking water, firewood, and pit toilets at **Carcross Campground,** 1km north of town on Hwy. 2 (follow signs for the dump).

Pirogies (Russian dumplings) are a local specialty. Two beef *pirogies* cost $8.50 at **The Golden Spike Restaurant** (821-3412), below the Caribou Hotel. Burgers cost $6.25 and up. (Open daily 7am-8pm.) Herbivores can get cheese and potato *pirogies* for $5-9 at the **Spirit Lake Restaurant** (821-4337), in the Spirit Lake Lodge (open daily 7am-10pm). If you've brought your mom's *pirogi* recipe from Russia, you can shop for ingredients at **Montana Services** (821-3708), at the Chevron station on Hwy. 2 (open daily May-Sept. 7am-11pm, Oct.-April 8am-8pm).

Sights and Outdoors South of town an old, rough mining road reaches part way up Montana Mountain. Legs and lungs carry the stalwart past the lichen, snow, and boulders to the spectacular view. To get there follow Hwy. 2 south. Take the first right across the bridges, then the first left, and then the first right again, then follow until the road becomes impassable; from there, walk up to gain an astounding **view** of the Yukon.

The tiny steam locomotive *Duchess,* built in 1878 to haul coal and passengers, is on display by the depot housing the Reception Centre (see above). Anglers can cast for lake trout and grayling from the footbridge that spans the river.

The **Carcross Desert** is 2km north of town on Hwy. 2. This desert, once the sandy bottom of a large glacial lake, was exposed by glacial retreat, and harsh winds from Lake Bennett have discouraged plant growth. Alternating shallows and deep pools create a mottled blue-and-green effect at **Emerald Lake,** 8km farther north. You can rent canoes ($5 per hr., $25 per day) from the **Spirit Lake Lodge** (821-4337), 7km north of town on Hwy. 2.

The **Museum of Yukon Natural History** (667-1055), 1km north of the desert, presents mounted animals in life-like settings, including the largest polar bear ever mounted (open mid-May to mid-Sept. daily 8am-5:30pm; $3, children $2).

■■■ KLUANE NATIONAL PARK

On St. Elias' Day 1741, Vitus Bering, a Danish captain in the Russian service, sighted the mountains of what is now **Kluane National Park** (kloo-AH-nee). "Kluane" is a Tutchone Native word, meaning "place of many fish." Kluane is Canadian wilderness at its most rugged, unspoiled, and beautiful. The "Green Belt" along the eastern park boundary, at the foot of the Kluane Range, supports the greatest diversity of plant and animal species in northern Canada. Beyond the Kluane loom the glaciers of the Icefield Range, home to Canada's highest peaks, including the tallest, 19,850-ft. Mt. Logan. These glaciers and mountains cover nearly two-thirds of the park and are accessible only to the most intrepid alpinist and adventurer. However, the Alaska Highway, near the northeastern boundary of the park, provides generally convenient park access.

Practical Information Pick up plenty of free information at the **Haines Junction Visitor Centre,** on Logan St. in Haines Junction (Canadian Park Service 634-2251; Tourism Yukon 634-2345; open mid-May to mid-Sept. daily 9am-9pm), or at the **Sheep Mountain Visitor Centre,** at Alaska Hwy. Km 1707 (841-5161; open June to mid-Sept. daily 9am-6:30pm). Visitors may also write to Superintendent, Kluane National Park and Preserve, Parks Service, Environment Canada, Haines Junction, YT Y0B 1L0 for information.

Kluane's 22,015 sq. km are bounded by Kluane Game Sanctuary and the Alaska Hwy. to the north, and the Haines Hwy. (Hwy. 3) to the east. The town of **Haines Junction** is at the eastern park boundary, 158km west of Whitehorse. **Alaska Direct** (800-770-6652, in Whitehorse 668-4833) runs three buses per week from Haines Junction to Anchorage (US$125), Fairbanks (US$100), Whitehorse (US$20), and Skagway (US$55).

The **visitor radio** station is FM 96.1. **Emergency numbers** in Haines Junction include: **medical,** 634-2213; **fire,** 634-2222; and **police,** 635-5555 (if no answer, call 1-667-5555). There is a **laundromat** in the Gateway Inn (see below; wash $1.50, 10-min. dry 25¢; open daily 7am-midnight). The **post office** (634-2706) is in Madley's General Store (open Mon., Wed., and Fri. 9-10am and 1-5pm, Tues. 9am-1pm, Thurs. 9am-noon, 1-5pm). The **Postal Code** is Y0B 1L0. The **area code** is 403.

Camping, Accommodations, and Food If you're seeking accommodations in Kluane, you have two choices: stay outdoors and fall victim to bloodthirsty mosquitoes, or head for shelter and fall victim to exorbitant hotel rates. Mosquitoes won't bother you if you buy some strong **insect repellent. Kathleen Lake Campground** (634-2251), 27km south of Haines Jct. off Haines Rd., is close to good hiking and fishing and features water, flush toilets, fire pits, firewood, and occasional "campfire talks" (sites $7.25; open June-Oct.). The Yukon government runs four campgrounds, all with hand-pumped cold water and pit toilets (sites $8; call Tourism Yukon at 634-2345 for more information): **Pine Lake,** 7km east of Haines Jct. on the Alaska Hwy.; **Congdon Creek,** 85km west of Haines Jct. on the Alaska Hwy.; **Dezadeash Lake,** 50km south of Haines Jct. on Haines Rd.; and **Million Dollar Falls,** 90km south of Haines Jct. on Haines Rd., near the BC border.

Indoor accommodations can be found at **Kathleen Lake Lodge,** 25km south of Haines Jct. (634-2319). Enormous rooms and private bathtub (singles $37, doubles $47; showers $3 or free with room). **The Gateway Inn,** at Haines Rd. and the Alaska

Hwy. in Haines Jct. (634-2371), offers clean, spare rooms with private bath and TV (singles $53.50, doubles $59, 8 RV sites $12.50).

Haines Junction restaurants offer standard highway cuisine; for groceries, head for **Madley's General Store,** at Haines Rd. and Bates (634-2200; open daily 8am-8pm; Oct.-April daily 8am-6:30pm). You could live for days on a monster croissant ($1) or tasty sourdough loaf ($2.25) from the **Village Bakery and Deli** (634-2867), on Logan St. across from the Visitor Centre. (Open May-June and Sept. daily 9am-6pm; July-Aug. daily 9am-9pm.) The **Cozy Corner Cafe** (634-2511), on the Alaska Hwy. 500 ft. west of Haines Hwy., draws highway crowds for big, cheap portions: burgers and fries from $6 (open daily 7am-10pm).

Outdoors in the Park Kluane National Park offers an opportunity to explore wild wilderness. There are few actual trails in the park; the major ones are the 4km **Dezadeash River Loop** (dez-a-DEE-ush), beginning at the Haines Junction Visitor Centre, the 15km **Auriol Trail** starting from Haines Hwy. (an excellent overnight hike), and the 85km **Cottonwood Trail,** a four-to-six-day trek beginning either 27 or 55km south of Haines Junction on Haines Hwy. Cottonwood is a loop trail offering 25km of trail above tree-line and a short detour up an adjacent ridge providing a view of the Icefield Ranges and Mount Logan on clear days.

The park also offers many **"routes"** following no formal trail and are not maintained by the park. These are reserved for more experienced hikers, since route finding, map reading, and compass skills may all be called for. Perhaps the most popular are the **Slims East** and **Slims West** routes, both beginning 3km south of the Sheep Mountain Information Center (see above); both follow the Slims River (each on its respective side) for 23-30km (one-way) to ridges overlooking the mighty **Kaskawalsh Glacier.** Both routes take 3-5 days; due to increased bear activity in this area, the park mandates the use of **bear canisters** for the storage of food on all overnight trips. These are available free of charge at both of the park's centres at Haines Junction and Sheep Mountain. The Sheep Mountain information centre is responsible for hikes from the north end of the park and the Slims Valley. All trekkers camping in the backcountry must register at one of the visitor centres. The park strongly encourages day hikers to do the same, especially in the **north end** and **Slims Valley** section of the park where trails are not as well marked and bear activity is more frequent. In late July when the soapberries bloom, the grizzlies come out of the highlands and feed directly along the trails. For the less adventurous, the park offers shorter **day hikes** and **walks** led by wardens concentrating on specific themes, ranging from bear habitats to the park's wildflowers. The park also offers campfire talks at the Sheep Mountain and Haines Junction Park Information Centres (the events are listed daily and weekly). Because the Slims Valley is semiarid, it receives less than 7 in. of precipitation annually; the two trailheads are frequently smothered by dust blowing down from the glacier. Travelers should avoid being caught in this area without a prearranged return ride, particularly since the road is not heavily traveled.

The **Kluane Park Adventure Center** is the central booking office for all outdoor activities going on in and around the park (634-2313, open daily 9am-6pm). The centre has **mountain bikes** ($20 per 24 hrs., $15 per ½-day, $5 per hr.) and canoes ($15 per ½-day, $25 per day) for rent. For $100, travelers can go from Copper Mine, BC to Dalton Post, YT through Class III and IV rapids along the Tatshenshini River. For the more serene, the centre offers a 2-hr. scenic interpretive float trip illustrating the park's ecology, fauna, and geology for $25.

Anglers are invited to put the park's name to the test. **Kathleen Lake** (see below) is home to lake and rainbow trout, arctic grayling, and Kokanee salmon. Grayling abound in **Jarvis Creek,** halfway between Haines Jct. and Sheep Mountain. Visitors can obtain a National Parks fishing permit ($7 weekly, $13 annually) at either visitor centre (see above). To maintain the natural stock, limits on both the size and number of fish which may be kept have been established. Anglers are required to use barbless hooks.

You can't miss (no matter how hard you try) the awful **Haines Junction Big Game Monument,** at the intersection of the Alaska Hwy. and Haines Rd. This *faux*-mountain landscape, fitted with crude wildlife sculptures, has the distressing appearance of a giant wild-animal-berry muffin. Next door, you can inscribe your name in the enormous **Alaska Highway Guest Book.**

BEAVER CREEK

176km north of Burwash Landing is **Beaver Creek,** Canada's westernmost community. (For the Alaska Hwy. in Alaska, see page 174). Because of permafrost, the Alaska Highway at Beaver Creek was not driveable in all weather until 1943; whether it will remain driveable is another question. **Ida's Hotel and Cafe** is *the* bar in Beaver Creek, and is a happening spot when the road crews finish up around midnight. During the day, Ida's runs a **restaurant** (862-7223) with some savory home cooking (open daily 6-10pm; bar is open 4pm-2am). Ida's has single rooms for $64.20 per night and doubles for $75, though travelers can camp out for free. The **Beaver Creek Motor Inn** also boasts home cooking (862-7600), and is open daily 6am-midnight; the "Monster Burger" is the meal of choice ($7.50 for cheeseburger with fries on a homemade bun). Have a monster snooze after the monster burger. Rooms at the motor inn are $45; $5 for each additional person. Before driving onto the border, travelers can check in at the **Beaver Creek Visitor Infocentre** (862-7321), which provides information on current road conditions (open mid-May to mid-Sept. daily 9am-9pm). The **post office** (862-7211; open Mon. 9am-5pm, Wed. 1-5pm, and Fri. noon-4pm; **Postal Code:** Y0B 1A0) is in the back of Community Hall. Going north on the highway, turn left immediately after the visitor's centre. The adjacent **swimming pool** is open Tuesday through Saturday in the afternoons and evenings (pick up a schedule there or at the post office; a day-pass is $3). The **health centre** can be reached at 862-7225. In an **emergency,** call the police at 862-5555.

■■■ KLONDIKE LOOP AND DEMPSTER HIGHWAY

These two roads intersect at Dawson City in northern Yukon Territory. The **Klondike Loop** connects the Yukon's two significant cities, Whitehorse to the south and Dawson City , 533km apart. The highway is entirely paved between the cities. Gas is available about every 90km; it's a good idea to fill up when you have the chance. The 741km **Dempster Hwy.,** named after Inspector W.J.D. Dempster, one of the most courageous officers to wear the red of the Royal Canadian Mounted Police, is the sole access road to Canada's isolated **Mackenzie River Delta** communities of **Fort McPherson, Arctic Red River,** and **Inuvik** (ih-NOO-vik) in the Northwest Territories. The first two are towns of the Dene (day-nay) Native people; the last, an administrative centre of about 3000 people. The Dempster Hwy. leads north from Dawson City to Inuvik. Halfway to Inuvik, 364km from Dawson City, gas, food, supplies, and accommodations are available at the well-kept **Eagle Plains Hotel,** and almost nowhere else, between Dawson City and Inuvik. You know what that means…brace yourself (singles $90, doubles $100; winter singles and doubles $75; prices are expected to rise soon). Gas 78¢ per liter, or $2.95 per gallon). It's a good thing the **ferries** are free: they cross the Peel and Arctic Red Rivers, in the Northwest Territories roughly 550 and 600km north of Dawson City, about 15 hours per day in summer (about mid-June-mid-Oct.). In winter, drive easily across the thick ice. **No crossing** is possible during fall freeze-in or spring thaw. Call 800-661-0752 for current status.

Clearly, the Dempster drive is not to be taken lightly. If you drive, you will be almost alone and enjoy stunning views of Arctic wilderness. Hitching the route is a poor idea. For 4½ days each autumn, the **Porcupine Caribou herd** (150,000 caribou!) migrates across the highway. Even if you're a seasoned veteran of the Massachusetts Turnpike, 150,000 caribou still have the right of way. Pick up the free pamphlet *The Dempster* at an information centre in Whitehorse or Dawson City before driving the Dempster Hwy. For conditions, **maps,** and information, contact the **Northwest Territories Visitors Centre** (993-6167), Front St. at King in Dawson city (open daily June-Sept. 9am-9pm). **Gold City Tours** (993-5175), on Front St. in Dawson City, provides bus service to Inuvik (2 per week; $198, round-trip $350).

■■■ DAWSON CITY

Gold. Gold! GOLD! Of all the insanity ever inspired by the lust for the dust, the creation of Dawson City must surely be ranked among the most amazing. For 12 glorious, crazy months, from July 1898 to July 1899, Dawson City, on the doorstep of the Arctic Circle and 1000 mi. from any other settlement, was the largest Canadian city west of Toronto and as cosmopolitan as San Francisco or Seattle. Its 30,000-plus residents, with names like Swiftwater Bill, Skookum Jim, Arizona Charlie Meadows, and The Evaporated Kid, had each somehow floated more than 1000 lb. of provisions down the Yukon River and made portages over some of the region's most rugged terrain, all driven by the desire to be filthy, stinkin' rich.

When the torrent of gold slowed to a trickle in 1900, the city proved less hardy than its inhabitants and quickly devolved into a ghost town. It wasn't until the early 1960s that the Canadian government, recognizing the historical importance of Dawson, brushed away the tumbleweeds and began to restore it. Here is a faithful recreation of the "Last Great Adventure." More than 75 years after its moment in the midnight sun, Dawson City is again the jewel of the Yukon.

PRACTICAL INFORMATION AND ORIENTATION

Visitors Information: Visitor Reception Centre (993-5566), Front and King St. Historic movies and extensive information. Open mid-May to mid-Sept. daily 9am-9pm. For information, write Box 40, Dawson City, YT Y0B 1G0. The **Northwest Territories Visitors Centre** (993-6167) is across the street and has plenty of advice on driving the Dempster Hwy. (open daily late May -early Sept. 9am-9pm). **Tourist radio** (96.1 FM) broadcasts weather, road conditions, and events.

Buses: Norline Coaches Ltd. (993-5331), at Gas Shack Chevron Station on 5th Ave. Service to Whitehorse 3 times per week (2 times in winter) for $72.75. **Gold City Tours** (993-5175) runs buses up the Dempster Hwy. Mon. and Fri. at 8am (round-trip to Inuvik $350).

Ferry: The **Yukon Queen** makes daily trips along the Yukon to and from Eagle, AK. The boat leaves Dawson daily at 8:30am. Make reservations at **Yukon Queen River Cruises** (993-5599), on Front St. next to the dock (one-way US$74; round-trip US$129). Yukon River Cruises offers 1½-hr. cruises aboard the **Yukon Lon** departing daily at 1pm ($15, children $7.50). Insomniacs can catch the Midnight Sun cruise, departing daily at 11pm ($20, children $10).

Canoe and Bike Rental: At the hostel (see Accommodations, below). Both $15 per day. Non-hostelers must present passport as deposit.

Library (993-5571), at 5th and Princess. Open in summer Tues.-Fri. noon-9pm, Sat. 11am-5pm; in winter Tues.-Wed. and Fri. 9am-7pm, Thurs. 1-8pm, Sat. noon-5pm.

Laundromat and Showers: River West, at Front and York. Wash $2.50, dry $2.50. 5-min. shower $1. Open daily 8am-11pm.

Pharmacy: Arctic Drugs (993-5331), on Front St. next to the visitors centre. Open Mon.-Fri. 9am-8pm, Sat.-Sun. 9am-6pm.

Medical Emergency: 993-2222.

Police (993-5555; if no answer 1-667-5555), on Front St. north of Craig St., in the southern part of town.

Post Office (993-5342), 5th Ave. and Princess St. Open Mon.-Fri. 8:30am-5:30pm, Sat. 8:30am-12:30pm. **Postal Code:** Y0B 1G0.

Area Code: 403.

To reach Dawson City, take the Klondike Hwy. 533km north from Whitehorse, or follow the **Top-of-the-World Hwy.** about 100km east from the Alaska border. (For the Top-of-the-World Hwy., see page 176).

ACCOMMODATIONS AND CAMPING

The hostel and the campground on the west side of town are the cheapest options. The **ferry** is free and runs 24 hrs.

Dawson City River Hostel (no phone). Across the river from downtown; take the 1st left when you come off the ferry. This is the hostel to end all hostels: brand-new bunks in brand-new log cabins with wood-heated "prospector's bath," refreshingly icy showers, cozy lounge with wood stove, and a beautiful hilltop view of the Yukon River and the city beyond. Friendly staff. Rates $12.50-15, tent sites $6 per person.

The Bunkhouse (993-6164), Front St. and Princess. Brand-new and in a great location. Wood-planked rooms and tiny shared bathrooms (singles $45, doubles $50).

Dawson City Bed and Breakfast, 451 Craig St. (993-5649). Fantastic rooms and wonderfully accommodating management. Singles $59. Doubles $69. Shared bath. Make reservations at least a week in advance, 2 weeks for a weekend stay.

Yukon River Campground. Ride the ferry to the west side of Dawson City and take the 1st right. A haven for budget travelers who want to return to nature. Remember to boil drinking water for 3 min. Pit toilets. RVs welcome, but no hookups available. Sites $8.

Gold Rush Campground (993-5247), 5th and York St. Gold Rush has a monopoly on RV sites anywhere close to downtown, so it's wise to phone ahead. Campsites are crowded and too rocky for tents. Laundromat, convenience store, showers, and dump station. Solicitous management. Sites $10, electric hookups $15, full hookups $18.

FOOD

There's not a lot around, but prices are reasonable by Yukon standards, especially compared to Thanksgiving Day in 1898, when a single turkey fetched over $100. Snag a bag of groceries at the **Dawson City General Store** (993-5475) at Front and Queen St. (open Mon.-Sat. 8am-8pm, Sun. 10am-6pm).

Nancy's (993-6901) at Front St. The Nancy's Breakfast is a gastronomic tour de force. $5 gets hungry travelers thick, thick toast, bacon, two eggs, and hash browns. Although the onion emphasis may cramp gregarious travelers' style, the German-style hashbrowns are to die for. Open daily 7am-10pm.

Big Bite Submarines (963-5607) on 2nd Ave. Enormous subs on tasty home-made rolls. 6-in. subs $4, 12-inch subs $7.75. As the only late-night eats place in Dawson, Big Bite is the place to be when the bars close for the city's "I can't believe it's not Eddie Vedder" crowd. In summer open 8am-3am daily, in winter 11am-11pm, weekends until 3am.

River West Food and Health (993-6339) on Front St. next to the visitors centre. The all-natural place to go for all-natural travelers. Sandwiches ($5) and "natural" coffees ($1.25-3.50). Open in summer 8:30am-7pm; in winter until 5:30pm.

The Jack London Grill (993-5346) in the Downtown Hotel at 2nd and Queen St. Don't be scared off by the well-furnished dining room. Terrific dinners start at $13. Open daily 6:30-10pm.

Klondike Kate's (993-6527) at 3rd and King St. The veggie sandwich ($5) should keep scurvy at bay. Open mid-May to mid-Sept. daily 7am-11pm.

SIGHTS AND ENTERTAINMENT

Perhaps to compensate for the cost of everything else, Dawson City sponsors many free tours and attractions. Free 90-minute **walking tours** leave from the visitors centre four times per day and from St. Paul's Church once per day. The guides are well-informed, and these tours are one of the best ways to appreciate the city.

The **Robert Service Readings** are in front of the cabin on 8th Ave. at Hanson where the Yukon Bard penned immortal ballads, including "The Cremation of Sam McGee" and "The Shooting of Dan McGrew" (shows daily at 10am and 3pm).

Down the street, on 8th Ave. at Grant, is the relocated **Jack London Cabin.** The great Yukon author's life and times are recounted during interpretive readings daily at 1pm. Tours of Arizona Charlie's marvelously restored **Palace Grand Theatre** at 2nd and King are given daily at 10am and noon. The **Gaslight Follies** (993-5575) are on display at the Palace Grand; an original vaudeville revue is shown Wednesday through Monday at 8pm. This show is perhaps the finest period performance available in the Yukon ($11.50 and $13.50, children $5.75).

The **Dawson City Museum** (993-5291), on 5th St. south of Church, elaborates on regional history with exhibits ranging from the mastodons to modern mining machinery. The museum holds shows by local artists and has hourly events, including the ½-hr. documentary **City of Gold** (which sparked Canada's interest in renovating Dawson City), showing daily at 10:30am and 4pm (open daily 10am-6pm; $3.50, children and seniors $2.50).

Nightlife in Dawson is dominated by **Diamond Tooth Gertie's,** at 4th and Queen, one of Canada's few legal gambling halls. For a $4.75 cover you can try your hand at roulette, blackjack, and Texas hold 'em; or just take in one of the three nightly floor shows at 8:30pm, 10pm, and 12:30am…a good bet (open nightly 7pm-2am).

The goldfields of **Bonanza** and **Eldorado Creeks** held some of the richest lodes discovered. Nearly 10 mi. of maintained gravel road follows Bonanza Creek to the former site of **Grand Forks,** chewed up when the dredges came through). Along the way are **Gold Dredge #4** and **Discovery Claim,** the site of George Carmack's discovery of August 16, 1896, that inspired the whole mad rush in the first place.

If you're interested in learning about the modern gold-mining operations (last year's take was over 3 tons) or panning on your own, check in with **Gold City Tours** (993-5175) on Front St. The three-hour tour (daily 1pm, $29) provides enough history and information to cause a mental meltdown (open daily 9am-6pm). The Park Service also maintains **Bear Creek,** 13km south of town on the Klondike Hwy. Mining here suddenly halted in 1966, leaving behind tools, machinery, and the haunting feeling that all the people should be *somewhere* nearby.

For those hunting their own fortunes in gold, many businesses let you pan gold for around $5, but anyone can pan for free at the confluence of the Bonanza and Eldorado Creeks (you need your own pan though). Panning anywhere else along the creeks could lead to a *very* unpleasant encounter with the owner/miner of the claim you're jumping.

■■■ INUVIK

Inuvik, "place of man" in Inuvialuktun, is a flourishing cultural centre, where three Arctic peoples live together in remarkable harmony: the Inuvialuit of the Beaufort sea coast, the Gwich'in of the Mackenzie River Delta, and transplants from southern Canada. Inuvik's 3200 inhabitants have adapted to the Arctic's peculiar seasonal rhythms, hibernating during the nine-month-long winter and emerging in the summer to celebrate their enduring place in the North.

Practical Information Stop by the **Inuvik Visitor Information Centre** (979-4518), on Mackenzie Rd. at Distributor St., to pick up information on tours of the Mackenzie Delta and the Beaufort Sea's coast (open June-Sept. daily 9am-8pm).

Inuvik is in the Mackenzie River Delta, 741km northeast of Dawson City and 100km south of the Beaufort Sea, in the Northwest Territories. The **Arctic Tour Co.,** 175 Mackenzie Rd. (979-4100 or 800-661-0721), runs buses (June to early Sept.) to Arctic Red River (2 per week, $45), Fort McPherson (2 per week, $60), and Dawson City, YT (2 per week, $198). Local transportation is provided by **Inuvik/Delta Taxi** (979-2525; 24 hrs.). For **ferry and road information,** call 800-661-0752.

Inuvik Rexall Drugs (979-2266) is at Mackenzie Rd. (open Mon.-Sat. 9am-6pm, Sun. 2-5pm). The **hospital** (979-2955) is also on Mackenzie Rd. at the south end of town. In an **emergency**, call 979-4357 or the **police** (979-2935), on Distributor St. at Mackenzie Rd. The **post office** (979-2252) is on Distributor St. at Mackenzie Rd. (open Mon.-Sat. 9am-5:30pm; **Postal Code: X0E 0T0**). The **area code** is 403.

Camping, Accommodations, and Food Inuvik offers two categories of accommodations: $100-per-night hotel rooms for the bored well-to-do and camp-grounds for the rugged adventurer (that's you). The **Happy Valley Campground** (979-7230), on Happy Valley Rd. in the northwestern part of town, has a play-ground, firepits, flush toilets, showers, and a laundromat ($2). The 37 gravelly sites feature a view of the Mackenzie River ($10, $5 for day use). The **Chuk Territorial Campground**, 3.5km south of town on the Dempster Hwy., has firepits, flush toi-lets, and showers, and a 20m observation tower with a spectacular view of the Mackenzie Delta (38 sites, $10).

Many of Inuvik's restaurants offer northern delicacies such as caribou and Arctic char. None of these tastes anything like chicken. **To Go's**, 71 Mackenzie Rd. in the town centre (979-3030), has beef and caribou burgers ($4.50) and musk ox burgers ($5.50; we warned you), and "the best pizza this side of the 60th parallel" (small $10). (Open Mon.-Thurs. 7am-midnight, Fri-Sat. 7am-4am, Sun. 10am-11pm.)

Sights, Outdoors, and Entertainment The visitors centre will help you make arrangements to visit **Our Lady of Victory Church,** on Mackenzie Rd. The "igloo church," built in the late 1950s without blueprints and on a shoestring bud-get, but winterproof nonetheless, reflects the blend of European and Arctic cultures that is Inuvik. **Inhamo Hall,** on Mackenzie Rd. at the northern end of town, is the meeting place and cultural centre of the Gwich'in; some celebrations and special events are open to the public.

As the days grow longer and longer (and longer), winter ski trails become sum-mer **hiking** trails. Several trails 3-5km in length depart from Loucheaux Rd. behind Grollier Hall. Prime birdwatching rewards those who make the short walk to the **Lagoon,** off Navy Rd. at the west end of town. You can rent a **bicycle** ($3 per hr., $20 per day) from **Northern Recreation,** 60 Franklin Rd. (open Mon.-Thurs. and Sat. 10am-6pm, Fri. 10am-8pm). If you want to get a little farther out of town, the **Arctic Tour Company** (979-4100) sponsors scenic wildlife tours and boating and fly-in excursions to the delta communities of Aklavik and Tuktoyaktuk.

Inuvik makes the most of its short, sunny summer with a host of festivals and spe-cial events. Street dancing and nocturnal chicanery accompany the summer solstice during **Midnight Madness.** The **Northern Games** in late July include three days of non-stop activity, including a blanket toss and seal skinning (with free tasting for hungry onlookers). The 10-day **Great Northern Arts Festival,** Box 2291, Inuvik, NWT X0E 0T0 (979-3536), also in July, attracts the Arctic's finest artists and artisans for workshops; media range from soapstone to antler. The two-day **MusicFest** (979-3111) coincides with the Arts Festival and offers free performances by way-northern bands.

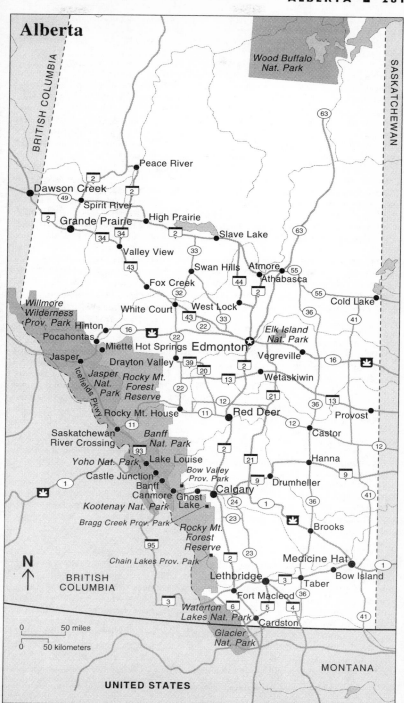

Alberta

WOOD BUFFALO Nat. Park

BRITISH COLUMBIA

SASKATCHEWAN

ALBERTA

Peace River

Dawson Creek

Spirit River

Grande Prairie

High Prairie

Slave Lake

Valley View

Swan Hills

Atmore

Athabasca

Fox Creek

White Court

West Lock

Cold Lake

Willmore Wilderness Prov. Park

Hinton

Pocahontas

Miette Hot Springs

Edmonton

Elk Island Nat. Park

Jasper

Drayton Valley

Vegreville

Jasper Nat. Park

Icefields Pkwy

Rocky Mt. Forest Reserve

Wetaskiwin

Rocky Mt. House

Red Deer

Provost

Saskatchewan River Crossing

Banff Nat. Park

Castor

Yoho Nat. Park

Lake Louise

Hanna

Castle Junction

Banff

Bow Valley Prov. Park

Drumheller

Canmore

Ghost Lake

Calgary

Kootenay Nat. Park

Bragg Creek Prov. Park

Brooks

Rocky Mt. Forest Reserve

Chain Lakes Prov. Park

Medicine Hat

Lethbridge

Taber

Bow Island

Fort Macleod

Waterton Lakes Nat. Park

Cardston

Glacier Nat. Park

N

BRITISH COLUMBIA

0   50 miles

0   50 kilometers

MONTANA

UNITED STATES

■ Alberta

The icy peaks and turquoise lakes of Banff and Jasper National Parks, in western Alberta, reign as Alberta's most breathtaking landscapes. Kananaskis country, between Banff and Calgary, is a hiker's paradise. To the east, less sublime vistas of farmland, prairie, and oil fields fill the yawning expanses. Alberta boasts thousands of prime fishing holes, world-renowned fossil fields, and centres of Native Canadian culture; many of the province's most fascinating attractions, such as Waterton Lakes National Park, Head-Smashed-In Buffalo Jump, and the Crowsnest Pass, are within easy traveling distance of the U.S. border.

Petrodollars have fostered the growth of gleaming, modern cities on the prairie. Partly due to Pierre Trudeau's National Energy Policy, an unpopular implicit tax on Alberta's oil prosperity in the 1970s, Alberta is widely recognized as the most conservative province in Canada. Calgary caught the world's eye when it hosted the XV Winter Olympics in 1988, and is annual host to the wild Stampede. The world's largest rodeo, the Stampede brings together the most skilled cowboys from all over the West. Edmonton is slightly larger than its intense civic and hockey rival. Edmonton has an undeserved reputation for dullness. Alberta's capital has been given little credit as a budget travel destination, but that situation is changing quickly. Of course, nobody knows which city will next reign as the "Hockey Capital of Alberta."

From Edmonton, coverage extends to Jasper and Banff, followed by Calgary and southern Alberta. Half the province lies north of Edmonton, and is sparsely inhabited. A drive to Grande Prairie toward the Alaska Highway might lure you north.

PRACTICAL INFORMATION

Capital: Edmonton.

Visitors Information: Alberta Tourism, 3rd floor, 10155 102 St., Edmonton T5J 4L6 (800-661-8888, 427-4321 in Alberta). Information on Alberta's provincial parks can be obtained from **Provincial Parks Information,** Standard Life Centre #1660, 10405 Jasper Ave., Edmonton T5J 3N4 (944-0313). For information on the province's national parks (Waterton Lakes, Jasper, Banff, and Wood Buffalo), contact the **Parks Canada,** Box 2989, Station M, Calgary T2P 3H8 (292-4401). The **Alberta Wilderness Association,** P.O. Box 6398, Station D, Calgary T2P 2E1, distributes information for off-highway adventurers.

Motto: *Fortis et Liber* (Strong and Free). **Provincial Bird:** Great Horned Owl, chosen by Albertan schoolchildren in a 1977 province-wide vote. **Provincial Flower:** Wild Rose. **Provincial Tree:** Lodgepole Pine.

Emergency: 911.

Time Zone: Mountain (2 hr. behind Eastern).

Postal Abbreviation: AB.

Drinking Age: 18.

Traffic Laws: Mandatory seatbelt law.

Area Code: 403.

GETTING AROUND

Hwy. 16 connects Jasper with Edmonton, while the **Trans-Canada Hwy.** (Hwy. 1) connects Banff with Calgary, 120km to the east. **Hwy. 3** runs from Medicine Hat to Vancouver, BC. The extensive highway system facilitates bus connections between major points of interest. Calgary is a convenient base. **Greyhound** runs from Calgary to Edmonton to Jasper, as well as from Calgary to Banff. **Brewster,** a subsidiary of Greyhound, runs an express bus between Banff and Jasper. Alberta's major **airports** are in Calgary and Edmonton. **Writing-On-Stone Provincial Park** and **Elk Island National Park,** two of the province's most intriguing destinations, lie off of the usual tourist trail. To reach out-of-the-way sights, consider renting a car.

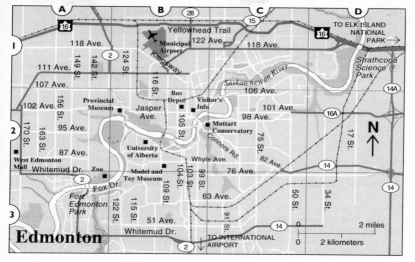

Edmonton

More adventurous travelers should have no problem discovering alternative methods of transportation in Alberta. **Hikers, mountaineers,** and **ice climbers** will find the best terrain in the Canadian Rockies of Banff and Jasper National Parks and Kananaskis Country. **Canoeing centres** adjoin the lakes of northern Alberta and the Milk River in the south. The wide shoulders of Alberta's highways make **bicycle** travel relatively easy; some highway segments, such as the stretch of the Trans-Canada that runs between Banff and Calgary, have special bike lanes marked on the right shoulder. Consider renting a mountain bike instead of a 10-speed; you and your bike will have an easier time on the rough rural roads, and you'll be able to enjoy the Rocky Mountain **backcountry.** The national parks have made an effort to improve Alberta's travel situation by erecting a string of **hostels** between Banff and Jasper and by establishing campsites that accommodate only hikers and bicyclists.

■■■ EDMONTON

Beyond Edmonton's superficial drabness, there is plenty to see and do. Edmonton boasts one of the few existing shops devoted exclusively to budget travel, and a funky conservatory which exhibits a large collection of tropical and desert plants north of 53°N latitude. Toss in a toy museum and a great alternative music festival, and it shouldn't take long for Edmonton to lose its dull image. Established as a trading post in 1806 in the magnificent valley of the North Saskatchewan River, Edmonton remained an insignificant dot on the vast plain until 1897, at the peak of the Klondike gold rush, when Edmonton opportunistically promoted itself as the starting point of an overland route to Yukon. While producing the desired economic explosion, the "Klondike Trail" had little basis in fact; many would-be prospectors perished trying to find it. As penance, the city wallowed in stagnation until 1942, when it flourished as a major supply centre while the Japanese threat to Alaska sparked construction of the Alaska Highway. With rows of refineries and towers of glass, concrete, and steel, Edmonton is now one of Big Oil's capital cities.

PRACTICAL INFORMATION AND ORIENTATION

Visitors Information: Edmonton Tourism, City Hall, 1 Sir Winston Churchill Square (426-4715), at 102A Ave., west of 99 St. Main floor. Information, maps, brochures, and directions. Helpful staff. Open Victoria Day-Labor Day Mon.-Fri. 9am-4pm, Sat.-Sun. 11am-5pm. Also at **Gateway Park** (800-463-4667 or 496-

8400), on Hwy. 2 south of the city. Open daily 8am-9pm; winter Mon.-Fri. 8:30am-4:30pm, Sat.-Sun. 9am-5pm. For information about the rest of the province, head to **Alberta Tourism,** Commerce Court, 10155 102 St. (427-4321; postal code T5J 4L6), on the 3rd floor. Open Mon.-Fri. 8:15am-4:30pm. Information by phone Mon.-Fri. 9am-4:30pm.

Budget Travel: The Travel Shop, 10926 88 Ave. (Travel 439-3096, Retail 439-3089). Regional office for **Alberta Hostels.** A travel agency with camping and hiking gear, serving youth and student travelers. Will make international and local hostel reservations. Open Mon.-Wed. and Fri.-Sat. 9am-6pm, Thurs. 9am-8pm.

American Express, 10305 Jasper Ave. (421-0608). Holds mail free of charge for cardholders. **Postal code:** T5J 1Y5. Open Mon.-Fri. 8:30am-5:30pm.

Greyhound, 10324 103 St. (421-4211). To: Calgary (nearly every hr. 8am-8pm, plus milk run for die-hards at midnight, $32), Jasper (4 per day, $43), Vancouver (3 per day direct via Jasper-Kamloops, 2 per day via Calgary, $111), Yellowknife (summer 1 per day Mon.-Fri.; winter Mon., Wed., and Fri.; $175). If you plan to travel extensively on bus, consider purchasing a 7-, 15-, 30-, or 60-day Canada Pass. Open daily 5:30am-1am. Locker storage $1.50 per 24 hrs.

VIA Rail, 10004 104 Ave. (422-6032 for recorded information, 800-501-8630 for reservations), in the CN Tower, easily identified by the huge red letters on the front of the building. To: Jasper ($82, students $73) and Vancouver ($194, students $175). No train service to Calgary. Open Mon., Thurs., and Sat. 7am-3:30pm, Tues. and Fri. 8:30am-9pm, Wed. 8:30am-4pm, Sun. 10:30am-9pm.

Edmonton Transit, 423-4636 for schedule information (Mon.-Fri. 6:30am-10:30pm, Sat 8am-5pm, Sun. 9am-5pm). Buses and light rail transit **(LRT)** run frequently all over this sprawling metropolis. LRT free in the downtown area Mon.-Fri. 9am-3pm and Sat. 9am-6pm (between Grandin Station at 110 St. and 98 Ave. and Churchill Station at 99 St. and 102 Ave.). Fare $1.60, over 65 and under 15 80¢. No bikes on LRT during peak hours (Mon.-Fri. 7:30-8:30am, 4-5pm). No bikes on buses. For information, stop by the **Downtown Information Centre,** 100 A St. and Jasper Ave. Open Mon.-Fri. 9:30am-5:30pm. Another information booth in the Churchill LRT station. Open Mon.-Fri. 8:30am-4:30pm.

Taxis: Yellow Cab, 462-3456. **Alberta Co-op Taxi,** 425-8310.

Car Rental: Rent-A-Wreck, 11225 107 Ave. (448-1234). Cars start at $27 per day, $25 in winter. 10¢ per km after 200km. Must be 21. Under 25 subject to $12 per day insurance surcharge and $500 deductible; over 25 $11 surcharge and $250 deductible. Insurance fees may be waived if driver is already covered. Open Mon.-Fri. 7:30am-6pm, Sat. 9am-5pm, Sun. 10am-4pm. AMA members receive a 10% discount. Hostel International (HI) members receive a $5 discount per rental; $25 on a rental of one week or more. Also rent at **Tilden,** 10135 100A St. (422-6097). Cars start at $33 per day, 12¢ per km after 100km. 3-day weekend specials start at $70 per day, 12¢ per km after 1000km. Must be 21 (open Mon.-Fri. 7am-6pm, Sat.-Sun. 8am-4pm).

Bike Rental: Edmonton Hostel (see Accommodations below) rents mountain bikes for $13 per day, $7.50 after 1pm.

Library: Edmonton Public Library, 7 Sir Winston Churchill Square (423-2331). Open Mon.-Fri. 9am-9pm, Sat. 9am-6pm, Sun. 1-5pm.

Gay/Lesbian Community Centre: 11745 Jasper Ave., #104 (basement), (488-3234). Community listings, on-site peer counseling. Open Mon.-Fri. 7-10pm, Wed. 1-5pm. **Womenspace,** 9930 106 St. #30 (425-0511). Edmonton lesbian group. Call for recording of local events.

Square Dancing: Edmonton and District Square Dance Association, 496-9136.

Weather Information: 468-4940.

Rape Crisis: Sexual Assault Centre (423-4121), 24 hrs. **Distress Line:** 482-HELP (4357).

Pharmacy: Mid-Niter Drugs, 11408 Jasper Ave. (482-1011). Open daily 8am-midnight.

Hospital: Royal Alexander Hospital, 10240 Kingsway Ave., 477-4111.

Emergency: 911.

Police: 423-4567.

Post Office: 9808 103A Ave. (495-4105), adjacent to the CN Tower. Open Mon.-Fri. 8am-5:45pm. **Postal Code:** T5J 2G8.
Area Code: 403.

Although Edmonton is the northernmost major city in North America, it's actually in the southern half of Alberta. Calgary is 294km south of Edmonton, an easy 3½-hr. drive on **Hwy. 2;** Jasper lies 362 km to the west, a 4-hr. drive on **Hwy. 16.** The **Greyhound** and **VIA Rail** stations are downtown. The **airport** sits 29km south of town, a prohibitively expensive cab fare away (flat rate $26 to city centre). The **Grey Goose Airporter Service** runs a shuttle to the downtown area for $11 ($18 round-trip). Those not willing to pay $11 are known to hop on an airport shuttle bus taking travelers to downtown hotels.

Edmonton's ridiculous **street system** dates from 1912, when Edmonton devoured its smaller neighbor Strathcona. A 1914 plebiscite was to have solved the problem of Edmonton and Strathcona's incompatible systems; the persistent incongruity calls into the question the merits of representative government. The basic concept is sound: streets run north-south, and avenues run east-west. Street numbers increase to the west, and avenue numbers increase to the north. The problem with the system is that "0 St." and "0 Ave." are not where they should be; "City Centre" sits at 105 St. and 101 (Jasper) Ave., while East Edmonton bears the ignominious distinction of having *negative* street addresses. Disoriented travelers can find solace, humor, and distraction in trying to imagine the street system the public rejected.

ACCOMMODATIONS

The liveliest place to stay in Edmonton is the hostel, though you'll have more privacy at St. Joseph's College or the University of Alberta.

Edmonton International Youth Hostel (HI-C), 10422 91 St. (429-0140), off Jasper Ave. Take bus #1 or #2. A long walk from the bus station. The area surrounding the hostel is seedy; you'll feel safer walking along busy, lighted Jasper Ave. Air-conditioned with common room, snack bar, showers, kitchen and laundry facilities. Family rooms available. Open daily 8am-midnight. $10, non-members $14.

St. Joseph's College (492-7681), 89 Ave. at 114 St., in the University of Alberta neighborhood. Take bus #43, or take the LRT and get off at University. The rooms here are smaller, quieter, less institutional, and cheaper than those at the university nearby. Shaded lawn out front. In summer, make reservations; rooms fill up fast. Singles $21.75, weekly $131. Full board plan available. Single with full board $34.75, or pay for meals separately: breakfast $3.25, lunch $4.50, dinner $6.50. Library facilities, TV lounge, pool table. Check-in desk open Mon.-Fri. 9am-5pm.

University of Alberta (492-4281), 87 Ave. between 116 and 117 St. on the ground floor of Lister Hall. Socialist-realist rooming units. Staff are friendly and helpful. Just try to (grrrf) move the (unnnngh!!) mattress. Singles $27. Doubles $36. Continental breakfast included. Weekly rates. Weight, steam and game rooms, dry-cleaning, and a convenience store on the premises. Suites available $30 per night; shared bathroom. Check-in after 3pm.

YWCA, 10305 100 Ave. (429-8707). Feels safe. Clean and quiet. Men not allowed on the residential floors. Women slumber in quiet rooms, many with balconies. Residence office on 3rd floor. Phone hook-up in room for 53¢ per day allows unlimited local calls. Dorm-style beds $13. Singles $30, with bath $37. Doubles $45. Very close to downtown. Quiet hours 11pm-7am.

YMCA, 10030 102A Ave. (421-9622), close to bus and rail stations. A lively, clean building with rooms available for both men and women. More secure rooms especially appropriate for women available on 4th floor. Free use of gym and pool facilities included with accommodation fee. Dorm bunk beds $15 per night, $13 with student ID. 3-night max. stay in dorm. Singles $30. Doubles $45. Student rates $85 per week, $235 per month.

FOOD

Little evidence can be found to support the theory that citizens of the self-labeled "City of Champions" kick off their day with a big bowl of Wheaties, but both **downtown** and **Old Strathcona,** a region along 82 (Whyte) Ave. between 102 and 105 St., snap, crackle and pop with eateries.

Lunch with politicians in the main cafeteria of the **Alberta Legislature Building** when the legislature is in session (cafeteria open 7am-3:30pm and 5-7pm). Or try the cheap cafeterias of the **YWCA** (men allowed; open Mon.-Fri. 7am-8:30pm, Sat. 9am-2pm, Sun. and holidays 10am-2pm) and the **YMCA** (open Mon.-Fri. 7am-6:30pm). **Lister Hall** at the University of Alberta also operates a cafeteria (Mon.-Fri.: breakfast 7-10am, lunch 11:30am-1:30pm, dinner 4:30-6:30pm).

The Silk Hat, 10251 Jasper Ave. (428-1551). Beside the Paramount theater. Diner motif with Rock-Ola's in every booth. One of the oldest restaurants in Edmonton. Tea leaves read daily from 1-7pm. Two eggs with two Northwest Territories-scale pancakes, $3.25. Hamburger Deluxe with choice of fries or potato salad $4.25. Open Mon.-Fri. 6:30am-10pm, Sat. 8am-9pm, Sun. and holidays 11am-7pm.

The Next Act, 8224 104 St. in Old Strathcona (433-9345). Good, solid, fun burger and beer establishment. Cheap daily lunch specials Mon.-Fri. 2-for-1 Burger or Burrito special ($5) Sat. Draft beer $1.25 a glass. Small stage features local bands every Wed.; used during the jazz festival in June. Open Sun.-Wed. 11:30am-midnight; Thu.-Sat. 11:30am-2am.

The Black Dog Freehouse, 10425 Whyte Ave., near 104 St. (439-1082) Good pub fare in a dark and smoky setting. Everything under $6. Open daily 11am-2am.

Veggies, 10331 82nd Ave. in Old Strathcona. Creative vegetarian cuisine. Hummus plate ($5.50). Open Mon.-Fri. 11am-10pm, Sat. 9am-10pm, Sun. 9am-9pm.

Real Pizza & Steaks, 9449 Jasper Ave. (428-1989), near hostel. Great breakfasts in a depressing atmosphere. Blueberry pancakes are superb (no wimpy soft berries! just good, firm ones). Good breakfast special: 2 eggs, toast, bacon, and hash browns $4.50. Open 10am-2am.

Polo's Cafe, 8405 112 St. (432-1371). Contemporary Asian cuisine in a predominantly pink setting. Large stir fry and noodle dishes $6-8, salads $3-6. The Malaysian Wave, a heaping helping of beef/chicken, vegetables, and spicy egg noodles, is a favorite of U. of Alberta students. Open Mon.-Fri. 11am-midnight.

Patisserie Kim's Cafe, 10217 97 St. (422-6754). No frills; just fast, cheap food. For $2.25 dine on 2 eggs, hash browns, toast, and coffee, or for $2.85, a hamburger and fries. Not the safest location, though the law courts are just across the street. Open Mon.-Fri. 6:30am-8pm, Sat.-Sun. 6:30am-7pm.

SIGHTS

The "oh-my-god-that's-*obscenely*-huge" **West Edmonton Mall** (444-5200 or 800-661-8890; open Mon.-Fri. 10am-9pm, Sat. 10am-6pm, Sun. noon-5pm) sprawls across the general area of 170 St. and 87 Ave. Within the Milky Way's second-largest assembly of retail stores, consumerism reigns unchecked. When It first landed, Its massive sprawl of boutiques and eateries seized 30% of Edmonton's retail business, choking the life out of the downtown shopping district. Encompassing a water park, an amusement park, and dozens of pathetically caged exotic animals, The World's Second-Biggest Mall appears even Bigger than It is thanks to the mirrors plastered on nearly every wall. Among Its many attractions, The Mall boasts twice as many submarines as the Canadian Navy, a full-scale replica of Columbus' *Santa Maria,* and **Lazermaze,** the world's first walk-through video game. You can get to The Mall via bus #10.

After sampling the achievements of late 20th-century malls, the Victorian era will seem a welcome relief as you head for **Fort Edmonton Park** (428-2992), off Whitemud Dr. near the Quesnell Bridge. Fort Edmonton was dismantled in 1907 to make room for the new legislature building. The Fort's timbers lay under the high-level bridge from 1914 to 1974, when it was reassembled at its present location. At the far end of the park sits the fort, a 19th-century "office building" for Alberta's first entrepreneurs: ruthless whiskey traders. Between the fort and the park entrance are three long streets (1885 St., 1905 St., and 1920 St.), each bedecked with period buildings, including apothecaries, blacksmith shops, and barns, keyed to the streets' respective years. Appropriately clothed park volunteers greet visitors with the inquisitiveness of a 19th-century schoolmarm or the geniality of a general-store owner. (Park open Victoria Day-late June, Mon.-Fri. 10am-4pm, Sat.-Sun. 10am-6pm; late June-Labor Day daily 10am-6pm; Labor Day-Thanksgiving Sun., Mon., and holidays 10am-6pm. $6.25, seniors and ages 13-17 $4.75. Discounts for HI members.) Bus #123 or #32 stops near the park.

After visiting the fort, stop in at the **John Janzen Nature Centre** next door to pet the salamanders (open late June-Labor Day Mon.-Fri. 9am-4pm, Sat.-Sun. 11am-6pm). Then, sprint across Hwy. 2 to the **Valley Zoo** (496-6911), at 134 St. and Buena Vista Rd.; yes, it *does* have more species than The Mall (zoo open daily early May-Sept. 10am-6pm. $4.75, seniors $3.50, youths $2.50; Oct.-March Sat.-Sun. noon-4pm. $3.25, seniors $2.40, children $1.65).

From the enclosed fauna of the Valley Zoo, turn to the enclosed flora of the **Muttart Conservatory,** 9626 96A St. (496-8755). Here plant species from around the world live in the climate-controlled comfort of four ultramodern glass-and-steel pyramids. Palm trees and banana plants tower over orchids and hibiscus in the humid Tropical Pavilion; cacti and desert shrubs flourish in the dry heat of the Arid Pavilion. (Cacti are awesome.) Take your wedding photos in the Show Pavilion, which presents brilliant floral displays that change seasonally. If you happen to be traveling with an ailing plant, Muttart will diagnose the problem for a "minimal" fee (open Sun.-Wed. 11am-9pm, Thurs.-Sat. 11am-6pm. Admission $4, seniors and youths $3, children $2.) Bus #51 whisks you to Muttart.

The **Alberta Legislature Building,** 97 Ave. and 109 St. (427-7362). Designed by American-educated architect A.M. Jeffers, Alberta's capitol building was roundly criticized when it was first completed in 1912 for too-closely resembling American state capitol buildings of the beaux-arts style. Free tours guide you to the cool "Magic Spot," where water sounds as if it's pouring down torrentially from above; it's only an echo from the fountain three floors below. (Tours every ½ hr. Victoria Day-Labor Day Mon.-Fri. 9am-8:30pm, Sat.-Sun. 9am-4:30pm; call in winter).

On sunny summer days, crowds throng to the magnificent fountains and greens that stretch before the steps of the capitol building. Check out the **AGT Vista 33** on the 33rd floor of the Alberta Telephone Tower, 10020 100 St. (493-3333). This lookout spot also includes a small **telephone museum.** A number of hands-on displays might make the elevator trip worth the nominal fee (open Mon.-Sat. 10am-8pm, Sun. noon-8pm. Admission $1, children 50¢, seniors and pre-schoolers free).

You can retrace the steps of Alberta's pioneers along **Heritage Trail.** The self-guided tour begins at 100 St. and 99 Ave. and winds past the Legislature Building, Edmonton's first schoolhouse, and other historic landmarks. Just follow the red brick road. Another self-guided tour, the **Walking Tour of Old Strathcona,** starts at 8331 104 St. (433-5866) in the Old Strathcona Foundation Building (open Mon.-Fri. 8:30am-4:30pm). The **Old Strathcona Model and Toy Museum,** McKenzie Historic House, 8603 104th St. (433-4512), is a pleasant way to spend a few minutes. Examine over 200 paper reconstructions of monumental buildings, including St. Basil's Cathedral and the Taj Mahal, and of great ships like the *Mayflower* and the *Titanic.* The paper caricatures of Canadian PMs are particularly well-done (open Wed.-Fri. noon-8pm, Sat. 10am-6pm, Sun. 1-5pm; free). Take bus #43.

More substantial artifacts may be found at the **Provincial Museum of Alberta,** 12845 102 Ave. (453-9100), which caches all kinds of Albertan relics. The museum's collection of Alberta's plants, animals, and minerals is impressive. A boon to local taxidermists, the habitat exhibit is a better way to get up-close and personal with Alberta's larger, more dangerous animals than surprising them in a forest or colliding with them on Hwy. 16. The museum's **Bug Room** is alive with a variety of insect species, some rodent-sized. Saturdays at 2pm the museum is alive with little kids, who have come to watch Godzilla-style bug flicks. Despite the impressive and enter-

ENTERTAINMENT

taining wildlife collection, the museum offers no cohesive picture of pioneer or Native life (open Victoria Day-Labor Day daily 9am-8pm; winter Tues.-Sun. 9am-5pm. Admission $3.25, children $1.25. Tues. free.) Take bus #1 or #2.

Farmers and artisans from the outlying area peddle their wares at the **Old Strathcona Farmer's Market,** located at the corner of 104 Ave. and 83rd St. (Tues. 1-6pm, Sat. 8am-3pm). The **Edmonton Art Gallery,** 2 Sir Winston Churchill Square (422-6223), is a small gallery showcasing Canadian and Albertan art. Admission is $3, students and seniors $1.50, Thursday evenings free (open Mon.-Wed. 10:30am-5pm, Thurs.-Fri. 10:30am-8pm, weekends and holidays 11am-5pm).

ENTERTAINMENT AND ACTIVITIES

Led by Wayne Gretzky, the NHL's **Edmonton Oilers** skated off with five Stanley Cups between 1984 and 1990. The Great One departed for the Los Angeles Kings, but the Oilers still play from October through April in the **Northlands Coliseum,** 7424 118 Ave. (471-2191). The Canadian Football League's **Edmonton Eskimos,** winners of the Grey Cup for five consecutive years in the late 70s and early 80s, play from July to November at **Commonwealth Stadium** (448-3757 for ticket information). Baseball fans can catch Triple-A professional baseball action at **John Ducey Park** (429-2934), home of the **Edmonton Trappers,** from April to August. Famous Trapper alumni include Chi-Chi Rodriguez of L.A. Dodgers and "WKRP in Cincinnati" fame.

Visitors hoping to catch a glimpse of Edmonton's dark underbelly should head to one of the bars in the downtown area. Homesick Brits hold support groups at **Sherlock Holmes,** 10012 101A Ave. (426-7784), an English-style pub known for its singalongs and a passel of staple British ales on tap. Country fans should mosey on over to **Cook County Saloon,** 8010 103 St. (432-2665), while Charlie Parker aficionados will dig **Yardbird Suite** at 10203 86 Ave. (432-0428). If you prefer a crowd with more grit, the **Blues on Whyte** at the Commercial Hotel, 10329 82 Ave. (439-3981) is a good blues club.

For a more cerebral evening, buy tickets to the **Princess Theatre,** 10337 82 (Whyte) Ave. (433-0979, 433-5785 for a recording). Watch for the Princess's **Grazing on Film** festival in June (tickets $7, seniors and children $2.25). Check the *Edmonton Bullet* (free) for theater, film, and music listings. The "Live-Line" (424-5483) updates the performance scene.

EVENTS

Edmonton proclaims itself "Canada's Festival City." Decide for yourself: experience the **International Street Performers Festival** (425-5162), which in mid-July attracts a plethora of international talent. Each summer, top alternative entertainment dominates the Old Strathcona district along 82nd (Whyte) Ave. The **Fringe Theatre Event** (448-9000; mid-Aug.) features 150 alternative theatre and music productions in area parks, theaters, and streets, including excellent Canadian talent (Crash Test Dummies, Sarah MacLachlan). The **Edmonton Folk Music Festival** (429-1899; early Aug.) brings country and bluegrass banjo-pickin' to the city. The **International Jazz City Festival** (432-7166; late June-early July) jams together 10 days of club dates and free performances by some of Canada's most noted jazz musicians. This musical extravaganza coincides with a visual arts celebration called **The Works** (426-2122).

■ NEAR EDMONTON

Wilderness beckons a mere 35km to the east at **Elk Island National Park.** In 1906, civic concern prompted creation of the park to protect endangered elk herds. Since then, all sorts of exotic mammals (plains bison, wood bison, moose, hikers) have moved in, along with 240 species of birds. Pick up your copy of *You Are in Bison Country* at the **Park Information Centre,** just off Hwy. 16. The shore of **Astotin Lake** is the centre of civilized activity in the park. The **Astotin Interpretive Centre** (992-6392) answers questions, screens films, and schedules activities (open Sat.-Sun.

3-6pm). The information office at the south gate (922-5833; open daily 10am-6pm) or the administration office of the park (992-6380) will also field questions. Admission to the park is $5 per vehicle. Backcountry **camping** is allowed in certain areas with a **free permit,** obtainable at the Information Centre. The park also features 12 well-marked **hiking trails,** most 3-17km in length, which double as cross-country and snowshoeing trails in the winter. If possible, visitors should try to catch a **small-town rodeo.** These are extremely entertaining; on any summer weekend there may be several near Edmonton, with admission ranging from $6-10, a negligible fee given the quality. Contemplate cowboys' enormous belt buckles; watch rodeo contestants grip bleating, bucking, powerful sheep; revel in the antics of rodeo clowns as they are nearly impaled by enraged bulls. Contact the tourist information office for a schedule of events; they publish a list of cities and towns that hold rodeos.

■■■ YELLOWHEAD HIGHWAY 16

Yellowhead Highway 16 stretches 3185km across western Canada from Manitoba to the Pacific Coast, but the most interesting and scenic 999km stretch connects Edmonton and Prince Rupert, BC. The highway is named after the Iroquois trapper and guide Pierre Bostonais, who led the European traders of the Hudson Bay Company across the Rockies and into the British Columbia interior in 1826. Lauded as the "less stress, more scenery" route, in Alberta and British Columbia Hwy. 16 is uncongested and user-friendly. (For Highway 16 in British Columbia, west of Jasper National Park, see the *Northern British Columbia and the Yukon* section preceding). Drivers should pick up a free copy of *Yellowhead It,* a map showing distances between major points that also offers a complete listing of all the radio stations along the way. The travel guidebook *The Legend of the Yellowhead,* also free, is more substantial, giving a province-by-province, city-by-city account of Hwy. 16's major, and not so major, tourist attractions. For **road conditions** along Hwy. 16 phone 1-800-222-6501. The **Yellow Emergency Shelter** offers confidential counseling and free accommodations and meals to women and children travelers in distress (800-661-0737, 24 hrs.).

In Alberta, the Yellowhead's two lanes, smooth surface, and 110kph (69 mph) speed limit make for fast, easy driving. An hour west of Edmonton, amid the gentle undulations of the surrounding farmlands, is the town of **Fallis.** A massive radio tower here testifies to the appropriateness of the town's appellation. (*Let's Go* cannot comment on the name Uren, Saskatchewan.) 189 km west of Edmonton, Hwy. 16 splits to acknowledge **Edson,** a sleepy town of 7500. A saw mill and two coal mines sustain Edson; except for some good fishing in the surrounding lakes and rivers, the town has little to offer. Hungry visitors should grab a bite to eat at the **Charbroiled Burger Shack** on 4th Ave. (Hwy. 16 West) on the way to Jasper.

Farther west, the many "Cold Beer" signs of downtown **Hinton** may distract travelers lacking the stamina necessary to complete the remaining 50km to Jasper. Like Edson, Hinton's 10,000 citizens depend mainly on a paper mill and a coal mine for their livelihood. For fishermen, plenty of pike, rainbow and cutthroat trout, Dolly Varden, and yellow perch lurk in nearby lakes and rivers. Consult the *Alberta Guide to Sportfishing* for a detailed listing of lake stocks, licensing fees, and regulations. The guide and other tourist information is available at the **Tourist Information Centre,** at 308 Gregg Ave., downtown (865-2777, open Mon.-Sat. 10am-5:30pm).

Just west of Hinton, Hwy. 16 begins its long downward progression toward the floor of the **Athabaskan River Valley** and into **Jasper National Park.** Jasper's scenic splendor can loosen the jaw muscles of even the most seasoned mountaineer. Mesmerized drivers are cautioned to pay close attention to **wildlife warnings** in the park. Free to roam throughout the park's 10,878 sq. km, Jasper's animal inhabitants invariably choose to graze in roadside ditches. In 1993, 138 large animals were killed in collisions with vehicles; it doesn't require much imagination to complete the other side of that equation. *Reduce driving speed in the park, especially at night.*

■■■ JASPER NATIONAL PARK

Before the Icefields Parkway was built, few travelers dared venture north from Banff into the untamed wilderness of Jasper. But those bushwhackers who returned came back with stunning reports, and the completion of the Parkway in 1940 paved the way for everyone to appreciate Jasper's astounding beauty. In contrast to its glitzy southern peer, Jasper townsite manages to maintain the look and feel of a real small town. The houses of Jasper's permanent residents rise away from Connaught Drive and blend peacefully with the surrounding landscape. The only conspicuous traces of Jasper's tourist trade are the blue-and-white signs advertising "approved accommodations" and the imitation totem pole at the VIA Rail station, which keeps its back turned to the town in a gesture of good taste.

PRACTICAL INFORMATION AND ORIENTATION

Visitors Information: Park Information Centre, 500 Connaught Dr. (852-6176). Trail **maps** and information on all aspects of the park. Open daily 8am-8pm; early Sept. to late Oct. and late Dec. to mid-May 9am-5pm; mid-May-mid-June 8am-5pm. **Alberta Tourism,** 632 Connaught Dr. (800-222-6501 in AB, 800-661-8888 elsewhere). Open Victoria Day-Labour Day daily 9am-8pm. **Jasper Chamber of Commerce,** 632 Connaught Dr. (852-3858). Open Mon.-Fri. 9am-5pm. For further information, write to **Park Headquarters,** Superintendent, Jasper National Park, 632 Patricia St., Box 10, Jasper T0E 1E0 (852-6161).

VIA Rail, 314 Connaught Dr. (800-852-3168). To: Vancouver (Mon., Thurs., Sat.; $130), Edmonton (Tues., Fri., Sun.; $76), and Winnipeg (Tues., Fri., Sun.; $207). 10% discount for seniors and students; children 50%. Coin-operated lockers $1 for 24 hrs.

Greyhound, 314 Connaught Dr. (852-3926), in the VIA station. To: Edmonton (4 per day; $43), Kamloops ($45), and Vancouver ($84).

Brewster Transportation Tours, 314 Connaught Dr. (852-3332), in the VIA station. To Banff (daily; 4¼hr.; $37) and Calgary (daily; 8hrs.; $49.50).

Taxi: Heritage Taxi, 611 Patricia (852-5558), offers a flat rate of $8 between town and Whistler's hostel, and a 30% discount from regular fares to HI members.

Car Rental: Tilden Car Rental, in the bus depot (852-4972). $46 per day with 100 free km. Must be 21 with credit card. $300 insurance deductible for drivers under 25.

Bike Rental: Freewheel Cycle, 611 Patricia Ave. (852-5380). Mountain bikes $5 per hr., $12 per 5 hr., $18 per day. Open in summer daily 9am-8pm; in spring and fall Tues.-Sun. 10am-6pm. **Whistlers Mountain Hostel** rents mountain bikes for $13 (non-members $17) per day (see Accommodations, below, for address).

Laundry and Showers: Jasper Laundromat and Showers, on Patricia St. near the Post Office. Wash $1.75, 5-min. dry 25¢. 5-min. showers $2. Open daily 8am-11pm.

Pharmacy: Whistler Drugs, 100 Miette Ave. (852-4411). Open daily 9am-10:30pm; early Sept. to mid-June 9am-9pm.

Hospital: 518 Robson St. (852-3344).

RCMP Emergency: 852-4848. **Ambulance and Fire:** 852-3100.

Police: 600 Pyramid Lake Rd. (852-4848).

Post Office: 502 Patricia St. (852-3041), across from the townsite green. Open Mon.-Fri. 9am-5pm. **Postal Code:** T0E 1E0.

Area Code: 403.

All of the above addresses are found in **Jasper townsite,** which is near the centre of the park, 362km west of Edmonton and 287km northwest of Banff. **Hwy. 16** transports travelers through the northern reaches of the park, while the **Icefields Parkway** (Hwy. 93) connects to Banff National Park in the south. Buses run to the townsite daily from Edmonton, Calgary, Vancouver, and Banff. Trains arrive from Edmonton and Vancouver. Renting a bike is the most practical option for short jaunts within the park; bikes can also be rented for one-way trips between Jasper and Banff. Hitching is popular along the Icefields Parkway, particularly among locals. (*Let's Go* does not recommend hitchhiking.)

ACCOMMODATIONS

Hotels in Jasper townsite are expensive. You may, however, be able to stay cheaply at a **bed and breakfast** (singles $20-35, doubles $25-45). Most are located right in town near the bus and train stations. Ask for the *Private Homes Accommodations List* at the Park Information Centre or the bus depot. Since few visitors know of the list, space in B&Bs may be available on short notice. If you have a car and would like to get away from the townsite, head for one of Jasper's hostels (listed below from north to south). Reservations, and information on closing days and on the winter "key system," are channeled through the Edmonton-based **Northern Alberta Hostel Association** (439-3139; fax 403-433-7781).

Maligne Canyon Hostel (HI-C), (852-3584), 11km east of the townsite on Maligne Canyon Rd. Small, recently renovated cabins on the bank of the Maligne River. An ideal place for viewing wildlife; the knowledgeable manager is happy to lead guided hikes through nearby Maligne Canyon. Accommodates 24. $9, non-members $12. Winter closed Wed.

Whistlers Mountain Hostel (HI-C), (852-3215), on Sky Tram Rd. , 7km south of the townsite. Closest to the townsite, this is the park's most modern (and crowded) hostel. Usually full in summer. Bring your own food, leave your shoes at the front door, and struggle to hold your own against the staff in an all-out game of volleyball. Accommodates 69. Curfew midnight. $13, non-members $18.

Mt. Edith Cavell Hostel (HI-C), on Edith Cavell Rd., off Hwy. 93A. The road is closed in winter, but the hostel welcomes anyone willing to ski 11km from Hwy. 93A; see reservations number above. Accommodates 32. $8, non-members $12. Open mid-June to early Oct., key system in winter.

Athabasca Falls Hostel (HI-C), on Hwy. 93 (852-5959), 30km south of Jasper townsite, 500m from Athabasca Falls. Huge dining/recreation room with wood-burning stove. Accommodates 40. $9, non-members $14. Closed Tues. in winter.

Beauty Creek Hostel (HI-C), on Hwy. 93, 78km south of Jasper townsite. Next to the stunning Sunwapta River. Accommodates 24. Accessible through a "key system" in winter (groups only). $8, non-members $12. Open May-mid-Sept. Thurs.-Tues.

CAMPING

The campsites below are listed from north to south. For campground updates, tune in 1450AM on your radio when nearing the townsite. For detailed information, call the Park Information Centre (852-6176).

Snaring River, 16km east of the townsite on Hwy. 16. Kitchen shelters, dry toilets. 56 sites, $8.50. Open mid-May to early Sept. Overflow site opened when the park sites are full. Pit toilets, no running water, great view. $6.

Pocahontas, on Hwy. 16, at the northern edge of the park, 46km east of the town-site. Closest campground to the Miette Hot Springs. Flush toilets, hot and cold running water. Wheelchair access. 140 sites, $11. Open mid-May to early Sept.

Whistlers, on Whistlers Rd., 3km south of the townsite. If you're intimidated by wilderness, the occupants of the 781 neighboring sites will keep you company. Hot and cold running water, showers. Wheelchair access. Tent sites $12, full hookups $18. Open early May to mid-Oct.

Wapiti, on Hwy. 93, 2km south of Whistlers. RV central. 366 Winnebago-packed sites. Hot and cold running water, showers. Sites $13, with electricity $15. Open mid-June to early Sept.

Wabasso, on Hwy. 93A, about 17km south of Jasper townsite. Flush toilets, hot and cold running water, showers, trailer sewage disposal. Wheelchair access. 238 sites, $11. Open late June to early Sept.

Mount Kerkeslin, on Hwy. 93, about 35km south of Jasper townsite. Kitchen shelters, dry toilets. 42 sites, $8.50. Open mid-June to early Sept.

JASPER NATIONAL PARK

Honeymoon Lake, on Hwy. 93, about 50km south of the townsite. Kitchen shelters, dry toilets, swimming. 35 sites, $8.50. Open mid-May-Oct.

Jonas Creek, on Hwy. 93, about 70km south of the townsite. Kitchen shelters, dry toilets. 25 sites, $8.50. Open mid-May-Oct.

Columbia Icefield, on Hwy. 93, 103km south of the townsite, at the southern border of the park. Close enough to the Athabasca Glacier to receive an icy breeze on the warmest summer night, but crowded nonetheless. Kitchen shelters, dry toilets. 33 sites, $8.50. Open mid-May-Oct.

Wilcox Creek, on Hwy. 93, at the southern park boundary. Kitchen shelters, dry toilets, trailer sewage disposal. 46 sites, $8.50. Open mid-June-mid-Sept.

FOOD

It's a good idea to stock up on food at a local market or bulk foods store before heading for the backcountry. For grocery supplies at any time of night or day, stop at **Wink's Food Store,** 617 Patricia St. (852-4223), or **Super A Foods,** 601 Patricia St. For bulk grains, nuts, and dried fruits, try **Nutter's,** 622 Patricia St. (852-5844). They also sell deli meats, canned goods, and freshly ground coffee. (Open Mon.-Sat. 9am-10pm, Sun. 10am-8pm.)

Mountain Foods and Cafe, 606 Connaught Dr. (852-4050). Stake out a table at this popular streetside cafe. The menu has both hot and cold sandwiches ($3), soups, and desserts. Pita melt with avocado, turkey, and tomato ($7). Hearty bowl of French Onion soup ($2.75). Frozen yogurt ($1.60). Prepare for the New Age by stocking up on bulk grains and holistic books. Open daily 8am-10pm.

Smitty's, 109 Miette Ave. (852-3111). Diner-type restaurant with huge menu and all-day breakfast. Veggie omelete ($6), burgers ($4-7). Open summer 6:30am-10:30pm; winter 6:30am-6:45pm.

Scoops and Loops, 504 Patricia St. (852-4333). Average food at great prices. Croissant sandwiches ($2.75-3.50) and bran muffins ($1.34) are fine for lunch, but definitely save room for dessert. Monstrous selection of hard and soft ice cream, pies, and pastries. Open daily 10am-10pm.

Mondi's, 632 Connaught Dr. Pasta dishes and entrees $10-13; 5pm-6pm all entrees are 2-for-1.

OUTDOORS

An extensive network of trails connects most parts of Jasper; many paths start at the townsite itself. Information Centres (see Practical Information for locations) distribute free copies of *Day Hikes in Jasper National Park* and a summary of longer hikes. The trails listed cover the park's three different ecological zones. The **montane zone** blankets the valley bottoms with lodgepole pine, Douglas fir, white spruce, and aspen. Subalpine fir and Engelmann spruce inhabit the middle part of the canopy, called the **subalpine zone,** which comprises 40% of the park. Fragile plants and wildflowers struggle for existence in the uppermost **alpine zone,** which covers another 40% of Jasper. Hikers should not stray from trails in the alpine area, so as to avoid trampling endangered plant species. Kick off any foray into the wilderness with a visit to the Information Centre in the townsite. Experts will direct you to appropriate hiking and mountain-biking trails. The Icefield Centre, on Hwy. 93 at the southern entrance to the park (see Icefields Parkway), provides similar services.

Mt. Edith Cavell, named after an English nurse who was executed during WWI by the Germans for providing aid to the Allies, will shake you to the bone with the thunderous roar of avalanches off the Angel Glacier. Take the 1.6km loop trail **Path of the Glacier** to the top or the 8km hike through **Cavell Meadows.** Edith rears her enormous head 30km south of the townsite on Mt. Edith Cavell Rd.

Not to be outdone by Banff, Jasper has a gondola of its own. The **Jasper Tramway** (852-3093), the longest and highest tramway in Canada, offers a panoramic view of the park as it rises 2.5km up the side of **Whistlers Mountain.** The gondola draws crowds and packs the parking lot. ($10, ages 5-14 $5, under 5 free. Open mid-April to early Sept. 8am-9:30pm; Sept.-mid-Oct. 9am-4:30pm.) A steep 10km trail starting from the Whistlers Mountain Hostel also leads up the slope; take the tram ride down ($5) to spare your quadriceps. No matter which way you go, be sure to bring along a warm jacket and sunglasses to protect against rapidly changing weather conditions at the summit.

Maligne Lake, the largest glacier-fed lake in the Canadian Rockies, is located 50km southeast of the townsite at the end of Maligne Lake Rd. In Maligne's vivid turquoise waters you can enjoy every conceivable water sport. Reservations for boat cruises and whitewater rafting trips can be made through the **Maligne Tours** office, 626 Connaught Dr. (852-3370). Farther north in the valley and 30km east of the townsite, the Maligne River flows into **Medicine Lake,** but no river flows out. The trick? The water escapes underground through tunnels in the easily dissolved limestone, re-emerging 16km downstream in the **Maligne Canyon,** 11km east of the townsite on Maligne Canyon Rd. (This is the longest known underground river in North America. Pretty sneaky, eh?)

Whitewater Rafting (Jasper) Ltd. (852-7238) offers several rafting trips from $35; a two-hour trip down the Maligne River costs $45. Register by phone or stop at the Esso station in the townsite. **Rocky Mountain River Guides** (852-3777), in On-Line Sport and Tackle, offers a three-hour trip ($50) and a calmer Athabasca trip ($35). **Sekani Mountain Tours** (852-5337) offers various trips with discounts to HI members. **Boat rental** is available at **Pyramid Lake** (852-3536; canoes $10 for 1 hr., $8 each additional hr., $25 per day; motorboats $15 for 1 hr., $12 each additional hr., $45 per day; $20 or a valid ID required for deposit) and **Maligne Lake** (852-3370; canoes $10 for 1 hr., $7 each additional hr., $30 per day; ID required for deposit). For a less strenuous tour of Maligne Lake, **Maligne Lake Scenic Cruises** offers narrated cruises in cozy, heated tour boats. Reservations are recommended ($29, seniors $26, children $14.50).

In May, trout and anglers abound in Jasper's spectacular lakes. The key to finding a secluded **fishing** spot at Jasper is to go someplace inaccessible by car. One such remote area is **Beaver Lake,** located about 1km from the main road at the tip of Medicine Lake. The lake is beautiful but never crowded, and even novice fisherfolk can hook themselves a dinner. Rent equipment at **Currie's,** in **The Sports Shop** at 416 Connaught Dr. (852-5650; rod, reel, and line $10; one-day boat rental $25, $18 if rented after 2pm).

Let your steed do the sweating on a **guided horseback trail ride.** Three-hour rides at Maligne Lake cost $45, $30 at the Jasper Park Lodge (852-5794). Guided rides at Pyramid Lake are $17 per hour (852-3562).

The saddle-sore can revive at **Miette Hot Springs** (866-3939), north of the townsite off Hwy. 16 along the clearly marked, 15km Miette Hotsprings Rd. The Hot Springs building contains lockers and two pools (one is wheelchair accessible; neither is especially mesmerizing). Free from nutrient-filled additives and the rotten-egg reek of sulfur, the pools are heated by external pipes through which the spring water is pumped from the smelly source. Unfortunately, the 40°C (104°F) water is off-limits in winter. (Open May 25-June 24 Mon.-Fri. 12:20-8pm, Sat.-Sun. 10:30am-9pm; June 25-Sept. 5 daily 8:30am-10:30pm. $2.50, children $1.50. Day passes $6.25, for children $5.50. Suit rental $1.25, towels $1, lockers 25¢.) Rotten-egg-lovers can wallow in the sulfur spring itself; a short trail leads south from a picnic area near the modern pool complex to one of the steamy outlets. Don't drink the water; it's 55°C (131°F) and full of microorganisms.

Intrepid hikers should attempt the three-faced **Mystery Lake Trail,** leading east, uphill from the pools. The trail changes from a paved path into a dirt road, and then into a serious trek in the course of the 11km journey to Mystery Lake. Be warned that you will need to ford a major river that becomes impassable after periods of heavy rainfall; contact the trail office at the Information Centre for a report on trail conditions.

Winter may keep you away from the hot springs, but you can always warm up on the ski slopes of **Marmot Basin,** near Jasper townsite (852-3816). A full-day lift ticket costs $34, ½-day $29. Ski rental is available at **Totem's Ski Shop,** 408 Connaught Dr.

(852-3078). A full rental package (skis, boots, and poles) runs $9.50 per day. (Open daily 9:30am-10pm; Labor Day-Victoria Day Sun.-Fri. 8am-6pm, Sat. 8am-9pm.) Maligne Lake offers cross-country ski trails from November through May.

The extra-adventurous who do not consider hiking, fishing, boating, skiing, and sightseeing stimulating enough will find Jasper a challenging site for feats of daredeviltry. **Jasper Climbing School,** 806 Connaught Dr. (852-3964), offers an introductory three-hour rappelling class ($25) for those who want a closer look at the imposing cliffs which surround Jasper. **Caving** is a little-talked-about and extremely dangerous pursuit, and is not permitted in the national parks without a permit; one should try it only with an experienced guide. Ben Gadd (852-4012), author of *Handbook of the Canadian Rockies,* leads tours to the **Cadomin Caves** and charges a flat rate of $250 for up to 15 people. Because these caves are outside the National Park, a permit is not required.

■ ICEFIELDS PARKWAY

The Icefields Parkway (Hwy. 93), dubbed the "window on the wilderness," is a glacier-lined, 230km road connecting Jasper townsite with Lake Louise in the south. The Parkway snakes past dozens of ominous peaks and glacial lakes; pull over at the head of one of 17 **trails** into the wilderness, or stop at one of 22 **scenic points** to take in a spectacular view. The 10-minute trail to **Bow Summit** affords a magnificent view of **Peyto Lake**, with its unreal fluorescent blue-green coloring, especially vivid at the end of June. Marvel at the **Weeping Wall,** where water seems to seep from the rock, or at **Bridal Veil Falls'** beautiful series of small cascades. Whether driving or biking, set aside at least three days for the Parkway; its challenging hikes and endless vistas are never monotonous. Thanks to the extensive campground and hostel networks which line the Parkway, extended trips down the entire length of Jasper and Banff National Parks are convenient and affordable. (See Accommodations and Camping under each park.) All points on the parkway are within 30km of a location where you can roll out your sleeping bag.

Before setting your wheels on the road, pick up a free map of the *Icefields Parkway,* available at park Information Centres in Jasper and Banff. The pamphlet is also available at the **Icefield Centre** (852-7030), at the boundary between Banff and Jasper, 103 km south of Jasper townsite. The Centre is within view of the **Athabasca Glacier,** the most prominent of the eight major glaciers which flow from the 325-sq.-km **Columbia Icefield,** one of the largest accumulations of ice and snow south of the Arctic Circle. Its meltwater runs into streams and rivers that terminate in three different oceans: north to the Arctic, east to the Atlantic, and west to the Pacific. Summer crowds have snowball fights on the vast icefields to the side of the road. **Brewster Transportation and Tours** (762-2241) carries visitors right onto the Athabasca Glacier in monster buses called "Snocoaches." This 75-min. trip is $18.50 (ages 6-15 $9). Explore the icy expanse on your own from the parking lot. (Tours given early May to mid-Oct. daily 9am-5pm; late Oct. 10am-4pm.)

If you have a bone-chilling curiosity to know about the geological history of the glaciers, sign up for a guided **interpretive hike** on the Athabasca (offered mid-June to mid-Sept.). A three-hour hike called "Ice Cubed" costs $21 (ages 7-17 $10), and the five-hour "Icewalk Deluxe" is $25 (ages 7-17 $12). Write **Athabasca Glacier Icewalks,** Attn.: Peter Lemieux, Box 216, Revelstoke, BC V0E 2S0.

A warmer alternative to journeying out onto the glacier is the 13-minute explanatory film inside the cozy Icefield Centre. (Open mid-June to Aug. daily 9am-7pm; mid-May to mid-June and Sept. 9am-4pm.) Although the Centre is closed in winter, the Parkway is closed only after heavy snowfalls, and then only until the plows clear the way.

If you only have time for a quickie, try the **Parker Ridge Trail.** The 2.4-km hike (one-way) guides you away from the Parkway, past the treeline, and over Parker Ridge. At the end of the trail awaits an amazing view of the **Saskatchewan Glacier.**

The trailhead is located 1km south of the **Hilda Creek Hostel,** which is itself located 8.5km south of the Icefields (see Banff: Accommodations).

■ LAKE LOUISE

Spectacular turquoise Lake Louise often serves North American filmmakers' need for "Swiss" scenery. Unfortunately, most visitors spend only enough time at the lake to snap photos. Few stay as long as explorer Tom Wilson did in the 1880s, when he wrote of its majesty, "I never in all my explorations...saw such a matchless scene."

To gain a deeper appreciation of the soothing blue lake and its surrounding glaciers, consult the **Lake Louise Information Centre** at Samson Mall (522-3833; open daily May 19-June 23 8am-6pm; June 24-Sept. 4 8am-8pm; Sept. 5-Oct. 9 10am-6pm; winter 9am-5pm). The brand-new $4.4 million complex is also a museum, with exhibits and a short film on the formation of the Rockies. Renting a canoe from the **Chateau Lake Louise Boat House** (522-3511) will give you the closest look at the lake ($20 per hr.; open 10am-8pm). Several hiking trails begin at the water; aim for the ends of the 3.4km **Lake Agnes Trail** and the 5.3km **Plain of Six Glaciers Trail.** The spectacular views, and the opportunity to leave the shutterbugs at the end of the lake, should be incentive enough to rent a boat and pull an oar for a while.

Many find **Lake Moraine** to be even more stunning than its sister Lake Louise, which lies nearby. The lake, also explorable by canoe or boat, lies in the awesome **Valley of the Ten Peaks,** including glacier-encrusted **Mount Temple.** Join the multitudes on the 1km **Rockpile Trail** for an eye-popping view of the lake and valley, or stroll along the lake-hugging **Lakeshore Trail.** If you're looking for a longer route, try the trail to **Larch Valley.** Continue along the same trail to **Sentinel Pass** for some of the best views in the area. You can cross the pass and make a long loop, connecting with the **Paradise Valley Trail;** get further information at the Lake Louise Visitor Centre. If you don't get a chance to visit Lake Moraine, just get your hands on a $20 bill; the Valley of Ten Peaks is pictured on the reverse.

Timberline Tours (522-3743), located off Lake Louise Dr. near Deer Lodge, offers guided horseback rides through the area. The 1½-hour tour costs $26; the daytrip, $70 (lunch included). The **Lake Louise Sightseeing Lift** (522-3555), which runs up Mt. Whitehorn across the Trans-Canada Hwy. from Lake Louise, provides another chance to gape at the landscape. (Open early June to late Sept. daily 8am-9pm. Fare $9, seniors and students $7, ages 6-16 $5). Like its counterpart at Sulphur Mountain, Lake Louise's lift offers a $9 breakfast deal, which includes a lift ticket. Coupons worth $1.50 off appear in the lift's brochure, available locally and at the park Information Centres.

■ ■ ■ BANFF NATIONAL PARK

Banff is Canada's best-loved and best-known natural preserve. It offers 2543 sq. mi. (6600 sq. km) of peaks and canyons, white foaming rapids and brilliant turquoise lakes, dense forests and open meadows. Yet it was not simple love of natural beauty that motivated Prime Minister Sir John MacDonald to establish Canada's first national park in 1885. Rather, officers of the Canadian Pacific Railroad convinced him of Banff's potential for "large pecuniary advantage," and were quick to add, "since we can't export the scenery, we shall have to import the tourists."

The millions who come to Banff every year can afford to dismiss such callous assessments, though. The Park's priceless greenery clearly does grow on trees, offering an abundance of unspoiled backcountry opportunities to novices and experts alike. And while every year the government gets its share of the millions of dollars poured into the overpriced, colorless shops of Banff townsite, it is still up to those who visit Banff to decide how much they want to buy and pay, how much comfort they require, and how much wilderness they wish to experience.

PRACTICAL INFORMATION AND ORIENTATION

Visitors Information: Banff Information Centre, 224 Banff Ave. (762-1550). Includes **Chamber of Commerce** (762-8421) and **Canadian Parks Service** (762-4256). Open daily 8am-8pm; Oct.-May 9am-5pm. **Lake Louise Information Centre** (522-3833). Open mid-May-mid-June daily 10am-6pm; mid-June-Aug. 8am-8pm; Sept.-Oct. 10am-6pm; winter 9am-5pm. Both Centres dispense detailed maps and brochures, and provide information about ski areas, restaurants, activities, accommodations, and cultural attractions.

Park Administration, Superintendent, Banff National Park, Box 900, Banff T0L 0C0 (762-1500). Open Mon.-Fri. 8am-4:30.

American Express: Brewster Travel, 130 Banff Ave., Box 1140 (762-3207). Holds mail free of charge for cardmembers. Open Mon.-Fri. 8am-6pm, Sat. 8am-5:30pm. **Postal code:** T0L 0C0.

Greyhound, 100 Gopher St. (762-6767). From the Brewster terminal. To: Lake Louise (5 per day, $7), Calgary (6 per day; $15), Vancouver (5 per day; $96).

Brewster Transportation, 100 Gopher St. (762-6767), near the train depot. Monopoly on tours of the area; runs 1 express daily to Jasper ($37). Does not honor Greyhound Ameripasses. Depot open daily 7:30am-10pm.

Banff Explorer, operated by the town, runs 2 routes stretching from the Banff Springs Hotel to the Hostel and Tunnel Mountain Campground. Fare $1.25. Exact change required. Operates mid-June-mid-Sept. daily 9am-9pm.

Taxis: Legion Taxi, 762-3353. 24 hrs. **Lake Louise Taxi,** 522-2020.

Car Rental: Banff Used Car Rentals, in the Shell Station at the junction of Wolf and Lynx (762-3352). $44 per day, 100km free, 10¢ per additional km. Must be 21with major credit card. **Avis,** Cascade Place on Wolf St. (762-3222). $45 per day with 100km free, 20¢ per additional km. HI-C members get 50km free bonus. Must be 21 with credit card. **Tilden Rent-a-Car,** at the corner of Caribou and Lynx (762-2688). $23 per day, plus 16¢ per km. Must be 21 with a credit card.

Bike Rental: Bactrax Rentals, 337 Banff Ave. (762-8177), in the Ptarmigan Inn . Mountain bikes $4-6 per hr., $15-20 per day. HI-C member discount: $1 off per hr., $4 off per day. Open daily 8am-8pm.

Equipment Rental: Performance Ski and Sport, 208 Bear St. (762-8222). Rents everything from tents to kayaks to crampons. 15% discount for HI-C members.

Laundry: Cascade Coin Laundry, downstairs in the Cascade Mall, 317 Banff Ave. (762-0165). Wash $1.75, 7-min. dry 25¢. Open daily 7:30am-10pm. **Lake Louise Laundromat,** Samson Mall (522-2143). $2 wash, 7min. dry 25¢. Showers $3. Open daily 7am-9pm.

Pharmacy: Harmony Drug, 111 Banff Ave. (762-5711). Open daily 9am-9pm.

Hospital: Mineral Springs, 316 Lynx St. (762-2222), near Wolf St.

Emergency: Banff Warden Office (762-4506), **Lake Louise Warden Office** (522-3866). Open 24 hrs. **Police:** (762-2226), on Railway St. by the train depot.

Post Office: 204 Buffalo St. (762-2586). Open Mon.-Fri. 9am-5:30pm. **Postal Code:** T0L 0C0.

Area Code: 403.

Banff National Park hugs the Alberta-British Columbia border, 120km west of Calgary. The **Trans-Canada Hwy.** (Hwy. 1) runs east-west through the park; **Icefields Parkway** (Hwy. 93) connects Banff to Jasper National Park in the north. Greyhound links the park to major points in Alberta and British Columbia. Civilization in the park centres around the towns of Banff and **Lake Louise,** 55km northwest of Banff on Hwy. 1. Hwy. 1A, the Bow Valley Parkway, parallels Hwy. 1 from Lake Louise to 8km west of Banff. Buses between the towns are expensive. Those who hitch report plenty of competition. (*Let's Go* does not recommend hitchhiking.)

ACCOMMODATIONS

Finding a cheap place to stay is easy in Banff. Fifteen residents of the townsite offer rooms in their own homes, often at reasonable rates, especially in the off-season. Check the list in the back of the Banff and Lake Louise Official Visitor's Guide, available free at the Banff Townsite Information Centre. Mammoth modern hostels at

Banff and Lake Louise anchor a chain of hostels stretching from Calgary to Jasper. The Pika Shuttle offers inexpensive transport among these hostels. Reserve a shuttle spot through the Banff International Hostel (800-363-0096). To reserve a bus seat, you must have a reservation at your destination hostel; six beds are held at each hostel for standby riders of the shuttle, which can be the only way to get a bed when they're booked. Shuttle rates vary from $5 to $51, depending on how far you're going.

Banff International Hostel (HI-C), Box 1358, Banff T0L 0C0 (762-4122 or 800-363-0096), 3km from Banff townsite on Tunnel Mountain Rd., among a nest of condominiums and lodges. BIH has the look and setting of a ski lodge. In winter, a large fireplace warms the lounge area for cross-country and downhill skiers. Clean quads with 2-4 bunk beds. Take the Banff Explorer from downtown, or join the many other hostelers hoofing it. Ski and cycle workshop. Cafeteria, laundry facilities, TVs, hot showers. Wheelchair-accessible. Accommodates 154. Open all day. No curfew; front desk closes at midnight. $16, non-members $21. Linen $1.

Banff YWCA, 102 Spray Ave. (762-3560). Welcomes both men and women. Meticulously clean; used to be a hospital. 48 private rooms, 100 bunks. Cafeteria downstairs. Complete ski packages available in winter. Winter rates include full breakfast. Unbeatable weekly rates. Singles $47. Doubles $53. Bunks $17, weekly $80. Prices for private rooms drop about $10 during winter (Oct. 1-May 15).

Castle Mountain Hostel (HI-C), on Hwy. 1A, 1.5km east of the junction of Hwy. 1 and Hwy. 93 between Banff and Lake Louise. Recently renovated. Accommodates 36. A common area with store and windows; frequent bear sightings. Call Banff International Hostel (see above) for reservations.$10, non-members $16.

Lake Louise International Hostel (HI-C), Village Rd. (522-2200 or 800-363-0096), ½km from Samson Mall in Lake Louise townsite. Brand-new super-hostel like Banff International, only cleaner. Accommodates 100. Cafeteria, full-service kitchen, hot showers. Wheelchair-accessible. The adjacent Canadian Alpine Centre sponsors various programs and events for hikers and skiers. $16, non-members $24. Private rooms $21.50, non-members $28.

Mosquito Creek Hostel (HI-C), 103km south of the Icefield Centre and 26km north of Lake Louise. Close to Wapta Icefield. Accommodates 38. Fireplace, sauna, full-service kitchen. $10, non-members $15. Call BIH for reservations.

Rampart Creek Hostel (HI-C), 34km south of the Icefield Centre. Rampart's proximity to several **world-famous ice climbs** (including Weeping Wall, 17km north on Icefields Parkway) makes it a favorite of winter mountaineers. Accommodates 30 in rustic cabins. Sauna, full-service kitchen, wood-heated bathtub. $9, non-members $14. Call BIH for reservations.

Hilda Creek Hostel (HI-C), 8.5km south of the Icefield Centre on the Icefields Parkway. The most noteworthy feature is a primitive **sauna** that holds about 4 people, uncomfortably. In the morning, guests must replenish the water supply with a shoulder-bucket contraption. Full-service kitchen. Accommodates 21. Excellent hiking and skiing nearby at Parker's Ridge. $8, non-members $13. Call BIH (above) for reservations.

CAMPING

There are hundreds of campers looking to be happy in Banff, and none of the campgrounds takes reservations, so arrive early in the day. Each site holds a maximum of two tents and six people. **Tunnel Mountain Village, Johnston Canyon, Lake Louise,** and **Mosquito Creek** have the best facilities and are nearest a townsite; contact the Banff or Lake Louise Information Centres (see Practical Information, above) for detailed information. The campgrounds below are listed from south to north.

Tunnel Mountain Village, 1km past the International Hostel, closest to Banff townsite. Flush toilets, showers. Self-guiding trail to Hoodoos. 811 (!) tent sites, $10.50. Open mid-May to late Sept.

Two Jack Main, 13km northeast of Banff. Flush toilets. Canoeing and cycling nearby. 381 tentsites, $11.50. Open late June to early Sept.

Johnston Canyon, 26km northwest of Banff on Hwy. 1A. Flush toilets, showers. Excellent trail access; cycling nearby. 132 sites, $14. Open mid-May-mid-Sept.

Castle Mountain, midway between Banff and Lake Louise along Hwy. 1A. Flush toilets. Cycling nearby. 43 sites, $11.50. Open late June to early Sept.

Protection Mountain, 11km west of Castle Junction on Hwy. 1A. Flush toilets. Cycling nearby. 89 sites, $11.50. Open late June to early Sept.

Lake Louise. Not on the lake, but the toilets flush. Hiking and fishing nearby. 220 tent sites, $12.50. Open mid-May to late Sept.

Mosquito Creek, 103km south of the Icefield Centre and 26km north of Lake Louise. Near the Mosquito Creek Hostel. 32 sites (20 during winter), $8 (free in winter). Open mid-June to early Sept.

Waterfowl, 57km north of Hwy. 1 on Hwy. 93. Flush toilets. Hiking and canoeing nearby. 116 sites, $11.50. Open mid-June to early Sept.

FOOD

Restaurants in Banff generally serve expensive, mediocre food. Luckily, the Banff **(Cafe Aspenglow)** and Lake Louise **(Bill Peyto's Cafe)** International Hostels and the Banff YWCA serve affordable, wholesome meals for $3-7. Or pick up a propane grill and a 10-lb. bag of potatoes and head for the mountains (baked potatoes, potato skins, hash browns, french fries, potato salad...). Shop at **Safeway** (762-5378), at Marten and Elk St., just off Banff Ave. (Open daily 8am-10pm; winter 9am-9pm.) If you're 18, some of the bars offer daily specials at reasonable prices.

Aardvark's, 304A Caribou St. (262-5500). This small pizza place does big business late at night, after the bars close. Excellent pizza anytime. Small $6-8, large $12-19. Huge subs (inc. veggie) $3-7, buffalo wings ("mild" through "suicide") $5. 10% discount with HI card. Open daily 11am-4am.

Jump Start, 206 Buffalo St. (762-0332). Refuel with all varieties of coffee, home-made soups ($5), and fresh, tasty sandwiches ($5). Save room for a slice of exquisite lemon-poppyseed loaf ($1.50). Open Mon.-Sat. 7am-8pm; Sun. 8am-8pm.

Laggan's Deli (522-3574), in Samson Mall at Lake Louise. Savor a thick sandwich on whole-wheat bread ($3.75) with a Greek salad ($1.75), or take home a freshly baked loaf ($2) for later. Always crowded; nowhere better in Lake Louise Village. Open daily 6am-8pm.

Btfsplk's Diner, 221 Banff Ave. (762-5529). A clssc dnr, wth a blck and wht tile flr and a rd everything else. For those who hate vwls but like meal-size Caesar salads ($7) and BBQ brgrs ($7).

ENTERTAINMENT

Banff's bartenders say the real wildliffe in Banff is at the bars. Most of the bars are along Banff Ave. where, iff you're 18, you can drink 'til you barff.

Rose and Crown, 202 Banff Ave. (762-2121). Waits of 1 hr. to get into this popular English-style pub are common on weekends. Live music almost every night. Happy hour (4:30-7:30pm) has $3 drafts, $2.75 highballs. Open daily 11am-2am.

Barbary Coast, upstairs at 119 Banff Ave. (762-4616). Sports paraphernalia dominates the decor at this fashionable, laid-back bar. The kitchen could stand on its own as an excellent restaurant; the pasta dishes are particularly good. Look for specials at lunch ($6-7). Live music every night ranges from blues to light rock. 15¢ chicken wings Wed.; happy hour 4:30-7:30pm. Open 11am-2am.

Silver City, 110 Banff Ave. (762-3337). Once notorious for countless drunken brawls, this "Hall of Fame Sports Bar" has mellowed with age and an unforeseen 100% staff turnover, but it still one of the most crowded in town. Billiards $1.25. Happy hour Mon.-Sat. 6-9pm, 6pm-2am Sun. Open daily 6pm-2am.

SIGHTS AND EVENTS

The palatial **Banff Springs Hotel** (762-6895) on Spray Ave. overlooks the town. In 1988, this 825-room castle celebrated its 100th birthday with a series of posh parties and its own special brand of beer (weakened at the request of hotel guests). You can enjoy a Centennial Ale, a basket of bread, and a fantastic view for $3.75 at the **Grapes Wine Bar** on the mezzanine level. Ride the guest elevator up to the 8th floor to see what kind of view you'd have if you could afford to stay here. In summer, the hotel offers free guided tours of the grounds daily at 4:30pm. The tour, a good pastime for a rainy day, offers a grand opportunity to view lavish architecture and museum-quality artifacts. The hotel offers horseback riding (daily 9am-5pm; $22 for 1 hr., $46 for 3 hrs.; reservations recommended by calling 722-2848).

Other rainy-day attractions include Banff's small museums. The **Whyte Museum of the Canadian Rockies,** 111 Bear St. (762-2291), offers a look at the history of Canadian alpinism. Exhibits in the museum's **Heritage Gallery** explain how Banff developed: very rapidly, unchecked, and catering to the whims of wealthy guests at the Banff Springs Hotel. The galleries downstairs display local artists' paintings of the mountains and their inhabitants. (Open daily 10am-6pm; mid-Oct.-mid-May Tues.-Sun. 1-5pm, Thurs. until 9pm. $3, seniors and students $2, children free, discounted rate within one hour of closing). The **Banff Park Museum** (762-1558), on Banff Ave. near the bridge, is a taxidermist's dream. Explore the well-stocked reading room and discover the differences between buffalo and bison, or peruse clippings that detail violent encounters between elk and automobiles. More impressive than the exhibits is the building itself, erected in 1903 before electric lights were widespread, and designed to maximize natural light with high windows and a wooden balcony (open daily 10am-6pm; Sept.-May daily 1-5pm. Admission $2, children $1). A block away on the second floor of the Clock Tower Mall is the **Natural History Museum,** 112 Banff Ave. (762-4747). The amateur private collection focuses on geology, but contains a little of everything. The complete tour includes a thrilling 20-minute video documentary focusing on the eruption of Mount St. Helens. (Unfortunately, the early-'80s soundtrack is not available for purchase). On your way out, be sure to make faces at the 8-ft. "authentic" model of Sasquatch. (Open daily May-June 10am-8pm, July-Aug. 10am-10pm, Sept. 10am-8pm, in winter 10am-6pm. $3, seniors and teens $2, under 10 free.)

The culture industry moves into Banff every year for the summer-long **Banff Festival of the Arts,** producing drama, ballet, jazz, opera, and other aesthetic commodities. Pick up a brochure at the Information Centre or call 762-6300 for details.

OUTDOORS

Hike to the **backcountry** for total privacy, intense beauty, over 1600km of trails, and trout that will bite anything. Pick up the complete *Backcountry Visitors' Guide* at Information Centres (see Practical Information). You need a permit to stay overnight; get one at the Information Centres for $5 per person per day, up to $25 per person, or $35 per year. All litter must leave the backcountry with you, and no live trees may be chopped in the parks. Both the Banff International Hostel (see Accommodations) and the Park Information Centre have the *Canadian Rockies Trail Guide,* with excellent information and maps. If you want your own copy, you can find it in almost any bookstore or outdoors shop. In general, the farther you get from a townsite, the further behind you'll leave people altogether. Day hiking does not require a permit. The pamphlet *Drives and Walks* describes day and overnight hikes in the Lake Louise and Banff areas.

Two easy trails lie within walking distance of the Banff. **Fenland** winds 2km through an area creeping with beaver, muskrat, and waterfowl. Follow Mt. Norquay Rd. out of Banff and look for signs either at the bridge just before the picnic area or across the railroad tracks on the left side of the road (the trail is closed in late spring and early summer due to elk calving). The summit of **Tunnel Mountain** provides a spectacular view of Bow Valley and Mt. Rundle. Follow Wolf St. east from Banff Ave. and turn right on St. Julien Rd. to reach the head of the 2.3km trail.

About 25km out of Banff toward Lake Louise along the Bow Valley Parkway, **Johnston Canyon** offers a popular half-day hike. The 1.1-km hike to the canyon's lower falls and the 2.7-km trip to the upper falls consist mostly of a catwalk along the edge of the canyon. Don't stop at the falls, though; proceed along the more rugged trail for another 3.1km to seven blue-green cold-water springs known as the **Inkpots.** The trail is packed with video-camera-toting tourists up to the lower falls, while beyond the upper falls it is relatively tourist-free.

After a strenuous day of hiking, consider driving one of the many scenic routes in the Banff area. **Tunnel Mountain Drive** begins at the intersection of Banff Ave. and Buffalo St. and proceeds 9km past Bow Falls and up the side of Tunnel Mountain. Several markers along the way point to splendid views of the Banff Springs Hotel, Sulphur Mountain, and Mt. Rundle. Turn right onto Tunnel Mountain Rd. to see the **hoodoos,** long, finger-like projections of limestone once part of the cliff wall and thought by Native Canadians to encase sentinel spirits. Or, drive west along Vermillion Lakes Drive, which branches off Mt. Norquay Rd. just before the overpass. When the sun sets gloriously over the snowy mountains and shimmering lakes, remember to keep both eyes on the road.

Bicycling is permitted on public roads and highways and on certain trails in the park. Spectacular scenery and the proximity to a number of hostels and campgrounds make the Bow Valley Parkway (Hwy. 1A) and the Icefields Parkway (Hwy. 92) perfect for extended cycling trips. The *Trail Bicycling Guide,* available at the Information Centres in Banff and Lake Louise, lists trails on which bikes are permitted. Trail cyclists should remember to dismount and stand to the downhill side if a horse approaches. Also be forewarned that the quick and quiet nature of trail bicycling is more prone to surprise a bear than is the tromping of hikers. **Hammerhead Mountain Bike Tours** (547-1566) offers a great deal: a day-long guided off-road tour, including transport from Banff, bike and helmet rental, and picnic lunch, all for $44 (June-Sept. Mon., Wed., and Fri.).

Banff National Park's original name was Hot Springs Reserve, and its featured attraction was the **Cave and Basin Hot Springs.** The **Cave and Basin National Historic Site** (762-1557), a refurbished resort circa 1914, now screens documentaries and stages exhibits. Walk along the **Discovery Trail** to see the original spring discovered over 100 years ago by three Canadian Pacific Railway workers. The Centre is southwest of the city on Cave Ave. (Open daily 9am-7pm; winter 9am-5pm. $2, children $1.) The pool was closed in 1993 because its cracking tile posed a danger to public health; while various proposals for the pool's future are considered, you can still investigate the original cave, or examine a series of exhibits which present a refreshingly enlightened viewpoint on the role of the National Parks. Free guided tours meet out front at 11am and 2pm in summer, 11am in winter.

A particularly scenic walk lies just beyond the Cave and Basin in **Sundance Canyon.** Allow about an 1½ hours for the uphill trail. Follow the rotten-egg smell to the **Upper Hot Springs pool** (762-1515), a 40°C (104°F) sulphurous cauldron up the hill on Mountain Ave. A soak in the pool is relaxing, but it will soak your wallet. (Open daily 8am-11pm; mid-Sept-mid-June Mon.-Fri. noon-9pm, Sat. and Sun. 10am-11pm. $4, seniors and children $3. Bathing suit rental (or plastic pants) $1.50, towel rental $1, locker rental 25¢.)

Taking a **gondola** to the top of a peak is an expensive way to see the park, but it saves your legs for hiking at the summit. The **Sulphur Mountain Gondola** (762-5438), next to the Upper Hot Springs pool, lifts you 700m to a view of the Rockies normally reserved for birds and mountain goats. You can hike all the way back down on a 6-km trail that deposits you right back at the parking lot (open daily 8:30am-8pm. Fare $8.50, ages 5-11 $4, under 5 free.) The **Summit Restaurant** (Canada's highest), perched atop Sulphur Mountain, serves an "Early Morning Lift" breakfast special for $4. Grab a table by the window.

Brewster Tours (762-6767) offers an extensive array of guided bus tours within the park. If you don't have a car, these tours may be the only way to see some of the main attractions, such as the Great Divide, the Athabasca Glacier, and the spiral railroad tunnel (trains are often so long that you can see them entering and exiting the mountain at the same time). The tour-guide/drivers are professional, knowledgeable, and entertaining. If you were planning on taking the regular Brewster bus from Banff to Jasper ($37), you might want to spend $24 more to see the sights in between. (One way 9½ hrs.; $59.50, round-trip 2 days, $83. A tour of the Columbia Icefields is $19.50 extra. Tickets can be purchased at the bus depot.)

If you'd prefer to look up at the mountains rather than down from them, the nearby lakes provide a serene vantage point. **Fishing** is legal virtually anywhere you can find water, but you must hold a National Parks fishing permit, available at the Information Centre ($6 for a 7-day permit, $13 for an annual permit good in all Canadian National Parks). A particularly feisty breed of brook trout rewards those willing to hike the 7km to **Bourgeau Lake.** Closer to the road, try **Herbert Lake,** off the Icefields Parkway between Lake Louise and the Columbia Icefield, or **Lake Minnewanka,** on Lake Minnewanka Rd. northeast of Banff townsite, rumored to be the home of a half-human, half-fish Indian spirit. You can find out about this myth during a 1½-hour guided tour sponsored by **Minnewanka Tours Ltd.** (762-3473; $24, children $8). Lake Minnewanka Rd. also passes **Johnson Lake,** where the sun warms the shallow water to a swimmable temperature, and **Two Jack Lake,** just beyond Lake Minnewanka, easily explored by boat or canoe.

Those who prefer more vigorous water sports can **raft** the waters of the **Kootenay River. Kootenay River Runners** (604-347-9210) offer half- and full-day trips for $49 and $69 respectively, as well as a more boisterous full-day trip on the **Kicking Horse River** for $69. Tickets are available at **Tickets** (762-5385), located on the corner of Caribou St. and Banff Ave. **Alpine Rafting Company's** day-long trip on the Kicking Horse ($72), includes a steak barbecue lunch (604-344-5016). A good deal is offered by the **Banff International Hostel** (see Accommodations): rafting on the Kicking Horse River (transportation included) for $44. A stop in a pub is promised afterwards.

■■■ KANANASKIS COUNTRY

Between Calgary and Banff lie 4000 sq. km of provincial parks, **Bow Valley, Peter Lougheed,** and **Bragg Creek,** and so-called "multi-use recreational areas" (**Ribbon/ Spray Lakes** and **Highwood/Cataract Creek** are two of the largest). Although use can be heavy in summer, the sheer size of Kananaskis and the dispersed nature of its attractions keeps it tranquil and unspoiled.

Kananaskis offers skiing, snowmobiles, windsurfing, golfing, biking, and hiking. Eager staff members at the five Park Information Centres can help design itineraries for visitors. Expect to be showered with maps and elaborate brochures describing your activity of choice. **Visitor Centres** lie within (or nearby) each of the three provincial parks. The **Bow Valley** centre (673-3663) is located north of Hwy. 1 between Seebe and Exshaw (open daily 9am-8pm); the **Elbow Valley** centre is located on Hwy. 66 near **Bragg Creek** (949-3754); the cozy, chalet-style centre in **Peter Lougheed Park** (591-7222), complete with a fireplace, a wooden deck, and informative displays and videos, is located on the Kananaskis Lakes Trail (hours vary from season to season). The Alberta Parks System has a central office on **Barrier Lake,** near the junction of Hwy. 40 and 68 (673-3985; open Mon.-Tues. 10am-5pm, Wed.-Sun. 9am-6pm; Mon.-Fri. 9am-7pm; winter Thurs.-Mon. 10am-5pm). **Travel Alberta** maintains a helpful office in **Canmore,** just off Hwy. 1A near the northwest border of K-Country (678-5508; open Sun.-Thurs. 9am-6pm, Fri.-Sat. 8am-8pm). In an emergency, call the **Canmore Police** (591-7707). Get free publications at any of the information centres. *Kanaskis Country at a Glance* is helpful for navigation; *Experience Kanaskis Country* is full of recreational information.

Kananaskis' **hiking trails** accommodate all kinds of nature lovers. Those with limited time or endurance will enjoy the hour-long interpretive hikes. The 1.9km **Canadian Mt. Everest Expedition Trail** in Peter Lougheed Provincial Park, for example, provides a majestic view of both Upper and Lower Kananaskis Lakes. More serious hikers will find Gillean Dafferns' *Kananaskis Country Trail Guide* (published by Rocky Mountain Books) the definitive source on area trails, detailing 337 hikes through the area. For additional hints and trail updates, ask a staff member at an Information Centre (see above for locations). Bikers will also find the park staff helpful in planning treks along the untraveled highways and trails. The **Canmore Nordic Centre** (678-2400), the 1988 Olympic Nordic skiing venue, offers world-class cross-country skiing in the winter and 60km of mountain bike trails in summer.

Greyhound buses stop at the **Rusticana Grocery,** 801 8th St. in Canmore (678-4465). Three buses pass each day from Calgary ($12) and Banff ($3). Or, take the **Pike Shuttle** (see Banff Accommodations, above) directly to the Ribbon Creek Hostel for $7 from Banff or $15 from Calgary. Once in Kananaskis, hitchhiking is difficult. (Let's Go does not recommend hitchhiking.)

No less than 3000 campsites are accessible via K-Country roads, and camping is unlimited in the backcountry as long as you set up camp at least 1km from a trail. Most established campsites in Kananaskis cost at least $11 per night. The **Ribbon Creek Hostel ,** near the Nakiska Ski Area, 24km south of the Trans-Canada Hwy. on Hwy. 40, accommodates 48 people. The hostel's private family rooms hold four beds each, and its living room has a fireplace. The remote location results in frequent sightings of bear, wolf, and cougar ($11, non-members $17). For reservations call the Banff International Hostel at 762-4122 or 800-363-0096. **William Watson Lodge** (591-7227), a few km north of the Information Centre in Peter Lougheed Park, accommodates disabled visitors. Though only disabled Alberta residents and resident Alberta seniors may make reservations, and anyone may drop by to enjoy the accessible local trails.

■ ■ ■ CALGARY

The Northwest Mounted Police were sent to Alberta in the 1870s to put an end to illegal whiskey trade and to discourage American expansion into the Canadian wilderness. In 1875, Inspector Denny described the Mounties' arrival at the confluence of the Bon and Elbon Rivers: "Before us lay a lovely valley, bordered to the west by towering mountains with their snowy peaks....The knowledge that a fort was to be built here gave us the greatest satisfaction." Ranchers and farmers were soon attracted by the low prices of the prairie land, and the population boomed in the 1880s with the arrival of the Canadian Pacific Railway.

Although "Calgary" is derived from the Gaelic for "clear running water," the city now thrives on a black, viscous liquid. Oil made the transformation from cowtown to major metropolis possible. In July, Calgarians forget the oil business and get all gussied up in cowboy boots, jeans, Western shirts, and ten-gallon hats for the "Greatest Outdoor Show on Earth," the **Calgary Stampede.** Grown men and women go to their professional jobs in full cowboy attire. Don't miss over a week of world-class rodeo action, chuckwagon races, country music, rides, pancake breakfasts, and "Loonie Madness". Yaaaahoooooooo!!!

PRACTICAL INFORMATION AND ORIENTATION

Visitors Information: Calgary Convention and Visitors Bureau, 237 8th Ave. SE, Calgary, AB T2G 0K8 (263-8510). Call or write for help finding accommodations, especially around Stampede time. Open daily 8am-5pm. For drop-in information, there are two **Information Centres** in the city: **Tower Centre,** ground floor of Calgary Tower at 101 9th Ave. SW (263-8510 x 397), open daily 8:30-5pm; and at **Calgary International Airport** on the arrivals level of the main terminal (292-8477), open daily 7am-10pm. The **Visitor Information Phone Line** (262-2766 Mon.-Fri. 8am-5pm, Sat.-Sun. 10am-5pm) provides more information. For the cost of a local call, the **"Talking Yellow Pages"** provides a wide range of information, from local events and attractions to the latest in vomit-stain removal techniques (no joke). Dial 521-5222 and the appropriate 4-digit code, listed in the front of the Yellow Pages (general visitor's info. is code 8950).

American Express, Canada Trust Tower, main floor, 421 7th Ave. SW (261-5085). **Postal Code:** T2P 4K9.

Greyhound, 877 Greyhound Way SW (outside Calgary 800-661-TRIP/-8747; 265-9111 in Calgary). Frequent service to Edmonton ($31) and Banff ($15), 2 buses

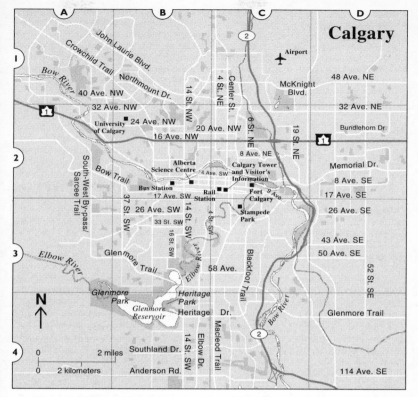

Calgary

daily to Drumheller ($16.70). Seniors 10% off. Free shuttle bus from C-Train at 7th Ave. and 10th St. to bus depot (every hr. on the ½-hr., 6:30am-7:30pm).

Other Buses: Brewster Tours, 221-8242. Operates buses from the airport to: Banff (3 per day; 12:30, 3, and 6pm; $26); Lake Louise (3 per day; 12:30, 3, and 5pm; $28), and Jasper (1 per day; 12:30pm; $49.50).

Calgary Transit: Information and Downtown Sales Centre, 240 7th Ave. SW. Bus schedules, passes, and maps. Open Mon.-Fri. 8:30am-5pm. Fare $1.50, ages 6-14 90¢, under 6 free. Exact change required. Day pass $4.50, children $2.50. Book of 10 tickets $12.50, children $8.50. **Information line** (262-1000) open Mon.-Fri. 6am-11pm, Sat.-Sun. 8am-9:30pm.

Taxi: Checker Cab, 299-9999. **Yellow Cab,** 974-1111.

Car Rental: Dollar, 221-1888 at airport, 269-3777 downtown (123 5th Ave. SE). Cars start at $37 per day with unlimited mileage. Weekend special for $29 per day. Must be 23 with a major credit card. If under 25, $9 per day surcharge for collision insurance. Open daily 7am-midnight at airport; Mon.-Fri. 7am-7pm, Sat. and Sun. 8am-7pm downtown. **Rent-A-Wreck,** 112 5th Ave, SE (287-9703). Cars start at $30 per day, 200km free, 13¢ each additional km. $5 per day discount to HI members. If under 25, $16 per day surcharge for collision insurance. Open Mon.-Fri. 8am-6pm, Sat.-Sun. 9am-5pm. Most companies increase rates during the summer, especially during the Stampede; call for exact rates.

Bike Rental: Budget Car Rental, 140 6th Ave. SE (226-1550). $12 per day. Must be 18 with a credit card. **Sports Rent,** 9250 Macleod Trail (252-2055). $17 per day. **The Bike Shop,** 1321 1st St. SW (264-0735). $20 per day.

Pharmacy: Shopper's Drug Mart, Chinook Centre, 6455 Macleod Trail S (253-2424). Open 24 hrs.

Laundromat: Beacon Speed Wash & Dry, 1818 Centre St. N (230-9828). Open daily 8am-11pm.

Environment Canada, Calgary & Banff weather, 275-3300.

Gay Lines Calgary: 223 12th Ave. SW (234-8973). Clearinghouse for gay community information from events to services to bars. Peer counseling available. Recorded information after hours. 700-volume library. Buzz #116 downstairs to be let in. Open Mon.-Fri. 10am-10pm, Sat.-Sun. 10am-5pm.

Women's Resource Centre, 325 10th St. NW (263-1550), 1 block west of the Sunnyside C-Train stop. Operated by the YWCA. For women of all ages seeking any kind of assistance. Open Mon.-Fri. 8:30am-4:30pm.

Sexual Assault Centre: 237-5888. Open daily 9:30am-5pm.

Crisis Line: 266-1605.

Poison Centre: 670-1414.

Hospital: Calgary General, 841 Centre Ave. E (268-9111).

Emergency: 911.

Police: 316 7th Ave. SE (266-1234).

Post Office: 220 4th Ave. SE (292-5512). Open Mon.-Fri. 8am-5:45pm. **Postal Code:** T2P 180.

Area Code: 403.

Calgary, on the **Trans-Canada Hwy.** (Hwy. 1), is very accessible by car. Planes fly into **Calgary International Airport** (292-8400 for the Airport Authority; 292-8477 for general information, Mon.-Fri. 8am-4:30pm), about 5km northwest of the city centre. **Cab** fare from the airport to the city is about $20. Bus #57 provides sporadic service from the airport to downtown (call for schedule). Unless you take a cab or have impeccable timing, you will probably end up taking the **Airporter Bus** (539-3909), which offers frequent and friendly service to major hotels in downtown Calgary for $7.50; if you ask nicely they just may drop you off at an unscheduled stop.

Calgary is divided into quadrants: **Centre Street** is the east-west divide; the **Bow River** divides the north and south sections. The rest is simple: avenues run east-west, streets run north-south. Pay careful attention to the quadrant distinctions (NE, NW, SE, SW) at the end of each address. You can derive the street from an avenue address by disregarding the last two digits of the first number: thus 206 7th Ave. is at 2nd St., and 2339 Macleod Trail is at 23rd St. Pick up a **city map** at convenience stores or at any of the Information Centres.

Public transportation within the city is inexpensive and efficient. **Calgary Transit** operates both buses and streetcars ("C-Trains"). Buses ($1.50) run all over the city. You need only call 262-1000 to find out how to get around. Though they cover less territory, C-Trains are free in the downtown zone (along 7th Ave. S; between 10th St. SW and 3rd St. SE); you pay the $1.50 fare only when you leave downtown. Most lodging, food, and sights are within the C-Train's free zone anyway.

ACCOMMODATIONS

Cheap lodging in Calgary is rare only when packs of tourists Stampede into the city's hotels. For stays in July, you cannot reserve too early. Contact the **B&B Association** of Calgary (531-0065) for information and availability on this type of lodging. Prices for singles begin around $30, doubles around $45.

Calgary International Hostel (HI-C), 520 7th Ave. SE (269-8239). Conveniently located several blocks east of downtown with access to the 3rd St. SE C-Train station and public buses. Snack bar, meeting rooms, cooking and barbeque facilities, laundry, and a cycle workshop. Employs an activities coordinator in summer, an invaluable resource for information about the city. Make reservations for the Stampede *way* in advance. Wheelchair accessible. Discount tickets for the Calgary Tower can be purchased by showing your hostel card at the Tower. Open 24 hrs., but the front desk closes at midnight. $13, non-members $18.

University of Calgary, in the NW quadrant. Out of the way, but easily accessible via bus #9 or the C-Train. If you can't make the Olympic squad, at least you can sleep in their beds; U of C was the Olympic Village home to 1988 competitors and offers clean rooms at competitive prices. More lavish suites with private bathrooms are available in Olympus Hall or Norquay Hall for approximately $35. Booking for all rooms coordinated through **Kananaskis Hall,** 3330 24th Ave. (220-3203), a 12-min. walk from the University C-Train stop (open 24 hr.). Rooms available May-Aug. only. Two types of rooms have shared bathrooms: 22 rooms are set aside for those with student ID: singles $21, doubles $31.50. These are first-come, first-serve only. A vastly greater number of rooms may be reserved in advance, and are often booked solid: singles $30, doubles $38.

St. Regis Hotel, 124 7th Ave. SE (262-4641). Friendly management and clean, comfortable rooms. Tavern and snack bar downstairs. Singles $37, with TV $40, with TV and bath $48. If you're feeling particularly ascetic, try an inside room with no TV, bath, or windows for $31.35. Same prices during Stampede, but usually has a few openings nonetheless. Weekly rates $96-117.

FOOD

Ethnic and cafe-style dining spots line the **Stephen Avenue Mall,** 8th Ave. S between 1st St. SE and 3rd St. SW. Good, reasonably-priced food is also readily available in the **"+15" Skyway System.** Designed to provide indoor passageways during bitter winter days, this futuristic mall-in-the-sky connects the second floors of dozens of buildings throughout downtown Calgary; look for the blue and white "+15" signs on street level. **Safeway** supermarkets dot the city.

For trendier, costlier restaurants, go to the **Kensington District,** along Kensington Rd., between 10th and 11th St. NW. Take the C-train to Sunnyside or use the Louise Bridge to reach the area. Other lively cafe-restaurants are on 4th St. SW (take #3 and #53 buses) and 17th Ave. SW (#7 bus). If you're at the University, the **MacEwen Student Centre** has a food court on the 2nd floor with every kind of cheap, quick food imaginable, from cheesesteaks to curry to chow mein to chimichangas. Fresh fruits, vegetables, seafood, baked goods, and flowers grace the plaza-style, upscale **Eau Claire Market** (264-6450), on 3rd St. SW near Prince's Island Park.

4th Street Rose, 2116 4th St. SW (228-5377). A fashionable, California-cool, relaxing restaurant on the outskirts of town: high ceilings, tile floors, and the positively groovy "Aztec Room" upstairs. Sit among cacti in the skylit interior or join the "in-crowd" on the patio. The house specialty is the "pro-size" Caesar Salad ($4.50), served in a large Mason jar. Gourmet pizzas and homemade pastas $7-10. Open Mon.-Thurs. 11am-1am, Fri. 11am-2am, Sat. 10am-2am, Sun. 10am-midnight.

City Hall Cafeteria, (268-2463) in the City Hall Municipal Building at 800 Macleod Trail SE, or take the back entrance to City Hall. Backpackers and briefcases guzzle coffee (50¢) and munch muffins (85¢). Stop by for a cheap breakfast special ($3.20) on your way downtown. Lunch specials $4-5. Open Mon.-Fri. 7am-4pm.

The Bread Line, 2120 4th St. SW (245-1888). Surround yourself with wood, plants, and racks of fresh-baked loaves of bread ($2-3), as you sip fresh-squeezed fruit and vegetable juices in this pleasant café. The light entrees ($4-5) are tasty, and you can follow them up with just about any designer coffee you desire ($1-4). Open Mon.-Fri. 6am-midnight, Sat.-Sun. 8am-midnight.

Hang Fung Foods Ltd., 119 3rd Ave. SE (269-5853), located in the rear of a Chinese market with the same name. The genuine article. Chinese clientele. Chopsticks; if you want to use a fork, bring your own. Enormous bowl of plain *congee* (rice broth) $1.50. Combination dinners include wonton soup, a spring roll, pork fried rice, and a large entree for $8.50. Open daily 9am-9pm.

Picadilly Grill, 216 7th Ave. SW (261-6699). A slightly upscale restaurant and bar in the heart of downtown with lots of dark wood and a bow-tied bartender. Burgers and sandwiches $6-8, entrees $10-14. Tuesday is pasta night: all you can eat for $8. On Fridays, any entree on the menu is $8. Open Mon.-Fri. 6:30am-9pm, Sat. 8am-10pm, Sun. 8am-9pm.

Take Ten Cafe, 304 10th St. NE (270-7010). Less trendy than other joints in the area, but the food is much less expensive, plentiful, and tasty. All burgers under $4, and the lunch specials (under $5) include large Chinese dishes on a heap of rice. They won't mind if you linger. Open Mon.-Wed. 8:30am-5pm, Thurs. 8:30am-6:30pm, Fri. 8:30am-7pm, Sat. 9am-5pm, Sun. 10am-4pm.

Island Experience, 314A 10th St. NW (270-4550). Specializes in Caribbean treats borrowed from India, including rotis (flat bread, filled with curry), Banana Date Chutney ($1), and Peanut Punch ($2). Entrees 6.25-7.50. Open Mon.-Thurs. 11am-9pm, Fri.-Sat. 11am-10pm, Sun. noon-9pm.

The Roasterie, 312 10th St. NW (270-3304), near Kensington Rd.; also 2212 4th St. SW (541-0960). Just cookies, muffins, and about 20 kinds of coffee, from Rioberry ($2.75) to HiTest ($1.50) to Vietnamese Iced Coffee ($3.25), served in giant bowls. Muffinhead would enjoy. Decide for yourself whether there's any truth to their claim that "caffeine saves the brain." Hot chocolate ($1.25); tea ($1). Open Mon.-Fri. 7am-midnight, Sat. 8am-midnight, Sun. 9am-11pm.

Golden Age Club Cafeteria, 610 8th Ave. SE (262-6342), upstairs from the club. Very convenient to the hostel, this centre for the retired welcomes the hungry of all ages. The young will not feel out of place at this friendly, laid-back establishment. Patio furniture and bright lights create a cheerful, relaxing atmosphere. Daily hot lunch specials ($4-5). Breakfast fare ranges from toast and jam (80¢) to the "Hungry Cowboy," which includes pancakes, eggs, ham, bacon, or sausage, and hashbrowns ($4.50). Open Mon.-Fri. 8am-3pm.

SIGHTS

Don't just gaze at the **Calgary Tower,** 101 9th Ave. SW (266-7171); ride an elevator to the top for a spectacular view of the Rockies ($5, seniors $3, ages 13-18 $3.25, ages 3-12 $2). The 190m tower also affords a 360° view of the city (elevator pass is valid throughout the day). (Rides daily 8am-11pm, shorter hours in winter.)

The **Glenbow Museum,** 130 9th Ave. SE (268-4100), just across the street from the Tower, is a nexus of cultural pride in this boomtown. There's something for everyone in the Glenbow's extensive and well-organized collection. From rocks and minerals to Native Canadian lifestyles to the art of Asia to the history of the Canadian West, the Glenbow has it all. Temporary exhibitions include frequent displays of modern art. You could easily spend an entire day in the museum. (Open Tues.-Sun. 10am-6pm. $4.50, seniors, students and children $3; under 7 free; free on Sat.) Less than a block northeast of the museum on 7th Ave. SE, the **Olympic Plaza** still attracts crowds on sunny days years after the flame left town. The site of the medal presentations during the 1988 Winter Games, this open-air park now hosts a variety of special events, including free concerts during the **Calgary Jazz Festival** in June. For an update on Olympic Plaza programming, call 268-3888 during business hours. One of the park's most interesting features, the **walkway,** was constructed out of more than 20,000 bricks, each purchased for $20-30 and engraved with the name or personal message of the patron. Try to decipher such cryptic messages as "NGF 1959 BN B IN YYC."

Five blocks down 8th Ave. to the west and about 50 ft. straight up are the **Devonian Gardens,** a cool, quiet oasis in an often hot and noisy city. Located on the fourth floor of Toronto Dominion Sq. (8th Ave. between 2nd and 3rd St. SW), this 2.5-acre indoor garden contains sculptures, fountains, waterfalls, bridges, and over 20,000 plants, representing 138 local and tropical species. Sit on a rock and feed the goldfish as you watch your reflection in the mirrored windows of the skyscrapers across the street. (Open daily 9am-9pm. Free.)

Prince's Island Park can be reached by footbridges from either side of the Bow River. Many evenings in summer at 7:30pm a local college puts on free Shakespeare plays in the park. When an airplane flies overhead, drowning out the actors, a bizarre whistle is blown and everyone on stage freezes until the plane is gone. Call 240-6359 for information. The park is laced with biking and fitness trails. The park sometimes hosts events such as the **Caribbean Cultural Festival** in June.

Calgary's other island park, **St. George's Island,** is accessible by the river walkway to the east and is home to the marvelous **Calgary Zoo** (232-9300). No matter how strongly you might disapprove of caging wild animals, you'll be impressed by the habitats' authenticity, the variety of animals, and how cute a baby hippo can be. The

Canadian Wilds exhibit re-creates the sights, sounds, and, yes, the smells of Canada's wilderness. A pamphlet available at the zoo entrance gate lists animal feeding times; visitors are invited to watch big animals eat little animals. The squeamish must content themselves with a stroll through the **botanical gardens** or the **prehistoric park,** or a visit to the **children's zoo.** (Gates open in summer 9am-6:30pm in summer; winter 9am-4pm; grounds open in summer until 8:30pm; winter until 5:30pm. $7.50, seniors $4.75, children $3.75. Seniors $2 on Tues. Refund if you leave within ½ hr. of arriving.)

Though the Olympic flame has left Calgary, the world-class athletic facilities are still there. The most impressive arena is the **Olympic Oval** (220-7954 or 220-7890), an indoor speed-skating track on the University of Calgary campus (open daily 8am-10pm, April-June Mon.-Fri. 8:30am-4:30pm). The Oval has the fastest ice in the world and a major international training facility. You can sit in the bleachers, marvel at the size of the building, and observe the action on the ice for free. The speed skaters work out in the early morning and late afternoon. During public skating times, you can take a spin for yourself ($3.25; speed skate rental $3.75). **Canada Olympic Park** (247-5452), 10 minutes from downtown Calgary on Hwy. 1 west, was the site of the bobsled, luge, and ski jumping competitions. A guided tour of Olympic Park costs $6 (seniors and children $3); the one-hour trip around the facilities includes a chance to stand in the bobsled track and to glance down the slope from atop the 90m ski jump tower (tours daily mid-Sept.-mid-May 9am-4pm). The **Olympic Hall of Fame** (268-2632), also at Olympic Park, honors Olympic achievements with displays, films, and videos. (Open daily 8am-5pm. $3.75; seniors, students, and children $2.70.) The Grand Olympic Tour includes a visit to the Park and the Olympic Hall of Fame for $8 (children and seniors $4). If you're looking to get into the action, you can cruise through the last six turns of the Olympic luge course on your own **luge ride** (June-Aug.; $12). Of course, you're free to stroll the grounds without paying anything.

For more downhill excitement, turn to the slopes of **Nakiska at Mt. Allan** (591-7777), 99 km west of Calgary on Hwy. 40 in Kananaskis Country, the site of Olympic alpine events and freestyle moguls. Nordic skiers can tread in the tracks of Olympians free at the **Canmore Nordic Centre** (678-2400), in Kananaskis Country just outside the town of Canmore. Of the 56km of trails, one is designed for beginners; the rest are all Olympic-level. If you have brought along your biathalon association membership card and a rifle, you are cordially invited to use the **shooting range** and, in summer, the **roller-ski course.** You can also mountain-bike on the trails (open daily 9am-5pm).

The **Energeum,** 640 5th Ave. SW (297-4293), is Calgary's shrine to oil. The 3,500 sq. ft. hall has lots of hands-on exhibits and photographs to enlighten you about Calgary's life-blood, and to allow you to "recapture the days of cheap gasoline and big, big cars." (Open Mon.-Fri. 10:30am-4:30pm, June-Aug. also open Sun.; always free.)

ENTERTAINMENT

Many young Calgarians like to pound bottles of local brew along **"Electric Avenue,"** the stretch of 11th Ave. SW between 5th and 6th St. Beware of Electric Avenue during hockey playoff time (IT'S HOCKEY NIGHT IN CANADAAAAA!!!): the streets are closed and the lines for bars and clubs wind around the block. Last call in Calgary is 2am, and is strictly observed.

   The King Edward Hotel, 438 9th Ave. SE (262-1680). The Eddy brings in true top bluesmen, including Clarence "Gatemouth" Brown and Matt "Guitar" Murphy. Great blues Mon.-Fri. 9:30pm-2am and jam sessions Sat. 2:30pm-7pm and Sun. 7pm-1am. Cover $3-6. Drinks from $2.75. A bit expensive, but worth it.
   Bottlescrew Bill's Pub, at 10th Ave. SW and 1st St. (263-7900). Take refuge from Electric Avenue in the mellow atmosphere of this "Old English Pub." Bill's offers the widest selection of beers in Alberta ($3-15). If you feel bold, try a pint of Bill's

own Buzzard Breath Ale ($3.50). Happy hour 4-7pm, all day on Sun. Open Mon.-Wed. 11am-1am, Thurs.-Sat. 11am-2am.

REpublik, 219 17th Ave. SW (244-1884). Grungeoids slam and grind with their Gap-clad brethren in Calgary's loudest nuclear bunker and biggest party zone. On the harder side of alternative, the REpublik is a favorite stage for hungry up-and-coming Western bands. The mosh pit likes its victims raw. Cover $2-7. Average drink $3.25; Thurs. night special "triple highballs" 3 for $4.25; Sat. night special "double highballs" 2 for $3.25. Open Mon.-Sat. 8:30pm-3am.

Ranchman's Steak House, 9615 Macleod Trail S (253-1100). One of Canada's greatest honky-tonks. Genuine cowboys. Yuppie-cowboys, stay away. Experience Calgary's Wild West tradition firsthand in the live C&W or with Calgary Stampede beer. Open Mon.-Wed. 9pm-2am, Thurs.-Sat. 8pm-2am. During the Stampede, look for the 18-wheeler full of kegs.

The Stadium Keg, 1923 Uxbridge Dr. NW (282-0020). Where the "Dinos" from the nearby U. of Calgary eat, drink, and be merry. Crowded with college students. Good rock blasted at a level which still allows you to hear yourself think. 2 large TVs. Drink specials nightly 6-9pm. Chicken wings 35¢ per basket on Thurs. Tues. is Tequila night ($1.75). Open Mon.-Sat. 4:30pm-2am-ish, Sun. 4:30-10pm.

THE STAMPEDE

Calgarians take great pride in their "Greatest Outdoor Show on Earth"; it seems that the more cosmopolitan the city becomes, the more firmly it clings to its frontier origins. Drawing millions every summer from across Alberta, Canada, and the world, the Stampede deserves your attention. Make the short trip out to **Stampede Park,** just southeast of downtown, for steer wrestling, saddle bronc, bareback and bull riding, pig racing, wild cow milking, and the famous chuckwagon races, involving four horses per wagon and nerves of steel. Visit an authentic Native encampment and a re-created Wild West town, perch yourself atop the wild, thrashing roller coaster at the **Stampede Midway,** or try the gaming tables in the **Frontier Casino.**

Parking is ample, but the crowd is always more than ample in July. Instead of driving, take the C-Train from downtown to the Stampede stop. For information and ticket mail-order forms, write **Calgary Exhibition and Stampede,** Box 1860, Station M, Calgary, AB T2P 2L8, or call 800-661-1260 (261-0101 in Calgary). Tickets are $16-42. Inquire about rush tickets, available for $8 (youth $7, seniors and children $4). Plan now. The Stampede takes place July 7-16 in 1995 and July 5-14 in 1996.

Even if you can't be there in July, Stampede Park has sights to amuse and educate. Jog over to **Lindsay Park Sports Centre,** 2225 Macleod Trail S (233-8393), across from Stampede Park. This bubble, often mistaken for the Saddledome, offers three swimming pools, an indoor track, basketball courts, a weight room, and aerobics. Built in 1983 for the Western Canada Summer Games, Lindsay Park is primarily a "competition and training" facility for Canadian athletes of all levels. Call ahead to inquire about hours. ($6.60, youths $4.65, children $2.65, seniors $3.25. 20% off Mon.-Fri. from 9-11am and 1:30-3:30pm.)

■ NEAR CALGARY: ALBERTA BADLANDS

You won't lose the crowds by going to the **Royal Tyrrell Museum of Paleontology** (TEER-ull; 403-823-7707), near Drumheller, but you will lose your sense of self-importance. Drumheller lies 100km northeast of Calgary; get there by driving east on Hwy. 1 and northeast on Hwy. 9. The world's largest display of dinosaur specimens forcibly reminds one that humanity is a mere crouton in the Caesar salad of Earth's history. From the Big Bang to the Quarternary Period (that's when we are), Royal Tyrrell covers it all with a dizzying array of displays and videos. If you're not slide-tackled by a hyperactive kindergartner who's run away from his class trip, you may get to build your own "Sillysaurus" on one of the museum's educational computers. The food at the museum cafeteria is inexpensive and tasty. Grab a seat beneath an umbrella on the patio and beat the heat with a breakfast or lunch special (about $5). To see every video, exhibit, and bone, you'll need most of the day. Leave and reenter without paying again (open in summer daily 9am-9pm; Labor Day-Victoria Day Tues.-Sun. 10am-5pm. $5.50, ages 7-17 $2.25, under 7 free; winter Tues. free.) To really get your hands on some fossils, you can participate in a **day dig.** These immensely popular day-long excursions include instruction in paleontology and excavation techniques and a chance to dig in a dinosaur quarry, all for $75 (ages 10-15, $50), including lunch and transportation (leaves daily at 8:30am during July and Aug.; reservations recommended). If that's a little expensive, consider a **Dig Watch,** a 2-hr. guided tour to the quarry, where you can look down upon the fortunate few (July-Aug. daily 10am and 1pm. $8, ages 7-17 $6, under 7 free). The museum is on **Secondary Hwy. 838,** or the **North Dinosaur Trail,** 6km from Drumheller. From Calgary, it's a 90-minute drive via Hwy. 2 north to Hwy. 72 and 9 east. Tyrrell isn't directly served by public transportation, but you can take Greyhound from Calgary to Drumheller (2 per day, one-way $16.70). From Drumheller, rent a bike or take a $3 shuttle bus from the Alexandra Hostel (see below).

Tyrrell lies in the heart of the Alberta **badlands,** where prehistoric wind, water, and ice carved weird, tortured landscapes out of the sedimentary rock. Tyrrell offers free 90-min. interpretive walks through the surrounding badlands (weekends and holidays only, 11am and 3pm), but **Horseshoe Canyon,** about 20km west of Drumheller on Hwy. 9, offers the most impressive landscapes. With its inhospitable terrain and grotesquely twisted rock formations, the canyon will give you a good idea of what hell must look like. Carry at least one quart of water if you want to explore the canyon during hot weather. Horseshoe Canyon is also a favorite **mountain biking** locale. It is possible to bike all the way from the overlook on Hwy. 9 to the Red Deer River northwest of Drumheller. Ask for information and directions at the Old Midland Mine Office.

While the staff at Tyrrell will tell you that the dinosaurs vanished from the earth 65 million years ago, a stroll through nearby **Drumheller** will reassure you that the "terrible lizards" continue to reign supreme at the heart of Drumheller's tourist economy. Tacky dinosaur statues on the edge of town threaten to ravage its few attractions, including a number of shops that sell dinosaur t-shirts, dinosaur mugs, and little plastic dinosaurs. There's even a "dinosaur adoption centre."

Flee the dino-monsters at the **Alexandra Hostel (HI-C),** 30 Railway Ave. N (403-823-6337), which has 55 beds in a converted hotel built during the 1930s coal boom. The hostel has a kitchen, laundry, and bicycle shed, and is wheelchair accessible. Check-in is 9am-11pm. ($15, non-members $19; includes linen.) The hostel also runs a shuttle service ($3 to Tureel) and rents mountain bikes ($4 per hr., $15 per day). There are two campgrounds in Drumheller, **Shady Grove Campground** (823-2576) and **Dinosaur Trailer Park** (823-3291), across from each other on North Dinosaur Trail at the intersection with Hwy. 9. Tent sites are about $15 per night.

The **Field Station** (378-4342) for the Tyrrell Museum is located 48km east of **Brooks** in **Dinosaur Provincial Park.** The station contains a small museum that complements Tyrrell, but the main attraction is the **Badlands Bus Tour,** which runs two to eight times per day between Victoria Day and Thanksgiving. For $4.50 (youth $2.25, children free), be chauffeured into this restricted archaeological hot spot of dinosaur discoveries and fossil finds. Many fossils still lie within the eroding rock; if you make a discovery, however, all you can take home with you are memories, Polaroids, and a coveted "Fossil Finder Certificate," but not the actual goods. The **campground** (378-4342) in the park is shaded from the summer heat, and grassy plots cushion most campsites. Although it stays open year-round, the campground is fully serviced only in summer. (Sites $11, $13 with power. Field Station open Victoria Day-Labour Day daily 8:15am-9pm; call for winter hrs.) For more information, contact the Field Station, Dinosaur Provincial Park, Box 60, Patricia T0J 2K0. To reach the field station from Drumheller, follow Hwy. 56 south for 65km, then take Hwy. 1 about 70km to Brooks. Once in Brooks, go north along the well-marked Hwy. 873 and east along Hwy. 544. Bikers should be especially cautious since much of the route from Brooks is loose gravel.

■■■ LETHBRIDGE

Amid minuscule prairie farming towns, this city of 60,000 is home to a university and a community college, an interesting historical park, and a lush Japanese garden. Lethbridge retains a tempered rustic pride that characterizes the whole region.

PRACTICAL INFORMATION AND ORIENTATION

Visitors Information: Chinook Country Tourist Association, 2805 Scenic Dr. (320-1222), at Scenic and Mayor Magrath Dr. The staff will gladly help you plan a tour of southern Alberta. Maps, brochures and guides to the city and the region. Open mid-May-Labour Day daily 9am-8pm; Labour Day-mid-Oct. daily 9am-5pm; winter Mon.-Sat. 9am-5pm. A newer **Information Centre,** located on Brewery Hill, at 1st Ave. S off Hwy. 3 (320-1223), provides the same maps and pamphlets and features an intoxicating vista of Brewery Gardens, a meticulously landscaped lawn and garden on a reclaimed disposal site for coal ashes. Open May-Labor Day daily 9am-8pm; Labour Day- mid-Oct. Tues.-Sat. 9am-5pm.

Greyhound, 411 5th St. S (327-1551). To: Calgary (5 per day, $25.65) and Edmonton (4 per day, $56.75). Lockers $1. Open daily 7:30am-7pm.

Buses: Lethbridge City Transit operates 9 routes which blanket the city. You can catch the buses at the intersection of 4th Ave. S and 6th St. S. Fare $1.20, senior citizens and ages 6-17 75¢, under 6 free. The "Ride Guide" (free at the info-centre) includes an excellent city map. For information call 320-3885 Mon.-Fri. 7:30am-4:30pm.

Taxi: Lethbridge Cabs, 327-4005. Senior discount 10%. 24 hrs.

Car Rental: Rent-A-Wreck, 2211 2nd Ave. N (328-9484). Must be 21 with credit card. $29 per day with 100km free, 12¢ per additional km. Open Mon.-Fri. 8:30am-5pm, Sat. 8:30am-3pm.

Bike Rental: Alpenland Ski and Cycle, 1202 3rd Ave. S (329-6094). Mountain bikes $25 per day. Open Mon.-Wed. and Sat. 9am-5:30pm, Thurs. and Fri.9am-9pm.

Women's Shelter: Harbour House, 604 8th St. S, run by the YWCA (320-1881; phone staffed 24 hrs.).

Poison Centre: 800-332-1414

Sexual Assault Crisis Line: 327-4545 or 800-552-8023.

Hospital: Lethbridge Regional Hospital, 960 19th St. S (382-6111).

Emergency: 911.

Police: 444 5th Ave. S (general business 327-2210; complaints 328-4444).

Post Office: 704 4th Ave. S (320-7133). Open Mon.-Fri. 8:30am-5pm. **Postal Code:** T1J 0N0.

Area Code: 403.

Lethbridge lies on Hwy. 3, also known as the **Crowsnest Trail.** Highways 4 and 5 enter the city from the south. From Calgary or Edmonton, drive south on Hwy. 2, then travel 50km east on Hwy. 3. Avenues run east-west; streets, north-south.

ACCOMMODATIONS

The reputable motels along Mayor Magrath Dr. run about $45 a night. Stay away from the sleazy, ultra-cheap hotels in the city centre. The most convenient local campground floods when it rains.

Chelsea House, 9 Dalhousie Rd. W, T1K 3X2 (381-1325). From the University, take University Dr. South, turn right on McGill, and right on Dalhousie (or take the #7 bus which stops at the corner of McGill and Dalhousie). Most of the houses in the neighborhood look similar, but one of these houses is not like the others. Wary travelers can enjoy a warm welcome, comfy beds in tastefully decorated rooms, a home-cooked breakfast, and a relaxed, homey atmosphere. You won't do better in Lethbridge. Singles $35. Doubles $50.

University of Lethbridge (329-2793), across the Oldman River from the city but easily reached by buses #7 and #8. In summer, the residence office, #K-100 in Kainai House (in Aperture Park, reached by the southern entrance to the university, or by bus #7), rents rooms to students and others. If you're hungry and unwilling to make the 15-min. trek to the West Village Mall, the University's vending machines in University Hall serve up a mean pizza sub for $2. Check-in 8:30am-11pm. Singles $28. Suites w/kitchen and private bath $34; $49 for two.

YWCA, 604 8th St. S (329-0088). Women traveling alone will feel safe here. Comfortable, homey place with shared kitchenette, TV room, and laundry on each floor. *Women only.* Male visitors restricted to lobby. Singles $22, weekly $80. Shared rooms $20.

Parkside Inn, 1009 Mayor Magrath Dr. (328-2366 or 800-240-1471), next to the Japanese Gardens, Henderson Lake, and the golf course. Take bus #1 from downtown. A cut above your standard budget motel. Large, luxurious rooms with A/C, cable TV, and unlimited local phone calls. Singles $43. Doubles $47.

FOOD

Lethbridge is not exactly a budget smorgasbord. Fast-food joints line Mayor Magrath Dr. and cluster near the city centre. Pick up groceries at the **Garden Market IGA,** 721 3rd Ave. S (320-2603; open Mon.-Fri. 9am-9pm, Sat. 8am-9pm, Sun. 9am-6pm).

Penny Coffee House, 331 5th St. S (320-5282). Every kind of coffee imaginable, excellent sandwiches ($4.45), unbelievable bread. Add a bowl of homemade soup for $1. Reading material glued to the walls ("We're all just pot roasts in the microwave of life") makes for deep philosophical conversation over cappuccino ($1.75). Open Mon.-Sat. 8am-10pm, Sun. 10am-5pm.

Top Pizza and Spaghetti House, 11th St. and 4th Ave. S (327-1952). Top-notch pizza, rock-bottom prices: small $5.60, medium with pepperoni and mushroom $9.20. Struggle with gobs of cheese in the $5.25 baked lasagna special. Open Mon.-Thurs. 11am-1am, Fri.-Sat. 11am-3am, Sun. noon-midnight.

The Duke of Wellington, 132 Columbia Blvd. W (381-1455), standing square in the West Village Mall. Close to the University; far from Flanders. Students, Napoleon, and Blucher dine here infrequently. The cool, dark interior offers a respite from the blazing prairie sun. Burgers and sandwiches $5-7, entrees $8-12. Daily sandwich specials ($5.50) include soup and fries. Open Mon.-Sat. 11am-10pm.

SIGHTS

Fort Whoop-Up (329-0444), located in **Indian Battle Park** on the east bank of the Oldman River, is a replica of the notorious whiskey trading outpost which once stood 10km from present-day Lethbridge. Guides at the **Interpretive Centre** explain the history of the whiskey and fur trades. Europeans introduced the Native Canadians and Americans to makeshift whiskey, a vile mix of pure grain firewater flavored with tobacco, lye, ink, and whatever else was handy at the time, and in the process bilked local tribesmen out of land. Visit the vintage working blacksmith's shop. A generally unbiased slide show is projected on request. (Interpretive Centre open May-Labor Day Mon.-Sat. 10am-6pm, Sun. noon-5pm. $2.50, students and seniors $1, children free.) No public transportation serves this area. Drive or trek 20 minutes down a regional trail which begins at 3rd and Scenic.

Young children and naturalists alike will appreciate the nature trails of **Helen Schuler Coulee Centre and Nature Reserve** (320-3064), a section of Indian Battle Park created to protect local vegetation, prairie animals, and the occasional great horned owl. (Open Sun.-Thurs. 10am-8pm, Fri.-Sat. 10am-6pm; spring and fall Tues.-Sat. 1-4pm, Sun. 1-6pm; winter Tues.-Sun. 1-4pm.) Outside the Reserve sits the **Coal Banks Kiosk,** which outlines the progress of Lethbridge's coal industry from the first excavation in 1881 through the city's incorporation in 1906. The kiosk lies beneath the spectacular **High-Level Bridge,** the longest and highest of its kind in the world. The black steel skeleton opened to trains in 1909 and is still in use today.

The **Nikka Yuko Japanese Garden** (328-3511) in the southeast corner of town in Henderson Park is the city's most trumpeted attraction. Constructed in Japan, then dismantled and shipped to Lethbridge, the main pavilion blends surprisingly well with Albertan placidity. An informative hostess appears at each point of interest to guide you through the garden. (Open mid-May-mid-June and late Aug.-late Sept. Mon.-Fri. 10am-5pm, Sat.-Sun. 9am-5pm; mid-June to late Aug. Mon.-Fri. 10am-8pm, Sat.-Sun. 9am-8pm. $3, seniors and youths $2, children free.) The **rose garden** immediately outside the Japanese garden is an ideal resting or picnicking spot. Take bus #1 to the garden.

■ HEAD-SMASHED-IN BUFFALO JUMP

Head-Smashed-In Buffalo Jump is west of Lethbridge and Fort Macleod on Secondary Rte. 785, about 30km west off Hwy. 2. Coveted as a source of fresh meat, sustenance, tools, and shelter, the buffalo was the victim of one of history's most innovative forms of mass slaughter: the buffalo jump, used by many Plains Native nations. While warriors maneuvered the herd into position, a few extremely brave young men, disguised in coyote skins among the buffalo, would spook hundreds of nearly-blind bison into a fatal stampede over a 10m cliff. Usually highly successful, though occasionally grotesquely fatal for a spooker, this created an instant all-you-can-eat-or-use buffet at the bottom of the cliff. The area earned its name about 150 years ago in memory of a young thrill-seeking warrior who was crushed against the cliff by a pile of buffalo as he watched the event from the base.

Although UNESCO will fine you $50,000 if you forage for souvenirs in the 10m-deep beds of bone, you can learn about buffalo jumps and local Native culture at the **Interpretive Centre** (553-2731), a $10-million, 7-story facility built into the cliff itself. The centre screens reenactments of the fatal plunge (not filmed with live buffalo). Extensive exhibits detail the lifestyle of the Native Canadians and the impact of their contact with Western civilization. 2km of walking trails lead to the top of the cliff and the kill site below. If all this talk of buffalo stirs your appetite, head to the cafe on the second floor, where you can munch Buffalo Burgers ($5) and "Buffalo Chips" ($1.80). (Open daily 9am-8pm; Labor Day-Victoria Day 9am-5pm. $5.50, youths $2.25, under 6 free).

■■■ CROWSNEST PASS

Crowsnest Pass, a convenient stop for travelers driving between Alberta and British Columbia, was the site of multiple cataclysmic mining disasters, frequent shootouts, and train robberies during the wild rum-running days of the 1920s. The grim history of Crowsnest Pass prompts many visitors to overlook its natural beauty; southern Alberta's "Gateway to the Rockies" remains surprisingly tourist-free. Moose, Dall sheep, and bears stroll among the area's stately pines and brilliant mountain wildflowers, and the towns of Crowsnest Pass are minutes away from opportunities for fishing, hiking, and mountain climbing.

ACCOMMODATIONS, CAMPING, AND FOOD

Chinook Lake Campground (Alberta Forest Service, 403-427-3582). Follow Hwy. 3 west from Coleman for 9km, then follow the signs up Allison Creek Rd. Virtually inaccessible to the traveler on foot. 70 sites. $7.50, seniors $5.50.

Lost Lemon Campground (562-2932), just off Hwy. 3A near Blairmore. More commercial than most in the Pass, this campground offers hot showers, a heated pool, laundry facilities, and 64 sites for RVs or tenters. Great fishing in the Crowsnest River. Sites $15, full hookups $17.

Chris and Irvin's Cafe, 7802 17 Ave. (563-3093), in downtown Coleman. This classic diner serves up the Miner's Deluxe ($4.65). Fantastic fries. Open Mon.-Fri. 6am-10pm, Sat. 7am-10pm, Sun. 8am-7pm.

Gramma's Cookie Box (562-2777), on Main Street in Blairmore. Don't leave Blairmore without stopping in for delicious baked goods of every conceivable variety. Try the poppy seed bun (55¢). Stock up on fresh, homemade bread ($7 for 11 loaves; smaller quantities available). Or, have Gramma slap together a sandwich ($3.75-4.25) or sub ($4.50-5.25) for you.

SIGHTS AND ACTIVITIES

Heavy mining turned Crowsnest Pass into a modern Pompeii in 1903, when one mining tunnel too many sent Turtle Mountain tumbling like a giant sandcastle. 90 million cubic feet of stone spilled into the town of Frank, burying 70 people and their houses in less than 2 min. The **Frank Slide Interpretive Centre** on Hwy. 3 details the dramatic collapse of the still-unstable mountain; ask Joey, who works there, about the book he's written on **hiking** in the area.

The Pass offers a host of diversions more cheerful than the mining disaster sites. The **trout fishing** in the **Crowsnest River, Castle River,** and **Oldman River** is reputed to be among the best in all of the Rockies. Crowsnest Pass is also home to the **Gargantua Cave,** the second longest and deepest cave in all of Canada. Known simply as "The Cave," Gargantua is located near the Alberta-British Columbia border at the site of Old Man River's spill into Crowsnest Lake. Drop by the Frank Slide Interpretive Centre (above) for a look at topographic maps and for information on how to safely explore the cave.

If heading west, take Hwy. 3 into the beautiful Kootenay country of British Columbia. If heading north into **Kananaskis** and **Banff,** consider taking the scenic but dusty **Forestry Trunk Rd.,** which meets Hwy. 3 near Coleman. The drive offers spectacular vistas of mountains colored in vibrant hues of green, red, brown, and purple. The road is lined with Forest Service campgrounds such as **Dutch Creek, Old Man River,** and **Cataract Creek** (sites $7.50, seniors $5.50). Call 562-7307 for information. An **Alberta Tourism Information Centre** (563-3888) is located 8km west of Coleman on Hwy. 3 and can provide further information on sights in the area. (Open May 15-Labor Day daily 9am-7pm.)

■■■ WATERTON LAKES NATIONAL PARK

Waterton Lakes National Park is only a fraction of the size of its Montana neighbor, Glacier National Park, but it offers spectacular scenery and activities and is less crowded than Glacier during the peak months of July and August. Part of an "International Peace Park" symbolizing the lasting peace between Canada and the United States, the park provides sanctuary for bears, bighorn sheep, mountain goats, moose, and the grey wolf.

Practical Information The only road from Waterton's park entrance leads 5 mi. south to **Waterton.** On the way, grab a copy of the *Waterton-Glacier Guide* to local services and activities, at the **Waterton Visitor Centre,** 215 Mountain View Rd. (859-2224), 5 mi. south of the park entrance (open mid-May-June daily 10am-5:30pm; July-mid-Sept.; 8am-8:30pm).

If you're on four wheels, drive either the **Akamina Parkway** or the less traveled **Red Rock Canyon Road.** Both leave the main road near Waterton and wind through magnificent mountain scenery, ending at spectacular viewpoints where backcountry trails begin. Rent bikes from **Pat's Texaco and Cycle Rental,** Mount View Rd., Waterton townsite (859-2266; mountain bikes $5.50 per hr. or $27 per day, plus $20 damage deposit; motor scooters cost $13 per hr. or $60 per day).

In a medical **emergency,** call an **ambulance** (859-2636). The **police station** (859-2244) is on Waterton Ave. at Cameron Falls Dr. Waterton's **post office** is on Fountain Ave. at Windflower, in Waterton town (open Mon., Wed., and Fri. 8:30am-4:30pm, Tues. and Thurs. 8:30am-4pm). The **postal code** is T0K 2M0. The **area code** is 403.

Accommodations, Camping, and Food As you enter the park, marvel at the enormous **Prince of Wales Hotel** (859-2231), where you can have tea while maintaining a proper distance from the common townsite. Pitch a tent at one of the park's three campgrounds. **Crandell** (sites $10.50), on Red Rock Canyon Rd., and

WATERTON LAKES NATIONAL PARK

Belly River (sites $7.25), on Chief Mountain Hwy., are cheaper and farther removed from the hustle and bustle characteristic of townsite life. **Backcountry camping** is free but requires a permit from the Visitor Centre (see above) or from **Park Headquarters and Information,** Waterton Lakes National Park, 215 Mount View Rd., Waterton AB T0K 2M0 (859-2224; open Mon.-Fri. 8am-4pm). The backcountry campsites are rarely full, and several, including beautiful **Crandell Lake,** are less than an hour's walk from the trailhead.

If you prefer to stay indoors, head straight for the **Mountain View Bed and Breakfast,** Box 82, Mountain View, AB T0K 1N0 (653-1882), 20km east of the park on Hwy. 5, where you'll enjoy comfy beds, true down-home hospitality, and a hearty breakfast, including homemade bread. Singles are $25, doubles $45. Don Anderson also runs a fishing guide service and can supply you with gear. Don will keep you entertained and educated with stories from more than 50 years of living in the area. If you insist on having a bed in Waterton, drop by the **Waterton Pharmacy,** on Waterton Ave. (859-2335), and ask to sleep in one of the nine rooms of the **Stanley Hotel** (singles or doubles $45; no shower or private bath).

Waterton is sorely lacking in budget restaurants; the most attractive option in the Townsite is **Zum's,** 116B Waterton Ave. (859-2388), which serves good cheeseburgers on a pleasant patio for $4 (open daily 8am-9pm). Stock up on dried meat and granola at the **Rocky Mountain Foodmart** (859-2526) on Windflower Ave. (open daily 8am-10pm; hours vary). Nothing gets cheaper by being trucked out to Waterton. Buy your groceries outside the park for substantial savings.

Outdoors If you've brought only hiking boots to Waterton, you can set out on the **International Lakeside Hike,** which leads along the west shore of Upper Waterton Lake and delivers you to Montana some 5 mi. after leaving the town. The **Crypt Lake Trail,** voted Canada's best hike in 1981, leads past waterfalls in a narrow canyon, and through a 20m natural tunnel bored through the mountainside to arrive after 4 mi. at icy, green Crypt Lake, which straddles the international border. To get to the trailhead, you must take the **water taxi** run by the **Emerald Bay Marina** (859-2632). The boat runs 4 times per day ($9, ages 4-12 $5). The Marina also runs a 2-hr. boat tour of Upper Waterton Lake (mid-May-mid-Sept.; 5 per day July-Aug., fewer outside these months. $15, ages 13-17 $11, ages 4-12 $7).

Anglers alike will appreciate Waterton's **fishing.** Fishing in the park requires a **license** ($6 per 7 days), available from the Park offices, campgrounds, wardens, and service stations in the area. Lake trout cruise the depths of **Cameron** and **Waterton Lakes,** while Northern Pike prowl the weedy channels of **Lower Waterton Lake** and **Maskinouge Lake.** Most of the backcountry lakes and creeks support populations of rainbow and brook trout. Try the nameless creek that spills from Cameron Lake about 200m to the east of the parking lot, or hike 1.5km in to Crandell Lake for plentiful, hungry fish. You can rent a **rowboat** or **paddleboat** at Cameron Lake for $8 per hour, or a canoe for $10 per hour. **Alpine Stables,** 2½ mi. north of the Townsite (859-2462, in winter 908-968-0247), conducts trail rides of varying lengths. (1-hr. ride $12.50, all-day $64.)

In the evening, take in a free **interpretive program** at the **Falls** or **Crandell Theatre.** These interesting programs change yearly and have funky titles, like *Bearying the Myths,* offering straight talk about bears. There are programs daily in summer at 8:30pm; contact the Information Office for schedule information.

Washington

Geographically and culturally, the Cascade Mountains divide Washington. The personality difference between the state's eastern and western halves is long-standing and often polarizing. The division stretches back to the 1840s, when Senator Stephen Douglas, chairman of the Committee on Boundaries, dragged his cane down the spine of the Cascade Range on a map of the Oregon Territory and sensibly urged the committee to make the range the border between any two new states.

Western Washington is lush and green. One of the world's only cold-temperate rainforests thrives in Olympic National Park as Pacific clouds constantly dump rain and snow on the Olympic Peninsula. Massive forests cover much of the land. Low clouds and fog hang over cultured, sophisticated Seattle and industrial Tacoma, coloring the sky grayish-white and usually obscuring the view of Mt. Olympus, Mt. Rainier, Mount St. Helens, and other huge peaks easily seen on clear days. It snows little in winter, but a constant drizzle falls in most months. To "wet-siders," the great majority of the state's population, the term "dry-siders" conjures images of rednecks tearing around in their pickup trucks through wheat farms and dry ranches, yahooing it up in clouds of dust.

Eastern Washington is dry and often brown. Though the Columbia's course and irrigation have made the region productive in wheat, apples and other fruits, and potatoes, few people live in the rural communities spread across the region. Most precipitation falls as winter snow. Though Spokane is a major trade center, "dry-siders" complain of being dominated in the capital, Olympia, by Puget Sound-controlled political interests. To them, a "wet-sider" might be a long-haired urban liberal who has lingered a few hours too long over a few cups too many in one of Seattle's coffeehouses, and pontificating endlessly and arrogantly, in a bored voice, about how those who make a living from the land should be thrown out of work.

Stereotypes are colorful, but unfair to Washingtonians, who are known for an independent frame of mind. Though as a whole usually left-of-center, state voters do not register their political affiliation. The spectrum of elected officials varies more widely than is usual in other parts of the country. Washingtonians also enjoy diverse local food. The palate of western Washington is sated by abundant seafood. Salmon and shellfish are available at the Pike Place Market in Seattle or closer to the source at spots like Dungeness, famous crab, on the Olympic Peninsula. Their meal would be incomplete, however, without supplement from the orchards of Wenatchee and Yakima, producing excellent wine, apples, apricots, and potatoes.

Washington's terrain is all-encompassing: deserts, volcanoes, farms, mountains, lakes, Pacific beaches, and rain forest all lie within state boundaries. You can raft on the Skagit and other wild rivers, sea kayak around the San Juan Islands, and build sand castles on the Strait of Juan de Fuca. Mount Rainier and the Olympic Peninsula have fantastic hiking, while the Cascades are perfect for winter skiing. Seattle, one of the world's cosmopolitan cities, has great food, a fantastic theater scene, and endless things to do. Best of all, Washington is a small, compact state by Western standards, and most destinations are within a day's trip.

This chapter is organized from complete coverage of Seattle, through the large cities of Puget Sound, then north through the Sound to the San Juan Islands. Coverage then crosses the Sound to the beautiful, easily-accessible Olympic Peninsula. After stopping in towns of the southern coast, the Cascade Range is covered from Mount St. Helens and Mt. Rainier in the south to the incredible North Cascades. Spokane, a budget traveler's dream-city, and the rest of Eastern Washington end the chapter.

PRACTICAL INFORMATION

Capital: Olympia.
Visitor Information: Dept. of Economic Development, Tourism Development Division, P.O. Box 42500, Olympia 98504-2500 (206-586-2088 or 206-586-2102, 800-544-1800 for vacation planning guide). Open Mon.-Fri. 9am-5pm. **Washington State Parks and Recreation Commission,** 7150 Cleanwater Lane, KY-11, Olympia 98504 (206-753-5755, May-Aug. in WA 800-562-0990). **Mt. Baker Information:** 206-220-7450. **Olympic National Forest Information:** 800-956-2400.
Fishing and Hunting: Dept. of Fish and Wildlife, 600 Capitol Way N, Olympia 98501-1091 (206-902-2200). Send away for their complete guides to Washington fishing and hunting, licensing fees, and regulations, including the *Sport Fishing Guide, Game Fish Regulations,* and *Hunting Seasons and Rules.*
State Motto: *"Alki,"* a Salishan word meaning "by and by," looking to the future greatness of the state. **Nickname:** Evergreen State. **State Song:** "Washington, My Home." **State Flower:** Coastal Rhododendron. **State Dance:** Square Dance. **State Rock:** Petrified Wood. **State Mollusk:** Geoduck. **State Bird:** Goldfinch. **State Tree:** Western Hemlock.
Area: 68,192 sq. mi.
Emergency: 911.
Time Zone: Pacific (3 hr. behind Eastern).
Postal Abbreviation: WA.
Drinking Age: 21.
Traffic Laws: Mandatory seatbelt law.
Area Codes: 206 in western Washington, 509 in eastern Washington.

GETTING AROUND

Bus remains the cheapest way to travel long distances in Washington. Greyhound (800-231-2222) serves the two main transportation centers, Spokane and Seattle, with other major cities in between. Local buses cover most of the remaining cities, although a few areas (such as the northwestern Olympic Peninsula) have no bus service. There is an **Amtrak train** line from Los Angeles to Vancouver with many stops in western Washington; another line extends from Seattle to Spokane and on to Chicago. Amtrak serves most large cities along these two lines.

Hitchhiking in the San Juans and on the southern half of Whidbey Island is locally accepted if not legal. Hitching on the Olympic Peninsula is less speedy; hitching in other parts of western Washington is neither speedy nor safe. "No hitchhiking permitted" signs are posted on all highways. Opportunities for thumbing decrease as one goes east. *Let's Go* does not recommend hitchhiking as a safe means of transportation. Women traveling alone should *never* hitchhike.

ACCOMMODATIONS AND CAMPING

With the exception of those in Seattle, Washington's **hostels** are generally uncrowded, even in summer. Cheap hotels exist in downtown areas of most large cities, but safety is not assured.

State park **campgrounds** have less expensive, more secluded sites than private campgrounds. They provide better access to trails, rivers, and lakes. Drivers will find state park campgrounds (standard sites $11) more accessible than Department of Natural Resources (DNR) and National Forest campgrounds. Most campgrounds have sites for hikers and bikers for $5.50 with vehicle access, $4 without. The state park system charges $14 for hookups and $4-5 for extra vehicles. Six-minute showers cost 25¢. Some parks allow self-registration; others have rangers register campers at their sites in the evening. Expect long, slow lines if the campground requires registration at the office. Campers who arrive after dusk need not register until a ranger checks the sites in the morning. The gates open at dawn (about 6:30am in summer and 8am October 16-March 31) and close at dusk (about 10pm in summer). Pets must be leashed and accompanied by owners at all times.

Be aware that several state parks, including Belfair, Birch Bay, Fort Flagler, Steamboat Rock, Fort Canby, Twin Harbors/Grayland Beach, Lake Chelan, Pearrygin Lake,

WASHINGTON

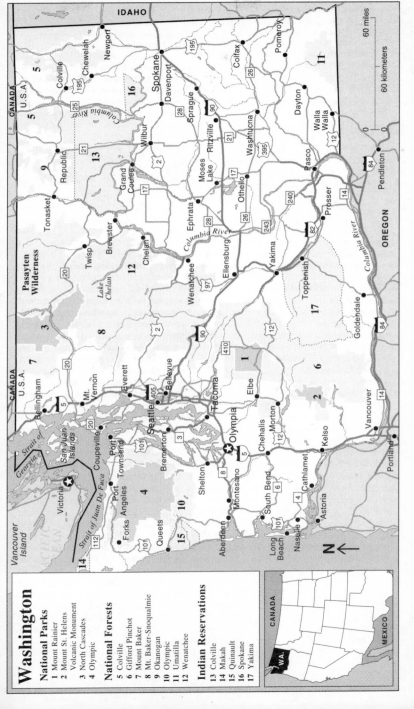

Washington

National Parks
1 Mount Rainier
2 Mount St. Helens
  Volcanic Monument
3 North Cascades
4 Olympic

National Forests
5 Colville
6 Gifford Pinchot
7 Mount Baker
8 Mt. Baker-Snoqualmie
9 Okanogan
10 Olympic
11 Umatilla
12 Wenatchee

Indian Reservations
13 Colville
14 Makah
15 Quinault
16 Spokane
17 Yakima

IDAHO

CANADA · U.S.A.

OREGON

Newport
Chewelah
Colville
Republic
Tonasket
Twisp
Brewster
Chelan
Wenatchee
Ellensburg
Yakima
Toppenish
Goldendale
Vancouver
Portland
Astoria
Cathlamet
Kelso
Naselle
Long Beach
South Bend
Aberdeen
Montesano
Queets
Forks
Port Angeles
Port Townsend
Coupeville
Bremerton
Shelton
Olympia
Chehalis
Morton
Elbe
Tacoma
Seattle
Bellevue
Everett
Mt. Vernon
Bellingham
Victoria
Spokane
Davenport
Sprague
Wilbur
Grand Coulee
Ephrata
Moses Lake
Othello
Ritzville
Washtucna
Pasco
Prosser
Walla Walla
Dayton
Pomeroy
Colfax
Pendleton
Nahcotta

Columbia River
Lake Chelan
Pasayten Wilderness
San Juan Islands
Vancouver Island
Strait of Georgia
Strait of Juan De Fuca
PACIFIC OCEAN

60 miles
60 kilometers

CANADA
WA.
MEXICO

and Moran, accept reservations for Memorial Day through Labor Day and may be filled up weeks in advance, especially during July and August. Reservations can be made in January, and must be made two weeks in advance.

Drivers can enjoy the solitude of the many National Forest and DNR sites. National Forest campsites cost from nothing up to $8 (most cost about $6). Call MIS-TIX at 800-365-2267 to reserve campsites in the national forests or national parks. National Park campgrounds accessible by road cost $8 on average and are generally in the best settings. Olympic National Park has some free campgrounds accessible by car. Campgrounds that can be reached only by trail are usually free.

■■■ SEATTLE

It seems everybody wants to come to Seattle, the Northwest's largest and most cosmopolitan city. Is it for the setting? Seattle is an isthmus, nearly surrounded by water, with mountain ranges to the east and west. Every hilltop in Seattle offers an impressive view of Puget Sound, Lake Washington, Mt. Olympus, Mt. Baker, Mt. Rainier, or Mt. St. Helens. Residents spend as much time as possible outdoors, biking in the parks or hiking, climbing, or skiing in the nearby Cascades and Olympic Peninsula. Incredible, sublime outdoor experiences are within a day's drive.

Or is it for the world-class theater, art, and music scene? The *New York Times* often complains that there is more good theater in Seattle than on Broadway (backhanded compliments are still compliments). The local theater is not to be missed; both first-run and creative experimental works mark the ever-changing Seattle theater scene as a center for semi-professional talent. Tickets are cheap, and theater options are plentiful. Opera performances consistently sell out. Musically, however, Seattle has *not* sold out: the same city that produced Jimi Hendrix and other rock greats has recently dominated the small-market rock scene with famous bands like Pearl Jam, the Screaming Trees, Nirvana, and Soundgarden, and many others, all noted for their artistic integrity as much as their unique sound. The alternative music scene is as lively as it was before the national mass media tripped and fell over it. Local bands keep pushing the envelope, and Seattle remains a great place to find a cool club and mosh with sheer abandon to good, fresh, young, loud rock music.

Seattle's many small newspapers and publications offer continual updates on artistic life. Read them for a full appreciation of what the city has to offer. Don't forget to eat out often, either, and sample the great food from any of the over 40 small, inexpensive restaurants listed all over the city. Amid the seafood of Pike Place, the bakeries and coffeeshops citywide, and the East Asian food in the International District, you'll neither go hungry no go broke. Great food and interesting clubs and theaters abound in the U-District near the University of Washington. Whatever you do, don't be dismayed by the drizzle, and bag the umbrella. Although the clouds may seem almost as permanent as the mountains they mask, the temperature is constant, too, hovering between 40°F and 70°F year-round. Even in winter, light drizzle is standard; it rarely snows. Sunny days, however, are far from rare. Occasionally the skies clear and "the mountain is out," and Seattlites run to the country.

PRACTICAL INFORMATION

Visitors Information: Seattle-King County Visitors Bureau, 8th and Pike St. (461-5840; fax 461-5855), on the 1st floor of the convention center. **Maps,** brochures, newspapers, and transit and ferry schedules. Helpful staff. Open Mon.-Fri. 8:30am-5pm; summer Mon.-Fri. 8:30am-5pm, Sat.-Sun. 10am-4pm. The **airport branch** (433-5218) fields questions from 5 to 7:30pm.

Parks Information: Seattle Parks and Recreation Department, 5201 Green Lake Way N, Seattle 98103 (684-4075). Open Mon.-Fri. 8am-6pm. **National Park Service, Pacific Northwest Region,** 915 2nd Ave. #442 (220-7450). Open Mon.-Fri. 8am-4:30pm.

Currency Exchange: Thomas Cook Foreign Exchange, 906 3rd Ave. (623-6203). Open Mon.-Fri. 9am-5pm. **Mutual of Omaha** (243-1231) behind the Continental Airlines ticket counter at **Sea-Tac Airport.** Open daily 6am-9:30pm.

Airport: Seattle-Tacoma International (Sea-Tac) (433-5217 for general information) on Federal Way, south of Seattle proper. **Sea-Tac Visitors Information Center** (433-5218), in the central baggage claim area, helps with basic transportation concerns for arriving visitors. Open daily 9:30am-7:30pm. Foreign visitors should contact **Operation Welcome** (433-5367), in the customs and immigration areas, where staff members answer questions on customs, immigration, and foreign language services in just about every language.

Amtrak (800-872-7245), King Street Station, 3rd and Jackson St. Trains daily to: Portland (3 per day; $23); Tacoma (3 per day; $8); Spokane (1 per day; $67); San Francisco (1 per day; $153, $88 special available). Station open daily 6am-5:30pm; ticket office open daily 6:30am-5pm.

Greyhound (800-231-2222 or 628-5526), 8th Ave. and Stewart St. Buses daily to: Sea-Tac Airport (2 per day; $3.75); Spokane (3 per day; $26); Vancouver, BC (4 per day; $22); Portland (11 per day; $19); Tacoma (8 per day; $5.75). Ticket office open daily 5:30am-9pm and midnight-2am.

Green Tortoise Bus Service (324-7433 or 800-227-4766); buses leave from 9th Ave. and Stewart St. Departs Thurs. and Sun. only, at 8am. To Portland, OR ($15); Eugene, OR ($25); Berkeley, CA ($52); San Francisco, CA ($52); and Los Angeles, CA ($89, Thurs. only). Reservations required, should be 5 days in advance.

Metro Transit: Customer Assistance Office, 821 2nd Ave. (24-hr. information 553-3000; TTD service 684-1739), in the Exchange Building downtown. Open Mon.-Fri. 8am-5pm. Fares are based on a 2-zone system. Zone 1 includes everything within the city limits ($1.10 during peak hours, 85¢ off-peak); Zone 2 comprises anything outside the city limits ($1.45 peak, $1.10 off-peak). Ages 5-18 75¢. With reduced fare permits ($1), over 64 and disabled pay 25¢ to go anywhere at any time. Peak hours in both zones are generally Mon.-Fri. 6-9am and 3-6pm. Exact fare required. Transfers valid for 2 hrs. and for Waterfront Streetcars. Weekend all-day passes $1.70. Ride free 4am-9pm within the **"Magic Carpet"** area downtown, bordered by Jackson St. on the south, 6th Ave. and I-5 on the east, Battery St. on the north, and the waterfront on the west. See Getting Around, below, for more information.

Ferries: Washington State Ferries, Colman Dock, Pier 52, downtown (see page 43 for complete **schedule and fare information**). Service from downtown to: Bainbridge Island (**A**), Bremerton in the Kitsap Peninsula (**B and N**), and Vashon Island (**G**). Service from Fauntleroy in West Seattle to: Southworth in the Kitsap Peninsula (**H**) and Vashon Island (**D**). Again, see page 43. Ferries leave daily, and frequently, about 5am-about 2am. A new ferry service is available directly from Seattle to Victoria. The **Victoria Line** leaves pier 48 daily at 1pm, and will have you in Victoria in 4½-5 hrs. This is the only auto ferry service available from Seattle to Victoria. One way: passengers CDN$25, car and driver CDN$49; round-trip passengers CDN$45, car and driver CDN$90. Under 12 ½-price.

Car Rental: A-19.95-Rent-A-Car, 804 N 145th St. (365-1995). $20 per day ($25 if under 21); 10¢ per mi. after 100 mi. Free delivery. Drivers under 21 welcome, but must have verifiable auto insurance. Credit card required. The cheapest is also worth a try: **Auto Driveaway** (235-0880) hires people to drive their cars to various locations across the U.S.

Ride Board: 1st floor of the Husky Union Building (the HUB), behind Suzallo Library on the University of Washington main campus. Matches cars and riders for destinations across the country. Check the bulletin board at the hostel as well.

Bike Rentals: The Bicycle Center, 4529 Sand Point Way (523-8300). $3 per hr. (2-hr. min.), $15 per day. Credit card or license required as deposit. Open Mon.-Fri. 10am-6pm, Sat. 9am-6pm, Sun. 10am-5pm. **Alki Bikes,** 2611 California Ave. (938-3322). Mountain bikes $9 per hr., $20 per 24 hrs. Credit card or license required as deposit. Open Mon.-Fri. 10am-7pm, Sat. noon-6pm, Sun. noon-5pm; winter Mon.-Fri. 3-7pm.

Seattle Public Library: 1000 4th Ave. (386-4636 for quick info.). Free newsletter with information on library and local free lectures, films and other programs. Free

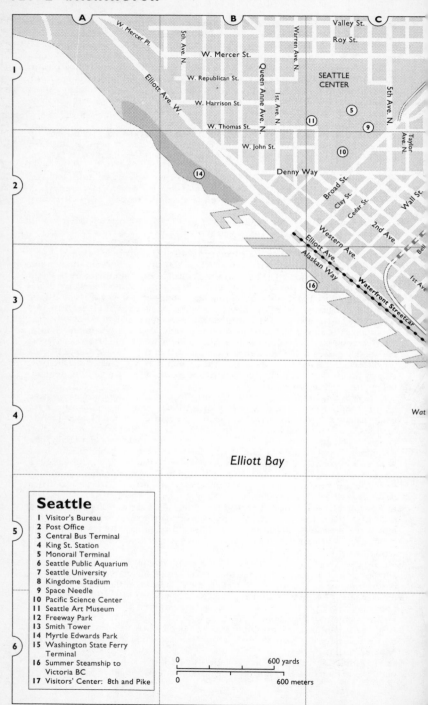

Seattle

1 Visitor's Bureau
2 Post Office
3 Central Bus Terminal
4 King St. Station
5 Monorail Terminal
6 Seattle Public Aquarium
7 Seattle University
8 Kingdome Stadium
9 Space Needle
10 Pacific Science Center
11 Seattle Art Museum
12 Freeway Park
13 Smith Tower
14 Myrtle Edwards Park
15 Washington State Ferry
   Terminal
16 Summer Steamship to
   Victoria BC
17 Visitors' Center: 8th and Pike

tours leave the information desk Wed. noon and Sat. 2pm. Open Mon.-Thurs. 9am-9pm, Fri.-Sat. 9am-6pm; Sept.-May also Sun. 1-5pm.

Ticket Agencies: Ticket Master, in every Tower Records store; hours depend on the store. **Ticket/Ticket,** 401 Broadway E (324-2744), on the 2nd floor of the Broadway Market. ½-price day-of-show tickets to local theater, music, concerts, comedy, and dance performances. Cash only. Open Tues.-Sun. 10am-7pm. Also in the Pike Place Market, open Tues.-Sun. noon-6pm.

Laundromat: Queen Anne Maytag Center, Queen Anne N and W Boston (282-6645). On the top of Queen Anne hill, north of downtown. Attended facility. Take bus #3, 4, or 13. Wash Tues.-Thurs. 75¢, Fri.-Mon. $1; 17-min. dry 25¢. Open daily 7:30am-10:30pm. **Downtown-St. Regis,** 116 Stewart St., attached to the St. Regis Hotel (see Accommodations). A somewhat scary area; bring a friend and watch your laundry. Wash $1.25, dry 75¢. 24 hrs.

Crisis Clinic: 461-3222. 24 hrs. **Seattle Rape Relief:** 1905 S Jackson St., #102 (632-7273). Crisis counseling, advocacy, and prevention training. 24 hrs.

University of Washington Women's Information Center: (685-1090), Cunningham Hall, in the main campus. Monthly calendar, networking, and referral for women's groups throughout the Seattle area. Open Mon.-Fri. 9am-5pm.

Senior Information and Assistance: 1601 2nd Ave., #800 (448-3110). Open Mon.-Fri. 9am-5pm.

Travelers' Aid: 909 4th Ave., #630 (461-3888), at Marion, in the YMCA. Free services for stranded travelers who have lost wallets, or their marbles. Open Mon. and Wed.-Fri. 9am-4:45pm, Tues. 9am-9pm, Sat. 9am-1pm.

Operation Nightwatch: 91 Wall St. (448-8804). Emergency aid in the downtown area. Street ministry operates nightly 10pm-1am. Answering machine 24 hrs.

International District Emergency Center: 623-3321. Medics with multilingual assistance available. 24 hrs.

Poison Information: 526-2121. 24 hrs.

AIDS Hotline: Open Mon.-Fri. 8am-5pm.

Gay Counseling: 200 W Mercer, #300 (282-9307). Open Mon.-Fri. noon-9pm.

Lesbian Resource Center: 1208 E Pine (322-3953). Support groups, drop-in center, lending library, workshops, and job referrals. Open Mon.-Fri. 2-7pm.

Health Care: Aradia Women's Health Center, 1300 Spring St. (323-9388). Appointments are necessary and should be made 1 wk. in advance; urgent cases are given priority. Staff will refer elsewhere when booked. Open Mon.-Fri. 10am-6pm. **Chec Medical Center,** 1151 Denny Way (682-7418). Walk-in; appointments helpful but unnecessary.

Emergency: 911. **Police Department,** 610 3rd Ave. (625-5011).

Post Office: (442-6340), Union St. and 3rd Ave. downtown. Open Mon.-Fri. 8am-5:30pm. **General Delivery ZIP Code:** 98101.

Area Code: 206.

GETTING THERE AND GETTING AROUND

Seattle is a long, skinny city, stretched north to south on an isthmus between **Puget Sound** to the west and **Lake Washington** to the east and linked by locks and canals. Downtown, avenues run northwest to southeast and streets southwest to northeast. Outside downtown, everything is simplified: avenues run north-south and streets east-west, with few exceptions. The city is split into many **quadrants:** 1000 1st Ave. NW is a long walk from 1000 1st Ave. S. The designation system takes getting used to, but is logical and extremely helpful.

The city is easily accessible by **car** via **I-5,** running north-south through the city, east of downtown; and by **I-90** from the east, ending at I-5 southeast of downtown. From I-5, get to downtown by taking any of the exits from James to Stewart St. (including **Pioneer Square, Pike Place Market,** and the **waterfront).** Take the Mercer St./Fairview Ave. exit to the **Seattle Center.** The Denny Way exit leads to **Capitol Hill,** and farther north, the 45th St. exit will take you to the **University District.** Getting onto the freeway from downtown is a challenge. The freeway is always visible; just drive around until you spot a blue I-5 sign. **Rte. 99** skirts the western side of downtown, offering some of the best views from the **Alaskan Way Viaduct.** Rte. 99

is less crowded than I-5, and is often the better choice when driving downtown, to Queen Anne, or generally to the northwestern part of the city.

Transportation options from the mammoth **Seattle-Tacoma International Airport (Sea-Tac)** abound. **Gray Line** coaches (626-5208) whisk you to and from downtown ($7 one way, $12 round-trip). **Metro buses** #174 and #194 are cheaper and run daily every half-hour from 6am to 1am. A taxi ride from the airport to downtown Seattle costs about $25.

Parking downtown is expensive; traffic, steep hills, and one-way streets make driving frustrating. A good strategy to get downtown quickly and save yourself money and trouble is to park at the **Seattle Center,** near the Space Needle, where parking is cheap and plentiful, then to take the **monorail** to the convenient **Westlake Center** downtown and walk. Seattle's **Metro Transit** bus system provides complete, reliable, and inexpensive service throughout the city and suburbs (see Practical Information for fares). The hassles of downtown traffic jams and expensive parking can be avoided by taking the bus. Buses operate daily from 6am to 1 or 2am, and a few buses offer "night owl service" from 1:30 to 4:30am. Express buses do not run on weekends. All passes, timetables, and a free, comprehensive **map,** are available from the **Metro Transit Customer Assistance Office** (see Practical Information). Timetables and maps are also available at public libraries, the hostel, the University Book Store, the visitors bureau, and on the buses.

Routes and buses equipped with lifts are marked by blue **wheelchair accessibility** signs. **Bike racks** holding two bikes are attached to the buses that run from downtown to Bellevue and Kirkland. Not all buses are equipped with racks, and bikes can be loaded only at designated stops; check out Metro's *Bike & Ride* pamphlet, available at the visitors center and hostel (see above, and below).

Metro extends into Seattle's outskirts, covering King County east to North Bend and Carnation, south to Enumclaw, and north to Snohomish County, where Metro bus #6 hooks up with **Community Transit.** This line runs to Everett, Stanwood, and well into the Cascades. Metro bus #174 connects in Federal Way to Tacoma's Pierce County System.

PUBLICATIONS

The city's major newspaper is the *Seattle Times* (464-2121). The paper's "Tempo" section, published on Fridays, lists upcoming events. The *Seattle Weekly* is the popular alternative to the dominant daily; it pumps out fresh opinions every Wednesday. *Arts Focus,* a free magazine available at most bookstores, carries information on the performing arts, and *Seattle Arts* published by the Seattle Arts Commission is especially good for events in the visual arts. Both are published monthly. The *Rocket,* the *Wire,* and *Hype* are sources of information on the music scene. *Seattle Gay News* is an established weekly catering to the gay community. The University of Washington puts out two papers that also list upcoming events and give a sense of Washingtonian attitudes: *University Herald* and *The Daily U of WA General.* Various suburban publications include the *Belltown/Brainfever Dispatch,* the *Capitol Hill Times,* and the *Ballard News Tribune;* though somewhat harder to find, most of these can be found in cafes and in bookstores. Many publications are free: for an excellent listing of upcoming events at the local art galleries, grab a copy of the *Pike Place Market News.* Available in many eating establishments in the marketplace area, this complimentary paper also includes a handy **map** of the market, a calendar of its upcoming events, and phone numbers of all Pike Place establishments. The *International Examiner* provides a free weekly news update of the local Asian-American community, and covers restaurants and upcoming community events. *Eastside Week* is a large, free events paper that offers everything from theatre, cinema, and restaurant reviews to esoteric want ads and local politics.

ACCOMMODATIONS

The **Seattle International Hostel** is the best option for the budget traveler staying downtown. For those tired of the urban scene, the **Vashon Island Hostel** (sometimes called "Seattle B") is ideal (see page 343). **Pacific Bed and Breakfast,** 701 NW 60th St., Seattle 98107 (784-0539), can set you up with a single room in a B&B in the $40-70 range (open Mon.-Fri. 9am-5pm).

Downtown

Seattle International Hostel (HI/AYH), 84 Union St. (622-5443), at Western Ave. Take Metro #174, 184, or 194 from the airport. 139 beds, common kitchen open 24 hrs., immaculate facilities, modern amenities, and a friendly, knowledgeable staff. Check-in may be tedious, but security is tight. Convenient location; alluring crowd. Loads of information about Seattle in the library and on the brochure racks. The view of the bay will mollify your temper when the traffic gets too loud. Hostel is always full in summer, so make reservations (participates in international reservations system). In summer, there is a supplemental hostel for overflow. Offers discount tickets for Aquarium and Omnidome. Sleep sacks required (linen rental $2). 5-day max. stay in summer. Front desk open 7am-2am. Checkout 10:30am. Room closeout 11am-2pm, but living areas open at all times. No curfew. $14, nonmembers $17. Members receive priority in summer.

YMCA, 909 4th Ave. (382-5000), near the Madison St. intersection. Men and women welcome; must be over 18. Small, well-kept rooms. Good location; tight security, staffed security desk. TV lounge on each floor, laundry facilities, and swimming pool and fitness facilities. Bring your own bedding for the bunk-room and your own lock for lockers. Check-out by noon. No curfew. HI/AYH members: bunk in a 4-person room $18, singles $30, doubles $34. Nonmembers: Singles $34, with bath $46. Doubles $43.50, with bath $51.

YWCA, 1118 5th Ave. (461-4888), near the YMCA. Take any 4th Ave. bus to Seneca St. *Women only, ages under 18 require advance arrangement.* Great security; front desk open and staffed 24 hrs. Good, central location. Shared kitchen facilities. 2-week max. stay. No curfew. Singles $31, with bath $36. Doubles $42, with bath $48. Weekly: singles $186, with bath $216. Health center use $5. Key deposit $2.

Green Tortoise Backpacker's Guesthouse, 715 2nd Ave. N (322-1222; fax 282-9075), on the southern slope of Queen Anne Hill, 3 blocks from the Space Needle. 40 beds in 11 rooms and a common kitchen with adjoining deck and garden. Library/reading room with view of the city. No curfew. Quiet hours after 11pm. Laundry $1. Rooms $11. Shared doubles $20. Private doubles $30. Call for pickup.

Commodore Hotel, 2013 2nd Ave. (448-8868), at Virginia. Clean, feels safe. Singles $42, with bath $47, with 2 beds and bath $54.

Moore Motel, 1926 2nd Ave. (448-4851 and 448-4852), at Virginia. Next to the historic Moore Theater. Big rooms include 2 beds, bath, and TV. Singles $34. Doubles $39. For those turned away from the full hostel, and with membership, singles $30, doubles $35.

St. Regis Hotel, 116 Stewart St. (448-6366), 2 blocks from the Pike Place Market. Pleasant management and good security, but the rooms are a little bare. No visitors after 10pm. Laundromat on the first floor. Singles $33, with bath $42. Doubles $42, with bath $49. $1 key deposit.

Other Neighborhoods

The College Inn, 4000 University Way NE (633-4441). European-style B&B in the University District. Antiques and individual wash basins in every room. The rooms facing 40th are the quietest. All rooms have shared shower and bath, but a cozy diner-style breakfast is included, served in a finely refurbished attic. Singles from $63. Doubles $63-75.

Park Plaza Motel, 4401 Aurora Ave. N (632-2101). Just north of the Aurora bridge; take bus #6 to 46th Ave. or #5 to 43rd and Fremont. Friendly and surprisingly quiet. Unfortunately, the external orange decor is replicated on the inside. Bare rooms and halls. Singles $30. Doubles from $32.

Nites Inn, 11746 Aurora Ave. N (365-3216). Take bus #6. One of the many motels that line Aurora north of 85th St., but the rooms are larger than most. Cable TV and free local calls. Singles $38. Doubles $42.

Motel 6, 18900 47th Ave. S (241-1648), exit 152 off I-5. Take bus #194. Near Sea-Tac Airport, but inconvenient to downtown. Crowded; make reservations. Singles $30. Doubles $36.

FOOD

If fresh seafood, sticky pastries, and strong, exotic coffee is your idea of a great meal, you'll never want to leave Seattle. The best fish, produce, and baked goods can be purchased from various vendors in **Pike Place Market** (see below for more information). If you have the facilities and faculties to cook for yourself, you can buy fish right off the boats at **Fisherman's Wharf,** at NW 54th St. and 30th Ave. NW in Ballard, along the route of bus #43. The wharf is usually open from 8am to 3 or 4pm. Or visit one of Seattle's active **food coops,** such as those at 6518 Fremont Ave. N (in Green Lake) and at 6504 20th NE (in the Ravenna District north of the university). Also in Ravenna is a fine produce stand, **Rising Sun Farms and Produce,** 6505 15th Ave. NE (524-9741; open daily 8am-8pm).

Seattlites are serious about coffee. **Uptown Espresso,** 525 Queen Anne Ave. N (281-8669) at the base of Queen Anne, has a well-established reputation. Most Seattlites develop strict loyalties to several obscure street corner carts for their espresso; brand-wise, the best bet is the locally roasted **Starbucks** or **SBC** (Stuart Bros. or "Seattle's Best"). Both have many shops downtown.

One final word for those culinary loonies with thin wallets and a high tolerance for greasy pizza: **Godfather's Pizza** has an all-you-can-eat lunch special for $3.75. They have locations throughout the city, including one at 1414 Alaskan Way (621-7835), downtown.

Pike Place Market

Farmers have been selling their own produce here since 1907, when angry Seattle citizens demanded the elimination of the middle-merchant. A nasty fire in 1941, the World War II draft, and the internment of Japanese-Americans almost did away with the market, but in the last 15 years a rehabilitation drive has restored it. Lunatic fish-and produce-mongers bellow at customers and at each other while street performers offer their own entertainment to the crowds. The market's restaurants allow you to escape the crowded aisles for space at a crowded table. Farmers and fishmongers are the mainstays of the market, although public personalities like Shawn Kemp of basketball's Seattle Supersonics occasionally sell fish to raise money for charity.

The best time to visit the market is between 7 and 9am, when the fish are yawning and the fruit is freshest. In summer (10am-5pm) tourists and locals flood the market, providing excellent people-watching opportunities in a thick crowd. You might want to show up late and hunt around for end-of-the-day specials on produce, or linger at **86 Pike Place** on the corner (you can't miss it), where they will sing your order in chorus and fling the immense fish among themselves (but they'll *hand* it to you). The monthly *Pike Place Market News,* available free in the market, has a **map** and the low-down on the market's latest events, new merchants, and old-timers. An information booth in front of the bakery in the main market can answer your questions. (Table open Mon.-Sat. 10am-6pm, Sun. noon-6pm. Market open Mon.-Sat. 6:30am-6pm, Sun. 6:30am-5pm.)

Soundview Cafe (623-5700), on the mezzanine level in the Main Arcade just to the left of the largest fish stall. This wholesome self-serve sandwich-and-salad bar offers fresh food, a spectacular view of Elliott Bay, and occasional poetry readings. Get a View Special (eggs and potatoes) for $2.90, egg salad for $3.25, or bring a brown-bag lunch: the cafe offers public seating. Open daily 7am-5pm.

Lowell's Restaurant, 1519 Pike Pl. (622-2036). Great view of the water, at least for those tall enough to see over the top of one of their immense seafood specials ($7). Head to the upper dining room to avoid the bustle of the market and the harried servers. Open Mon.-Fri. 7am-5pm, Sat. 7am-5:30pm, Sun. 8am-3pm.

Three Girls Bakery (622-1045), at Post and Pike Pl. Order to go or sit in the cafe. The rows of bread and pastry will make you drool, not to mention the fresh-bread aroma. Mammoth apple fritters (95¢). Open Mon.-Sat. 7am-6pm, Sun. 8am-6pm.

Copacabana, 1520½ Pike Pl. (622-6359). Music and passion are always in fashion. The outdoor tables are probably the best place in the market to watch the harried crowds go by. Try the Bolivian *salteña* ($3), a meat and raisin pastry and the house specialty. Open Mon.-Sat. 11:30am-9pm, Sun. 11:30am-5pm.

Athenian Inn, 1517 Pike Pl. (622-4881). Great Greek food. Try the Athenian steak ($6), the spinach salad ($7), or any other item off the huge menu. Open Mon.-Sat. 10am-7pm.

Emmett Watson's Oyster Bar, 1916 Pike Pl. (448-7721). Watson is a local newspaper columnist and California-basher who founded the Lesser Seattle movement in order to dissuade tourists and new residents with the candid motto, "Keep the Bastards Out." The restaurant isn't as interesting as the wise old huckster himself, but the patio is pretty and the oysters plentiful. You haven't really experienced a vitamin E high until you've tried the Oyster Bar Special ($5.65). Open Mon.-Sat. 11:30am-9pm, Sun. 11:30am-6pm.

Delcambre's Ragin' Cajun, 1523 1st Ave. (624-2598). Good food, tremendous portions. Open Tues.-Sat. 11am-3pm and 5-9pm.

International District

Along King and Jackson St., between 5th and 8th Ave., Seattle's International District crowds together immigrants, some of them excellent chefs, from China, Japan, the Philippines, and Southeast Asia. Fierce competition keeps prices low and quality high. Any choice here will probably be a good one, as three out of any four restaurants have been named (at one time or another) the best in town by a *Seattle Times* reviewer. Don't shy away from a shabby exterior; the quality of the facade is often inversely proportional to the quality of the food. **Uwajimaya,** 519 6th Ave. S (624-6248), is the largest East Asian retail store in the Pacific Northwest. A huge selection of Japanese staples, fresh seafood (often still swimming), a wide variety of dried and/or instant foods (great for camping), a sushi bar, and a bakery make this Seattle institution a must-visit. (Also sells toys, books, furniture, clothes, and jewelry. Open daily 9am-8pm. Take bus #7 or #14.)

Tai Tung, 655 S King St. (622-7372). A Chinese diner. The busiest hours at Tai Tung are 1-3am, when the munchies take hold of university students. Waiters here rise to the occasion; they're likely to learn your name by the second night you're in. 10-page menu taped up around the dining room, with entrees $7-8. Open Mon.-Sat. 10am-3:30am, Sun. 10am-1:30am.

Ho Ho Seafood Restaurant, 653 S Weller St. (382-9671). Casually elegant. Generous portions. Great seafood. Check the blackboard list for daily specials. Entrees $7-11.50. Open Sun.-Thurs. 11am-1am, Fri.-Sat. 11am-3am.

House of Hong Restaurant, 409 8th Ave. S (622-7997), at Jackson. The most popular *dim sum* in town at $1.80-3 per dish; served daily 11am-3pm. Open Mon.-Thurs. 11am-10pm, Fri. 11am-midnight, Sat. 10:30am-midnight, Sun. 10:30am-10pm. Reservations and proper dress (not coat and tie, but close) recommended. Cocktail lounge Mon.-Fri. 11am-midnight, Sat. 10:30am-midnight, Sun. 10:30am-11pm.

Phnom Penh Noodle Soup House, 414 Maynard Ave. S (682-5690). Phnomenal Cambodian cuisine. Head to the tiny upstairs dining room for a view of the park and a large bowl of noodles. Try the Phnom Penh Noodle Special; some people come here weekly and never order anything else (well, there are only six items on the menu). Everything $3.90. Open Mon.-Tues. and Thurs.-Sun. 8:30am-6pm.

Viet My Restaurant, 129 Prefontaine Pl. S (382-9923), near 4th and Washington. Hard to find, but the consistently delicious Vietnamese food at great prices is worth the search. Try *bo la lot* (beef in rice pancakes, $3.50) or shrimp curry ($4.25). Avoid the lunch rush. Open Mon.-Sat. 11am-9pm.

Chau's Chinese Seafood Restaurant, 310 4th St. (621-0006), at 4th and Jackson. The best in late night seafood, though not in decor. Try the geoduck with ginger sauce ($6.50). Open Mon.-Thurs. 11am-midnight, Fri. 11am-1am, Sat. 4pm-1am, Sun. 4-11pm.

Mon Hei Bakery, 669 Main St. Some of the best finds in the international district can be had in tiny bakeries like this. Pastries (from 35¢) and gloriously sweet rice cakes (50¢). Open daily 11am-8pm.

Pioneer Square and the Waterfront

Budget eaters beware of Pioneer Square. The Waterfront lures tourists with wharf-side fare that's more suited to be thrown to the seagulls. The best option is a picnic in Occidental Park or Waterfall Park.

Panchitos, 704 1st Ave. (343-9567). This Mexican cafeteria may lack table service and big prices, but nothing is lacking in the food. Enchiladas ($2.50), burritos with all the fixings ($4). Open daily 11:30am-8pm.

Seattle Bagel Bakery, 1302 Western Ave. (624-2187). Two blocks in from the waterfront, 1 block west of Pier 56. The best buy in Seattle. Yummy, fat bagels (40¢) that could take over Manhattan. Also bagel sandwiches (from $3.25). Open Mon.-Thurs. 7am-5:30pm, Fri. 7am-6:30pm, Sat.-Sun. 8:30am-5:30pm.

Ivar's Fish Bar, Pier 54 (624-6852), on the waterfront. One of a string of seafood restaurants founded by and named for the late Seattle celebrity and shipping magnate Ivar Haglund. For years Ivar donated the fireworks to Seattle's 4th of July celebration. Fish and chips ($4.25), or definitive Seattle clam chowder ($1.40). Dine with the gulls and pigeons in covered booths outside. Open daily 11am-10pm.

Trattoria Mitchelli, 84 Yesler Way (623-3883), at Yesler and Western. A cozy pizza place that evolves into an elegant late-night cafe as the sun sets. Also relaxing brunch spot (Sun. until 3pm). Open Mon. 7am-11pm, Tues.-Fri. 7am-4pm, Sat. 8am-4am, Sun. 8am-11pm.

Grand Central Bakery, 214 1st Ave. S (622-3644). Walk-up cafe and deli in the Grand Central Arcade. Buy a loaf of bread ($2.90) or Irish soda bread (85¢). Come early. These famous pastries sell out fast. Eat at outdoor tables in the attractive antique arcade or just outside in Occidental Park. Open Mon. 7am-11pm, Tues.-Thurs. 7am-4am, Fri.-Sat. 8am-4am, Sun. 8am-11pm.

Capitol Hill

With dance steps paved into the sidewalks, Capitol Hill offers a chance to sashay away from tourist traps to the imaginative shops, elegant clubs, and espresso houses of **Broadway Avenue.** The eclectic array of restaurants that lines the avenue provides opportunities for patrons to watch the parade of people walking by. The food is some of the best in the city. **15th Street,** also on the hill, is more sedate. Bus #7 runs along Broadway; #10, along 15th St. Unless taking-out, ignore the metered parking on Broadway and head east for the free angle spots behind the reservoir at Broadway Field.

Dick's, 115 Broadway Ave. E (323-1300). A Broadway institution, recently made famous in Sir Mix-A-Lot's rap "Broadway." This local drive-in burger chain also has locations in Wallingford, Queen Anne, and Lake City. Try Dick's Deluxe Burger ($1.60), and a good shake ($1.10). Open daily 10:30am-2am.

Hamburger Mary's, 401 Broadway E (325-6565), in the ritzy Broadway Market. Rockin' and racin' with the Broadway Ave. step, this branch of Portland's famous H.M. is a hot-spot for the gay community. Nightly specials offer less meaty options than the obvious fare. Hamburgers around $5. Entrees under $12. Open Mon.-Fri. 10am-2am, Sat.-Sun. 9am-2am.

Cafe Paradiso, 1005 E Pike (322-6960). A bit off the geographical beaten-path, this proud-to-be-alternative cafe gives you your RDA of both caffeine and counter-culture, but not much in the way of food. Muffin and croissant fare. Open Mon.-Sat. 7am-1am, Sun. 9am-1am.

Deluxe Bar and Grill, 625 Broadway E (324-9697). An indoor/outdoor joint where you can enjoy great breakfasts for under $6. Watch out for the ravenous "potato crowd." The humongous spuds have been a favorite here since the 1930s. Don't try to get food here after midnight. Grill open Sun.-Thurs. 11am-midnight, Fri. 11am-1am, Sat. 10am-1am. Bar open Mon.-Wed. 10am-1am, Thurs.-Fri. 10am-2am, Sat.-Sun. 9am-2am.

Rocket Pizza, 612 Broadway E (329-4405). A slice here will set you back $1.35, but the prime location for people-watching makes this a popular hang-out within and without. Open Mon.-Sat. 10am-11:30pm, Sun. 10am-10pm.

The Gravity Bar, 415 Broadway E (325-7186), also in the Broadway Market. New-ton's Own fruit and vegetable juices. Blast off from a table or kneel at the bar. Among the infamous fruit and vegetable drinks are Daily Planets, Moonjuice (a lemon/lime concoction, $3.50), and Mr. Rogers on Amino Acid (16 fl. oz., $3.75). Also has a small closet outlet in Pike Place Market off Pine St. (443-9674). Open Mon.-Sun. 9am-10pm.

Siam, 616 Broadway E (324-0892). The interior may lack the old-world atmosphere of Thai Garden, but the food is equally good and less expensive. Did you know that *pad thai* ($5.25) translates from the Thai as "Delicious Thai food every Thai restaurant everywhere shall sell"? Open Mon.-Thurs. 11:30am-10pm, Fri. 11:30am-11:30pm, Sat. 5-11pm, Sun. 5-10pm.

Hana Japanese Restaurant, 219 Broadway Ave. E (328-1187). This small and ele-gant spot gets packed early with sushi fanatics out for the $1-per-plate deal. Open Mon.-Sat. 11am-10:30pm, Sun. 2-10pm.

Matzoh Mamma's, 509 15th E (324–6262), at Republican. Kosher-style (not *glatt* kosher) deli and restaurant. Try the chicken soup ($2.75) or the *Nudnik* sand-wich ($7 for a triple-decker). Eat, eat, eat! Put a little fat on your bones! Open Sun.-Thurs. 8am-9pm, Fri. 9am-9pm, Sat. 4-9pm.

Giorgina's Pizza, 131 15th Ave. E (329-8118). Great New York-style pizza, across the street from Group Health. Varied veggie toppings in addition to the usual stuff. 13-in. cheese ($7.50), 16-in. ($10). Slices ($1.40) also available. Open Mon.-Fri. 11am-10pm, Sat. 5-10pm. Delivery Mon.-Sat. until 9:45pm.

Espresso Roma, 202 Broadway Ave. E (324-1866). The pleasant service and propi-tious placement of this light and airy cafe make it a cut above the plethora of Seat-tle espresso bars and cafes. Open Mon.-Thurs. 7am-11pm, Fri.-Sun. 8am-midnight.

Kokeb Restaurant, 926 12th Ave. (322-0485). Behind Seattle University at the far south end of Capitol Hill, near the First Hill neighborhood. This Ethiopian eatery serves hot and spicy meat or vegetable stews on spongy *injera* bread. Watch Ethi-opian videos while you eat. Entrees $7-11. Open daily 5-10pm.

University District

The immense **University of Washington** (colloquially known as "U-Dub"), north of downtown between Union and Portage Bays, supports a colorful array of funky shops, ethnic restaurants, and a slew of coffeehouses. Most of the good restaurants, jazz clubs, cinemas, and cafes are within a few blocks of **University Way.** Ask for "University Way," however, and be prepared for puzzled looks; it's known around here as **"Th'Ave"** (one contracted syllable). To reach the University, take any one of buses #70-74 from downtown, or bus #7 or 43 from Capitol Hill.

Flowers, 4247 University Way NE (633-1903). This local landmark has been here since the 1920s, except that it was a florist for about 70 years. Now an English-style pub, with the notable exception of its all-you-can-eat vegetarian buffet ($5), including vegan options. Also open Mon.-Thurs. 10am-10pm, Fri.-Sat. 10am-mid-night, Sun. noon-5pm.

Last Exit, 5211 University Way NE (no phone, by choice). One block west of Uni-versity Way at NE 40th St. The Exit was established in 1967 and never quite left the '60s; aging hippies watch aspiring chessmasters battle it out in a large smoky room. Dirt-cheap espresso (65¢) and coffee (80¢). Try the espresso float ($2) or the cream cheese cupcakes (85¢). Sandwiches $2-5. Open mike for music as announced. Open Mon.-Fri. 10am-2am, Sat. 11am-2am, Sun. 11am-midnight.

Silence-Heart Nest, 5247 University Way NE (524-4008). Vegetarian and Indian food served up by followers of Sri Chinmoy. Try *calananda* (described as an East Indian calzone) or the Bliss-Burger ($4.75 for either). Open Thurs.-Tues. 10am-9pm, Wed. 10am-3pm.

Asia Deli, 4235 University Way NE (632-2364). Quick service and generous portions of delicious Vietnamese and Thai food. Noodle central. Try the sauteed chicken and onions ($3.75). Almost all the dishes are under $4, and all are prepared without MSG. Open daily 11am-9pm.

Grand Illusion Cinema and Espresso, 1405 50th St. NE (525-9573), at University Way. Relaxing coffeehouse with an overstuffed green couch in front of the working fireplace. Small, beachy wooden terrace and in-house theater (see Entertainment). Hot and cold coffees (95¢-$2.15) to make both Jean and his *père*, Auguste, proud. Try the whole wheat cream scone (85¢). Open Mon.-Sat. 8:30am-11pm, Sun. 8:30am-10:30pm.

Tandoor Restaurant, 5024 University Way (523-7477). Their all-you-can-eat lunch buffet ($4.50) is a *superfind!* Open Mon.-Fri. 11am-2:30pm and 4:30-10pm, Sat.-Sun. 11am-10:30pm.

Pizzeria Pagliacci, 4529 University Way NE (632-0421). Voted Seattle's best pizza, at $1.15 a slice it's also one of the city's best values. Open Sun.-Thurs. 11am-11pm, Fri.-Sat. 11am-1am.

Dankens, 4507 University Way NE (932-4774). Known nationally for their "Chocolate Decadence" ice cream (made in the store) and for their infamous "Seattle Sludge." Get a 2-for-1 special by showing the scoopers a picture of your parents, or try your luck at Trivial Pursuit. During happy hour every afternoon (5-7pm), one scoop is $1. (Normally $1.45 per scoop.) Open daily 8am-6pm.

Black Cafe and Vegetarian Collective Kitchen, 4110 Roosevelt Way NE (547-3887). Away from the fray behind a dry cleaners. A sunny, nonsmoking alternative to the Last Exit that seems to exist in a world of its own, without additives or preservatives. Small vegetarian menu, laid back atmosphere; sandwiches $3-5. Have a light bite in the outdoor seating area. Open Tues.-Sun. 10am-9pm.

Other Neighborhoods

Cafe D'Arte, 101 Denny Way (448-6263), near the Seattle Center. Classy 24-hr. diner about 15 min. walk from downtown. Beer, burgers, and fettucine alfredo ($8) menu draws diverse clientele from the well-heeled to the young and flannel-shirted. Great people-watching opportunities in the evening.

Burk's Cafe-Creole and Cajun, 5411 Ballard Ave. NW (782-0091), in (surprise) Ballard. A relaxed Creole cafe. Lunch sandwiches reasonably priced at $5, dinners $7-11. Try the crawfish with *remoulade* sauce ($5). A bowl of pickled okra sits on every table. Open Tues.-Sat. 11am-10pm.

Spud, 6860 E Green Lake Way N (524-0565), across the lake from Green Lake Jake's. Serving the Seattle staple of fish and chips ($2.60) for 51 years. Clams and chips ($2.90). Open daily 10:30am-9:30pm. Also in **West Seattle** right on the beach at 266 Alki SW (938-0606).

Zesto's Burger and Fish House, 6416 15th NW (783-3350). This Ballard High hangout has been serving students and frying fish since 1952, and even local fishermen rave about Zesto's "oriental-style" batter. Filling fish and chips dinners run $6.25, and the distinctive "snowshoe" fries make the deal a good one. Good burgers ($2.20-3.10), too. Open Sun.-Thurs. 11am–10pm, Fri.-Sat. 11am-11pm.

Green Lake Jake's, 7918 E Green Lake Dr. N (523-4747), on the north shore of Green Lake. Great breakfasts: 2 blueberry muffins ($1.70). Large lunches with salads $6-7. Open daily 6:30am-9pm.

Honey Bear, 2106 N 55th St. (545-7296), near Green Lake in Meridian. *The* best cinnamon rolls in town ($1.60). Green Lake exercisers come here to refuel. Dinners are simple soup-and-pizza style (around $3). Open daily 6am-11pm.

Julia's 14 Carrot Cafe, 2305 Eastlake Ave. E (324-1442), between Lake Union and I-5 at Lynn St. Only Julia's could make edible nut burgers that don't crumble, dry up, or stick in the back of your throat ($3.50). Great baked goods, too. Open Mon.-Fri. 7am-3pm, Sat.-Sun. 7am-4pm.

SIGHTS AND ACTIVITIES

The best way to take in the city skyline is from any one of the **ferries** that leave from the waterfront at frequent intervals. The finest view of Seattle, however, is a bit of a secret, and an exclusively female privilege. The athletic club on the top floor of the

Columbia Tower (the big black building at 201 5th Ave.) has floor-to-ceiling windows in the ladies room, overlooking the entire city.

It takes only two frenetic days to get a closer look at most of the city sights, as most are within walking distance of one another or are within Metro's Free Zone (see Getting Around, above). Just be sure not to ignore the more relaxing natural sights. Take a rowboat out on Lake Union, bicycle along Lake Washington, or hike through the wilds of Discovery Park.

Downtown

The new **Seattle Art Museum,** 100 University Way (654-3100 for a recording, 345-3121 Wed.-Fri. 1-5pm for a live voice), near 1st and University Way, boasts a stunning design by Philadelphian architect Robert Venturi. There's art *inside* the building, too. Call for current information on films and lectures. (Free tours Tues.-Sat. 2pm, Sun. 1pm, Thurs. 7pm; special exhibitions 30 min. later. Museum open Fri.-Wed. 10am-5pm, Thurs. 10am-9pm. $6, students and seniors $4, under 12 free. Occasional additional charges for special events.) One block north of the museum on 1st Ave., inside the Alcade Plaza Building, is the **Seattle Art Museum Gallery,** featuring current art, sculpture, jewelry, and prints by local artists. Browse for free.

Westlake Park, with its Art Deco brick patterns and Wall of Water, is a good place to kick back and listen to steel drums. This small triangular park, on Pike St. between 5th and 4th Ave., is bordered by the original **Nordstrom's** and the gleaming new **Westlake Center.** Nordstrom's is an upscale department store emphasizing superlative customer service. (Travelers toting *Let's Go* may find **Nordstrom's Rack,** at 2nd and Pine, more appealing.)

Many of the business-district high-rises warrant a closer look. **The Pacific First Center** at 5th and Pike displays a breathtaking collection of glass art commissioned from the prestigious Pilchuk School. Other notable buildings include the **Washington Mutual Tower** on 3rd Ave. and the complex of buildings around 6th and Union.

Bristling with excitement, and only a short walk down Pike St., is the **Pike Place Market,** a public market frequented by tourists and natives in equal proportions. (See Pike Place Market in the Food section, above.)

The Waterfront

The **Pike Place Hillclimb** descends from the south end of the Pike Place market down a set of staircases, leading past more chic shops and ethnic restaurants to Alaskan Way and the **waterfront.** (An elevator is also available.) The excellent **Seattle Aquarium** (386-4320) sits at the base of the Hillclimb at Pier 59, near Union St. Outdoor tanks re-create the ecosystems of salt marshes and tide pools, employing marine birds, mammals, and fish. The aquarium's star attraction, the underwater dome featuring the fish of the Puget Sound, is alone worth the admission price. See the world's only aquarium salmon ladder and an excellent fur seal exhibit. Don't miss the daily 11:30am feeding. (Open daily 10am-5pm. $6.75, seniors $5.25, ages 6-18 $4.25, ages 3-5 $1.75.)

Next to the Aquarium is **Omnidome** (622-1868). The only good thing about this large wrap-around movie screen is that you get to watch two movies for the price of one. The theater and the screen are of marginal quality, and neither film shown uses the Omnidome format particularly well. *The Eruption of Mt. St. Helens* offers striking photography but little else. (Films shown daily 9:30am-10pm. Tickets to 2 movies $6.25, seniors and students $5.25, ages 3-12 $4.25; with admission to aquarium $9, seniors and ages 13-18 $8, ages 6-12 $7.25.).

Pier 59 and the aquarium sit smack in the middle of the waterfront district. Explore north or south by foot or by **streetcar.** The 1920s cars were imported from Melbourne in 1982 because Seattle had sold its original streetcars to San Francisco, where they now enjoy international fame as cable cars. (Streetcars run every 20 min. Mon.-Sat. 7am-11pm, Sun. 10:15am-9:45pm; winter every ½-hr. until 6pm. 75¢ for 1½ hrs. of unlimited travel. Metro passes are good on the streetcar. On Sun., children under 12 ride free if accompanied by 1 paying passenger.)

North of Pier 70's pricey shopping arcade, **Myrtle Edwards Park** stretches along the water to the granaries on Piers 90 and 91. Despite lovely grassy areas and equally good views, Myrtle Edwards affords more seclusion than other downtown parks.

The Seattle Center

Although Seattlites generally disdain the Center (leaving it to tourists and suburbanites), there's actually a lot going on there. Take the **monorail** from the third floor of the Westlake Center; for 90¢ (ages 5-12 60¢, seniors 35¢) it will ferry passengers to the Seattle Center, every 15 min. from 9am to midnight. Between Denny Way and W Mercer St., and 1st and 5th Ave., the Center has eight gates, each with a model of the Center and a **map** of its facilities. The **Pacific Science Center** (443-2001), within the park, houses some of Seattle's best entertainment: a **laserium** (443-2850) and an **IMAX theater** (443-4629). Evening IMAX shows run Wednesday through Sunday (tickets to IMAX *and* the museum $8, seniors and ages 6-13 $7, ages 2-5 $5.50). The evening laser shows quake to music by groups like U2, Genesis, Metallica, and Led Zeppelin (Tues. $2.50; Wed.-Sun. $5.50).

The renowned **Pacific Northwest Ballet Company,** the **Opera,** and the **Seattle Symphony** all perform at the Seattle Center (see the Entertainment: Music and Dance section below). Locals flock to the frequent performances, special exhibits, and festivals. For information regarding special events and permanent attractions at the Center, call 684-8582 or 684-7200. The Center has a **customer service** desk in the Center House (open 7am-5pm; call 684-8582 7am-11pm). See Events, below, for information on the ever-popular **Seafair,** the **Folklife Festival,** the **Seattle International Children's Festival,** and the **Bite of Seattle,** all held annually at the Center. Over Labor Day weekend, Seattlites demonstrate their partygoing endurance at the four-day **Bumbershoot,** a festival of folk, street, classical, and rock music. Free concerts are also held during the summer at the **Seattle Center Mural Amphitheater,** and feature a variety of local rock bands. Check the "Tempo" section of the *Seattle Times* for listings.

The **Space Needle** (443-2111), sometimes known as "the world's tackiest monument," is a useful landmark for the disoriented, and houses an observation tower and an expensive, mediocre, dizzy restaurant.

Pioneer Square and Environs

From the waterfront or downtown, it's just a few blocks to historic Pioneer Square, at Yesler Way and 2nd Ave. Here, 19th-century warehouses and office buildings were restored in the 1970s. The *Complete Browser's Guide to Pioneer Square,* available in area bookstores, includes a short history and walking tour of the area, plus listings of all the shops, galleries, restaurants, and museums in the square. The earliest Seattlites settled on the site of Pioneer Square. "Doc" Maynard, a notorious early resident, gave a plot of land here to one Henry Yesler on the condition that he build a steam-powered lumber mill. Logs dragged down the steep grade of Yesler Way fed the mill, earning that street the epithet **"Skid Row."** Years later, the center of activity moved north, precipitating the decline of Pioneer Square and giving the term "skid row" its present meaning as a neighborhood of poverty and despair.

At the **Klondike Gold Rush National Historic Park,** 117 S Main St. (553-7220), the "interpretive center" depicts the lives and fortunes of miners. A slide show weaves together seven photographers' recordings of the miners' mostly unsuccessful ventures. To add some levity to this history of shattered dreams, the park screens Charlie Chaplin's 1925 classic, *The Gold Rush,* on the first Sunday of every month at 3pm (open daily 9am-5pm; free).

While in Pioneer Square, browse through the local art galleries, distributors for many of the Northwest's prominent artists. The first Thursday evening of each month, the art community sponsors **First Thursday,** a well-dressed and well-attended gallery walk. Call a Pioneer Square gallery for information. A few of the Square's notable galleries are **Flury and Co. Gallery,** 322 1st Ave. S (587-0260), featuring vintage photographic portraits of Native American life (open Mon.-Sat. 10am-

6pm, Sun. 11am-5pm, and by appt.); **Linda Farris Gallery,** 322 2nd Ave. S. (623-1110), promoting innovative Seattle artists (open Tues.-Sat. 11am-5:30pm, Sun. 1-5pm); **Native Design Gallery,** 108 Jackson St. (624-9985), housing imported art from Africa, South America, and India (open Tues.-Sat. 11am-5pm); and **Sacred Circle Gallery,** 607 1st Ave. (285-4425), guardian of an acclaimed collection of contemporary Native art (open Wed.-Sat. 10am-5pm, Sun. noon-5pm). Stop in also at the **Seattle Indian Arts and Crafts Shop,** 113 Cherry St. (621-0655), run by the American Indian Women's Service League. A non-profit business, the shop features Native art of the Northwest. Proceeds benefit the local Native American community (open Mon.-Sat. 10am-6pm, Sun. noon-6pm). For a different twist on American art, visit **Animation USA, Inc.,** 104 1st St. (625-0347). Tours of **In Public: 1991,** a project for which the Seattle Arts Commission hired 37 artists and spent $567,000 in public arts funds, leave from the Convention Center (Visitors Info.) at noon ($5). Another landmark of the Pioneer Square area is the **Smith Tower,** for many years the tallest building west of the Mississippi. The 21-story tower was commissioned in 1911 by L. C. Smith at a cost of $1,500,000, and was later owned by local celebrity and fish-and-ships mogul Ivar Haglund.

The Seattle professional sports scene is truly odd. Uglier and less productive than the Boeing factory, the **Kingdome,** 201 S King St. (340-2100 or 340-2128), down 1st Ave., where the **Mariners** play, ranks second only to the Astrodome in sunny Houston as an insult to baseball. Seattle is the only city in America where fans might prefer the game on TV rather than see it live, under poor, purplish, insipid light, on artificial turf, amid unearthly sounds and echoes. Now the roof is falling in. Forget the rain, tear it down, and build a decent outdoor ballpark, Seattle, or the **Tampa Bay Mariners** will be playing AL baseball by 1997! For a schedule, call 800-950-FANS (-3267). Tickets for Mariners games are cheap; $15 on the 3rd base line (206-628-0888 or 292-5454; open Mon.-Sat. 8am-9pm, Sun. 8am-6pm). Sunday is seniors discount day. By the way, the **Seahawks** play football here.

Besides the action in the Kingdome, there's also pro basketball in town. The **Seattle** Supersonics (281-5800) (the "**Sonics**") is the only Seattle team ever to win a national title, and their basketball games in the Coliseum in Seattle Center attract a religious following. Unfortunately, last year they became the first #1 team in NBA playoff history to be eliminated by #8, the Denver Nuggets. The **University of Washington Huskies** football team has dominated the PAC-10 recently. Call the **Athletic Ticket Office** (543-2200) for schedules and price information.

The International District

Three blocks east of Pioneer Square, up Jackson on King St., is Seattle's International District. Though sometimes still called "Chinatown" by Seattlites, this area is now home to immigrants from all over Asia, and their descendants.

Start off your tour of the district by ducking into the **Wing Luke Memorial Museum,** 414 8th St. (623-5124). This tiny museum houses a permanent exhibit on the different Asian nationalities in Seattle, and temporary exhibits by local Asian artists. There are occasional free demonstrations of traditional crafts. Thursdays are always free. (Open Tues.-Fri. 11am-4:30pm, Sat.-Sun. noon-4pm. $2.50, seniors and students $1.50, ages 5-12 75¢.) Other landmarks of the International District include the **Tsutakawa sculpture** at the corner of S Jackson and Maynard St. and the gigantic dragon mural in **Hing Hay Park** at S King and Maynard St. The community gardens at Main and Maynard St. provide a peaceful and well-tended retreat from the downtown sidewalks.

Capitol Hill

Capitol Hill inspires extreme reactions from both its residents and its neighbors. In any case, the former wouldn't live anywhere else. The district's Leftist and gay communities set the tone for its nightspots (see Entertainment below), while the retail outlets include collectives and radical bookstores. The coffee shops and restaurants offer the best sites for people-watching. Explore Broadway or its cross streets in order to window-shop and experience the neighborhood, or walk a few blocks east and north for a stroll down the hill's residential streets, lined with well-maintained Victorian homes. Bus #10 runs along 15th St. and #7 cruises Broadway.

Volunteer Park, between 11th and 17th Ave. at E Ward St., north of the main Broadway activity, welcomes tourists away from the City Center. Named for the "brave volunteers who gave their lives to liberate the oppressed people of Cuba and the Philippines" during the Spanish-American War, the park boasts lovely lawns and an outdoor running track. The park has an unsavory reputation after dark. Climb the water tower at the 14th Ave. entrance for a stunning 360° panorama of the city and the Olympic Range. The views beat those from the Space Needle, and they're free. On rainy days, hide out amid the orchids inside the glass **conservatory** (free).

The **University of Washington Arboretum** (543-8800), 10 blocks east of Volunteer Park, houses the Graham Visitors Center, with exhibits on local plant life. It also shelters superb **cycling** and **running** trails, including Lake Washington Blvd., a smooth bicycling road running the length of the arboretum from north to south and continuing along the western shore of Lake Washington as far south as Seward Park. The Arboretum boasts 4000 species of trees and shrubs and 43 species of flowers, making for an Edenesque stroll. A tranquil, beautiful **Japanese Garden** (684-4725) is at the southern end of the arboretum at E Helen St. Take bus #11 from downtown. The nine acres of sculpted gardens encompass fruit trees, a reflecting pool, and a traditional tea house. (Park open March-Nov. daily 10am-8pm. Arboretum open daily dawn-dusk. Greenhouse open Mon.-Fri. 10am-4pm. $2; seniors, disabled, and ages 6-18 $1; under 6 free.)

University District

With 33,000 students, the **University of Washington** is the state's cultural and educational center of gravity. The "U District" swarms with students year-round, and Seattlites of other occupations take advantage of the area's many bookstores, shops, taverns, and restaurants. To reach the district, take buses #71-74 from downtown, or #7, #43, or #48 from Capitol Hill. Stop by the friendly, helpful **visitors center,** 4014 University Way NE (543-9198), to pick up a campus **map** and to obtain information about the University (open Mon.-Fri. 8am-5pm).

On the campus, visit the **Thomas Burke Memorial Washington State Museum** (543-5590), at NE 45th St. and 17th Ave. NE, in the northwest corner of the campus. The museum exhibits a superb collection about the Pacific Northwest's Native nations. The scrimshaw displays and the long-house front are memorable. (Open daily 10am-5pm. Suggested donation $3, seniors and students $2.) The astronomy department's **observatory** (543-0126) is open to the public for viewings on clear nights. The grounds and gardens of the University are a popular and beautiful place to stroll, and enormous **Red Square** is a great meeting place and relaxation area.

The **Henry Art Gallery**, 15th Ave. NE and NE 41st St. (543-2280), has excellent exhibits. Stop in before you stroll the campus lawns. (Open Tues.-Wed. and Fri.-Sun. 11am-5pm, Thurs. 10am-9pm. $3.50, seniors and students $2, under 12 and Thurs. free.) The **UW Arts Ticket Office,** 4001 University Way NE (543-4880), has information and tickets for all events (open Mon.-Fri. 10:30am-4:30pm).

Students often cross town for drinks in the **Queen Anne** neighborhood (see below), and the intervening neighborhood, **Fremont** basks in the jovial atmosphere. A statue entitled "Waiting for the Inner-city Urban" depicts several people waiting in bus-purgatory, and, in moments of inspiration and sympathy, is frequently dressed up by passers-by. Another interesting comment on civilization is the statue of a large, mean **troll** who sits beneath the Fremont Bridge (on 35th St.) grasping a Volkswagen Bug, recently covered in cement to prevent vandalism. Fremont is also the home of **Archie McPhee's,** 3510 Stone Way (545-8344), a shrine to pop culture and plastic absurdity. People of the punk and funk persuasion make pilgrimages from as far as the record stores of Greenwich Village in Manhattan just to handle the notorious **slug selection.** You can get to Archie's on the Aurora Hwy.

(Rte. 99), or take bus #26. The store is east of the Hwy. between 35th and 36th, two blocks north of Lake Union (open Mon.-Fri. 10am-6pm, Sat. 10am-5pm).

Waterways and Parks

A string of attractions festoon the waterways linking Lake Washington and Puget Sound. Houseboats and sailboats fill **Lake Union.** Here, the **Center for Wooden Boats,** 1010 Valley St. (382-2628), maintains a moored flotilla of new and restored small craft for rent (rowboats $8-12 per hr., sailboats $10-15 per hr.; open daily 11am-6pm). **Kelly's Landing,** 1401 NE Boat St. (547-9909), below the UW campus, rents canoes for outings on Lake Union. (Sailboats $10-20 per hr., also day rates. 2-hr. min. Hours determined by weather, but normally Mon.-Fri. 10am-dusk, Sat.-Sun. 9am-dusk.) **Gasworks Park,** a much-celebrated kite-flying spot at the north end of Lake Union, was reopened a few years ago by the EPA after being shut for a time due to an excess of toxins. Don't be daunted by the climb up a large hill. At the top is a gorgeous view and an "interactive sundial," where your shadow acts as the pointer. **Gasworks Kite Shop,** 1915 N 34th St. (633-4780), is one block north of the park. (Kite shop open Mon.-Fri. 10am-6pm, Sat. 10am-5pm, Sun. noon-5pm. Park open dawn-dusk.) To reach the park, take bus #26 from downtown to N 35th St. and Wallingford Ave. N. The popular **Burke-Gilman Trail** runs from Latona St. at NE Northlake, just next to the Washington Ship Canal Bridge and I-5, through the university, past Sand Point and Magnuson Park, north to NE 145th.

Farther west, the **Hiram M. Chittenden Locks** (783-7001) draw good-sized crowds to watch Seattle's boaters jockey for position in the locks. A circus atmosphere develops at peak hours, as all the boats traveling between Puget Sound and Lake Washington try to cross over (viewing hrs. daily 7am-dusk). If listening to the cries of frustrated skippers ("Gilligan, you nitwit!") doesn't amuse you, climb over to the **fish ladder** on the south side of the locks to watch trout and salmon hurl themselves over 21 concrete steps on their journey from the sea. Take bus #43 from the U District or #17 from downtown. The busiest salmon runs occur from June to November; steelhead trout run in the winter; cutthroat trout, in the fall. Afterwards, you can listen to summertime lectures held in the **visitors center** (783-7059) on Tuesdays at 7:30pm. The Army Corps of Engineers gives talks with captivating titles like "The Corps Cares About Fish" and "A Beaver in Your Backyard?" (Visitors center open daily 11am-8pm; Sept. 16-June 14 Thurs.-Mon. 11am-5pm.)

Farther north, on the northwestern shore of the city, lies the **Golden Gardens Park,** in the Loyal Heights neighborhood, between NW 80th and NW 95th St. A small boat ramp lies at the southern end; an ideal spot for a picnic, especially as the sun sets over Shilshole Bay. Several expensive restaurants line the piers to the south, and unobstructed views of the Olympic Mountains almost justify the prices of their uniformly excellent seafood.

Directly north of Lake Union, exercisers run, roller skate, and skateboard around **Green Lake.** Take bus #16 from downtown Seattle to Green Lake. The lake is also given high marks by windsurfers, but woe to those who lose their balance. Whoever named Green Lake wasn't kidding; even a quick dunk results in gobs of green algae clinging to your body and hair. A more pleasant way to experience the lake is by renting a boat from **Green Lake Rentals** (527-0171) on the eastern side of the lake (sailboards $12 per hr., pedalboats, rowboats, canoes, and kayaks $8 per hr., rowboats $6 per hr.). But watch out: on sunny afternoons the boat-renters, the windsurfers, and energetic scullers can make the lake feel more like rush hour on I-5. Next to the lake is Woodland Park and the **Woodland Park Zoo,** 5500 Phinney Ave. N (684-4034), best reached from Rte. 99 or N 50th St. Take bus #5 from downtown. The park itself is shaggy, but this makes the animals' habitats seem realistic. The African Savannah and Gorilla Houses reproduce the wilds, while the Nocturnal House reveals what really goes on when the lights go out. The newly opened **elephant habitat** has enhanced the zoo's international reputation for creating natural settings. It's one of only three zoos in the U.S. to receive the Humane Society's highest standard of approval. (Open daily 9:30am-6pm, $6.50; ages 6-17, seniors and disabled $5, ages 3-5 $4.)

Discovery Park, on a lonely point west of the Magnolia District and south of Golden Gardens Park, at 36th Ave. W and Government Way W, is comprised of acres of minimally tended grassy fields and steep bluffs atop Puget Sound. Take bus #24. At the park's northern end is the **Indian Cultural Center** (285-4425), operated by the United Indians of All Tribes Foundation. (Open Wed.-Fri. 8:30am-5pm, Sat.-Sun. 10am-5pm. Free.) The Cultural Center also houses the **Sacred Circle Gallery,** a rotating exhibit of older and contemporary pieces of Native American artwork. (Open Tues.-Sat. 10am-5pm, Sun. noon-5pm.)

Seward Park (723-5780) is the southern endpoint of a string of beaches and forest preserves along the western shore of Lake Washington. Take bus #39. The park has beaches, wooded areas, and walking and biking trails, a fishing pier, picnic shelters, tennis courts, and an arts center. After exercising in the park, refresh yourself with a tour of the **Rainier Brewery Co.,** 3100 Airport Way S (622-2600), off I-5 at the West Seattle Bridge. Take bus #123. Attentiveness is rewarded with complimentary beer (root beer for those under 21) and cheese and crackers (30-min. tours Mon.-Sat. 1-6pm; free).

Directly across town, on Puget Sound, is **Alki Beach Park,** a thin strip of beach wrapped around residential West Seattle. Take bus #36. The water is chilling, but the **views** of downtown and the Olympics are outstanding. The first white settlers of Seattle set up camp here in 1851, naming their new home New York Alki, meaning "New York By and By" in the local Native language. By the time the settlement moved to Pioneer Square, parvenu Doc Maynard suggested that perhaps "New York By and By" was too deferential a name and that the city should be named for his friend Chief Sealth. Because the Suquamish people did not believe in pronouncing the names of the deceased, the city's name became "Seattle." A monument to the city's birthplace is found along Alki Beach at 63rd Ave. SW, south of Alki. Just south of **Lincoln Park,** along Fauntleroy Way in Fauntleroy, is the departure point for **passenger and auto ferries** to **Vashon Island** and **Southworth** (see Practical Information). Take bus #18 to Lincoln Park. The park has playing fields, tennis courts, picnic tables, swimming beaches, bicycling trails, and the Colman Pool, open in summer.

SPORTS AND RECREATION

Pick up a copy of the pamphlet *Your Seattle Parks and Recreation Guide,* available at the visitors bureau or the Parks Department (see Practical Information), or the monthly *Sports Northwest,* available at most area sports outfitters (free). The paper includes calendars of competitive events in the Northwest, book reviews, and recreation suggestions.

Road bicyclists should gear up for the 192-mi., 1600-competitor **Seattle to Portland Race.** Call the **bike hotline** (522-2453) for more information. The Seattle Parks Department also holds a monthly **Bicycle Sunday** from May to September, when Lake Washington Blvd. is open only to cyclists from 10am to 5pm. Contact the Parks Department's Citywide Sports Office (684-7092) for more information. **Marymoor Velodrome** (282-8356), in Redmond off Rte. 520 at the Rte. 901 exit, is open to the public when not in use for competition, and offers classes on the ways of the track. Pack a picnic supper and sit on the lawn to watch the sweaty races, sponsored by the Washington State Bicycling Association from May through August on Friday nights at 7:30pm. All buses that cross Lake Washington have bike racks; call Metro (447-4800) for more information.

Many **whitewater rafting** outfitters are based in the Seattle area, even though the rapids are hours away by car. Over 50 companies compete for a growing market. A good way to secure an inexpensive trip is to call outfitters and quote competitors' prices at them; they are often willing to undercut one another. Scour the "Guides" section in the Yellow Pages. In recent years rafting companies have attempted to subject themselves to a regulatory bureaucracy of their own making, **River Outfitters of Washington (ROW)** (485-1427), which sets safety guidelines for its members. Even if your outfitter does not belong to ROW, be sure it lives up to ROW's basic safety standards. Don't hesitate to spend the extra dollars to ensure the highest level of safety. Private boaters should remember that whitewater is unpredictable and potentially dangerous; *always* scout out new rivers before running them. ROW has a list of tips for private boaters, and outfitters can give you the scoop on navigable Washington rivers.

The **Northwest Outdoor Center,** 2100 Westlake Ave. (281-9694), on Lake Union, holds instructional programs in **whitewater** and **sea kayaking** during the spring, summer, and fall. (Two-evening introduction to sea kayaking $40 if you have your own boat. Equipment rentals available.) The center also leads excursions, sea kayaking through the San Juan Islands or **backpacking and paddling** through the North Cascades (open Mon.-Fri. 10am-8pm, Sat.-Sun. 10am-6pm).

Skiing near Seattle is every bit as good as the mountains look. **Alpental, Ski-Acres,** and **Snoqualmie** co-sponsor an information number (232-8182), which can give out conditions and lift ticket rates for all three. **Crystal Mountain** (663-2265), the region's newest resort, can be reached by Rte. 410 south out of Seattle and offers ski rentals, lessons, and lift ticket packages.

Since the Klondike gold rush, Seattle has been one of the foremost cities in the world for outfitting wilderness expeditions. Besides Army-Navy surplus stores and campers' supply shops (try **Federal Army and Navy Surplus,** 2112 1st Ave.; 443-1818; open Mon.-Sat. 9:30am-6pm), the city is home to many world-class outfitters. **Recreational Equipment Inc. Coop (REI Coop),** 1525 11th Ave. (323-8333), is the favored place to buy high-quality mountaineering and water recreation gear. Take bus #10. For a few dollars you can join the Coop and receive a year-end rebate on your purchases. REI has a bulletin board where lone hikers advertise for hiking companions. The company also offers its own backpacking and climbing trips and clinics, in addition to presenting free slide shows and lectures on topics such as trekking through Nepal, bicycling in Ireland, or improving your fly-fishing techniques. Call or stop by the store for a full schedule. (Open Mon.-Tues. 10am-6pm, Wed.-Fri. 10am-9pm, Sat. 9:30am-6pm, Sun. noon-5pm.)

Opening Day (the first Sat. in May) in the U of W's Montlake Cut, the channel between Lake Washington and Portage Bay, is a big spring **rowing** event. Crowds flood the banks to watch streams of sailboats (usually dressed up to follow a theme), and, most importantly, to watch the University of Washington crews challenge Harvard and other competitors in 2km sprint races. Take the Bellevue exit off I-5.

ENTERTAINMENT

During lunch hours in the summertime, the free, city-sponsored **"Out to Lunch"** series (623-0340) brings everything from reggae to folk dancing to the parks and squares of Seattle. The **Seattle Public Library** (386-4636) shows free films as part of the program, and has a daily schedule of other free events, such as poetry readings and children's book-reading competitions. *Events,* published every two months, is a calendar of the library's offerings (available at libraries throughout the city).

Music and Dance

The **Seattle Opera** (389-7676, open Mon.-Fri. 9am-5pm, or ticketmaster at 292-2787) performs in the Opera House in the Seattle Center throughout the winter. The popularity of the program requires that you order tickets well in advance, although rush tickets are sometimes available 15 minutes before curtain time ($8 and up). Write to the Seattle Opera, P.O. Box 9248, Seattle 98109. The **Seattle Symphony Orchestra** (443-4747), also in Seattle Center's Opera House, performs a regular subscription series from September through June (rush tickets $4 and up) and a special pops and children's series. The symphony plays the summer series in the gorgeous, renovated **Fifth Avenue Theater.** The **Pacific Northwest Ballet** (441-9411) starts its season at the Opera House in December with the spectacular Maurice Sendak-designed version of the *Nutcracker.* The season continues through May with four or five slated productions (tickets $10 and up). The **University of Wash-**

ington offers its own program of student recitals and concerts by visiting artists. Call the Meany Hall box office (543-4880, open Mon.-Fri. 10:30am-4:30pm).

For a truly off-beat but rewarding experience, try a concert at the **Paramount Theatre,** 911 Pine St. (682-1414 from 9am-6pm); the theater hosts artists ranging from Bonnie Raitt to the Butthole Surfers. Ticket prices vary as widely as the performers. Also check out the **Moore Theater,** 1932 2nd Ave. (443-1744), for punk to pop to hypnotism. Ticket prices vary.

Theater

Seattle theater is outstanding. With the second-largest number of professional companies in the U.S., Seattle hosts an exciting array of first-run plays and alternative works, particularly in the many talented semi-professional groups. Although touring companies do pass through, they are nowhere near as interesting as the local scene.

You can often get **rush tickets** at nearly half price on the day of the show (with cash only) from **Ticket/Ticket** (324-2744; see page 322).

Seattle Repertory Theater, 155 W Mercer St. (443-2222, Mon.-Fri. 9am-7pm or 10pm-2am), in the wonderful **Bagley Wright Theater** in Seattle Center. Artistic director Daniel Sullivan and the repertory company won the 1990 Tony for Regional Excellence. Their winter season combines contemporary, original, and classic productions (usually including Shakespeare). Recent plays that eventually reached Broadway but got their start at the Rep include *The Heidi Chronicles* and *Fences.* Tickets for weekends and opening nights range $16-31.50. Other nights and Sun. Matinee $13.50-29.50. Ten min. before each show senior and variable student rates are available with ID.

A Contemporary Theater (ACT), 100 W Roy St. (285-5110), at the base of Queen Anne Hill. A summer season of modern and off-beat premieres. Tickets $13-23. Open Tues.-Thurs. noon-7pm, Fri.-Sat. noon-8pm, and Sun. noon-7:30pm.

Annex Theatre, 1916 4th Ave. (728-0933). Refreshing emphasis on company-generated material. New "1-week wonders" are a good bet; they're experimental shows staged between the regular 4-week-long productions. Every Fri. during the summer sees an "Improv. Night" at 11pm for $2, or free with a ticket from the evening's show. Regular tickets $10-16. Open Tues.-Fri. noon-7:30pm.

The Empty Space Theatre, 3509 Fremont Ave. N (547-7500), 1½ blocks north of the Fremont bridge. It almost folded a few years ago, but this space is not empty yet; the zany comedies rollick onward. Tickets $13-20, preview tickets (first 4 performances of any show) $10.

Intiman Theater at the Playhouse in Seattle Center (626-0782). Their season (May-Dec. 1) usually snags the most talented local actors for a classical repertoire. Tickets $13.50-21. Open Tues.-Wed. noon-7pm, Thurs.-Sat. noon-8pm.

Bathhouse Theater, 7312 W Green Lake Dr. N (524-9108). This small company is known for its popular restaging of radio skits and transplanting Shakespeare to unexpected locales (e.g., a Wild West *Macbeth,* Kabuki *King Lear,* and *Midsummer Night's Dream* set in the 50s). Tickets $13-20. Open Tues.-Sun. noon-7pm.

Seattle Group Theatre, 3940 Brooklyn Ave. NE (441-1299), in the U District. Home to **The Group,** one of Seattle's most innovative small theater ensembles, performing original, interactive, and avant-garde works. Tickets $14-20, seniors ½-price, students $6. Call Tues.-Sat. noon-7pm, Sun. noon-6pm.

Alice B. Theater, Broadway Performance Hall (322-5423), at Broadway and Pine. This gay/lesbian theater company keeps getting better. Witty musicals. Tickets $10-14.

New City Theater, 1634 11th Ave. (323-6800 or 323-6801), on Capitol Hill. The farthest gone of the alternative theaters, the size and type of their offerings swings wildly. Ticket prices change accordingly. Offers occasional "parties," featuring champagne, beer, free food, and live interactive acting performances for a $2 admission fee. Free Parking.

University of Washington School of Drama Theaters (543-4880 or 543-5986). The Penthouse, Meany Hall, and Glenn Hughes Playhouse, the three U of W theaters, offer a wide variety of works, from children's shows to classical and contemporary theater. Of particular interest is the free open-air Shakespeare in the summer. Call for information on the wide variety of UW cultural activities. Tickets $22-35. Open Mon.-Fri. 10:30am-4:30pm.

Clubs and Taverns

One of the joys of living in Seattle is the abundance of community tavern, where downing alcohol and scoping is frowned upon. These taverns look instead to providing a relaxed environment for dancing and spending time with friends. In Washington, taverns may serve only beer and wine; a fully-licensed bar or cocktail lounge must adjoin a restaurant. You must be 21 to enter bars and taverns. The Northwest produces a variety of local beers, some sold in area stores but most only on tap in bars. Popular brews include **Grant's, Imperial Russian Stout, India Pale Ale, Red Hook, Ballard Bitter, Black Hook,** and **Yakima Cider.**

The best spot to go for guaranteed good beer, live music, and big crowds is **Pioneer Square.** Most of the bars around the Square participate in a **joint cover** ($10) that will let you wander from bar to bar and sample the bands you like. **Fenix Cafe and Fenix Underground** (343-7740), **Central Tavern** (622-0209), and the **Swan Cafe** (343-5288) all rock and roll consistently, while **Larry's** (624-7665) and **New Orleans** (622-2563) feature great jazz and blues nightly. The **J and M Cafe** (624-1670) is also in the center of Pioneer Square but has no music. All the Pioneer Square clubs shut down at 2am Friday and Saturday nights, and at around midnight during the week. Another option is to catch an evening of live **stand-up comedy** in one of Seattle's many comedy clubs, such as Pioneer Square's **Swannie's Comedy Underground,** 222 S Main St. (628-0303 or 622-4550 after 7:30pm), the oldest all-comedy club in Seattle and deemed by *Rolling Stone* to be the best in the entire Northwest. (Must be 21 to enter. Tickets $5 or so; acts daily at 9 and 11pm.)

Red Door Alehouse, 3401 Fremont Ave. N (547-7521), at N 34th St., across from the Inner-Urban Statue. Throbbing with University students who attest to the good local ale selection. Open daily 11am-1:30am. Kitchen closes at midnight.

The Trolleyman Pub, 3400 Phinney Ave. N (548-8000). In the back of the Red Hook Ale Brewery, which rolls the most popular kegs on campus to U of W students. Early hours make it a mellow spot to listen to good acoustic music and contemplate the newly-made bubbles in a fresh pint, especially if it is a pint of Nut Brown Ale. Open Mon.-Thurs. 8:30am-11pm, Fri. 8:30am-midnight, Sat. noon-midnight, Sun. noon-7pm.

Kells, 1916 Post Alley (728-1916), at Pike Place. A raging Irish pub with nightly Irish tunes and a crowd that guarantees good "crack," as the Irish would say. Live music Wed.-Sat. Open Wed.-Sat. 11:30am-2am. $3 cover Fri. and Sat. only.

Off Ramp, 109 Eastlake Ave. E (628-0232). Among the most popular venues of the local music scene. Always loud; wild at times. Open 5pm-2am daily. Cover varies.

Under the Rail (448-1900), 5th and Battery. This newest and largest downtown club offers local music (cover $4-5) and the occasional national tour. DJ and dancing on nights without concerts. Loud. Hours change nightly according to show times. Often open past 2am. Always open Sat. midnight-5am.

OK Hotel, 212 Alaskan Way S (621-7903). One cafe, one bar, one building. All-ages establishment serves beer and wine, and coffee and dessert. Just below Pioneer Square toward the waterfront. Lots of wood, lots of coffee. Great live bands with hot alternative sound. Grab breakfast here and rub elbows with the many local artists who live in the Pioneer Sq. area. Open Sun.-Thurs. 6am-3am, Fri.-Sat. 8am-4am. Occasional cover charge up to $6. Call 386-9934 for the coffee house.

Comet Tavern, 922 E Pike (323-9853), in the Capitol Hill area. Mixed crowd, no cover, and you can add your tip to the growing sculpture of dollar bills stuck to the ceiling. Open daily noon-2am.

Weathered Wall, 1921 5th Ave. (448-5688). An audience as diverse and artistic as its offerings (poetry readings to punk). The Weathered Wall is always interesting, and promotes audience interaction. Open Tues.-Sun. 9pm-2am. Cover $3-7.

The University Bistro, 4315 University Way NE (547-8010). Live music (everything from blues to reggae) nightly. Happy hours (4-7pm) feature pints of Bud for

$1.25, pitchers $4. Cover $2 Tues., $3-5 Wed.-Sat., free Sun.-Mon. Open Mon.-Fri. 11am-2am, Sat. 6pm-2am.

Murphy's Pub (634-2110), at Meridian Ave. N and N 45th St., in Wallingford, west of the U District. Take bus #43. A classic Irish pub with a mile-long beer list. Popular with a young crowd, Murphy's has live Irish and folk music Fri. and Sat. (cover $2). Open mike on Wed. Open daily 11:30am-2am.

Re-Bar, 1144 Howell (233-9873). A gay bar for those who like dancing on the wild side, depending on the night. Open daily 9pm-2am. Cover $5.

The Vogue, 2018 1st Ave. (443-0673). A rockin' dance place for the black-clad and/or angst-ridden. Features local alternative music. Open daily 9pm-2am

Cinema

Seattle is a *Cinema Paradiso*. Most of the theaters that screen non-Hollywood films are on Capitol Hill and in the University District. Most matinee shows (before 6pm) cost $4; after 6pm, expect to pay $6.50. Seven Gables has recently bought up the Egyptian, the Metro, the Neptune, and others. $20 buys admission to any five films at any of their theaters.

The Egyptian, 801 E Pine St. (323-4978), at Harvard Ave., on Capitol Hill. This handsome Art Deco theater shows artsy films and is best known for hosting the **Seattle Film Festival** (although some films are screened at other theaters) held the last week of May and the first week of June. The festival includes a retrospective of one director's work with a personal appearance by the featured director. Festival series tickets are available at a discount. Regular tickets $6.50, seniors and children $4, first matinee $4.

The Harvard Exit, 807 E Roy St. (323-8986), on Capitol Hill. Quality classic and foreign films. Half the fun of seeing a movie here is the theater itself, a converted residence. The lobby was once someone's living room. Arrive early for complimentary cheese and crackers over a game of chess, checkers, or backgammon. $6.50, seniors and children $4, first matinee $4.

Neptune, 1303 NE 45th St. (633-5545), just off University Way. A repertory theater, with double features that change daily. *Rocky Horror* has been playing at midnight for as many Saturdays as anyone can remember. $6.50, seniors and children $4, first matinee $4.

Seven Gables Theater, 911 NE 50th St. (632-8820), in the U District, just off Roosevelt, a short walk west from University Way. Another cinema in an old house. Independent and classic films. $6.50; first matinee, seniors, children $4.

Guild 45th, 2115 N 45th (633-3353). Shows slightly off the beaten track features, but the real attraction is the neon pink stucco building, a prominent fixture in the landscape and local art. $6.50, first matinee $4.

Grand Illusion Cinema, 1403 NE 50th St. (523-3935), in the U District at University Way. A tiny theater attached to an espresso bar, showing films made on 1930s-type budgets. $6, matinees $4, seniors and children $3.

Metro Cinemas, 45th St. and Roosevelt Way NE (633-0055), in the U District. A large, modern 10-theater complex. Half the screens show mainstream movies; the other half are reserved for contemporary art films. $6.50, first matinee, seniors, and under 12 $4.

Bookstores

University Book Store, 4326 University Way NE (634-3400). The second-largest college bookstore in the country. Textbooks are in the basement. Good collection of children's books. Open Mon.-Wed. and Fri.-Sat. 9am-6pm, Thurs. 9am-9pm, Sun. noon-5pm.

Left Bank Books, 92 Pike St. (622-0195), in the Pike Place Market. A Leftist bookstore, quietly awaiting the Revolution. Mostly political selection. Good prices on new and used books. Open Mon.-Sat. 10am-9pm, Sun. noon-6pm.

Shorey's Book Store, 1411 1st Ave. (624-0221), downtown. One of the oldest and largest bookstores in the Northwest, Shorey's sells new, used, and rare books. Open Mon.-Sat. 10am-6pm, Sun. noon-5pm.

Elliott Bay Books, 101 S Main St. (624-6600), in Pioneer Sq. Vast collection; 150, 000 titles. The store sponsors frequent reading and lecture series. Coffee house in the basement. Open Mon.-Sat. 10am-11pm, Sun. noon-6pm.

Red and Black Books, 432 15th Ave. E (322-7323). Features multicultural, gay, and feminist literature and frequent readings. Open Mon.-Thurs. 10am-8pm, Fri.-Sat. 10am-9pm, Sun. 11am-7pm.

Beyond the Closet, 1501 Belmont Ave. E (322-4609). Exclusively gay/lesbian material. Open Sun.-Thurs. 10am-10pm, Fri.-Sat. 10am-11pm.

EVENTS

Pick up a copy of the Seattle-King County visitors center's *Calendar of Events,* published every season, for event coupons and an exact listing of innumerable area happenings. One of the most notable events is the **Northwest Folklife Festival,** held on Memorial Day weekend at the Seattle Center. Artists, musicians, and dancers congregate to celebrate the heritage of the area. The Japanese community celebrates the third week of July with the traditional **Bon Odori** festival in the International District, when temples are opened to the public and dances fill the streets. **Street fairs** throughout the city are popular conglomerations of crafts and food stands, street music, and theater. Especially of note are those in the University District during mid- to late May, the Pike Place Market over Memorial Day weekend, and the Fremont District (633-4409) in mid-June.

The **Bite of Seattle** (232-2980) is a celebration of food, held in mid-July in the Seattle Center (free). The summer is capped by the massive **Bumbershoot** (622-5123), held in the Seattle Center over Labor Day weekend. This fantastic four-day arts festival attracts big-name rock bands, street musicians, and a young, exuberant crowd (Fri. free, Sat.-Sun. $4 at the door or $3 in advance). The Seattle Center is also home to the **Seattle International Children's Festival.** This week-long event in mid-May is targeted to entertaining children, but its featured performers from Canada, Colombia, Ghana, China, and other countries have wide appeal. Call the Seattle Center (443-20001) or write 305 Harrison St., Seattle 98109-4695.

If you're looking for **live music,** the City Hall Park Concert Series presents free reggae, blues, jazz, and other concerts nearly every day in summer. Call 781-3590 for information, or stop by the park at 516 3rd Ave, south of the King County Courthouse.

The **International District** holds its annual two-day bash in mid-July, featuring traditional (and nontraditional) arts & crafts booths, East Asian and Pacific food booths, and exhibits ranging from the Radical Women/Freedom Socialist Party to the Girl Scouts. **Maps** and admission free. For information call **Chinatown Discovery,** Inc., at 236-0657 or 583-0460, or write P.O. Box 3406, Seattle 98114. They will also be offering free International District tours during the festival.

Puget Sound's **yachting** season falls in May. **Maritime Week** (467-6340 or 329-5700), during the third week of May, and the **Seattle Boats Afloat Show** (634-0911) in mid-August, gives area boaters a chance to show off their craft. At the beginning of July, the Center for Wooden Boats sponsors the free **Wooden Boat Show** (382-2628) on Lake Union. Don't go without your blue blazer and deck shoes. Size up the entrants (over 100 traditional wooden boats) and then watch a demonstration of boat-building skills. The year-end blow-out is the **Quick and Daring Boatbuilding Contest.** Hopefuls go overboard trying to build and sail wooden boats of their own design using a limited kit of tools and materials. Plenty of music, food, and alcohol make the sailing smooth.

The biggest, baddest festival of them all is the **Seattle Seafair** (728-0123), spread out over three weeks from mid-July to early August. All of the city's neighborhoods contribute with street fairs, parades large and small, balloon races, musical entertainment, and a seafood fest. The festival ends with the totally insane **Emerald City Unlimited Hydroplane Races.** Everybody grabs anything that will float and heads to Lake Washington for front row seats. As the sun shines more often than not during these weeks, half the city seems to turn out in inner-tubes.

The year ends with the annual **Christmas Cruise** in early December. Sparkling boats promenade along Lake Washington and Elliott Bay, with local choirs singing seasonal music nightly.

■ NEAR SEATTLE

Cross **Lake Washington** on the two floating bridges to arrive in a biker and picnicker's dream vision. The spacious parklands and miles of country roads delight those who enjoy being outdoors. In the much-maligned, built-up suburb of **Bellevue,** the July **Bellevue Jazz Festival** (455-6885) attracts both local jazz cats and national acts. If nothing else, a jaunt to suburbia grants a fine view of Seattle against a mountainous backdrop. The hills due east of the city are full of good hiking trails.

Head farther out for lovely country excursions. Take I-90 east to **Lake Sammamish State Park,** off exit 15, for excellent swimming and water-skiing facilities, volleyball courts, and playing fields. You might want to continue onward to the towns of **Snoqualmie** and **North Bend,** 29 mi. east of Seattle. In Snoqualmie, the **Puget Sound Railroad Museum,** 109 King St. (746-4025), on Rte. 202, houses a collection of functional early steam and electric trains in the old Snoqualmie Depot. Train rides on these antique beasts run to North Bend, offering views of **Snoqualmie Falls.** Trips run on the hour, and the full round-trip takes an hour. (Open April-Sept. Sat.-Sun. 11am-4pm. Round-trip rides $6, seniors $5, children $4.) In North Bend, the **Snoqualmie Valley Museum,** 320 North Bend Blvd. S (888-3200 or 888-0062), resurrects a turn-of-the-century parlor and kitchen. (Open Thurs.-Sun. 1-5pm and occasionally during the week; call for information.) Call the **Snoqualmie Chamber of Commerce** at 888-4440.

From North Bend, take bus #210 or Rte. 202 north to view the astounding **Snoqualmie Falls.** Formerly a sacred place for local Native people, the falls now work for Puget Power; the utility acquired the ability to turn the falls on and off in 1898. Puget Power maintains public picnic facilities in the vicinity. The falls were featured in David Lynch's cult TV series *Twin Peaks,* and the small town of Snoqualmie has been host to hordes of "Peaks freaks" (mostly Japanese) since the release two summers ago of the show's big-screen flick, *Fire Walk With Me.*

U-pick berry farms line Rte. 202 north along the Snoqualmie River and are open in the spring and summer. In **Woodinville** is the **Ste. Michelle Vintners,** 14111 145th St. NE (488-4633), a leader in the recent movement to popularize Washington **wines.** 45-minute tours of the facility, resembling a French chateau, end with wine tasting for those 21 and over (tours daily 10am-4:30pm; free). To reach Woodinville from downtown Seattle, take bus #310 during peak hours only.

The Seattle area is surrounded by the vast factories of **Boeing,** Seattle's most prominent employer. At Boeing Field south of Seattle is the **Museum of Flight,** 9404 E Marginal Way S (767-7373). Take I-5 south to exit 158 and turn north onto E Marginal Way S, or take bus #123. The museum is in the restored red barn where William E. Boeing founded the company in 1916. Inside, photographs and artifacts trace the history of flight from its beginnings through the 1930s, including an operating replica of the Wright Brothers' wind tunnel. Explore the B-17 bomber; it's surprisingly small. **Rare aircraft** sometimes participate in special events on the grounds nearby. The July 13-14 **Airshow** is always a soaring success. (Open Fri.-Wed. 10am-5pm, Thurs. 10am-9pm; $5, ages 6-15 $3.)

Just south of **Des Moines** on Rte. 509 off Rte. 99 is **Saltwater State Park** (764-4128). Take bus #130. The park has extensive foot trails through the Kent Smith Canyon, a beach for swimming and clamming, and 52 campsites with pay showers and flush toilets (sites $11).

BAINBRIDGE ISLAND

Ferries (see page 319) depart from Colman Dock downtown for **Bainbridge Island,** a rural idyll homesteaded by late-19th-century Swedish and late-20th-century Californian immigrants. Eat at the firecracker- and flower-festooned **Streamliner Diner,**

397 Winslow Way (842-8595), where natural foods and rich pies (slice $2.50) tempt the traveler. (Open Mon.-Fri. 7am-3pm, Sat.-Sun. 8am-2:30pm.) Wash it down with a bottle of Ferry Boat White from the **Bainbridge Island Vineyards & Winery** (842-9463). Here you can sample the local grapes or tour the fields where they are grown; just turn right at the first white trellis on Rte. 305 as you come from the ferry. Bottles range in price from $7.50 to $22.50 (open Wed.-Sun. noon-5pm, tours Sun. 2pm; free).

Head for one of Bainbridge Island's state parks. **Fort Ward,** southwest of Bainbridge Island, offers boat launches, picnic facilities, and an underwater scuba diving area (day-use only). **Fay-Bainbridge,** (842-3931) on the northern tip of the island just 1½ mi. from **Cliffhaven,** has good fishing and 36 **campsites** with pay showers and flush toilets (sites $11, walk-in sites $8).

PUGET SOUND

According to Native American legend, Puget Sound was created when Ocean, wishing to keep his children Cloud and Rain close to home, gouged a trough and molded the dirt into the Cascade Range. Since then, Cloud and Rain have stayed close to Ocean, rarely venturing east of the mountain wall. Millions of Washington's people live along Puget Sound, in the Seattle-Tacoma-Olympia belt or in Bremerton to the north, but with the pristine, rural setting and great hostel of Vashon Island, the Kitsap Peninsula and its cycling trails, and the scenic, berry-bushed bluffs of Whidbey Island, outdoor adventure is never far from urban sophistication.

■■■ VASHON ISLAND

Only a short ferry ride from Seattle and an even shorter ferry hop from Tacoma, Vashon Island has remained inexplicably invisible to most Seattlites. One in every ten islanders is a professional artist. The small-town lifestyle of the islanders is virtually unaffected by the proximity to city speedways, and so is Vashon's wealth of natural beauty. Most of the island is undeveloped. Green forests of Douglas firs, rolling cherry orchards, strawberry fields, and wildflowers cover the island during the summer. The island includes a tiny town and several unimposing factories. Taking a trip to Vashon from Seattle is like taking a breath of fresh air on the back porch: necessary at times, no matter how nice the house.

Practical Information Vashon Island stretches between Seattle and Tacoma on its eastern side and between Southworth and Gig Harbor on its western side. From Seattle, drive south on I-5, take exit 164 down to Western Ave. and the waterfront or exit 163A (West Seattle/Spokane St.) down Fauntleroy Way to Fauntleroy Cove. From Tacoma, off I-5, take exit 132 (Bremerton/Gig Harbor) to Rte. 16, Pearl St., and Point Defiance Park.

Four different **Washington State Ferries** (see page 43 for **complete schedule and fare information**) can get you to Vashon Island. Ferries leave from Fauntleroy in West Seattle (**D**), from downtown Seattle (**G**), and from Southworth in the Kitsap Peninsula (**F**) for the northern tip of Vashon Island; ferries leave from Point Defiance in Tacoma (**E**) for the southern tip. Hostels give discounts on ferry tickets.

Buses #54, #118, and #119 serve the island ferries from downtown Seattle (call 800-542-7876 for bus info.); vans also service the island, beginning their runs from the ferry landing. Unlike the buses, the vans can be flagged down anywhere. Fares are the same as in the rest of the system: $1 for travel in one zone, $1.50 for two-zone travel. The island is all within one zone. Buses #54 and #55 from the Fauntleroy ferry to downtown Seattle are the only ones that run on Sunday. Buses #118 and #119 are the way to get to the town of Vashon.

The **Vashon Manny Senior Center** (463-5173) is downtown on Bank Rd. So is **Joy's Village Cleaner,** 17500 Vashon Hwy. (463-9933; wash and dry 75¢ each; open Mon.-Sat. 7am-10pm, Sun. 7am-9pm). **Emergency numbers:** 911; **police,** 463-3618; **Coast Guard,** 463-2951. Vashon's **post office** is on Bank Rd. (463-9390; open Mon.-Fri. 9am-5pm; **General Delivery ZIP code:** 98070). The **area code** is 206 (from Seattle, dial 1 and then the 7-digit number).

Accommodations and Food The **Vashon Island Ranch/Hostel (HI/AYH)** (sometimes called **"Seattle B"**) is really the island's only accommodation, and it is in itself one of the main reasons to come here. The hostel is at 12119 SW Cove Rd. (463-2592); to get there, jump on any bus at the ferry terminal, ride it until it gets to **Thriftway Market,** and call from the pay phone inside the market, marked with an HI/AYH sticker. Judy will come pick you up if the hour is reasonable, and she has never turned a hosteler away. "Seattle B" is a wonderful retreat from "Seattle A," with all the comforts of home: free pancakes for breakfast, free use of old bikes, free campfire wood, free volleyball games in the afternoon, and a caring manager. The hostel accommodates 14 in bunk rooms, but those are for the weak of heart. Go for the huge tepees or covered wagons under the stars. When all beds are full, you can pitch a tent (open year-round; tents and beds $9, non-members $12). If, for some reason, you can't make it to the hostel, call for information on **B&Bs** (463-3556).

Most hostelers get creative in the kitchen with supplies from **Thriftway** downtown (open daily 8am-9pm). However, there are other options for those allergic to dishwashing. **Cafe Tosca,** 9924 Bank Rd. (463-2125), has the best food in town and a charming, low-key atmosphere. Entrees will run you $10 to $15. (Open Mon.-Thurs. 11am-2pm and 5-8pm, Fri.-Sun. 11am-2pm and 5-9pm.) You'll find better-than-average Chinese and American cuisine at **Happy Gardens,** Vashon (463-9109). Vegetable chow mein ($4.75) is popular. (Open daily 7:30am-11pm, popular lounge open till 2am.) The **Dog Day Café and Juice Bar,** 17530 Vashon Hwy. in the Vashon Mall, offers a Seattle-style coffee-house and restaurant. If you're in town on the weekends, you can grab dinner there too. (Sandwiches are $3.50-5, entrees $5-7. Open Tues.-Wed. 10am-4pm, Thurs.-Sat. 10am-4pm and 5-9pm, Sun. 10am-4pm).

Sights and Events The island is wonderful for **biking.** Don't be deceived by the short distances; Vashon's hills will turn even a short jaunt into an arduous affair. A sweaty exploration will be rewarded, however, with rapturous scenery. **Point Robinson Park** is a gorgeous spot for a picnic (from Vashon Hwy. take Ellisburg to Dockton to Pt. Robinson Rd.); check out the mysterious old lighthouse. **Wax Orchards** is also a fulfilling destination (take 204 to 111 Ave. SW to SW 220, then to Wax Orchard Rd.). More than 500 acres of hiking trails weave their way through the woods in the middle of the island, and several lovely walks start from the hostel.

Count on some culture no matter when you visit. **Blue Heron Arts Center** (463-5131) coordinates most activities. Call for information on upcoming classes and events (gallery and craft shop open Tues.-Fri. 11am-5pm, Sat. 10am-5pm).

On a calm day at **Tramp Harbor** you can rent a sea kayak or rowboat at the **Quartermaster Marina** (463-3624). The **Strawberry Festival,** held during the second weekend in July, seems to awaken even the mainland to Vashon's existence, and people flood the island to cheer soap derby races down those infamous Vashon hills. Local and national bands inspire street dancing well into the night, and small children are known to metamorphose into giant strawberries among the miles of food and craft stands.

■■■ TACOMA

Though spending time in Tacoma rather than Seattle is somewhat like hanging out in Newark instead of New York, Tacoma has a few worthwhile outdoor attractions suitable for a daytrip.

Practical Information Visitors Information in Tacoma can be obtained at the **Pierce County Visitor Information Center**, 906 Pacific Ave. (627-2836), downtown on the 4th floor of the Seafirst Center; open Mon.-Fri. 8:30am-5pm). Useful phone numbers: **Greyhound Bus Terminal** (333-3629), at the corner of Pacific and 14th, in downtown Tacoma. (Station open 5:30am to 7pm daily.) **Emergency,** 911; **Crisis Line,** 759-6700; **Rape Relief,** 474-7273; **Safeplace,** 279-8333. The Tacoma **post office** is on 11th at A St. (Open Mon.-Fri. 8am-5:30pm. **General Delivery ZIP Code:** 98402.) The **area code** is 206. There is regular **ferry service** to Vashon Island from Tacoma (see Sights).

Tacoma lies on I-5 about 35 mi. south of Seattle and about 35 mi. east of Olympia. Rte. 7 offers quick access to Mt. Rainier, the Cowlitz Valley, and Mount St. Helens. Rte. 16 links Tacoma with Bremerton and the Kitsap Peninsula.

Accommodations and Food If you're staying the night in Tacoma, don't go out alone. One of the city's best hotels is the **Valley Motel,** 1220 Puyallup Ave. (272-7720), which is clean and feels safe (singles $25, doubles $29). Large rooms are $1 more and include kitchenettes ($2 key deposit).

Stop in at **Antique Sandwich Company,** 5102 N Pearl St. (752-4069), near Point Defiance, for some great natural food, an open mike on Tuesday nights, and live music on Friday night. The "poor boy" sandwich is $5.75; espresso shakes are $3.25. (Open Mon. and Wed.-Thurs. 7am-8pm, Tues. 7am-10pm, Fri. 7am-9pm, Sat. 7am-7pm, Sun. 8am-7pm.) On your way home, you might want to visit the monkeys (named Java and Jive) at **Bob's Java Jive,** 2102 S Tacoma Way (475-9843), south of downtown, directly beneath the I-5 Skyway. The Java Jive is a locals-only hangout and at 9pm the cabaret starts up. Hamburgers and sandwiches around $3 (open Mon.-Thurs. noon-11pm, Fri. noon-2am, Sat. 3pm-2am).

Sights Tacoma's waterfront is home to **Point Defiance Park** (591-3681), one of the most attractive parks in the Puget Sound area. Point Defiance is Tacoma's **ferry** terminal; the ferry runs regularly to Vashon Island (**E**; see page 43 for **complete schedule and fare information**). To reach the park, take a short detour off I-5 onto **Ruston Way** north of downtown; the route replaces the stifling clouds of Tacoma's smokestacks with views of Mt. Rainier. Continue toward Point Defiance Park; a 5-mi. loop passes by all the park's attractions and offers postcard views of the Puget Sound and access to miles of woodland **trails.** In the spring, stop to smell the flowers; the enormous **tulip and daffodil garden** can be overwhelming. **Owen Beach** looks across at **Vashon Island** and is a good starting place for rambles down the beach. The loop then brushes by the spot where Captain Wilkes of the U.S. Navy proclaimed in 1841 that if he had guns on this and the opposite shore (Gig Harbor) he could defy the world ("Point Defiance").

The park's prize possession is the **Point Defiance Zoo and Aquarium** (591-5335). Penguins, polar bears, and scary sharks populate the tanks of the aquarium. Attend a "Mature Mammal Talk," taking place intermittently from 11am- 4pm. (Open daily 10am-7pm; Labor Day-Memorial Day 10am-4pm. $6.50, seniors $6, ages 5-17 $4.75, ages 3-4 $2.50, under 3 free.) The meticulously restored **Fort Nisqually** (591-5339), in the park, also merits a visit. Hudson's Bay Company built the fort in 1832 to offset growing commercial competition from Americans. (Fort open daily 11am-6pm; in winter Wed.-Fri. 9am-4:30pm, Sat.-Sun. 12:30-4:30pm. Museum open daily noon-6pm; in winter Tues.-Sun. 1-4pm. Free.) **Camp Six Logging Museum** (752-0047), also in the park, retrieves an entire 19th-century logging camp from the dustbin of history. The camp includes buildings and equipment and offers a 1-mi. ride ($2, seniors and children $1) on an original steam-powered logging engine. (Open Memorial Day-Labor Day Wed.-Fri. 10am-6pm, Sat.-Sun. 10am-7pm. $2, seniors and children $1.) For those traveling with small children, Port Defiance Park also contains **Never Never Land** (591-5845). This park winds along a path and allows youngsters to look at display scenes from famous nursery rhymes and fairytales, and costumed characters and puppet shows ($2, ages 13-17 $1.50, 3-12 $1, under 3 free.

The **Tacoma Art Museum** (272-4258), on the northeast corner of 12th and Pacific, has a stupendous collection of photographs upstairs by the eccentric Weegee upstairs (open Tues.-Sat. 10am-5pm, Thurs. 10am-7pm, Sun. noon-5pm; $3, seniors and students $2, ages 6-12 $1).

■■■ OLYMPIA

While still peaceful and easy-going, Olympia has smoothly made the transition from small fishing-and-oyster port to growing state capital. The sprawling Capitol Campus, with its whitewashed buildings and manicured lawns, dominates the downtown. Listen to politicians argue from the Capitol gallery and sample beer at the local brewery. The city is a center for small-market alternative rock. Olympia also draws on its natural environment for picturesque Japanese gardens and two wildlife refuges, one a haven for endangered wolves.

PRACTICAL INFORMATION AND ORIENTATION

Visitors Information: Chamber of Commerce, 1000 Plum St. (357-3362 or 800-753-8474), next to the City Hall. Pleasant, competent staff will help you sort through an array of brochures. A page of crisis line listings is available. Open Mon.-Fri. 9am-5pm. An information booth is set up at the **Farmer's Market,** 401 N Capitol Way. **Olympia State Capitol Visitors Center,** P.O. Box 41020 (586-3460), on Capitol Way between 12th and 14th Ave. The signs on I-5 will direct you to this visitors center. Brochures for Olympic National Park (see page 369) and the Olympic Peninsula (see page 364). A few photos of historic Olympia on the walls, and a VCR available for viewing travel videos of the Northwest area. Open Mon.-Fri. 8am-5pm, Sat.-Sun. 10am-4pm; Labor Day-Memorial Day Mon.-Fri. 8am-5pm. **Department of Trade and Economic Development, Tourism Division,** General Administration Bldg., #G-3 (800-544-1800 or 586-2088). Open Mon.-Fri. 9am-4pm. **City of Olympia Parks and Recreation Department,** 222 N Columbia Ave. (753-8380). Information on community activities. Open Mon.-Fri. 8am-8pm.
Washington State Parks and Recreation Commission, 7150 Cleanwater Lane (753-5755).Write to P.O. Box 42650, Olympia WA, 98504-2650 for information/reservation packet. All the latest on the state parks. Immensely helpful staff. Open Mon.-Fri. 8am-5pm.
Department of Natural Resources (DNR), 1111 Washington St. (902-1000). The *Guide to Camp and Picnic Sites* shows free DNR sites statewide. Ask for their guide to waterfront areas around Puget Sound. The **maps department,** P.O. Box 47031 (902-1234), offers both publications. Open Mon.-Fri. 8am-4:30pm.
Department of Fish and Wildlife, 1111 Washington St. (902-2200 or 753-5700). Information on saltwater fishing and shellfish, including season and limit designations, fish and wildlife regulations. Write 600 Capital Way N, Olympia 98501-1091. Open Mon.-Fri. 8am-5pm.
Trains: Amtrak, 6600 Yelm Hwy. (800-872-7245). To: Seattle (3 per day, $13); Portland (3 per day, $19).
Greyhound, 107 E 7th Ave. (357-5541), at Capitol Way. To: Seattle (7 per day, $10); Portland (8 per day, $19); Spokane (3 per day, $49). Open daily 6:30am-8pm; in winter, hours are restricted.
Buses: Intercity Transit, 526 S Pattison St. (943-7777). Office open Mon.-Fri. 8am-5pm. Phone staffed Mon.-Fri. 7am-7pm, Sat. 8am-5pm, Sun. 7:30am-6pm. Buses run Mon.-Fri. 6am-11:30pm, Sat. 8am-10pm, Sun. 8am-7pm. Fare 50¢, seniors and the disabled 25¢. Day passes $1. The **Capitol Shuttle** is free to the public. Buses run from the Capitol Campus to downtown, or to East side and West side, every 15 min. between 6:30am and 6:15pm. The free **State Office Shuttle** runs between the Insurance Building on Capitol Campus and Lacey/Tumwater every ½-hr. between 6:50am and 6pm. **Custom buses** continue on from where normal fixed routes stop. These run Mon.-Sat. (Standard fares from 7pm on; call 943-7777 for info.) Supplementary transport is provided for seniors and travelers with dis-

abilities by **Special Mobility Services,** 320 Dayton SE (754-1200 or 754-9430), but you must complete an application first. **Olympia Express** (Intercity Transit) runs between Olympia and Tacoma Mon.-Fri. 5:50am-6pm. Buses leave every ½-hr.; fare $1.50. Transferring to a Seattle bus in Tacoma costs an additional $1.25; total time to Seattle just under 2 hrs. If all of this info. has you thoroughly befuddled, the friendly **Customer Service Department** (786-1881 or 800-287-6348) will be delighted to straighten you out.

Taxi: Red Top Taxi, 357-3700. **Capitol City Taxi,** 357-4949. Both 24 hrs.

Car Rental: U-Save Auto Rental, 3015 Pacific Ave. (786-8445). $26 per day plus 20¢ for each additional mi. over 100. Must be at least 21 with credit card.

Equipment and Bike Rental: Olympic Outfitters, 407 E 4th Ave. (943-1997). Mountain bikes $25 per day. $100 deposit, or leave a credit card number. This enormous sports shop also rents tents, skis, and mountain climbing gear. Open Mon.-Fri. 10am-8pm, Sat. 10am-6pm, Sun. noon-5pm. **Big Foot Outdoor,** 518 Capital Way S (352-4616), rents 3-person tents ($30 per week), backpacks ($50 per week). $50 deposit, or leave a credit card. Open Mon.-Sat. 7:30am-6pm, Sun. 9am-4pm. **River Rat,** 215 7th Ave. SW (705-1585), rents kayaks ($27 per day), canoes ($5 per hr. or $27 per day), double kayaks ($10 per hr.), and whitewater rafts ($64 per day). Convenient to Capital Lake. Open Mon.-Fri. 10am-10pm, Sat. 10am-midnight, Sun. noon-6pm.

Olympia Timberland Library, 313 8th Ave. SE (352-0595), at Franklin St. Open Mon.-Thurs. 10am-9pm, Fri.-Sat. 10am-5pm; winter Sun. 1-5pm.

Laundromat: The Wash Tub, 2103 Harrison Ave. NW (953-9714). Wash $1.10, 8-min. dry 25¢. Open Mon.-Fri. 7am-10pm, Sat. 8am-10pm, Sun. 8am-11pm.

Crisis Clinic, 352-2211 or 800-627-2211. 24-hr. hotline for info. and referral.

Women's Shelter: Safeplace, 754-6300. 24-hr. counseling, housing referrals.

Emergency: 911. **Police:** 753-8300. **Fire:** 753-8348.

Post Office: 900 S Jefferson SE (357-2286). Open Mon.-Fri. 7:30am-6pm, Sat. 9am-4pm. **General Delivery ZIP Code:** 98501.

Area Code: 206.

Olympia, located where I-5 meets U.S. 101, is a logical stopping point for those heading north to the Olympic Peninsula or Seattle, or south to the Cascade peaks or Portland. The city is visibly creeping toward big-city status. The west side of the downtown area borders Capital Lake and West Bay; part of the city's northwest section is directly accessible only by bridge. Olympia is divided into four quadrants with ambiguous boundaries.

ACCOMMODATIONS AND CAMPING

The motels in Olympia generally cater to lobbyists and lawyers rather than to budget tourists. The local universities reserve rooms only for their own students, so your choices here are limited. Camping is the cheapest option.

Bailey Motor Inn, 3333 Martin Way (491-7515), exit 107 off I-5. Clean, comfortable rooms and an indoor pool. The heaters stuffed with fake wood are slightly absurd. Restaurant (espresso!) next door. Singles from $34. Doubles from $41.

The Golden Gavel Motor Hotel, 909 Capitol Way (352-8533). Immaculate, almost-elegant rooms geared toward lower-budget businessmen. Cable TV, morning coffee, and phones. Singles $41. Doubles $44.

Motel 6, 400 W Lee St. (754-7320; fax 705-0655), in Tumwater. Take Exit 102 off I-5 and head east on Trosper Rd., then south 1 block on Capitol Blvd., and west on W. Lee St. Reliably clean rooms. Color TV and swimming pool. Singles $36. Doubles $42. Each additional person $6. Under 17 free with parent.

Millersylvania State Park, 12245 Tilly Rd. S. (753-1519), 10 mi. south of Olympia. Take Exit 99 off I-5, then head south on Rte. 121, or exit 95 off I-5 and head north on Rte. 121. 216 tree-shrouded, reasonably spacious sites overrun by irrepressible children on bicycles, with pay showers and flush toilets. Facilities for the disabled. Primitive hiker/biker sites available. Standard sites $11, RV hookups $16.

Capital Forest Multiple Use Area, 15 mi. southwest of Olympia, off I-5 exit 95. Administered by the DNR. 50 campsites scattered among 6 campgrounds. Camping is free and requires no notification or permit. Pick up a forest **map** at the visitors bureau or at the state Department of Natural Resources office (see Practical Information). The area is unsupervised; lone women might be better off paying the $11 for Millersylvania. Grab a space early in the summertime; "free" is a magic word for a lot of campers.

FOOD

There is potential for good eating along bohemian 4th Ave., east of Columbia, especially when the pace picks up during the school year. Vegetarians fill up here before heading north to Burgerland. When that 2am urge for carrot sticks hits you (it will...you think you can resist too, but it's *hopeless* so just *give in to the carrot sticks now*) try 24-hr. **Top Foods & Drug,** 1313 Cooper Pt. Rd. SW (754-1428), in the wee hours. The **Olympia Farmer's Market,** 401 N Capital Way (352-9096), has a great selection of in-season fruits and berries; you can buy a fantastic cheap lunch here. Try the grilled salmon burger (mmmm...$3.75). (Open early May-Sept. Thurs.-Sun.10am-3pm; April Sat.-Sun. 10am-3pm; Oct.-mid-Dec. Fri.-Sun. 10am-3pm.)

   The Spar Cafe & Bar, 111 E 4th Ave. (357-6444). Feel a touch of nostalgia as you down a grilled oyster sandwich ($6) or a Spar burger ($5.50) in this old logger haunt. Old pictures, polished wood, and a long counter send you back to the age of Bogart. Mellow bar in back, with live jazz Sat. nights (no cover). Restaurant open daily 6am-9pm; bar open daily 11am-2am.
   Smithfield Cafe, 212 W 4th Ave. (786-1725). The relaxed, mixed straight/gay crowd digs the deluxe burrito ($4.50) and the vegetarian and vegan options. Check the board inside for the word on local band action. Free condoms in the bathroom. Open Mon.-Fri. 7am-8pm, Sat.-Sun. 8am-8pm.
   Jo Mama's Restaurant, 120 N Pear St. (943-9849), in an old house at State St. Homemade pizza served in an all-wood, "old-tavern" atmosphere. The food is somewhat pricey (the 10-in. vegetarian pizza for $14.75 feeds 2 hungry travelers), but the ambience compensates. Cheerful, convivial staff. Open Mon.-Thurs. 11am-10pm, Fri. 11am-11pm, Sat. 4-11pm, Sun. 4-10pm.
   Bayview Deli & Bakery, 516 W 4th (352-4901), in the rear of Thriftway. Cheap and extensive deli selection, but the real draw is the tables right on the waterfront. Finish up with an ice cream "kiddie cone;" 60¢. Open daily 7am-9pm.

SIGHTS, ACTIVITIES, AND EVENTS

The focal point of Olympia is the **State Capitol Campus,** where, Madonna fans will be delighted to know, part of the movie *Body of Evidence* was filmed in 1991. Take a free tour of the **Legislative Building** (586-8677) to sneak a peek of the public sphere. Only the tours can usher you in to the legislative chambers, which are otherwise off-limits (except during the legislative session between January and March).

An enormous wool, velvet, and velour carpet covers over 1200 sq. ft. of the State Reception Room's teakwood floor; when the handpainted rug was completed, the original pattern was destroyed so it could not be replicated elsewhere. To frustrate state employees' tendency to roll back the carpet and dance the Charleston after work, many pieces of heavy furniture were purchased in 1929 and placed on the carpet's perimeter (45-min. tours daily 10am-3pm; building open Mon.-Fri. 8am-5pm, Sat.-Sun. 10am-4pm).

Unfortunately, the building's spectacular **dome** is indefinitely closed to the public. Built for maintenance purposes only, the 200-step staircase up was quivering under the pounding of tourists tramping up and down. But although this panoramic view of Olympia is no longer available, the rest of the magnificent building is certainly worth a wander. The newly revamped **State Capitol Museum,** 211 W 21st Ave. (753-2580), due to reopen in May 1995, has historical and political exhibits, including an informative display on the lives of Native children in boarding schools. (Open Tues.-Fri. 10am-4pm, Sat.-Sun. noon-4pm; free, but donation encouraged.)

   Capitol Lake Park is a favorite retreat for runners, sailors, and swimmers. Spawning salmon head for Tumwater Falls late August through October; you can spot the leaping lox as they cross the lake. Canoe and kayak rentals are available at **River Rat's** (see Practical Information). Or stroll on the boardwalk at **Percival Landing Park** (743-8379); various boats jam the Port, a reminder of Olympia's oyster-filled past. The **Yashiro Japanese Garden** (753-8380), open daily from 10am to dusk by the Chamber of Commerce (see Practical Information), is tiny but beautiful, a perfect spot for a picnic.

As in Transylvania, budget deals in Olympia come out after dark. The **State Theater,** 204 E 4th Ave. (357-4010), shows recent movies for $1. During the summer, the city schedules free jazz, ensemble, and symphony concerts at **Sylvester Park** (Fri. at noon; call 953-2375 for info.). Since 1985 the band Beat Happening and their label, K Records, have made Olympia one of the centers of the international **rock music underground.** The Kill Rock Stars label, and their flagship feminist band Bikini Kill, live here too. Ask in record shops about shows or look for posters.

Capital Lakefair is a not-to-be-missed bonanza the third week in July, with an overwhelming array of food, carnival rides, and booths staffed by non-profit organizations. Contact the Chamber of Commerce for other festivals in Olympia.

■ NEAR OLYMPIA

Olympia Beer (754-5177), actually brewed south of the capital city in **Tumwater,** has been taken over by the Pabst Company, which now produces several different beers on the premises. You can tour the facility and have a brew on the house (open daily 8am-4:30pm; free). The brewery, highly visible from I-5, can be reached from exit 103 in Tumwater. Nearby **Tumwater Falls Park** practically begs for picnickers.

The **Mima Mounds** (753-2400), unusual geologic formations, are preserved in a Department of Natural Resources prairie park 10 mi. south of Olympia. The self-guided interpretive trails are wheelchair-accessible (open daily 8am-dusk). Take I-5 south to exit 95; 1 mi. west of Littlerock, follow Wadell Creek Rd. west, and look for a tiny sign about 1½ mi. up the road pointing left.

The **Nisqually National Wildlife Refuge** (753-9467), off I-5 between Olympia and Tacoma (at exit 114), has recently pitted neighbor against neighbor in the quiet Nisqually delta. Environmentalists seek to preserve the delta's diverse marsh and marine life, but developers hope to cast some of their bread upon the water and its environs. For the time being, you can still view the protected wildlife from blinds or walk the trails that wind through the preserve. Trails open daily during daylight hours (office open Mon.-Fri. 7:30am-4pm; $2).

Ten mi. south of the city is **Wolfhaven,** 3111 Offut Lake Rd. (264-4695 or 800-448-9653). The haven now preserves 40 wolves of six different species. Tour the grounds ($5, children $2) or take part in the Howl-In (every Fri. and Sat. 6-9pm; $6, children $4). Groups tell stories 'round a campfire to the accompaniment of the howling residents (open May-Sept. daily 10am-5pm; Oct.-April Wed.-Sun. 10am-4pm).

■■■ KITSAP PENINSULA

The Kitsap Peninsula occupies much of the area between the Olympic Peninsula and Seattle. With natural deep-water inlets, it is an excellent naval base, holding eight nuclear-powered Trident submarines. Aesthetic quirks aside, travelers without Top Secret clearance can still enjoy the area's forested, green, hilly terrain. The peninsula's back roads and campgrounds are a **cycling** paradise. Explore Northwest Native history at the grave of Chief Sealth, the Suquamish Chief after whom Seattle is named. For a cultural shift, enjoy the May "Viking Fest" in **Poulsbo.**

Bremerton is the hub of the Kitsap Peninsula. You'll swear you've stepped into a Tom Clancy novel; every third person has a Navy security pass swinging from his or her neck. The Navy Yard here is immense. President Clinton only added to the local flavor by hosting his 1993 meeting with East Asian leaders at nearby **Tillicum Village.** The town contains few sights but is a good base for exploring the peninsula and Hood Canal. **Kingston,** at the northern tip about 20 mi. from Bremerton on Rte. 3 and Rte. 104, is linked by ferry to **Edmonds** on the mainland. **Southworth,** about 10 mi. east of Bremerton on Rte. 16 and Rte. 160, is connected to West Seattle and Vashon Island by ferry. For ferry information, see below. Rte. 3 and Rte. 104 lead north to the Olympic Peninsula across the **Hood Canal Bridge.** Rte. 16 leads south to Tacoma.

Practical Information The Bremerton Kitsap County Visitor and Convention Bureau, 120 Washington St. (479-3588), is just up the hill from the ferry terminal, and will help you navigate the area. The office puts out a flotilla of pamphlets on Bremerton and nearby towns, and the lively staff tries hard to cover up the city's fundamental drabness. (Open Mon.-Fri. 9am-5pm, Sat. 10am-4pm; Labor Day-Memorial Day Mon.-Fri. 9am-5pm.) The **post office** (373-1456) is stationed at 602 Pacific Ave. (open Mon.-Fri. 9am-5pm; **General Delivery ZIP Code:** 98310).

Frequent **ferry service** to the Kitsap Peninsula arrives at three points (see page 43 for **complete schedule and fare information**). From Bremerton, ferries run to downtown Seattle (**B** and **N**); from Southworth, to Fauntleroy in West Seattle (**H**) and Vashon Island (**F**); and from Kingston to Edmonds on the mainland (**C**).

Once there, **Kitsap Transit** (373-BUSS, or 373-2877), at 234 Wycott St., about one and a half blocks from the Bremerton Information Bureau, maintains several buses connecting population centers. Call ahead for times or pick up schedules at the Winslow, Bremerton, or Kingston ferry terminals (75¢ peak times, 50¢ off-peak, seniors 25¢ off-peak.) Keep in mind, however, that the buses are designed to serve commuters, and that many lines stop running after 6pm and do not service the Winslow terminal Saturday or Sunday. However, the area is compact, and a **bike** will get you most places.

Accommodations, Camping, and Food If you're intent on spending the night here, your best bet is to camp. Those traveling by foot will find **Illahee State Park** (478-6460) wonderfully convenient. To get there, hop on bus #29 at the ferry terminal in Bremerton and take it to the corner of Perry and Sylvan. From there, walk ¼ mi. up the hill on Sylvan until you reach the entrance. The park has 51 campsites replete with water, bathrooms, and hot showers (sites $10, walk-in sites $5). Another possibility is **Scenic Beach State Park** (830-5079), near the village of Seabeck on the west coast of the peninsula. The park has 52 campsites with water and bathrooms (sites $10, walk-in sites $5). From Silverdale, take Anderson Hill Rd. or Newberry Hill Rd. west to Seabeck Hwy., and then follow the highway 7 mi. south to the Scenic Beach turnoff. **Cyclists** should be prepared for the staggering hills along this route.

Culinary choices in Bremerton are about as appealing as those on a ship. Locals head for the slightly upscale **Boat Shed,** 101 Shore Dr. (377-2600), on the water immediately below the northeast side of the Manette Bridge. The Shed has terrific seafood, sandwiches, and super nachos, all in the $5 range (open daily Mon.-Sat. 11am-11pm).

Sights and Events Next to the Visitor's Center (see above), you'll find the excellent **Bremerton Naval Museum** (479-7447). Thrill to the sight of large action photos from WWII and transparent models of destroyers and aircraft carriers measuring up to 10 ft. (Open Tues.-Sat. 10am-5pm, Sun. 1-5 pm; free, though donations requested.) In Bremerton, guide yourself through the destroyer **USS Turner Joyce,** a floating museum (792-2457; $4, ages 5-12 $3, under 5 free). The **Naval Undersea Museum,** 610 Donell St. (396-4148) in **Keyport,** exhibits undersea artifacts, including a K-10 torpedo and a Japanese Kamikaze aircraft (open June-Sept. Tues.-Sun.10am-4pm; Oct.-May Tues.-Sun. 10am-4pm). The **foot ferry** across the Sinclair Inlet to **Port Orchard** affords an excellent view of the shipyards (ferry leaves every hr., on the ¼-hr. The fare is 70¢, and the ferry leaves from the Bremerton terminal.)

If you ask nicely, the driver of bus #90 will let you off at the Longhouse Convenience Store. Follow the road 1 mi. to the fascinating **Suquamish Museum** (598-3311). The museum is on the north side of the **Agate Pass (Hood Canal) Bridge** on Rte. 305. Run by the Port Madison Reservation, this small museum is devoted entirely to the history and culture of the Puget Sound Salish Native people. Striking photographs, artifacts, and quotations from respected elders piece together the lives of those who inhabited the peninsula before the great invasion (open daily 10am-5pm; $2.50, seniors $2, under 12 $1). **Chief Sealth,** for whom Seattle was named, belonged to the Suquamish people. His grave is up the hill, about a 15-minute walk away. The Chief's memorial, constructed of cedar war canoes over a Christian headstone is an excellent example of the melding of Catholic and Native religions attempted briefly in the 19th century. Next to the gravesite is a Suquamish city park that was once the site of **Old Man House,** a cedar longhouse burned by Federal agents in 1870 in an attempt to destroy the communal lifestyle of the Native people, regarded as immoral and conducive to smallpox.

Be sure to visit striking **Tillicum Village;** tours depart three times daily from Seattle May 1st through Oct. 31 (reservations necessary; call 443-1244). Tillicum offers beautiful views of the Seattle Skyline, Mt. Rainier, Mt. Baker, and the Cascade and Olympic Mountain ranges. The tour of the village itself presents a traditional Northwest Native longhouse, a salmon dinner, and Native dance performances.

■■■ WHIDBEY ISLAND

Clouds, wrung dry by the time they finally pass over Whidbey Island, release a scant 20 in. of rain each year. Rocky beaches lead back to bluffs crawling with wild roses and blackberry brambles. Visitors drawn to this sunny island will discover that, because it is a long island, the points of interest on Whidbey are widely distributed. Explore Whidbey's berry picking, arts and crafts festivals, scuba diving, wine tasting, forests, beaches, and Bufflehead-watching by bike or car.

PRACTICAL INFORMATION

Chambers of Commerce: Oak Harbor, 5506 Rte. 20, P.O. Box 883, Oak Harbor 98260 (675-3535), about 1½ mi. north of the town center. Open Mon.-Fri. 9am-5pm, Sat. 9am-6pm, Sun. 10am-4pm; Sept.-May Mon.-Fri. 9am-5pm. **Coupeville,** 5 S Main St., P.O. Box 152, Coupeville (678-5434). Open Mon.-Fri. 9am-noon and 2-5pm. **Langley,** 124½ 2nd St. (321-6765), behind the Star Bistro Cafe (see Food), fronting the alley between 1st and 2nd St. Open Mon.-Fri. 10am-3pm.
Ranger Station: Deception Pass, 5175 N Rte. 20, Oak Harbor (675-2417). **Fort Ebey State Park,** Coupeville (678-4636).
Bike Rental: See Getting There and Getting Around below.
Library: Oak Harbor Public Library, 7030 70th St. E (675-5115), in City Hall, lower level. Open Mon.-Thurs. 10am-9pm, Fri.-Sat. 10am-5pm.
Crisis Center: 678-5555 or 321-4868. 24 hrs.
Pharmacy: Langley Drug, 105 1st St. (221-4359), across from the Post Office. Open Mon.-Fri. 9am-7pm, Sat. 9am-5pm, Sun. 10am-4pm.
Hospital: Whidbey General, 101 N Main St. (678-5151), in Coupeville.
Emergency/Police/Fire: 911.
Post Offices: Oak Harbor, 7035 70th St. NW (675-6621). Open Mon.-Fri. 8:30am-5pm. **General Delivery ZIP Code:** 98277. **Coupeville,** 201 NW Coveland (678-5353). Open Mon.-Fri. 9:30am-4:30pm, Sat. 11am-1pm. **General Delivery ZIP Code:** 98239. **Langley,** 115 2nd St. (321-4113). Open Mon.-Fri. 8:30am-5pm. **General Delivery ZIP Code:** 98260.
Area Code: 206.

GETTING THERE AND GETTING AROUND

The southern tip of Whidbey Island lies 40 mi. north of Seattle, as the Bufflehead flies. Two **ferry** lines run from the mainland to the island (see page 43 for **complete fare and schedule information**). One ferry (**I**) connects **Mukilteo,** a tiny community just south of Everett, with **Clinton**, a town on the southern end of Whidbey. The other (J) connects **Port Townsend** on the Olympic peninsula with the terminal at **Keystone State Park**, at the "waist" of the island on the western side. Service is frequent; again, see page 43.

Public transportation from Seattle is slightly more difficult. Take Metro Bus #6 from downtown Seattle to the Aurora Transit Center ($1, during rush-hour $1.50). From there, catch the Community Transit Bus #170 to the Mukilteo ferry terminal (fare 40¢). The last bus from the ferry terminal back to Aurora leaves at 6:30pm.

There is no hostel on the island, and inexpensive motels are few; those that do exist are often run-down. Making reservations is always sensible, especially in rain-free July and August. Some B&Bs offer pleasant, homey rooms for a few dollars more. Contact **Whidbey Island Bed and Breakfast Association,** P.O. Box 259, Langley 98260 (321-8323) for a full listing; reservations are necessary. Four **state parks** on a 50-mi.-long island can hardly be missed. They are listed south to north.

Tyee Motel and Cafe, 405 S Main St., Coupeville (678-6616), across Rte. 20 from the town proper, toward the Keystone ferry. Clean, standard motel rooms, with showers but no tubs. The setting is bleak; you might forget you're on an island, but it's within walking distance of Coupeville and the water. Cafe open Mon.-Sat. 6:30am-8:30pm. Singles and doubles from $45. You can also check in at the lounge (open 11:30am-2am) if the cafe is closed.

Crossroads Motel, 5622 Rte. 20 (675-3145), on northern edge of Oak Harbor. Cinderblock construction suggests cheap military housing, but the rooms are immaculately kept and the ship-shape management adds a feeling of security. Senior and military discounts. Singles $32. Doubles $45. Rooms with kitchens $50.

Fort Ebey State Park, 395 N Fort Ebey Rd. (678-4636). North of Fort Casey and just west of Coupeville. Take the Libbey Rd. turn-off from Rte. 20. Miles of hiking trails and easy access to a pebbly beach make this newest of Whidbey's campground also its best. 50 sites for cars and RVs; $11 (Oct.-April $6). Three hiker/biker sites $5. Pay showers.

South Whidbey State Park, 4128 S Smuggler's Cove Rd. (331-4559), 7 mi. northwest of Freeland via Bush Point Rd. and Smuggler's Cove Rd. Deer browse by RVs. On a cliff in a virgin stand of Douglas fir. Steep ¼-mi. trail leads down to a broad but rocky beach. 54 sites; sites $11. Open year-round.

Fort Casey State Park, 1280 S Fort Casey Rd. (678-4519), right next to the Keystone ferry terminal, 3 mi. south of Coupeville on Fort Casey Rd. 35 sites in an open field. This campground doesn't fill because of its aesthetic appeal; the ferry is 2 steps away. Sites $11. Open year-round.

Deception Pass State Park, 5175 N Rte. 525 (675-2417), 8 mi. north of Oak Harbor. The highway passes right through the park on Deception Pass Bridge. The park has 8½ mi. of hiking trails and freshwater fishing and swimming. Jets flying overhead from Oak Harbor Naval Air Station will lull you right to sleep. 250 standard sites $11. Four rustic hiker/biker sites $5. Open year-round.

FOOD

Smoked salmon is the dish of choice on Whidbey. In Oak Harbor, your best bet is the **Safeway** grocery store on Rte. 20 (open 24 hrs.).

Toby's Tavern, 8 Front St. (678-4222), Coupeville, in the 1890 Whidbey Mercantile Company Bldg. Like everything else in Coupeville, a historical landmark. Inside, the tavern (a favorite with locals) serves burgers ($4.25), sandwiches ($4.50), and beer ($1). Open daily 11am-11pm, until 2am Sat.-Sun.

Doghouse Tavern, 230 1st St. (321-9996), in Langley, on the main drag of a 1-block town. A local hangout that serves 10¢ 6-oz. beers with lunch (limit 2). Eat $5 sandwiches, burgers, burritos, and BBQ, either in the tavern or around the back in the "family restaurant." Open Mon.-Fri. 11am-9pm. Sat.-Sun. 11am-10pm. Bar open till 1-2am.

WHIDBEY ISLAND

SIGHTS AND ACTIVITIES

You could spend days exploring Whidbey Island, or only a few hours as you wait for transport connections. Whichever interval you choose, spend no more time in **Clinton** than is required to get off the ferry, scratch your mosquito bites, and get up the hill. Keep an eye out for **loganberries** and **Penn Cove mussels,** Whidbey's biggest exports. The island's interior regions are uninspiring; Whidbey's real beauty lies in its circle of beaches.

On the west side of **Useless Bay,** toward the south end of the island on the side opposite Clinton, 1½ mi. of uninterrupted **beach** along **Double Bluff Park** wait to be combed. The bay can be reached by Double Bluff Rd., about 5 mi. west of Langley Rd. and 1 mi. east of Freeland on Rte. 525. Perhaps the single most impressive **view** on the island is of Seattle and Mt. Rainier from the parking lot at the southern end of Double Bluff Rd. Another great nature spot is **South Whidbey State Park,** 4128 S Smuggler's Cove Rd. (331-4559), about 7 mi. north of Freeland off Rte. 525. The park's 87 acres of virgin **forest** and **beach** wrap around the west coast of the island, from Lagoon Point in the north to a **lighthouse** on Bush Point in the south.

Around the bend to the north lies **Fort Casey State Park,** 1280 S Fort Casey Rd. (678-4519), right next to the Keystone ferry terminal, 3 mi. south of Coupeville. The park is situated on the site of an 1890s fort designed to defend against naval attack from the Pacific. Tours of the fort's remnants are given on weekends at 2pm and start at the main gun sites. Fort Casey also operates shower rooms for **scuba divers.**

Fort Ebey State Park, 395 N Fort Ebey Rd. (678-4636), is accessible by taking Rte. 20 north from Coupeville and turning West onto Libbey Rd. by the Valley Drive park entrance. The way from the highway to the park is well-marked, but the way back to the highway is not; leave a trail of breadcrumbs or remember your route. The park is also the driest spot on the island; prickly pear cacti grow on the parched bluffs. Public beach lands, perfect for all-day expeditions, stretch from the southern tip of Fort Casey to Partridge Point, north of Fort Ebey.

Both parks and the town of **Coupeville** are contained within **Ebey's Landing National Historical Reserve,** established by the Federal government for the "preservation and protection of a rural community." Many of Coupeville's homes and commercial establishments date from the 19th century. Two fortified buildings at the west end of town, the **John Alexander Blockhouse** and the **Davis Blockhouse,** stand as reminders of the early settlement's standoff with the Skagit Native people. **Rhododendron Park,** 2 mi. southeast of Coupeville on Rte. 20, has picnic areas and six free campsites that fill early in summer. During the second weekend in August, Coupeville's **Arts and Crafts Festival** draws artists from all over the Northwest. For information, contact the **Central Whidbey Chamber of Commerce,** P.O. Box 152, Coupeville 98239 (678-5434).

Oak Harbor, on Rte. 20 facing Oak Harbor Bay at the northern end of the island, was named for the Garry Oaks that once dominated the landscape. Fast-food restaurants dominate the town. **City Beach Park,** downtown, maintains a free swimming pool. kitchens, and tennis courts. (Buildings and facilities open April-Nov.; park open year-round.) In mid-July the city sponsors **Whidbey Island Race Week,** a colorful **yacht** regatta. A few mi. north on Rte. 20, the sword and plough share the field at **U-Pick Strawberry Farms,** where the roar from low-flying Navy jets virtually rattles the fruit from the plants.

When the Skagit people lived and fished around Deception Pass, the area was often raided by the Haida people from the north. A bear **totem** of the Haidas now occupies the north end of West Beach in **Deception Pass State Park,** 5175 N Rte. 20 (675-2417), at the northern tip of the island. The pass itself was named by veteran explorer Captain George Vancouver, who found the tangled geography of Puget Sound as confusing as most visitors do today. This is the most heavily used of Whidbey's four state parks, and its **views** are magnificent. A brand-new **interpretive center** in the Bowman area, just north of the WPA bridge on Rte. 20 E, describes the army that built so many of the parks in the Northwest during the Depression. There are camping facilities, a saltwater boat launch, and a freshwater lake for **swimming,**

fishing, and **boating.** A **fishing license,** available at most hardware stores, is required for fishing in the lake; the season runs from mid-April to October.

■■■ BELLINGHAM

Between Seattle and Vancouver on I-5, Bellingham is a paper-milling industrial town in a strategic location. The ferries of the **Alaska Marine Highway** (see page 44) serve Bellingham regularly, with connections once or twice a week in summer to Ketchikan, AK and Prince Rupert, BC. The Alaska Marine Highway is the Alaska state ferry service, and docks in Bellingham as its mainland port. Another ferry offers access to rural **Lummi Island.** The city is also convenient to towering, volcanic **Mt. Baker,** a major skiing and hiking area. Most events in Bellingham revolve around Western Washington University. If you travel enough in the Puget Sound/Georgia Strait area, you will almost certainly be spending some time in Bellingham.

PRACTICAL INFORMATION AND ORIENTATION

Visitors Information, 904 Potter St. (671-3990). Take exit 253 (Lakeway) from I-5. Prepare yourself for a flood of Whatcom County trivia and non-trivial information. Extremely helpful staff. Open daily 9am-6pm; winter 8:30am-5:30pm.

Greyhound, 1329 N State St. (733-5251). To: Seattle (4 per day, $1); Vancouver (4 per day; $12); Mt. Vernon (4 per day; $5.75). Open Mon.-Fri. 7:30am-11am and noon-5:15pm, Sat.-Sun. 7:30-9am and noon-5:15pm.

Whatcom County Transit: 676-7433. All buses originate at the terminal in the Railroad Ave. mall on Magnolia St., where **maps** and schedules are available. Fare 25¢, seniors 10¢; no free transfers. Buses run every 15-30 min. Mon.-Fri. 7am-7pm, reduced service until 11pm and Sat. 9am-6pm.

Lummi Island Ferry (676-6730), at Gooseberry Pt. off Hackston Way. 26 trips back and forth each day. The first leaves the island at 6:20am; the last departs the mainland at 12:10am. Round-trip fare $1, with car $3.

Taxi: Superior Cabs, 734-3478. **Bellingham Taxi,** 676-0445. Both open 24 hrs.

Car Rental: U-Save Auto Rental, 1100 Iowa (671-3688). Cars from $18 per day; 15¢ per mi. after 100 mi. Must be 21, with credit card or $250 deposit. Open Mon.-Fri. 9am-5:30pm, Sat. 9am-noon.

Laundromat: Bellingham Cleaning Center, 1010 Lakeway Dr. (734-3755). Wash $1, 10-min. dry 25¢. Open daily 7am-10pm.

Public Library: 210 Central (676-6860), in the central business district. Open Mon.-Thurs. 10am-9pm, Fri.-Sat. 10am-6pm.

Ride Board: Viking Union at Western Washington University. Rides most often to Seattle and eastern Washington.

Senior Services: Information and assistance 733-4033 (city) or 398-1995 (county); take bus 10B to the corner of Ohio and Cornwall St. Open 8:30am-4pm daily.

Crisis Centers: Bellingham (734-7271). Whatcom County (384-1485). Both 24 hrs.

Pharmacy: Payless Drug, 1400 Cornwall St. (733-0580). Open Mon.-Fri. 8am-7pm, Sat. 9am-6pm. Pharmacy closes ½-hr. before store.

Hospital: St. Joseph's General, 2901 Squalicum Pkwy. (734-5400). Open 24 hrs.

Post Office: 315 Prospect (676-8303). Open Mon.-Fri. 8am-5pm, Sat. 9:30am-noon. **General Delivery ZIP Code:** 98225.

Area Code: 206.

Bellingham lies along I-5, 90 mi. north of Seattle and 57 mi. south of Vancouver. Downtown is a small shopping and business area centered on Holly St. and Cornwall Ave., dominated by the Georgia Pacific paper plant. Western Washington University climbs a hill to the south along Indian St. The South Side fronts the south end of the bay along South State St. suburbs. 130 acres of city parks encircle Bellingham. **Whatcom County Transit** provides service throughout the area.

ACCOMMODATIONS AND CAMPING

For both aesthetics and budget, the hostel is the best bet. For help with accommodations, try **Babs**, P.O. Box 5025, Bellingham, WA 98225, the local bed & breakfast association. Bed & Breakfast doubles average around $60 per night (though some are at least $20 less).

Fairhaven Rose Garden Hostel (HI/AYH), 107 Chuckanut Dr. (671-1750), next to Fairhaven Park, about ¾-mi. from the ferry terminal. Take exit #250 from I-5, west on Fairhaven Parkway to 12th St.; bear left onto Chuckanut Dr. Alternatively, take bus lines 1A and 1B. If stranded after buses stop running, the hostel itself will sometimes pick up from depot or ferry terminal. Only 10 beds. The hostel itself rests in a rose garden. Open Jan. 2-Dec. 23. Check-in 5-9pm. Check-out 10am. No curfew, but living room closes at 10:30pm. $9, non-members $12. Call ahead, especially if you plan to stay a Wed. or Thurs. night, as Alaska-bound travelers fill the hostel quickly. Reservations mandatory Nov.-Feb.

Mac's Motel, 1215 E Maple St. (734-7570), at Samish. Large clean rooms. Pleasant management, and cats all over the place. Mac loves cats. Singles $25. Double occupancy $33. Two beds $40. Open 7am-11:30pm.

Bell Motel, 208 N Samish Way (733-2520), on the strip. Hard beds and plain decor. Free local calls. Refrigerator in most rooms. Singles $45. Doubles from $55.

YWCA, 1026 N Forest St. (734-4820), up the hill, 1 block east of State St., about 4 blocks from Greyhound. *Only women over 18 allowed;* priority given to long-term residents. A pleasant, older building. Bathroom on the hall. Check-in Mon.-Fri. 8am-9pm, Sat. 9am-5pm. Private singles $20, adjoining singles $15.

Larrabee State Park, Chuckanut Dr. (676-2093), 7 mi. south of Bellingham. 86 sites on Samish Bay, a half-hidden flatland outside of the city. Check out the nearby tide pools or hike to alpine lakes. The 8 walk-in tentsites are the best option. Sites $11.25. Hookups $16.

FOOD

The **Community Food Co-op,** 1220 N Forest St. (734-8158), at Maple, has the natural food essentials. Buy in bulk. (Open Mon.-Sat. 9am-8pm, Sun. 11am-6pm). If you're in town on a Saturday, give the **Bellingham Farmer's Market** a peek for the fruit and vegetable stands and homemade donuts (Sat., April-Oct. 10am-3pm; Chestnut St. and Railroad Ave.) For information call 647-2060.

Bullie's Restaurant, 1200 Harris Ave. (734-2855), in the Fairhaven Marketplace. Burgers ($4.75-6.50), entrees more expensive; massive beer selection, including micro-brews. Sports play on three TVs simultaneously. Open Mon.-Thurs. 7am-11pm, Fri.-Sat. 7am-midnight, Sun. 8am-10pm.

Tony's Coffees and Tea Shop, 1101 Harris Ave. (733-6319), in Fairhaven Village, just down the hill from S State St. Dining garden complete with old railway car. Some tables are inlaid with hand-painted tiles. Coffee, ice cream, bagels, soup. Stop by the separate **coffeehouse/retail store** (738-4710) and give the Toxic Milkshake a whirl (if you dare.). Smalls $2. Free live music at random. Open daily 7:30am-11pm, garden open 7am-11pm. Same cinnamon rolls for ½-price at the **Great Harvest Bakery** in the Bellingham Mall (671-0873), on Samish Way. Bakery open Tues.-Sat. 9:30am-6pm.

Pepper Sisters, 1055 N State (671-3414). ½ mi. north of Fairhaven village. Mexican food with a yuppie ambiance. Heaping portions (Vegetarian burrito $4.75, Pork and Bean Burrito $6.50) and cheap beer. Outdoor seating with a lovely view (of a parking lot). Open Tues.-Thurs. and Sun. 4:30-9pm, Fri.-Sat. 4:30-9:30pm.

SIGHTS AND ACTIVITIES

Except in summer, **Western Washington University** (650-3000) is the nexus of much activity. The campus ornaments its sylvan setting with 16 pieces of outdoor sculpture, commissioned from local and nationally-known artists. A free brochure, available at the visitor information center, guides the visiting critic around campus from piece to piece. Friday nights during the academic year, a program of concerts called **Mama Sundays** heats up the Viking Union on campus. Top-notch folk and bluegrass are the norm ($3-5). In the summer, there are free weekday lunchtime concerts. The **Western Visitors Center** (650-3424) is at the entrance to the college on South College Dr., and information is also available at the Whatcom County Visitors Center in Blaine. Here you can pick up a schedule for the Faculty of Dramatic Arts **Summer Stock Theater,** running from July to August. Take bus #3B, 7B, or 8A to reach the campus. Smart, bouncy, and basic, Bellingham natives **Crayon** are one of the world's best rock and roll bands. See them if possible. Garage-rock label Estrus and their rockin' Mono Men also live and perform here.

EVENTS

Whatcom County hosts annual fairs and festivals that celebrate its modestly colorful past. Held on Gooseberry Point in the Lummi Island Reservation, the **Lummi Stommish Water Carnival** (734-8180) is entering its 46th year. The three-day carnival at the end of June stages traditional dances, war-canoe races, arts and crafts sales, and a salmon barbecue.

For the **Deming Logging Show** (676-1089), tree-fellers converge here from throughout the region to compete in axe-throwing, log-rolling, and speed climbing. To reach the Showgrounds, take Mt. Baker Hwy. Twelve mi. east to Cedarville Rd. and head north. Signs lead you to the grounds.

The **Northwest Washington Fairgrounds** (354-4111), in Lynden, hosts blow-out wing-dings throughout the summer, including the **Northwest Washington Fair** in mid-August.

OUTDOORS

Hike up **Chuckanut Mountain** through a quiet forest to overlook the islands that fill the bay. You can occasionally spot Mt. Rainier to the south. A 2½-mi. hike uphill leaves from Old Samish Hwy. about 1 mi. south of the city limits. The beach at **Lake Padden Park,** 4882 Samish Way (676-6989), delights those who find Puget Sound a little chilly. Take bus #5B or #10A 1 mi. south of downtown. A lifeguard keeps watch from Memorial Day through Labor Day. The park also has miles of hiking trails, a boat launch (no motors allowed), tennis courts, and playing fields. The park is wheelchair-accessible (open daily 6am-10pm).

Whatcom Falls Park, 1401 Electric Ave., due east of town, also has fantastic **hiking trails,** picnic facilities, and tennis courts. Upper Whatcom Falls Trail (1.6 mi.) leads to the falls themselves, converted into a waterslide by locals. Take bus #4A or 11A (open daily 6am-10pm). The fishing is good in both these lakes and also in **Lake Samish** and **Silver Lake,** north of the town of Maple Falls off the Mt. Baker Hwy. The lake trout season opens on the third Sunday in April. **Fishing licenses** ($3) are available from the Department of Fisheries (902-2464), at any sporting goods store, and at some hardware stores.

Popular with South Side residents, **Interurban Trail** runs 6.6 mi. from Fairhaven Park to Larrabee State Park along the route of the old Interurban Electric Railway. The trail is less developed than those at Padden and Whatcom Lakes and follows a creek through the forest. Occasional breaks in the trees permit a glimpse of the San Juan Islands. You may stumble onto **Teddy Bear Cove,** along the Interurban Trail, accessible from Chuckanut Drive, 2 mi. south of Fairhaven. This clothing-optional beach offers revealing views of the local wildlife.

■ NEAR BELLINGHAM

MT. BAKER

To reach the volcano, take exit 255 off I-5, just north of Bellingham, to Rte. 542, the **Mt. Baker Hwy.** Fifty-six mi. of roadway traverse the foothills, affording spectacular views of Baker and the other peaks in the range. Crowning the Mt. Baker-Snoqualmie National Forest, Mt. Baker contains excellent downhill and cross-country skiing facilities, usually open late October to mid-May. On your way to the mountain, stop at the **Mount Bakery,** 3706 Mt. Baker Hwy. (592-5703), for gigantic apple fritters, donuts, and pastries for around 50¢ (open Mon.-Sat. 5am-5pm).

Silver Lake Park, 9006 Silver Lake Rd. (599-2776), is 28 mi. east of Bellingham on the Mt. Baker Hwy. and 3 mi. north of Maple Falls on Silver Lake Road. The park tends 113 **campsites** near the lake with facilities for swimming, hiking, and fishing. Tentsites are $6, with hookups $7.50.

LUMMI ISLAND

Lummi Island, off the coast of Bellingham, was for centuries the fishing and hunting ground of the Lummi Native nation. Now the Lummi have been moved to a reservation, and the island has been overrun by hermits. Lummi is rural, with paved roads only on the northern half. The old logging roads that cross the rest of the island are ideal for **hiking** up to Lummi Mountain or down to the island's various **tide pools. Bicyclists** will find the island roads peaceful.

Lummi Island can be reached by **ferry** (see Practical Information in the Bellingham section, above) from **Gooseberry Point** on the Lummi Reservation, 15 mi. from Bellingham. Take I-5 north to exit 260; left on Rte. 540 will lead you west about 3½ mi. to Haxton Way. Turn south and follow signs to the ferry terminal. For 10 days in June each year, the ferry is sent to Seattle for maintenance. During this interlude a walk-on ferry is substituted, so call before taking your car.

BLAINE

A border town 20 mi. north of Bellingham, Blaine is the busiest port of entry between Canada and the U.S. Those who get turned away from the Canadian border for insufficient identification or funds (you need CDN$500 per car and $50 per extra passenger if you're headed for Alaska) often head for Blaine, and the border patrol prides itself on catching these undesirables with blanket stop-checks.

The main attraction in Blaine is the **Peace Arch Park Heritage Site** (332-8221; open for day use only). Built in 1921 with nickels and dimes volunteered by school children in Washington and British Columbia, the arch commemorates the 1814 signing of the Treaty of Ghent, terminating the War of 1812 and inaugurating an era of peace between Canada and the U.S. The two legs of the arch straddle the international border. With two gates, one hinged on the U.S. side, the other on the Canadian, the gate can be closed only by mutual consent. Summer-time happenings include "hands across the border" events with kids, balloons, and Rotarians (open daily 6:30am-dusk; Oct. 16-March 8am-5pm; toilets, kitchen facilities).

The spit of land encompassing **Semiahmoo Park** (371-5513), 5 mi. southwest of Blaine, was first inhabited by the coastal Salish people, who harvested shellfish when the tide was low. Clam digging is still a popular activity. Buckets and shovels may be rented from the park; no license is required. Take Drayton Harbor Rd. around to the southwestern side of Drayton Harbor (open mid-Feb. to Dec. Wed.-Sun. 1-5pm; free). The **Blaine Visitors Center,** 900 Peace Portal Dr. (332-4544), is a storehouse of information on these parks and American and Canadian points of interest in the area. (Open Mon-Fri. 9am-5pm, Sat.-Sun. 9am-4pm.)

The **Birch Bay Hostel (HI/AYH),** building #630 on the former Blaine Air Force Base (371-2180), is one of the Pacific Northwest's biggest (HI/AYH members only), with TV and full cooking facilities. The rooms are spotless, and the manager helpful. Take either the Birch Bay-Lynden Rd. exit or the Grandview Rd. exit off I-5 and head west. Blaine Rd. will take you to the Alderson Rd. entrance to the Air Force base (open April-Sept.; $9, non-members $12). The **Westview Motel,** 1300 Peace Portal Dr. (332-5501), also offers excellent lodgings (singles $29, doubles $32).

For campers, **Birch Bay State Park,** 5105 Helwig Rd. (371-2800), 10 mi. south of Blaine, operates 167 sites near the water. The Semiahmoo Native people used this area and the marshland at the southern end of the park to harvest shellfish and hunt waterfowl; today, 300 species of birds live in the park's **Terrell Creek Estuary.** The park is also a good area for crabbing, scuba diving, water-skiing, and swimming. To reach the park, take the Birch Bay-Lynden exit off I-5 and turn south onto Blaine

Rd. When you run out of road, turn east onto Bay Rd. Turn south on Jackson Rd. and take it to Helwig Rd. The way is well-marked from the freeway (open year-round; sites $11, with hookup $16).

The best seafood in town, fresh daily, is at the **Harbor Cafe,** on Marine Dr. (332-5176), halfway down the pier. The $7 fish and chips, salad bar and roll included, is hard to resist.

The Blaine **Greyhound Station** uses a drop-off point at the Burger King on the truck route junction. For more information, call the station in Bellingham (733-5251). There is one bus to Seattle per day ($13.50).

SAN JUAN ISLANDS

If you live in pursuit of the picturesque Northwest, begin by looking in the San Juan Islands. Bald eagles spiral above green hillsides, pods of killer whales spout offshore, and, despite the lush vegetation, it never seems to rain. The San Juans are home to abundant populations of great horned owls, puffins, sea otters, sea lions, and killer whales. Experience it firsthand in a relaxed, beautiful setting.

Although the population of San Juan, the main island in the chain, has doubled in the last five years, there are still fewer than 3000 permanent residents. The populations of the other three main inhabited islands are far lower. The parks and coast lines of the islands offer the promise of serene seclusion. Over 1.5 million visitors come ashore the San Juans each year, however, usually in July and August; to avoid the rush but still enjoy good weather, try the islands in late spring or early fall. Although tension is starting to build between locals and transplants from Seattle and California who are buying up huge chunks of the islands at exorbitant prices, well-behaved tourists and their dollars are still welcome on the San Juans.

An excellent guide to the area is *The San Juan Islands Afoot and Afloat* by Marge Mueller ($10), available at bookstores and outfitting stores on the islands and in Seattle. *The San Juans Beckon* is published annually by the *Islands Sounder,* the local paper, and provides **maps** and up-to-date information on island recreation; you can pick it up free on the ferries and in island stores. The *San Juanderer* also has useful information, including tide charts and ferry schedules (free on ferries or at the tourist centers).

FERRIES

Washington State Ferries serve the islands daily from **Anacortes** on the mainland. To reach Anacortes, take I-5 north from Seattle to Mt. Vernon. From there, Rte. 20 heads west to Anacortes, and the way to the ferry is well-marked. **Gray Line** (624-5077) buses to Anacortes depart Seattle from the Greyhound depot at 8th Ave. and Stewart St. at 5:55am daily ($13.25). Call for more information.

Of the 172 islands in the San Juan archipelago, only four are accessible by ferry. **Washington State Ferries** depart Anacortes about nine times daily on a route that stops at **Lopez, Shaw, Orcas,** and **San Juan** (see page 43 for **complete fare and schedule information;** refer to ferry (**K**)). In summer, two additional ferries per day travel directly to San Juan Island, and one ferry per day (**L**) continues to the town of **Sidney, BC,** 32km north of Victoria on Vancouver Island. Not every ferry services all the islands, so check the schedule (see page 43). The ferry system revises its schedule seasonally. You can purchase **ferry tickets** in Anacortes. Pay only on westbound trips to or between the islands; no charge is levied on eastbound traffic. A money-saving tip: to see more islands and save on ferry fares, travel directly to the westernmost island on your itinerary and then make your way back to the mainland island by island. Foot passengers travel in either direction between the islands free of charge. Some car spaces are available from the islands to Sidney. Reservations for Sidney are strongly recommended; call before noon the day before your trip to ensure a space. The San Juan ferries (**K** and **L**) are packed in summer. On peak travel

SAN JUAN ISLAND

days, arrive with your vehicle at least one hour prior to scheduled departure. The ferry authorities accept only cash or in-state checks as payment.

■■■ SAN JUAN ISLAND

Made part of Washington by an act of Kaiser William I of Germany, San Juan Island has a bizarre history. The 1846 Treaty of Oregon, setting the 49th parallel and the center of the Georgia and Juan de Fuca Straits as the international boundary, left control ambiguous. Rival claims by Whitehall in London and the Territorial Legislature in Oregon City eventually climaxed with the cold-blooded shooting of a British pig found rooting one morning in an American's potato patch, leaving both countries with no choice but to send in troops. For 12 years, two thoroughly bored garrisons spent the "Pig War" yawning, occasionally rousing to join in horse races and Christmas dances, until both sides agreed in 1872 to seek the good offices of Kaiser William as arbitrator. Not surprisingly, he awarded the islands to the U.S.

Lime Kiln State Park provides the best ocean vista for **whale-watching** of all of the islands. San Juan may be the last stop on the ferry route, but it is still the most frequently visited island, and provides the traveler with all the beauty of San Juan and all the comforts of **Friday Harbor,** the largest town in the archipelago. Since the ferry docks right in town, this island is also the easiest to explore.

PRACTICAL INFORMATION AND ORIENTATION

Visitors Information: Chamber of Commerce (468-3663), on Front St. at the Ferry Terminal. **National Park Service Information Center** (378-2240), northeast corner of 1st and Spring. Both answer questions about San Juan National Historic Park. Park Service open Mon.-Fri. 8:30am-5pm, 8am-4pm in the off-season.

U.S. Customs, 271 Front St. (378-2080 or 800-562-5943 for 24-hr. service). Open 8am-5pm.

Ferry Terminal: 378-4777. Information line open 24 hrs. Waiting room opens ½-hr. before scheduled departures.

Taxi: Primo Taxi, 378-3550. Open daily 5am-3am.

Car Rental: Friday Harbor Rentals, 410 Spring St. (378-4351), in the Inn at Friday Harbor. $45 per day, unlimited mileage. Major credit card required. Only rents to people 21 and over with insurance.

Bike Rental: Island Bicycles, 380 Argyle St., Friday Harbor (378-4941). One-speeds (kids only) $10 per day, 6-speeds $15 per day, 12-speeds $20 per day, mountain bikes $25 per day. Locks and helmets included. Also rents child carriers and trailers. Provides **maps** of the island and suggests bike routes. Credit card required. Open daily 10am-5:30pm; Labor Day-Memorial Day Thurs.-Sat. 10am-5:30pm.

Moped Rental: Susie's Mopeds (378-5244), 1st and A St. Mopeds $12 per hr., $45 per day. Credit card required. Open March-Oct. daily 9am-6pm. Also available at Roche Harbor July 4-Labor Day.

Kayak Tours: San Juan Kayak Expeditions, P.O. Box 2041, Friday Harbor, WA 98250. Equipment, gear, and food included in the $160 cost of a 2-day tour. Three- and 4-day tours offered.

Tours: The Inn at Friday Harbor, 410 Spring St. (378-4351), takes 10-12 people on a bus around the island via English Camp and Lime Kiln Park (for whale-watching) daily at 2pm ($12).

Laundromat: Wash Tub Laundromat (378-2070), in the San Juan Inn on Spring St., ½ block from the ferry dock. Wash $1.50, 11-min. dry 25¢. Open daily 7:30am-9pm.

Senior Services: at the Gray Top Inn (378-2677). Open Mon.-Fri. 9am-4pm.

Red Tide Hotline: 800-562-5632 in WA only.

Pharmacy: Friday Harbor Drug, 210 Spring St. (378-4421). Open Mon.-Sat. 9am-7pm, Sun. 10am-4pm.

Medical Services: Inter-Island Medical Center, 550 Spring St. (378-2141). Open Mon.-Fri. 9am-5pm, Sat. 10am-noon.

Emergency: 911. **Sheriff:** 135 Rhone St., at Reed St. (non-emergency 378-4151).

Post Office: (378-4511), Blair and Reed St. Open Mon.-Fri. 8:30am-4:30pm. **General Delivery ZIP Code:** 98250.
Area Code: 206.

With bicycle, car, and boat rentals all within a few blocks of the ferry terminal, Friday Harbor is a convenient base for exploring the islands. Miles of road make all corners of the island accessible, but the roads are poorly marked. It's smart to plot your course carefully on one of the free **maps** available at the information center in town (see above). If the information center is closed, stop at one of the island's real estate offices. They often distribute free **maps** outside their doors.

ACCOMMODATIONS AND CAMPING

Cheap accommodations in the San Juans, outside of camping, are nearly non-existent. You will not find bargains in the busy-season. If you plan to stay overnight and camping is not your style, try one of the many Bed & Breakfasts: although expensive, they are often beautiful. San Juan's campgrounds have become wildly popular; show up early in the afternoon to make sure you get a spot.

Lakedale Campgrounds, 2627 Roche Harbor Rd. (378-2350), 4 mi. from Friday Harbor. Attractive grounds are surrounded by 50acres of lakes. Rowboats ($3.50 per hour, $14 per day), canoe rentals ($4.50 per hr., $18 per day), and paddle boats ($5.50 per hr., $24 per day). Pay showers ($1 per 5 min.), fishing in nearby fertile waters ($4), and swimming in freshwater lakes (non-campers $1.50, under 12 $1). Sites with vehicle access for 1-2 people $15 (July-Aug. $18), plus $3.50 per each additional person. Hiker/biker sites $5 (July-Aug. $5.50). Open April 1-Oct. 15.

San Juan County Park, 380 Westside Rd. (378-2992), 10 mi. west of Friday Harbor on Smallpox and Andrews Bays. Cold water and flush toilets. No RV hookups. Sites for those with vehicles $14. Hiker/biker sites $4.50.

FOOD

Stock up at **King's Market,** 160 Spring St. (378-4505; open daily 8am-10pm).

San Juan Donut Shop, 225 Spring St. (378-2271). Cheap eats. For endless coffee, inexpensive breakfast, and lunch sandwiches, this is the place in San Juan. Coffee 60¢; grilled cheese, bacon and chips $3.50. Unhurried service; get an early start (open Mon.-Sat. 5am-5pm, Sun. 7am-3pm).

Vic's Driftwood Drive-In (378-8427), at 2nd and Court. Amiable management with great burgers ($1.60) and shakes so thick you'll get dimples trying to drink them ($1.50). Open Mon.-Fri. 6am-7pm, Sat. 6am-2pm.

Katrina's, 65 Nichols St. (378-7290), behind the Funk 'n Junk "antique" store. Hard to find, but worth it. The tiny kitchen cooks up a different menu every day, but they always have local organic salads, freshly baked bread, and gigantic cookies (50¢) to fill a picnic basket. Open Mon.-Sat. noon-5pm.

SIGHTS AND ACTIVITIES

Friday Harbor is crowded when the tourists are out in full force, but appealing at other times, especially in spring and fall. Take time to poke around the galleries, craft shops, and bookstores. The **Whale Museum,** 62 1st St. (378-4710), stars skeletons, sculptures, and information on new research. The museum even operates a toll-free **whale hotline** (800-562-8832) to report sightings and strandings. (Open daily 10am-5pm; in winter daily 11am-4pm. $3, seniors and students $2.50, under 12 $1.50.) The **San Juan Historical Museum,** 405 Price St. (378-3149), in the old King House across from the St. Francis Catholic Church, explodes with exhibits, furnishings, and photographs from the late 1800s. Pick up the pamphlet mapping out a free walking tour of Friday Harbor. (Open Wed.-Sat. 1-4:30pm; Labor Day-May Thurs.-Fri. 1-4pm. Free.)

A drive around the perimeter of the island takes about 90 minutes, and the route is flat for cyclists. The **West Side Rd.** traverses gorgeous scenery and provides the best chance for sighting **orcas** ("killer whales") offshore.

To begin a tour of the island, head south and west out of Friday Harbor on Mullis Rd. This will merge with Cattle Point Rd. and take you straight into **American Camp** (378-2907), on the south side of the island. The camp dates to the Pig War of 1859, when the U.S. and Britain were at loggerheads over possession of the islands. Two of the camp's buildings still stand. An interpretive shelter near the entrance to the park explains the history of the conflict, and a self-guided trail leads from the shelter through the buildings and past the site of the British sheep farm. Every weekend (June-Sept. noon-3pm), volunteers in period costume reenact daily life at the camp (free). If the sky is clear, make the ½-mi. jaunt farther down the road to **Cattle Point** for views of the distant Olympic Mountains.

Returning north on Cattle Point Rd., consider taking the gravel **False Bay Rd.** to the west. The road will guide you to **False Bay,** a true bay that is home to nesting **bald eagles** and a great spot for watching them. During the spring and summer, walk along the northwestern shore (to your right as you face the water) at low tide to see the eagles nesting.

Farther north on False Bay Rd., you'll run into **Bailer Hill Rd.,** turning into West Side Rd. when it reaches Haro Straight. You can also reach Bailer Hill Rd. by taking Cattle Point Rd. to Little Rd. Slopes overflowing with wildflowers rise to one side, while rocky shores descend to the ocean on the other.

Lime Kiln Point State Park is known as the best whale-watching spot in the area. Before you head out, gauge your chances of actually seeing **orcas** by inquiring at the Whale Museum for day-to-day information on whale-sightings. For those truly determined to see whales, a whale-watching cruise may be best. Be prepared to shell out serious cash; most operations charge about $40 for adults and $30 for children on a three- to four-hour boat ride. For information pick up one of the abundant brochures, or else stop by the National Park Service Information Center, 100 Spring St. (378-2240; open 3am-4:30pm in the fall, 8am-5:30pm June-Aug.).

The Pig War casts its comic pallor over **British Camp,** the second half of **San Juan National Historical Park.** The camp lies on West Valley Rd. on the sheltered **Garrison Bay** (take Mitchell Bay Rd. east from West Side Rd.). Here, four original buildings have been preserved, including the barracks, now used as an **interpretive center.** The center chronicles the "War" and sells guides to the island. It also shows a relatively interesting 13-minute slide show on the epic, decisive struggle. (Park open year-round; buildings open Memorial Day-Labor Day daily 8am-4:30pm. Free.)

Stop by the information kiosk in front of the **Hotel de Haro** at the **Roche Harbor Resort,** Roche Harbor Rd. (378-2155), on the northern side of the island, for a copy of the $1 brochure, *A Walking Tour of Historic Roche Harbor.* Don't miss the bizarre mausoleum; the Masonic symbolism that garnishes the structure is explained in the *Walking Tour.*

If you're eager to **fish** or **clam,** pick up a copy of the Department of Fisheries pamphlet, *Salmon, Shellfish, Marine Fish Sport Fishing Guide,* for details on regulations and limits. The guide is available free at **Friday Harbor Hardware and Marine,** 270 Spring St. (378-4622). Hunting and fishing licenses are required on the islands, and can be obtained from the hardware store (open Mon.-Sat. 8am-6pm, Sun. 10am-4pm). Check with the **red tide hotline** (800-562-5632) if you'll be gathering shellfish; the nasty bacteria can wreak deadly havoc on your intestines.

The annual **San Juan Island Traditional Jazz Festival** brings several swing bands to Friday Harbor in August. A $45 badge ($40 if purchased before July 1) will gain you admission to all performances, but you'll have just as much fun for free by joining the crowds of revelers in the streets outside the clubs. Single performance tickets range from $10 to $25. For more information, contact San Juan Island Goodtime Classic Jazz Association, P.O. Box 1666, Friday Harbor 98250 (378-5509). The other annual festival of the island is the mid-June **Pig War BBQ Jamboree,** complete with

Beer Garden, 10K race, live bands, and a pork BBQ cook-off. For information call 378-3818, or write PIG WAR, P.O. Box 366, Friday Harbor 98250.

■■■ ORCAS ISLAND

Mt. Constitution overlooks much of Puget Sound from its 2409-ft. summit atop Orcas Island, the largest island of the San Juan chain. In the mountain's shadow dwells a small population of retirees, artists, and farmers in understated homes surrounded by the red bark of madrona trees and greenery. With an enchanting state park and funky youth hostel, Orcas has perhaps the best budget tourist facilities of all the islands. The one problem is that much of the beach access is occupied by private resorts and is closed to the public. The trail to **Obstruction Pass Beach** is the best of the few ways to clamber down to the rocky shores.

PRACTICAL INFORMATION AND ORIENTATION

Visitors Information: 206-468-3663 Mon.-Fri. 9am-4pm, on North Beach Rd., ½ block north of Horseshoe Hwy. next to the museum. An unstaffed shack with racks of pamphlets. Call the **Chamber of Commerce** (376-2273) for other information, or stop at a real-estate office along North Beach Rd. for free **maps.** For lodging, call the hotline at 376-8888.

Ferries: Washington State Ferry, 376-4389 or 376-2134. 24 hrs. **Island Shuttle Express,** 671-1137. Service to Anacortes and Friday Harbor (1 per day; $33). Walk-on or bike passengers only. Departs from Obstruction Pass dock at 8:15am. Refer to page 43 for total ferry information.

Taxi: Adventure Taxi, 376-4994.

Bike Rental: Wildlife Cycle (376-4708), A St. and North Beach Rd., in Eastsound. 21-speeds $5 per hr., $20 per day. Open Mon.-Sat. 10:30am-5pm.

Moped Rental: Key Moped Rentals (376-2474), just north of the fire station on Prune Alley in Eastsound; also at ferry landing. $12 per hr., $45 per 8-hr. day. Drivers license and $10 deposit required. Helmets, gas, and **maps** included. Open May-Sept. daily 10am-6pm.

Library: (376-4985), at Rose and Pine in Eastsound. Open Tues.-Thurs. 10am-7pm, Fri.-Sat. 10am-4pm.

Senior Services Center: (376-2677), across from the museum on North Beach Rd. in Eastsound. Open Mon.-Fri. 9am-4pm.

Pharmacy: Ray's (376-3693, after-hours emergencies 476-4756), in Templin Center. Open Mon.-Sat. 9am-6pm, Sun. 10am-6pm.

Emergency: 911.

Post Office: (376-4121), A St. in Eastsound Market Place, ½-block north of the Chamber of Commerce. Open Mon.-Fri. 9am-4:30pm. **General Delivery ZIP Code:** 98245.

Area Code: 206.

Because Orcas is shaped like a horseshoe, getting around is a chore. The ferry lands on the southwest tip. Travel 9 mi. northeast to the top of the horseshoe to reach **Eastsound,** the island's main town. Olga and Doe Bay are an additional 8 and 11 mi. from Eastsound, respectively, down the eastern side of the horseshoe. Stop in one of the shops at the landing to get a free **map** (most are open daily 8:30am-6:30pm).

ACCOMMODATIONS AND CAMPING

Avoid the bed and breakfasts (upwards of $60 per day) of the "Healing Island" and stay at the Doe Bay Resort. If full, try a campground.

Doe Bay Village Resort, Star Rte. 86, Olga 98279 (376-2291 or 376-4755), off Horseshoe Hwy. on Pt. Lawrence Rd., 8 mi. out of Moran State Park. On a secluded bay. The resort comes with kitchen facilities, a health food store, an organic cafe, and plenty of grounds on which to wander. The crowning attraction is the steam sauna and mineral bath ($3 per day, nonlodgers $6; bathing suits optional). Beds $12.50, nonmembers $14.50. Camping $10.50. Cottages from $32.50. Enjoy the imaginative and flexible work-trade program. Guided kayak trips $35 per 3 hrs. (see Sights). Reservations recommended (only 8 bunks). Open year-round.

Outlook Inn (376-2200), P.O. Box 210, Eastsound 98245. On the north side of Horseshoe Hwy. in the center of Eastsound. If the island's many beach-cabin resorts don't appeal to you, this elegant inn by the shore is a good alternative. Singles from $64. Doubles $69. Reservations required. Rates $10 less in winter.

Moran State Park, Star Rte. 22, Eastsound 98245 (376-2326). Follow Horseshoe Hwy. straight into the park. All the best of San Juan fun: swimming, fishing, and hiking. Arresting grounds, amiable staff. Four different campgrounds with a total of 151 sites. About 12 sites remain open year-round, as do the restrooms. Back-country camping is prohibited. Rowboats and paddleboats $8-9 for the 1st hr., $6 per hr. thereafter. Standard sites with hot showers $12. Hiker/biker sites $5. **Information booth** at park entrance open Memorial Day-Labor Day daily 2-11pm. Park open daily 6:30am-dusk; Sept.-March 8am-dusk. Reservations are strongly recommended May-Labor Day. Send $16 ($11 per site plus a $5 reservation fee).

Obstruction Pass: Accessible only by boat or on foot. Just past Olga, turn off Horseshoe Hwy. and hang a right to head south on Obstruction Pass Rd. Soon you'll come to a dirt road marked "Obstruction Pass Trailhead." Follow the road for about 1 mi. The sites are a ½-mi. hike from the end of the road. No drinking water, so bring plenty. Pit toilets. A rocky but well-maintained trail to a beach overhang. 9 sites; free.

FOOD

All the essentials can be found at **Island Market,** on Langdell St. (376-6000; open Mon.-Sat. 8am-9pm, Sun. 10am-8pm). For loads of fresh local produce, try the **Farmer's Market** in front of the museum (every Sat. 10am).

Night Heron, behind the only gas station in Eastsound, off Horseshoe Hwy. Coffee, music, food, and live music shows with an oceanside view. Local hangout for the counter-cultural crowd. Most interesting find in town, but more of a coffeehouse. Open Mon.-Wed. 6pm-midnight, Fri.-Sun. 6pm-midnight.

Portofino Pizzeria, Prune Alley (376-2085). 10-in. pizza $7.50; only 93¢ per slice. Open Tues.-Thurs. noon-9pm, Fri.-Sat. noon-10pm.

Bilbos Festivo (376-4728), Prune Alley and A St. Good Mexican cooking and *great* salsa, but the hot sauce is severely lacking in zing. You can try the peppy Christmas burrito year-round ($7). Homemade chocolate desserts $3-4. Artistic decor, patio dining. Open Mon.-Fri. noon-2:30pm and 5-9:30pm, Sat.-Sun. 5-9:30pm.

The Lower Tavern (376-4848), on Langdell St. behind the Island Market, Eastsound. Boasts the town's best burgers (with fries, $4.75). Avoid the lunchtime rush. Open Mon.-Sat. 11am-midnight, Sun. noon-7pm.

Rose's Bakery Cafe (376-4220), in Eastsound Sq. Upbeat, offbeat staff serves up croissants ($1) and sandwiches ($6). Buy bags of day-old pastries at ½-price. Open Mon.-Sat. 8am-5pm, Sun. 10am-3pm.

Cafe Olga (376-5098), in the Orcas Island Artworks Bldg. at the Olga crossing, a few mi. beyond Moran State Park. A cooperative gallery converted into an artsy-pricey coffeehouse. Soup and sandwich special $5.50, blackberry pie $3.25. Open March-Dec. daily 10am-6pm.

SIGHTS AND ACTIVITIES

Trippers on Orcas Island don't need to travel with a destination in mind. At least half the fun lies in simply tramping about: pick a side road, select a particularly moving vista, and meditate on llife, llove, and llamas.

Moran State Park is unquestionably Orcas's greatest attraction. Over 21 mi. of hiking trails cover the park, ranging in difficulty from a one-hour jaunt around Mountain Lake to a day-long constitutional up the south face of **Mt. Constitution,** the highest peak on the islands. Pick up a copy of the trail guide from the **rangers**

station (376-2837). From the summit of Constitution, you can see other islands in the group, the Olympic and Cascade Ranges, Vancouver Island, and Mt. Rainier. The stone tower at the top was built in 1936 by the Civilian Conservation Corps as an observation tower for tourists and a fire lookout. Rental mopeds are not powerful enough to reach the summit. To shorten the hike, park your car along the way at any one of tree-lined car parks and proceed from there. For an abbreviated jaunt, drive up Mt. Constitution and hike part-way down to **Cascade Falls,** spectacular in the spring and early summer. Down below, you can swim in two freshwater lakes easily accessible from the highway or rent rowboats ($8 per hr.) and paddleboats ($9 per hr.) from the park. Head from the lake to the lagoon for an oceanside picnic.

Eastsound offers great views from the highway and from the adjacent beach. Stop in at the picturesque and peaceful **Emmanuel Church** (376-2352), on Main St., just across from the library. Built in 1885, the islanders transcend their sectarian differences and worship in this one building. A path behind the church leads to a rock-ledge seat that hangs over the surfline.

Olga is a minuscule collection of buildings that challenges the definition of "town." Off Horseshoe Hwy., on West Beach Rd., is **The Right Place,** giving you an eyewitness view of glass-blowers in action. Continue along Horseshoe Hwy. to **Doe Bay Village Resorts** (376-2291), where you can soak in the natural mineral waters, sweat in the sauna, and have prophetic visions as you jump into the cold bath (bathing suits are the exception; see Accommodations and Camping). The **Sea Kayak Tour** of the surrounding islands is a fascinating, albeit expensive, "water-hike" of the north end of Puget Sound. ($35 per 3-hr. tour. Tours leave June-Sept. Mon.-Fri. at 1pm, Sat.-Sun. at 10am and 2pm, and include a ½-hr. of dry-land training.) The resort grounds are secluded and make for good wandering. Check first with the manager to learn the perimeters and parameters of the resort.

■■■ SMALLER ISLANDS

LOPEZ ISLAND

Smaller than either Orcas or San Juan, Lopez (or "Slow-pez") lacks some of the tourist facilities of the other islands; hence, it also lacks tourists. Keep a hand free while you're passing through. You'll need it to return the genial waves of the locals.

Lopez Island is ideal for those seeking solitary beach-walking or tranquil bicycling. It is, for the most part, free of both imposing inclines and heavy traffic. Since **Lopez Village,** the largest "town," is 3½ mi. from the ferry dock, it's best to bring your own bicycle. If you need to rent a bike, head to **Lopez Bicycle Works** (468-2847), south of the village next to the island's Marine Center. The cheerful staff will give you a detailed **map** of island roads, complete with distances, even if you don't rent (10-speeds $4.50 per hr. and $18 per day; mountain bikes $5 per hr. and $23 per day; open June-Aug. daily 10am-6pm; call in winter). **Cycle San Juan,** Rte. 1 Box 1744, Lopez Island 98261 (468-3251), offers bicycle tours of all of the islands. A half day costs $35, a full day $75. Prices include meals and water-bottle souvenirs. Call ahead, as you never know on which island the tours will be (rentals also available).

Once you've obtained a bike or car, **Shark Reef** and **Agate Beach Park,** small parks on the south end of the island that are meant for daytime use, offer a change from mainland campgrounds. Shark Reef features tranquil and well-maintained hiking trails, and Agate's beaches are calm and desolate. The only other "sight" is the **Lopez Island Historical Society Museum** in Lopez Village (468-2049), one and a half blocks from the New Bay, across from the San Juan County Bank. Besides exhibits on island history, this facility boasts an open shed filled with old canoes and obsolete farm equipment. (Open Wed.-Sun. noon-4pm; May-June and Sept. Fri.-Sun. noon-4pm; closed Oct.-April. Free.)

If you do decide to spend the night on the island, camping is your only hope for a good deal. **Odlin Park** (468-2496), is close (1 mi.) to the ferry terminal, south along Ferry Rd. The park offers 30 sites, a kitchen with a wood stove, and cold running water. There are a boat launch, volleyball net, and payphone on the grounds. ($10 per vehicle up to 4 people, each additional person $3; hiker/biker sites $2.50. Dogs $3 each.) **Spencer Spit State Park** (468-2251), on the northeast corner of the island, about 3½ mi. from the ferry terminal, has 51 sites along 1 mi. of beachfront with good clamming year-round ($10; 2 8-bunk covered shelters $14 per person).

Bring a lunch to Lopez Island; nobody's promising low prices. If you're in a pinch, the **Lopez Village Pharmacy** off Fisherman Bay Road (468-3801) hides a little soda fountain in the back room (Egg Salad $2.75, Veggie Sandwich $3.75) with inexpensive lunch foods (open Mon.-Sat. 8am-7pm, Sun. 9am-5pm). To sample the local fares, hang at **Greggs Smokehouse,** Shoal Bay Lane, which smokes fresh salmon. The **Lopez Island Vineyards** (468-3644) are a must-see; for $1 you can sample all of their wines, and for $8-12 you can have a bottle/souvenir of your own. (Free tours of the grounds and equipment; open June 1-Sept. 7 Wed.-Sun. noon-5pm; Sept. 8-Dec. 23 Fri.-Sat. noon-5; March 5-May 31 Fri.-Sat. noon-5pm.) Or sample fresh pastries and bread at **Holly B's** (from 85¢) and day-olds at a discount (open Wed.-Mon. 8am-5pm). **Madiona Farms** (468-3441), at Davis Bay and Richardson Rd., is a good place to pick up a snack of seasonal fruits and berries (open Mon.-Fri. 8am-5pm). **Laundry** facilities can be found along Fisherman's Bay Road, 100 yards south of the winery. (Wash $1.50, 7-min. dry for 25¢.) The **seniors' helpline** is 468-2421 (open Mon.-Fri. 9am-4pm). The **emergency number** is 911. You can reach the **post office** at 468-2282. **General Delivery ZIP Code:** 98261.

OTHER ISLANDS

With one store and 100 residents, **Shaw Island** was not designed with tourists in mind. One eclectic building serves island visitors: a combination ferry terminal/general store/post office/dock/gas station run by Franciscan nuns. However, the island's 11 mi. of public roads are endearing to hikers and bikers. The library and museum, near the center of the island, at the intersection of Blind Bay and Hoffman Cove Rd., are open only on Mondays and Saturdays. **Shaw Island County Park,** on the south side of the island, has eight campsites ($6) that fill quickly. There are no other accommodations on the island.

Washington State Parks operates over 15 **marine parks** on some of the smaller islands in the archipelago. These islands, accessible by private transportation only, have anywhere from one to 51 mainly primitive campsites. The park system publishes a pamphlet on its marine facilities, available at parks or hardware and supply stores on the larger islands. One of the most popular destinations is **Sucia Island,** site of gorgeous scenery and rugged terrain. Canoes and kayaks can easily navigate the archipelago when the water is calm, but when the wind whips up the surf, only larger boats (at least 16 ft.) go out to sea. **Navigational maps** are essential to avoid the reefs and nasty hidden rocks that surround the islands. The Department of Natural Resources operates three parks; each has three to six free campsites with pit toilets but no drinking water. Cypress Head on **Cypress Island** has wheelchair-accessible facilities.

OLYMPIC PENINSULA AND PACIFIC COAST

North of the Columbia estuary, small resort, timber, and fishing towns, economically maimed by the state's recent ban on commercial salmon fishing, cluster at the mouth of the river and around the wide bays to the north. Wild marshlands and grasslands run up against one another, and several stunning state parks and wildlife refuges harbor a variety of coastal fauna. For information on the area, contact the **Tourist Regional Information Program,** SW Washington, P.O. Box 128, Longview 98632. In **emergencies** call the state **police** at 911 or 206-577-2050.

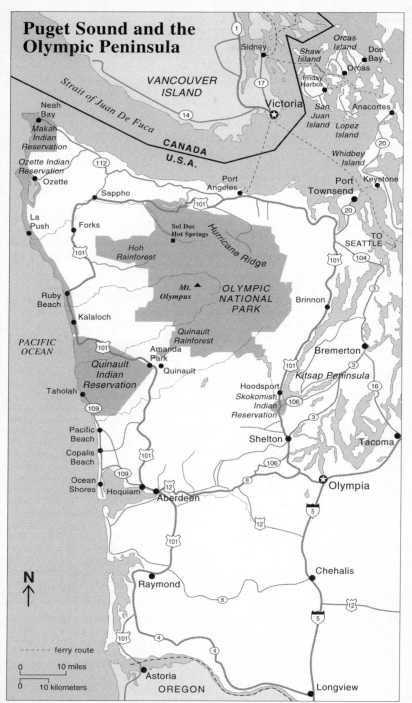

Puget Sound and the Olympic Peninsula

VANCOUVER ISLAND

Strait of Juan De Fuca

CANADA
U.S.A.

Sidney

Shaw Island

Orcas Island

Doe Bay

Friday Harbor

Orcas

Victoria

San Juan Island

Lopez Island

Anacortes

Whidbey Island

Keystone

Neah Bay

Makah Indian Reservation

Ozette Indian Reservation

Ozette

Sappho

Port Angeles

Port Townsend

TO SEATTLE

La Push

Forks

Sol Duc Hot Springs

Hoh Rainforest

Hurricane Ridge

Mt. Olympus

OLYMPIC NATIONAL PARK

Brinnon

Ruby Beach

Kalaloch

PACIFIC OCEAN

Quinault Rainforest

Amanda Park

Quinault

Quinault Indian Reservation

Bremerton

Kitsap Peninsula

Taholah

Hoodsport

Skokomish Indian Reservation

Pacific Beach

Copalis Beach

Ocean Shores

Hoquiam

Aberdeen

Shelton

Tacoma

Olympia

Raymond

Chehalis

N

- - - - - ferry route

0   10 miles
0   10 kilometers

Astoria
OREGON

Longview

■■■ PORT TOWNSEND

The Victorian splendor of Port Townsend's buildings, unlike the salmon industry, has survived the progression of time and weather. The entire business district has been restored and declared a national landmark. Port Townsend is a genuine cultural oasis on an otherwise untamed peninsula. Walk down Water Street, and you'll be lured by countless cafes, book shops, and an immense ice cream parlor. Port Townsend is one of the few places west of Seattle where espresso stands outnumber live bait shops. After taking in the town, rent a sailboat and cruise into Puget Sound.

Practical Information and Orientation The town's **Chamber of Commerce,** 2437 E Sims Way, Port Townsend 98368 (385-2722), lies about 10 blocks from the center of town on Rte. 20. Ask the helpful staff for a free **map** and visitors guide (open Mon.-Fri. 9am-5pm, Sat. 10am-4pm, Sun. 11am-4pm). Find the **Public Library** at 1220 Lawrence (385-3181), uptown (open Mon. 11am-5pm, Tues.-Thurs. 11am-9pm, Fri.-Sat. 11am-5pm).

By land, Port Townsend can be reached either from **U.S. 101** or from the **Kitsap Peninsula** across the Hood Canal Bridge. **Greyhound's** daily Seattle-to-Port Angeles run connects with Jefferson County Transit in the town of Port Ludlow for the last leg to Port Townsend. By water, Port Townsend can be reached via the **Washington State Ferry** (see page 43), crossing frequently to and from Keystone (**J**) on Whidbey Island. Ferries dock at Water St., west of downtown.

Jefferson County Transit (JCT), 1615 W Sims Way (385-4777), operates Port Townsend's public transportation and connects the city with nearby destinations. To reach Port Angeles from Port Townsend, hop on JCT bus #8 (at Water and Quincy St.), to Sequim (30 min.), and from there you can catch Clallam Transit System bus #30 to Port Angeles (30 min.). JCT also sends the #1 bus to Brinnon and Quilcene (Mon.-Fri.) and the #7 bus to Poulsbo, Winslow, and Bremerton via Kitsap Transit (Mon.-Sat.) (Fares 50¢ and 25¢ per zone, seniors and passengers with disabilities 25¢ and 25¢ per zone, ages 6-18 10¢. Day passes $1.50.) A Port Townsend **shuttle bus** loops around the town itself, and other service extends west along the strait to Sequim (50¢, seniors and students 25¢, under 6 free; daily passes $1.50). For a **taxi,** call Key City Transport (385-5972; open 24 hr.).

P.T. Cyclery, 100 Tyler St. (385-6470), rents mountain bikes. Helmets and locks are included (open Mon.-Sat. 10am-5:30pm, Sun 11am-3pm; closed Sun. after Labor Day; $6 per hr., $22.50 per day). **Field Dock,** Port Ludlow Marina (437-0513), in Port Ludlow, south of Port Townsend, rents 14-ft. sailboats ($6 per hr., $18 per 3 hrs., $36 per day). **Sport Townsend,** 1044 Water St. (379-9711), rents camping equipment by the day. A two-person tent is $13 for the first day, $5 per additional day, $40 per week (open Mon.-Thurs. 10am-6pm, Fri.-Sat. 10am-7pm, Sun. 11am-4pm).

A local pharmacy is **Don's,** 1151 Water St. (385-2622; open Mon.-Fri. 9am-7pm, Sat. 9am-5pm). The Hospital is **Jefferson General,** 385-2200. **Emergency Medical Care** (385-4622) is on the corner of Sheridan and 9th St. in the west end of town. In an **emergency,** call 911. The **police,** at 607 Water St. , can be reached at 385-2322. The **Jefferson County Crisis Line** is 385-0321; 24-hrs. mental health counseling is available. **Senior Assistance,** at 385-2552, is open Monday through Friday from 8:30am to 4:30pm. Port Townsend's **post office** is at 1322 Washington St. (385-1600. Open Mon.-Fri. 9am-5pm; **General Delivery ZIP Code:** 98368). The **area code** is 206.

Accommodations and Camping That there are so many cheap places to stay in such a small town doesn't make sense, but who's complaining? **Fort Worden Youth Hostel (HI/AYH),** Fort Worden State Park (385-0655), 2 mi. from downtown, has bulletin boards and trekkers' logs, good if dated sources of information on budget travel around the Olympics. The hostel also has kitchen facilities.

(Open Feb.-Dec. 21. Call ahead for Nov.-Feb. Check in 5-10pm; check-out 9:30am; no curfew. $9, non-members $12. Cyclists $7-10. Family rates available.) **Fort Flagler Youth Hostel (HI/AYH),** Fort Flagler State Park (385-1288), lies on handsome Marrowstone Island, 20 mi. from Port Townsend. From Port Townsend head south on Rte. 19, which connects to Rte. 116 east and leads directly into the park. It's fantastic for cyclists and solitude-seekers: miles of pastoral bike routes weave through Marrowstone, and the hostel is virtually unoccupied, even in summer. (Open year-round by reservation only. Check in 5-10pm, lockout 10am-5pm. $8.50, non-members $11.50. Cyclists $6.) **Point Hudson Resort,** Point Hudson Harbor (385-2828 or 800-826-3854), at the end of Jefferson St., is a collection of faded wooden structures recalling a time when Point Hudson was the major resort in the area. Today, amateur boat-builders hammer away outside your window, and a buoy clangs incessantly. Well-kept rooms. (Singles and doubles start at $45, with bath $53.)

Campers should try **Fort Worden State Park** (385-4730) for $15 per night, or **Old Fort Townsend State Park** (385-4730) for $10 per night, $14 with hookup ($5-7 for primitive hiker/biker sites). The latter is 5 mi. south of Port Townsend just off Rte. 20, and is open mid-May to mid-Sept. Fort Worden is open year-round. You can also camp on the beach at **Fort Flagler State Park** (753-2027).

Food Strap on your Birkenstocks and grab your organic food at **Abundant Life Seed,** 1029 Lawrence (385-5660), at Polk. A **Safeway,** 442 Sims Way (385-2806), south of town along Rte. 20, serves the less macrobiotically inclined. **Burrito Depot,** 609 Washington St. (385-5856), at Madison, offers huge Mexican servings. Try the mouth-watering veggie fajita ($3.85), or fill up on big burritos from just $3 (open Mon.-Sat. 10am-9pm, Sun.11am-4pm). **Bread and Roses Bakery and Deli,** 230 Quincy St. (385-1044), offers gargantuan raspberry croissants ($1.50), currant scones ($1.10), and a dozen varieties of muffins for your morning (open daily 6am-5pm).

Port Townsend's first and finest pizza fills the tiny **Waterfront Pizza,** 951 Water St. (385-6629). 16-in. pies start at $10 (open 11am-10pm daily). **Landfall,** 412 Water St. (385-5814), on Point Hudson, cooks up seafood, salads, and Mexican food. Dinners are expensive; go for breakfast or lunch ($4-6). A huge bowl of homemade fish and chips rings in at a salty $5.75, and tasty sourdough French toast at $3. The boat-making crowd hangs out here, seasoning their food with shoptalk about hulls and wind resistance (open Mon.-Thurs. 7am-3pm, Fri.-Sun. 7am-9pm). **Elevated Ice Cream Co.,** 627 Water St. (385-1156), is owned by friendly people receptive to the scruffy traveler. Perhaps the largest ice cream shop in the U.S., the Elevated serves delicious homemade ice cream and decent espresso (90¢). One scoop of ice cream or two mini-scoops of Italian ice are $1.15 (open daily 9:30am-10pm; winter 11am-10pm).

Sights and Events Port Townsend is full of huge Queen Anne and Victorian mansions. Of the over 200 restored homes in the area, some have been converted into bed and breakfasts; others are open for tours. The 1868 **Rothschild House** (355-2722), at Franklin and Taylor St., has period furnishings and herbal and flower gardens. (Open daily 10am-5pm; Sept. 16-May 14 Sat.-Sun. 11am-4pm. Requested donation $2.) Or peek into the **Heritage House** at Pierce and Washington (open daily 12:30-3pm; $1.50).

Go down the steps on Taylor St. down to **Water Street,** the town's quaint main artery. This is reputedly the place where Jack London spent a night in jail on the way to the Yukon. Brick buildings of the 1890s are interspersed with newer shops and cafes with the old-style motif. The **Jefferson County Museum** (385-1003), at Madison and Water St., showcases vestiges of the town's wild past. Highlights include a dazzling kayak parka made of seal intestines (open Mon.-Sat. 11am-4pm, Sun. 1-4pm; donations $2).

The red **bell tower** on Jefferson St. called firefighters to their work in Port Townsend for 80 years. The base of the grand tower overlooks the town. An old

Romanesque clock tower hovers over the **County Courthouse,** at Jefferson and Walker St. Farther southwest is the **Manresa Castle** (385-5750), on 7th and Sheridan St., built in 1892 and used as a Jesuit school for 42 years. It's now a hotel and open for exploration.

Point Hudson, the hub of the small shipbuilding area, forms the corner of Port Townsend, where Admiralty Inlet and Port Townsend Bay meet. North of Point Hudson are several mi. of beach, **Chetzemolka Park,** and the larger **Fort Worden State Park.** Don't let the tide sneak up on you as you walk along the pretty coastline; you could easily find yourself on your own private island with no escape. **Fort Worden** (385-4730), a strategic military post dating from the 1890s, guards the mouth of Puget Sound and commands views of Puget Sound. The fort was pressed back into service in 1981 as a set for the movie *An Officer and a Gentleman.*

Twenty mi. south of town on Marrowstone Island, **Fort Flagler State Park,** another discharged military post, has slightly more run-down barracks than Fort Worden, but only a fraction of the tourists. Explore the gun emplacements, watch the sailboats on Puget Sound from the outpost high above the water, or stroll along the almost-deserted beach down below.

From mid-June to early September, the **Centrum Foundation** sponsors a series of festivals in Fort Worden Park. The foundation supports bluegrass, jazz, folk, and classical music, along with poetry readings, dance performances, and painting displays. Two of the most popular events are the **Fiddle Tunes Festival** in early July and **Jazz Port Townsend** later in the same month. Tickets are $8 to $15 for most single events; combination tickets can be purchased to cover the whole of each festival. For a schedule, write the Centrum Foundation, P.O. Box 1158, Port Townsend 98368 (385-3102). Other annual attractions include the **Wooden Boat Festival,** held the first weekend after Labor Day, and the **House Tour,** held the following weekend, when all the mansions are open to visitors free of charge. For more information, contact the Chamber of Commerce.

■■■ PORT ANGELES

Port Angeles is ideally situated between Olympic National Park and a gorgeous blue bay. The town's character is indistinct; the era of domination by paper and plywood mills has ended, and Port Angeles joins the leagues of small locales hungering after the tourist dollar. Stop in town for information and transportation connections or before driving up to the stupendous Hurricane Ridge, but don't stay around long; the rest of the peninsula awaits.

Practical Information Visitors information is at the **Chamber of Commerce,** 121 E Railroad (452-2363), next to the ferry terminal, 2 blocks from the intersection of Lincoln and Front St. The center provides a free telephone for local calls (open daily 8am-9pm; winter Mon.-Fri. 10am-4pm, Sat.-Sun. 10am-noon).

Port Angeles is served by **Greyhound,** 1115 E Front (452-8311 or 800-366-3380; to Seattle twice daily (once Sun.) $15.25, seniors $13.75). **Black Ball Transport,** 101 E Railroad Ave. (457-4491), has ferry service to Victoria ($6.25, $9.25 with bicycle, $25 with car, $3.15 for children). **Clallam Transit System,** 2419 W 19th St. (800-858-3747 or 452-4511), serves the Port Angeles area (buses run Mon.-Fri. 6:30am-7:30pm, Sat. 10am-6pm; fare within downtown 50¢, ages 6-19 35¢, disabled 25¢). **Car Rental** is available at **All-Star,** 602 E Front St. (452-8001), in Aggie's Motel complex (must be 21; cars from $25 per day; 100 free mi. per day, 20¢ each additional mi.). Every conceivable type of mountain equipment (except sleeping bags) can be rented from **Olympic Mountaineering, Inc.,** 221 S Peabody St. (452-0240). Tents cost $24 per day; external frame packs are $14 per day, cross-country ski gear is $15 per day. The list goes on and on, and weekly rates are lower (open Mon.-Sat. 9am-6pm, Sun. 9am-3pm). **Pedal 'n Paddle,** 120 E Front St. (457-1240), rents mountain bikes (helmets included, $6 per hour, $20 per day).

The local **laundromat** is the **Peabody Street Coin Laundry,** 212 Peabody St. (452-6493; open 24 hrs.; wash $1, dry 25¢ for 10 min.). The **post office** sits at 424 E 1st St. (452-9275), at Vine. (Open Mon.-Fri. 9am-5pm, Sat. 9am-noon. **General Delivery ZIP Code:** 98362.)

Accommodations, Camping, and Food A night indoors in Port Angeles is costly, especially in the summer (winter rates drop $5-15). The least expensive options line noisy U.S. 101. The **All-View Motel** (ignore the name), 214 E Lauridsen Blvd. (457-7779) has fairly spacious, well-furnished rooms with morning coffee, HBO, and direct dial phones (singles $39; 2 double beds $47). A few mi. west of town, the **Fairmont Motel,** 1137 U.S. 101 W (457-6113), has decent, cable-equipped rooms with a food mart next door (queen bed $37.50).

Heart o' the Hills is the closest campground (see Olympic Peninsula: Northern Rim, above). The closest free campground is **Boulder Creek Campground,** at the end of Elwha River Rd., 8 mi. past Altaire. Park at the end of the road, and hike 2 mi. along an abandoned road. You'll need a free **backcountry permit,** available at the trailhead, to pitch at one of the 50 sites. Be sure to bring your own water.

Seafood is abundant, but grill the waiters to be sure it's fresh. An excellent place to sample the local catch is **La Casita,** 203 E Front St. (452-2289). This Mexican restaurant stuffs its seafood burrito ($7) with generous amounts of crab, shrimp, and fish, and has free all-you-can-eat tortilla chips and salsa (open Mon.-Thurs. 11am-10pm, Fri. 11am-11pm, Sat. 11am-10pm, Sun. noon-9pm). Or duck into bustling **First Street Haven,** 107 E 1st St. (457-0352; open Mon.-Fri. 7am-4pm, Sat. 8am-4pm, Sun. 8am-2pm) for some strawberry Belgian waffles. Espresso fiends should try the **Coffeehouse Gallery,** 118 E 1st (452-1459). The coffeehouse offers a variety of entrees, local artwork, and live folk music most weekends (free, with an occasional cover of up to $5; coffeehouse open Mon.-Sat. 7am-8pm, Sun. 8am-5pm). Picnickers can peruse the shelves of **Safeway,** 115 E 4th St. at Lincoln St. (Open 24 hrs.)

Sights Port Angeles correctly bills itself as the "Gateway to the Olympics;" the city itself has little to offer. For those without a vehicle and disinclined to ride a bike uphill for 20 mi., **Olympic Van Tours** runs three-hour or all-day excursions to Hurricane Ridge. (Check out the kiosk on the sidewalk by the ferry docks, or call 452-3858; $12.75-16.) The **Olympic National Park Visitors Center,** 3002 Mt. Angeles Rd. (452-0330), at Race St., dispenses free **maps,** and will acquaint you with the majestic environs (open July-Aug. daily 8:30am-6pm; winter 9am-4pm). More accessible by foot is the **Arthur D. Feiro Marine Laboratory** (452-9277), offering a large classroom of touch tanks and aquariums with local marine life. The lab is operated by Peninsula College Students (open June 15-Sept. daily 10am-8pm; winter Sat.-Sun. noon-4pm; $1, seniors 50¢, under 12 50¢). Also on the pier is an observation tower with great views of the port and the Olympic Mountains that overlook the town (open daily 6am-10pm). Passing through the pier is the 6-mi. **Waterfront Trail,** a handicapped-accessible path that provides a full and colorful overview of the city's portside activities.

In a funky round building with great views of the water rests the **Fine Arts Center,** 1203 E 8th St. (457-3532), which has small but excellent exhibits from regional artists (free; open Thurs.-Sun. 11am-5pm).

■■■ OLYMPIC NATIONAL PARK

The Olympic Peninsula is dominated by Olympic National Park and ringed by small logging, fishing, and Native towns connected near the coast by U.S. 101. West lies the Pacific; north, the Strait of Juan de Fuca separates the Olympic Peninsula from Vancouver Island in Canada; and east, Hood Canal and the Kitsap Peninsula isolate this sparsely inhabited wilderness from Seattle sprawl. The spectacular, rugged scenery of Olympic National Park, with its unique **cold-temperate rainforest** and its rocky, untouched coast, is accessible to both day-trippers from Seattle or Victoria and hard-core backcountry explorers. The best time to visit the area is in the summer months, when it rains less. Plan to bring complete waterproof gear at all times, but also pack a camera loaded with film to capture the splendid natural beauty and wildlife along the peninsula.

The Olympic Mountains in the Park's center wring huge quantities of moisture from the heavy Pacific air. Average precipitation in the Park varies, but 12 ft. of rain and snow yearly is common; some areas average over 17 ft. The mountains take so much of the clouds' water that some areas northeast of the Park get less than 1½ ft., making them among the driest in Washington. The rainforests lie on the west side of the Park, along the coast and in the Hoh, Queets, and Quinault river valleys, where moderate temperatures, lots of rain, and summer fogs support a fantastic Northwestern jungle dominated by Sitka spruce and western red cedar. The rest of the park includes fir and hemlock lowland forest, silver fir at higher elevations, and flower-filled mountain meadows offering stunning views.

The coast is a wild, unspoiled wilderness, too. Forests cover rocky headlands as the surf pounds the wide, driftwood-strewn beaches. Bird and animal prints are everywhere. The only evidence of human existence you might see is another hiker or a **Japanese glass float,** loose from the net of a fishing boat across the Pacific and washed up on the American coast after a year's travel.

Visitors to the Peninsula may be stunned by the extensive devastation caused by **logging,** particularly on the western side. The National Park is totally protected from logging, and within the Park scarred views will disappear, but both the private land and the National Forest surrounding it are harvested by timber companies. The State of Washington manages huge tracts along the Hoh and Clearwater Rivers, near the western shore. Until recently, private and state policies pursued a "liquidation of old growth," a phrase illuminated by the western segment of U.S. 101, at times a corridor through clearcuts, with placards indicating the dates of harvest and replanting. Due to the spotted owl uproar and federal regulations banning logging on public land, the Forest Service ceased to harvest any Olympic timber in the late 1980s; private and state harvesting has also slowed. Environmentally-motivated travelers should probably avoid discussing the issue with locals. Those who earn a living harvesting forest resources might not appreciate lectures on how to manage them.

PRACTICAL INFORMATION AND ORIENTATION

This pristine rainforest wilderness is most easily and safely reached by **car,** only a few hours from Seattle, Portland, or Victoria. Bicycling on U.S. 101 would be ideal if safe, but is extremely dangerous. Long stretches of U.S. 101 have no shoulders. Immense log trucks speed heedlessly along the winding road, and drivers blinded by sudden sunshine or paying too much attention to the breathtaking views may not anticipate a cyclist's presence. Secondary park access roads are usually gravel and unsuited to cycling. Hitchhiking is poor in the Olympic Peninsula, generally very dangerous in the U.S., and illegal on most of U.S. 101. **Greyhound** runs to Port Angeles north of the park and Aberdeen southwest of it, but neither of these towns offers the most convenient access. Driving suits the Peninsula and Park best.

Few roads attempt to penetrate the interior, but the roads that exist are easily accessible from U.S. 101 and serve as trailheads for over 600 mi. of hiking. No roads cross the park. Bring a waterproof, all-weather coat, good boots, and a waterproof tent. Waterproof to the extreme to stay warm.

July, August, and September are the best months to visit Olympic National Park, since much of the backcountry remains snowed-in until late June, and only the summer provides rainless days regularly. Backpackers should be prepared for a mix of weather conditions at any time. Always have waterproof hiking boots with good traction; trails can become rivers of slippery mud. Bring a warm, waterproof coat and a wool hat. In summer, competition for campground space can be fierce, particularly on weekends. From late June to late September, most sites are taken by 2pm, so start hunting early; in the more popular areas and along the Hoh River, find a site before noon. The **map** distributed at Park gates and most ranger stations gives an excellent overview of the entire Park, the inland and coastal sections, and the major trails through it. If you plan to do any beach exploration, pick up a **tide table** and the useful guide *Strip of Wilderness* with your map.

> **Visitors Information: Olympic Visitors Center,** 3002 Mt. Angeles Rd., Port Angeles (452-0330), off Race St. Main information center. Fields questions about the whole park, including camping, backcountry hiking, and fishing, and displays a **map** of locations of other park ranger stations. Also houses the **Pioneer Memorial Museum** (open daily July-Aug. 8:30am-6pm; Sept.-May 9am-4pm).
>
> **Park Superintendent,** 600 E Park Ave., Port Angeles (452-4501, ext. 311). Open Mon.-Fri. 8am-4:30pm.
>
> **Entrance Fee:** $5 per car is charged at the developed entrances, such as the Hoh, Heart o' the Hills, Sol Duc, Staircase, and Elwha, all with paved roads and toilet facilities. The fee buys an entrance permit good for 7 days. A similar pass for hikers and bikers costs $3.
>
> **Park Weather:** 452-0329. 24 hrs.
>
> **Park Radio:** 530 AM for road closures and general weather conditions.
>
> **Park Emergency:** 452-4501. Operates daily 8am-5pm; at other times phone 911.

EXPLORING THE BEACHES AND COAST

Fifty-seven mi. of pristine coastline await visitors on the Park's western coast. Piles of driftwood, imposing sea stacks, sculptured arches, and abundant wildlife frame a perfect sunset, cloud cover permitting. The rugged and deserted beaches are especially magnificent during winter storms. Bald eagles are often out on windy days, and whales and seals tear through the sea. Where U.S. 101 hugs the coast between the Hoh and Quinault Reservations, the beaches are easily accessible. The 15-mi. stretch of beaches begins in the north with **Ruby Beach** near Mile 165 on U.S. 101. South of Ruby Beach at Mile 160 is Beach #6, a favorite whale-watching spot. Another three mi. south is Beach #4, with its beautiful tidepools. South of Beaches #4 and #6 is **Kalaloch** (KLAY-lok) **Center,** with 177 sites near the ocean, including a lodge, a general store, a gas station, and a ranger station. Gather in the morning hours for interpretive talks on the tidepools; contact the Park Service West District Headquarters (374-5450), 3 mi. north of Forks on U.S. 101, for specific times. North of this strip, between the Hoh and Quileute lands, is a 17-mi. strip dominated by rocky headlands. At the north end of this strip, **Mora** (374-5460), due west of Forks near the Quileute Reservation, has a campground (sites $8) and a ranger station. From **Rialto Beach** near Mora, you can hike 21 mi. north along the coast to a free campground and roadhead at **Ozette Lake.**

The whole beach strip is a protected coastal wilderness for hiking and **backcountry camping.** Camping is permitted all along the beaches, except along the Kalaloch strip by U.S. 101. Pick up use **permits** at trailheads. Before hiking or camping along the coast, pick up a Park **map,** a **tide table,** and the useful folder *Strip of Wilderness* at a ranger station. The map will help you find coastal trails, estimate distances, and negotiate headlands. Some headlands are impassable at all times; trails run slightly inland behind them. Others, marked by purple dots on the map, are passable only at low tide. At high tide, those stretches of beach will be submerged and you'll hike behind them too; use your tide table to accurately predict your margin of tidal safety. At low tide, it may be perfectly safe to hike between the headland and ocean, but if you have any doubt, *do not risk drowning by trying to race against the incoming tide.* Your tide table will prove extremely useful in these situations. Several stretches of beach lie within land belonging to the Makah, Ozette, Quileute, Hoh, and Quinault Native nations. A continuous 57-mi. beach trek is impossible; reservation land is private and may not be crossed by hikers without permission.

BACKCOUNTRY AND RAINFOREST EXPLORATION

Backcountry camping in the Park requires a free **backcountry permit,** available at any ranger station and most trailheads. Four destinations within the park have issued only a limited number of backcountry permits in response to the area's popularity. These are North Beach by Lake Ozette (452-0300), the Soleduck District (327-3534), and Lake Constance and Flapjack Lakes, both overseen by the **Hood Canal Ranger Station** in **Hoodsport** (877-5254). Reservations for the last two are crucial; call for a summer permit in the early spring.

Between the coast and rainforest, the proud logging town of **Forks** on U.S. 101 offers cheap motels and food for the tired, hungry traveler. **Visitors Information** (374-2531) is on U.S. 101 on the southern end of town. The **Town Motel** has clean, well-kept rooms (singles $29, doubles $35). For good food from a huge menu, drop in at the **Raindrop Cafe,** 111 E A St. (374-6612), at S Forks Ave. for a $6 gourmet burger (open Mon.-Sat. 6am-9pm, Sun. 6am-8pm; in winter Mon.-Sat. 5am-8pm, Sun. 5am-6pm). Grab groceries at **Forks Thrifty Mart,** on U.S. 101 (374-6161; open Mon.-Sat. 8am-10pm; Sun. 9am-9pm).

Olympic National Park is home to one of the **world's only temperate rainforests.** Gigantic, thick old-growth trees, ferns, and mosses blanket the valleys of the Hoh, Queets, and Quinault Rivers, all on the west side of the Park. Although the forest floor is thickly carpeted with unusual foliage and fallen trees, rangers keep the many walking trails clear and well-marked. Many travelers seek out the **Hoh Rainforest Trail** for an incredible rainforest experience. Perfect for longer expeditions, the trail parallels the Hoh River for 18 mi. to Blue Glacier on the shoulder of Mount Olympus. Shy Roosevelt elk and Northern spotted owl inhabit the area. The first two campgrounds along the Hoh River Rd., which leaves U.S. 101 13 mi. south of the town of Forks, are administered by the state Department of Natural Resources (DNR), accept no reservations, and are free. Drinking water is available at the **Minnie Peterson** site only. DNR sites are usually uncrowded; stay at one and drive to the Hoh trailhead to get a **map** and begin your rainforest exploration. You can obtain a separate **map** of the Hoh-Clearwater Multiple Use Area from the DNR main office, just off U.S. 101 on the north side of Forks, or at Minnie Peterson. The **Hoh Rainforest Visitors Center** (374-6925) provides posters and permits (open July-Aug. daily 9am-6:30pm, winter 9am-5pm). Just south of Hoh River Rd., the Oil City Rd. leads west to the coast. Cottonwood, another free DNR site with drinking water, is 2.3 mi. down this road and 1 mi. down a gravel road leading left.

Trailheads to seek out for relative solitude are **Queets, North Fork,** and **Graves Creek,** in the west and southwest of the Park. These more remote, less crowded options offer excellent opportunities to explore more **rainforest** amid surrounding ridges and mountains. The Queets Trail follows the Queets River east from a free campground (20 sites for tents only; open June-Sept.). Treks along the Queets River Trail are generally thwarted by the high waters of the river, which must be crossed. The best chance is August, but there's still a risk that you'll be cut off. A shorter, 3-mi. loop is as much as most visitors can see of the Queets rainforest. The Park and Forest Services and the Quinalt Reservation, which owns the lake, share the land surrounding **Quinault Lake and River.** The Forest Service operates a day-use beach and an information center in the **Quinault Ranger Station,** South Shore Rd. (288-2444; open daily 9am-4:30pm; winter Mon.-Fri. 9am-4:30pm). From the Quinalt Ranger Station, it's 20 mi. to the North Fork trailhead; enterprising hikers can journey 44 mi. north across the entire park, finishing up at Whiskey Bend.

Never drink even one mouthful of untreated **water** in the park. *Giardia,* a nasty bacteria, lives in all these waters and causes severe diarrhea and abdominal cramps. Symptoms often don't appear for weeks after ingestion. Carry your own water supply or boil local water for five minutes before drinking it. You can also buy water purification tablets at the visitors center (see above) or at most camping supply stores. **Black bears,** eager to share your granola and peanuts, are another potential hazard for backcountry campers. To prevent mishaps, ranger stations will give lessons on hanging food out of reach when they issue your backcountry permit. Some stations have free rope available, but don't count on it. Bring your own 50-100 ft. of thin, sturdy rope. A map will tell you whether **open fires** are permitted in the backcountry area.

Mountain climbing is tricky in the Olympic Range. Although the peaks are not high (Mt. Olympus is only 7965 ft.), they are steep and prone to wet, cold, unpredictable weather. The quality of rock is poor, and most ascents require sophisticated equipment. Climbers are required to check in at a ranger station before any summit attempt. The rangers urge novices to buddy up with experienced climbers who are "wise in the ways of Northwest mountaineering."

Fishing within park boundaries requires no permit, but you must obtain a state game department punch card for salmon and steelhead at local outfitting and hardware stores, or at the Fish and Game Department in Olympia. The **Elwha River,** coursing through the northeastern part of the Park, is best for **trout.** The **Hoh River,** flowing west through the Park, is excellent for **salmon.**

CAMPING ON THE PENINSULA

Why pay to stay in a motel when you can camp for only a few bucks within walking distance of one of the world's three cold-temperate rainforests? Olympic National Park, Olympic National Forest, and the State of Washington all maintain free campgrounds. Pick up the **map** of the park and area from a ranger station for comprehensive information. The free **National Park campgrounds** include Deer Park, Dosewallips, Graves Creek, July Creek, Ozette (all with drinking water), and Queets (no water). In addition, the National Park has many standard campgrounds (sites $8). Fees in the **National Forest campgrounds** range from $4-12; six campgrounds in the Hood Canal Ranger District are free. Reservations can be made for three Forest Service campgrounds: Seal Rock, Falls View, and Klahowga, by calling 800-280-CAMP. Any ranger station can provide a list of both Park and Forest Service campgrounds, fees, and facilities. Several **State Parks** are scattered along Hood Canal and the eastern rim of the peninsula (sites $10-16; occasionally only $4-5).

Washington's **Department of Natural Resources (DNR)** manages the huge tracts near the western shore along the Hoh and Clearwater Rivers, and smaller, individual campsites sprinkled around the peninsula. DNR camping is free, first-come, first-served; and uncrowded except in mid-summer. Some sites allow RVs, some lack drinking water, and most have good fishing. Many sites cannot be found without a map. The DNR publishes a guide to all its Washington sites and displays additional **maps** of its Multiple Use Areas (MUAs).

The perimeters of the park are well-defined. The Park Service runs **interpretive programs** such as guided forest walks, **tidepool walks,** and campfire programs out of its various ranger stations (all free). For a full schedule of events obtain a copy of the park newspaper from ranger stations or the visitors center.

HOODSPORT AND EASTERN PARK RIM

The eastern and northern sections of the Park are the most heavily developed and used sites. Hikers use auto campgrounds as trailheads to the interior of the park. **Staircase Campground** (877-5569) is a major camping hub 16 mi. northwest of **Hoodsport** at the head of Lake Cushman in **Lake Cushman State Park** (877-5491); turn off U.S. 101, go past the joint Park/Forest Service **Hood Canal Ranger Station** (P.O. Box 68, Hoodsport, WA 98548 (877-5552); open Mon.-Fri. 7am-4:30pm, Sat.-Sun. 8am-4:30pm; mid-Sept.-mid-May Mon.-Fri. 7am-4:30pm), take a left after 9 mi. and follow the signs. The ranger station offers interpretive programs on weekends (59 sites, $8 on top of the $5 entrance fee; RV accessible). Lake Cushman is a popular base camp for extended backpacking trips into the National Forest and Park. With good swimming beaches, the park offers showers (6 min. for 25¢) and flush toilets (50 sites for $10; 30 with full hookup $15). Super-tough hikers should tackle the steep 3-mi. trail up **Mt. Ellnor,** 17 mi. east of Hoodsport. Get directions from the ranger station. On a clear day, the **view** from the top is unreal: the Olympic range unfolds to the northwest, and a head-turn away, Puget Sound, Seattle, Mt. Rainier, Mt. Adams, and the rim of Mt. St. Helens tower to the southeast. Back down at sea level, reward yourself with a giant double-scoop ice cream cone from **Fuddy Duddy's** (877-9344) on U.S. 101 in Hoodsport. Hoodsport also has a few small **gro-**

cery stores; it might be wise to stock up, because the next ones are 50 mi. north in Sequim. Drop by the Hoodsport Winery, N 23501 Hwy. 101 (877-9894), just south of town for tasting and tours (open daily 10am-6pm). Adjacent to the ranger station in Hoodsport is a **post office** (877-5552; open Mon.-Fri. 8am-12:30pm and 1:30-5pm, Sat. 8:30am-11:30pm; **General Delivery ZIP Code:** 98548).

Dosewallips (doh-see-WALL-ups), on a road that leaves U.S. 101 27 mi. north of Hoodsport, has 32 free but less developed sites for cars. The **ranger station** (summer only), has no electricity or telephones. A spectacular trail leads from Dosewallips across the Park to **Hurricane Ridge.**

Thirty mi. north of Hoodsport, the **Quilcene Ranger Station,** 20482 U.S. 101 S (765-3368) can point you to the **Mt. Walker View Point,** 3 mi. south of Quilcene on U.S. 101. A one-lane gravel road takes you 4 mi. to the lookout, the highest viewpoint accessible by car. The road is steep, has sheer drop-offs, and should not be attempted in foul weather. A breathtaking view of Hood Canal, Puget Sound, Mt. Rainier, and Seattle, awaits intrepid travelers on top. Picnic tables are provided on the east side; feast as you gaze at 7743-ft. **Mt. Constance** from the north side.

NORTHERN PARK RIM

The most developed part of Olympic National Park is along the northern rim near Port Angeles. **Heart o' the Hills Campground** (452-2713; 105 sites), 5½ mi. from Port Angeles up Race Rd. inside Olympic National Park, is filled with vacationers poised to take **Hurricane Ridge** by storm the next day (sites $8, plus the $5 entrance fee), where interpretive programs and a ranger station await. Clear days bring splendid views of Mt. Olympus and Vancouver Island, and the foreground is a haze of indigo lupine. The ridge can be crowded; the ideal time to go is sunrise, but after the herds arrive, more seclusion can be found on the many trails that originate here, including some for seniors and the disabled. On weekends in late December through late March, the Park Service organizes guided **snowshoe walks** (free, snowshoes free) atop the ridge. Call the Visitors Center at 452-0330 for details.

Further west on U.S. 101, **Elwha Valley** (452-9191; 41 sites), 5 mi. south off U.S. 101, has a ranger station accessible also to nearby **Altaire** (30 sites). Both have drinking water (sites $8). **Fairholm Campground** (928-3380; 87 sites), 30 mi. west of Port Angeles at the western tip of Lake Crescent, has sites with drinking water ($8). **The Storm King Information Station** (open June-Aug. daily 9am-5pm) runs interpretive evening programs at Fairholm Campground, but has no camping. The lake is huge and magnificent. Jump on a **paddlewheeler** for a 75 min. cruise over the icy blue waters ($15; seniors $14; under 17 $10). Call 452-4520 to make reservations, or drop by the **Shadow General Store** on the east side of Crescent Lake. A shuttle to the boat leaves every half hour beginning at 10:30am from the general store (first cruise 11:30am; last cruise 6pm in summer, 4:30pm otherwise).

The **Marymere Falls Trail** loops 2 mi. through old-growth Douglas firs, western hemlock, and red cedar. Further west on U.S. 101, an entrance fee of $5 and 13 mi. of paved road will get you through to the **Sol Duc Hot Springs Campground** (327-3534). A roving naturalist is on duty in the afternoon, and there are scheduled programs in the evening (sites $8). The grounds close when it snows. The Sol Duc trailhead is also a route for those heading for the heights; stop by the **Sol Duc Ranger Station** (327-3534; open July-Aug. daily 8am-5pm) for information and free backcountry permits. The **Sol Duc Trail** draws many hikers, but crowds thin considerably above Sol Duc Falls. The ridges above Sol Duc offer great views.

At nearby **Sol Duc Hot Springs** (327-3583; $5.50 per day, seniors $4.50), the cement docks, chlorine smell, and "shower before you enter" signs detract from this pristine source of naturally hot water (open mid-May-Sept. daily 9am-9pm; closes at 8pm in Sept.; April and Oct. 9am-5pm). A better and less well-known way to harness the region's geothermal energy is to hike up to **Olympic Hot Springs.** Turn off at the Elwha River Road and follow it 12 mi. to the trailhead. The natural springs are about a 2½-mi. hike, but well worth it. As you go higher up on the mountain, the springs get warmer and give off a sulfurous aroma.

CAPE FLATTERY AND NEAH BAY

The Olympic Peninsula contains the northwesternmost point in the contiguous U.S. In 1778, the area caught the attention of explorer James Cook, who named the tip Cape Flattery because it "flattered us with the hopes of finding a harbor." It still flatters the visitor with pristine beaches. At the westernmost point on the strait is Neah Bay, the only town in the **Makah Reservation.** Rte. 112 leads there west from Port Angeles; from the south, take the short road north from **Sappho.** The **Clallam Transit System** (800-858-3747 or 452-4511) reaches Neah Bay via Sappho. Take bus #14 from Oak St. in Port Angeles to Sappho (60 min.). Then take bus #16 to Neah Bay (75 min.). Check schedules at the Port Angeles Greyhound Station to avoid long layovers. (75¢, ages 6-19 60¢, seniors free). In case of **emergency** in Neah Bay, call 911 (645-2236 in a **marine emergency**). **General Delivery ZIP Code:** 98357. **Area code:** 206.

Cape Flattery sits in the corner of Neah Bay's backyard, but the dirt road out is a pothole party. Drive slowly, and drive during the day, to avoid the deep ruts. Follow the road past the Cape Flattery Resort. The road becomes dirt; stay on it for another 4 mi. until you reach a small, circular parking area. A well-marked trailhead sends you toward Cape Flattery. The half-hour hike rewards those willing to risk twisted ankles with fantastic views of Tatoosh Island just off the coast and Vancouver Island across the strait. A few mi. south of Cape Flattery is **Hobuck Beach,** where camping and picnicking are within car's reach. Coming from Neah Bay, turn left just before you reach Cape Flattery resort, cross the bridge, and take the first right to the **Hobuck Beach Park** (645-6422), with outhouses, running water, and camping space for $10 per night. No reservations are allowed. To the south lie the more secluded beaches, reachable only by foot. The whole beach is private property, but visitors are welcome. Slightly more opulent accommodations can be had at the Cape Flattery Resort (645-2251), 2 mi. west of Neah Bay; just follow the signs to the 36 comfortable but no-frills dormitory beds ($12.50 per night; RV hookup $15) in this converted Air Force station owned by the Makah. Call for reservations; the facility is a hot spot for conference groups.

Back in Neah Bay, the **Makah Cultural and Research Center** (645-2711) on Hwy. 112 houses artifacts from the archaeological site at Cape Alava, where a huge mudslide 500 years ago buried and preserved an entire settlement. The downstairs of a 70-ft.-long house, with a sloped roof ideally suited to the rainy environment, has been replicated at the museum. (Open daily 10am-5pm; Oct.-April Wed.-Sun. 10am-5pm. $4, seniors and students $3.) The salmon smell in the Makah house is authentic enough to inspire you to dash over to **Rosie's II Cafe** (645-2789), also on Hwy. 112, for a big helping of fish and chips ($7). This is an informal place for hobnobbing with the locals; dine as you admire the ocean (open daily 5am-10pm; winter 5am-9pm). The Makah nation, whose recorded history goes back 2000 years, still lives, fishes, and produces magnificent artwork on its original land. During the last full weekend of August, Native Americans from around the region come to participate in canoe races, traditional dances and bone games (a form of gambling) during the **Makah Days.** The delicious salmon bake is a definite highlight. Contact the cultural center for more information.

■■■ GRAYS HARBOR

North of Willapa Bay, at the southwest corner of the Olympic Peninsula, the restless waters of Grays Harbor make a large triangular dent in Washington's coastline. The long sandbars that protect the harbor extend north and south of the bay, forming wide, fine-grained beaches that stretch for miles. Take advantage of the many beach accesses on Rte. 105 between Willapa Bay and Gray's Harbor. The long, isolated stretches of sand are perfect for beachcombing; be sure to scan the horizon for pieces of driftwood or highly coveted **Japanese glass floats.** These vibrantly colored glass balls have been carried by the Kuroshio Current across thousands of mi.

of Pacific Ocean from Japan, where they were used to support fishing nets. Having traveled an average of 10 years before arriving on American shores, the floats may be older than those who claim them. The best time to look is after a storm, but finds are rare. Digging for **razor clams** on the beaches from October to mid-March is a far safer bet. Licenses are available at local establishments; contact the Washington State Dept. of Fisheries (268-0623) for the opening date of the clam season.

On your way north along Rte. 105, take a right at Cranberry Rd. and observe the huge **cranberry bogs** giving the area its nickname: the "Cranberry Coast." Harvesting runs from late September through Thanksgiving. Local pride for the cranberries is warranted; the tart fruit is one of only three fruits native to North America (Concord grapes and blueberries are the others).

Westport, on Grays Harbor's southern spit, has been efficiently fishing salmon for many years, so efficiently that there are no more salmon to fish. Given the state moratorium on salmon fishing, Westport minus salmon equals tourists. Despite the scarcity of salmon, charter fishing companies grow thick and ugly on Westhaven Dr. near the waterfront, offering tuna, halibut, and bottom fishing. **Whale-watching trips** are the activity of choice between March and May, when the huge gray ones weave through the waters. **BraLee Charters** (268-9177) runs trips daily at 11am and 2pm ($17.50, children $10). The floats in the Westport Marina are some of the best places on the coast to go **crabbing**. The season runs from December through September 15, and the sport is simple: just rent a crab ring (a hula-hoop-like contraption with nets attached) for $3-5, load it with dead fish, put it in the water, and check every 15 minutes (but don't forget a "seaweed license," $6). If you'd like to pay the crabs a visit, **scuba gear and lessons** are available at **Harbor Dive,** 100 N Montesano St. (268-0080).

Dozens of cheap motels line Rte. 105 in Westport; the best deal is at **Breakers Motel,** 971 N Montesano St. (268-0848). The "sleeping rooms," with bathrooms down the hall, are large and have twin beds and cable TV. Reserve early, or you'll lose the rooms to surfers. (Singles $22, with private bath $34. Doubles $27, with private bath $44.) The **Chamber of Commerce,** 2985 S Montesano St. (268-9422), has seemingly infinite lists and brochures on accommodations and charter boats (open Mon.-Fri. 9am-5pm, Sat.-Sun. 10am-2pm). Catch **buses** for Taholah (25¢), Westport (25¢), and Olympia ($1) just across Hwy. 105 from the visitors center.

Twenty mi. northeast of Westport on Hwy. 105 puff **Aberdeen** and **Hoquiam,** heavily industrialized mini-cities at the mouth of the Chehalis River. Upon seeing the mills and malls of Aberdeen, alternative-rock fans will easily see how it could have produced the angst-ridden artistry of Kurt Cobain. Their strategic location and low prices make them good places to rest and refuel, if not to linger, between Puget Sound, the beaches and forests of the Olympic Peninsula, and the coast.

The **Grays Harbor Historical Seaport** (532-8611), 813 East Heron St. in Aberdeen, is a working shipyard that constructs and maintains vintage vessels, including replicas of Robert Gray's *Columbia Rediviva* (the first American ship to circumnavigate the world) and *Lady Washington* (the first American ship to visit Japan). (Open daily 10am-5pm. $3, seniors and students $2, under 12 $1.) Frequent cruises to Westport and around the harbor are $20-25. If you haven't been camping long enough to yearn for the comforts of a cheap motel, make a stop in **Montesano,** a small town about 20 minutes east of Aberdeen on U.S. 12. From Montesano, you can enjoy an stay and a swim at **Lake Sylvia** (249-3621; sites $10).

Grays Harbor National Wildlife Refuge, 1 mi. south of Rte. 109 in Hoquiam, is a Hitchcockian nightmare: over one million birds gather here in spring. Put on your boots and hike the muddy 1-mi. trail to Bowerman Basin, the best place to watch species such as sandpipers and dunlin. During peak migration times (late April), a **shuttle bus** provides round-trip service from Hoquiam High School (25¢). For information call the **refuge office** at 100 Brown Farm Rd. in Olympia (532-6237).

A string of inexpensive but amenity-filled motels is the best reason to linger overnight. The family-run **Snore & Whisker,** 3031 Simpson Ave. in Hoquiam (532-5060) has small but beautiful rooms with mini-fridges, cable TV, fans, and free local calls.

(Singles $30. Doubles $35.) The **Grays Harbor Chamber of Commerce,** 506 Duffy, Aberdeen 98520 (532-1924 or 800-321-1924), can provide information on the area (open Mon.-Fri. 8am-5pm, Sat.-Sun. 10am-5pm).

A resort area creeps north to Moclips near the **Quinault Reservation** (KWE-nelt). Mobs of vacationers had invaded the turf of the Quinault Nation until 1969, when the Quinault people booted the littering and vandalizing visitors off their beaches. This bold move brought a flood of supportive letters to the Quinault's mailboxes. A tiny museum up the coast in **Taholah,** 50 mi. north of Aberdeen on Hwy. 101, in the office of the **Quinault Historical Foundation** (276-8211 for the museum), exhibits the 1969 event, and baskets, carvings, and artifacts (open Mon.-Fri. 8am-5pm). The staff is rarely on hand to answer questions, but visitors are welcome. Take **Grays Harbor Transit** bus #50, which stops in Taholah.

■■■ WILLAPA BAY

Willapa Bay, dividing the Long Beach peninsula from the mainland, is known for its wildlife. The drive up U.S. 101, culminating with a turn west on Rte. 105 at **Raymond,** is a feast for the eyes and compensates for the protected bay's prohibitions on swimming and sunning. The highlight of the area is just off U.S. 101, the headquarters of the **Willapa National Wildlife Refuge** (484-3482), the last unpolluted estuary in the United States and a sanctuary for seabirds and waterfowl. The refuge is comprised of several "units" scattered through the Willapa Bay region, including a unit at Leadbetter Point on the tip of the Long Beach Peninsula and one on **Long Island** in Willapa Bay. The refuge offers the rare opportunity to observe Canada geese, loons, grebes, cormorants, trumpeter swans, and other birds. The greatest diversity of birds descends upon the area during the fall and winter months. Long Island is Willapa Bay's most superlative attraction. Not only is the island teeming with deer, bear, elk, beaver, otter, and grouse, it's also home to a 274-acre cedar grove, one of the Northwest's last climax forests, still growing new trees after 4000 years. The cedars average 160 ft. in height; some are 11 ft. in diameter.

Long Island is home to five limited-use **campgrounds** inaccessible by car. Reaching the island is a problem; you'll have to find your own boat. If you don't have a boat, you may be able to bum a ride. Don't try to swim the channel; the water is too muddy. Boats should be launched from the Wildlife Refuge Headquarters; the channel at this point is only about 100 yd. wide. After reaching the island and tying up your boat, hike 2½ mi. along the island's main road to reach the **Trail of Ancient Cedars.** The **office** at the Refuge furnishes advice on getting to the island and **maps** marked with campgrounds. Try your hand at digging **razor clams;** a two-day license costs $6. Dig at morning low tide; spring and fall are best.

Thirty mi. farther north and accessible by **Pacific Transit, South Bend's** world is the oyster, harvested from Willapa Bay's 25,000 acres of oyster beds. For a panoramic view of the Willapa River and its surrounding meadows and hills, stop by the teal-and-cream **Pacific County Courthouse,** up Memorial St. off U.S. 101.

■■■ LONG BEACH PENINSULA

Long Beach Peninsula, with 28 mi. of unbroken beach accessible by Hwy. 101, is an overwhelming combination of kites, souvenir shops, beaches, and more kites. Fishing, swimming, boating, and kite-flying fill the warmer months, allowing residents to recuperate from the pounding winter storms. You can beachcomb for peculiar pieces of driftwood and glass balls from Japanese fishing nets. (Permits are required for gathering driftwood in state parks.) Driving on the beach is legal (and common) on the hard, wet sand above the lower **clam beds.** Be sure to get up speed before driving from the road to the hard sand, or somebody may have to pull you out. From October to mid-March, look for people chasing the limit of 15 tasty razor clams. To find the fast-digging bivalves, look for dimples or bubbles in the sand. If you're willing to shell out $10.50 for an annual non-resident license (Washington residents $3.50) and spend a few days learning the ropes, you can harvest a seafood feast. The *Chinook Observer's Long Beach Peninsula Guide* and the **state fisheries** (753-6600) in Ocean Park both offer advice on technique. Consult fisheries' regulations before digging in. Free tide tables are available at information centers and many places of business. These are useful both for finding clams and escaping island status when the tide comes in.

You can fill up by **berry picking** in late summer; look for wild varieties in the weeds along the peninsula's roadsides. The peninsula contains nearly 500 acres of cranberry bogs, but be careful about picking on private property.

The **Long Beach Visitors Bureau** (642-2400 or 800-451-2542), five minutes south of Long Beach on Hwy. 101, has pamphlets galore on activities in Long Beach and other Northwest hot spots. **Pacific Transit** buses (in Raymond 642-9418, in Naselle 484-7136, farther north 875-9418) provide cheap local transportation. For 85¢ and a transfer, you can take a bus as far north as **Aberdeen,** home of Nirvana's talented but suicidal singer, Kurt Cobain. Bus schedules are available in post offices and visitors centers (service Mon.-Fri. 2-3 times per day). Past the town of Long Beach, check out the immense **boardwalk,** 10 mi. north on Long Beach itself. The seemingly infinite walkway stretches along the sand and provides a relaxing perch for watching the surf, the kites, and the sunset over the Pacific. On 10th St., a block from the beach, you can rent a horse from **Back Country Horse Rentals** (642-2576) for $11 per hour (a wrangler goes with you; open daily in summer 9am-6:30pm). Moped rentals for beach cruising are across the street at **OWW Inc.** (642-4260; $12 per hr., 40¢ for a helmet; drivers license required).

The city of Long Beach invites kite flyers from Thailand, China, Japan, and Australia to the **International Kite Festival** (642-2400) during the third week of August. Late July brings the **Sand Castle Festival** to the town. In 1989, a world record trembled when participants built a 3-mi.-long fortress of sand. Call the Long Beach Peninsula Visitor's Bureau (800-451-2541) for more information.

Among the cheapest places in town to sleep is the **Sand-Lo-Motel,** 1906 Pacific Hwy. (642-2600; singles and doubles $36). The beds are all raised on pedestals so that the high tide won't sweep you away (or so goes the owner's little joke). Call early for reservations. For your choice of delicious homemade cookies (30¢) or a sandwich ($3), go to the **Cottage Bakery and Deli** (642-4441), just south of the intersection of Rte. 103 and Bolstad St. in Long Beach (open daily 4am-8pm, in winter 4am-6pm). A slab of fresh, flaky berry pie ($3) at **Mom's Pie Kitchen** (642-2342) at 12th and Pacific, is a must. Mmmm. Specials are cheap ($2 for half a sandwich, salad, and half a pie; open Tues.-Sat. 11am-4pm, Sun. 11am-4pm).

Nearby **Nahcotta** relies on the oyster for financial solvency. Nahcotta's claim to fame is **The Ark** (665-4133), easily the finest restaurant in the area. Dinner might cost upwards of $15, but you'll be overwhelmed with fresh seafood, homemade baked goods and pastries, and Northwestern specialties, all elegantly prepared and presented (open for dinner Tues.-Sat. 5-10pm and for brunch Sun. 11am-8pm for brunch). Make reservations several days ahead. Rent a kayak for $25 per day at **Willapa Bay Kayak Rentals** (642-4892) in Nahcotta.

Leadbetter Point State Park, on the Long Beach peninsula's northernmost tip, is a favorite of photographers, nature lovers, and bird watchers. Over 100 species of birds enjoy this slice of the **Willapa Bay Wildlife Refuge** on the northernmost tip of the peninsula. Enjoy hiking through the varied terrain, but watch for black bears. Bring bug repellent so you don't lose limbs to the carnivorous mosquitoes. Farther down the peninsula, **Pacific Pines** and **Loomis Lake State Parks** are also perfect spots for hiking, picnicking, and surf-fishing, and are less crowded than Long Beach.

■■■ COLUMBIA RIVER ESTUARY

In 1788, British fur trader Captain John Meares, frustrated by repeated failures to cross the treacherous Columbia River sandbar, named the water now known as

Baker Bay **Deception Bay** and the large promontory guarding the river's mouth **Cape Disappointment.** Since then, more than 230 vessels have been wrecked, stranded, or sunk where the Columbia meets the ocean, a region aptly named "the graveyard of the Pacific."

Fort Columbia State Park (777-8221) lies on U.S. 101 northwest of the Astoria Megler Bridge, 1 mi. east of Chinook. The fort was built in 1896 and armed with huge guns to protect the mouth of the river from enemies who never showed up. The park's **interpretive center** entertainingly recreates life at the fort, and includes an exhibit on the Chinook Native people who once occupied this land. A 1-mi.-long woodland trail takes you past several historical sites, including an abandoned observation station. (Park open daily 6:30am-dusk; Oct. 16-March Wed.-Sun. 8am-dusk. Center open Wed.-Sun. 9am-5pm.) What was once the area's hospital is now the fantastic **Fort Columbia Youth Hostel,** P.O. Box 224, Chinook (777-8755) (see page 430).

In nearby **Ilwaco, Fort Canby State Park** offers camping and a megadose of Lewis and Clark. Super-cheap **Pacific Transit** buses (642-9418) connect Ilwaco with points north on the Washington coast, the Long Beach Peninsula, and Astoria, Oregon (daypass $1.50). From Ilwaco, walk 2 mi. to reach the park. The park's 190 tentsites and 60 RV sites are crowded on summer weekends (sites $11, with hookup $16, hiker/biker $5, full facilities include hot showers). To reserve a site, call the **park office** (642-3078).

The U.S. Coast Guard maintains a **lifeboat station** and **surf school** in the park. The students often have to abandon their maneuvers to attend to a real rescue of swimmers or vessels. This is one of the busiest search-and-rescue stations in the United States. The **North Head Lighthouse,** built in 1898, is in the northwest corner of the park and is accessible by a paved path. A clear day affords an incredible view of the Pacific cliffs. The **Cape Disappointment Lighthouse,** built in 1856 and the oldest in the Northwest, is in the southeast corner of the park and can be reached by puffing ¼ mi. up a steep hill from the Coast Guard station parking lot. Tours of the interior of North Head Lighthouse are given Saturdays in summer at 7pm; tours of Cape Disappointment Lighthouse, Fridays at 7pm ($1-2; call the park office for tour information). For a magnificent beach-level view of the Cape Disappointment Lighthouse, drive through the campground area past **Waikiki Beach** onto the **North Jetty.** Though not quite Honolulu, Waikiki Beach is ideal for swimming in summer, beachcombing after storms in winter, and year-round ship-watching. **Benson Beach,** north of the Jetty, is even less crowded. At the end of the main road sits the **Lewis and Clark Interpretive Center,** above the ruins of the fort. Beware the crowds of teenage rollerbladers whizzing through the fort. Inside, follow the trail through the wonderful displays of journal entries, photos, and equipment (beaches and interpretive center free; open summer daily 9am-5pm, call for winter hrs.).

Enjoy 3-D models, simulated wave action, and working miniature trains at the fun, highly worthwhile **Ilwaco Museum,** 115 Lake St. (642-3446); open summer Mon.-Sat. 9am-5pm, Sun. 10am-2pm; winter Mon.-Sat. 9am-4pm, Sun. 10am-2pm; $1.25, seniors $1, under 12 75¢).

The 1990s is one period of history Ilwaco would like to forget, quickly. The 1993 Endangered Species Act and record-low salmon counts have stopped salmon fishing, the town's chief livelihood, indefinitely. The boats still run, but engage in only sturgeon and bottom-fishing now. One of many charter organizations is **Pacific Salmon Charters,** P.O. Box 519, Ilwaco 98624 (642-3466), in the Port of Ilwaco, where eight-hour fishing tours (providing coffee and tackle) start at $59 (trips run daily at 6am). Wander further down the Port of Ilwaco to **Smalley's Galley** (642-8700), serving tasty clam chowder ($2), fish and chips ($5.50), and hamburgers with fries ($3.75). (Open Sun.-Mon. 4am-4pm, Wed. 5am-4pm, Thurs.-Fri. 4am-4pm, Sat. 4am-7pm.)

CASCADE RANGE

In 1859, the first white explorer to record his observations of the Cascade Range, gushed, "Nowhere do the mountain masses and peaks present such strange, fantastic, dauntless, and startling outlines as here." Native people summed up their admiration more succinctly, dubbing the Cascades "The Home of the Gods."

Intercepting the moist Pacific air, the Cascades divide Washington into the lush, wet green of the west and the low, dry plains of the east. The tallest white-domed peaks of Mt. Baker, Vernon, Glacier, Rainier, Hood, Adams, and St. Helens are accessible by four major roads offering good trailheads and impressive scenery. **U.S. 12** through White Pass approaches Mt. Rainier National Park and offers access to Mount St. Helens from the north; **I-90** sends four lanes past the major ski resorts of Snoqualmie Pass; scenic **U.S. 2** leaves Everett for Stevens Pass and descends along the Wenatchee River, a favorite of whitewater rafters.

But **Rte. 20, the North Cascades Hwy.,** is the most breathtaking of the trans-Cascade highways, possibly one of the most amazing drives in North America. From spring to fall it provides access to the wilderness of **North Cascades National Park.** Rte. 20 and U.S. 2 are often traveled in sequence as the **Cascade Loop.**

Greyhound runs the I-90 and U.S. 2 routes to and from Seattle (3-hr. round-trip), while **Amtrak** parallels I-90. Rainstorms and evening traffic can slow hitchhiking; locals warn against thumbing across Rte. 20, as a few hitchers apparently have vanished over the last few years. (*Let's Go* does not recommend hitchhiking). This corner of the world can only be explored properly with a car. The mountains are most accessible in the clear months of July, August, and September; many high mountain passes are snowed in the rest of the year. The best source of general information on the Cascades is the joint **National Park/National Forest Information Service,** 915 2nd Ave., Seattle 98174 (206-220-7450).

■■■ MOUNT ST. HELENS

On May 18, 1980, in a single cataclysmic blast, the summit of Washington's beautiful Mount St. Helens exploded into dust, creating a hole 2 mi. long and 1 mi. wide in what had once been a perfect cone. The force of the blast is almost impossible to imagine; it robbed the mountain of 1300 ft. in height (an immense volume of rock) and razed entire forests, leaving a stubble of trunks on nearby slopes. The explosion was directed laterally northward; no energy was dissipated fighting gravity. Ash from the crater blackened the sky for days and hundreds of miles, and fell in a blanketing black powder over towns as far as Yakima, 80 mi. away. Debris spewed from the volcano-flooded Spirit Lake, choking rivers with mud.

The **Mount St. Helens National Volcanic Monument,** administered by the Forest Service, is now steadily recovering from the explosion that, in minutes, transformed 150 sq. mi. of prime forest land into gray wasteland. The spectacle of disaster is now freckled by signs of returning life; saplings push their way up past their fallen brethren, while insects and small mammals are returning to the blast zone. The area surrounding the monument is now the **Gifford Pinchot National Forest.** Much of the monument area is off-limits to the public because of ongoing delicate geological experiments and the unpredictability of the volcanic crater. The mountain is, like many other Cascade peaks, still considered active and could erupt again, though risk is now low.

PRACTICAL INFORMATION AND ORIENTATION

Visitors Information: Mount St. Helens National Volcanic Monument Visitor Center, (206-274-2100, or 206-274-2103 for 24-hr. recorded information), on Rte. 504, 5 mi. east of Castle Rock. Take exit 49 off I-5, and follow the signs. The center is an excellent introduction to the mountain, with displays on eruption and regeneration. Information on highway access and camping. A list of area lodgings is also available. The keynote is the free 22-min. film *The Eruption of Mt. St. Helens,* showing graphic footage of the eruption and its aftermath. The captioned film is shown every hour on the hour. Interpretive naturalist activities take place mid-June-Aug. There is no actual viewing of the volcano from here, however. (Open daily 9am-6pm; Oct.-March 9am-5pm.) **Coldwater Ridge Visitors Center** (247-2131; fax 274-2129), 43 mi. east from exit 49 off I-5. This brand-new, modern building on a windy ridge has a deck with a superb view of the collapsed cavity where the mountain's north side used to be. Emphasis on the recolonization of living things. No accommodations; hiking and picnic areas, interpretive talks, and a gift shop/snack bar. Open daily 9am-6pm; Oct.-March 9am-5pm.

Information Inside the Monument: Several stations are staffed to answer visitor questions. At **Woods Creek Information Station,** 6 mi. south of Randle on Rd. 25, you not only will find **maps** and brochures, but you can also have an attendant answer your questions without leaving your car. Open June-Sept. daily 9am-5pm. The **Pine Creek Information Station,** 17 mi. east of Cougar on Rd. 90, shows a short movie to prepare visitors for their monumental excursion. Open June-Sept. daily 9am-6pm. **Apes' Headquarters,** at Ape Cave on Rd. 8303, is the place to go with questions on the lava tube. Interpretive walks through the caves daily. Open May-Sept. daily 10am-5pm. The **Monument Headquarters** (750-3900, or 750-3903 for 24-hr. recorded message), 3 mi. north of Amboy on Rte. 503, can fill you in on just about anything. They are in charge of **crater-climbing permits.** Not a visitors center, but call for info. Open Mon.-Fri. 7:30am-5pm.

The Volcano Review, a yearly publication available free at all visitors centers and ranger stations, is the tourist's bible for Mount St. Helens. Contains a **map,** copious info., and schedules concerning activities at the National Monument.

Gifford Pinchot National Forest Headquarters, 6926 E 4th Plain Blvd., P.O. Box 8944, Vancouver, WA 98668 (206-750-5000). Camping and hiking information within the forest. Additional **ranger stations** at: **Randle** (206-497-7565), north of the mountain on U.S. 12 and east of the visitors center; **Packwood** (206-494-5515), farther east on U.S. 12; **Wind River** (509-427-5645), south of the mountain on Forest Service Rd. 30 and north of the town of Carson in the Columbia River Gorge; and **Mt. Adams** (509-395-2501), at Trout Lake, southeast of the mountain on Rte. 141 and above White Salmon in the Columbia River Gorge. All stations are open Mon.-Fri. 8am-5pm; some are open on weekends.

Climbing Permits: Between May 16 and Oct. 31, the Forest Service allows only 100 people to hike to the crater each day. Reservations can be made in person or by writing to **The Monument Headquarters,** 1 hr. north of Portland off Rte. 503 at 42218 NE Yale Bridge Rd., Amboy, WA 98601 (750-3900). Sixty permits are available on reserve; the Forest Service begins accepting applications Feb. 1. Write early; weekends are usually booked before March, and weekdays often fill up as well. Climbers who procrastinate should head for **Jack's Restaurant and Country Store** (231-4276), Rte. 503, 5 mi. west of Cougar, where 40 unreserved permits are available per day on a first-come, first-served basis. Each day at 11am, a list is made of those wanting permits for the next day. Weekend climbers should arrive at Jack's by 7am and hang out for 4 hrs. to hold a place in line. On weekdays, there is rarely a line; stop by any time the day before your climb before 6pm. If you're confused, call the Monument Headquarters (750-3900).

Climbing Hotline: 247-5800. Information on snow, temperature, visibility, wind, and other vital factors that might affect climbing the volcano.

Radio Station: 530 AM. Road closures and station hours.

Emergency: 911.

Area Code: 206.

A basic, invaluable **map** of the area is on the back of the *Volcano Review.* Also, drivers should fill up their **gas** tanks before an excursion into Mount St. Helens, as fuel is not sold in the monument. The main access routes skirt the monument widely; actually getting there takes time. Visitors must prioritize and cannot view the mountain from all angles in one day. The monument is roughly bounded on the north by U.S. 12, on the east by Rd. 25 which connects to U.S. 12, and on the south by Rd. 99 which connects to Rd. 25. From the west, Rte. 504 and Rte. 503 offer access to the monument; Rte. 503 connects with Rd. 99 near the hamlet of **Cougar** and its neighbor, **Yale.** Despite what this town's unfortunate name might lead the traveler to believe, it is not at all inferior, deficient, inadequate, execrable, insufferable, imbecilic, flawed, doomed, low, or second-rate. U.S. 12, reached by Rte. 7 south from Tacoma or exit 68 off I-5, offers no direct mountain access but is the quickest way to Windy Ridge and offers stunning views of blasted forest. Rte. 504 is the most scenic road, offering gorgeous mountain views with plenty of turnouts. Rte. 504 can be reached by exiting I-5 at exit 49. Rte. 503 is for climbers.

For a close-up view of the volcano, plan to spend the whole day in the monument and visit either the **Pine Creek Information Center** in the south or the **Woods Creek Information Center** in the north. These two centers are each within a mi. of excellent viewpoints. There are three main access points for the monument. 37 mi. further east on Rte. 504, a splendid view of the collapsed north face can be seen at the Coldwater Ridge Visitors Center. Bear in mind that Rte. 504 dead-ends at Coldwater Lake, and there are no access roads to other state highways in the monument; you must return to I-5. About 25 mi. further south, Rte. 503 runs east through Cougar, where climbers want to go, with eventual access to Rd. 99 and Windy Ridge.

The **Coldwater Ridge Visitors Center** (274-2131; fax 274-2129), 43 mi. east of Castle Rock and I-5 on Rte. 504., is an angular triumph of modern architecture and practically a free museum unto itself. The deck, flooded with photographs, has a superb view of the cavity where the mountain's north side used to be and two lakes created by the eruption's aftermath. There are lots of button-pushing displays on the eruption, with emphasis on the recolonization of living things. Check out the hiking and picnic areas, interpretive talks, snack bar, and gift shop. (Open daily 9am-6pm; Oct.-March 9am-5pm.)

CAMPING

Although the monument itself contains no campgrounds, many are scattered throughout the surrounding national forest. Free dispersed camping *is* allowed within the monument, meaning that if you stumble upon a site on an old forest service road you can camp out there, but finding a site is a matter of luck; contact a ranger for information. The closest campsite to the scene of the explosion is the **Iron Creek Campground,** just south of the Woods Creek Information Center on Forest Service Rd. 25, near the junction with Rd. 76 (98 sites, $8). For reservations call 800-280-2267. Only 15 sites can be reserved; the rest are first-come, first-served. Farther south is **Swift Campground,** on Forest Service Rd. 90, just west of the Pine Creek Information Station. Swift is run by Pacific Power & Light (503-464-5023) on a first-come, first-pitched basis (93 sites, $8). West of Swift Campground on Yale Reservoir lie two other PP&L campgrounds; both accept reservations and have flush toilets and showers. **Beaver Bay,** with 63 RV and tent sites ($8), lies 2 mi. east of **Cougar,** which offers 45 tentsites ($8).

Seaquest State Park (274-8633), on Rte. 504, 5 mi. east of the town of Castle Rock at exit 49 off I-5 and across from the visitors center, has 92 sites ($10), four of which are primitive and reserved for the hiker/biker set.

OUTDOOR EXPLORATION

The first stop for visitors traveling south on Rd. 25 from Randle and U.S. 12 should be the **Woods Creek Information Station.** Viewpoints are listed on various handouts at the visitors center and include the **Quartz Creek Big Trees** and **Ryan Lake.** Continue south 9 mi. farther until you reach Rd. 99 going west. The newly paved, two-lane Rd. 99 passes through 17 mi. of curves, clouds of ash, and cliffs. Those with trailers should leave them in the **Wakepish Sno-park,** the designated trailer drop at the junction of Rds. 25 and 99. Allow a few hrs. to complete this stretch of road. Without stops it takes nearly one hour to travel out and back on Rd. 99, but the many talks, walks, and views along the way make stops worthwhile.

On the way west along Rd. 99, **Bear Meadow** provides the first interpretive stop and an excellent view of Mount St. Helens, and the last restrooms before Rd. 99

ends at **Windy Ridge.** The monument begins just west of here, where Rds. 26 and 99 meet, at **Meta Lake.** Forest interpreters lead 45-minute walks to this emerald lake from June through September (daily at 12:30pm and 3pm); meet at the old **Miners' Car.** Farther west along Rd. 99, frequent roadside turnouts offer interpretive information on the surroundings, unbeatable photo opportunities, and trailheads for hikers. **Independence Pass Trail #227** (3½ mi., 4-hr. round-trip) is a difficult hike with overlooks to **Spirit Lake** and superb views of the crater and dome that improve as you go farther along the trail. Farther west, **Harmony Trail #224** (2 mi., 1½-hr. round-trip) provides the only public access to Spirit Lake. Forest interpreters lead a hike from the Harmony Viewpoint to Spirit Lake along this trail during the summer daily at 1:30pm. This trail may be a breeze going down, but the return trip is tough and steep.

Windy Ridge, at the end of Rd. 99, is worth enduring the winding trip. From here, you can climb atop an ash hill for a magnificent view of the crater from 3½ mi. away. In summer, forest interpreters describe the eruption during talks held in the Windy Ridge amphitheater (every hr. on the ½ hr., daily 11:30am-4:30pm).

The **Pine Creek Information Station** lies 25 mi. south of the Rd. 25-Rd. 99 junction. Take Rd. 25 to Rd. 90. From here continue 12 mi. west and then 2 mi. north on Rd. 83 to reach **Ape Cave,** a broken 2½-mi.-long lava tube formed in an ancient eruption. Wear a jacket and sturdy shoes. Lanterns may be rented for $3, or bring your own flashlights (minimum of 2) or Coleman lanterns. Forest interpreters lead 30-minute guided lantern walks during the summer through the Western Hemisphere's longest known lava tube (every hr. on the ½ hr.; Mon.-Fri. 12:30-2:30pm, Sat.-Sun. 11:30am-4:30pm).

Rd. 83 continues 9 mi. farther north, ending at **Lahar Viewpoint,** site of terrible mudflows following the eruption. Interpretive signs show travelers how life is slowly returning to a devastated area. Nearby, **Lava Canyon Trail #184** offers three hikes with views of the **Muddy River waterfall.**

Those with a taste for conquest and the proper equipment should scale the new, stunted version of the mountain to glimpse the lava dome from the crater's rim. Although not a technical climb, the route up the mountain is steep, a pathway of ash strewn with picnic boulders. Often the scree is so thick that a step forward brings a half-step back. The view from the top is magnificent. As you perch on the lip of the crater, listening to rumbling rockfalls, there are incredible **views** of Mt. Rainier, Mt. Adams, Mt. Hood, and Spirit Lake and the lava dome directly below. Average time up is five hrs. Climbers are encouraged to bring sunglasses, sunscreen, sturdy climbing boots, foul-weather clothing, plenty of water, and gaiters to keep your boots from filling with ash. Free camping is available at the **Climber's Bivouac,** the trailhead area for the **Ptarmigan Trail #216A,** which starts the route up the mountain. Check Practical Information for permit information.

■■■ COWLITZ VALLEY

The **Cowlitz River** originates from the tip of a Rainier glacier and cuts a long, deep divot west between Mt. Rainier and Mount St. Helens, then turns south to flow into the Columbia. Although your view of St. Helens and Rainier will be obscured when you sink into the Cowlitz Valley, your loss will be compensated with miles of lush foothills and farmland.

The river forms part of the watershed for both the **Mt. Adams** and **Goat Rocks Wilderness Areas,** to the west and northwest of Mt. St. Helens. Both areas are excellent hiking country, accessible only by foot or horseback, and include sections of the **Pacific Crest Trail** among their extensive trail networks. The rugged Goat Rocks area is famed for its herd of mountain goats, while Mt. Adams seduces hundreds of climbers each year with its snow-capped summit (12,307 ft.). Two **ranger stations** in the valley are at 13068 U.S. 12, **Packwood** (206-494-5515), and at 10024 U.S. 12, **Randle** (206-497-7565). Contact the Forest Service at one of these locations for trail guides and other information on the wilderness areas.

The Cowlitz passes closest to Mt. St. Helens near the town of **Morton.** This logging town is accessed by U.S. 12 from the east and west (I-15 exit 68), Rte. 508 from the west (I-5 exit 71), and Rte. 7 from the north. The **Morton Chamber of Commerce** (496-6086), in the log cabin just off U.S. 12 as you enter town, can fill you in on local events, including the **Loggers Jubilee** in mid-August. The **Cody Cafe** (496-5787), on Main St., serves a Helenic stack of three pancakes ($2.25). Lunches run from $3 to $5 (open Mon.-Fri. 4am-10pm, Sat. 5am-10pm, Sun. 6am-10pm). If you are staying overnight in the area, head for the lime-green **Evergreen Motel** (496-5407), at Main and Front St. The rooms may be plain, but they're still cheap and clean (singles $27, doubles and triples $32-45). Morton's **post office** (496-5316) is at 2nd and Bingham (open Mon.-Fri. 8am-5pm; **General Delivery ZIP code:** 98356).

The Cowlitz River, once wild and treacherous, has been tamed considerably by a Tacoma City Light hydroelectric project. The **Mayfield** and **Mossyrock Dams** back up water into the river gorge to create two lakes, **Mayfield** and **Riffe,** both much-used recreation areas. **Ike Kinswa State Park** and **Mayfield Lake County Park,** on Mayfield Lake off U.S. 12, offer camping and excellent **rainbow** and **silver trout** fishing year-round. Ike Kinswa (983-3402) has over 100 sites with showers (sites $11, full hookups $16). Mayfield Lake (985-2364) offers 54 tentsites ($10); no RVs. Public boat launches provide access to Mayfield, the lower of the two lakes.

Riffe Lake, much larger than Mayfield Lake, was named to memorialize **Riffe,** a town flooded by the building of the enormous Mossyrock Dam. Campers at **Mossyrock Park** (983-3900) on the south shore can drop by the display at Hydro Vista next to the dam (sites $10, hookup $10-13). Tacoma City Light offers free guided tours of the **Cowlitz River Dams.**

One of the more intriguing aspects of the complex is the **Cowlitz Salmon Hatchery,** south of the town of Salkum just off U.S. 12. The free self-guided tours of the facility include views of fish ladders, the spawning center, and the tanks where the salmon are kept. This facility releases 17½ million young **chinook salmon** each year. Hatcheries like this one have been constructed all over the Northwest, both to encourage salmon fishing and to attempt to compensate for changes in the environment wrought by hydroelectric projects.

Below the dams, the Cowlitz River courses through farmland, flowers, and blueberries. Hosts of local farms dot the hillside along the road, many offering **U-pick berry bargains** during the summer harvest season (late June-Aug.).

Two free **publications,** *The Lewis County Visitors Guide* and *The Morton Journal View,* are available throughout the Cowlitz Valley and provide up-to-date information on local parks, camping, hiking, food, and lodging.

■■■ MOUNT RAINIER NATIONAL PARK

14,411-ft. Mt. Rainier (ray-NEER) presides over the Cascade Range. The Klickitat Native people called it *Tahoma,* "mountain of God," but Rainier is simply "the mountain" to most Washington residents. Due to its height, Rainier creates its own weather, jutting into the warm, wet air and pulling down vast amounts of snow and rain. Clouds mask the mountain up to 200 days per year, frustrating visitors who come to see the summit. 76 glaciers (only 26 are named) patch the slopes and combine with sharp ridges and steep gullies to make Rainier an inhospitable place for the thousands of determined climbers who attempt its summit each year.

Those who don't feel up to scaling the mountain can find outdoor enjoyment in the old-growth forests and alpine meadows of Mt. Rainier National Park. With over 305 mi. of trails, solitude is just a step away, whether you choose to hike past hot springs, across rivers, or alongside wildflowers.

PRACTICAL INFORMATION AND ORIENTATION

Visitors Information: Each **visitors center** has displays, brochures on everything from hiking to natural history, postings on trail and road conditions, and rangers to help point visitors in the right direction, whether on foot, in a wheelchair, or driving. Guided trips and talks, campfire programs, and slide presentations are given at the visitors centers and vehicle campgrounds throughout the park. Check at a visitors center or get a copy of the free guide, *Tahoma*. The **Longmire Hiker Information Center** distributes **backcountry permits.** Open Sun.-Thurs. 8am-4:30pm, Fri. 8am-7pm, Sat. 7am-7pm; closed in winter. The **Paradise Visitors Center** (589-22275) offers lodging, food, and souvenirs. Open daily 9am-7pm; late Sept. to mid-Oct. 9:30am-6pm; mid-Oct.-winter 10am-5pm. The **Sunrise Visitors Center** contains exhibits, snacks, and a gift shop. Open daily June 25-mid-Sept. 9am-6pm. The **Ohanapecosh Visitors Center** offers information and wildlife displays. Open summer daily until mid-Oct. 9am-6pm and Sat.-Sun. May-June 9am-6pm. All centers can be contacted by writing c/o Superintendent, Mt. Rainier National Park, Ashford 98304, or by telephoning the park's central operator (569-2211). Additional backpacking and camping information can be obtained by writing or calling the **Backcountry Desk,** Mt. Rainier National Park, Tahoma Woods, Star Route, Ashford 98304 (569-2211 ext. 3317).

Park Administrative Headquarters, Tahoma Woods, Star Route, Ashford 98304 (569-2211). Open Mon.-Fri. 8am-4:30pm.

Entrance Fee: $5 per car, $3 per hiker. Gates are open 24 hrs.; free evenings.

Gray Line Bus Service, 720 S Forest St., Seattle 98134 (624-5077). Excursions daily from Seattle to Rainier May-Oct. 13 (single-day round-trip $46, under 13 $17). Buses leave from the Sheraton Hotel in Seattle at 8:15am and return around 6pm, giving you about 1½ hr. at Paradise and about 3½ hrs. total at the mountain, ample time to tramp through the trails.

Hiking Supplies: Rainier Mountaineering Inc. (RMI) (569-2227), in Paradise. Rents ice axes ($7), crampons ($7.25), boots ($15), packs ($15), and helmets ($5) by the day. Expert RMI guides also lead summit climbs, seminars, and special schools and programs. Open May-Oct. daily 10am-5pm. Winter office: 535 Dock St. #209, Tacoma 98402 (206-627-6242). You must have experience to climb Mt. Rainier. Otherwise you must buy a 3-day package that includes a day of teaching and 2 days of climbing.

Ski Supplies: White Pass Sports Hut, U.S. 12, Packwood (494-7321). Alpine package $11.50 per day, Nordic package $9. Also rents snowshoes and snowboards and sells camping equipment. Open daily 8am-6pm; winter Mon.-Thurs. 8am-6pm, Fri.-Sun. 7am-6pm.

Park Emergency: 569-2211, or 911. 24 hrs.

Post Office: In the **National Park Inn,** Longmire. Open Mon.-Fri. 8:30am-noon and 1-5pm. Also in the **Paradise Inn,** Paradise. Same hours as Longmire. **General Delivery ZIP Code:** 98398.

Area Code: 206.

To reach Mt. Rainier from the west, drive south from Seattle on I-5 to Tacoma, then go east on Rte. 512, south on Rte. 7, and east on Rte. 706. This scenic road meanders through the town of **Ashford** and into the park by the Nisqually entrance. **Rte. 706** is the only access road open throughout the year; snow usually closes all other park roads from November through May. Mt. Rainier is about 65 mi. from Tacoma and about 90 mi. from Seattle.

The park covers over 350 sq. mi., and the only **gas station** is in **Longmire,** where supplies are often limited. The distance from the Nisqually entrance to the first visitors center is considerable. Get gas before entering the park.

A car tour is a good introduction to the park. All major roads offer scenic views of the mountain and have roadside sites for camera-clicking and general gawking. The roads to Paradise and Sunrise are especially picturesque. **Stevens Canyon Road** connects the southeast corner of the national park with Paradise, Longmire, and the Nisqually entrance, unfolding spectacular vistas of Rainier and the rugged Tatoosh

Range. The accessible roadside attractions of **Box Canyon, Bench Lake,** and **Grove of the Patriarchs** line the route.

Many visitors say that **hitchhiking** opportunities along the mountain roads are exceptionally good. (*Let's Go* does not recommend hitchhiking.) Contrary to what rangers say, Park Service employees will sometimes give lifts to stranded hikers. Be careful, though, to avoid getting marooned in the middle of nowhere. Those who need help should ask a ranger for assistance; park employees are helpful and friendly, especially on rare sunny days when the peak is visible and spirits are high.

Summer temperatures are warm during the day but drop sharply at night. Be prepared for changing weather. Pack warm clothes and cold-rated equipment. Before setting out, ask rangers for the two **brochures** on **mountain-climbing** and **hiking** that contain helpful hints and a list of recommended equipment for the Rainier explorer. Party size is limited in many areas, and campers must carry all trash and waste out of the backcountry. Piped water (potable) is available at most backcountry campsites, but carry a canteen for day use. All stream and lake water should be treated for *giardia* before drinking. The park is staffed with EMTs and owns several emergency vans. Rangers can provide first aid. The nearest **medical facilities** are in **Morton** (40 mi. from Longmire) and **Enumclaw** (50 mi. from Sunrise).

The **Gifford Pinchot National Forest** is headquartered at 6926 E Fourth Plain Blvd., P.O. Box 8944, Vancouver, WA 98668 (206-750-5000). The section of the **Mt. Baker-Snoqualmie National Forest** that adjoins Mt. Rainier is administered by the **Wenatchee National Forest,** 301 Yakima St., Wenatchee 98807 (509-662-4314). Closer **ranger stations** are at 10061 U.S. 12, Naches 98937 (509-965-8005), and Packwood Ranger Station, P.O. Box 559 Packwood 98361 (206-494-5515).

ACCOMMODATIONS AND FOOD

Longmire, Paradise, and **Sunrise** offer accommodations and food that are usually too costly for the budget traveler. The general stores sprinkled throughout the area sell only last-minute trifles like bug repellant and marshmallows, and items are charged an extra state park tax. Stock up and stay in **Ashford** or **Packwood** if you must have a roof over your head. Otherwise, camp…isn't that what you're here for?

Gateway Inn Motel, 38820 Rte. 706 E, Ashford 98304 (569-2506). Roadside motel with private cabins and traditional motel rooms. Cabin for two with fireplace $59, without fireplace $49. Singles and doubles with bath $40; shared bath $34.50.

Paradise Inn (569-2413, reservations 569-2275), Paradise. This rustic inn, built in 1917 from Alaskan cedar, offers paradisiacal views of the mountain. Wake up early to hike the heavenly **Skyline Trail,** starting in the heavenly parking lot. Singles and doubles with shared bath from $66, each additional person $10. Open late May-early Oct. Reservations required in summer; call at least a month ahead.

Hotel Packwood, 104 Main St. (494-5431), Packwood. Old motel; reasonable prices. Singles $20, with bath $38. Doubles $30.

Sweet Peaks, 38104 Rte. 706 (569-2720), on the way to the Nisqually Entrance. Stop off for a killer cinnamon roll ($1.25) or a loaf of fresh bread ($1.25-2). The bakery also sells an assortment of camping gear. Open Mon.-Thurs. 7:30am-8pm, Fri.-Sun. 7am-8pm.

Ma & Pa Rucker's (494-2651), Packwood. This local favorite serves piping hot pizza (small $5, large $9) and typical burgers and chicken sandwiches. A single scoop of their divine peppermint candy ice cream is $1. Stick around long enough and Ma & Pa will tell you about their son, Fudd. Open Mon.-Thurs. 9am-9pm, Fri.-Sun. 9am-10pm.

CAMPING

Camping at the auto-accessible campsites between mid-June and late September requires a permit ($8-10), available at campsites. **Alpine** and **cross-country camping** require free permits year-round and are subject to certain restrictions. Be sure to pick up a copy of the *Wilderness Trip Planner* pamphlet at a ranger station or hikers' center before you set off. Alpine and cross-country access is strictly controlled to prevent forest damage, but auto camping permits are relatively easy to get.

Drive to **Ohanapecosh** for the gorgeous and serene high ceiling of **old-growth trees;** to **Cougar Rock,** near Longmire, for the strictly maintained quiet hours; and to both **White River** in the northeastern corner and **Sunshine Point** near the Nisqually entrance for the panoramas. Open on a first-come, first-camped basis, the grounds fill only on the busiest summer weekends. Sunshine Point is the only auto campground open year-round.

With a **backcountry permit,** hikers can use any of the free, well-established trailside camps scattered in the park's backcountry. Most camps have toilet facilities and a nearby water source, and some have shelters as well. Most of these sites are in the low forests, though some are high up the mountain on the glaciers and snow fields. Adventurous hikers can test their survival skills in the vast cross-country zones at any of the low forests and in the sub-alpine zone. *Fires are prohibited in both areas,* and there are limits to the number of members in a party. Talk to a ranger for details. **Glacier climbers** and **mountain climbers** intending to go above 10,000 ft. must always register in person at ranger stations to be granted permits.

The **National Forests** outside Rainier Park provide both developed sites (free-$5) and thousands of acres of freely campable countryside. When free-camping, be sure to avoid eroded lakesides and riverbanks; flash floods and debris flows can catch unwary campers in their paths. Minimum-impact **campfire permits,** allowing hikers to burn small fires that don't sterilize the soil, are available at National Forest ranger stations (see Practical Information). Don't count on receiving one, however, since the small number of backcountry sites limits the supply of permits. All permits are issued on a first-come, first-served basis.

OUTDOORS

Mt. Adams and Mount St. Helens, not visible from the road, can be seen clearly from such mountain trails as **Paradise** (1½ mi.), **Pinnacle Peak** (2½ mi.), **Eagle Peak** (7 mi.), and **Van Trump Peak** (5½ mi.). For more information on these trails, pick up *Viewing Mount St. Helens* at one of the visitors centers.

Several less-developed roads reach isolated regions, often meeting trailheads that cross the park or lead to the summit. Hiking and camping outside designated campsites is permissible in most regions of the park, but a permit is required for overnight backpacking trips. The **Hiker Centers** at Carbon River and Longmire have information on day and backcountry hikes through the park, and dispense necessary camping permits (see Practical Information for hours).

A segment of the **Pacific Crest Trail (PCT),** running between the Columbia River and the Canadian border, crosses through the southeast corner of the park. Geared to hikers and horse riders, the PCT is maintained by the Forest Service. Primitive campsites and shelters line the trail; a permit is not required for camping, although you should contact the nearest ranger station for information on site and trail conditions. Food may be stored at designated food-cache areas in the park. Call 569-2211 x 3317 for details. The trail, offering glimpses of the snow-covered peaks of the Cascades, leads through delightful wildlife areas.

A trip to the **summit** of Mt. Rainier requires substantial preparation and expense. The ascent is a vertical rise of more than 9000 ft. over a distance of 8 or more mi., usually taking two days, with an overnight stay at **Camp Muir** on the south side (10,000 ft.) or **Camp Schurman** on the north side (9500 ft.). Camp Muir provides a public shelter, but climbers should be prepared to camp if it is full. Each camp has a ranger station, rescue cache, and some form of toilet. Climbers must melt snow for drinking water.

Experienced climbers may form their own expeditions upon satisfactory completion of a detailed application; consult a climbing ranger at the Paradise, Carbon River, or White River stations. Solo climbing requires the consent of the superintendent. Novices can sign up for a summit climb with **Rainier Mountaineering, Inc. (RMI),** offering a one-day basic-climbing course followed by a two-day guided climb;

the package costs $320 and requires strength and physical fitness. You must bring your own sleeping bag, headlamp, rain jacket, corset, and pants and carry four meals in addition to hiking gear. For more information, contact Park Headquarters or RMI (see above).

Less ambitious, ranger-led **interpretive hikes** delve into everything from area history to local wildflowers. Each visitors center (see Practical Information) conducts its own hikes on its own schedule. These free hikes complement evening campfire programs, also conducted by each visitors center.

If you are llooking to spend an unusual day in a llovely llocation, **Llama Wilderness Pack Trips,** Tatoosh Motel, Packwood (491-5262) offers a llunch with the llamas in the park for $25 per person (4 to 5-hr. trip). They also llease their llamas for pack trips and have guided trips of their own.

Longmire

Longmire's **museum,** in the visitors center, dwells on Rainier's past. The rooms are filled with exhibits on natural history and the history of human encounters with the mountain (open summer daily 9am-5:30pm; off-season daily 9am-4:30pm).

Programs run by the visitors center in the Longmire area typically include night meadow walks and hikes into the surrounding dense forest. The **Hikers Center** is an excellent source of information and guidance for all backcountry trips except summit attempts. Free information sheets about specific day and overnight hikes are available throughout the park. The **Rampart Ridge Trail** (a 2½-hr., 4.6-mi. loop) has excellent views of the Nisqually Valley, Mount Rainier, and Tumtum Peak. The path of the **Kaetz Creek Mudflow** of 1947 and **Van Trump Park & Comet Falls Trail** (a steep 4-hr., 5-mi. hike) passes Comet Falls and, in early July, often a mountain goat or two. Check out the Center's relief model of the mountain before plunging into the woods. Remember that a permit is required for backcountry camping. The **Eagle Peak Saddle Trail** (a 7-mi. round-trip) ends with a **view** of Mt. Rainier and the Gifford Pinchot National Forest.

Longmire remains open during the winter as a center for snowshoeing, cross-country skiing, and other alpine activities. **Guest Services, Inc.** (569-2275) runs a **cross-country ski center** (rental $15 per day, $9.75 for children, lessons available Sat. and Sun. only 10am and 1:30pm. Group lessons $16 per hr., private lessons $30. Day tour $20, moonlight tour $12). The trails are difficult, but you can snowshoe eight months out of the year. Some diehards even enjoy winter hiking and climbing out of Longmire.

Paradise

One of the most visited places in the park, Paradise is perhaps the only place in Rainier where the sound of bubbling brooks and waterfalls might be drowned out by screaming children. Summer weekends bring city dwellers and families trying to escape to the wilderness; nearby inner-tubing runs attract many to visit just for the day. Nevertheless, if you can manage to avoid the hustle and bustle and arrive on a clear, sunny weekday, the name Paradise won't seem meant to mock you.

Above the timberline, the sparkling snowfields can blind visitors staring down at the forest canyons thousands of feet below, even in mid-June. The road from the Nisqually entrance to Paradise is open year-round, but the road east through Stevens Canyon is open only from mid-June through October, weather permitting. The **Paradise Visitors Center** offers audiovisual programs and an observation deck for viewing the heavens. From January to mid-April, park naturalists lead **snowshoe hikes** to explore winter ecology around Paradise (Sat.-Sun. at 10:30am, 12:30, and 2:30pm; snowshoe rental $1). You'll need the snowshoes; winter has brought snowfalls of over 90 ft.

Paradise is the starting point for several **trails** heading through the meadows to the nearby Nisqually Glacier or up the mountain to the summit. Many trails allow close-up views of Mt. Rainier's glaciers, especially the two closest to Paradise, the **Paradise** and the **Stevens** glaciers. The 5-mi. **Skyline Trail** is the longest of the loop trails out of Paradise (4-hr. walk). The marked trail starts at the Paradise Inn, climbing above the treeline. Skyline is probably the closest a casual hiker can come to climbing the mountain. The first leg of the trail is often hiked by climbing parties headed for **Camp Muir** (the base camp for most ascents to the summit). The trail turns off before reaching Camp Muir, rising to its highest elevation at **Panorama Point.** Although only halfway up the mountain, the point is within view of the glaciers, and the summit appears deceptively close. Turn around to behold rows of blue-gray mountaintops, with Mount St. Helens and Mt. Adams dominating the horizon. Heading back down the trail, you will cross a few snowfields and do some boulder-hopping. Since route conditions vary, contact a ranger station in Paradise, White River, Sunrise, or Longmire for information on crevasse and rockfall conditions.

The mildly strenuous, 2½-mi. half-day hike up to **Pinnacle Peak,** beginning across the road from Reflection Lakes (just east of Paradise), features a clear view of Mount Rainier, Mt. Adams, Mount St. Helens, and Mt. Hood. One of the most striking aspects of hikes out of Paradise are the expanses of wildflowering alpine meadows; they are some of the largest and most spectacular in the park.

Hikers should be especially careful to stay on the trails, since the meadows are extremely fragile. Erosion and hiker damage can take years to repair; some of the plants in the area bloom only once in several years.

Ohanapecosh and Carbon River

Though in opposite corners of the park, the Ohanapecosh and Carbon Rivers are in the same ranger district. The **Ohanapecosh Visitors Center** and campground are in a lush forest along a river valley in the park's southeast corner. Here grows the **Grove of the Patriarchs,** one of the oldest stands of original trees in Washington. An easy 2-mi., 1½-hour walk will take you to these 500- to 1000-year-old Douglas firs, cedars, and hemlocks. The visitors center has displays on the forest and naturalist programs, including walks to the Grove, **Silver Falls,** and **Ohanapecosh Hot Springs,** a trickle of warm water in an area returning to the wild after commercialization as a therapeutic resort in the 1920s. For serious hiking, the **Summerland** and **Indian Bar Trails** are excellent.

Carbon River Valley, in the northwest corner of the park, is one of the only **rainforests** in the continental U.S., and its trails are on every ranger-in-the-know's top 10 list for hiking. **Spray Park** and **Mystic Camp** are superlative free backcountry campsites. Carbon River also has access to the **Wonderland Trail** (see Sunrise, below). Most visitors to the park miss Carbon River, however, because they don't find out about it until they reach one of the more popular visitors centers and then can't stomach the three-hour drive. If you arrive at the park through Carbon River (via Rte. 165), however, the region is more easily accessible. Your time here will no doubt leave you hoping that Carbon River remains one of the best-kept secrets.

Sunrise

The winding road to Sunrise, the highest of the four visitors centers, swims with visions of the Pacific Ocean, Mt. Baker, and the heavily glaciated eastern side of Mt. Rainier. The mountain views from Sunrise are among the best in the park.

Trails vary greatly in difficulty; the visitors center has details on hikes ranging from ½ to 13 mi. Two favorites are **Burrough's Mt. Trail,** a 5-mi., three-hour walk affording excellent views of the glaciers, and **Mt. Fremont Trail,** a 5.6-mi., four-hour hike with views of the Cascades, Grand Park, and quite possibly mountain goats.

The **Wonderland Trail** passes through Sunrise on its way around the mountain. A popular 95-mi. trek circumscribing Rainier, the trail traverses ridges and valleys. The lakes and streams near the path are full of **trout.** The entire circuit takes 10 to 14 days and includes several brutal ascents and descents. Beware of early snowstorms in September, snow-blocked passes in June, and muddy trails in July, all of which can force hikers to turn back. Rangers can provide information on weather and trail conditions; they also can store food caches for you at ranger stations along the trail.

In case of an emergency, you would be at most one hiking day away from a park road or ranger station.

The hike from **Fryingpan Creek Bridge** (3 mi. from the White River entrance) to Summerland is popular for its views of Mt. Rainier; behold elk and mountain goats grazing on the surrounding slopes. The circuit runs 4.2 mi. from the road along Fryingpan Creek to the Sunrise campground, ranger station, and meadows.

ROSLYN

On Rte. 903 at the edge of Wenatchee National Forest, a few years ago **Roslyn** was a sleepy little town. The mines responsible for the town's existence had closed, and no new source of income had yet emerged to take up the economic slack. Then came *Northern Exposure*, the wildly popular television show, which chose tiny Roslyn to be the set for the fictitious town of **Cicely, Alaska** (the moose was imported). Tourists quickly followed, welcomed by most longtime residents as the source for much-needed revenue, though some curmudgeons, mostly recent transplants, curse the city folk who have spoiled their backwoods paradise. Souvenir shops have sprung up, with several new restaurants. In symbolic homage to the impact of network TV on Roslyn, many businesses display photographs of their owners with the stars of the program.

While in town, fight your way through the crowd snapping pictures of a mural at 2nd and Pennsylvania to eat some terrific food at the **Roslyn Cafe** (649-2763).

You can sample the local brew, Roslyn Beer, at the Brick Tavern, 1 Pennsylvania Ave. (649-2643), the oldest operating saloon in Washington. Or go straight to the source and visit the **Roslyn Brewing Company,** 33 Pennsylvania Ave. (649-2232), where the brewery is open to the public (Sat.-Sun. noon-5pm). **Gray Line Bus Tours** (624-5077) runs a Northern Exposure tour to Roslyn with a stopover at Snoqualmie Falls on the way back ($30). Buses depart from 8th Ave. and Stewart.

■■■ LEAVENWORTH

"*Willkommen zu* Leavenworth" proclaims the decorous wooden sign at the entrance to this resort/theme-park. After the logging industry exhausted Leavenworth's natural resources and the railroad switching station moved to nearby Wenatchee, the town was forced to invent a tourist gimmick to survive. By the mid-1960s, "Project Alpine," as this kitschy endeavor was called, had placed a Bavarian veneer over Leavenworth. One can only wonder at the planners' *Weltanschauung*. Today, an estimated one million people visit this living Swiss Miss commercial each year, with massive influxes during the city's three annual festivals. Waiters in *lederhosen* work in restaurants with freakish names fused from German and English. The sidewalks are lined with expensive stores. Loudspeakers pump the musical theme from the wedding scene of *Deer Hunter* into the streets. Never mind that no one knows any German; this town is an experience in bizarre, pseudo-cultural American vacation tackiness. Rent a mountain bike and head for the mountains and forest.

PRACTICAL INFORMATION AND ORIENTATION

Visitors Information: Chamber of Commerce, 894 U.S. 2 (548-5807), in the Clocktower Bldg. Helpful staff, many of whom see absolutely nothing amusing in their town's *töricht* gimmick. Open Mon.-Sat. 9am-6pm, Sun. 10am-4pm.

Ranger Station, 600 Sherbourne (782-1413 or 548-4067), just off U.S. 2. The source for information on recreation in the dramatic mountains surrounding Leavenworth. Pick up a list of the 9 developed campgrounds within 20 mi. of Leavenworth. Open daily 7:45am-4:30pm; winter Mon.-Fri. 7:45am-4:30pm.

Greyhound, 662-2183. Stops west of town on U.S. 2 at the Department of Transportation. One bus per day to Spokane ($32) and 3 to Seattle ($25).

Link, (662-1155 or 800-851-5465). Free bus service! Runs 16 buses per day between Wenatchee and Leavenworth, with 3 stops around Leavenworth. Pick up a schedule at the Chamber of Commerce, or call for assistance. All buses have bike racks.

Bike Rental: Der Sportsmann, 837 Front St. (548-5623). Das mountain bike $6 per hr. or $20 per day, und der Kross-kountry skis $10 der day. Hiking and biking **maps** too. Open summer daily 9am-7pm; off-season Sun.-Thurs. 10am-6pm, Fri.-Sat. 10am-7pm.

Weather: 884-2982. **Cascade Snow Report:** 353-7440.

Seniors Center, 423 Evans (548-6666), across from Chamber.

Pharmacy: Village Pharmacy, 821 Front St. (548-7731). Open Mon.-Fri. 8:30am-6:30pm, Sat. 9am-5:30pm, Sun. 11am-5pm.

Hospital: Cascade Medical Center, 817 Commercial Ave. (548-5815). Clinic open Mon.-Fri. 8am-5pm, Sat. 8am-1pm. Emergency Room 24 hrs.

Emergency: 911.

Post Office: 960 U.S. 2 (548-7212). Open Mon.-Fri. 9am-5pm, Sat. 9-11am. **General Delivery ZIP Code:** 98826.

Area Code: 509.

Leavenworth is on the eastern slope of the Cascades, near Washington's geographical center. U.S. 2 bisects Leavenworth within 200 ft. of the main business district. The main north-south route through the area is U.S. 97, intersecting U.S. 2 about 6 mi. southeast of town. Leavenworth is approximately 121 mi. east of Seattle, 190 mi. west of Spokane.

ACCOMMODATIONS AND CAMPING

For hotels, forget it. Most start at above $40 for a single (an exception is listed below). **Camping** is plentiful, inexpensive, and spectacular in **Wenatchee National Forest.** Ten mi. from town along **Icicle Creek Road,** a series of Forest Service campgrounds squeeze between the creek and the road. To get there, take the last left in town on U.S. 2 heading west. All have drinking water; the closest to town is $8, all others $7. The last campground in the group is for horse campers only. Another option is **Tumwater,** 10 mi. west of Leavenworth on U.S. 2, with 84 sites ($8) with water, flush toilets, and wheelchair access. If you seek solitude, avoid weekend stays after Memorial Day. In any case, come early, or you may not find a spot at any of the campgrounds.

Hotel Edelweiss, 843 Front St. (548-7015), downtown. Plain and run-down but clean rooms; bar and cocktail lounge downstairs. "Room" 14 (solitary confinement...they have ways of making you talk!) has no TV, bath, or windows, but it's only $17. Room 10 is graced with a TV and a window, but no bath or sink ($18). Other singles with sink and TV from $25. For your own bathroom, you'll have to shell out at least $40. Make reservations for weekends.

FOOD

Predictably, Leavenworth's food mimics German cuisine; surprisingly, it often succeeds. Those who wish to avoid burgers and hot dogs and scarf some *schnitzel,* however, should be prepared to pay at least $8-16 for a full dinner. If you're heading into the wilderness, shop at **Safeway,** 940 U.S. 2 (548-5435; open daily 7am-11pm).

Oberland Bakery and Cafe, 703 Front St. (548-7216). The "Europeans" painted on the walls keep you company as you nibble on your Bavarian almond pretzel. Crunch outside on the patio. Hunt for merchant ships with your generous $4 sub; pocket-battleships unavailable. Open daily 9am-5:30pm.

Casa Mia Restaurant, 703 U.S. 2 (548-5621). The food is excellent, and meals are preceded by chips and salsa. The lunch menu offers enchiladas and burritos from $4. The dinners are expensive, but authentic; if you join their side, they'll give you Arizona, New Mexico, and Texas back. *Arroz con pollo* is $9.50. Lunch served noon-4pm. Open Sun.-Thurs. noon-9pm, Fri.-Sat noon-10pm.

Bavarian Beer Garden, Bar-B-Que and Sausage Haus, 226 8th St. (548-5998). The place to go for *wurst* ($3-4). Open 11am-10pm or when it starts to rain.

Mini-Market, 285 U.S. 2 (548-5027). This run-of-the-mill convenience store merits mention for 10¢ and 25¢ coffee, 50¢ hot cider or egg nog, and 25¢ hot chocolate. Today, the Cascades! Tomorrow the World! Open daily 6am-midnight.

SIGHTS AND ENTERTAINMENT

Except perhaps for tourist-watching, the most compelling reason to come to Leavenworth is for the extensive **hiking** opportunities in the **Wenatchee National Forest.** The heavily-visited Alpine Lakes Wilderness stretches south of town, attracting hikers from everywhere. The **ranger station** in Leavenworth hands out several brief, free descriptions of hikes near town. Families may wish to consult the page-long list of "relatively easy, short hikes," while more experienced walkers can check out the "moderate to difficult" list. The ranger station also sells an informative, well-organized guide to all the area's trails for $1.25. The most complete hike descriptions can be found in the well-written *100 Hikes in Washington's Alpine Lakes,* by Harvey Manning, on sale at the ranger station for $13 (or contact **The Mountaineers Books,** 1011 SW Klickitat Way, #107, Seattle WA 98134; 800-553-4453). One pleasant day-hike is the moderately sloping 3.5-mi. trail to picturesque **Eightmile Lake,** a great spot for a picnic. To reach the trailhead, travel 9.4 mi. up Icicle Creek Rd., make a left onto Eightmile Rd., and continue to the trailhead on your right.

Permits are required to enter the popular **Stuart Lake, Colcheck Lake, Snow Lakes,** and **Enchantment Lakes** areas. If you're a day-hiker only, the permits are free and "self-issuing," meaning you just have to fill out a form, either at the ranger station or at trailheads. For overnights, permits cost $1 per person per day, and can be obtained in two ways. First, you can file an application for a permit starting March 1 for the upcoming summer (write to or call the ranger station to obtain an application). Second, you can participate in a lottery for a limited number of permits each morning at 7:45am (at the ranger station).

On your way up Icicle Rd., stop at the **Leavenworth National Fish Hatchery** (548-7641) to immerse yourself in exhibits about local river life. In the summer, adult chinook salmon, sometimes reaching 30 lbs., fill the holding ponds waiting to be butchered. (Open daily 7:30am-3:30pm.) If you are in a riding mood, try the **Eagle Creek Ranch** (548-7798), north on Rte. 209, then right on Eagle Creek Rd. for 5½ mi. The ranch offers horseback rides ($15 per hr.), hay rides ($12), and winter horse-drawn sleigh rides. On your way south to the U.S. 97 junction, be sure to stop in **Cashmere** at their **Aplets and Cotlets Factory,** 117 Mission St. (782-2191), for free tours of the plant and ample samples of their gooey candies. You have to wear a hat during the tour, but they'll give you a goofy paper one if you don't bring your own. (Open Mon.-Fri. 8am-5:30pm, Sat.-Sun. 10am-4pm; Jan.-March Mon.-Fri. 8:30am-4:30pm.) The **Washington State Leaf Festival,** a celebration of autumn, lasts for nine days during the last week in September and the first week in October. It includes a Grand Parade, art shows, flea markets, and street dances. "Smooshing," a four-person race run on wooden two-by-fours, is the highlight of the **Great Bavarian Ice Fest,** held on the weekend of Martin Luther King, Jr. Day.

■■■ LAKE CHELAN

The serpentine body of Lake Chelan (sha-LAN) winds over 50 mi. northwest from the Columbia River and U.S. 97 into the eastern Cascades. Although the lakeshores around the faded resort town of **Chelan** are an unimpressive dry brown, the shores farther north are handsome indeed. The lake, at points 1500 ft. deep, extends far into Wenatchee National Forest and pokes its northwesternmost tip into the Lake Chelan Recreation Area, a section of North Cascades National Park. While Chelan has become an overpriced tourist trap, **Stehekin,** at the other end of the lake, offers plenty of solitude, open space, and access to a vast wilderness.

Sights and Practical Information The **Chelan Ranger Station,** 428 W Woodin Ave. (682-2576, or 682-2549 for the National Park Service), just south of

Chelan on the lakeshore, will tell you all about the area, forests, and recreation areas (open daily 7:45am-4:30pm; Oct.-May Mon.-Fri. 7:45am-4:30pm). If you'll be in Chelan for a while, stop by the **Lake Chelan Chamber of Commerce,** 102 E Johnson (682-3503 or 800-424-3526); it offers plenty of information on Chelan and nearby Manson, but not much on the surrounding wilds (open Mon.-Fri. 9am-5pm, Sat. 10am-3pm, Sun. 10am-1pm; winter Mon.-Fri. 9am-5pm).

Empire Bus Lines stops at 115 S Emerson St. (682-4147), by the pony mailbox, and sends one bus daily south to Wenatchee, with connections to Seattle ($28) and Spokane ($32); and one bus daily north to British Columbia. Rent a bike at **Nature Gone Wild,** 106 S Emerson (682-8680), for $5 per hr., or $25 per 24 hrs. (open Mon.-Fri. 9am-6pm, Sat. 8am-5pm, Sun. noon-?, says the sign). Chelan's pharmacy is **Green's Drugs,** 212 E Woodin Ave. (682-2566; open Mon.-Sat. 9am-5:30pm, Sun. as posted). The **Lake Chelan Community Hospital** (682-2531) is open 24 hrs. Important phone numbers: **emergency,** 911; **24-hr. Crisis Line,** 662-7105; **Police,** 207 N Emerson St. (682-2588). Wash that grey right out of your clothes ($1 a load; 10-min. dry 25¢) at **Chelan Cleaners,** 127 E Johnson (open daily 7am-10pm; winter 7am-8pm). The **post office** (682-2625) is at 144 E Johnson at Emerson (open Mon.-Fri. 8:30am-5pm; **General Delivery ZIP Code:** 98816). The **area code** is 509.

Accommodations, Camping, and Food Exploiting sun-starved visitors from Puget Sound, Chelan has jacked up the prices on just about everything. Most motels and resorts in town are unaffordable during the summer. An exception is **Mom's Montlake Motel,** 823 Wapato (682-5715) at Clifford, a mom-and-pop operation with clean rooms for $40-55. Another option is the **Travelers Motel,** 204 E Wapato Ave. (682-4215), around the corner from the bus depot (no single rooms; doubles $35, with kitchen $69; prices $10 higher on weekends). Most campers head for **Lake Chelan State Park** (687-3710), a pleasant grassy campground 9 mi. from Chelan up the south shore of the lake. (Open April-Sept.; 144 sites $12, with hookup $16. Reservations necessary: write Lake Chelan State Park, Rte. 1, P.O. Box 90, Chelan WA 98816.) Nine mi. farther up the shore, **Twenty-Five Mile Creek State Park** (687-3610) is more tightly packed, but still a better deal than the commercial parks around Chelan (open Memorial Day-late Oct. Tents $12, with hookup $16). **Ramona Park,** a free, primitive campground, is reached by turning left onto Forest Rd. 5900 near the end of the South Shore Rd. (just beyond 25 Mile Creek), then left onto Forest Rd. 8410 after 2.5 mi. Continue another ½ mi. Campers may also pitch tents anywhere they please, free, in the National Forest and in this area.

The cheapest eats in Chelan can be had at local fruit stands, the **Safeway** (106 W Manson Rd., 682-2615; open daily 6am-11pm), or the *fantastic* **Golden Florin's Bear Foods,** 125 E Woodin Ave. (682-5535), selling a wide variety of natural foods in industrial quantities (open Mon.-Sat. 9am-7pm, Sun. noon-5pm). **Judy Jane Bakery,** 216 Manson Rd. (682-2151), sells delicious baked goods and deli foods. The sandwich of the day and salad special costs $2.70 (open daily 7am-8pm).

Outdoors One mi. east of Chelan in Lakeside is **Lake Chelan Butte Lookout.** Take a hike to the top for a great view of the lake and the hang-gliders taking the easy way down. For other hiking try **Twenty-Five Mile Creek.** Better, find your way to **Stehekin,** a town inaccessible by road. The **Lake Chelan Boat Company,** 1418 W Woodin, Chelan 98816 (682-2224), runs one round-trip to Stehekin daily (April 15-Oct. 15; leaving at 8:30am and arriving at 12:30pm, with a 1½-hr. stop). Don't miss the return trip unless you're prepared to camp out (or shell out a small fortune for a cabin) in Stehekin. The dock is 1 mi. south of Chelan on U.S. 97. (Boats also run Oct. 16-April 14 Mon., Wed., Fri., and Sun. $14 one-way, $21 round-trip. Ages 6-11 ½ price; under 6 free.)

STEHEKIN

For less than the price of a motel room in Chelan, you can take a ferry from Chelan 50 mi. over sparkling turquoise waters to Stehekin (ste-HEE-kin), a tiny town at the mouth of a magnificent valley. From Stehekin, you can catch a shuttle bus a few mi. up the valley, camp for free on the banks of a rushing, crystal green river beneath snow-capped peaks, spend days exploring some of the most beautiful country in the Cascades, and return to Chelan.

A **lodge, ranger station,** and **campground** cluster around Stehekin. An unpaved road and many trails probe north into the **North Cascades National Park.** A **Park Service shuttle** ($10, see page 396) operates along the Stehekin Valley Rd., linking Stehekin to the National Park (buses leave Stehekin Landing at 8am and 2pm. Reservations are required to ride the shuttle; call 206-856-5703 x 14 more than 2 days in advance). At the end of the Park Service shuttle route, it is a 9-mi. hike through the National Park to Rte. 20. Another **shuttle** runs to **High Bridge** ($4). Either shuttle will drop you off anywhere along the way for full fare. You can also rent a bike; instead of renting from the Stehekin Lodge, save a few dollars by walking several hundred yards up-valley to the **bike rental stand** outside the Courtney Log Office ($3.50 per hour, $10 per day 8am-5pm, $15 per 24 hrs.). All walk-in campgrounds in North Cascades National Park are open May through October (free). **Backcountry permits** are mandatory in the park throughout the year and are available on a first-come, first-served basis. Pick one up at the Chelan or Stehekin ranger stations. (For more information, see North Cascades National Park.) An excellent resource for the entire Stehekin area is *The Stehekin Guidebook* (free).

The **Lake Chelan Boat Company** (see Chelan above), about 1 mi. west of town on Woodin Ave., runs the *Lady of the Lake II,* a 350-person ferry making one round trip to Stehekin per day. For the same fare, you can catch the ferry at Chelan (parking $4.50 per day, $25 per week) at 8:30am; or at **Fields Point,** 16 mi. up the South Shore Rd. (parking $3.25 per day, $17 per week) at 9:45am. The scenery gets increasingly spectacular as the boat proceeds "uplake;" the views on the ride alone are worth the price ($14 one way, $21 round-trip, ages 6-11 ½-price, under 6 free). Indeed, when the ferry arrives at Stehekin at 12:30pm, most people choose to stay only until the boat's departure at 2pm. If that's your plan, the **Rainbow Falls Tour,** leaving as soon as the *Lady* arrives, is a good way to see the valley and its major sights: the one-room **Stehekin School,** the **Stehekin Pastry Company,** a **bakery** in a log cabin off in the woods that sells wonderful baked goods at high prices (all the ingredients must come in by boat); and **Rainbow Falls,** a misty 312-ft. waterfall. The narrated bus tour includes natural and human history ($4.25).

To truly appreciate Stehekin, let the tourists take the boat back to Chelan. Camping is the cheapest way to stay in the valley overnight; a room at the **North Cascades Stehekin Lodge** (P.O. Box 457, Chelan; 682-4494), right at the landing, is $55 and sleeps two. For larger groups, a **log cabin** rental can be a good deal. Cragg and Roberta Cortney (Box 67, Stehekin, WA 98852; 682-4677) rent a completely furnished cabin with a full kitchen that sleeps up to nine, and comes with a vehicle. It goes for $80 per day plus $10 for each person over two.

The Park Service maintains primitive campgrounds along the Stehekin Valley Road. You need a free **permit** to use these campgrounds. Get one at the Ranger Station in Chelan or at the **Golden West Visitor Center,** up the hill from the landing (open daily 7:30am-4pm).

If you want a meal in the valley, you have three options. The **grocery/convenience store** at the landing has hearty soups and chili ($1.50) and big, thick slices of pizza they'll microwave for you ($2). Next door, the **Lodge Restaurant** serves expensive burgers ($6-7) and dinners ($8-12) in a more elegant setting. Or, you can catch a bus up to the **Stehekin Valley Ranch** for dinner. You'll need reservations (made at the Courtney Log Office; see above), and the delicious country meal will set you back about $12. Bring groceries from Chelan; the store in Stehekin has only a small selection of expensive groceries.

Two dramatically different **dayhikes** start from High Bridge. The mellow **Agnes Gorge trail** begins 200 yds. beyond the bridge, and travels a level 2.5 mi. through forests and meadows with great views of Agnes Mountain, ending where Agnes Creek takes a dramatic plunge into Agnes Gorge. Starting behind the ranger cabin, the **McGregor Mountain Trail** takes a straight shot up the side of McGregor Mountain (8124 ft. in elevation), climbing 6525 vertical ft. over 8 horizontal mi. The last ½-mi. is a scramble up ledges. This extremely difficult trail is often blocked by snow into July; check at the visitor center before starting out. The persevering hiker is rewarded with unsurpassed **views** of the high North Cascades peaks.

For **backpackers,** a good two-day hike combines the **Purple Creek Trail,** beginning behind the Golden West visitor center, with the **Boulder Creek Trail.** A longer loop from Harlequin Campground combines the **Company Creek Trail** and the **Devore Creek Trail.**

■■■ NORTH CASCADES (RTE. 20)

A favorite stomping ground for Jack Kerouac (*The Dharma Bums*), deer, mountain goats, black bears, and grizzlies, the North Cascades remain one of the last great expanses of untouched land in the continental U.S. The dramatic peaks north of Stevens Pass on U.S. 2 occupy land administered by several different government agencies. **Pasayten** and **Glacier Peak** are designated wilderness areas, each attracting backpackers and mountain climbers. **Ross Lake Recreation Area** surrounds the Rte. 20 corridor, and **North Cascades National Park** extends north and south of Rte. 20. The **Mt. Baker/Snoqualmie National Forest** borders the park on the west, the **Okanogan National Forest** to the east, and **Wenatchee National Forest** to the south. **Rte. 20** (open April-Nov., weather permitting) is the primary means of access to the area and awards jaw-dropping views around each curve; a road designed for unadulterated driving pleasure.

Books can assist in planning an expedition in the North Cascades. Ira Springs's *100 Hikes in the North Cascades* (The Mountaineers Press) is among the most readable for recreational hikers, while Fred Beckley's *Cascade Alpine Guide* (The Mountaineers Press) targets the more serious high-country traveler and mountain climber.

PRACTICAL INFORMATION AND ORIENTATION

North Cascades National Park, 2105 Rte. 20, Sedro Woolley 98284 (206-856-5700). Open June-Sept. Sat.-Thurs. 8am-4:30pm, Fri. 8am-6:30pm; Oct.-April Mon.-Fri. 8am-4:30pm.

National Park/National Forest: Outdoor Recreation Information Office, Jackson Federal Building, 915 2nd Avenue, Room 442, Seattle 98174 (206-220-7450). Open Mon.-Fri. 8:30am-5:30pm.

Wenatchee National Forest, 301 Yakima St., P.O. Box 811, Wenatchee 98801 (509-662-4335).

Snow Avalanche Information: 206-526-6677.

Area Code: 206 west of the Cascades, 509 to the east.

Rte. 20 (exit 230 on I-5) follows the Skagit River to the Skagit Dams and lakes, whose hydroelectric energy powers Seattle. It then enters the Ross Lake Recreation Area, offering access to North Cascades National Park and nearby wilderness areas, before crossing Washington Pass (5477 ft.) and finally descending to the Methow River and the dry Okanogan rangeland of eastern Washington.

Greyhound stops in Burlington once per day on the Seattle-Bellingham route, and **Empire Lines** (affiliated with Greyhound) serves Okanogan, Pateros, and Chelan on the eastern slope. The fare is about $15 from Seattle to the East Cascades. No public transportation lines run within the park boundaries or along Rte. 20.

SEDRO WOOLLEY TO MARBLEMOUNT

Sedro Woolley, though situated in the rich farmland of the lower Skagit Valley, is primarily a logging town. The main attraction of this village is the annual **Sedro Woolley Loggerodeo.** The festivities are dominated by a carnival, parade, and rodeo queen contest. Axe-throwing, pole-climbing, and sawing competitions vie for center stage with beer and rodeo events such as bronco-busting and calf-roping. Call or write the Sedro Woolley **Chamber of Commerce,** P.O. Box 562, Sedro Woolley 98284 (855-1841), at 116 Woodsworth St. for more information (open Mon.-Sat. 9am-5pm "with an hour break for lunch"). Sedro Woolley also houses the **North Cascades National Park Headquarters.** Rte. 9 leads north of town through forested countryside, providing indirect access to **Mt. Baker** via the forks at the Nooksack River and Rte. 542. (For information about Mt. Baker, see page 355).

As it continues east, Rte. 20 forks at **Baker Lake Road,** which dead-ends 25 mi. later at **Baker Lake.** There are several campgrounds along the way, but only **Horseshoe Cove** and **Panorama Point** offer toilets and potable water (sites $10, plus $6.50 for each additional vehicle). All other grounds are free. Call 800-280-CAMP for reservations.

To the east, **Rockport** borders **Rockport State Park** (853-8461) along with its magnificent Douglas firs, a trail that accommodates wheelchairs, and 62 fully developed campsites in a densely wooded area ($8, with full hookup $12, each extra vehicle $3). The surrounding **Snoqualmie National Forest** permits free camping closer to the high peaks. From Rockport, Rte. 530 stems south to **Darrington,** home to a large population of displaced North Carolinians and a well-attended **Bluegrass Festival** on the third weekend of June. Darrington's **ranger station** (436-1155) is on Rte. 530 at the north end of town. (Open Mon.-Fri. 7am-5pm, Sat.-Sun. 8am-4:30pm; Oct.-April Mon.-Fri. 7am-4:30pm. Call for information about Rockport State Park.) If Rockport is full, continue 1 mi. east to Skagit County's **Howard Miller Steelhead Park** on the Skagit River, ideal for fishing and rafting, with 10 tentsites (tents $7, hookups $10).

At **Marblemount,** try stopping at **Good Food,** a small family diner at the east edge of town along Rte. 20. This pithy eatery boasts not only riverside, outdoor picnic tables with incredible views but also a great vegetarian sandwich ($3.25). Boost your caffeine level with a shot of espresso. For dessert, the shake is tasty. (Open Mon.-Fri. 8am-8pm. No phone.)

From Marblemount, it's 22 mi. up Cascade River Rd. to the trailhead for a 9-mi. hike to **Cascade Pass.** From the pass, the **Park Service Shuttle** runs the 26 mi. between **Cottonwood** and the isolated town of **Stehekin** (ste-HEE-kin) to the southeast and at the north tip of Lake Chelan, reachable only by by boat, plane, or foot. (Shuttle runs June-Sept. twice per day at 8am and 2pm, 2 hr., one-way $10; see page 394). Shuttle reservations are required; call or check in at the **Marblemount Ranger Station,** P.O. Box 10, Marblemount 98267 (873-4590), 1 mi. north of Marblemount on a well-marked road from the west end of town (open daily 7am-8pm; in winter Mon.-Fri. 8am-4:30pm). Marblemount is the last place to buy supplies before **Winthrop,** 90 mi. further east.

ROSS LAKE & NORTH CASCADES NATIONAL PARK

Newhalem is the first town on Rte. 20 as you cross into the **Ross Lake National Recreation Area,** a buffer zone between the highway and North Cascades National Park. A small grocery store and **hiking** trails to the dams and lakes nearby are the highlights of Newhalem. Information is available at the **visitors center** (386-4495), on Rte. 20 (open late June-early Sept. daily 8:30am-5:30pm; late Sept. 9am-4:30pm; call for winter hours).

The artificial expanse of **Ross Lake,** behind Ross Dam, extends into the mountains as far as the Canadian border. The lake is ringed by 15 campgrounds, some accessible by trail, others only by boat. The trail along **Big Beaver Creek,** at Mile 134 on Rte. 20, leads from Ross Lake over Ross Dam into the Picket Range and eventually all the way to Mt. Baker. The **Sourdough Mountain** and **Desolation Peak lookout towers** near Ross Lake offer eagle's-eye views of the range.

The National Park's **Goodell Creek Campground,** just south of Newhalem, has 22 sites suitable for tents and trailers with drinking water and pit toilets, and a launch site for **whitewater rafting** on the Skagit River (sites $7; after Oct., no water, and sites are free). **Colonial Creek Campground,** 10 mi. to the east, is a fully developed, vehicle-accessible campground with flush toilets, a dump station, and campfire programs every evening. Colonial Creek is also a trailhead for several hikes into the southern unit of the North Cascades National Park (open mid-May to Nov.; 164 sites, $7). **Newhalem Creek Campground,** near the visitors center, is another similarly developed National Park facility (129 sites, $7).

Diablo Lake lies southwest of Ross Lake; the foot of Ross Dam acts as its eastern shore. The town of Diablo Lake is the main trailhead for hikes into the southern unit of North Cascades National Park. The **Thunder Creek Trail** traverses Park Creek Pass to Stehekin River Rd., in Lake Chelan National Recreation Area south of the park. Diablo Lake supports a boathouse and a lodge that sells groceries and gas, an interpretive center, and several boat-in or hike-in campsites. For some areas, a free **backcountry permit** is required and available from park ranger stations.

EAST TO MAZAMA AND WINTHROP

Thirty mi. of jaw-dropping views east on Rte. 20, the **Pacific Crest Trail** crosses **Rainy Pass** on one of the most scenic and difficult legs of its 2500-mi. Canada-to-Mexico route. The trail leads north through **Pasayten Wilderness** and south past **Glacier Peak** (10,541 ft.) in the **Glacier Peak Wilderness.** Near Rainy Pass, groomed **scenic trails** 1 to 3 mi. long can be hiked in sneakers, provided the snow has melted (about mid-July). An overlook at **Washington Pass** rewards a short hike with one of the state's most dramatic panoramas, a flabbergasting **view** of the red rocks of upper **Early Winters Creek's Copper Basin.** It's only a five-minute walk on a wheelchair-accessible paved trail. The popular 2.2-mi. walk to **Blue Lake** begins just east of Washington Pass. The deep turquoise lake is surrounded by cliffs. An easier 2-mi. hike to **Cutthroat Lake** departs from an access road 4.6 mi. east of Washington Pass. From the lake, the trail continues 4 mi. further (and almost 2,000 ft. higher) to **Cutthroat Pass,** giving the persevering hiker a breathtaking view of towering, rugged peaks.

The spectacular, hair-raising 19-mi. road to **Hart's Pass** begins at **Mazama,** 10 mi. east of Washington Pass. The narrow gravel road snakes up to the highest pass crossed by any road in the state. Breathtaking views reward the steel-nerved driver, both from the pass and from **Slate Peak** beyond the pass, site of a fire lookout station. The road is usually open early July-late Sept. and is **closed to trailers.**

The Forest Service maintains a string of campgrounds along Rte. 20 (sites $8), between Washington Pass and Mazama. Explore the other, more remote campgrounds along the Forest Rd. northwest of Mazama. The **Early Winters Visitor Center** (996-2534), just outside **Mazama,** is aflutter with information about the **Pasayten Wilderness,** an area whose rugged terrain and mild climate endear it to hikers and equestrians. Take yourself on a hard-core five-day backcountry excursion to really experience it (open daily 9am-5pm; in winter, Sat.-Sun. 9am-5pm).

WINTHROP TO TWISP

Farther east is the town of **Winthrop,** child of an unholy marriage between the old television series *Bonanza* and Long Island yuppies (lawn-GUY-land) who would eagerly claim a rusty horseshoe as an antique. Find the **Winthrop Information Station** (996-2125), on the corner of Rte. 20 and Riverside (open early May-mid-Oct. daily 10am-5pm). For homemade soups and great sandwiches, stop in at the **Trail's End Way Station** (996-2303), tucked into a corner of the Trail's End Motel. Follow Riverside from Rte. 20; the Trail's End is the last old-west style building on the right. The racks upon racks of videos for rent don't improve the ambience, but nothing can detract from the delicious sandwiches ($4-5). The half-sandwich and cup of soup is $4.50. Most entrees are $8-9 (open daily 7am-9pm).

The summer is bounded by **rodeos** on Memorial and Labor Day weekends. Late July brings the top **Winthrop Rhythm and Blues Festival** (996-2111); 1994 featured Bo Diddley, J. J. Cale, and John Hammond. Tickets for the great 4-day event cost around $30. You can take a guided trail ride at the **Rocking Horse Ranch** (996-2768), 9 mi. north of Winthrop on the North Cascade Hwy. ($20 per 1½ hrs.). Or rent a bike ($5 per hr., $20 per day), or try you hand at an indoor climbing wall at

Winthrop Mountain Sports, 257 Riverside Ave. (996-2886). The **Winthrop Ranger Station,** P.O. Box 579 (996-2266), at 24 W Chewuch Rd., off Rte. 20 in the west end of town, knows all about campgrounds, hikes, and fishing spots (open Mon.-Fri. 7:45am-5pm, Sat. 8:30am-5pm; closed Sat. in winter).

One mi. south of Winthrop, the **National Fish Hatchery** raises 1½ million spring chinook salmon and ¾ million trout. Visitors can guide themselves through between 7:30am and 4:30pm daily. The fish are fed between 8am and 10pm. Between Winthrop and Twisp on the East Country Road (9129), the **North Cascades Smokejumper Base** (997-2031) is a center for folks who get their kicks by parachuting into forest fires in an effort to fight them. The courageous smokejumpers will give you a tour of the base and explain the procedures and equipment (open June-Oct. daily 8am-5pm; Nov.-May call for a tour).

Flee Winthrop's prohibitively expensive hotels and sleep in **Twisp,** the town that should have been a breakfast cereal. Nine mi. south of Winthrop on Rte. 20, this peaceful hamlet offers low prices and far fewer tourists than its neighbor. Stay at **The Sportsman Motel,** 1010 E Rte. 20 (997-2911), a hidden jewel, where a barracks-like facade masks tastefully decorated rooms and kitchens (singles $31, doubles $36). The **Twisp Ranger Station,** 502 Glover St. (997-2131), employs an extremely helpful staff ready to strafe you with trail and campground guides (open Mon.-Sat. 7:45am-4:30pm; winter Mon.-Fri. 7:45am-4:30pm). The **Methow Valley Tourist Information Office,** in the community center/karate school at Rte. 20 and 3rd, has area brochures (open Mon.-Fri. 8am-5pm, Sat. 9am-4pm, Sun. 11am-4pm). From Twisp, Rte. 20 continues east to Okanogan, and Rte. 153 runs a short distance south to **Lake Chelan.**

Locals frequent **Rosey's Branding Iron,** 123 Glover St. (997-3576), in the center of town. The Iron usually has really cheap specials on the menu (under $3.50) and offers special menus for dieters, seniors, and children. All-you-can-eat soup and salad is only $6 (open Mon.-Sat. 5am-8pm, Sun. 6am-3pm).

EASTERN WASHINGTON

In the rain-shadow of the Cascades, the hills and valleys of the Columbia River Basin once fostered little more than sagebrush and tumbleweed. With irrigation and the construction of several dams, the basin now yields bumper crops of many kinds of fruit. The same sun that ripens the region's orchards also bronzes flocks of visitors from Puget Sound. East of the river, ranching, wheat and fruit farming, and mining dominate the economy. **Spokane** is the largest city east of the Cascades.

U.S. 97, running north-south along the eastern edge of the Cascades, strings together the main fruit centers and mountain resorts of the Columbia River Basin. **I-90** emerges from Seattle and the Cascades to cut a route through Ellensburg, Moses Lake, and Spokane, while **I-82** dips south from Ellensburg through Yakima and Richland to Hermiston, OR. **Greyhound** (509-624-5251) runs along both interstates. **Empire Lines** (509-624-5116) runs from Spokane to Grand Coulee and Brewster, and along U.S. 97 from Oroville on the Canadian border to Ellensburg, passing by Lake Chelan. **Amtrak** (509-624-5144) runs its "Empire Builder" through Spokane, Richland, along the Columbia River to Portland, and through Ellensburg to Tacoma and Seattle.

■ ■ ■ SPOKANE

Spokane was the first pioneer settlement in the Northwest. The economy is based on agriculture, lumber, and mining, and Spokane is one of the Northwest's major trade centers. The area achieves urban sophistication without typical big-city hassles; the downtown thrives, but the pace is slow. The legacy of Expo '74 includes a museum and theater in **Riverfront Park.** With a three-diamond, inexpensive motel and lots of delicious, cheap food, Spokane is a budget-travel legend.

PRACTICAL INFORMATION AND ORIENTATION

Visitors Information: Spokane Area Convention and Visitors Bureau, W 926 Sprague Ave. (747-3230), exit 280 off I-90. Overflowing with literature extolling every aspect of Spokane. Open Mon.-Fri. 8:30am-5pm, and most summer weekends, Sat. 8am-4pm, Sun. 9am-2pm. At the Idaho state line, exit 299 off I-90, the **Spokane River Rest Area Visitor Center** (226-3322) offers similar pamphlets and enthusiasm. Open daily May 1-Sept. 30 8am-5pm).

Amtrak, W 221 1st St. (624-5144, after business hours 800-872-7245), at Bernard St., downtown. To: Chicago (1 per day; $217); Seattle (1 per day; $65); Portland (1 per day; $65). Depot open Mon.-Fri. 11am-3:30am, Sat.-Sun. 7:15pm-3:30am.

Greyhound, W 1125 Sprague (624-5251), at 1st Ave. and Jefferson St., downtown. **Empire Lines** (624-4116) and **Northwest Stage Lines** (800-826-4058 or 838-4029) share the terminal with Greyhound, serving other parts of Eastern Washington, northern Idaho, and British Columbia. Greyhound to Seattle (5 per day; $26). Station open 24 hrs., though ticket office hours are limited.

Spokane Transit System, W 1229 Boone Ave. (328-7433). Serves all of Spokane, including Eastern Washington University in Cheney. Fare 75¢, over 64 and travelers with disabilities 35¢. Operates until 12:15am downtown, 9:15pm in the valley along E Sprague Ave. Call 325-6084 for 24-hr. public information.

Taxi: Checker Cab, 624-4171. **Yellow Cab,** 624-4321. Both open 24 hrs.

Car Rental: U-Save Auto Rental, W 918 3rd St. (455-8018), at Monroe. Cars from $23 per day; 20¢ per mi. after 150 mi. $250 deposit or major credit card required. Must be over 21. Open Mon.-Fri. 7am-7pm, Sat. 8am-5pm, Sun. 10am-5pm.

AAA Office, W 1717 4th (455-3400). Open Mon.-Fri. 8am-5pm.

Camping Equipment: White Elephant, N 1730 Division St. (328-3100) and E 12614 Sprague (924-3006). Every imaginable piece of equipment at bargain prices. Open Mon.-Thurs. and Sat. 9am-6pm, Fri. 9am-9pm. **Outdoor Sportsman,** N 1602 Division St. (328-1556). Prices are even lower. Open Mon.-Thurs. 9am-6:30pm, Fri. 9am-7pm, Sat. 9am-6pm, Sun. 9am-5pm.

Public Library: W 906 Main St. (838-3361). Open Mon.-Thurs. 10am-9pm, Fri.-Sat. 10am-6pm.

Laundromat: Ye Olde Wash House Laundry and Dry Cleaners, E 4224 Sprague (534-9859). Wash (electric, not ye olde tub) 75¢, 12-min. dry 25¢.

Events Line: 747-3230. 24-hr. recorded information.

Travelers Aid Service, W 1017 1st (456-7164), near the bus depot. Kind staff, adept at helping stranded travelers find lodgings. Open Mon.-Fri. 1-4:30pm.

Crisis Hotline: 838-4428. 24 hrs.

Urgent Care Center: Rockwood Clinic, E 400 5th Ave. (838-2531). Open Mon.-Fri. 8am-8pm, Sat.-Sun. 9am-5pm. No appointment necessary.

Poison Information: 747-1077. 24 hrs.

Senior Center: W 1124 Sinto (327-2861). Mon.-Sat. 8:30am-5pm, Sun. 2-5pm.

Elderly Services Information and Assistance: 458-7450.

Gay & Lesbian Community Services: 489-2206.

Pharmacy: Hart and Dilatush, W 501 Sprague at Stevens (624-2111). Open Mon.-Fri. 8am-midnight, Sat.-Sun. noon-8pm.

Hospital: Deaconess Medical Center, W 800 5th (458-7100; emergency info. 458-5800).

Emergency: 911.

Police: 456-2233. **Ambulance: Lifefleet** 328-6161. Both 24 hrs.

Post Office: W 904 Riverside (459-0230), at Lincoln. Open Mon.-Fri. 8:30am-5pm. **General Delivery ZIP Code:** 99210.

Area Code: 509.

Spokane lies 280 mi. east of Seattle on I-90. The **Spokane International Airport** (624-3218) is off I-90 8 mi. southwest of town. Avenues run east-west parallel to the river, streets north-south, and both alternate one-way. The city is divided north and south by **Sprague Ave.,** east and west by **Division St.** Downtown is the quadrant north of Sprague and west of Division, wedged between I-90 and the Spokane River. I-90 exits 279 to 282 access to Spokane. As in many cities in the Interior West, street addresses begin with the compass point first, list the number second, and the street name third (W 1200 Division). All Spokane Transit System buses start and finish their routes two blocks south, at Riverside and Howard St.

ACCOMMODATIONS AND CAMPING

Don't try to sleep in Riverfront Park; the Spokane police *don't* like it. Stay indoors. Spokane is good to budget travelers.

Hosteling International Spokane (HI/AYH), S 930 Lincoln (838-5968). A steep climb up Lincoln brings you to a large, warm, Victorian house with a spacious porch and delightfully creaky wooden floorboards. Cozy kitchens, laundry, and baths complete the nostalgic atmosphere. The hostel fills in July and Aug., so make reservations. 22 beds. Check-in 4-10pm, no curfew. $10, nonmembers $13.

Town Centre Motor Inn, W 901 1st St. (747-1041), at Lincoln St. in the heart of downtown, 4 blocks from the bus depot. Large, luxurious, sparkling-clean rooms, including a refrigerator and a microwave. Exercise room and "steam room." The 3-diamond rating by AAA tells you how fancy this place is. Save 20-25% by exchanging your US$ for CDN$ at one of the downtown banks beforehand; to attract Canadian business, the Motor Inn accepts north-of-the-border currency at par. Surprisingly, this is not unusual in Spokane. Singles $44. Doubles $49.

Suntree 8 Inn, S 123 Post. St. (838-8504). Clean, modern, comfortable rooms hide behind this motel's drab exterior. If you're feeling spry or you brought your ear plugs, you can save $6 by taking a room (identical to the others) on the 3rd floor, or next to the railroad tracks. Join the "V.I.P. Club" for $4, and you can pay with CDN$ at par. Singles $40. Doubles $44.

Motel 6, S 1580 Rustle St. (459-6120), off of I-90 at exit 277 (follow signs for West Spokane), far from downtown. TV, pool, and A/C. More spartan, less convenient, and less expensive. Singles $33. Doubles $39. Reserve 2-3 weeks ahead.

Riverside State Park (456-3964), 6 mi. northwest of downtown on Rifle Club Rd., off Rte. 291 or Nine Mile Rd. Take Division north and turn left on Francis, then follow the signs. 101 standard sites in a pleasant, open Ponderosa forest. Kitchen, shower, bath, and the Spokane River running by. Wheelchair access. Sites $11.

Mt. Spokane State Park (456-4169), 35 mi. northeast of the city. Take U.S. 395 5 mi. north to U.S. 2, then go 7 mi. north to Hwy. 206, which leads into the park. Popular with winter athletes for its cross-country skiing and snowmobiling trails. Views of 2 states and Canada from the Vista House. 12 sites. Flush toilets; no showers, cold water only. Sites $11.

Park Washington Ponderosa Hill, (747-9415 or 1-800-494-7275 ext. 801), 5 mi. west of the city. Take I-90 to exit 272. Follow the signs along Hallett Rd. east to Thomas-Mallon Rd., then 1 mi. south. A brand-new hi-tech campground with separate tent and RV sections, showers, and laundry facilities. Sites $14, full hookup $22. 10% discount for AAA or "Good Sam" members.

FOOD

Spokane, Washington's agricultural center, is a great place to get fresh produce. The **Spokane County Market** at Division St. and Riverside Ave. (482-2627) sells fresh fruit, vegetables, and baked goods (open May-Oct. Wed. 9am-5pm, Sat.-Sun. 11am-4pm). The **Green Bluff Growers Cooperative,** E 9423 Green Bluff Rd., Colbert, WA 99005, is an organization of 20-odd fruit and vegetable farms, marked with the big red apple sign 16 mi. northwest of town off Day-Mountain Spokane Rd. Many farms have "u-pick" arrangements and are near free picnic areas.

For a variety of interesting eateries downtown, head to **The Atrium,** on Wall St. near 1st. Ave. **Europa Pizzeria,** one of the restaurants in this small brick building, bakes the best pizza in town. Another center for restaurants and shops is the **Flour Mill,** just across the Spokane River to the north of Riverfront Park. The unique building is a 100-year-old mill containing individually owned and operated shops and eateries. The famished should eat in bulk; many of the chain restaurants clustered along 3rd. Ave. advertise all-you-can-eat specials and buffets.

Dick's, E 103rd Ave. (747-2481), at Division. Look for the pink panda sign near I-90. This takeout burger phenomenon, in an inexplicably inflation-free pocket of Washington, has been permanently enshrined in the *Let's Go: Did You Know?* Hall of Fame. Burgers 55¢, fries 43¢, sundaes 65¢, soft drinks 43-75¢. The more substantial "Whammy" ($1.07) has twice the meat and twice the cheese. Take the panda's advice and buy by the bagful. Dick's is always crowded, but battalions of workers move the lines along quickly. Open daily 9am-1:30am.

Cyrus O'Leary's, W 516 Main St. (624-9000), in the Bennetts Block complex at Howard St. A Spokane legend. Something like a carnival inside, with lots of carved animals (real and imaginary) and servers in costumes. Devour delicious food from a creative 25-page menu offering enormous meals ($7-15). Sandwiches $5.75 and up. Happy hour 4:30-6:30pm. Open Mon.-Thurs. 11:30am-11pm, Fri.-Sat. 11:30am-midnight, Sun. 11:30am-10pm.

Thai Cafe, W 410 Sprague (838-4783). This tiny restaurant adds plenty of spice (or only a little, your choice) to Spokane's American fare. The traditional *pad thai* and *gai pad* are $5. Curries are under $6. Open Mon.-Fri. 11:30am-1:30pm and 5-8:30pm, Sat 5-8:30pm.

Benjamin's Restaurant (455-6771), in the Parkade Plaza on Howard between Riverside and Main. This popular alternative to Dick's sells larger, juicer, more expensive burgers ($2). Get a little crazy with the curly fries (90¢) or one of their other home-cookin' menu items. The fresh baked hamburger buns are worth nearly $2 themselves. Open Mon.-Fri. 7am-5:30pm, Sat. 8am-4pm.

Milford's Fish House and Oyster Bar, N 719 Monroe (326-7251). Don't be fooled by the dingy neighborhood. Milford's is one of the finest restaurants in the Pacific Northwest. And though it may sink your budget, the freshest seafood in town will certainly buoy your spirits. Choose from a placard of fresh specials ($12-18) rotated daily; each includes a bowl of clam chowder or a dinner salad along with bread and vegetables. Open Mon. 5-9pm, Tues.-Sat. 5-10pm, Sun. 4-9pm.

SIGHTS

Spokane is too down-to-earth to aspire to flashy art or high-flown architecture. The city's best attractions concentrate on local history and culture. The **Cheney Cowles Memorial Museum,** W 2316 1st Ave. (456-3931), houses displays on the animals and pioneers of Eastern Washington. The museum's exhibits on Native North and South American art and artifacts have recently been augmented. One gallery is also devoted to contemporary Northwest art. (Open Tues. and Thurs.-Sat. 10am-5pm, Wed. 10am-9pm, Sun. 1-5pm.)

Riverfront Park, N 507 Howard St. (625-6600), just north of downtown, is Spokane's civic center. If the park hadn't been built for the 1974 World's Fair, the populace would have nowhere to stroll on leisurely weekend afternoons. The **IMAX Theater** (625-6686) boasts a five-story movie screen and a projector the size of a Volkswagen. (Tues.-Sun. 11am-9pm, shows on the hr. $5, seniors $4.50, under 18, $4.) Another section of the park offers a full range of kiddie rides, including the exquisitely hand-carved **Looff Carousel** (open daily 11am-9pm, summer 10pm; $1 a whirl). A one-day pass ($12, children and seniors $11) covers admission to the whole works. The park offers ice-skating in the winter ($4, skate rental $1.25) and often hosts special programs and events.

Hard-core Bingsters will be drawn to the **Crosby Student Center,** E 502 Boone St. (328-4220 ext. 4279), at Gonzaga University. Here, in the Crosbyana Room, the faithful exhibit the Bingmeister's relics and gold records. (Open daily, but call for hours. Free.)

Manito Park (625-6622), on S Grand Ave. between 17th and 25th Ave. south of downtown, encompasses a flower garden, tennis courts, and a duck pond. The **Dr. David Graiser Conservatory** cultivates many tropical and local plant species (open daily 8am-dusk; winter 8am-3:30pm; free). Adjacent to Manito Park is the

Nishinomiya Garden, a lush Japanese garden consecrating the friendship of Spokane and her Japanese sister city, Nishinomiya (same hours as Manito Park; free).

ENTERTAINMENT AND EVENTS

The *Spokane Spokesman-Review's* Friday "Weekend" section and the *Spokane Chronicle's* Friday "Empire" section give the lowdown on area happenings. During the summer, the city parks present a free **Out-to-Lunch** concert series at noon on weekdays at various locations around town. (Call 625-6200, Mon.-Fri. 8:30am-4:30pm for schedule information.)

Spokane supports two minor league sports teams. The **Indians** play ball at N 602 Havana (328-0450) from June to August (tickets $4-6), while the **Chiefs** skate at the Coliseum (535-2922) from October through March. All city-sponsored events are ticketed by Select-A-Seat. Call 325-7469 for information or 325-7328 for reservations.

The Opera House, W 334 Spokane Falls Blvd. (353-6500). Home to the Spokane Ballet and the Spokane Symphony Orchestra; also stages special performances ranging from rock concerts to chamber music. Open Mon.-Fri. 8:30am-5pm.

Civic Theater, N 1020 Howard St. (325-1413; for calendar information, call 1-800-248-3230 or 747-3230), opposite the Coliseum. Locally produced shows; has a downstairs theater for more risqué productions. Tickets Fri.-Sat. $16, Wed.-Thurs. $12, seniors and students $9.

Spokane Interplayers Ensemble, S 174 Howard (455-7529). A resident professional theater performing a broad range of plays. Seven productions a season, 20 public performances each. Oct.-June.

Magic Lantern Theatre, S 123 Wall St. (838-8276). Foreign and independent films with an occasional major release. $5.50, seniors and students $4.50, and for matinees and *Rocky Horror* $3.

Fox Theatre, W 1005 Sprague, (624-0105). The most convenient of several theatres showing major releases anywhere from one month to a year after mainstream release, $1.

The Quarterhorse, W 321 Sprague Ave. (456-3778). The place to be among Spokane's younger, monied crowd. Sports cars and vanity plates out front. Drink specials in a relaxed atmosphere. Occasional pool and dart tournaments. $1 beers on Thurs.-Sun. Cover Thurs.-Sat. $2. Hosts local bands on Fri. and Sat.

Mother's Pub, W 230 Riverside Ave. (624-9828). *The* place for live rock Fri.-Sat. nights. Cover charge varies from $2-6 depending on the band. Local and out-of-town bands, including Beggar's Opera, Rhinestone, and New Rules, slam and thrash here. Soul Patch (rest its soul) played its last show here on July 15, 1994. Draft beer $1.50-25. Open Wed.-Sat. 7pm-2am.

On the first Sunday in May, Riverfront Park hosts its premature, annual **Bloomsday Road Race,** the second biggest footrace on the West Coast. The race is the highlight of the **Lilac Festival,** a week-long hoopla of car shows, art fairs, house tours, and Special Olympics. For information on these and other events, contact the Chamber of Commerce (see above).

OUTDOORS

Riverside State Park (456-3964) embroiders the Spokane River with 12 sq. mi. of volcanic outcroppings, hiking trails (especially good in **Deep Creek Canyon,** the fossil beds of a forest that grew there seven million years ago), and equestrian trails in nearby Trail Town (horse rides $12.50 per hr., by appointment only; 456-8249). A July, 1994 wildfire charred much of the park, but the blackened trees blend in well with the volcanic rock, yielding a stark and beautiful effect. **Mount Spokane State Park** (456-4169) stands 35 mi. to the northeast of the city. A well-paved road extends to the summit, affording **views** of the Spokane Valley and (on clear days) the distant peaks of the Rockies and Cascades. Mt. Spokane is a **skiing** center with free cross-country trails and downhill ski packages (from $20). The area is also good for **hiking, horseback riding** (no rentals here), and **camping** (see Accommodations).

Lucky visitors may catch a glimpse of trumpeter swans at the **Turnbull National Wildlife Refuge** (235-4723), 21 mi. south of Spokane. Blinds have been set up for photographing at this happy breeding ground for bird species of the Pacific flyway. To get there, take the Four Lakes exit off I-90 in Cheney, and go left on Badger Rd. (open daily until dusk. $2 per vehicle).

Don't leave Spokane without tasting a fine Eastern Washington wine. The **Arbor Cliff House,** N 4705 Fruithill Rd. (927-9463), offers a tour of the vineyards, a view of the city, and free wine (daily from noon-5pm). It's worth the trip: take I-90 to the Argonne north exit, travel north on Argonne over the Spokane River, turn right on Upriver Dr., proceed 1 mi., and then bear left onto Fruithill Rd. Take a sharp right at the top of the hill. If you can't get out of town, stop in at **Knipprath Cellars,** S 163 Lincoln St. (624-9132), in downtown Spokane. Their elegant Victorian tasting room seems out of place in the hot downtown (open Tues.-Sun. 11:30am-5:30pm).

■■■ PULLMAN

Virtually everything in Pullman revolves around the enormous **Washington State University,** whose grassy expanses stretch out east of town.

Practical Information The **Pullman Chamber of Commerce,** N 415 Grand Ave. (334-3565), doles out free **maps** and can tell you about Pullman's favorite vegetable, the lentil. (Open Mon.-Sat. 9am-5pm.)

Pullman lies at the junction of Rte. 27 and 272. U.S. 195, running from Spokane south to Lewiston, bypasses the city to the west. Spokane lies 70 mi. north. Pullman lies 9 mi. *zapad* of Moscow, Idaho, home to the **University of Idaho. Northwestern Trailways,** NW 1002 Nye (334-1412), runs buses to Boise (1 per day; $39), Seattle (2 per day; $35), and Spokane (2 per day; $13). (Open Mon.-Fri. 8:30am-4:30pm.) Within the town itself, the two lines of **Pullman Transit,** 775 Guy St. (332-6535), mostly run between the WSU campus and the downtown area. (Operates Mon.-Fri. 6:50am-5:50pm. Fare 35¢, seniors and under 18 20¢.) **Evergreen Taxi Inc.** (332-7433) runs 24 hrs. **U-Save Car Rental,** S 1115 Grand Ave. (334-5195), rents cars for $25 per day, 20¢ per mi. after 100 mi. No minimum age (open Mon.-Fri. 8am-6pm, Sat. 8am-5pm).

Cleanse your clothes at **Betty's Brite and White,** N 1235 Grand Ave. (332-3477). A load of wash is 50¢, and a dryer costs 25¢ (open daily 7am-11pm).

The **Pullman Senior Center,** City Hall (332-1933) is available to seniors (open Mon.-Fri. 11am-4pm). **Pullman Memorial Hospital** is at NE 1125 Washington Ave. (332-2541). **Corner Drug Store,** on E Main St. at Kamiaken (334-1565). Useful phone numbers: **Rape Resource,** 332-4357, 24 hrs.; **Emergency,** 334-2131; **Ambulance and Police,** 332-2521. The **Post Office** (334-3212) is on Grand Ave. (open Mon.-Fri. 8:30am-5pm, Sat. 8:30-11:30am; **General Delivery ZIP Code:** 99163). **Area Code:** 509.

Accommodations and Camping The consistent stream of student travelers through Pullman fosters a decent selection of moderately priced, no-frills motels. Rooms are easy to find, except on home football weekends and during commencement (the first week of May). **Lodge Motel** (334-2511), SE 455 Paradise at Main, three blocks from the Greyhound station, is clean, comfortable, and occupies a great location. Try to get a room with a refrigerator, couch, and bathtub (open 7am-11pm, after hours ring night bell. Singles $20, doubles $26.) **The American Travel Inn Motel,** S. 515 Grand Ave. (334-3500) has 35 spacious rooms, with A/C, cable TV, and a pool. (Single $34. Doubles $37.) **Kamiak Butte Park,** 10 mi. north of Pullman on U.S. 27, offers 10 forested campsites with water and toilets for $5.

Food Ferdinand's (335-4014), on WSU campus next to the tennis courts in the Food Quality Bldg., makes everything with milk from WSU's dairy. Their Cougar Gold cheese ($10 for a 30-oz. tin) may be Pullman's biggest attraction. An ice cream cone ($1) and a large glass of milk (55¢) will do your body good. Sneak around back to their "observation room" and see cheese being made. (Open Mon.-Fri. 9:30am-4:30pm.) Motor through the drive-through or slide into a booth inside at **Cougar Country Drive-In,** N 760 Grand Ave. (332-7829), a 10-minute walk from downtown. This popular student hang-out offers burgers (from $1.40) and shakes (dozens of flavors, $1.40). Enjoy the best Chinese food in the area at the **Mandarin Wok Restaurant,** N 115 Grand Ave. (332-5863). Dinners can get expensive, but try the $4 lunch specials (main dish and soup). They have good vegetarian specials, too. (Open lunch Mon.-Fri. 11:30am-1pm. Dinner Mon.-Thurs. 5-9pm, Fri.-Sat. 5-9:30pm, Sun. 5-8:30pm.) **The Combine** (332-1774), 215 E Main St., in the Combine Mall, is the town's best coffee house with sandwiches ($2.75) and has a great space upstairs for relaxing. Live bands and poetry readings during the school year (open Mon.-Sat. 7am-midnight, Sun. 9am-10pm).

Sights and Entertainment Most of Pullman's enterprises lie along Main St. and Grand Ave. Grand runs north to south; Main travels west to east, terminating at the **Washington State University** campus. The campus has consumed the eastern half of town and is Pullman's primary pull. Call or stop by the **University Relations Office** in the French Administration Building, Room 442 (335-4527). The office offers guided tours of the 100-year-old campus every weekday at 1pm. Pick up a copy of *Museums and Collections at Washington State University.* All campus museums are free. If you follow the signs to the "Visitor Center," you'll end up at the **parking office** (335-9684), which may not be a bad thing; if you don't go there voluntarily to buy a $1 parking permit good for one day, you may have to go there with a parking ticket in your hand. For an outdoor attraction, head out from WSU to the end of Grimes Way to see **grizzly bears** and **bighorn sheep** (in separate pens!) up close. Good viewing hours are from 9am to 8pm, or call 335-1119 for information.

Pullman's surrounding gentle terrain and the broad vistas of Washington's **Palouse region** make the area ideal for exploration by bicycle or automobile. **Kamiak** and **Steptoe Buttes,** north of town off Rte. 27, both make enjoyable day trips. Pack a picnic lunch and head for the hills.

There are nearly as many bars as Cougar signs in the Palouse. Two local favorites are **Rico's,** E 200 Main (332-6566) and **Pete's Bar and Grill,** SE 1100 Johnson Ave. (334-4200). Near the end of August of each year, the **National Lentil Fesitival** burst onto the Pullman scene, with a parade, live music, and a 5-km fun run. The center piece of the festival remains the lentil food fair, showcasing lentil pancakes and lentil ice cream. The festival gained national recognition a few years back when it became the first engagement ever cancelled by Jerry Seinfeld. The festival remains a small-town tribute to a major player in the local economy (nearly all the lentils grown in the U.S. come from the Palouse). For more information, write National Lentil Festival, P.O. Box 424, Pullman WA 99163, or call 334-3565 or 800-365-6948.

Outdoors A glimpse of the **Blue Mountains** 25 mi. south of Pullman may spark a yearning for high, cool forests to replace the baking summer temperatures of the Palouse. A good approach is along Rte. 128 from the town of **Pomeroy,** 20 mi. southwest (but over 40 mi. by car, by U.S. 195 south to Clarkston, and U.S. 12 west) . This area, including the vast, remote **Wenaha-Tucannon Wilderness,** is administered by the **Pomeroy Ranger District** of Umatilla National Forest, Rte. 1, Box 53-F, Pomeroy, WA 99347 (843-1891; open Mon.-Fri. 7:45am-4:30pm). Information is also available at the **Walla Walla Ranger District** office at 1415 W Rose St, Walla Walla 98362 (522-6290; open Mon.-Fri. 7:45am-4:30pm.)

■■■ YAKIMA

With 300 days of sunshine per year, volcanic soil, and a fresh groundwater supply, Yakima and the Yakima Valley have earned the title "fruit bowl of the nation" by producing the most apples, mint, and hops (used to brew beer) of any U.S. county.

Unfortunately, things in downtown Yakima are not exactly peachy. Yakima has an extremely high crime rate. Visitors, especially women traveling alone, should keep this while planning their itineraries, although the areas frequented by tourists are not particularly dangerous. Most of the attractions of the Yakima Valley (other than two great restaurants) are wineries and orchards, and hence lie outside of the city proper.

Practical Information Yakima is on I-82, 145 mi. southeast of Seattle and 145 mi. northwest of Pendleton, OR. The Yakima Valley lies mostly southeast of Yakima, along I-82. Pick up one of the local handouts at the **Yakima Valley Visitor's and Convention Bureau,** 10 N 8th St. (575-1300), at E Yakima (open Mon.-Fri. 8am-5pm, Sat.-Sun. 9am-5pm), or ask a native for tips on good car and bike loops. A great path follows the Yakima River through the Yakima Greenway, a corridor of preserved land, from Robertson Landing (exit 34 off I-82) to Harlan Landing in Selah Grove (exit 31 off I-82).

Numbered streets are east of Front St., while numbered avenues are west of Front. **Yakima Transit** buses trace 10 convenient routes; there is also a downtown trolley (operates Mon.-Fri. 5:30am-6:30pm, Sat. 7am-6:30pm; fare 35¢, seniors 15¢, children 20¢). For specific route information, call 575-6175. **Greyhound,** 602 E Yakima (457-5131; open Mon.-Fri. 8am-5pm), stops in Yakima on the way to and from Seattle (2 per day, $22 one-way). There is no service from Yakima to Mt. Rainier. For a taxi, call **Diamond Cab,** 904 S 3rd St. (453-3113), open 24 hrs. It's worth renting a car to see the Blue Mountains when you can get a great deal at **Savemore Auto Rentals,** 615 S 1st St. (575-5400; $16 per day with 100 free mi.; 15¢ each additional mi. Must be 21.) For **senior information and assistance** call 454-5475 (Mon.-Fri. 8:30am-5pm). The **crisis line** is 575-4200 (24 hrs.) Seniors get a discount on all prescriptions at **Medicine Mart Downtown,** 306 E Yakima Ave. (248-9061; open Mon.-Fri. 9am-6pm, Sat. 9am-1pm). Yakima has two **hospitals,** both open 24 hrs.: **Yakima Valley Memorial,** 2811 Tieton Dr. (575-8000), and **St. Elizabeth Medical Center,** 110 S 9th Ave. (575-5000). In an **emergency,** call 911. The **police** are at 204 E B St. (575-6200). Rinse your rags at **K's Coin Laundry,** at the corner of N 6th and Fruitvale (452-5335; open daily 7am-9pm). The **post office** is at 205 W Washington Ave. on the corner of 6th Ave. (575-5823 or 575-5827; open Mon.-Fri. 8:30am-5pm; **General Delivery Zip Code:** 98903-9999). The **area code** is 509.

Accommodations and Food Finding a cheap bed in the fruit bowl of the nation is often difficult. The YWCA, 15 N Naches Ave. (248-7796), near the **Greyhound** station, serves women only. The nine single rooms (shared baths) are often full, so call ahead. You can only stay during the weekend if you arrived during the week ($10 per night, $65 per week, $200 per month; $25 key deposit). A good bet for clean and comfortable rooms is the **Red Apple Motel,** 416 N 1st St. (248-7150), where the friendly management does its best to keep out the bad apples. Stop in and inquire even if the "no vacancy" sign is on. (21 and over. A/C, cable TV, apple-shaped pool. Singles $32. Doubles $36. Prices slightly higher on weekends.) **Motel 6,** 1104 N 1st St. (454-0080), a 20-minute walk from downtown, is more reliable and professional than most of the string of budget motels along 1st St. A 1994 renovation left the rooms virtually brand new, and the pool provides welcome relief from the scorching Yakima heat. (Singles $32, Doubles $36.)

Yakima's few **campgrounds** are overcrowded and noisy. Less expensive, more pleasant campgrounds a lie on U.S. 12, about 30 mi. west of town on the way to Mt. Rainier. Sites with drinking water are $5; those without are free.

Santiago's, 111 E Yakima Ave. (453-1644), was named the best Mexican restaurant in the region by *Pacific Northwest* magazine in 1989. Santiago's dishes up their gourmet interpretations of classic Mexican dishes in a quiet, elegant setting. Try a filling burrito for lunch ($5.50). Their delicious salsa and chips (free with a meal or drinks at the bar) are almost better than their entrees ($9-10). (Open for lunch Mon.-Fri. 11am-2:20pm, Sat. noon-2:30pm; for dinner Mon.-Thurs. 5-10pm, Fri.-Sat. 5-

11pm, Sun. 5-9pm.) For a less adventurous meal, stop by **Kemper's,** 306 S 1st St. (453-6362), a gaudy purple burger joint where George Jetson would feel at home, for standard burgers (deluxe cheese $1.25) and intriguing shakes ($1). True junkies can order a sack of fries (serves 6, $3.10; open Mon.-Thurs. 9am-midnight, Fri.-Sat. 9am-12:30am, Sun. 9:30am-midnight). **Grant's Brewery Pub,** 32 N Front St. (575-2992), on the north end of the train station, is the only worthwhile attraction in Yakima. Call to arrange a tour of the microbrewery, the oldest in the Northwest (575-1900). Pint of Grant's Scottish Ale $2.50, of Yakima cider $3. Small lunch menu varies, but usually includes fish and chips. Live jazz, blues, or folk on weekends. (Open Mon.-Thurs. 11:30am-midnight, Fri.-Sat. 11:30am-1am, Sun. 11:30am-10pm.)

Sights and Events The *Yakima Valley Farm Products Guide,* distributed at the Visitor's Bureau and at regional hotels and stores, lists local fruit sellers and u-pick farms. Pounds of **peaches** often cost less here in season than do single peaches in other parts of the country. Fruit stands are common on the outskirts of town, particularly on 1st St. and near interstate interchanges. A good fruit stop for interstate travelers is the **Donald Fruit and Mercantile,** at 4461 Yakima Valley Hwy. in Wapato, 11 mi. southeast of Yakima, at exit 44 off I-82 (877-3115; open Memorial Day-Oct. 31 Mon.-Sat. 9am-6pm, Sun. 10am-6pm). **Johnson Orchards,** 4906 Summitview Ave. (966-7479), is the **u-pick farm** closest to town, specializing in **cherries** (June-July) and **apples** (Aug.-Nov.). A slightly longer jaunt can yield a wider range of u-pick produce, from **cantaloupes** to **jalapeno peppers.** Farms generally stay open in summer from 8am to 5pm, but check in the *Farm Products Guide* or call ahead to be sure. Wear gloves and sturdy shoes, and bring as many empty containers as you can. U-picks are good deals and fun, but you can save almost as much by buying directly from the farms themselves. **Snokist Growers,** 10 W Mead Ave. (457-8444), sells apples (open Mon.-Fri. 8am-5pm, Sat. 9am-2pm).

Toppenish, 19 mi. southeast of Yakima, is the jump-off town for the **Yakima Reservation.** The **Yakima Nation Cultural Center** (865-2800), 22 mi. south on U.S. 97 in Toppenish, offers cultural events about the 14 tribes that once inhabited the Yakima Valley. The museum concentrates on the oral tradition of the Yakima Natives, and includes a restaurant. ($4, students and seniors $2. Open Mon.-St. 9am-6pm, Sun. 10am-5pm.) The **Toppenish Powwow Rodeo and Pioneer Fair** (865-3262) occurs during the first weekend of July on Division Ave. in Toppenish, and features games, dancing, live music, a rodeo, and fair food (fair admission $2, rodeo $10). The **Central Washington State Fair** is held in Yakima in late September. The nine-day event includes agricultural displays, rodeos, big-name entertainers, and horse racing (call 248-7160 for more information).

■ NEAR YAKIMA: WINE COUNTRY

A television commercial a few years ago showed an incredulous Frenchman, glass of wine in hand, staring at a globe and wondering aloud: "Washington State?" At one time, wine connoisseurs would have turned up their *nez* at pedestrian Washington labels. But the state is now the second-largest producer of wine in the nation, and local vineyards have been garnering international acclaim.

The majority of wineries are situated in the Yakima, Walla Walla, and Columbia Valleys. These areas, just east of the Cascades, benefit from a rain shield that keeps the land naturally dry (and thus easily controlled by irrigation) with a mineral-rich soil bequeathed by ancient volcanoes. Sunlight produces grape sugars, and the cool nights protect acids. And, as almost every wine brochure points out, this region is at exactly the same latitude as Burgundy.

Wineries abound in the small towns between Yakima and the Tri-Cities. Almost all offer tours and tastings and many boast spectacular scenery that you don't have to be buzzed to appreciate. Common varieties of grape grown in the region are *Chardonnay, Riesling, Chenin Blanc, Gewürztraminer, Merlot, Semillon, Pinot Noir, Lemberger, Muscats,* and *Cabernet Sauvignon.* The following wineries are listed in geographical order leading from Yakima to the Tri-Cities (Pasco, Richland, and Kennewick; 88 mi. east of Yakima). Almost all are near I-82. Hours vary, but most are open 10am-5pm, some with shorter hours on Sunday; call ahead for hours or make an appointment. **Yakima:** Thurston Wolfe. **Wapato:** Staton Hills. **Zillah:** Zillah Oakes, Bonair, Hyatt Vineyards, Covey Run, Portteus, Horizon's Edge. **Granger/Sunnyside:** Eaton Hill, Stewart Vinyards, Tefft Cellars, Washington Hills Cellars, Tucker Cellars. **Grandview/Prosser:** Chateau Ste. Michelle, Yakima River Winery, Pontin Del Rosa, Hinzerling Winery, Chinook Wines, The Hogue Cellars. **Paterson (take Rte. 221 south from Prosser):** Columbia Crest. **Benton City:** Seth Ryan Winery, Oakwood Cellars, Kiona Vinyards, Blackwood Canyon. Useful guides are available free in visitor centers across the region. Of particular value are the *Winery Tour: Tri-Cities Area* and the *Yakima Valley Wine Tour,* overflowing with **maps.**

■■■ GRAND COULEE

Eighteen thousand years ago, the weather warmed, and a little glacier blocking a lake in Montana slowly melted and gave way. The resulting flood swept across eastern Washington, gouging out layers of loess and basalt to expose the granite below. The washout, believed to have occurred over a month, carved massive canyons called "coulees" out of a region now known as the **Channeled Scab Lands.** Geologists, who generally assume that changes in the earth's surface take place gradually, were at first baffled by the coulees, but the area is now acknowledged as a striking example of potential for violent, rapid geological change. The largest of the coulees is named, appropriately enough, Grand Coulee. The construction of the **Grand Coulee Dam** created the massive **Franklin D. Roosevelt Lake** and **Banks Lake.**

Practical Information and Sights The Dam and its surrounding cities, Grand Coulee, Coulee Dam, and Electric City, constitute the hub of the **Coulee Dam National Recreation Area,** stretching along the Columbia River from Banks Lake north to the Canadian border. The Dam was a local cure for the economic woes of the Great Depression. From 1934 to 1942, 7000 workers were employed in constructing this engineering marvel. Today the dam irrigates the previously parched Columbia River Basin and generates more power than any other hydroelectric plant in the United States.

The rotund **Visitors Arrival Center** (633-9265), on Rte. 155 just north of Grand Coulee, is full of exhibits about the construction, operation, and legacy of the Dam, area history, and recreational opportunities. During the day you can see a 15-minute film (it plays every ½-hr.) called "The Columbia: A Fountain of Life" featuring vintage 1930s footage of the dam's construction, accompanied by Woody Guthrie's music. This sentimental look at the Dam is not strongly based on hard fact. For a more in-depth look at the construction and operation of the Dam, watch the 50-minute film "The Grand Coulee Dam" each night at 7:30 and 8:45 (schedule changes with laser show). The visitors center also provides information on fishing and motorboating on the two enormous lakes, hiking and biking **trail maps,** camping guides, and self-guided tours through the power plants. (Open late-May-July daily 8:30am-11pm; Aug. 8:30am-10:30pm; Sept. 8:30am-9:30pm; Oct.-late May 9am-5pm.) Free guided tours of the dam leave from atop the monolith at the third power plant (station #5) on the half-hour every day in summer between 10am and 5pm. The dam is impressive from any angle, but standing on top is perhaps the most awe-inspiring viewpoint. Return to the dam when night falls during the summer to see a spectacular, multicolored **laser show** on the concrete walls, with a narration of the area's natural and human history (late May-late July 10pm, Aug. 9:30pm, Sept. 8:30pm; free).

The **Midway Mini Mart** in the Exxon station at 212 Midway (633-0230) is Grand Coulee's bus terminal. **Empire Bus Lines** runs to Spokane (1 per day, $18). Midway Mini Mart has schedule information and tickets inside. **C&B Cab** (633-3565) charges $4 for a trip from downtown Grand Coulee to the Dam.

T&T Bowling and Laundry, 412 Midway (633-2695), has $1 washers and 75¢ dryers (open daily 8am-8pm); you can bowl while waiting for laundry (open Fri.-Sun. 1-8pm; $1.50 per game). In an **emergency,** dial 911. To reach the **police,** call 633-1411. **Coulee Community Hospital** is found at 404 Fortuyn Rd. (633-1911). The **post office** is on Midway Ave. across from the Safeway (see below; open Mon.-Fri. 8:30am-4:45pm, Sat. 8:30-11:30am). The **General Delivery ZIP Code** is 99133.

Accommodations, Camping, and Food Spokane Way in Grand Coulee is the place for budget motels. **Center Lodge Motel,** 508 Spokane Way (633-0770), has plain rooms furnished for munchkins: low beds and tiny sinks. If you're lucky you might meet the owner, Wizard Max. (Singles $30, doubles $35 (rates slightly higher July-Aug.). The **Umbrella Motel,** 404 Spokane Way (633-1691), in Grand Coulee, is also a good deal: smaller rooms, bigger beds (singles $25, doubles $30).

Campers should head to **Spring Canyon** (633-9118), 2 mi. east of Grand Coulee off Rte. 174, in a gorgeous setting on the banks of Franklin D. Roosevelt Lake, with 89 sites and a beach area (sites $10, seniors with Golden Age Passport $5). Eight mi. south of the dam on Rte. 155 by the banks of Banks Lake, busy **Steamboat Rock State Park** (633-1304; write P.O. Box 370, Electric City, WA 99123 for summer reservations) has 168 sites set beneath dramatic rock walls (tentsites $11, RV hookup $16). Both campgrounds are wheelchair-accessible and have flush toilets. Steamboat Park has pay showers. Campsites east of Spring Canyon are accessible by boat.

Free camping areas line Rte. 155 south of Electric City; information is available at Steamboat Rock State Park. Pull onto any of several unmarked dirt roads that lead to Banks Lake, but keep an eye (and an ear) out for rattlesnakes. The **Coulee Playland Resort** (633-2671), in Electric City 4 mi. from the Dam, offers more amenities than the free campsites nearby, but you'll have to pay $17 for a tent site or $16 for an RV hookup. Call the State Parks summer hotline for general information (800-562-0990; open May 1-Labor Day Mon.-Fri. 8am-5pm).

New owners Pat and Emily pack 'em in for country cooking and great breakfasts at **New Flo's Place,** 316 Spokane Way (633-3216), in Grand Coulee, and the only thing on the menu over $5 is steak and eggs (open Mon.-Sat. 5:30am-2pm, Sun. 7am-noon). **That Italian Place** (633-1818), a mi. east of Grand Coulee on Rte. 174, serves inexpensive pizza and good calzones ($4) in a more elegant dining atmosphere (open daily 11am-10pm). Find a **Safeway** (633-2411) in Grand Coulee at 101 Midway Ave. (open daily 7am-midnight; winter 7am-10pm).

OREGON

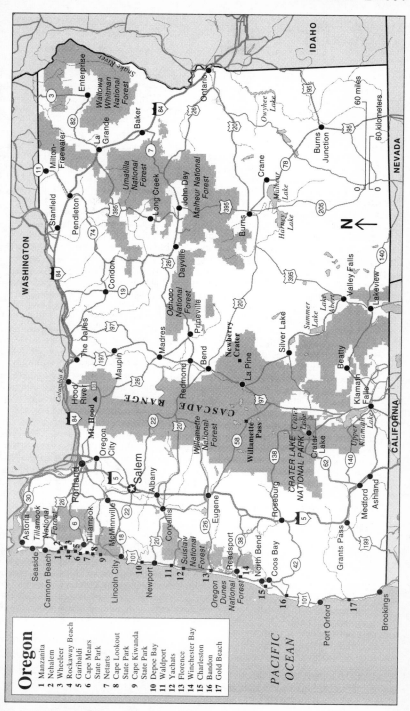

Oregon

1 Manzanita
2 Nehalem
3 Wheeler
4 Rockaway Beach
5 Garibaldi
6 Cape Mears
   State Park
7 Netarts
8 Cape Lookout
   State Park
9 Cape Kiwanda
   State Park
10 Depoe Bay
11 Waldport
12 Yachats
13 Florence
14 Winchester Bay
15 Charleston
16 Bandon
17 Gold Beach

Oregon

Have you ever wondered why, over 150 years ago, entire families liquidated their possessions, sank their life's fortunes into covered wagons, oxen, horses, flour, bacon, and small arms, and trekked 1500 mi. from the edge of civilization (Missouri) across harsh, boundless, rugged, hostile, and totally unfamiliar country just to get to Oregon? Once you visit Oregon, you'll realize why. Thousands of visitors are drawn each year by unparalleled natural beauty, including North America's deepest gorge and the towering Wallowa Mountains in the northeast; the vast, desolate Steens country in the southeast, solitary and begging for outdoor exploration; the forested peaks of the Cascade Range, with Crater Lake, Mt. Hood, and the Pacific Crest Trail; the awesome Columbia River Gorge; and the rugged coast with its brilliant tide pools. Hikers, cyclists, anglers, climbers, skiers, windsurfers, trekkers, and explorers all find themselves reveling in Oregon.

Oregon is divided by the Cascade Range. East of the Cascades, in the drier interior, ranchers, farmers, and loggers work the sparsely populated land. Rain is scarce, but winters are cold and snowy. This is a vast, open country. Visit one of America's best rodeos in Pendleton and poke around for dinosaur bones near John Day. Take up windsurfing at Hood River or ski Mt. Bachelor, home of the U.S. Ski Team. In the west, where trees are thick and rain frequent, get on the road and cycle south along U.S. 101 or through the Willamette Valley. Take your rod, have a mountain stream all to yourself for a while, and breakfast on some fresh fish. After exhausting yourself in the outdoors, enjoy world-class Shakespearean acting in Ashland, or hang out with college friends in diverse Eugene or tiny, laid-back Corvallis.

The state's social factionalism, however, runs deeper than mere east-west land divisions. There is a sharp gap between progressive, urban areas and provincial, rural districts. The traveler exploring the whole state should be aware that, though Oregon's reputation for tolerance is earned statewide, several tiny towns (none listed in this *Guide*) have attempted to pass local legislation based on prejudice and fear, excluding those they deem undesirable. These areas are known for bigoted, xenophobic attitudes. However, the views of a small, intolerant minority do not reflect the character of most Oregonians, on either the political Right or Left.

Portland, for example, is considered one of the most progressive cities in America. After exploring the outdoors, head here for a cheap stay at the hostel and treat yourself to great ethnic food. Take your meal to Washington Park and eat lunch over a view of the entire city. Wash up, iron your clothes, and get a dose of culture at the symphony, or catch a free outdoor jazz concert. Linger with friends until morning over Belgian beer or one of Portland's best microbrews. From Portland south along the coast, along the Willamette Valley, and across the Cascades, by the time you've explored this amazing state, you, too, will want to park the wagon and settle here.

PRACTICAL INFORMATION

Capital: Salem.
Visitors Information: State Tourist Office, 775 Summer St. NE, Salem 97310 (800-547-7842). **Oregon State Parks,** 1115 Commercial St. SE, Salem 97310-1001 (378-6305). **Department of Fish and Wildlife,** P.O. Box 59, Portland 97207 (229-5404). For a complete list of licensing restrictions and fees, send away for the *Sport Fishing Regulations, Ocean Salmon Sport Fishing Regulations, Game Bird Regulations,* and *Big Game Regulations.* **Oregon State Marine Board,** 435 Commercial St. NE, Salem 97310 (378-8587). **Statewide Road Conditions,** 889-3999.
State Motto: The Union. **Nickname:** Beaver State. **State Song:** "Oregon, My Oregon." **State Flower:** Oregon Grape. **State Animal:** Beaver. **State Fish:** Chinook Salmon.
Emergency: 911.

Time Zone: Mostly Pacific (1 hr. behind Mountain, 2 behind Central, 3 behind Eastern). A small southeastern section is Mountain (1 hr. ahead of Pacific, 1 hr. behind Central, 2 behind Eastern).
Postal Abbreviation: OR.
Drinking Age: 21.
Traffic Laws: Seatbelts required. Also, no self-serve gas stations, by law.
Area Code: 503.

■■■ PORTLAND

Portland is casual, tolerant, and idiosyncratic, the quietest and mellowest big city on the West Coast. Unhurried, uncongested, and without pretension, the downtown is spotless but clearly not designed to exclude, while the city wears its sketchier and industrial districts on its sleeve. A few short blocks north of the West Hills, Portland's upper-income residential district, huge factories puff away by the freight and rail yard. Building height is regulated to preserve views of the river, hills, and mountains and prevent a feeling of urban alienation. Like the old, popular poster depicting local tavern-owner "Bud" Clark in a trenchcoat flashing a public sculpture (he was shortly thereafter elected mayor), Portland has nothing to hide.

Funded by a one-percent tax on this new construction, Portland has fostered a growing body of outdoor sculpture and outdoor jazz concerts. Improvisational theaters are in constant production, and the Center for the Performing Arts is widely known for Shakespearean talent. This varied artistic scene is anchored by Portland's venerable Symphony Orchestra, the oldest in the country. Knowing that good beverages are essential to full enjoyment of any event, the city's first-rate flock of small breweries pump out barrels of some of the nation's finest ale. The stuffed interior of Powell's Books, the largest bookstore in the country, is full of casually-dressed people devouring the 500,000 volumes. The immense gardens of Washington Park overlook the city.

Though there is plenty to do in the city, Portlanders take full advantage of their area's natural endowments. Drawn by a common need to escape the urban, they are consummate hikers, bikers, and runners. The Willamette River and its wide park border the downtown, and dense forests at the city's edge cloak miles and miles of well-maintained hiking trails. Attractions within an easy drive of the city are still more satisfying, on any July day you can ski Mt. Hood in the morning, watch the sun drop into the Pacific Ocean from the cool sand of an empty beach, and still return to town in time to catch an outdoor jazz concert at the zoo.

PRACTICAL INFORMATION

Visitors Information: Portland/Oregon Visitors Association, 25 SW Salmon St. (222-2223 or 800-962-3700), at Front St., in the Two World Trade Center complex. From I-5, follow the signs for City Center. Distributes extensive information on the city and surrounding area. The free *Portland Book* is a magazine containing **maps,** general information, and historical trivia. Open Mon.-Fri. 8am-6:30pm, Sat. 8:30am-5pm, Sun. 10am-4pm; in winter Mon.-Fri. 8:30am-5pm, Sat. 9am-3pm.
Airport: Portland International Airport, 7000 NE Airport Way (335-1234). For transportation to and from the airport, see Orientation and Getting Around.
Portland Parks and Recreation, 1120 SW 5th Ave. #1302 (823-2223 or 823-5100). Open 8am-5pm.
Local Events Hotline: 233-3333. Recording.
Amtrak, 800 NW 6th Ave. (273-4866 or 800-872-7245, Union Station 273-4865), at Hoyt St. To: Seattle (4 per day, $23); Eugene (1 per day, $24); Spokane (1 per day, $67), Boise (1 per day, $83). Open daily 6:45am-6pm.
Greyhound, 550 NW 6th Ave. (800-231-2222) at Glisan. To: Seattle (12 per day; $19); Eugene (11 per day, $13); Spokane (5 per day, $42); Boise (3 per day, $61). Lockers available, $2 for 6 hrs. Ticket window daily open 5am-midnight. Station open 24 hrs.

Green Tortoise, 225-0310 for reservations. Pick-up point 616 SW College Ave. at 6th Ave. To: Seattle (Tues. and Sat., 4pm; $15) and San Francisco (Sun. and Thurs., 12:30pm; $39).

City Buses: Tri-Met, Customer Service Center, #1 Pioneer Courthouse Sq., 701 SW 6th Ave. (238-7433; open Mon.-Fri. 7:30am-5:30pm). Several 24-hr. recorded information numbers are available: how to use the Call-A-Bus information system (231-3199); fare information (231-3198); updates, changes, and weather-related problems (231-3197); TDD information (238-5811); senior and disabled services (238-4952); lost and found (238-4855, Mon.-Fri. 9am-5pm). Service generally 5am-midnight, reduced Sat.-Sun. Fare 95¢-$1.25, ages 7-18 70¢, over 65 and handicapped 45¢; no fare in Fareless Square downtown. All-day pass $3.25. All buses have bike racks (a $5 2-year permit can be obtained at an area bike store) and are wheelchair accessible. **MAX** (228-7246) is an efficient, light-rail train running between Gresham to the east and downtown, stopping at points along the way. **MAX** is also based at the Customer Service Center and has the same fares as Tri-Met. More MAX lines planned and under construction.

Taxi: Broadway Cab, 227-1234. **New Rose City Cab Co.,** 282-7707. Airport to downtown $21-24. Airport to hostel $18-20. 24 hrs.

Car Rental: Avis Rent-A-Car, at airport (800-331-1212 or 249-4950). $30 per day, unlimited free mi. $120 weekly rate. Must be 25 or older with credit card. **Practical Rent-A-Car,** 1315 NE Sandy Blvd. (224-8110). From $24 per day, 15¢ per mi. after 100 mi. Must be 21 or older with credit card.

AAA Automobile Club of Oregon, 600 SW Market St., 97201 (222-6734). Open Mon.-Fri. 8am-5pm.

Library: 801 SW 10th (248-5123). Open Mon.-Thurs. 10am-8pm, Fri-Sat 10am-5:30pm, Sun. 1am-5pm.

Tickets: Ticketmaster Information/Charge by Phone (224-4400), for Oregon and Washington events only.

Laundromat: Springtime Cleaners and Laundry, 2942 SE Hawthorne Blvd. (235-5080), across from the hostel. Wash $1, 10-min. dry 25¢. Open daily 8am-8:30pm.

Ski Conditions: Timberline, 222-2211. **Ski Bowl,** 222-2695. **Mt. Hood Meadows,** 227-7669.

Weather/Road Conditions: 222-6721.

Crisis Line: 223-6161. **Women's Crisis Line:** 235-5333. Both 24 hrs.

Women's Services: West Women's Hotel Shelter, 2010 NW Kearney St. (224-7718).

AIDS Hotline: 223-2437.

Gay and Lesbian Information: Phoenix Rising, 620 SW 5th #710 (223-8299). Counseling and referral for gays and lesbians. Open Mon.-Fri. 9am-5pm.

Senior Services: Senior Helpline, 248-3646, 8am-5pm. **Oregon Retired Persons' Pharmacy,** 9800 SW Nimbus Ave., Beaverton (646-0591 for orders, 646-3500 for information). Open Mon.-Fri. 8:30am-5pm, Sat. 9am-1pm.

Emergency: 911. **Police:** 1111 SW 2nd (230-2121) for non-emergency response, 823-4636 for information. **Fire:** 55 SW Ash (823-3700).

Post Office: 715 NW Hoyt St. (294-2300). **General Delivery ZIP Code:** 97208-9999. Open Mon.-Sat. 7am-6:30pm.

Area Code: 503.

ORIENTATION AND GETTING AROUND

Portland is in the northwest corner of Oregon, near where the Willamette (wi-LAM-it) River flows into the Columbia River. By car, Portland lies about 70 mi. from the Pacific Ocean, 635 mi. north of San Francisco, 170 mi. south of Seattle, and 430 mi. west of Boise. I-5 connects Portland with San Francisco and Seattle; I-84 follows the route of the Oregon Trail through the Columbia River Gorge toward Boise. West of Portland, U.S. 30 follows the Columbia downstream to Astoria, but U.S. 26 is the fastest way to reach the coast. I-405 runs just west of downtown to link I-5 with U.S. 30 and 26.

Portland is a major link for both **Amtrak** and **Greyhound.** Both the train and bus stations are inside Tri-Met's Fareless Square (see Practical Information).

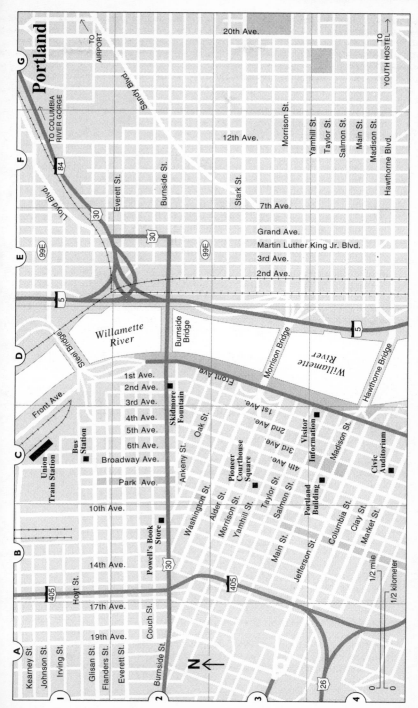

Portland

TO AIRPORT

TO COLUMBIA RIVER GORGE

TO YOUTH HOSTEL

Sandy Blvd.

Lloyd Blvd.

20th Ave.

12th Ave.

7th Ave.

Grand Ave.

Martin Luther King Jr. Blvd.

3rd Ave.

2nd Ave.

Morrison St.

Yamhill St.

Taylor St.

Salmon St.

Main St.

Madison St.

Hawthorne Blvd.

Everett St.

Burnside St.

Stark St.

Willamette River

Willamette River

Burnside Bridge

Morrison Bridge

Hawthorne Bridge

Steel Bridge

Front Ave.

Front Ave.

Skidmore Fountain

Oak St.

Ankeny St.

Washington St.

Alder St.

Morrison St.

Yamhill St.

Taylor St.

Salmon St.

1st Ave.

2nd Ave.

3rd Ave.

4th Ave.

Visitor Information

Madison St.

Civic Auditorium

Portland Building

Jefferson St.

Columbia St.

Clay St.

Market St.

Main St.

1st Ave.

2nd Ave.

3rd Ave.

4th Ave.

5th Ave.

6th Ave.

Broadway Ave.

Park Ave.

10th Ave.

14th Ave.

17th Ave.

19th Ave.

Bus Station

Union Train Station

Powell's Book Store

Pioneer Courthouse Square

Kearney St.

Johnson St.

Irving St.

Glisan St.

Flanders St.

Everett St.

Hoyt St.

Couch St.

Burnside St.

1/2 mile

1/2 kilometer

N

A B C D E F G

1 2 3 4

The cheapest way to reach downtown from **Portland International Airport** is to take Tri-Met bus #12 (a 45-min. ride), which arrives going south on SW 5th Ave. (95¢). **Raz Tranz** (246-3301 for taped information) provides an airport shuttle. It stops at most major hotels downtown. Fare $7, 6-12 $1. Taxis cost $21-24 to downtown.

Portland is divided into five districts. **Burnside St.** divides the city into north and south, while east and west are separated by the Willamette River. **Williams Ave.** cuts off a corner of the northeast sector, called simply "North." All street signs are labeled by their districts: N, NE, NW, SE, and SW. **Southwest Portland** is usually known as **downtown,** but also includes the southern end of historic Old Town and a slice of the wealthier West Hills. The center of downtown is the **transit mall** between SW 5th and 6th Ave., closed to all but pedestrian and bus traffic and the center of the extensive bus network. Almost all downtown streets are one-way. Parking is plentiful but expensive: meters are 75¢ per hour. The downtown is clean, pleasant, and seems designed for walking. Jaywalking is risky: cars will definitely stop for you, but the police may ticket you. Worse, jaywalking is a bit like using an umbrella: everyone will know you're not from Portland. Streets in **Northwest Portland** also offer metropolitan trendiness; NW 21st and NW 23rd are hot-spots for yuppie boutique shopping. **Southeast Portland** is a mixed neighborhood, with residential areas of all classes, parks, factories, and local businesses. The wide green quads and brick halls of beautiful Reed College lie at the core of Southeast Portland. The city's best ethnic restaurants line **Hawthorne Boulevard,** along with small cafes and theaters with a progressive, intellectual atmosphere supported by the college and Southeast residents. **North** and **Northeast Portland** are chiefly residential, punctuated by a few quiet, small parks. North Portland is the site of the University of Portland, a great place to watch good soccer matches. Drug traffickers base their operations in Northeast Portland; parts of the area are dangerous and there is almost no reason to go there. Just across the Burnside Bridge in lower NW is also a seedy neighborhood.

The award-winning **Tri-Met bus system** weaves together Portland's districts and suburbs. In the transit mall, 31 covered passenger shelters serve as both stops and information centers. Southbound buses pick up passengers along SW 5th Ave.; northbound passengers board on SW 6th Ave. Bus routes fall into seven regional service areas, each with its own individual "Lucky Charm": orange deer, yellow rose, green leaf, brown beaver, blue snow, red salmon, and purple rain. Shelters and buses are color-coded for their region. A few buses with black numbers on white backgrounds cross town north-south or east-west, ignoring color-coded boundaries.

Most of downtown, from NW Irving St. in the north to I-405 in the west and south and the Willamette River in the east, constitutes **"Fareless Square."** As the name suggests, the buses and MAX are free in this zone. For fares outside this zone, see Practical Information. Pick up monthly passes, **bus maps,** and schedules at the visitors center (see Practical Information), or at the Tri-Met Customer Assistance Office.

ACCOMMODATIONS AND CAMPING

Downtown is studded with Marriott-esque hotels, and the smaller motels are slowly raising their prices. But Portland is still great for the budget traveler, especially for those willing to share a room. The **Portland Hostel** (see below) is an old standby, and smaller establishments offer low-cost, pleasant overnight housing.

It's always wise to make reservations early, because places can fill in a flash, especially during the Rose Festival or a convention. Camping, though distant, is available in natural settings; no gravel-only RV spots around Portland.

Portland International Hostel (HI/AYH), 3031 SE Hawthorne Blvd. (236-3380), at 31st Ave. Take bus #14 (brown beaver). Cool people come to Portland; this is the place to meet them. Cheerful, clean, and crowded. Sleep inside or on the back porch when it's dry. Kitchen facilities; laundromat across the street. Fills up early in the summer (particularly the women's rooms), so make reservations (credit card required) or plan to arrive at 5pm to get one of the 12-15 beds saved for walk-ins. Don't miss the all-you-can-eat pancakes every morning (a paltry $1, and if you're lucky, a tub of free bagels lurks in the kitchen). Open daily 7:30-10am and 5-11pm. No curfew. $12, non-members $15.

Ondine, 1912 SW 6th Ave. (725-4336), between College and Hall St. Budget travel experience of a lifetime! Settle down among Portland State University students. 5 clean, spacious rooms, each with 2 twin beds. Linen and towels provided. Private bathrooms. Microwaves available; no kitchen. Laundry facilities. Excellent views down 6th St. from the window. The dormitory is in Fareless Square, so you can hop on the bus and be downtown in a minute. Parking nightmarish. Reservations required, 1-2 wks. in advance. Cash or out-of-state checks accepted. $20 for one person, $25 for two.

Aladdin Motor Inn, 8905 SW 30th St. (246-8241 or 800-292-4466; fax 244-1939), behind the shopping center at Barbur Blvd., a 10-min. ride from downtown. Take bus #12 (yellow rose) from 5th Ave., exit 294 from northbound I-5, or exit 296a and turn left off the exit if coming south. Stellar rooms with cable TV, free local calls, A/C, kitchens. Laundry facilities. Double-digit discount if you mention *Let's Go:* Singles $35-40. Doubles $39-49.

YWCA, 1111 SW 10th St. (223-6281). Women only. Situated on the park blocks, close to major sights. Clean and comparatively safe. Small rooms. Bathroom, shower, laundry and small kitchen down the hall. Hostel has 7 beds ($10); singles $19, with semi-private bath $24. $2 key deposit.

McMenamins Edgefield Hostel, 2126 SW Halsey St., Troutdale (669-8610 or 800-669-8610), 20 minutes east of Portland off I-84. Elegant, dark wood bunks and vast rooms. Two rooms, single-sex, each with 12 beds. Shower facilities down the hall; two claw-footed tubs. $18 per night. Save money by bringing food. Wine tasting, $1 movies, bar also on the property.

Ben Stark Hotel International Hostel, 1022 SW Stark St. (274-1223; fax 274-1033). Ascend the imposing, dark staircase to find 3 decent hostel rooms, mostly for international travelers. 12 beds. $15 per night, $12 in winter. No curfew; 24-hr. desk service. Fantastic location, just blocks from downtown. Call for reservations.

Midtown Motel, 1415 NE Sandy Blvd. (234-0316). Take bus #12, 19, or 20 from 6th Ave. Standard rooms fairly close to downtown with TV and A/C. Singles from $22. Doubles from $26.

Rose Manor Inn, 4546 SE McLoughlin Blvd. (236-4175 or 800-252-8333, fax 232-5201). Bus #19 (brown beaver). Clean, well-kept rooms 10 min. from downtown. Mention *Let's Go* to get the commercial rate: $31 for a single, $36 for a double.

Motel 6, 3104 SE Powell Blvd. (238-0600). Take bus #9 (brown beaver) from 5th Ave. What do you expect from a Motel 6? Singles $37. Doubles $44. Always full; call 3-4 days in advance. Wheelchair access.

Fourth Avenue Motel, 1889 SW 4th Ave. (226-7646). Just blocks from the center of town. Clean rooms with A/C and TV. Singles from $38. Doubles from $43.

Milo McIver State Park, 25 mi. southeast of Portland, off Rte. 211, 5 mi. west of the town of Estacada. Fish, swim, or bicycle along the Clackamas River. Hot showers, flush toilets. Sites $12.

Champoeg State Park, 8239 Champoeg Rd. NE (678-1251). Hike, bike, or visit the historic home and log cabin museum. Sites $16, "primitive" tent sites $9.

Ainsworth State Park, 37 mi. east of Portland off I-84, in the Columbia Gorge. Hot showers, flush toilets, and hiking trails. Sites with full hookup $13.

FOOD

Portland has more restaurants per capita than any other American city. It's a budget traveler's paradise. Great food is widely available at reasonable prices. You'll never get tired of eating out in Portland, and you'll also never go broke. Espresso bars are everywhere; some gas stations serve espresso.

Southwest

Panini, 620 SW 9th Ave. (224-6001). Pizza, pasta and espresso blend perfectly in this well-priced indoor/outdoor Italian panini bar. The cafe's small size belies its popularity; the line grows exponentially at noon. Delicious fresh calzones ($5.50). Extensive selection of Italian wines and beverages. Excellent service. Open Mon.-Fri. 7am-7pm, Sat. 8am-5pm.

Brasserie Montmartre, 626 SW Park Ave. (224-5552). Beautiful, fun, yet classy restaurant. Paper tablecloths and crayons and live jazz nightly offer diverse diversions for dull dates and similarly-awkward social situations. The playing cards tastefully scattered on the ceiling come courtesy of the nightly musician. Lunch entrees around $6, dinner $9 for chicken or steak. See and be seen as you sit in the bistro section: order the *Mange-á-trois,* a trio of *pâtés* ($5.75). Open Mon.-Thurs. 11:30am-2am, Fri. 11:30am-3am, Sat. 10am-3am, Sun. 10am-2am.

Western Culinary Institute Chef's Corner, 1239 SW Jefferson (242-2422). The testing ground for the cooking school's creative adventures. Students in tall white hats will whip up a delicious, cheap meal. Sandwiches ($3.50) are small; the best bet is a hearty, homemade loaf ($1) or a mouth-watering pastry. All lunches under $6. For breakfast, try the gourmet hash browns. Assorted breads $1 per loaf. Cheerful atmosphere. Open Mon. 8am-2:30pm, Tues.-Fri. 8am-6pm.

Kent's, 1022 SW Morrison St. (221-4508). Of the dozen *bento* (Japanese: "in a box") places that have opened recently in Portland, Kent's is *ichi-ban.* Chicken and vegetable bento $5. Pretend you're an on-the-go *sarariman* in need of refueling and guzzle the vitamin beverage Lipovitan-D ($1.75). Open Mon.-Sat. 11:30am-9pm.

Chang's Mongolian Grill, 1 SW 3rd St. (243-1991), at Burnside. After one of their all-you-can-eat lunches ($6) or dinners ($9), you, too, will feel fit to conquer most of Asia. Select your meal from a buffet of fresh vegetables, meat, and fish, mix your own sauce to taste, and watch your chef make a wild show of cooking it on a domed grill the size of a Volkswagen beetle. Rice and hot-and-sour soup included. Open daily 11:30am-2:30pm and 5-10pm.

Heathman Bakery & Pub, 901 SW Salmon St. (227-5700). The second home of many Portland State students. Delicious grill. Oven pizza ($8) and beer, beneath fish hangings. Consider the higher prices a tribute to the relaxed yet elegant ambience. Open Sun.-Fri. 7am-11pm, Sat. 8am-11pm.

Northwest

If the lunch or dinner hours find you prowling NW 21st and 23rd streets, you are, sadly, far from unique. In a city full of wonderful, cheap food, the trendy, expensive eating establishments are mobbed. **Food Front,** 2375 NW Thurman St. (223-6819), has a superb deli selection amid a wonderland of natural foods, fruit, and baked goods. Mmmm. (Open daily 9am-9pm, summer 9am-10pm.)

Kornblatt's, 628 NW 23rd Ave. (242-0055). Take bus #15 (red salmon), not the F train. A delicatessen haven for homesick New Yorkers. "What, you're not eating? You look so thin!" Endless menu includes matzoh ball soup ($3), knishes ($2.25), latkes ($3.50). Crowded, but worth the wait. Open Mon.-Fri. 7am-9pm, Sat. 7:30am-10pm, Sun. 7:30am-9pm

Shaker's Cafe, 1212 NW Glisan St. (221-0011). One of the best diners in Portland. Features blue corncakes ($4.75) and a wonderful staff. Great breakfasts. Open Mon.-Fri. 6:30am-3:30pm, Sat. 7:30am-3:30pm.

Fong Chong, 301 NW 4th Ave. (220-0235), in the heart of Chinatown. Portland's best dim sum (served daily 11am-3pm), but be prepared to move quickly as the harried waiters whiz by with their carts. Expect to spend about $7 for a dim sum meal. The ginger chicken is fabulous. Open daily 10:30am-10pm.

Old Town Pizza, 226 NW Davis St. (222-9999). Relax on a couch, or at a table, if you must be civilized, in this former whorehouse. Elegant wooden interior. Reported ghost sightings by the staff have not affected their pizza-crafting abilities (small cheese, $4.55). Grab a beer to complete the effect.

Garbonzo's, 2074 NW Lovejoy (227-4196), at 21st. Seek refuge from the mad boutique-seekers on the street at this quite, delicious falafel bar. The falafel pita ($3.50) is a superb choice. All items below $7. Open Sun.-Thurs. 11:30am-1:30am, Fri.-Sat. 11:30am-3am.

Southeast and Northeast

Southeast, especially along Hawthorne Blvd. and Belmont St., has tasty coffee and dessert places that become college hangouts as the night creeps on. **People's Food Store Co-op,** 3029 SE 21st, is the place for granola-seekers. Open daily 9am-9pm.

Montage, 301 SE Morrison St. (234-1324). Take bus #15 (brown beaver). Famed mac & cheese has exploded into a mac & cheese bar. What else could you want at 3am? Menu jammed with eclectic entrees, and the music jams as the night grows long. Open daily 6pm-4am.

Cafe Lena, 2239 SE Hawthorne Blvd. (238-7087). Take bus #5 (brown beaver). The Portland intelligentsia reverently frequent this cafe, known for its open-mike poetry every Tues. at 7:30pm. Live music accentuates an appetizing menu. Try the Birkenstock Submarine ($5). Breakfast served Tues.-Sun. until 4pm. Open Tues.-Sat. 7am-11pm, Sun. 8am-2pm. Closed Mondays.

Thanh Thao Restaurant, 4005 SE Hawthorne Blvd. (238-6232). You may walk out the door, you may leave Portland, but you'll be back eventually for a second helping of this fabulous Thai cuisine. The menu is long, ranging from cashew beef ($6.75) to eggplant in black bean sauce ($6.25). There's often a wait for dinner, so go early. Open Mon.-Fri. 11am-2:30pm and 5-10pm., Sat.-Sun. 11am-10pm.

Rimsky-Korsakoffee House, 707 SE 12th Ave. (232-2640). Take bus #15 (brown beaver) to 12th, then walk 2 blocks north. Big red Victorian house converted into a cozy salon. Bacchanalian frenzy of desserts. Cool. Ask for a mystery table. Live classical music nightly. Open Sun.-Thurs. 7pm-midnight, Fri.-Sat. 7pm-1am.

Pied Cow Coffeehouse, 3244 SE Belmont St. (230-4866). Take bus #15 (brown beaver) right to the front door. Bring that hot date from the hostel, 6 blocks away, for latte and chocolate cake by candlelight in the outdoor garden. When it starts raining, bring it inside the Victorian house, if you like. Open Tues.-Thurs. 6pm-midnight, Fri. 6pm-1am, Sat. 10am-1am, Sun. 10am-11pm.

Nicholas' Restaurant, 318 SE Grand Ave. (235-5123). Take bus #15 (brown beaver) across the bridge to Grand, then walk 5 blocks north. Don't let the unassuming facade fool you. Nicholas serves tantalizing Lebanese and Mediterranean food at incredibly inexpensive prices. Try Meezza ($6), the I'll-try-a-little-bit-of-everything platter, or the Phoenician pizza ($2). Open Mon.-Sat. 11am-6pm.

Cup & Saucer, 3566 SE Hawthorne Blvd. (236-6001). Take bus #5 (brown beaver). Friendly, frantic neighborhood restaurant famous for its pancakes ($3.25) and garden burgers ($4.25). Open Sun.-Wed. 7am-8pm, Thurs.-Sat. 7am-9pm.

PaRaDoX Palace Cafe, 3439 SE Belmont St. (232-7508). Homemade food, with healthy, clean ingredients. Bring a newspaper; it's acceptable to come alone. Quiet and uncrowded, a novelty in Southeast. Try the artichoke heart dip ($3.50), or their homemade granola with yogurt and fruit ($2.50).

Saigon Kitchen, 835 NE Broadway (281-3669). Take bus #9 (purple raindrops). Quite possibly the best Vietnamese restaurant in town. The *chazio* rolls ($3.50) are a perennial favorite. Most entrees $6-8. Open Mon.-Sat. 11am-10pm, Sun. noon-9pm.

SIGHTS AND ACTIVITIES

Shaded parks, magnificent gardens, innumerable museums and galleries, and bustling open-air markets beckon the city's tourists and residents alike. Catch the best of Portland's dizzying dramatic and visual arts scene on **"First Thursday"** (of each month), when the small galleries in the Southwest and Northwest all stay open until 9pm. For information contact the **Metropolitan Arts Commission,** 1120 SW 5th Ave. (823-5111), or go to the museum to latch onto a **Public Art Walking Tour** at the **Portland Art Museum,** 1219 SW Park Ave. (226-2811; museum open Tues.-Sat. 11am-5pm, Sun. 1-5pm).

Downtown

Portland's downtown area is centered on the pedestrian and bus **mall,** running north-south between 5th and 6th Ave., bounded on the north by W Burnside St. and on the south by SW Madison St. At 5th Ave. and Morrison St. sits **Pioneer Court-**

house, the original downtown landmark. The monument is still a Federal court-house and is the centerpiece for **Pioneer Courthouse Square,** 701 SW 6th Ave. (223-1613), which opened in 1983. Portland and area citizens purchased personal-ized bricks to support the construction of an amphitheater in the square for live jazz, folk, and ethnic music. During the summer (Tues. and Thurs. noon-1pm) the **Peanut Butter and Jam Sessions** draw thousands to enjoy the music.

Certainly the most controversial building in the downtown area is Michael Graves' postmodern **Portland Building** (823-4000), on the mall. The building's 1984 opening was attended by King Kong (full-sized and inflatable), perched on the roof. Since then, this amazing confection of pastel tile and concrete has been both praised to the stars and condemned as an overgrown jukebox. Make sure to visit the interior, which looks like something out of the film *Blade Runner.* On a niche out-side the building's second floor, *Portlandia* reaches down to crowds below. This immense bronze statue portrays the trident-bearing woman on the state seal, that to many looks like a man with breasts brandishing a large salad fork. The **Standard Insurance Center,** nearby at 900 SW 5th Ave., has also engendered controversy for the white marble sculpture out front, *The Quest.* The sculpture is more commonly known to locals as *Three Groins in the Fountain.* Also notable is the glass **Equita-ble Building,** at SW 6th and Alder, designed by Pietro Belluschi.

There is room for romping just west of the mall on the **South Park Blocks,** a series of cool, shaded parks down the middle of Park Ave., enclosed on the west by **Portland State University.** Facing the parks is the **Oregon Art Institute,** 1219 SW Park Ave. (226-2811), at Jefferson St., whousing the **Portland Art Museum, The Pacific Northwest College of Art** (226-4391), and the **Northwest Film Center** (221-1156), showing classics and offbeat flicks. Tickets are available at the box office, 921 SW Morrison. The Art Museum has a fine exhibit of Pacific Northwest Native American art, including masks, textiles, and sacred objects. International exhibits and local artists' works are interspersed (Open Tues.-Sept. 11am-5pm, Sun. 1-5pm. $4.50, seniors $3.50, students $2.50. 2 for 1 AAA discount. 1st Thurs. of each month free from 4-9pm. Thurs. seniors free.) **Museum After Hours** is a jazz and blues concert series (Oct.-April, 5:30-7:30pm). Popular with execs and the after-work crowd; $4.50.

Across the street, the **Oregon Historical Society Museum and Library,** 1200 SW Park Ave. (222-1741), stores photographs, artifacts, and records of Oregon's past 200 years. (Open Tues.-Sat. 10am-5pm., Sun. noon-5pm. $4.50, students $1; Thurs. seniors free; 1st Thurs. of every month all are free. 2 for 1 AAA discount.

Four separate theaters make up the **Portland Center for the Performing Arts,** 1111 SW Broadway (248-4496), on the eastern side of the Park Blocks. The **Schnitzer Concert Hall** (274-6564), a recently refurbished marble-and-granite won-der, shares the corner of SW Broadway and Main with the brick and glass **Winning-stad Theatre** (274-6566) and the **Intermediate Theater** (274-6566). The **Civic Auditorium,** 222 SW Clay St., is the Center's fourth component. The modern, glass-fronted, 3000-seat auditorium plays host to opera, ballet, and the occasional jazz or folk concert. Call the center for tickets and schedules.

The view from the Civic Auditorium includes Lawrence Halprin's Forecourt Foun-tain (better known as **Ira's Fountain**), Portland's most popular foot-soaking oasis. Retreat to a secluded niche behind the terraced waterfall at SW 3rd Ave. and Clay St.

Old Town, north of the mall, resounded a century ago with the clamor of sailors whose ships filled the ports. The district has been revived by the large-scale restora-tion of store fronts, new "old brick," polished iron and brass, and a bevy of recently opened shops and restaurants. A popular people-watching point, the **Skidmore Fountain,** at SW 1st Ave. and SW Ankeny St., marks the entrance to the quarter. Had the city accepted resident brewmeister Henry Weinhard's offer to run draft beer through the fountain, it would have been a truly cordial watering hole indeed (and much much popular). Old Town also marks the end of **Waterfront Park.** This 20-block-long swath of grass and flowers along the Willamette River provides locals with an excellent place to picnic, fish, stroll, and enjoy major community events.

The eclectic, festive **Saturday Market** (222-6072), 108 W Burnside St., under the Burnside Bridge between 1st and Front St., is overrun with street musicians, artists, craftspeople, chefs, and greengrocers clogging the largest open-air crafts market in the country. Many of these artists sell their work in the city's studios and galleries during the week. (March-Christmas Sat. 10am-5pm, Sun. 11am-4:30pm.)

The Portland Children's Museum, 3037 SW 2nd Ave. (823-2227), at Wood St. (take bus #1, 12, 40, 41, 43, 45, or 55, all yellow rose), schedules organized games, races, arts activities, and hands-on exhibits (open daily 9am-5pm; $3.50 for all ages). Tour the facilities and sample some local lager at the **Blitz Weinhard Brewing Co.,** 1133 W Burnside St. (222-4351).

West Hills

Less than 2 mi. west of downtown, the posh neighborhoods of West Hills form a manicured buffer zone between the soul-soothing parks and the turmoil of the city below. Take the animated "zoo bus" (#63) or drive up SW Broadway to Clay St. and turn right onto U.S. 26 (get off at zoo exit).

Washington Park and its nearby attractions are perhaps the most soulful sites in Portland. The park's gates are open daily 7am to 9pm in an attempt to close out lawless types. Definitely sketchy after 9pm, by day Washington Park is beautiful. The **Bristlecone Pine Trail** is wheelchair accessible. Obtain **maps** at the information stand near the parking lot of the arboretum, or refer to those posted on the windows. **Hoyt Arboretum,** 4000 SW Fairview Blvd. (228-8733 or 823-3655), at the crest of the hill above the other gardens, features 200 acres of trees and trails. Free nature walks (April-Nov. Sat.-Sun. at 2pm) last 60-90 min. and cover 1-2 mi. The 3-mi. **"Wildwood" Trail** connects the arboretum to the zoo in the south (trails open daily 6am-10pm; visitors center open daily 9am-3pm).

Below the Hoyt Arboretum lie many of Portland's most popular attractions. The **Rose Garden,** 400 SW Kingston Ave., on the way to the zoo entrance, is packed with flowers and a gorgeous place to stroll on a lazy day or cool evening. Clear days afford a spectacular view of the city and distant **Mount Hood.** Stunning views are also seen at the **Japanese Gardens,** 611 SW Kingston Ave., are spectacular and the most authentic outside Japan. Although they can be crowded on hot summer days, both are worth seeing. The **Washington Park Zoo,** 4001 SW Canyon Rd. (226-1561 or 226-7627), is renowned for its successful elephant-breeding and its scrupulous re-creation of natural habitats. Whimsical murals decorate the #63 "zoo" bus from the park to SW Morrison St. in the downtown mall. A miniature **railway** also connects the Washington Park gardens with the zoo (fare $2.50, seniors and ages 3-11 $1.75). The zoo features a number of interesting "animal talks" at various times on weekends and has a pet-the-animals **children's zoo.** If you have time, pull up a seat in the grassy amphitheater and watch as huge birds of prey swoop down over you in a demonstration. (Open summer daily 9:30am-6pm. $5.50, seniors $4, children $3.50. 2nd Tues. of each month free 3-6pm.) If you're around in late June, July, or August, grab your picnic basket, head to the Washington Park amphitheatre to catch **Your Zoo and All That Jazz** (234-9695 or 226-1561), a nine-week series of open-air jazz concerts (Wed. 7-9pm), free with zoo admission. **Rhythm and Zoo Concerts** (234-9694) also features a series of concerts (Thurs. 7-9pm), also free with admission.

The **World Forestry Center,** 4033 SW Canyon Rd. (228-1367), specializes in exhibits on Northwestern forestry and logging, although it is now taking on the entire world. The eavesdropping trees in *The Wizard of Oz* would have gone bonkers if they had to listen to the Forestry Center's "talking tree" all day long; the 70-ft. plant never shuts up. (Open daily 9am-5pm, Labor Day-Memorial Day 10am-5pm. $3, students $2.)

Northwest, North, and Northeast

From Washington Park, you have easy access to sprawling **Forest Park,** a favorite of hikers and bikers, the largest park completely within the confines of an American city. The park is laced with trails and scenic picnic areas. The **Pittock Mansion,**

3229 NW Pittock Dr. (823-3624), within Forest Park, was built by Henry L. Pittock, the founder of Portland's daily, the *Oregonian*. From the lawn of the 80-year-old French Renaissance mansion, you can take in a striking panorama of the city. To reach the mansion from downtown, take crosstown bus #20 (orange deer) to NW Barnes and W Burnside St., and walk ½ mi. up Pittock Ave. (open daily noon-4pm; $4, seniors $3.50, under 18 $1.50).

Downtown on the edge of the Northwest district is **Powell's City of Books,** 1005 W Burnside St. (228-4651 or 800-878-7323), a cavernous establishment with more volumes than any other bookstore in the U.S. (almost 500,000). If you tend to dawdle in bookstores, bring a sleeping bag and rations. It's so huge, they even provide a **map** of the store; you'll need it. The **Anne Hughes Coffee Room,** inside Powell's, is haven for such campers. Enjoy bagels and cookies and sip coffee while devouring any book, free. Powell's also features frequent poetry and fiction readings in the afternoons and an extensive travel section on Portland and the Northwest (open Mon.-Sat. 9am-11pm, Sun. 9am-9pm).

Farther out, geographically and spiritually, is the **Grotto,** 8840 NE Skidmore, at the Sanctuary of Our Sorrowful Mother, NE 85th Ave. and NE Sandy Blvd. (254-7371). Take bus #12 (purple rain). The splendid grounds are decorated with depictions of the Stations of the Cross and Mary's Seven Sorrows. You can behold the Columbia River Gorge from the cliff (open daily 9am-8pm, winter 9am-5:30pm; $1.50 to view the Gorge).

Some find shopping a religious experience in the **Nob Hill** district. Fashionable boutiques run from Burnside to Thurman St., between NW 21st and NW 24th Ave. Or make the pilgrimage to NE Broadway and 15th Ave. to shop at **Lloyd Center** (288-6073). Dodge crowbar-wielding thugs at the open-air ice-skating rink ($4, under 17 $3.50, skate rental $1.25). Also noteworthy is **Lloyd Cinema** (248-6938), an ultramodern multiplex equipped with comfortable contour chairs.

Southeast

Southeast Portland is largely a residential district with the exception of two colorful, eclectic strips. **Reed College,** 3203 SE Woodstock (771-1112), a small liberal arts school founded in 1909, sponsors many cultural events. The ivy-draped grounds, encompassing a lake and a state wildlife refuge, make up what is certainly one of the most attractive college campuses in the country. In 1968 this enclave of progressive politics became the first undergraduate college to open its own nuclear reactor. One-hour tours, geared mainly to prospective students, leave Eliot Hall #220, 3203 Woodstock Blvd. at SE 28th, twice per day during the school year (Mon.-Fri. 10am and 2pm; individual tours are available by appointment in summer. Call 777-7511). The **Chamber Music Northwest Summer Festival** (294-6400 or 223-3202) holds concerts at the college and at Catlin Gabel School in Portland every summer from late June to late July (Mon. and Thurs.-Sat. at 8pm). Concerts sell out quickly; call ahead for tickets ($12-17). Open, free rehearsals are held in July at the Reed College Commons; call 223-3202 for full details. Across the street, in the lovely **Crystal Springs Rhododendron Test Gardens,** SE 28th Ave., at Woodstock (take bus #19), 2500 rhododendrons surround a lake. The rhododendrons and azaleas are in full bloom April and May. (Open "in season" daily during daylight hours. $2 Thurs.-Mon. 10am-6pm, but gardens open daily 6am-9pm.)

The **Oregon Museum of Science and Industry (OMSI),** 1945 SE Water Ave. (228-2828), at SE Clay, will keep children and adults mystified with do-it-yourself science exhibits, including an earthquake-simulator chamber. The museum also houses an impressive OmniMax theater. (Open Thurs.-Fri 9:30am-9pm, Sat.-Wed. 9:30am-7pm; in winter Sat.-Wed. until 5:30pm. $7, seniors $6, 3-17 $4.50, same prices for the theater.) OMSI also features popular evening laser light shows set to bands like Metallica or Led Zeppelin. Times vary; check with the museum ($6.50). While at OMSI, check out the **USS Blueback,** the Navy's last diesel submarine. This amazing sub set a record by traversing the Pacific Ocean underwater, never failed to complete a mission, and starred in the 1990 hit film *The Hunt for Red October* (remember the sub that jumped nose-first out of the water?) The sub is now open for exploration. ($3.50.)

Hawthorne Boulevard (take bus #5 from downtown) has a high concentration of quiet cafes, antique shops, used book stores, and theaters useful for dodging the sporadic Portland rainfall. It ends at the bottom of **Mt. Tabor Park,** one of two city parks in the world on the site of an extinct volcano. Take bus #15 (brown beaver) from downtown, or hunt it down at SE 60th Ave. and Salmon St.

ENTERTAINMENT

Once an uncouth and rowdy port town, Portland manages to maintain an irreverent attitude. Many waterfront pubs have evolved into upscale bistros and French bakeries. Nightclubs cater to everyone from the casual college student to the hard-core rocker. Upon request, the Portland Oregon Visitors Association will hand over a thick packet outlining that month's events, but that's only part of it. Portland is a tower of culture and activity. The best shows will drain your pocket, but the community also sponsors many free and well-attended events. The best entertainment listings are in the Friday edition of the *Oregonian* and in a number of free handouts: *Willamette Week* (put out each evening and catering to students), the *Main Event, Clinton St. Quarterly, Just Out* (catering to gay and lesbian interests), the *Portland Guide,* and the *Downtowner* (friend of the upwardly mobile). All are available in restaurants downtown and in boxes on street corners.

Music

Portland has its share of good, formally presented concerts, but why bother with admission fees? You'll find the most exciting talent playing for free in various public facilities around the city. Call the Park Bureau (796-5193) for info, and check the *Oregonian* (see above) for **Brown Bag Concerts,** free public concerts given around the city in a six-week summer series (at noon during the week and Tues. evenings).

Oregon Symphony Orchestra plays a classical and pop series in Arlene Schnitzer Concert Hall, 1111 SW Broadway Ave. (800-228-7343 or 228-1353), Sept.-June. Tickets $8-46. "Symphony Sunday" afternoon concerts $18.

Portland Civic Auditorium, 222 SW Clay St. (248-4496). Attracts the usual hard rockin' arena acts, and a few jazz and opera stars. Ticket prices vary ($8-30).

Sack Lunch Concerts, 1422 SW 11th Ave. and Clay St. (222-2031), at the Old Church. Free organ concert every Wed. at noon during the summer.

Chamber Music Northwest performs summer concerts from late June through July at Reed College Commons, 3203 SE Woodstock Ave. (223-3202) at 28th St. Classical music Mon., Thurs., and Sat. at 8pm. $17, ages 7-14 $9. College students can call 294-6900 for a discount.

Lewis & Clark Summer Concert Series, Lewis and Clark College, 0615 SW Palatine Hill Rd. (768-7297), 8 mi. south of downtown. Free classical concerts throughout June and July. Wed. noon-1pm.

Starbucks by Starlight (223-1613), at Pioneer Courthouse Square, hosts blues and jazz during the summer. Mon. 5:30-7pm.

Peanut Butter and Jam Sessions (223-1613) at Pioneer Courthouse Square from noon to 1pm every Tues. and Thurs. during the summer months. A potpourri of rock, jazz, folk, and world music. Always jammed.

Aladdin Theatre, 3017 SE Milwaukee Ave. (233-1994). A popular arena for alternative music acts.

Theater

Theater in Portland covers all tastes, all ages, and all budgets while maintaining high quality. Tickets for most productions can be charged by phone at 244-4400, a Ticketmaster number for Oregon events only.

Portland Center Stage (274-6588), at the Intermediate Theater of **PCPA,** at SW Broadway and SW Main. Oct.-April 5-play series, featuring classics and modern adaptations. Tickets: Fri.-Sat. $11-33, Sun. and Tues.-Thurs. 10% higher. Half-price tickets sometimes available at the Intermediate Theater 1 hr. before showtime.

Portland Repertory Theater, 25 SW Salmon St. in Two World Trade Center, 3rd level (224-4491). 6 plays per year. Professionally done, professional prices. Tickets start at $24. A cheaper production, featuring local playwrights, shows at 815 NW 12th. Tickets range $15-19; this theatre has only 160 seats, so reserve early.

Oregon Ballet Theater (241-8316), at the Civic Auditorium at 3rd and Clay and at the Intermediate Theater at Main and Broadway. 4 Ballet productions per season, from Oct.-May. Tickets $10-60, student rush 1 hr. before Civic Auditorium shows.

Artists Repertory Theater (242-9403), SW 10th, on the 3rd floor of the YMCA. This small theater puts on excellent low-budget productions, many of them experimental. Tickets $15.

Portland State University Summer Festival Theater (229-4440), at the Lincoln Hall Auditorium. Schedules at the box office or the Portland Public Library. Performances mid-June to mid-July. Tickets $8-15.

Portland Civic Auditorium, 222 SW Clay St. (248-4496). Occasional big splashy opera and touring shows, now part of the Performing Arts Center. Tickets $25-55.

Cinema

Most of Portland's countless movie theaters have half-price days or matinee shows. With the help of the *Oregonian,* it's sometimes possible to dodge the $7.25 ticket price for the average "major motion picture."

Baghdad Theater and Pub, 3702 SE Hawthorne (230-0895). This magnificently renovated theater shows second run movies and boasts an excellent beer menu (pint $2.90). Evening shows are popular; have a pizza delivered to you right in the theater. Doors open 5pm, Sun. 2pm matinee; $1.

Mission Theatre and Pub, 1624 NW Glisan (223-4031). Serves excellent home-brewed ales, and delicious and unusual sandwiches ($4.50). Also offers showings of double features nightly. Relax in the balcony of this old moviehouse with a pitcher of Ruby, a fragrant raspberry ale named after one of Mick Jagger's creations. Showtimes 5:30, 8:05, 10:30pm.

Cinema 21, 616 NW 21st (223-4515). Clean, attractive cinema showing mostly documentary, independent, and foreign films. Highly acclaimed student haunt. Tickets $5; students, seniors, and matinee $2.

Clinton Street Theater, 2522 SE Clinton St. (238-8899). Classic and foreign films $3.50. Do the time-warp again with the *Rocky Horror Picture Show* every Sat. at midnight $4.

Laurelhurst Theater, 2735 E Burnside (232-5511). Multimedia theater, showing inexpensive, second-run films. $1.50-3 all seats.

Northwest Film Center, 1219 SW Park Ave. (221-1156), in the Berg Swann Auditorium at the Portland Art Museum. Mostly documentary films on little-known places and peoples. Films rotated every 3 months on a thematic basis. Tickets $5.50, seniors $4.50. Box office opens 30 min. before each show.

Sports

Contact the **Portland Park Bureau,** 1120 SW 5th Ave., #502 (796-5150 for indoor athletics or 823-5132 for outdoor recreation), for a complete guide to Portland's many parks, containing hiking and cycling trails and lakes for swimming and sailing. Forty parks have outdoor **tennis courts,** many lighted for night play and free to the public. The following parks have **swimming pools:** Columbia, Creston, Dishman, Grant, Mt. Scott, Montavilla, Peninsula, Pier, Wilson, and Sellwood (pool $1.50, children 50¢). Special facilities and programs are provided for seniors and people with disabilities (call 248-4328).

The **Coliseum,** 1401 N Wheeler (235-8771), is home to the **Trail Blazers** (231-8000), Oregon's beloved NBA team. The hard-working Blazers have won multiple Western Conference titles and become a regular fixture in post-season play. The **Winter Hawks** (238-6366) of the Western Hockey League also play at the Coliseum. Take bus #9 (brown beaver) or MAX. The **Beavers** play Class AAA baseball (and aspire to become Minnesota Twins) at Civic Stadium, 1844 SW Morrison St. (248-4345; tickets $4.50, seniors and students $2.50).

Clubs and Bars

The best clubs in Portland are the hardest ones to find. Neighborhood taverns and pubs may be hidden, but they have the most character and best music. The most accessible clubs from downtown are in Northwest Portland. Flyers advertising upcoming shows are always plastered on telephone poles around town. Pubs featuring McMenamin's microbrew have almost monopolized the brew scene; locals sometimes abscond to other bars simply for a taste of something new.

Produce Row Cafe, 204 SE Oak St. (232-8355). Bus #6 (red salmon) to SE Oak and SE Grand, then walk west along Oak toward the river. 28 beers on tap, 72 bottled domestic and imported beers, from China and Belgium and everywhere else. Backporch seating a big draw in summer. Ask one of the friendly bartenders to mix you the house special, a Black and Tan (Guinness Stout and Watney's, $3). Live music Sat.-Mon., $1 cover. Open Mon.-Fri. 11am-midnight or 1am, Sat. noon-1am, Sun. noon-midnight.

La Luna, 215 SE 9th Ave. (241-LUNA /-5862). Take bus #20 (purple raindrops), get off at 9th, walk 2 blocks south. Too much going on here: live concerts, 2 bars, 1 non-smoking coffee room, and an anything-goes Generation X crowd. All ages admitted (well, except to the bars). Call ahead for concert listings. The Living Room bar open Thurs.-Sat. 8pm-2:30am, concerts and special events other nights.

Panorama, 341 SW 10th St. (221-RAMA/ -7262) at Stark St. Cavernous dance floor studded with elegant Mediterranean pillars. Thriving club; friendly owner. Gay and straight; dance till you drop. Adjacent to Brigg and Boxx's. Thurs.-Sat. tech-notrance. Sun. retro-disco. Cover $3. Sundays 50¢ draft beer. Open Thurs. and Sun. 9pm-2:30am, Fri.-Sat. 9pm-4am.

Bridgeport Brew Pub, 1313 NW Marshall (241-7179). The zenith of beer and pizza joints. The pizza is locally famous, the atmosphere as relaxed as you can get without using controlled substances. Lots o' space for lots o' people. Open Mon.-Thurs. 2-11pm, Fri. 2pm-midnight, Sat. noon-midnight, Sun. 1-9pm. Much-acclaimed homebrew and great pizza in a old, wood-beamed former rope factory that actually fills on weekend nights.

Mission Theater and Pub, 1624 NW Glisan (223-4031). Serves excellent home-brewed ales and delicious and unusual sandwiches ($4.50). Also offers free showings of double features (everything from Bogart to Allen) twice nightly. Relax in the balcony of this old moviehouse with a pitcher of Ruby, a fragrant raspberry ale named after one of Mick Jagger's creations ($1.50 glass, $7 pitcher). Open daily 5pm-1am.

East Avenue Tavern, 727 E Burnside St. (236-6900). Bus #12, 19, or 20 (all brown beaver). Bluegrass and flok bands send out Irish vibes. Upbeat live performances. Cover Thurs.-Sun. $2-5. Guiness on tap, $2.75 per pint. Open Mon.-Sat. noon-1:30am.

Dot's Cafe, 2612 SE Clinton St. (235-0203). Take bus #4 (brown beaver) to 26th, and walk 3 blocks south. The place burned down in 1993, but now Dot's business is all aflame. Can be crowded and smoky. Monkey madness on all sides. Pool tables. Popular with Reed College students and their bohemian brethren. Open daily 9am-2am.

Lotus Card Room and Cafe, 932 SW 3rd Ave. (227-6185), at SW Salmon St. 20-something crowd laps up 80s wave music each Thurs. Techno, house, and hip-hop attract a collegiate crowd on Fri. and Sat. Disco on Sun. is the grooviest dance experience in the city. Lots of food. Dance floor open Wed.-Sun. 10pm-2am. Cover $3, Thurs.-Sun. $1. Open daily 7am-2am.

Gypsy, 625 NW 21st Ave. (796-1859). Take bus #17 (red salmon). Fabulous David Lynch-ian decor wasted on unmistakably American crowd. Bring your cool friends for moral support. Groovy hour Mon.-Fri. 4-7pm features beer for $1.50 and appetizers at ½ price. Open Mon.-Fri. 9am-2am, Sat.-Sun. 8am-2am.

The Laurelhurst Public House, 2958 NE Glisan (232-1504). Take Bus #19. Welcoming, relaxed atmosphere. When the local acoustic acts tune-up each night, forget your conversation and just jam. Free pool Sun. Features Sierra Nevada: glass $1.65, pint $3. Cover $1, Fri.-Sat. $2. Open daily 9am-2:30am.

Barley Mill Pub, 1629 SE Hawthorne (231-1492). A colorful, slightly smoky temple to Jerry Garcia and his entourage. Fantastic murals and random decorations. McMenamin's beer. Open Mon.-Sat. 11am-1am, Sun. 11:30am-midnight.

Red Sea, 318 W 3rd Ave. (241-5450). Harry Belafonte's happy hunting ground. Calypso galore. Live reggae on Thurs. Bring an escort; seedy area. Cover $2-3. Henry Weinhard's $2.24. Vicious carding. Open Thurs. 9pm-1:30am, Fri.-Sat. 9pm-2:30am.

X-Ray Cafe, 214 W Burnside St. (721-0115). The romping ground for generation X. Cheap meals, loud music. Cover $3-5. Open Tues.-Sun. noon-midnight.

Caribou Cafe, 503 W Burnside St. (227-0245). Two caribou from 1927 oversee this bar. 125 drinks for $1 each(!!!) from Thurs. through Sat. Eclectic clientele (businesspeople to drag queens) and varied music (Rolling Stones to Porno for Pyros) make for one loud and crowded fiesta. Private security always on hand. Cover Sun.-Wed. $1, Thurs.-Sat. $2. Open Mon.-Sat. 11:30am-1:30pm.

Embers, 110 NW Broadway (222-3082). Hot dancing until 2:30am. Mostly gay clientele. Beer 75¢, well drinks $2.50.Open Sun.-Thurs. 11am-2:30am, Fri.-Sat. 11am-4am.

The Space Room, 4800 SE Hawthorne Blvd. (235-8303). Take bus #14 (brown beaver). Judy Jetson smoked way too many cigarettes inside this space-age joint. The cutting-edge, neighborhood crowd contemplate the vintage-clothing possibilities. Under 21? Don't bother. One bloody mary ($3) will put you over the edge. Open daily 6am-2:30am.

Brigg and Boxx's Video Bar, 1035 SW Stark (226-4171). Male-dominated, primarily gay bar with dancing beginning at 9pm. Boxx open daily, noon-2:30am, Brigg open daily 8am-2:30am.

Key Largo, 31 NW 1st Ave. (223-9919). Airy, tropical atmosphere. Dance out on the patio when it's not raining. Variety of local and national bands. Rock, rhythm & blues, zydeco, jazz. Yuppie enclave. Cover $3-7, depending on the band. Poetry on Sunday evenings. Open Mon.-Sat. 11am-2:30am, Sun. 11am-10pm.

EVENTS

Cinco de Mayo Festival (823-4000 or 292-5752). May 5th. Mexican Independence Day celebration complete with fiery food, entertainment, and crafts at SW Front and Salmon.

Rose Festival (call 248-7923 for recording, 277-2681 at NW 2nd Ave. for offices). First 3 weeks of June. U.S. Navy sailors flood the street while the city decks itself in all its finery for Portland's premier summer event. Waterfront concerts, art festivals, celebrity entertainment, auto racing, parades, an air show, Navy ships, and the largest children's parade in the world (the Rose Junior Parade). Great during the day. At night, women should exercise caution; locals have dubbed this event the "rape festival." Many of the events require tickets; call 224-4400 to order.

Waterfront Blues Festival (282-0555). Early July. Outrageously good. International celebrities and some of the finest regional blues artists participate in this 3-day event.

Oregon Brewers Festival (281-2437 or 241-7179). Mid-July. The continent's largest gathering of independent brewers makes for one incredible party at Waterfront Park. Brew expensive; admission charged.

Mt. Hood Festival of Jazz, first weekend in Aug. at Mt. Hood Community College in Gresham (666-3810). Overpriced (tickets start at $25 per night), but this is the premier jazz festival of the Pacific Northwest, with 20 hrs. of music over the course of a weekend. Wynton Marsalis and the late Stan Getz have been regulars in the past. Reserve tickets well in advance. Write Mt. Hood Festival of Jazz, P.O. Box 696, Gresham 97030. To reach the festival, take I-84 to Wood Village-Gresham exit and follow the signs, or follow the crowd on MAX to the end of the line.

Artquake (227-2787). Labor Day weekend. Music, mime, food, and neo-situationist hoopla in and around Pioneer Courthouse Square.

Portland Marathon (226-1111). Late-Sept. Feeling in shape? Join the thousands who run this 26.2-mi. race. Many shorter runs and walks are also held.

■ NEAR PORTLAND

Many Portland residents wouldn't consider relocating—not only is the city a cultural giant, but it is also near some of America's most fantastic natural attractions. The burned-out, truncated shell of Mt. St. Helens is a short drive north into Washington State; the Columbia River Gorge, full of colorful windsurfers and breathtaking views, is only a 30-minute drive up I-84; Mt. Hood, year-round host to skiers, is one and a half hours away. You can retrace the footsteps of early pioneers east along the Oregon Trail in the Mount Hood National Forest or in the Gorge. West of Portland, a two-hour jaunt west will take you to the rugged rocks and cliffs lining the Pacific, and a slightly longer drive north or south will land you in such coastal towns as Cannon Beach, Seaside, Astoria, or Tillamook.

OREGON CITY

Take bus #32, 33, or 35 (all green leaf) to Oregon City from 5th Ave. in downtown Portland, or drive approximately 20 minutes south down Rte. 43, Rte. 99E, or I-205. The first capital of the Oregon Territory, the town is expanding its "Interpretive Center" to a full-scale **museum,** equipped with artifacts and photographs and featuring a film documenting the pioneers' journey to Oregon. Could be good; due to open in December 1994, at 1725 Washington St. (657-9336; $4, seniors and under-12 discounts.

SAUVIE ISLAND

Twenty minutes from downtown Portland, Sauvie Island is a peaceful rural hideaway at the confluence of the Columbia and Willamette Rivers. The island offers great views of the city from its vast sandy stretches. On winter mornings, eagles and geese congregate along the roads, and in spring and summer, berries are everywhere. For many Portlanders, a summer trip to the island's **u-pick farms** (family operations announced by hand-lettered signs along the roads) is an annual tradition. The island's beaches are another star attraction, and understandably so, since at night many visitors feel free to swim without a suit. **Oak Island,** at the North East end, is the best beach area. In light of all these possibilities, it might be an easy thing to forget yourself; don't forget ample supplies of gas and drinking water. Gas is unavailable on the island, and water can only be found in private campgrounds.

MOUNT HOOD

Magnificent, glacier-topped Mt. Hood is at the junction of U.S. 26 and Rte. 35, 90 min. east of Portland and 1 hr. from Hood River. The 11,235-ft. active volcano doesn't steam, has no crater, and seems dormant because open vents keep internal pressure low. Skiers can take advantage of the winter trails at three great ski areas: Timberline, Mt. Hood Ski Bowl, and Mt. Hood Meadows. All three offer night skiing. **Timberline** (272-3311 or 231-7979) is the only North American resort to offer summer skiing. Rental of skis, poles, and boots runs $19 per day ($13 for children) and lift tickets generally cost around $26 per day ($25 in the summer). Snowboard rental $32 with boots, $24 without. **Mount Hood Ski Bowl,** 87000 E Highway 26, in Government Camp, 2 mi. west of the junction with Hwy. 35, rents ski equipment for $16, juniors $10. Lift tickets are $22, $15 for juniors. (Night skiing Sun.-Thurs. 4:30 - 10pm, and Fri.-Sat. 4-11pm.) **Mount Hood Meadows** (337-2222), 11 mi. west on Hwy. 35, has ski equipment rentals for $16, juniors $14; lift tickets are $31, juniors $30 (night skiing Wed.-Sat. 4-10pm-Sun. 4-7pm. All three areas offer ski lessons averaging $35 per hour or $15 per person for group lessons. Special packages including rental, lesson, and lift tickets are often available at a much-reduced price; call for current deals. Timberline's **Magic Mile** lift carries nonskiers up above the clouds for spectacular views of the Cascades ($6, children $3).

For adventurers who wish to tackle the mountain on foot, **Timberline Mountain Guides**, P.O. Box 23214, Portland (636-7704), offers mountain, snow, and ice climbing courses led by experts. Climbs last one to three days, with one-day trips starting at $80. Even if you decide to ski at Ski Bowl or Mt. Hood Meadows, turn up the 6-mi. road just off **Government Camp** to the Depression-era **Timberline Lodge** (800-547-1406, 231-5400 from Portland), site of the outdoor filming of Stanley Kubrick's *The Shining*. The road to the lodge also offers arresting views of the valley below, and Mt. Jefferson and the Three Sisters to the south. Next door is the Wy'east **Day Lodge**, where skiers can store equipment without staying overnight, and the **Wy'east Kitchen,** a cafeteria alternative to Timberline's expensive dining (entrees $2-6; open daily 6:30am-4pm in summer; 7:30am-4pm in winter; 7:30-10pm when there is night skiing). Ski Bowl runs an alpine slide ($5 per slide), a go-kart course, and groomed mountain-bicycle trails. In addition, **hiking** trails circle the mountain. The most popular is **Mirror Lake,** a 4-mi. loop open June through October. Start from the parking lot off U.S. 26, 1 mi. west of Government Camp. For permits and more information, drop in at the well-stocked **Mt. Hood Visitors Information Center,** 65000 E U.S. 26., Welches 97067 (622-4822, 30 min. west of Mt. Hood). The **Mt. Hood Village** (622-4011, 253-9445 from Portland, or 800-255-3069) also contains pleasant, shaded campgrounds (tents $16, RV $18, full hookup $21. Full facilities, including a heated pool). Call the **Hood River Ranger Station,** 67805 Rte. 35, Parkdok 97041 (352-6002), for information about the area. Camping spots in the Mt. Hood National Forest cluster near the junction of U.S. 26 and Rte. 35. Less than 1 mi. below Timberline is **Alpine,** accessible only in the summer. Choose one of 16 sites, all with water and toilets. Reservations are essential (the U.S. Ski Team is fond of Alpine), and should be made through Timberline at 800-547-1406, or 231-5400 in Portland ($7 per night). **Trillin Lake Campground,** just east of the Timberline turn-off on U.S. 26, has scenic trails, campgrounds. and 55 sites with water and toilets. 10 mi. further east on Rte. 35 are **Sherwood and Robinwood Campgrounds,** where sites are $10 per night. All Mt. Hood National Forest campground reservations should be made by calling 800-280-CAMP.

COLUMBIA RIVER GORGE

Only an hour from Portland, close enough for a great daytrip, the spectacular Columbia Gorge stretches 20 to 90 mi. east of Portland. Here the Columbia carves a canyon 1000 ft. deep through rumpled hills and sheer, rocky cliffs. Mt. Hood and Mt. Adams loom nearby while waterfalls from streams plunge hundreds of feet over cliffs toward the Columbia. Both banks are heavily forested, although eastward the trees give way to drier grasslands and farms. Some of man's most immense structures, the dams that harness electricity from the Columbia, look puny compared to the sheer expanse and depth of the Gorge. Free publications, including *Gorge Vistas, The Visitor's Guide to Gorge Fun,* and for windsurfers, *Northwest Sailboard,* offer excellent information on local sights, camping, accommodations, history, and events. Also useful for backpackers is the $2 USFS **map** of the Columbia Wilderness. These are available at visitor centers and chambers of commerce along the Gorge.

Practical Information To follow the Gorge, which divides Oregon and Washington, take I-84 20 mi. east to the Troutdale exit onto the **Columbia River Scenic Highway.** Bring a camera. This road follows the crest of the gorge walls and affords unforgettable views. The largest town in the Gorge is **Hood River,** at the junction of I-84 and Rte. 35, leading south to Mt. Hood. Take **Greyhound** from Portland ($11) or Seattle ($30); the **station** (386-1212) is at 1203 B Ave. in Hood River. **Amtrak** also runs trains from Portland for less than $15. Summer winds sweeping through the Gorge make Hood River a well-known **windsurfing** mecca. The town is packed with board-rental shops. Boards are available for a range of abilities; contact the **Hood River County Chamber of Commerce** (386-2000 or 800-366-3530) in

Port Marine Park for information on Hood River (open Mon.-Thurs. 9am-5pm; mid-April-mid-Oct. Fri. 9am-4pm, Sat.-Sun. 10am-4pm; mid-Oct.-mid-April Fri. 9am-5pm). It is the center for information on **mountain biking** and **hiking** trails. **Discover Bicycles,** at 1020 Wasco St. (386-4820) rents mountain bikes starting at $3 per hr., $15 per day (open daily Mon.-Sat. 9am-8pm, Sun. 9am-5pm).

19 mi. east of Hood River on I-84, **The Dalles** (DALZ) was the last stop on the agonizing Oregon Trail. Lewis and Clark camped here at Fort Rock on Bargeway Rd. in 1805. French trappers named the area *Le Dalle* (the trough) after the rapids around that section of the river. **Fort Dalles** (296-4547), at 14th and Garrison, a historical museum housed in the original 1856 surgeon's quarters, displays memorabilia of these historical events. For a free **map** including a walking tour, go to the **Convention and Visitor's Bureau,** 404 W 2nd St. (296-6616 or 800-255-3385). The visitors center at the **Dalles Lock and Dam** (296-1181) offers free public viewing of its fish ladders (tours every half hour) and a train tour around the facilities (open June-Labor Day daily 9am-5pm).

Accommodations and Camping   Cheap lodging is available at the **Bingen School Inn Hostel,** 3 min. away across the Columbia in White Salmon, WA (50¢ toll bridge) at Humbolt and Cedar St. (509-493-3363). Sleep, this time without guilt, in front of the blackboards in this converted old schoolhouse. 42 hostel beds ($11 per night) and 18 private bedrooms ($29 per night). The wonderful, outdoors-obsessed staff is full of suggestions for activities. **Mountain bikes** ($15 per day) and **surfboards** ($30 per day) are available for rent. Campgrounds also surround Hood River; the **Wind Ranch Camping & Lodging,** a virtual windsurfers' colony, has tent space ($8 per night) at the base of a steep hill. Electricity ($2), coffee, valet parking, and all other amenities are available.

Sights and Outdoors   The magnificent power of the Columbia's water and 30mph winds make Hood River a **windsurfing** paradise. Vibrantly colored sailboards decorate the Gorge, engaging in obsessive, zany competitions like the "Killer Loop Classic." Sublime **hiking** experiences and **views** are accessible all the way down the Columbia River Scenic Hwy. Trails usually begin at the Scenic Hwy. Four great trails include the shorter **Horsetail** and **Oneonta Trails,** the medium-length **Wyeth Trail** near the hamlet of Wyeth, and the long (13 mi.) but incredible **Eagle Creek Trail,** literally chiseled into cliffs high above Eagle Creek, passing four waterfalls before joining the Pacific Crest Trail. For information on trails and a friendly earful of local lore, call Columbia Gorge National Scenic Area Headquarters (386-2333).

About 20 **waterfalls** line the Scenic Hwy. At **Latourell Falls** you can clamber over jagged black rock to stand behind a plume of falling spray. 6 mi. farther, take the steep trail to the top of the beautiful, crowded **Multnomah Falls** (Exit 31 off I-84). The falls crash 620 ft. into a tiny pool at the bottom. Wading is allowed in the pool, but be aware of the sometimes sharp, slippery rocks along the bottom. Because it's the highest, it's the one tourists visit. It shouldn't be missed, but those who push up the trail will be rewarded and left alone with a series of smaller but spectacular waterfalls. Hikers can follow other paths into **Mt. Hood National Forest;** the **information center** at the base of Multnomah Falls is full of alternative suggestions.

The famous **Vista House** (695-2240), completed in 1918 in Crown Point State Park as a memorial to Oregon's pioneers, is now a visitors center. The house hangs on the edge of an outcropping high above the river. A trail leaves the road a few yards down from the house, ending in a secluded view of both the house and the gorge. Reach Crown Point from the Scenic Hwy. or from exit 22 eastbound off I-84.

44 mi. east of Portland is the oldest of the Columbia River hydroelectric projects, the **Bonneville Dam** (Exit 40 off I-84). Woody Guthrie was working for the Bonneville Power Co. when he wrote "Roll On Columbia," a salute to river development: "Your power is turning our darkness to dawn, so roll on Columbia, roll on." Across the river on the Washington side, the **Bradford Island Visitors Center** (374-8820) shows tourists a fish ladder, the dam's powerhouse, and the generator room. Also

on this side of the river, don't miss dramatic **Beacon Rock,** the 848-ft.-high neck of an old volcano, the largest monolith in the U.S.

At the **Cascade Locks** (Exit 44 off I-84), 4 mi. past Bonneville, take a two-hour, narrated **sternwheeler ride** aboard the *Columbia Gorge* (374-8427, in Portland 223-3928), a replica of the sternwheelers that used to ply the Columbia and Willamette Rivers (2-hr. rides, 3 per day; fare $12, seniors $11, children $6).

You can also cross the Columbia over the **Bridge of the Gods** (75¢ toll) here. The bridge was constructed at the site where, according to Native legend, a natural bridge once stood. It collapsed when the two warrior gods, Klickitat (Mt. Adams) and Wy'east (Mt. Hood), erupted in a fight for the honor of Sleeping Beauty Mountain. (Mt. Adams and Sleeping Beauty are in Washington, north of the town of White Salmon. Mt. Adams, at 12,307 ft., is easy to spot; Sleeping Beauty is 4568 ft. high). The bridge seems fragile even now; if you drive slowly, you can see through the bridge grating to the river below. Just across the bridge in Washington is the town of **Carson,** where visitors can go to the **Hot Mineral Springs Resort** (509-427-8292) and relax in a hot mineral bath ($8 for a bath and wrap).

From the Gorge, take **Rte. 35** south from Hood River, through apple, pear, and cherry orchards. The drive is beautiful in April when the trees are in bloom. Mt. Hood lies ahead, while Mt. Adams looms in the rearview mirror. The Mt. Hood loop offers wine-tasting during the summer and fall at the area's vineyards. **Hood River Vineyard** is open to the public Sat.-Thurs. 1-5pm. **Gray Line Tours,** 4320 N Suttle Rd. in Portland (285-9845), offers an 8½-hr. ride around Mt. Hood and through the Columbia River Gorge ($30, under 12 $17). Tours leave from Union Station at 800 NW 6th Ave. (mid-May to late-Oct. Tues., Thurs., and Sat. at 9am). The **Mt. Hood Railroad** (386-3556), also connects the mountain and Gorge. Trains leave daily at 10am and 3pm ($20, seniors $17, ages 2-11 $12).

East of Hood River, across the Columbia on U.S. 97, lies the **Mary Hill Museum of Art,** 35 Maryhill Museum Dr. in Goldendale, WA (509-773-3733). European and American paintings, including works by Native Americans, and over 100 funky hand-made chess sets make the museum an interesting visit. $4, seniors $3.50, ages 6-16 $1.50. Open mid-March through mid-Nov. daily 9am-5pm.

OREGON COAST

The renowned coastal highway **U.S. 101** hugs the shore, occasionally rising to lofty viewpoints. From Astoria in the north to Brookings in the south, the highway laces together the resorts and fishing villages clustering around the mouths of rivers feeding into the Pacific. Its most breathtaking stretch lies between the coastal towns, where hundreds of miles of state and national parks allow direct access to the beach. Wherever the highway leaves the coast, look for a beach loop road—these quiet byways afford some of the finest scenery on the western seaboard. Stop and wander along the huge stretches of unspoiled beach and observe the ocean's more comfortable inhabitants—the seals, sea lions, and waterfowl just offshore.

GETTING AROUND

For the most extensive and rewarding encounter with the coast, travel by car or bike. Cyclists should write to the Oregon Dept. of Transportation, Salem 97310, or to virtually any visitors center or Chamber of Commerce on the coast for the free *Oregon Coast Bike Route Map;* it provides invaluable information on campsites, hostels, bike repair facilities, temperatures, and wind conditions. Remember that Portlanders head down-road to vacation, so most traffic flows south. In summer, the prevailing winds will be at your back if you **cycle** south.

For those without a car or bike, transportation becomes a bit tricky. **Greyhound** offers only two coastal runs from Portland per day; one of those takes place under cover of night, when the coast's beautiful scenery is hidden. Along the southern coast, the 10-hour Portland-Brookings route stops at Lincoln City, Newport, Florence, Reedsport, Coos Bay, Bandon, Port Orford, Gold Beach, and every suburb between Portland and the coast. The northern route connects Portland with Tillamook, Cannon Beach, Seaside, and Astoria. Local public transportation links Astoria to Cannon Beach, but vanishes south of Cannon Beach.

Gasoline and grocery **prices** on the coast are about 20% higher than in the inland cities. Motorists should try to stock up and fill up before reaching the coastal highways. When searching for a site to pull in for the night, look to the small villages, as they tend to be the most interesting (and often the cheapest) places to stay. From north to south, Nehalem, Wheeler, Depoe Bay, Winchester Bay, Charleston, Bandon, and Port Orford offer escape from the larger and more commercialized towns of Seaside, Tillamook, Lincoln City, Newport, and Coos Bay. State parks along the coast offer 17 major campgrounds with electricity and showers.

■■■ ASTORIA

Peer down the streets, mentally removing the Golden Arches and the espresso-bar signs, and you'll have an excellent outline of turn-of-the-century Astoria. Lewis and Clark arrived here in 1805 at the end of their transcontinental trek; six years later, John Astor, scion of one of 19th-century America's most famously wealthy families, established a fur-trading post, making Astoria the first permanent U.S. settlement on the West Coast.

Astoria's Victorian small-town appearance has made it a favorite for movie shootings. *Kindergarten Cop,* with Arnold Schwarzenegger, was filmed here. Movies like *Goonies, Free Willy,* and even *Teenage Mutant Ninja Turtles III* (do you see a pattern here?) also use Astoria's panoramic view of the Columbia River and Pacific Ocean. The firefighters' museum and the model boats in the maritime museum are both worth seeing. Explore the genuinely preserved forts; the military history of the Astoria area is bizarre. In the evening, relax with samples of local wine.

PRACTICAL INFORMATION AND ORIENTATION

Visitors Information: Astoria/Warrenton Area Chamber of Commerce, 111 W Marine Dr. (325-6311; fax 325-6311), just east of the bridge to Washington. P.O. Box 176, Astoria, OR 97103. Stocked with information on Astoria, the Coast, and southwest Washington. Open Mon.-Sat. 8am-6pm, Sun. 9am-5pm; Sept.-May Mon.-Fri. 8am-5pm, Sat.-Sun. 11am-4pm. Also operates a small summer **information hut** at the base of Astoria Column. Open daily June-Labor Day 11am-6pm.

Greyhound (RAZ Transportation), 364 9th St. (325-5641), at Duane St. To: Portland (2 per day, 9:30am and 7:30pm; $15); leaves Portland for Astoria (2 per day, 6:30am and 4:30pm; $15). Open Mon.-Sat. 9:30-noon and 4:30-7:30pm.

Sunset Empire Transit (800-452-2085), at Greyhound depot in Seaside (738-7083). Round-trip Astoria-Seaside, serving towns between. One departure per day, Mon.-Fri.

Pacific Transit System, at the Greyhound depot (206-642-9418 or 206-875-9418). To Chinook and Ilwaco, WA (50¢). Buses leave Astoria Mon.-Fri. at 7:30, 11:30am, 3:05 and 5:45pm.

Astoria Transit System, 364 9th St. (325-0563 or 800-452-2085). Local bus service. Makes a full city loop every 20 min. (75¢, students 50¢). Service Mon.-Fri. 6:50am-6:10pm, Sat. 9am-6:30pm.

Taxi: Yellow Cab, 325-3131. 24 hrs.

AAA: 5 N U.S. 101, Warrenton (861-3118). Open Mon.-Fri. 8am-5pm.

Laundromat: Coin Laundry, 823 W Marine Dr. (325-2027), next to Dairy Queen. Wash $1, 8½ min. dry 25¢. Open daily 7:30am-10pm.

General Crisis Line: 325-3426, Mon.-Fri. 9am-5pm.

Clatsop County Women's Crisis Service: 10 6th St. #104, (325-5735) at Marine Dr. 24 hrs.

Seniors Information Service: 800 Exchange St. (325-0123). Legal services and community center. Open Mon.-Fri. 8:30am-noon and 1-3pm.

Pharmacy: Astoria Pharmacy, 840 Exchange St. (325-1123). In the Astoria Family Clinic Building. Open Mon.-Fri. 9:30am-5:30pm, Sat. 9:30am-12:30pm.
Hospital: Columbia Memorial, 2111 Exchange St. (325-4321 or 800-962-2407).
Emergency: 911. **Police:** 555 30th St. (325-4411). **Clatsop County Sheriff:** 911 Center St. (325-2061). **Coast Guard:** Tongue Pt. (861-6100).
Post Office: 750 Commercial St. (325-2141), in the Federal Bldg. at 8th St. Open Mon.-Fri. 8:30am-5pm. **General Delivery ZIP Code:** 97103.
Area Code: 503.

Astoria is the most convenient connection between the Oregon coast and Washington. Two bridges run from the city: the **Youngs Bay Bridge,** to the southwest, on which Marine Drive becomes U.S. 101, and the **Astoria Bridge,** a 4-mi. span over the Columbia River into Washington. The Astoria Bridge has extremely narrow and hazardous bike lanes. Drivers might prefer to ferry you across rather than swerve around you on the narrow bridge. (*Let's Go* does not recommend hitchhiking.)
   Warrenton lies a few mi. west of Astoria. U.S. 30 runs to Portland, 100 road mi. east. Astoria can also be reached from Portland via U.S. 26 and U.S. 101 at Seaside.

ACCOMMODATIONS AND CAMPING

Motels are crowded and expensive. The area has a great, almost unknown hostel, though, and is a paradise for campers; Hwy. 101, south of Astoria, is littered with campgrounds. **Fort Stevens State Park** is by far the best.

Fort Columbia State Park Hostel (HI/AYH), Fort Columbia, Chinook, WA (206-777-8755), within the park boundaries. Across the 4-mi. bridge into Washington, then 3 mi. north on U.S. 101. Take the 50¢ Pacific Transit System bus on weekdays (see Practical Information). In this 1896 military hospital-turned-hostel, coffee filters double as hats on festive occasions, and 50¢ stuff-your-face pancakes rule the mornings. A fire on chilly evenings, coffee, tea, and snacks in the kitchen, and laundry and barbecue facilities. Why isn't this wonderful place mobbed? Lockout 9:30am-5pm, check-in 5-10pm. $9, non-members $12, bicyclists $7, under 18 (with parent) $4.50. Open March 1-Oct. 31.

Astoria City Center Motel, 495 Marine Dr. (325-4211). Nothing fancy, but clean and comfortable. In-room coffee, TV, some refrigerators. Singles $38. Doubles $49; two beds $62. Senior discount $2. Rates drop $6-10 in winter.

Grandview Bed and Breakfast, 1574 Grand Ave. (325-0000 or 800-488-3250). Cheery rooms with shared bath (unless you've got $70 to spare). "Continental breakfast plus" includes fresh muffins, smoked salmon, bagels, and more. Cheapest room $39, the rest start at $53. Off-season: 2 rooms for the price of 1.

Lamplighter Motel, 131 W Marine (325-4051). Attractive rooms with multiple amenities. Coffee in lobby, copy and fax machines available, cable TV. Singles $42. Doubles $52. Rates drop $10 lower in winter. Senior discounts. Reserve at least 1 week in advance.

Fort Stevens State Park (861-1671), over Youngs Bay Bridge on U.S. 101 S, 10 mi. west of Astoria. For reservations, write Fort Stevens, Hammond, OR 97121. A huge park with rugged, empty beaches. Near cool historic attractions. 605 sites with hot showers; facilities for the disabled. Sites $16-18. If you're fresh off a hike or a bike: $4.

FOOD

Escape the expensive seafood and chain restaurants at **Safeway,** 1153 Duane (325-4662; open 24 hrs.). A limited selection of natural foods and organic produce is available at the tiny **Community Store,** 1389 Duane St. (325-0027; open Mon.-Sat. 10am-6pm).

Columbian Cafe, 1114 Marine Dr. (325-2233). The best show in town is the crepe-flipping action of this lively, charismatic chef. The pasta dishes ($8-9) and crepes ($5) are divine. Watch the time: dinner is too popular for the cafe's tiny size. A morning option is "Mercy Food:" Chef's choice ($5.50). One local has so much faith that he has ordered Mercy Food over 1200 times. Open for lunch Mon.-Fri. 8am-2pm, Sat. 10am-2pm; dinner Wed.-Sat. 5-9pm.

Ship Inn, One 2nd St. (325-0033). A harbor for seafood lovers, this popular restaurant admirably replicates an English fish and chips establishment. No wimpy fries here; it's "potato planks" heaped on high with your order. The squid is tender and delicious; half an entree ($5-25) will fill you up. Some tables look out on the river, and there is an excellent bar adjoining with plenty of English and Irish draughts on tap ($1.75 per glass). Open daily 11:30am-9:30pm.

Victoria Dahl's Cafe, 2921 Marine Dr. (325-7109). It is a universally acknowledged truth that anyone in search of a "Zesty Italian" meal should dine at Victoria's. Return to 19th-century England, with dark wood panelling, romantically low lighting, and an antique shop to stroll in if your companion proves boring. A full dinner runs about $10; lunch with pastrami sandwiches and salads, $5-6. Open Tues.-Wed. 11am-5pm, Thurs-Fri. 11am-9pm, Sat. 11am-4pm.

Peri's, 915 Commercial St. (325-5560). A friendly indoor/outdoor deli that serves only a few items, but serves them well. Bagel sandwiches ($2.50), regular sandwiches ($4.25). Open Mon. 9am-4pm, Tues.-Fri. 9am-7pm, Sat. 11am-4pm.

SIGHTS AND EVENTS

Astoria's prime location is best appreciated from the top of the **Astoria Column,** on Coxcomb Hill Rd., affording a view of Saddle Mtn. and lush forests to the south and the Columbia River estuary to the north. Completed in 1926, the column is wrapped by 166 steps on the exterior, passing faded, storm-worn friezes which depict the history of the area. Tableaux of historic Astoria include the discovery of the Columbia River by intrepid English sea captain Robert Grey, the arrival of Lewis and Clark, and the settling of Astoria (open from dawn to 10pm).

The Historical Society maintains three **museums** in Astoria; the most unique is the **Uppertown Firefighters' Museum** (325-6920), 30th and Marine Dr., with its displays of vintage firefighting equipment (open Fri.-Sun. 10am-5pm; Nov.-April 11am-4pm).

Astoria's most unique attraction is the wave-shaped **Columbia River Maritime Museum,** 1792 Marine Dr. (325-2323), on the waterfront. The prize of the model boat collection is Robert Gray's 1792 vessel, in which he "discovered" the Columbia River mouth. This large museum is packed with marine lore, from displays on the salmon fisheries that once dominated Astoria to a diving suit with a mask that looks like Darth Vader. The Coast Guard also gives excellent 45-min. tours of the *Columbia,* the last lightship to see active duty at the mouth of the Columbia (museum open daily 9:30am-5pm; $5, seniors $4, ages 6-17 $2).

One block up from the Maritime Museum, the owner of the **Shallon Winery,** 1598 Duane St. (325-5978), will give you a tour of his small winemaking facilities, provide his interpretation of the area's history, and proudly display his extraordinary repetoire of wines. A self-proclaimed connoisseur of fine food, he insists you call him "anytime of day or night" before you consider eating at any restaurant within a 50-mi. radius. He'll treat you to a taste of wines made from local berries and the only commercially produced **whey wines** (from Tillamook cheese) in the world. Approach the cranberry and whey wine with caution; its fruity taste belies its alcohol content. Sampling **lemon meringue pie wine** is likely to be the highlight of any trip to the Oregon Coast; the taste is so uncanny that you'd swear you were drinking a puree of grandma's special. The owner even serves the wine with a small cracker to ensure that you receive the correct proportion of crust to pie (open daily noon-6pm; gratuities appreciated).

The **Astoria Regatta** (325-5139), held the second week in August, is one of the longest running community events in the Northwest, dating back to 1894. The regatta tradition remains strong and features food and craft booths, a watershow, scenic boat rides, fireworks, dances, and even a sailboat race or two. At the end of the day, unwind with an hour of pore-cleansing steam from **Union Steam Baths,** 285 W. Marine Dr. (325-0651). The establishment is entirely reputable and unaffiliated with the "Adults Only" sleaze-fest upstairs ($9 per bath, $11 per couple. Open Thurs.-Sun. 4:30-10:30pm).

The Scandinavian Festival on the second weekend in June attracts a large following to enjoy the crafts, dancing, and Scandinavian food. Contact the Chamber of Commerce (325-6311) for information.

■ NEAR ASTORIA

Five mi. south of Astoria, the **Fort Clatsop National Memorial** (861-2471) reconstructs the winter headquarters of the Lewis and Clark expedition, based on descriptions in their detailed journal. The log fort housed Lewis, Clark, their interpreter Sacajawea, Clark's black servant York, three officers, 24 enlisted men, several Northwest Natives, and plenty of fleas. The **visitors center** has an impressive collection of exhibits, movies, and a slide show. Talks and demonstrations by historically-clothed rangers are delivered daily, including a demonstration of the fragile-looking muzzle-loading guns the expedition relied on for hunting and defense (open mid-June to Labor Day daily 8am-6pm; winter 8am-5pm; $2, under 17 free, family $4).

Fort Stevens State Park (campground 861-1671; historical area 861-2000), off U.S. 101 on a narrow peninsula 10 mi. west of Astoria, has excellent swimming, fishing, boating facilities, beaches, and hiking trails. Fort Stevens was constructed in 1864 to prevent Confederate naval raiders from entering the Columbia. (It seems odd, but the last military engagement of the Civil War was a naval battle, fought in the summer of 1865 off the coast of Russian Alaska between a New England whaler and a Southern commerce raider. Of course, the combatants blasting away at each other in the Gulf of Alaska didn't know that General Lee had already surrendered in Virginia. During the war, Confederate commerce raiders ranged across the world's oceans.) It also showed American strength in the Northwest to prevent the more threatening British from attempting to take local advantage of the U.S. preoccupation with the war back East. From 1897 to 1904, the fort underwent a massive development program, including the construction of eight concrete-gun batteries. Although the guns have all been removed, nearly all the batteries remain and are the primary focus of a self-guided historical walking tour (about two hours), which begins up the road from the day-use and campground areas. Between Memorial Day and Labor Day, a restored 1954 Army cargo truck takes visitors on narrated tours given daily at 11am, 12:30, 2:30, and 4pm ($2.50, children $1.25). Guided tours of **Battery Mishler** are also available at the same times ($2, children $1). The tours leave from the **Fort Stevens Military Museum and Interpretive Center** (861-2000), which contains displays and artifacts spanning the history of the fort (open daily 10am-6pm; winter Wed.-Sun. 10am-4pm). The **Memorial Rose Garden,** with 150 commemorative roses, is in the same area ($3).

Battery Russell (861-2471), in the park ½ mi. south of the historical area, bears the dubious distinction of being the only mainland American fort to see active defensive duty since the War of 1812. At 11:30pm on June 21, 1942, a Japanese submarine surfaced offshore (lost, or just searching for immortality in this Guide?) and shelled the fort with 17 rounds. The fort was undamaged and did not return fire. Today it is a military monument, and allows free access to the wanderer. Another historical marker, the 287-ft. British schooner *Peter Iredale,* lost in 1906, lies near a soothing beach. Colorful kites offset the gloom of the skeletal remains.

Bike paths weave their leisurely way through the park. **Fort Stevens Bicycle Rentals** (861-0937) rents bikes next to the Historical Area (open June-Sept. 10am-6pm; $4 per hour, $20 per 24 hrs.). And if a dip in the ocean sounds a bit icy, try **Coffenbury Lake,** a warmer spot for swimming and fishing. The fee is only $3, and encompasses both the interpretive center and the lake.

■■■ SEASIDE

Near Seaside in the winter of 1805-6, explorers Lewis and Clark made their western-most camp. They'd be appalled to see what has become of the area; you too might feel a strong desire to turn around and head back up the Columbia. Built into a resort in the 1870s, the years and tourists have eroded Seaside's charm. With crowds, fast food, video arcades, a developed beach, and screeching kids and teen-agers, Seaside has ambitions to be the Jersey shore; it lacks only sunshine, warm water, and a Trump casino.

PRACTICAL INFORMATION AND ORIENTATION

Visitors Information: Chamber of Commerce, 7 N Roosevelt St. (738-6391; in OR 800-444-6740), on U.S. 101 and Broadway. Well-versed staff ready for any question about the town. Also a referral service for most local motels. Open Mon.-Sat. 8am-6pm, Sun. 9am-5pm.; Oct.-May Mon.-Fri. 9am-5pm, Sat.-Sun. 10am-4pm.

Greyhound (RAZ Transportation), 201 S Holladay (738-5121). Leaves Portland at 4:30am for Seaside and Astoria. Returns to Portland at 8:45am ($13).

Taxi: Yellow Cab, 738-3131. 24 hrs.

Bike Rental: Prom Bike Shop, 622 12th Ave. (738-8251), at 12th and Holladay; also at 80 Ave. A, downtown. Bikes, roller skates, and beach tricycles $15 per hr. and $25 per 24 hr.; tandem bicycles $8 per hr. ID held during rental. Open daily 10am-6pm.

Laundromat: Holladay Coin Laundry, 57 N Holladay St. (738-3458), at 1st Ave. Wash $1.25, 8-10 min. dry 25¢. Open daily 7am-11pm, last load in at 10pm.

Library, 60 N Roosevelt Dr. (738-6742). Open Tues.-Thurs. 9am-8pm, Fri.-Sat. 9am-5pm, Sun. 1-5pm. Closed Mondays.

Senior Citizen's Information Service: 1225 Ave. A (738-7393). Information and referral. Open Mon.-Fri. 9am-4:30pm.

Women's Crisis Service: 325-5735. 24 hr.

Hospital: Providence Seaside Hospital, 725 S Wahanna Rd. (738-8463).

Emergency: 911. **Police:** 1091 Holladay Dr. (738-6311).

Post Office: 300 Ave. A (738-5462). Open Mon.-Fri. 8:30am-5pm, Sat. (for pickup only) 8-10:30am. **General Delivery ZIP Code:** 97138.

Area Code: 503.

Seaside lies 17 mi. south of Astoria and 8 mi. north of Cannon Beach along U.S. 101. The most direct route between Seaside and Portland is U.S. 26, which intersects U.S. 101 just south of Seaside along Saddle Mountain State Park. The **Necanicum River** runs north-south through Seaside, approximately two blocks from the coastline, paralleled by U.S. 101 and Holladay Dr. to the east. All three are bisected by **Broad-way,** the main street. As the center for gift shops and restaurants, Broadway is usu-ally clogged with tourists; cars should be abandoned for the day, because all of Seaside's attractions are within easy walking distance.

ACCOMMODATIONS AND CAMPING

Seaside's dismally expensive motel scene has been greatly remedied by the opening of a large hostel. Reservations are essential in this tourist mob scene. The prices of motels are directly proportional to their proximity to the beach. Though there are seemingly thousands of motels, the cheapest hover near $40 per night (and they're cheaper during the off-season). Rooms are invariably full by 5pm; get ahead of the game and ask the Chamber of Commerce for availability listings. They won't reserve a room for you, but they'll offer advice.

Seaside International Hostel (HI/AYH), 930 N Holladay Dr. (738-7911). Like a phoenix rising from the ashes, this new hostel sprung up in 1994 from the remains of an old hotel and a law library. The friendly manager, a former Assistant Director of AYH/HI, will recommend hikes, and two canoes are available for hos-tellers' free use. Espresso bar in the office. Each room has its own shower. Gor-geous river view; 48 large bunks. $12, nonmembers $15.

Mariner Motel, 429 S Holladay Dr. (738-8254). Fine rooms, many newly recarpeted. Free coffee (8:30-10am) in the office. Singles $41. Double bed $42, 2 double beds $50. Oct. 15-June 1 rates are $6 lower, plus an additional $5 discount if you whip out a *Let's Go*.

Royale Motel, 531 Ave. A (738-9541), Friendly staff and large, clean rooms. Full-length windows would be amazing if the view were of the ocean and not the parking lot. Cable TV and phones. Singles $36 (in spring $39). Two double beds $51, $41 in winter and $45 in spring. Coffeemakers in the office. Make reservations 2 wks. in advance.

Riverside Inn, 430 S Holladay Dr. (738-8254 or 800-826-6151), next to the Holladay. Small bedrooms, with bookshelves, fresh flowers, and raftered ceilings. All rooms have private bath and TV. If you ask nicely, the owners will serve you the included full breakfast on the riverfront deck. Singles from $49, $45 in winter.

Circle Creek RV Park & Campground, the sole nearby tent spot, is phasing over to RVs (preferring sedate recreating types to crazy tent partiers.) They may still have tent sites available; call to be sure. The sites are grassy, the shower area pristine (25¢ per 8 min. shower). Tents $11-13, RVs $15, full hookup $17 per night.

The closest state parks are **Fort Stevens,** 21 mi. north (see Astoria: Accommodations and also Near Astoria) and **Saddle Mountain** (861-1671), 14 mi. southeast of Seaside off U.S. 26, 8 mi. northeast of Necanicum Junction. Saddle Mountain has ten "primitive" campsites ($9) with flush toilets (but no showers), near the base of the Saddle Mountain hiking trail. Closer to Seaside is **Kloochie Creek,** about 300 yd. off U.S. 26, 6 mi. southeast of town. Pitch a tent at the base of the world's largest Sitka Spruce tree (9 sites, $6). Sleeping on the beach in Seaside is illegal, and police enforce this rule.

FOOD

Broadway, especially toward the beach, becomes a madhouse at lunchtime. Restaurant prices are high; the best bet may be **Safeway,** 401 S. Roosevelt (738-7122), which is still expensive, but meals for under $9 can be concocted (open daily 6am-midnight).

Dooger's Seafood and Grill, 505 Broadway St. (738-3773). The best clam chowder in town ($1.50), unadulterated by flour or cornstarch thickeners. Enormous platefuls. Try the lunch special of sea scallops, salad, and garlic toast ($7.50). Open Mon.-Fri. 11am-9:30pm, Sat.-Sun. 11am-10pm.

Pacific Way Cafe & Bakery, 601 Pacific Way in Gearhart (738-0245). Worth the 2-mi. drive north on Hwy. 101. A cafe with class. Dine in the rainforest on a huge, fresh manonberry scone, or take a picnic to the Gearhart Beach ¼ mi. away. Sandwiches with homemade bread ($6-9), espresso, and pastries. Open Wed.-Sun. 9:30am-4:30pm.

Bee Bop Burgers, 111 Broadway (738-3271). Classic 50s tunes rock around the clock while you enjoy your choice of Bopper ($2.75), Big Bopper ($3.95), or Teeny Bopper ($1.25). Wash it down with a cherry, chocolate, vanilla, or lemon coke (75¢). Open Sun.-Thurs. 10am-10pm, Fri.-Sat. 10am-11pm.

Miguel's Mexican and Seafood, 412 Broadway (738-0171). A tiny restaurant which fills up fast for $9 dinners. Appetizer can double as light lunch- try the cheese and chile quesadilla ($3.50). Open Mon.-Thurs. noon-10pm, Sun. 12:30-9pm.

Little New York on Broadway, 604 Broadway (738-5992). Seaside's interpretation of Italian cuisine in a "back-East" setting. It works pretty well: sandwiches $5 and pastas $7-9 are tasty and substantial, but the 5¢ coffee (with any order) works best. Open Mon. 8am-6pm, Tues. 8am-4pm, Wed.-Thurs. 8am-6pm, Fri.-Sat. 8am-8pm.

SIGHTS AND EVENTS

Seaside revolves around **Broadway,** a garish strip of arcades, shops, and salt water taffy joints running the ½ mi. from Roosevelt (U.S. 101) to the beach. Indoor miniature golf, bumper cars, and video games are some of the "highlights." The **Turn-around** at the end of Broadway signals the "official" (read: arbitrary) end of the Lewis and Clark Trail. In 1986, the Turnaround underwent a facelift to add to the $1.3 million spent on street improvements in 1982-3, and a statue of Lewis and Clark was erected at the end of the Trail. Eight blocks south of the Turnaround lies the **Saltworks,** a replica of the cairn used by the Lewis and Clark expedition to hold sea water. Using fires, members of the expedition boiled away the water and used the salt to preserve their food, which was mostly meat and fish. The tiny **Seaside Museum,** 570 Necanicum Dr. (738-7065), brims with tasty tidbits about Lewis and Clark, and other artifacts and displays.

A recent addition to the downtown beachfront culture is along the Necanicum River. **Quatat Marine Park** (from the Clatsop Native word meaning "village by the sea") spans four blocks between First Ave. and Broadway and boasts peaceful dock walkways and benches removed from the teeming sidewalks of Broadway. Quatat Park also offers water sports of sorts: **Monkey Business** has bumper boats (inner tubes with motors) at $3 for 5 minutes, and paddle boats at $8 per ½-hour for two people (open daily 11am-6pm). The authentic Seaside experience requires "Sun Cycles": rent them for $14 per ½-hour from **Sun Cycle Express,** 407 S Holladay Dr. (738-8447), and view tacky Seaside from a motor-scooter.

Explore the wonders of the sea at the **Seaside Aquarium,** 200 N Promenade (738-6211). Marvel at the 20-ray starfish and the Leopard Shark, or feed fish to the spirited harbor seals. (Open Wed.-Sun. 9am-5pm; March-Oct. Mon.-Fri. 9am-6pm, Sat.-Sun. 9am-7pm. $4.50, ages 6-11 $2.25.)

Seaside's beach front is large, but crowded nonetheless. Lifeguards are on duty from Memorial Day to Labor Day (daily 10am-6pm), even though the water is always too cold for swimming. Don't even think about taking a dip on "red flag" days: the surf is too rough. Exercise caution at all times, due to strong undertows. For a quieter beach, head to **Gearhart,** approximately two mi. north of downtown off U.S. 101. The beach has no lifeguard, and town officials strongly discourage swimming. You can, however, explore the long stretch of sand and dunes on foot or by car.

Farther east on U.S. 26 lies the **Jewell Meadows Wildlife Area,** a wintering habitat for Roosevelt elk. Parking spaces throughout the refuge allow you to get out and wander about with the elk, present mostly in fall and winter. Black-tailed deer often appear in the spring and summer, and a coyote may turn up any time of year. Take U.S. 26 to Jewell Junction, then head north on the unmarked state road for 9 mi. to Jewell. Turn left and travel 1½ mi. on Rte. 202 to the refuge area.

The **Seaside Beach Run, Promenade Walk,** and **Sand Games** are held in the third week of July. The 8-mi. beach race leaves from Seaside's Turnaround. Contact Sunset Empire Park & Recreation, 1140 E Broadway (738-3311), for more information. This organization also oversees **"Where the Stars Play,"** a free concert series every Saturday from late June through early September. Everything from folk to Caribbean is blasted at Quatat Marine Park at 2pm. The real kicker comes at the end of August, when the **Hood to Coast Race** finishes in Seaside to the cheers of 25,000 spectators. Some 750 12-person teams run this two-day relay race from Mt. Hood in 5-mi. shifts. Contact the Oregon Road Runners' Club in Portland (646-7867) for more information. The evening of the finish, **Johnny Limbo and the Lugnuts** shake up the city with some swinging songs.

■■■ CANNON BEACH

A rusty cannon from the shipwrecked schooner *Shark* washed ashore at Arch Cape, giving this town its name. Resist the urge to find a cannon of your own to aim at the highbrow art galleries and expensive craft stores. The maxim for budget travelers is "look but don't touch;" an elevated aesthetic doesn't come cheap. But if you arrive during the Sand Castle Festival or spend a day at the beach among the wildlife-packed tide pools in nearby Ecola State Park, you'll have too good a time to notice the yuppie hordes.

PRACTICAL INFORMATION AND ORIENTATION

Visitors Information: Cannon Beach Chamber of Commerce, 207 N Spruce St. (436-2623), at 2nd St. P.O. Box 64, Cannon Beach 97110. Emblematic of the city, this visitors center stocks T-shirts, postcards, and a small stock of brochures. Open Mon.-Sat. 9am-5pm, Sun. 11am-5pm.

Buses: Sunset Transit System (325-0563 or 800-452-2085). To: Seaside ($1.50); Astoria ($3.50). **Local Transit: Cannon Beach Shuttle,** a natural-gas powered bus service. Traverses the downtown area; board at any point. Service Fri.-Tues. 10am-1pm and 2-6pm. Ask the Chamber of Commerce for the schedule.

Bike Rental: Mike's Bike Shop, 248 N Spruce St. (436-1266 or 800-492-1266), around the corner from the Chamber of Commerce. Offers **maps** of routes that follow old logging roads. Mountain bikes ($6 per hr. and $20 per day), beach tri-cycles ($7 per 90 min). Credit card deposit required. Open daily 10am-6pm.

Lifeguard Service: 436-2345. July-Aug. daily 10am-8pm.

Weather: 861-2722.

Hospital: Providence Seaside Hospital, 725 S Wahanna Rd. in Seaside (738-8463). **Cannon Beach** (436-1142), walk-in clinic at 171 Larch St. in Sandpiper Sq. Mon.-Fri. 9am-midnight.

Emergency: 911. **Police:** 163 Gower St. (436-2811). **Fire Dept.:** 436-2949.

Post Office: 155 N Hemlock St. (436-2822). Open Mon.-Fri. 9am-5pm. **General Delivery ZIP Code:** 97110.

Area Code: 503.

Cannon Beach lies 7 mi. south of Seaside and 42 mi. north of Tillamook on U.S. 101, which does not run through the center of town. Watch for signs; Hemlock, Cannon Beach's main drag, connects with U.S. 101 in four places. Cannon Beach is 79 mi. from Portland via U.S. 26.

ACCOMMODATIONS AND CAMPING

Hemlock St. is lined with pleasant motels, none of which cost less than $40 in the summer, though family units are often available for less. Book early on summer weekends. In the winter, inquire about specials; most motels offer "two nights for one" deals in an effort to stay afloat. Camping is clearly the best (perhaps the only) option for the budget traveler. Many people ignore the "no camping" signs at the incredibly gorgeous **Ecola State Park** (436-2844). Like all Oregon state parks, Ecola has sites for hiker/bikers. To reach them, follow the long, paved road into the park and, heeding the signs, turn right into Indian Beach. A 2-mi.-long trail leads to the camp. Overnight parking is the park is illegal, however, so have someone drop you off. Less rugged camping is available at **Oswald West** (see Cannon Beach to Tillamook, below), 10 mi. south of town. Just north of Cannon Beach proper, the **Sea Ranch RV Park,** 415 N Hemlock St., P.O. Box 214 (436-2815), has 35 tent sites and over 30 hookup sights in a safe field and tree-studded area. (Showers included. Tents $12; full hookup $16, hiker/biker sites $4. Reservations recommended, and a one-night's deposit is required.)

Blue Gull Inn, 487 S Hemlock St. (436-2714 or 800-507-2714). Big, clean rooms decorated with expensive oil paintings of crashing surf. Set back from the street. TV with cable and laundry facilities. Singles and doubles from $45 in summer; in winter from $40. Ask about the winter specials; the family units, which sleep 4, are a good bulk deal.

The Sandtrap Inn, 539 S Hemlock St. (436-0247 or 800-400-4106 from Portland). Picturesque, tastefully furnished rooms start at $50, $40 off-season. Working fire-places, cable TV. 2-nights-for-1 off-season special.

FOOD

Cafe-style dining, with plenty of outdoor seating, has proliferated in Cannon Beach to serve the store-hopping tourist clientele. Surprisingly, food prices are not as sky-high as everything else in town. For the basics, **Mariner Market,** 139 N Hemlock St.

(436-2442), has a broad, inexpensive selection of foodstuffs. You can have peanut butter ground while you wait ($3 per lb.). (Open May-Sept. Sun.-Thurs. 9am-10pm, Fri.-Sat. 9am-11pm; Oct.-April Sun.-Thurs. 9am-9pm, Fri.-Sat. 9am-10pm.

Lazy Susan Cafe, 126 N Hemlock St. (436-2816). A cozy wood restaurant serving yummy homemade food. Sandwiches $5-6; seafood salads $8-9; variety of omelets $5-7.25. Open Mon. and Wed.-Sat. 8am-3pm, Sun. 8am-2pm.

Bill's Tavern, 188 N Hemlock (436-2202). If you're 21-plus in Cannon Beach, Bill's is the place to be. Down-home pub grub ranges from $3 to $5, pints $1.75-2.75. Open Thurs.-Tues. 11:30am-midnight.

Midtown Cafe, 1235 S Hemlock St. (436-1016) in the Haystack Sq. Complex. Relax with a tub of potatoes deluxe ($4.75) in the morning, and stay for the lunchtime lentil burger ($6.50). Open Wed.-Fri. 7am-3pm, Sat. 7am-2pm, Sun. 8am-2pm.

Osburn's Deli and Grocery, 240 N Hemlock St. (436-2234). Hearty sandwiches to go ($4.50, available 10am-7pm, winter 11am-5pm). Open daily 8:30am-8:30pm; Labor Day-June 9am-8pm. **Osburn's Ice Creamery** (436-2578), next door, scoops cones for $1.25. The fresh raspberry shake ($3.50), available in season, is nectar of the gods. Open daily 10am-10pm; winter 11am-7pm.

SIGHTS, EVENTS, AND OUTDOORS

Put on silver slippers, clap your hands three times, and you can be transported to yuppieland to browse at your leisure through diverse, elegant, expensive art galleries and gift shops. Or flee for a morning stroll along the 7-mi. long stretch of beach. Picnickers and hikers can follow the narrow, winding road to **Ecola State Park** (436-2844; $3 entrance fee). **Ecola Point** offers a spectacular vantage point of the hulking **Haystack Rock,** which is spotted with (and splattered by) gulls, puffins, barnacles, anemones, and the occasional sea lion. The Rock's **tide pools** teem with colorful sea life. Digging for mussels and clams is now prohibited and enforced by the City Police. In an effort to educate the public about the Rock's remarkable self-contained ecosystem, guides are present on weekends during unusually low tides.

Ecola Point also affords views of the Bay's 235-ft. centerpiece, the **Tillamook Lighthouse,** which clings like a barnacle to a wave-swept rock. Construction of the lighthouse, begun in 1879, continued for years in Sisyphean fashion, as storms kept washing the foundations away. Decommissioned in 1957 because of damage caused by storm-tossed rocks, the now privately-owned lighthouse can be reached only by helicopter and only for the purpose of depositing ashes of the dead. From Ecola State Park, take the 12-mi. round-trip hike to **Tillamook Head,** from which you can sometimes glimpse migrating whales. In the fall, ask a knowledgeable local to point out chanterelle mushrooms along the path. The trail is open year-round, and the top provides an excellent view of the coast. If you want to tear up the water, **Cleanline Surf,** 171 Sunset Blvd. (436-9726) rents complete surfing gear for $35 per day. Indian Beach, in Ecola State Park, is a favorite with surfers.

Fill your evenings with cultural stimulation at the **Coaster Theater,** 1087 N Hemlock St. (436-1242), which stages theater productions, music concerts, ballet and modern dance concerts, comedy, and musical revues throughout the year. Write to Coaster Theater, P.O. Box 643, Cannon Beach 97110 for information (tickets $12-15; may be purchased by phone, at the Box Office Wed.-Sat. 1-5pm, or an hour before showtime).

In late spring, catch the annual **Sand Castle Competition.** Contestants pour in from hundreds of miles away and begin construction early in the morning, creating ornate sculptures from wet sand. By evening the high tide washes everything away, leaving photographs as the sole testimony to the staggering creative energy expended during the day. Photos are prominently displayed in the Chamber of Commerce; call them for more information.

During the first weekend in November, the community gathers for the **Stormy Weather Arts Festival.** Highlights include gallery shows, a theater production, and a free choral concert during Sunday brunch. Contact the Chamber of Commerce for more information. **Saddle Mountain State Park,** 14 mi. east of Cannon Beach on

U.S. 26, is named for the highest peak in the Coast Range. A strenuous 6-mi., 4 hr. hike up to Saddle Mountain's 3283-ft. summit rewards the fit with an astounding view of the Nehalem Bay and the Pacific to the west and the Cascades to the north (summit trail open March-Dec.)

■ CANNON BEACH TO TILLAMOOK

In the summer of 1933, the "Tillamook Burn" reduced 500 sq. mi. of forest to charcoal. While Nature has restored Tillamook State Forest to health, humanity has been crowding the small coastal towns with espresso bars and dime-a-dozen gift shops. Tourist information for the area is available at the visitors information bureau in Tillamook (see Tillamook: Practical Information) or the **Rockaway Beach Chamber of Commerce,** 405 S U.S. 101 (355-8108; open Mon.-Fri. 9am-5pm, Sat. 10am-3pm).

Oswald West State Park, 10 mi. south of Cannon Beach, is a tiny headland **rainforest** with huge spruce and cedar trees. The park is accessible only on foot on a ¼-mi. trail off U.S. 101. This doesn't quite qualify as "roughing it," as the State Parks Division provides hulking, wooden wheelbarrows for transporting gear from the parking area to the 36 primitive campsites near the beach (open mid-May-Oct.; sites $9). No electricity or showers, but water and toilets. The sites are beautiful and secluded, just minutes away from the beach. Surfers love it; they occupy every other campsite. Fall asleep to the sound of gently rustling water. Arrive early, even on a summer weekday; these are the cheapest sites around. From the park, take the 4-mi. **Cape Falcon** hiking trail farther out toward the water, or just follow the path from the campground down to one of Oregon's few surfing beaches.

Five mi. south of Oswald West State Park, self-consciously quaint **Manzanita** reclines across a long expanse of uncrowded beach. The **Sand Dune Motel,** 428 Dorcas Lane (368-5163), just off Laneda St., the main drag through town, has pleasant rooms a mere 5 blocks from the shore (singles and doubles $40, winter $30).

Scenic coastal hiking trails are close to Cannon Beach. The **Tillamook Head Trail,** 6 mi. north near **Ecola State Park,** is a 1000-ft. climb up a huge piece of land jutting into the ocean, and affords incredible photo opportunities. 20 mi. south of Cannon Beach, just north of Nehalem, **Nehalem Bay State Park** (368-5154 or 368-5943) offers 291 sites with electricity ($16), including some hiker/biker sites ($4 per person) and 17 horse campsites with individual corrals for your steed ($9, plus $1 per horse; they've got to make money somehow). Facilities include hot showers.

Nehalem, a few mi. south of Manzanita, consists of little more than a handful of "made in Oregon" shops marshalled along U.S. 101. On the northern boundary of Nehalem, the **Bunk House** (368-6183), at 36315 U.S. 101, offers one of the Oregon Coast's best indoor deals. The rooms are reasonably clean, and for just $15 (singles) to $35 (doubles). Some rooms have complete kitchens, and there's a coffee house next door. Call two weeks ahead to make reservations. Stop in at the **Bayway Eatery,** 25870 7th St. (368-6495), for an excellent fish and chips meal ($4.50) or an enormous order of fries ($1.25). This well-worn diner is a favorite Nehalem hangout (open daily 6am-9pm). Three mi. away, south on U.S. 101 to Rte. 53, the **Nehalem Bay Winery,** 34965 Rte. 53 (368-WINE/9463), distributes samples of local specialties, including cranberry and blackberry wines, for a $2 tasting fee collected on the honor system (open daily 10am-6pm).

In **Wheeler,** a short jog south from Nehalem, shove off in one of **Annie's Kayaks,** 487 U.S. 101 (368-6005). Lessons are available on Saturday mornings for $15 per person (minimum of two; call in advance). Single kayaks run $10 per hour, $25 per day; add $5 for doubles (open Tues.-Sun. 10am-5pm; reservations suggested on those hot summer weekends). After a grueling paddle-trip, grab some grub in the town of **Garibaldi.** Try to ignore the garish G scarring the hillside above town. The **Bayfront Bakery and Deli,** 302 Garibaldi (322-3787), on U.S. 101, has barbecued ribs, pizza, and salads. The pies and baked goods can't be beaten; thick loaves of bread go for $1.25 (open Wed.-Sat. 4:30am-5:30pm, Sun. 4:30am-4pm; winter Tues.-Sat. 4:30am-5:30pm). The **Old Mill Restaurant** (322-0222), at 3rd and Americana St.

overlooks the boats and water. Turn west off U.S. 101 over the railroad tracks and follow the signs to the left. Sit in brilliant blue seats and enjoy the daily lunch special ($4-6), a bowl of clam chowder ($2), or a razor clam dinner ($13). (Open daily 8am-9pm).

■ ■ ■ TILLAMOOK

Ever seen a cheese factory at work? Some of Oregon's finest, most famous cheeses are cultured on the shore of Tillamook Bay, where cow pastures predominate. Some visitors enjoy a brief jaunt through the countryside, but most just hanker for a hunk of cheese and a look at the funky Tillamook Cheese Factory.

PRACTICAL INFORMATION AND ORIENTATION

Visitors Information: Tillamook Chamber of Commerce, 3705 U.S. 101 N (842-7525), next to the Tillamook Cheese Factory. Open Mon.-Fri. 9am-5pm, Sat. 10am-4:30pm, Sun. 10am-2pm. **Parks and Recreation:** Regional Office, 2505 U.S. 101 N (842-5501). Open Mon.-Fri. 9am-5pm.
Taxi: Tillamook Taxi, 842-4567. 24 hrs.
Seniors' Information: 842-7988. Open daily 8am-5pm.
Tillamook Women's Crisis Center: 2515 11th St., 842-9486. 24 hrs.
Laundromat: Little Cheese (842-2211), on the corner of 3rd and Pacific. 75¢ wash, 7½-min. 25¢ dry.
Hospital: Tillamook County General Hospital, 1000 3rd St. (842-4444).
Emergency: 911. **Police:** 842-2522, in City Hall. **Fire:** 2310 4th St. (842-7587). **County Sheriff:** 201 Laurel St. (842-2561), in the courthouse.
Post Office: 2200 1st St. (842-4711). Open Mon.-Fri. 8:30am-5pm. **General Delivery ZIP Code:** 97141.
Area Code: 503.

Tillamook lies 49 mi. south of Seaside and 44 mi. north of Lincoln City on U.S. 101. The most direct route from Portland is U.S. 26 to Rte. 6 (74 mi.). U.S. 101 is the main drag, and splits into two one-way streets in the downtown area. The Tillamook Cheese Factory is almost a downtown in itself, but is north of the major shops.

ACCOMMODATIONS AND CAMPING

The visitors center has a **map** of all the camping spots in the area; it's worth a look. Most motel prices are exorbitant. Prices are especially inflated in summer, and some motels will cheese you out of a few extra bucks on weekends.

Tillamook Inn, 1810 U.S. 101 N (842-4413), between the center of town and the Tillamook Cheese Factory. Generic motel rooms. Free coffee. Rates may be lower in the off-season. Senior citizen discount. Singles $34. Doubles $46. Winter rates lower. Call a few days in advance.
MarClair Inn, 11 Main Ave. (842-7571or 800-331-6857). Convenient, downtown location. Big, tastefully decorated rooms, pool, and jacuzzi. $4 AAA discount. Singles $56, off-season $46. Doubles $62, off-season $52.
Kilchis River Park (842-6694), 8 mi. northeast of Tillamook at the end of Kilchis River Rd. 40 primitive sites in a county park near the river and the county ball field. Tent sites $10. Hiker/biker $2.

FOOD

If you like cheese and ice cream, you're in Paradise. Collect other picnic supplies at **Safeway,** 955 N Main (842-4831; open daily 6am-midnight).

Tillamook Cheese Factory, 4175 U.S. 101 N (842-4481). Fun just to see; visit when hungry, too. Cheese aside, they have divine homemade ice cream, including Brown Cow, French Silk, and other exotic flavors ($1.25). Deli sandwiches $2-5; cheap breakfasts 8-11am. Open daily 8am-8pm; Sept.-mid-June 8am-6pm.

Main St. Pizza Company, 2205 N Highway 101 (842-7277) in the Cornet shopping area. More cheese: think hot and gooey. Popular locally for homemade pizza and salad bar, and because local kids play video games in the back. Junior 8-in. pizza serves one ($3.30). Open Sun.-Thurs. 11am-10pm, Fri.-Sat. 11am-11pm.

La Casa Medello, 1160 U.S. 101 N (842-5768). Good family dining, with mild Mexican food prepared to order. Lunch specials $4-5. Massive 12-in. tacos ($6), burritos ($5). Dinners ($6-9) come with rice, beans, and chips. Extremely busy. Open Mon.-Fri. 11am-8:30pm, Sat.-Sun. 11am-9:30pm.

SIGHTS AND ACTIVITIES

The **Tillamook Cheese Factory,** a temple to dairy delights, is usually packed in summer. Watch from glass windows as the stuff is made, stirred, cut, weighed, and packaged. Sample a tidbit in the tasting room. Try their ice cream too. Less crowded is the friendly **Blue Heron French Cheese Factory,** 2001 Blue Heron Dr. (842-8281), 1 mi. south of the Tillamook factory on the east side of U.S. 101 (but north of town). The "factory" no longer produces cheese, but the sales room is fortified with free samples of brie and wine (open daily 8am-8pm, winter 9am-6pm).

West of the highway, downtown, the **Tillamook County Pioneer Museum,** 2106 2nd St. (842-4553), features all manner of household and industrial goods from the pioneer era. The museum's prized treasure, however, is an impressive collection of animals, considered the best in the state, preserved by taxidermist Alex Walker. (Open Mon.-Sat. 8am-5pm, Sun. noon-5pm; Oct.-March Tues.-Sat. 8am-5pm, Sun. noon-5pm. $2, seniors $1.50, ages 12-17 50¢, families $5, under 12 free.)

Tillamook's largest attraction is the **Tillamook Naval Air Station Museum,** 6030 Hangar Rd. (842-1130), 2 mi. south of Tillamook. This behemoth was used during World War II to house a fleet of U.S. Navy blimps. Considered the largest standing wooden structure in the world, the building covers more than 7 acres. The chilly cavern contains WWII navigation nostalgia; sometimes a working blimp is even present. The price is a bit high ($5, ages 6-12 $2.50), but the experience is novel (open summer daily 9am-8pm; winter 9am-5pm). 5 mi. south of the hangars off U.S. 101, one can admire the sublime **Munson Creek Falls** which, cascading 266 ft. over spectacularly rugged cliffs, is the highest waterfall in the Coast Range. A 1½-mi. road leads to a parking lot from which two trails are accessible. The lower trail is ¼ mi. long and ends at the base of the falls. The upper trail is a bit longer (½ mi.) and a bit more difficult. Passing over rotting wooden catwalks and obstructed by the twisted trunks of uprooted trees, its end rewards hikers with a close view of the wispy, white foam slipping into the canyon.

■■■ TILLAMOOK TO LINCOLN CITY

Between Tillamook and Lincoln City, U.S. 101 wanders eastward into wooded land, losing contact with the coast. Instead of staying on the highway, consider taking the **Three Capes Loop,** a 35-mi. circle to the west that connects a trio of spectacular promontories: **Cape Meares, Cape Lookout,** and **Cape Kiwanda State Parks.** The beaches are secluded, and the scenery makes the uncrowded drive worthwhile. Cyclists should beware of the narrow twists and poor condition of the roads.

Cape Meares, at the tip of the promontory jutting out from Tillamook, is home to the **Octopus Tree,** a gnarled Sitka spruce with several trunks (a tree-climber's dream). The **Cape Meares Lighthouse,** built in 1890, also stands in the park and now operates as an illuminating on-site interpretive center. Another climbing opportunity: struggle to the top for sweeping views and a peek at the original lens of the big light (open May-Sept. daily 11am-4pm; Oct.-March Fri.-Sat. 11am-4pm; free).

From Cape Meares one can make out the three lonely **Arch Rocks** in the distance. Jutting out of the water like the humps of a ghastly sea monster, the Arch Rocks are a Federal refuge for sea lions and birds. You can gain a better view of the sea lions a bit farther south, toward **Netarts Bay.**

Continue 12 mi. southwest and get out of your car at **Cape Lookout,** which has trails and facilities for people with disabilities (842-4981; see Tillamook: Accommodations). South of Cape Lookout, the loop undulates through sand dunes, where the sound of the rushing wind competes with the intermittent roar of all-terrain vehicles. A 2.5-mi. trail to the end of the lookout will reward you with a spectacular panorama, including **Tillamook Head, Three Arches Rock,** and **Haystack Rock.** From south of Cape Lookout, the loop undulates through sand dunes, where the sound of the rushing wind competes with the intermittent roar of all-terrain vehicles.

Cape Kiwanda, the third promontory on the loop, is for day-use only (open 8am-dusk). On sunny, windy days, hang gliders gather to test their skill at negotiating the wave-carved sandstone cliffs. The sheltered cape also draws skin divers, and beachcombers come to sink their toes into the dunes. A state park trail overlooks the top of the cape before reaching the ocean. On the cape, just barely north of Pacific City, massive rock outcroppings in a small bay mark the launching pad of the flat-bottomed **dory fleet,** one of the few fishing fleets in the world that launches beachside, directly onto the surf. If you bring your own fishing gear down to the cape most mornings around 5am, you can probably convince someone to take you on board; the fee will nearly always be lower than that of a commercial outfitter. Six mi. north of Pacific City is the USDA Forest Service's popular **Sandbeach Campground,** only a short walk to the beach, with flush toilets and drinking water. Arrive early in the summer or make a reservation at 800-280-226 (10 sites; $8).

Pacific City, a delightful town missed by most travelers on U.S. 101, is home to the other **Haystack Rock,** just as impressive as its sibling to the north. The mammoth rock has a handle jutting out from its northern edge, suggesting that some prehistoric giant left it here when he grew tired of carrying it. The **Chamber of Commerce** (965-6161) does not operate an office, but does have a complete information sign and map posted at 34960 Brooten Rd., in the middle of nowhere.

The **Anchorage Motel,** 6585 Pacific Ave. (965-6773) offers large, simple singles for $32 and doubles for $35. A two-room bedroom complex, with a fully equipped kitchen, is a bargain for $54. All rooms have cable and in-room coffee. Overlooking the Nescutta River, the **Riverhouse Restaurant,** 34450 Brooten Rd. (965-6722), features seafood and homemade desserts. Chowder and piled-high sandwiches cost $5-7. (Open Sun.-Thurs. 11am-9pm, Fri.-Sat. 11am-10pm).

Back on U.S. 101, six mi. north in **Hebo,** the ranger district operates a **ranger station** for the **Siuslaw National Forest** at 31525 Rte. 22 (392-3161). Lists of hiking and camping options are available. Five mi. along winding Forest Service Road #14 is **Hebo Lake Campground,** with sixteen gorgeous and outhouse-equipped sites rimming **Small Hebo Lake** ($6; open mid-April-mid-Oct.). Two mi. further up the road, the summit of **Mt. Hebo** offers excellent views of the coastline and, on clear days, Mt. Hood to the east.

Other Forest Service Campgrounds include the **Mt. Hebo Campground,** 2 mi. beyond the summit (primitive, no drinking water, free); **Rocky Bend campground,** 15 mi. east of Beaver on paved Nestuccca River Road (free; primitive; no drinking water) and **Castle Rock Campground,** 4.2 mi. south of Hebo on Rte. 22 (4 primitive sites; hand-pumped well for drinking water; free).

U.S. 101 crosses Rte. 18 at **Otis** (about 2 mi. east on Rte. 18). The **Otis Cafe** (994-2813) serves excellent home-style strawberry-rhubarb pie for $1.75 a slice. The cafe is often crowded; your patience will be rewarded with sandwiches on freshly baked bread ($3.10-5) and breakfast specials ($2.50-6). (Open Mon.-Wed. 7am-3pm, Thurs.-Sat. 7am-9pm, Sun. 8am-9pm.)

A dozen wineries line Rte. 18 on the way to Portland. A 9-mi. detour via Rte. 99 W and Rte. 47 will take you far from the coast to **Carlton,** home of the **Chateau Benoit Winery,** Mineral Springs Rd. (864-2991 or 864-3666). From Rte. 47 in Carlton, take Road 204 1.3 mi. east, then go 2½ mi. south on Mineral Springs. The winery specializes in Pinot Noir, Sparkling Brut, and Riesling (open daily 10am-5pm).

■■■ LINCOLN CITY

Lincoln City is actually five towns incorporated into one, all conspiring to force you to crawl at 30 mph past a 7-mi. strip of motels, gas stations, and tourist traps. Bicyclists will find Lincoln City hellish, and hikers should cut 3 blocks west to the seashore. Although it is perhaps the most commercialized town on the Oregon coast (boasting more than 1000 ocean-front motel rooms), Lincoln City is a convenient base from which to explore nearby capes, beaches, and waterways.

PRACTICAL INFORMATION

Visitors Information: Lincoln City Visitor and Convention Bureau, 801 SW U.S. 101 #1 (800-452-2151 or 994-8378). Offers brochures covering everything to do in Lincoln City and beyond. Open Mon.-Sat. 8am-6pm, Sun. 10am-5pm; mid-Sept.-June Mon.-Sat. 8am-5pm, Sun. 10am-5pm. **City Parks and Recreation Dept.,** P.O. Box 50 (994-2131).

Buses: Greyhound, S 14th St. at U.S. 101 (265-2253 in Newport), behind the bowling alley. To: Portland (2 per day, $11) and Newport (2 per day, $4.75). A stop only; no depot. **Lincoln Century Transit** (265-4900) based in Newport. To: Newport ($2).

Taxi: Lincoln Cab Company, (996-2003). 24 hrs.

Car Rental: Robben-Rent-A-Car, 3232 NE U.S. 101 (994-5530). $22 per day plus 15¢ per mi. after 50 mi. Must be 21 with major credit card. Office open Mon.-Sat. 8am-5pm.

Laundry: Coin Laundry, 2164 NE U.S. 101. Wash 1$, 10-min. dry 25¢. Open daily 9am-10pm.

Library: Driftwood Library, 801 SW U.S. 101 (996-2277), near the visitors center. They have books, too. Open Mon.-Thurs. 9am-9pm, Fri.-Sat. 9am-5pm.

Swimming and Showers: Community Pool, 2150 NE Oar Place (994-5208). Pool $1.75, showers 75¢.

Senior Citizen Center: 2150 NE Oar Place (994-2722 or 994-2131).

Hospital: North Lincoln Hospital, 3043 NE 28th St. (994-3661).

Emergency: 911. **Police:** 1503 E Devils Lake Rd. (994-3636). **Fire:** 2525 NW U.S. 101 (994-3100). **Coast Guard:** In Depoe Bay (765-2124).

Post Office: 1501 SE Devils Lake Rd. (994-2148). 2 blocks east of U.S. 101. Open Mon.-Fri. 9am-5pm. **General Delivery ZIP Code:** 97367.

Area Code: 503.

ACCOMMODATIONS

Camping near Lincoln City can be crowded; a stay here is a good time to opt for a roof over your head. Several inexpensive motels lie along U.S. 101.

Sea Echo Motel, 3510 NE U.S. 101 (994-2575). A bit removed from the hwy. atop a steep slope. Standard rooms with phones and Showtime. Singles and doubles $32; 2 beds $41.

Bel-Aire Motel, 2945 NW U.S. 101 (994-2984), at the north end of town. The decrepit exterior masks large, pleasant rooms. One bed $27, weekends $32; 2 beds from $43.

Budget Inn, 1713 NW 21st St. (994-5281). A huge, blue complex with fairly large rooms. Right on the highway. One bed $34, 2 beds $40; rates higher on weekends. 5 rooms for $30; request at least 2 weeks in advance.

Captain Cook Inn, 26 NE U.S. 101 (994-2522 or 800-994-2522). Judging from the exterior, the famous explorer must have reveled in pale yellow. Gracious, remodelled rooms with queen beds starting at $43, $38 in winter. One room with double bed $33. Reservations at least two weeks in advance.

FOOD

Head down to Depoe Bay or Newport for good seafood. But Lincoln City has a few classy spots, if you can navigate the fast-food shoals. The **Safeway** and **Thriftway** markets, both on U.S. 101, are open 24 hrs.

Lighthouse Brew Pub, 4157 N Highway (994-7238), in Lighthouse Sq. at the north end of town. Renowned for its good beer and relaxed atmosphere. 10 beers are brewed here, not to mention the beer shake ($3); say the word and someone will give you a tour of the brewery (Capt. Neon's Fermentation Chamber). The food is cheap and good. Open Sun.-Thurs. 11am-11pm, Fri.-Sat. 11am-1pm; winter daily 11am-11pm.

Foon Hing Yuen, Inc., 3138 SE U.S. 101 (996-3831). Generous portions of good Chinese food. Lunches can be had for $3.50; the specials will run you $6-9. Despite the name, the *pork chow yuk* ($6.50) is delicious. This is one of few restaurants in town that doesn't close before 10pm. Take-out available. Bar and restaurant open Sun.-Thurs. noon-11pm, Fri.-Sat. noon-1am.

Kyllo's, 1110 NW First Ct. (994-3179), at U.S. 101. Dinners are expensive but the seafood is good; the view overlooking the ocean is even better. Try the Manilla clams in white wine ($9).

Williams' Colonial Bakery, 1734 NE U.S. 101 (994-5919). Wrong ocean, but a definite score for early birds. Vast array of fantastic pastries and baked goods. Grab some buttermilk bars (40¢), apple fritters (55¢), and glazed doughnuts (50¢), and take them back for your still-snoozing friends. Open daily 5am-6pm.

SIGHTS, ACTIVITIES, AND EVENTS

Drive or cycle along **East Devil's Lake Road,** which leads around the lake to quiet, clearly marked fishing and picnic sites. **Road's End Park,** a couple of mi. past the Lighthouse Square turn-off at the north end of town, features yet another of Oregon's beautiful beaches.

Film buffs should know that *Sometimes a Great Notion,* based on the Ken Kesey novel, was filmed in Lincoln City. The mock old house that was used as the set can be seen by turning east off U.S. 101 onto the Siletz River Hwy. You can enjoy some of Oregon's fine wines, coffee, and food at **Chateau Benoit,** Wine & Food Center, 1524 E Devils Lake Rd. (996-3981), in the Factory Stores.

One of only three sanctioned road races in Oregon and Washington, the **Soap Box Derby** zooms through Lincoln City every Father's Day weekend. During the **Fall International Festival** in the first part of October, Lincoln City is overrun by kite-flyers. Call the Vistor and Convention Bureau for information.

■■■ LINCOLN CITY TO NEWPORT

Between Lincoln City and Newport, there are rest stops and beach access parking lots every few mi., one with overnight camping. The free **North Creek Campground,** a small area within the Siuslaw National Forest with no drinking water, is off County Rte. 229 on Forest Service Rd. 19.

A few mi. south on U.S. 101, diminutive **Depoe Bay** boasts the best **gray whale viewing points** along the seawall in town, at the **Depoe Bay State Park Wayside,** and at the **Observatory Lookout,** 4½ mi. south of town. Go out early in the morning on a cloudy, calm day between Dec. and May for the best chance of spotting the huge grays. Several outfitters charter fishing trips from Depoe Bay. **Deep Sea Trollers** (765-2248) offers five-hour trips for $40 per person (trips leave daily at 7am). **Dockside Charters** (765-2545 or 800-733-8915) offers similar trips for $45; a one-hour whale-watching excursion goes for $9, under 13 $6.

Just south of Depoe Bay, take a detour from U.S. 101 to the famous **Otter Crest Loop,** a twisting 4-mi. drive high above the shore which affords spectacular vistas at every bend. A lookout over **Cape Foulweather** has telescopes (25¢) for spotting sea lions on the rocks below. Captain James Cook first saw the North American mainland here in 1778; it greeted him with gale-force winds. Wind speeds at this 500-ft. elevation still often reach 100 mph. The incredible **Devil's Punchbowl** is also on the loop. This collapsed seaside cave is best viewed at high tide, when the heavy waves form a frothing cauldron beneath your feet.

Just south of the Punchbowl, the road returns to U.S. 101 and brings eager campers to the much-trafficked **Beverly Beach State Park,** 198 NE 123rd St. (265-9278), a year-round campground in gorgeous, rugged terrain. Cold water and frequent riptides should discourage even the most intrepid swimmers. The views from the hiking trails will satisfy most visitors. Hot showers and facilities for people with disabilities are available, and a few hiker/biker spots (sites $15, hookups $17). Reservations during the summer are strongly advised.

Just south of Beverly Beach is the **Yaquina Head Lighthouse** (265-2863), a photogenic coastal landmark. Large decks provide good views of the offshore rocks that are home to one of the few seabird colonies close to the U.S. mainland. Western gulls, tufted puffins, and cormorants, among others, can be seen in fine detail. The low, flat rock to the south of the headland is home to harbor seals, sea lions, and many small pebbles. Gray whales are sometimes spotted in the waters beyond. The top of the lighthouse itself can be reached only through free tours (daily June- mid-Sept. every ½ hr. 9-11:30am. The first 15 people get to go; arrive early to assure a spot. The public can guide themselves through the lighthouse daily noon-4pm, but the top is closed then.

■ ■ ■ NEWPORT

Part tourist mill, part fishing village, and part logging town, Newport seems typically Oregonian. The recently renovated waterfront area provides a rare escape from the malls and gas stations, offering the sights and smells of a classic seaport with kitschy shops and bizarre, garish tourist attractions.

PRACTICAL INFORMATION AND ORIENTATION

Visitors Information: Chamber of Commerce, 555 SW Coast Hwy. (265-8801 or 800-262-7844). Large, friendly office with bus schedules, lots of free **maps,** and guides to Newport and surrounding areas. Open Mon.-Fri. 8:30am-5pm, Sat.-Sun. 10am-4pm; Oct.-April Mon.-Fri. 8:30am-5pm.

Newport Parks and Recreation Office, 169 SW Coast Hwy. (265-7783). Open Mon.-Fri. 8am-4:30pm.

Greyhound, 956 SW 10th St. (265-2253) at Bailey St. To: Portland (3 per day; $17.25; $42 to Seattle) and San Francisco (4 per day; $79). Open Mon.-Fri. 8am-5pm, Sat. 8am-1pm.

Local Transit: Lincoln County Transit, 821 SW Lee St. (265-4900), reaches south as far as Yachats and north as far as Otis (beyond Lincoln City). Fares within Newport 50¢, outside Newport variable, depending on destination.

The Newport Connection (265-4900). June-Labor Day 1 per hr. Free.

Taxi: Yaquina Cab Company, 265-9552. 24 hrs.

Car Rental: Surfside Motors, 27 S Coast Hwy. (265-6686). From $27 per day with 50 free mi., 20¢ per extra mi. Reservations necessary, major credit card required for deposit. Must be 25 or older. Open Mon.-Fri. 8am-5pm, Sat. 9am-5pm.

Bike Rental: Embarcadero, 1000 SE Bay Blvd. (265-5435). Bikes $4 per hour, $25 per day; $25 deposit or major credit card held. No helmets. Also rents crab rings ($5 per day); clam shovels ($3.50 per day); and boats ($12.50 per hour).

Newport Public Library, 34 W Olive St. (265-2153). Open Mon.-Thurs. 10am-8pm, Fri.-Sat. 1-6pm, Sun. 1-4pm.

Laundry: Eileen's Coin Laundry, 1078 N Coast Hwy. Open daily 5am-midnight.

Weather: 265-5511.

Crisis Line: Contact, 132 W Olive St. (265-9234). 24-hr. helpline.

Hospital: Pacific Communities Hospital, 930 SW Abbey (265-2244).

Emergency: 911. **Police:** 810 SW Alder, (265-5331). **Fire:** 245 NW 10th St., 265-9461. **Coast Guard:** 265-5831.

Post Office: 310 SW 2nd St. (265-5542). Open Mon.-Fri. 9am-5pm. **General Delivery ZIP Code:** 97365.

Area Code: 503.

U.S. 101 divides East and West Newport, while U.S. 20 bisects North and South. Corvallis lies 50 mi. east on U.S. 20. Newport is bordered on the west by the foggy

Pacific Ocean, and on the south by Yaquina Bay. A sweeping suspension bridge ferries U.S. 101 travelers across the bay.

ACCOMMODATIONS AND CAMPING

The strip along U.S. 101 provides plenty of affordable motels, with predictably noisy consequences. Weekend rates generally rise a couple of dollars, and winter rates improve what are already good deals. Ask the Chamber of Commerce for a list and further advice on accommodations.

Brown Squirrel Hostel (HI/AYH), 44 SW Brook St. (265-3729). This hostel has a cavernous living room adjacent to the kitchen. You can be out the door and at the beach in 2 min. Lockout 10am-4pm. Doors locked at 11:30pm, mid-Sept.-May at 10pm. Laundry and kitchen facilities. Members and non-members $10.

El Rancho Motel, 1435 N U.S. 101 (265-5192 or 800-765-7671). The red and white ranch-like decor is indisputably cheesy, but the motel has fine, cheap rooms. Cable TV, direct-dial phones. Singles $25. Doubles $35.

Newport Bay Motel, 1823 N Coast Highway (265-4533). Clean, inexpensive rooms with cable TV. Plenty of counter space on which to spread out. Singles from $27, doubles from $40. Prices slightly higher on weekends and for newly redone rooms. Call 4 days in advance.

Summerwind Budget Motel, 728 N Coast Hwy. (265-8076). Unremarkable rooms with TV, phones, free coffee. Singles $36. Doubles $40, less in winter.

City Center Motel, 538 SW Coast Hwy. (265-7381). Small but clean rooms with queen beds, cable TV, and coffee; across from the visitors center. Singles $37. Doubles $41.

Finding a place to pitch your tent in or around Newport can be tricky. The few private campgrounds are overrun by RVs, and campground owners have established facilities geared exclusively to these monstrosities. Campers should escape to the many state campgrounds along U.S. 101, where sites average $14 and hookups go for $16. **South Beach State Park,** 5580 S Coast Hwy., South Beach 97366 (867-4715), 2 mi. south of town, has 254 electrical hookup sites ($12) and showers. Just north of town lies the best option, **Beverly Beach State Park,** 198 N 123rd St., Newport (265-9278), which has 151 sites specifically for tents ($14) and 53 full hookup sites. Reserve a site.

FOOD

Food in Newport is decent, particularly along the bay, where tourists cluster. **Oceana Natural Foods Coop,** 159 SE 2nd St. (265-8285), has a small selection of reasonably priced natural foods and produce (open daily 9am-7pm). **J.C. Sentry,** 107 N Coast Hwy. (265-6641), sells standard supermarket stock 24 hrs. per day.

The Chowder Bowl, 728 NW Beach Dr. (265-7477), at Nye Beach. Renowned bowls of chowder ($2.75). Fill your boiler with a "Mate's Portion" of Fish & Chips ($6). The chips are round (and so may you be, if you finish the Whale Platter.) A fresh salad bar and cheap sandwiches ($3.50-5) are available for those averse to fried food. Open June-mid-Sept. 11am-8pm, Fri.-Sat. 11am-9pm.

The Whale's Tale, 452 SW Bay Blvd. (265-8660), on the bayfront at Hurbert St. This famous place is great fun, carved out of driftwood and decorated with local art and mismatched old wooden chairs and tables. For breakfast, the celebrated poppy seed pancakes ($4 for two) are a must-try. Dinners can be expensive (*cioppino* $14), but good seafood and vegetarian sandwiches can be harpooned for $4.50 and come with soup. Open Mon.-Fri. 8am-10pm, Sat.-Sun. 9am-10pm. In winter open daily 9am-9pm (but closed around 3pm Wed. Closed Jan.).

Boardwalk Cafe, 1000 SE Bay Blvd. (265-5028). A healthful selection of vegetarian sandwiches, soups, and tempting baked goods (scones $1.25). Plenty of picnic tables on the boardwalk outside for a scenic bayside meal. Try the chowder/salad/hunk of homemade bread combo for $4.25. Open daily 8am-2pm, in winter Wed.-Mon. 8am-2pm. Closed in Dec.

Bayfront Brewery & Public House, 748 SW Bay Blvd. (265-3188). All hail the local ale: plenty of brew on tap, and and ale bread ($1.50) to boot. Much-prized "secret recipe" pizza (small from $6.75, large from $12) and sandwiches with chips ($4.75) also available. Open daily Mon.-Fri. 11:30am-11pm or midnight Sat.-Sun. 11am-11pm or midnight.

SIGHTS, ACTIVITIES, AND EVENTS

Just stay away from the eminently tacky **Wax Works Museum,** the **Undersea Gardens** across the street, and the similarly garish **Ripley's Believe It or Not**.

The **Oregon Coast Aquarium,** 2820 SE Ferry Slip Rd. (867-3474), is unquestionably number one on Newport's greatest hits list. This vast, well-designed building features 2½ acres of wild, wet indoor and outdoor exhibits. The museum is a living classroom, teaching visitors about the wondrous wildlife of the Oregon Coast. Stroll through the galleries, where kelp sways, waves crash, and anemones "stick" to your hands. Peer at a tank of jellyfish, who resemble small pink umbrellas. Wander through the aviary, home of the tufted puffin, or peer into the sea otter tank through the underwater windows. The whale theater shows a 10-minute video on those huge, breezy denizens of the deep, the gray whales. ($7.75, seniors and ages 13-18 $4.50, under 13 $3.30. Open daily 9am-6pm; winter 10am-4:30pm.)

Just beyond the aquarium, the **Mark O. Hatfield Marine Science Center** (867-0100) on Marine Science Dr., is the hub of Oregon State University's coastal research. The Center's museum explains its research and displays Northwest marine animals in their natural environments. Talks, show films, and nature walks led by marine educators are available as part of a year-round program entitled **Seatauqua.** Fees range from $8 to $30, Call 867-0246 for details (open daily 10am-6pm; Nov.-mid-June 10am-4pm; free).

Observe more refined culture in a wander through Newport's many elegant **art galleries;** ask the Chamber of Commerce for help in locating them. The **Newport Performing Arts Center,** 777 W Olive (265-2787) has some excellent orchestral and band concerts. The Chamber has a seasonal schedule; tickets range from $5-13 with a few freebies). Popular festivals in Newport include the **Newport Seafood and Wine Festival** on the last full weekend in February, showcasing Oregon wines, food, music, and crafts; and **Newport Loyalty Days and Sea Fair Festival,** the first weekend in May, with rides, parades, fried chicken, and sailboat races. The second week in October, the **Microbrew Festival** features the tiniest beers in the Northwest. Be sure to try a Widmer Hekewiezen. Contact the Newport Chamber of Commerce (see Practical Information) for information on all seasonal events. To sample some local beer, cross the bay bridge, follow the signs to the Hatfield Center and turn off into the **Rogue Ale Brewery,** 2320 SE Oregon State University Dr. (867-3663). Unfortunately, the Brewery found free tasting to be unprofitable and began to charge 50¢ for a 3-oz. glass of full-bodied brew. Request a tour (open in summer daily 11am-8pm; winter hours cut back slightly).

Yaquina Bay State Park, 46 SW Government St. at the southwest end of town but the north side of the bay, is home to the **Yaquina Bay Lighthouse.** The dark lighthouse (in operation from 1871-1874) presides over the fleets of fishing boats that cruise in and out of the bay daily. It's also haunted. The legend is verified in a 20-minute video screened within the lighthouse; the video also features footage of the Coast Guard's dramatic rescue of the crew of the *Blue Magpie* in 1983. The crew was salvaged, but not the ship, a portion of which can be seen from the lighthouse on clear days (open daily 11am-5pm; Sept.-May Sat.-Sun. noon-4pm; free). Call 867-7451 for tour information.

If you have time and money, try **bottom-fishing** with one of Newport's charter companies. Salmon and halibut are no longer plentiful, but you can try to net some tuna with **Newport Tradewinds,** 653 SW Bay Blvd. (265-2101), which runs five, six, and eight-hour trips for $10 per hour. A 3-hr. crabbing trip costs $30; a 2½-hr. whale-watching trip is $27. **Yaquina Birdwatchers Club** (265-2965), welcomes guests to its free field trips (usually on the 3rd weekend of each monthSept.-June). Open meetings are held the third Tuesday of each month.

Some of the sheltered coves in the area, especially those to the north around Depoe Bay, are excellent for **scuba diving.** Rent equipment and get tips from **Newport Water Sports,** 1441 SW 26th St., South Beach (867-3742), at the south end of the bridge. (Open daily Mon.-Thurs. 9am-6pm, Fri. 8am-6pm, Sat.-Sun. 8am-8pm. Top-of-the-line gear rental about $25 during the week, $30 on weekends.)

■■■ NEWPORT TO REEDSPORT

From Newport to Reedsport, U.S. 101 passes beautiful campgrounds, beaches, and beachside attractions. The **Waldport Ranger District Office,** 1049 SW Pacific Hwy. (563-3211), in **Waldport,** is not far from U.S. 101 and worth a stop if you're considering going **hiking** in the **Siuslaw National Forest,** a patchwork of wilderness areas along the Oregon Coast. The office provides **maps** of area campgrounds and trails and directs bikers to appropriate spots (open Mon.-Fri. 7:45am-4:30pm).

Continuing south, U.S. 101 passes through Yachats, a town not particularly notable except for the **New Morning Coffeehouse** (547-3848), at 4th and U.S. 101 beside the Back Porch Gallery. With a relaxed atmosphere, this place is a favorite coffee-stop for U.S. 101 travelers. Try one of the sweet pastries (scones $1.25) and an espresso ($1; open Wed.-Sun. 9am-4pm).

Cape Perpetua, at 803 ft. the highest point on the coast, lies 2-3 mi. south of Yachats. Take a break from U.S. 101 and drive (or hike 1.6 mi. up a steep trail from the visitors center) to the top of Cape Perpetua. The view of the coast is spectacular; you can see the **Devil's Churn** frothing 800 ft. below. **Cape Perpetua Campground** has 37 beautiful, drinking-water-equipped sites. The next campground heading south is **Rock Creek Campground,** with 16 sites and drinking water. Both are excellent alternatives to more expensive, RV-filled campgrounds, and both offer $10 tent sites, flush toilets, and drinking water. The largest sea caves on the coast, **Sea Lion Caves,** 91560 U.S. 101 (547-3111), are a permanent home to a sizeable colony of sea lions. Viewpoints from within the caves and above ground allow visitors to observe the lions feeding and being beastly during the breeding fights of June and July (wheelchair access; open daily 9am-dusk; $5.50, children $3.50). 1 mi. north of the caves lies **Devil's Elbow.** The day-use beach requires a $3 parking permit; get your money's worth by walking from the lot up to an amazing and uncrowded viewpoint on the cliffs of the **Heceta Head Lighthouse.**

Florence is a far-too-long strip of fast-food joints and expensive motels. Fifteen mi. west of Florence, at the junction of U.S. 36 and U.S. 126 (to Eugene) is **Mapleton,** a tiny community home to a **Ranger Station,** 10692 U.S. 126 (268-4473), which can give tips to prospective **hikers** or **bikers** in the **Siuslaw National Forest** (open Mon.-Fri. 8am-4:30pm). Road-trip-induced hunger can be assuaged at the **Alpha Bits Cafe** (268-4311) on U.S. 126, just beyond the ranger station. Owned and staffed by a commune, the store is part cafe, part browsable book store. Falafel Pita Pockets are $4, grainburgers are $3 (open Mon.-Thurs. 10am-6pm, Fri. 10am-9pm, Sat. 10am-6pm). For a full, free experience in community living, push thirty minutes east to **Alpha Farm** (964-5102), 7 mi. up Deadwood Creek Rd. The farm, in scenic Nowheresville, offers an unusual, distinctively communal alternative to the bourgeois tourism of the coast. In exchange for a day of labor on the farm, visitors can camp out or stay in the sparse but comfortable bedrooms. Visitors are welcome from Monday to Friday for stays of up to three days; call ahead. Be prepared to kiss the hands of your fellows in a warm post-dinner ritual.

■■■ REEDSPORT AND THE DUNES

For 50 mi. between Florence and Coos Bay, the beach widens to form the **Oregon Dunes National Recreation Area.** Shifting hills of sand rise to 500 ft. and extend up to 3 mi. inland (often to the shoulder of U.S. 101), clogging mountain streams and forming small lakes. Hiking trails wind around the lakes, through the coastal forests, and up to the dunes themselves. In many places, no grasses or shrubs grow, and the vista holds only bare sand and sky, but campgrounds fill up early with dune buggy and motorcycle junkies, especially on summer weekends. The blaring radios, thrumming engines, and staggering swarms of tipsy tourists might drive you Jim Morrison-like into the sands to seek eternal truth, or at least a quiet place to crash. The dune-buggy invasion is increasingly controversial, but the **National Recreation Area Headquarters** in Reedsport refuses to take sides. They can tell visitors just how many decibels a dune-buggy engine can produce, but they will also provide the **trail maps** necessary for quiet, serene escape.

PRACTICAL INFORMATION AND ORIENTATION

Visitors Information: Oregon Dunes National Recreation Area Information Center, 855 USDA. 101, Reedsport (271-3611), just south of the Umpqua River Bridge. The Forest Service runs this center and will happily answer your questions or provide you with *Sand Tracks,* the area recreation guide, and hiking and camping tips. **Map** $3. Open daily 8am-4:30pm; Sept.-May Mon.-Fri. 8am-4:30pm.
Reedsport Chamber of Commerce (271-3495 or 800-247-2155 in OR), P.O. Box 11, U.S. 101 and Rte. 38, a pointy log shack across the street from the Recreation Area office. Dune buggy rental information and motel listings are available. Open daily 9am-6pm; Oct.-April 10am-4pm; May 9am-5pm.
Greyhound runs through Reedsport; call 756-4900 in Coos Bay for a schedule.
Taxi: Coastal Cab, 139 N 3rd St. (271-2690). About $7 to Windy Bay (in the dunes), $3 more to the beach. Service daily 6am-3pm. $1 for each extra person 12 and older.
Sand Buggy Rentals: Sandland Adventures (997-8087) at 10th St. and U.S. 101. Rental rate is $25 per hr., or take a tour for $25 per hr. Open daily.
Bike Rentals: Rent-All Center, 75303 U.S. 101 (271-4011) in Winchester, has tandems ($5 per hr.); single-speed bikes ($3 per hr.); and, mountain bikes ($5 per hr.). Open daily 8am-5:30pm; Nov.-Feb. Thurs.-Tues. 8am-5:30pm.
Laundromat: Coin Laundry, 420 N 14th St. (271-3587) next to the Umpqua Shopping Center in Reedsport. Wash $1, 7½-min. dry 25¢, Open daily 8am-9pm.
Library: 395 Winchester Ave. (271-3500). Open Mon. 2-8:30pm, Tues.-Wed. 10am-6pm, Thurs. 2-8:30pm, Fri. 10am-6pm, Sat. 10am-1pm.
Police: 136 N 4th, Reedsport (271-2109). **Fire:** 124 N 4th, Reedsport (271-2423).
Coast Guard: near the end of the harbor, at the foot of the mountain in Winchester Bay (271-2137).
Emergency: 911.
Post Office: 301 Fir St. (271-2521). Open Mon.-Fri. 8:30am-5pm. **General Delivery ZIP Code:** 97467.
Area Code: 503.

The dunes' shifting grip on the coastline is broken only once along the expanse, when the Umpqua and Smith Rivers empty into Winchester Bay about 1 mi. north of town. Reedsport, 21 mi. south of Florence, is a typical small highway town of motels, banks, and flashy restaurants, neatly subdivided by U.S. 101 and Rte. 38, which connects with I-5 60 mi. to the east.

ACCOMMODATIONS

Four mi. makes a significant difference in price: **Winchester Bay,** just south of Reedsport, has rooms for $30 or under, while the Reedsport average is about $40. Reservations are advisable in summer, particularly for weekends.

Harbor View Motel (271-3352), U.S. 101 in Winchester Bay. Spitting distance from the boats. The brown and white exterior is mildly depressing, but rooms are clean and comfortable, and there is no lack of mirrors. All rooms have small refrigerators. Huge glossy pictures of Marilyn Monroe and John Wayne in the lobby.

Clean, comfortable rooms are popular with anglers. Singles $26. Doubles $29. Rooms with 2 beds $34. Off-season rates $4 lower.

Fir Grove Motel, 2178 U.S. 101, Reedsport (271-4848). Quiet, comfortable rooms with coved ceilings and archways. Outdoor heated pool, cable TV, and coffee, donuts and fruit available from 6-9:30am. Queen bed $40, queen and twin bed $44, kitchen-equipped suite of 3 double beds and one twin for $65. Fantastic senior discounts: $6-10 off.

Tropicana Motel, 1593 U.S. 101 (271-3671), Winchester Bay. A respectable, clean motel with comfortable rooms; no tropical fruit in evidence. Continental breakfast, color TV with HBO, and a small trapezoidal swimming pool. Queen bed $43.

CAMPING

The national recreation area is administered by the Siuslaw National Forest. The campgrounds that allow dune buggy access, **Spinreel, Lagoon** (with Fri. and Sat. night campfire programs), **Waxmyrtle,** parking-lot style **Driftwood II,** and **Horsfall** (with showers), are generally loud and rowdy in the summer (sites $10). Limited reservations for summer weekends are available; call 800-280-CAMP more than 10 days prior to arrival. **Carter Lake** (22 sites) and **Tah Kenitch** (36 sites), both $10, are quieter sites designed for tenters and small RVs. The sites closest to Reedsport are in Winchester Bay and are either ugly, RV-infested, or both. The best campgrounds are between 1 and 4 mi. south of the Bay.

During the summer, RVs dominate all the campsites around Reedsport and Winchester Bay. Summer campers with tents don't have much hope of finding a legal campground free of screaming children. Flee to Eel Creek and Carter Lake.

Eel Creek Campground, 9 mi. south of Reedsport on U.S. 101. Excellent sites, some semi-sandy and many secluded by a border of tall bushes. The Forest Service runs interpretive programs at the tiny six-bench amphitheatre on Fri. nights. Sites $10.

Umpqua Lighthouse State Park (271-3546), 5 mi. south of Reedsport on U.S. 101. Quiet spots with hot showers, boat launch, hiker/biker sites ($4). Nearby **Lake Marie** is cold, but swimmable, with beach to boot. Sites $13, hookup $15.

William H. Tugman State Park, 8 mi. south of Reedsport on U.S. 101. Quiet, shady sites with a pleasant smattering of sand. Very close to gorgeous Eel Lake. All sites have water and electricity. Showers and facilities for campers with disabilities. Sites $14, hiker/biker $4.

Carter Lake Campground, 12 mi. north of Reedsport on U.S. 101. As quiet as it gets north of Reedsport; pleasant sites ($10). No ATVs.

Surfwood Campground, ½ mi. north of Winchester Bay off U.S. 101 on the beach side (271-4020). Sites have grassy parking areas, and are accessed by a painfully patched road. Sites separated by large, unidentifiable vegetation. RV Central. But the luxuries are all there: laundromat, heated pool, grocery store, tennis court, and hot showers. Call a week in advance during the summer. Sites for 2 people $12, full hookups $14. $2 each extra person.

FOOD

Cheap, greasy options prevail in Winchester Bay and Reedsport; vegetarians are advised to seek sustenance at **Safeway,** in the Umpqua Shopping Center in Reedsport (open daily 7am-11pm).

Don's Diner and Ice Cream Parlor, 2115 Winchester Ave. (271-2032) on U.S. 101. The restaurant may look like a fast-food chain, but don't take flight: the food is cheap and good, the menu extensive. Burgers (including a $3 gardenburger) are $2-5, sandwiches $3, salad $4. Save plenty of room for dessert: one scoop of ice cream (75¢) is phenomenally huge and absolutely delicious. Open daily 10am-10:30pm, winter 10am-10pm.

Seafood Grotto and Restaurant (271-4250), 115 8th St. at Broadway, Winchester Bay. An unexpected find: excellent seafood restaurant showcasing a large Victorian doll house. Lunches $4-7; for dinner splurge on the large salmon steak ($14). Open daily 11am-9pm.

Sugar Shack Bakery, at 2 locations: 145 N 3rd in **Reedsport** and in the **Umpqua Shopping Center** (271-3514). The latter is called **Leona's Restaurant** and has selection enough for a real meal; try the chili ($1.75) with a biscuit (75¢), or a sandwich ($3-5.50). Open Mon.-Thurs. 5am-9pm, Fri.-Sat. 5am-9:30pm. The actual bakery, which does a good business with chatty locals in the early hours, showcases excellent, fresh baked goods loaded with sugar. Fresh loaves of bread ($1.30) also available. Open daily 4am-8:30pm, in winter 4am-7:30pm.

OUTDOORS

Romp in the dunes. Why else are you here?

Those with little time or low noise tolerance should at least stop at the **Oregon Dunes Overlook,** off U.S. 101, about halfway between Reedsport and Florence. Steep wooden ramps lead to the gold and blue swells of the dunes and the Pacific. Trails wander off from the overlook, as they do at several other points on U.S. 101. The *Sand Tracks* brochure (available at the Information Center) has a free detailed **map** of the dunes. The Overlook is staffed daily from Memorial Day to Labor Day between 10am and 3pm. Guided hikes, brochures, and talks are available. A pamphlet on trails for dune-bound **hikers** is also available at the information center; an excellent, easy choice is the **Taylor Dunes** trail. This gentle, ½-mi. trail brings you to a good view of the dunes without the crowds. The trail is barrier-free and closed to off-road vehicles. Enjoy the cloying poetry on viewpoints along the way.

For a true dune experience, venture out on wheels. An ever-greater number of shops offer **dune-buggy** rentals or guided tours. **Oregon Dunes Tours** (759-4777) on Wildwood Dr., 10 mi. south of Reedsport off U.S. 101, gives 30-minute ($18) and hour-long ($30) dune-buggy rides (open daily 9am-6pm). The buggy rides are more fun than the tacky base camp would suggest, and the drivers have lots of good stories. If you really want to tear up the dunes, shell out $25 for 1 hr. on your own dune buggy. Rent from **Dune's Odyssey,** on U.S. 101 in Winchester Bay (271-4011; open Mon.-Sat. 8am-5:30pm, Sun. 9am-5:30pm, in winter closed Wed. in), **Sandland Adventures** (997-8087) at 10th St. and U.S. 101. (open daily), or **Spinreel Park,** 9122 Wildwood Dr., 8 mi. south on U.S. 101 (759-3313; open daily 9am-6pm, winter 9am-sunset). A host of other dune-buggy hot spots will be glad to rent their vehicles; ask at the Reedsport Chamber of Commerce.

When you tire of dune dawdling, you could try **deep-sea fishing** with one of the many charter companies that operate out of **Salmon Harbor,** Winchester Bay. Like everywhere else on the coast, you can virtually forget salmon fishing, but tuna and bottom-fishing are still available for die-hard enthusiasts. **Gee Gee Charters, Inc.** offers five-hour bottom-fishing trips ($50) daily at 6am and 1pm. Call the 24-hr. phone service several days before you wish to go to secure a reservation (271-3152). The required one-day license ($6.75) may be purchased at any of the charter offices. Trips leave daily at 6, 10am, and 2pm. Three-hour crabbing trips are also available for $30.

Water enthusiasts can take a two-hour cruise of Winchester Bay with **Umpqua Jet Adventures,** 423 Riverfront Way (271-5694 or 800-353-8386), in Reedsport. Trips run $15 a pop, ages 4-11 $8. The penniless should take in the wildlife at the **Dean Creek Elk Viewing Area,** 2 mi. east of Reedsport on Rte. 38. Here, you can observe the Roosevelt Elk, Oregon's largest land mammal, which was named after antler-toting Rough Rider Teddy Roosevelt. Large herds gather in an isolated spot off the road behind and to the right of the viewing area, into which few tourists venture.

Bird watching (lists are available at the National Recreation Area headquarters, across from the tourist office) and **whale watching** (across from the lighthouse in April, November, and December) are also popular. If you would rather catch animals than watch them, you can rent huge nets to nab crabs in Salmon Harbor. Around Labor Day every summer, Winchester Bay merchants sponsor a crabbing contest; the first competitor to find the tagged crab wins $1000. Plant-watching can, apparently, be interesting as well. At the **Darlington Botanical Gardens,** just off U.S. 101 a few mi. north of Reedsport, you can see an array of bug-eating plants.

■■■ COOS BAY AND NORTH BEND

The largest city on the Oregon Coast, Coos Bay is making an economic turnaround in the face of environmental regulations which have decimated the local lumber industry. The tourist trade has expanded economic opportunity, and businesses are returning to the once-deserted downtown shopping mall. Huge iron-sided tankers have begun to replace quaint fishing boats, and U.S. 101 passes through a bustling strip of shops and espresso bars.

PRACTICAL INFORMATION AND ORIENTATION

Visitors Information: Bay Area Chamber of Commerce, 50 E Central (269-0215 or 800-824-8486), off Commercial Ave. in Coos Bay, between the one-way thoroughfares of U.S. 101. Plenty of free brochures, but shell out $1.50 for a good county **map.** Open Mon.-Fri. 8:30am-6:30pm, Sat. 10am-4pm, Sun. noon-4pm; winter Mon.-Fri. 9am-5pm, Sat. 10am-4pm. **North Bend Information Center,** 1380 Sherman Ave. (756-4613), on U.S. 101, just south of the harbor bridge in North Bend. Open Mon.-Fri. 9am-5pm, Sat. 10:30am-4pm, Sun. 10am-4pm; closed winter. Closed Sun. Both are large and helpful.
Oregon State Parks Information, 365 N 4th St., Coos Bay (269-9410). Open Mon.-Fri. 8am-5pm. **Coos County Parks Department:** Open Mon.-Fri. 8am-noon and 1-5pm.
Greyhound, 2007 Union St. (756-4900). To Portland (3 per day, $24) and San Francisco (2 per day, $66). Open Mon.-Thurs. 9am-5pm, Fri. 9am-4pm, Sat. 9am-3pm.
Car Rental: Verger, 1400 Ocean Blvd. (888-5594). Cars from $20 per day; 15¢ per mi. after 50 mi. Open Mon.-Fri. 8am-6pm, Sat. 9am-6pm.
Taxi: Yellow Cab, 267-3111. 24 hrs. Seniors discount.
AAA Office: 1705 Ocean Blvd. SE (269-7432). Open Mon.-Fri. 8am-5pm.
Laundromat: Wash-A-Lot, 1921 Virginia Ave. Wash $1, 10-min. dry 25¢. 24 hrs.
Coos Bay Public Library: 525 W Anderson (269-1101). Open Mon.-Thurs. 10am-8pm, Fri.-Sat. 10am-5:30pm.
Crisis Line: 888-5911. 24-hr. information and referral. **Women's Crisis Service:** 756-7000, 24 hrs.
Hospital: Bay Area Hospital, 1775 Thompson Rd. (269-8111), in Coos Bay. **Medical Emergency:** 269-8085.
Emergency: 911. **Police:** 500 Central Ave. (269-8911). **Fire:** 150 S 4th St. (269-1191). **Coast Guard:** 4645 Eel Ave. (888-3266), in Charleston.
Post Office: 470 Golden Ave. (267-4514), at 4th St. Open Mon.-Fri. 8:30am-5pm. **General Delivery ZIP Code:** 97420.
Area Code: 503.

U.S. 101 again jogs inland south of Coos Bay, rejoining the coast at Bandon. Route 42 heads 85 mi. from Coos Bay to I-5 and U.S. 101 continues north into dune territory. U.S. 101 skirts the east side of both Coos Bay and North Bend, and the Cape Arago Hwy. continues west to **Charleston,** at the mouth of the bay.

ACCOMMODATIONS AND CAMPING

You have lots of options in Coos Bay and North Bend. Non-camper types should also consider the wonderful **hostel,** 23 mi. south on U.S. 101 in **Bandon.** Campers, be psyched: the state-run and private campgrounds allow you to take full advantage of the breathtaking coast.

Bluebill Forest Service Campground, off U.S. 101, 4 mi. northwest of North Bend. Follow the signs to the Horsfall Beach area. 19 sites with flush toilets. Trails lead to the ocean and dunes. Sites $10.
Bastendorff Beach Park (888-5353). A county park 11 mi. southwest of Coos Bay Cape off Arago Hwy. Highly developed sites include hot showers (25¢), flush toi-

lets, and hiking trails. No reservations accepted, but the park fills early; arrive before 5pm. Open year-round. 25 sites $11, 57 with full hookup $13.

Sunset Bay State Park 10965 Cape Arago Hwy., Coos Bay 97420 (888-4902), 12 mi. south of Coos Bay and 3½ mi. west of Charleston on the Coos Bay/Bandon loop. Akin to camping in a parking lot, but the cove makes the scene feel like Club Med. 138 sites with hot showers and wheelchair-accessible facilities. The phone booths actually have doors here. Reservations accepted by mail. Open mid-April through Oct. Hiker/biker sites $4, tent sites $15. Electrical hookup $16, full hookup $17.

Itty Bitty Inn Motel Bed and Breakfast, 1504 Sherman Ave., North Bend (756-6398), on U.S. 101. Tiny, comfortable rooms with cable TV, refrigerators, and freezers have been refurbished in cozy Adobe style. The aesthetic even extends to a pale purple and yellow exterior. For $2 more receive a gift-certificate for $10 at the Virginia St. Diner. Singles $35. Doubles $40. In winter about $3 less. Reservations recommended.

2310 Lombard, guess where, (756-3857) at the corner of Cedar St. An excellent choice. Two small, simple, and pleasant rooms with a smattering of African and Korean art on the walls, one with two twin beds, one with a double bed; shared bath. Large, comfortable common room with TV and magazines. Full breakfast from a wonderful hostess. Singles $30, doubles $35. Reservations recommended.

Captain John's Motel, 8061 Kingfisher Dr., Charleston (888-4041). Next to the small boat basin in Charleston, 9 mi. from the crowds at Coos Bay. The ranch-like red and white exterior gives this large, professional motel a feel-good air. Within walking distance of the decks. Queen beds $40-45, $2 student discount.

Timber Lodge, 1001 N Bayshore Dr., Coos Bay (267-7066), on U.S. 101. Downtown. Big rooms, restaurant, lounge. Morning coffee. Singles $39. Doubles $43. Business rates $10 lower a few weeks in advance. July-Aug. prices higher.

Parkside Motel, 1490 Sherman Ave. (756-4124), on U.S. 101 on the north edge of town. Plastic seagulls perched on every door. Rooms with cable TV and phones. Kitchenettes and laundry facilities available. Singles $38. Doubles $42.

FOOD

The Blue Heron Bistro, 100 Commercial St., Coos Bay (267-3933), at U.S. 101, Charleston turn-off. Almost upscale atmosphere and a well-stocked magazine and newspaper rack. Gigantic muffins ($1.25); lunches ($4.50-7). Dinners a bit more, but sublime. Try the seafood on a bed of spinach fettuccine ($12.45). Open daily 9am-10pm.

Kaffe 101, 134 S Broadway St. (267-5894) in Coos Bay. The fireplace, comfortable chair, and atmosphere echo an English tea house. The food is limited to the likes of cinnamon rolls ($1.75), so suck up lots of espresso ($1.25) or their twelve-oz. specialty drinks, like French Vanilla Nut ($2.50). A local harpist tunes in on Thurs. nights; an acoustic guitarist Tues. and Fri. nights. Open Mon.-Thurs. 6am-9pm, Fri. 6am-10pm, Sat. 8am-10pm; in winter Mon.-Thurs. 7:30am-8pm, Fri. 7:30am-10pm, Sat. 8am-10pm.

Cheryn's Seafood Restaurant and Pie House (888-3251), at the east end of Charleston Bridge, in Charleston. A baby-blue and pink building. The menu is jammed with inexpensive, grilled, or fried seafood ($6-10), sandwiches ($4-6), and even garden burgers ($4.25). Diffuse awkward moments of silence by studying the county maps conveniently located beneath the glass on every table. Open daily 8am-9pm; in winter daily 8am-8pm.

Virginia Street Diner, 1430 Virginia St., North Bend (756-3475). Uplift your soul with the 50s music in this locally popular diner. A 65¢ coffee at breakfast means the whole pot. Entrees $6-7. Try the honey-dipped chicken ($6.35). Open daily 6am-10pm.

SIGHTS AND ACTIVITIES

Those who need to fill a rainy day or are simply tired of water should make a beeline for **Cranberry Sweets,** 1005 Newmark (888-9824) in Coos Bay. This sucrose wonderland is half-factory, half-shop. Free candy samples are tiny but abundant; nibble as you watch formless chocolate sludge miraculously transformed into shapely pieces of candy (open Mon.-Sat. 9am-5:30pm, Sun. 11am-4pm).

South of Coos Bay is the **Marshfield Sun Printing Museum,** 1049 N Front St. (269-1363), at Front St. and U.S. 101, across from the Timber Inn. The first floor remains in its early 20th-century state; some of the equipment dates to the paper's birth in 1891. Upstairs are exhibits on the history of printing, American newspapers, and early Coos Bay (open June-Aug. Tues.-Sat. 1-4pm; free; call 756-6418 to arrange a winter tour).

In North Bend, the **Little Theatre on the Bay** (756-4336), at Sherman and Washington St., presents musical cabaret with a regional flavor on Saturday nights.

Coos Bay is one of the few places on the coast where life slows down as you near the shore. Escape the industrial chaos by following Cape Arago Hwy. from Coos Bay to **Charleston.** (The highway signs alternately say Charleston and Ocean Beaches.) A town where crusty old sea salts seem at home, Charleston is a more authentic place to stay for an extended period than its two bigger neighbors.

Make arrangements to tour the **Coast Guard Lifeboat Station** (888-3266) in the Charleston Marina (tours available anytime by prior reservation) or hop on board one of the many charters nearby. **Betty Kay Charters,** P.O. Box 5020 (888-9041 or 800-752-6303), and **Bob's Sportfishing,** P.O. Box 5018 (888-4241 or 800-628-9633), operate out of the same building in the Charleston Boat Basin. Both companies run six-hour bottom fishing trips daily at 6am and noon for $55 with a $6.75 daily license. Crab rings are rented for $3 each (with a $15 deposit), and the clamming is good, but bring your own shovel or rake.

OUTDOORS

Charleston is a convenient stop on the way to **Shore Acres State Park** (888-3732). Once the estate of local lumber lord Louis J. Simpson, the park contains botanical gardens that survived when the mansion was razed. The well-cared-for flowers are a refreshing change of scenery from endless seashell-strewn beaches. The egret sculptures are a more recent addition, courtesy of some artistically-inclined inmates from the state penitentiary. A lovely rose garden lies hidden in the back. In the week before Christmas, the flowers are festooned with strings of lights, and the park serves complimentary cocoa and hot cider. (Open daily 8am-dusk. $3 per car on weekends. Wheelchair access.)

Farther down the same highway is **Cape Arago,** notable mainly for its wonderful **tide pools.** Large sand bars rise and fade for some distance from the actual shore, giving a illusory impression of water depth.

Four mi. up off the Cape Arago Hwy., the **South Slough National Estuarine Research Reserve** (888-5558) is one of the most dramatic and underappreciated spots on the central coast. The Reserve protects over almost 7 sq. mi. of estuaries, where salt and fresh water mix. The Slough area teems with wildlife, from sand shrimp to deer. **Hiking trails** weave through the sanctuary; take a lunch and commune with the blue heron. **Hidden Creek** (3 mi. round-trip), **Winchester,** and **Wasson Creek Trails** give access to the upper reaches of the freshwater marsh. The trails are usually quiet, but beware: during the academic year, schools of children on field trips swarm into the reserve.

Travel 4 mi. to the new **visitors center** and headquarters which explains the ecology of the estuarine environment. Guided walks are given during the summer (Fri. 2-4pm). Canoe tours ($5) are also available, depending on the tides and provided you have your own canoe. For a summer calendar, write P.O. Box 5417, Charleston, OR 97420 (open daily 8:30am-4:30pm; trails open dawn to dusk daily).

Freshwater fanatics should drive northeast from Eastside on the Coos River Rd. past the town of Allegany to **Golden and Silver Falls State Park.** There, ¾ mi. up a beautiful trail crossed with downed logs, twin falls (about 1 mi. apart each) crash 100 ft. into groves of red alder and Douglas fir.

EVENTS

The **Oregon Coast Maritime Festival** hits Coos Bay in mid-July, during the opening weekend of the **Oregon Coast Music Festival,** P.O. Box 663, Coos Bay 97420 (269-0938), which is itself the most popular event on the coast. Art exhibits, vessel tours, and a free concert virtually treble the options for activities in Coos Bay. The Music Festival itself draws a variety of musical performances to Coos Bay and North Bend (and Bandon and Reedsport). Unreserved tickets range from $7 to $10; for a few dollars extra, tickets can be renewed and charged by phone at 267-0938. Ask at the Chamber of Commerce (see Practical Info.) about unreserved ticket outlets.

In the second week of August, Charleston hosts a refined but nevertheless decadent **Seafood and Wine Festival** in the Boat Basin. In late August, Coos Bay touts a native fruit with the **Blackberry Arts Festival.** Downtown rocks with square dancing, wine tasting, concerts, and crafts. Contact the Chamber of Commerce for more details. In September, Oregon remembers one of its favorite sons in the **Steve Prefontaine 10K Road Race,** named after the great Olympic athlete who died in an automobile accident in the bell lap of his career. The race attracts dozens of world-class runners to the area (entrance $12-15). For information on these events, contact the Bay Area Fun Festival, P.O. Box 481 Coos Bay (269-7514).

■■■ COOS BAY TO BROOKINGS

BANDON

The McDonald's-free town of Bandon lies twenty-four mi. south of Coos Bay on U.S. 101. **Greyhound** (756-4900) stops twice daily by **McKay's Market** on U.S. 101. The **Bandon Chamber of Commerce,** P.O. Box 1515 (347-9616) on U.S. 101 has departure times and plenty of brochures and assistance (open daily 10am-5pm; Sept.-May 10am-4pm).

The rambling **Sea Star Hostel (HI/AYH),** 375 2nd St. (347-9632), in Old-Town Bandon, adds a budget element to town accommodations. Comfortable bunkrooms, a kitchen, a laundry room, and an open-24-hours policy combine to make this hostel a relaxed and fun place to pass a night on the coast. No smoking. The Bistro downstairs offers expensive but good gourmet cuisine and espresso. The hostel costs $12, non-members $15, under 12 ½-price. Private rooms are also available ($26, non-members $32). Alternatively, find your way to the **Bandon Wayside Motel** (347-3421) on Hwy. 42. Each room contains a magazine selection and cable TV (singles from $29, doubles from $34).

Free cheese? Head for the **Bandon Cheese Inn** (347-2456), on U.S. 101. The quantity of free samples will astound; remember, though, that this retail store will expect you to buy something (open Mon.-Sat. 8:30am-5:30pm, Sun. 9am-5pm). Factory viewing is possible on Tuesday, Thursday, and Saturday mornings.

Outdoor activities near Bandon abound. Trolling around Old-town Bandon is picturesque and pleasant, as is exploring the beaches with a horse from **Bandon Stables** (347-3423); one-hour rides cost $20. Or drive through **Bullard's Beach State Park,** 2 mi. north of town off U.S. 101, and scramble to the top of the 1986 **Coquille River Lighthouse** (open daily during daylight hours).

The State Park has 192 sites (tent $15; electrical hookup $16; full hookup $17; hiker/biker $4; primitive campsites $9). For a bit of peace, tenters should grab a spot in the horse-camp, tucked away from the main camp. Campfire talks are given Tuesday through Saturday nights.

The **post office** in Bandon is at 105 12th St. (347-3406; open Mon.-Fri. 8:30am-4:30pm). The **General Delivery ZIP Code** is 97411.

PORT ORFORD

Tiny Port Orford is near **Cape Blanco,** the westernmost point in the continental U.S. In **Cape Blanco State Park,** the Cape reaches out from the coast far enough for you to see forever. The park's flower-carpeted hills are topped by a postcard-perfect lighthouse. The **information center,** P.O. Box 637 (332-8055), at Battle Rock, on the south side of town, dispenses more brochures than one would expect a town this size could produce (open daily 9am-5pm). U.S. 101 zips through Port Orford so quickly that unless you know where Battle Rock is, you'll miss the town entirely. Port Orford is 45 mi. south of Bandon and 30 mi. north of Gold Beach. **Greyhound** (247-7710) stops at the Circle K store, across from the Port Orford Motel, with service to Portland ($29) and San Francisco ($60). The **Post Office** is at 311 W 7th St. (332-4251) at Jackson (open Mon.-Fri. 8:30am-1pm and 2-5pm). **General Delivery ZIP Code:** 97465. **Area code:** 503.

While in Port Orford, admire the sunburnt-pink buildings and beautiful landscaping of the **Port Orford Motel,** 1034 Oregon St. (332-1685), at U.S. 101 or, for $30-35 a night, admire them from the inside. The Port Orford Motel is closer to the bus line than the waterfront motels, and only 10 minutes from the beach. The Shoreline Motel, P.O. Box 26 (332-2903), across U.S. 101 from the visitors center, has large rooms equipped with coffee and cable (singles $36, doubles $38, winter rates drop $10). If you must stay on the beach, stay at one of the three campgrounds. **Humbug Mountain State Park** (332-6774), 6 mi. south of Port Orford, has 108 sites with stunning scenery ($15, full hookup $17, hiker/biker $4). You'll also find magnificent views at **Cape Blanco State Park** (332-6774), 9 mi. north of Port Orford, off U.S. 101 (58 sites; tent $15, full hookup $17, hiker/biker $4). A bit more off the beaten path lies the **Elk River Campground,** 93363 Elk River Rd. (332-2255), off U.S. 101. You'll be rewarded for your trip with clean sites and great fossil-hunting nearby at Butler Bar (sites $8, full hookups $12).

For other magnificent views, take a walk through **Humbug Mountain State Park,** 7 mi. south of town. Survivors of the 3-mi. hike up the mountain win a tremendous panorama of the entire area. **Fishing** in the two nearby rivers (the Sixes and the Elk) is fantastic. Ask at the information center for details. **Scuba divers** come to the area for Port Orford's protected coves, where the water temperature rises to a mild 65°F and water clarity ranges from 10 to 50 ft. in summer. Water clarity is even better during the winter, when lower water temperatures (45-60°F) drive the plankton away.

GOLD BEACH

Twenty-five mi. north of Brookings, the town of Gold Beach has a commercial bent worthy of its name. The brochure-fortified **Chamber of Commerce,** 1225 S Ellensburg Ave. (247-7526 or 800-525-2334; open Mon.-Fri. 8am-7pm, Sat.-Sun. 10am-5pm), shares a building with the **Gold Beach Ranger District** (247-6655; open Mon.-Fri. 8am-5pm, Sat.-Sun. 8am-4pm).

The best in Gold Beach's budget accommodations is the **Oregon Trail Lodge,** 550 N Ellensburg Ave. (U.S. 101), which has tiny but respectable rooms for $33 in summer. The $37 rooms are worth the extra $4; a little annex contains a stove (bring your own pots). Locals love the **Port Hole Cafe;** it's not at all the typical greasy coastal cafe. Feast on their famous salads ($7) or a tempting assortment of fresh seafood, burgers, or sandwiches (try the "Gold Digger:" deep fried snapper for $6). The atmosphere is light, with refreshing tunes and porthole-wanna-be-mirrors lining the walls (open daily 11am-8pm).

Earn your dinner money by **panning for gold** along the beach. The town didn't get its name for nothing; equipment can be purchased for $4 from the **Rogue Outdoor Store,** 560 N Ellensburg Ave. (247-7142).

Greyhound, 310 Colvin St. (247-7710) runs through Gold Beach ($5.50 to Port Orford or Brookings). The **Post Office** is at 32865 Nesika Rd. (247-7610; open Mon.-Fri. 8am-5pm, Sat. 8:30-10:30am). The **General Delivery ZIP Code** is 97464.

■■■ BROOKINGS

Brookings, the southernmost stop before California, is one of the few coastal towns that has remained relatively tourist-free. Here trinket shops do not elbow out hardware stores and warehouses. Although gorgeous beaches and parks surround

Brookings, it is accessible only by U.S. 101 and tends to be more of a stopover than a destination. So while good restaurants and lodgings are not abundant, the beaches are among the most unspoiled on the Oregon coast. Brookings sits in a region often called the "Banana Belt" due to its mild climate: summery weather is not uncommon in January, and Brookings' beautiful blossoms bloom early.

Practical Information The **Brookings State Welcome Center,** 1650 U.S. 101 maintains an exceptionally well-stocked office just north of Brookings and answers questions regarding the Oregon coast (open April-Oct. Mon.-Sat. 8am-6pm, Sun. 9am-5pm). The town's **Chamber of Commerce,** 16330 Lower Harbor Rd. (469-3181 or 800-535-9469; fax 469-4094), is across the bridge to the south, a short way off the highway. City **maps** are $1 (open Mon.-Fri. 9am-5pm, Sat. 9am-1pm). The **Chetco Ranger Station,** 555 5th St. (469-2196), distributes information on this area of the **Siskiyou National Forest** (open daily 7:30am-4:30pm).

The **Greyhound** station, 601 Railroad Ave. (469-3326), at Tanburk, sends 2 buses north and 2 south each day. (To: Portland, $32; San Francisco, $53); open Mon.-Fri. 8:30am-6:30pm, Sat. 8:30am-noon.) The **Maytag Laundry** (469-3975), is known to locals as "The Old Wash House"; you'll find it in the Brookings Harbor Shopping Center (open daily 7am-11pm; wash $1, 10-min. dry 25¢). The **Post Office** (469-2318), is at 711 Spruce St. (Open Mon.-Fri. 9am-4:30pm. **General Delivery ZIP Code:** 97415.)

Accommodations, Camping, and Food Bed down at the **Chetco Inn,** 417 Fern St. (469-5347), a hotel on a hill (behind the Chevron gas station overlooking the town). The red-carpeted hallways lead to an almost-hostel-like bargain: fairly plain but adequate singles for $28, doubles $29 (both with hall bathrooms). Rooms with private baths run $35 for singles, $37 doubles. In winter prices drop $7-10 in winter.

Harris Beach State Park (469-2021), at the north edge of Brookings, has 69 tent sites in the midst of a grand natural setting. The park lies on the beach across from the 21-acre **Goat Island** and is equipped with showers, hiker/biker sites ($2), and facilities for people with disabilities (open year-round; sites $15, with hookup $17). Make reservations if you plan to stay between Memorial Day and Labor Day. **Loeb State Park,** 8 mi. east of Brookings, has good swimming and fishing. A 1-mi. trail leads to a soothing redwood grove. Tent sites ($13) include electricity and water (open year-round; no reservations accepted). For more campsites off the beaten path, continue east another 7 mi. past Loeb to the charming **Little Redwood** campground. Redwood picnic grove, alongside a burbling and salamander-filled creek, has about 35 sites ($4), with pit toilets. For more information contact the **Chetco Ranger District** (see Practical Information, above).

Sights, Activities, and Events Brookings is known statewide for its beautiful flowers. In **Azalea Park,** downtown, lawns are encircled by large native azaleas, some of which are more than 300 years old (bloom-time is April-June). Two rare weeping spruce trees also grace the park's grounds. Picnic areas and facilities for the disabled are provided. The **Chetco Valley Historical Society Museum,** 15461 Museum Rd. (469-6651), 2½ mi. south of the Chetco River, occupies the oldest building in Brookings. Exhibits include the patchwork quilts of settlers and Native American basketwork. The museum is hard to miss; the nation's largest cypress tree stands in front (open Wed.-Sun. noon-4pm; $1, children 50¢). The pride of Brookings is its annual **Azalea Festival,** held in the Azalea Park during Memorial Day weekend. March brings the **Beachcomber's Festival,** which showcases art created from driftwood and other material found on the beach.

If you're heading north from Brookings by bicycle, take scenic **Carpenterville Rd.,** which was the only highway out of town before U.S. 101 was built. The twisty, 13½-mi. road features beautiful ocean views. Watch for cattle and sheep; the road crosses an open grazing range. Boardman State Park enfolds U.S. 101 for 8 mi. north of Brookings; overlooks and picnic sites provide fantastic views of the coast. North of Bookings, you can ride a mail boat up the **Rogue River. Mail Boat Hydro-Jets** (247-7033 800-458-3511) offers 64-, 80-, and 104-mi. daytrips abounding in scenic views, history, and whitewater (from $27.50, children from $10).

INLAND VALLEYS

While the jagged cliffs and coastal surf draw tourists and nature lovers to the Oregon coast, more Oregonians live in the lush Willamette and Rogue River Valleys. Vast tracts of fertile land support productive agriculture. For decades, the immense forest resources also supported a healthy timber industry, but a few years ago, Congress passed legislation to protect the endangered northern spotted owl. A federal court injunction then banned logging in the public forests of the Pacific Northwest, crippling the local economy, leaving mills idle, and throwing many out of work. In June 1994, however, after a review of a complex new forest-use-and-protection plan created by the Clinton Administration, another Federal court ruling lifted the ban and permitted limited logging. Environmental groups and timber interests will likely contest the forest plan in court. But while the fortunes of the timber industry appear uncertain, tourism is definitely a growth industry in southern Oregon.

Interstate 5 (I-5), which runs north-south through Oregon, traverses rolling agricultural and forest land punctuated by a few urban centers. Farthest south, the **Rogue River Valley,** from Ashland to Grants Pass, is generally hot and dry in the summer, which brings a lucrative business to the whitewater rafting and kayaking outfitters. **Eugene,** Oregon's second-largest city and bawdiest college town, rests at the southern end of the temperate **Willamette Valley.** This carpet of agricultural land extends 20 mi. on either side of the river and runs 80 mi. north until it bumps into Portland's bedroom communities.

It is possible to travel Oregon's 305-mi. stretch of I-5 from tip to toe in less than six hours, but pedal-happy out-of-staters should be wary—most Oregonians obey speed limits, and fines for speeding have recently skyrocketed. But don't despair; the Oregon Parks and Recreation Department maintains rest areas every 30 to 40 mi. along the interstate. Public rest rooms, phones, picnic tables, and "animal exercise areas" are available. Rest areas are shaded, grassy, and generally well-kept, but travelers should bring their own toilet paper. Tents may not be pitched in public rest areas, but those motorists who can stick it out on a back seat may park for up to 18 hours.

■■■ ASHLAND

With an informal, rural setting near the California border, Ashland mixes hippiness and history, making it the perfect locale for the world-famous **Shakespeare festival** (see below). From mid-February to October, drama devotees can choose from a repertoire of 11 plays, all performed in Ashland's three elegant theaters. The plays are neatly incorporated into the town itself; Ashland's balmy climate allows for nightly summertime performances in the outdoor Elizabethan theater and refunds in case of rain. Though Ashland can be crowded with visitors in the summer, the town has not sold its soul to the tourist trade. It has preserved a genuine identity, and the Shakespearean acting is quite possibly world-class. Internationally famous theater companies make Ashland a regular stop. In its 60-year history, the festival has fostered delightful shops, lodgings, and restaurants within the city. Culture comes with a price, but low-cost accommodations and tickets reward those who investigate.

October's rains see the last of the Shakespeare buffs and return the students of **Southern Oregon State College.** By Thanksgiving, the nearby Siskiyou Mountains are blanketed with snow and sprinkled with cross-country skiers, while alpine skiers swarm to Mt. Ashland. Spring thaw brings hikers, bikers, and rafters.

A S H L A N D

PRACTICAL INFORMATION AND ORIENTATION

Visitors Information: Chamber of Commerce, 110 E Main St. (482-3486). A harried, busy staff frantically answers phones and dishes out free play schedules and brochures, several of which contain small but adequate **maps.** The Chamber of Commerce does *not* sell tickets to performances. Open Mon.-Fri. 9am-5pm.

Oregon Shakespearean Festival Box Office, P.O. Box 158, Ashland 97520 (482-4331; fax 482-8045), at 15 S Pioneer St. next to the Elizabethan Theater. Rush tickets (½-price) occasionally available ½ hr. before performances that aren't sold out. Ask at the box office for more options; the staff is full of tips for desperate theater-goers. (See **The Shakespeare Festival** below.)

US Forest Service at 645 Washington St. (482-3333). Hiking and other outdoor information, including the Pacific Coast Trail.

Rogue Valley Transportation (779-2877), in Medford. Schedules available at the Chamber of Commerce. Base fare 75¢. Over 65 and ages 6-11 ½-price. The #15 bus serving Ashland runs every ½ hr. Mon.-Fri. 5am-7:30pm, Sat. 7am-6pm. Service Mon.-Sat. to Medford ($1.25), and from there to Jacksonville (on bus #30, $1.50). Also loops through downtown Ashland every 15 min. (25¢).

Greyhound: There is no depot in Ashland. Pick-up and drop-off at 2nd St. and Lithia Way, in front of Rocket Photo. To: Portland (2 per day; $33) and Sacramento (3 per day; $44) with service to San Francisco.

Taxi: Ashland Taxi, 482-3065. 24 hr.

Car Rental: Budget, 2525 Ashland St., at the Windmill Ashland Hills Inn (488-7741 for reservations, phone or fax 482-0626 for information). Mid-sized cars $40 per day on weekdays, $33 per day on weekends, or $189 per week. Unlimited mileage. 10% AARP discount, $2 off for *Let's Go* users. Under 25 $7.50 per day extra, no under-21 rentals. Accepts all major credit cards.

Library: Ashland Branch Library, 410 Siskiyou Blvd. (482-1197). Open Mon.-Tues. 10am-8pm, Wed.-Thurs. 10am-6pm, Fri.-Sat. 10am-5pm.

Laundromat: Main St. Laundromat, 370 E Main St. (482-8042). Wash $1, 10-min. dry for 25¢. Open daily 8am-9pm.

Public Toilets: At Tudor Guild & S Pioneer St., Lithia Park; also try the library.

Equipment Rental: Ashland Mountain Supply, 31 N Main St. (488-2749). Internal frame backpacks $7.50 per day for the first 2 days, $5 per additional day ($100 deposit). External frame backpacks $5 per day for the first 2 days, $3.50 per additional day ($50 deposit). Mountain bikes $10 for 2 hr., $25 per day. **The Adventure Center,** 40 N Main St. (488-2819). Mountain bikes $20 per day. Guided bike tours from $34.

Road Conditions: 1-976-7277.

Crisis Intervention Services: 779-4490.

Emergency: 911. **Police:** 1155 E Main St. (482-5211). **Fire:** 422 Siskiyou Dr. (482-2770).

Post Office: 120 N 1st St. (482-3986), at Lithia Way. Open Mon.-Fri. 9am-5pm.
General Delivery ZIP Code: 97520.
Area Code: 503.

Ashland is 15 mi. north of the California border. Rte. 66 traverses 64 mi. of stunning scenery between Klamath Falls and Ashland. Downtown Ashland centers around E Main St.; a medley of restaurants and shops rings the Plaza, where E becomes N Main St. About 1½ mi. west down Siskiyou Blvd. is Southern Oregon State College (SOSC), which supports another, smaller grouping of eating and sleeping establishments.

ACCOMMODATIONS AND CAMPING

"Now spurs the lated traveler apace to gain the timely inn"
Macbeth, III.iii.6.

In winter, Ashland is a budget traveler's paradise of vacancy and low rates, but in summer, rates double in virtually every hotel, and the hostel is impenetrable. Only a rogue or knave would arrive without a reservation. Mid-summer nights see vacant accommodations only in nearby Medford. Note: the bathroom in your hotel or accommodation may (or may not) smell strongly of rotten eggs. Almost all municipal water supplies everywhere contain traces of dissolved salts and compounds; at least part of Ashland's water supply contains dissolved sulfurous compounds. It is perfectly safe to drink and bathe in but lends some bathrooms a characteristically repugnant, and nearly permanent, odor.

Ashland Hostel (HI/AYH), 150 N Main St. (482-9217). Well-kept and cheery, this hostel is run by a wonderful staff that is ready to advise you on the ins and outs of Shakespeare ticket-hunting. Breakfast each morning is a great opportunity to enthuse over the plays with other happy hostel guests. Laundry facilities, game room. $11, non-members $13. $1 discounts for Pacific Coast Trail hikers, touring cyclists, or recognized groups. Check-in 5-11pm. Curfew at midnight. Lockout 10am-5pm. Reservations essential March-Oct; large groups sometimes fill the hostel.

Columbia Hotel, 262½ E Main St. (482-3726). A European-style home 1½ blocks from the theaters. Splendid 1940s decor, with wood panelling, old pictures, muted colors and a magnificent sitting room lifted from the pages of a Jane Austen novel. Friendly staff. Bathroom down the hall. Singles and doubles $46 June-Oct., March-May $39, Nov.-Feb. $28. 10% discount for HI/AYH members in the off-season, children under 12 free.

Timbers Motel, 1450 Ashland St. (482-4242; fax 482-8723), 5 min. from downtown. Good-sized rooms, with a thick carpet for weary feet. Pool, color TV, phone in room. Singles and doubles $52 in summer, add $5 for each additional person. Winter rates $40 for singles and doubles. 10% discount for AAA members.

Vista 6 Motel, 535 Clover Lane (482-4423), on I-5 at exit 14. Small rooms. Not center-stage for main attractions. Friendly staff. TV, A/C, small pool. Singles $23. Doubles $26. Winter and spring discounts.

Palm Motel, 1065 Siskiyou Blvd. (482-2636). Small but pleasantly furnished rooms, pool and picnic area. Singles $39. Doubles $48 in summer.

Jackson Hot Springs, 2253 Hwy. 99 N (482-3776), off exit 19 from I-5, down Valley View Rd. to Rte. 99 N for about ½ mi. Nearest campground to downtown. Separate tent area in a grassy, open field encircled by RV sites, which might make you feel like you're camping in front of an apartment building. Laundry facilities, hot showers, and mineral baths ($5 per person, $8 for a couple). Tent sites $12, RV sites $15, with full hookup $17.

Emigrant Lake (776-7001), 6 mi. southeast on Rte. 66, exit 14 off I-5. Sites $12 for 2 adults and children under 16 years; $2 per additional adult. Nearby swimming in Emigrant Lake. Hot showers. No hookup available.

FOOD

> *"Give them great meals of beef and iron and steel, they will eat like wolves and fight like devils"*
>
> Henry V, III.vii.166.

Ashland cooks up an equally impressive, and somewhat more digestible, spread for its festival guests. Beware the pre-show rush; a downtown dinner planned at 6:30pm can easily become a later affair. The hostel has kitchen facilities (see Accommodations). **Ashland Community Food Store COOP,** 237 3rd St. (482-2237), has a great selection of organic produce and natural foods, ideal to supply a picnic or hike (5% discount for seniors; open Mon.-Sat. 8am-9pm, Sun. 9am-9pm). Groceries are available at **Sentry Market,** 310 Oak St. (482-3521; open daily 8am-10pm), and **Safeway,** 585 Siskiyou Blvd. (482-4495; open daily 6am-midnight).

Geppetto's, 345 E Main St. (482-1138). A local favorite, Geppetto's is the place to get late-night nosh. A large, eclectic straw-basket collection on the walls complements the large, eclectic dinner crowd. All produce organically grown. Loosely Italian cuisine, with burgers randomly included. Mostly healthful; fantastic eggplant veggie-burger on a bun ($3.75). Dinners average $10; breakfasts less—try the pesto omelette ($6.50). Lunches $4-6. Open daily 8am-midnight.

The Bakery Cafe, 38 E Main St. (482-2117). *The* breakfast place. A menu as unique as Ashland itself. Blueberry buckwheat pancakes ($4.25) or scrambled tofu options ($6) for those who can't resist tofu before noon. Always crowded, always delicious. Open Mon. 7am-4pm, Tues.-Sun. 7am-8pm.

Great American Pizza Company, 1448 Ashland St. (Rte. 66), (488-7742). A fairly standard, pizza parlor-esque interior is home to "the best pizza in town." Large, cheese-smothered slices. Locals whisper reverently of the Mediterranean pizza with spinach, garlic, and artichoke hearts (small $6.50, large $16). Ben & Jerry's Peace Pops ($1.75) on the dessert list.

Greenleaf Restaurant, 49 N Main St. (482-2808). Healthy, delicious food, right on the plaza near the creek. Scones, interlaced with strawberry jam, are a breakfast treat ($1.20); pasta entrees ($4.50-7) are a sure bet for dinner. Carry-out for a picnic in nearby Lithia Park. Open Tues.-Sun. 8am-9pm, Mon. 8am-7pm.

Brothers Restaurant and Delicatessen, 95 N Main St. (482-9671). A traditional New York-style deli and cafe, with some offbeat selections (zucchini burger $4). Open Sun.-Mon. 7am-3pm, Tues.-Sat. 7am-8pm.

Backporch BBQ, 92½ N Main St. (482-4131), north of the plaza, above the creek. Texas-style barbecue ($9-12) and margaritas ($3.25) consumed outside to the tune of a bubbling creek. Restaurant open June-Aug. daily 11:30am-9pm. Bar open until 2am on weekends. Closed in winter, but the adjacent **Senor Gator** remains open and carries the BBQ torch through the cold season.

Omar's, 1380 Siskiyou Blvd. (482-1281). A complete dining experience in Ashland's oldest operating restaurant and lounge. Seafood lovers' mouths will water, especially at the daily specials, including baked sturgeon and chinook salmon. Steak fans will also be pleased with top sirloin offerings. Entrees $10-15; sandwiches $4-6. Lunch Mon.-Fri. 11:30am-2pm; dinner 5-10pm, until 10:30 on Fri. and Sat. nights. Bar open until 2:30am every night.

Fine Rivers, 139 E Main St. (488-1883), upstairs from street level. Slip upstairs, away from the madness of Shakespeare aficionados, to spicy and delicious Indian cuisine. Elegant Indian artwork. Entrees $5.50-11.50; vegetarian options all below $6.50. Daily lunch buffet $5.50. Open daily 11am-2:30pm, 5:30-10pm.

North Light Vegetarian Restaurant, 120 E Main St. (482-9463). Great Mexican and Oriental vegetarian fare. The outdoor patio is a relaxed, pleasant environment where you can savor the bean and tofu offerings. Bean burrito ($4) and curried tofu with noodles ($6.25) are good bets. Open Mon.-Fri. 11am-8:30pm, Sat.-Sun. 9am-8pm.

THE SHAKESPEARE FESTIVAL

"This is very midsummer madness"

Twelfth Night, III.iv.62.

The **Shakespeare Festival,** the 1935 brainchild of local college teacher Angus Bowmer, began with two plays performed in the Chautauqua theater by schoolchildren as an evening complement to daytime boxing matches. Today, professional actors perform eleven plays in repertory. As the selections have become more modern, Shakespeare's share has shrunk to three plays; the other eight are classical and contemporary dramas. Performances run on the three Ashland stages from mid-February through October, and any boxing now is over the extremely scarce tickets ("Lay on, Macduff! And damned be him that first cries, 'Hold, enough!'" *Macbeth,* V.vii.62). On the side of the Chautauqua theater stands the **Elizabethan Stage,** an outdoor theater modeled after one in eighteenth-century London. Open only from mid-June through early October, the Elizabethan hosts two Shakespeare plays per season. The **Angus Bowmer** is a 600-seat indoor theater that stages one Shakespeare play and several classical dramas. Modeled after a 17th-century London theater, the Elizabeth is open only June to September. The newest of the three theaters is the intimate **Black Swan,** home to small-scale, offbeat productions. The house is dark on Mondays.

Due to the tremendous popularity of the productions, ticket purchases are recommended six months in advance. General mail-order ticket sales begin in January, but phone orders are not taken until February ($17-23 spring and fall, $20-26 in summer). For complete ticket information, write Oregon Shakespeare Festival, P.O. Box 158, Ashland 97520; call 482-4331; or fax 482-8045. Though obtaining tickets can be difficult in the summertime, spontaneous theater-goers should not abandon hope. The **box office** at 15 S Pioneer St. opens at 9:30am on theater days; prudence demands arriving a few hours early. Local patrons have been known to leave their shoes to hold their places in line, and you should respect this tradition. At 9:30am, the box office releases any unsold tickets for the day's performances. If no tickets are available, you will be given a priority number, entitling you to a place in line when the precious few tickets that festival members have returned are released (12:30pm for 1pm matinees, 1pm for 2pm matinees, and 6pm for evening performances). The box office also sells twenty clear-view standing-room tickets for sold-out shows on the Elizabethan Stage ($9, obtained only on the day of the show). At these times, unofficial ticket transactions also take place just outside the box office, though scalping is illegal. ("Off with his head!" —*Richard III,* III.iv.75). From March to May, half-price rush tickets are often available an hour before every performance that is not sold out. Additionally, some half-price student-senior matinees are offered. Spring and summer previews (pre-critic, full-performance shows) are offered early in the season at the Black Swan and Elizabethan Stage for a discounted price ($14-21).

The **Greenshaw** provides a relaxed way to warm up to Shakespeare; each show offers 1½ hours professional folk dancing and singing, free. Held at 15 S Pioneer St., on the lawn outside the box office. It holds three shows in rotation, one per day. No tickets are necessary. (June-Oct. Sun.-Tues. 7pm, spring and fall Sun.-Tues. 6:30pm.) The **backstage tours** ($8, ages 5-7 $6) provide a wonderful glimpse of the festival from behind the curtain. Tour guides (usually actors or technicians) divulge all kinds of anecdotes—from bird songs during an outdoor *Hamlet* to the ghastly events which take place every time they do "that Scottish play." Tours last almost two hours and leave from the Black Swan (Tues.-Sun., 10am). Admission fee includes a trip to the **Exhibit Center** for a close-up look at sets and costumes (otherwise $2, children under 12 $1). Bring a camera to record your own role in the dress-up room (open Tues.-Sun. 10am-4pm; fall and spring 10:30am-1:30pm). Further immersion in Shakespeare can be had at two-hour summer seminars offered on selected Fridays (9:30-11:30am) by Southern Oregon State College ($5). Call 552-6904 for further information. The Shakespeare festival also includes special events, such as the **Feast of Will** in mid-June, a celebration honoring the opening of the Elizabethan Theater. Dinner and merrie madness are held in Lithia Park starting at 6pm (tickets $16; call 482-4331 for exact date. Tickets are hard to obtain, so call early). The **Palo Alto Chamber Orchestra** performances in late June ($10) are also a hit (482-4331).

"Give me excess of it, that, surfeiting, the appetite may sicken and so die" (*Twelfth Night,* I.i.2-3). Still haven't had enough theater? The **Cabaret Theater,** P.O. Box 1149 (488-2902), at 1st and Hagarcline, stages light musicals in a wonderful pink former church with drinks and hors d'oeuvres (tickets $9-15.50; box office open Mon. and Wed.-Sat. 1-8pm, Sun. 3-8pm). Small groups, such as **Actor's Theater of Ashland, Studio X,** and the theater department at **Southern Oregon State College,** also raise the curtains sporadically throughout the summer.

SIGHTS AND ACTIVITIES

Before it imported Shakespeare, Ashland was naturally blessed with lithia water—water containing dissolved lithium salts. This water was reputed to have miraculous healing powers. The mineral springs have given their name to the well-tended **Lithia Park,** west of the plaza off Main St. To quaff the vaunted water itself, head for the circle of fountains in the center of the plaza, under the statue of horse and rider. It's a good idea to hold your nose, since the water also contains dissolved sulfur salts. Guided historical tours are given by **Old Ashland Story Tours** (488-3281 or

488-1993; June-Sept. Mon.-Sat. 10am; $5, children under 12 $2). Daily events are listed in brochures at the Chamber of Commerce (see Practical Information). The park itself has hiking trails, picnic grounds, a Japanese garden, duck and swan ponds, and a creek that trips over itself in ecstatic little waterfalls.

If the park and mineral waters fail to refresh you, find your way to the **Chateulin Selections,** 52 E Main St. (488-WINE or 9463), for free wine tasting. Since a sip is never enough, the wines, along with gourmet cheese and specialities, are also available for sale (open daily noon-6pm; in winter Tues.-Sun. 11am-6pm). Or duck into **Gard's Java House** (376 E Main St., 482-2267) for a bowl of coffee ($1) and relax among the college students. Cool jazz musicians every Sunday night attract a crowd (open Mon.-Tues. 8am-11pm., Thurs.- Fri. 8am-midnight, Sat. 9am-midnight, Sun. 9am-11pm).

If your muscles are demanding a little abuse after all this R&R, you can join the **Pacific Crest Trail** at Grouse Gap where it passes near Ashland. Take exit 6 off I-5 and follow the signs along the Mt. Ashland Access Rd. Contact the **Forest Service** (see Practical Information) for further information. **The Adventure Center** (488-2819 or 800-444-2819) has a kiosk on the plaza downtown at 40 N Main St. and organizes rafting, fishing, rock climbing, and horseback riding trips. Daily raft trips on the Rogue River start at $46. The Center also rents bikes, jet skis, and hot air balloons (open Mon.-Sat. 8am-8pm, Sun. 8am-6pm; winter daily 10am-5pm). For a tamer experience, try the double-flumed, 280-ft. **waterslide** at **Emigrant Lake Park** (10 slides for $4), or just practice your freestyle in the lake for free. **Jackson Hot Springs,** 2 mi. north of Ashland on Rte. 99 (482-3776), offers swimming in a pool filled by the hot springs (½-day for $2, all day for $3) and private hot mineral baths ($5, or $8 per couple). **Mount Ashland** is a community-owned ski area with 23 ski runs of varying difficulty, four chair lifts, and over 100 mi. of cross-country trails. (Open Thanksgiving Day-April, daily 9am-4pm; night skiing Thurs.-Sat. 4-10pm. Day ticket weekdays $16, weekends $24. Full rental $15.) Contact **Ski Ashland,** P.O. Box 220, Ashland 97520 (482-2897). For **snow conditions,** call 482-2754.

The **Schneider Museum of Art,** at Siskiyou Blvd. and Indiana St. on the Southern Oregon State campus (552-6245), displays college-sponsored contemporary art exhibits that change every six weeks (open Tues.-Fri. 11am-5pm, Sat. 1-5pm; free). The much-heralded **Pacific Northwest Museum of Natural History,** opened in July 1994, focuses on the interesting geology of Ashland and the surrounding areas ($6, ages 5-15 $4.50. Open April-Oct. 9am-5pm, Nov.-March 10am-4pm). In July and August, the **Ashland City Band** sets up every Thursday at 7:30pm in Lithia Park (488-5340).

ENTERTAINMENT

The Black Sheep, 51 N Main St. (482-6414), upstairs on the Plaza. Celebrate Shakespeare with a pint of his native brew. With the opening of this lively hangout, the British pub scene has arrived in America. Jolly good scene, too. Fish & chips, and other, more healthful options, make up the "traditional English fayre" served; fortunately, it doesn't taste like traditional English pub food. Homemade ice cream. Open daily 11am-1am; minors welcome, to eat, until 11pm.

Rogue Brewery and Public House, 31B Water St. (488-5061; fax 488-4450). If you're dining in the Rogue during an earthquake, you're one unhappy camper. An impressive array of beer bottles lines the walls of this microbrewery. Popular with off-beat and older crowds, the Rogue has chess, TV, and darts, and local bands perform twice a week. Pizza is homemade. Spacious outdoor deck. Open Mon.-Thurs. 4pm-midnight, Fri.-Sun. 11:30am-midnight.

Mark Antony Hotel, 212 E Main St. (482-1721). "The Mark" has cozy wooden booths, a large circular bar, and eclectic artwork lining the walls. Occasional $3 cover. Weekend dancing, to live entertainment. Open July-Sept. noon-2am, Oct.-June 3pm-2am. Open daily 11am-2am.

Cook's Tarem, 66 E Main St. (482-4626). Gay and straight crowds flock to Cook's. Mostly for dancing with a DJ on Thursday through Saturday nights. Open Sun.-Wed. 2pm-2am, Thurs.-Sat. 2pm-2:30am.

■■■ MEDFORD

Once a mere satellite to Jacksonville, Medford lured the 19th-century railroad barons with $25,000 in under-the-table cash. The result: Medford got the railroad lines and the county seat, while Jacksonville was left in the dust with outmoded horse-and-buggy transport. Today, Medford is a rapidly expanding but nondescript community. The town motto is "We hug Visitors in Medford;" accept your hug, rest up in an inexpensive motel, but then slip off to nearby Jacksonville or Ashland for some real action.

PRACTICAL INFORMATION

Visitors Information: Chamber of Commerce, 101 E 8th St. (779-4847), at Front St. Stacks of **maps** and directories. Open Mon.-Fri. 9am-5pm. Also see the **Visitors Information Center,** 1315 Maple Grove Rd. (776-4021), in a log cabin just off I-5 at exit 27. A plethora of free brochures. The volunteer staff is armed with fluorescent highlighters, the better to mark up the maps they will give you. Open daily June-Sept. 8:30am-6:30pm, Oct.-May 9am-5pm.

Greyhound, 212 N Bartlett St. (779-2103), at 5th St. To: Portland (7 per day; $33), Sacramento (5 per day; $46), and San Francisco ($53). Open daily 6am-6:30pm.

Rogue Valley Transportation, 3200 Crater Lake Ave. (779-2877). Connects Medford with: Jacksonville, Phoenix, White City, Talent, and Ashland. Buses leave from 6th and Bartlett, Mon.-Fri. 8am-5pm. Limited service Sat. 9am-5pm. Service to Ashland every half-hour, hourly service to all other destinations. Fare 75¢ plus 25¢ per zone crossed, seniors and under 18 pay ½ price, under 6 free.

Taxi: Metro Cab Co., 773-6665. 24 hrs.

Car Rental: Budget (773-7023), at the airport or (779-0488) at Biddle Rd. Cars from $30 per day (on weekends), $39 per day mid-week. 5% AAA, AARP discounts. Must be at least 21 with credit card. $7.50 extra charge for ages 21-25.

Equipment Rental: McKenzie Outfitters, 130 E 8th St., off Central Ave. (773-5145 or 683-2038 for central office in Eugene). Backpacks from $15 per day; tents $25 per day for 1-3 days; $15 per day for 4-7 days; ice axes $5 per day; crampons $5 per day. Open Mon.-Sat. 10am-6pm, Sun. 11am-4pm.

Public Library: 413 W Main St. (776-7281), at Oakdale Ave. Open Mon.-Thurs. 9:30am-8pm, Fri.-Sat. 9:30am-5pm.

Crisis Intervention Services: 779-4357.

Hospital: Providence, 111 Crater Lake Ave., at Woodrow St. (773-6611). Emergency care 24 hr.

Emergency: 911. Police and Fire: City Hall, 411 W 8th St., at 8th and Oakdale (770-4783).

Post Office: 333 W 8th (776-1326), at Holly St. Open Mon.-Fri. 8:30am-5:30pm. **General Delivery ZIP Code:** 97501.

Area Code: 503.

Medford straddles I-5 in southern Oregon, at its intersection with Rte. 238, or Main St. in Medford. Grants Pass is 30 mi. northwest, Ashland 12 mi. to the southeast. Central Ave. and Riverside Ave., both one-way, have a number of cheap motels. Find food near E Main St., on the other side of I-5. Main St. intersects Central in the heart of the city and then proceeds west to Jacksonville.

ACCOMMODATIONS

The small, clean motels that line Central Ave. and Riverside Ave. are depressingly similar, but the prices will cheer up the weary visitor coming from the overpriced Ashland or Jacksonville. All prices *decrease* about $10 in summer, and many places drop their rates on weekdays. There are no campgrounds within 15 mi. of town, just several "day-use parks"— grassy areas with wooden picnic tables.

Village Inn, 722 N Riverside (773-5373). Clean, well-kept rooms for an excellent price. Singles $25. Doubles $30.

MEDFORD

Motel Orleans, 850 Alba Dr. (779-6730 or 800-626-1900), south of town at exit 27 off I-5. A night in this three-story, mansionesque white motel is worth being ten minutes away from the city center. Rooms well-furnished, and all upstairs rooms have balconies. Singles $29. Doubles with one bed $32, with two beds $42.50. AARP discounts.

Capri Motel, 250 Barnett Rd., just off I-5 exit 27 (773-7796). Blue building with large clean rooms and blue or soft pink bathtubs next to a blue-bottomed pool. Quiet. A/C, phones, and cable. Hot pot with instant coffee packets in each room. Singles $34. Doubles $39.

Cedar Lodge, 518 N Riverside Ave. (773-7361 or 800-773-7361; fax 776-1033). Spacious rooms, with complimentary coffee and fruit served in the office in the morning. Friendly and efficient staff. Singles $40. Doubles $44. 15% AAA and senior discounts make prices even more reasonable.

Sierra Inn Motel, 345 S Central Ave. (773-7727). Better-than-average rooms. TV, A/C. Laundry and kitchen facilities available. Singles $36. Doubles $40. Reservations recommended.

FOOD

If you've been contemplating a fast, Medford is the place to begin. It's essentially burger or bust, though a few spacious sandwich shops do serve up some less hearty and more healthful fare. You're better off grabbing dinner in Ashland (a mere 12 mi. away). Safeway, at 1003 Medford Shopping Center off Crater Lake Ave. (773-7162), is well-stocked, with a bakery, deli, and low prices (open daily 6am-midnight).

C.K. Tiffins, 226 E Main St. (779-0480). "Naturally good" health food and pastries served cafeteria-style in an airy renovated warehouse. Great place to bring your newspaper for breakfast. Daily lunch specials range from Enchilada Bake ($5 with fruit salad) to Greek spinach and artichoke pasta ($5). Open Mon.-Fri. 7:30am-3pm.

Deli Down, 406 E Main St. (772-4520), in the Main St. Market downstairs from Country Things. A bustling business fills two large rooms. You can't miss the counter. It's on a black-and-white checkerboard floor. Large sandwich selection; soup and salad combos for $4.25. All-you-can-eat hot pasta bar for $4.25. Open Mon.-Fri. 10am-4pm.

Squeeze-Inn Sandwich Shop, 616 Crater Lake Ave. (772-7489). Not downtown, but cheap sandwiches ($4 whole; $2.50 half) served deli-style. A haven for salami and cheese lovers. There's often a short line around lunch time, but you can entertain yourself by gazing at pinwheels, sunshine balloons, and ferns that sprout up on the walls. Open Mon.-Fri. 11am-5pm, Sat. 11am-4pm.

Las Margaritas, 12 N Riverside (779-7628). This cavernous Mexican restaurant serves up large and delicious portions. Enchiladas and burritos in full ($3.75) and reduced ($2.50) sizes. One of the few decent dinner places in town. Receive an additional 10% off 3-5pm. Open Sun.-Tues. 11am-10pm, Fri.-Sat. 11am-11pm.

SIGHTS AND ACTIVITIES

Medford's location on I-5 between Grants Pass and Ashland makes it the hub of southern Oregon. But don't leave town yet. Medford does offer some interesting (and cost-free) alternatives for the history buff. The **Medford Railroad Park** (770-4586), at the junction of Table Rock Rd. and Berrydale Ave., offers Medford's closest brush with Disneyworld; for no charge, you can chug around in cars pulled by a miniature steam engine. (Open April-Oct. Mon.-Sat. and the fourth Sunday of each month, 11am-3pm). More free glimpses of the past can be had at the **South Oregon History Center,** 106 N Central Ave. (773-6536), at 6th St., with a research library, a history store, and various exhibits on Oregon history (open Mon.-Fri. 9am-5pm).

In April, the **Pear Blossom Festival,** P.O. Box 339 (734-7327) lures runners to its 10K race. Other activities include a street fair, a band festival, a golf tournament and, of course, a parade. A more recent addition to the Medford social calendar is the **Medford Jazz Jubilee** (770-6972), held for three days in October. Bands come from across the nation to blow their horns in Medford.

Harry and David's Original Country Store, off Exit 27 south (776-2277), is the L.L. Bean of the fruit world, selling produce, nuts, candies, and gift items. (Open Mon.-Sat. 11am-5pm, Sun. 10am-6pm.) One mi. south of Medford on Rte. 99 is the 43,000-sq.-ft. show garden of **Jackson & Perkins,** the world's most prolific rose growers (open Mon.-Sat. 9am-5pm, Sun. 10am-6pm).

■■■ JACKSONVILLE

The biggest of Oregon's gold boomtowns, Jacksonville played the role of rich and lawless frontier outpost with appropriate licentious zeal. But the gold dwindled, the railroad and stagecoach lines took Jacksonville off their routes, and, in the final *coup de (dis)grâce*, the city lost the county seat to Medford. On the brink of oblivion, Jacksonville was revitalized by nostalgia. During the '50s, the town was rehabilitated; today, it is a national historic landmark, one of only eight towns in Oregon on the National Register of Historic Places. A stroll down Main St. unveils views of balustraded, century-old buildings: the United States Hotel, the Methodist-Episcopal Church, the old courthouse, and others. Residents are rightfully proud of their friendly, interesting town, and are eager to give you their perspectives on its history, a particularly convenient resource if you want to skip over the thousands of Jacksonville brochures.

Practical Information To reach Jacksonville (or "J-ville," as residents affectionately call it), take Rte. 238 southwest from Medford or catch the #30 bus at 5th and Bartlett St. in Medford (buses run Mon.-Sat.; see Medford: Practical Information). Jacksonville can be reached by bus from Ashland only via Medford.

Drop by the **visitors center** in the old railway station at 185 N Oregon St., at C St. (899-8118), where you will be well-supplied with directions and pamphlets (open daily 10am-4pm). The **post office** (899-1563) is next door at 175 N Oregon St. (Open Mon.-Fri. 8:30am-5pm. **General Delivery ZIP Code:** 97530.)

Accommodations and Food Try to avoid spending the night in town. There are no campgrounds, and the **Jacksonville Inn,** 175 E California St. (899-1900 or 800-231-9544), for all its charm, free Belgian waffle breakfasts, and free mountain bikes, has rooms starting at $60 for a single. For a classy, though casual, dining experience, go to the **Bella Union,** 170 W California St. (899-1770). The Bella Union serves American favorites like pizza, pasta, and chicken, at relatively high prices ($8-$14), but the opportunity to dine beneath a tapestry of vines is unique. Part of the Bella Union **saloon** becomes a stage Thursday through Saturday nights for live band performances (restaurant hours Mon.-Fri. 11:30am-10pm, Sat. 11am-10pm, Sun. 10am-10pm). A cheaper and equally delightful dining experience can be had at **The Cafe,** upstairs in the **Terra Firma Store** at 135 W California St. (899-1097 or 899-8565). Enjoy soup, salad, and sandwiches at reasonable prices. On street level at the Terra Firma is the **Jacksonville Ice Cream & Soda Company,** which will fix your ice cream sodas the old-fashioned way. $1.50 will buy you a huge single cone, and the more adventurous and historically-minded can sip lime or cherry phosphates for 60¢. (Open summer Mon.-Sat. 10am-6pm, Sun. 11am-5pm; winter Mon.-Sat. 11am-5pm, Sun. noon-5pm).

Sights and Events Jacksonville is history; walk down California St. and instantly flash back to the 19th-century. At the **Beekman House,** on the corner of Laurelwood St. and California St., costumed hosts will be quite charmed, my dear, to guide you through the residence. The delightful interactive tour lasts 35 minutes, and costs $2 ($1 for ages 6-11; open 1-5pm; call 773-6536 for more information). No, it isn't a history-induced hallucination if you see a well-dressed 19th-century gentleman in the middle of the street; "Mr. Beekman" often gets the random urge to wander the streets of Jacksonville.

The **Jacksonville Museum** (773-6536) in the Old County Courthouse at 206 N 5th St., is a treasure-trove of history. As you explore the museum's fantastic 3-D exhibits, leave the kids locked up in the jail next door (now the **Children's Museum**). All artifacts are hands-on. The kids may head straight for the Bozo the Clown exhibit, an authentic Jacksonville native (born 1892). Life-size figures, train noises, and great murals by local artists make the museum a delight. Exhibits change constantly. A $2 ticket will gain entrance to both exhibits. (Both are open in summer daily 10am-5pm, in winter closed Monday.)

Stan the Man (535-5617), a community legend, runs a 50-minute trolley-tour, which provides an excellent overview of the town's attractions and a chance (finally) to sit down ($4, under 12 $2, runs daily from 10am-4pm from 3rd and California St.). The vast **Jacksonville Cemetery** (filled with wildflowers in the spring) is a short walk uphill from the intersection of N Oregon and E St. Dotted with haunting madrone trees, the cemetery provides a peaceful and somber reminder that, indeed, much time has passed since the age of the hoop skirt.

Jacksonville goes schizo every summer (mid-June to early Sept.) under the influence of the **Peter Britt Music Festivals,** P.O. Box 1124, Medford 97501 (800-882-7488, or 773-6077 in OR; fax 503-776-3712), named after the pioneer photographer whose hillside estate is the site of the fest. Now in its 33rd year, the festivals feature jazz, classical, folk, country, and pop acts, dance theater and musicals. 1994 saw the Neville Brothers, Joan Baez, and Arlo Guthrie perform for the crowded outdoor amphitheater (tickets for single events $10-$30, 12 and under $6-10. Order tickets starting early in May; don't wait or the best acts may pass you by. On performance days, tickets are available at the Main Britt Pavilion in Jacksonville. Advance-purchase group discounts available; $2 senior discounts for classical events.) Many people bring picnic dinners as they watch.

One weekend in mid-July, the amphitheater is overrun by kids on the loose at the **Children's Festivals** (889-1665). Entertainment includes story-telling, crafts, ballet, and puppet theater, all geared toward the pre-adolescent crowd (parents can come, too; $1.50). Jacksonville in September slows down, bringing a respite from the parching work of reliving the past. Sample free wine from the **Wests' Tasting Room,** 690 N 5th St. (899-1829). The place offers vintages from the nearby Valley View Vineyard (open daily 8am-7pm; winter 10am-6pm). Also in mid-September is the unofficial town-wide garage sale; locals (including people from Medford and Ashland) cast their earthly possessions into their yards and the wheeling and dealing begins.

■■■ GRANTS PASS

Workers building a road through the Oregon mountains in 1863 were so excited by the news of General Ulysses Grant's victory at Vicksburg that they named the town after the burly President-to-be. Grants Pass is a base to discover the Rogue River Valley and the Illinois Valley regions, which have parks offering camping, swimming, and fishing.

PRACTICAL INFORMATION AND ORIENTATION

Visitors Information: Visitor and Convention Bureau (800-547-5927 or 476-7717 in OR), at 6th and Midland. Loads of brochures covering all of Josephine County. Eager and pleasant volunteer staff. Open Mon.-Fri. 8am-5pm, in summer also Sat.-Sun. 9am-5pm.

Greyhound, 460 NE Agness Ave. (476-4513), at the east end of town. To: Portland ($31.25, 5 departures daily 4am-6:25pm) and Sacramento (4 departures daily 5:10am-9:55pm; $44), continued service to San Francisco ($55). A few storage lockers (75¢ per 24 hr.) lurk next to the station. Open Mon.-Fri. 6:30am-6pm, Sat. 6:45am-1pm. Closed holidays.

Taxi: Grants Pass Taxi, 476-6444. 24 hr.

Car Rental: Discount Rent-a-Car, 1470 NE 7th St. (471-6411). Cars from $28 per day, with 20¢ for each mile over 100 mi. per day. Open Mon.-Fri. 7:30am-5:30pm.
Laundromat: MayBelle's Washtub, 306 SE I St. (471-1317), at 8th St. Open daily 7am-9pm. Washer 75¢, 10-min. dry 25¢.
Crisis Hotline: 479-4357.
Seniors' Information: Senior Community Center, 3rd and B St. (474-5440). **Senior Citizen Helpline,** 479-4357. 24 hrs.
Information for Travelers with Disabilities: Handicapped Awareness and Support League, 290 NE C St. (479-4275).
Hospital: Josephine Memorial Hospital, 715 NW Dimmick (476-6831), off A St.
Emergency: 911. **Police:** Justice Building at 101 NW A St. (474-6370) at 6th St.
Post Office: 132 NW 6th St. (479-7526). Open Mon.-Fri. 9am-5pm. **General Delivery ZIP Code:** 97526.
Area Code: 503.

I-5 curves around Grants Pass to the northeast, heading north to Portland; south of the city, U.S. 199 runs along the Rogue River before making the 30-mi. trip south to Cave Junction. The two main north-south arteries are 6th St. (one-way south) and 7th St. (one-way north). 6th St. is the divider between streets labeled East and West, and the railroad tracks (between G and F St.) divide North and South addresses. The Rogue River lies just south of the city.

ACCOMMODATIONS AND CAMPING

Grants Pass supports a number of ugly jello-molded motels that vary greatly in price (but they don't jiggle when you shake them). Since Grants Pass is a favorite highway stop, rooms fill up quickly, especially on weekends and in August, when rates (not by coincidence) hit their peak. Most of the motels are strung along 6th St.

Grants Pass is not a camper's dream town. **Rogue Valley Overnighters RV Park,** 1806 NW 6th St. (479-2208) has sites within city limits. Not beautiful, but ample and convenient ($18.55 for full hookup, restrooms, showers available). Summer reservations recommended at least one week in advance. Another option is **Schroeder Campgrounds,** 605 Schroeder Lane, (474-5285), 4 mi. south of town; take U.S. 199 Southwest, angle right on Redwood Ave., turn right onto Willow Lane, then follow the signs 1 mi. to the campground. Excellent, spacious sites by the Rogue River. A pier offers fishing access for the disabled (playground, showers 25¢. Sites $12, with hookups $17). 2 mi. south on Rte. 99, **River RV Park,** 2956 Rogue River Highway (479-0046), offers grassy, quiet sites for $20. Check with Visitors Information (see above) for further camping sites.

Fordson Home Hostel (HI/AYH), 250 Robinson Rd., Cave Junction 97523 (592-3203), 37 mi. southwest of Grants Pass on U.S. 199. Accessible only by car; call for directions. This rambling old house is the headquarters of Nowhere, but you won't be lonely. Companions include at least 20 antique tractors, a saw mill, a few other hostel guests, and an owner who will gladly give you a tour of his beautiful property. Free bicycle loans, comfortable accommodations, 33% discounted admission to the Oregon Caves National Monument. Five beds and camping available. $8, non-members $10.
Motel Townhouse 839 NE 6th St. (479-0892). Superb rooms for superb prices-One three-bed, two room unit could hold five for only $45. Prices vary according to number of occupants. Singles $25. Doubles $30. Two-bed quads $38. Seniors $1 discount. $5 for kitchenette (found only in some rooms). Reservations advised.
Hawks Inn Motel 1464 NW 6th St. (479-4057). Clean, pleasant rooms. Friendly staff. Pool with gazebo. A/C, HBO. Small singles $30. Doubles $33. Two-room, 2-bed triple or quad for $43. Reservations advised in summer.
Knight's Inn Motel, 104 SE 7th St. (800-826-6835 or 479-5595). Huge rooms with cable TV (plus HBO) and A/C. Knight shields on the railings definitely a cheesy touch. In summer, singles $37. Doubles $43 in summer, $6 for use of kitchen with microwave. Reservations advised.

GRANTS PASS

Motel 6, 1800 NE 7th St. (474-1331; fax 474-0136). Low prices for antiseptic rooms. Cable TV, swimming pool, A/C. Complimentary morning coffee served at front desk. Singles $35. Doubles $41. Reserve 1 or 2 days ahead.

FOOD

Good dining in Grants Pass is an ethnically enlightening experience, unless McDonald's or Bee-Gees makes your mouth water. You might also try the **Safeway,** among other grocery stores, at 115 SE 7th St. (479-4276; open daily 6am-midnight). **The Growers' Market** (476-5375) on C St. between 4th and 5th is the largest open-air market in the state, vending everything a produce-lover could imagine. (Open March 15-Thanksgiving Tues. and Sat. 9am-1pm; July-Halloween on Sat. only.)

Pongsri's, 1571 NE 6th St. (479-1345). Combines a down-home atmosphere with spicy Thai food. Thai cuisine aficionados will love it; meat-and-potatoes lovers can focus on the slatted wood booths and ornate Thai decorations. Large portions. Entrees $6-8, lunch special $4, served Tues.-Fri. 11am-2pm. Open Tues.-Sun. 11am-9:30pm, 11am-9pm in winter.

Matsukaze, 1675 NE 7th St. (479-2961). Japanese food that Americans will recognize in a simple and tasteful setting. Bonding opportunities in booths sunk into the floor. Daily lunch specials are $3.50-4.50. Chicken, beef, vegetable, and seafood offerings. Light dinners $5-6, full entrees $8-13. Daily lunch specials (try chicken teriyaki, $3.50). Open Mon.-Sat. 11am-2pm; also open Mon.-Thurs. 5-9pm and Fri.-Sat. 5-9:30pm.

Sunshine Cafe, 128 SW H St. (474-5044). Set in a natural foods store, this is the Grants Pass variation on the Green Theme. Simple but delicious vegetarian sandwiches (the Vegecstasy, $5.25, with avocado, sprouts, artichoke hearts, and soy cheese, deserves applause). There are burger options here: tofu or tempeh burgers, that is ($4.75). Mexican entrees also available. Open Mon.-Fri. 9am-6pm, Sat. 10am-5pm.

SIGHTS AND OUTDOORS

While the town of Grants Pass itself offers few attractions, **Wildlife Images,** at 11845 Lower River Rd. (476-0222), is worth a visit. This private, non-profit organization is practical environmentalism in action: it treats, rehabilitates, and releases a wide variety of injured and orphaned wild animals from all over the West. Free tours are given (Tues.-Sun. at 11am and 1pm year-round), though baby animals are more frequent in summer. Reservations required.

A few miles east of Grants Pass in the town of **Rogue River** lies **Valley of the Rogue State Park** (see Accommodations and Camping). You can enjoy the nearby Rogue (one of the few federally-protected rivers designated as a "Wild and Scenic River") by raft, jetboat, mail boat, or simply by fishing or walking along its banks. If you fish, you'll be in good company: Zane Grey and Clark Gable reportedly roamed the Rogue River with tackle and bait. More enterprising (and affluent) souls can hop on a two-hour scenic tour given by **Hellgate Excursions, Inc.** (479-7204; $20, ages 4-11 $10). Those in search of longer trips should try the half-day ($35) and full-day ($50) whitewater rafting and inflatable-kayaking trips run by **Orange Torpedo Trips,** 209 Merlin Rd., north of Grants Pass off Rte. 61 (479-5061 or 800-635-2925; daily May 15-Sept. 15; full day trip includes lunch). **Whitewater Cowboys,** also at 209 Merlin Rd., rents inflatable kayaks for $15 per day (open daily 8am-6pm).

Dry off with a **hike** in the **Rogue State Park** or head south if you have a car. While **Gold Hill** (20 mi. south on I-5) is famous for the large cave of bat guano kept under constant watch by local police, it also houses the **Oregon Vortex/House of Mystery,** 4303 Sardine Creek Rd. (855-1543). Here, balls roll uphill, pendulums hang at an angle, and people seem to vary in height depending on where they stand. The bizarre phenomena are supposedly due to a local perturbation of the earth's magnetic field. The owners apologize for any crude imitations of this house that tourists may have seen across the country, and assure visitors that this is the *real* thing.

Decide for yourself. Open daily 8:30am-6pm; March-May and Sept.-Oct. 9am-4:30pm. $6 (ages 5-11 $4. 50% off each ticket for groups of 15 or more).

The **Oregon Caves National Monument** (592-3400) can be reached by heading 30 mi. south along U.S. 199 to Cave Junction, and then following Rte. 46 as it winds east for 20 mi. Here in the belly of the ancient Siskiyous, acidic waters carved out limestone that had been compressed to marble. Dissolved and redeposited, the limestone filled cavernous chambers with exotic formations, whose slow growth is nurtured by the constant 41°F (5°C) climate. Bring a jacket. 75-min. tours are conducted as groups of 16 form. (Tours given daily 8am-7pm; mid-Oct. to April at 8:30am, 10am, 11:30am, 1pm, 2:30pm, and 4pm; and mid-Sept.-mid.-Oct. daily 8:30am-5pm. $5.75, ages 6-11 $3.50, under 6 $3.) Children must be over 42 in. (107cm) tall to take a tour. No child care is provided.

The town of **Cave Junction,** about 35 mi. south of Grants Pass along U.S. 199, has one foot in cowboy-hat culture and the other firmly planted in the age of supermarkets and fast-food chains. The **Visitors Information Center,** 201 Caves Hwy. (592-2631), has many more brochures than the town has attractions. You can catch some z's at the **Kerbyville Inn Bed and Breakfast,** 24304 Redwood Hwy., in Kerby. Rooms start at $50 and include a complimentary half-bottle of wine from the nearby **Bridgeview Winery,** 4210 Holland Loop Rd. (592-4688), which operates the inn. The winery is open for free tasting (daily 9am-5pm). The **hostel** is nearby (see Accommodations above). For RV drivers, the pleasant **Town & Country RV Park** lies 2 mi. out of town at 28288 Redwood Hwy. (592-2656; $15 per site; full hookup.)

■■■ EUGENE

Situated between the **Siuslaw** (see-YU-slaw) and the **Willamette** (wil-LAM-it) **National Forests,** Oregon's second-largest city sits astride the Willamette River, touching tiny Springfield (BART!!) to the east. Eugene is an experience. More mellow and less serious than Berkeley, tolerance defines this large college town. Set that blender to "liquefy": hippies and rednecks, Birkenstocks and hunting boots, students, Deadheads, professionals, professional Deadheads, amateur and elite runners, frat boys, organically-grown food, pickup trucks, track teams, mountain bikes, tourists, locals, guns, bohemians, outfitters, loggers...usually peacefully emulsified in a small city (pop. 110,000; swelling to 350,000 when the Grateful Dead play). Compared to Eugene, post-destruction Babel was a model of uniformity. Yet in Eugene no one pretends; everyone mixes and one simply and genuinely *is*.

Eugene is trying hard to shake an image of being stuck in the '70s, but doesn't seem to know where to go next; unregulated diversity, by popular consent, rules the city. City slickers can shop and dine in downtown's pedestrian mall and **5th St. Market.** Outdoor types can raft the river, bike and run on its banks, or hike in one of the large parks near the city. Home to the **University of Oregon,** Eugene teems with art museums, pizza joints, and all the other trappings of a college town. Fraternities spawn a meat-market night scene near the University, but better nightlife is only a short walk away.

The fleet-footed and free-spirited have dubbed Eugene the running capital of the universe." Only in this city could the annual **Bach Festival,** in late June, be accompanied by the "Bach Run," a 1 to 5km dash through the city's downtown area. The Nike running shoe company, founded in Eugene, sponsors the event, which culminates in a performance of the so-called "Sports Cantata" (BWV 12 *"Weinen, Klagen, Laufen,"* or "Weeping, Lamenting, Running").

PRACTICAL INFORMATION AND ORIENTATION

Visitors Information: Eugene-Springfield Convention and Visitors Bureau, 305 W 7th (484-5307; outside OR 800-547-5445), at Lincoln St. between Lincoln and Lawrence St. downtown. **Maps,** brochures, listings, and guides to absolutely everything. (Open June-Aug. Mon.-Fri. 8am-5pm, Sat. and Sun. 10am-4pm.)

Park Information: Willamette National Forest Service, 211 E 7th Ave. (465-6522). **Maps** ($3), brochures ($1), and advice (free!) on the campgrounds, recreational areas, and wilderness areas in the National Forest. Open Mon.-Fri. 8am-4:30pm.

University of Oregon Switchboard, 1585 E 13th Ave. (346-3111). Referral for almost anything—rides, housing, emergency services. Open Mon.-Fri. 7am-6pm.

Amtrak, 433 Willamette St. (800-872-7245), at 4th St. To: Seattle (1 per day; $50), Portland (1 per day; $24), Oakland (1 per day; $104, with service to San Francisco). 15% senior discount, 24% handicapped discounts.

Greyhound, 987 Pearl St. (344-6265 or 800-231-2222) at 9th St. Eight buses north, 5 south per day. To: Seattle ($32), San Francisco ($71), Portland ($13). Open daily 6am-10pm. Storage lockers $1 per day.

Green Tortoise (937-3603), at 14th and Kincaid. To: San Francisco ($39), Portland ($10), and Seattle ($25). Reservations required. Open daily 8am-8pm.

Lane Transit District (LTD): (687-5555), at 10th and Willamette St. Provides public transportation throughout Eugene. Pick up a **map** and timetables at the Convention and Visitors Bureau, or the LTD Service Center. All routes wheelchair-accessible. Fares Mon.-Fri. 75¢; Mon.-Fri. after 7pm and Sat.-Sun. 50¢; seniors and children 35¢. Main route service Mon.-Fri. 6am-11:30pm, Sat. 7:30am-10:30pm, Sun. 8:30am-7:30pm.

Ride Board: Erb Memorial Union (EMU) Basement, University of Oregon. Open Mon.-Thurs. 7am-7pm, Fri. 7am-5pm.

Taxi: Yellow Cab, 746-1234. 24 hr.

Car Rental: Away Rent-a-Car, 110 W 6th St. (683-0874). $20 per day; first 100 mi. free, 18¢ per mi. thereafter.

AAA Office, 983 Willagillespie Rd. (484-0661). Open Mon.-Fri. 8am-5pm.

Laundromat: Club Wash, 595 E 13th St. (342-1727), at Patterson. Open daily 7am-2am. Wash 75¢, 10-min. dry 25¢.

Bike Rental: Bicycle Way of Life, 152 W 5th Ave. (344-4105). Friendly staff offers city/mountain bikes for $15 per day, $8 for 4 hrs., $2 per additional hour. Tandems $25 per day, $15 per ½ day. Major credit card or $100 deposit. Open Mon.-Fri. 9am-7pm, Sat.-Sun. 10am-5pm. **Pedal Power,** 535 High St. (687-1775), downtown. 6-speeds $3 per hr., $15 per day. Mountain bikes $20 for 4 hrs., $30 per day. Tandems $6 per hour, $30 per day. Open Mon.-Fri. 9am-7pm, Sat. 9am-6pm, Sun. 10am-5pm.

Crisis Line: White Bird Clinic, 341 E 12th Ave. (800-422-7558). Free crisis counseling and low-cost medical care. Open Mon.-Fri. 8am-5pm with 24-hr. backup.

Rape Crisis: Sexual Assault Support Services, 630 Lincoln St. (485-6700). Open Mon.-Fri. 9am-5pm. Hotline and answering service 24 hrs.

Emergency: 911. **Police/Fire:** 777 Pearl St. (687-5111), at City Hall.

Post Office: In **Eugene** (341-3611) at 5th and Willamette St., or in the **EMU Bldg.** (341-3692) at the university. Open Mon.-Fri. 8:30am-5:30pm, Sat. 10am-2pm. **General Delivery ZIP Code:** 97401.

Area Code: 503.

Eugene is 111 mi. south of Portland on the I-5 corridor. The University of Oregon campus lies in the southeastern corner of town, bordered on the north by Franklin Blvd., which runs from the city center to I-5. 1st Ave. runs alongside the winding Willamette River; Willamette Ave. intersects the river, dividing the city into east and west. Be sure you know whether your destination is east or west! Willamette Ave. is the main drag and is interrupted by the pedestrian mall on 7th, 8th, and 9th St. The city is a motorist's nightmare of one-way streets; free parking is virtually nonexistent in the downtown area.

ACCOMMODATIONS

Eugene has the usual assortment of motels. The cheapest are on E Broadway and W 7th St. Make reservations early; motels can be packed on big football weekends, or when the Dead appear in town. The **hostel,** though far from downtown, is the least expensive and most interesting place to stay. The closest legal camping is 7 mi.

away, although it is said that people camp by the river (especially in the wild and woolly northeastern side near Springfield). Most park hours are officially 6am to 11pm. Lone women should avoid the university campus vicinity at night.

Lost Valley Educational Center (HI/AYH), 81868 Lost Valley Lane, near the tiny town of Dexter (937-3351; fax 937-3646). Take Rte. 58 east for 8 mi. toward Oakbridge, turn right on Rattlesnake Creek Rd.; after 4 mi., turn right on Lost Valley Lane, and 1 mi. later you're there. Eco-enthusiasts unite! Complete with water-conserving toilets and comprehensive recycling guidelines, the hostel brings together a fascinating group of individuals. Sleep in large cabins and wake yourself up with a dip in the swimming hole. Come in at night for the organic dinner. Call ahead for reservations or to sign up for a variety of ecology retreats and conferences. This oasis of idealism is a perfect spot to contemplate anything and everything. Beautiful countryside. Members $7, non-members $10. Campsites $5 per person. Dinner (Mon.-Fri.) $6.

Talray Holdings Inc., 1810 Harris St. (344-2657 or 344-9763; fax 344-0365), at 18th in Woodside Manor. A plain gray building 10 min. from downtown hides the best deal in town. Talray offers dormitory-style living accommodations: you'll get a single room that shares a kitchen and a tiny bathroom with three other rooms to comprise a quad. Rooms are small but well worth the price: $15 per night. Each room has a sink and a mattress; bring your own sheets. $50 deposit, money order or cashiers check preferred. No credit cards or cash accepted. Reserve one week in advance. Call Tues.-Sat. 9am-6pm.

Downtown Motel, 361 W 7th Ave. (345-8739). Singles $28.50. Doubles (1 bed) $39.50, 2-beds $44. Reservations advised one week in advance. Spacious and beautiful rooms; dreary bathrooms. Free coffee in the morning. Next to the Visitors Center for those requiring extra guidance. Cable TV, A/C.

66 Motel, 755 E Broadway (342-5041). Very professional, cheap and crowded. Large bathrooms, cable TV, A/C, and phones. Singles $31. Doubles $34 ($2 per additional person).

Executive House Inn, 1040 W 6th Ave. (683-4000). No A/C, but huge rooms with TV, phones, and sink. Singles $27. Doubles $32.

Timbers Motel, 1015 Pearl St. (343-3345 or 800-643-4167; fax 343-3345 x 300), ½ block from Greyhound. Newly refurbished. Complimentary coffee, tea, or cocoa in the morning. Perfect for late-night bus arrivals. Cable TV, A/C. Singles $28-35 (the cheaper rooms are in the basement), doubles $38. Seniors $1 off, AAA 10% off.

CAMPING

Unfortunately, KOAs and RV-only parks monopolize the camping scene around Eugene, but further east on Rtes. 58 and 126 the immense **Willamette National Forest** is packed with forested campsites. Around the beautiful, mysterious **Black Canyon** campground 28 mi. east of Eugene on Hwy. 58 ($3-7), a swamp sometimes gives the tree bark and ferns an eerie phosphorescence.

Eugene Mobile Village, 4750 Franklin Blvd. (747-2257). 3 mi. from downtown Eugene; RV-only park. $15 per night for 2 with full hookup; 75¢ per additional person. 30 spaces, free showers. Reserve 3 nights ahead.

Sherwood Forest Campground, just off I-5 exit 182, 9 mi. south of Eugene. Lulled by roaring freeway traffic, you can pay an exorbitant tent fee ($12) and seek the company of RVs ($16, with full hookup $19). Don't all stampede at once! Pool, showers, laundry facilities.

Dorena Lake and Cottage Grove Lake (942-5631), 20 mi. south of Eugene on I-5. Equipped for camping. **Pine Meadows** campground (942-6857) has sites with showers for $10. **Schwarz Park** (942-1418), at the west end of Dorena Lake, has sites for $8.

FOOD AND ENTERTAINMENT

Cheap ethnic food and hamburger joints are tough to find in this down-to-earth, health-oriented "track city." Outdoor cafe dining, or grab-and-go, are common options. The downtown area specializes in trendy, gourmet food; regular grocery stores circle the city, but the radius is large. The granola crowd does its shopping at **Sundance Natural Foods,** 748 E 24th Ave. (343-9142), at 24th and Hilyard. This vegetarian wonderland specializes in fruits and vegetables, baked goods, and local dairy products; you can create a salad for $3.89 per pound (open daily 9am-11pm). Right in town, **Kiva,** 125 W 11th (342-8666) supplies a smaller array of organic produce and natural foods. Open Mon.-Sat. 9am-8pm, Sun. 9am-5pm.

Keystone Cafe, 395 W 5th St. (342-2075). An eclectic co-op which serves up incredible vegetarian and vegan food made from home-grown ingredients. Draws from a large local following. A small kitchen makes for slow service, but one mouthful of their famous pancakes ($2, organic toppings 70¢) and all will be forgiven. Vegetarian burgers, sandwiches, and chili served 11am-3pm, and other breakfast foods served all day. Open daily 7am-3pm.

Cafe Navarro, 454 Willamette St. (344-0943). Caribbean and Latin cuisine and decor. Vegetarian dishes complement a selection of creative dishes ($8.50-13). Open Tues.-Sat. 11am-2pm and 5-9:30pm. Also breakfast Sat.-Sun. 9am-2pm.

Pizza Stop Cafe, 1478 Willamette St. (345-4811). Locally renowned pizza in a friendly, well-lit cafe. Sold by the pan or by the slice ($1.75, 40¢ toppings). Vegans can take the soy cheese option ($2.15 per slice). Sandwiches ($3.50) and salads also available. 10% discount for seniors, pregnant women (remember: you're in Eugene). Open Mon.-Thurs. 10am-9pm, Fri. 10am-10pm, Sat. 11am-10pm, and Sun. 11am-9pm.

Prince Puckler's Ice Cream Parlor, 861 Willamette St. (343-2621). Homemade ice cream from all-natural ingredients. Best ice cream in Eugene. Experience the "euphoria ultra chocolate" sundae ($2.10), made with locally-produced chocolate sauce and truffles. Pizza parlor in back of store (343-1372) —a slice of cheese is $1.60, but the pesto pizza special ($2.40) is worth the splurge. Open Mon.-Fri. 7am-6pm, Sat. 10am-6pm, Sun. noon-6pm.

West Bros. Bar-B-Que, 844 Olive St. (345-8489). If you have an appetite for bizarre vegetarian or seafood dishes, or you're simply aching for some good old Texas barbecued beef ($6.75) served the Oregon way, grab a seat and relax with a beer. A bit expensive (lunch $7-8, dinner $6-11), but a worthwhile deviation from Eugene's sandwich obsession. Homemade bread. Open Sun.-Thurs. 11:30am-9pm, Fri.-Sat. 11:30am-10pm.

Rainy Day Cafe, 50 E 11th Ave. (343-8108). Inexpensive vegetarian pizza and sandwich selections. Entrees run to $6. Wed., Fri., and Sat. nights this spacious cafe plays host to reggae, folk, and rock bands for $1 cover. Open Sun.-Thurs. 11am-midnight, Fri.-Sat. 10am-1am.

New Day Bakery, 345 Van Buren (345-1695). The best bread in town is served with a hearty bowl of soup ($2.50) in this quiet cafe. Open Mon.-Sat. 7am-7pm, Sun. 7am-3pm.

University Area

The university-area hangout is near 13th and Kincaid. A squadron of cafes along 13th serve cheap food and coffee by day and jam hard by night.

The Glenwood Restaurant, 1340 Alder (687-0355), at 13th St. Locals love this place for its excellent vegetarian selection and hearty breakfasts. Eggs Benedict ($5.35) is captioned "please forgive us if we sell out." Dinners $4.50-6. Open 24 hrs., except Sun. (closes at 9pm).

Sandino's, 854 E 13th St. (342-2241). This sanctuary for smokers dishes up Mexican and Middle Eastern food. Burritos ($4.25) are a hot item. Live bands, mainly acoustic, on Fri.-Sat., and occasional spontaneous poetry readings occur on mellow evenings. Open Mon.-Thurs. 7:30am-12am, Fri. 7:30am-11am, Sat. 9am-4am, Sun. 10am-4am.

Taylor's Collegeside Inn, 894 E 13th St. (344-6174), right across from the university. Low-key, low-priced, friendly waiters, plenty of beer. Burgers and sandwiches ($3-4). This mild-mannered restaurant tunes in to the blues on Wed.-Sat. at the former haunt of John Belushi (cover $4-8). Restaurant open daily 8am-10pm, nightclub 8pm-2am.

CLUBS AND BARS

Live music is everywhere in Eugene. Not surprisingly, the band-toting string of cafes along 13th St. by the university is dominated by fraternity beer bashes. Refugees from this scene will find an amazingly diverse cross-section of nightlife in Eugene. A good time will be had by all when the tempo picks up after 10pm.

High St. Brewery Cafe, 1243 High St. (345-4905). Proudly sells McMenamins and seasonal fruit ale. Slap on jeans and a T-shirt, relax, and enjoy their great brew in this wooden, mellow atmosphere. Open Mon.-Sat. 11am-1am, Sun. noon-1am.

Doc's Pad, 165 W 11th St. (683-8101). The drinks are strong, the music is loud, and the place can be packed and smoky —take a deep breath and unbuckle your seat belt. Classic rock until 9pm; "alternative" rock after. Happy hour Mon.-Fri. 4-7 pm. Friday special brings you Long Island Iced Teas for $3. Open daily 10am-2:15am.

Club Arena, 959 Pearl St. (683-2360). Underneath Perry's Restaurant. The only gay dance club in town. High-tech lights, top-40 music of the '80s and '90s, and on-the-edge drinks: "Screaming Orgasm" $4.50. Monday is men's night. Fri.-Sat. $1.50 cover. Open daily 7pm-2:30am.

Jo Federigo's, 259 E 5th St. (343-8488). A bit expensive, but attracts classy jazz bands 5 nights a week. Table-top art opportunity with crayons—if you're lucky (and a good artist) your creation may go on the wall. No cover, but $5 minimum, and an additional surcharge of 50¢ per drink. Open Mon.-Thurs. 2pm-midnight, Fri. 2pm-2am, Sat. 5pm-2am, Sun. 5pm-midnight.

New Max's, 550 E 13th Ave. (342-6365). Oldest pub in town (despite the name). Great blues and other regional bands (cover $2-5). Open mike on Sunday night. Reputedly a frat-magnet. Open Mon.-Sat. noon-2:30am, Sun. 4pm-3:30am.

SIGHTS AND ACTIVITIES

Oregon track and football are practically festivals in themselves, but the city's dedication to the Great Outdoors also offers ample opportunities for those out of the athletic loop. If you're looking to get closer to nature, **River Runner Supply,** 2222 Centennial Blvd. (343-6883 or 800-223-4326), organizes outdoor experiences from fishing to whitewater rafting on the Willamette River. A four-hour rafting trip costs $40 per person (with a 4-person minimum), two to three hours $30 per person. They also rent out kayaks ($25 per day), canoes ($20 per day), and rafts ($40 per day). The visitors information center can supply a list of several other outfitters. Reservations recommended on weekends. Check local river conditions and **maps,** since there are some relatively dangerous areas on the Willamette near Eugene.

If you just have an afternoon hour to spare, canoe or kayak the **Millrace Canal,** which parallels the Willamette for 3 mi. This shallow waterway passes under many small foot bridges and through a tunnel under the road. Rent canoes or kayaks from **The Canoe Shack,** 1395 Franklin Blvd. (346-4386), run by University of Oregon students (open summer Mon.-Fri. 12:30-dusk, Sat.-Sun. 10:30am-dusk. $4 per hour, $15 for 24 hrs.). Or join the ranks of cyclists and joggers at **Amazon Park;** head south on Pearl St. and it will become Amazon Dr. just beyond E 19th St. This small, peaceful park has paved and dirt trails along the Amazon River. To the northwest of the city, the **Owen Memorial Rose Garden,** just after the I-5 overpass, is perfect for a picnic, replete with rumbling traffic. Any frolicking should take place in full daylight, for the surrounding Whitewater neighborhood is considered unsafe.

High-brow culture resides at the $26-million **Hult Performing Arts Center,** the city's crown jewel, at One Eugene Center, 7th and Willamette St. (**ZIP Code:** 97401). The two theater halls host a spectrum of music from the blues to Bartók.

(Free tours Thurs. and Sat. at 1pm. Call 687-5087 or fax 687-5246 for information, 687-5000 for the ticket office, and 342-5746 for 24-hr. event info.) Locals young and old leave the Hult to the society types who can afford tickets, and instead head to the Community Center for the Performing Arts, better known as **WOW Hall,** 291 W 8th St. (687-2746). WOW Hall is an old Wobblie (International Workers of the World) meeting hall that for years has sponsored concerts by lesser-known artists. Brochures announcing these offbeat acts are plastered everywhere. Tickets available at WOW Hall (open Tues.-Fri. 3-6pm), CD World (3215 W 11th St.) and various other locations. Tickets occasionally available at the door for less raging acts.

The average hair length in Eugene extends about a foot when the Grateful Dead roll into the University's Autzen Stadium in the early summer. Banned for a year by the University (you have one guess to figure out why), the Dead were back in 1994 to probe their Eugene roots and to light up the night. If you're interested in hanging out near the stadium in a more permanent capacity, head to the reception centers for the **University of Oregon** at **Oregon Hall** (346-3014), E 13th Ave. and Agate St., and at the visitors parking and information booth, just left of the main entrance on Franklin Blvd., for tours and **campus maps.** Take time to admire the ivy-covered halls that set the scene for National Lampoon's *Animal House.* The **University Museum of Art** (346-3027), on 13th St. between Kincaid and University St., houses a changing repertoire of Northwest and American art, and an extensive permanent collection of art and artifacts from Southeast Asia. (Open Wed.-Sun. noon-5pm. Free. Tours given Sat. and Sun. at 2pm.) A few blocks away, the **Museum of Natural History,** 1680 E 15th Ave. (346-3024), at Agate, shows a collection of relics from indigenous cultures worldwide that includes a 7000-year-old pair of shoes (opportunistically billed by Nike as sneakers); a primitive "swoosh" is still visible (open Wed.-Sun. noon-5pm; free).

Only a beat away from the heart of tourist country lurks the highly acclaimed **Fifth Street Market** (484-0383), at 5th and High St. (open Mon.-Sat. 7am-7pm, Sun. 7am-6pm). This collection of artsy, overpriced boutiques and eateries attracts those who are under the mystifying impression that British cuisine is "gourmet." Instead of falling victim to this labyrinth of pseudo-sophistication, head to the **Saturday Market** (686-8885), at 8th and Oak, held weekly April through December. The food here, ranging from blintzes to berries to burritos, is tastier, healthier, and cheaper than that at 5th St. Organic foods are available at the Farmer's Market section.

EVENTS

The two-week **Oregon Bach Festival** at the Hult and U. of O's Beall Concert Hall beginning the last week of June (346-5666) brings Helmuth Rilling, world-renowned authority on Baroque music, to lead some of the country's finest musicians in performances of Bach's cantatas and concerti. (Contact the Hult Center Ticket Office, listed above, for information. Tickets $4-25, students 6-16 $6, senior discount for selected events.) **Art and the Vineyard,** at Alton Baker Park (345-1571), is a happy food, wine, and culture fest held for three days in July. The large park is taken over by West Coast artisans and local vineyards, complete with a food festival and live music. (Suggested donation $3.)

The enormous **Oregon Country Fair,** 13 mi. west of Eugene on Rte. 126 (343-6554), takes place for three days ($6 per day; $5 for first day only). To alleviate the yearly traffic jams, LTD provides free bus service to and from the fairgrounds in Veneta. Buses leave every half-hour in the morning from the LTD Customer Service Center and take off again before the fairgrounds close at 7pm. The fair is a huge crafts-and-music happening, characterized by a unique mellow spirit and hailed by many as a Woodstock-like reprise. The **Oregon Festival of American Music** (687-6526) takes place during one week in late summer, and often features big-name singers and musicians. (Tickets range from $4.50-34.50 depending on the event. 5% discount for pre-June 21 purchases.)

OUTDOORS

Eugene lies at the southern end of the Willamette Valley, whose fertile floor and richly forested hills attracted waves of pioneers. To see country that hasn't changed since the human invasion, take Rte. 126 east from Eugene; the highway runs adjacent to the beautiful McKenzie River, and on a clear day the mighty snowcapped **Three Sisters** of the Cascades are visible. Rte. 126 surveys the McKenzie Valley and the **McKenzie Pass,** where lava outcroppings served as a training site for astronauts preparing for lunar landings.

Forty mi. east of Eugene, Rte. 58 enters the **Willamette National Forest.** Ten miles later (1.2 mi. past the McKenzie Bridge) is the start of the 26-mi. **McKenzie River Trail.** The first 6 mi. of the trail are easily accessible, sandwiched between the highway and the river; the trail then crosses the river and continues up past **Clear Lake.** Three **campgrounds** are available for overnight use.

More ambitious hikers can sign up for an overnight permit at the **McKenzie Ranger Station,** on Rte. 126 (822-3381) and head for the high country. U.S. 242 branches off 126 about 3 mi. beyond the ranger state and winds up into the Three Sisters' Wilderness; trails that will carry you above treeline begin about 15 mi. up the road. The McKenzie Ranger Station is a well-spring of advice; name your abilities and goals, and they'll direct you to a great trail.

Tramping the trails is dusty work, so head off for some free pleasure at the **Terwilliger Hot Springs** (call the Blue River Ranger District for information at 822-3914). Six mi. east of Blue River on Rte. 126, turn right onto Auterheide Drive (Forest Service Rd. #19), and follow the road as it winds on the right side of Cougar Reservoir. Clothing is optional, and these two lovely rock pools have become the Willamette Forest's hippie hotspot. Other hot springs are scattered through the area; the Forest Service can suggest sulfur baths for the more modest.

Rte. 58 also leads east into beautiful and undeveloped country. Mountain biking is the sport of choice in **Oakridge,** 35 mi. southeast of Eugene. The **Fat Tire Festival,** (P.O. Box 127, or call Paul Kemp at 782-4228) held annually the third weekend in July, features family-oriented mountain-bike rides and races, and food and live music, without which no Oregon festival is complete. Entry fees for individual events are $10-20, $45 for all events. **Pathfinders,** 47470 Rte. 58 in Oakridge (484-4838), rents out mountain bike year-round ($20 for ½-day, $30 for a full day) and has a great stock of suggested routes (open Wed.-Sun. noon-6pm).

The small-town scenes in National Lampoon's *Animal House* and parts of the Rob Reiner film *Stand By Me* were filmed in **Cottage Grove,** 20 mi. south of Eugene off I-5; this sleepy town was typecast for its big-screen debut. **Maps** for self-guided car tours of the "Covered Bridge Capital of Oregon" are available at the **Chamber of Commerce,** 710 Row River Rd. (942-2411). Nearby Dorena and Cottage Grove Lakes are popular spots for water sports, hiking, and picnicking.

■ ■ ■ CORVALLIS

This peaceful residential community, 15 mi. east of I-5 in the northern Willamette Valley, makes no pretense of overplaying its history. It has no need to. Home to **Oregon State University** of forestry and engineering fame, this unassuming town lives in the present, particularly when it comes to outdoor frolicking. Mountain bikes dominate the roads and trails, and those without wheels can enjoy the wonderful parks scattered throughout the city. Most importantly, Corvallis is the hometown of the Maraschino cherry that tops every proper cocktail and sundae. Corvallis is a good place to relax and hang with your OSU friends.

PRACTICAL INFORMATION

Chamber of Commerce (757-1505), and the Convention and Visitors Bureau (757-1544 or 800-334-8118), 420 NW 2nd St. Advice and brochures dispensed freely; city **maps** are $1. Open Mon.-Fri. 8am-5pm.

Greyhound, 153 NW 4th St. (757-1797). To Portland (5 per day; $11) , Seattle (5 per day; $42), Newport (3 per day; $10), and Eugene (5 per day; $5.25). 24 hr. lockers for $1. Open Mon.-Fri. 7am-7pm, Sat. 7am-1pm.

Corvallis Transit System (757-6998). Fare 35¢, ages 5-17, seniors, and disabled 25¢. Service runs Mon.-Fri. 6:37am-7pm, Sat. 10am-4:43pm. Bus schedule available free from the Chamber of Commerce.

Oregon State University (737-0123 or 737-1000). Main entrance and information booth at Jefferson and 14th St.

Laundromat: Campbell's Cleaners, 1120 NW 9th St. $1 wash, 10 min. dry 25¢. Open daily 7am-11pm.

Taxi: A-1 Taxi, 754-1111. 24-hr. service.

Library: 645 NW Monroe (757-6927). Open Mon.-Wed. 10am-9pm, Thurs.-Sat. 10am-5:30pm, Sun. 1-5pm.

Emergency: 911. Police: 757-6924.

Post Office: 311 SW 2nd St. (758-1412). Open Mon.-Fri. 8am-5:30pm.

General Deliver Zip Code: 97333.

Area Code: 503.

Corvallis is laid out in checkerboard fashion, with numbered streets running north-south and streets named for the Presidents running east-west. College students hang out along SW Monroe St. when they aren't hitting the trails.

ACCOMMODATIONS AND CAMPING

With its new downtown youth hostel and easily accessible scenic campgrounds (which are *not* RV mini-cities), Corvallis gives the budget-conscious traveler a break. Motels are few and spaced throughout the city.

Cheshire Moon HI/AYH Hostel, 351 NW Jackson Ave. (753-9036), right across from the Greyhound bus station. Check in all day (8am-10pm) at the Juice Bar, same address next door. 12 beds and overflow space available. $10, $13 non-members.

Jason Inn, 800 NW 9th St. (753-7326 or 800-346-3291). Standard, pleasant rooms with cable TV and A/C. Singles $34. Doubles $38.

Budget Inn, 1480 SW 3rd St. (752-8756). Thick carpet and bathrooms big enough to waltz around in. 1 bed $35, senior/AAA discount $3. Reserve 2 wks. ahead.

Benton County Fairgrounds, 110 SW 53rd St. Follow Hamson west through Corvallis, and left onto 53rd St. about 2 mi. out. A pleasant, tree-lined campspot by the fairgrounds. Faint aroma brings horses to mind. First come, first served. Full hookup $9 per night, 50 outlets. Tents $4.50 per night.

Willamette Park, on SE Goodnight Rd. (757-6918). Follow Rte. 99W toward Eugene, after 2 mi. turn left on Goodnight Rd. 15 lovely camping sites on a horse-shoe-shaped field lined with trees 200 yards from the Willamette River. $7 per night, no hookup. First come, first served.

FOOD AND ENTERTAINMENT

Corvallis has a selection of collegiate pizza parlors and several different interpretations of Mexican food. OSU students usually prowl Monroe St. on their restaurant beat. Prices are marvelously cheap for tasty, filling food. Place your orders at the counter. The natural foods connection is **First Alternative Inc.,** 1007 SE 3rd St. (753-3115). Run by volunteers, this store stocks a range of well-priced produce, baked goods, and granola-esque groceries.

Nearly Normal's, 109 NW 15th (753-0791). Good Mexican meals. Arboreal aura. Large servings of anything and everything vegetarian for $4-7. Dine under apple trees out back, or beside tree-like projections upstairs. Open Mon.-Fri. 8am-9pm, Sat. 9am-9pm.

American Dream Pizza, 2525 NW Monroe St. (757-1713). The pizza-by-the-slice ($1.40, toppings 35¢ each) option draws a following of cafeteria-weary college students. Superb homemade pizza in oversized, enveloping wooden booths or painted chairs beneath bicycles and colorful mobiles dangling from the ceiling. Open Mon.-Thurs. 11am-10pm, Fri. 11am-11pm, Sat.-Sun. 4-10pm. Will deliver.

Bombs Away Café, 2527 NW Monroe (757-7221). Where Mexican food and multicolored geometric art combust, Slurp down their "Wet Burrito" specialty for $5. Open Mon.-Sat. 11am-10pm, Sun. 4-10pm.

New Morning Bakery, 219 SW 2nd St. (752-8549). A befuddling array of pastries, breads, and cookies greets happy patrons. Entrees $4, also serve breakfast and lunch. Fri. and Sat. nights bring local bands. Open Sun. 8am-7pm, Mon.-Thurs. 7am-9pm, Fri.-Sat. 7am-11pm.

Clubs and Bars

Squirrel's Tavern, 100 SW 2nd (753-8057). Although plastered with sports banners, the live action here comes from relaxing around the bar or wood tables. 2 pool tables upstairs. Live music Sat. nights for a $2 cover.

Murphy's Tavern, 2740 SW 2nd Ave. (754-3508). Corvallis is practically rural, so why not partake of a little country culture? Live country music Fri. and Sat., and brave the crowds for Trivia Night on Thurs. Beers 25¢ every Wed. noon-8pm. Open Sun.-Thurs. noon-midnight, Fri.-Sat. noon-2am.

Clodfelters, 1501 NW Monroe (758-4452). Cheap beer. Domestic pitcher $4.50. Grab a burger before heading back to campus to get wild. Happy Hour Thurs. 5-8pm is packed. Open daily 11am-1am.

Peacock Tavern, 125 SW 2nd (754-8552). Pool tables and an oh-so-bored fraternity crowd. Live bands Tues.-Sun. Open daily 7am-1am.

OUTDOORS

Mountain-biking is a way of life in Corvallis. Set off in any direction, and you're bound to hit some good trails. Many people head for the **McDonald Forest** owned by OSU; just drive west out of town on Harrison about 2 mi., and angle right on Oak Creek Rd. The road dead ends at OSU's Lab, and multiple trails lead from there into the forest. **Mary's Peak,** off of Hwy. 34 14 mi. from Corvallis, is also a popular area. The downhill-only crowd can drive up Mary's Peak and speed down on two wheels. **Peak Sports,** 129 NW 2nd St. (757-0545), rents out bikes for $15 per day.

City parks, well-maintained expanses of fields and trails, are fantastic areas for a mosey or a picnic. 74-acre **Avery Park,** just south of the city, draws frisbee players, sun bathers, and kids clambering on the full-size locomotive model. The vast campus of **Oregon State University,** marked by buildings of widely varying architectural style, is worth exploring. Arrange a tour through the admissions office at 737-4411. Parking is available behind the information booth at Jefferson and 15th.

The third weekend in July, the heart rate of sleepy Corvallis picks up fifty beats with the **da Vinci Days festival.** Only in Corvallis could one celebrate Art, Science, and Technology, and have a blast. If your interest in technology extends only to those who blast out music best, don't despair: the festival brings in nationally known bands, from jazz to folk to cajun to rock ($5, $3 ages 4-12).

Fifteen mi. east in Albany (just off I-5), thousands of people gather from mid-July through August each Thursday night for the **River Rhythms** concert series. Concerts are free, and are held in the Monteith River Park. Call the Albany Visitors Center (928-0911) for further information.

■■■ SALEM

Despite state-capital status and the presence of Willamette University, Salem seems barely able to register a pulse. Travelers stopping or staying in Salem might check out the impressive **Capitol,** but the city offers few options for budget travelers.

Practical Information and Orientation The **Visitors Association and Salem Convention,** 1313 Mill St. SE (581-4325), part of the Mission Mill Village complex, stocks brochures on Salem and other parts of the state (open Mon.-Fri. 8:30am-noon and 1-5pm, Sat.-Sun. 10am-4pm; fall and winter Mon.-Fri. 8:30am-5pm). The

Chamber of Commerce, 220 Cottage St. NE (581-1466). has free **maps** and phone books available. Open Mon.-Fri. 8:30am-5pm.

Amtrak, 500 13th St. SE (588-1551 or 800-872-7245), is at 12th and Mill St. SE, across from Willamette University. Trains run daily to Portland ($12), Seattle ($35), and San Francisco ($129). **Greyhound,** 450 Church St. NE (362-2428), at Center St., run buses north and south, with service eight times daily to Portland ($7.50; open daily 6:30am-8:30pm). Local transportation is managed by **Cherriots** (588-2877). Buses originate from High St.; terminals are in front of the courthouse. (Fare 50¢, under 18 35¢, seniors and disabled 25¢. Service Mon.-Fri. 6:15am-6:15pm about every ½-hr., Sat. 7:45am-5:45pm hourly.) Fares and schedule will change slightly in late 1994. For an update, call 588-2885. For a taxi, call **Salem Yellow Cab Co.** (362-2411; 24 hrs.). Rent a car from **National,** 695 Liberty St. NE (800-624-2997 or 585-4226; cars from $35; 30 ¢ per mi. after 100 mi.; open Mon.-Fri. 8am-5:30pm).

Wash your clothes at **Laundromat: Suds City Depot,** 1785 Lancaster Dr. NE (362-9845; open daily 7:30am-9pm; wash 75¢, $1 on weekends after 10am, dry 50¢-75¢). The **Women's Crisis Center** phone number is 399-7722 (24 hrs.). The **library** is at 585 Liberty St. SE (588-6315; open Mon., Fri., and Sat. 10am-6pm, Tues.-Thurs. 10am-9pm). In an **emergency,** dial 911; find the **police** at 555 Liberty St. SE (588-6123), in City Hall. The **Post Office** is at 1050 25th St. SE (370-4700; open Mon.-Fri. 8:30am-5:30pm; **General Delivery ZIP Code:** 97301). The **area code** is 503.

Salem is bordered on the west by the Willamette River and on the east by I-5, 47 mi. south of Portland. The downtown area centers around Liberty St., several blocks west of the capitol. Street addresses are arranged by the quadrant system, with State St. as the north-south divider, and the Willamette River as the east-west divider. The roads downtown are in good condition, but the rest of Salem begs for road work.

Accommodations and Camping In the far, faraway galaxy of Northwestern budget travel, the Manichean battle continues: if Spokane were the Force, Salem would be the Dark Side. For camping, struggle valiantly against the tractor beam of KOA and stay at Silver Falls. B&Bs are more affordable here than anywhere else in the state (starting at $40 per room), so spending the extra $10 might not be a bad idea. The Visitors Center has a list of area B&Bs. The **Holiday Lodge,** 1400 Hawthorne Ave. NE (585-2323 or 800-543-5071), has large, comfortable rooms, as close to downtown as you can hope to get. (Singles $35. Doubles $42. $3 per additional person. Under 15 free). The **Hampshire House Bed & Breakfast,** 975 D St. NE (370-7181), has two comfortable rooms, both with TVs. Honeymooners (or pretenders) should ask for the bridal room, with a soft pink bedspread and filmy white curtains. Full breakfast is served (rooms $40). Seek Yoda and Jedi instruction at **Silver Falls State Park,** 20024 Silver Falls SE (Rte. 214) (873-8681), 26 mi. from Salem, is Oregon's largest state park, offering swimming, hiking, and views of waterfalls, including a trail leading behind one of the falls. The tallest, spectacular Double Falls, crashes 178 ft. (sites $14, with electricity and water $15).

Food The Salem sandwich is two pieces of bread with whatever you want in the middle. It isn't expensive, and it isn't very good. A decent dinner is only a dream— there are fifteen dollar meals, and there is Taco Bell. The bars that proliferate throughout the downtown area may be the best bet for dinner. An exception is the **Off-Center Cafe,** 1741 Center NE (363-9245), in the aqua-green building. It's appreciably pioneering, with a leftist approach and generally delicious food that has become a local favorite. Start the morning off with a hearty dose of "bibble and squib" ($4) or scrambled tofu ($5.25; open Tues.-Fri. 7am-2:30pm, Sat.-Sun. 8am-2pm. Dinner Thurs.-Sat. 6-9pm.) Locals stock up at **Heliotrope Natural Food,** 2060 Market St. NE (362-5487). It's a small store, but prices are decent, and there's a good selection of bread and produce. Join the locals at the yellow counter or booths at the **Courth Street Dairy,** 347 Court St. NE (363-6433), for a taste of the '50s. An antique cash register will ring up your order of old-fashioned burgers or shakes. Old photos of Depression-era Salem cover the walls. (It used to be worse!) (Open Mon.-

Fri. 7am-2pm, Sat. 8am-noon.) Follow the executive crowd into **Deja Bree'z,** 1210 State St. (364-6246), just one block from the capital. The Salem Sandwich, plus fruit or salad, goes for $4.50. A bowl of soup ($2) and homemade bread (50¢) is a more dynamic option. (Open Mon.-Fri. 7am-7pm, Sat. 11am-5pm.)

Sights and Events The **State Capitol,** 900 Court St. NE (378-4423), on Court St. between W Summer and E Summer St., is capped by a 23-ft. gold-leaf statue of the quintessential "Oregon Pioneer," giving the building an imposing, temple-like appearance. Artwork and sculptures depicting the great Westward Push through the frontier ornament the interior. But nature is still wild 150 years later: the Capitol's rotunda is closed off for two years due to damage inflicted by a 5.6 earthquake in March, 1993. Nothing collapsed, but the structure was significantly weakened. Wander in, it's free and impressive inside. In the legislative chambers, check out the evergreen motif in the House and the salmon motif in the Senate chamber. If you're looking for real excitement, try to observe a floor debate on gun control in this politically evenly-divided state (open Mon.-Fri. 7:30am-5:30pm, Sat. 9am-4pm, Sun. noon-4pm. Free tours in June-Aug. leave on the hour).

Across the street is **Willamette University,** 900 State St. (370-6303). Founded by Methodist missionaries in 1842, this good private school is the oldest university in the West. **Tours** leave from the admissions office in George Putnam University Center (370-6303) daily at 10am and 2pm; call ahead. **The Historic Deepwood Estate,** 1116 Mission St. SE (363-1825),gives house tours for the same prices (summer Sun.-Fri. noon-4:30pm; winter Sun.-Fri. 1-4pm). The real joy of Deepwood is in admiring the extensive, well-manicured gardens.

The **Honeywood Winery,** 1350 Hines St. SE (362-4111), Salem's only urban winery, is Oregon's oldest (open for tours and tasting by appointment Mon.-Fri. 9am-5pm, Sat. 10am-5pm, Sun. 1pm-5pm). Other wines can be found by contacting Visitors Information. For a sample of something drier, check out the **Salem Art Fair and Festival** (581-2228), held during the third week of July in Bush's Pasture Park, 2330 17th St. NE. The Festival showcases the works of Northwestern artists. Free band performances jam or strum away the afternoons, and anyone with extra energy can join the 5K **Run for the Arts,** held during the festival. ($5 for entrance. Write to the Salem Arts Association, 600 Mission St. SE, or call 581-2228). Salem gears up for the annual **Oregon State Fair** (378-3247 or 800-833-0011), when people, farm animals, craft booths, and chaos come hurtling simultaneously into the city.

CENTRAL AND EASTERN OREGON

Most people visualize Oregon as a verdant land of sweeping rains and rich forests. This is true enough of western Oregon, where most Oregonians live, but it's a poor description of Oregon's high desert region east of the Cascade Range. The low, forested Coast Range and the high, jagged, volcanic, forested Cascades are natural rain barriers, trapping moisture from Pacific winds and making the western coast and valleys green, densely forested, and wet while leaving the eastern basin hot and arid.

Eastern Oregon is known as the High Desert, but the "desert" is somewhat misleading. The eastern slope of the Cascades is still full of life, with high peaks, world-class skiing, volcanic flows, Crater Lake, and the fun, energetic town of Bend, an outdoor mecca. The southeastern region near Burns is the driest, full of beautiful, empty country, dramatic mountains, expansive skies, vast grasslands, lava beds, deserts, marshes, and lakes. Northeastern Oregon, near Pendleton and Baker City, offers the Wallowa Mts., pine and fir forests, fossil beds, 8000-ft.-deep Hells Canyon, and fascinating Oregon Trail history. But despite all of the outdoor activity, eastern Oregon is sparsely populated and seldom visited. It's easy to lose yourself in the pristine forests or desert wildernesses.

For generations, this arid region has challenged its human inhabitants, from the Cayuse, Shoshone, Nez Perce, and others who first occupied it, to the pioneers who crossed it on foot and in wagons, to the modern farmers, ranchers, loggers, and town-dwellers who live there today. Fast rivers and streams flow through the region, and heavy winter snows nourish forests. Eastern Oregon is a great place to enjoy the outdoors, bask in the sun, expand your sky, explore uncrowded forests, and find solitude. In this vast and largely undeveloped region, a car is almost a must. Distances are great, and the few buses take roundabout routes.

■■■ CRATER LAKE AND KLAMATH FALLS

Mirror-blue Crater Lake, the namesake of Oregon's only national park, was regarded as sacred by Native American shamans, who forbade their people to look upon it. Iceless in winter and flawlessly circular, the lake plunges from its 6000-ft. elevation to a depth of nearly 2000 ft., making it the nation's deepest lake. Klamath (kuh-LAH-math) Falls offers a few diversions for those making a pit stop, but time and money are better spent at Crater Lake.

PRACTICAL INFORMATION AND ORIENTATION

Visitors Information: William G. Steel Center (594-2211 x 402), next to park headquarters on the south access road. Pick up backcountry camping **permits** here or at Rim Village (free). Also screens a free 17-min. movie on Crater Lake every ½ hr. 9am-4:30pm. Open daily 9am-5pm. **Crater Lake National Park Visitors Center** (524-2211 x 415), on the lake shore at **Rim Village.** Pamphlets and advice regarding trails and campsites. Open daily July-Aug. 9:30am-4:30pm. The **Klamath County Department of Tourism** runs a visitor information center at 1451 Main St. (884-0666 or 800-445-6738). Open daily June-Sept. 9am-5:30pm, Oct.-May 8am-5:30pm.

Park Admission: Admission is charged only in summer. Cars $5, hikers and bikers $3, 62 and over free with Golden Age Passport.

Amtrak, S Spring St. depot (884-2822; reservations 1-800-USA-RAIL or 872-7245). One train per day north, 1 per day south. To Portland: $64. Open daily 7-10:30am and 8:45-10pm.

Greyhound, 1200 Klamath Ave. (882-4616). To: Bend (1 per day; $19.25); Redding, CA (1 per day; $31); Eugene (1 per day; $21). Lockers $1 per 24 hrs. Open Mon.-Fri. 6am-5pm, Sat. 6am-4pm.

Basin Transit Service: (883-2877), runs 6 routes around Klamath Falls Mon.-Fri. 6am-7pm, Sat. 10am-5pm. Fare 70¢.

Roadmaster Transportation: (884-9990), runs a 5-hr. tour from Klamath Falls to Crater Lake ($50). You can make 2 reservations, be dropped off in the park, and cancel your second reservation if you can find a ride by talking it up at the Mazama campground.

Taxi: AB Taxi, (885-5607). 24 hrs.

Car Rental: Budget, at Airport (885-5421), take S 6th and turn right on Altamonta. $30-44 per day Thurs.-Mon. 150 free mi. per day, 25¢ per additional mi. Open Mon.-Fri. 7am-7:30pm, Sat.-Sun. 8am-5pm.

Equipment Rental: All Seasons Sports, 714 Main St., Klamath Falls (884-3863). Rents all kinds of skis (winter, downhill, cross-country) for $15 first day, $10 additional days. In-line skates $12 per day or $6 for 4 hr. Open Mon.-Sat. 9am-6pm, Sun. noon-5pm.

Laundromat: Main Street Laundromat, 1711 Main St. (883-1784). Wash $1, 12-min. dry 25¢. Open daily 8am-7pm.

Weather and Road Conditions: Park Information, including weather and road conditions, is broadcast continuously on radio station 1610 AM in Crater Lake.

Crisis: Red Cross, 884-4125. **Poison Control,** 800-452-7165. **Rape Crisis,** 884-0390.

Hospital: Merle West Medical Center, 2885 Doggett St. (883-6176), from U.S. 97 northbound, turn right on Campus Dr., then right on Dogget.
Emergency: 911. **Police: Klamath Falls,** 452 Walnut (883-5336). **Fire:** 885-2056, non-emergency.
Post Office: Klamath Falls, 317 S 7th St. (884-9226). Open Mon.-Fri. 7:30am-5:30pm, Sat. 9am-noon. **Zip Code:** 97601. **Crater Lake,** in the Steel Center. Open Mon.-Fri. 10am-4pm. **Zip Code:** 97604.
Area Code: 503.

Rte. 62 through Crater Lake National Park and the south access road up to the Rim are open year-round, but the park's services and accommodations are available only after the snow has melted, typically July and August. After skirting the southwestern edge of the lake, Rte. 62 heads southwest to Medford and southeast to Klamath Falls. To reach the park from Portland, take I-5 to Eugene, then Rte. 58 east to U.S. 97 south. Many roads leading to the park are closed or dangerous during the winter. Crater Lake averages over *44 ft.* of snow per year, so some roads could be closed as late as July; call the Steel Center for road conditions (see Practical Information). Rte. 138 heads west from U.S. 97 and approaches the lake from the north, but this route can only be used during the summer. All of Crater Lake's services and operating hours are based on changing funding levels, which are not determined until April. Call the Steel Center to verify services and hours.

Klamath Falls lies 24 mi. south of the intersection of Rte. 62 and U.S. 97, at the southern tip of Upper Klamath Lake. Many roads lead to this small town: Rte. 66 heads east from Ashland; Rte. 39 goes south to Redding; Rte. 140 runs east to Lakeview; and U.S. 97 continues south to Weed, CA. Main St. is the historic center of town with many of the restaurants and motels on it or only a few blocks distant. For more recent strip development, S 6th St. is a crowded thoroughfare. The area around Klamath Falls and Crater Lake is quiet in the winter. The lake is effectively, if not officially, closed then, and Klamath Falls motels have lots of room.

ACCOMMODATIONS AND CAMPING

Klamath Falls has several affordable hotels; you may be wise to sack out in the town and make your forays to Crater Lake from there. The national park contains two campsites: **Mazama Campground** and the smaller **Lost Creek Campground,** which is often closed when roads are impassable (see below). Backcountry camping is allowed within the park; pick up permits (free) from Rim Village Visitors Center or at the Steel Center (see Practical Information). Food must be stored properly to prevent hungry bears from investigating; talk to the rangers for more details. Make sure you treat any stream water before ingesting (boiling thoroughly is the most foolproof method), as nasty microscopic critters often lurk.

Fort Klamath Lodge Motel (381-2234), on Rte. 62, 6 mi. from the southern entrance to Crater Lake National Park. The closest motel to the lake, the 6-unit lodge is in historic Fort Klamath, which consists of little more than a grocery store, post office, restaurant, and tons of wildflowers in the spring. Cozy but aging countrified motel rooms with knotted-pine walls. TV; no phones in the rooms. Laundry available. Singles $30. Doubles $35.

Townhouse Motel, 5323 S 6th St. (882-0924). The shaggy red rugs may remind you of a basement rec. room, but the rooms are clean, and the price can't be beat. 16 units. Singles $22. Doubles $25.

Maverick Motel, 1220 Main St. (882-6688), down the street from Greyhound in Klamath Falls. A bit north of the action but only a short walk. Ask the manager about rides to Crater Lake. Basic, standard motel rooms, but well kept-up. TV, A/C, and a postage stamp-sized pool. Singles $30. Doubles $35.

Mazama Campground (594-2511), in Crater Lake National Park. RVs swarm into the 198 sites in this monster facility in mid-summer, but fortunately a sprinkling of sites throughout are reserved for tents only. **Loop G,** reserved for tents only, has denser timber and more spacious sites, offering greater seclusion. Rarely fills completely. Firewood for sale. No hookups, but flush toilets, telephones. Pay laundry facilities and shower. Wheelchair accessible. Sites $11. No reservations.

Lost Creek Campground (594-2211 x 402), in Crater Lake National Park. Hidden at the southwest corner of the park, this campground has only 16 sites. Try to secure a spot in the morning. Drinking water and pit toilets. Usually open by mid-July. Tents only, sites $5. No reservations.

FOOD

Eating inexpensively in Crater Lake is difficult. Crater Lake Lodge has a small dining room, and Rim Village establishments charge high prices for a skimpy array of food-stuffs. If you're coming from the south, **Fort Klamath** is the final food frontier before you trek into the park. If you've already looked in Klamath Falls and can't find the food you need, try the **Old Fort Store** (381-2345; open summer daily 9am-7pm). There are several affordable restaurants in Klamath Falls and a number of large grocery stores, including a 24-hour **Safeway** (882-2660) at Pine and 8th St., one block from Main St. (open 6am-11pm daily).

Llao Rock Cafe, in the Rim Village has deli sandwiches for $4-6. Open daily 8am-8pm. Upstairs, **The Watchman Eatery and Lounge** has burgers ($6 with potato salad) you can munch while looking out on the stillness of Crater Lake, plus a salad bar—all you can eat $6. Open June 10-Sept. 4 daily noon-10pm.

Hobo Junction, 636 Main St. (882-8013), at 7th St. The place to stock up for a picnic or to simply relax among the potted plants. Good deli fare, with hearty bowls of chili ($1.65) and 22 varieties of hot dogs. Pass the Pepto! Try #8, the Hobo Dog (cheddar and Swiss cheese, bacon, and salsa, $2.65). Open Mon.-Fri. 11am-5pm.

The Blue Ox, 535 Main St. (884-5495). Slow service but portions of Bunyanic proportions. $4.25 buys a mammoth Oxburger, and the Chili burger ($4.25) comes open-faced with so much chili that it's best tackled with a knife and fork. Just $1.65 gets you 2 eggs, hashbrowns, and toast. Bottomless cup of coffee 75¢. Breakfast served all day. Open daily 7am-9pm.

Cattle Crossing Cafe, (381-9801) on Hwy. 62 in Fort Klamath. Step over the silver-plated cow pie into this cool, clean restaurant for hearty, rib-sticking breakfasts ($3-6) and burgers ($4-6). Don't roll out until you've had a slice of homemade pie ($2). Open daily 6am-9pm.

SIGHTS

As you approach **Crater Lake,** you won't see anything remarkable; it could be any lake. The sky and mountains are initially what capture your attention. As you ascend, however, the lake's reflected blue becomes almost unreal in its placidity. The fantastic depth of the lake (1932 ft.), combined with the extreme clarity of its waters, creates its amazingly serene and intensely blue effect. About 7700 years ago, Mt. Mazama created this pacific scene by means of one of the Earth's most destructive cataclysms. A massive eruption buried thousands of square miles in the western U.S. under a thick layer of ash and left a deep caldera to be filled with still waters. The lake is rightfully the center of attention and activity in the park.

Rim Drive, a route open only in summer, is a 33-mi. loop around the rim of the caldera, high above the lake, along which the Park Service has thoughtfully scattered pull-outs at every point where a view of the lake might cause an awe-struck tourist to drive right off the road. A vast majority of visitors stay in their vehicles as they tour the lake, so it's relatively easy to get away from the shifting crowds. Just stop at any of the trailheads scattered around the rim, and hike away from the road to another awesome view. Among the most spectacular are **Discovery Point Trail,** from which the first pioneer saw the lake in 1853 (1.3 mi. one way), **Garfield Peak Trail** (1.7 mi. one way), and **Watchman Lookout** (.8 mi. one way).

The hike up **Mt. Scott,** the park's highest peak (a tad under 9000 ft.), begins from the drive near the lake's eastern edge. Although steep, the 2½-mi. trail to the top gives the persevering hiker a unique view of the lake and its surroundings that justifies the sweaty ascent. Steep **Cleetwood Trail,** a 1-mi. switchback, is the only route to the lake's edge. From here, the **Lodge Company** (594-2511) offers two-hour boat tours on the lake. (Tour schedule varies; 3-9 tours leave per day June 18-Sept. 17; fare $10, under 12 $6). Both **Wizard Island,** a cinder cone 760 ft. above lake level, and **Phantom Ship Rock** are fragile, tiny specks when viewed from above, yet they are surprisingly large when viewed from the surface of the water. If you take an early tour, you can be left on Wizard Island to be picked up later. Picnics and fishing are allowed, as is swimming, but surface temperature reaches a maximum of only 50°F (10°C). Six species of fish have been introduced artificially into the lake, but the water is too pure to support much life; only rainbow trout and kokanee have survived. Park rangers lead free walking tours daily in the summer and periodically during the winter (on snowshoes). Call the Steel Center for schedules (see Practical Information).

If pressed for time, walk the easy 100 yd. from the visitors center down to the **Sinnott Memorial Overlook.** The view is the area's most panoramic and accessible. For a short lecture on the area's geology and history, attend one of the nightly ranger talks (held July-Labor Day daily at 9pm in the Mazama Campground Amphitheater) or catch the 12-minute film at the Steel Center, which is refreshing for its Native American perspective.

After you've seen the lake from every possible angle, consider a **hiking** trip into the park's vast **backcountry.** Leave the vehicles and all but the hardiest people behind, and explore the Pacific Crest Trail where it passes through the park, or any of the other trails that cross the terrain. Best of all, the tall forests and high peaks of the backcountry feel like a different national park. One excellent route makes a loop of the **Crater Springs, Oasis Butte,** and **Boundary Springs** trails. Acquire information and permits (free) at the Steel Center.

■■■ BEND

Sun and snow make Bend busy all year, yielding the best of both weather worlds: temperatures as high as 100°F (36°C) in summer and over 5 ft. of snow in the winter (at the lower elevations!) Bordered by Mt. Bachelor, part of the Cascade Range and home of the U.S. Ski Team, the Deschutes River, a favorite of rafters, and a national forest, the city is an ideal focal point for hikers and bicyclists, too. Put on the map in the 1820s by pioneers who found "Farewell Bend" a convenient river ford, the city has grown to become the state's largest urban population east of the Cascades (21,000) and offers more cultural, culinary, and athletic options than its neighbors. Bend is a hub of central Oregon's highway system, where U.S. 97 and U.S. 20 intersect, and here you will find what the rest of eastern Oregon is missing: people, fast food, even some traffic. Bend is growing extremely fast, as young people seeking the outdoors and refugees from California push Bend toward urban status. Yet cheap food and places to stay are easy to find in Bend, and the young, athletic crowd make the town one of the liveliest, especially for its size, in the Northwest.

PRACTICAL INFORMATION AND ORIENTATION

Visitors Information: Central Oregon Welcome Center, 63085 N U.S. 97 (382-3221). In a spacious new building. Read the State Park Guide, Events Calendar, National Forest Information, and free **maps** while you drink a complimentary cup of steaming coffee. Open Mon.-Sat. 9am-5pm, Sun. 11am-3pm.

Parks and Recreation Dept., 200 Pacific Park Ln. (389-7275). Information on everything about parks. Open Mon.-Fri. 8am-5pm.

Deschutes National Forest Headquarters, 1645 E U.S. 20 (388-2715). General forest, recreation, and wilderness information. Peruse the *Recreation Opportunity Guide* for each of the four Ranger Districts. Open Mon.-Fri. 7:45-4:30pm.

Greyhound, 2045 E U.S. 20 (382-2151), a few mi. east of town. One bus per day to: Portland ($20.50) and Klamath Falls ($19.50). Open Mon.-Fri. 7:30am-noon and

12:30-5:30pm, Sat. 7:30am-noon, Sun. 8-11:30am. Several other bus and van lines stop herel, with different destinations; call the above number for information.

Taxi: Owl Taxi, 1917 NE 2nd St. (382-3311). 24 hr.

AAA, 20350 Empire Ave. (382-1303). Open Mon.-Fri. 8am-5pm. For AAA members.

Car Rental: Rent-A-Wreck, 315 SE 3rd St. (385-3183). $25 per day with 100 free mi., or $125 per week with 700 free mi. Must be 21 with a major credit card.

Bicycle Rental: Hutch's Bicycles, 725 NW Columbia Ave. (382-9253). Mountain bikes $15 per day or $50 per week. Open Mon.-Fri. 9am-7pm, Sat.-Sun. 9am-6pm.

Laundromat: Nelson's, 407 SE 3rd St. (388-2140). Wash $1, 12 min. dry 25¢. Open daily 7am-10:30pm.

Library: Deschutes County Library, 507 NW Wall (388-6679). Open Mon.-Fri. 10am-6pm, Tues.-Thurs. 10am-8pm, Sat. 10am-5pm.

Central Oregon Battering and Rape Alliance (COBRA): 800-356-2369.

Poison Control: 800-452-7165.

Teen Crisis Line: 800-660-0934.

Alcohol and Drug Help Line: 800-621-1646.

Hospital: St. Charles Medical Center, 2500 NE Neff Rd. (382-4321), for major emergencies only. For routine cuts, scrapes, fractures and illnesses, go to either of two **St. Charles Immediate Care Centers,** at 1302 NE U.S. 97 (388-7799; open Mon.-Fri. 8am-8pm, Sat.-Sun. 10am-6pm) and 1245 S U.S. 97 #C-3, in the Village Shopper Mall off Division Street (385-6388).

Emergency: 911. **Police:** 711 NW Bond (388-5550). **Fire:** 388-5533.

Post Office: 2300 NE 4th St. (388-1971), at Webster. Open Mon.-Fri. 8:30am-5:30pm, Sat. 10am-1pm. **General Delivery ZIP Code:** 97701.

Area Code: 503.

U.S. 97 (3rd St.) bisects Bend. The downtown area lies to the west along the Deschutes River; Wall and Bond St. are the two main arteries.

ACCOMMODATIONS AND CAMPING

Most of the cheapest motels are just outside town on 3rd St., but don't let the distance deter you; for a tourist town, the rates are surprisingly low. The hostel and bed and breakfast provide phenomenal deals for tired travelers. **Deschutes National Forest** maintains a huge number of campgrounds in the Cascades to the west of town. All have pit toilets; those with drinking water cost $8-12 per night; those without are free. Contact the **Bend Ranger District Office** at 1230 NE 3rd St., Suite A-262 (388-5664) for more information.

Mill Inn, 642 NW Colorado (389-9198), on the corner of Bond St. This bed & breakfast in a recently rebuilt hotel and boarding house is the labor of love of Ev and Carol Stiles, who keep the place sparkling clean. Hearty home-cooked breakfast included. $15 gets you a bunk in the dorm-style "Locker Room" (capacity 4), or splurge for a trim, elegant private room for $32 for one or $36 for two, with shared bath. Reservations recommended.

Bend Alpine Hostel (HI/AYH), 19 SW Century Dr., Bend 97702 (389-3813). From 3rd St., take Franklin west, and follow the Cascade Lakes Tour signs to Century Drive (14th St.). Go to the Bend Alpine Hostel. Go directly to the Bend Alpine Hostel. Do not pass Go. Do not collect $200. Brand new and impeccably clean. The personable and friendly managers can tell you everything there is to know about the Bend area. Two blocks from ski and bike rentals and the free shuttle to Mt. Bachelor. Laundry and kitchen, linen rental available. Lockout 9:30am-4:30pm, curfew 11pm. Members $12, non-members $15.

Holiday Motel, 880 SE 3rd St. (382-4620 or 800-252-0121). Small rooms with thin walls, but the folks are really friendly and the beds really comfortable. Really. Cable and A/C. Singles $30. Doubles $34.

Hosmer Lake Campground is just over 1 mi. up Forest Rd. 4625, which diverges from the Cascade Lake Highway 35 mi. west of Bend. One of the better Forest Service campgrounds, featuring 22 secluded sites and tiny Hosmer Lake in which to play. No water; free.

Edelweiss Motel, 2346 NE Division St. (382-6222), at Xerxes St. near the northern intersection with 3rd St. Old building, and there are no phones or A/C, but it's kept clean, and you won't find a cheaper room in Bend. Singles $25. Doubles $28.

FOOD

The diversity of food in Bend gives travelers a welcome respite from the surrounding beef-and-potatoes monotony. You won't go hungry here; restaurants generally maintain high standards, and there are a number to choose from. While downtown Bend offers many pleasant cafes, 3rd St. also proffers a variety of good eateries. No fewer than four mega-markets line the east side of 3rd St.- for example, the **Safeway** at 642 NE 3rd St. (382-7341), open daily 6am-midnight.

Nature's General Store, in the Wagner Mall on 3rd St. (382-6732), has bulk food, organic produce, and healthy sandwiches (open Mon.-Fri. 9:30am-9pm, Sat. 9:30am-6pm, Sun. 11am-6pm).

West Side Bakery and Cafe, 1005 NW Galveston (382-3426). Locally famous for its breakfasts, the West Side Cafe's lunches should soon extend its reputation. Served among stuffed animals and toy trains are lots of healthy sandwiches ($4.75), including "the Natural," a vegetarian favorite with two kinds of cheese and every imaginable kind of vegetable. Virtually everything here is homemade, including the bread, which is so good you'll want to bring away whole loaves of it ($2 each). Open breakfast and lunch only, Mon.-Sat. 7am-3pm, Sun. 7am-2pm.

Pilt Butte Drive-In Restauarant, 917 NE Greenwood (U.S. 20) (382-2972). Home of the 18-oz. "Pilot Butte Burger," ("It's BIG:" $9.50), and many of more manageable size. Breakfasts are huge—for example, #3 (2 eggs, 2 hotcakes for $2.75). Open daily 6am-9pm.

Deschutes Brewery and Public House, 1044 NW Bond St. (382-9242). Tasty pub food and home-brewed beer. Daily specials $4-7. Pint of ale, bitters, or stout brewed on the premises ($2). Homemade root beer $1.50. Live music many weekends. No smoking. Wheelchair access. Open Mon.-Thurs. 11am-11:30pm, Fri.-Sat. 11am-12:30am, Sun. noon-10pm. Minors not allowed after 8:30pm.

Sargent's Cafe, 719 SE 3rd St. (382-3916). A crowded, friendly diner with abundant portions. One pancake ($1.50) is a full meal. All-you-can-eat spaghetti plate $5.50. Wheelchair access. Open daily 5:30am-9:30pm.

Rolaine's Cantina, 785 SE 3rd St. (382-4944), across from Albertson's. Frighteningly large Mexican specials. The vegetarian tostada ($6.50) comes smothered in so much lettuce, carrots, tomatoes, sprouts, red cabbage, and cucumbers, you'll wonder if there's a tostada under it all. Try their specialty, the *burrito rolaine* ($6.25), and garnish it with gobs of "killer" salsa (available upon request). Wheelchair access. Open Mon.-Fri. 11:30am-10pm, Sat. noon-10pm, Sun. noon-9pm.

Goody's, 975 NW Wall St. (389-5185). A generous scoop of phenomenal ice cream is $1.20 on a cone, or $1.50 in a homemade waffle cone or "waffle dish." Open Mon.-Thurs. 10am-9pm, Fri.-Sat. 10am-10pm, Sun. noon-8pm.

Cafe Paradiso, 945 NW Bend (385-5931). Good coffee (75¢), espresso ($1.25), and cappucino ($1.50) in a cafe that would be at home in Cambridge or Greenwich Village. Relax in comfy couches and catch up on some reading while you sip. Occasional live music on a tiny stage. Open Mon.-Thurs. 8am-11pm, Fri. 8am-midnight, Sat. 10am-midnight, Sun. 10am-6pm.

SIGHTS AND OUTDOORS

Six mi. south of Bend on U.S. 97, the **High Desert Museum** (382-4754) is great, offering exhibits on the fragile ecosystem of the Oregon plateau, realistic and audio-visual exhibitions of the West in days past, and refreshing temporary exhibitions. A new wing opened in 1991 with a "Desertarium," where seldom-seen animals like burrowing owls and collared lizards are presented in a simulated desert habitat. Outside, paved paths wind past exhibits on otters, porcupines, birds of prey, a settler's cabin, sheepherder's wagon, and an old-time sawmill. Packed with 1300 visitors daily in mid-summer. Coming early in the day is your only hope of beating the crowds. Allow at least a few hours for the visit. Lack of funding has kept the price of admission high, but it's worth it. (Open daily 9am-5pm. $5.50, seniors $5, ages 5-12 $2.75.)

In November, 1990, **Newberry National Volcanic Monument** was established to link together and preserve the volcanic features south of Bend. For an introduction to the area, visit the **Lava Lands Visitor Center** (593-2421), 5 mi. south of the High Desert Museum on U.S. 97. The center has exhibits on the volcanism that created the Cascade Range and shaped the local geography. (Open March to mid-October 10am-4pm daily, Memorial Day-Labor Day 9am-5pm.)

Immediately behind the visitor center is **Lava Butte**, a 500-ft. cinder cone from which many of the nearby lava flows, and the High Cascades to the west, can be viewed. Between Memorial Day and Labor Day, one can take a shuttle bus ($1.50) or walk the 1.5-mi. road. In the off-season, individuals may drive their own cars up the incline.

One mi. south of the Visitor Center on U.S. 97 is **Lava River Cave** (593-1456), a 1-mi.-long subterranean lava tube. The entrance to the cave is in a stand of gigantic ponderosa pines, perfect for a picnic. The cave temperature hovers at 42°F (5°C) year-round, so come bundled in warm clothes, and bring a flashlight or propane lantern. For real fun, turn off your lantern to experience the utter blackness, but don't forget to bring an extra match. The entire length of the cave is over 2 mi. (Open May-Oct. 10, 9am-6pm. $2, ages 13-17 $1.50, under 13 free. Lantern rental $1.50.)

The central component of the monument is **Newberry Crater,** 18 mi. south of Lava Butte on U.S. 97, then about 15 mi. east on Rte. 21. This diverse volcanic region was formed by many eruptions of Newberry Volcano over millions of years (Newberry is one of three volcanoes in Oregon expected to possibly erupt again "soon"). The caldera in the center of the volcano covers some 500 sq. mi. and contains two lakes, **Paulina Lake** and **East Lake**, whose azure waters are popular for fishing (rainbow, brown, kokanee, and brown trout), sailing, and boating. The crater also contains an enormous **Obsidian Flow**, deposited by an eruption only 1300 years ago; a 1-mi. trail winds among the huge chunks of volcanic glass. Over 150 mi. of trails cross the area, including a 21-mi. loop that circumnavigates the caldera rim. More than 250 campsites line the shores of the lakes in five different campgrounds.

West of Bend, **Century Drive** (Cascade Lakes Hwy.; follow the signs throughout town) makes a dramatic 89-mi. loop past Mt. Bachelor, through the forest, and past the Crane Prairie Reservoir before rejoining U.S. 97. Thirty campgrounds, trout fishing areas, and hiking trails dot the countryside. Allow a full day for the spectacular drive, and pack a picnic lunch. Pick up the "Highway of the Cascades: Cascade Lakes Tour" brochure describing points of interest at the Central Oregon Welcome Center or Bend Ranger District Office (see Practical Information and Orientation; drive open Memorial Day to snow-in, usually in Oct.)

Mountain biking is one of the predominant forms of transportation in and around Bend. Many roads have bike lanes or wide shoulders. The Bend Ranger District Office has a new, slick guide to the vast array of mountain bike trails around Bend. A mountain bike might be the perfect way to explore the Cascade-Lakes Highway, making the day-long auto tour into a week-long adventure.

If you can ski the 9075-ft. **Mt. Bachelor,** with its 3100-ft. vertical drop, you're in good company; Mt. Bachelor is one of the home mountains of the U.S. Ski Team. (Daily lift passes $33, ages 7-12 $18, or ski by a "point system" where you pay only for the runs you ski. Many nearby lodges offer 5-night ski packages. Call 800-800-8334 or 382-8334. For general information call 800-829-2442; for ski report and summer events call 382-7888.) The ski season often extends to the first of July. Ticket prices rise and fall in proportion to the number of trails open. From Christmas through Easter, free morning and afternoon shuttle bus service is offered for the 22 mi. between the Mt. Bachelor corporate office (in Bend) and the West Village Guest Services Building at the mountain. Chairlifts are open for sightseers during the summer (open 10am-4pm; $9, kids $4.50, seniors $6.50) and in the summer a U.S. Forest Service naturalist gives free presentations on local natural history on the summit daily at 11:30am and 2:30pm.

The Three Sisters Wilderness Area, north and west of the Cascade Lakes Highway, is one of Oregon's largest and most popular wilderness areas. A permit (free) is required to go into the wilderness, but day-hikers can issue themselves permits at most trailheads. No bikes allowed in the wilderness. Permits and information are available at Bend Ranger District Office or Central Oregon Welcome Center (see Practical Information).

Would-be cowpokes can get their fix on **horseback rides** offered by local resorts. **Nova Stables** (389-9558), at Inn of the Seventh Mountain several miles west of Bend on Century Drive, leads trail rides (1 hr. $15, 2 hr. $25). **Sun River Lodge** (593-1221). though more expensive, will arrange longer rides (1 hr. $22, 2 hr. $38). **Whitewater rafting,** although costly, is the number one local recreational activity. Most resorts offer half- to three-day whitewater rafting expeditions, and most companies will pick you up in town. Trips usually run around $65 per person per day, $25 per half day. Two of the most highly regarded are **Hunter Expeditions** (389-8370); ½ day $27, full day $65) and **Inn of the Seventh Mountain** (382-8711; ½ day $22, ages 12 and under $18).

In Bend, you can get up-close-and-personal with ducks and geese, or just enjoy a picnic lunch, on the rolling lawns of aptly-named **Drake Park.** The park is sandwiched between Mirror Pond, a dammed part of the Deschutes River, and Franklin St., a block from downtown. The park also plays host to a number of events and festivals, most significantly the **Cascade Festival of Music,** a 10-day event in mid-June that brings world-class performers (including, in 1994, the prominent Cajun band Beausoeil) to Bend (for information, write 842 NW Wall St. #6, Bend, OR 97701, or call 383-2202).

Baseball fans bemoaning the dearth of live action in Oregon can stop in on the single-A farm team of the National League's Colorado Rockies, the **Bend Rockies.** From mid-June through September, games take place at the Vince Genna Stadium, 401 SE Roosevelt, just off 3rd St. (382-8011; $4, kids $3).

■ NEAR BEND: SISTERS

Nestled against the Cascades, twenty miles northwest of Bend, is the charming, restored western village of **Sisters.** Somehow, the tiny town has managed to take an Old West look in order to attract tourist dollars without falling victim to tacky commercialism (yet!). Still, the plan seems to have worked, and Sisters can get overrun in midsummer by the camera-snapping and souvenir-buying set. While Cascade St. (Sisters' main drag) is good for a stroll or snack, the real reasons to come to this corner of Central Oregon are the massive mountains to the west of town, which are covered with dense forest, interspersed with spring-fed creeks, alpine lakes, and a sizable river. Although this is a popular part of the Cascades, it isn't hard to find somewhere to be alone, if that's your fancy.

Practical Information Sisters rests 20 mi. northeast of Bend on U.S. 20. From Sisters, Rte. 126 heads east to Redmond (20 mi.) and Prineville (39 mi.), and joins U.S. 20 for the trip over the Cascades to the west. Rte. 242 heads southwest out of town and over McKenzie Pass to rejoin Rte. 126 on the other side of the Cascades. The highways all blend in town into one street, Cascade St. Almost everything in Sisters is within a block or two of it. The **Sisters Ranger District Station (Deschutes National Forest)** (P.O. Box 249; 549-2111) on Cascade St. at the west edge of town is the place to go for all kinds of recreation information, including a list of nearby campgrounds and the *Day Hike Guide* (free), a catalogue of five nearby hikes from 2 to 10 mi. long (open in summer Mon.-Fri. 7:45am-4:30pm, Sat. 11am-3pm). The **Chamber of Commerce,** at 151 N. Spruce St. (549-0251; open Mon.-Sat. 10am-4pm). provides more general tourist information.

Accommodations, Camping, and Food A cheap bed is hard to find in Sisters. One option is the **Silver Spur Motel,** on the highway at the west end of town (P.O. Box 415; 549-6591), an old building with dim, undistinguished rooms, some with free kitchens. Singles $33, doubles $36. Next door, the **Sisters Motor Lodge,** 600 W Cascade (549-2551), is a step up in both quality and price, with clean, classy rooms for $43-60 in summer, $36-50 in winter. Groups of 3-7 people can rent a dorm-style room at **Conklin's Guest House,** 69013 Camp Polk Rd., off Cascade at the east end of town (549-0123). The room costs a flat $90, which includes breakfast.

　　Camping is plentiful and spectacular near Sisters. The Sisters Ranger District (see above) maintains 26 campgrounds in the area. Many of these cluster near **Camp Sherman,** a small community on the Metolius River, 15 mi. northwest of Sisters. The Metolius River campgrounds tend to be the most crowded, and virtually all charge an $8 fee. For free and less frequented camping spots, take Elm St. south from Sisters. The street becomes Forest Rd. 16 and leads to two free campgrounds, **Black Pine Springs** (8 mi. out; 4 sites) and **Driftwood** (17 mi. out; 16 sites). Better yet, cruise 14 mi. west on Rte. 242 to **Lava Camp Lake,** a magnificently isolated, free campground just off of the lava fields of McKenzie Pass.

　　Restaurants in Sisters will tickle a variety of palates. For good soup and tasty sandwiches on a bagel or pita for around $4, pop into **Ali's** (mmm! turrrkeeey!) 100 W Cascade St. (549-2545), in the town square mall. The **Sisters Bakery** (549-0361) has all kinds of delectable baked goods, including maple-covered "pinecones" (85¢). The bakery is also a good place to stock up on loaves of top-quality bread ($1-2).

Sights and Outdoors The **Sisters Rodeo,** the "Biggest Little Show in the World," takes place annually on the second weekend in June and packs an astonishing purse: some $170,000 total attracts big-time wranglers for three days and nights of saddle bronco riding, calf-roping, and steer wrestling, among other events. Tickets are $8-12, and the show usually sells out. (Write the Sisters Rodeo Association, P.O. Box 1018, Sisters, OR 97759, or call 549-0121 for more information, or call 800-827-7522 for tickets.)

　　Hundreds of miles of **hiking** trails loop through the forests and mountains around Sisters. An easy, level walk along the **Metolius River** will give you time to ponder the debate over the origin of the river's name (some say "metolius" means "white fish," some, "spawning salmon," and others, "stinking water"). Drive past Camp Sherman to the Wizard Falls Fish Hatchery to catch the trail. A slightly more challenging hike is the 4-mi. round-trip up **Black Butte,** the near-perfect cone looming over the west end of town. The steep, steady climb leads up to a terrific view of the Cascades and a fire lookout, still in service. To get to the trailhead, go 6 mi. west from Sisters on U.S. 20, turn right onto Forest Rd. 11, then turn onto Forest Rd. 1110 after 4 mi. Proceed another 4 mi. to the trailhead. Deeper in the mountains, the strenuous 7.6 mi. round-trip hike up **Black Crater** offers unsurpassed views of snow-capped peaks and the unreal lava flows on McKenzie Pass, and an up-close-and-personal experience with volcanism: the last part of the trail crosses open pumice slopes. The trail departs from the left-hand side of U.S. 242 about 11 mi. west of Sisters.

　　The Metolius River is the focal point for **fishing** in the area, supporting a top notch fishery for rainbow and brook trout, kokanee, and the under-appreciated whitefish. Special regulations apply, requiring catch-and-release and fly-fishing only, in certain areas. Contact the Sisters Ranger District Office (see Practical Information) for details. Lakes and streams in the area offer more solitary fishing opportunities, primarily for trout. **Suttle Lake** supports a warm-water fishery, including bass.

　　McKenzie Pass, 15 mi. west of Sisters on U.S. 242, was the site of a relatively recent lava flow, creating ranging, barren fields of black *aa* (AH-ah) lava (which is the sharp kind, as opposed to *pahoehoe,* which is smooth and...well, we publish a *Let's Go* Guide to Hawaii!) Look for the hill the lava flowed around, creating an island. A tall, quasi-medieval tower built of lava chunks affords a panoramic view of the high Cascades. A ½-mile, paved trail winds among the basalt boulders, cracks, and crevices, while interpretive signs tell what happened here. Foot travel directly across the lava fields can be attempted either with extreme care or in a cares-to-the-wind spirit (at your own risk). Either way, the fields yield many a secluded nook, perfect for a lunar picnic lunch (bring something to protect yourself...lava is *sharp!*)

Mountain biking opportunities abound near Sisters. Some trails are open to bikes, as are the many miles of little-used dirt roads in the area. A recently constructed mountain bike trail departs from behind the ranger station and runs west for 10 mi., featuring portions specifically designed to challenge mountain biking skills, Ask at the ranger station for details. **Eurosports,** at 115 W. Hood (P.O. Box 1421; 549-2471) rents mountain bikes for $10 per day, $50 per week.

■■■ PRINEVILLE

At the junction of U.S. 26 and Rte. 126, about 40 mi. northeast of Bend, the quiet, slow-paced town of Prineville claims about 5500 residents, which makes it a virtual metropolis compared to the rest of eastern Oregon. This close-knit, forest-and-timber-oriented town drew national attention after sustaining a grave shock in the summer of 1994. In a single explosion, a Colorado wildfire claimed the lives of 14 young, courageous, front-line firefighters; nine of them (five men, four women) lived in Prineville.

As is often the case in eastern Oregon, Prineville itself is less compelling as a final destination than as a jumping-off point for exploring the surrounding wilderness.

Practical Information and Orientation U.S. 26 and Rte. 126 join west of Prineville and run east to become 3rd St. in town. Main St. intersects 3rd at the center of town and runs north-south. **The Prineville-Crook County Chamber of Commerce,** 390 N Fairview (447-6304), provides typical tourist information, and leaves brochures on the porch after hours (open Mon.-Fri. 9am-5pm). The **Prineville Ranger District Office,** 155 N Court (447-9641), has lots of handouts on trails, wilderness areas, and campgrounds (open Mon.-Fri. 7:45am-4:30pm). The Prineville district office of the **Bureau of Land Management,** 185 4th St. (447-4115) administers a huge area of Eastern Oregon, including the lower Deschutes, Crooked, and John Day rivers. Stop in for information on fishing these rivers. (Open Mon.-Fri. 7:45am-4:30pm.) In an **emergency,** dial 911. The **police station** is at 400 E 3rd (447-4168). **Pioneer Hospital** is at 1201 N Elm St. (447-6254). The **senior center,** 180 N Belknap (447-6844), is open Mon.-Fri. 8am-5pm. The **post office** is at 155 N Court (447-5652; open Mon.-Fri. 8:30am-5pm). The **General Delivery Zip Code** is 97754; the **Area Code** is 503.

Accommodations, Camping, and Food Hot **camping** opportunities in **Ochoco National Forest** make the limited lodging options (both in number and appeal) of Prineville seem even less desirable. Stop in at the ranger station (see above) for information and directions. **Wildcat Campground** has 17 sites under towering pines with Mill Creek burbling by. To reach Wildcat, head east from Prineville on U.S. 26. Travel 9 mi., turn left on Mill Creek Rd., and continue for 11 mi. to the campground. You might also try the lovely **Ochoco Campground**. To get there, go 16 mi. east of Prineville on U.S. 26, turn at the sign for Ochoco Ranger Station, and proceed 9 mi. Both campsites have $6 sites with drinking water and pit toilets. **Ochoco Lake State Park,** 7 mi. east of Prineville on U.S. 26, offers gorgeous picnic sites and a refreshing lake for swimming and boating. Primitive campsites with flush toilets and water are also available ($11). **Prineville Reservoir State Park** (17 mi. southeast of Prineville; take the signed exit off U.S. 26 at the east edge of town) provides more extensive outdoor opportunities, plus improved campsites ($12, full hookups $15) and showers.

Campers may also pitch tents for free anywhere on **National Forest** land, but there are parcels of private land interspersed with the public, and grazing allotments harbor cattle. Watch for the "No Trespassing" signs, and don't cross fence lines.

If you must have a bed, try the **Carolina Motel,** 1050 E 3rd St. (447-4152), which has dark, panelled rooms with super-soft beds. It won't compare to a mountain camp, but it's clean and offers A/C, color TV (free HBO and ESPN), and some kitchens. (Rates range from $27 to $40.)

Prineville is short on exciting food. Closet Craig Claibornes would do well to risk their own culinary creations. **Erickson's Sentry,** 315 W 3rd (447-6291), is the place for groceries, and has its own bakery (open daily 7am-10pm). **Gee's Family Restaurant** dishes up surprisingly good Chinese food. Try the sizable Szechuan chicken ($7), or fried rice ($5.50). Avoid the pork noodles ($5.25), a mere bowl of ramen with sliced pork on top. Traditional breakfasts and lunches in moderate proportion can be had at **Dad's Place,** 229 N Main (447-7059; open Mon.-Fri. 5am-2pm, Sat. 7am-1pm).

Sights and Outdoors In an instance of excusable civic solipsism, the folks at the **Chamber of Commerce** call Prineville the "rockhounding capital of the world." While that may be a slight exaggeration, rockhounds do come from all over in search of agates, jasper, petrified wood, and thunder eggs. Free and commercial digs abound; the Chamber of Commerce publishes a *Rockhound's Guide,* which will tell you where to plant your shovel. The climax of rockhounding activity is the **Rockhound Powwow** (447-5564), an enormous festival of rockhounds and merchants that takes place on the Crook County Fairgrounds south of town in mid-June. Only during the Powwow and the **Crooked River Roundup** (447-4479), a rough-and-tumble rodeo in early July, does Prineville come alive. (Tickets $6-10).

Covering nearly 850,000 acres of land east of Prineville, **Ochoco National Forest** (OACH-a-co) includes vast pine forests, canyons, stunning views, antelope, wild horses, golden and bald eagles, mule deer, elk, and wildcats. Rockhounds, mountain bikers, horse riders, campers, and hikers escape the pressures of civilization in this immense wild country. The Ochoco National Forest also contains three federal wilderness areas, all of which are small but little-used. The **Mill Creek Wilderness,** the largest of the three at 17,400 acres, is the closest to Prineville and the most frequently explored. The creeks and forested ridges of the area are usually overlooked by visitors in favor of **Twin Pillars,** two basalt spires formed by volcanic intrusion into a surrounding rock that later disintegrated. The popular Twin Pillars Trail begins at the Wildcat campground (see above), winding its way through steep canyons, around bluffs and through a pristine forest, arriving at the pillars after about 6 mi. The **Black Canyon Wilderness,** some 80 mi. east of Prineville, is 13,400 acres of rugged country, dominated by the steep canyons and sharp ridges of the Black Canyon. Black Canyon Creek offers good trout fishing, and the entire area is a great point from which to spot deer and elk. The Black Canyon Trail, the primary means of access to the area, leads through the canyon for 11.6 mi. To reach the trailhead, follow U.S. 26 east from Prineville for about 80 mi. to Dayville, then take Forest Rd. 47 south about 10 mi. The **Bridge Creek Wilderness** is the place to go if you want to avoid all signs of civilization. Over 5000 acres in size, the Bridge Creek area is remote, trailless, and virtually unused, except during hunting season (fall). To head for the ultimate in naturalistic escapism, proceed past the Ochoco Campground (see above) on Forest Rd. 22, make a left onto Rd. 150, which will become Rd. 2630 and eventually lead to the wilderness area.

Mountain bikers can enjoy some 3,700 mi. of little-used forest service roads and an additional 600 mi. of blocked or closed roads with no motor vehicle traffic. What these areas lack in raw scenic beauty, they make up for in isolation. Many trails are also open to bikes; in particular, **Lookout Mountain** provides challenging terrain. Contact the Prineville Ranger District Office (see Practical Information) for more information.

■ NEAR PRINEVILLE: JOHN DAY FOSSIL BEDS NATIONAL MONUMENT

The **John Day Fossil Beds National Monument** records the history of life well before the Cascade Range was formed, depicting a land of lush, tropical vegetation and ambling dinosaurs. The park exists in three parts, each representing a different epoch, each at least as impressive for its scenery as for its fossils. **Clarno,** the oldest, is on Rte. 218 (accessible by U.S. 97 to the west and Rte. 19 to the east), 20 mi. west of Fossil. Leave the developed area and be humbled as you confront the embarrassing insignificance of our species in the grand geological scheme—mere tadpoles in the Great Lake of time. And watch out for snakes. **Painted Hills,** 3 mi. east of Mitchell off U.S. 26, focuses on an epoch circa 30 million years ago when the land was in geologic transition. The ½-mi. trail to the overlook gives a hawk's perspective sure to impress, especially at dawn or after a rain, when the whole gorge glistens. **Sheep Rock,** 25 mi. west of Mitchell and 5 mi. east of Dayville at the U.S. 26-Rte. 19 junction, houses the monument's **visitors center** and will satiate all angry demands for fossils you can see and touch. The **Sheep Rock Overlook,** up the hill, offers a view of the valley. (All 3 units keep the same hours: open daily 8:30am-6pm; Sept.-Nov. 8:30am-5pm; Dec.-Feb. Mon.-Fri. 8:30am-5pm.) The **Parks Department,** 420 W Main St., John Day (575-0271), will also field fossil questions (open Mon.-Fri. 8am-4:30pm). After a stop in the visitor center, don't miss the **Island in Time Trail,** a ½-mi. trail that leads into the middle of Blue Basin, a fossil-rich and strikingly beautiful canyon of eroded badland spires. (Park always open; **visitors center** open March-Aug. daily 8:30am-6pm; Sept.-Nov. 8:30-5pm; Dec.-Feb. Mon.-Fri. 8:30am-5pm). The **Park Headquarters** is at 420 W Main St., John Day (575-0271), but the office staff here is only equipped to answer orientation questions.

The AAA-approved **Dreamer's Lodge,** 144 N Canyon Blvd. (575-0526; reservations 800-654-2849, fax 575-2733) is a great place to relax. The clean, comfortable rooms all have La-Z-Boy recliners (singles $38, doubles $42.) The **Gold Country Motel,** 250 E Main (575-2100), has large, attractive rooms with HBO on the tube (singles from $38, doubles from $45, less if they're not full). Seven mi. west of John Day on U.S. 26, **Clyde Holliday State Park** (575-2773) offers 30 campsites with electricity and showers ($15), and a hiker/biker camp ($8). For hearty, basic fare, tap into the **Mother Lode Restaurant,** 241 W Main (575-2714). Sandwiches cost $5-7. A special menu offers selections for seniors (open daily 5am-9pm; winter daily 5am-8pm). **The Cave Inn,** 830 S Canyon Blvd. (575-1083), has good pizza ($7.30-13) and seems to be the hoppin' local hangout, where every pair of teenagers has a pitcher of Pepsi, and every couple a pitcher of beer.

In John Day, the **Kam Wah Chung and Co. Museum,** on Canton St. near City Park, showcases the personal possessions that Chinese immigrants brought with them to Grant County during the 1862 Gold Rush. The highlight is a large collection of herbal medicines. The building, once the community center of Chinese miners in eastern Oregon, dates back to the 1860s. (Open May 1-Oct. 31 Mon.-Thurs. 9am-noon and 1-5pm, Sat.-Sun. 1-5pm. $2, seniors $1.50, ages 13-17 $1, under 12 50¢.)

John Day is surrounded on three sides by the massive **Malheur National Forest** (mal-HERE). Information is available at the Malheur National Forest **ranger station** (575-1731) on the eastern edge of John Day at 139 NE Dayton (open Mon.-Fri. 7:15am-5pm). Most of the time, this vast, wild region of timbered hills and jagged ridges gets little use, creating prime opportunities for solitude and great hiking, particularly in the Forest's two designated wilderness areas, **Strawberry Mountain** and **Monument Rock.** All of that changes during hunting season (Sept.-Nov.), when the whole of John Day heads for the hills. The ranger station in town knows next to nothing about licenses to kill black bears, bighorn sheep, or mule deer. If you're hoping to bag a black bear or catch some salmon and trout, you can obtain licenses at several local stores. Camp wherever you please in the forest, except, of course, near "No Trespassing" signs. Some areas in the forest have cantilever toilets and drinkable water. **Magone Lake** is one of the forest's most popular campgrounds, and the only one with a user fee ($3). The **John Day River** presents a range of water conditions suitable for everything from placid float trips (or **fishing;** the John Day supports a huge smallmouth bass population) to moderate (class III) whitewater adventures. Inflatable kayaks for one to two people are available for $20 per day at **John Day River Outfitters** (575-2386) which also organizes two- to five-day trips.

■■■ BURNS

Visit Burns in the context of exploring the vast, unspoiled, virtually uninhabited wilderness that fills southeastern Oregon. Burns is the seat of Harney County, a county larger than Vermont in area but with fewer residents than Montpelier. Tiny Burns and its even tinier neighbor Hines serve as way-stations and supply centers for travelers. Ideally situated between the **Ochoco** and **Malheur National Forests, Steens Mountain,** the **Alvord Desert,** and the **Malheur National Wildlife Refuge,** there's plenty of open country around Burns in which to flee civilization and bask under the big sky beneath beaming sun and occasional towering thunderheads. (See the several Near Burns sections following for information on outdoor areas and accommodations.) Stock up on gas, water, information, and supplies in Burns and head for forest, mountain, desert, or marsh.

PRACTICAL INFORMATION AND ORIENTATION

Visitors Information: Harney County Chamber of Commerce, 18 W D St. (573-2636), on the corner of N Broadway. Pamphlets and brochures blanket one large wall. Open June-Sept. Mon.-Fri. 9am-5pm, Sat. 9am-5pm.

Parks and Recreation: Burns Ranger District (Malheur National Forest) and **Snow Mountain Ranger District (Ochoco National Forest),** HC 74, Box 12870, Hines, OR 97738 (573-7292). About 4½ mi. south of the center of Burns, these two jurisdictions share the same office and provide information on hiking, fishing, and camping. **Burns District Office (BLM),** HC 74-12533 U.S. 20 West, Hines, OR 97738 (573-5241), a few mi. west of Hines. Rife with information on public lands SE of Burns.

Van Service: Pacific Stage Lines. $18 one-way to Bend (11am) or Ontario (3:45pm). No reservations. Stops at BP station, 682 N Broadway (573-2891).

Laundromat: Jiffy Wash, S Diamond St., 1 block south of W Monroe. Wash $1, 12½-min. dry 25¢. Open daily 7am-10pm.

Pharmacy: Payless Drug, 629 N U.S. 20 in Hines (573-1525). Open Mon.-Sat. 9am-8pm, Sun. 10am-6pm.

Crisis Hotline: H Hope Hotline (573-7176).

Emergency: 911.

Police: 242 S Broadway (573-6028).

Hospital: Harney District Hospital, 557 W Washington St., at the end of W Adams St.

Post Office: 100 S Broadway (573-2931). Open Mon.-Fri. 8:30am-5pm.

ZIP Code: Burns 97720; Hines 97738.

Area Code: 503.

U.S. 20 from Ontario and U.S. 395 from John Day converge about 2 mi. north of Burns. They continue through Burns and Hines as one highway and diverge about 30 mi. west of town, U.S. 20 continuing west to Bend and the Cascade Range, U.S. 395 south to Lakeview, OR and California.

ACCOMMODATIONS AND CAMPING

Though Burns provides several good budget motels, the **Frenchglen Hotel** and the **Malheur Field Station** (see Near Burns: Outdoors) both provide unique, attractive options to experience more closely the natural beauty of southeastern Oregon. Camping is the cheapest way to enjoy the breathtaking open country around Burns (see Near Burns: Outdoors). While the RV parks all appear unappealing, the U.S. Forest Service maintains three campgrounds in the area. Contact their office in Hines (see Practical Information, above) for more information.

Bontemps Motel, 74 W Monroe (573-2037). At the center of Burns, the Bontemps is the best deal in town. The rooms, though small and spare, are neat and trim, and each one is different. No phone in rooms; pay phone on premises. Refrigerators at no extra cost, and $35 extra for 1 of the 4 rooms with a kitchen. Color TV,

A/C, garage. 15 units. Singles $23.55. Doubles with one bed $27.85; with two, $32.10. Pets $1 extra.

Silver Spur Motel, 789 N Broadway at D St. (537-2077). Standard budget motel rooms, clean bathrooms, knowledgable owner. 26 units. Cable TV w/ HBO, A/C, coffee, and continental breakfast included. Singles $28.15. Doubles with 1 bed $35.50; with 2, $39. Seniors' discount.

FOOD

Beef is king here; with few exceptions, restaurants serve traditional, uninspired American fare. Vegetarians or health-conscious eaters will want to stop at the **Wayside Delicatessen,** while perhaps the most appetizing food in town is do-it-yourself: groceries can be had at **Safeway,** 246 W Monroe (573-6767; open daily 5am-11pm).

Wayside Delicatessen, 530 N Broadway (573-7020). Step no further than this inviting wooden storefront for large sandwiches made with fresh ingredients, including mmmm turrrkeeey. The "vegi deluxe" comes piled with all kinds of green stuff, including cucumbers and sprouts. Top off your meal with a slice of drop-dead delish fruit-swirled cheesecake ($2) and a cappucino ($1.50). Soups and salads, too. Most sandwiches $3-5. Open Mon.-Fri. 7:30am-4pm, Sat. 10am-4pm.

Jerry's, 937 Oregon Ave. (537-7000). Though a chain, Jerry's has the atmosphere of a down-home local diner. Besides, you can sidle up to the counter and suck down all-you-can-eat buttermilk pancakes for $3.50 anytime. Bottomless cup of coffee 89¢. Open 24 hrs.

OUTDOORS

Burns itself offers few sights and attractions to visitors. The surrounding open country, however, beckons to the outdoor adventurer. Thirty mi. southeast of Burns, water oozes inexplicably into the desert, sagebrush country becomes marshland, and thousands of birds drop out of their migratory flight paths to join the thousands more that make their year-round home here. This improbable marsh is **Malheur Lake,** protected as part of the 185,000-acre **Malheur National Wildlife Refuge.** Home to some 300 species of birds, the refuge contains enough grebes, ibis, plovers, shrikes, vireos, and wigeons not only to satisfy the most serious bird-watchers and photographers, but also to interest even the least bird-conscious traveler. The best times to see birds are during the fall and spring migration, early or late in the day, but there is no wrong time to bird-watch. The **visitors center** (open Mon.-Fri. 7am-3:30pm) helps provide a general orientation to the area, and merits a trip. The **museum** (open daily sunrise-sunset) contains an enormous selection of mounted birds. The refuge is open year-round during daylight hours. **Malheur Field Station,** HC 72 Box 260, Princeton, OR 97721 (493-2629), offers room and board to visitors staying overnight in the refuge. Accommodations are spartan, but clean and inexpensive; $13 for dorm or private accommodations. Meals cost $6-7. Laundry and cooking facilities, gym, vehicle rentals, and gas available. Bring a sleeping bag or bedroll. (Reservations strongly encouraged.) To reach the field station or the refuge from Burns, travel 3 mi. east on Rte. 78 (E. Monroe St. in Burns), 26 mi. south on Rte. 205, then 5 mi. east at a marked turnoff on a gravel road.

Continue on Rte. 205 south for another 34 mi., however, and you will not only realize why you came all the way to southeastern Oregon, but you may never want to leave. The **Frenchglen Hotel,** Rte. 205, Frenchglen, OR 97736 (493-2825), serves up genuine homemade food better than your mother's in a quaint, historic building owned by Oregon State Parks. The enormous breakfasts ($2.75-5.75) will keep you going all day (the pancakes measure eight inches across), and the "family-style" dinner (by reservation only) is not to be forgotten ($11-15). If you're thinking about splurging on some quality accommodation, this is the place to do it. Trim, cozy rooms with wood-frame full beds, patchwork quilts and shared bath go for $42. Whether you come to eat, sleep, or both, John Ross, the hotel operator, will make you feel right at home—you'll never want to leave (open March 1-Nov. 15; breakfast 7:30am-9:30am; lunch 11:30am-2:30pm).

About 60 mi. southeast of Burns lies **Steens Mountain,** a 30-mi.-long fault-block whose east face rises an abrupt, dramatic vertical mile above the surrounding desert. At 9773 ft. in elevation, Steens is the highest mountain in southeastern Oregon, and the view from the top includes parts of four states on a clear day. The **Steens Mountain Loop Road** is a 66-mi. dirt road which climbs the gradual west slope of the mountain to several viewpoints above deep glacier-carved gorges. The road is rough, but the view magnificent. The mountain offers many recreational opportunities, including wildlife watching (notably bighorn sheep and pronghorn antelope) and hiking. The mountain's remoteness keeps it relatively uncrowded, and nearly all visitors are vehicle-shackled sightseers; a willingness to walk even a short distance from the road brings real solitude. To get to Steens, continue 34 mi. past the Malheur Wildlife Refuge, turn off on Rte. 205 to Frenchglen, then turn east onto a dirt road at a signed junction. The road is open when snow-free; typically July 1 to October 31. Contact the Burns District BLM office (See Practical Information) for up-to-date road information and guidance about recreational opportunities.

East of Steens stretches the bone-dry, mirror-flat **Alvord Desert.** Lying in the rain shadow of the Steens, which squeezes virtually all the moisture out of the east-bound clouds, the Alvord gets less than 6 in. of precipitation a year. Desert hikers, glider pilots, and wind sailors all enjoy this driest and emptiest part of the entire Pacific Northwest. In winter, snowmelt from Steens can inundate the desert. To get there, head south from Frenchglen for about 50 mi. to Field, then turn left onto the dirt road toward the settlement of Andrews.

Winding its way north from Nevada through the Alvord Desert and up Steens Mountain is the **Desert Trail,** an arid hiking route planned to run from the Mexican border to the Canadian border on the desert lands east of the Sierras and Cascades. This little-known trail stretches 150 mi. through southeastern Oregon, offering some beautifully empty, desolate exploration. Trail guides and information are available from the Desert Trails Association. Contact the Membership and Hike Chairman Keith Sheerer at P.O. Box 346, Madras, OR 97741, or call 475-2960.

Anglers will be pleased with the fishing opportunities in the area. Prime areas for rainbow trout include the **Little Blitzen River, Fish Lake** and **Wildhorse Lake** on the east side of Steens Mountain, and **Yellow Jacket Lake** in the Malheur National Forest and **Delintment Lake** in the Ochoco National Forest, both northwest of Burns and both the sites of Forest Service campgrounds. The campground at Delintment Lake offers 24 sites with drinking water and pit toilets for $4. To get to either lake, take a marked turnoff north from U.S. 20 a short distance west of the Forest Service office in Hines. **Krumbo Reservoir** in Malheur National Wildlife Refuge contains both rainbow trout and largemouth bass. **Mann Lake,** north of the Alvord Desert on the east side of Steens, is well known for cutthroat trout. For information, stop by **B&B Sporting Goods** on U.S. 20 at Conley Ave. in Hines (573-6200; open Mon.-Sat. 8am-6pm).

Geology buffs will want to head for **Diamond Craters,** where a series of basaltic burps by the Earth's mantle have created a diverse landscape of volcanic features. But if you go, be careful, or "you might spend some time stuck in loose cinder, volcanic ash or clay," warns a BLM publication. Pick up a self-guided auto tour of the area, along with other information, at the Burns District BLM office in Hines.

About 4 mi. east of Frenchglen, two campgrounds provide more primitive sleeping arrangements. The **Steens Mountain Resort** (also called the **Camper Corral;** 493-2415) offers a variety of sites and amenities, but, unfortunately, also steep prices and lots of RVs (tent site $10, RV hookup $14, open March-Nov.). For reservations, call 800-542-3765. Just down the road, the BLM-administered **Page Springs** campground has 30 sites of varying seclusion and cover, drinking water, and vault toilets. (No reservations, $4.) There are two more similar BLM campgrounds, **Fish Lake** and **Jackman Park,** about 15 mi. up the Steens Loop Road from Page Springs.

■■■ PENDLETON

For most of the year, Pendleton is typical of Eastern Oregon's towns, offering little more than a quiet night's sleep for the weary traveler. During the day porch swings are actually used here, and lawn care seems to be the primary recreation. At night, teens and wanna-bes slowly cruise the streets in jacked-up muscle cars, careful not to make too much noise, 'cause everybody knows everybody. All that changes in mid-September, however, when 50,000 yahoos descend on the town for the Pendleton Round-Up. Downtown, men gussied up in Stetson hats drink whiskey shots, swagger in dusty leather boots, and talk horses, as Pendleton becomes a macho town.

PRACTICAL INFORMATION AND ORIENTATION

Visitors Information: Pendleton Chamber of Commerce, 25 SE Dorion Ave. (276-7411 or 800-547-8911). Open Mon.-Fri. 9am-5pm, summer Sat. 9am-2pm.

Greyhound, 320 SW Court Ave. (276-1551), a few blocks west of the city center. To: Portland (2 per day, $27); Boise, ID (2 per day; $40); Walla Walla (2 per day; $12.25). Open Mon-Sat. 8:30am-noon, 1-5pm, 12:30-3am.

Amtrak: Unstaffed shelter and boarding area at 108 S Frazer. To: Portland (3 per week) and Denver (3 per week). Call 800-872-7245 for prices and additional info.

Taxi: Elite Taxi (276-8294). Open 4:30am-3am.

Car Rental: Ugly Duckling Rent-A-Car, 309 SW Emigrant Ave. (276-1498). The only way to enjoy the Blue or Wallowa Mts. from Pendleton without your own car. $20 per day with 50 free mi., 15¢ each additional mi. Unlimited free mileage for weekly rental. Credit card required. Must be over 21. Open Mon.-Fri. 8am-5pm, Sat. 8am-noon.

Hospital: St. Anthony's, 1601 SE Court Ave. (276-5121).

Emergency: 911. **Police:** 109 SW Court Ave. (276-4411). **Fire:** 276-1442.

Post Office: Federal Building, 104 SW Dorion Ave. (278-0203), at SW 1st. Open Mon.-Fri. 9am-5pm, Sat. 10am-1pm. **General Delivery ZIP Code:** 97801.

Area Code: 503.

Pendleton is at the junction of I-84 and Rte. 11, just south of the Washington border, roughly equidistant (200-230 mi.) from Portland, Spokane, and Boise. **Raley Park,** right next to the Round-Up Grounds, is the spiritual center of town, while Main Street is the geographic hub.

Pendleton's streets were named to facilitate navigation for airmen from a nearby base (now closed). The east-west streets have names and are arranged in alphabetical order moving south. From Main St., north-south streets are numbered, increasing in both directions (there are hence two 2nd Streets, for example, 2nd SE and 2nd SW, parallel to each other).

ACCOMMODATIONS AND CAMPING

During most of the year, lodging in Pendleton is inexpensive. To stay here during the Round-Up, however, you must reserve rooms *up to two years* in advance. Rates double, and prices on everything from hamburgers to commemorative cowboy hats are jacked up. The nearest decent camping is 25 mi. distant, though the Round-Up provides 1500 camping spots. (Call the Chamber of Commerce after April 1 for reservations.)

Longhorn Motel, 411 SW Dorion Ave. (276-7531), around the corner from the bus station. Clean, comfy rooms right in downtown Pendleton. Some rooms have HBO; some wheelchair access. Singles $28. Doubles $32.

Pioneer Motel, 1807 SE Court Pl. (276-4521), just off Rte. 11. Large, pleasant rooms. Singles $22. Doubles $25.

7 Inn, 6 mi. west of town at exit 202 off I-84 (outside the reach of the city's motel tax). Horribly inconvenient for travelers without a car, but amid sublime rolling farmlands, and by far the best deal in the area. Large, clean rooms with more chairs and closets than you'll ever know what to do with. Cable TV, A/C. Singles $20. Doubles $28.

Motel 6, 325 SE Nye Ave. (276-3160), on the south side of town. Not in the middle of things, but easy access to I-84. Motel 6 is the only place in town whose rates don't increase for the Round-Up. They offer current Round-Up guests the chance to renew their reservations for the following year, then take calls to book the remaining rooms on the Sunday following Round-Up, at 7am. There are usually only about 20 rooms open, and they go fast. Cable TV, A/C, and heated pool. Singles $30. Doubles $36.

Emigrant Springs State Park, (983-2277) 26 mi. southeast of Pendleton on I-84. Excellent proximity to Pendleton. 41 sites (18 with hookup) in a shady grove of evergreens at a historic camp on the Oregon Trail. Unfortunately, lots of noise. Hot showers. Sites $13, with hookup $16.

FOOD

Vegetarians will have more luck grazing in the outlying wheat fields than in selecting from the restaurant menus. This is steak country. Exceptions are **Cakreations** (see below) and, for staples, the huge **Albertson's** on SW Court across from the Round-Up grounds (276-1362, open daily 6am-11pm).

Cakreations, 16 SE Court (276-7978). Originally started as a specialty cake bakery, now expanded to include a full line of bakery products, deli sandwiches, and soups. The enormous store lurks behind a tiny storefront, and all the freezers, ovens, and bakers are situated where you can watch the activity. Delicious, healthy food to write home about. Sandwiches come on fresh bakery bread. The "vegi" ($3.25) has an entire garden in it. Other sandwiches $3-4, add $1 for soup or salad. Top it off with a tasty cookie (60¢) or muffin (85¢), and take at least one loaf of fresh-baked bread ($2) with you. Open Mon.-Sat. 7:30am-6pm.

Bread Board, 141 S Main St. (276-4520). Great $2-4 sandwiches and $1 cinnamon rolls in a friendly atmosphere, with national newspapers strewn about. Try the ham, egg, and cheese croissant for breakfast ($2.75). Open Mon.-Fri. 8am-3pm.

The Circle S, 210 SE 5th St. (276-9637). Don't let the 3-ft. axe door-handle scare you away from this great Western barbecue restaurant. Drink beverages from Mason jars while you enjoy a teriyaki burger and fries ($5) and a *creme de menthe* sundae ($1.75). If you can eat the 4-lb. sirloin ($45) in an hour, like John Candy in *The Great Outdoors,* it's free (but only weekdays before 8pm). Thankfully, smaller portions also available. Open Tues.-Sat. 7am-10pm, Sun. 7am-3pm.

Rainbow Cafe, 209 S Main St. (276-4120). Where the cowboys chow down. Classic American bar/diner with rodeo decor, including rainbow neon. Good, hearty lunch foods, but breakfast is wimpy. Burger and beer $3-4. Open daily 6am-2:30am. Minors allowed only in the "fine foods" area in back, 6am-3pm.

SIGHTS AND ACTIVITIES

The **Pendleton Round-Up** (276-2553 or 800-524-2984), a premier event on the nation's rodeo circuit, draws ranchers from all over the U.S. for "four glorious days and nights" (always the second full week in Sept.; Sept. 13-16, 1995; Sept. 11-14, 1996). Steer-roping, saddle-bronc riding, bulldogging, and bareback riding are featured, not to mention buffalo-chip tosses, wild cow milking, and greased-pig chases. For information or tickets ($6-12), write to the Pendleton Round-Up Association, P.O. Box 609, Pendleton 97801. The **Round-Up Hall of Fame** (276-2553), under the south grandstand area at SW Court Ave. and SW 13th St., gives tours by appointment during the week (open in summer daily 9am-5pm). There's usually someone knowledgeable around to answer questions. The hall has captured some of the rodeo's action for all eternity, including Pendleton's best preserved Round-Up hero, a stuffed horse named "War Paint." Lifetime memberships only $100.

Unless you have some special interest in wool you may want to bag the hyper-hyped tour of the **Pendleton Woolen Mills,** 1307 SE Court Ave. (276-6911; tours Mon.-Fri. at 9 and 11am, 1:30 and 3pm; open Mon.-Fri. 8am-4:45pm, Sat. 8am-2pm; Oct.-April Mon.-Fri. 8am-4:45pm, Sat. 9am-1pm; free).

At **Hamley's Western Store,** 30 SE Court Ave. (276-2321), ask in front for someone to show you part (but not all) of the 80-hour saddle-making process that goes on in the back of the store (open Mon.-Sat. 8:30am-5:30pm; free).

The **Umatilla County Historical Society Museum,** 108 SW Frazer (276-0012), includes a working railroad telegraph (open Tues.-Sat. 10am-4pm; admission by donation). Pendleton is also a good jumping-off point for exploration of the northern **Blue Mountains** and **Umatilla National Forest** (yoo-ma-TILL-uh). The **Forest Headquarters** in Pendleton, 2517 SW Hailey Ave. (278-3716), has the friendliest, most helpful staff you could ever want in a land management agency. Go there for information on hiking, camping, fishing, and biking in the vast forested plateaus and canyons of the Blues (visible from exit 210 off I-84; open Mon.-Fri. 7:45am-4:30pm). The main access to the area is found at Rte. 204, reached by heading north out of Pendleton on Rte. 11 for 21 mi. After 41 mi., the highway loops up over the Blues to meet Rte. 82 at Elgin on the east side of the mountains. Along the way, the road winds through dense timber, past campgrounds, creeks, and lakes, and near two wilderness areas, the small **North Fork Umatilla** and the larger, more remote **Wenaha-Tucannon** wilderness. Both are little-used and offer real solitude, though Wenaha-Tucannon offers more challenging hiking. There are four campgrounds along this route. Woodward ($4 per night) and Woodland (free) are two tiny campgrounds just off Rte. 242. Better bets are **Target Meadows** ($3 per night), an isolated spot only 2 mi. off of the highway, or **Jubilee Lake** ($5-7 per night), a developed (and crowded) wheelchair-accessible campground on a lovely lake. To reach these two, make a left onto Forest Rd. 46 at Tollgate, 22 mi. east of the Rte. 242-Rte. 11 junction, and follow the signs. The Forest Service operates an **information booth** just off of the highway on Rd. 46 (open in summer daily 9am-4pm).

■■■ BAKER CITY

When Oregon Trail pioneers discovered gold, they got excited enough not only to settle, but to build a city at the base of the Blue Mountains. Tossing their tents aside, Baker City's first residents poured their riches into Victorian houses and grand hotels. Today, mining plays no larger a role in the local economy than do agriculture, wood products, and (gulp) tourism. Convenient to the Wallowa-Whitman National Forest and Hells Canyon, Baker City has a deep legacy rooted in the Oregon Trail. The interesting, high-quality museums will appeal even to the independent traveler who ordinarily avoids crowds of tourists and the road-tripper or outdoor-seeker with a day to spend and an interest in American history.

PRACTICAL INFORMATION

Visitors Information: Baker County Visitor Convention and Convention Bureau, 490 Campbell St. (523-3356, 800-523-1235 outside OR). Everything a visitors center should be in a little wooden house. The lower level is stockpiled with enough brochures for 3 states, and the upper level is a small museum of delightful antique furniture and photos. The friendly volunteers seem to be on a first-name basis with everyone in town. Open Mon.-Fri. 8am-6pm, Sat. 8am-4pm, Sun. 9am-1pm; winter Mon.-Fri. 8am-5pm.

Greyhound: 515 Campbell St. (523-5011) in the Truck Corral Café. Buses east to Boise (2 per day) and west to Portland (2 per day). Open daily 7-9:30am and 4-7pm.

Amtrak: Shelter and boarding area at west end of Church St. To Portland (3 per week) and Denver (3 per week). Call 1-800-872-7245 for up-to-the-minute fare and scheduling information.

Taxi: Baker Cab Co., 990 Elm St. (523-6070). Up to $3.75 within Baker City, $1 per mi. outside city limits.

Laundromat: Baker City Laundry, 815 Cambell St. (523-9817). The mother of all laundromats, with showers ($3.50), the cheapest fountain drinks around (32 oz. 69¢), and a **Subway** sub shop next door. What more could you want? Wash $1, 12-min. dry 25¢. Open daily 7am-10pm.

Senior Services: Community Connection (523-6591). Open Mon.-Fri. 8am-5pm.
Hospital: St. Elizabeth, 3325 Pocahontas Rd. (523-6461). Open 24 hrs.
Police: 1655 1st St. (523-3644).
Post Office: 1550 Dewey Ave. (523-4327). Open Mon.-Fri. 8:30am-5pm, Sat. 11am-noon. **General Delivery ZIP Code:** 97814.
Area Code: 503.

Baker City lies 43 mi. south of La Grande and 137 mi. west of Boise, ID, on I-84 in northeastern Oregon. Rte. 86 leads east from the city to Hells Canyon and Rte. 7 leads west, connecting with U.S. 26 to John Day and Prineville. Campbell and Main St. are the principal thoroughfares: Main runs parallel to I-84, and Campbell intersects I-84 just east of the city. Other important streets are Broadway Ave., which intersects Main St. downtown, and Bridge St., an offshoot of Main St. to the southeast.

ACCOMMODATIONS AND CAMPING

Baker City has several reasonably priced motels. Most places will knock off a few dollars if you nudge. Generally, the deals get better the further you get from the interstate.

Eldorado Motel, 695 Campbell St. (523-6494), right next to Greyhound. Polished motel, with neo-conquistador architecture. Big rooms with matador paintings. Indoor pool and jacuzzi, TV, A/C. Singles $41.

Oregon Trail Motel, 211 Bridge St. (523-5844). Clean, spacious rooms are a great excuse not to spend another night in the covered wagon. Pool, cable TV, A/C. Seniors' discount. Singles $32. Doubles $40.

Union Creek Campground, Box 54, Baker (894-2210), at Phillips Lake. Follow signs to Sumpter, and go 20 mi. down Rte. 7 to this lovely park. Beach and toilets, but no showers. Tent area $8, sites $10. Full hookup, $14. Heater or A/C $1 per day. Senior Citizen discount. 58 sites.

FOOD

Baker City is a breakfast bonanza for those beaten by the morning blues. There are a number of great cafes strung along Main St. Several restaurants here offer alternatives to the ubiquitous Oregon meat and potatoes fare. Take time to grab Mexican food or gourmet pizza while you can.

The Brass Parrot, 2190 Main at Church St. (523-4266). Polly wanna taco? Try the Mexican food for a refreshing change from Eastern Oregon's often-slimy hamburgers. Relax in a cool wood-and-brick dining room with a delicious frozen peach-wine margarita ($3.25) and a monstrous burrito ($5). Open daily 11am-10pm.

Baker City Cafe, 1915 Washington Ave. (523-3641). Phenomenal gourmet pizza in a small, friendly cafe. The prices may look steep: slices go for $2-2.50, pies for $9.20, but are well worth it. Besides, 2 thick, wide slices are a meal. Open Mon.-Thurs. 11am-8pm, Fri. 11am-9pm, Sat. noon-9pm.

Klondike's Pizza, 1726 Campbell St. (523-7105). Good pizza in what looks like a reclaimed bordello. Cutely named pizzas, including Pyrite Pete's Pleaser. Pies come in 4 sizes from the microscopic "mini" to the gargantuan "giant" and range in price from $2.20-18.65. Try the Mother Lode Deli pizza topped with "everything but the ovens." The "economy pizza," the best deal, costs $7 for a medium, $8 for a giant, and comes with one topping. The all-you-can-eat salad bar ($3.60) is an equally inviting option. Open Sun.-Thurs. 11am-10pm, Fri.-Sat. 11am-11pm.

Oregon Trail Restaurant, 211 Bridge St. (523-5844, x 179). Good, hearty American fare. Caters to the senior set, but the portions are not bird-like. (They are, on the other hand, cheap.) Try the enormous hotcakes (2 for $2.50, or 3, if you can manage it, for $3.) At dinner, sample a 6-oz. steak sandwich for $7. Senior dinners all under $5.25. Open daily 6am-9pm.

SIGHTS AND EVENTS

The hills 5 mi. east of Baker City have recently been invaded by the multi-million dollar **National Historic Oregon Trail Interpretive Center** at Flagstaff Hill. Volunteers in pioneer vesture will cordially greet you at the door, ushering you on to a walk-through tour that recreates the times with videos and more. The tour depicts all the joys and sorrows of life on the trail, not only for the pioneers, but for the miners, fur traders, and Native Americans who lived here. Demonstrations of pioneer arts and skills are held outside at the wagon station encampment and the lode mining operation. Over 4 mi. of trails, some accessible to the disabled, lead to scenic overlooks and interpretive sites. In some places you can actually walk alongside the wagon ruts of the original Trail. Highly recommended; set aside at least a few hours for this informative look at the past. Free!

The **Oregon Trail Regional Museum,** 2490 Grove St. (523-9308), off Campbell St., is worth a trip even if it isn't raining. The world's largest cluster of fluorite and quartz is accompanied by other specimens of superlative geological interest and visual impact. At the back of the museum is a room illuminated only by its shelf of phosphorescent rocks. (Open May-Oct. daily 9am-4pm. Suggested donation $1.50, children 50¢.)

If the kids get bored, take them to **Geiser Pollman Park** on Campbell St., a big lawn with a playground, two blocks from Main St. along the river. Next to the park, the **Public Library** (523-6419), on Resort St., has a huge selection of children's books. (Open Mon. and Thurs. 10:30am-8pm, Tues.-Wed. 10:30am-6pm, Fri. 10:30am-5pm, Sat.-Sun. noon-4pm.) The festivities at the **Miners' Jubilee,** on the 3rd weekend of July, include a hotly-contested mining competition, "Arts in the Park," a show and sale of arts and crafts with live music; and **single-jack,** where one man pounds a chisel through solid granite for five minutes (7 inches!).

Elkhorn Ridge, towering steeply over Baker City to the west, is the local manifestation of the Blue Mountains. While this jagged line of peaks was avoided by Oregon Trail pioneers, today a paved loop, designated a National Scenic Byway, leads over the range, providing drivers of the 106 mi. route with lofty views and hiking and fishing opportunities. The drive takes four to eight hours, though it's well worth taking the extra time for a picnic or short hike. For more information, stop at the Visitor and Convention Bureau, or contact **Wallowa National Forest,** 1550 Dewey Ave. (523-6391; open Mon.-Fri. 7:45am-4:30pm). If you're heading west on I-84, a wonderful complement to the Oregon Trail Interpretive Center in Baker City is the **Blue Mountain Crossing.** A ½-mi., paved, wheelchair-accessible path leads through the open forest to the original ruts (still there) of the Oregon Trail. Interpretive signs provide emigrant diary excerpts and commentary on the sights. Two self-guided paths afford a longer look at the Trail. On summer weekends, a pioneer encampment offers a living-history glimpse of life on the trail. It's all free, and highly recommended. To reach the site, leave I-84 at exit 248 (12 mi. west of La Grande; nearly 60 mi. from Baker City) and follow the signs. (Open daily during daylight hours.)

■ ■ ■ HELLS CANYON AND THE WALLOWA MOUNTAINS

In the northeast corner of Oregon is the state's most rugged, remote, and arresting country, with jagged granite peaks, glacier-gouged valleys, and azure lakes. East of La Grande, the Wallowa Mountains rise abruptly, towering over the plains from elevations of over 9000 ft. Thiry mi. farther east, the deepest gorge in North America plunges 5500 ft. to the Snake River below. The barren and dusty slopes, lack of water, and scorching heat give credence to the name Hells Canyon. Here is a vast, isolated, untrammeled wilderness; here you can lose yourself in the land and find yourself in it. Locals are welcoming to tourists, but the peaceful Wallowa Valley seems immune to life outside its tiny corner of heaven.

PRACTICAL INFORMATION AND ORIENTATION

Visitor Information: The Wallowa Mountains Visitor Center, 88401 Rte. 83 (426-4978), just outside Enterprise to the west, is a Forest Service Information extraordinaire, packed with information and displays about the Wallowas and Hells Canyon. The $3 **forest map** is a virtual necessity for navigating the elaborate network of roads in the area. Competent, friendly staff can help you plan everything from an afternoon's drive to a week-long backpacking trek. Movies; slide shows of the Wallowa Mountains and Hells Canyon shown upon request. Open Mon.-Sat. 7:30am-5pm, Sun. 10am-5pm; winter Mon.-Fri. 7:30am-5pm. **The Wallowa County Chamber of Commerce,** in the Mall at SW 1st St. and W Greenwood Ave. (426-4622), in Enterprise (P.O. Box 427), offers general tourist information with an emphasis on local business establishments and the comprehensive $1 *Wallowa County Visitor's Guide.* Open Mon.-Fri. 9am-5pm. The **Hells Canyon Chamber of Commerce,** in the office of Halfway Motels in Halfway (P.O. Box 841, Halfway OR 97834; 742-5722), can provide information on accommodations, outfitters, and guides; a welcome orientation to the area as seen from its southern entrance.

Bus Line: Moffit Brothers Transportation, P.O. Box 156, Lostine OR 97857 (569-2284), runs the **Wallowa Valley Stage Line,** which makes one round-trip run from Wallowa Lake to La Grande, Mon.-Sat. Stops at the Chevron station in Joseph and the Texaco station in Enterprise. One-way fare from La Grande to: Enterprise ($8), Joseph ($8.80), Wallowa Lake ($10.60). Stops at the Greyhound terminal in La Grande. Reservations recommended.

Bike Rental: Crosstown Traffic, 101 W McCully in Joseph OR (432-2453). $15 per day, discounts for multiple days' rental. Open daily 10am-6pm, and by arrangement.

Laundromat: Enterprise Homestyle Laundromat, 110 Greenwood St. 75¢ wash, 45 min. dry 75¢. Open daily 6am-10pm.

Road and Trail Conditions: 426-4978 or 426-5591. Open 24 hrs.

Hospital: Wallowa Memorial, 401 NE 1st St. (426-3111), in Enterprise.

Emergency: 911.

Police: 426-3036 (State), 426-3131 (County).

Post Office: 101 NE 1st, on Hwy. 82 in Enterprise. Open Mon.-Fri. 9am-5pm. Zip Code: 97828.

Area Code: 503.

Hells Canyon and the Wallowa Mountains sandwich the Wallowa Valley, which can be reached in three ways. From Baker City, Rte. 86 heads east through Halfway to connect with Forest Rd. 39, which winds over the southern end of the Wallowas, meeting Rte. 350 9 mi. east of Joseph. From La Grande, Rte. 82 arcs around the north end of the Wallowas, through the small towns of **Elgin, Minam, Wallow,** and **Lostine,** continuing through **Enterprise** and **Joseph,** and terminating at Wallowa Lake. From Clarkston, WA, Rte. 129 heads south, taking a plunge through the valley of the Grande Ronde River, becoming Rte. Three in Oregon, to end at Rte. 82 in Enterprise. Within the area, the only two major roads are Rte. 350, a paved route from Joseph northeast 30 mi. to Imnaha River, and Forest Rd. 3955, or the Imnaha River Rd., a good gravel road which runs south from Imnaha to reconnect with Forest Service 39 about 50 mi. southeast of Joseph. The free pamphlet *Look Into Hells Canyon* is worth picking up. It includes a clear **map** of area roadways showing campgrounds and points of interest.

ACCOMMODATIONS AND CAMPING

Most of the little towns along Rte. 82 have little motels, and most of the little motels have little vacancy signs during the week. On weekends, things get a little more crowded and rooms a little scarce. Make a little reservation.

There's no reason to come to the Wallowa Valley if you don't love nature, and if you love it, live it. Campgrounds here are plentiful, inexpensive, and sublime. Pick up a complete listing of campgrounds from the Wallowa Mountains Visitors Center.

Indian Lodge Motel, (432-2651), on Rte. 82 in Joseph. Truly elegant rooms: recently renovated, and tastefully decorated with lots of dark wood. Air conditioning and TV make this the best deal around. Singles $35. Doubles $45 (rates considerably lower in winter).

Melody Ranch Motel, on Rte. 82 in Enterprise (426-4022). This friendly motel's decorations suggest a county farm. The lack of air conditioning is not a problem-even on the hottest summer days the rooms stay remarkably cool. Singles $34. Doubles $44.

Halfway Motels, just off Rte. 86 in Halfway (742-5722). Verging on a monopoly, this dynasty includes three separate locations. The units in the "old" part of the motel are getting worn with age, but are kept clean. Singles $32. Doubles $37. "New" rooms considerably better. Singles $37. Doubles $47.

Saddle Creek Campground, 7 spectacular sites perched right on the lip of Hells Canyon. Unbelievable views of the canyon, especially at dusk and dawn. Bring your own water. Pit toilets. Free. To get there, drive 18 mi. up the rough, steep narrow road to Hat Point from Imnaha.

Hidden Campground, shaded by giant conifers and bordered by the clear, cool South Fork of the Inmaha River, from which you may be able to pull a trout for your dinner. Head southwest of Joseph on Forest Rd. 39 for about 40 mi., then turn up Forest Rd. 3960 toward Indian Crossing for 9 mi. (gravel). 13 sites, pit toilets, drinking water, $4.

Two Pan Campground, with 8 pleasant sites, some right on the Lostine River. From Lostine, follow the Lostine River Rd. (Forest Rd. 8210) to its end after 18 mi. The last 5 mi. are on a rough gravel road. Bring your own water. Free.

Hurricane Creek Campground, a quiet campground at a trailhead with Hurricane Creek bubbling by. From Joseph, take Forest Rd. 8205 west 6 mi. to its end (the gravel road gets a little rough). Bring your own water. Free.

FOOD

A few affordable restaurants hide out in the small towns of the Wallowa Valley, and one place is definitely worth a special trip. If you're heading out onto the chassis-shaking roads of Hells Canyon, bring along some provisions. You never know when a flat or breakdown will leave you stranded. Stock up at **Safeway,** 601 W North St. (Hwy. 82), in Enterprise (462-3722; open daily 6am-11pm).

Vali's Alpine Delicatessen Restaurant (432-5691), in Wallowa Lake. Ask any local where to get a good meal and they will unhesitatingly tell you "Vali's." This restaurant serves a different authentic European dish every night. Reservations are required, and the offerings increase in cost from stuffed cabbage on Tuesday ($7) to schnitzel on Sunday ($10.25). Continental breakfast from 10am-noon (no reservations necessary). Dinner Tues.-Sun. 5:30pm.

Cloud 9 Bakery, 105 SE 1st St., (426-3790), in Enterprise. Hang out with friendly local folks while enjoying heavenly baked goods. Try an apple fritter (75¢) and a cup of coffee (50¢). Homemade soups and sandwiches ($3.50-5) grace the lunch menu. Open Mon.-Fri. 7am-4pm, Sat.-Sun. 7am-2:30pm.

The Common Good Marketplace, 100 W Main (426-4125), in Enterprise. This health food store sells bulk food, herbs, and books on holstic living. They also build enormous sandwiches ($3.95, ½ for $2.95) and cook up "Un Canny" soups (get it?). The full service juice bar is the only place in the valley you can tank up on carrot or beet juice ($3). Open for lunch Mon.-Fri. 10:30am-4:30pm.

Wagon Wheel Restaurant, 500 N Main St. (432-9300), in Joseph. The atmosphere is more elegant than in the other joints in the valley, but the food is the same, generally uninspiring American fare. The all-you-can-eat soup and salad bar comes with a fresh dinner roll (lunch $5, dinner $6). Open Mon.-Fri. 6am-11pm, Sat.-Sun. 7am-11pm.

OUTDOORS

Any direction you head from the Wallowa Valley you'll find endless rugged, pristine, isolated country. You can't go wrong out here.

The Wallowa Mountains

Without a catchy, Federally-approved name like "Hells Canyon National Recreation Area", the Wallowas often take second place to the canyon in the minds of travelers from beyond Eastern Oregon. This is a shame; the mountains possess a scenic beauty of a diametrically opposed nature to that of Hells Canyon, but every bit as magnificent. The jagged peaks, towering in stately splendor over the Wallowa Valley, beg to be explored. The resort town of **Wallowa Lake** sits at the south end of its namesake, a brilliantly blue, deep body of water that stretches south from Joseph for 4 mi. Wallowa Lake is the center of tourist activity in the Wallowas, which is a good reason to avoid it. Unless you want to try your luck for the rainbow or brook trout, kokanee, or dolly varden cruising the lake, the view is better, the swimming is as good, and the crowds are gone at the north end of the lake. Although there are lots of fish in the lake, there are even more anglers. If you want to join the fray, the **Wallowa Lake Marina** (432-9115) is open daily 8am-8pm and rents paddleboats ($6 per hr.), canoes and rowboats ($5 per hr.), and six-horsepower motorboats ($10 per hr.) with discounts for longer rentals. If you're on time, you can catch a ride on the **Wallowa Lake Tramway** (432-5331), which will whisk you up 3,700 feet in 15 minutes on North America's steepest gondola. The views on the ride up, and at the top of 8200 ft. Mt. Howard, are extraordinary. Two km of walking trails at the top lead to different viewpoints. Unfortunately, the lofty views come with a lofty price ($10, seniors $9, under 11 $5; open daily 10am-4pm).

Over 500 mi. of hiking trails cross the **Eagle Cap Wilderness.** Deep glacial valleys and high granite passes make hiking this wilderness tough going; it often takes more than a day to get into the most picturesque and remote areas. Still, several high alpine lakes are accessible to the dayhiker. A 5-mi. hike from the **Lillyville** trailhead on the Lostine River Road (Rd. 8210) leads to **Chimney Lake.** The **Two Pan** trailhead at the end of the Lostine River Road is the start of the popular 6-mi.hike to **Minam Lake.** Or, hike the 6 mi. from the **Wallowa Lake** trailhead up the East Fork of the Wallowa River to **Aneroid Lake.** By far the most popular area in the Eagle Cap Wilderness is the **Lakes Basin,** where unsurpassed scenery and many lakes draw huge crowds. While it is possible to find solitude in the basin during the week, on weekends it is something like a spectacular Central Park. For more secluded **backpacking,** try the strenuous hike into little-visited **Wood Lake,** or investigate the alpine trio of **Steamboat, Long,** and **Swamp Lakes.** The trailheads for those hikes are both on the Lostine River Road. Rangers at the visitor's center can also recommend alternative, secluded routes. For a hefty fee, you can hire a **llama** to carry your supplies. **Hurricane Creek Llama Treks** (432-4455) offers a range of trips into the Wallowa Mountains and Hells Canyon.

Hells Canyon

"The government bet you 160 acres that you couldn't live there three years without starving to death," said one early white settler of the region. Hells Canyon's endearing name comes from its legendary inaccessibility and hostility to human inhabitants. It is North America's deepest gorge: in some places the walls drop 5500 ft. to **Snake River** below. The fault and fold lines in the canyon walls make the cliffs seem to melt into great wrinkles of grass and rock.

Accessing the area without four wheels or a horse is difficult. One can hitchhike in from the gateway towns of Joseph or Halfway, and talking it up with people at campsites can get one out. (*Let's Go* does not recommend hitchhiking.) The **Area Headquarters** (208-628-3916 or 426-4978) is at 88401 Rte. 82, on the west side of Enterprise. This is a good place to start, for the rangers can provide extensive practical information on the area and tips on the best things to see. Detailed **maps** are worth the $3 price (open Mon.-Sat. 7:30am-5pm, Sun. 10am-5pm).

Camping in the region can be a spiritual experience for those who have made adequate preparations. You should stock up on food, drinking water, and gas, and remember that there are no showers or flush toilets anywhere. If you plan to hike down into the canyon, insect repellent is a must. Because of adverse road conditions, most campsites are only open from July to September. **Copperfield Park,** with 132 sites (a few of them developed) near the Oxbow Dam, is the only campsite open all year. From Halfway, take Rte. 86 to the Snake River.

Inaccessibility poses a problem when exploring Hells Canyon. The few roads are notoriously poor. The only way to even get close to the canyon without taking at least a full day is to drive the **Hells Canyon National Scenic Loop Drive,** which will only give you the vaguest conception of what Hells Canyon is all about. Still, this is the extent of most tourists' experiences of the area. The drive begins and ends in Baker City, following Rte. 86, Forest Rd. 39 and 350, Rte. 82, and finally I-84. Even this entirely paved route takes six hours to two days to drive (and it covers nearly every mile of pavement in the area). Lookout Points provide dramatic views of the rugged canyons. **Hells Canyon Overlook,** the most accessible, is reached by driving up Forest Rd. 3965, 3 mi. of the smoothest, most luxurious pavement in Wallowa County. Enjoy it while you can. The road departs Rd. 39 about 5 mi. south of the Imnaha River crossing. The broadest and most eye-popping **views** are from the **Hat Point Overlook,** where visitors can climb a 90-ft. wooden fire lookout to vastly improve the view. But there's hell to pay for this heavenly view: a 24-mi. drive on a narrow, steep, rough road from Imnaha, which takes one-and-a-half to two hours one-way (no trailers). The first 7 mi. from Imnaha are by far the worst, so don't get fed up and turn back early. There are pit toilets and six campsites at the overlook. More campsites line the lower Imnaha River along Forest Rd. 3980 (dirt) and 3965 (dirt). Both are accessible from Rd. 39 (also dirt), and both allow easy access to the **Hell's Canyon Overlook** on Rd. 3965. Those wishing to descend into the canyon could make base camp at **Hat Point Overlook,** about a two-hour drive (24 mi.) from Imnaha (from Joseph, take Rte. 350 to Imnaha, then Rd. 4240 to Rd. 315, rough but still negotiable, dirt roads). Campsites have self-registration kiosks, although you should let a ranger know you're going in for emergency purposes. **Campfires** are illegal from July to September, and in all other months can only be made in a metal pan to up within ¼ mi. of Snake River. No permit is required for either camp or fire.

The **Buckhorn Lookout** lies far off the beaten path, 42 mi. northeast of Joseph, and offers lofty views of the Imnaha River Valley. To get there, take Rd. 350 east out of Joseph for 4 mi., turn north on Crow Creek Road (Rd. 799), and make a right onto Zumwalt Road (Rd. 697). Follow Zumwalt road to its end. The rough roads take a full day to drive round-trip, or you can camp at the lookout.

Hiking is perhaps the best way to fully comprehend the vast emptiness of Hells Canyon, but to really get into the canyon requires a backpacking trip of at least a few days. There are over 1000 mi. of trail in the canyon, only a fraction of which are maintained regularly by the Forest Service. A wide array of dangers lurk below the rim: huge elevation gains and losses, poison oak, rattlesnakes, blistering heat, and lack of water, to name a few. Still, if you're prepared, a backpacking trip into the Canyon can provide a great one-on-one experience with the land. Discuss your plans with rangers before heading out.

For something a little less intense, you can hike along the bottom of the canyon on the **Snake River Trail,** starting from Dug Bar. The problem here is that the drive to the trailhead is intense: 25 mi. of bone-rattling road recommended only for 4-WD or high-clearance vehicles (though passable, with care, in passenger vehicles). **Hells Canyon Bicycle Tours,** P.O. Box 483, Joseph OR 97846 (432-2453), operates out of the Crosstown Traffic Bike Shop in Joseph (see Practical Information, above). With the encouraging motto "We bring 'em back alive," the outfit offers one- to four -day tours of the National Recreation Area. Day rides ($75) include transportation and lunch, while overnight trips (2 days $175; each additional day $75) include everything but sleeping bags and personal gear. Rides of varying difficulty can be arranged, though mountain biking experience is necessary for rides which drop into the canyon. Most canyon-bottom rides are in spring or fall.

Probably the best way to see the canyon by either jet boat tour or raft. A panoply of outfitters run trips through the canyon. The Forest Service visitor center (see above) has a list of all the permittees, or pick up a brochures at any Chamber of Commerce office (see above). **Hells Canyon Adventures** runs a wide range of jet boat and raft trips through the Canyon. You can take a full day jet boat tour ($70), or a three-hour tour for $30. A full day of whitewater rafting ($90) includes a jet boat ride back upstream.

Index

★ FREE T-SHIRT ★

JUST ANSWER THE QUESTIONS ON THE FOLLOWING PAGES AND MAIL TO:

Let's Go Survey
Macmillan Ltd.
18-21 Cavaye Place
London SW10 9PG

WE'LL SEND THE FIRST 1,500 RESPONDENTS A LET'S GO T-SHIRT!
(Make sure we can read your address.)

■ LET'S GO 1995 READER ■ QUESTIONNAIRE

1) Name _____

2) Address _____

3) Are you: female   male

4) How old are you?   under 17   17-23   24-30   31-40   41-55   over 55

5) Are you (circle all that apply):   at school   at college or university
                                        employed   unemployed   retired

6) What is your annual income?
£10,000-£15,000   £15,000 - £25,000   £25,000 - £40,000   Over £40,000

7) Have you used *Let's Go* before?

   Yes   No

8) How did you hear about *Let's Go* guides?

   Friend or fellow traveller
   Recommended by bookshop
   Display in bookstore
   Advertising in newspaper/magazine
   Review or article in newspaper/ magazine

9) Why did you choose *Let's Go*?

   Updated every year
   Reputation
   Prominent in-store display
   Price
   Content and approach of books
   Reliability

10) Is *Let's Go* the best guidebook?

   Yes
   No (which is?) _____
   Haven't used other guides

11) When did you buy this book?

   Jan   Feb   Mar   Apr   May   Jun
   Jul   Aug   Sep   Oct   Nov   Dec

12) When did you travel with this book? (Circle all that apply)

   Jan   Feb   Mar   Apr   May   Jun
   Jul   Aug   Sep   Oct   Nov   Dec

13) Roughly how much did you spend per day on the road?

   Under £10   £45-£75
   £10-£25   £75-£100
   £25-£40   Over £100

14) What were the main attractions of your trip?
(Circle top three)

   Sightseeing
   New culture
   Learning language
   Sports/Recreation
   Nightlife/Entertainment
   Local cuisine
   Shopping
   Meeting other travellers
   Adventure/Getting off the beaten path

15) How reliable/useful are the following features of *Let's Go*?

   v = very, u = usually, s = sometimes
   n = never, ? = didn't use

Feature	v	u	s	n	?
Accommodations	v	u	s	n	?
Camping	v	u	s	n	?
Food	v	u	s	n	?
Entertainment	v	u	s	n	?
Sights	v	u	s	n	?
Maps	v	u	s	n	?
Practical Info	v	u	s	n	?
Directions	v	u	s	n	?
"Essentials"	v	u	s	n	?
Cultural Intros	v	u	s	n	?

16) Would you use *Let's Go* again?

Yes
No (why not?) _____

_____

_____

17) Which of the following destinations
are you planning to visit as a tourist
in the next five years?
(Circle all that apply)

Australasia
Australia
New Zealand
Indonesia
Japan
China
Hong Kong
Vietnam
Malaysia
Singapore
India
Nepal

Europe And Middle East
Middle East
Israel
Egypt
Africa
Turkey
Greece
Scandinavia
Portugal
Spain
Switzerland
Austria
Berlin
Russia
Poland
Czech/Slovak Republic
Hungary
Baltic States

The Americas
Caribbean
Central America
Costa Rica
South America
Ecuador
Brazil
Venezuela
Colombia
Canada
British Columbia
Montreal/Quebec
MaritimeProvinces

18) What **major** destinations (countries, regions, etc.) covered in this
book did you visit on your trip?

_____

_____

_____

_____

_____

_____

_____

_____

_____

_____

_____

_____

_____

19) What other countries did you visit
on your trip?

_____

_____

_____

_____

_____

20) How did you get around on your
trip?
Car   Train   Plane
Bus   Ferry   Hitching
Bicycle   Motorcycle

Mail this to:

Let's Go Survey

Macmillan Ltd.
18-21 Cavaye Place
London SW10 9PG

Many Thanks For Your Help!